Caravan &
Camping Guide
2013

AA Lifestyle Guides

This 45th edition published 2013
© AA Media Limited 2012
AA Media Limited retains the copyright in the current edition
© 2012 and in all subsequent editions, reprints and amendments to editions.

To contact us:
Advertisement Sales: advertisingsales@theAA.com
Editorial: lifestyleguides@theAA.com

Co-ordinator, AA Caravan & Camping Scheme: David Hancock
Editors: David Hancock and Lin Hutton

Typeset and colour organisation by Servis Filmsetting Ltd, Manchester
Printed and bound by Printers Trento srl, Italy

Published by AA Publishing, a trading name of AA Media Limited, whose registered office is Fanum House, Basing View, Basingstoke, Hampshire, RG21 4EA. Registered number 06112600

A CIP catalogue record for this book is available from the British Library
ISBN: 978-0-7495-7395-9
A04892

Maps prepared by the Mapping Services Department of AA Publishing.

Maps © AA Media Limited 2012.

Contains Ordnance Survey data © Crown copyright and database right 2012

Land & Property Services. This is based upon Crown Copyright and is reproduced with the permission of Land & Property Services under delegated authority from the Controller of Her Majesty's Stationery Office.
© Crown copyright and database rights 2012
Licence number 100,363.
Permit number 110097

Ordnance Survey Ireland Ireland's National Mapping Agency
Republic of Ireland mapping based on © Ordnance Survey Ireland/Government of Ireland Copyright Permit number MP000611

Information on National Parks in England provided by the Countryside Agency (Natural England).

Information on National Parks in Scotland provided by Scottish Natural Heritage.

Information on National Parks in Wales provided by The Countryside Council for Wales.

Contents

How to Use the Guide

1 LOCATION

Place names are listed alphabetically within each county.

2 MAP REFERENCE

Each site is given a map reference for use in conjunction with the atlas section at the back of the guide. The map reference comprises the guide map page number, the National Grid location square and a two-figure map location reference.

For example: **Map 4 ST85**.

4 refers to the page number of the map section at the back of the guide.

ST is the National Grid lettered square (representing 100,000sq metres) in which the location will be found.

8 is the figure reading across the top or bottom of the map page.

5 is the figure reading down each side of the map page.

3 PLACES TO VISIT

Suggestions of nearby places to visit for adults and children.

4 AA CAMPING CARD SCHEME

See explanation on page 7.

5 RATING & SITE NAME

Campsites are listed in descending order of their Pennant Quality rating (see pages 10 & 11). Sites are rated from one to five pennants and are also awarded a score ranging from 50-100% according to how they compare with other parks within the same pennant rating. Some sites are given a Holiday Centre grading. For a fuller explanation see page 10. A category for parks catering only for recreational vehicles (**RV**) has been created (no toilet facilities are provided at these sites).

NEW indicates that the site is new in the guide this year. Where the name appears in *italic* type the information that follows has not been confirmed by the campsite for 2013.

6 6-FIGURE MAP REFERENCE

Each entry also includes a 6-figure National Grid reference as many sites are in remote locations. To help you find the precise location of a site the 6-figure map reference, based on the National Grid, can be used with the relevant Ordnance Survey maps in conjunction with the atlas at the back of the guide.

7 CONTACT DETAILS

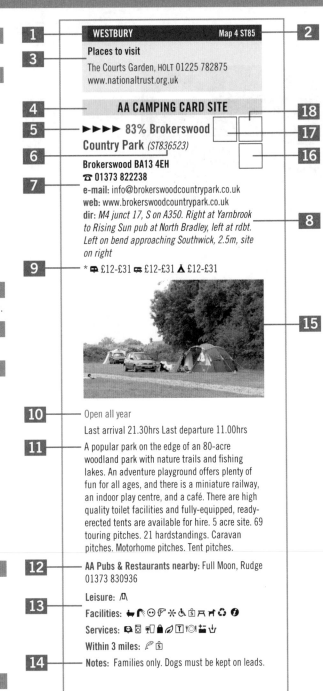

1 **WESTBURY** Map 4 ST85

3 **Places to visit**
The Courts Garden, HOLT 01225 782875
www.nationaltrust.org.uk

4 **AA CAMPING CARD SITE**

5 ▶▶▶▶ 83% Brokerswood **18**
6 Country Park *(ST836523)* **17**

Brokerswood BA13 4EH **16**
7 ☎ 01373 822238
e-mail: info@brokerswoodcountrypark.co.uk
web: www.brokerswoodcountrypark.co.uk
dir: *M4 junct 17, S on A350. Right at Yarnbrook to Rising Sun pub at North Bradley, left at rdbt. Left on bend approaching Southwick, 2.5m, site on right* **8**

9 * ⊕ £12-£31 ⊕ £12-£31 ▲ £12-£31

15

10 Open all year
Last arrival 21.30hrs Last departure 11.00hrs

11 A popular park on the edge of an 80-acre woodland park with nature trails and fishing lakes. An adventure playground offers plenty of fun for all ages, and there is a miniature railway, an indoor play centre, and a café. There are high quality toilet facilities and fully-equipped, ready-erected tents are available for hire. 5 acre site. 69 touring pitches. 21 hardstandings. Caravan pitches. Motorhome pitches. Tent pitches.

12 **AA Pubs & Restaurants nearby:** Full Moon, Rudge 01373 830936

13 Leisure: ⌿
Facilities: ➼ ⋔ ☺ ☞ ✳ ⓰ 🝔 ⚲ 🛒 ♺ ❶
Services: 🚾 🗑 🍴 🛢 ⌀ 🅣 🍽 🛒 ⛟
Within 3 miles: 🖉 ⓢ

14 **Notes:** Families only. Dogs must be kept on leads.

8 DIRECTIONS

Brief directions from a recognisable point, such as a main road, are included in each entry. Please contact the individual site for more detailed directions or try the online AA Route Planner, **theAA.com**, and enter the postcode.

9 CHARGES

Rates are given after each appropriate symbol (🚐 Caravan, 🚐 Campervan, ▲ Tent) and are the overnight cost for one caravan or tent, one car and two adults, or one motorhome and two adults. The prices vary according to the number of people in the party, but some parks have a fixed fee per pitch regardless of the number of people. Please note that some sites charge separately for certain facilities, including showers; and some sites charge a different rate for pitches with or without electricity. Prices are supplied to us in good faith by the site operators and are as accurate as possible. They are, however, only a guide and are subject to change during the currency of this publication.
* If this symbol appears before the prices, it indicates that the site has not advised us of the prices for 2013; they relate to 2012.

10 OPENING, ARRIVAL & DEPARTURE TIMES

Parks are not necessarily open all year and while most sites permit arrivals at any time, checking beforehand is advised (see page 12).

11 DESCRIPTION

Descriptions are based on information supplied by the AA inspector at the time of the last visit.
Please note: The AA pennant classification is based on the touring pitches and the facilities only. AA inspectors currently do not visit or report on statics or chalets for hire under the AA Caravan & Camping quality standards scheme. However the AA has introduced the new category of Holiday Homes 🏠 and will be inspecting these in the future; unfortunately we were unable to inspect the 11 new Holiday Parks included in this guide before our deadlines.
For sites other than those marked with 🏠 we only include the number of static caravan pitches in order to give an indication of the nature and size of the site.

12 AA PUBS & RESTAURANTS

An entry may include suggestions for nearby pubs and/or restaurants recognised by the AA. Some of these establishments will have been awarded Rosettes for food excellence.

13 SYMBOLS & ABBREVIATIONS

These are divided into Leisure, Facilities, Services and Within 3 miles sections. Explanations can be found on page 9 and at the bottom of the pages throughout the guide.

14 NOTES

This includes information about any restrictions the site would like their visitors to be aware of and any additional facilities.
🏧 As most sites now accept credit and debit cards, we have only indicated those that don't accept cards.

15 PHOTOGRAPH

Optional photograph supplied by the campsite.

16 COUNTRYSIDE DISCOVERY

 A group of over 30 family-run parks with fewer than 150 pitches, each sharing a common theme of tranquillity. **www.countryside-discovery.co.uk**

17 BEST OF BRITISH

 A group of over 50 parks, both large and small, which focus on high quality facilities and amenities. **www.bob.org.uk**

18 DAVID BELLAMY AWARDS

 Many AA recognised sites are also recipients of a David Bellamy Award for Conservation. The awards are graded Gold, Silver and Bronze. The symbols we show indicate the 2011/12 winners as this was the most up-to-date information at the time of going to press. For the 2012/13 winners please contact:
British Holiday & Homes Parks Association
Tel: 01452 526911

Facilities for disabled guests

The Equality Act 2010 provides legal rights for disabled people including access to goods, services and facilities, and means that service providers may have to consider making adjustments to their premises.
For more information about the Act see: **www.equalities.gov.uk** or **www.direct.gov.uk/en/DisabledPeople/RightsAndObligations/DisabilityRights/DG_4001068**
♿ If a site has told us that they provide facilities for disabled visitors their entry in the guide will include this symbol. The sites in this guide should be aware of their responsibilities under the Act. However, we recommend that you always telephone in advance to ensure the site you have chosen has facilities to suit your needs.

CASTLE CARY HOLIDAY PARK

Creetown, Nr Newton Stewart, Wigtownshire DG8 7DQ
Telephone: 01671 820264
Fax: 01671 820670
www.castlecary-caravans.com
enquiries@castlecarypark.f9.co.uk

For that quiet relaxing holiday in the heart of romantic Galloway, Castle Cary has much to offer, and constantly adds to and improves its facilities year after year. It has views over fields, woodlands and the estuary of the River Cree.

Having your very own luxurious holiday home on Castle Cary Holiday Park is no longer a dream. It has became a reality for more and more customers who are aware of the advantages of having your own holiday home. We have a comprehensive selection of new and used caravans, and a wide range of luxury lodges for sale.

FACILITIES

- Shower and toilets; Family room
- Outdoor heated swimming pool; Games room; Shop
- Indoor heated swimming pool; Donkey park
- Snooker room; Restaurant/Inn
- Giant Draughts; Crazy Golf
- Coarse Fishing; New for 2011 – Glamping
- Children's Play Park; C.W. Points
- Tourers, tents, motor homes all welcome
- Special 10% discount for weekly bookings

AA Camping Card Scheme

THE AA CAMPING CARD

In this edition of the AA Caravan & Camping Guide you will find some sites highlighted with the **AA CAMPING CARD SITE** banner. This indicates that the site has signed up to the AA Camping Card Scheme, and means they have agreed to offer reduced rates to campers who book in advance, citing the AA Camping Card, and show the card on arrival at the site. The offers are provided by and are available entirely at the discretion of participating campsites. Offers may include, for example, reduced pitch prices at certain times of the week or year. These discounts will only be available to those booking in advance, stating at the time of booking that an AA Camping Card is being used, and showing the card on arrival. Scheme terms and campsite terms of booking will apply.

You'll need to contact the site to find out what they are offering. We hope this will encourage you to visit sites and explore parts of the country you may not have considered before.

Terms and conditions

This card may be used at any campsite specified as accepting the AA Camping Card within the AA Caravan & Camping Guide 2013 and is valid for and may be applied to stays that expire before 31.1.2014.

To make use of the benefits of the AA Camping Card Scheme you must notify any participating campsite that you are a cardholder at your time of advance booking and provide details. Scheme Cards are issued and enclosed with your copy of the AA Caravan & Camping Guide 2013 at the point of initial purchase.

The card entitles the bearer to any discount or other benefits being offered by the campsite under the scheme at the time of making an advance booking. Participating campsites may formulate, provide, vary or withdraw offers at their discretion. Offers may vary from campsite to campsite. Acceptance by you of any offer made by a campsite is an agreement between you and the campsite. Offers are subject to availability at time of booking and presentation of the booker person's AA Camping Card on arrival. Photocopies will not be accepted. Campsite terms and conditions will apply.

Only one card per person or party accepted. No change given. This card is valid during the period(s) specified by the campsites concerned, and will not be valid after 31 Jan 2014. This card cannot be used in conjunction with any other discount voucher or special offer. No cash alternative available.

This scheme will be governed by English law.

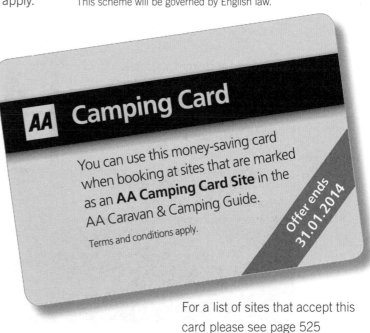

AA Camping Card

You can use this money-saving card when booking at sites that are marked as an **AA Camping Card Site** in the AA Caravan & Camping Guide.

Terms and conditions apply.

Offer ends 31.01.2014

For a list of sites that accept this card please see page 525

Windblocker Shades
by Lillypad Leisure Ltd

The lightweight alternative to heavy safari rooms.

Windblocker Shades provide a good degree of privacy without blocking the view, in addition to offering shade and protection from the wind and rain. When not in use Windblocker Shades pack into a space equivalent to half a carrier bag.

In addition to our standard sizes we also offer a bespoke 'made-to-measure' service and alterations to standard ends to create wrap around ends for existing customers.

We also sell tie down straps, draught skirts, wheel arch covers, separate front and end panels and fly screen doors.

Lillypad Leisure is a family run business and we are proud to offer the highest standard of customer service.
Your satisfaction is our business

lillypadleisure.com
0845 230 5260

Give us a ring and ask to speak with Anthony

Lillypad Leisure Ltd

Tie Down Straps

Easy On/Easy Off
Wheel Arch Covers & Draught Skirts

Now with wrap around corners

For Fiamma & Orminster Canopies

Custom Sizes & Bespoke Service

Symbols & Abbreviations

Facilities

- Bath
- Shower
- Electric Shaver
- Hairdryer
- Ice Pack Facility
- Disabled Facilities
- Public Telephone
- Shop on Site or within 200yds
- Mobile Shop (calling at least 5 days per week)
- BBQ Area
- Picnic Area
- Wi-fi Access
- Internet Access
- Recycling Facilities
- Tourist Information
- Dog Exercise Area

Leisure

- Indoor Swimming Pool
- Outdoor Swimming Pool
- Tennis Court
- Games Room

- Children's Playground
- Kid's Club
- Stables & Horse Riding
- 9/18 hole Golf Course
- Boats for Hire
- Cinema
- Entertainment
- Fishing
- Mini Golf
- Watersports
- Gym
- Sports Field
- Spa
- Separate TV room

Services

- Toilet Fluid
- Café or Restaurant
- Fast Food/Takeaway
- Baby Care
- Electric Hook Up
- Motorvan Service Point
- Launderette
- Licensed Bar

- Calor Gas
- Camping Gaz
- Battery Charging

Abbreviations

BH	bank holiday/s
Etr	Easter
Whit	Whitsun
dep	departure
fr	from
hrs	hours
m	mile
mdnt	midnight
rdbt	roundabout
rs	restricted service
RV	Recreational Vehicles
U	rating not confirmed
wk	week
wknd	weekend

- no dogs
- no credit or debit cards
- children of all ages accepted

AA Pennant Classification

AA Pennant Rating and Holiday Centres

AA parks are classified on a 5-point scale according to their style and the range of facilities they offer. As the number of pennants increases, so the quality and variety of facilities is generally greater. There is also a separate category for Holiday Centres which provide full day and night holiday entertainment as well as offering complete touring facilities for campers and for caravanners.

What can you expect at an AA-rated park?

All AA parks must meet a minimum standard: they should be clean, well maintained and welcoming. In addition they must have a local authority site licence (unless specially exempted), and satisfy local authority fire regulations.

The AA inspection

Each campsite that applies for AA recognition receives an unannounced visit each year by one of the AA's highly qualified team of inspectors. They make a thorough check of the site's touring pitches, facilities and hospitality. The sites pay an annual fee for the inspection, the recognition and rating, and receive a text entry in the AA Caravan & Camping Guide. AA inspectors pay when they stay overnight on a site. The criteria used by the inspectors in awarding the AA Pennant rating is shown on the opposite page.

AA Quality % Score

AA Rated Campsites, Caravan Parks and Holiday Centres are awarded a percentage score alongside their pennant rating or holiday centre status. This is a qualitative assessment of various factors including customer care and hospitality, toilet facilities and park landscaping. The % score runs from 50% to 100% and indicates the relative quality of parks with the same number of pennants. For example, one 3-pennant park may score 60%, while another 3-pennant park may achieve 70%. Holiday Centres also receive a % score between 50% and 100% to differentiate between quality levels within this grading. Like the pennant rating, the percentage is reassessed annually.

Holiday Centres

In this category we distinguish parks which cater for all holiday needs including cooked meals and entertainment.

They provide:
- A wide range of on-site sports, leisure and recreational facilities
- Supervision and security at a very high level
- A choice of eating outlets
- Facilities for touring caravans that equal those available to rented holiday accommodation
- A maximum density of 25 pitches per acre
- Clubhouse with entertainment provided
- Laundry with automatic washing machines

Holiday Home Parks

Parks in this category are static only parks offering holiday caravans for hire and catering for all holiday needs.

They provide:
- Quality holiday hire caravans ranging from 'Standard' caravans to ultra-modern and luxurious 'Platinum' caravans
- A wide range of on-site sports, leisure and recreational facilities
- Supervision and security at a very high level
- A choice of eating outlets
- Clubhouse with entertainment provided

AA Pennant Rating Guidelines

 ## One Pennant Parks
These parks offer a fairly simple standard of facilities including:
- No more than 30 pitches per acre
- At least 5% of the total pitches allocated to touring caravans
- An adequate drinking water supply and reasonable drainage
- Washroom with flush toilets and toilet paper provided, unless no sanitary facilities are provided in which case this should be clearly stated
- Chemical disposal arrangements, ideally with running water, unless tents only
- Adequate refuse disposal arrangements that are clearly signed
- Well-drained ground, and some level pitches
- Entrance and access roads of adequate width and surface
- Location of emergency telephone clearly signed
- Emergency telephone numbers fully displayed

 ## Two Pennant Parks
Parks in this category should meet all of the above requirements, but offer an increased level of facilities, services, customer care, security and ground maintenance. They should include the following:
- Separate washrooms, including at least 2 male and 2 female WCs and washbasins per 30 pitches
- Hot and cold water direct to each basin
- Externally-lit toilet blocks
- Warden available during day, times to be indicated
- Whereabouts of shop/chemist clearly signed
- Dish-washing facilities, covered and lit
- Reception area

 ## Three Pennant Parks
Many parks come within this rating and the range of facilities is wide. All parks will be of a very good standard and will meet the following minimum criteria:
- Facilities, services and park grounds are clean and well maintained, with buildings in good repair and attention paid to customer care and park security
- Evenly-surfaced roads and paths
- Clean modern toilet blocks with all-night lighting and containing toilet seats in good condition, soap and hand dryers or paper towels, mirrors, shelves and hooks, shaver and hairdryer points, and lidded waste bins in female toilets
- Modern shower cubicles with sufficient hot water and attached, private changing space
- Electric hook-ups
- Some hardstanding/wheel runs/firm, level ground
- Laundry with automatic washing and drying facilities, separate from toilets

- Children's playground with safe equipment
- 24 hours public telephone on site or nearby where mobile reception is poor
- Warden availability and 24-hour contact number clearly signed

 ## Four Pennant Parks
These parks have achieved an excellent standard in all areas, including landscaping of grounds, natural screening and attractive park buildings, and customer care and park security.
Toilets are smart, modern and immaculately maintained, and generally offer the following facilities:
- Spacious vanitory-style washbasins, at least 2 male and 2 female per 25 pitches
- Fully-tiled shower cubicles with doors, dry areas, shelves and hooks, at least 1 male and 1 female per 30 pitches
- Availability of washbasins in lockable cubicles, or combined toilet/washing cubicles, or a private/family room with shower/toilet/washbasin
Other requirements are:
- Baby changing facilities
- A shop on site, or within reasonable distance
- Warden available 24 hours
- Reception area open during the day, with tourist information available
- Internal roads, paths and toilet blocks lit at night
- Maximum 25 pitches per campable acre
- Toilet blocks heated October to Easter
- Minimum 50% electric hook-ups
- Minimum 10% hardstandings where necessary
- Late arrivals enclosure

 ## Five Pennant Premier Parks
Premier parks are of an extremely high standard, set in attractive surroundings with superb mature landscaping. Facilities, security and customer care are of an exceptional quality. As well as the above they will also offer:
- First-class toilet facilities including several designated self-contained cubicles, ideally with WC, washbasin and shower.
- Electricity to most pitches
- Minimum 20% hardstandings (where necessary)
- Some fully-serviced 'super' pitches: of larger size and with water and electricity supplies connected
- A motorhome service point
Many Premier Parks will also provide:
- Heated swimming pool
- Well-equipped shop
- Café or restaurant and bar
- A designated walking area for dogs (if accepted)

Useful Information

Booking Information

It is advisable to book in advance during peak holiday seasons and in school or public holidays. It is also wise to check whether or not a reservation entitles you to a particular pitch. It does not necessarily follow that an early booking will secure the best pitch; you may simply have the choice of what is available at the time you check in.

Some parks may require a deposit on booking which may be non-returnable if you have to cancel your holiday. If you do have to cancel, notify the proprietor at once because you may be held legally responsible for partial or full payment unless the pitch can be re-let. Consider taking out insurance such as AA Travel Insurance, tel: 0800 085 7240 or visit the AA website: **theAA.com** for details to cover a lost deposit or compensation. Some parks will not accept overnight bookings unless payment for the full minimum period (e.g. two or three days) is made.

Last Arrival – Unless otherwise stated, parks will usually accept arrivals at any time of the day or night, but some have a special 'late arrivals' enclosure where you have to make temporary camp to avoid disturbing other people on the park. Please note that on some parks access to the toilet block is by key or pass card only, so if you know you will be late, do check what arrangements can be made.

Last Departure – Most parks will specify their overnight period – e.g. noon to noon. If you overstay the departure time you can be charged for an extra day.

Chemical Closet Disposal Point (CDP)

You will usually find one on every park, except those catering only for tents. It must be a specially constructed unit, or a WC permanently set aside for the purpose of chemical disposal and with adjacent rinsing and soak-away facilities. However, some local authorities are concerned about the effect of chemicals on bacteria in cesspools etc, and may prohibit or restrict provision of CDPs in their areas.

Complaints

Speak to the park proprietor or supervisor immediately if you have any complaints, so that the matter can be sorted out on the spot. If this personal approach fails, you may decide, if the matter is serious, to approach the local authority or tourist board. AA guide users may also write to:
The Co-ordinator, AA Caravan & Camping Scheme,
AA Lifestyle Guides, 13th floor, Fanum House, Basingstoke,
RG21 4EA

The AA may at its sole discretion investigate any complaints received from guide users for the purpose of making any necessary amendments to the guide. The AA will not in any circumstances act as representative or negotiator or undertake to obtain compensation or enter into further correspondence or deal with the matter in any other way whatsoever. The AA will not guarantee to take any specific action.

Dogs

Dogs may or may not be accepted at parks, and this is entirely at the owner's or warden's discretion (assistance dogs should be accepted). Even when the park states that they accept dogs, it is still discretionary, and certain breeds may not be considered as suitable, so we strongly advise that you check when you book.* Dogs should always be kept on a lead and under control, and letting them sleep in cars is not encouraged.

*Some sites have told us they do not accept dangerous breeds.
The following breeds are covered under the Dangerous Dogs Act 1991 – Pit Bull Terrier, Japanese Tosa, Dogo Argentino and Fila Brazilerio.

Electric Hook-Up

This is becoming more generally available at parks with three or more pennants, but if it is important to you, you should check before booking. The voltage is generally 240v AC, 50 cycles, although variations between 200v and 250v may still be found. All parks in the AA scheme which provide electric hook-ups do so in accordance with International Electrotechnical Commission regulations. Outlets are coloured blue and take the form of a lidded plug with recessed contacts, making it impossible to touch a live point by accident. They are also waterproof. A similar plug, but with protruding contacts which hook into the recessed plug, is on the end of the cable which connects the caravan to the source of supply, and is dead. This equipment can usually be hired on site, or a plug connector supplied to fit your own cable. You should ask for the male plug; the female plug is the one already fixed to the power supply. This supply is rated for either 5, 10 or 16 amps and this is usually displayed on a triangular yellow plate attached to source of supply. If it is not, be sure to check at the site reception. This is important because if you overload the circuit, the trip switch will operate to cut off the power supply. The trip switch can only be reset by a park official, who will first have to go round all the hook-ups on park to find the cause of the trip. This can take a long time and will make the culprit distinctly unpopular with all the other caravanners deprived of power, to say nothing of the park official. Tents and trailer tents are recommended to have a Residual Circuit Device (RCD) for safety reasons and to avoid overloading the circuit.

It is a relatively simple matter to calculate whether your appliances will overload the circuit. The amperage used by an appliance depends on its wattage and the total amperage used is the total of all the appliances in use at any one time. If you are not sure whether your camping or caravanning equipment can be used at a park, check beforehand.

Average amperage

Portable black & white TV 50 watts approx.	0.2 amp
Small colour TV 90 watts approx.	0.4 amp
Small fan heater 1000 watts (1kW) approx.	4.2 amp
One-bar electric fire NB each extra bar rates 1000 watts (1kW)	4.2 amp
60 watt table lamp approx.	0.25 amp
100 watt light bulb approx.	0.4 amp
Battery charger 100 watts approx.	0.4 amp
Small fridge 125 watts approx.	0.4 amp
Domestic microwave 600 watts approx.	2.5 amp

Motor Caravans

At some parks motor caravans are only accepted if they remain static throughout the stay. Also check that there are suitable level pitches at the parks where you plan to stay.

Overflow Pitches

Campsites are legally entitled to use an overflow field which is not a normal part of their camping area for up to 28 days in any one year as an emergency method of coping with additional numbers at busy periods. When this 28 day rule is being invoked site owners should increase the numbers of sanitary facilities accordingly. In these circumstances the extra facilities are sometimes no more than temporary portacabins.

Parking

Some park operators insist that cars be put in a parking area separate from the pitches; others will not allow more than one car for each caravan or tent.

Park Restrictions

Many parks in our guide are selective about the categories of people they will accept on their parks. In the caravan and camping world there are many restrictions and some categories of visitor are banned altogether. Where a park has told us of a restriction/s this is included in notes in their entry.

On many parks in this guide, unaccompanied young people, single-sex groups, single adults, and motorcycle groups will not be accepted. The AA takes no stance in this matter, basing its pennant classification on facilities, quality and maintenance. On the other hand, some parks cater well for teenagers and offer magnificent sporting and leisure facilities as well as discos; others have only very simple amenities. A small number of parks in our guide exclude all children in order to create an environment aiming at holiday makers in search of total peace and quiet. (See page 49)

Pets Travel Scheme

The importation of animals into the UK is subject to strict controls. Penalties for trying to avoid these controls are severe. However, the Pet Travel Scheme (PETS) allows cats, dogs, ferrets and certain other pets coming from the EU and certain other countries to enter the UK without quarantine provided the appropriate conditions are met. For details:
www.defra.gov.uk/wildlife-pets/pets/travel/pets/index.htm
PETS HELPLINE on 0870 241 1710
E-mail: quarantine@animalhealth.gsi.gov.uk
Pets resident in the British Isles (UK, Republic of Ireland, Isle of Man and Channel Islands) are not subject to any quarantine or PETS rules when travelling within the British Isles.

Seasonal Touring Pitches

Some park operators allocate a number of their hardstanding pitches for long-term seasonal caravans. These pitches can be reserved for the whole period the campsite is open, generally between Easter and September, and a fixed fee is charged for keeping the caravan on the park for the season. These pitches are in great demand, especially in popular tourist areas, so enquire well in advance if you wish to book one.

Shops

The range of food and equipment in shops is usually in proportion to the size of the park. As far as our pennant requirements are concerned, a mobile shop calling several times a week, or a general store within easy walking distance of the park is acceptable.

Unisex Toilet Facilities

An ever-increasing number of parks now offer unisex toilet facilities instead of (or sometimes as well as) separate units for men and women. If the type of toilet facility is important to you, please check what the park has to offer at the time of booking.

After Bite

Fast relief from bites and stings.

Don't let bites and stings stop the family fun
– take After Bite away with you.

Easy-to-apply, fast-acting After Bite provides
instant relief from the effects of mosquitoes,
bees, wasps, nettles and jellyfish.

From Boots, Superdrug, Tesco, Lloydspharmacy
and good chemists everywhere.
Online at **www.afterbite.co.uk**
Contains ammonia 3.5% w/v. Always read the label.

Island Camping

Channel Islands

Tight controls are operated because of the narrow width of the mainly rural roads. On all of the islands tents can be hired on recognised campsites.

Alderney

Neither caravans nor motor caravans are allowed, and campers must have a confirmed booking on the one official camp site before they arrive.

Guernsey

Only islanders may own and use towed caravans, but a limited number of motor caravans are now permitted on the island. The motor caravan, used for overnight accommodation, must be not more than 6.9mtrs long, must be booked into an authorised site (Fauxquets Valley Campsite or Le Vaugrat Camp Site) and must obtain a permit from the site operator before embarking on a ferry for Guernsey – Condor Ferries will not accept motor caravans without this permit. A window sticker must be displayed, motor caravans must return to the site each night, and the visits are limited to a maximum of one month. Permission is not required to bring a trailer tent to the island. For further details see www.visitguernsey.com/faqs.aspx

Herm and Sark

These two small islands are traffic free. Herm has a small campsite for tents, and these can also be hired. Sark has two campsites. New arrivals are met off the boat by a tractor which carries people and luggage up the steep hill from the harbour. All travel is by foot, on bicycle, or by horse and cart.

Jersey

Visiting caravans are allowed into Jersey, provided they are to be used as holiday accommodation only. Caravans will require a permit for travelling to and from the port and campsite on their arrival and departure days only. Motorvans may travel around the island on a daily basis, but must return to the campsite each night. Bookings should be made through the chosen campsite, who will also arrange for a permit. Early booking is strongly recommended during July and August.

Isle of Man

Motor caravans may enter with prior permission. Trailer caravans are generally only allowed in connection with trade shows and exhibitions, or for demonstration purposes, not for living accommodation. Written application for permission should be made to the Secretary, Planning Committee, Isle of Man Local Government Board, Murray House, Mount Havelock, Douglas. The shipping line cannot accept caravans without this written permission.

Isles of Scilly

Caravans and motor caravans are not allowed, and campers must stay at official sites. Booking is advisable on all sites, especially during school holidays.

Scottish Islands

Inner Isles (including Inner Hebrides)

Skye is accessible to caravans and motor caravans, and has official camping sites, but its sister isles of **Rhum** and **Eigg** have no car ferries, and take only backpackers. On the **Isle of Bute** only official camping is allowed. The islands of **Mull**, **Islay**, **Coll** and **Arran** have official campsites, and welcome caravans, motor caravans and tenters; offsite camping is also allowed with the usual permission. **Iona**, a backpacker's paradise, does not permit non-residents' vehicles. Wild camping is permitted on **Tiree** in accordance with the Scottish Outdoor Access Code (see www.isleoftiree.com). Prior arrangements must be made if you wish to camp with a motor vehicle, or go wild camping on **Colonsay** or **Cumbrae** (see www.colonsay.org.uk) and **Great Cumbrae** does not permit caravanning or camping, although organized groups may stay with official permission. **Jura** and **Gigha** allow neither camping nor caravanning, and **Lismore** bans caravans but permits camping, although there are no official sites and few suitable places.

Orkney

There are no camping and caravanning restrictions, and plenty of beauty spots in which to pitch camp.

Shetland

There are four official campsites on the Shetlands, but visitors can camp anywhere with prior permission. Caravans and motor caravans must stick to the main roads. Camping 'böds' offer budget accommodation in unisex dormitories for campers with their own bed rolls and sleeping bags. There is a campsite on **Fetler** (see www.fetler.org), but no camping or caravanning is permitted on **Noss** and **Fair Isle**.

Western Isles (Outer Hebrides)

There are official campsites on these islands, but wild camping is allowed within reason, and with the landowner's prior permission.

Save up to 50%* on 2013 UK holidays

Haven

Britain's Favourite Seaside Holiday

Come and stay in one of our comfortable, roomy self-catering caravans...

...or bring your own. We welcome tourers, motorhomes, tents and trailer tents

You can't beat a good seaside holiday

- Splash around in our heated pools - some with flumes and slides
- Be adventurous - try out our many sports activities and facilities
- Dazzling family entertainment and fun packed kids' clubs
- There's tasty food and drink on the menu at all our parks
- Most of our parks are right beside the sea - so don't forget your buckets and spades

To find out more, order a brochure and to book

Call: 0843 658 0450 Quote: AA2013 **Visit: haven.com/aa2013**

Calls cost 5p per minute plus network extras. Open 7 days a week, 9am-9pm

*Save up to 50% discount is available on selected spring and autumn dates in 2013. Full booking terms and conditions apply. Haven Holidays is a trading name of Bourne Leisure Limited, 1 Park Lane, Hemel Hempstead, HP2 4YL. Registered in England No. 04011660.

AA Campsites of the Year

ENGLAND & OVERALL WINNER OF THE AA BEST CAMPSITE OF THE YEAR

▶▶▶▶▶ 97% THE OLD OAKS TOURING PARK

GLASTONBURY, SOMERSET PAGE 288

Since winning the South West regional award several years ago this impressive adult's only park has been developed further by the White family. The attention to detail is exceptional in all areas of the park – even the dog wash has hot water – and the overall quality is stunning, earning it a Quality Score of 97%, the highest in the 2013 guide. Set on a working farm on the outskirts of the town, close to Glastonbury Tor and with panoramic views towards the Mendip Hills, Old Oaks offers sophisticated services whilst retaining a farming atmosphere. The park is divided up into several beautifully landscaped areas, each adding to the quality and overall feel of the park, and the spacious super pitches can really be classed as luxurious. The addition of a new state-of-the-art toilet block in 2012 has taken this park to the next level. Apart from being very well appointed and modern it boasts the highest quality fittings and has excellent fully equipped rooms with walk in showers, toilet and wash hand basins. The new building is very tastefully built using traditional materials, stonework and tiles as well as being very eco friendly. The park caters for caravans, motorhomes and tents and has several luxury camping cabins for hire. A genuine warm welcome and an enjoyable stay are assured by the White family and their attentive team – it is perfect place to relax on holiday.

SCOTLAND

▶▶▶▶ 88% MILTON OF FONAB CARAVAN SITE

PITLOCHRY, PERTH & KINROSS PAGE 395

Anyone wishing to be located in the centre of Scotland should choose Pitlochry and stay at this lovely site, which has been owned by the Stewart family for generations. Set on the banks of the River Tummel, just a short walk from the town and with views of the Tummel Valley and the surrounding hills, it makes an ideal base from which to tour Scotland. Expect excellent facilities and mature trees and hedges dividing the two main areas of the park, with the grass manicured to bowling green standard and the colourful flowers beds, baskets and tubs enhancing the tranquil and spacious feel of this traditional caravan site. The shop and reception are modern and clean, well maintained toilets blocks are far in excess of requirements. The static hire caravans are modern and provide all the comforts of home and Wi-fi is free to all customers. Fishing is available on the river and on the surrounding lochs and rivers, just ask Fiona Stewart, who displays a photo of her record salmon catch at the site shop. Overall, this is an excellent site, with spotlessly maintained facilities, supervised by a caring team of dedicated staff who will do their best to ensure a stay at Milton of Fonab is unforgettable.

WALES

▶▶▶▶▶ 86% CAERFAI BAY CARAVAN & TENT PARK

ST DAVIDS, PEMBROKESHIRE PAGE 434

Magnificent coastal scenery and an outlook over St Bride's Bay can be enjoyed from this delightful site set high on the cliffs beside the Pembrokeshire Coastal Path near St Davids. If that wasn't enough to make this friendly, family run park popular, it is located just 300 yards from a glorious bathing beach, which is ideal for families. Comprising three separate field enclosures, linked by upgraded roadways, the park offers first-class toilet facilities, which include four smart family rooms, which are a huge asset during high season, and two, equally popular solar-heated wet suit shower rooms. A new geo-thermal underground water heating system supplements the solar panels and ensures the toilets have piping hot water. Recent improvements to the park include a superb new amenity building, which was completed in 2011 and houses the launderette, dishwashing and the information/rest room under one roof. Campers appreciate the small kitchen area with microwave, kettle, toaster, fridge and breakfast bar, and the area also boasts a computer area with internet access, lockers for phone charging, a play pen for small children, and a conservatory seating area with sea views. There's an excellent organic farm shop across the road and summer coastal buses stop outside the park. A worthy winner.

AA Campsites of the Year – Regional Award Winners

SOUTH WEST ENGLAND

▶▶▶▶▶ **93%** CARNON DOWNS CARAVAN & CAMPING PARK

TRURO, CORNWALL PAGE 116

Located just off the A39, just three miles west of Truro, this beautifully mature park is set in 33 acres of meadowland and woodland close to the village amenities of Carnon Downs and provides easy access to the magnificent beaches of north and south Cornwall. First impressions on arrival are very positive, from the modern wooden lodge-style reception, which is festooned with colourful floral displays, to the excellent landscaping across the park. Numerous hedged paddocks, all linked by good tarmac drives, feature tightly mown grass, neat shrubbery, and spacious, well laid out pitches, including over 100 fully serviced hardstanding pitches. In addition, room has been found for an exciting children's play area, a football pitch and good walks through adjoining bluebell woods. There are four toilets blocks, all are very modern, extremely well decorated and cleaned to a very high standard and, in addition to the normal toilet and shower amenities, they include 23 excellent fully-serviced unisex cubicles, each with shower, toilet and wash hand basins. A new 'drive-over' motorhome service point for large RVs to empty grey and black water was built for the 2012 season.

SOUTH EAST ENGLAND

▶▶▶▶▶ **87%** KLOOFS CARAVAN PARK

BEXHILL, EAST SUSSEX PAGE 311

Hidden away down a quiet lane, just inland from Bexhill and the coast, Kloofs is a friendly, family-run park surrounded by farmland and oak woodlands, with views extending to the South Downs from the prime hilltop pitches. Lovingly developed by the Terry and Helen Griggs over the past 17 years, the site is well landscaped and thoughtfully laid out, with raised beds full of colourful flowers and shrubs, and spacious pitches, each with mini patio, bench and barbecue stand. There are also excellent terraced hardstanding pitches, some of which are fully serviced and large enough to accommodate American-style RVs. Spotless, upmarket toilet facilities include a family shower room and a unique unisex pine cabin facility containing privacy cubicles (one with bidet and another with a kiddies' toilet), a dog shower, a drying room, and the rare luxury provision of a dishwasher, all of which underline the level of attention to detail on this park. In addition, there is a well-equipped reception/shop selling essential food items and camping spares, and the adjoining conservatory is chock-full of local information. Campers can expect high levels of customer care from the hands-on owners and well trained staff.

HEART OF ENGLAND

▶▶▶▶▶ 85% WOODHALL COUNTRY PARK

WOODHALL SPA, LINCOLNSHIRE PAGE 245

Woodhall Country Park is a stunning operation. The touring park, situated a short walk from Woodhall Spa, is just two years old and the owners have spared no expense in transforming part of the woodland area into a countryside retreat for campers who wish to escape from a hectic lifestyle. A commitment to providing a 'back to nature' experience is matched by quality facilities for both tourers and campers, creating a memorable camping experience. There is also a strong ethos towards sustainability, with a bio mass boiler providing heating and hot water to the three superb log cabin amenity blocks, which are spotlessly clean and equipped with excellent modern fixtures and fittings. The park is well organised and well laid out, and the spacious, fully serviced pitches are attractively set amongst mature trees, while the lush tent pitches are also well screened. In 2012 bird hides and camping pods were strategically placed around park. Activities on the park include a fishing lake and, as there is formal play equipment, children are encouraged to embark on a wildlife experience by exploring the wild areas to seek out the wide variety of fauna and flora. Campers can expect high levels of customer care from park manager, Ian Edmondson and his team.

NORTH WEST ENGLAND

▶▶▶▶▶ 91% LAMB COTTAGE CARAVAN PARK

WHITEGATE, CHESHIRE PAGE 57

Located close to historic Chester and for motor racing fans, a few minutes' drive from Oulton Park, this long established all-level park provides lush grassed spacious touring pitches, including spacious serviced pitches with wide grass borders, within beautifully landscaped hedge-screened areas. Arboretum standard coniferous and deciduous trees surround the park and mature shrubs and pretty floral displays ensure a colourful presentation for every season. The amenities block has that 'wow' factor with superb modern fixtures and fittings and the private shower/wc/wash basin suites are of an excellent standard. A regular detailed cleaning schedule ensures a spotless presentation of all areas and a high level of customer care is guaranteed by progressive resident owners and caring wardens. In addition to the reception office with generous opening hours, a separate comprehensively stocked information kiosk is also available. Peace and tranquility are assured, with just the dovecot's residents being the only welcome distraction. Lamb Cottage Caravan Park is an ideal destination for those wishing to escape the pressures of everyday life and enjoy a break in a beautiful part of the Cheshire countryside, with excellent access to nearby woodland walks and cycle trails.

AA Campsites of the Year *continued*

NORTH EAST ENGLAND

▶▶▶▶▶ 82% VALE OF PICKERING CARAVAN PARK

ALLERSTON, NORTH YORKSHIRE PAGE 341

Peacefully located east of Pickering and within easy reach of the North York Moors and Scarborough and its many attractions, this well maintained and spacious family park benefits from year on year investment by hands-on owners and their dedicated resident wardens to provide positive improvements to enhance the customer experience. The lush grassed touring areas are beautifully landscaped with mature trees, shrubs and seasonal flowers and many of the generously sized pitches are hedge screened to ensure optimum privacy. A woodland walk is an additional benefit and children of all ages are offered a choice of quality play equipment and a ball games field. The well stocked shop, reception and amenities blocks are surrounded by pretty seasonal floral arrangements and the spotlessly clean toilet and shower areas are equipped with modern efficient fittings and good additional privacy options. Customer care is a real strength with all the team genuinely pleased to help and despite the wet summer last year, staff were always on hand to assist guests who experienced difficulty, especially on the day our inspector stayed on site when three inches of rain fell overnight, proving that the 'customer is king' at this memorable holiday destination.

HOLIDAY CENTRE

 91% FRESHWATER BEACH HOLIDAY PARK

BRIDPORT, DORSET PAGE 190

Situated on Dorset's World Heritage Coast between Bridport and the delightful village of Burton Bradstock, this well managed, family-run holiday centre really does offer the perfect place to take the family. The touring area is spacious and has large grass pitches plus some serviced hardstanding pitches for caravans and motorhomes, plus there is a terraced section reserved mainly for tents. Touring facilities include the provision of three modern and well-appointed toilet and shower blocks, all with excellent family rooms. Occupying a prime location of the park are quality holiday homes for hire, many have superb views out to sea and along the coast. The park has the unique benefit of its own private beach as well as both indoor and outdoor swimming pools. Recent additions include the new indoor leisure complex, the Jurassic Fun Centre, which includes indoor pools and water slides, a gym, sauna and hot tub, plus 10-pin bowling and an excellent bar and restaurant, which has great views over the park and coast. There is a very good entertainment programme and a wealth of activities for children to enjoy on site. Weymouth, Lyme Regis and Abbotsbury are close by and the park adjoins the South West Coast Path for superb walking.

ROGER ALMOND AWARD – MOST IMPROVED CAMPSITE

►►►► **87%** HOLLINS FARM CAMPING & CARAVANNING

FAR ARNSIDE, LANCASHIRE PAGE 234

Hollins Farm is a long established campsite and offered a very traditional camping experience before the Holgates Group, who also own the nearby award-winning Silverdale Holiday Park, acquired it in 2008. Since then the touring areas have been completely transformed with all aspects of the campsite being seriously upgraded to modern-day expectations, yet without losing the traditional 'back to nature' feel of a farm campsite, with farm animals to entertain children and chickens roaming free. Firstly, 2,500 shrubs were planted for future pitch screening and privacy and then, following discussions with the planning authorities, it was decided to reduce the overall number of pitches and the new-look touring field now has 50 spacious, fully serviced hardstanding pitches for tourers and 25 tent pitches with water, with most enjoying stunning views towards Morecambe Bay. Not content just to a have 'decent' toilet block, in typical Holgates style a brand new amenity block was built from local stone and opened in 2012. It has a definite 'wow' factor, with an excellent design to blend in with the surrounding countryside, and a superb interior, replete with smart cladding, quality fittings, underfloor heating, and fully serviced cubicles. Campers staying on Hollins Farm have full use of the leisure and entertain facilities at Silverdale Holiday Park, just a 5-minute walk away across fields.

Gamekeeper
turned
poacher

AA Campsite Inspector Brian Jones takes up site duties at an AA rated campsite to find out what goes on behind the scenes...

Who would be willing to employ me on a temporary basis I wondered? It was vitally important that the park owner and the staff should treat me as one of the employees, without any deference in respect of my 'day job'. The best operators take the view that they and the AA work in partnership to drive standards up and they look forward to our annual inspections, which give them direct, confidential and personal feedback on AA Quality Standards and how they apply them.

I was successful at my first attempt to find willing owners. Martyn and Sara Merckel, who own two very different sites in Cumbria, both franchised to The Camping and Caravanning Club, were happy to take me on. Eskdale Camping & Caravanning Site was to be my place of employment.

It was agreed with Martyn and Sara that I would join the team for a weekend in August, when the site was sure to be full of families, hopefully enjoying some good weather – but I decided to pack my wellies and waterproofs just in case. Two thoughts crossed my mind –

will they supply me with Marigolds to clean the toilets or shall I bring my own, but more worrying, whilst I am experienced at assessing standards under AA criteria, could I live up to their high employee expectations?

Friday, 10th August – Getting the hang of it all

The day had arrived and I must confess that I had not slept very well, with all thoughts of what lay ahead of me preying on my mind. On opening the curtains, I was greeted with glorious sunshine; had summer arrived at last? Surely this was a good omen. I knew from speaking with Martyn on the phone that Eskdale had suffered three weeks of continuous rain, with a very heavy downpour earlier in the week, but happily, the weekend forecast was good. I arrived at noon and was warmly greeted by Martyn, Sara and duty wardens Lisa and Rowan, who made me feel very welcome. After donning my distinctive Camping & Caravanning Club polo shirt, I immediately started work in the shop. As the computer booking system is complex and requires ▷

"I must have passed this initial test because Lisa promoted me to family bathroom cleaning on my own – success at last!"

training, I was relieved to learn I could opt out of this task if I wanted to – I had visions of crashing the entire Club website, so I declined.

Martyn left us to begin mowing the grass to make a final cut before the hoard of afternoon and evening arrivals; they were expecting 55 additional tents and motorhomes, which would take them to full capacity. In between serving in the

Brian & Lisa

shop, my jobs on the first day included emptying bins, checking the gents' toilets and explaining to new arrivals the site's facilities and giving them the emergency contact details. Sara trusted me to personally escort new arrivals to the backpackers' field, and it was good to see the delight on their faces as we crossed the free running beck over slate bridges to the adults-only camping areas.

The phone was constantly ringing and I could see the disappointment on Sara's face as she informed countless customers that the site was fully booked; business for campsite owners this wet year has either been feast or famine. As it happened, that afternoon some families turned up without a reservation and had to be turned away. Martyn, who was personally allocating pitches, did not wish to spoil the enjoyment of the majority in favour of his own short term financial gain. An exception was made in the late afternoon for two backpackers, one who had walked from Ambleside and the other from Tarn Hows; Sara told me that they will always find room for a backpacker, and it was a pleasure for me to personally escort those two hardy souls to a sheltered area on the field.

The shop was constantly busy, as customers purchased everything from

wine and beer to locally-sourced Cumberland sausage and bacon, and given the glorious weather, ice creams, ice cubes and chilled drinks too. Sara's previous experience in the retail industry is very evident in the variety of the items she has on sale. She knows full well that some visitors are bound to forget to pack an essential item, be it a can opener, or even a mug for their coffee – no worries, they will find them here.

It was good to interact with new arrivals and learn about their journeys, however frustrating – I heard about the usual problems on the M6 from south to north and of the Sat Nav users who discovered that the 'quick way' from M6 junction 36 took them over the Hardknott Pass, a route, some say, not dissimilar to the Italy's Amalfi coastal road – a rollercoaster ride that can test the nerves of both drivers and passengers!

It had been agreed that I would do the late shift the following day, so at 8.30pm Sara suggested that I finish my first day. Apart from a quick sandwich lunch at the house, I had been working for eight hours and the time had just flown by. As I departed for a shower and then a tasty meal at the nearby hostelry, Sara told me that with Martyn's skill they had managed to accommodate 65 new arrivals. On returning from the pub at 10.30pm, I noticed that the shop/reception was still open and found Martyn patiently waiting for three very late arrivals, even though at the time of booking they were asked to arrive by 8pm. I turned in for the night certain that the latecomers would still be greeted with a smile. Next day I found out that poor Martyn had finally retired to bed at 1.30am!

Saturday 11th August – New duties

I woke naturally, at 8am, and was surprised that I had slept for nine hours! After showering and shaving and with time to spare before my 10am start, on what was another sunny morning, I walked around the site observing happy couples and families who were enjoying their breakfasts alfresco, be it barbecued bacon and sausages or rolls and hot coffee.

The shop was already busy when I arrived to start my shift and after serving customers for a short time, Sara asked me to assist Rowan in cleaning two recently vacated camping pods. I quickly realised that at Eskdale, when it comes to cleaning there is a set of rules covering everything, from designated cleaning materials to a demanding attention to detail. First the pods are brushed out, then the portable vacuum is used, not only to pick up floor debris, but also to run along grooves in ceilings to catch potential stray spiders (apologies here to conservationist and Club President, David Bellamy). The windows and doors are then cleaned with a different solution, before a final mop to the interior and the decking. I must admit that the result was sweet smelling and very inviting.

Before I knew it, it was 11am and time to clean the amenities block. It was

Brian, Rowan, Martyn, Lisa & Sara

agreed that while Rowan was emptying the bins after breakfast, Lisa and I would start in the ladies' toilet and shower facilities. By now I was getting slightly confused with all the additional chemicals to be used. Lisa was very patient though and after demonstrating the procedure in the first toilet cubicle, I happily got the hang of it. First the bowl chemical was sprayed, followed by a different solution for exterior and seats, leaving a smear-free presentation. The shower cladding, both inside and outside, was next on the list, not forgetting the tops of doors and rails. Any slightly stained interior curtains were replaced with new ones, and the chrome fittings were cleaned with another different product to leave a sparkling finish. After sinks and mirrors, the final mopping was carried out with a solution that left a lingering citrus scent. I must have passed this initial test because Lisa promoted me to family bathroom cleaning on my own – success at last!

In the meantime, Rowan had started on the gents' facilities and I joined him to finish the cleaning. I noticed that he burst into song while working and wondered if it was a compulsory requirement, but decided to keep my vocal chords in check; I thought maybe I'd practice the next week by singing in the shower!

Whilst the more adventurous campers were now absent from the site, either walking or climbing in this Area of Outstanding Natural Beauty, many families remained on site, relaxing and enjoying the rare sunny weather. Lisa summed up the situation by saying that with no mobile signal, no TV signal and no Wi-fi, guests had to 'revert to nature' and engage in conversation or play games, without the distractions of social networking sites and other engineered forms of entertainment.

The day progressed with new visitors turning up, which included backpackers and pod users and, whilst it still required the professionalism and expertise of Martyn and Rowan to allocate the larger tent pitches, I was now the inductor of the smaller tent owners and was really ▷

beginning to feel like part of the team. At 6.30pm, Sara sent me off duty but asked me to join her and Martyn later for the nightly close down.

At about 10pm, after tackling the rapidly filling bins, I joined Sara and Martyn for the last amenities clean of the day. It was carried out with the same scrutiny as previously – the only difference to the day routine was the absence of chrome polishing! Campers were still using the showers while we were cleaning and expressed surprise that anyone would carry out such duties so late at night. An hour and half later Martyn and I took the final patrol to ensure there was no excess noise or fires alight, ending at the front barrier gate, which was locked for the night. And so, finally to bed!

Sunday 12th August – Up with the early birds

My earliest start yet, and the day began by observing Sara walking down to open the main gate just before 7am, with her eyes peeled to the left and right, obviously looking for anything out of the ordinary, perhaps unleashed dogs or discarded litter. One of the great things about Eskdale is that it is litter free. With a pristine appearance throughout the site, it would take a brave or ignorant soul to mar the presentation and, throughout my stay, I observed that even the little ones dropped their lolly wrappers and sticks in the bins provided.

On entering the shop as it opened, I met Charlie and Adrian, both teachers by profession, who had replaced Rowan and Lisa for a well-earned day off. Adrian, with my assistance on occasions, seemed to spend most of the time emptying bins as a large number of campers made ready to depart and, even though we had carried out a thorough clean of the amenities block late the previous night, regular checks by Charlie and Adrian ensured that toilet roll holders were refilled and showers mopped dry.

Saying Goodbye

All the effort and dedication put in by everyone at Eskadale doesn't go unnoticed and it was heartwarming to observe just how many departing campers made an effort to personally thank Sara, Martyn and the team (including me) for a memorable weekend.

So, all too soon my exceptional visit came to an end. Just before noon, I bid farewell to all as I started on my trek back home to north Wales, grateful for the opportunity to have toiled in such a friendly and industrious environment and hoping that my brief involvement had assisted the team in their demanding workload. I will have many happy memories of my time as a campsite worker, which has undoubtedly enhanced my respect and admiration for those who provide such a delightful countryside escape, and make a real difference to those who suffer the pressures of everyday life in the fast lane.

Below: The touring area. Right: Eskdale Pods

Eskdale Camping and Caravanning Site, is stunningly located on an unusually level area, surrounded by mountains, mature trees and with a beck running through, the only welcome distractions are the sounds of running water and birdsong. Although there are some spaces for motorhomes, this site is a haven for campers with facilities that include a lush backpackers' field, a camping barn and ten pods for hire. The top notch modern amenities block includes a fully serviced wet room-style family room with power showers, and a well-stocked shop. This site holds an AA Five Pennant rating with a very good AA Quality Score of 83%. See page 127

Ravenglass Camping & Caravanning Club Site, attractively terraced site amongst mature trees, colourful shrubs and pretty seasonal flowers, is geared towards caravans and motorhomes. This site is managed by dedicated wardens and holds an AA Three Pennant rating with a high AA Quality Score of 85%, demonstrating that it is an excellent example within its approved rating. See page 136

Shepherd's Delight

David Hancock discovers a new and enchanting way of getting away from it all in the Stour Valley

The growing trend for staying in quirky, often unusual places in wild and remote locations, perhaps an old windmill, a cliff-top lighthouse, or a secluded beach hut has become very popular. Luxury camping is increasingly a viable alternative to the choice of just another hotel room or cottage rental.

Despite some wet summers, camping can still be 'chic and cool', and many traditional camping parks have developed 'glamping' areas to lengthen their season and broaden their appeal to a wider cross-section of society. Wooden camping pods, replete with gravel terraces, are popping up everywhere, while Mongolian-style yurts on raised wooden floors, mini-reservations of tipis, solar-powered bell tents, and the odd 1950s Airstream trailer are increasingly found alongside traditional grass tent pitches and fully-serviced hardstanding pitches for caravans and motorhomes.

However, it's the new breed of quirky, eco-friendly boutique campsites, often found on isolated farms where such diversification has been key to their survival, that lead the glamping trend. On these you will now find refurbished gypsy caravans, elaborate, multi-roomed treehouses, luxuriously kitted-out yurts with king-size beds, en suite facilities and, perhaps, a hot tub. Posh shepherd's huts in peaceful glades are the latest trend, although two traditional campsites listed in this guide have them too – Harford Bridge Holiday Park near Tavistock, Devon, and Blackmore Vale Caravan and Camping Park near Shaftesbury, Dorset.

Borleymere – a little bit of paradise

To find Borleymere shepherd's hut first locate tiny Borley Green, a sleepy hamlet lost down meandering lanes in gently rolling and totally unspoilt Suffolk countryside, a world away but surprisingly close to Long Melford and the busy market town of Sudbury. Totally secluded and private, the wooden hut stands beside a lake and is surrounded by hazel woodland and glorious wild flower meadows in nine acres of land behind Jeremy and Charlotte Hamps's equally idyllic thatched cottage. With its own gated entrance down the lane and private access track through woodland, it really is the perfect spot to relax and escape the pressures of daily life. ▷

Above and below: Shepherd's hut interior

offer a unique 'glamping' experience for two people in a gorgeous hand-built shepherd's hut set in four acres. Traditionally these huts were temporary shelters for shepherds while they tended their sheep particularly at lambing time, and as they were on wheels they could be moved around the hillsides. The Borleymere hut (not moveable!) is bespoke-built by a craftsman from Framlingham, it is longer and wider than its forerunner, so as to accommodate a 6-foot long bed, but really looks the part with thick, rustic wooden axles, cast iron wheels, and a stable door.

It has been strategically placed beside a weeping willow tree at one end of the lake, with views across the lake to a small pontoon, and direct access to mown paths through the woodland and around the lake. In addition to the hut your secluded hideaway has a fully equipped kitchen cabin, smart decking with barbecue, posh teak chairs and bench, facing a brazier and the lake, a hammock under the willow tree, and a shower/compost loo cabin tucked into the edge of the woodland. You're not overlooked and it's totally private.

Chic retreat – all the comforts of home

Jeremy and Charlotte have been meticulous in planning, designing and kitting out the hut and kitchen cabin, so guests can really enjoy the tranquillity of the wild with all the comforts of home. However, don't expect mains power, wireless connection or a television, although phones can be charged at the nearby pump house, reached via a meandering path through the wild flower meadows. Here, you will also find two bikes for exploring the traffic-free lanes, a freezer full of ice packs for the kitchen

Having bought and split the vast field behind their cottage with a neighbour in 1997, they drained the area, planted the wild flower meadows and 3,400 trees, and began digging and developing the lake in 2001, planting natural reeds, shrubs and water-loving plants around the edge and introducing carp and trout. A decade on and the area is fully mature and a haven for wildlife, including moorhens, duck, hovering dragonflies and the occasional heron and kingfisher.

In 2012 Charlotte and Jeremy decided to share their little bit of paradise and cold box, and ready meals, if you can't face leaving this rural idyll to find a supermarket.

As for the hut, step through the stable door and be completely wowed by the design and quality of the interior and the general attention to detail that make it so snug and cosy. The roof is curved like a traditional hut, the decor is a tasteful cream with dark sage green window frames, the floor is laminate wood, and it is immaculately presented.

There's a proper built-in bed at the far end, beautifully made up with quality linen, a tweed wool throw, vintage floral print cushions, and the mattress is super comfortable. Underneath, in two wooden compartments are stored extra throws for cooler autumn nights and a hammock. On the long cream-painted shelf above the bed you'll find a DAB Roberts solar radio, a vintage-style clock, and an assortment of quirky local interest books. To read them, there is a bright rechargeable light under the shelf.

Under the window is a solid wood drop-leaf table, where you'll find the excellent information pack detailing local walks and cycle rides, places to visits and eat locally, and a jug filled with fresh wild flowers. There are also two simple wooden chairs, and you can sit and eat in comfort at the table if the weather is too inclement to eat alfresco. At the same time why not light the tiny wood-burning stove, set on a granite base in one corner, as it's stoked ready for use and you have all the necessary kit at hand – mini bellows, steel pan and brush, brass poker, and an iron pale for the ash.

Finally, along the wall opposite the table is a wooden two-door cabinet topped with a work surface containing single hob, which is perfect for brewing up tea first

"...be completely wowed by the design and quality of the interior..."

thing in the morning, a small round porcelain sink, and brass Victorian lamp. The cabinet stores all the essentials one needs in an electricity-free zone – spare tea light candles and an array of torches to choose from for the night time trek to the loo hut – as well as a hot water bottle with cover, a selection of games, a clothes line and pegs, a tablecloth, a first aid kit and a pair binoculars. A further shelf above the cabinet is where you will find the tea lights, a decorative red box containing spare matches, and essential reading material, including a guide to 'Self Sufficiency' and the Campervan Cookbook.

Surprisingly, the Hamps still found room for more detailed touches like a straw broom and an umbrella by the door, a wooden coat rack with padded hangers, tissues, chamomile and vanilla hand wash, and a make-up mirror.

Field kitchen heaven

Realising that living, cooking and eating in the hut could become cramped, let alone the lingering smell of food and, perhaps, the single hob being a little limiting on what you can prepare and cook, Jeremy and Charlotte decided to construct a wooden kitchen cabin

alongside the shepherd's hut. It complements the hut perfectly and their approach to kitting it out is as detailed as the hut, nothing has been forgotten and every conceivable luxury added to make cooking food in a field beside a lake as comfortable as possible.

Hidden away behind a thick, sliding plastic curtain (to keep the rain out) is a fully equipped field kitchen. Wooden shelves, the tiled work surface and plastic boxes are filled with everything you need. There's an old Belfast sink, a cooker with two gas hobs and an oven, a cool box lined with ice blocks for your food (another for your beer and wine), shelves laden with plates, glasses, cafetière, mugs, various oils and condiments, candles and re-chargeable torches, and jars of tea bags and fresh coffee. Neatly stored boxes are filled with cutlery, pots and pans and one for essentials like tea towels, foil, cling film, matches, candles and fire lighters. Batteries and gas containers are boxed in wood and recycling bins are tucked away behind the cabin.

On arrival you find a welcome basket of goodies containing fresh fruit, a loaf of bread, eggs, bacon and milk – perfect for your first morning's breakfast. ▷

Above: Shepherd's hut and field kitchen

which toilet is for 'pee' and which toilet is for 'poo', and that gents are welcome to wee in the woods..!

Alfresco living

When the sun shines on Borleymere your living space extends to acres rather than the confines of the hut when the weather is inclement. The hut and kitchen cabin are gorgeous and ooze home-from-home comforts, but combine them with hot and sunny weather and it's the outdoor space that makes a stay at Borleymere so memorable.

Under the shade of the willow tree you can doze or read a book in the hammock, stroll the lakeside and woodland paths, feed the fish from the pontoon, go for a swim in the lake, or potter around in the tiny dinghy that is moored on the bank.

Come evening, the decked area that links the hut with the kitchen cabin is where you can cook supper on the barbecue, then with the sun setting you can fire up the brazier and, with glass in hand, gaze across the lake from the bench beneath the willow tree, watching the arriving ducks and the fish rising to feed, or the magical Milky Way on a clear, starlit night.

If you can bear to leave...

You might not want to leave the tranquillity of Borleymere, a good book and comfy hammock may be all you need to relax and unwind. But, if the weather's not up to much, then there's a host of things to see and do and the excellent information folders in the hut are chock full of ideas.

Borrow the bikes and pootle along traffic-free lanes through rolling Suffolk farmland and wonderfully named villages, perhaps taking in the historic church at Belchamp Water, noted for its wall

The ablution cabin

Accessed via a small wooden bridge over a ditch and path (watch out for slugs at night) beside the woods, the eco-friendly wooden toilet and shower cabin blends into the trees, with hazel trunks used as the upright poles on the verandah. Instant gas-heated hot water is pumped

to an invigorating rain shower in a spacious wood-clad cubicle and washbasins in both cubicles, where you will find Charlotte's fragrant handmade soaps. Loos are of the compost variety, namely dry waterless toilets where no chemicals or cleaners are used.

Charlotte's witty notices inform you

paintings, en route to Gestingthorpe and a delicious lunch at The Pheasant. If a gentle walk is more your thing, take one of Charlotte's marked-up maps and explore the surrounding footpaths and hamlets.

A short drive, or a gentle bike ride away, is the historic village of Long Melford, noted for its fine timbered buildings, its many antique shops and galleries, and two stately homes and gardens, Kentwell Hall and Melford Hall. Lavenham is one of England's finest surviving medieval villages with a wealth of ancient timber-framed buildings and is not to be missed, especially The Guildhall on the Market Square and the grand church of St Peter and St Paul, which dominates the surrounding landscape. The picture-postcard villages of Cavendish, famous for its thatched cottages, and Clare, with its 13th-century Augustinian priory and range of independent shops, are well worth exploring.

In Sudbury you will find weekly markets and artist Thomas Gainsborough's birthplace, now a museum exhibiting collections of his work. Further east is Dedham Vale, often referred to as Constable Country as the area was famously the subject of John Constable's art. Flatford Mill features in some of his most famous paintings, including *The Hay Wain* and *Willy Lot's Cottage*.

There is much to enjoy is this tranquil, unspoilt area on the Suffolk/Essex border and Borleymere makes the perfect base, if you can bear to leave your private piece of paradise.

Essential Information
Borleymere Shepherd's Hut –
www.borleymereshepherdshuts.co.uk
Marketed through –
www.grove-cottages.co.uk

Above: Hammock beside the lake

Below: Ablution cabin

The Quiet Site

CAMPSITES
go green

By CLIVE GARRETT

Without doubt, camping has become more sophisticated as it follows market demands and works to cater for the needs of the modern camper. Gear has developed to such a degree that many traditional camping skills have become redundant, yet growing interest in the environment has led to something of a return to traditional camping values. This has created some interesting challenges, and campsites are at the fore when it comes to addressing these trends.

Camping back then

My early need to camp was driven by the desire to watch the wildlife and explore the countryside further afield from my home town. Given the fact that many places I visited did not have any sort of accommodation and, as a young teen with little money, my options were limited to an old cotton tent on a campsite or to finding a youth hostel.

Camping was a different beast in those days. Campsites were fields with a tap. You learnt vital skills like digging a 'lat trench' for the toilet and wet and dry pits for the kitchen, choosing the right wood for your cooking fire and, above all, how to leave the land so that there was little to no evidence of your passing. The camping gear used then appears unsophisticated to the modern eye but it was perfect for the style of the time. However, camping skills were far more advanced – and much was made about

the need to protect the countryside that provided so much enjoyment.

I love tent camping and consider it the true outdoor experience. It places you so close to nature, such as the time when a hedgehog foraging for its night time meal passed centimetres from my head, separated by less than a millimetre of material. Like me, you may be lucky enough to see a creature from the comfort of your sleeping bag if the doors are open or you have access to a low-level window from your bedroom compartment. With the possible exception of boating enthusiasts, is there anyone so close to the effects of the weather as those living under canvas?

Return to nature

Alongside financial considerations, escaping the daily grind by returning to nature is one of the key factors that is driving camping's popularity today. ▷

"…holidays in Britain's green and pleasant land work their wonders."

The Camping and Caravanning Club's ('The Club') President and celebrity botanist David Bellamy, says: "There are many research papers proving that patients in hospitals surrounded by trees and greensward get well quicker than those surrounded by concrete. Likewise, holidays in Britain's green and pleasant land work their wonders. Surely the 12 million people who pack their tents, caravans and motorhomes to find solace in the countryside cannot be wrong?"

Yet, while camping has proven benefits to health and wellbeing, the educational infrastructure to assist the millions who now enjoy camping to get the most out of our pastime is only just starting to meet the challenge. Much is down to the work carried out by campsite owners and organisations such as The Club. For instance, as the popularity of cotton tents has grown it has become apparent how few campers understand that such tents require different skills to use and maintain, compared to the synthetic tents that generations of campers are now familiar with. While Club data sheets help fill this knowledge gap, not many will understand how other techniques such as brailing a tent, or airing the ground, will benefit their camping experience.

Thankfully campsite owners do understand. Modern, large family tents with their full sewn-in groundsheets play havoc with grass over the time span of a family holiday – especially during rainy weather. Such is the damage from these groundsheets that site owners may have to re-turf the pitch or leave it fallow until the ground recovers.

Some owners are now introducing hardstandings for tents. Although this might sound horrendous, the benefits are obvious: a level pitch, a clean entry into the tent in bad weather, no grass cuttings or mud on the tent carpet etc. Once tried, campers seem to appreciate the 'comfort' provided by pea gravel on the hardstanding, and I, for one, am always happy to use such a pitch.

Any campsite owner tackling environmental issues will soon find that there is much to be gained. The local economic environment will be improved if the site creates new jobs and supports local suppliers; the natural environment will be improved if vast tracts of the countryside are managed to encourage wildlife, and the global environment will be improved if they implement policies that include energy and water conservation, waste management and sustainable tourism.

Encouraging wildlife
Ten years ago many campsites were considered pioneers in implementing solutions to many of these environmental issues. Now owners are reporting that 'green' features are expected because their visitors are accustomed to recycling, using energy efficient lighting and power supplies at home. However, sites continue to be recognised for their hard work and investment by schemes like the British Holiday & Home Parks Association, David Bellamy Conservation Awards, Green Tourism validation and various sustainable tourism awards.

Bellamy again: "Over the past 15 years I have received thousands of postcards from campers telling me in glowing terms that they have seen so much flora and fauna living on campsites. This is followed by a string of questions asking about a park's Bellamy rating because they want to see wildlife. Questions range from 'where can we see glow worms' to 'can we see the Milky Way?'"

Even simple changes can influence the amount of wildlife and also improve the camping experience. Bellamy says: "Hedges allow spacing and the right trees and bushes planted in the right places will encourage wildlife. They can also help protect and give privacy to pitches. ▷

Right: David Bellamy

Solar panels at The Quiet Site

Indeed, there are many campsites where the tent and caravan pitches face outwards so campers can watch the wildlife." He also points out the benefits to wildlife of the various water features like ponds and lakes that are often created on campsites – they are also a natural focus for campers to congregate and enjoy.

New schemes

Many site owners are now working on schemes that go far beyond simple landscape improvements – they combine a desire to improve visitor experience with firm business acumen. Take *The Quiet Site* in Cumbria. Here farmer and site owner Daniel Holder manages the site's waste water by using two reed beds, in the process creating wildlife sanctuaries and, by pumping back treated waste water to fulfil functions like flushing the toilets, helps save this valuable resource

while reducing overall costs. Such forward thinking is not always appreciated and it was only Daniel's determination and thorough research of the project that turned a sceptical planning authority in his favour.

Daniel, whose business is a recipient of Cumbria Tourism's 2012 Stainable Tourism Award, believes that operating a sound environmental policy makes good business sense and, just two of his many ideas are thermal solar panels to heat the washroom water, and tap aerators that halve water consumption.

No doubt there are big savings to be made through efficient waste management. Toilet flushing and watering the trees, bushes and plants use up a tremendous amount of water during the summer months and this strain can be alleviated through rainwater harvesting. Chris Woods of the *Teversal Camping and Caravanning Club Site* in Nottinghamshire

stores 9,000 litres of rainwater under his patio for use in the toilet block. However, instead of thermal solar power Chris has found that investing in the latest energy-saving boilers and storage facilities is the most efficient way to save resources while ensuring campers always have a ready supply of hot water. The block's chic interior is lit by sun tubes, while high speed hand dryers save more energy, and the underfloor heating keeps things warm and cosy. Environmentally-friendly and practical it may be, but the block also has a big wow factor.

For farmer Dominic Fairman of *South Penquite Farm* in Cornwall, an environmentally-friendly campsite naturally complements his organic business and work as a Countryside Steward. With this background he is very aware of non-renewable products and how chemicals like phosphates can affect the land and a water course. He is keen to recycle as much as possible and even his old silage wrap goes back to the manufacturer who turns it into picnic benches for the campsite.

While saving resources is important, as a camper himself Dominic also knows the value of providing a stress-free environment, as well as supporting his local community. Like many owners he is keen on sourcing locally-produced items while not competing with community resources like the local shop and pub. His yurts are made locally and the craftsman, being a trained 'backwoods man' now runs bushcraft courses from the site. Everything is geared towards education, and Dominic also runs field trips for schools, and classes for photographers and painters.

The support of local and camping communities is a vital role for the campsite owner. Over the years the Club's popular Eat Local campaign has grown to the point where most campsites promote local produce, so expect to find a selection of such goodies in the site shop – especially if camping on a working farm. It's always great to find something out of the ordinary. Such as Josh 'Guyrope Gourmet' Sutton (web: guyropegourmet. com) who enthusiastically preaches the culinary delights of outdoor cooking and runs an 'under canvas' cookery school on a campsite.

Continuing the good work
So what does the future hold? Recycling has now become the norm so other schemes are being thought of – owners can encourage cars and motorhomes to be left at the site for the duration of a holiday; they can assist in the creation of local bus routes to take campers out for the day; offer bike hire; supply details of cycling and walking routes, and, of

Above: South Penquite Farm

Right: Teversal's amenity block

course, provide seasonal pitches to reduce the need of towing a unit to and fro.

For Dominic Fairman the key will be a campsite's ability to demonstrate that they are a good neighbour and that they respect all aspects of the environment. He hopes that campers will take such messages on board and when back home will appreciate how much benefit was gained on their holiday – a belief shared by David Bellamy, who thinks good communication is vital.

It would appear that many campsite owners are singing from the same hymn sheet and that campers can expect an even greener experience over the next few years as various, and sometimes ground breaking, projects are implemented. Daniel Holder believes it could and should spread further: "I would

like to see other branches of the camping industries join us. An environmental policy walks hand-in-hand with business, and all benefit from the sustainable approach to camping. It is a no-brainer."

My thanks to David Bellamy; The Camping and Caravanning Club & Teversal Camping & Caravanning Club Site (www.campingandcaravanningclub. co.uk); The Quiet Site (www.thequietsite. co.uk); South Penquite Farm (www.southpenquite.co.uk)

Best for...

The AA thinks these are the best sites for...

...waterside pitches

ENGLAND

PENTEWAN SANDS HOLIDAY PARK,
Pentewan, Cornwall
SOUTH END CARAVAN PARK,
Barrow-in-Furness, Cumbria
SLENINGFORD WATERMILL CC PARK,
North Stainley, North Yorkshire
SWALE VIEW CARAVAN PARK,
Richmond, North Yorkshire

SCOTLAND

INVER MILL FARM CARAVAN PARK,
Dunkeld, Perth & Kinross
SKYE C&C CLUB SITE,
Edinbane, Isle of Skye

WALES

RIVERSIDE CAMPING,
Caernarfon, Gwynedd

NORTHERN IRELAND

DRUMAHEGLIS MARINA & CARAVAN PARK, Ballymoney, Co Antrim

...stunning views

ENGLAND

TRISTRAM C&C PARK,
Polzeath, Cornwall
TROUTBECK C&C CLUB SITE,
Troutbeck, Cumbria
SYKESIDE CAMPING PARK,
Patterdale, Cumbria
GALMPTON TOURING PARK,
Brixham, Devon
HIGHLANDS END HOLIDAY PARK,
Bridport, Dorset
NEW HALL FARM TOURING PARK,
Southwell, Nottinghamshire
WIMBLEBALL LAKE,
Dulverton, Somerset
HOWGILL LODGE,
Bolton Abbey, North Yorkshire
WOLDS WAY CARAVAN PARK,
West Knapton, North Yorkshire

CHANNEL ISLANDS

ROZEL CAMPING PARK,
St Martin, Jersey

SCOTLAND

OBAN C&C PARK, Oban, Argyll & Bute
LINNHE LOCHSIDE HOLIDAYS,
Corpach, Highland
INVERCOE C&C PARK,
Glencoe, Highland
JOHN O'GROATS CARAVAN SITE,
John O'Groats, Highland

WALES

BRON-Y-WENDON CARAVAN PARK,
Llanddulas, Conwy
BODNANT CARAVAN PARK,
Llanrwst, Conwy
BEACH VIEW CARAVAN PARK,
Abersoch, Gwynedd
TRAWSDIR TOURING C&C PARK,
Barmouth, Gwynedd
EISTEDDFA, Criccieth, Gwynedd
BARCDY TOURING C&C PARK,
Talsarnau, Gwynedd
CARREGLWYD C&C PARK,
Port Einon, Swansea

...good on-site restaurants

ENGLAND

STROUD HILL PARK,
St Ives, Cambridgeshire
TRISTRAM C&C PARK,
Polzeath, Cornwall
BINGHAM GRANGE T&C PARK,
Bridport, Dorset
HIGHLANDS END HOLIDAY PARK,
Bridport, Dorset
BAY VIEW HOLIDAY PARK,
Bolton-Le-Sands, Lancashire
THE OLD BRICK KILNS,
Barney, Norfolk
BEACONSFIELD FARM CARAVAN PARK, Shrewsbury, Shropshire

CHANNEL ISLANDS

BEUVELANDE CAMP SITE,
St Martin, Jersey

SCOTLAND

GLEN NEVIS C&C PARK,
Fort William, Highland

...top toilets

ENGLAND

CARNON DOWNS C&C PARK,
Truro, Cornwall
BEECH CROFT FARM,
Buxton, Derbyshire
RIVERSIDE C&C PARK,
South Molton, Devon
SHAMBA HOLIDAYS,
St Leonards, Dorset
TEVERSAL C&CC SITE,
Teversal, Nottinghamshire
DELL TOURING PARK,
Bury St Edmunds, Suffolk
MOON & SIXPENCE,
Woodbridge, Suffolk
RIVERSIDE CARAVAN PARK,
High Bentham, North Yorkshire
WAYSIDE HOLIDAY PARK,
Pickering, North Yorkshire
MOOR LODGE PARK,
Bardsey, West Yorkshire

SCOTLAND

SKYE C&C CLUB SITE,
Edinbane, Isle of Skye
BEECRAIGS C&C SITE,
Linlithgow, West Lothian

...on-site fishing

ENGLAND

FIELDS END WATER CP,
Doddington, Cambridgeshire
BACK OF BEYOND TOURING PARK,
St Leonards, Dorset
BLACKMORE VALE C&C PARK,
Shaftesbury, Dorset
WOODLAND WATERS,
Ancaster, Lincolnshire
SALTFLEETBY FISHERIES,
Saltfleetby by Peter, Lincolnshire
LAKESIDE CARAVAN PARK & FISHERIES, Downham Market, Norfolk
THORNEY LAKES CARAVAN PARK,
Langport, Somerset

MARSH FARM CARAVAN SITE, & CARLTON MERES COUNTRY PARK Saxmundham, Suffolk
SUMNERS PONDS FISHERY & CAMPSITE, Barns Green, West Sussex

SCOTLAND

HODDOM CASTLE CARAVAN PARK, Ecclefechan, Dumfries & Galloway
MILTON OF FONAB CARAVAN SITE, PITLOCHRY, Perth & Kinross
GART CARAVAN PARK, Callander, Stirling

WALES

AFON TEIFI C&C PARK, Newcastle Emlyn, Carmarthenshire
YNYSYMAENGWYN CARAVAN PARK, Tywyn, Gwynedd

...the kids

ENGLAND

TREVORNICK HOLIDAY PARK, Holywell Bay, Cornwall
EDEN VALLEY HOLIDAY PARK, Lostwithiel, Cornwall
GOLDEN VALLEY C&C PARK, Ripley, Derbyshire
FRESHWATER BEACH HOLIDAY PARK, Bridport, Dorset
SANDY BALLS HOLIDAY CENTRE, Fordingbridge, Hampshire
HEATHLAND BEACH CARAVAN PARK, Kessingland, Suffolk
GOLDEN SQUARE TOURING PARK, Helmsley, North Yorkshire
RIVERSIDE CARAVAN PARK, High Bentham, North Yorkshire
GOOSEWOOD CARAVAN PARK, Sutton-on-the-Forest, North Yorkshire

SCOTLAND

BLAIR CASTLE CARAVAN PARK, Blair Atholl, Perth & Kinross

WALES

HOME FARM CARAVAN PARK, Marian-Glas, Isle of Anglesey
HENDRE MYNACH TOURING C&C PARK, Barmouth, Gwynedd

TRAWSDIR TOURING C&C PARK, BARMOUTH, Gwynedd

...being eco-friendly

ENGLAND

SOUTH PENQUITE FARM, Blisland, Cornwall
RIVER DART COUNTRY PARK, Ashburton, Devon
BROOK LODGE FARM C&C PARK, Cowslip Green, Somerset

SCOTLAND

SHIELING HOLIDAYS, Craignure, Isle of Mull

WALES

CAERFAI BAY CARAVAN & TENT PARK, St David's, Pembrokeshire

...glamping it up
and staying in a pod or wigwam

ENGLAND

TREGOAD PARK, LOOE, Cornwall
RUTHERN VALLEY HOLIDAYS, Ruthernbridge, Cornwall
LOW WRAY NATIONAL TRUST CAMPSITE, Ambleside Cumbria
WILD ROSE PARK, Appleby-in-Westmorland, Cumbria (wigwams)
ESKDALE C&C CLUB SITE, Boot, Cumbria
GREAT LANGDALE NATIONAL TRUST CAMPSITE, Great Langdale, Cumbria
WOODCLOSE CARAVAN PARK, Kirkby Lonsdale, Cumbria (wigwams)
WASDALE HEAD NATIONAL TRUST CAMPSITE, Wasdale Head, Cumbria
THE QUIET SITE, Watermillock, Cumbria
LEE VALLEY CAMPSITE, London E4
BELLINGHAM C&C CLUB SITE, Bellingham, Northumberland
COTSWOLD VIEW TOURING PARK, Charlbury, Oxfordshire

SCOTLAND

LINWATER CARAVAN PARK, East Calder, West Lothian

...or staying in a yurt

ENGLAND

SOUTH PENQUITE FARM, Blisland, Cornwall
TREVELLA TOURIST PARK, Crantock, Cornwall
GREAT LANGDALE NATIONAL TRUST CAMPSITE, Great Langdale, Cumbria
BLACKMORE VALE C&C PARK, Shaftesbury, Dorset
ACTON FIELD CAMPING SITE, Swanage, Dorset
HERSTON C&C PARK, Swanage, Dorset

...or staying in a tipi

ENGLAND

LOW WRAY NATIONAL TRUST CAMPSITE, Ambleside, Cumbria
SYKESIDE CAMPING PARK, Patterdale, Cumbria
BLACKMORE VALE C&C PARK, Shaftesbury, Dorset
SANDY BALLS HOLIDAY CENTRE, Fordingbridge, Hampshire
ROEBECK CAMPING & CARAVAN PARK, Ryde, Isle of Wight

WALES

EISTEDDFA, Criccieth, Gwynedd

...or staying in a safari tent

ENGLAND

TREVELLA TOURIST PARK, Crantock, Cornwall
BURNHAM-ON-SEA HOLIDAY VILLAGE, Burnham-on-Sea, Somerset

...or staying in a shepherd's hut

ENGLAND

HARFORD BRIDGE HOLIDAY PARK, Tavistock, Devon
BLACKMORE VALE C&C PARK, Shaftesbury, Dorset

Premier Parks ▶▶▶▶▶

ENGLAND

BERKSHIRE
HURLEY
Hurley Riverside Park

CAMBRIDGESHIRE
DODDINGTON
Fields End Water C P & Fishery
ST IVES
Stroud Hill Park

CHESHIRE
CODDINGTON
Manor Wood Country Caravan Park
WHITEGATE
Lamb Cottage Caravan Park

CORNWALL
BUDE
Wooda Farm Holiday Park
CARLYON BAY
Carlyon Bay Caravan & Camping Park
CRANTOCK
Trevella Tourist Park
GOONHAVERN
Silverbow Park
LEEDSTOWN
Calloose Caravan & Camping Park
LOSTWITHIEL
Eden Valley Holiday Park
MEVAGISSEY
Seaview International Holiday Park
PADSTOW
Padstow Touring Park
PENTEWAN
Sun Valley Holiday Park
REDRUTH
Globe Vale Holiday Park
REJERRAH
Newperran Holiday Park
ST AUSTELL
River Valley Holiday Park
ST IVES
Ayr Holiday Park
Polmanter Touring Park
ST JUST-IN-ROSELAND
Trethem Mill Touring Park
ST MERRYN
Atlantic Bays Holiday Park
ST MINVER
Gunvenna Caravan Park

TRURO
Carnon Downs Caravan & Camping Park
Cosawes Park
Truro Caravan and Camping Park
WATERGATE BAY
Watergate Bay Touring Park

CUMBRIA
AMBLESIDE
Skelwith Fold Caravan Park
APPLEBY-IN-WESTMORLAND
Wild Rose Park
BOOT
Eskdale C & C Club Site
KESWICK
Castlerigg Hall Caravan & Camping Park
KIRKBY LONSDALE
Woodclose Caravan Park
TROUTBECK [NEAR KESWICK]
Troutbeck C & C Club Site
WINDERMERE
Park Cliffe Camping & Caravan Estate

DEVON
BRAUNTON
Hidden Valley Park
CLYST ST MARY
Crealy Meadows C& C Park
DARTMOUTH
Woodlands Grove C & C Park
DAWLISH
Cofton Country Holidays
KINGSBRIDGE
Parkland Caravan and Camping Site
NEWTON ABBOT
Dornafield
Ross Park
SIDMOUTH
Oakdown Country Holiday Park
TAVISTOCK
Woodovis Park

DORSET
ALDERHOLT
Hill Cottage Farm C & C Park
BRIDPORT
Bingham Grange T & C Park
Highlands End Holiday Park
CHARMOUTH
Wood Farm Caravan & Camping Park
CHRISTCHURCH
Meadowbank Holidays

LYTCHETT MINSTER
South Lytchett Manor C & C Park
ST LEONARDS
Shamba Holidays
WAREHAM
Wareham Forest Tourist Park
WEYMOUTH
East Fleet Farm Touring Park
WIMBORNE MINSTER
Merley Court
Wilksworth Farm Caravan Park

HAMPSHIRE
ROMSEY
Hill Farm Caravan Park

HEREFORDSHIRE
PEMBRIDGE
Townsend Touring Park

KENT
ASHFORD
Broadhembury Caravan & Camping Park
MARDEN
Tanner Farm Touring C & C Park

LANCASHIRE
SILVERDALE
Silverdale Caravan Park
THORNTON
Kneps Farm Holiday Park

LINCOLNSHIRE
WOODHALL SPA
Woodhall Country Park

NORFOLK
BARNEY
The Old Brick Kilns
BELTON
Rose Farm Touring & Camping Park
CLIPPESBY
Clippesby Hall
NORTH WALSHAM
Two Mills Touring Park

NORTHUMBERLAND
BELLINGHAM
Bellingham C & C Club Site
BERWICK-UPON-TWEED
Ord House Country Park

NOTTINGHAMSHIRE
TEVERSAL
Teversal C & C Club Site

OXFORDSHIRE
HENLEY-ON-THAMES
Swiss Farm Touring & Camping
STANDLAKE
Lincoln Farm Park Oxfordshire

SHROPSHIRE
BRIDGNORTH
Stanmore Hall Touring Park
SHREWSBURY
Beaconsfield Farm Caravan Park
Oxon Hall Touring Park
TELFORD
Severn Gorge Park

SOMERSET
GLASTONBURY
The Old Oaks Touring Park
PORLOCK
Porlock Caravan Park
WELLS
Wells Holiday Park
WIVELISCOMBE
Waterrow Touring Park

SUFFOLK
WOODBRIDGE
Moon & Sixpence

SUSSEX, EAST
BEXHILL
Kloofs Caravan Park

WIGHT, ISLE OF
NEWBRIDGE
The Orchards Holiday Caravan Park
RYDE
Whitefield Forest Touring Park
WROXALL
Appuldurcombe Gardens Holiday Park

WORCESTERSHIRE
HONEYBOURNE
Ranch Caravan Park

YORKSHIRE, NORTH
ALLERSTON
Vale of Pickering Caravan Park
ALNE
Alders Caravan Park
HARROGATE
Ripley Caravan Park
Rudding Holiday Park

HELMSLEY
Golden Square Touring Caravan Park
HIGH BENTHAM
Riverside Caravan Park
OSMOTHERLEY
Cote Ghyll Caravan & Camping Park
SCARBOROUGH
Jacobs Mount Caravan Park
SUTTON-ON-THE-FOREST
Goosewood Caravan Park
WYKEHAM
St Helens Caravan Park

CHANNEL ISLANDS

JERSEY
ST MARTIN
Beuvelande Camp Site

SCOTLAND

ABERDEENSHIRE
HUNTLY
Huntly Castle Caravan Park

DUMFRIES & GALLOWAY
BRIGHOUSE BAY
Brighouse Bay Holiday Park
CREETOWN
Castle Cary Holiday Park
ECCLEFECHAN
Hoddom Castle Caravan Park

EAST LOTHIAN
DUNBAR
Thurston Manor Leisure Park

FIFE
ST ANDREWS
Craigtoun Meadows Holiday Park
FIFE
Cairnsmill Holiday Park

HIGHLAND
CORPACH
Linnhe Lochside Holidays

PERTH & KINROSS
BLAIR ATHOLL
Blair Castle Caravan Park
River Tilt Caravan Park

STIRLING
ABERFOYLE
Trossachs Holiday Park

WALES

ANGLESEY, ISLE OF
DULAS
Tyddyn Isaf Caravan Park
MARIAN-GLAS
Home Farm Caravan Park

CARMARTHENSHIRE
LLANDOVERY
Erwlon Caravan & Camping Park
NEWCASTLE EMLYN
Cenarth Falls Holiday Park

CONWY
LLANDDULAS
Bron-Y-Wendon Caravan Park
LLANRWST
Bron Derw Touring Caravan Park

GWYNEDD
BARMOUTH
Hendre Mynach Touring C & C Park
Trawsdir Touring Caravans & C P
TAL-Y-BONT
Islawrffordd Caravan Park

MONMOUTHSHIRE
USK
Pont Kemys Caravan & Camping Park

PEMBROKESHIRE
ST DAVIDS
Caerfai Bay Caravan & Tent Park

POWYS
BRECON
Pencelli Castle Caravan & Camping Park

WREXHAM
EYTON
The Plassey Leisure Park

NORTHERN IRELAND

CO ANTRIM
BALLYMONEY
Drumaheglis Marina & Caravan Park
BUSHMILLS
Ballyness Caravan Park

CO FERMANAGH
BELCOO
Rushin House Caravan Park

AA Holiday Centres

ENGLAND

CORNWALL
BUDE
Sandymouth Holiday Park
HAYLE
St Ives Bay Holiday Park
HOLYWELL BAY
Holywell Bay Holiday Park
Trevornick Holiday Park
LOOE
Tencreek Holiday Park
MULLION
Mullion Holiday Park
NEWQUAY
Hendra Holiday Park
Newquay Holiday Park
PERRANPORTH
Perran Sands Holiday Park
ST MERRYN
Harlyn Sands Holiday Park
WIDEMOUTH BAY
Widemouth Bay Caravan Park

CUMBRIA
FLOOKBURGH
Lakeland Leisure Park
POOLEY BRIDGE
Park Foot C&C Park
SILLOTH
Stanwix Park Holiday Centre

DEVON
CROYDE BAY
Ruda Holiday Park
DAWLISH
Lady's Mile Holiday Park
EXMOUTH
Devon Cliffs Holiday Park
MORTEHOE
Twitchen House Holiday Park
PAIGNTON
Beverley Parks C&C Park
SHALDON
Coast View Holiday Park
WOOLACOMBE
Golden Coast Holiday Park
Woolacombe Bay Holiday Park
Woolacombe Sands Holiday Park

DORSET
BRIDPORT
Freshwater Beach Holiday Park
West Bay Holiday Park
HOLTON HEATH
Sandford Holiday Park
POOLE
Rockley Park
WEYMOUTH
Littlesea Holiday Park
Seaview Holiday Park

ESSEX
CLACTON-ON-SEA
Highfield Grange
Martello Beach Holiday Park
MERSEA ISLAND
Waldegraves Holiday Park
ST LAWRENCE
Waterside St Lawrence Bay
ST OSYTH
The Orchards Holiday Park
WALTON ON THE NAZE
Naze Marine

CO DURHAM
BLACKHALL COLLIERY
Crimdon Dene

HAMPSHIRE
FORDINGBRIDGE
Sandy Balls Holiday Centre

KENT
EASTCHURCH
Warden Springs Caravan Park

LANCASHIRE
BLACKPOOL
Marton Mere Holiday Village

LINCOLNSHIRE
CLEETHORPES
Thorpe Park Holiday Centre
MABLETHORPE
Golden Sands Holiday Park
SALTFLEET
Sunnydale

MERSEYSIDE
SOUTHPORT
Riverside Holiday Park

NORFOLK
BELTON
Wild Duck Holiday Park
BURGH CASTLE
Breydon Water
CAISTER-ON-SEA
Caister Holiday Park
GREAT YARMOUTH
Vauxhall Holiday Park
HUNSTANTON
Manor Park Holiday Village
Searles Leisure Resort

NORTHUMBERLAND
BERWICK-UPON-TWEED
Haggerston Castle
NORTH SEATON
Sandy Bay

SOMERSET
BREAN
Holiday Resort Unity
Warren Farm Holiday Centre
BRIDGWATER
Mill Farm C&C Park
BURNHAM-ON-SEA
Burnham-on-Sea Holiday Village
CHEDDAR
Broadway House Holiday Park

SUFFOLK
KESSINGLAND
Kessingland Beach Holiday Park

SUSSEX, EAST
CAMBER
Camber Sands

SUSSEX, WEST
SELSEY
Warner Farm Touring Park

WIGHT, ISLE OF
COWES
Thorness Bay Holiday Park
SHANKLIN
Lower Hyde Holiday Park
ST HELENS
Nodes Point Holiday Park
WHITECLIFF BAY
Whitecliff Bay Holiday Park

YORKSHIRE, EAST RIDING OF
SKIPSEA
Skirlington Leisure Park
TUNSTALL
Sand le Mere Holiday Village
WITHERNSEA
Withernsea Sands

YORKSHIRE, NORTH
FILEY
Blue Dolphin Holiday Park
Flower of May Holiday Park
Primrose Valley Holiday Park
Reighton Sands Holiday Park

SCOTLAND
DUMFRIES & GALLOWAY
GATEHOUSE OF FLEET
Auchenlarie Holiday Park
SOUTHERNESS
Southerness Holiday Village

EAST LOTHIAN
LONGNIDDRY
Seton Sands Holiday Village

HIGHLAND
DORNOCH
Grannie's Heilan Hame HP
NAIRN
Nairn Lochloy Holiday Park

NORTH AYRSHIRE
SALTCOATS
Sandylands

PERTH & KINROSS
TUMMEL BRIDGE
Tummel Valley Holiday Park

SCOTTISH BORDERS
EYEMOUTH
Eyemouth

SOUTH AYRSHIRE
AYR
Craig Tara Holiday Park
COYLTON
Sundrum Castle Holiday Park

WALES
CEREDIGION
BORTH
Brynowen Holiday Park

CONWY
TOWYN
Ty Mawr Holiday Park

DENBIGHSHIRE
PRESTATYN
Presthaven Sands

GWYNEDD
PORTHMADOG
Greenacres
PWLLHELI
Hafan Y Mor Holiday Park

PEMBROKESHIRE
TENBY
Kiln Park Holiday Centre

SWANSEA
SWANSEA
Riverside Caravan Park

Adults – No Children Parks

Over 40 of the parks in the AA pennant rating scheme have opted to provide facilities for adults only, and do not accept children. The minimum age for individual parks may be 18, or 21, while one or two pitch the limit even higher. For more information please contact the individual parks.

ENGLAND

CAMBRIDGESHIRE
Fields End Water CP & Fishery, Doddington
Stroud Hill Park, St Ives

CHESHIRE
New Farm Caravan Park, Wettenhall
Lamb Cottage Caravan Park, Whitegate

CORNWALL
St Day Touring Park, St Day
Wayfarers C & C Park, St Hilary

CUMBRIA
Green Acres Caravan Park, Carlisle
Larches Caravan Park, Mealsgate

DERBYSHIRE
Clover Fields Touring CP, Buxton

DEVON
Woodland Springs Adult TP, Drewsteignton
Zeacombe House CP, East Anstey
Widdicombe Farm TP, Torquay

DORSET
Bingham Grange T&CP, Bridport
Fillybrook Farm TP, Hurn
Back of Beyond TP, St Leonards

HEREFORDSHIRE
Arrow Bank Holiday Park, Eardisland
Cuckoo's Corner Campsite, Moreton on Lugg

LINCOLNSHIRE
Orchard Park, Boston
Long Acres Touring Park, Boston

NORFOLK
Two Mills Touring Park, North Walsham
The Rickels C&C Park, Stanhoe
Breckland Meadows TP, Swaffham
Lode Hall HP, Three Holes

NOTTINGHAMSHIRE
New Hall Farm Touring Park, Southwell

SHROPSHIRE
Beaconsfield Farm CP, Shrewsbury

SHROPSHIRE
Severn Gorge Park, Telford

SOMERSET
Exe Valley Caravan Site, Bridgetown
Cheddar Bridge Touring Park, Cheddar
The Old Oaks Touring Park, Glastonbury
Long Hazel Park, Sparkford
Greenacres Touring Park, Wellington
Homestead Park, Wells
Wells Holiday Park, Wells
Waterrow Touring Park, Wiveliscombe

SUFFOLK
Moat Barn Touring CP, Woodbridge

WEST MIDLANDS
Somers Wood Caravan Park, Meriden

WIGHT, ISLE OF
Riverside Paddock Camp Site, Newport

YORKSHIRE, EAST RIDING OF
Blue Rose Caravan Country Park, Brandesburton

YORKSHIRE, NORTH
Shaws Trailer Park, Harrogate
Foxholme Caravan Park, Helmsley
Maustin Caravan Park, Netherby

YORKSHIRE, WEST
Moor Lodge Park, Leeds
St Helena's Caravan Park, Leeds

WALES

PEMBROKESHIRE
Rosebush Caravan Park, Rosebush

POWYS
Riverside C&C Park, Crickhowell
Dalmore C&C Park, Llandrindod Wells

England

The Westbury White Horse, Wiltshire

ISLE OF - Places incorporating the words 'Isle of' or 'Isle' will be found under the actual name, eg Isle of Wight is listed under Wight, Isle of. Channel Islands and Isle of Man, however, are between England and Scotland, and there is also a section in the guide for Scottish Islands.

BERKSHIRE

FINCHAMPSTEAD — Map 5 SU76

Places to visit

West Green House Gardens, HARTLEY WINTNEY 01252 844611 www.westgreenhouse.co.uk

Museum of English Rural Life, READING 0118 378 8660 www.merl.org.uk

Great for kids: The Look Out Discovery Centre, BRACKNELL 01344 354400 www.bracknell-forest.gov.uk/be

▶▶▶ 79% California Chalet & Touring Park *(SU788651)*

Nine Mile Ride RG40 4HU
☎ 0118 973 3928
e-mail: enquiries@californiapark.co.uk
dir: From A321 (S of Wokingham), right onto B3016 to Finchampstead. Follow Country Park signs on Nine Mile Ride

* 🚐 £23-£30 🚐 £23-£30 ▲ £17-£45

Open all year

Last arrival flexible Last departure noon

A simple, peaceful woodland site with secluded pitches among the trees, adjacent to the country park. Several pitches have a prime position beside

the lake with their own fishing area. Two new large hardstandings have been created, with more planned for 2013, the chalet accommodation has been upgraded and the toilet block revamped with quality vanitory units and fully tiled showers. Trees have been thinned to allow more sun onto pitches and future investment plans are very positive for this well located park. 5.5 acre site. 44 touring pitches. 44 hardstandings. Caravan pitches. Motorhome pitches. Tent pitches.

AA Pubs & Restaurants nearby: The Broad Street Tavern, Wokingham 0118 977 3706

L'ortolan, Shinfield 0118 988 8500

Facilities: 🎣 ⊙ ☕ 🅿 & 🚿 ᴡɪꜰɪ ♻ 🔵

Services: 🔌 🔟 🔒 🇹 📮 ♻

Within 3 miles: ⛳ 🏇 🎣 ◎ 🍴 🔵 U

Notes: No ground fires, no washing of caravans. Dogs must be kept on leads.

HURLEY

Places to visit

Cliveden, CLIVEDEN 01628 605069 www.nationaltrust.org.uk/cliveden

The Hell-Fire Caves, WEST WYCOMBE 01494 524411 (office) www.hellfirecaves.co.uk

Great for kids: Bekonscot Model Village and Railway, BEACONSFIELD 01494 672919 www.bekonscot.co.uk

PREMIER PARK

▶▶▶▶▶ 82% Hurley Riverside Park *(SU826839)*

Park Office SL6 5NE
☎ 01628 824493 & 823501
e-mail: info@hurleyriversidepark.co.uk
dir: Signed off A4130 (Henley to Maidenhead road), just W of Hurley

* 🚐 £15-£27 🚐 £15-£27 ▲ £13-£24

Open Mar-Oct

Last arrival 20.00hrs Last departure noon

A large Thames-side site with a good touring area close to river. A quality park with three beautifully appointed toilet blocks, one of which houses quality, fully-serviced unisex facilities. Level grassy pitches are sited in small, sectioned areas, and this is a generally peaceful setting. There are furnished tents for hire. 15 acre site. 200 touring pitches. 18 hardstandings. Caravan pitches. Motorhome pitches. Tent pitches. 290 statics.

LEISURE: 🏊 Indoor swimming pool 🏊 Outdoor swimming pool 🎢 Children's playground 🧒 Kid's club 🎾 Tennis court 🎱 Games room 📺 Separate TV room ⛳ 9/18 hole golf course 🚣 Boats for hire 🎬 Cinema 🎵 Entertainment 🎣 Fishing ◎ Mini golf 🎿 Watersports 🏋 Gym 🏟 Sports field Spa U Stables
FACILITIES: 🛁 Bath 🚿 Shower ⊙ Electric shaver 🅿 Hairdryer ❄ Ice Pack Facility & Disabled facilities ☎ Public telephone 🛒 Shop on site or within 200yds 🏪 Mobile shop (calls at least 5 days a week) 🍴 BBQ area 🌳 Picnic area ᴡɪꜰɪ Wi-fi 💻 Internet access ♻ Recycling 🔵 Tourist info 🐕 Dog exercise area

AA Pubs & Restaurants nearby: Black Boys Inn, Hurley 01628 824212

Hotel du Vin & Bistro Henley-on-Thames 01491 848400

Hurley Riverside Park

Leisure:

Facilities:

Services:

Within 3 miles:

Notes: No unsupervised children, no young groups, no commercial vehicles, quiet park policy, max 2 dogs. Dogs must be kept on leads. Fishing in season, slipway, nature trail, riverside picnic grounds.

see advert on opposite page

NEWBURY

Places to visit

Highclere Castle & Gardens, HIGHCLERE 01635 253210 www.highclerecastle.co.uk

West Berkshire Museum, NEWBURY 01635 519231 www.westberkshiremuseum.org.uk

Great for kids: The Living Rainforest, HAMPSTEAD NORREYS 01635 202444 www.livingrainforest.org

NEWBURY Map 5 SU46

►►► 80% *Bishops Green Farm Camp Site* *(SU502630)*

Bishops Green RG20 4JP
☎ 01635 268365
dir: *Exit A339 (opposite New Greenham Park) towards Bishops Green & Ecchinswell. Site on left, approx 0.5m by barn*

Open Apr-Oct

Last arrival 21.30hrs

A sheltered and secluded meadowland park close to the Hampshire/Berkshire border, offering very clean and well-maintained facilities, including a toilet block with a disabled/family room. There are woodland and riverside walks to be enjoyed around the farm, and coarse fishing is also available. The site is very convenient for visiting the nearby market town of Newbury with its attractive canal in the town centre. 1.5 acre site. 30 touring pitches. 6 hardstandings. Caravan pitches. Motorhome pitches. Tent pitches.

AA Pubs & Restaurants nearby: The Yew Tree Inn, near Highclere 01635 253360

Facilities:

Services:

Within 3 miles:

Notes: Dogs must be kept on leads.

RISELEY

Places to visit

Basildon Park, LOWER BASILDON 0118 984 3040 www.nationaltrust.org.uk/basildonpark

Mapledurham House, MAPLEDURHAM 0118 972 3350 www.mapledurham.co.uk

Great for kids: Beale Park, LOWER BASILDON 0870 777 7160 www.bealepark.co.uk

RISELEY Map 5 SU76

►►► 84% Wellington Country Park *(SU728628)*

Odiham Rd RG7 1SP
☎ 0118 932 6444
e-mail: info@wellington-country-park.co.uk
web: www.wellington-country-park.co.uk
dir: *M4 junct 11, A33 south towards Basingstoke. M3 junct 5, B3349 north towards Reading*

Open Mar-Nov

Last arrival 17.30hrs Last departure noon

A peaceful woodland site, popular with families, set within an extensive country park, which comes complete with lakes and nature trails, and these are accessible to campers after the country park closes. There's also a herd of Red and Fallow deer that roam the meadow area. This site is ideal for those travelling on the M4. 80 acre site. 72 touring pitches. 10 hardstandings. Caravan pitches. Motorhome pitches. Tent pitches.

AA Pubs & Restaurants nearby: The George & Dragon, Swallowfield 0118 988 4432

Leisure:

Facilities:

Services:

Within 3 miles:

Notes: No open fires, latest arrival time 16.30hrs low season. Dogs must be kept on leads. Miniature railway, crazy golf, maze, animal corner, access to Country Park.

BRISTOL

BRISTOL

See Cowslip Green, Somerset

CAMBRIDGESHIRE

COMBERTON Map 12 TL35

Places to visit

Imperial War Museum Duxford, DUXFORD 01223 835000 www.iwm.org.uk/duxford

Audley End House & Gardens, AUDLEY END 01799 522842 www.english-heritage.org.uk

Great for kids: Linton Zoological Gardens, LINTON 01223 891308 www.lintonzoo.co.uk

►►►► 91% Highfield Farm Touring Park *(TL389572)*

Long Rd CB23 7DG
☎ 01223 262308
e-mail: enquiries@highfieldfarmtouringpark.co.uk
dir: *From M11 junct 12, take A603 (Sandy) for 0.5m, then right onto B1046 to Comberton*

🚐 🚌 ⛺

Open Apr-Oct

Last arrival 22.00hrs Last departure 14.00hrs

Run by a very efficient and friendly family, the park is on a well-sheltered hilltop, with spacious pitches including a cosy backpackers/cyclists' area, and separate sections for couples and families. There is a one and a half mile marked walk around the family farm, with stunning views. 8 acre site. 120 touring pitches. 52 hardstandings. Caravan pitches. Motorhome pitches. Tent pitches.

AA Pubs & Restaurants nearby: The Three Horseshoes, Madingley 01954 210221

Restaurant 22, Cambridge 01223 351880

Leisure: 🛝

Facilities: 🚿 ⊙ 💨 ❄ ☎ [S] 🐕 [Wi-fi] ℹ

Services: 🧺 ⊡ 🔒 🔥 [T] 🍴 ⚓

Within 3 miles: ⛳ 🎣 [S] ⊡ U

Notes: ⊘ Dogs must be kept on leads. Postbox.

DODDINGTON Map 12 TL49

Places to visit

WWT Welney Wetland Centre, WELNEY 01353 860711 www.wwt.org.uk

Flag Fen Archaeology Park, PETERBOROUGH 01733 313414 www.flagfen.org

PREMIER PARK

►►►►► 83% Fields End Water Caravan Park & Fishery *(TL378908)*

Benwick Rd PE15 0TY
☎ 01354 740199
e-mail: info@fieldsendfishing.co.uk
dir: *Exit A141, follow signs to Doddington. At clock tower in Doddington turn right into Benwick Rd. Site 1.5m on right after sharp bends*

* 🚐 £16-£20 🚌 £16-£20 ⛺ £14-£17

Open all year

Last arrival 20.30hrs Last departure noon

This meticulously planned and executed park makes excellent use of its slightly elevated position in The Fens. The 33 fully serviced pitches, all with very generous hardstandings, are on smart terraces with sweeping views of the countryside. The two toilet blocks contain several combined cubicle spaces and there are shady walks through mature deciduous woodland adjacent to two large and appealingly landscaped fishing lakes. 20 acre site. 52 touring pitches. 16 hardstandings. Caravan pitches. Motorhome pitches. Tent pitches.

AA Pubs & Restaurants nearby: The Crown, Broughton 01487 824428

The Old Bridge Hotel, Huntingdon 01480 424300

Facilities: 🚿 ⊙ 💨 ❄ ♿ [S] 🐕 [Wi-fi] ♻ ℹ

Services: 🧺 ⊡ 🔒 [T] 🍴

Within 3 miles: ⛳ 🎣 ◎ [S] ⊡

Notes: Adults only. Dogs must be kept on leads. Fishing lakes.

HEMINGFORD ABBOTS Map 12 TL27

►►► 79% Quiet Waters Caravan Park *(TL283712)*

PE28 9AJ
☎ 01480 463405
e-mail: quietwaters.park@btopenworld.com
web: www.quietwaterscaravanpark.co.uk
dir: *Follow village signs from A14 junct 25, E of Huntingdon, site in village centre*

* 🚐 £15.50-£19.50 🚌 £15.50-£19.50 ⛺ £15.50-£19.50

Open Apr-Oct

Last arrival 20.00hrs Last departure noon

This attractive little riverside site is found in a most charming village just one mile from the A14, making an ideal centre to tour the Cambridgeshire area. There are nine holiday statics for hire. 1 acre site. 20 touring pitches. 18 hardstandings. Caravan pitches. Motorhome pitches. Tent pitches. 40 statics.

AA Pubs & Restaurants nearby: The Cock Pub & Restaurant, Hemingford Grey 01480 463609

The Old Bridge Hotel, Huntingdon 01480 424300

Facilities: 🚿 ⊙ 💨 ❄ ♿ ☎ [Wi-fi] ℹ

Services: 🧺 ⊡ 🔒 🔥

Within 3 miles: ⛳ 🚣 🎬 🎣 [S] ⊡ U

Notes: Dogs must be kept on leads. Fishing, boating.

LEISURE: 🏊 Indoor swimming pool 🏊 Outdoor swimming pool 🛝 Children's playground 👋 Kid's club 🎾 Tennis court 🎱 Games room 📺 Separate TV room ⛳ 9/18 hole golf course 🚣 Boats for hire 🎬 Cinema 🎵 Entertainment 🎣 Fishing ◎ Mini golf 🏄 Watersports 🏋 Gym ⚽ Sports field Spa U Stables
FACILITIES: 🛁 Bath 🚿 Shower ⊙ Electric shaver 💨 Hairdryer ❄ Ice Pack Facility ♿ Disabled facilities ☎ Public telephone [S] Shop on site or within 200yds 🚚 Mobile shop (calls at least 5 days a week) 🍖 BBQ area 🧺 Picnic area [Wi-fi] Wi-fi 💻 Internet access ♻ Recycling ℹ Tourist info 🐕 Dog exercise area

HUNTINGDON Map 12 TL27

Places to visit

Ramsey Abbey Gatehouse, RAMSEY 01480 301494 www.nationaltrust.org.uk

Fitzwilliam Museum, CAMBRIDGE 01223 332900 www.fitzmuseum.cam.ac.uk

Great for kids: The Raptor Foundation, WOODHURST 01487 741140 www.raptorfoundation.org.uk

►►► 80% Huntingdon Boathaven & Caravan Park *(TL249706)*

The Avenue, Godmanchester PE29 2AF
☎ 01480 411977
e-mail: boathaven.hunts@virgin.net
dir: *S of town. Exit A14 at Godmanchester junct, through Godmanchester on B1043 to site (on left by River Ouse)*

Open all year (rs Open in winter when weather permits)

Last arrival 21.00hrs

A small, well laid out site overlooking a boat marina and the River Ouse, set close to the A14 and within walking distance of Huntingdon town centre. The toilets are clean and well kept. A pretty area has been created for tents beside the marina, with wide views across the Ouse Valley. Weekend family activities are organised throughout the season. 2 acre site. 24 touring pitches. 18 hardstandings. Caravan pitches. Motorhome pitches. Tent pitches.

AA Pubs & Restaurants nearby: The Old Bridge Hotel, Huntingdon 01480 424300

King William IV, Fenstanton 01480 462467

Facilities:

Services:

Within 3 miles:

Notes: No cars by tents. Dogs must be kept on leads.

►►► 79% The Willows Caravan Park

(TL224708)

Bromholme Ln, Brampton PE28 4NE
☎ 01480 437566
e-mail: willows@willows33.freeserve.co.uk
dir: *Exit A14/A1 signed Brampton, follow Huntingdon signs. Site on right close to Brampton Mill pub*

* £18-£20 £18-£20 £15-£18

Open all year

Last arrival 20.00hrs Last departure noon

A small, friendly site in a pleasant setting beside the River Ouse, on the Ouse Valley Walk. Bay areas have been provided for caravans and motorhomes, and planting for screening is gradually maturing. There are launching facilities and free river fishing. 4 acre site. 50 touring pitches. 10 hardstandings. 10 seasonal pitches. Caravan pitches. Motorhome pitches. Tent pitches.

AA Pubs & Restaurants nearby: The Old Bridge Hotel, Huntingdon 01480 424300

Leisure:

Facilities:

Services:

Within 3 miles:

Notes: No cars by tents. Ball games on field provided, no generators, no groundsheets, 5mph one-way system. Dogs must be kept on leads. Free book lending/exchange.

ST IVES

Places to visit

The Farmland Museum and Denny Abbey, WATERBEACH 01223 860988 www.dennyfarmlandmuseum.org.uk

Oliver Cromwell's House, ELY 01353 662062 www.visitely.org.uk

ST IVES Map 12 TL37

PREMIER PARK

►►►►► 95% Stroud Hill Park

Best of British

(TL335787)

Fen Rd PE28 3DE ☎ 01487 741333
e-mail: stroudhillpark@btconnect.com
dir: *Exit B1040 in Pidley follow signs for Lakeside Lodge Complex, into Fen Rd, site on right*

Open all year

Last arrival 20.00hrs Last departure noon

A superb adults-only caravan park designed to a very high specification in a secluded and sheltered spot not far from St Ives. A modern timber-framed barn houses the exceptional facilities. These include the beautifully tiled toilets with spacious cubicles, each containing a shower, washbasin and toilet. A bar and café, restaurant, small licensed shop, tennis court and course fishing are among the attractions. There are three pay-as-you-go golf courses plus ten-pin bowling nearby. 6 acre site. 60 touring pitches. 44 hardstandings. Caravan pitches. Motorhome pitches. Tent pitches.

AA Pubs & Restaurants nearby: The Old Ferryboat Inn, Holywell 01480 463227

Leisure:

Facilities:

Services:

Within 3 miles:

Notes: Adults only. No large motorhomes. Dogs must be kept on leads.

WISBECH
Map 12 TF40

Places to visit

Peckover House & Garden, WISBECH 01945 583463 www.nationaltrust.org.uk/peckover

Sandringham House, Gardens & Museum, SANDRINGHAM 01485 545408 www.sandringhamestate.co.uk

Great for kids: Butterfly & Wildlife Park, SPALDING 01406 363833 www.butterflyandwildlifepark.co.uk

►►► 82% Little Ranch Leisure
(TF456062)

Begdale, Elm PE14 0AZ
☎ 01945 860066
dir: *From rdbt on A47 (SW of Wisbech) take Redmoor Lane to Begdale*

* ➡ fr £17 ⇌ fr £17 ▲ fr £12

Open all year

A friendly family site set in an apple orchard, with 25 fully-serviced pitches and a beautifully designed, spacious toilet block. The site overlooks a large fishing lake, and the famous horticultural auctions at Wisbech are nearby. 10 acre site. 25 touring pitches. 25 hardstandings. Caravan pitches. Motorhome pitches. Tent pitches.

AA Pubs & Restaurants nearby: The Crown Lodge Hotel, Wisbech 01945 773391

The Hare Arms, Stow Bardolph 01366 382229

Facilities: ↿ ⊙ ⌕ ✳ ⅙ 🐕 ♻ ❶
Services: ⊕ 🖸 ⅄
Within 3 miles: 🖉 🖺
Notes: ⊗

CHESHIRE

CODDINGTON
Map 15 SJ45

Places to visit

Cholmondeley Castle Gardens, CHOLMONDELEY 01829 720383 www.cholmondeleycastle.com

Hack Green Secret Nuclear Bunker, NANTWICH 01270 629219 www.hackgreen.co.uk

Great for kids: Dewa Roman Experience, CHESTER 01244 343407 www.dewaromanexperience.co.uk

PREMIER PARK

►►►►► 88% Manor Wood Country Caravan Park (SJ453553)

Manor Wood CH3 9EN
☎ 01829 782990 & 782442
e-mail: info@manorwoodcaravans.co.uk
dir: *From A534 at Barton, turn opposite Cock O'Barton pub signed Coddington. Left in 100yds. Site 0.5m on left*

* ➡ £12-£24 ⇌ £12-£24 ▲ £12-£24

Open all year (rs Oct-May swimming pool closed)

Last arrival 19.00hrs Last departure 11.00hrs

A secluded landscaped park in a tranquil country setting with extensive views towards the Welsh Hills across the Cheshire Plain. The park offers fully serviced pitches, a heated outdoor swimming pool and all weather tennis courts. Wildlife is encouraged and lake fishing, with country walks and pubs are added attractions. Generous pitch density provides optimum privacy and new for the 2012 season has been a total refurbishment of the amenities block — it has excellent decor, under-floor heating and smart modern facilities and very good privacy options. 8 acre site. 45 touring pitches. 38 hardstandings. Caravan pitches. Motorhome pitches. Tent pitches. 12 statics.

AA Pubs & Restaurants nearby: The Calveley Arms, Handley 01829 770619

1851 Restaurant at Peckforton Castle, Peckforton 01829 260930

Leisure: ⇌ ⋀ 🏊 ☻ 🔍
Facilities: ↿ ⊙ ⌕ ✳ ⅙ ⊕ 🞠 🐕 📶 🖥 ♻ ❶
Services: ⊕ 🖸 ⅄
Within 3 miles: 🖈 🖉 🖺 🖸
Notes: No cars by caravans. No cycles, no noise after 23.00hrs. Dogs must be kept on leads.

DELAMERE
Map 15 SJ56

Places to visit

Jodrell Bank Discovery Centre, JODRELL BANK 01477 571766 www.jodrellbank.net

Little Moreton Hall, CONGLETON 01260 272018 www.nationaltrust.org.uk

Great for kids: Chester Zoo, CHESTER 01244 380280 www.chesterzoo.org

►►►► 83% Fishpool Farm Caravan Park (SJ567672)

Fishpool Rd CW8 2HP
☎ 01606 883970 & 07501 506583
e-mail: enquiries@fishpoolfarmcaravanpark.co.uk
dir: *From Tarporley take A49 towards Cuddington. Left onto B5152. Continue on B5152 (Fishpool Rd). Site on right*

* ➡ fr £22 ⇌ fr £22 ▲ fr £20

Open 15 Feb-15 Jan

Last arrival 19.00hrs Last departure noon

Developed on a former hay field on the owner's farm, this excellent park has a shop/reception, a superb purpose-built toilet block with laundry facilities, a picnic area, and 50 spacious pitches, all with electric hook-up. There is a lakeside lodge, coarse fishing and a nature walk. 5.5 acre site. 50 touring pitches. Caravan pitches. Motorhome pitches. Tent pitches.

AA Pubs & Restaurants nearby: The Dysart Arms, Bunbury 01829 260183

Alvanley Arms Inn, Tarporley 01829 760200

Leisure: ⋀
Facilities: ↿ ⊙ ⌕ ✳ ⅙ 🖺 🞠 🐕 ♻
Services: ⊕ 🖸 🖴 ⅄
Within 3 miles: 🖈 🖉 ⊚ 🛥 🖺 🖸 ∪
Notes: Dogs must be kept on leads. Dog walks available, fresh eggs from own hens.

KNUTSFORD
Map 15 SJ77

►►► 77% Woodlands Park (SJ743710)

Wash Ln, Allostock WA16 9LG
☎ 01565 723429 & 01332 810818
dir: *M6 junct 18 take A50 N to Holmes Chapel for 3m, turn into Wash Ln by Boundary Water Park. Site 0.25m on left*

* ➡ £14 ⇌ £14 ▲ £12

Open Mar-6 Jan

LEISURE: 🏊 Indoor swimming pool 🏊 Outdoor swimming pool ⋀ Children's playground 🎣 Kid's club 🎾 Tennis court 🎱 Games room 📺 Separate TV room ⛳ 9/18 hole golf course 🚣 Boats for hire 🎦 Cinema 🎵 Entertainment 🎣 Fishing ⊚ Mini golf 🏄 Watersports 🏋 Gym 🏟 Sports field Spa ∪ Stables
FACILITIES: 🛁 Bath 🚿 Shower ⊙ Electric shaver ⌕ Hairdryer ✳ Ice Pack Facility ⅙ Disabled facilities 🕾 Public telephone 🖺 Shop on site or within 200yds 🖥 Mobile shop (calls at least 5 days a week) 🍖 BBQ area 🞠 Picnic area 📶 Wi-fi 🖥 Internet access ♻ Recycling ❶ Tourist info 🐕 Dog exercise area

Last arrival 21.00hrs Last departure 11.00hrs

A very tranquil and attractive park in the heart of rural Cheshire, and set in 16 acres of mature woodland. Tourers are located in three separate wooded areas that teem with wildlife and you will wake up to the sound of birdsong, plus the rhododendrons look stunning in the spring. This park is just three miles from Jodrell Bank. 16 acre site. 40 touring pitches. Caravan pitches. Motorhome pitches. Tent pitches. 140 statics.

AA Pubs & Restaurants nearby: The Dog Inn, Knutsford 01625 861421

The Duke of Portland, Lach Dennis 01606 46264

Facilities: ⚡⚐⚓

Services: ⚡⚓

Within 3 miles: ⚓⚓⚓⚓

Notes: ⚓ No skateboards or rollerblades. Dogs must be kept on leads.

SIDDINGTON
Map 15 SJ87

Places to visit

Capesthorne Hall, CAPESTHORNE 01625 861221
www.capesthorne.com

Gawsworth Hall, GAWSWORTH 01260 223456
www.gawsworthhall.com

Great for kids: Jodrell Bank Discovery Centre, JODRELL BANK 01477 571766
www.jodrellbank.net

▶▶▶▶ 87% NEW Capesthorne Hall
(SJ841727)

Congleton Rd SK11 9JY
☎ 01625 861221
e-mail: info@capesthorne.com
dir: Exit A34. Telephone site for detailed directions

⚓ £25-£30 ⚓ £25-£30

Open Apr-Oct

Last arrival 22.00hrs Last departure noon

Located within the grounds of the notable Jacobean Capesthorne Hall, this lush all level site provides generous sized pitches, all with electricity and most with hard standings. A new Scandanavian-style amenities block was introduced for the 2013 season, with smart quality modern interior and very good privacy levels. Guests also have the opportunity to visit the award winning gardens on certain days and there are many extensive walking opportunities directly from the camping areas. 5 acre site. 50 touring

---

pitches. 30 hardstandings. Caravan pitches. Motorhome pitches.

AA Pubs & Restaurants nearby: The Wizard Inn, Nether Alderley 01625 584000

Facilities: ⚡✳⚓⚓⚓⚓⚓⚓⚓⚓

Services: ⚡⚓⚓

Within 3 miles: ⚓⚓⚓⚓

Notes: No motorised scooters or skateboards, minimum 3 night stay on BH wknds. Dogs must be kept on leads. Access to historic house & gardens at additional cost for hall only.

WETTENHALL
Map 15 SJ66

▶▶▶ 83% New Farm Caravan Park
(SJ613608)

Long Ln CW7 4DW
☎ 01270 528213 & 07970 221112
e-mail: info@newfarmcheshire.com
dir: M6 junct 16, A500 towards Nantwich, right onto Nantwich bypass (A51). At lights turn right, follow A51 Caster & Tarporely signs. After Calveley right into Long Ln (follow site sign). Site in 2m

* ⚓ £19-£24 ⚓ £19-£24

Open all year

Last arrival 20.00hrs Last departure 14.00hrs

Diversification at New Farm led to the development of four fishing lakes, quality AA-listed B&B accommodation in a converted milking parlour, and the creation of a peaceful small touring park. The proprietors provide a very welcome touring destination within this peaceful part of Cheshire. Expect good landscaping, generous hardstanding pitches, a spotless toilet block, and good attention to detail throughout. Please note there is no laundry. 40 acre site. 24 touring pitches. 17 hardstandings. 6 seasonal pitches. Caravan pitches. Motorhome pitches.

AA Pubs & Restaurants nearby: The Nags Head, Haughton Moss 01829 260265

The Brasserie at Crewe Hall, Crewe 01270 253333

Facilities: ⚡⚓✳⚓⚓⚓

Services: ⚡⚓⚓⚓

Within 3 miles: ⚓⚓⚓⚓⚓

Notes: Adults only. Dogs must be kept on leads.

WHITEGATE
Map 15 SJ66

Places to visit

The Cheshire Military Museum, CHESTER 01244 327617
www.cheshiremilitarymuseum.co.uk

Chester Cathedral, CHESTER 01244 500961
www.chestercathedral.com

Great for kids: Blue Planet Aquarium, ELLESMERE PORT 0151 357 8800
www.blueplanetaquarium.com

PREMIER PARK

REGIONAL WINNER - NORTH WEST ENGLAND AA CAMPSITE OF THE YEAR 2013

▶▶▶▶▶ 91% Lamb Cottage
Caravan Park (SJ613692)

Dalefords Ln CW8 2BN
☎ 01606 882302
e-mail: info@lambcottage.co.uk
dir: From A556 turn at Sandiway lights into Dalefords Ln, signed Winsford. Site 1m on right

* ⚓ £21-£26 ⚓ £20-£25

Open Mar-Oct

Last arrival 20.00hrs Last departure noon

A secluded and attractively landscaped adults-only park in a glorious location where the emphasis is on peace and relaxation. The serviced pitches are spacious with wide grass borders for sitting out and the high quality toilet block is spotlessly clean and immaculately maintained. A good central base for exploring this area, with access to nearby woodland walks and cycle trails. 6 acre site. 45 touring pitches. 45 hardstandings. 14 seasonal pitches. Caravan pitches. Motorhome pitches. 26 statics. See also page 21.

AA Pubs & Restaurants nearby: The Bear's Paw, Warmingham 01270 526317

Facilities: ⚡⚓⚓⚓⚓⚓⚓⚓⚓

Services: ⚡⚓⚓

Within 3 miles: ⚓⚓⚓⚓

Notes: Adults only. No tents (except trailer tents), no commercial vehicles. Dogs must be kept on leads.

Cornwall

Known for its wild moorland landscapes, glorious river valleys, quaint towns and outstanding coastline, Cornwall is one of the country's most popular holiday destinations. Boasting the mildest and sunniest climate in the United Kingdom, as a result of its southerly latitude and the influence of the Gulf Stream, the county benefits from more than 1,500 hours of sunshine each year.

Bordered to the north and west by the Atlantic and to the south by the English Channel, the county boasts prehistoric sites, colourful mythology, a wealth of ancient traditions, a legacy of tin mining and impressive cultural diversity. Cornwall is acknowledged as one of the Celtic nations by many locals and use of the revived Cornish language has increased.

St Piran's flag is regarded by many as the national flag of Cornwall and an emblem of the Cornish people. It is said that St Piran, who is alleged to have discovered tin, adopted the flag's two colours – a white cross on a black background – after spotting the white tin amongst the black coals and ashes.

The coast

The Cornish coastline offers miles of breath-takingly beautiful scenery. The northern coast is open and exposed; the 735-ft High Cliff, between Boscastle and St Gennys, represents the highest sheer drop cliff in the county. In contrast are long stretches of golden sandy beaches, including those at St Ives, and Newquay, now an internationally renowned surfing destination. ▶

The Lizard, at Cornwall's most southerly point, is a geological masterpiece of towering cliffs, stacks and arches as is Land's End, on the county's south-west corner. The legendary 603-mile (970km) walk from this point to John O'Groats at the northern tip of Scotland creates a daunting challenge that numerous people, including sportsmen and TV personalities, have tackled with varying degrees of success over the years.

Truro is Cornwall's great cathedral city, with a wealth of Georgian buildings, quaint alleyways and historic streets adding to its charm. Compared to many cathedrals throughout the country, Truro's is relatively young; the foundation stones were laid in 1880 and the western towers were finally dedicated some thirty years later.

● Tate St Ives

Inspirational Cornwall

Mysterious Bodmin Moor lies at the heart of Cornwall. In 1930 the writer Daphne du Maurier spent a night at Jamaica Inn in Bolventor, which inspired the famous novel of the same name; *Menabilly*, her home near Fowey, on Cornwall's south coast, was the inspiration for '*Manderley*', the house in *Rebecca*, almost certainly her best-known and best-loved book. It is said that one day while out walking she spotted a flock of seagulls diving and wheeling above a newly ploughed field, which gave her the idea for the short story *The Birds*, which Alfred Hitchcock memorably turned into a horror film.

Walking and Cycling

Naturally, walking and cycling are very popular pursuits in Cornwall. The South West Coast Path offers many miles of rugged coastal grandeur and stunning views, while inland there is the chance to combine this most simple of outdoor pursuits with suitably green and environmentally friendly train travel. Tourist information centres provide leaflets showing a variety of linear or circular walks incorporating branch line stations; easy-to-follow maps are included. One popular route involves taking the train along the scenic Atlantic Coast line to Luxulyan, then cutting across country on foot for 2.5 miles (4km) to reach the Eden Project.

Festivals and Events

- The Newlyn Fish Festival takes place on August Bank Holiday Monday.
- Penzance hosts the Golowan Festival and Mazey Day for two weeks in mid-June.
- St Ives has its Feast Day in early February and the St Ives Festival of Music and the Arts for two weeks in early September.
- Victorian Day on Cotehele Quay near Calstock in mid-August is family fun and involves dressing up.

● Newquay beach

CORNWALL & ISLES OF SCILLY

See Walk 1 & Cycle Ride 1 in the Walks & Cycle Rides section at the end of the guide

ASHTON   Map 2 SW62

Places to visit

Godolphin House,
GODOLPHIN CROSS 01736 763194
www.nationaltrust.org.uk/godolphin

Poldark Mine and Heritage Complex, WENDRON 01326 573173 www.poldark-mine.com

Great for kids: The Flambards Theme Park, HELSTON 01326 573404 www.flambards.co.uk

▶▶▶ 76% *Boscrege Caravan & Camping Park* (SW595305)

TR13 9TG
☎ 01736 762231
e-mail: enquiries@caravanparkcornwall.com
dir: *From Helston on A394 turn right in Ashton by Post Office into lane. Site in 1.5m, signed*

⬛ ⬛ ⛺

Open Mar-Nov

Last arrival 22.00hrs Last departure 11.00hrs

A quiet and bright little touring park divided into small paddocks with hedges, and offering plenty of open spaces for children to play in. The family-owned park offers clean, well-painted toilets facilities and neatly trimmed grass. In an Area of Outstanding Natural Beauty at the foot of Tregonning Hill, this site makes an ideal base for touring the southern tip of Cornwall; Penzance, Land's End, St Ives and the beaches in between

are all within easy reach. 14 acre site. 50 touring pitches. Caravan pitches. Motorhome pitches. Tent pitches. 26 statics.

AA Pubs & Restaurants nearby: The Victoria Inn, Perranuthnoe 01736 710309

New Yard Restaurant, Helston 01326 221595

Leisure: ⬛ ⬛ ⬛ ⬛
Facilities: ⬛ ⬛ ⬛ ⬛ ⬛ ⬛ ⬛ ⬛ ⬛ ⬛ ⬛ ⬛
Services: ⬛ ⬛ ⬛ ⬛ ⬛ ⬛
Within 3 miles: ⬛ ⬛ ⬛ ⬛ ⬛ ⬛ ⬛ ⬛ ⬛

Notes: Dogs must be kept on leads. Microwave available. Nature trail.

BLACKWATER   Map 2 SW74

Places to visit

Royal Cornwall Museum, TRURO 01872 272205 www.royalcornwallmuseum.org.uk

East Pool Mine, POOL 01209 315027 www.nationaltrust.org.uk

Great for kids: National Maritime Museum Cornwall, FALMOUTH 01326 313388 www.nmmc.co.uk

▶▶▶▶ 83% **Chiverton Park**
(SW743468)

East Hill TR4 8HS
☎ 01872 560667 & 07789 377169
e-mail: chivertonpark@btopenworld.com
dir: *Exit A30 at Chiverton rdbt (Starbucks) onto unclassified road signed Blackwater (3rd exit). 1st right, site 300mtrs on right*

⬛ ⬛ ⛺

Chiverton Park

Open Mar-end Oct

Last arrival 19.00hrs Last departure noon

A small, well-maintained site with some mature hedges dividing pitches, sited midway between Truro and St Agnes. Facilities include a good toilet block and a steam room, sauna and gym. All touring pitches are fully serviced. There is a games room with pool table, and the children's outside play equipment proves popular with families. 4 acre site. 12 touring pitches. 10 hardstandings. Caravan pitches. Motorhome pitches. Tent pitches. 50 statics.

AA Pubs & Restaurants nearby: Driftwood Spars, St Agnes 01872 552428

Leisure: ⬛ ⬛ ⬛ Spa
Facilities: ⬛ ⬛ ⬛ ⬛ ⬛ ⬛ ⬛ ⬛ ⬛
Services: ⬛ ⬛ ⬛
Within 3 miles: ⬛ ⬛ ⬛ ⬛ ⬛ ⬛ ⬛

Notes: No ball games. Dogs must be kept on leads. Drying lines.

LEISURE: 🏊 Indoor swimming pool 🏊 Outdoor swimming pool 🎠 Children's playground 🪁 Kid's club 🎾 Tennis court 🎱 Games room 📺 Separate TV room
⛳ 9/18 hole golf course 🚣 Boats for hire 🎬 Cinema 🎵 Entertainment 🎣 Fishing ⛳ Mini golf 🏄 Watersports 🏋 Gym ⚽ Sports field **Spa** ♨ Stables
FACILITIES: 🛁 Bath 🚿 Shower 🔌 Electric shaver 💈 Hairdryer ❄ Ice Pack Facility ♿ Disabled facilities 📞 Public telephone 🏪 Shop on site or within 200yds
🛒 Mobile shop (calls at least 5 days a week) 🍖 BBQ area 🪑 Picnic area 📶 Wi-fi 💻 Internet access ♻ Recycling ℹ Tourist info 🐕 Dog exercise area

►►►► 80% *Trevarth Holiday Park*

(SW744468)

TR4 8HR

☎ 01872 560266

e-mail: trevarth@btconnect.com

web: www.trevarth.co.uk

dir: *Exit A30 at Chiverton rdbt onto B3277 signed St Agnes. At next rdbt take road signed Blackwater. Site on right in 200mtrs*

Open Apr-Oct

Last arrival 22.00hrs Last departure 11.30hrs

A neat and compact park with touring pitches laid out on attractive, well-screened high ground adjacent to the A30/A39 junction. This pleasant little park is centrally located for touring, and is maintained to a very good standard. There is a large grassed area for children to play on which is away from all tents. 4 acre site. 30 touring pitches. 10 hardstandings. 2 seasonal pitches. Caravan pitches. Motorhome pitches. Tent pitches. 20 statics.

AA Pubs & Restaurants nearby: Driftwood Spars, St Agnes 01872 552428

Leisure: ⚠ 🔍

Facilities: 🐾 ⊙ 🅿 ✳ 🕐 📶 ♻ ❶

Services: 🔌 🔲 🛢 🧴 ➡

Within 3 miles: 🎣 ♨ 🛒 🐕

Notes: Dogs must be kept on leads.

BLISLAND   Map 2 SX17

Places to visit

Tintagel Old Post Office, TINTAGEL 01840 770024 www.nationaltrust.org.uk/main/w-tintageloldpostoffice

---

►►► 85% *South Penquite Farm*

(SX108751)

South Penquite PL30 4LH

☎ 01208 850491

e-mail: thefarm@bodminmoor.co.uk

dir: *From Exeter on A30 exit at 1st sign to St Breward on right, (from Bodmin 2nd sign on left). Follow narrow road across Bodmin Moor. Ignore left & right turns until South Penquite Farm Lane on right in 2m*

* 🚐 £7-£8 ▲ £7-£8

Open May-Oct

Last arrival dusk Last departure 14.00hrs

This genuine 'back to nature' site is situated high on Bodmin Moor on a farm committed to organic agriculture. As well as camping there are facilities for adults and children to learn about conservation, organic farming and the local environment, including a fascinating and informative farm trail (pick up a leaflet); there is also a Geocaching trail. Toilet facilities are enhanced by a timber building with quality showers and a good disabled facility. The site has designated areas where fires may be lit. Organic home-reared lamb burgers and sausages are for sale, and one field contains four Mongolian yurts, available for holiday let. 4 acre site. 40 touring pitches. Motorhome pitches. Tent pitches. 4 bell tents/yurts.

AA Pubs & Restaurants nearby: The Blisland Inn, Blisland 01208 850739

The Old Inn & Restaurant, St Breward 01208 850711

Leisure: ⚠ 🔍

Facilities: 🐾 ⊙ 🅿 ✳ 🛢 🪑 ♻ ❶

Services: 🔲

Within 3 miles: 🛶 ♨ 🛒 🐕

Notes: ⊘ No caravans, no pets.

BODMIN   Map 2 SX06

AA CAMPING CARD SITE

►►► 83% Mena Caravan & Camping Park *(SW041626)*

PL30 5HW
☎ 01208 831845
e-mail: mena@campsitesincornwall.co.uk
dir: *Exit A30 onto A389 N signed Lanivet & Wadebridge. In 0.5m 1st right & pass under A30. 1st left signed Lostwithiel & Fowey. In 0.25m right at top of hill. 0.5m then 1st right. Entrance 100yds on right*

Open all year

Last arrival 22.00hrs Last departure noon

Set in a secluded, elevated location with high hedges for shelter, and plenty of peace. This grassy site is about four miles from the Eden Project and midway between the north and south Cornish coasts. There is a small coarse fishing lake on site, hardstanding pitches, a shop selling take-away snacks, and two static caravans for holiday hire. The site is on the Saint's Way, and nearby is Helman Tor, a Neolithic hill fort, and the highest point on Bodmin Moor. There is a fish and chip restaurant in Lanivet (approximately 1 mile); from here there is a bus service to Bodmin. 15 acre site. 25 touring pitches. 4 hardstandings. Caravan pitches. Motorhome pitches. Tent pitches. 2 statics.

AA Pubs & Restaurants nearby: The Borough Arms, Dunmere 01208 73118

Trehellas House Hotel & Restaurant, Bodmin 01208 72700

Leisure: ⚫ ⚫
Facilities: ⚫⚫⚫⚫⚫⚫⚫⚫⚫⚫
Services: ⚫⚫⚫⚫⚫⚫⚫⚫
Within 3 miles: ⚫⚫⚫⚫⚫⚫

BOSCASTLE   Map 2 SX09

Places to visit

Tintagel Castle, TINTAGEL 01840 770328
www.english-heritage.org.uk

Tintagel Old Post Office, TINTAGEL 01840 770024 www.nationaltrust.org.uk/main/w-tintageloldpostoffice

Great for kids: The Milky Way Adventure Park, CLOVELLY 01237 431255
www.themilkyway.co.uk

►► 80% Lower Pennycrocker Farm *(SX125927)*

PL35 0BY
☎ 01840 250613
e-mail: karyn.heard@yahoo.com
dir: *Exit A39 at Marshgate onto B3263 towards Boscastle, site signed in 2m*

Open Etr-Oct

Last arrival anytime Last departure anytime

Mature Cornish hedges provide shelter for this small, family-run site on a dairy farm. Spectacular scenery and the nearby coastal footpath are among the many attractions, along with fresh eggs, milk and home-made clotted cream for sale. The excellent toilets and showers enhance this site's facilities. Two traditional Cornish cottages are available to let. 6 acre site. 40 touring pitches. Caravan pitches. Motorhome pitches. Tent pitches.

AA Pubs & Restaurants nearby: The Port William, Trebarwith 01840 770230

The Wellington Hotel, Boscastle 01840 250202

Facilities: ⚫⚫⚫⚫⚫⚫⚫⚫
Services: ⚫⚫⚫⚫
Within 3 miles: ⚫⚫⚫⚫
Notes: Dogs must be kept on leads.

BRYHER (ISLES OF SCILLY)   Map 2 SV81

►►► 79% Bryher Camp Site *(SV880155)*

TR23 0PR
☎ 01720 422559
e-mail: relax@bryhercampsite.co.uk
web: www.bryhercampsite.co.uk
dir: *Accessed by boat from main island of St Marys*

* ⚫ fr £20

Open Apr-Oct

Set on the smallest inhabited Scilly Isle with spectacular scenery and white beaches, this tent-only site is in a sheltered valley surrounded by hedges. Pitches are located in paddocks at the northern end of the island, which is only a short walk from the quay. There is a good modern toilet block, and plenty of peace and quiet. There is easy boat access to all the other islands. 2.25 acre site. 38 touring pitches. Tent pitches.

AA Pubs & Restaurants nearby: Hell Bay Hotel, Bryher 01720 422947

Leisure: ⚫
Facilities: ⚫⚫⚫⚫⚫⚫ ⚫
Services: ⚫⚫⚫⚫
Within 3 miles: ⚫⚫⚫⚫⚫⚫⚫⚫
Notes: No cars by tents. No pets.

BUDE   Map 2 SS20

See also Kilkhampton & Bridgerule (Devon)

89% *Sandymouth Holiday Park (SS214104)*

Sandymouth Bay EX23 9HW
☎ 08442 729530
e-mail: enquiries@sandymouthbay.co.uk
web: www.sandymouthbay.co.uk
dir: *Signed from A39 approx 0.5m S of Kilkhampton, 4m N of Bude*

Open Mar-26 Nov (rs 16 May-9 Jul (excl half term week) closed for private booking)

Last arrival 21.00hrs Last departure 10.00hrs

A bright and friendly holiday park with glorious and extensive sea views from all areas. The park offers modern and well maintained touring facilities, alongside excellent leisure and entertainment facilities, notably the eye-catching pirate galleon in the fabulous children's play area. 24 acre site. 22 touring

LEISURE: 🏊 Indoor swimming pool   🏊 Outdoor swimming pool   🛝 Children's playground   🧒 Kid's club   🎾 Tennis court   🎱 Games room   📺 Separate TV room   ⛳ 9/18 hole golf course   🚣 Boats for hire   🎬 Cinema   🎵 Entertainment   🎣 Fishing   ⛳ Mini golf   🏄 Watersports   💪 Gym   ⚽ Sports field   Spa   ⛎ Stables
FACILITIES: 🛁 Bath   🚿 Shower   ⊙ Electric shaver   🔲 Hairdryer   ❄ Ice Pack Facility   ♿ Disabled facilities   📞 Public telephone   🏪 Shop on site or within 200yds   🚐 Mobile shop (calls at least 5 days a week)   🍖 BBQ area   🪑 Picnic area   Wi-fi   💻 Internet access   ♻ Recycling   ℹ Tourist info   🐕 Dog exercise area

pitches. 22 hardstandings. Caravan pitches. Motorhome pitches. Tent pitches.

AA Pubs & Restaurants nearby: The Bush Inn, Morwenstow 01288 331242

The Castle Restaurant, Bude 01288 350543

Sandymouth Holiday Park

Leisure: ⚽ 🅰 🏊 ☀ ♨ 🎵

Facilities: 🍴 ☉ 🅿 ☼ 🕐 📷 💻 ♻ 🛈

Services: 🔌 🔲 🍺 🔋 🇹 🍽 🛒

Within 3 miles: 🎣 ⛳ 🐎 🛒 ♨ 🍽 🛒 🎱 ↻

Notes: Dogs must be kept on leads. Sauna.

see advert below

► ► ► ► ► **90% Wooda Farm Holiday Park**

(SS229080)

Poughill EX23 9HJ
☎ **01288 352069**
e-mail: enquiries@wooda.co.uk
web: www.wooda.co.uk
dir: *2m E. From A39 at outskirts of Stratton follow unclassified road signed Poughill*

✳ 🚐 £17-£30 🚌 £14-£30 ⛺ £14-£26

Open Apr-Oct (rs Apr-May & mid Sep-Oct shop hours limited, bar & takeaway)

Last arrival 20.00hrs Last departure 10.30hrs

An attractive park set on raised ground overlooking Bude Bay, with lovely sea views. The park is divided into paddocks by hedges and mature trees, and offers high quality facilities in extensive colourful gardens. A variety of activities is provided by way of the large sports hall and hard tennis court, and there's a super children's playground. There are holiday static caravans for hire. At the time of our last inspection the site was planning to install a fully interactive information screen in the reception area, for customer use. 50 acre site. 200 touring pitches. 80 hardstandings. Caravan pitches. Motorhome pitches. Tent pitches. 55 statics.

AA Pubs & Restaurants nearby: The Bush Inn, Morwenstow 01288 331242

The Castle Restaurant, Bude 01288 350543

Wooda Farm Holiday Park

Leisure: ⚓ 🅰 🏊 ⚽ ♨ ▭

Facilities: 🛁 🍴 ☉ 🅿 ☼ 🕐 📷 🪑 📧 WiFi ♻ 🛈

Services: 🔌 🔲 🍺 🔋 🚐 🇹 🍽 🛒 🛢 🛠

Within 3 miles: 🎣 ⛳ 🎾 🐎 ◎ ♨ 🍽 🛒 🎱 ↻

Notes: Restrictions on certain dog breeds, skateboards, rollerblades & scooters. Dogs must be kept on leads. Coarse fishing, clay pigeon shooting, pets' corner, woodland walks.

see advert on page 66

SERVICES: 🔌 Electric hook up 🔲 Launderette 🍺 Licensed bar 🅰 Calor Gas ⊘ Camping Gaz 🇹 Toilet fluid 🍽 Café/Restaurant 🛒 Fast Food/Takeaway 🔋 Battery charging Baby care 🛠 Motorvan service point **ABBREVIATIONS:** BH/bank hols-bank holidays Etr-Easter Whit-Whitsun dep-departure fr-from hrs-hours m-mile mdnt-midnight rdbt-roundabout rs-restricted service wk-week wknd-weekend No credit cards no dogs See page 7 for details of the AA Camping Card Scheme

BUDE *continued*

►►►► 85% Budemeadows Touring Park *(SS215012)*

Widemouth Bay EX23 0NA
☎ 01288 361646
e-mail: holiday@budemeadows.com
dir: *3m S of Bude on A39. Follow signs after turn to Widemouth Bay. Site accessed via layby from A39*

* ⊞ £14.50-£27 ⊞ £14.50-£27
▲ £10.50-£27

Open all year (rs Sep-late May shop, bar & pool closed)

Last arrival 21.00hrs Last departure 11.00hrs

This is a very well kept site of distinction, with good quality facilities, hardstandings and eight fully-serviced pitches. Budemeadows is set on a gentle sheltered slope in nine acres of naturally landscaped parkland, surrounded by mature hedges. The internal doors in the facility block have all been painted in pastel colours to resemble beach huts. The site is just one mile from Widemouth Bay, and three miles from the unspoilt resort of Bude. 9 acre site. 145 touring pitches. 24 hardstandings. Caravan pitches. Motorhome pitches. Tent pitches.

AA Pubs & Restaurants nearby: Bay View Inn, Widemouth Bay 01288 361273

The Castle Restaurant, Bude 01288 350543

Budemeadows Touring Park

Leisure: ⊛ ⚑ ⚲ ⊡
Facilities: ⛴ ⎀ ⊙ ☞ ※ ⅁ ⓢ ⑤ ⊓ ⟦Wi-fi⟧ ▣ ♻ ❶
Services: ⊡ ⑤ ⊞ ⌀ ⊓ ⛴ ⬛ ⬆
Within 3 miles: ⌕ ⊁ ⊟ ⚡ ◎ ⊱ ⑤ ⑤ ∪

Notes: No noise after 23.00hrs, breathable groundsheets. Dogs must be kept on leads. Table tennis, giant chess. baby changing facility.

►►►► 85% Widemouth Fields Caravan & Camping Park *(SS215010)*

Park Farm, Poundstock EX23 0NA
☎ 01288 361351 & 01489 781256
e-mail: enquiries@widemouthbaytouring.co.uk
dir: *M5 junct 27 (signed Barnstaple). A361 to rdbt before Barnstaple. Take A39 signed Bideford & Bude. (NB do not exit A39 at Stratton). S for 3m, follow sign just past x-rds to Widemouth Bay. Into lay-by, entrance on left*

* ⊞ £16-£26 ⊞ £16-£26 ▲ £14-£19

Open Apr-Sep

Last arrival dusk Last departure noon

In a quiet location with far reaching views over the rolling countryside, this site is only one mile from the golden beach at Widemouth Bay, and just three miles from the resort of Bude. The park has a shop and small café/takeaway, and offers many hardstanding pitches. The toilets are of outstanding quality with a wealth of combined fully-serviced cubicles. All the buildings resemble log cabins which certainly adds to the appeal of the site. The owner, having acquired Widemouth Bay Holiday Village, runs courtesy shuttle buses into Bude and to the Holiday Village, where the facilities can be used by the touring campers. 15 acre site. 156 touring pitches. 156 hardstandings. 20 seasonal pitches. Caravan pitches. Motorhome pitches. Tent pitches.

LEISURE: ⊛ Indoor swimming pool ⊛ Outdoor swimming pool ⚑ Children's playground ⚓ Kid's club ⚲ Tennis court ⚲ Games room ⊡ Separate TV room ⌕ 9/18 hole golf course ⊁ Boats for hire ⊟ Cinema ⚡ Entertainment ☞ Fishing ◎ Mini golf ⊱ Watersports ⚐ Gym ⊕ Sports field **Spa** ∪ Stables
FACILITIES: ⛴ Bath ⎀ Shower ⊙ Electric shaver ☞ Hairdryer ※ Ice Pack Facility ⅁ Disabled facilities ⓢ Public telephone ⑤ Shop on site or within 200yds ⑤ Mobile shop (calls at least 5 days a week) ⬛ BBQ area ⊓ Picnic area ⟦Wi-fi⟧ Wi-fi ⬛ Internet access ♻ Recycling ❶ Tourist info ⬆ Dog exercise area

AA Pubs & Restaurants nearby: Bay View Inn, Widemouth Bay 01288 361273

Leisure: ⚙️☀️🎏

Facilities: 🍴🐾☀️📮✳️♿🛁🔥🚮📶♻️🛒ℹ️

Services: 🔌🎲⚗️Ⓣ🍴🔋↯

Within 3 miles: 🚴🏇⚓🎣◎⛳🏕️🎲↻

Notes: Entry to site by swipecard only, deposit taken when booking in.

AA CAMPING CARD SITE

NEW ▶▶▶▶ 84% **Pentire Haven Holiday Park** *(SS246111)*

Stibb Rd, Kilkhampton EX23 9QY
☎ 01288 321601
e-mail: holidays@pentirehaven.co.uk
dir: A39 from Bude towards Bideford, in 3m turn left signed Sandymouth Bay

🚐 £9-£23 🚚 £9-£23 ⛺ £9-£23

Open 31 Mar-3 Nov

Last arrival 23.30hrs Last departure 10.30hrs

A very open grassed site handy for many beautiful beaches, but in particular the surfing beach of

Bude only four miles away. The site has been taken over by new management and the staff are making a real impression. There are excellent toilet facilities in addition to a new children's playground and a small swimming pool which is open during the busy season. 23 acre site. 120 touring pitches. 46 hardstandings. 40 seasonal pitches. Caravan pitches. Motorhome pitches. Tent pitches.

AA Pubs & Restaurants nearby: Bay View Inn, Widemouth Bay 01288 361273

The Castle Restaurant, Bude 01288 350543

Pentire Haven Holiday Park

Leisure: 🏊⚙️🎠👶🏐🎵

Facilities: 🐾📮✳️♿🛁🔥📶♻️

Services: 🔌🎲🍴🚿⚗️Ⓣ🍴🔋🛒↯

Within 3 miles: 🚴🏇⚓🎣⛳🏕️🎲↻

Notes: No fires. Dogs must be kept on leads.

see advert below

▶▶▶▶ 78% *Willow Valley Holiday Park* *(SS236078)*

Bush EX23 9LB
☎ 01288 353104
e-mail: willowvalley@talk21.com
dir: On A39, 0.5m N of junct with A3072 at Stratton

🚐 🚚 ⛺

Open Mar-end Oct

Last arrival 21.00hrs Last departure 11.00hrs

A small sheltered park in the Strat Valley with level grassy pitches and a stream running through it. The friendly family owners have improved all areas of this attractive park, including a smart toilet block and an excellent reception/shop. The park has direct access off the A39, and is only two miles from the sandy beaches at Bude. There are four pine lodges for holiday hire. 4 acre site. 41 touring pitches. Caravan pitches. Motorhome pitches. Tent pitches. 4 statics.

AA Pubs & Restaurants nearby: The Bickford Arms, Holsworthy 01409 221318

The Castle Restaurant, Bude 01288 350543

Leisure: ⚙️

Facilities: 🐾☀️📮✳️♿🛁🔥🚮♻️ℹ️

Services: 🔌🎲🔋⚗️Ⓣ🔋

Within 3 miles: 🚴🏇⚓🎣◎⛳🏕️🎲↻

Notes: 🚫 Dogs must be kept on leads.

BUDE *continued*

▶▶▶ 80% Upper Lynstone Caravan Park *(SS205053)*

Lynstone EX23 0LP
☎ **01288 352017**
e-mail: reception@upperlynstone.co.uk
dir: *0.75m S of Bude on coastal road to Widemouth Bay*

🚐 🚆 ⛺

Open Apr-Oct

Last arrival 22.00hrs Last departure 10.00hrs

There are extensive views over Bude to be enjoyed from this quiet, sheltered family-run park, a terraced grass site suitable for all units. There is a reception/shop selling basic food supplies and camping spares, a children's playground, and static caravans for holiday hire. A path leads directly to the coastal footpath with its stunning sea views, and the old Bude Canal is a stroll away. 6 acre site. 65 touring pitches. Caravan pitches. Motorhome pitches. Tent pitches. 41 statics.

AA Pubs & Restaurants nearby: The Castle Restaurant, Bude 01288 350543

Leisure: 🛝

Facilities: 🚿☉📮☀🚻🏧🛒🏛🎪

Services: 🔌🔽🛒📶ⓣ🍴🧺

Within 3 miles: ↕🏇📅📌◎🛟🛒🎱🐴

Notes: No groups. Baby changing room.

CAMELFORD   Map 2 SX18

▶▶▶▶ 85% *Juliot's Well Holiday Park (SX095829)*

PL32 9RF
☎ **01840 213302**
e-mail: holidays@juliotswell.com
web: www.juliotswell.com
dir: *Through Camelford, A39 at Valley Truckle turn right onto B3266, 1st left signed Lanteglos, site 300yds on right*

🚐 🚆 ⛺

Open all year

Last arrival 20.00hrs Last departure 11.00hrs

Set in the wooded grounds of an old manor house, this quiet site enjoys lovely and extensive views across the countryside. A rustic inn on site offers occasional entertainment, and there is plenty to do, both on the park and in the vicinity. The superb, fully-serviced toilet facilities are very impressive. There are also self-catering pine lodges, static caravans and five cottages. 33 acre site. 39 touring pitches. Caravan pitches. Motorhome pitches. Tent pitches. 82 statics.

AA Pubs & Restaurants nearby: The Mill House Inn, Trebarwith 01840 770200

Leisure: 🛥 🛝 🎣

Facilities: 🛁🚿☉📮☀🛒🔧🏧🛒📶

Services: 🔌🔽🛒ⓣ🍴🧺

Within 3 miles: ↕📌🛒🎱🐴

Notes: Complimentary use of cots & high chairs.

AA CAMPING CARD SITE

▶▶▶ 78% Lakefield Caravan Park *(SX095853)*

Lower Pendavey Farm PL32 9TX
☎ **01840 213279**
e-mail: lakefieldcaravanpark@btconnect.com
dir: *From A39 in Camelford onto B3266, then right at T-junct, site 1.5m on left*

* 🚐 £11-£13.50 🚆 £11-£13.50 ⛺ £11-£13.50

Open Etr or Apr-Sep

Last arrival 22.00hrs Last departure 11.00hrs

Set in a rural location, this friendly park is part of a specialist equestrian centre, and offers good quality services. All the facilities are immaculate and spotlessly clean. Riding lessons and hacks always available, with a BHS qualified instructor. Newquay, Padstow and Bude are all easily accessed from this site. 5 acre site. 40 touring pitches. Caravan pitches. Motorhome pitches. Tent pitches.

AA Pubs & Restaurants nearby: The Old House Inn & Restaurant, St Breward 01208 850711

Facilities: 🚿☉📮☀🔧🏧📶

Services: 🔌🛒🍴ⓣ🍴🧺

Within 3 miles: ↕📌🛒🎱🐴

Notes: Dogs must be kept on leads. On-site lake.

CARLYON BAY   Map 2 SX05

Places to visit

Charlestown Shipwreck & Heritage Centre, ST AUSTELL 01726 69897
www.shipwreckcharlestown.com

Eden Project, ST AUSTELL 01726 811911
www.edenproject.com

Great for kids: Wheal Martyn Museum & Country Park, ST AUSTELL 01726 850362
www.wheal-martyn.com

PREMIER PARK

▶▶▶▶▶ 89% Carlyon Bay Caravan & Camping Park *(SX052526)*

Bethesda, Cypress Av PL25 3RE
☎ **01726 812735**
e-mail: holidays@carlyonbay.net
dir: *Exit A390 W of St Blazey, left onto A3092 for Par, right in 0.5m. On private road to Carlyon Bay*

* 🚐 £15-£29 🚆 £15-£29 ⛺ £15-£29

Open Etr-28 Sep (rs Etr-mid May & mid-end Sep swimming pool, takeaway & shop closed; Jul-Aug only - children's entertainment)

Last arrival 21.00hrs Last departure 11.00hrs

An attractive, secluded site set amongst a belt of trees with background woodland. The spacious grassy park is beautifully landscaped and offers quality toilet and shower facilities and plenty of on-site attractions, including a well-equipped games room, TV room, café, an inviting swimming pool, and occasional family entertainment. It is less than half a mile from a sandy beach and the Eden Project is only two miles away. 35 acre site. 180 touring pitches. 12 hardstandings. Caravan pitches. Motorhome pitches. Tent pitches.

AA Pubs & Restaurants nearby: Austells, St Austell 01726 813888

Leisure: 🛥 🛝 🏊 🎱 🎮 🖵

Facilities: 🚿☉📮☀🛒🔧🏧🛒📶♻🛒

Services: 🔌🔽🛒📶ⓣ🍴🧺🛒♿

Within 3 miles: ↕🏇📅📌◎🛟🛒🎱🐴

Notes: No noise after 23.00hrs. Dogs must be kept on leads. Crazy golf.

see advert on page 91

LEISURE: 🛀 Indoor swimming pool 🛥 Outdoor swimming pool 🛝 Children's playground 🚩 Kid's club 🎾 Tennis court 🎯 Games room 🖵 Separate TV room ↕ 9/18 hole golf course 🚤 Boats for hire 🎬 Cinema 🎵 Entertainment 🎣 Fishing ◎ Mini golf 🏄 Watersports 💪 Gym 🌀 Sports field Spa ♨ Stables
FACILITIES: 🛁 Bath 🚿 Shower ☉ Electric shaver 📮 Hairdryer ☀ Ice Pack Facility ♿ Disabled facilities 🕐 Public telephone 🛒 Shop on site or within 200yds 🏪 Mobile shop (calls at least 5 days a week) 🍴 BBQ area 🎪 Picnic area 📶 Wi-fi 🌐 Internet access ♻ Recycling ❶ Tourist info 🐕 Dog exercise area

►►► 83% East Crinnis Camping & Caravan Park (SX062528)

Lantyan, East Crinnis PL24 2SQ
☎ **01726 813023 & 07950 614780**
e-mail: eastcrinnis@btconnect.com
dir: *From A390 (Lostwithiel to St Austell) take A3082 signed Fowey at rdbt by Britannia Inn, site on left*

🚐 £10-£20 🚐 🅰

Open Etr-Oct

Last arrival 21.00hrs Last departure 11.00hrs

A small rural park with spacious pitches set in individual bays about one mile from the beaches at Carlyon Bay, and just two miles from the Eden Project. The friendly owners keep the site very clean and well maintained, and also offer three self-catering holiday lodges and two yurts for hire. It is a short walk to Par where restaurant food can be found. 2 acre site. 25 touring pitches. 6 hardstandings. Caravan pitches. Motorhome pitches. Tent pitches. 2 yurts.

AA Pubs & Restaurants nearby: Britannia Inn, Par 01726 812 889

The Rashleigh Inn, Polkerris 01726 813991

Austells, St Austell 01726 813888

Leisure: 🅰 🌀
Facilities: 🇳 ⊙ 🍴 ✳ ⅙ 🛉 🚻 🖙 💻 ♻ ❶
Services: 🔌 🗑 🛒
Within 3 miles: ↓ ⅃ 🍴 🎱 ◎ ⅒ 🏧 🗑 ↺

Notes: Dogs must be kept on leads. Coarse fishing, wildlife & pond area with dog walk.

COVERACK — Map 2 SW71

Places to visit

Trevarno Estate Garden & Museum of Gardening, HELSTON 01326 574274 www.trevarno.co.uk

Goonhilly Satellite Earth Station Experience, HELSTON 0800 679593 www.goonhilly.bt.com

Great for kids: National Seal Sanctuary, GWEEK 0871 423 2110 www.sealsanctuary.co.uk

---

►►► 80% Little Trevothan Caravan & Camping Park (SW772179)

Trevothan TR12 6SD
☎ **01326 280260**
e-mail: sales@littletrevothan.co.uk
web: www. littletrevothan.co.uk
dir: *A3083 onto B3293 signed Coverack, approx 2m after Goonhilly ESS, right at Zoar Garage onto unclassified road. Approx 1m, 3rd left. Site 0.5m on left*

* 🚐 £12-£15 🚐 £12-£15 🅰 £12-£15

Open Mar-Oct

Last arrival 21.00hrs Last departure noon

A secluded site, with excellent facilities, near the unspoilt fishing village of Coverack, with a large recreation area and good play equipment for children. The nearby sandy beach has lots of rock pools for children to play in, and the many walks both from the park and the village offer stunning scenery. 10.5 acre site. 70 touring pitches. 10 hardstandings. 9 seasonal pitches. Caravan pitches. Motorhome pitches. Tent pitches. 22 statics.

AA Pubs & Restaurants nearby: The New Inn, Manaccan 01326 231323

Leisure: 🅰 🌀 🎣 🖵
Facilities: 🇳 ⊙ 🍴 ✳ 🕐 ⅙ 🛉 ♻ ❶
Services: 🔌 🗑 🛢 ⊘ 🇹 🛒
Within 3 miles: 🎱 ⅒ 🏧 🗑

Notes: ⊛ No noise between 22.00hrs & 08.30hrs. Dogs must be kept on leads.

CRACKINGTON HAVEN — Map 2 SX19

►►► 77% *Hentervene Holiday Park* (SX155944)

GOLD

EX23 0LF
☎ **01840 230365**
e-mail: contact@hentervene.co.uk
dir: *Exit A39 approx 10m SW of Bude (1.5m beyond Wainhouse Corner) onto B3263 signed Boscastle & Crackington Haven. 0.75m to Tresparret Posts junct, right signed Hentervene. Site 0.75m on right*

🚐 🚐

Open Mar-Oct

Last arrival 21.00hrs Last departure 11.00hrs

This much improved park is set in a rural location a short drive from a golden sandy beach. It is in an Area of Outstanding Natural Beauty, and pitches are in paddocks which are bordered by mature hedges, with a small stream running past. Some pitches are on level terraces, and there are also hardstandings. A new lake has been created which has a woodland walk around it. Static caravans and three pine lodges are available for self-catering holiday hire. 11 acre site. 8 touring pitches. 8 hardstandings. Caravan pitches. Motorhome pitches. 24 statics.

Leisure: 🅰 🎣 🖵
Facilities: 🇳 ⊙ 🍴 ✳ 🕐 🛉 🖙 ♻ ❶
Services: 🔌 🗑 🛢 ⊘ 🇹
Within 3 miles: 🎱 ⅒ 🏧 🗑 ↺

Notes: Microwave & freezer for campers.

CRANTOCK (NEAR NEWQUAY)   Map 2 SW76

PREMIER PARK

► ► ► ► ► 88% *Trevella Tourist Park* (SW801599)

TR8 5EW
☎ **01637 830308**
e-mail: holidays@trevella.co.uk
dir: *Between Crantock & A3075*

Open Etr-Oct

A well established and very well run family site, with outstanding floral displays. Set in a rural area close to Newquay, this stunning park boasts three teeming fishing lakes for the both experienced and novice angler, and a superb outdoor swimming pool and paddling area. The toilet facilities include excellent en suite wet rooms. All areas are neat and clean and the whole park looks stunning. Yurts, eurotents and safari tents for hire are now available. 15 acre site. 313 touring pitches. 53 hardstandings. Caravan pitches. Motorhome pitches. Tent pitches.

AA Pubs & Restaurants nearby: The Smugglers' Den Inn, Cubert 01637 830209

The Lewinnick Lodge Bar & Restaurant, Newquay 01637 878117

Leisure: 🏊 ⚲ ♜ ▢
Facilities: ⬤ ⊙ ⌿ ✳ ⓒ 🚽 ♿
Services: 🔌 🛢 🔥 🍴 🛒 ♨ 🚮
Within 3 miles: ⚓ 🎣 🎿 🏌 🎯 🏊 🛍 💷 ♻ ⛲
Notes: Crazy golf, badminton.

see advert on page 92

► ► ► ► 85% **Treago Farm Caravan Site** (SW782601)

TR8 5QS
☎ **01637 830277**
e-mail: info@treagofarm.co.uk
dir: *From A3075 (W of Newquay) turn right for Crantock. Site signed beyond village*

Open mid May-mid Sep

Last arrival 22.00hrs Last departure 18.00hrs

A grass site in open farmland in a south-facing sheltered valley. This friendly family park has direct access to Crantock and Polly Joke beaches, National Trust land and many natural beauty

spots. 5 acre site. 90 touring pitches. Caravan pitches. Motorhome pitches. Tent pitches. 10 statics.

AA Pubs & Restaurants nearby: The Smugglers' Den Inn, Cubert 01637 830209

The Lewinnick Lodge Bar & Restaurant, Newquay 01637 878117

Leisure: ⚲ ▢
Facilities: ⬤ ⊙ ⌿ ✳ ⓒ 🚽 ♿ 🐾 ♻ ❶
Services: 🔌 🛢 🔥 🛢 🍴 🛒
Within 3 miles: ⚓ 🎣 ♜ 🎣 🏊 🛍 💷 ⛲
Notes: Dogs must be kept on leads.

► ► ► 82% **Quarryfield Holiday Park** (SW793608)

TR8 5RJ
☎ **01637 872792 & 830338**
e-mail: quarryfield@crantockcaravans.orangehome.co.uk
dir: *From A3075 (Newquay-Redruth road) follow Crantock signs. Site signed*

Open Etr to end Oct (rs May-Oct pool open)

Last arrival 23.00hrs Last departure 10.00hrs

This park has a private path down to the dunes and golden sands of Crantock Beach, about ten minutes away, and it is within easy reach of all that Newquay has to offer, particularly for families. The park has very modern facilities, and provides plenty of amenities including a great swimming pool. Extensive improvements have been made to the bar and the children's play area. 10 acre site. 145 touring pitches. Caravan pitches. Motorhome pitches. Tent pitches. 43 statics.

AA Pubs & Restaurants nearby: The Smugglers' Den Inn, Cubert 01637 830209

The Lewinnick Lodge Bar & Restaurant, Newquay 01637 878117

Leisure: 🏊 ⚲ ♜
Facilities: ⬤ ⊙ ⌿ ✳ ⓒ 🚽 ♿ 🐾 ♻
Services: 🔌 🛢 🔥 🍴 🛒 🍴 🛒 ♨ 🚮
Within 3 miles: ⚓ 🎿 🎣 ♜ 🎣 🏊 🛍 💷 ⛲
Notes: No campfires, quiet after 22.30hrs. Dogs must be kept on leads.

► ► ► 80% **Crantock Plains Touring Park** (SW805589)

TR8 5PH
☎ **01637 830955 & 07967 956897**
e-mail: crantockplainstp@btconnect.com
dir: *Exit Newquay on A3075, 2nd right signed to park & Crantock. Site on left in 0.75m on narrow road*

Open mid Apr-end Sep

Last arrival 22.00hrs Last departure noon

A small rural park with pitches on either side of a narrow lane, surrounded by mature trees for shelter. This spacious, family-run park has good modern toilet facilities and is ideal for campers who appreciate peace and quiet and is situated approximately 1.2 miles from pretty Crantock, and Newquay is within easy reach. 6 acre site. 60 touring pitches. 20 seasonal pitches. Caravan pitches. Motorhome pitches. Tent pitches.

AA Pubs & Restaurants nearby: The Smugglers' Den Inn, Cubert 01637 830209

The Lewinnick Lodge Bar & Restaurant, Newquay 01637 878117

Leisure: ♜ ❀ ⚲
Facilities: ⬤ ⊙ ⌿ ✳ ⓒ 🚽 🐾 ❶
Services: 🔌 🛢 🛒
Within 3 miles: ⚓ 🎣 🏊 🛍 💷 ⛲
Notes: No skateboards. Dogs must be kept on leads.

CUBERT   Map 2 SW75

Places to visit

Blue Reef Aquarium, TYNEMOUTH 0191 258 1031
www.bluereefaquarium.co.uk

Trerice, TRERICE 01637 875404
www.nationaltrust.org.uk

Great for kids: Dairy Land Farm World,
NEWQUAY 01872 510246
www.dairylandfarmworld.com

►►► 81% Cottage Farm Touring Park *(SW786589)*

Treworgans TR8 5HH
☎ 01637 831083
e-mail: info@cottagefarmpark.co.uk
web: www.cottagefarmpark.co.uk
dir: *From A392 towards Newquay, left onto A3075 towards Redruth. In 2m right signed Cubert, right again in 1.5m signed Crantock, left in 0.5m*

* 🚐 £12-£17 🚐 £12-£17 ▲ £12-£17

Open Apr-end Sep

Last arrival 22.30hrs Last departure noon

A small grassy touring park nestling in the tiny hamlet of Treworgans, in sheltered open countryside close to a lovely beach at Holywell Bay. This quiet family-run park boasts very good quality facilities including a new fenced playground for children, with a climbing frame, swings, slides etc. 2 acre site. 45 touring pitches. 2 hardstandings. Caravan pitches. Motorhome pitches. Tent pitches. 1 static.

AA Pubs & Restaurants nearby: The Smugglers' Den Inn, Cubert 01637 830209

The Plume of Feathers, Mitchell 01872 510387

Facilities: 🍴⊙☂✳♻ ❶
Services: 🔌🔥🛒
Within 3 miles: ↨🐾🎌🔎◎🛁🔵🔴∪
Notes: No noise after 23.00hrs. Dogs must be kept on leads.

EDGCUMBE   Map 2 SW73

Places to visit

Poldark Mine and Heritage Complex, WENDRON 01326 573173 www.poldark-mine.com

Trevarno Estate Garden & Museum of Gardening, HELSTON 01326 574274
www.trevarno.co.uk

Great for kids: National Seal Sanctuary, GWEEK 0871 423 2110 www.sealsanctuary.co.uk

The Flambards Theme Park, HELSTON 01326 573404 www.flambards.co.uk

►►► 79% Retanna Holiday Park *(SW711327)*

TR13 0EJ
☎ 01326 340643
e-mail: retannaholpark@btconnect.com
web: www.retanna.co.uk
dir: *On A394 towards Helston, site signed on right. Site in 100mtrs*

* 🚐 £16.50-£22.50 ▲ £16.50-£22.50

Open Apr-Oct

Last arrival 21.00hrs Last departure noon

A small family-owned and run park in a rural location midway between Falmouth and Helston, and only about eight miles from Redruth. Its well-sheltered grassy pitches make this an ideal location for visiting the lovely beaches and towns nearby. For a fun day out the Flambards Experience is only a short drive away, and for sailing enthusiasts, Stithians Lake is on the doorstep. 8 acre site. 24 touring pitches. Caravan pitches. Tent pitches. 23 statics.

AA Pubs & Restaurants nearby: Trengilly Wartha Inn, Constantine 01326 340332

Leisure: 🎱♻🎣🖵
Facilities: 🍴⊙✳♻🕒🍴📶 🔥 ♻ ❶
Services: 🔌🔥🛒🚿Ⓣ🛒🍼
Within 3 miles: ↨🐾🔎◎🛁🔵🔴∪
Notes: No pets, no disposable BBQs, no open fires. Free use of fridge/freezer in laundry room, free air bed inflation, free mobile phone charging.

FALMOUTH   Map 2 SW83

Places to visit

Pendennis Castle, FALMOUTH 01326 316594
www.english-heritage.org.uk

Trebah Garden, MAWNAN SMITH 01326 252200
www.trebah-garden.co.uk

Great for kids: National Maritime Museum Cornwall, FALMOUTH 01326 313388
www.nmmc.co.uk

►►► 74% Pennance Mill Farm Touring Park *(SW792307)*

Maenporth TR11 5HJ
☎ 01326 317431
dir: *From A39 (Truro to Falmouth road) follow brown camping signs towards Maenporth Beach. At Hill Head rdbt take 2nd exit for Maenporth Beach*

* 🚐 £20-£23 🚐 £20-£23 ▲ £20-£23

Open Etr-Nov

Last arrival 22.00hrs Last departure 10.00hrs

Set approximately half a mile from the safe, sandy bay at Maenporth, accessed by a private woodland walk direct from the park, this is a mainly level, grassy park in a rural location sheltered by mature trees and shrubs and divided into three meadows. It has a modern toilet block. 6 acre site. 75 touring pitches. 12 hardstandings. Caravan pitches. Motorhome pitches. Tent pitches. 4 statics.

AA Pubs & Restaurants nearby: Trengilly Wartha Inn, Constantine 01326 340332

Budock Vean - Hotel on the River, Mawnan Smith 01326 252100

Leisure: 🎱♻🎣
Facilities: 🍴⊙✳🕒🍴🔥♻ ❶
Services: 🔌🔥🛒🚿🛒🛒🍼
Within 3 miles: ↨🐾🎌🔎◎🛁🔵🔴∪
Notes: 🚫 No noise after 23.00hrs. 0.5m private path to walk or cycle to beach.

FALMOUTH *continued*

►► 78% Tregedna Farm Touring Caravan & Tent Park *(SW785305)*

Maenporth TR11 5HL
☎ 01326 250529
e-mail: enquiries@tregednafarmholidays.co.uk
dir: *Take A39 from Truro to Falmouth. Turn right at Hill Head rdbt. Site 2.5m on right*

Open Apr-Sep

Last arrival 22.00hrs Last departure 13.00hrs

Set in the picturesque Maen Valley, this gently-sloping, south-facing park is part of a 100-acre farm. It is surrounded by beautiful wooded countryside just minutes from the beach, with spacious pitches and well-kept facilities. 12 acre site. 40 touring pitches. Caravan pitches. Motorhome pitches. Tent pitches.

AA Pubs & Restaurants nearby: Trengilly Wartha Inn, Constantine 01326 340332

Budock Vean - Hotel on the River, Mawnan Smith 01326 252100

Leisure: ⚲
Facilities: ⬙⊙✳️🕗🗑️🛒♻️ ❶
Services: ⬛🗑️⚗️
Within 3 miles: ⬩🎋🎡⚲◎⮕🗑️🗑️

Notes: ⬤ One dog only per pitch. Dogs must be kept on leads.

►►► 83% Penmarlam Caravan & Camping Park *(SX134526)*

Bodinnick PL23 1LZ
☎ 01726 870088
e-mail: info@penmarlampark.co.uk
dir: *From A390 at East Taphouse take B3359 signed Looe & Polperro. Follow signs for Bodinnick & Fowey, via ferry. Site on right at entrance to Bodinnick*

✱ ⬙ £15.50-£26.50 ⬛ £15.50-£26.50
⬙ £15.50-£26.50

Open Apr-Oct

Last departure noon

This tranquil park set above the Fowey Estuary in an Area of Outstanding Natural Beauty, with access to the water, continues to improve. Pitches are level, and sheltered by trees and bushes in two paddocks, while the toilets are spotlessly clean and well maintained. The shop is licensed and sells local and other Cornish produce. Good walks surrounding site include one to the Penruan passenger ferry, and one to the Bodinnick car ferry giving easy access to Fowey (charge £4.50 for car

and two passengers). 4 acre site. 63 touring pitches. 20 seasonal pitches. Caravan pitches. Motorhome pitches. Tent pitches.

AA Pubs & Restaurants nearby: The Ship Inn, Fowey 01726 832230

The Fowey Hotel, Fowey 01726 832551

Facilities: ⬙⊙☈✳️⬩🗑️🎏🛒 📺 🗑️♻️ ❶
Services: ⬛🗑️🔋⚗️🚽🚼
Within 3 miles: ⬩🎋🎡🎡◎⮕🗑️🗑️⟳

Notes: Dogs must be kept on leads. Private slipway, small boat storage.

LEISURE: 🏊 Indoor swimming pool 🏊 Outdoor swimming pool ⚲ Children's playground ⚲ Kid's club ⚲ Tennis court ⚲ Games room ⬜ Separate TV room ⬩ 9/18 hole golf course ⚲ Boats for hire ⬚ Cinema ♪ Entertainment ⚲ Fishing ◎ Mini golf ⚲ Watersports ⚲ Gym ⚲ Sports field Spa ⟳ Stables
FACILITIES: ⬙ Bath ⬙ Shower ⊙ Electric shaver ⚲ Hairdryer ✳️ Ice Pack Facility ⬩ Disabled facilities ⚲ Public telephone 🗑️ Shop on site or within 200yds 🗑️ Mobile shop (calls at least 5 days a week) ⬙ BBQ area ⬙ Picnic area ⬙ Wi-fi ⬙ Internet access ♻️ Recycling ❶ Tourist info 🎏 Dog exercise area

GOONHAVERN   Map 2 SW75

PREMIER PARK

▶▶▶▶▶ 84% Silverbow Park

(SW782531)

Perranwell TR4 9NX
☎ 01872 572347
e-mail: silverbowhols@btconnect.com
dir: *Adjacent to A3075, 0.5m S of village*

🚐 🚃 Å

Open May-end Sep

Last arrival 22.00hrs Last departure 10.30hrs

This park, on the main road to Newquay, has a quiet garden atmosphere, and appeals to families with young children. The superb landscaped grounds and good quality toilet facilities, housed in an attractive chalet-style building, including four family rooms, are maintained to a very high standard with attention paid to detail. Leisure facilities include two inviting swimming pools (outdoor and indoor), a bowling green, and a nature walk around small lakes, with a summer house where children can take part in a number of nature activities. 14 acre site. 100 touring pitches. 2 hardstandings. 24 seasonal pitches. Caravan pitches. Motorhome pitches. Tent pitches. 15 statics.

AA Pubs & Restaurants nearby: The Smugglers' Den Inn, Cubert 01637 830209

Silverbow Park

Leisure: 🏊 🚴 ⚽ 🎯 🎣
Facilities: 🚿 🛁 ⊙ 📶 ✳ ♿ 🛒 🏪 🚻 🛫 ♻ ❓
Services: 🔌 🗑 🛢 🚿 🅣
Within 3 miles: 🎣 ✈ 🏊 ◎ 🍴 🛒 🏧 U

Notes: ⊘ No cycling, no skateboards. Short mat bowls rink, conservation/information area, indoor/ outdoor table tennis.

see advert on opposite page

▶▶▶▶ 86% Penrose Holiday Park

(SW795534)

TR4 9QF
☎ 01872 573185
e-mail: info@penroseholidaypark.com
web: www.penroseholidaypark.com
dir: *From Exeter take A30, past Bodmin & Indian Queens. Just after Wind Farm take B3285 towards Perranporth, site on left on entering Goonhavern*

* 🚐 £14.35-£26.65 🚃 £14.35-£26.65
Å £14.35-£26.65

Open Apr-Oct

Last arrival 21.30hrs Last departure 10.00hrs

A quiet sheltered park set in five paddocks divided by hedges and shrubs, only a short walk from the village. Lovely floral displays enhance the park's appearance, and the grass and hedges are neatly trimmed. Four cubicled family rooms are very popular, and there is a good laundry, and a smart reception building. A new internet café is now available. 9 acre site. 110 touring pitches. 48 hardstandings. Caravan pitches. Motorhome pitches. Tent pitches. 24 statics.

AA Pubs & Restaurants nearby: The Plume of Feathers, Mitchell 01872 510387

Leisure: 🅰
Facilities: 🛁 ⊙ 📶 ✳ ♿ 🕐 🚻 🛫 🖥 ♻ ❓
Services: 🔌 🗑 🛢 🚿 🅣 🍴 🏧 🔋 ⚓
Within 3 miles: 🎣 ✈ 🏊 ◎ 🍴 🛒 🏧 U

Notes: Families & couples only. Dogs must be kept on leads. Campers' kitchen.

▶▶▶ 77% Sunny Meadows Tourist Park *(SW782542)*

Rosehill TR4 9JT
☎ 01872 571333
dir: *From A30 onto B3285 signed Perranporth. At Goonhavern turn left at T-junct, then right at rdbt to Perranporth. Site on left*

🚐 🚃 Å

Open Etr-Oct

Last arrival 22.30hrs Last departure 10.30hrs

A gently-sloping park in a peaceful, rural location, with mostly level pitches set into three small hedge-lined paddocks. Run by a friendly family, the park is just two miles from the long sandy beach at Perranporth; Newquay is only a 20-minute drive away. 14.5 acre site. 100 touring pitches. 1 hardstanding. Caravan pitches. Motorhome pitches. Tent pitches. 4 statics.

AA Pubs & Restaurants nearby: The Smugglers' Den Inn, Cubert 01637 830209

The Plume of Feathers, Mitchell 01872 510387

Leisure: 🅰
Facilities: 🛁 ⊙ ✳ ♿ 🚻 🛫 ♻ 🕐
Services: 🔌 🛢 🚿 🅣 🔋
Within 3 miles: 🎣 🏊 🛒 🏧 U

Notes: ⊘ One car per pitch. Dogs must be kept on leads. Pool table & family TV room; washing machine & tumble dryer.

see advert on page 74

SERVICES: 🔌 Electric hook up 🗑 Launderette 🍺 Licensed bar 🛢 Calor Gas 🚬 Camping Gaz 🅣 Toilet fluid 🍴 Café/Restaurant 🍟 Fast Food/Takeaway 🔋 Battery charging
🚼 Baby care ⚓ Motorvan service point **ABBREVIATIONS:** BH/bank hols-bank holidays Etr-Easter Whit-Whitsun dep-departure fr-from hrs-hours m-mile mdnt-midnight
rdbt-roundabout rs-restricted service wk-week wknd-weekend ⊘ No credit cards 🚫 no dogs   See page 7 for details of the AA Camping Card Scheme

GOONHAVERN *continued*

▶▶▶ 75% Roseville Holiday Park

(SW787540)

TR4 9LA

☎ 01872 572448

dir: *From mini-rdbt in Goonhavern follow B3285 towards Perranporth, site 0.5m on right*

Open Whit-Oct (rs Apr-Jul, Sep-Oct shop closed)

Last arrival 21.30hrs Last departure 11.00hrs

A family park set in a rural location with sheltered grassy pitches, some gently sloping. The toilet facilities are modern, and there is an attractive outdoor swimming pool complex. This park is approximately two miles from the long sandy beach at Perranporth. 8 acre site. 95 touring pitches. Caravan pitches. Motorhome pitches. Tent pitches. 5 statics.

AA Pubs & Restaurants nearby: The Smugglers' Den Inn, Cubert 01637 830209

The Plume of Feathers, Mitchell 01872 510387

Leisure: 🏊 ⚠ 🔍
Facilities: 🎣 ☺ 🅿 ✳ 👤 🐎
Services: 🔌 🗑 🛢 🧹 T 🚐
Within 3 miles: 🎣 🏌 ◎ 🚣 🅑 🕭 ♻
Notes: 🐾 Families only. Off-licence in shop.

▶▶ 82% *Little Treamble Farm Touring Park* *(SW785560)*

Rose TR4 9PR

☎ 01872 573823 & 07971 070760

e-mail: info@treamble.co.uk

dir: *A30 onto B3285 signed Perranporth. Approx 0.5m right into Scotland Rd signed Newquay. Approx 2m to T-junct, right onto A3075 signed Newquay. 0.25m left at Rejerrah sign. Site signed 0.75m on right*

Open all year

Last departure noon

This site, within easy reach of Padstow, Newquay and St Ives, is set in a quiet rural location with extensive countryside views across an undulating valley. There is a small toilet block, a new disabled facility and a well-stocked shop. This working farm is next to a Caravan Club site. 1.5 acre site. 20 touring pitches. Caravan pitches. Motorhome pitches. Tent pitches.

AA Pubs & Restaurants nearby: The Smugglers' Den Inn, Cubert 01637 830209

The Plume of Feathers, Mitchell 01872 510387

Facilities: 🎣 ✳ 🅑
Services: 🔌 T 🚐
Within 3 miles: 🎣 🏌 ◎ 🕭 ♻

▶▶▶ 80% Treveague Farm Caravan & Camping Site *(SX002410)*

PL26 6NY

☎ 01726 842295

e-mail: treveague@btconnect.com

web: www.treveaguefarm.co.uk

dir: *B3273 from St Austell towards Mevagissey, pass Pentewan at top of hill, right signed Gorran. Past Heligan Gardens towards Gorran Churchtown. Follow brown tourist signs from fork in road. (NB roads to site are single lane & very narrow. It is advisable to follow guide directions & not Sat Nav)*

* 🚐 £7.50-£22 🚍 £7.50-£22 🛖 £6-£20

Open Apr-Sep

Last arrival 21.00hrs Last departure noon

Spectacular panoramic coastal views can be enjoyed from this rural park, which is set on an organic farm and well equipped with modern facilities. A stone-faced toilet block with a Cornish slate roof is an attractive and welcome feature, as is the building that houses the smart reception, café and shop, which sells meat produced on the farm. There is an aviary with exotic birds, and also

LEISURE: 🏊 Indoor swimming pool   🏊 Outdoor swimming pool   ⚠ Children's playground   👦 Kid's club   🎾 Tennis court   🔍 Games room   📺 Separate TV room   🏌 9/18 hole golf course   🚣 Boats for hire   🎬 Cinema   🎵 Entertainment   🎣 Fishing   ◎ Mini golf   🚤 Watersports   👟 Gym   🏟 Sports field   Spa   ♻ Stables
FACILITIES: 🛁 Bath   🚿 Shower   ☺ Electric shaver   🅿 Hairdryer   ✳ Ice Pack Facility   ♿ Disabled facilities   📞 Public telephone   🛒 Shop on site or within 200yds   🚐 Mobile shop (calls at least 5 days a week)   🍖 BBQ area   🧺 Picnic area   WiFi Wi-fi   💻 Internet access   ♻ Recycling   ℹ Tourist info   🐕 Dog exercise area

chinchillas. A footpath leads to the fishing village of Gorran Haven in one direction, and the secluded sandy Vault Beach in the other. The site is close to a bus route. 4 acre site. 40 touring pitches. Caravan pitches. Motorhome pitches. Tent pitches.

AA Pubs & Restaurants nearby: The Ship Inn, Mevagissey 01726 843324

The Crown Inn, St Ewe 01726 843322

Leisure: ⚑ ⚽

Facilities: ⬦⊙☞❊♿🛓🔥🚽 WiFi 🖥 ♻ ❶

Services: ⬛🔲 T 🍽 🛒 🏧

Within 3 miles: 🛶 ⚓ 🛶 🏧🔲

Notes: Bird hide with observation cameras.

►►► 80% Treveor Farm Caravan & Camping Site *(SW988418)*

PL26 6LW
☎ **01726 842387**
e-mail: info@treveorfarm.co.uk
web: www.treveorfarm.co.uk
dir: From St Austell bypass left onto B3273 for Mevagissey. On hilltop before descent to village turn right on unclassified road for Gorran. Right in 3.5m, site on right

* ⬛ £7.50-£16.50 ⬛ £7.50-£16.50
▲ £4.50-£13.50

Open Apr-Oct

Last arrival 20.00hrs Last departure 11.00hrs

A small family-run camping park set on a working farm, with grassy pitches backing onto mature hedging. This quiet site, with good facilities, is close to beaches and offers a large coarse fishing lake. 4 acre site. 50 touring pitches. Caravan pitches. Motorhome pitches. Tent pitches.

AA Pubs & Restaurants nearby: The Ship Inn, Mevagissey 01726 843324

The Crown Inn, St Ewe 01726 843322

Leisure: ⚑ **Facilities:** ⬦⊙☞❊♻ ❶

Services: ⬛🔲 **Within 3 miles:** 🛶 🛶 🏧

Notes: No hard balls, kites or frizbees. Dogs must be kept on leads.

GORRAN HAVEN   Map 2 SX04

Places to visit

Caerhays Castle Gardens, GORRAN
01872 501144 www.caerhays.co.uk

The Lost Gardens of Heligan, PENTEWAN
01726 845100 www.heligan.com

Great for kids: Wheal Martyn Museum & Country Park, ST AUSTELL 01726 850362
www.wheal-martyn.com

►► 74% Trelispen Caravan & Camping Park *(SX008421)*

PL26 6NT
☎ **01726 843501**
e-mail: trelispen@care4free.net
dir: B3273 from St Austell towards Mevagissey, on hilltop at x-roads before descent into Mevagissey turn right on unclassified road to Gorran. Through village, 2nd right towards Gorran Haven, site signed on left in 250mtrs (NB it is advisable to use guide directions not Sat Nav)

* ⬛ £14-£20 ⬛ £12-£18 ▲ £12-£16

Open Etr & Apr-Oct

Last arrival 22.00hrs Last departure noon

A quiet rural site set in three paddocks, and sheltered by mature trees and hedges. The simple toilets have plenty of hot water, and there is a small laundry. Sandy beaches, pubs and shops are nearby, and Mevagissey is two miles away. There is a bus stop 100yds from the site with a regular service to Mevagissey and St Austell. 2 acre site. 40 touring pitches. Caravan pitches. Motorhome pitches. Tent pitches.

AA Pubs & Restaurants nearby: The Ship Inn, Mevagissey 01726 843324

The Crown Inn, St Ewe 01726 843322

Leisure: ⚑ **Facilities:** ⬦⊙❊

Services: ⬛🔲 **Within 3 miles:** 🛶 ⚓ 🏧🔲

Notes: 🌐 30-acre nature reserve.

GWITHIAN   Map 2 SW54

Places to visit

East Pool Mine, POOL 01209 315027
www.nationaltrust.org.uk

►►►► 89% Gwithian Farm Campsite *(SW586412)*

Gwithian Farm TR27 5BX
☎ **01736 753127**
e-mail: camping@gwithianfarm.co.uk
dir: Exit A30 at Hayle rdbt, take 4th exit signed Hayle, 100mtrs. At 1st mini-rdbt turn right onto B3301 signed Portreath. Site 2m on left on entering village

⬛ £14-£27 ⬛ £14-£27 ▲ £14-£27

Open 31 Mar-1 Oct

Last arrival 21.00hrs Last departure 17.00hrs

An unspoilt site located behind the sand dunes of Gwithian's golden beach, which can be reached by footpath directly from the site, making this an ideal location for surfers. The site boasts stunning floral displays, a superb toilet block with excellent facilities, including a bathroom and baby-changing unit, and first-class hardstanding pitches. Each attractive pitch has been screened by hedge planting. There is a good pub opposite. 7.5 acre site. 87 touring pitches. 26 hardstandings. Caravan pitches. Motorhome pitches. Tent pitches.

AA Pubs & Restaurants nearby: The Basset Arms, Portreath 01209 842077

Porthminster Beach Restaurant, St Ives 01736 795352

Leisure: ⚽

Facilities: ⬦⊙☞❊♿🛓📷🔥 WiFi ♻ ❶

Services: ⬛🔲 🅿 ⊘ T 🛒 🏧

Within 3 miles: 🛶⚓◎🛶🔲🔲 U

Notes: No ball games after 21.00hrs, no noise after 22.30hrs, payment by debit card only. Dogs must be kept on leads. Surf board & wet suit hire, table tennis.

SERVICES: ⬛ Electric hook up 🔲 Launderette 🍷 Licensed bar 🅿 Calor Gas ⊘ Camping Gaz T Toilet fluid 🍽 Café/Restaurant 🛒 Fast Food/Takeaway 🔋 Battery charging 🛒 Baby care 🏧 Motorvan service point **ABBREVIATIONS:** BH/bank hols-bank holidays Etr-Easter Whit-Whitsun dep-departure fr-from hrs-hours m-mile mdnt-midnight rdbt-roundabout rs-restricted service wk-week wknd-weekend 🌐 No credit cards 🚫 no dogs   See page 7 for details of the AA Camping Card Scheme

HAYLE
Map 2 SW53

Places to visit

Tate St Ives, ST IVES 01736 796226
www.tate.org.uk/stives

Barbara Hepworth Museum & Sculpture
Garden, ST IVES 01736 796226
www.tate.org.uk/stives

►►► 88% St Ives Bay Holiday Park

(SW577398)

73 Loggans Rd, Upton Towans TR27 5BH
☎ **01736 752274**
e-mail: stivesbay@btconnect.com
web: www.stivesbay.co.uk
dir: *Exit A30 at Hayle then immediate right onto B3301 at mini-rdbts. Site entrance 0.5m on left*

* ⊞ £10-£32 ⊞ £10-£32 ▲ £10-£32

Open Etr-1 Oct

Last arrival 21.00hrs Last departure 09.00hrs

An extremely well maintained holiday park with a relaxed atmosphere situated adjacent to a three mile beach. The various camping fields are set in hollows amongst the sand dunes and are very tastefully set out; the high fields have stunning views over St Ives Bay. The touring sections are in a number of separate locations around the extensive site. The park is specially geared for families and couples, and as well as the large indoor swimming pool there are two pubs with seasonal entertainment. 90 acre site. 240 touring pitches. Caravan pitches. Motorhome pitches. Tent pitches. 250 statics.

AA Pubs & Restaurants nearby: White Hart, Ludgvan 01736 740574

Porthminster Beach Restaurant, St Ives 01736 795352

Leisure: 🏊 🛝 🎣 ⚓ 🖵 🎵
Facilities: ⌐ ⊙ 𝓟 ✳ ⅗ 🕓 ⑤ 🛒 📶 ▬ ♻ 𝒊
Services: 🔌 ⑤ 🍴 🛢 🚿 ⊤ 🍽 🛒 🚮 🚾 ↯
Within 3 miles: ↕ 🏌 ⊚ ⑤ 🎣 ⑤ ♒

Notes: No pets. Crazy golf, video room.

see advert on page 90

AA CAMPING CARD SITE

►►► 83% Higher Trevaskis Caravan & Camping Park *(SW611381)*

Gwinear Rd, Connor Downs TR27 5JQ
☎ **01209 831736**
dir: *At Hayle rdbt on A30 take exit signed Connor Downs, in 1m turn right signed Carnhell Green. Site 0.75m just past level crossing*

* ⊞ £12-£20 ⊞ £12-£20 ▲ £12-£20

Open mid Apr-Sep

Last arrival 20.00hrs Last departure 10.30hrs

An attractive paddocked and terraced park in a sheltered rural position on a valley side with views towards St Ives. The terrace areas are divided by hedges. This secluded park is personally run by owners who keep it quiet and welcoming. Three unisex showers are a great hit with visitors. Fluent German is spoken. 6.5 acre site. 82 touring pitches. 3 hardstandings. Caravan pitches. Motorhome pitches. Tent pitches.

AA Pubs & Restaurants nearby: White Hart, Ludgvan 01736 740574

Porthminster Beach Restaurant, St Ives 01736 795352

Leisure: 🛝 ⚽
Facilities: ⌐ ⊙ 𝓟 ✳ 🕓 ⑤ ♻ 𝒊
Services: 🔌 ⑤ 🛢 🚿 ⊤ 🛒
Within 3 miles: ↕ 🏌 ⊚ 🎣 ⑤ ⑤

Notes: ⚫ Max speed 5mph, max 2 dogs, no dangerous dogs, balls on field only. Dogs must be kept on leads.

►►► 82% *Atlantic Coast Caravan Park* (NW580400)

53 Upton Towans, Gwithian TR27 5BL
☎ **01736 752071**
e-mail: enquiries@atlanticcoastpark.co.uk
dir: *From A30 into Hayle, turn right at double rdbt. Site 1.5m on left*

⊞ ⊞ ▲

Open Mar-early Jan

Last arrival 20.00hrs Last departure 11.00hrs

Fringed by the sand-dunes of St Ives Bay and close to the golden sands of Gwithian Beach, the small, friendly touring area offers fully serviced pitches. There's freshly baked bread, a takeaway and a bar next door. This park is ideally situated for visitors to enjoy the natural coastal beauty and attractions of south-west Cornwall. The entrance and exit roads to the touring park have been widened to improve the access. Static caravans for holiday hire. 4.5 acre site. 15 touring pitches. 5 seasonal pitches. Caravan pitches. Motorhome pitches. Tent pitches. 50 statics.

AA Pubs & Restaurants nearby: White Hart, Ludgvan 01736 740574

Porthminster Beach Restaurant, St Ives 01736 795352

Facilities: ⌐ ⊙ 𝓟 ✳ ⅗ 🕓 ⑤ 📶 ♻ 𝒊
Services: 🔌 ⑤ ⊤ 🍽 🚾
Within 3 miles: ↕ 🏌 ⊚ 🎣 ⑤ ⑤ ♒

Notes: No commercial vehicles, gazebos or day tents. Dogs must be kept on leads.

LEISURE: 🏊 Indoor swimming pool 🏊 Outdoor swimming pool 🛝 Children's playground 🧒 Kid's club 🎾 Tennis court ⚔ Games room 🖵 Separate TV room ↕ 9/18 hole golf course ⛵ Boats for hire 🎬 Cinema 🎵 Entertainment 🎣 Fishing ⊚ Mini golf ⚓ Watersports 🏋 Gym ⑤ Sports field **Spa** ♒ Stables
FACILITIES: 🛁 Bath 🚿 Shower ⊙ Electric shaver 𝓟 Hairdryer ✳ Ice Pack Facility ⅗ Disabled facilities 🕓 Public telephone ⑤ Shop on site or within 200yds ⑤ Mobile shop (calls at least 5 days a week) 🍴 BBQ area 🏕 Picnic area 📶 Wi-fi ▬ Internet access ♻ Recycling 𝒊 Tourist info 🐕 Dog exercise area

▶▶▶ 79% Parbola Holiday Park
(SW612366)

Wall, Gwinear TR27 5LE
☎ 01209 831503
e-mail: bookings@parbola.co.uk
dir: At Hayle rdbt on A30 take Connor Downs exit. In 1m turn right signed Carnhell Green. In village right to Wall. Site in village on left

🚐 🚌 ⛺

Open Etr-Sep (rs Etr-end of Jun & Sep shop closed, pool unheated)

Last arrival 21.00hrs Last departure 10.00hrs

A spacious touring park set in woodland with the reception and shop in the centre. Pitches are provided in both wooded and open areas. The park is centrally located for touring the seaside resorts and towns in the area, especially nearby Hayle with its three miles of golden sands. 16.5 acre site. 110 touring pitches. 4 hardstandings. Caravan pitches. Motorhome pitches. Tent pitches. 28 statics.

AA Pubs & Restaurants nearby: White Hart, Ludgvan 01736 740574

Porthminster Beach Restaurant, St Ives 01736 795352

Leisure: ⚓ 🎢 ☼ 🔍
Facilities: 📡 ☉ 🏳 ❅ ⚒ 🛅 📶 🖥 ♻ ❶
Services: 🔌 🔲 🔋 🍴 🔋 🛒
Within 3 miles: 🎣 🚶 ⊚ 🛝 🐴 ∪

Notes: Dogs not allowed Jul-Aug. Dogs must be kept on leads. Crazy golf & table tennis, giant chess & draughts, hairdresser, make-up room, herb garden.

▶▶▶ 79% Treglisson Touring Park
(SW581367)

Wheal Alfred Rd TR27 5JT
☎ 01736 753141
e-mail: enquiries@treglisson.co.uk
dir: 4th exit off rdbt on A30 at Hayle. 100mtrs, left at 1st mini-rdbt. Approx 1.5m past golf course, site sign on left

* 🚐 £10-£14 🚌 £10-£14 ⛺ £10-£14

Open Etr-Sep

Last arrival 20.00hrs Last departure 11.00hrs

A small secluded site in a peaceful wooded meadow, and a former apple and pear orchard. This quiet rural site has level grass pitches and a well-planned modern toilet block, and is just two miles from the glorious beach at Hayle with its vast stretch of golden sand. 3 acre site. 26 touring pitches. 3 hardstandings. Caravan pitches. Motorhome pitches. Tent pitches.

AA Pubs & Restaurants nearby: White Hart, Ludgvan 01736 740574

Porthminster Beach Restaurant, St Ives 01736 795352

Leisure: ⚓ 🎢
Facilities: 📡 ☉ 🏳 ❅ ⚒ 🛅 📶 ♻ ❶
Services: 🔌 🔲 🔋
Within 3 miles: 🎣 🚶 ⚓ 🛝 🔋

Notes: Max 6 people to one pitch. Dogs must be kept on leads. Milk deliveries.

🏕 ⋃ NEW Riviere Sands Holiday
hh **Park** (SW556386)

Riviere Towans TR27 5AX
☎ 01736 752132
e-mail: rivieresands@haven.com
web: www.haven.com/rivieresands
dir: A30 towards Redruth. Follow signs into Hayle, cross double mini rdbt. Turn right opposite petrol station towards Towans and beaches. Park 1m on right

Open Mar-Oct

Close to St Ives and with direct access to a safe, white sandy beach, Riviere Sands is an exciting holiday park with much to offer families. Kids can enjoy the crazy golf, amusements, swimming pool complex and the beach; evening entertainment for adults is extensive and lively. There are a good range of holiday caravans and apartments. At the time of going to press the quality rating for this site had not been confirmed. For up-to-date information please see the AA website: theAA.com.

Change over day: Mon, Fri, Sat
Arrival & departure times: Please contact the site

Statics 295 **Sleep** 6-8 **Bedrms** 2-3 **Bathrms** 1-2 **Toilets** 1-2 **Freezer** TV Sky/FTV **Elec** included **Gas** included **Grass area** Parking

Children 🚼 **Cots Leisure:** ⚓ ⚓ 🤚 🎢

AA Pubs & Restaurants nearby: The Queens, St Ives 01736 796468

The Sloop Inn, St Ives 01736 796584

Carbis Bay Hotel, St Ives 01736 795311

see advert on page 62

HELSTON   Map 2 SW62

See also Ashton

Places to visit

Trevarno Estate Garden & Museum of Gardening, HELSTON 01326 574274 www.trevarno.co.uk

Goonhilly Satellite Earth Station Experience, HELSTON 0800 679593 www.goonhilly.bt.com

Great for kids: The Flambards Theme Park, HELSTON 01326 573404 www.flambards.co.uk

►►►► 85% *Lower Polladras Touring Park* (SW617308)

Carleen, Breage TR13 9NX
☎ 01736 762220
e-mail: lowerpolladras@btinternet.com
web: www.lower-polladras.co.uk
dir: *From Helston take A394 then B3302 (Hayle road) at Ward Garage, 2nd left to Carleen, site 2m on right*

Open Apr-Jan

Last arrival 22.00hrs Last departure noon

An attractive rural park with extensive views of surrounding fields, appealing to families who enjoy the countryside. The planted trees and shrubs are maturing, and help to divide the area into paddocks with spacious grassy pitches. The site has a dishwashing area, a games room, a dog and nature walk, and also Wi-fi, with plans for a campers' kitchen and two fully-serviced family rooms. 4 acre site. 39 touring pitches. 23 hardstandings. Caravan pitches. Motorhome pitches. Tent pitches. 3 statics.

AA Pubs & Restaurants nearby: The Ship Inn, Porthleven 01326 564204

The Kota Restaurant with Rooms, Porthleven 01326 562407

The New Yard Restaurant, Helston 01326 221595

Leisure: 🎠 🔍

Facilities: ℮ ⊙ 🗪 ⚓ ❄ ⚑ 🛒 🚻

Services: 🚉 🔌 🧹 🚿 ⊤ 🛒 ⚒

Within 3 miles: ⚓ ✈ 🎣 ⊙ 🏊 🍴 🏪 ⛎

Notes: ⊛ Caravan storage area.

AA CAMPING CARD SITE

►►► 77% Poldown Caravan Park

(SW629298)

Poldown, Carleen TR13 9NN
☎ 01326 574560
e-mail: stay@poldown.co.uk
dir: *From Helston follow Penzance signs for 1m, right onto B3302 to Hayle, 2nd left to Carleen, 0.5m to site*

* 🚍 £13.50-£20.50 🚐 £11.50-£17 🏕 £11.50-£17

Open Apr-Sep

Last arrival 21.00hrs Last departure noon

Ideally located for visiting the towns of Helston, Penzance and St Ives, this small, quiet site is set in attractive countryside. The park is sheltered by mature trees and shrubs. All the level grass pitches have electricity, and there are toilet facilities. 2 acre site. 13 touring pitches. 2 hardstandings. Caravan pitches. Motorhome pitches. Tent pitches. 7 statics. 2 bell tents/yurts.

AA Pubs & Restaurants nearby: The Ship Inn, Porthleven 01326 564204

The Kota Restaurant with Rooms, Porthleven 01326 562407

The New Yard Restaurant, Helston 01326 221595

Leisure: 🎠

Facilities: ℮ ⊙ 🗪 ❄ ⚓ ⊙ ⚑ 🛒 🚻 🖥 ♻ ⓘ

Services: 🚉 🔌 🛒 ⚒

Within 3 miles: ⚓ ✈ 🎣 ⊙ 🏊 🍴 🏪 ⛎

Notes: No credit cards, only debit cards accepted. Dogs must be kept on leads. Table tennis.

AA CAMPING CARD SITE

►►► 76% Skyburriowe Farm

(SW698227)

Garras TR12 6LR
☎ 01326 221646
e-mail: bkbenney@hotmail.co.uk
web: www.skyburriowefarm.co.uk
dir: *From Helston A3083 to The Lizard. After Culdrose Naval Airbase continue straight at rdbt, in 1m left at Skyburriowe Ln sign. In 0.5m right at Skyburriowe B&B/Campsite sign. Pass bungalow to farmhouse. Site on left*

🚍 £14-£18 🚐 £14-£18 🏕 £12-£15

Open Apr-Oct

Last arrival 22.00hrs Last departure 11.00hrs

A leafy no-through road leads to this picturesque farm park in a rural location on the Lizard Peninsula. The toilet block offers excellent quality facilities, and most pitches have electric hook-ups. There are some beautiful coves and beaches nearby, and for a great day out Flambards Experience is also close by. Under the supervision of the owner, children are permitted to watch his herd of Friesian cows being milked. 4 acre site. 30 touring pitches. 2 hardstandings. Caravan pitches. Motorhome pitches. Tent pitches.

AA Pubs & Restaurants nearby: The Ship Inn, Porthleven 01326 564204

Facilities: ℮ ⊙ ❄ ⚓ ⚑ ♻ ⓘ   Services: 🚉 🛒
Within 3 miles: ⚓ ✈ 🎣 🏊 🍴 🏪 ⛎

Notes: ⊛ Quiet after 23.00hrs. Dogs must be kept on leads.

LEISURE: 🏊 Indoor swimming pool 🏊 Outdoor swimming pool 🎠 Children's playground 🧒 Kid's club 🎾 Tennis court 🔍 Games room 🖵 Separate TV room ⛳ 9/18 hole golf course ⛵ Boats for hire 🎬 Cinema 🎵 Entertainment 🎣 Fishing ⊙ Mini golf 🏄 Watersports 🏋 Gym ⚽ Sports field **Spa** ⛎ Stables
FACILITIES: 🛁 Bath 🚿 Shower ⊙ Electric shaver 🗪 Hairdryer ❄ Ice Pack Facility ♿ Disabled facilities ☎ Public telephone 🏪 Shop on site or within 200yds 🛒 Mobile shop (calls at least 5 days a week) 🍴 BBQ area ⚑ Picnic area 🚻 Wi-fi 🖥 Internet access ♻ Recycling ⓘ Tourist info 🐕 Dog exercise area

HOLYWELL BAY   Map 2 SW75

Places to visit

Trerice, TRERICE 01637 875404
www.nationaltrust.org.uk

Blue Reef Aquarium, NEWQUAY 01637 878134
www.bluereefaquarium.co.uk

Great for kids: Newquay Zoo, NEWQUAY
0844 474 2244 www.newquayzoo.org.uk

 94% Trevornick Holiday Park
(SW776586)

TR8 5PW
☎ 01637 830531
e-mail: info@trevornick.co.uk
web: www.trevornick.co.uk
dir: 3m from Newquay exit A3075 towards
Redruth. Follow Cubert & Holywell Bay signs
* ⊞ £13.65-£24.15 ⊞ £13.65-£24.15
▲ £13.65-£24.15

Open Etr & mid May-mid Sep

Last arrival 21.00hrs Last departure 10.00hrs

A large seaside holiday complex with excellent
facilities and amenities. There is plenty of
entertainment including a children's club and
an evening cabaret, adding up to a full holiday
experience for all the family. A sandy beach is
just a 15-minute footpath walk away. The park
has 68 ready-erected tents for hire. 20 acre
site. 688 touring pitches. 53 hardstandings. 8
seasonal pitches. Caravan pitches. Motorhome
pitches. Tent pitches.

AA Pubs & Restaurants nearby: The Smugglers'
Den Inn, Cubert 01637 830209

Leisure: ⇔ ⋔ ⬇ ☺ ☜ ♫ Spa
Facilities: ⊶ ⋒ ⊙ ☞ ⚹ ⚄ ☺ ☒ ☐ ☢ WI-FI
♻ ❂

Services: ⊞ ⊟ ☎ ⚄ ⚗ ⒯ ⦿ ⛿ ⊕ ⚓

Within 3 miles: ⌁ ✛ ☰ ⚲ ◎ ≋ ☒ ☐ ⟲

Notes: Families & couples only. Dogs must
be kept on leads. Fishing, golf course,
entertainment, fun park, Eurotents.

see advert on page 87

 **79% Holywell Bay
Holywell Park** (SW773582)

TR8 5PR
☎ 0844 335 3756
e-mail: touringandcamping@parkdeanholidays.
com
web: www.parkdeantouring.com
dir: Exit A30 onto A392, take A3075 signed
Redruth, right in 2m signed Holywell/Cubert.
Through Cubert past Trevornick to site on left
* ⊞ £11-£42 ⊞ £11-£42 ▲ £8-£37

Open Mar-Oct (rs 4 May-16 Sep pool open)

Last arrival 23.00hrs Last departure 10.00hrs

Close to lovely beaches in a rural location,
this level grassy park borders on National
Trust land, and is only a short distance from
the Cornish Coastal Path. The touring area
is at the rear in a very quiet and flat area.
The park provides a popular entertainment
programme for the whole family (including
evening entertainment), and there is an outdoor
pool with a water slide and children's clubs.
Newquay is just a few miles away. 16 acre site.
39 touring pitches. Caravan pitches. Motorhome
pitches. Tent pitches. 156 statics.

AA Pubs & Restaurants nearby: The Smugglers'
Den Inn, Cubert 01637 830209

Leisure: ⇔ ⋔ ⬇ ☜ ♫
Facilities: ⋒ ⊙ ⚄ ☺ ☒ ☐
Services: ⊞ ⊟ ☎ ⒯ ⦿ ⊕ ⚓

Within 3 miles: ⌁ ⚲ ◎ ≋ ☒ ☐ ⟲

Notes: No pets. Surf school & hire shop,
adventure playground.

SERVICES: ⊞ Electric hook up ⊟ Launderette ☎ Licensed bar 🗎 Calor Gas ⊘ Camping Gaz ⒯ Toilet fluid ⦿ Café/Restaurant ⊕ Fast Food/Takeaway ⚓ Battery charging
⛭ Baby care ⚓ Motorvan service point **ABBREVIATIONS:** BH/bank hols-bank holidays Etr-Easter Whit-Whitsun dep-departure fr-from hrs-hours m-mile mdnt-midnight
rdbt-roundabout rs-restricted service wk-week wknd-weekend ⊗ No credit cards ⊗ no dogs   See page 7 for details of the AA Camping Card Scheme

INDIAN QUEENS — Map 2 SW95

Places to visit

Lanhydrock, LANHYDROCK 01208 265950
www.nationaltrust.org.uk

Charlestown Shipwreck & Heritage Centre,
ST AUSTELL 01726 69897
www.shipwreckcharlestown.com

Great for kids: Eden Project, ST AUSTELL
01726 811911 www.edenproject.com

▶▶▶ 76% *Gnome World Caravan & Camping Park* (SW890599)

Moorland Rd TR9 6HN
☎ 01726 860812 & 860101
e-mail: gnomesworld@btconnect.com
dir: *Signed from slip road at A30 & A39 rdbt in village of Indian Queens - site on old A30, now unclassified road*

🚐�90🅰

Open Mar-Dec

Last arrival 22.00hrs Last departure noon

Set in open countryside, this spacious park is set on level grassy land only half a mile from the A30 (Cornwall's main arterial route) and in a central holiday location for touring the county. Please note that there are no narrow lanes to negotiate. 4.5 acre site. 50 touring pitches. 25 hardstandings. Caravan pitches. Motorhome pitches. Tent pitches. 60 statics.

AA Pubs & Restaurants nearby: The Plume of Feathers, Mitchell 01827 510387

Gnome World Caravan & Camping Park

Leisure: 🅰
Facilities: 🌂⊙✳&🎇🛁
Services: 🚐🖐🛍
Within 3 miles: ♨🖐🛍🛍∪
Notes: Dogs must be kept on leads. Nature trail.

see advert below

JACOBSTOW — Map 2 SX19

Places to visit

Launceston Castle, LAUNCESTON 01566 772365
www.english-heritage.org.uk

Tamar Otter & Wildlife Centre, LAUNCESTON
01566 785646 www.tamarotters.co.uk

Great for kids: Launceston Steam Railway,
LAUNCESTON 01566 775665
www.launcestonsr.co.uk

▶▶▶ 76% Edmore Tourist Park

(SX184955)

Edgar Rd, Wainhouse Corner EX23 0BJ
☎ 01840 230467
e-mail: enquiries@cornwallvisited.co.uk
dir: *Exit A39 at Wainhouse Corner onto Edgar Rd, site signed on right in 200yds*

🚐 £14-£16 �90 £14-£16 🅰 £14-£16

Open 1 wk before Etr-Oct

Last arrival 21.00hrs Last departure noon

A quiet family-owned site in a rural location with extensive views, set close to the sandy surfing beaches of Bude, and the unspoilt sandy beach and rock pools at Crackington Haven. The friendly owners keep all facilities in a very good condition including the lovely grounds, and the site has hardstanding pitches and gravel access roads. There is an excellent children's play area. The site is handy for bus routes as it is close to the A39. 3 acre site. 28 touring pitches. Caravan pitches. Motorhome pitches. Tent pitches.

LEISURE: 🏊 Indoor swimming pool 🏊 Outdoor swimming pool 🅰 Children's playground 🧒 Kid's club 🎾 Tennis court 🎱 Games room ☐ Separate TV room ♨ 9/18 hole golf course ⛵ Boats for hire 🎬 Cinema 🎵 Entertainment 🎣 Fishing ⊙ Mini golf 🏄 Watersports 🏋 Gym ⚽ Sports field **Spa** ∪ Stables
FACILITIES: 🛁 Bath 🌂 Shower ⊙ Electric shaver 🪮 Hairdryer ✳ Ice Pack Facility & Disabled facilities 📞 Public telephone 🛍 Shop on site or within 200yds 🛒 Mobile shop (calls at least 5 days a week) 🍖 BBQ area 🎇 Picnic area **Wi-Fi** Wi-fi ▬ Internet access ♻ Recycling 🛈 Tourist info 🐕 Dog exercise area

AA Pubs & Restaurants nearby: Bay View Inn, Widemouth Bay 01288 361273

Leisure: �

Facilities: ♜⊙☐☀☺❂

Services: ⊑⊠❚⚊

Within 3 miles: ⓢ

Notes: ☺ Dogs must be kept on leads.

KENNACK SANDS   Map 2 SW71

Places to visit

National Seal Sanctuary, GWEEK 0871 423 2110
www.sealsanctuary.co.uk

Trevarno Estate Garden & Museum of Gardening, HELSTON 01326 574274
www.trevarno.co.uk

Great for kids: Goonhilly Satellite Earth Station Experience, HELSTON 0800 679593
www.goonhilly.bt.com

The Flambards Theme Park, HELSTON 01326 573404 www.flambards.co.uk

---

►►►► 86% *Chy Carne Holiday Park*
(SW725164)

Kuggar, Ruan Minor TR12 7LX
☎ 01326 290200 & 291161
e-mail: enquiries@camping-cornwall.com
web: www.chycarne.co.uk
dir: *From A3083 onto B3293 after Culdrose Naval Air Station. At Goonhilly ESS right onto unclassified road signed Kennack Sands. Left in 3m at junct*

⊞ ⊟ ⚊

Open Etr-Oct

Last arrival dusk

This spacious 12-acre park is in a quiet rural location and has excellent family facilities. There are extensive sea and coastal views over the sandy beach at Kennack Sands, less than half a mile away. Food is available from the site takeaway, or the local hostelry is not far away in the village. 12 acre site. 30 touring pitches. 4 hardstandings. Caravan pitches. Motorhome pitches. Tent pitches. 18 statics.

AA Pubs & Restaurants nearby: Cadgwith Cove Inn, Cadgwith 01326 290513

Leisure: � ✎

Facilities: ♜⊙☐☀♿⚲☐⚟ ﹅ WiFi

Services: ⊑⊠❚⊘☐⊠⚊⊞

Within 3 miles: ⚴⚘⚲◎☐⚲↺

►►► 84% Silver Sands Holiday Park (SW727166)

Gwendreath TR12 7LZ
☎ 01326 290631
e-mail: info@silversandsholidaypark.co.uk
dir: *From Helston follow signs to Future World Goonhilly. After 300yds turn right at x-roads signed Kennack Sands, 1m, left at Gwendreath sign, site 1m (NB it is recommended that guide directions are followed not Sat Nav)*

⊞ £14.50-£21 ⊟ £14.50-£21 ⚊ £12.50-£21

Open 22 Mar-3 Nov

Last arrival 21.00hrs Last departure 11.00hrs

A small, family-owned park in a remote location, with individually screened pitches providing sheltered suntraps. The owners continue to upgrade the park, improving the landscaping, access roads and toilets; lovely floral displays greet you on arrival. A footpath through the woods leads to the beach and the local pub. One of the nearby beaches is the historic Mullion Cove, and for the children a short car ride will ensure a great day out at the Flambards Experience. 9 acre site. 16 touring pitches. Caravan pitches. Motorhome pitches. Tent pitches. 17 statics.

AA Pubs & Restaurants nearby: Cadgwith Cove Inn, Cadgwith 01326 290513

Leisure: �☺☐

Facilities: ♜⊙☐☀♿⚲⚟⚟⚟﹅❂

Services: ⊑⊠❚⊘

Within 3 miles: ⚴⚘⚲↺

Notes: No noise after 23.00hrs. Dogs must be kept on leads.

►►► 72% Gwendreath Farm Holiday Park (SW738168)

TR12 7LZ
☎ 01326 290666
e-mail: tom.gibson@virgin.net
dir: *From A3083 turn left past Culdrose Naval Air Station onto B3293. Right past Goonhilly Earth Station signed Kennack Sands, left in 1m. At end of lane turn right over cattle grid. Right, through Seaview to 2nd reception*

⊞ ⚊

Open May-Sep

Last arrival 21.00hrs Last departure 10.00hrs

A grassy park in an elevated position with extensive sea and coastal views, and the beach just a short walk through the woods. Campers can use the bar and takeaway at an adjoining site. It is advisable to phone ahead and book before arrival. 5 acre site. 10 touring pitches. Caravan pitches. Tent pitches. 17 statics.

AA Pubs & Restaurants nearby: Cadgwith Cove Inn, Cadgwith 01326 290513

Leisure: � Facilities: ♜⊙☀☺☐⚟♺ ❂

Services: ⊑⊠⊘⚊

Within 3 miles: ⚘⚲☐⚲↺

Notes: ☺ Dogs must be kept on leads.

KILKHAMPTON   Map 2 SS21

Places to visit

Dartington Crystal, GREAT TORRINGTON 01805 626242 www.dartington.co.uk

RHS Garden Rosemoor, GREAT TORRINGTON 01805 624067 www.rhs.org.uk/rosemoor

Great for kids: The Milky Way Adventure Park, CLOVELLY 01237 431255
www.themilkyway.co.uk

►► 75% Upper Tamar Lake (SS288118)

Upper Tamar Lake EX23 9SB
☎ 01288 321712
e-mail: info@swlakestrust.org.uk
dir: *From A39 at Kilkhampton onto B3254, left in 0.5m onto unclassified road, follow signs approx 4m to site*

* ⊟ £11-£19 ⚊ £11-£19

Open Apr-Oct

A well-trimmed, slightly sloping site overlooking the lake and surrounding countryside, with several

continued

KILKHAMPTON *continued*

signed walks. The site benefits from the excellent facilities provided for the watersports centre and coarse anglers, with a rescue launch on the lake when the flags are flying. A good family site, with Bude's beaches and surfing waves only eight miles away. 2 acre site. 28 touring pitches. 2 hardstandings. Motorhome pitches. Tent pitches. 3 wooden pods.

AA Pubs & Restaurants nearby: The Bush Inn, Morwenstow 01288 331242

Leisure: ⚙

Facilities: 🌂🍽⚙✳♿🏬♻ ❶

Services: ⊘🍽🏭

Within 3 miles: 🚴🐾🎣🚣🛒♨

Notes: No swimming in lake. Dogs must be kept on leads. Canoeing, sailing, windsurfing.

LANDRAKE — Map 3 SX36

Places to visit

Cotehele, CALSTOCK 01579 351346 www.nationaltrust.org.uk

Mount Edgcumbe House & Country Park, TORPOINT 01752 822236 www.mountedgcumbe.gov.uk

Great for kids: The Monkey Sanctuary, LOOE 01503 262532 www.monkeysanctuary.org

▶▶▶▶ **88% Dolbeare Park Caravan and Camping** (SX363616)

St Ive Rd PL12 5AF
☎ 01752 851332
e-mail: reception@dolbeare.co.uk
web: www.dolbeare.co.uk
dir: *A38 to Landrake, 4m W of Saltash. At footbridge over A38 turn right, follow signs to site (0.75m from A38)*

🚐 🚍 Å

Open all year

Last arrival 18.00hrs Last departure noon

Set in meadowland close to the A38 and the Devon/Cornwall border, this attractive touring park is run by innovative, forward-thinking owners, who have adopted a very 'green' approach to running the park. The smart toilet block is very eco-friendly - electronic sensor showers, an on-demand boiler system, flow control valves on the taps, and low-energy lighting, as well as an

impressive family room. The park is extremely well presented, with excellent hardstanding pitches, a good tenting field, offering spacious pitches, and good provision for children with a separate ball games paddock and nature trail. Expect high levels of customer care and cleanliness. The on-site shop sells fresh bread and local produce. One pre-erected, full equipped Eurotent is available for hire. 9 acre site. 60 touring pitches. 54 hardstandings. Caravan pitches. Motorhome pitches. Tent pitches.

AA Pubs & Restaurants nearby: The Crooked Inn, Saltash 01752 848177

The Farm House, Saltash 01752 854661

Leisure: ⚙⚽

Facilities: 🌂🍽⚙✳♿🏬🕙🛒🍴📶 🖥
♻ ❶

Services: ⊘🍽🏭⊘T🚽🏬⛽

Within 3 miles: 🚴🐾🎣🛒♨

Notes: No cycling, no kite flying, late arrival fee payable after 18.00hrs. Dogs must be kept on leads. Off licence, free use of fridge & freezer.

see advert on page 91

LEEDSTOWN (NEAR HAYLE) — Map 2 SW63

Places to visit

East Pool Mine, POOL 01209 315027 www.nationaltrust.org.uk

Godolphin House, GODOLPHIN CROSS 01736 763194 www.nationaltrust.org.uk/godolphin

PREMIER PARK

▶▶▶▶▶ **82% Calloose Caravan & Camping Park** (SW597352)

TR27 5ET
☎ 01736 850431 & 0800 328 7589
e-mail: calloose@hotmail.com
dir: *From Hayle take B3302 to Leedstown, turn left opposite village hall, before entering village. Site 0.5m on left at bottom of hill*

🚐 🚍 Å

Open all year

Last arrival 22.00hrs Last departure 11.00hrs

A comprehensively equipped leisure park in a remote rural setting in a small river valley. This very good park is busy and bustling, and offers bright, clean toilet facilities, an excellent games room, an inviting pool, a good children's play area,

and log cabins and static caravans for holiday hire. 12.5 acre site. 109 touring pitches. 29 hardstandings. Caravan pitches. Motorhome pitches. Tent pitches. 25 statics.

AA Pubs & Restaurants nearby: Mount Haven Hotel & Restaurant, Marazion 01736 710249

Leisure: 🏊⚙🏊🎱🖵

Facilities: 🌂🍽⚙✳♿🕙🛒🍴

Services: ⊘🍽🖊🏭⊘T🍽🏬⛽

Within 3 miles: 🐾🛒🍴

Notes: No noise after mdnt, no pets in statics or lodges. Crazy golf, skittle alley.

LOOE — Map 2 SX25

Places to visit

Antony House, TORPOINT 01752 812191 www.nationaltrust.org.uk/antony

Mount Edgcumbe House & Country Park, TORPOINT 01752 822236 www.mountedgcumbe.gov.uk

Great for kids: The Monkey Sanctuary, LOOE 01503 262532 www.monkeysanctuary.org

AA CAMPING CARD SITE

79% Tencreek Holiday Park (SX233525)

Polperro Rd PL13 2JR
☎ 01503 262447
e-mail: reception@tencreek.co.uk
web: www.dolphinholidays.co.uk
dir: *Take A387 1.25m from Looe. Site on left*

✱ 🚐 £11.50-£21.50 🚍 £11.50-£21.50 Å £11.50-£21.50

Open all year

Last arrival 23.00hrs Last departure 10.00hrs

Occupying a lovely position with extensive countryside and sea views, this holiday centre is in a rural spot but close to Looe and Polperro. There is a full family entertainment programme, with indoor and outdoor swimming pools, an adventure playground and an exciting children's club. The superb amenities blocks include several private family shower rooms with WC and washbasin. 24 acre site. 254 touring pitches. 12 hardstandings. 120 seasonal pitches. Caravan pitches. Motorhome pitches. Tent pitches. 101 statics.

LEISURE: 🏊 Indoor swimming pool 🏊 Outdoor swimming pool ⚙ Children's playground 🪁 Kid's club 🎾 Tennis court ♞ Games room 🖵 Separate TV room 🏌 9/18 hole golf course 🚣 Boats for hire ▤ Cinema 🎵 Entertainment 🎣 Fishing ◉ Mini golf 🏄 Watersports 🏋 Gym 🎯 Sports field Spa ♨ Stables
FACILITIES: 🛁 Bath 🌂 Shower ⊙ Electric shaver 🖊 Hairdryer ✳ Ice Pack Facility ♿ Disabled facilities 🕙 Public telephone 🛒 Shop on site or within 200yds 🛒 Mobile shop (calls at least 5 days a week) 🍴 BBQ area 🍽 Picnic area 📶 Wi-fi 🖥 Internet access ♻ Recycling ❶ Tourist info 🐾 Dog exercise area

AA Pubs & Restaurants nearby: Barclay House, Looe 01503 262929

Trelaske Hotel & Restaurant, Looe 01503 262159

Leisure: 🏊🎡🎯🎱🏐🎣🎵

Facilities: 📶☉🅿☀♿🛁🚻📶🖥♻🛈

Services: 🔌🗑🍺🔋🔥🚰🚽🍽📷🎮🔌🔧

Within 3 miles: 🏇🏌🛒⚓🛥🎣🏧🎬⛳

Notes: Families & couples only. Dogs must be kept on leads. Nightly entertainment.

►►►► 82% Polborder House Caravan & Camping Park (SX283557)

Bucklawren Rd, St Martin PL13 1NZ
☎ 01503 240265

e-mail: reception@polborderhouse.co.uk
dir: Approach Looe from E on A387, follow B3253 for 1m, left at Polborder & Monkey Sanctuary sign. Site 0.5m on right

🚐 🚍 ⛺

Open all year

Last arrival 22.00hrs Last departure 11.00hrs

A very neat and well-kept small grassy site on high ground above Looe in a peaceful rural setting. Friendly and enthusiastic owners continue to invest in the park. The toilet facilities have upmarket fittings (note the infra-red operated taps and under floor heating). A bus stops at the bottom of the lane, but you must flag down the driver. A coastal walk runs by the site, and it is a 20-minute walk to the beach at Looe. 3.3 acre site. 31 touring pitches. 19 hardstandings. Caravan pitches. Motorhome pitches. Tent pitches. 5 statics.

AA Pubs & Restaurants nearby: Barclay House, Looe 01503 262929

Trelaske Hotel & Restaurant, Looe 01503 262159

Leisure: 🎡

Facilities: 📶☉🅿☀♿🛁🚻📶♻🛈

Services: 🔌🗑🔋🚰🚽🍽

Within 3 miles: 🏇🏌⚓🛥🏧🎬⛳

Notes: Dogs must be kept on leads.

►►►► 81% Camping Caradon Touring Park (SX218539)

Trelawne PL13 2NA
☎ 01503 272388

e-mail: enquiries@campingcaradon.co.uk
dir: Site signed from B3359 near junct with A387, between Looe & Polperro. Also signed on junct A387/B3359 (NB access roads are narrow)

🚐 🚍 ⛺

Open all year (rs Nov-Mar by booking only)

Last arrival 22.00hrs Last departure noon

Set in a quiet rural location between the popular coastal resorts of Looe and Polperro, this family-run and developing eco-friendly park is just one and half miles from the beach at Talland Bay. The site, run by hands-on owners, has a bar and restaurant (food can also be delivered to your pitch), and two fully-serviced family/disabled wet rooms. 3.5 acre site. 75 touring pitches. 23 hardstandings. Caravan pitches. Motorhome pitches. Tent pitches.

AA Pubs & Restaurants nearby: Old Mill House Inn, Polperro 01503 272362

Barclay House, Looe 01503 262929

Leisure: 🎡🎣🖥

Facilities: 📶☉🅿☀♿🛁🚻📶♻🛈

Services: 🔌🗑🍺🔋🔥🚰🚽🍽📷🚽

Within 3 miles: 🏌⚓🎬🛥🏧🎬

Notes: No noise 23.00hrs-07.00hrs & barrier not operational. Dogs must be kept on leads.

►►►► 79% Tregoad Park (SX272560)

St Martin PL13 1PB
☎ 01503 262718

e-mail: info@tregoadpark.co.uk
web: www.tregoadpark.co.uk
dir: Signed with direct access from B3253, or from E on A387 follow B3253 for 1.75m towards Looe. Site on left

🚐 🚍 ⛺

Open all year (rs low season bistro closed)

Last arrival 20.00hrs Last departure 11.00hrs

Investment continues at this smart, terraced park with extensive sea and rural views, about a mile and a half from Looe. All pitches are level. The facilities are well maintained and spotlessly clean, and there is a swimming pool with adjacent jacuzzi and sun patio, and a licensed bar where bar meals are served in the conservatory. The site

has fishing lakes stocked with carp, tench and roach. There is a bus stop at the bottom of the drive for the Plymouth and Truro routes. Static caravans, holiday cottages and two camping pods are available for holiday hire. 55 acre site. 200 touring pitches. 60 hardstandings. Caravan pitches. Motorhome pitches. Tent pitches. 7 statics.

AA Pubs & Restaurants nearby: Barclay House, Looe 01503 262929

Trelaske Hotel & Restaurant, Looe 01503 262159

Leisure: 🏊🎡🎣🖥

Facilities: 🐕📶☉🅿☀♿🛁🚻📶📶

Services: 🔌🗑🍺🔋🔥🚰🚽🍽🚽

Within 3 miles: 🏇🏌🛒⚓🛥🎣🏧🎬⛳

Notes: Pets on leads at all times. Crazy golf, ball sports area.

►►► 82% Trelay Farmpark (SX210544)

Pelynt PL13 2JX
☎ 01503 220900

e-mail: stay@trelay.co.uk
dir: From A390 at East Taphouse, take B3359 S towards Looe. After Pelynt, site 0.5m on left (NB due to single track roads it is advisable to follow guide directions not Sat Nav)

🚐 £7.50-£17.50 🚍 £7.50-£17.50
⛺ £7.50-£17.50

Open Dec-Oct

Last arrival 21.00hrs Last departure 11.00hrs

A small site with a friendly atmosphere set in a pretty rural area with extensive views. The good-size grass pitches are on slightly-sloping ground, and the toilets are immaculately kept, as is the excellent washing-up room. Looe and Polperro are just three miles away. 4.5 acre site. 66 touring pitches. 3 hardstandings. 7 seasonal pitches. Caravan pitches. Motorhome pitches. Tent pitches. 54 statics.

AA Pubs & Restaurants nearby: Old Mill House Inn, Polperro 01503 272362

Barclay House, Looe 01503 262929

Leisure: 🎡

Facilities: 📶☉🅿☀♿🛁🚻📶♻🛈

Services: 🔌🗑🔋🚰🚽🍽🚽

Within 3 miles: 🏌⚓🛥🎬🏧⛳

Notes: No skateboards, ball games or kites. Dogs must be kept on leads. Fridge & freezer.

LOSTWITHIEL — Map 2 SX15

Places to visit

Restormel Castle, RESTORMEL 01208 872687
www.english-heritage.org.uk

Eden Project, ST AUSTELL 01726 811911
www.edenproject.com

AA CAMPING CARD SITE

PREMIER PARK

▶▶▶▶▶ 80% **Eden Valley Holiday Park** (SX083593)

SILVER

PL30 5BU
☎ 01208 872277
e-mail: enquiries@edenvalleyholidaypark.co.uk
dir: 1.5m SW of Lostwithiel on A390 turn right at brown/white sign in 400mtrs (NB it is advisable to follow guide directions not Sat Nav)

🚐 £13-£17 🚍 £13-£17 ▲ £13-£17

Open Etr or Apr-Oct

Last arrival 22.00hrs Last departure 11.30hrs

A grassy park set in attractive paddocks with mature trees. A gradual upgrading of facilities continues, and both buildings and grounds are carefully maintained and contain an impressive children's play area. This park is ideally located for visiting the Eden Project, the nearby golden beaches and sailing at Fowey. There are also two self-catering lodges. The bus to St Austell and Truro stops at the entrance. 12 acre site. 56 touring pitches. 25 hardstandings. 20 seasonal pitches. Caravan pitches. Motorhome pitches. Tent pitches. 38 statics.

AA Pubs & Restaurants nearby: The Crown Inn, Lanlivery 01208 872707

Leisure: ⋒ ⊙ ⬤ ⬜

Facilities: ⬛ ⊙ ⬤ ✳ ⬛ ⬤ ⬤ ⬤ ⬤ ⬤

Services: ⬛ ⬛ ⬛ ⬤ ⊤ ⬛ ⬛

Within 3 miles: ⬛ ⬛ ⬤ ◎ ⬛ ⬛ ⬛ ⬛ ⬛

Notes: Dogs must be kept on leads. Table football, pool, table tennis, putting green, football.

LUXULYAN — Map 2 SX05

Places to visit

Restormel Castle, RESTORMEL 01208 872687
www.english-heritage.org.uk

Eden Project, ST AUSTELL 01726 811911
www.edenproject.com

▶▶▶ 77% **Croft Farm Holiday Park** (SX044568)

GOLD

PL30 5EQ
☎ 01726 850228
e-mail: enquiries@croftfarm.co.uk
dir: Exit A30 at Bodmin onto A391 towards St Austell. In 7m left at double rdbt onto unclassified road towards Luxulyan/Eden Project, continue to rdbt at Eden, left signed Luxulyan. Site 1m on left. (NB do not approach any other way as roads are very narrow)

🚐 🚍 ▲

Open 21 Mar-21 Jan

Last arrival 18.00hrs Last departure 11.00hrs

A peaceful, picturesque setting at the edge of a wooded valley, and only one mile from The Eden Project. Facilities include a well-maintained toilet block, a well-equipped dishwashing area, replete with freezer and microwave, and a revamped children's play area reached via an attractive woodland trail. There is a good bus service to St Austell and Luxulyan (the bus stop is at the site's entrance) and trains run to Newquay. 10.5 acre site. 52 touring pitches. 42 hardstandings. 32 seasonal pitches. Caravan pitches. Motorhome pitches. Tent pitches. 45 statics.

AA Pubs & Restaurants nearby: The Crown Inn, Lanlivery 01208 872707

Leisure: ⋒ ⬤

Facilities: ⬛ ⋒ ⊙ ⬤ ✳ ⬤ ⬛ ⬛ ⬛ ⬛ ⬤ ⬤

Services: ⬛ ⬛ ⬛ ⬤ ⊤ ⬛

Within 3 miles: ⬛ ⬛ ⬛ ⬛ ⬤ ⬛ ⬛ ⬛

Notes: No skateboarding, ball games only in playing field, quiet between 23.00hrs-07.00hrs. Woodland walk, information room.

MARAZION — Map 2 SW53

See also St Hilary

Places to visit

St Michael's Mount, MARAZION 01736 710507
www.stmichaelsmount.co.uk

Trengwainton Garden, PENZANCE 01736 363148
www.nationaltrust.org.uk

▶▶▶ 80% **Wheal Rodney Holiday Park** (SW525315)

Gwallon Ln TR17 0HL
☎ 01736 710605
e-mail: reception@whealrodney.co.uk
dir: Exit A30 at Crowlas, signed Rospeath. Site 1.5m on right. From Marazion centre turn opposite Fire Engine Inn, site 500mtrs on left

🚐 🚍 ▲

Open Etr-Oct

Last arrival 20.00hrs Last departure 11.00hrs

Set in a quiet rural location surrounded by farmland, with level grass pitches and well-kept facilities. Within half a mile are the beach at Marazion and the causeway or ferry to St Michael's Mount. A cycle route is within 400 yards; Penzance is only a short car or cycle ride away. 2.5 acre site. 30 touring pitches. Caravan pitches. Motorhome pitches. Tent pitches.

AA Pubs & Restaurants nearby: Godolphin Arms, Marazion 01736 710202

Leisure: ⬆

Facilities: ⋒ ⊙ ⬤ ✳ ⬤ ⬛ ⬛ ⬤ ⬤

Services: ⬛ ⬛ ⬛

Within 3 miles: ⬛ ⬤ ◎ ⬛ ⬛ ⬛ ⬛

Notes: Quiet after 22.00hrs. Dogs must be kept on leads.

LEISURE: ⬆ Indoor swimming pool ⬇ Outdoor swimming pool ⋒ Children's playground ⬤ Kid's club ⬤ Tennis court ⬤ Games room ⬜ Separate TV room ⬤ 9/18 hole golf course ⬤ Boats for hire ⬛ Cinema ⬤ Entertainment ⬤ Fishing ◎ Mini golf ⬤ Watersports ⬤ Gym ⬤ Sports field Spa ⬤ Stables
FACILITIES: ⬛ Bath ⋒ Shower ⊙ Electric shaver ⬤ Hairdryer ✳ Ice Pack Facility ⬤ Disabled facilities ⬤ Public telephone ⬛ Shop on site or within 200yds ⬛ Mobile shop (calls at least 5 days a week) ⬛ BBQ area ⬛ Picnic area ⬛ Wi-fi ⬛ Internet access ⬤ Recycling ⬤ Tourist info ⬛ Dog exercise area

MAWGAN PORTH   Map 2 SW86

AA CAMPING CARD SITE

►►►► 81% Sun Haven Valley Holiday Park

(SW861669)

TR8 4BQ
☎ 01637 860373
e-mail: sunhaven@sunhavenvalley.com
dir: *Exit A30 at Highgate Hill junct for Newquay; follow signs for airport. At T-junct turn right. At beach level in Mawgan Porth take only road inland, then 0.25m. Site 0.5m beyond S bend*

🚐 🚍 ▲

Open Apr-Oct

Last arrival 22.00hrs Last departure 10.30hrs

An attractive site with level pitches on the side of a river valley; being just off the B3276 this makes an ideal base for touring the Padstow and Newquay areas.The very high quality facilities include a TV lounge and a games room in a Swedish-style chalet, and a well-kept adventure playground. Trees and hedges fringe the park, and the ground is well drained. 5 acre site. 109 touring pitches. 11 hardstandings. Caravan pitches. Motorhome pitches. Tent pitches. 38 statics.

AA Pubs & Restaurants nearby: The Falcon Inn, St Mawgan 01637 860225

The Scarlet Hotel, Mawgan Porth 01637 861800

Leisure: Λ 🔍 🖵
Facilities: 🖕 🏷 ☉ ℗ ✷ 🕹 ⓢ 🔣 🚾 ♻ ❶
Services: 🔌 🗑 🔋 🧺 🛒
Within 3 miles: ⌇ ℘ ◎ ⛴ ⓢ 🗑 ∪

Notes: Families and couples only. Dogs must be kept on leads.

►►► 79% *Trevarrian Holiday Park*

(SW853661)

TR8 4AQ
☎ 01637 860381 & 0845 2255910
e-mail: holiday@trevarrian.co.uk
dir: *From A39 at St Columb rdbt turn right onto A3059 towards Newquay. Fork right in approx 2m for St Mawgan onto B3276. Turn right, site on left*

🚐 🚍 ▲

Open all year

Last arrival 22.00hrs Last departure 11.00hrs

A well-established and well-run holiday park overlooking Mawgan Porth beach. This park has a wide range of attractions including a free entertainment programme in peak season and a 10-pin bowling alley with licensed bar. It is only a short drive to Newquay and approximately 20 minutes to Padstow. 7 acre site. 185 touring pitches. 10 hardstandings. Caravan pitches. Motorhome pitches. Tent pitches.

AA Pubs & Restaurants nearby: The Falcon Inn, St Mawgan 01637 860225

Leisure: 🚣 Λ ☺ 🔍 🖵 🎵
Facilities: 🖕 🏷 ☉ ℗ ✷ 🕹 ⓢ 🔣 🚾 ♻ ❶
Services: 🔌 🗑 🔋 🧺 🍴 🛒 🚽 ⌅
Within 3 miles: ⌇ ✛ 🏇 ℘ ◎ ⓢ 🗑 ∪

Notes: No noise after mdnt. Dogs must be kept on leads. Crazy golf.

MEVAGISSEY   Map 2 SX04

See also Gorran & Pentewan

AA CAMPING CARD SITE

PREMIER PARK

►►►►► 92% Seaview International Holiday Park

(SW990412)

Best of British

Boswinger PL26 6LL
☎ 01726 843425
e-mail: holidays@seaviewinternational.com
web: www.seaviewinternational.com
dir: *From St Austell take B3273 signed Mevagissey. Turn right before entering village. Follow brown tourist signs to site (NB very narrow lanes to this site; it is advisable to follow guide directions not Sat Nav)*

* 🚐 £8-£45 🚍 £8-£45 ▲ £8-£45

Seaview International Holiday Park

Open Mar-Oct (rs Late May-Early Sep swimming pool opens late)

Last arrival 20.00hrs Last departure 10.00hrs

An attractive holiday park set in a beautiful environment overlooking Veryan Bay, with colourful landscaping, including attractive flowers and shrubs. It continues to offer an outstanding holiday experience, with its luxury family pitches, super toilet facilities, takeaway, shop and an alfresco eating area complete with a TV screen. A new addition is the 'off the lead' dog walk. The beach is just half a mile away. There is a 'ring and ride' bus service to Truro, St Austell and Plymouth which stops at the park gate. Static caravans are available for holiday hire. 28 acre site. 201 touring pitches. 23 hardstandings. 8 seasonal pitches. Caravan pitches. Motorhome pitches. Tent pitches. 39 statics.

AA Pubs & Restaurants nearby: The Ship Inn, Mevagissey 01726 843324

Seaview International Holiday Park

Leisure: 🚣 Λ ⛱ ☺ 🔍
Facilities: 🖕 🏷 ☉ ℗ ✷ 🕹 ⓢ 🔣 🚾 ♻ ❶
Services: 🔌 🗑 🔋 🧺 T 🍴 🛒 🚽 ⌅
Within 3 miles: ✛ ℘ ◎ ⛴ ⓢ 🗑

Notes: Restrictions on certain dog breeds. Crazy golf, volleyball, badminton, scuba diving.

see advert on page 86

MULLION
Map 2 SW61

Places to visit

Trevarno Estate Garden & Museum of Gardening, HELSTON 01326 574274 www.trevarno.co.uk

Goonhilly Satellite Earth Station Experience, HELSTON 0800 679593 www.goonhilly.bt.com

Great for kids: National Seal Sanctuary, GWEEK 0871 423 2110 www.sealsanctuary.co.uk

The Flambards Theme Park, HELSTON 01326 573404 www.flambards.co.uk

 75% Mullion Holiday Park *(SW699182)*

Ruan Minor TR12 7LJ
☎ 0844 335 3756 & 01326 240428
e-mail: touringandcamping@parkdeanholidays.com
web: www.parkdeantouring.com
dir: *A30 onto A39 through Truro towards Falmouth. A394 to Helston, A3083 for The Lizard. Site 7m on left*

* 🚐 £9-£41 🚙 £9-£41 ⛺ £7-£32

Mullion Holiday Park

Open Apr-Oct (rs 4 May-16 Sep outdoor pool open)

Last arrival 22.00hrs Last departure 10.00hrs

A comprehensively-equipped leisure park geared mainly for self-catering holidays, and set close to the sandy beaches, coves and fishing villages on The Lizard peninsula. There is plenty of on-site entertainment for all ages, with indoor and outdoor swimming pools and a bar and grill. 49 acre site. 105 touring pitches. 9 hardstandings. Caravan pitches. Motorhome pitches. Tent pitches. 305 statics.

AA Pubs & Restaurants nearby: The Halzephron Inn, Gunwalloe 01326 240406

Leisure: 🏊🏊⛱️⚽🎣🕹️📺🎵

Facilities: 📶💇‍♀️🚿✂️♿🕐🚾🧴📶💻♻️🅿️

Services: 🔌🚿🚽🛁🚮🍽️🛒🛍️

Within 3 miles: 🚣⛳🎡🚲🎿♿🚤⛵

Notes: Dogs must be kept on leads. Scuba diving, football pitch, surf & cycle hire, multi-sports court.

▶▶▶ **75% 'Franchis' Holiday Park** *(SW698203)*

Cury Cross Lanes TR12 7AZ
☎ 01326 240301
e-mail: enquiries@franchis.co.uk
web: www.franchis.co.uk
dir: *Exit A3083 on left 0.5m past Wheel Inn PH, between Helston & The Lizard*

* 🚐 £13-£18 🚙 £13-£18 ⛺ £11-£18

Open Apr-Oct

Last arrival 20.00hrs Last departure 10.30hrs

A mainly grassy site surrounded by hedges and trees, located on Goonhilly Downs and in an ideal position for exploring the Lizard Peninsula. The site is divided into two paddocks for tourers, and the pitches are a mix of level and slightly sloping. There are good facilities for families, and for a fun-filled family day out Flambards Experience is less than 20 minutes' drive away in Helston. 16 acre site. 65 touring pitches. 5 seasonal pitches. Caravan pitches. Motorhome pitches. Tent pitches. 12 statics.

LEISURE: Indoor swimming pool  Outdoor swimming pool 🅰 Children's playground 🚩 Kid's club 🎾 Tennis court 🎱 Games room 📺 Separate TV room ⛳ 9/18 hole golf course 🚣 Boats for hire 🎬 Cinema 🎵 Entertainment 🎣 Fishing ⛳ Mini golf 🏄 Watersports 🏋 Gym 🏟 Sports field **Spa** ⛵ Stables
FACILITIES: 🛁 Bath 🚿 Shower ⚡ Electric shaver ✂ Hairdryer ❄ Ice Pack Facility ♿ Disabled facilities 📞 Public telephone 🏪 Shop on site or within 200yds 🚐 Mobile shop (calls at least 5 days a week) 🍖 BBQ area 🍽 Picnic area 📶 Wi-fi 💻 Internet access ♻ Recycling ℹ Tourist info 🐕 Dog exercise area

AA Pubs & Restaurants nearby: The Halzephron Inn, Gunwalloe 01326 240406

Facilities: 🅟☉✳🚿💧🅆WI-FI ♻ 🛈

Services: 🔌🗑🍺💧🛒🅣🔋

Within 3 miles: 🚶🚲🏇🛒🏪🎣⛳

Notes: Dogs must be kept on leads.

NEWQUAY

See also Rejerrah

Places to visit

Blue Reef Aquarium, NEWQUAY 01637 878134
www.bluereefaquarium.co.uk

Newquay Zoo, NEWQUAY 0844 474 2244
www.newquayzoo.org.uk

Great for kids: Dairy Land Farm World, NEWQUAY 01872 510246
www.dairylandfarmworld.com

NEWQUAY

Map 2 SW86

AA CAMPING CARD SITE

 92% Hendra Holiday Park

(SW833601)

TR8 4NY
☎ 01637 875778
e-mail: enquiries@hendra-holidays.com
dir: A30 onto A392 signed Newquay. At Quintrell Downs over rdbt, signed Lane, site 0.5m on left

* 🚐 £12.10-£21.35 �caravan £12.10-£21.35
⛺ £12.10-£21.35

Open 25 Mar-4 Nov (rs Apr-Spring BH, Sep-Oct outdoor pool closed)

Last arrival dusk Last departure 10.00hrs

A large complex with holiday statics and superb facilities including an indoor fun pool and an outdoor pool. There is a children's club for the over 6s, evening entertainment during high season, a new skateboard park, fish and chip shop and a fantastic coffee shop. The touring pitches are set amongst mature trees and shrubs, and some have fully-serviced facilities. All amenities are open to the public. This site generates most of its own electricity from a 1.5 megawatt solar farm. There are camping pods available for hire. 80 acre site. 548 touring pitches. 28 hardstandings. Caravan pitches. Motorhome pitches. Tent pitches. 307 statics. 3 wooden pods.

AA Pubs & Restaurants nearby: Lewinnick Lodge Bar & Restaurant, Pentire Headland, Newquay 01637 878117

Leisure: 🏊♨♿🎱🎮👶🎯🎪🎵

Facilities: 🅟☉🅟✳♿🅒🚿💧🅆WI-FI 🖥 ♻ 🛈

Services: 🔌🗑🍺💧🛒🅣🍴🔋🚮♿

Within 3 miles: 🚶🚲🏇🛒🏪🎣🎯🏪🎣⛳

Notes: Families and couples only. Solarium, train rides, skate & scooter park.

see advert on page 90

SERVICES: 🔌 Electric hook up 🗑 Launderette 🍺 Licensed bar Calor Gas 🛢 Camping Gaz 🅣 Toilet fluid 🍴 Café/Restaurant 🍟 Fast Food/Takeaway 🔋 Battery charging 👶 Baby care ♿ Motorvan service point **ABBREVIATIONS:** BH/bank hols-bank holidays Etr-Easter Whit-Whitsun dep-departure fr-from hrs-hours m-mile mdnt-midnight rdbt-roundabout rs-restricted service wk-week wknd-weekend No credit cards no dogs See page 7 for details of the AA Camping Card Scheme

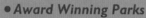

Hendra
HOLIDAY PARK
camping ★ touring ★ holiday homes

Quite simply a five star holiday

01637 875778
www.hendra-holidays.com
Hendra Holidays, Newquay, Cornwall, TR8 4NY

enjoyEngland.com
HOLIDAY, TOURING & CAMPING PARK

St Ives Bay
HOLIDAY PARK

Right on the beach!

- CHALETS
- CARAVANS
- CAMPING

www.stivesbay.co.uk • tel: 0800 317713

Treloy
Touring Park

The friendly park
in beautiful Cornwall

Telephone: **01637 872063**

Website: www.treloy.co.uk

Email: stay@treloy.co.uk

Address: Newquay, Cornwall TR8 4JN

Heated swimming pool	Licensed family bar	On site shop
Free entertainment	TV and games room	Treloy golf course nearby
Adventure playground	Electric hook-ups	Café/takeaway

NEWQUAY *continued*

81% Newquay Holiday Park *(SW853626)*

TR8 4HS
☎ 0844 335 3756
e-mail: touringandcamping@parkdeanholidays.com
web: www.parkdeantouring.com
dir: *From Bodmin on A30, under low bridge, right towards RAF St Mawgan. Take A3059 towards Newquay, site past Treloy Golf Club*

* ⊞ £8-£44 ⊞ £8-£44 Å £8-£42

Open Mar-Oct (rs May-19 Sep outdoor pool complex open)

Last arrival 21.00hrs Last departure 10.00hrs

A well-maintained park with a wide range of indoor and outdoor activities. A children's playground and bar and grill enhance the facilities, and the club and bars offer quality entertainment. Three heated outdoor pools and a giant waterslide are very popular. 60 acre site. 53 touring pitches. 10 hardstandings. Caravan pitches. Motorhome pitches. Tent pitches. 312 statics.

AA Pubs & Restaurants nearby: Lewinnick Lodge Bar & Restaurant, Pentire Headland, Newquay 01637 878117

Leisure: ☜ ⋒ ⅏ ⋟ ☐ ⎓
Facilities: ⋔ ⊙ ⌕ ⋇ ᚳ ☾ ⓢ ⌤ ⊀ ▥
Services: ⊡ ⓢ ⛽ ⌷ ⌀ ⊤ ⎚ ⌸ ⎗
Within 3 miles: ⌁ ⅙ ⅌ ⌕ ◎ ⓢ ⛽ ∪

Notes: Pool room, family entertainment, children's clubs.

►►►► 84% Trencreek Holiday Park *(SW828609)*

Hillcrest, Higher Trencreek TR8 4NS
☎ 01637 874210
e-mail: trencreek@btconnect.com
dir: *A392 to Quintrell Downs, right towards Newquay, left at 2 mini-rdbts into Trevenson Rd to site*

⊞ ⊞ Å

Open Whit-mid Sep (rs Etr-Whit swimming pool closed)

Last arrival 22.00hrs Last departure noon

An attractively landscaped park in the village of Trencreek, with modern toilet facilities of a very high standard. Two well-stocked fishing lakes, and evening entertainment in the licensed clubhouse, are extra draws. Located about two miles from Newquay with its beaches and surfing. 10 acre site. 194 touring pitches. 8 hardstandings. Caravan pitches. Motorhome pitches. Tent pitches. 6 statics.

AA Pubs & Restaurants nearby: Lewinnick Lodge Bar & Restaurant, Pentire Headland, Newquay 01637 878117

Leisure: ☜ ⋒ ⋟ ☐
Facilities: ⋔ ⊙ ⌕ ⋇ ᚳ ☾ ⓢ ⊀ ❶
Services: ⊡ ⓢ ⛽ ⌷ ⌀ ⊤ ⎚ ⌸ ⎗
Within 3 miles: ⌁ ⅙ ⅌ ⌕ ◎ ⓢ ⛽ ∪

Notes: ⊘ ⊗ Families and couples only. Free coarse fishing.

►►►► 79% Treloy Touring Park *(SW858625)*

TR8 4JN
☎ 01637 872063 & 876279
e-mail: stay@treloy.co.uk
web: www.treloy.co.uk
dir: *On A3059 (St Columb Major-Newquay road)*

⊞ ⊞ Å

Open May-15 Sep (rs Sep pool, takeaway, shop & bar)

Last arrival 21.00hrs Last departure 10.00hrs

An attractive site with fine countryside views, that is within easy reach of resorts and beaches. The pitches are set in four paddocks with mainly level but some slightly sloping grassy areas. Maintenance and cleanliness are very high. There is a very nice swimming pool. 18 acre site. 223 touring pitches. 24 hardstandings. Caravan pitches. Motorhome pitches. Tent pitches.

AA Pubs & Restaurants nearby: Lewinnick Lodge Bar & Restaurant, Pentire Headland, Newquay 01637 878117

Leisure: ☜ ⋒ ⅏ ☺ ⋟ ☐ ⎓
Facilities: ⋔ ⊙ ⌕ ⋇ ᚳ ☾ ⓢ ⊀ ▥ ♻ ❶
Services: ⊡ ⓢ ⛽ ⌷ ⌀ ⊤ ⎚ ⌸ ⎗ ⅄
Within 3 miles: ⌁ ⅙ ⅃ ⅌ ◎ ⅙ ⓢ ⛽ ∪

Notes: Concessionary green fees for golf.

see advert on opposite page

NEWQUAY *continued*

AA CAMPING CARD SITE

▶▶▶▶ 79% Trethiggey Touring Park *(SW846596)*

GOLD

Quintrell Downs TR8 4QR
☎ **01637 877672**
e-mail: enquiries@trethiggey.co.uk
dir: A30 onto A392 signed Newquay at Quintrell Downs rdbt, left onto A3058, pass Newquay Pearl centre. Site 0.5m on left

* 🚐 £11.10-£17.90 🚐 £9.70-£16.40
▲ £11.10-£17.90

Open Mar-Dec

Last arrival 22.00hrs Last departure 10.30hrs

A family-owned park in a rural setting that is ideal for touring this part of Cornwall. It is pleasantly divided into paddocks with maturing trees and shrubs, and offers coarse fishing and tackle hire. This site has a car park for campers as the camping fields are set in a car-free zone for children's safety. 15 acre site. 145 touring pitches. 35 hardstandings. Caravan pitches. Motorhome pitches. Tent pitches. 12 statics.

AA Pubs & Restaurants nearby: Lewinnick Lodge Bar & Restaurant, Pentire Headland, Newquay 01637 878117

Leisure: � 🔍 🖵

Facilities: 🛏 🞋 ☉ 🎱 ☀ ♿ ⓢ 🍴 🎿 🐕 📶 🖵 ♻ ❶

Services: 🔌 🗑 🎱 ❸ 🚰 ⬍

Within 3 miles: 🛴 🎣 🖹 🎱 ◎ 🚣 ⓢ 🎱 ∪

Notes: No noise after mdnt. Dogs must be kept on leads. Off licence, recreation field.

see advert on page 92

▶▶▶▶ 78% Porth Beach Tourist Park *(SW834629)*

BRONZE

Porth TR7 3NH
☎ **01637 876531**
e-mail: info@porthbeach.co.uk
dir: 1m NE off B3276 towards Padstow

🚐 🚐 ▲

Open Mar-Nov

Last arrival 18.00hrs Last departure 10.00hrs

This attractive, popular park offers level, grassy pitches in neat and tidy surroundings. It is a well-run site set in meadowland in a glorious location adjacent to Porth Beach's excellent sands. 6 acre

---

site. 200 touring pitches. 19 hardstandings. Caravan pitches. Motorhome pitches. Tent pitches. 18 statics.

AA Pubs & Restaurants nearby: Lewinnick Lodge Bar & Restaurant, Pentire Headland, Newquay 01637 878117

Leisure: 🅰

Facilities: 🞋 ☉ ♿ ⓢ 📶 ♻ ❶

Services: 🔌 🗑 🎱 ❸ 🚰 ⬍

Within 3 miles: 🛴 🎣 🖹 🎱 ◎ 🚣 ⓢ 🎱 ∪

Notes: Families and couples only. Dogs must be kept on leads.

see advert on page 88

▶▶▶▶ 76% Trenance Holiday Park *(SW818612)*

Edgcumbe Av TR7 2JY
☎ **01637 873447**
e-mail: enquiries@trenanceholidaypark.co.uk
dir: Exit A3075 near viaduct. Site by boating lake rdbt

* 🚐 £16-£20 🚐 £16-£20 ▲ £16-£20

Open 21 Apr-22 Sep

Last arrival 22.00hrs Last departure 10.00hrs

A mainly static park popular with tenters, close to Newquay's vibrant nightlife, and serving excellent breakfasts and takeaways. Set on high ground in an urban area of town, with cheerful owners and clean facilities. The local bus stops at the site entrance. 12 acre site. 50 touring pitches. Caravan pitches. Motorhome pitches. Tent pitches. 190 statics.

AA Pubs & Restaurants nearby: Lewinnick Lodge Bar & Restaurant, Pentire Headland, Newquay 01637 878117

Leisure: 🔍

Facilities: 🞋 ☉ ☀ ♿ ⓢ 📺 ♻ ❶

Services: 🔌 🗑 🎱 ❸ 🚰 🎱 🍴 ⬍ ⚱

Within 3 miles: 🛴 🎣 🖹 🎱 ◎ 🚣 ⓢ 🎱 ∪

Notes: No pets.

▶▶▶ 80% Trebellan Park *(SW790571)*

Cubert TR8 5PY
☎ **01637 830522**
e-mail: enquiries@trebellan.co.uk
dir: 4m S of Newquay, turn W off A3075 at Cubert sign. Left in 0.75m onto unclassified road

* 🚐 £18.50-£25 🚐 £18.50-£25 ▲ £14-£20

Open May-Oct

Last arrival 21.00hrs Last departure 10.00hrs

A terraced grassy rural park within a picturesque valley with views of Cubert Common, and adjacent to the Smuggler's Den, a 16th-century thatched inn. This park has a very inviting swimming pool and three well-stocked coarse fishing lakes. 8 acre site. 150 touring pitches. Caravan pitches. Motorhome pitches. Tent pitches. 7 statics.

AA Pubs & Restaurants nearby: Lewinnick Lodge Bar & Restaurant, Pentire Headland, Newquay 01637 878117

Leisure: 🏊 🅰 🖵

Facilities: 🞋 ☉ 🎱 ☀ ♿ ⓢ 🎱

Services: 🔌 🗑 ⚱

Within 3 miles: 🛴 🎱 ◎ 🚣 ⓢ 🎱 ∪

Notes: Families and couples only. Dogs must be kept on leads.

▶▶▶ 78% Riverside Holiday Park *(SW829592)*

Gwills Ln TR8 4PE
☎ **01637 873617**
e-mail: info@riversideholidaypark.co.uk
web: www.riversideholidaypark.co.uk
dir: A30 onto A392 signed Newquay. At Quintrell Downs cross rdbt signed Lane. 2nd left in 0.5m onto unclassified road signed Gwills. Site in 400yds

🚐 £14-£19 🚐 £14-£19 ▲ £14-£19

Open Mar-Oct

Last arrival 22.00hrs Last departure 10.00hrs

A sheltered valley beside a river in a quiet location is the idyllic setting for this lightly wooded park; the site is well placed for exploring Newquay and Padstow. The park caters for families and couples only. There is a lovely swimming pool. The site is close to the wide variety of attractions offered by this major resort. Self-catering lodges, cabins and static vans are for hire. 11 acre site. 65 touring

---

LEISURE: 🏊 Indoor swimming pool   🏊 Outdoor swimming pool   🅰 Children's playground   🧒 Kid's club   🎾 Tennis court   🔍 Games room   🖵 Separate TV room
🏌 9/18 hole golf course   ⛵ Boats for hire   🎬 Cinema   🎵 Entertainment   🎣 Fishing   ◎ Mini golf   🚣 Watersports   🏋 Gym   ⚽ Sports field   **Spa**   ∪ Stables
FACILITIES: 🛁 Bath   🞋 Shower   ☉ Electric shaver   🔲 Hairdryer   ☀ Ice Pack Facility   ♿ Disabled facilities   ⓒ Public telephone   ⓢ Shop on site or within 200yds
🏪 Mobile shop (calls at least 5 days a week)   🍴 BBQ area   🞕 Picnic area   📶 Wi-fi   🖥 Internet access   ♻ Recycling   ❶ Tourist info   🐕 Dog exercise area

pitches. Caravan pitches. Motorhome pitches. Tent pitches. 65 statics.

AA Pubs & Restaurants nearby: Lewinnick Lodge Bar & Restaurant, Pentire Headland, Newquay 01637 878117

Leisure: 🏊 🅰 ♨ 🖵

Facilities: 🅿 ☉ ☝ ☀ ⅋ ⊙ 🛒 ⎝wi-fi⎠ ♻ ❶

Services: 🔌 🔋 🍽 🛢 🚿 T 🛄 ⚒

Within 3 miles: ⤴ ≒ 🗒 🖉 ◎ ⚓ 🛍 🛍 ⟲

Notes: Families and couples only. Dogs must be kept on leads.

OTTERHAM   Map 2 SX19

Places to visit

Launceston Castle, LAUNCESTON 01566 772365 www.english-heritage.org.uk

Launceston Steam Railway, LAUNCESTON 01566 775665 www.launcestonsr.co.uk

Great for kids: Tamar Otter & Wildlife Centre, LAUNCESTON 01566 785646 www.tamarotters.co.uk

►►► 83% St Tinney Farm Holidays

(SX169906)

PL32 9TA
☎ **01840 261274**
e-mail: info@st-tinney.co.uk
dir: From A39 follow Otterham sign onto unclassified road. Then follow site signs

🚐 🚌 🅰

Open Etr-Oct

Last arrival 21.00hrs Last departure 10.00hrs

A family-run farm site in a rural area with nature trails, lakes, valleys and offering complete seclusion. Visitors are free to walk around the farmland lakes and lose themselves in the countryside. 34 acre site. 20 touring pitches. Caravan pitches. Motorhome pitches. Tent pitches. 6 statics.

AA Pubs & Restaurants nearby: The Wellington Hotel, Boscastle 01840 250202

Leisure: 🏊 🅰 ♨

Facilities: 🅿 ☉ ☝ ☀ ✂ ⎝wi-fi⎠ ♻ ❶

Services: 🔌 🔋 🍽 🛢 🚿 T 🍴 ⚒

Within 3 miles: 🖉 🛍

Notes: No open fires, noise restrictions. Dogs must be kept on leads. Coarse fishing.

PADSTOW   Map 2 SW97

See also Rumford

Places to visit

Prideaux Place, PADSTOW 01841 532411 www.prideauxplace.co.uk

PREMIER PARK

►►►►► 93% Padstow Touring Park (SW913738)

PL28 8LE
☎ **01841 532061**
e-mail: bookings@padstowtouringpark.co.uk
dir: 1m S of Padstow, on E side of A389 (Padstow to Wadebridge road)

* 🚐 £15-£24.50 🚌 £15-£24.50 🅰 £11-£20

Open all year

Last arrival 21.00hrs Last departure 11.00hrs

Improvements continue at this popular park set in open countryside above the quaint fishing town of Padstow, which can be approached by footpath directly from the park. It is divided into paddocks by maturing bushes and hedges to create a peaceful and relaxing holiday atmosphere. 13.5 acre site. 150 touring pitches. 39 hardstandings. Caravan pitches. Motorhome pitches. Tent pitches.

AA Pubs & Restaurants nearby: The Cornish Arms, St Merryn 01841 532700

Paul Ainsworth at No 6, Padstow 01841 532093

Leisure: 🅰

Facilities: 🅿 ☉ ☝ ☀ ⅋ 🛒 🍴 ⎝wi-fi⎠ 🖥 ♻ ❶

Services: 🔌 🔋 🛢 🚿 T 🛄 🚚 ⚒

Within 3 miles: ⤴ ≒ 🖉 ◎ ⚓ 🛍 🛍 ⟲

Notes: No groups, no noise after 22.00hrs. Dogs must be kept on leads.

►►► 76% Dennis Cove Camping

(SW919743)

Dennis Ln PL28 8DR
☎ **01841 532349**
dir: Approach Padstow on A389, right at Tesco into Sarah's Ln, 2nd right to Dennis Ln, follow to site at end

🚐 🚌 🅰

Open Etr-end Sep (rs Etr opening confirmed 2 wks in advance)

Last arrival 21.00hrs Last departure 11.00hrs

Set in meadowland with mature trees, this site overlooks Padstow Bay, with access to the Camel Estuary and the nearby beach. The centre of town is just a 10-minute walk away, and bike hire is available on site, with the famous Camel Trail beginning right outside. 3.5 acre site. 40 touring pitches. Caravan pitches. Motorhome pitches. Tent pitches.

AA Pubs & Restaurants nearby: Margot's, Padstow 01841 533441

The Seafood Restaurant, Padstow 01841 532700

Facilities: 🅿 ☉ ☝ ☀ ⅋ ❶

Services: 🔌 🔋 🛢 🚿 🛄

Within 3 miles: ⤴ ≒ 🗒 🖉 ◎ ⚓ 🛍 🛍 ⟲

Notes: 🐾 Arrivals from 14.00hrs, no groups, no open fires. Dogs must be kept on leads.

►►► 74% Padstow Holiday Park

(SW009073)

Cliffdowne PL28 8LB
☎ **01841 532289**
e-mail: mail@padstowholidaypark.co.uk
dir: Exit A39 onto either A389 or B3274 to Padstow. Site signed 1.5m before Padstow

🚐 🚌 🅰

Open Mar-Dec

Last arrival 17.00hrs Last departure noon

An excellent and quiet site of exceptional quality within a mile of Padstow which can be reached via a footpath. It is mainly a static park with some touring pitches in a small paddock and others in an open field. Three holiday letting caravans are available. 5.5 acre site. 27 touring pitches. Caravan pitches. Motorhome pitches. Tent pitches. 74 statics.

AA Pubs & Restaurants nearby: The Cornish Arms, St Merryn 01841 532700

Leisure: 🅰

Facilities: ➰ 🅿 ☉ ☝ ☀ ⊙ 🛒 ⎝wi-fi⎠ ♻ ❶

Services: 🔌 🔋 🛢 🖉 T

Within 3 miles: ⤴ ≒ 🗒 🖉 ◎ ⚓ 🛍 🛍 ⟲

Notes: ⊗

PENTEWAN   Map 2 SX04

Places to visit

The Lost Gardens of Heligan, PENTEWAN
01726 845100 www.heligan.com

Charlestown Shipwreck & Heritage Centre,
ST AUSTELL 01726 69897
www.shipwreckcharlestown.com

Great for kids: Eden Project, ST AUSTELL
01726 811911 www.edenproject.com

PREMIER PARK

►►►►► 84% Sun
Valley Holiday Park

(SX005486)

Pentewan Rd PL26 6DJ
☎ 01726 843266 & 844393
e-mail: reception@sunvalleyholidays.co.uk
dir: *From St Austell take B3273 towards
Mevagissey. Site 2m on right*

* ♠ £15-£32.50 ♠ £15-£32.50 ▲ £15-£32.50

Open all year (rs Winter pool, restaurant & touring
field)

Last arrival 22.00hrs Last departure 10.30hrs

In a picturesque wooded valley, this neat park is
kept to a high standard. The extensive amenities
include tennis courts, indoor swimming pool,
takeaway, licensed clubhouse and restaurant. The
sea is just a mile away, and can be accessed via a
footpath and cycle path along the river bank.
Bicycles can be hired on site. A public bus stops
at the site entrance. 20 acre site. 29 touring
pitches. 13 hardstandings. Caravan pitches.
Motorhome pitches. Tent pitches. 75 statics.

AA Pubs & Restaurants nearby: The Crown Inn,
St Ewe 01726 843322

Leisure: 🏊 ⚿ 🎱 🎣 🎵
Facilities: 🚿 ⊙ ⚡ ✳ ⛐ 🕐 🏠 🛒 💤 WI-FI ♻ 🛈
Services: 🔌 🗑 🔧 🛢 🚿 🍽 🛒 🚽 ⚡
Within 3 miles: 🚴 🚤 🎭 🎣 ⚓ 🛒 🐎 ∪

Notes: Certain pet restrictions apply, please
contact the site for details. No motorised scooters,
skateboards or bikes at night. Dogs must be kept
on leads. Pets' corner, bike hire, outdoor & indoor
play areas.

►►► 83% Heligan Woods *(SW998470)*

PL26 6BT
☎ 01726 842714 & 844414
e-mail: info@pentewan.co.uk
dir: *From A390 take B3273 for Mevagissey at
x-roads signed 'No caravans beyond this point'.
Right onto unclassified road towards Gorran, site
0.75m on left*

♠ ♠ ▲

Open 16 Jan-26 Nov (rs 9-11am & 5-6pm
Reception open)

Last arrival 22.00hrs Last departure 10.30hrs

A pleasant peaceful park adjacent to the Lost
Gardens of Heligan, with views over St Austell Bay,
and well-maintained facilities. Guests can also
use the extensive amenities at the sister park,
Pentewan Sands, and there's a footpath with
direct access to Heligan Gardens. 12 acre site. 89
touring pitches. 24 hardstandings. 3 seasonal
pitches. Caravan pitches. Motorhome pitches. Tent
pitches. 17 statics.

AA Pubs & Restaurants nearby: Austells,
St Austell 01726 813888

Leisure: ⚿
Facilities: 🚿 ⊙ ⚡ 🕐 🛒 🐕
Services: 🔌 🗑 🛢 🚿 🍽 🚽 ⚡
Within 3 miles: 🚴 🚤 🎭 🎣 ⚓ 🛒 🐎 ∪

PENZANCE   Map 2 SW43

See also Rosudgeon

Places to visit

Trengwainton Garden, PENZANCE 01736 363148
www.nationaltrust.org.uk

St Michael's Mount, MARAZION 01736 710507
www.stmichaelsmount.co.uk

►►► 78% Bone Valley Caravan &
Camping Park *(SW472316)*

Heamoor TR20 8UJ
☎ 01736 360313
e-mail: wardmandie@yahoo.co.uk
dir: *Exit A30 at Heamoor/Madron rdbt. 4th on
right into Josephs Ln. 800yds left into Bone Valley.
Entrance 200yds on left*

♠ ♠ ▲

Open all year

Last arrival 22.00hrs Last departure 10.00hrs

A compact grassy park on the outskirts of
Penzance, with well maintained facilities. It is
divided into paddocks by mature hedges, and a
small stream runs alongside. 1 acre site. 17
touring pitches. 6 hardstandings. Caravan
pitches. Motorhome pitches. Tent pitches. 3
statics.

AA Pubs & Restaurants nearby: Dolphin Tavern,
Penzance 01736 364106

Harris's Restaurant, Penzance 01736 364408

Leisure: ☐
Facilities: 🚿 🕐 ⊙ ⚡ ✳ ⚡ 🕐 🛒 🛒 WI-FI
Services: 🔌 🗑 🛢 🅃
Within 3 miles: 🚴 🎭 🛒 🐎 ∪

Notes: Dogs must be kept on leads. Campers'
lounge, kitchen & laundry room.

PERRANPORTH   Map 2 SW75

See also Rejerrah

Places to visit

Royal Cornwall Museum, TRURO 01872 272205
www.royalcornwallmuseum.org.uk

Trerice, TRERICE 01637 875404
www.nationaltrust.org.uk

Great for kids: Blue Reef Aquarium, NEWQUAY
01637 878134 www.bluereefaquarium.co.uk

84% Perran Sands
Holiday Park *(SW767554)*

TR6 0AQ
☎ 0871 231 0871
e-mail: perransands@haven.com
web: www.haven.com/perransands
dir: *A30 onto B3285 towards Perranporth. Site
on right before descent on hill into Perranporth*

♠ ♠ ▲

Open mid Mar-end Oct (rs mid Mar-May & Sep-
Oct some facilities may be reduced)

Last arrival 22.00hrs Last departure 10.00hrs

LEISURE: 🏊 Indoor swimming pool ⚿ Outdoor swimming pool 🎢 Children's playground 👧 Kid's club 🎾 Tennis court 🎱 Games room 📺 Separate TV room 🏌 9/18 hole golf course ⚓ Boats for hire 🎬 Cinema 🎵 Entertainment 🎣 Fishing ⊙ Mini golf 🏄 Watersports 💪 Gym 🏟 Sports field Spa ∪ Stables
FACILITIES: 🛁 Bath 🚿 Shower ⊙ Electric shaver 🕐 Hairdryer ✳ Ice Pack Facility ⚡ Disabled facilities 🕐 Public telephone 🛒 Shop on site or within 200yds 🚐 Mobile shop (calls at least 5 days a week) 🍖 BBQ area 🌲 Picnic area WI-FI Wi-fi 💻 Internet access ♻ Recycling 🛈 Tourist info 🐕 Dog exercise area

Situated amid 500 acres of protected dune grassland, and with a footpath through to the surf and three miles of golden sandy beach, this lively park is set in a large village-style complex. It offers a complete range of on-site facilities and entertainment for all the family, which makes it an extremely popular park. There are two new top-of-the-range facility blocks. 550 acre site. 363 touring pitches. Caravan pitches. Motorhome pitches. Tent pitches. 600 statics.

AA Pubs & Restaurants nearby: Driftwood Spars, St Agnes 01872 552428

Leisure: 🎿🏊🎡⚽🎵
Facilities: 🚿🍴🌳🔥🛒🔥📶♻️❓
Services: 🔌📺🍺🪫🍷🍴🍔
Within 3 miles: ⬇️🐴◎🐕🐟🎣🛒♨️⛳

Notes: Max 2 dogs per booking, certain dog breeds banned, no commercial vehicles, no bookings by persons under 21yrs unless a family booking.

see advert on page 63

▶▶▶▶ **81% Tollgate Farm Caravan & Camping Park** *(SW768547)*

Budnick Hill TR6 0AD
☎ 01872 572130 & 0845 166 2126
e-mail: enquiries@tollgatefarm.co.uk
dir: *Exit A30 onto B3285 to Perranporth. Site on right 1.5m after Goonhavern*

🚗🚐⛺

Open Etr-Sep

Last arrival 21.00hrs Last departure 11.00hrs

A quiet site in a rural location with spectacular coastal views. Pitches are divided into four paddocks sheltered and screened by mature hedges. Children will enjoy the play equipment and pets' corner. The three miles of sand at Perran Bay are just a walk away through the sand dunes,

or by car it is a three-quarter mile drive. 10 acre site. 102 touring pitches. 10 hardstandings. 12 seasonal pitches. Caravan pitches. Motorhome pitches. Tent pitches. 5 wooden pods.

AA Pubs & Restaurants nearby: Driftwood Spars, St Agnes 01872 552428

Tollgate Farm Caravan & Camping Park

Leisure: 🛝⚽
Facilities: 🚿◎🌳🔥🛒🔥🏠🛝📶♻️❓
Services: 🔌📺🪫🍷🛠️🍔🚙⛽
Within 3 miles: ⬇️🐴🐴🎣◎🐕🐟🎣🛒⛳
Notes: No large groups. Dogs must be kept on leads.

see advert below

SERVICES: 🔌 Electric hook up 📺 Launderette 🍺 Licensed bar 🪫 Calor Gas 🌀 Camping Gaz 🚰 Toilet fluid 🍴 Café/Restaurant 🍔 Fast Food/Takeaway 🔋 Battery charging 🚼 Baby care ⛽ Motorvan service point **ABBREVIATIONS:** BH/bank hols-bank holidays Etr-Easter Whit-Whitsun dep-departure fr-from hrs-hours m-mile mdnt-midnight rdbt-roundabout rs-restricted service wk-week wknd-weekend 🚫 No credit cards 🐕 no dogs   See page 7 for details of the AA Camping Card Scheme

PERRANPORTH *continued*

AA CAMPING CARD SITE

▶▶▶ 82% **Higher Golla Touring & Caravan Park** *(SW756514)*

Penhallow TR4 9LZ
☎ **01872 573963 & 07800 558407**
e-mail: trevor.knibb@gmail.com
web: www.highergollatouringpark.co.uk
dir: *A30 onto B3284 towards Perranporth. (Straight on at junct with A3075). Approx 2m. Site signed on right*

⚐ £13-£21 ⊕ £13-£21 ▲ £9-£21

Open Etr-end Sep

Last arrival 20.00hrs Last departure 10.30hrs

Extensive country views can be enjoyed from all pitches on this quietly located site, which now has high quality and immaculate toilet facilities. Every pitch has electricity and a water tap and this peaceful park is just two miles from Perranporth and its stunning beach. 1.5 acre site. 18 touring pitches. 2 hardstandings. 4 seasonal pitches. Caravan pitches. Motorhome pitches. Tent pitches. 2 statics.

AA Pubs & Restaurants nearby: Driftwood Spars, St Agnes 01872 552428

Facilities: �📷 ☉ ⚒ ✱ 🚿 👤 🚻 🛜 ♻ ❶
Services: 🔌 🖥 🚽 ⚱
Within 3 miles: ⬇ 🏌 ◎ 🏊 🛥 🐎 ⛵ ∪

Notes: No kite flying, quiet between 21.00hrs-08.00hrs. Dogs must be kept on leads.

▶▶▶ 67% **Perranporth Camping & Touring Park** *(SW768542)*

Budnick Rd TR6 0DB
☎ **01872 572174**
dir: *0.5m E off B3285*

* ⚐ £18-£22 ⊕ £18-£22 ▲ £18-£22

Open Whit-Sep (rs Etr & end Sep shop, swimming pool & club facilities closed)

Last arrival 23.00hrs Last departure noon

A mainly tent site with few level pitches, located high above a fine sandy beach, which is much-frequented by surfers. The park is attractive to young people, and is set in a lively town on a spectacular part of the coast. 9 static caravans for holiday hire. 6 acre site. 120 touring pitches. 4 hardstandings. Caravan pitches. Motorhome pitches. Tent pitches. 9 statics.

AA Pubs & Restaurants nearby: Driftwood Spars, St Agnes 01872 552428

Perranporth Camping & Touring Park

Leisure: 🏊 ⛰ 🎱 ▢
Facilities: 🛁 📷 ☉ ⚒ ✱ 👤 ♿ 🛍 🚻 🐕 ❶
Services: 🔌 🖥 🍴 🏪 🛢 ⚡ 🚽 ⚱
Within 3 miles: ⬇ 🎣 🏌 ◎ 🏊 🛥 🐎 ∪

Notes: No noise after 23.00hrs. Dogs must be kept on leads.

see advert below

LEISURE: 🏊 Indoor swimming pool 🏊 Outdoor swimming pool ⛰ Children's playground 🎣 Kid's club 🎾 Tennis court 🎱 Games room ▢ Separate TV room ⬇ 9/18 hole golf course 🚣 Boats for hire 🎬 Cinema 🎵 Entertainment 🎣 Fishing ◎ Mini golf 🏊 Watersports 🏋 Gym 🏑 Sports field Spa ∪ Stables
FACILITIES: 🛁 Bath 📷 Shower ⊙ Electric shaver ⚒ Hairdryer ✱ Ice Pack Facility ♿ Disabled facilities 🕿 Public telephone 🛍 Shop on site or within 200yds 🖥 Mobile shop (calls at least 5 days a week) 🍴 BBQ area 👤 Picnic area 🛜 Wi-fi 🖳 Internet access ♻ Recycling ❶ Tourist info 🐕 Dog exercise area

POLPERRO · Map 2 SX25

Places to visit

Restormel Castle, RESTORMEL 01208 872687
www.english-heritage.org.uk

Great for kids: The Monkey Sanctuary, LOOE
01503 262532 www.monkeysanctuary.org

►► 77% Great Kellow Farm Caravan & Camping Site *(SX201522)*

Lansallos PL13 2QL
☎ 01503 272387
e-mail: kellow.farm@virgin.net
dir: *From Looe to Pelynt. In Pelynt left at church follow Lansallos sign. Left at x-rds, 0.75m. At staggered x-rds left, follow site signs. (NB Access is via single track lanes. It is advisable to follow guide directions not Sat Nav)*

🚐 £11-£15 �"£11-£15 ▲ £11-£15

Open Mar-3 Jan

Last arrival 22.00hrs Last departure noon

Set on a high level grassy paddock with extensive views of Polperro Bay, this attractive site is on a working dairy and beef farm, and close to National Trust properties and gardens. It is situated in a very peaceful location close to the fishing village of Polperro. 3 acre site. 30 touring pitches. 25 seasonal pitches. Caravan pitches. Motorhome pitches. Tent pitches. 10 statics.

AA Pubs & Restaurants nearby: Old Mill House Inn, Polperro 01503 272362

Barclay House, Looe 01503 262929

Facilities: 🏕⊙✳🛁♻ 𝒊

Services: 🔌

Within 3 miles: ⚲🎣🎿💰

Notes: ⊛ No noise after 23.00hrs. Dogs must be kept on leads.

POLRUAN · Map 2 SX15

Places to visit

Restormel Castle, RESTORMEL 01208 872687
www.english-heritage.org.uk

Great for kids: The Monkey Sanctuary, LOOE
01503 262532 www.monkeysanctuary.org

►►► 87% Polruan Holidays-Camping & Caravanning *(SX133509)*

Polruan-by-Fowey PL23 1QH
☎ 01726 870263
e-mail: polholiday@aol.com
web: www.polruanholidays.co.uk
dir: *A38 to Dobwalls, left onto A390 to East Taphouse. Left onto B3359. Right in 4.5m signed Polruan*

🚐🚐▲

Open Etr-Oct

Last arrival 21.00hrs Last departure noon

A very rural and quiet site in a lovely elevated position above the village, with good views of the sea. The River Fowey passenger ferry is close by, and the site has a good shop, and barbecues to borrow. The bus for Polperro and Looe stops outside the gate, and the foot ferry to Fowey, which runs until 11pm, is only a 10-minute walk away. 3 acre site. 47 touring pitches. 7 hardstandings. Caravan pitches. Motorhome pitches. Tent pitches. 10 statics.

AA Pubs & Restaurants nearby: The Ship Inn, Fowey 01726 832230

The Fowey Hotel, Fowey 01726 832551

Leisure: 🅰

Facilities: 🏕⊙🏪✳🕭🛁🎪📶🖥♻𝒊

Services: 🔌🅾🛢🚿🚽🍴

Within 3 miles: ⚲🎣🎿💰🛍U

Notes: No skateboards, rollerskates, bikes, water pistols or water bombs. Dogs must be kept on leads.

POLZEATH · Map 2 SW97

►►► 86% Tristram Caravan & Camping Park *(SW936790)*

PL27 6TP
☎ 01208 862215
e-mail: info@tristramcampsite.co.uk
web: www.polzeathcamping.co.uk
dir: *From B3314 onto unclassified road signed Polzeath. Through village, up hill, site 2nd right*

🚐🚐▲

Open Mar-Nov (rs mid Sep reseeding the site)

Last arrival 21.00hrs Last departure 10.00hrs

An ideal family site, positioned on a gently sloping cliff with grassy pitches and glorious sea views, which are best enjoyed from the terraced premier pitches, or over lunch or dinner at the Café India adjacent to the reception overlooking the beach. There is direct, gated access to the beach, where surfing is very popular, and the park has a holiday bungalow for rent. The local amenities of the village are only a few hundred yards away. 10 acre site. 100 touring pitches. Caravan pitches. Motorhome pitches. Tent pitches.

AA Pubs & Restaurants nearby: Restaurant Nathan Outlaw, Rock 01208 863394

Facilities: 🏕⊙🏪✳🕭🛁📶♻𝒊

Services: 🔌🛢🚿🍴🔋

Within 3 miles: 🏌⚲🎯🎣◎🛍🛍U

Notes: No ball games, no disposable BBQs, no noise between 23.00hrs-07.00hrs. Dogs must be kept on leads. Surf equipment hire.

see advert on page 100

SERVICES: 🔌 Electric hook up 🅾 Launderette 🍸 Licensed bar 🛢 Calor Gas ⊘ Camping Gaz 🚽 Toilet fluid 🍴 Café/Restaurant 🍔 Fast Food/Takeaway 🔋 Battery charging 🍼 Baby care 🚐 Motorvan service point **ABBREVIATIONS:** BH/bank hols-bank holidays Etr-Easter Whit-Whitsun dep-departure fr-from hrs-hours m-mile mdnt-midnight rdbt-roundabout rs-restricted service wk-week wknd-weekend ⊛ No credit cards ⊗ no dogs See page 7 for details of the AA Camping Card Scheme

LEISURE: Indoor swimming pool Outdoor swimming pool Children's playground Kid's club Tennis court Games room Separate TV room 9/18 hole golf course Boats for hire Cinema Entertainment Fishing Mini golf Watersports Gym Sports field **Spa** Stables
FACILITIES: Bath Shower Electric shaver Hairdryer Ice Pack Facility Disabled facilities Public telephone Shop on site or within 200yds Mobile shop (calls at least 5 days a week) BBQ area Picnic area Wi-fi Internet access Recycling Tourist info Dog exercise area

POLZEATH *continued*

►►► 85% South Winds Caravan & Camping Park *(SW948790)*

Polzeath Rd PL27 6QU
☎ 01208 863267 & 862215
e-mail: info@southwindscamping.co.uk
web: www.polzeathcamping.co.uk
dir: *Exit B3314 onto unclassified road signed Polzeath, site on right just past turn to New Polzeath*

Open May-mid Sep

Last arrival 21.00hrs Last departure 10.30hrs

A peaceful site with beautiful sea and panoramic rural views, within walking distance of a golf complex, and just three quarters of a mile from beach and village. There's an impressive reception building, replete with tourist information, TV, settees and a range of camping spares. 16 acre site. 165 touring pitches. Caravan pitches. Motorhome pitches. Tent pitches.

AA Pubs & Restaurants nearby: Restaurant Nathan Outlaw, Rock 01208 863394

Facilities: 🔥☉🅿✳🔥🔥🔥🔥🔥🔥🔥🔥🔥 ♻ ❶
Services: 🔋🔥🔥🔥🔥🔥🔥
Within 3 miles: 🔥🔥🔥🔥🔥🔥🔥🔥🔥🔥U

Notes: Families & couples only. No disposable BBQs, no noise 23.00hrs-07.00hrs. Dogs must be kept on leads. Restaurant & farm shop adjacent, Stepper Field open mid Jul-Aug.

see advert on opposite page

►►►► 93% Porthtowan Tourist Park *(SW693473)*

Mile Hill TR4 8TY
☎ 01209 890256
e-mail: admin@porthtowantouristpark.co.uk
web: www.porthtowantouristpark.co.uk
dir: *Exit A30 at junct signed Redruth/Porthtowan. Take 3rd exit at rdbt. 2m, right at T-junct. Site on left at top of hill*

* 🚐 £10-£18 🚗 £10-£18 ▲ £10-£18

Open Apr-Sep

Last arrival 21.30hrs Last departure 11.00hrs

A neat, level grassy site on high ground above Porthtowan, with plenty of shelter from mature trees and shrubs. The superb toilet facilities considerably enhance the appeal of this peaceful rural park, which is almost midway between the small seaside resorts of Portreath and Porthtowan, with their beaches and surfing. There is a new, purpose-built games/meeting room with a good library where tourist information leaflets are available. 5 acre site. 80 touring pitches. 5 hardstandings. 8 seasonal pitches. Caravan pitches. Motorhome pitches. Tent pitches.

AA Pubs & Restaurants nearby: Driftwood Spars, St Agnes 01872 552428

Leisure: 🎠🎯🎱
Facilities: 🔥☉🅿✳🔥🔥🔥🔥🔥🔥🔥🔥 ♻ ❶
Services: 🔋🔥🔥🔥🔥🔥🔥
Within 3 miles: 🔥🔥🔥🔥🔥🔥🔥U

Notes: No bikes or skateboards during Jul & Aug. Dogs must be kept on leads.

►►►► 72% Wheal Rose Caravan & Camping Park *(SW717449)*

Wheal Rose TR16 5DD
☎ 01209 891496
e-mail: whealrose@aol.com
dir: *Exit A30 at Scorrier sign, follow signs to Wheal Rose. Site 0.5m on left (Wheal Rose to Porthtowan road)*

* 🚐 £12-£17 🚗 £12-£17 ▲ £12-£17

Open Mar-Dec

Last arrival 21.00hrs Last departure 11.00hrs

A quiet, peaceful park in a secluded valley setting, central for beaches and countryside, and two miles from the surfing beaches of Porthtowan. The friendly owners work hard to keep this park immaculate, with a bright toilet block and well-trimmed pitches. There is a swimming pool and a new games room. 6 acre site. 50 touring pitches. 6 hardstandings. Caravan pitches. Motorhome pitches. Tent pitches. 3 statics.

AA Pubs & Restaurants nearby: Bassett Arms, Portreath 01209 842077

Leisure: 🏊🎠🎯🎱
Facilities: 🔥☉🅿✳🔥🔥🔥🔥🔥🔥🔥 ♻ ❶
Services: 🔋🔥🔥🔥🔥🔥
Within 3 miles: 🔥🔥🔥🔥🔥🔥U

Notes: 5mph speed limit, minimum noise after 23.00hrs, gates locked 23.00hrs. Dogs must be kept on leads.

PORTREATH — Map 2 SW64

Places to visit

East Pool Mine, POOL 01209 315027
www.nationaltrust.org.uk

►►►► 84% Tehidy Holiday
Park *(SW682432)*

GOLD

Harris Mill, Illogan TR16 4JQ
☎ 01209 216489
e-mail: holiday@tehidy.co.uk
web: www.tehidy.co.uk
dir: *Exit A30 at Redruth/Portreath junct onto A3047 to 1st rdbt. Left onto B3300. At junct straight over signed Tehidy Holiday Park. Past Cornish Arms pub, site 800yds at bottom of hill on left*

* ☞ £12-£21 ☞ £12-£21 ▲ £12-£21

Open all year (rs Nov-Mar part of shower block & shop closed)

Last arrival 20.00hrs Last departure 10.00hrs

An attractive wooded location in a quiet rural area only two and half miles from popular beaches. Mostly level pitches on tiered ground, and the toilet facilities are bright and modern. Holiday static caravans for hire. 4.5 acre site. 18 touring pitches. 11 hardstandings. 4 seasonal pitches. Caravan pitches. Motorhome pitches. Tent pitches. 32 statics. 2 wooden pods.

AA Pubs & Restaurants nearby: The Basset Arms, Portreath 01209 842077

Leisure: ⚠ 🎡 🎱 ⬛
Facilities: 🚿 ⊙ 🪒 ✳ ♿ 🕐 🛄 🎌 🛒 ♻ ❶
Services: 🚰 🗑 🚿 🍴 🍺
Within 3 miles: ⚓ ⛵ 🎍 🎣 ◎ ⛷ 🛒 🖫 🐎 ♻
Notes: No pets, no noise after 23.00hrs. Trampoline, off-licence.

see advert on page 88

PORTSCATHO — Map 2 SW83

Places to visit

St Mawes Castle, ST MAWES 01326 270526
www.english-heritage.org.uk

Trelissick Garden, TRELISSICK GARDEN
01872 862090 www.nationaltrust.org.uk

►►► 80% Trewince Farm Touring
Park *(SW868339)*

TR2 5ET
☎ 01872 580430
e-mail: info@trewincefarm.co.uk
dir: *From St Austell take A390 towards Truro. Left on B3287 to Tregony, following signs to St Mawes. At Trewithian, turn left to St Anthony. Site 0.75m past church*

* ☞ £11.50-£18.50 ☞ £11.50-£18.50
▲ £11.50-£18.50

Open May-Sep

Last arrival 23.00hrs Last departure 11.00hrs

A site on a working farm with spectacular sea views from its elevated position. There are many quiet golden sandy beaches close by, and boat launching facilities and mooring can be arranged at the nearby Percuil River Boatyard. The village of Portscatho with shops and pubs and attractive harbour is approximately one mile away. 3 acre site. 25 touring pitches. Caravan pitches. Motorhome pitches. Tent pitches.

AA Pubs & Restaurants nearby: The New Inn, Veryan 01872 501362

The Quarterdeck at The Nare, Veryan
01872 500000

Facilities: 🚿 ⊙ 🪒 ✳ 🖫 🎌 🐎 ♻ ❶
Services: 🚰 🗑 🚿
Within 3 miles: 🎍 🎣 ⛷ 🖫 🐎 ♻
Notes: 🐕 Dogs must be kept on leads.

REDRUTH — Map 2 SW64

Places to visit

East Pool Mine, POOL 01209 315027
www.nationaltrust.org.uk

Pendennis Castle, FALMOUTH 01326 316594
www.english-heritage.org.uk

Great for kids: National Maritime Museum Cornwall, FALMOUTH 01326 313388
www.nmmc.co.uk

PREMIER PARK

►►►►► 85% Globe Vale Holiday
Park *(SW708447)*

Radnor TR16 4BH
☎ 01209 891183
e-mail: info@globevale.co.uk
dir: *A30 take Redruth/Porthtowan exit then Portreath/North Country exit from rdbt, right at x-rds into Radnor Rd, left after 0.5m, site on left after 0.5m*

☞ ☞ ▲

Open all year

Last arrival 20.00hrs Last departure 10.00hrs

A family owned and run park set in a quiet rural location yet close to some stunning beaches and coastline. The park's touring area has a number of full facility hardstanding pitches, a high quality toilet block, a comfortable lounge bar serving bar meals, and holiday static caravans. 13 acre site. 138 touring pitches. 19 hardstandings. Caravan pitches. Motorhome pitches. Tent pitches. 10 statics.

AA Pubs & Restaurants nearby: The Basset Arms, Portreath 01209 842077

Leisure: ⚠ 🎱
Facilities: 🚿 ✳ ♿ 🐎 ♻ ❶
Services: 🚰 🗑 🍴 🛢 🖫 🚰 🍺 ⚡
Within 3 miles: ⚓ 🎍 ⛷ 🖫
Notes: Dogs must be kept on leads. Heated shower block in winter.

see advert on page 89

►►►► 80% *Lanyon Holiday Park*
(SW684387)

Loscombe Ln, Four Lanes TR16 6LP
☎ 01209 313474
e-mail: info@lanyonholidaypark.co.uk
dir: *Signed 0.5m off B2397 on Helston side of Four Lanes village*

🚐 🚏 Å

Open Mar-Oct

Last arrival 21.00hrs Last departure noon

Small, friendly rural park in an elevated position with fine views to distant St Ives Bay. This family owned and run park continues to be upgraded in all areas, and is close to a cycling trail. There is a well-stocked bar and a very inviting swimming pool. Stithian's Reservoir for fishing, sailing and windsurfing is two miles away. Two holiday cottages are available. 14 acre site. 25 touring pitches. Caravan pitches. Motorhome pitches. Tent pitches. 49 statics.

AA Pubs & Restaurants nearby: The Basset Arms, Portreath 01209 842077

Leisure: 🏊 🎪 🎣 🎱 🏓

Facilities: 🚿 📮 ⊙ 🅿 ✳ 🌲 🪠 Wi-Fi

Services: 🔌 🗑 🍽 🎱 🔋 ⚡

Within 3 miles: 🚴 ⛷ 🎿 🅿 ⊙ 🏊 🛒 🗑 ⛳

Notes: Family park. Take-away service, all-day games room.

see advert on page 89

►►► 79% *Cambrose Touring Park*
(SW684453)

Portreath Rd TR16 4HT
☎ 01209 890747
e-mail: cambrosetouringpark@supanet.com
dir: *A30 onto B3300 towards Portreath. Approx 0.75m at 1st rdbt right onto B3300. Take unclassified road on right signed Porthtowan. Site 200yds on left*

🚐 🚏 Å

Open Apr-Oct

Last arrival 22.00hrs Last departure 11.30hrs

Situated in a rural setting surrounded by trees and shrubs, this park is divided into grassy paddocks. It is about two miles from the harbour village of Portreath. The site has an excellent swimming pool with a sun bathing area. 6 acre site. 60 touring pitches. Caravan pitches. Motorhome pitches. Tent pitches.

AA Pubs & Restaurants nearby: The Basset Arms, Portreath 01209 842077

Leisure: 🏊 🎪 ⚽ 🎣

Facilities: 📮 ⊙ 🅿 ✳ ♿ 🛒 🗑 🪠 Wi-Fi ♻ 🛈

Services: 🔌 🗑 🔋 🧪 T 🔋 ⚡

Within 3 miles: 🚴 🎿 🅿 ◎ 🗑 🛒 ⛳

Notes: Mini football pitch.

►►► 72% Stithians Lake Country Park (SW705369)

Stithians Lake, Menherion TR16 6NW
☎ 01209 860301
e-mail: stithianswatersports@swlakestrust.org.uk
dir: *From Redruth take B3297 towards Helston. Follow brown tourist signs to Stithians Lake, entrance by Golden Lion Inn*

✳ 🚐 £13-£15 🚏 £13-£15 Å £13-£15

Open all year

Last arrival 17.30hrs Last departure noon

Opened just a couple of year's ago this simple campsite is a two-acre field situated adjacent to the Watersports Centre, which forms part of a large activity complex beside Stithians Lake. Campers have to use the functional toilet/shower facilities at the centre, and there is an excellent waterside café that also serves breakfasts. This is the perfect campsite for water sport enthusiasts. 2.1 acre site. 40 touring pitches. Caravan pitches. Motorhome pitches. Tent pitches.

AA Pubs & Restaurants nearby: Bassett Arms, Portreath 01209 842077

Leisure: 🎪

Facilities: 📮 ♿ 🛒 🪠 ♻ 🛈

Services: 🔌 🗑 🍽

Within 3 miles: 🎿 🅿 🏊 🗑 🛒

Notes: Dogs must be kept on leads.

REJERRAH — Map 2 SW75

Places to visit

Trerice, TRERICE 01637 875404
www.nationaltrust.org.uk

Blue Reef Aquarium, NEWQUAY 01637 878134
www.bluereefaquarium.co.uk

Great for kids: Newquay Zoo, NEWQUAY
0844 474 2244 www.newquayzoo.org.uk

PREMIER PARK

▶▶▶▶▶ 87% Newperran Holiday Park (SW801555)

TR8 5QJ
☎ 01872 572407
e-mail: holidays@newperran.co.uk
dir: 4m SE of Newquay & 1m S of Rejerrah on
A3075. Or A30 Redruth, exit B3275 Perranporth,
at 1st T-junct right onto A3075 towards Newquay,
site 300mtrs on left

* 🚐 £10.70–£18.50 🚎 £10.70–£18.50
🅰 £10.70–£18.50

Open Etr-Oct

Last arrival mdnt Last departure 10.00hrs

A family site in a lovely rural position near several
beaches and bays. This airy park offers screening
to some pitches, which are set in paddocks on
level ground. High season entertainment is
available in the park's high quality country inn,
and the café has an extensive menu. There is also
a swimming pool with a separate toddlers'
paddling area. 25 acre site. 357 touring pitches.
20 hardstandings. Caravan pitches. Motorhome
pitches. Tent pitches. 16 statics.

AA Pubs & Restaurants nearby: The Smugglers'
Den Inn, Cubert 01637 830209

Leisure: 🏊 🄌 ☺ ♠ ♫
Facilities: 🎿 ☉ 🖫 ✳ ☺ 🄌 🖼 ♻ ❶
Services: 🔌 🗄 🍴 🛢 ⊘ ⊤ 🍴 ⚒ 🛒 ↯
Within 3 miles: ⚓ 🚣 🎬 🎣 ☺ 🛳 🅿 🅱 ♨

Notes: Families & couples only. No skateboards.
Dogs must be kept on leads. Adventure
playground.

see advert on page 89

ROSUDGEON — Map 2 SW52

Places to visit

Trengwainton Garden, PENZANCE 01736 363148
www.nationaltrust.org.uk

Goonhilly Satellite Earth Station Experience,
HELSTON 0800 679593 www.goonhilly.bt.com

Great for kids: The Flambards Theme Park,
HELSTON 01326 573404 www.flambards.co.uk

▶▶▶▶ 87% Kenneggy Cove Holiday Park (SW562287)

Higher Kenneggy TR20 9AU
☎ 01736 763453
e-mail: enquiries@kenneggycove.co.uk
web: www.kenneggycove.co.uk
dir: On A394 between Penzance & Helston, turn S
into signed lane to site & Higher Kenneggy

🚐 🚎 🅰

Open 12 May-Sep

Last arrival 21.00hrs Last departure 11.00hrs

Set in an Area of Outstanding Natural Beauty with
spectacular sea views, this family-owned park is
quiet and well kept, with a well-equipped
children's play area, superb toilets, and a
takeaway food facility offering home-cooked
meals. A short walk along a country footpath leads
to the Cornish Coastal Path, and on to the golden
sandy beach at Kenneggy Cove. It's a half mile
walk to the main road to pick up the local bus
which goes to Penzance or Helston, with many
pretty Cornish coves en route. There is a fish and
chip shop and Chinese restaurant with takeaway a
short drive away. 4 acre site. 45 touring pitches.
Caravan pitches. Motorhome pitches. Tent pitches.
7 statics.

AA Pubs & Restaurants nearby: The Victoria Inn,
Perranuthnoe 01736 710309

The Ship Inn, Porthleven 01326 564204

Leisure: 🄌 ☺
Facilities: 🎿 ☉ 🖫 ✳ ☺ 🄌 🖼 ♻ ❶
Services: 🔌 🗄 🛢 ⊘ ⊤ ⚒ ↯
Within 3 miles: ⚓ 🚣 🅿 🛳 🅱 🅱 ♨

Notes: ⊘ No large groups, no noise after
22.00hrs. Dogs must be kept on leads. Fresh
bakery items, breakfasts.

RUMFORD — Map 2 SW87

Places to visit

Prideaux Place, PADSTOW 01841 532411
www.prideauxplace.co.uk

▶▶▶ 80% Music Water Touring Park (SW906685)

PL27 7SJ
☎ 01841 540257
dir: A39 at Winnards Perch rdbt onto B3274
signed Padstow. Left in 2m onto unclassified road
signed Rumford & St Eval. Site 500mtrs on right

* 🚐 £11–£15 🚎 £11–£15 🅰 £11–£15

Open Apr-Oct

Last arrival 23.00hrs Last departure 10.30hrs

Set in a peaceful location yet only a short drive to
the pretty fishing town of Padstow, and many
sandy beaches and coves. This family owned and
run park has grassy paddocks, and there is a
quiet lounge bar and a separate children's games
room. 8 acre site. 55 touring pitches. 2
hardstandings. Caravan pitches. Motorhome
pitches. Tent pitches. 2 statics.

AA Pubs & Restaurants nearby: The Cornish
Arms, St Merryn 01841 532700

Leisure: 🏊 🄌 ♠
Facilities: 🎿 ☉ 🖫 ✳ 🄌 🚜
Services: 🔌 🗄 🍴 ⊘ ⚒
Within 3 miles: 🎬 🅿 🛳 🅱 🅱 ♨

Notes: ⊕ Maximum 2 dogs per pitch, one tent per
pitch. Pets' corner (ponies, chickens).

RUTHERNBRIDGE — Map 2 SX06

Places to visit

Prideaux Place, PADSTOW 01841 532411 www.prideauxplace.co.uk

Cornwall's Regimental Museum, BODMIN 01208 72810

Great for kids: Pencarrow, BODMIN 01208 841369 www.pencarrow.co.uk

►►► 78% *Ruthern Valley Holidays* (SX014665)

PL30 5LU

☎ 01208 831395

e-mail: camping@ruthernvalley.com

web: www.ruthernvalley.com

dir: *A389 through Bodmin, follow St Austell signs, then Lanivet signs. At top of hill turn right on unclassified road signed Ruthernbridge. Follow signs*

🚐 🚌 ⛺

Open all year

Last arrival 20.30hrs Last departure noon

An attractive woodland site peacefully located in a small river valley west of Bodmin Moor. This away-from-it-all park is ideal for those wanting a quiet holiday, and the informal pitches are spread in four natural areas, with plenty of sheltered space. There are also 12 lodges, heated wooden wigwams, camping pods, and static holiday vans for hire. 7.5 acre site. 26 touring pitches. 2 hardstandings. Caravan pitches. Motorhome pitches. Tent pitches. 3 statics. 3 tipis. 3 wooden pods.

AA Pubs & Restaurants nearby: The Swan, Wadebridge 01208 812526

Trehellas House Hotel & Restaurant, Bodmin 01208 72700

Leisure: 🛝

Facilities: 🚿 ⊙ ✳ 📞 🛒 🪑 [Wi-Fi] ℹ

Services: 🔌 🧺 🛢 🍃 [T] 🔋

Within 3 miles: ⛳ 🎣 🛒 🧺 🐴

Notes: No dogs in camping pods or wigwams. No fires, no noise 22.30hrs-07.00hrs. Woodland area, farm animals.

ST AGNES — Map 2 SW75

Places to visit

Royal Cornwall Museum, TRURO 01872 272205 www.royalcornwallmuseum.org.uk

Trerice, TRERICE 01637 875404 www.nationaltrust.org.uk

AA CAMPING CARD SITE

►►►► 78% Beacon Cottage Farm Touring Park (SW705502)

Beacon Dr TR5 0NU

☎ 01872 552347 & 07879 413862

e-mail: beaconcottagefarm@lineone.net

web: www.beaconcottagefarmholidays.co.uk

dir: *From A30 at Threeburrows rdbt take B3277 to St Agnes, left into Goonvrea Rd, right into Beacon Drive, follow brown sign to site*

🚐 £16-£22 🚌 £16-£22 ⛺ £16-£22

Open Apr-Oct (rs Etr-Whit shop closed)

Last arrival 20.00hrs Last departure noon

A neat and compact site on a working farm, utilizing a cottage and outhouses, an old orchard and adjoining walled paddock. The unique location on a headland looking north-east along the coast comes with stunning views towards St Ives, and the keen friendly family owners keep all areas very well maintained. 5 acre site. 70 touring pitches. 2 seasonal pitches. Caravan pitches. Motorhome pitches. Tent pitches.

AA Pubs & Restaurants nearby: Driftwood Spars, St Agnes 01872 552428

Leisure: 🛝 ⚽

Facilities: 🚿 ⊙ 💨 ✳ 🛒 🪑 🐕 ♻ ℹ

Services: 🔌 🧺 🛢 🍃 🔋 🚰

Within 3 miles: ⛳ 🪁 🎣 🎯 🏄 🛒 🧺 🐴

Notes: No large groups. Dogs must be kept on leads. Secure year-round caravan storage.

►►► 82% Presingoll Farm Caravan & Camping Park (SW721494)

TR5 0PB

☎ 01872 552333

e-mail: pam@presingollfarm.co.uk

dir: *From A30 Chiverton rdbt take B3277 towards St Agnes. Site 3m on right*

* 🚐 fr £14 🚌 fr £14 ⛺ fr £14

Open Etr & Apr-Oct

Last departure 10.00hrs

An attractive rural park adjoining farmland, with extensive views of the coast beyond. Family owned and run, with level grass pitches, and a modernised toilet block in smart converted farm buildings. There is also a campers' room with microwave, freezer, kettle and free coffee and tea, and a children's play area. This is an ideal base for touring the Newquay and St Ives areas. 5 acre site. 90 touring pitches. 6 hardstandings. Caravan pitches. Motorhome pitches. Tent pitches.

AA Pubs & Restaurants nearby: Driftwood Spars, St Agnes 01872 552428

Leisure: 🛝

Facilities: 🚿 ⊙ 💨 ✳ ♿ 🛒 🚚 🪑 🐕 ♻ ℹ

Services: 🔌 🧺 🔋

Within 3 miles: 🎣 🛒 🐴

Notes: 🚫 No large groups. Dogs must be kept on leads. Microwave & freezer facility, tea & coffee.

SERVICES: 🔌 Electric hook up 🧺 Launderette 🍷 Licensed bar 🛢 Calor Gas 🍃 Camping Gaz [T] Toilet fluid 🍴 Café/Restaurant 🍔 Fast Food/Takeaway 🔋 Battery charging 👶 Baby care 🚰 Motorvan service point **ABBREVIATIONS:** BH/bank hols-bank holidays Etr-Easter Whit-Whitsun dep-departure fr-from hrs-hours m-mile mdnt-midnight rdbt-roundabout rs-restricted service wk-week wknd-weekend 🚫 No credit cards 🐕⃠ no dogs See page 7 for details of the AA Camping Card Scheme

ST ALLEN
Map 2 SW85

Places to visit

Royal Cornwall Museum, TRURO 01872 272205
www.royalcornwallmuseum.org.uk

Trerice, TRERICE 01637 875404
www.nationaltrust.org.uk

Great for kids: Dairy Land Farm World,
NEWQUAY 01872 510246
www.dairylandfarmworld.com

▶▶▶ 82% *Tolcarne Campsite*

(SW826513)

Tolcarne Bungalow TR4 9QX
☎ 01872 540652 & 07881 965477
e-mail: dianemcd@talktalk.net
dir: *A30 towards Redruth. Approx 1m W of Carland
Cross rdbt 2nd left to St Allen. 1m, 3rd left to site*

⛟ ⛟ ▲

Open all year

Last arrival 22.00hrs Last departure noon

A rural site with fantastic countryside views from
the terraced pitches. Expect level, beautifully
mown pitches and a spotlessly clean and purpose-
built facilities block. New bathrooms have been
built, together with a campers' kitchen and fully
equipped laundry room. 1 acre site. 10 touring
pitches. 5 seasonal pitches. Caravan pitches.
Motorhome pitches. Tent pitches.

AA Pubs & Restaurants nearby: Plume of
Feathers, Mitchell 01872 510387

Facilities: ⛟ ☉ ✻ ⛟ ⑤ ⌂ ⛟ ❶

Services: ⛟ ⊘ ⛟

Within 3 miles: ⛟ ⛟ ⑤

Notes: ⊗ No noise after 22.30hrs. Dogs must be
kept on leads.

ST AUSTELL

See also Carlyon Bay

Places to visit

Charlestown Shipwreck & Heritage Centre,
ST AUSTELL 01726 69897
www.shipwreckcharlestown.com

Eden Project, ST AUSTELL 01726 811911
www.edenproject.com

Great for kids: Wheal Martyn Museum &
Country Park, ST AUSTELL 01726 850362
www.wheal-martyn.com

ST AUSTELL
Map 2 SX05

PREMIER PARK

▶▶▶▶▶ 84% River Valley Holiday
Park (SX010503)

London Apprentice PL26 7AP
☎ 01726 73533
e-mail: mail@cornwall-holidays.co.uk
web: www.rivervalleyholidaypark.co.uk
dir: *Direct access to site signed on B3273 from
St Austell at London Apprentice*

⛟ £13-£34 ⛟ £13-£34 ▲ £13-£34

Open Apr-end Sep

Last arrival 21.00hrs Last departure 11.00hrs

A neat, well-maintained family-run park set in a
pleasant river valley. The quality toilet block and
attractively landscaped grounds make this a
delightful base for a holiday. All pitches are
hardstanding, mostly divided by low fencing and
neatly trimmed hedges, and the park offers a good
range of leisure facilities, including an inviting
swimming pool, a games room, an internet room,
and an excellent children's play area. There is

LEISURE: 🏊 Indoor swimming pool 🏊 Outdoor swimming pool 🛝 Children's playground 🪁 Kid's club 🎾 Tennis court 🎱 Games room 📺 Separate TV room
⛳ 9/18 hole golf course ⛵ Boats for hire 🎬 Cinema 🎵 Entertainment 🎣 Fishing ◎ Mini golf 🏄 Watersports 🏋 Gym ⚽ Sports field Spa ♻ Stables
FACILITIES: 🛁 Bath 🚿 Shower ☉ Electric shaver 💈 Hairdryer ✻ Ice Pack Facility ⛟ Disabled facilities ⏰ Public telephone ⑤ Shop on site or within 200yds
🏪 Mobile shop (calls at least 5 days a week) 🍖 BBQ area 🍴 Picnic area Wi-Fi Wi-fi ▮ Internet access ♻ Recycling ❶ Tourist info ⛟ Dog exercise area

direct access to river walks and the cycle trail to the beach at Pentewan. Site is on bus route to St Austell. 2 acre site. 45 touring pitches. 45 hardstandings. Caravan pitches. Motorhome pitches. Tent pitches. 40 statics.

AA Pubs & Restaurants nearby: Austells, St Austell 01726 813888

River Valley Holiday Park

Leisure:

Facilities:

Services:

Within 3 miles:

Notes: Off-road cycle trail to beach.

see advert on opposite page

AA CAMPING CARD SITE

►►►► 81% Meadow Lakes *(SW966485)*

Hewas Water PL26 7JG
☎ 01726 882540
e-mail: info@meadow-lakes.co.uk
web: www.meadow-lakes.co.uk
dir: *From A390 4m SW of St Austell onto B3287, Tregony. 1m, site on left*

£7.50-£24 £7.50-£24 £7.50-£24

Open mid Mar-end Oct

Last arrival 20.00hrs

Set in a quiet rural area, this extensive park is divided into paddocks with mature hedges and trees, and with its own coarse fishing lakes. This friendly, family park has enthusiastic and hands-on owners - all facilities are immaculate and spotlessly clean. The park offers organised activities for children indoors (there is a well-equipped games room) and out in the summer holidays, and at other times caters for adult breaks. There are animals in pens which children can enter. Self-catering lodges, static caravans and nine bungalows are also found at this site. The bus to Truro and St Austell stops within half a mile of the site. 56 acre site. 190 touring pitches. 11 hardstandings. 30 seasonal pitches. Caravan pitches. Motorhome pitches. Tent pitches. 32 statics. 3 wooden pods.

AA Pubs & Restaurants nearby: Austells, St Austell 01726 813888

Leisure:

Facilities:

Services:

Within 3 miles:

Notes: Dogs must be kept on leads. Table tennis, fishing.

►►► 78% Court Farm Holidays

(SW953524)

St Stephen PL26 7LE
☎ 01726 823684
e-mail: info@courtfarmcornwall.co.uk
dir: *From St Austell take A3058 towards Newquay. Through St Stephen (pass Peugeot garage). Right at St Stephen/Coombe Hay/Langreth/Industrial site sign. 400yds, site on right*

Open Apr-Sep

Last arrival by dark Last departure 11.00hrs

Set in a peaceful rural location, this large camping field offers plenty of space, and is handy for the Eden Project and the Lost Gardens of Heligan. Coarse fishing and star-gazing facilities at the Roseland Observatory are among the on-site attractions. It is a five-minute walk to a Co-op store, and also to the bus stop on the Newquay to St Austell route. 4 acre site. 20 touring pitches. 5 hardstandings. Caravan pitches. Motorhome pitches. Tent pitches.

AA Pubs & Restaurants nearby: Austells, St Austell 01726 813888

Leisure:

Facilities:

Services:

Within 3 miles:

Notes: No noise after dark. Astronomy lectures, observatory, solar observatory.

ST BLAZEY GATE **Map 2 SX05**

Places to visit

Eden Project, ST AUSTELL 01726 811911 www.edenproject.com

St Catherine's Castle, FOWEY 0870 333 1181 www.english-heritage.org.uk

Great for kids: Wheal Martyn Museum & Country Park, ST AUSTELL 01726 850362 www.wheal-martyn.com

►►► 84% Doubletrees Farm

(SX060540)

Luxulyan Rd PL24 2EH
☎ 01726 812266
e-mail: doubletrees@eids.co.uk
dir: *On A390 at Blazey Gate. Turn by Leek Seed Chapel, almost opposite BP filling station. After approx 300yds turn right by public bench into site*

Open all year

Last arrival 22.30hrs Last departure 11.30hrs

A popular park with terraced pitches offering superb sea and coastal views. Close to beaches, and the nearest park to the Eden Project (a 20-minute walk), it is very well maintained by friendly owners. There is a Chinese restaurant, a fish and chip shop and bus stop in St Blazey Gate within 300 yards of the entrance. 1.57 acre site. 32 touring pitches. 6 hardstandings. Caravan pitches. Motorhome pitches. Tent pitches.

AA Pubs & Restaurants nearby: Austell's, St Austell 01726 813888

Facilities:

Services:

Within 3 miles:

Notes: No noise after mdnt. Dogs must be kept on leads.

ST BURYAN
Map 2 SW42

AA CAMPING CARD SITE

►►► 87% **Treverven Touring Caravan & Camping Park** *(SW410237)*

Treverven Farm TR19 6DL
☎ 01736 810200 & 810318
e-mail: trevervenpark@btconnect.com
dir: *A30 onto B3283 1.5m after St Buryan, left onto B3315. Site on right in 1m*

Open Etr-Oct

Last departure noon

Situated in a quiet Area of Outstanding Natural Beauty, with panoramic sea and country views, this family-owned site is located off a traffic-free lane leading directly to the coastal path. The toilet facilities are very good, and Treverven is ideally placed for exploring west Cornwall. There is an excellent takeaway facility on site. 6 acre site. 115 touring pitches. Caravan pitches. Motorhome pitches. Tent pitches.

AA Pubs & Restaurants nearby: Old Success Inn, Sennen 01736 871232

Lamorna Wink, Lamorna 01736 731566

Leisure: ⅍

Facilities: ⎀⊙⌀⚡⁎ﬞ☉ʰ᪤☐ﬞⅅ᪢

Services: ⌑☐ᵇ🛢⌀☐🗑⌂

Within 3 miles: ⊟⌀⋚ﬞ🔔᪑

Notes: No noise after 22.00hrs. Dogs must be kept on leads. Toaster & kettle available.

ST COLUMB MAJOR
Map 2 SW96

Places to visit

Prideaux Place, PADSTOW 01841 532411
www.prideauxplace.co.uk

Cornwall's Regimental Museum, BODMIN
01208 72810

Great for kids: Pencarrow, BODMIN
01208 841369 www.pencarrow.co.uk

►►► 87% *Southleigh Manor Naturist Park (SW918623)*

TR9 6HY
☎ 01637 880938
e-mail: enquiries@southleigh-manor.com
dir: *Exit A30 at junct with A39 signed Wadebridge. At Highgate Hill rdbt take A39. At Halloon rdbt take A39. At Trekenning rdbt take 4th exit. Site 500mtrs on right*

Open Etr-Oct (rs Peak times shop open)

Last arrival 20.00hrs Last departure 10.30hrs

A very well maintained, naturist park in the heart of the Cornish countryside, catering for families and couples only. Seclusion and security are very well planned, and the lovely gardens provide a calm setting. There are two lodges and static caravans for holiday hire. A new bus stop has been placed at the entrance gate which gives easy access to Newquay, Padstow or St Ives. 4 acre site. 50 touring pitches. Caravan pitches. Motorhome pitches. Tent pitches.

AA Pubs & Restaurants nearby: The Falcon Inn, St Mawgan 01637 860225

Leisure: ⋚ ⅍

Facilities: ⎀⊙⌀⚡⁎ﬞ☉᪤☐

Services: ⌑☐🍴🛢⌀☐🍲🛒

Within 3 miles: ⌀🔔᪑

Notes: ᪲ Sauna, spa bath, pool table, putting green.

►►► 80% NEW **Trewan Hall** *(SW911646)*

TR9 6DB
☎ 01637 880261 & 07900 677397
e-mail: enquiries@trewan-hall.co.uk
dir: *From A39 N of St Columb Major (do not enter town) turn left signed Talskiddy & St Eval. Site 1m on left*

* 🚐 £9.70-£18.60 🚐 £9.70-£18.60
▲ £9.70-£18.60

Open 11 May-17 Sep (rs Low season shop open shorter hours)

Last arrival 22.00hrs Last departure noon

Trewan Hall lies at the centre of a Cornish estate amongst 36 acres of wooded grounds. The site's extensive amenities include a 25-metre swimming pool and a free, live theatre during most of July and August, plus the campsite shop stocks everything from groceries to camping equipment. The site also has fine gardens, four acres of woodland for dog walking and a field available for ball games. St Columb is just a short walk away. 14.27 acre site. 200 touring pitches. Caravan pitches. Motorhome pitches. Tent pitches.

AA Pubs & Restaurants nearby: The Falcon Inn, St Mawgan 01637 860225

Leisure: ⋚⋚⅍᪲🔔᪑

Facilities: ⎀⎀⊙⌀⚡⁎ﬞ☉᪤☐ﬞﬞ᪢ ♻ ❶

Services: ⌑☐🛢⌀☐🍲🛒

Within 3 miles: ⌀⋚⊙⋚🔔᪑

Notes: No cycling, no driving on fields from mdnt-08.00hrs, no noise after mdnt, families & couples only. Dogs must be kept on leads. Library, billiard room.

LEISURE: 🏊 Indoor swimming pool 🏊 Outdoor swimming pool ⅍ Children's playground 🪀 Kid's club 🎾 Tennis court ♣ Games room ⧠ Separate TV room ⛳ 9/18 hole golf course ⛵ Boats for hire 🎬 Cinema 🎵 Entertainment 🎣 Fishing ⊙ Mini golf 🏄 Watersports 🏋 Gym 🏐 Sports field **Spa** ᪑ Stables
FACILITIES: 🛁 Bath ⎀ Shower ⊙ Electric shaver ⌀ Hairdryer ⁎ Ice Pack Facility ☉ Disabled facilities ℂ Public telephone 🏪 Shop on site or within 200yds 🏪 Mobile shop (calls at least 5 days a week) 🍲 BBQ area 🏕 Picnic area 📶 Wi-fi 🖥 Internet access ♻ Recycling ❶ Tourist info 🐾 Dog exercise area

ST DAY — Map 2 SW74

Places to visit

Royal Cornwall Museum, TRURO 01872 272205
www.royalcornwallmuseum.org.uk

East Pool Mine, POOL 01209 315027
www.nationaltrust.org.uk

►►► 82% St Day Touring Park

(SW733422)

Church Hill TR16 5LE
☎ 01209 821086
e-mail: holidays@stdaytouring.co.uk
dir: *From A30 at Scorrier onto B3298 towards Falmouth. Site signed on right in 2m*

Open Etr & Apr-Oct

Last departure 11.00hrs

A very good touring area with modern toilet facilities. This rurally located park run by keen friendly owners is situated in a quiet area between Falmouth and Newquay and within close walking distance of the attractive village of St Day. 2 acre site. 30 touring pitches. 9 hardstandings. 9 seasonal pitches. Caravan pitches. Motorhome pitches. Tent pitches.

Facilities: ♠⊙♀✻ॐ 🚾 ♻ ❶
Services: ⚡🔆🔋
Within 3 miles: ⚑🔫🛒◎≈🔒🔅∪

Notes: Adults only. ⊛ No ball games. Dogs must be kept on leads.

ST GILES-ON-THE-HEATH

See Chapmans Well (Devon)

ST HILARY — Map 2 SW53

Places to visit

Godolphin House, GODOLPHIN CROSS
01736 763194
www.nationaltrust.org.uk/godolphin

Great for kids: The Flambards Theme Park, HELSTON 01326 573404 www.flambards.co.uk

AA CAMPING CARD SITE

►►►► 83% Wayfarers Caravan & Camping Park *(SW558314)*

Relubbus Ln TR20 9EF
☎ 01736 763326
e-mail: elaine@wayfarerspark.co.uk
dir: *Exit A30 onto A394 towards Helston. Left at rdbt onto B3280 after 2m. Site 1.5m on left on bend*

🚐 £19-£26 🚏 £19-£26 ⚑ £18-£24

Open May-Sep

Last arrival 19.00hrs Last departure 11.00hrs

Located in the centre of St Hilary, two and half miles from St Michael's Mount, this is a quiet sheltered park in a peaceful rural setting. It offers spacious, well-drained pitches and very well cared for facilities. It has a separate car park for campers which makes the camping area safer. 4.8 acre site. 39 touring pitches. 25 hardstandings. Caravan pitches. Motorhome pitches. Tent pitches. 3 statics.

AA Pubs & Restaurants nearby: Trevelyan Arms, Goldsithney 01736 710453

Godolphin Arms, Marazion 01736 710202

Facilities: ♠⊙♀✻ॐ🕓🔒🚻♻ ❶
Services: ⚡🔆🛢🖉🅣🔋⛟
Within 3 miles: ⚑🔫🛒◎≈🔒🔅∪

Notes: Adults only. ⊛ ⊗ No pets.

►►► 77% Trevair Touring Park

(SW548326)

South Treveneague TR20 9BY
☎ 01736 740647
e-mail: info@trevairtouringpark.co.uk
dir: *A30 onto A394 signed Helston. 2m to rdbt, left onto B3280. Through Goldsithney. Left at brown site sign. Through 20mph zone to site, 1m on right*

Open Etr-Nov

Last arrival 22.00hrs Last departure 11.00hrs

Set in a rural location adjacent to woodland, this park is level and secluded, with grassy pitches. Marazion's beaches and the famous St Michael's Mount are just three miles away. The friendly owners live at the farmhouse on the park. 3.5 acre site. 40 touring pitches. Caravan pitches. Motorhome pitches. Tent pitches. 2 statics.

AA Pubs & Restaurants nearby: Trevelyan Arms, Goldsithney 01736 710453

Godolphin Arms, Marazion 01736 710202

Facilities: ♠⊙✻♻ ❶
Services: ⚡🔆🔋
Within 3 miles: ⚑🔫🔅🔒∪

Notes: ⊛ No noise after 23.00hrs. Dogs must be kept on leads.

ST IVES   Map 2 SW54

Places to visit

Barbara Hepworth Museum & Sculpture Garden, ST IVES 01736 796226
www.tate.org.uk/stives

Tate St Ives, ST IVES 01736 796226
www.tate.org.uk/stives

PREMIER PARK

►►►►► 96% **Polmanter Touring Park** (SW510388)

Best of British

Halsetown TR26 3LX
☎ 01736 795640
e-mail: reception@polmanter.com
dir: Signed from B3311 at Halsetown

* ⊞ £18.50-£36 ⊞ £18.50-£36 ▲ £15-£28

Open Whit-10 Sep (rs Whit shop, pool, bar & takeaway food closed)

Last arrival 21.00hrs Last departure 10.00hrs

A well-developed touring park on high ground, Polmanter is an excellent choice for family holidays and offers high quality in all areas, from the immaculate modern toilet blocks to the outdoor swimming pool and hard tennis courts. Pitches are individually marked and sited in meadows, and the park has been tastefully landscaped, which includes a field with full-facility hardstanding pitches to accommodate larger caravans and motorhomes. The fishing port and beaches of St Ives are just a mile and a half away, and there is a bus service in high season. 20 acre site. 270 touring pitches. 60 hardstandings. Caravan pitches. Motorhome pitches. Tent pitches.

AA Pubs & Restaurants nearby: The Tinners Arms, Zennor 01736 796927

The Gurnard's Head, Zennor 01736 796928

Leisure: ⋞ ⚠ ⌣ ☺ ✺

Facilities: ⋔ ☉ ⚑ ✳ ⅙ ⌙ ⓢ ⊀ ⅏ 🖳 ♻ ❶

Services: ⊞ ⓢ ⊪ ⌀ Ⓣ ◎ ⌸ ⌲ ↯

Within 3 miles: ↧ ⅟ 日 ⌇ ◎ ≚ ⓢ ⓢ ∪

Notes: Family camping only. No skateboards, roller blades or heelys. Dogs must be kept on leads. Putting.

see advert on page 91

PREMIER PARK

►►►►► 86% **Ayr Holiday Park** (SW509408)

GOLD

TR26 1EJ
☎ 01736 795855
e-mail: recept@ayrholidaypark.co.uk
dir: From A30 follow St Ives 'large vehicles' route via B3311 through Halsetown onto B3306. Site signed towards St Ives town centre

* ⊞ £16.50-£33.50 ⊞ £16.50-£33.50
▲ £16.50-£33.50

Open all year

Last arrival 22.00hrs Last departure 10.00hrs

A well-established park on a cliff side overlooking St Ives Bay, with a heated toilet block that makes winter holidaying more attractive. There are stunning views from most pitches, and the town centre, harbour and beach are only half a mile away, with direct access to the coastal footpath. This makes an excellent base for surfing enthusiasts. 4 acre site. 40 touring pitches. 20 hardstandings. Caravan pitches. Motorhome pitches. Tent pitches.

AA Pubs & Restaurants nearby: The Watermill, Hayle, near St Ives 01736 757912

Leisure: ⚠ ✺

Facilities: ⌦ ⋔ ☉ ⚑ ✳ ⅙ ⌙ ⓢ ⊀ ⅏ 🖳 ♻ ❶

Services: ⊞ ⓢ ⋔ ⌀ Ⓣ ⌲ ↯

Within 3 miles: ↧ ⅟ 日 ⌇ ◎ ≚ ⓢ ⓢ ∪

Notes: No disposable BBQs. Dogs must be kept on leads.

see advert on opposite page

►►►► 80% *Penderleath Caravan & Camping Park* (SW496375)

Towednack TR26 3AF
☎ 01736 798403 & 07840 208542
e-mail: holidays@penderleath.co.uk
dir: From A30 take A3074 towards St Ives. Left at 2nd mini-rdbt, approx 3m to T-junct. Left then immediately right. Next left

⊞ ⊞ ▲

Open Etr-Oct

Last arrival 21.30hrs Last departure 10.30hrs

Set in a rugged rural location, this tranquil park has extensive views towards St Ives Bay and the north coast. Facilities are all housed in modernised granite barns, and include spotless toilets with fully-serviced shower rooms, and there's a quiet licensed bar with beer garden, a food takeaway, breakfast room and bar meals. The owners are welcoming and helpful. 10 acre site. 75 touring pitches. Caravan pitches. Motorhome pitches. Tent pitches.

AA Pubs & Restaurants nearby: The Watermill, Hayle, Nr Ives 01736 757912

Leisure: ⚠ ✺

Facilities: ⋔ ☉ ⚑ ✳ ⅙ ⌙ ⓢ ⊀ ♻ ❶

Services: ⊞ ⓢ ⋔ ⌀ Ⓣ ◎ ⌲ ⌸

Within 3 miles: ↧ ⅟ 日 ⌇ ◎ ≚ ⓢ ⓢ ∪

Notes: No campfires, no noise after 23.00hrs, dogs must be well behaved. Dogs must be kept on leads. Bus to St Ives in high season.

►►►► **79% Trevalgan Touring Park** *(SW490402)*

Trevalgan TR26 3BJ
☎ **01736 792048**
e-mail: recept@trevalgantouringpark.co.uk
dir: From A30 follow holiday route to St Ives. B3311 through Halsetown to B3306. Left towards Land's End. Site signed 0.5m on right

* ⬛ £14.50-£25 ⬛ £14.50-£25 ▲ £14.50-£25

Open Etr-Sep

Last arrival 22.00hrs Last departure 10.00hrs

An open park next to a working farm in a rural area on the coastal road from St Ives to Zennor. The park is surrounded by mature hedges, but there are extensive views over the sea. There are very good toilet facilities including family rooms, and a large TV lounge and recreation room with drinks machine. There is a safari tent with tables and chairs so that campers can eat outside during inclement weather. 4.9 acre site. 120 touring pitches. Caravan pitches. Motorhome pitches. Tent pitches.

AA Pubs & Restaurants nearby: The Tinners Arms, Zennor 01736 796927

The Gurnard's Head, Zennor 01736 796928

Leisure: ⚄ ✿ 🔍 ▢
Facilities: ⚫☉ℙ✳ᕒ☉ⓢ⊟✿ ❶
Services: ⚡ⓢ 🔋⊘ T 🎣 🛖 ⚒
Within 3 miles: ⏚ ✚ 日 ⚲ ◎ ⬒ ⓢ ⓢ ∪
Notes: Dogs must be kept on leads. Farm trail.

►► **87% Balnoon Camping Site**
(SW509382)

Halsetown TR26 3JA
☎ **01736 795431**
e-mail: nat@balnoon.fsnet.co.uk
dir: From A30 take A3074, at 2nd mini-rdbt 1st left signed Tate/St Ives. In 3m turn right after Balnoon Inn

* ⬛ £11.50-£15 ⬛ £11.50-£15 ▲ £11.50-£15

Open Etr-Oct

Last arrival 20.00hrs Last departure 11.00hrs

Small, quiet and friendly, this sheltered site offers superb views of the adjacent rolling hills. The two paddocks are surrounded by mature hedges, and the toilet facilities are kept spotlessly clean. The beaches of Carbis Bay and St Ives are about two miles away. 1 acre site. 23 touring pitches. Caravan pitches. Motorhome pitches. Tent pitches.

AA Pubs & Restaurants nearby: The Tinners Arms, Zennor 01736 796927

The Gurnard's Head, Zennor 01736 796928

Facilities: ⚫☉ℙ✳ⓢ
Services: ⚡⊘T🎣
Within 3 miles: ⏚✚日⚲◎ⓢⓢ∪
Notes: ⊗ No noise between 23.00hrs-07.30hrs. Dogs must be kept on leads.

SERVICES: ⚡ Electric hook up ⓢ Launderette ▭ Licensed bar 🔋 Calor Gas ⊘ Camping Gaz T Toilet fluid 🍴 Café/Restaurant 🛖 Fast Food/Takeaway 🎣 Battery charging ⚒ Baby care ⚒ Motorvan service point **ABBREVIATIONS:** BH/bank hols-bank holidays Etr-Easter Whit-Whitsun dep-departure fr-from hrs-hours m-mile mdnt-midnight rdbt-roundabout rs-restricted service wk-week wknd-weekend ⊗ No credit cards ⊗ no dogs   See page 7 for details of the AA Camping Card Scheme

ST JUST (NEAR LAND'S END) Map 2 SW33

Places to visit

Geevor Tin Mine, PENDEEN 01736 788662 www.geevor.com

Carn Euny Ancient Village, SANCREED 0870 333 1181 www.english-heritage.org.uk

►►► 83% *Roselands Caravan and Camping Park* *(SW387305)*

Dowran TR19 7RS
☎ 01736 788571
e-mail: info@roselands.co.uk
dir: *From A30 Penzance bypass turn right for St Just on A3071. 5m, turn left at sign after tin mine chimney, follow signs to site*

🚐 🚌 ⛺

Open all year

Last arrival 21.00hrs Last departure 11.00hrs

A small, friendly park in a sheltered rural setting, an ideal location for a quiet family holiday. The owners continue to upgrade the park, and in addition to the attractive little bar there is an indoor games room, children's playground and good toilet facilities. 3 acre site. 15 touring pitches. Caravan pitches. Motorhome pitches. Tent pitches. 15 statics.

AA Pubs & Restaurants nearby: The Wellington, St Just 01736 787319

Harris's Restaurant, Penzance 01736 364408

The Navy Inn, Penzance 01736 333232

Leisure: 🛝 🏓 📺

Facilities: 🚿 🪒 💨 ❄ 📞 [$] 🧺 [Wi-fi]

Services: 🔌 🧼 🍸 🔒 🍃 [T] 🛒

Within 3 miles: ⛳ 🎣 🏄 [$] 🧼 🐴

Notes: No cars by caravans.

►►► 80% *Kelynack Caravan & Camping Park* *(SW374301)*

Kelynack TR19 7RE
☎ 01736 787633
e-mail: kelynackholidays@tiscali.co.uk
dir: *1m S of St Just, 5m N of Land's End on B3306*

🚐 🚌 ⛺

Open all year

Last arrival 22.00hrs Last departure 10.00hrs

A small secluded park that sits alongside a stream in an unspoilt rural location. The level grass pitches are in two areas. The park is within reach of Land's Ends, Sennen Cove, Minack Theatre and Penzance. 3 acre site. 28 touring pitches. 3 hardstandings. Caravan pitches. Motorhome pitches. Tent pitches. 13 statics.

AA Pubs & Restaurants nearby: The Wellington, St Just 01736 787319

Harris's Restaurant, Penzance 01736 364408

The Navy Inn, Penzance 01736 333232

Leisure: 🛝 🏓

Facilities: 🚿 🪒 💨 ❄ ♿ 📞 [$] 🧺 [Wi-fi] ♻ ℹ

Services: 🔌 🧼 🔒 🍃 [T] 🛏 🐕

Within 3 miles: ⛳ 🎣 🏄 [$] 🐴

Notes: Dogs must be kept on leads. Dining & cooking shelter.

►►► 80% Trevaylor Caravan & Camping Park *(SW368222)*

Botallack TR19 7PU
☎ 01736 787016 & 07816 992519
e-mail: trevaylor@cornishcamping.co.uk
dir: *On B3306 (St Just-St Ives road), site on right 0.75m from St Just*

* 🚐 £11-£16 🚌 £11-£16 ⛺ £11-£16

Open Mar-Oct

Last arrival 21.00hrs Last departure 11.00hrs

A sheltered grassy site located off the beaten track in a peaceful location at the western tip of Cornwall; it makes an ideal base for discovering Penzance and Land's End. The dramatic coastline and the pretty villages nearby are truly unspoilt. Clean, well-maintained facilities and a good shop are offered along with a bar serving meals. The open-top bus stops at the entrance to the site. The new owners are planning positive changes to this popular park. 6 acre site. 50 touring pitches. Caravan pitches. Motorhome pitches. Tent pitches. 5 statics.

AA Pubs & Restaurants nearby: The Wellington, St Just 01736 787319

Harris's Restaurant, Penzance 01736 364408

The Navy Inn, Penzance 01736 333232

Leisure: 🛝 🏓 📺

Facilities: 🚿 💨 ❄ [$] [Wi-fi] ♻ ℹ

Services: 🔌 🧼 🍸 🔒 🍃 [T] 🍴 🛏 🛒

Within 3 miles: ⛳ 🎣 🏄 [$] 🧼 🐴

Notes: Quiet after 220hrs. Dogs must be kept on leads.

LEISURE: Indoor swimming pool · Outdoor swimming pool · 🛝 Children's playground · Kid's club · Tennis court · 🏓 Games room · 📺 Separate TV room · ⛳ 9/18 hole golf course · Boats for hire · Cinema · Entertainment · 🎣 Fishing · Mini golf · 🏄 Watersports · Gym · Sports field · Spa · 🐴 Stables
FACILITIES: Bath · 🚿 Shower · 🪒 Electric shaver · 💨 Hairdryer · ❄ Ice Pack Facility · ♿ Disabled facilities · 📞 Public telephone · [$] Shop on site or within 200yds · Mobile shop (calls at least 5 days a week) · BBQ area · 🧺 Picnic area · [Wi-fi] Wi-fi · Internet access · ♻ Recycling · ℹ Tourist info · Dog exercise area

AA CAMPING CARD SITE

►►► 75% Secret Garden Caravan & Camping Park *(SW370305)*

Bosavern House TR19 7RD
☎ 01736 788301
e-mail: mail@bosavern.com
web: www.secretbosavern.com
dir: *Exit A3071 near St Just onto B3306 (Land's End road). Site 0.5m on left*

* 🚐 fr £15.75 🚚 fr £15.75 **Å** fr £15.75

Open Mar-Oct

Last arrival 22.00hrs Last departure noon

A neat little site in a walled garden behind a guest house, where visitors can enjoy breakfast, and snacks in the bar in the evening. This site is in a fairly sheltered location with all grassy pitches. Please note that there is no children's playground. 1.5 acre site. 12 touring pitches. Caravan pitches. Motorhome pitches. Tent pitches.

AA Pubs & Restaurants nearby: The Wellington, St Just 01736 787319

Harris's Restaurant, Penzance 01736 364408

The Navy Inn, Penzance 01736 333232

Leisure: 🖵
Facilities: 🌂 ⊙ ☀ ⊙ WiFi 🖥 🐾 ♻ ❼
Services: 🔌 🗑 🔧 🏪 🚮 ⬇
Within 3 miles: ⬇ 🎣 🐎 🛒 Notes: No pets.

ST JUST-IN-ROSELAND   Map 2 SW83

Places to visit

St Mawes Castle, ST MAWES 01326 270526
www.english-heritage.org.uk

Trelissick Garden, TRELISSICK GARDEN
01872 862090
www.nationaltrust.org.uk

PREMIER PARK

►►►►► 90% Trethem Mill Touring Park

(SW860365)

TR2 5JF
☎ 01872 580504
e-mail: reception@trethem.com
dir: *From Tregony on A3078 to St Mawes. 2m after Trewithian, follow signs to site*

* 🚐 £18-£26 🚚 £18-£26 **Å** £18-£26

Open Apr-mid Oct

Last arrival 20.00hrs Last departure 11.00hrs

A quality park in all areas, with upgraded amenities including a reception, shop, laundry, and disabled/family room. This carefully-tended and sheltered park is in a lovely rural setting, with spacious pitches separated by young trees and shrubs. The very keen family who own the site are continually looking for ways to enhance its facilities. 11 acre site. 84 touring pitches. 61 hardstandings. Caravan pitches. Motorhome pitches. Tent pitches.

AA Pubs & Restaurants nearby: The Victory Inn, St Mawes 01326 270324

Hotel Tresanton, St Mawes 01326 270055

Driftwood, Porthscatho 01872 580644

Leisure: ⚠ ⚽
Facilities: 🌂 ⊙ ☀ ⅗ ⊙ 🗑 🐾 WiFi ♻ ❼
Services: 🔌 🗑 🔧 🏪 T 🏪 ⬇
Within 3 miles: 🎣 🐎 🛒 🛒
Notes: No skateboards or rollerblades. Information centre.

ST MARY'S (ISLES OF SCILLY)   Map 2 SV91

Places to visit

Isles of Scilly Museum, ST MARY'S 01720 422337
www.iosmuseum.org

►►► 80% Garrison Campsite

(SV897104)

Tower Cottage, The Garrison TR21 0LS
☎ 01720 422670
e-mail: tedmoulson@aol.com
dir: *10 mins' walk from quay to site*

* **Å** £16.30-£22

Open Etr-Oct

Last arrival 20.00hrs Last departure 19.00hrs

Set on the top of an old fort with superb views, this park offers tent-only pitches in a choice of well-sheltered paddocks. There are modern toilet facilities (with powerful showers), a superb children's play area, and a good shop at this attractive site, which is only ten minutes from the town, the quay and the nearest beaches. There is easy access to the other islands via the direct boat service from the Hugh Town quay; the campsite owners will transport all luggage, camping equipment etc to and from quay. Good

food available in many hostelries in the main town.

9.5 acre site. 120 touring pitches. Tent pitches.

Facilities: 🌂 ⊙ 🗑 ☀ ⊙ 🗑 WiFi ♻ ❼
Services: 🔌 🗑 🔧 🏪 🚮
Within 3 miles: ⬇ 🎣 🐎 🛒 🛒 U

Notes: No cars on site, no open fires, no pets.

ST MERRYN (NEAR PADSTOW)   Map 2 SW87

Places to visit

Prideaux Place, PADSTOW 01841 532411
www.prideauxplace.co.uk

78% Harlyn Sands Holiday Park *(SW873752)*

Lighthouse Rd, Trevose Head PL28 8SQ
☎ 01841 520720 & 01752 841485
e-mail: enquiries@harlynsands.co.uk
web: www.harlynsands.co.uk
dir: *Exit B3276 in St Merryn centre onto unclassified road towards Constantine Bay & Trevose Golf Club. Through golf club, left to site*

* 🚐 £8-£35 🚚 £8-£35 **Å** £8-£35

Open Etr-end Oct

Last arrival 22.00hrs Last departure 10.00hrs

A family park for 'bucket and spade' holidays, surrounded by seven bays each with its own sandy beach. On site entertainment for children and adults is extensive, and there is an indoor swimming pool complex, excellent restaurant and takeaway, and a quiet over-30s lounge bar. 21 acre site. 160 touring pitches. 6 hardstandings. 60 seasonal pitches. Caravan pitches. Motorhome pitches. Tent pitches. 350 statics.

AA Pubs & Restaurants nearby: The Cornish Arms, St Merryn 01841 532700

Leisure: 🏊 ⚠ 🎣 🎱 🖵 🎵
Facilities: 🌂 ⊙ 🗑 ☀ ⅗ ⊙ 🗑 🐾 WiFi ♻ ❼
Services: 🔌 🗑 🔧 🏪 🛢 🏪 T 🍽 🚮 ⬇
Within 3 miles: ⬇ 🐎 🛒 🛒 U

Notes: Families only. Dogs must be kept on leads. Arcade, clubhouse, chip shop.

ST MERRYN (NEAR PADSTOW) *continued*

PREMIER PARK

▶▶▶▶▶ **85% Atlantic Bays Holiday Park** *(SW890717)*

St Merryn PL28 8PY
☎ **01841 520855**
e-mail: info@atlanticbaysholidaypark.co.uk
dir: *From A30 SW of Bodmin take exit signed Victoria/Roche, 1st exit at rdbt. At Trekenning rdbt 4th exit signed A39/Wadebridge. At Winnards Perch rdbt left B3274 signed Padstow. Left in 3m, follow signs*

🚐 ⛺ 🏕

Open Mar- 2 Jan

Last arrival 21.00hrs Last departure noon

Atlantic Bays has a mix of hardstanding and grass pitches, a high quality toilet/shower block and a comfortable bar/restaurant. The park is set in a rural area yet only two miles from the coast and beautiful sandy beaches, and within easy reach of the quaint fishing village of Padstow, and Newquay for fantastic surfing. 27 acre site. 70 touring pitches. 50 hardstandings. Caravan pitches. Motorhome pitches. Tent pitches. 171 statics.

AA Pubs & Restaurants nearby: The Cornish Arms, St Merryn 01841 532700

Leisure: 🄰 😊 🎱

Facilities: 🎇 ⊙ 🅿 ✳ & 🏧 🖾 🛗 🚻 🌁 🖥 ♻ ❶

Services: 🔌 🗑 🍽 🔳 🧺 🚮 ↯

Within 3 miles: ⌦ ⅓ 🎱 🏇 🗓 ◎ 🛥 🖾 🛥 U

Notes: Dogs must be kept on leads.

▶▶▶▶ **82% Carnevas Holiday Park & Farm Cottages** *(SW862728)*

Carnevas Farm PL28 8PN
☎ **01841 520230 & 521209**
e-mail: carnevascampsite@aol.com
dir: *From St Merryn on B3276 towards Porthcothan Bay. Approx 2m turn right at site sign onto unclassified road opposite Tredrea Inn. Site 0.25m on right*

* 🚐 £10.50-£18 ⛺ £10.50-£18 🏕 £10.50-£18

Open Apr-Oct (rs Apr-Whit & mid Sep-Oct shop, bar & restaurant closed)

A family-run park on a working farm, divided into four paddocks on slightly sloping grass. The toilets are central to all areas, and there is a small licensed bar serving bar meals. An ideal base for exploring the fishing town of Padstow or the surfing beach at Newquay. 8 acre site. 195 touring pitches. Caravan pitches. Motorhome pitches. Tent pitches. 14 statics.

AA Pubs & Restaurants nearby: The Cornish Arms, St Merryn 01841 532700

Leisure: 🄰 🎱

Facilities: 🎇 ⊙ 🅿 ✳ & 🏧 🖾 🚻 ♻ ❶

Services: 🔌 🗑 🍽 🧺 🚽 📺 🍴 🛥 ↯

Within 3 miles: ⌦ 🏇 🛥 🖾 🛥

Notes: No skateboards. Dogs must be kept on leads.

▶▶▶ **78% Trevean Caravan & Camping Park** *(SW875724)*

Trevean Ln PL28 8PR
☎ **01841 520772**
e-mail: trevean.info@virgin.net
dir: *From St Merryn take B3276 to Newquay for 1m. Turn left for Rumford. Site 0.25m on right*

🚐 ⛺ 🏕

Open Apr-Oct (rs Whit-Sep shop open)

Last arrival 22.00hrs Last departure 11.00hrs

A small working farm site with level grassy pitches in open countryside. The toilet facilities are clean and well kept, and there is a laundry and good children's playground. 1.5 acre site. 68 touring pitches. 35 seasonal pitches. Caravan pitches. Motorhome pitches. Tent pitches. 3 statics.

AA Pubs & Restaurants nearby: The Cornish Arms, St Merryn 01841 532700

Leisure: 🄰

Facilities: 🎇 ⊙ 🅿 ✳ & 🏧 🖾 🚻 🌁 🚻 ♻ ❶

Services: 🔌 🗑 🧺 🚮 🛥

Within 3 miles: ⌦ ⅓ 🏇 ◎ 🖾 🛥

Notes: Dogs must be kept on leads.

▶▶ **80% Tregavone Touring Park** *(SW898732)*

Tregavone Farm PL28 8JZ
☎ **01841 520148**
e-mail: info@tregavone.co.uk
dir: *From A389 towards Padstow, right after Little Petherick. In 1m just beyond Padstow Holiday Park turn left into unclassified road signed Tregavone. Site on left, approx 1m*

* 🚐 £10-£12 ⛺ £10-£12 🏕 £10-£12

Open Mar-Oct

Situated on a working farm with unspoilt country views, this spacious grassy park, run by friendly family owners, makes an ideal base for exploring the north Cornish coast and the seven local golden

---

LEISURE: 🏊 Indoor swimming pool 🏊 Outdoor swimming pool 🄰 Children's playground 🛝 Kid's club 🎾 Tennis court 🎱 Games room 📺 Separate TV room
⌦ 9/18 hole golf course 🚣 Boats for hire 🎬 Cinema 🎵 Entertainment 🎣 Fishing ◎ Mini golf 🛥 Watersports 🏋 Gym 🏐 Sports field Spa U Stables
FACILITIES: 🛁 Bath 🚿 Shower ⊙ Electric shaver 🅿 Hairdryer ✳ Ice Pack Facility & Disabled facilities 🕐 Public telephone 🗄 Shop on site or within 200yds
🖾 Mobile shop (calls at least 5 days a week) 🍖 BBQ area 🌁 Picnic area 🚻 Wi-fi 🖥 Internet access ♻ Recycling ❶ Tourist info 🚮 Dog exercise area

beaches with surfing areas, or for enjoying quiet country walks from the park. 3 acre site. 40 touring pitches. Caravan pitches. Motorhome pitches. Tent pitches.

AA Pubs & Restaurants nearby: The Cornish Arms, St Merryn 01841 532700

Facilities: ⌂ ⊙ ✳ ⌁

Services: ⊡ ⊙ ⚍

Within 3 miles: ⅃ ⌁ ☰ ⌒ ⊚ ⅀ ⓢ ⑥ ∪

Notes: ⊛

ST MINVER   Map 2 SW97

AA CAMPING CARD SITE

PREMIER PARK

▶▶▶▶▶ **82% Gunvenna Caravan Park** *(SW969782)*

PL27 6QN
☎ 01208 862405
e-mail: gunvenna.bookings@gmail.com
dir: *From A39 N of Wadebridge take B3314 (Port Isaac road), site 4m on right*

⊡ ⊟ Å

Open Etr-Oct

Last arrival 20.30hrs Last departure 11.00hrs

An attractive park with extensive rural views in a quiet country location, yet within three miles of Polzeath. This popular park is family owned and run, and provides good facilities in an ideal position for touring north Cornwall. The park has excellent hardstanding pitches, maturing landscaping and a beautiful indoor swimming pool with a glass roof. Two wooden mini glamping lodges, a holiday cottage and static caravans are for hire. The beach at Polzeath is very popular with the surfers. 10 acre site. 75 touring pitches. 23 hardstandings. 10 seasonal pitches. Caravan pitches. Motorhome pitches. Tent pitches. 44 statics. 2 wooden pods.

AA Pubs & Restaurants nearby: The Swan, Wadebridge 01208 812526

Restaurant Nathan Outlaw, Rock 01208 863394

Leisure: ☜ ⋔ ⚲

Facilities: ⌁ ⌂ ⊙ ⊘ ✳ ⚷ ⊕ ⓢ ⊟ ⌁ ⅏ ☶ ♻ ⓘ

Services: ⊡ ⊙ ⚓ ⊘ ⊤ ⚍ ⅃

Within 3 miles: ⅃ ☰ ⌒ ☰ ⅀ ⓢ ⑥ ∪

Notes: Owners must clear up after their dogs, no under 16yrs in pool unless accompanied by an adult. Dogs must be kept on leads.

SENNEN   Map 2 SW32

Places to visit
Geevor Tin Mine, PENDEEN 01736 788662
www.geevor.com

Carn Euny Ancient Village, SANCREED
0870 333 1181 www.english-heritage.org.uk

▶▶▶ **82% Trevedra Farm Caravan & Camping Site** *(SW368276)*

TR19 7BE
☎ 01736 871818 & 871835
e-mail: trevedra@btconnect.com
dir: *Take A30 towards Land's End. After junct with B3306 turn right into farm lane. (NB Sat Nav directs beyond site entrance to next lane which is unsuitable for caravans)*

⊡ £15.50-£18.50 ⊟ £15.50-£18.50
Å £15.50-£18.50

Open Etr or Apr-Oct

Last arrival 19.00hrs Last departure 10.30hrs

A working farm with dramatic sea views over to the Scilly Isles, just a mile from Land's End. The popular campsite offers well-appointed toilets, a well-stocked shop, and a cooked breakfast or evening meal from the food bar. There is direct access to the coastal footpath, and two beautiful beaches are a short walk away. 8 acre site. 100 touring pitches. Caravan pitches. Motorhome pitches. Tent pitches.

AA Pubs & Restaurants nearby: The Old Success Inn, Sennen 01736 871232

Facilities: ⌂ ⊙ ⊘ ✳ ⚷ ⓢ ⅏ ♻ ⓘ

Services: ⊡ ⊙ ⚓ ⊘ ⊤ ⓘ ⚍ ⊞ ⅃

Within 3 miles: ⅃ ⌒ ☰ ⅀ ⓢ ⑥

Notes: No open fires, no noise between 22.00hrs & 08.00hrs. Dogs must be kept on leads.

SUMMERCOURT   Map 2 SW85

Places to visit
Trerice, TRERICE 01637 875404
www.nationaltrust.org.uk

Blue Reef Aquarium, NEWQUAY 01637 878134
www.bluereefaquarium.co.uk

Great for kids: Dairy Land Farm World,
NEWQUAY 01872 510246
www.dairylandfarmworld.com

RV ▶▶▶▶ **95% *Carvynick Country Club*** *(SW878564)*

TR8 5AF
☎ 01872 510716
e-mail: info@carvynick.co.uk
web: www.carvynick.co.uk
dir: *Accessed from A3058*

⊟

Open all year (rs Jan-early Feb restricted leisure facilities)

Set within the gardens of an attractive country estate this spacious dedicated American RV Park (also home to the 'Itchy Feet' retail company) provides all full facility pitches on hardstandings. The extensive on-site amenities, shared by the high quality time share village, include an indoor leisure area with swimming pool, fitness suite and badminton court. 47 touring pitches. Motorhome pitches.

AA Pubs & Restaurants nearby: The Plume of Feathers, Mitchell 01872 510387

Leisure: ☜ ⅄ ⋔ ⚲

Facilities: ⌂ ⊙ ⊘ ♻ ⓘ

Services: ⊡ ⊙ ⅏ ⓘ ⅃

Within 3 miles: ⅃ ⓢ ⑥

Notes: Dogs must be exercised off site.

TINTAGEL
Map 2 SX08

See also Camelford

Places to visit

Tintagel Castle, TINTAGEL 01840 770328
www.english-heritage.org.uk

Tintagel Old Post Office, TINTAGEL
01840 770024 www.nationaltrust.org.uk/main/
w-tintageloldpostoffice

Great for kids: Tamar Otter & Wildlife Centre,
LAUNCESTON 01566 785646
www.tamarotters.co.uk

►►► 75% Headland Caravan & Camping Park (SX056887)

Atlantic Rd PL34 0DE
☎ 01840 770239
e-mail: headland.caravan@talktalkbusiness.net
dir: From B3263 follow brown tourist signs
through village to Headland

🚐 🚏 Å

Open Etr-Oct

Last arrival 21.00hrs

A peaceful family-run site in the mystical village
of Tintagel, close to the ruins of King Arthur's
Castle. There are two well terraced camping areas
with sea and countryside views, immaculately
clean toilet facilities, and good, colourful planting
across the park. The Cornish coastal path and the
spectacular scenery are just two of the attractions
here, and there are safe bathing beaches nearby.
There are holiday statics for hire. 5 acre site. 62
touring pitches. Caravan pitches. Motorhome
pitches. Tent pitches. 28 statics.

AA Pubs & Restaurants nearby: The Port William,
Trebarwith 01840 770230

Leisure: 🅰 **Facilities:** 🅿⊙🅿✳🖻📶 **❸**
Services: 🔌🔋🔧🖍📅🛒🖑
Within 3 miles: 🚴🎣🛶🍴🛍🛍🐴

Notes: Dogs must be kept on leads & exercised
off site. Quiet after 23.00hrs.

TORPOINT
Map 3 SX45

Places to visit

Antony House, TORPOINT 01752 812191
www.nationaltrust.org.uk/antony

Mount Edgcumbe House & Country Park,
TORPOINT 01752 822236
www.mountedgcumbe.gov.uk

Great for kids: The Monkey Sanctuary, LOOE
01503 262532 www.monkeysanctuary.org

AA CAMPING CARD SITE

►►►► 80% Whitsand Bay Lodge & Touring Park (SX410515)

Millbrook PL10 1JZ
☎ 01752 822597
e-mail: enquiries@whitsandbayholidays.co.uk
dir: From Torpoint take A374, turn left at Anthony
onto B3247 for 1.25m to T-junct. Turn left, 0.25m,
right into Cliff Rd. Site 2m on left

🚐 £15-£30 🚏 £15-£30 Å £5-£30

Open all year (rs Sep-Mar opening hours at shop,
pool & bar restricted)

Last arrival 19.00hrs Last departure 10.00hrs

A very well equipped park with panoramic coastal,
sea and countryside views from its terraced
pitches. A quality park with upmarket toilet
facilities and other amenities. There is a guided
historic walk around The Battery most Sundays,
and there is a bus stop close by. 27 acre site. 49
touring pitches. 30 hardstandings. 15 seasonal
pitches. Caravan pitches. Motorhome pitches. Tent
pitches. 5 statics.

AA Pubs & Restaurants nearby: The Halfway
House Inn, Kingsand 01752 822279

Leisure: 🏊🎯🅰🛝♠🎵
Facilities: 🅿⊙🅿✳🖻🖻🎣🛟📶🖥♻**❸**
Services: 🔌🔋🔧🖍📅🛒🖑
Within 3 miles: 🚴🎣🎿◎🛍🛍🐴

Notes: Families & couples only. Dogs must be
kept on leads. Putting, chapel, library, amusement
arcade, guided tours of monument.

TRURO
Map 2 SW84

See also Portscatho

Places to visit

Royal Cornwall Museum, TRURO 01872 272205
www.royalcornwallmuseum.org.uk

Trewithen Gardens, PROBUS 01726 883647
www.trewithengardens.co.uk

Great for kids: Pencarrow, BODMIN
01208 841369 www.pencarrow.co.uk

PREMIER PARK

REGIONAL WINNER - SOUTH WEST ENGLAND CAMPSITE OF THE YEAR 2013

►►►►► 93% Carnon Downs Caravan & Camping Park

(SW805406)

Carnon Downs TR3 6JJ
☎ 01872 862283
e-mail: info@carnon-downs-caravanpark.co.uk
dir: Take A39 from Truro towards Falmouth. Site
just off main Carnon Downs rdbt, on left

* 🚐 £19.50-£29 🚏 £19.50-£29 Å £19.50-£29

Open all year

Last arrival 22.00hrs Last departure 11.00hrs

A beautifully mature park set in meadowland and
woodland close to the village amenities of Carnon
Downs. The four toilet blocks provide exceptional
facilities in bright modern surroundings. An
extensive landscaping programme has been
carried out to give more spacious pitch sizes, and
there is an exciting children's playground with
modern equipment, and a football pitch. 33 acre
site. 150 touring pitches. 80 hardstandings.
Caravan pitches. Motorhome pitches. Tent pitches.
2 statics. See also page 20.

AA Pubs & Restaurants nearby: The Pandora Inn,
Mylor Bridge 01326 372678

Tabb's, Truro 01872 262110

Leisure: 🅰🖵
Facilities: 🛁🅿⊙🅿✳🖻🕓🎣♻**❸**
Services: 🔌🔋🔧🖍📅🛒🖑
Within 3 miles: 🚴🎣🍴🎿◎🛍🛍🐴

Notes: No children's bikes in Jul & Aug. Baby &
child bathroom.

LEISURE: 🏊 Indoor swimming pool 🏊 Outdoor swimming pool 🅰 Children's playground 🛝 Kid's club 🎾 Tennis court ♠ Games room 🖵 Separate TV room
🏌 9/18 hole golf course 🚣 Boats for hire 🎬 Cinema 🎵 Entertainment 🎣 Fishing ◎ Mini golf 🎿 Watersports 🏋 Gym 🎯 Sports field Spa 🐴 Stables
FACILITIES: 🛁 Bath 🚿 Shower ⊙ Electric shaver 🅿 Hairdryer ✳ Ice Pack Facility 🎣 Disabled facilities ♻ Public telephone 🛍 Shop on site or within 200yds
🖪 Mobile shop (calls at least 5 days a week) 🍴 BBQ area 🅿 Picnic area 📶 Wi-fi 🖥 Internet access ♻ Recycling ❸ Tourist info 🐕 Dog exercise area

PREMIER PARK

▶▶▶▶▶ 82% *Truro Caravan and Camping Park* (SW772452)

TR4 8QN
☎ **01872 560274**
e-mail: info@trurocaravanandcampingpark.co.uk
dir: *Exit A390 at Threemilestone rdbt onto unclassified road towards Chacewater. Site signed on right in 0.5m*

⊟ ⊞ Å

Open all year

Last arrival 19.00hrs Last departure 10.30hrs

An attractive south-facing and well laid out park with spacious pitches, including good hardstandings, and quality modern toilets that are kept spotlessly clean. It is situated on the edge of the city of Truro yet close to many beaches, with St Agnes being just ten minutes away by car. It is equidistant from both the rugged north coast and the calmer south coastal areas. There is a good bus service from the gate of the park to Truro. 8.5 acre site. 51 touring pitches. 26 hardstandings. Caravan pitches. Motorhome pitches. Tent pitches. 49 statics.

AA Pubs & Restaurants nearby: The Wig & Pen Inn, Truro 01872 273028

Probus Lamplighter Restaurant, Probus, Nr Truro 01726 882453

Facilities: ⊷ ⋔ ⊙ ⌖ ✷ ⚲ ⊛ ⧕ ⊞ Ⓦⓘⓕ ▬ ♻ ❶
Services: ⊞ ⊠ ⚋ ⌀ Ⓣ ⚏ ⇖
Within 3 miles: ↓ ⊟ ⌀ ◎ ⓵ ⓹ ∪
Notes: Dogs must be kept on leads.

PREMIER PARK

▶▶▶▶▶ 81% *Cosawes Park* (SW768376)

Perranarworthal TR3 7QS
☎ **01872 863724**
e-mail: info@cosawes.com
dir: *Exit A39 midway between Truro & Falmouth. Direct access at site sign after Perranarworthal*

⊟ £15-£23 ⊞ £15-£23 Å £13-£19

Open all year

Last arrival 22.00hrs Last departure 10.00hrs

A small touring park, close to Perranarworthal, in a peaceful wooded valley, midway between Truro and Falmouth, with a two-acre touring area. There

are spotless toilet facilities that include two smart family rooms. Its stunning location is ideal for visiting the many nearby hamlets and villages close to the Carrick Roads, a stretch of tidal water, which is a centre for sailing and other boats. 2 acre site. 59 touring pitches. 25 hardstandings. 15 seasonal pitches. Caravan pitches. Motorhome pitches. Tent pitches.

AA Pubs & Restaurants nearby: The Pandora Inn, Mylor Bridge 01326 372678

Facilities: ⋔ ⊙ ⌖ ✷ ⚲ ⊛ ⧕ ⋔ Ⓦⓘⓕ ♻ ❶
Services: ⊞ ⊠ ⚋ Ⓣ ⚏ ⇖
Within 3 miles: ↓ ⚲ ⊟ ⌀ ◎ ⓵ ⓸ ⓹ ∪
Notes: Dogs must be kept on leads. Underfloor heating, vanity cubicles. Fish & chips every Thursday evening.

▶▶▶ 80% Summer Valley (SW800479)

Shortlanesend TR4 9DW
☎ **01872 277878**
e-mail: res@summervalley.co.uk
dir: *3m NW off B3284*

*⊟ £12-£19 ⊞ £12-£19 Å £12-£19

Open Apr-Oct

Last arrival 20.00hrs Last departure 11.00hrs

A very attractive and secluded site in a rural setting midway between the A30 and the cathedral city of Truro. The keen owners maintain the facilities to a good standard. 3 acre site. 60 touring pitches. Caravan pitches. Motorhome pitches. Tent pitches.

AA Pubs & Restaurants nearby: Old Ale House, Truro 01872 271122

Bustophers Bar Bistro, Truro 01872 279029

Leisure: ⚠
Facilities: ⋔ ⊙ ⌖ ✷ ⊛ ⓢ ⧕ Ⓦⓘⓕ ♻ ❶
Services: ⊞ ⊠ ⚋ ⌀ Ⓣ ⚏
Within 3 miles: ↓ ⊟ ⌀ ◎ ⓵ ⓹ ∪
Notes: Dogs must be kept on leads. Campers' lounge.

WADEBRIDGE   Map 2 SW97

Places to visit
Prideaux Place, PADSTOW 01841 532411
www.prideauxplace.co.uk

Cornwall's Regimental Museum, BODMIN 01208 72810

Great for kids: Pencarrow, BODMIN 01208 841369 www.pencarrow.co.uk

▶▶▶▶ 90% *St Mabyn Holiday Park* (SX055733)

Longstone Rd, St Mabyn PL30 3BY
☎ **01208 841677**
e-mail: info@stmabyn.co.uk
web: www.stmabynholidaypark.co.uk
dir: *S of Camelford on A39, left after BP garage onto B3266 to Bodmin, 6m to Longstone, right at x-rds to St Mabyn, site approx 400mtrs on right*

⊟ ⊞ Å

Open 15 Mar-Oct (rs 15 Mar-Spring BH & mid Sep-Oct swimming pool may be closed)

Last arrival 22.00hrs Last departure noon

A family run site ideally situated close to the picturesque market town of Wadebridge, and within easy reach of Bodmin, and centrally located for exploring both the north and south coasts of Cornwall. The park offers peace and tranquillity in a country setting and at the same time provides plenty of on-site activities including a swimming pool and children's play areas. Holiday chalets and fully-equipped holiday homes are available to rent, along with a choice of pitches. 12 acre site. 120 touring pitches. 49 hardstandings. Caravan pitches. Motorhome pitches. Tent pitches. 20 statics. 1 wooden pod.

AA Pubs & Restaurants nearby: The Swan, Wadebridge 01208 812526

The Borough Arms, Dunmere 01208 73118

Leisure: ⚽ ⚠ ⚲ ▢
Facilities: ⋔ ⊙ ⌖ ✷ ⚲ ⊛ ⓢ ⧕ ⋔ Ⓦⓘⓕ ▬ ♻ ❶
Services: ⊞ ⊠ ⚋ ⌀ Ⓣ ⚏
Within 3 miles: ↓ ⌀ ⓵ ⓹ ∪
Notes: Quiet from 23.00hrs-07.00hrs. Information book given on arrival. Small animal area with goats.

WADEBRIDGE *continued*

▶▶▶▶ 89% *The Laurels Holiday Park*

(SW957715)

Padstow Rd, Whitecross PL27 7JQ
☎ 01209 313474
e-mail: info@thelaurelsholidaypark.co.uk
dir: *From A39 take A389 signed Padstow, follow signs. Site entrance 1st right*

🚐 🚈 Å

Open Apr or Etr-Oct

Last arrival 20.00hrs Last departure 11.00hrs

A very smart and well-equipped park with individual pitches screened by hedges and young shrubs. The enclosed dog walk is of great benefit to pet owners, and the Camel cycle trail and Padstow are not far away. An excellent base if visiting the Royal Cornwall Showground. 2.2 acre site. 30 touring pitches. 2 hardstandings. Caravan pitches. Motorhome pitches. Tent pitches.

AA Pubs & Restaurants nearby: The Swan, Wadebridge 01208 812526

Leisure: ⅄

Facilities: 🏕⊙🎇☀🛒🐾

Services: 🔌🅖🛄

Within 3 miles: ⅃🛶🎠🎣🏊🎱🎰🏇U

Notes: No group bookings, family park. Dogs must be kept on leads. Wet suit dunking bath & drying area.

see advert on page 89

▶▶▶ 84% Little Bodieve Holiday Park (SW995734)

Bodieve Rd PL27 6EG
☎ 01208 812323
e-mail: info@littlebodieve.co.uk
dir: *From A39 rdbt on Wadebridge by-pass take B3314 signed Rock/Port Isaac, site 0.25m on right*

🚐 🚈 Å

Open Apr-Oct (rs Early & late season pool, shop & clubhouse closed)

Last arrival 21.00hrs Last departure 11.00hrs

Rurally located with pitches in three large grassy paddocks, this family park is close to the Camel Estuary. The licensed clubhouse provides bar meals, with an entertainment programme in high season, and there is a swimming pool with sun terrace plus a separate waterslide and splash pool. This makes a good base from which to visit the Royal Cornwall Showground. 22 acre site. 195

touring pitches. Caravan pitches. Motorhome pitches. Tent pitches. 75 statics.

AA Pubs & Restaurants nearby: The Swan, Wadebridge 01208 812526

Leisure: 🏊⅄🎱🎵

Facilities: 🛁🏕⊙🎇☀🛒🐾🛄🎠♻🛈

Services: 🔌🅖🍽🐾🚰🅣🍴🛄🚽

Within 3 miles: ⅃🎿🎣🏊🎱🎰U

Notes: Families & couples only. Dogs must be kept on leads. Crazy golf, pets' corner.

WATERGATE BAY · Map 2 SW86

AA CAMPING CARD SITE

PREMIER PARK

▶▶▶▶▶ 85% Watergate Bay Touring Park (SW850653)

TR8 4AD
☎ 01637 860387
e-mail: email@watergatebaytouringpark.co.uk
web: www.watergatebaytouringpark.co.uk
dir: *From Bodmin on A30 follow signs for Newquay airport. Continue past airport, turn left at T-junct, site 0.5m on right*

✱ 🚐 £11-£20 🚈 £11-£20 Å £11-£20

Open Mar-Nov (rs Mar-Spring BH & Sep-Oct restricted bar, café, shop & pool)

Last arrival 22.00hrs Last departure noon

A well-established park above Watergate Bay, where acres of golden sand, rock pools and surf are seen as a holidaymakers' paradise. The toilet facilities are appointed to a high standard, and there is a well-stocked shop and café, an inviting swimming pool, and a wide range of activities including tennis courts and other outdoor facilities for all ages, plus regular entertainment in the clubhouse. 30 acre site. 171 touring pitches. 14 hardstandings. Caravan pitches. Motorhome pitches. Tent pitches. 2 statics.

AA Pubs & Restaurants nearby: Fifteen Cornwall, Watergate Bay 01637 861000

Watergate Bay Touring Park

Leisure: 🏊🏊⅄🛶🎠🎱🎰🎵

Facilities: 🛁🏕⊙🎇☀🛒🐾🛄🎠wifi 🖥♻🛈 Services: 🔌🅖🍽🐾🚰🅣🍴🛄🚽

Within 3 miles: ⅃🎣🏊🎱🎰

Notes: Dogs must be kept on leads. Free minibus to beach during main school holidays.

see advert on opposite page

WIDEMOUTH BAY · Map 2 SS20

72% Widemouth Bay Caravan Park (SS199008)

EX23 0DF
☎ 01271 866766
e-mail: bookings@jfhols.co.uk
dir: *From A39 take Widemouth Bay coastal road, turn left. Site on left*

🚐 🚈 Å

Open Etr-Oct

Last arrival dusk Last departure 10.00hrs

A partly sloping rural site set in countryside overlooking the sea and one of Cornwall's finest beaches. Nightly entertainment in high season with an emphasis on children's and family club programmes. This park is located less than half a mile from the sandy beaches of Widemouth Bay. A superb base for surfing. 58 acre site. 220 touring pitches. 90 hardstandings. Caravan pitches. Motorhome pitches. Tent pitches. 200 statics.

AA Pubs & Restaurants nearby: The Bay View Inn, Widemouth Bay 01288 361273

Castle Restaurant, Bude 01288 350543

Leisure: 🏊⅄🛶🎱🎵

Facilities: 🏕⊙🎇☀🛒🐾🛄🎠🐾wifi

Services: 🔌🅖🍽🍴🚽

Within 3 miles: ⅃🎿🎣🏊🎱🎰U

Notes: Crazy golf.

►►► 78% Cornish Coasts Caravan & Camping Park (SS202981)

Middle Penlean, Poundstock, Bude EX23 0EE
☎ 01288 361380
e-mail: enquiries5@cornishcoasts.co.uk
dir: 5m S of Bude on A39, 0.5m S of Rebel Cinema on right

🚐 🚗 Å

Open Apr-Oct

Last arrival 22.00hrs Last departure 10.30hrs

Situated on the A39 midway between Padstow and the beautiful surfing beaches of Bude and Widemouth Bay, this is a quiet park with lovely terraced pitches that make the most of the stunning views over the countryside to the sea. The reception is in a 13th-century cottage, and the park is well equipped and tidy, with the well maintained and quirky toilet facilities (note the mosaic vanity units) housed in a freshly painted older-style building. 3.5 acre site. 46 touring pitches. 8 hardstandings. Caravan pitches. Motorhome pitches. Tent pitches. 4 statics.

AA Pubs & Restaurants nearby: The Bay View Inn, Widemouth Bay 01288 361273

Castle Restaurant, Bude 01288 350543

Leisure: ⚠

Facilities: 🐾 ☺ ⚒ ☀ ⚿ 💲

Services: 🔌 🗄 🛢 🖊 🚽 🛒

Within 3 miles: 🚴 🎣 ◎ 🛶 🏰 ∪

Notes: Quiet after 22.00hrs. Post office.

►►► 75% Penhalt Farm Holiday Park (SS194003)

EX23 0DG
☎ 01288 361210
e-mail: denandjennie@penhaltfarm.fsnet.co.uk
web: www.penhaltfarm.co.uk
dir: From Bude on A39 take 2nd right to Widemouth Bay road, left at end by Widemouth Manor signed Millook onto coastal road. Site 0.75m on left

🚐 🚗 Å

Open Etr-Oct

Splendid views of the sea and coast can be enjoyed from all pitches on this sloping but partly level site, set in a lovely rural area on a working farm. About one mile away is one of Cornwall's finest beaches which proves popular with all the family as well as surfers. 8 acre site. 100 touring pitches. Caravan pitches. Motorhome pitches. Tent pitches.

AA Pubs & Restaurants nearby: The Bay View Inn, Widemouth Bay 01288 361273

Castle Restaurant, Bude 01288 350543

Leisure: ⚠ 🔍

Facilities: 🐾 ☺ ⚒ ☀ ⚿ 🕐 💲 🐕

Services: 🔌 🗄 🖊 🛒

Within 3 miles: 🚴 🎣 ⚙ 🛶 🏰 ∪

Notes: Pool table, netball & football posts, air hockey & table tennis.

Cumbria

Think of Cumbria and you immediately picture a rumpled landscape of magical lakes and mountains and high green fells. For sheer natural beauty and grandeur, the English Lake District is hard to beat, and despite traffic congestion and high visitor numbers, this enchanting corner of the country manages to retain its unique individuality and sense of otherness.

Even on a glorious summer's day, you can still escape the 'madding crowd' and discover Lakeland's true heart and face. It is a fascinating place, characterised by ever changing moods and a timeless air of mystery. By applying a little effort and leaving the tourist hotspots and the busy roads far behind, you can reach and appreciate the Lake District that inspired William Wordsworth, Samuel Taylor Coleridge, Arthur Ransome and Robert Southey.

Derwentwater – the 'Queen of the English Lakes' is one of the most popular lakes in the region and certainly the widest. Shelley described it as 'smooth and dark as a plain of polished jet.' Windermere, to the south, is the largest lake and the town of the same name is a popular tourist base; this is one of the few places in the Lake District that has a railway. Away from the lakes and the various watersports are miles of country for the adventurous to explore. The towering summits of Helvellyn, Scafell, Scafell Pike and Great Gable are the highest peaks in England.

Along the eastern edge of the 866-square mile National Park and handy for the West Coast main line and the M6 are several well-known towns – Kendal and Penrith.

▶

Lakeside and
Haverthwaite Railway

CUMBRIA

To the north is the ancient and historic city of
Carlisle; once a Roman camp – its wall still runs
north of the city – it was captured during the
Jacobean rising of 1745. The cathedral dates back
to the early 12th century.

The southern half of Cumbria is often
bypassed and overlooked in favour of the
more obvious attractions of the Lake District.
Visitors who do journey beyond the park
boundaries are usually impressed and inspired
in equal measure by its wealth of delights.
The Lune Valley, for example, remains as lovely
as it was when Turner came here to paint, and
the 19th-century writer John Ruskin described
the view from 'The Brow,' a walk running behind
Kirkby Lonsdale's parish church, as 'one of the
loveliest scenes in England.'

Walking and Cycling

Walkers are spoilt for choice in Cumbria and the Lake District. Numerous paths and trails crisscross this rugged mountain landscape. That is part of its appeal – the chance to get up close and personal with Mother Nature. For something even more ambitious and adventurous, there are several long-distance trails.

The 70-mile (112km) Cumbria Way follows the valley floors rather than the mountain summits, while the 190-mile (305km) Coast to Coast has just about every kind of landscape and terrain imaginable. The route, pioneered by the well-known walker and writer, Alfred Wainwright, cuts across the Lake District, the Yorkshire Dales and the North York Moors, spanning the width of England between St Bees on the Cumbrian west coast, and Robin Hood's Bay on the North Yorkshire and Cleveland Heritage Coast.

The region also offers a walk with a difference and one which brings a true sense of drama and adventure. At the extreme southern end of Cumbria, in the reassuring company of official guide Cedric Robinson, MBE, you can cross the treacherous, deceptively beautiful sands of Morecambe Bay on foot. The bay, which is Britain's largest continuous intertidal area, is renowned for its quick sand and shifting channels. Many lives have been lost here over the years but in Cedric's expert hands, it is safe to cross.

The region is also popular with cyclists with lots of cycle hire outlets and plenty of routes to choose from. The 12-mile Wast Water to Santon Bridge cycle route passes England's deepest lake and is reputed to offer the finest view of the Lake District. It's quite a tough challenge and not suitable for under-11s.

There are also waymarked bike trails in Grizedale Forest and Whinlatter Forest.

Festivals and Events

Cumbria offers something in the region of 500 festivals and events throughout the year. The choice includes:

- Ambleside Daffodil and Spring Flower Festival in late March.
- Ulverston Walking Festival at the end of April and beginning of May.
- In July there is the Coniston Water Festival, famous for its Duck Race at Church Bridge; the Carlisle Summer Classical Music Festival at the cathedral.
- The Westmorland County Show takes place at Crooklands, near Kendal, in early September while the Dickensian Festival is staged in Ulverston in late November.
- Model Railway and Transport Exhibition at Barrow-in-Furness, in October.
- There are winter lighting events along Hadrian's Wall in November and December; and Christmas at the Castle at Muncaster Castle, Ravenglass.

● Loughrigg Fell

CUMBRIA

See Walk 2 & Cycle Ride 2 in the Walks & Cycle Rides section at the end of the guide

AMBLESIDE   Map 18 NY30

Places to visit

The Armitt Collection, AMBLESIDE 015394 31212 www.armitt.com

Beatrix Potter Gallery, HAWKSHEAD 015394 36269 www.nationaltrust.org.uk

Great for kids: Lakes Aquarium, LAKESIDE 015395 30153 www.lakesaquarium.co.uk

PREMIER PARK

▶▶▶▶▶ 86% Skelwith Fold Caravan Park (NY355029)

GOLD

LA22 0HX
☎ 015394 32277
e-mail: info@skelwith.com
dir: From Ambleside on A593 towards Coniston, left at Clappersgate onto B5286 (Hawkshead road). Site 1m on right

* ⊟ £20.50-£38.50 ⊟ £20.50-£38.50

Open Mar-15 Nov

Last arrival dusk Last departure noon

In the grounds of a former mansion, this park is in a beautiful setting close to Lake Windermere. Touring areas are dotted in paddocks around the extensively wooded grounds, and the all-weather pitches are set close to the many facility buildings. The premium pitches are quite superb. There is a five-acre family recreation area, which has spectacular views of Loughrigg Fell. 130 acre site. 150 touring pitches. 150 hardstandings. 30 seasonal pitches. Caravan pitches. Motorhome pitches. 300 statics.

AA Pubs & Restaurants nearby: Wateredge Inn, Ambleside 015394 32332

Drunken Duck Inn, Ambleside 015394 36347

Leisure: � ⚽ ☺
Facilities: ⌐ ⊙ 🌣 ❄ & 🕒 🖼 🎁 ➡ 🐾 WiFi ♻
Services: 🔲 🔄 🛢 ⊘ T 🍴 ⚘
Within 3 miles: ⚴ ☕ ⊟ 🖊 ◎ ⚓ 🐟 🎁 ↻
Notes: Dogs must be kept on leads.

▶▶▶ 78% Low Wray National Trust Campsite (NY372013)

Low Wray LA22 0JA
☎ 015394 32733
e-mail: campsite.bookings@nationaltrust.org.uk
dir: 3m SW of Ambleside on A593 to Clappersgate, then B5286. Approx 1m turn left at Wray sign. Site less than 1m on left

⊟ Å

Open wk before Etr-Oct

Last arrival variable Last departure 11.00hrs

Picturesquely set on the wooded shores of Lake Windermere, this site is a favourite with tenters and watersports enthusiasts. The toilet facilities are housed in wooden cabins, and tents can be pitched in wooded glades with lake views or open grassland; here there are wooden camping pods, and a mini-reservation of tipis and solar-heated bell tents. In partnership with Quest 4 Adventure, many outdoor activities are available for families. Fresh bread is now baked daily on site in addition

LEISURE: 🏊 Indoor swimming pool 🏊 Outdoor swimming pool 🛝 Children's playground 🏸 Kid's club 🎾 Tennis court 🎱 Games room 📺 Separate TV room ⛳ 9/18 hole golf course 🚤 Boats for hire 🎬 Cinema 🎵 Entertainment 🎣 Fishing ◎ Mini golf 🏄 Watersports 💪 Gym ⚽ Sports field 💆 Spa ♨ Stables
FACILITIES: 🛁 Bath 🚿 Shower ⊙ Electric shaver ✂ Hairdryer ❄ Ice Pack Facility ♿ Disabled facilities 📞 Public telephone 🏪 Shop on site or within 200yds 🏪 Mobile shop (calls at least 5 days a week) 🍴 BBQ area 🎋 Picnic area WiFi Wi-fi 💻 Internet access ♻ Recycling ℹ Tourist info 🐕 Dog exercise area

to visits from the hot-food van in season. 10 acre site. 140 touring pitches. Motorhome pitches. Tent pitches. 10 wooden pods.

AA Pubs & Restaurants nearby: Wateredge Inn, Ambleside 015394 32332

Drunken Duck Inn, Ambleside 015394 36347

Kings Arms, Hawkshead 015394 36372

Low Wray National Trust Campsite

Leisure: ⚲

Facilities: ⚲☺✳&🕙💲♻🛈

Services: 🔲

Within 3 miles: ⚲🗓✐◎⚲🛒

Notes: No cars by tents. No groups of more than 4 unless a family group with children. Outdoor activities bookable during school holidays. Dogs must be kept on leads. Launching for sailing craft, orienteering course.

see advert below

►►► 77% The Croft Caravan & Campsite *(SD352981)*

North Lonsdale Rd, Hawkshead LA22 0NX
☎ **015394 36374**
e-mail: enquiries@hawkshead-croft.com
dir: *From B5285 in Hawkshead turn into site opposite main public car & coach park*

⚲ ⚲ Å

Open Mar-Nov

Last arrival 21.30hrs Last departure noon

In the historic village of Hawkshead, which is now a popular destination for Beatrix Potter fans, this former working farm has a large tent field that borders a beck, and the sound of running water and birdsong are welcome distractions. A well maintained amenities block and games room are additional benefits. 5 acre site. 75 touring pitches. 15 hardstandings. Caravan pitches. Motorhome pitches. Tent pitches. 20 statics.

AA Pubs & Restaurants nearby: The Queen's Head, Hawkshead 015394 36271

Kings Arms, Hawkshead 015394 36372

Leisure: ⚲

Facilities: ⚲☺🅿✳&🕙&🛒♻🛈

Services: 🔲🔲

Within 3 miles: ✐🛒🔲

Notes: No noise 23.00hrs-07.00hrs. Dogs must be kept on leads.

►►► 75% Hawkshead Hall Farm *(SD349988)*

Hawkshead LA22 0NN
☎ **015394 36221**
e-mail: enquiries@hawksheadhall-campsite.com
dir: *From Ambleside take A593 signed Coniston, then B5286 signed Hawkshead. Site signed on left just before Hawkshead. Or from Coniston take B5285 to T-junct. Left, then 1st right into site*

* ⚲ £17-£19.50 ⚲ £15-£16.50 Å £15-£16.50

Open Mar-Oct

Last arrival 21.00hrs Last departure noon

A mainly camping site a few minutes' walk from village centre in a landscape of gentle rolling hills. The pitch sizes are generous, and there's a very well-equipped, purpose-built amenities block. There is no laundry on this site, but there's direct access to the adjacent Croft site, under same ownership, where this facility can be used. 55 touring pitches. Caravan pitches. Motorhome pitches. Tent pitches.

AA Pubs & Restaurants nearby: The Queen's Head, Hawkshead 015394 36271

Kings Arms, Hawkshead 015394 36372

Facilities: ⚲☺🅿✳&♻🛈

Services: 🔲

Within 3 miles: ⚲✐🛒🔲🔲U

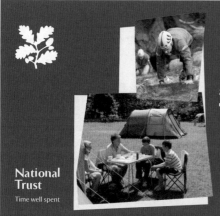

APPLEBY-IN-WESTMORLAND — Map 18 NY62

Places to visit

Brougham Castle, BROUGHAM 01768 862488
www.english-heritage.org.uk

Acorn Bank Garden and Watermill, TEMPLE
SOWERBY 017683 61893
www.nationaltrust.org.uk

Great for kids: Wetheriggs Animal Rescue &
Conservation Centre, PENRITH 01768 866657
www.wetheriggsanimalrescue.co.uk

AA CAMPING CARD SITE

PREMIER PARK

▶▶▶▶▶ 86% Wild Rose Park (NY698165)

Ormside CA16 6EJ
☎ 017683 51077
e-mail: reception@wildrose.co.uk
web: www.wildrose.co.uk
dir: Signed on unclassified road to Great Ormside,
off B6260

* 🚐 £18-£22 🚑 £18-£22 ▲ £18-£22

Open all year (rs Nov-Mar shop closed, restaurant
rs, pool closed 6 Sep-27 May)

Last arrival 22.00hrs Last departure noon

Situated in the Eden Valley, this large leisure
group-run park has been carefully landscaped and
offers superb facilities maintained to an extremely
high standard, including four wooden wigwams
for hire. There are several individual pitches, and
extensive views from most areas of the park.
Traditional stone walls and the planting of lots of
indigenous trees help it to blend into the
environment, and wildlife is actively encouraged.
The contemporary Cock-a-Hoop bar, lounge and
bistro is a superb addition for the 2012 season. 85
acre site. 226 touring pitches. 140 hardstandings.
Caravan pitches. Motorhome pitches. Tent pitches.
273 statics. 4 tipis.

AA Pubs & Restaurants nearby: The Royal Oak
Appleby, Appleby-in-Westmorland 017683 51463

Tufton Arms Hotel, Appleby-in-Westmorland
017683 51593

Wild Rose Park

Leisure: 🏊 🎱 🎣 🗔 🎵
Facilities: 🚿 ⊙ 🧴 ☀ ♿ 🕐 🛎 🖥 🚽 ♻ ❔
Services: 🔌 🗑 🍽 🍴 💧 🛒 🚐 🗑 🛍 ♻ ⚓
Within 3 miles: 🚴 ⚲ ◎ 🛍 🛍

Notes: No unaccompanied teenagers, no group
bookings, no dangerous dogs, no noise after
22.30hrs. Dogs must be kept on leads. Pitch &
putt, fishing.

AYSIDE — Map 18 SD38

Places to visit

Hill Top, NEAR SAWREY 015394 36269
www.nationaltrust.org.uk

Levens Hall, LEVENS 015395 60321
www.levenshall.co.uk

Great for kids: Lakes Aquarium, LAKESIDE
015395 30153 www.lakesaquarium.co.uk

▶▶▶ 78% Oak Head Caravan Park

(SD389839)

LA11 6JA
☎ 015395 31475
web: www.oakheadcaravanpark.co.uk
dir: M6 junct 36, A590 towards Newby Bridge,
14m. From A590 bypass follow signs for Ayside

* 🚐 £18 🚑 £18 ▲ £16-£18

Open Mar-Oct

Last arrival 20.00hrs Last departure noon

A pleasant terraced site with two separate areas -
grass for tents and all gravel pitches for caravans
and motorhomes. The site is enclosed within
mature woodland and surrounded by hills. This
site is located in a less busy area but convenient
for all the Lake District attractions. 10 acre site.
60 touring pitches. 30 hardstandings. Caravan

pitches. Motorhome pitches. Tent pitches. 71
statics.

AA Pubs & Restaurants nearby: Cavendish Arms,
Cartmel 015395 36240

Masons Arms, Cartmel 015395 68486

Rogan & Company Bar & Restaurant, Cartmel
015395 35917

Leisure: ✪ Facilities: 🚿 ⊙ 🧴 ☀ ♿ 🕐 🛎
Services: 🔌 🗑 🛍 ✎ 🛒
Within 3 miles: 🚴 ⚲ ⚲ 🚣 🛍 🚶

Notes: ⊛ No open fires. Dogs must be kept on
leads.

BARROW-IN-FURNESS — Map 18 SD26

Places to visit

The Dock Museum, BARROW-IN-FURNESS
01229 876400 www.dockmuseum.org.uk

Furness Abbey, BARROW-IN-FURNESS
01229 823420 www.english-heritage.org.uk

Great for kids: South Lakes Wild Animal Park,
DALTON-IN-FURNESS 01229 466086
www.wildanimalpark.co.uk

▶▶▶ 82% South End Caravan Park

(SD208628)

Walney Island LA14 3YQ
☎ 01229 472823 & 471556
e-mail: enquiries@secp.co.uk
web: www.walneyislandcaravanpark.co.uk
dir: M6 junct 36, A590 to Barrow, follow signs for
Walney Island. Cross bridge, turn left. Site 6m
south

* 🚐 £16-£22.50 🚑 £16-£22.50

Open Mar-Oct (rs Mar-Etr & Oct pool closed)

Last arrival 22.00hrs Last departure noon

A friendly family-owned and run park next to the
sea and close to a nature reserve, on the southern
end of Walney Island. It offers an extensive range

LEISURE: 🏊 Indoor swimming pool 🏊 Outdoor swimming pool 🛝 Children's playground 🛝 Kid's club ⛳ Tennis court 🎱 Games room 🗔 Separate TV room
🏌 9/18 hole golf course 🚣 Boats for hire 🎬 Cinema 🎵 Entertainment 🎣 Fishing ◎ Mini golf 🏄 Watersports 🏋 Gym 🏐 Sports field **Spa** ♨ Stables
FACILITIES: 🛁 Bath 🚿 Shower ⊙ Electric shaver 🧴 Hairdryer ☀ Ice Pack Facility ♿ Disabled facilities 🛎 Public telephone 🛍 Shop on site or within 200yds
🛒 Mobile shop (calls at least 5 days a week) 🍴 BBQ area 🍽 Picnic area 🛜 Wi-fi 🖥 Internet access ♻ Recycling ❔ Tourist info 🐕 Dog exercise area

of quality amenities including an adult lounge, and high standards of cleanliness and maintenance. 7 acre site. 50 touring pitches. 20 hardstandings. 29 seasonal pitches. Caravan pitches. Motorhome pitches. 250 statics.

South End Caravan Park

AA Pubs & Restaurants nearby: The Stan Laurel Inn, Ulverston 01229 582814

Leisure: ⛱ ⛰ ♨ ♣ ▭

Facilities: ⚶ ⊙ ✳ ⚖ ⊙ 🐕 ♻

Services: 🔌 🧺 🍺 🛢 ⊘ ⛟ 🚰

Within 3 miles: 🛊 ⚓ 🏧 🛒 ⛳

Notes: Dogs must be kept on leads. Bowling green, snooker table.

BASSENTHWAITE LAKE

See map for locations of sites in the vicinity

BOOT

Places to visit

Steam Yacht Gondola, CONISTON 015394 41288 www.nationaltrust.org.uk/gondola

The Ruskin Museum, CONISTON 015394 41164 www.ruskinmuseum.com

Great for kids: Ravenglass & Eskdale Railway, RAVENGLASS 01229 717171 www.ravenglass-railway.co.uk

BOOT Map 18 NY10

PREMIER PARK

►►►►► 83% Eskdale Camping & Caravanning Club Site *(NY178011)*

CA19 1TH
☎ 019467 23253 & 0845 130 7633
e-mail: eskdale.site@thefriendlyclub.co.uk
dir: *Exit A595 at Gosforth or Holmrook to Eskdale Green, then signs for Boot. Site on left towards Hardknott Pass after railway, 150mtrs after Brook House Inn*

* 🚐 £12.30-£19.90 ▲ £12.30-£19.90

Open Mar-14 Jan

Last arrival 20.00hrs Last departure noon

Stunningly located in Eskdale, a feeling of peace and tranquillity prevails at this top quality campsite, with the sounds of running water and birdsong the only welcome distractions. Although mainly geared to campers, the facilities here are very impressive, with a smart amenities block, equipped with efficient modern facilities including an excellent fully-serviced wet room-style, family room with power shower, and the surroundings of mountains, mature trees and shrubs create a wonderful 'back to nature' feeling. There's a nest of camping pods under the trees, with gravel access paths and barbeques, a super backpackers' field and a self-catering camping barn. Expect great attention to detail and a high level of customer care. The park is only a quarter of a mile from Boot station on the Ravenglass/Eskdale railway (La'al Ratty). 8 acre site. 100 touring pitches. Motorhome pitches. Tent pitches. 10 wooden pods. See also '*Gamekeeper turned Poacher*' on page 24.

AA Pubs & Restaurants nearby: Brook House Inn, Boot 019467 23288

Leisure: ⛰ ⚽

Facilities: ⚶ ⊙ ℉ ✳ ⚖ ⊙ 🏧 🐕 ♻ ❶

Services: 🔌 🧺 🛢 ⊘ T ⛟ 🚰 ⛟

Within 3 miles: 🛊 ⚓ 🏧 🛒 ⛳

Notes: Site gates closed & no noise 23.00hrs-07.00hrs, no open fires. Dogs must be kept on leads. 1 camping barn, free drying room.

BOWNESS-ON-WINDERMERE

Sites are listed under Windermere

CARLISLE Map 18 NY35

Places to visit

Carlisle Castle, CARLISLE 01228 591992 www.english-heritage.org.uk

Tullie House Museum & Art Gallery Trust, CARLISLE 01228 618718 www.tulliehouse.co.uk

Great for kids: Trotters World of Animals, BASSENTHWAITE 017687 76239 www.trottersworld.com

►►►► 84% Green Acres Caravan Park *(NY416614)*

High Knells, Houghton CA6 4JW
☎ 01228 675418 & 07720 343820
e-mail: info@caravanpark-cumbria.com
dir: *M6 junct 44, A689 E towards Brampton for 1m. Left at Scaleby sign. Site 1m on left*

* 🚐 £15-£19 🚐 £15-£19 ▲ £10-£14

Open Apr-Oct

Last arrival 21.00hrs Last departure noon

A small touring park in rural surroundings close to the M6 with distant views of the fells. A convenient stopover, this pretty park is run by keen, friendly owners who maintain high standards throughout. The site has a caravan and motorhome pressure-washer area, a field and woodland dog walk and two superb unisex shower rooms which include toilet and wash basin. 3 acre site. 30 touring pitches. 30 hardstandings. 12 seasonal pitches. Caravan pitches. Motorhome pitches. Tent pitches.

Leisure: ⚽

Facilities: ⚶ ⊙ ℉ ✳ 🐕 ♻ ❶

Services: 🔌 🧺 **Within 3 miles:** ⚓ 🏧

Notes: Adults only. ⊘ Dogs must be kept on leads.

CARLISLE *continued*

►►► 86% Dandy Dinmont Caravan & Camping Park *(NY399620)*

Blackford CA6 4EA
☎ 01228 674611
e-mail: dandydinmont@btopenworld.com
dir: *M6 junct 44, A7 N. Site 1.5m on right, after Blackford sign*

🚐 £15 🚐 £15 ▲ £13-£14

Open Mar-Oct

Last arrival 21.00hrs Last departure noon

A sheltered, rural site, screened on two sides by hedgerows and only one mile from the M6 and Carlisle. The grass pitches are immaculately kept, and there are some larger hardstandings for motor homes. This park attracts mainly adults; please note that cycling and ball games are not allowed. Touring customers are invited to view the private award-winning garden. 4.5 acre site. 47 touring pitches. 14 hardstandings. Caravan pitches. Motorhome pitches. Tent pitches. 15 statics.

Facilities: 🐾 ⊙ ✳ 🛱 ♻ ❶
Services: 🚐 🗑 🛢
Within 3 miles: ⅃ 🖋 ◎ 🏪 🛢 ∪

Notes: Dogs must be exercised off site. Children's activities are restricted. Dogs must be kept on leads. Covered dishwashing area.

CARTMEL — Map 18 SD37

►►► 76% Greaves Farm Caravan Park *(SD391823)*

Field Broughton LA11 6HR
☎ 015395 36329 & 36587
dir: *M6 junct 36, A590 signed Barrow. Approx 1m before Newby Bridge, turn left at x-roads signed Cartmel/Staveley. Site 2m on left just before church*

* 🚐 fr £16 🚐 fr £16 ▲ fr £16

Open Mar-Oct

Last arrival 21.00hrs Last departure noon

A small family-owned park close to a working farm in a peaceful rural area. Motorhomes are parked in a paddock which has spacious hardstandings, and there is a large field for tents and caravans. This simple park is carefully maintained, offers electric pitches (6amp), and there is always a sparkle to the toilet facilities. Static holiday caravans for hire. 3 acre site. 12 touring pitches. 6 hardstandings. Caravan pitches. Motorhome pitches. Tent pitches. 20 statics.

AA Pubs & Restaurants nearby: Cavendish Arms, Cartmel 015395 36240

Masons Arms, Cartmel 015395 68486

Rogan & Company Bar & Restaurant, Cartmel 015395 35917

Facilities: 🐾 ⊙ 🖋 ✳ ⓒ ① 🔥 ♻ ❶
Services: 🚐 🛢
Within 3 miles: ⅃ ⅄ 🖋 ⅀ 🏪 ∪

Notes: ☺ Couples & families only, no noise after 23.00hrs, no open fires. Dogs must be kept on leads. Separate chalet for dishwashing. Small freezer & fridge available.

►►►► 81% Waters Edge Caravan Park *(SD533838)*

LA7 7NN
☎ 015395 67708 & 67527
e-mail: info@watersedgecaravanpark.co.uk
dir: *M6 junct 36 take A65 towards Kirkby Lonsdale, at 2nd rdbt follow signs for Crooklands/Endmoor. Site 1m on right at Crooklands garage, just beyond 40mph limit*

* 🚐 £16.50-£23.80 🚐 £16.50-£23.80 ▲

Open Mar-14 Nov (rs Low season bar not always open on week days)

Last arrival 22.00hrs Last departure noon

A peaceful, well-run park close to the M6, pleasantly bordered by streams and woodland. A Lakeland-style building houses a shop and bar, and the attractive toilet block is clean and modern. This is ideal either as a stopover or for longer stays. 3 acre site. 26 touring pitches. 26 hardstandings. 8 seasonal pitches. Caravan pitches. Motorhome pitches. Tent pitches. 20 statics.

AA Pubs & Restaurants nearby: The Plough Inn, Lupton 015395 67700

Leisure: 🎣 ▢
Facilities: 🐾 ⊙ 🖋 ✳ 🚻 🏪 🛱 ❶
Services: 🚐 🛢 🍴 🛢 ⌀ 🅣
Within 3 miles: 🖋 🏪 ∪

Notes: No cars by tents. Dogs must be kept on leads.

LEISURE: 🏊 Indoor swimming pool 🏊 Outdoor swimming pool ⚠ Children's playground 🧒 Kid's club ⚟ Tennis court 🎣 Games room ▢ Separate TV room ⅃ 9/18 hole golf course ⛵ Boats for hire ▤ Cinema 🎵 Entertainment 🎣 Fishing ⓜ Mini golf 🏄 Watersports 💪 Gym ⊕ Sports field **Spa** ∪ Stables
FACILITIES: 🛁 Bath 🐾 Shower ⊙ Electric shaver 🖋 Hairdryer ✳ Ice Pack Facility ♿ Disabled facilities ☏ Public telephone 🏪 Shop on site or within 200yds 🏪 Mobile shop (calls at least 5 days a week) 🍴 BBQ area 🛱 Picnic area 🆆🅸🅵🅸 Wi-fi ▦ Internet access ♻ Recycling ❶ Tourist info 🐕 Dog exercise area

CUMWHITTON Map 18 NY55

Places to visit

Nenthead Mines, ALSTON 01434 382294
www.npht.com/nentheadmines

Lanercost Priory, BRAMPTON 01697 73030
www.english-heritage.org.uk

►►► 69% Cairndale Caravan Park

(NY518523)

CA8 9BZ
☎ 01768 896280
dir: *Exit A69 at Warwick Bridge on unclassified road through Great Corby to Cumwhitton, left at village sign, site 1m*

* 🚐 £10-£11 🚙 £10-£11

Open Mar-Oct

Last arrival 22.00hrs

Lovely grass site set in the tranquil Eden Valley with good views to distant hills. The all-weather touring pitches have electricity, and are located close to the immaculately maintained toilet facilities. Static holiday caravans for hire. 2 acre site. 5 touring pitches. 5 hardstandings. Caravan pitches. Motorhome pitches. 15 statics.

AA Pubs & Restaurants nearby: String of Horses Inn, Faugh 01228 670297

Facilities: 🚿 ☉ ✲ ♻ **Services:** 🔌 🛢 🔋
Within 3 miles: ⛳ 🎣 🏇 🏊 **Notes:** 💳

FLOOKBURGH Map 18 SD37

Places to visit

Holker Hall & Gardens, HOLKER 015395 58328
www.holker.co.uk

Hill Top, NEAR SAWREY 015394 36269
www.nationaltrust.org.uk

Great for kids: Lakes Aquarium, LAKESIDE 015395 30153 www.lakesaquarium.co.uk

80% Lakeland Leisure Park *(SD372743)*

AA HOLIDAY CENTRE

DAVID BELLAMY CONSERVATION AWARD GOLD

Moor Ln LA11 7LT
☎ 0871 231 0883
e-mail: lakeland@haven.com
web: www.haven.com/lakeland
dir: *On B5277 through Grange-over-Sands to Flookburgh. Left at village square, site 1m*

🚐 🚙 ⛺

Lakeland Park

Open mid Mar-end Oct (rs mid Mar-May & Sep-Oct reduced activities, outdoor pool closed)

Last arrival anytime Last departure 10.00hrs

A complete leisure park with full range of activities and entertainments, making this flat, grassy site ideal for families. The touring area, which includes 24 fully serviced pitches, is quietly situated away from the main amenities, but the swimming pools, all-weather bowling green and evening entertainment are just a short stroll away. 105 acre site. 185 touring pitches. Caravan pitches. Motorhome pitches. Tent pitches. 800 statics.

AA Pubs & Restaurants nearby: Cavendish Arms, Cartmel 015395 36240

Masons Arms, Cartmel 015395 68486

Rogan & Company Bar & Restaurant, Cartmel 015395 35917

Leisure: 🏊 🏊 ⛹ ✋ 🎾 ⚽ ♫
Facilities: 🚿 ☉ ♿ [$] 🐕 Wi-fi 💻 ♻ ℹ
Services: 🔌 🧺 🍷 🛢 [T] 🍴 🍔
Within 3 miles: ⛳ 🎣 ◎ 🏊 [$] 🧺 U

Notes: No cars by caravans or tents. Family park, max 2 dogs per booking, certain dog breeds banned, no commercial vehicles, no bookings by persons under 21yrs unless a family booking.

see advert on page 124

GRANGE-OVER-SANDS

See Cartmel

GREAT LANGDALE Map 18 NY20

Places to visit

Dove Cottage and The Wordsworth Museum, GRASMERE 015394 35544
www.wordsworth.org.uk

Honister Slate Mine, BORROWDALE 01768 777230 www.honister-slate-mine.co.uk

►►► 77% *Great Langdale National Trust Campsite* *(NY286059)*

LA22 9JU
☎ 015394 63862 & 32733
e-mail: campsite.bookings@nationaltrust.org.uk
web: www.ntlakescampsites.org.uk
dir: *From Ambleside, A593 to Skelwith Bridge, right onto B5343, approx 5m to New Dungeon Ghyll Hotel. Site on left just before hotel*

🚙 ⛺

Open all year

Last departure 11.00hrs

Nestling in a green valley, sheltered by mature trees and surrounded by stunning fell views, this site is an ideal base for campers, climbers and fell walkers. The large grass tent area has some gravel parking for cars, and there is a separate area for groups, and one for families with a children's play area. Attractive wooden cabins house the toilets, the reception and shop (selling fresh baked bread and pastries), and drying rooms, and there are wooden camping pods and two yurts for hire. Additionally, it is a gentle ten-minute walk to The Sticklebarn Tavern, the only National Trust run pub. 9 acre site. 220 touring pitches. Motorhome pitches. Tent pitches. 3 wooden pods.

AA Pubs & Restaurants nearby: New Dungeon Ghyll Hotel, Great Langdale 015394 37213

Britannia Inn, Elterwater 015394 37210

Leisure: ⛹
Facilities: 🚿 ☉ ✲ ♿ ☎ [$] ♻
Services: 🧺 🛢 🔥
Within 3 miles: 🎣 [$]

Notes: No cars by tents. No noise between 23.00hrs-07.00hrs, no groups of 4 or more unless a family with children. Dogs must be kept on leads.

HOLMROOK Map 18 SD09

Places to visit

The Beacon, WHITEHAVEN 01946 592302 www.thebeacon-whitehaven.co.uk

The Rum Story, WHITEHAVEN 01946 592933 www.rumstory.co.uk

Great for kids: Ravenglass & Eskdale Railway, RAVENGLASS 01229 717171 www.ravenglass-railway.co.uk

►►► 75% Seven Acres Caravan Park

(NY078014)

CA19 1YD
☎ 01946 822777
e-mail: reception@seacote.com
dir: *Site signed on A595 between Holmrook & Gosforth*

🚐 £18-£21 🚌 £18-£21 ⛺ £10-£24

Open Mar-15 Jan

Last arrival 21.00hrs Last departure 10.30hrs

This sheltered park is close to the quiet West Cumbrian coastal villages and beaches, and handy for Eskdale and Wasdale. There is a good choice of pitches, some with hedged bays for privacy, and some with coastal views. The park has a heated toilet block, and a children's play area, and there is plenty to do and see in the area. 7 acre site. 37 touring pitches. 20 hardstandings. Caravan pitches. Motorhome pitches. Tent pitches. 16 statics.

AA Pubs & Restaurants nearby: Bower House Inn, Eskdale Green 019467 23244

Cumbrian Lodge, Seascale 019467 27309

Facilities: 🚿 ⊙ 💨 ❄ ⛩ 🐕 ♻ ℹ

Services: 🚐 🧺 ⚡

Within 3 miles: ⛳ 🎣 ◎ 🧺 ∪

Notes: Dogs must be kept on leads.

KESWICK

Places to visit

Cumberland Pencil Museum, KESWICK 017687 73626 www.pencilmuseum.co.uk

Honister Slate Mine, BORROWDALE 01768 777230 www.honister-slate-mine.co.uk

Great for kids: Mirehouse, KESWICK 017687 72287 www.mirehouse.com

KESWICK Map 18 NY22

PREMIER PARK

►►►►► 86% *Castlerigg Hall Caravan & Camping Park*

(NY282227)

Castlerigg Hall CA12 4TE
☎ 017687 74499
e-mail: info@castlerigg.co.uk
dir: *1.5m SE of Keswick on A591, turn right at sign. Site 200mtrs on right past Heights Hotel*

🚐 🚌 ⛺

Open mid Mar-7 Nov

Last arrival 21.00hrs Last departure 11.30hrs

Spectacular views over Derwentwater to the mountains beyond are among the many attractions at this lovely Lakeland park. Old farm buildings have been tastefully converted into excellent toilets with private washing cubicles and a family bathroom, reception and a well-equipped shop, and there is a kitchen/dining area for campers, and a restaurant/takeaway. There is a superb toilet block, and wooden camping pods and a further ten all-weather pitches are located in the tent field. 8 acre site. 48 touring pitches. 48 hardstandings. Caravan pitches. Motorhome pitches. Tent pitches. 30 statics.

AA Pubs & Restaurants nearby: Kings Head, Keswick 017687 72393

Leisure: 📺

Facilities: 🛁 🚿 ⊙ 💨 ❄ ♿ 📞 [$] 🐕 [Wi-fi]

Services: 🚐 🧺 ⛽ 🍃 [T] 🍴 🥡 🍼 ⚡

Within 3 miles: ⛳ ⛵ 🎬 🎣 ◎ 🌊 [$] 🧺 ∪

Notes: Dogs not be left unattended. Dogs must be kept on leads. Campers' kitchen, sitting room.

►►►► 78% Gill Head Farm Caravan & Camping Park *(NY380269)*

Troutbeck CA11 0ST
☎ 017687 79652
e-mail: enquiries@gillheadfarm.co.uk
web: www.gillheadfarm.co.uk
dir: *M6 junct 40, A66, A5091 towards Troutbeck. Right after 100yds, then right again*

🚐 🚌 ⛺

Open Apr-Oct

Last arrival 22.00hrs Last departure noon

A family-run park on a working hill farm with a wide variety of trees and shrubs in addition to pretty seasonal floral displays; the site has lovely fell views. It has level touring pitches, and a log cabin dining room that is popular with families. Tent pitches are gently sloping in a separate field with glorious views towards Keswick. 5.5 acre site. 42 touring pitches. 21 hardstandings. Caravan pitches. Motorhome pitches. Tent pitches. 17 statics.

AA Pubs & Restaurants nearby: The George, Keswick 017687 72076

Leisure: 🛝 📺

Facilities: 🚿 ⊙ 💨 ❄ 📞 [$] ⛩ 🐕

Services: 🚐 🧺 ⛽ 🍃

Within 3 miles: ⛳ ⛵ 🎣 🌊 [$] ∪

Notes: No fires.

►►► 82% *Castlerigg Farm Camping & Caravan Site* (NY283225)

Castlerigg Farm CA12 4TE
☎ 017687 72479
e-mail: info@castleriggfarm.com
dir: *From Keswick on A591 towards Windermere, turn right at top of hill at camping sign. Farm 2nd site on left*

Open Mar-Nov (rs At quiet times café & shop restricted hours)

Last arrival 21.30hrs Last departure 11.30hrs

Nestling at the foot of Walla Crag, this tranquil fell-side park enjoys lake views, and is popular with families and couples seeking a quiet base for fell walking. The modern facilities include a shop, laundry and spotless toilet facilities, and a café in a converted barn. Castlerigg Stone Circle and the attractions of Keswick are nearby. 3 acre site. 48 touring pitches. Caravan pitches. Motorhome pitches. Tent pitches.

AA Pubs & Restaurants nearby: Horse & Farrier Inn, Keswick 017687 79688

The Swinside Inn, Keswick 017687 78253

Facilities: ⬚⊙☐✳⬚⬚☐☐ⴲ⬚
Services: ⬚☐☐⬚⬚☐⬚⬚⬚⬚⬚
Within 3 miles: ⬚⬚☐⬚⬚⬚⬚⬚

Notes: No noise after 22.30hrs, no fires on the ground. Dogs must be kept on leads. Cycle storage.

AA CAMPING CARD SITE

►►► 77% Burns Farm Caravan Park (NY307244)

St Johns in the Vale CA12 4RR
☎ 017687 79225 & 79112
e-mail: linda@burns-farm.co.uk
dir: *Exit A66 signed Castlerigg Stone Circle/Youth Centre/Burns Farm. Site on right in 0.5m*

Open Mar-4 Nov

Last departure noon

Lovely views of Blencathra and Skiddaw can be enjoyed from this secluded park, set on a working farm which extends a warm welcome to families. This is a good choice for exploring the beautiful and interesting countryside. Food can be found in the pub at Threlkeld. 2.5 acre site. 32 touring pitches. Caravan pitches. Motorhome pitches. Tent pitches.

AA Pubs & Restaurants nearby: Farmers Arms, Keswick 017687 72322

Facilities: ⬚⊙☐✳⬚⬚⬚⬚
Services: ⬚☐☐⬚
Within 3 miles: ⬚⬚☐⬚⬚⬚⬚☐☐U

Notes: ⬚ No noise after mdnt.

Places to visit

Sizergh Castle & Garden, SIZERGH
015395 60951 www.nationaltrust.org.uk

Kendal Museum, KENDAL 01539 815597
www.kendalmuseum.org.uk

Great for kids: Dales Countryside Museum & National Park Centre, HAWES 01969 666210
www.yorkshiredales.org.uk/dcm

PREMIER PARK

►►►►► 82% Woodclose Caravan Park (SD618786)

High Casterton LA6 2SE
☎ 015242 71597
e-mail: info@woodclosepark.com
web: www.woodclosepark.com
dir: *On A65, 0.25m after Kirkby Lonsdale towards Skipton, on left*

Open Mar-Oct

Last arrival 21.00hrs Last departure noon

A peaceful park with excellent toilet facilities set in idyllic countryside in the beautiful Lune Valley. Ideal for those seeking quiet relaxation, and for visiting the Lakes and Dales, with the riverside walks at Devil's Bridge, and historic Kirkby Lonsdale both an easy walk from the park. There are ten fully serviced pitches, and wigwam cabins for hire including one with en suite toilet. 9 acre site. 29 touring pitches. 28 hardstandings. Caravan pitches. Motorhome pitches. Tent pitches. 65 statics. 11 wooden pods.

AA Pubs & Restaurants nearby: Sun Inn, Kirkby Lonsdale 015242 71965

The Whoop Hall, Kirkby Lonsdale 015242 71284

Pheasant Inn, Kirkby Lonsdale 015242 71230

Leisure: ⬚⬚
Facilities: ⬚⊙☐✳⬚⬚☐☐ⴲ⬚⬚⬚⬚
Services: ⬚☐☐⬚
Within 3 miles: ⬚⬚☐☐U

Notes: No arrivals before 13.00hrs. Dogs must be kept on leads. Cycle hire, crock boxes for hire.

KIRKBY LONSDALE *continued*

▶▶▶▶ 79% New House Caravan Park *(SD628774)*

LA6 2HR
☎ 015242 71590
e-mail: colinpreece9@aol.com
dir: *1m SE of Kirkby Lonsdale on A65, turn right into site entrance 300yds past Whoop Hall Inn*

* ➡ £17 ⬅ £17

Open Mar-Oct

Last arrival 20.00hrs

A very pleasant base in which to relax or tour the surrounding area, developed around a former farm. The excellent toilet facilities are purpose built, and there are good roads and hardstandings, all in a lovely rural setting. 3 acre site. 50 touring pitches. 50 hardstandings. Caravan pitches. Motorhome pitches.

AA Pubs & Restaurants nearby: Sun Inn, Kirkby Lonsdale 015242 71965

The Whoop Hall, Kirkby Lonsdale 015242 71284

Pheasant Inn, Kirkby Lonsdale 015242 71230

Facilities: ➟ ☉ ☊ ☼ ☊ ☊ ☊ ☊ ☊ ☊ ☊ ☊
Services: ☊ ☊ ☊ ☊ ☊ ☊ ☊ ☊
Within 3 miles: ☊ ☊ ☊ ☊
Notes: ☊ No cycling.

LONGTOWN Map 21 NY36
Places to visit
Carlisle Castle, CARLISLE 01228 591992 www.english-heritage.org.uk
Tullie House Museum & Art Gallery Trust, CARLISLE 01228 618718 www.tulliehouse.co.uk

▶▶ 75% Camelot Caravan Park

(NY391666)

CA6 5SZ
☎ 01228 791248
dir: *M6 junct 44, A7, site 5m N & 1m S of Longtown*

➡ ⬅ ⛺

Open Mar-Oct

Last arrival 20.00hrs Last departure noon

A very pleasant level grassy site in a wooded setting near the M6, with direct access from the A7, and simple, clean toilet facilities. The park is an ideal stopover site. 1.5 acre site. 20 touring pitches. Caravan pitches. Motorhome pitches. Tent pitches. 2 statics.

Facilities: ➟ ☉ ☼ ☊ ☊
Services: ☊
Within 3 miles: ☊ ☊ ☊
Notes: ☊

MEALSGATE Map 18 NY24
Places to visit
Jennings Brewery Tour and Shop, COCKERMOUTH 0845 129 7190 www.jenningsbrewery.co.uk
Wordsworth House and Garden, COCKERMOUTH 01900 820882 www.nationaltrust.org.uk

▶▶▶▶ 80% Larches Caravan Park

(NY205415)

CA7 1LQ
☎ 016973 71379 & 71803
dir: *On A595 (Carlisle to Cockermouth road)*

➡ ⬅ ⛺

Open Mar-Oct (rs Early & late season)

Last arrival 21.30hrs Last departure noon

This over 18s-only park is set in wooded rural surroundings on the fringe of the Lake District National Park. Touring units are spread over two sections. The friendly family-run park offers constantly improving facilities, including a small swimming pool, and a well-stocked shop that also provides a very good range of camping and caravanning spares. 20 acre site. 35 touring pitches. 30 hardstandings. Caravan pitches. Motorhome pitches. Tent pitches.

AA Pubs & Restaurants nearby: Oddfellows Arms, Caldbeck 016974 78227

Leisure: ☊
Facilities: ➟ ☉ ☼ ☼ ☊ ☊ ☊ ☊
Services: ☊ ☊ ☊ ☊ ☊ ☊
Within 3 miles: ☊ ☊ ☊ ☊
Notes: Adults only. ☊

MILNTHORPE Map 18 SD48
Places to visit
Levens Hall, LEVENS 015395 60321 www.levenshall.co.uk
RSPB Leighton Moss Nature Reserve, SILVERDALE 01524 701601 www.rspb.org.uk/leightonmoss
Great for kids: Lakes Aquarium, LAKESIDE 015395 30153 www.lakesaquarium.co.uk

▶▶▶▶ 75% Hall More Caravan Park *(SD502771)*

GOLD

Hale LA7 7BP
☎ 01524 781453
e-mail: enquiries@pureleisure-holidays.co.uk
dir: *M6 junct 35, A6 towards Milnthorpe for 4m. Left at Lakeland Wildlife Oasis, follow brown signs*

➡ £17-£20 ⬅ £17-£20 ⛺ £16-£19

Open Mar-Jan

Last arrival 22.00hrs Last departure 10.00hrs

Set on former meadowland and surrounded by mature trees, this constantly improving rural park provides neat, well-spaced pitches with colourful hedged areas enhanced by pretty seasonal flowers. The site is adjacent to a fishery where fly fishing for trout is possible, and near a farm with stables offering pony trekking. There are seven wooden camping pods for hire. 4 acre site. 44 touring pitches. 7 hardstandings. Caravan pitches. Motorhome pitches. Tent pitches. 60 statics.

AA Pubs & Restaurants nearby: The Wheatsheaf, Beetham 015395 62123

Facilities: ➟ ☉ ☼ ☼ ☊ ☊
Services: ☊ ☊ ☊ ☊ ☊
Within 3 miles: ☊ ☊ ☊ ☊ ☊

LEISURE: ☊ Indoor swimming pool ☊ Outdoor swimming pool ☊ Children's playground ☊ Kid's club ☊ Tennis court ☊ Games room ☊ Separate TV room ☊ 9/18 hole golf course ☊ Boats for hire ☊ Cinema ☊ Entertainment ☊ Fishing ☊ Mini golf ☊ Watersports ☊ Gym ☊ Sports field Spa ☊ Stables
FACILITIES: ☊ Bath ☊ Shower ☊ Electric shaver ☊ Hairdryer ☊ Ice Pack Facility ☊ Disabled facilities ☊ Public telephone ☊ Shop on site or within 200yds ☊ Mobile shop (calls at least 5 days a week) ☊ BBQ area ☊ Picnic area ☊ Wi-fi ☊ Internet access ☊ Recycling ☊ Tourist info ☊ Dog exercise area

PATTERDALE   Map 18 NY31

►►► 78% Sykeside Camping Park

(NY403119)

Brotherswater CA11 0NZ
☎ 017684 82239
e-mail: info@sykeside.co.uk
dir: *Direct access from A592 (Windermere to Ullswater road) at foot of Kirkstone Pass*

* 🚐 £17.50-£25 🚐 £17.50-£25 ▲ £13.50-£23.50

Open all year

Last arrival 22.30hrs Last departure 14.00hrs

A camper's delight, this family-run park is sited at the foot of Kirkstone Pass, under the 2,000ft Hartsop Dodd in a spectacular area with breathtaking views. The park has mainly grass pitches with a few hardstandings, an area with tipis for hire, and for those campers without a tent there is bunkhouse accommodation. There's a small campers' kitchen and the bar serves breakfast and bar meals. There is abundant wildlife. 10 acre site. 86 touring pitches. 5 hardstandings. Caravan pitches. Motorhome pitches. Tent pitches.

AA Pubs & Restaurants nearby: The Queen's Head, Troutbeck 015394 32174

Inn on the Lake, Glenridding 017684 82444

Leisure: ⚙
Facilities: ⬛⊙☂☼☺⬛⬛⬛♻ ❶
Services: ⬛⬛⬛⬛⬛⬛⬛⬛⬛
Within 3 miles: ⬛⬛⬛⬛⬛
Notes: No noise after 23.00hrs. Laundry & drying room.

PENRITH   Map 18 NY53

Places to visit
Dalemain Mansion & Historic Gardens, DALEMAIN 017684 86450 www.dalemain.com

Shap Abbey, SHAP 0870 333 1181
www.english-heritage.org.uk

Great for kids: The Rheged Centre, PENRITH 01768 868000 www.rheged.com

►►►► 86% Lowther Holiday Park (NY527265)

GOLD

Eamont Bridge CA10 2JB
☎ 01768 863631
e-mail: alan@lowther-holidaypark.co.uk
web: www.lowther-holidaypark.co.uk
dir: *3m S of Penrith on A6*

* 🚐 £19-£30 🚐 £19-£30 ▲ £19-£30

Open mid Mar-mid Nov

Last arrival 22.00hrs Last departure 22.00hrs

A secluded natural woodland site with lovely riverside walks and glorious countryside surroundings. The park is home to a rare colony of red squirrels, and trout fishing is available on the two-mile stretch of the River Lowther which runs through it. A birdwatch scheme with a coloured brochure has been introduced inviting guests to spot some of the 30 different species that can be seen on the park. 50 acre site. 180 touring pitches. 50 hardstandings. 80 seasonal pitches. Caravan pitches. Motorhome pitches. Tent pitches. 403 statics.

AA Pubs & Restaurants nearby: Yanwath Gate Inn, Yanwath 01768 862386

Queen's Head Inn, Tirril 01768 863219

Cross Keys Inn, Penrith 01768 865588

Lowther Holiday Park

Leisure: ⚙☺⬛🎵 **Facilities:** ⬛⬛⊙☂☼☺
⬛⬛⬛⬛⬛♻ ❶
Services: ⬛⬛⬛⬛⬛⬛⬛⬛⬛⬛
Within 3 miles: ⬛⬛⬛⊙⬛⬛⬛⬛
Notes: Families only, no cats, rollerblades, skateboards or commercial vehicles. Dogs must be kept on leads.

see advert on page 134

AA CAMPING CARD SITE

►►►► 81% Flusco Wood

GOLD

(NY345529)

Flusco CA11 0JB
☎ 017684 80020
e-mail: info@fluscowood.co.uk
dir: *From Penrith to Keswick on A66 turn right signed Flusco. Approx 800mtrs, up short incline to right. Site on left*

* 🚐 £18.50-£21.50 🚐 £18.50-£21.50

Open 22 Mar-Oct

Last arrival 20.00hrs Last departure noon

Flusco Wood is set in mixed woodland with outstanding views towards Blencathra and the fells around Keswick. It combines two distinct areas, one of which has been designed specifically for touring caravans in neat glades with hardstandings, all within close proximity of the excellent log cabin-style toilet facilities. 24 acre site. 46 touring pitches. 46 hardstandings. 24 seasonal pitches. Caravan pitches. Motorhome pitches.

AA Pubs & Restaurants nearby: Yanwath Gate Inn, Yanwath 01768 862386

Queen's Head Inn, Tirril 01768 863219

Cross Keys Inn, Penrith 01768 865588

Leisure: ⚙
Facilities: ⬛⬛⊙☂☼☺⬛⬛⬛⬛♻ ❶
Services: ⬛⬛⬛⬛ **Within 3 miles:** ⬛
Notes: Quiet site, not suitable for large groups. Dogs must be kept on leads.

SERVICES: 🔌 Electric hook up 🔵 Launderette 🍸 Licensed bar 🔵 Calor Gas ⬛ Camping Gaz ⬛ Toilet fluid 🍽 Café/Restaurant ⬛ Fast Food/Takeaway ⬛ Battery charging
⬛ Baby care ⬛ Motorvan service point **ABBREVIATIONS:** BH/bank hols-bank holidays Etr-Easter Whit-Whitsun dep-departure fr-from hrs-hours m-mile mdnt-midnight
rdbt-roundabout rs-restricted service wk-week wknd-weekend ⬛ No credit cards ⬛ no dogs   See page 7 for details of the AA Camping Card Scheme

LOWTHER
HOLIDAY PARK

Lowther Holiday Park Limited
Eamont Bridge, Penrith, Cumbria CA10 2JB

Set in 50 acres of woodland and parkland, this river fronted park abounds with wildlife and easy reach of charming Lakeland villages and five miles from the best lake of them all, Ullswater.

The park is a mix of caravan holiday homes and timber lodges that are all for private use and available for sale as per our sales list on the web site. The touring area is served by two toilet/shower blocks and is a mix of hard standing and grass, all with electric hook up.

There is a well stocked mini market for all your needs and the Squirrel Inn will satisfy your thirst and hunger.

www.lowther-holidaypark.co.uk
Email sales@lowther-holidaypark.co.uk
Phone 01768 863631

Holiday Homes and lodges for sale
E-mail sales@lowther-holidaypark.co.uk

LEISURE: 🏊 Indoor swimming pool 🏊 Outdoor swimming pool 🎠 Children's playground 🛝 Kid's club 🎾 Tennis court 🎱 Games room 📺 Separate TV room ⛳ 9/18 hole golf course ⛵ Boats for hire 🎬 Cinema 🎵 Entertainment 🎣 Fishing ⛳ Mini golf 🏄 Watersports 🏋 Gym ⚽ Sports field **Spa** ♨ Stables

FACILITIES: 🛁 Bath 🚿 Shower 🪒 Electric shaver 💨 Hairdryer ❄ Ice Pack Facility ♿ Disabled facilities ☎ Public telephone 🛒 Shop on site or within 200yds 🛒 Mobile shop (calls at least 5 days a week) 🍖 BBQ area 🧺 Picnic area **Wi-fi** Wi-fi 💻 Internet access ♻ Recycling ℹ Tourist info 🐕 Dog exercise area

PENRUDDOCK Map 18 NY42

►►► 78% Beckses Caravan Park
(NY419278)

CA11 0RX
☎ 01768 483224
dir: *M6 junct 40, A66 towards Keswick. Approx 6m, at caravan park sign turn right onto B5288. Site on right in 0.25m*

🚐 🚌 ⛺

Open Etr-Oct

Last arrival 20.00hrs Last departure 11.00hrs

A small, pleasant site on sloping ground with level pitches and views of distant fells, on the edge of the National Park. This sheltered park is in a good location for touring the North Lakes. 4 acre site. 23 touring pitches. Caravan pitches. Motorhome pitches. Tent pitches. 18 statics.

AA Pubs & Restaurants nearby: Queen's Head, Troutbeck 015394 32174

Facilities: 🚿 ⊙ 💨 🐕 ♻

Services: 🔌 🛢 🍃 [T] 🔋 **Within 3 miles:** 🎣 🐎

Notes: No noise after 23.00hrs.

PENTON Map 21 NY47

AA CAMPING CARD SITE

►►► 76% Twin Willows *(NY449771)*

The Beeches CA6 5QD
☎ 01228 577313 & 07850 713958
e-mail: davidson_b@btconnect.com
dir: *M6 junct 44, A7 signed Longtown, right into Netherby St, 6m to Bridge Inn pub. Right then 1st left, site 300yds on right*

* 🚐 £20-£25 🚌 £20-£25 ⛺ £20

Open all year

Last arrival 22.00hrs Last departure 10.00hrs

Twin Willows is a spacious park in a rural location on a ridge overlooking the Scottish border. All facilities, including all-weather pitches, are of a high quality. The park is suited to those who enjoy being away-from-it-all yet at the same time being able to explore the rich history of this area. The attractive city of Carlisle is 20 miles from the park. 3 acre site. 16 touring pitches. 16 hardstandings. 10 seasonal pitches. Caravan pitches. Motorhome pitches. Tent pitches.

Leisure: 🏊 🛝 ⚽

Facilities: 🚿 ⊙ 💨 ❄ ♿ ☎ [$] 🧺 🐕 [Wi-fi] 💻 ♻ ℹ

Services: 🔌 🧼 🛢 🍃 [T] 🍴 🔋 🍔 🚰

Within 3 miles: 🎣 [$] 🧼 🐎

Notes: 🚫💳 Dogs must be kept on leads.

POOLEY BRIDGE Map 18 NY42

AA CAMPING CARD SITE

85% Park Foot Caravan & Camping Park *(NY469235)*

Howtown Rd CA10 2NA
☎ 017684 86309
e-mail: holidays@parkfootullswater.co.uk
web: www.parkfootullswater.co.uk
dir: *M6 junct 40, A66 towards Keswick, then A592 to Ullswater. Turn left for Pooley Bridge, right at church, right at x-roads signed Howtown*

* 🚐 £21-£38 🚌 £14-£29 ⛺ £14-£29

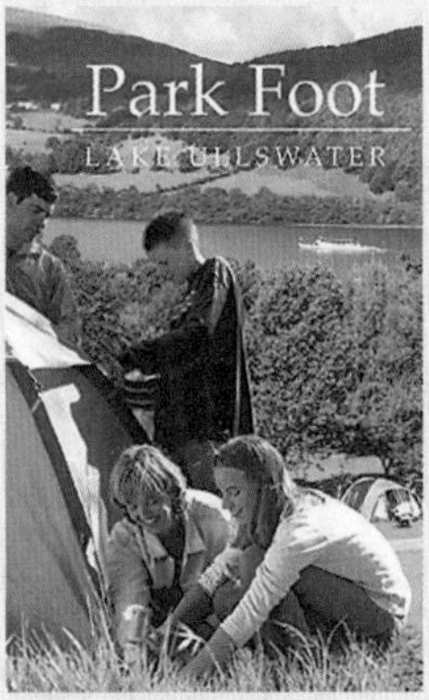

Open Mar-Oct (rs Mar-Apr, mid Sep-Oct clubhouse open wknds only)

Last arrival 22.00hrs Last departure noon

A lively park with good outdoor sports facilities, and boats can be launched directly onto Lake Ullswater. The attractive mainly tenting park has many mature trees, lovely views across the lake, and a superb amenities block in the family-only field. The Country Club bar and restaurant provides good meals, as well as discos, live music and entertainment in a glorious location. There are lodges and static caravans for holiday hire. 18 acre site. 323 touring pitches. 32 hardstandings. Caravan pitches. Motorhome pitches. Tent pitches. 131 statics.

AA Pubs & Restaurants nearby: Yanwath Gate Inn, Yanwath 01768 862386

Queen's Head Inn, Tirril 01768 863219

Leisure: 🛝 ✋ 🎾 🔍 🎮 🎵

Facilities: 🚿 ⊙ 💨 ❄ ♿ ☎ [$] 🧺 🐕 [Wi-fi] 💻 ♻ ℹ

Services: 🔌 🧼 🍷 🛢 🍃 [T] 🍴 🔋 🍔 🚰

Within 3 miles: ⛵ 🎣 🚤 [$] 🧼 🐎

Notes: Families & couples only. Dogs must be kept on leads. Boat launch, pony trekking, pool table, table tennis, bike hire, kids' club in summer holidays.

►►► 82% Waterfoot Caravan Park *(NY462246)*

GOLD

CA11 0JF
☎ 017684 86302
e-mail: enquiries@waterfootpark.co.uk
web: www.waterfootpark.co.uk
dir: *M6 junct 40, A66 for 1m, then A592 for 4m, site on right before lake. (NB do not leave A592 until site entrance; Sat Nav not compatible)*

🚐 🚌

Open Mar-14 Nov

Last arrival dusk Last departure noon

A quality touring park with neat, hardstanding pitches in a grassy glade within the wooded grounds of an elegant Georgian mansion. Toilet facilities are clean and well maintained, and the lounge bar with a separate family room enjoys lake views, and there is a path to Ullswater. Aira Force waterfall, Dalemain House and Gardens and Pooley Bridge are all close by. Please note that there is no access via Dacre. 22 acre site. 34 touring pitches. 30 hardstandings. Caravan pitches. Motorhome pitches. 146 statics.

AA Pubs & Restaurants nearby: Yanwath Gate Inn, Yanwath 01768 862386

Queen's Head Inn, Tirril 01768 863219

Leisure: 🛝 ⚽ 🔍

Facilities: 🚿 ⊙ 💨 ❄ ♿ ☎ [$] 🧺 🐕 [Wi-fi] 💻 ♻ ℹ

Services: 🔌 🧼 🍷 🛢 [T] 🔋 🚰

Within 3 miles: ⛳ ⛵ 🏋 🎣 🚤 [$] 🧼 🐎

Notes: Families only, no tents, no large RVS. Dogs must be kept on leads.

RAVENGLASS Map 18 SD09

►►► 85% *Ravenglass Camping & Caravanning Club Site* *(SD087964)*

CA18 1SR
☎ 01229 717250
dir: *From A595 turn W for Ravenglass. Before village turn left into site*

🚐 🚙 ⛺

Open 12 Jan-11 Nov

Last arrival 21.00hrs Last departure noon

A pleasant wooded park peacefully located in open countryside, a short stroll from the charming old fishing village of Ravenglass and the Eskdale/Ravenglass Steam Railway. Owners/franchisees Martyn & Sarah Merckel have improved the park to a very high standard, offering level gravel pitches, an upgraded toilet block and a smart reception. The enthusiastic young site management team will ensure that your visit is a memorable one. Muncaster Castle, the Lakeland Fells and stunning coastal drives are all within easy reach. 5 acre site. 66 touring pitches. 56 hardstandings. Caravan pitches. Motorhome pitches. Tent pitches.

Facilities: 🚿 ⊙ 💨 ✻ ♿ ✆ 🛒 [Wi-fi]

Services: 🔌 🧺 🔒 🧊 [T] 🍳 ⛽

Within 3 miles: ⛳ 🎣 🌊 🛒

Notes: Site gates closed 23.00hrs-07.00hrs, tents must book with site directly.

SANTON BRIDGE Map 18 NY10

Places to visit

Brantwood, CONISTON 015394 41396
www.brantwood.org.uk

►►► 75% The Old Post Office Campsite *(NY110016)*

CA19 1UY
☎ 01946 726286 & 01785 822866
e-mail: enquiries@theoldpostofficecampsite.co.uk
dir: *From A595 at Holmrook follow Santon Bridge signs, at T-junct left, site on right before river (NB Sat Nav may suggest a route via Wrynose & Hardknott Passes which may not be suitable for your vehicle at night or in bad weather)*

🚐 🚙 ⛺

Open all year

Last departure noon

A family-run campsite in a delightful riverside setting next to an attractive stone bridge, with very pretty pitches. The enthusiastic owner is steadily upgrading the park. Five camping pods are now available. Permits for salmon, sea and brown trout fishing are available, and there is an adjacent pub. 2.2 acre site. 40 touring pitches. 5 hardstandings. Caravan pitches. Motorhome pitches. Tent pitches. 5 wooden pods.

AA Pubs & Restaurants nearby: Bower House Inn, Eskdale Green 019467 23244

Wasdale Head Inn, Wasdale Head 019467 26229

Leisure: 🛝

Facilities: 🚿 ⊙ 💨 ✻ ♿ 🛒 🐕

Services: 🔌 🧺 ⛽

Within 3 miles: 🎣 🛒 ∪

Notes: Dogs must be kept on leads.

LEISURE: 🏊 Indoor swimming pool 🌊 Outdoor swimming pool 🛝 Children's playground 👋 Kid's club 🎾 Tennis court ♠ Games room 📺 Separate TV room ⛳ 9/18 hole golf course ⛵ Boats for hire 🎬 Cinema ♫ Entertainment 🎣 Fishing ◎ Mini golf 🌊 Watersports 🏋 Gym ⚽ Sports field **Spa** ∪ Stables
FACILITIES: 🛁 Bath 🚿 Shower ⊙ Electric shaver 💨 Hairdryer ✻ Ice Pack Facility ♿ Disabled facilities ✆ Public telephone 🛒 Shop on site or within 200yds 🚚 Mobile shop (calls at least 5 days a week) 🍖 BBQ area ⛩ Picnic area [Wi-fi] Wi-fi 💻 Internet access ♻ Recycling ℹ Tourist info 🐕 Dog exercise area

SILLOTH
Map 18 NY15

AA CAMPING CARD SITE

90% Stanwix Park Holiday Centre *(NY108527)*

Greenrow CA7 4HH
☎ 016973 32666
e-mail: enquiries@stanwix.com
dir: *1m SW on B5300. From A596 (Wigton bypass), follow signs to Silloth on B5302. In Silloth follow signs to site, approx 1m on B5300*

* ⊡ £21.15-£26.20 ⊟ £21.15-£26.20
▲ £21.15-£26.20

Open all year (rs Nov-Feb (ex New Year) no entertainment, shop closed)

Last arrival 21.00hrs Last departure 11.00hrs

A large well-run family park within easy reach of the Lake District. Attractively laid out, with lots of amenities to ensure a lively holiday, including a 4-lane automatic, 10-pin bowling alley. Excellent touring areas with hardstandings, one in a peaceful glade well away from the main leisure complex, and there's a campers' kitchen and clean, well maintained toilet facilities. 4 acre site. 121 touring pitches. 100 hardstandings. Caravan pitches. Motorhome pitches. Tent pitches. 212 statics.

Stanwix Park Holiday Centre

Leisure: ⌕ ⛵ 🏇 ⚑ ⚘ ↓ ⌕ 🎱 ⛳ ♫ Spa
Facilities: ⛟ ⋔ ☉ ℘ ✳ ㊡ Ⓢ 🏠 📶 ♻ ❶
Services: ⊡ 🔲 🍴 🛢 T 🍽 🛒 ☕ ⚕
Within 3 miles: ↓ ℘ ◎ 🏠 🔲
Notes: Families only. Dogs must be kept on leads. Amusement arcade.

see advert on opposite page

AA CAMPING CARD SITE

▶▶▶▶ **87% Hylton Caravan Park** *(NY113533)*

Eden St CA7 4AY
☎ 016973 31707 & 32666
e-mail: enquiries@stanwix.com
dir: *On entering Silloth on B5302 follow signs for site, approx 0.5m on left, (at end of Eden St)*

* ⊡ £18.80-£21 ⊟ £18.80-£21 ▲ £18.80-£21

Open Mar-15 Nov

Last arrival 21.00hrs Last departure 11.00hrs

A smart, modern touring park with excellent toilet facilities including several bathrooms. This high quality park is a sister site to Stanwix Park, which is just a mile away and offers all the amenities of a holiday centre, which are available to Hylton tourers. 18 acre site. 90 touring pitches. Caravan pitches. Motorhome pitches. Tent pitches. 213 statics.

AA Pubs & Restaurants nearby: Queen's Head, Troutbeck 015394 32174

Leisure: ⚑
Facilities: ⛟ ⋔ ☉ ℘ ㊡
Services: ⊡ 🔲 🛢 ⚕
Within 3 miles: ↓ ℘ ◎ 🏠 🔲
Notes: Families only. Dogs must be kept on leads. Use of facilities at Stanwix Park Holiday Centre.

TEBAY
Map 18 NY60

▶▶▶ **75% Westmorland Caravan Park** *(NY609060)*

GOLD

Orton CA10 3SB
☎ 01539 711322
e-mail: caravans@westmorland.com
web: www.westmorland.com/caravan
dir: *Exit M6 at Westmorland Services, 1m from junct 38. Site accessed through service area from either N'bound or S'bound carriageways. Follow park signs*

⊡ £18.50-£22 ⊟ £18.50-£22

Open Mar-Nov

Last arrival anytime Last departure noon

An ideal stopover site adjacent to the Tebay service station on the M6, and handy for touring the Lake District. The park is screened by high grass banks, bushes and trees, and is within walking distance of the excellent farm shop and restaurant within the services complex. 4 acre site. 70 touring pitches. 70 hardstandings. 43 seasonal pitches. Caravan pitches. Motorhome pitches. 7 statics.

AA Pubs & Restaurants nearby: Fat Lamb Country Inn, Ravenstonedale 015396 23242

Black Swan, Ravenstonedale 015396 23204

Facilities: ⋔ ☉ ℘ ✳ ㊡ Ⓢ 🏠 🏕 ♻ ❶
Services: ⊡ 🔲 🍴 🛢 T 🍽 🛒
Within 3 miles: ℘ 🏠 🔲

TROUTBECK (NEAR KESWICK) Map 18 NY32

PREMIER PARK

►►►►► 81% Troutbeck Camping and Caravanning Club Site *(NY365271)*

Hutton Moor End CA11 0SX
☎ 017687 79149
dir: *M6 junct 40, A66 towards Keswick. In 9.5m sharp left for Wallthwaite. Site 0.5m on left*

🚐 🚌 ⛺

Open 9 Mar-11 Nov & 26 Dec-2 Jan

Last arrival 20.00hrs Last departure noon

Beautifully situated between Penrith and Keswick, this quiet, well managed Lakeland campsite offers two immaculate touring areas, one a sheltered paddock for caravans and motorhomes, with serviced hardstanding pitches, and a maturing lower field, which has spacious hardstanding pitches and a superb and very popular small tenting area that enjoys stunning and extensive views of the surrounding fells. The toilet block is appointed to a very high standard and includes two family cubicles, and the log cabin reception/shop stocks local and organic produce. A luxury caravan, sleeping six, is available for hire. The enthusiastic franchisees offer high levels of customer care and are constantly improving the park, which is well-placed for visited Keswick, Ullswater and the north lakes. Non-members are also very welcome. 5 acre site. 54 touring pitches. 36 hardstandings. Caravan pitches. Motorhome pitches. Tent pitches. 20 statics.

Leisure: 🛝

Facilities: 🚿 🪒 💨 ❄ ♿ 🛒 🧺 [Wi-fi] ♻ ℹ

Services: 🔌 🫧 🛢 🍃 [T] 🔋 🚰

Within 3 miles: ⛳ 🛒 🐴

Notes: Site gates closed 23.00hrs-07.00hrs. Dogs must be kept on leads. Dog walk.

ULVERSTON Map 18 SD27

Places to visit

The Dock Museum, BARROW-IN-FURNESS 01229 876400 www.dockmuseum.org.uk

Furness Abbey, BARROW-IN-FURNESS 01229 823420 www.english-heritage.org.uk

Great for kids: South Lakes Wild Animal Park, DALTON-IN-FURNESS 01229 466086 www.wildanimalpark.co.uk

►►►► 85% Bardsea Leisure Park *(SD292765)*

Priory Rd LA12 9QE
☎ 01229 584712 & 484363
e-mail: reception@bardsealeisure.co.uk
dir: *M6 junct 36, A590 towards Barrow. At Ulverston take A5087, site 1m on right*

* 🚐 £14.50-£21.50 🚌 £14.50-£21.50

Open all year

Last arrival 21.00hrs Last departure 18.00hrs

An attractively landscaped former quarry, making a quiet and very sheltered site. Many of the generously-sized pitches offer all-weather full facilities, and a luxury toilet block provides plenty of fully-serviced cubicles. Set on the southern edge of the town, it is convenient for both the coast and the Lake District and there's an excellent caravan accessories shop on site. Please note that this site does not accept tents. 5 acre site. 83 touring pitches. 83 hardstandings. 50 seasonal pitches. Caravan pitches. Motorhome pitches. 88 statics.

AA Pubs & Restaurants nearby: Farmers Arms, Ulverston 01229 584469

Leisure: 🛝 ⚽

Facilities: 🚿 🪒 💨 ❄ ♿ 📞 🛒 🧺 🐕 [Wi-fi] 💻

Services: 🔌 🫧 🛢 🍃 [T] 🔋 ▦ 🚰

Within 3 miles: ⛳ 🎬 🎣 🛒 ◎ 🐴

Notes: No noise after 22.30hrs. Dogs must be kept on leads.

WASDALE HEAD Map 18 NY10

►►► 76% *Wasdale Head National Trust Campsite* *(NY183076)*

CA20 1EX
☎ 015394 63862 & 32733
e-mail: campsite.bookings@nationaltrust.org.uk
web: www.ntlakescampsites.org.uk
dir: *From A595(N) left at Gosforth; from A595(S) right at Holmrook for Santon Bridge, follow signs to Wasdale Head*

🚌 ⛺

Open all year (rs Wknds Nov-Feb shop open)

Last departure 11.00hrs

Set in a remote and beautiful spot at Wasdale Head, under the stunning Scafell peaks at the head of the deepest lake in England. Clean, well-kept facilities are set centrally amongst open grass pitches and trees, where camping pods are also located. There are eight hardstandings for motorhomes and eight electric hook ups for tents. The renowned Wasdale Head Inn is close by. 5 acre site. 120 touring pitches. 6 hardstandings. Motorhome pitches. Tent pitches. 3 wooden pods.

AA Pubs & Restaurants nearby: Wasdale Head Inn, Wasdale Head 019467 26229

Facilities: 🚿 🪒 💨 ❄ ♿ 📞 🛒 ♻

Services: 🔌 🫧 🍃

Notes: No cars by tents. No groups of more than 4 unless a family with children. Dogs must be kept on leads.

WATERMILLOCK Map 18 NY42

▶▶▶▶ 87% *The Quiet Site*

(NY431236)

GOLD

Ullswater CA11 0LS
☎ 07768 727016
e-mail: info@thequietsite.co.uk
dir: *M6 junct 40, A592 towards Ullswater. Right at lake junct, then right at Brackenrigg Hotel. Site 1.5m on right*

🚐 🚙 ⛺

Open all year (rs Low season bar open some wkdays only)

Last arrival 22.00hrs Last departure noon

A well-maintained site in a lovely, peaceful location, with good terraced pitches offering great fells views, very good toilet facilities including family bathrooms, and a charming 'olde-worlde' bar. There are 13 wooden camping pods for hire and a self-catering stone cottage. 10 acre site. 100 touring pitches. 60 hardstandings. Caravan pitches. Motorhome pitches. Tent pitches. 23 statics.

AA Pubs & Restaurants nearby: Macdonald Leeming House, Watermillock 0870 400 8131

Rampsbeck Country House Hotel, Watermillock 017684 86442

Leisure: ⚙ ⌂ 🎣 ▢
Facilities: 🚾 🏕 ⊙ 🅿 ✳ ⚡ 🕐 🕤 🎾 🏓 🛜 🖥 ♻ ℹ
Services: 🔌 🗑 🍺 🔋 ⛽ 🅃 🛒 ⚓
Within 3 miles: 🎣 🚴 ⛵ 🎣 🎰 🏇

Notes: Quiet from 22.00hrs onwards. Pool table, soft play area for toddlers, caravan storage.

AA CAMPING CARD SITE

▶▶▶▶ 80% Cove Caravan & Camping Park (NY431236)

Ullswater CA11 0LS
☎ 017684 86549
e-mail: info@cove-park.co.uk
dir: *M6 junct 40, A592 for Ullswater. Right at lake junct, then right at Brackenrigg Inn. Site 1.5m on left*

* 🚐 £18-£30 🚙 £18-£30 ⛺ £14-£25

Open Mar-Oct

Last arrival 21.00hrs Last departure noon

A peaceful family site in an attractive and elevated position with extensive fell views and glimpses of Ullswater Lake. The ground is gently sloping grass, but there are also eight fully serviced hardstandings for motorhomes and caravans. The amenities block was refurbished for the 2012 season. 3 acre site. 50 touring pitches. 21 hardstandings. 10 seasonal pitches. Caravan pitches. Motorhome pitches. Tent pitches. 39 statics.

AA Pubs & Restaurants nearby: Macdonald Leeming House, Watermillock 0870 400 8131

Cove Caravan & Camping Park

Leisure: ⚙
Facilities: 🏕 ⊙ 🅿 ✳ ⚡ 🎾 🏓 ♻ ℹ
Services: 🔌 🗑 🔋 ⛽
Within 3 miles: 🎣 🚴 ⛵ 🎰 🏇

Notes: No open fires, no noise after 22.30hrs. Dogs must be kept on leads.

see advert below

SERVICES: 🔌 Electric hook up 🗑 Launderette 🍺 Licensed bar 🔋 Calor Gas 🚿 Camping Gaz 🅃 Toilet fluid 🍴 Café/Restaurant 🍔 Fast Food/Takeaway ⚓ Battery charging 🍼 Baby care ⚙ Motorvan service point **ABBREVIATIONS:** BH/bank hols-bank holidays Etr-Easter Whit-Whitsun dep-departure fr-from hrs-hours m-mile mdnt-midnight rdbt-roundabout rs-restricted service wk-week wknd-weekend ⊘ No credit cards 🚫 no dogs See page 7 for details of the AA Camping Card Scheme

WATERMILLOCK *continued*

►►► 84% Ullswater Caravan, Camping & Marine Park *(NY438232)*

High Longthwaite CA11 0LR
☎ 017684 86666
e-mail: info@ullswatercaravanpark.co.uk
web: www.ullswatercaravanpark.co.uk
dir: *M6 junct 40, A592, W towards Ullswater for 5m. Right, alongside Ullswater for 2m, right at phone box. Site 0.5m on right*

* 🚐 £14-£27 🚌 £14-£27 ⛺ £14-£27

Open Mar-Nov (rs Low season bar open wknds only)

Last arrival 21.00hrs Last departure noon

A pleasant rural site with its own nearby boat launching and marine storage facility, making it ideal for sailors. The family-owned and run park enjoys fell and lake views, and there is a bar, café and shop on site. Many of the pitches are fully serviced and there are wooden cabins with barbecues. Please note that the Marine Park is one mile from the camping area. 12 acre site. 160 touring pitches. 58 hardstandings. Caravan pitches. Motorhome pitches. Tent pitches. 55 statics. 4 wooden pods.

AA Pubs & Restaurants nearby: Macdonald Leeming House, Watermillock 0870 400 8131

Rampsbeck Country House Hotel, Watermillock 017684 86442

Leisure: 🛝 🏓

Facilities: 🚿 ⊙ 💨 ❄ ♿ [$] 🐕 [Wi-fi] ♻

Services: 🔌 🧼 🍷 🛢 🧪 [T] 🔋

Within 3 miles: 🚣 🎣 🏄 [$] 🧼 🐴

Notes: No open fires, no noise after 23.30hrs. Dogs must be kept on leads. Boat launching & moorings 1m.

WINDERMERE

Places to visit

Holehird Gardens, WINDERMERE 015394 46008 www.holehirdgardens.org.uk

Blackwell The Arts & Crafts House, BOWNESS-ON-WINDERMERE 015394 46139 www.blackwell.org.uk

Great for kids: Lake District Visitor Centre at Brockhole, WINDERMERE 015394 46601 www.lake-district.gov.uk

WINDERMERE — Map 18 SD49

PREMIER PARK

►►►►► 84% Park Cliffe Camping & Caravan Estate *(SD391912)*

Birks Rd, Tower Wood LA23 3PG
☎ 01539 531344
e-mail: info@parkcliffe.co.uk
dir: *M6 junct 36, A590. Right at Newby Bridge onto A592. 3.6m right into site. (NB due to difficult access from main road this is only advised direction for approaching site)*

* 🚐 £25-£30 🚌 £25-£30 ⛺ £20-£35

Open Mar-10 Nov (rs Wknds & school hols facilities open fully)

Last arrival 22.00hrs Last departure noon

A lovely hillside park set in 25 secluded acres of fell land. The camping area is sloping and uneven in places, but well drained and sheltered; some pitches have spectacular views of Lake Windermere and the Langdales. The park offers a high level of customer care and is very well equipped for families (family bathrooms), and there is an attractive bar and brasserie restaurant serving quality food, and three static holiday caravans for hire. 25 acre site. 60 touring pitches. 60 hardstandings. 25 seasonal pitches. Caravan pitches. Motorhome pitches. Tent pitches. 56 statics. 5 wooden pods.

AA Pubs & Restaurants nearby: Eagle & Child Inn, Staveley 01539 821320

Jerichos, Windermere 015394 42522

Leisure: 🛝 🏓

Facilities: 🚿 ⊙ 💨 ❄ ♿ 📞 [$] 🧺 🐕 [Wi-fi] ♻ ℹ

Services: 🔌 🧼 🍷 🛢 🧪 [T] 🍽 🛍 🍼 ⚓

Within 3 miles: ⛳ 🚣 🎬 🎣 ◎ 🏄 [$] 🧼 🐴

Notes: No noise 23.00hrs-07.30hrs. Dogs must be kept on leads. Off-licence.

►►►► 87% Fallbarrow Park *(SD401973)*

Rayrigg Rd LA23 3DL
☎ 015395 69835
e-mail: enquiries@southlakelandparks.co.uk
dir: *0.5m N of Windermere on A591. At mini-rdbt turn left to Bowness Bay & the Lake. Site 1.3m on right*

🚐 £18.50-£35 🚌 £18.50-£35

Open Mar-mid Nov

Last arrival 22.00hrs Last departure 12.00hrs

A park set in impressive surroundings just a few minutes' walk from Bowness on the shore of Lake Windermere. There is direct access to the lake through the park. The site has good, hedged, fully serviced pitches, quality toilet facilities, a deli and café serving meals using locally sourced produce, and a comfortable lounge bar for adults only with a wood burning stove. The site has 30 holiday hire statics. 32 acre site. 32 touring pitches. 32 hardstandings. Caravan pitches. Motorhome pitches. 269 statics.

AA Pubs & Restaurants nearby: Eagle & Child Inn, Staveley 01539 821320

Jerichos, Windermere 015394 42522

Leisure: 🛝 🏓 📺

Facilities: 🚿 ⊙ 💨 ♿ 📞 [$] 🧺 🐕 [Wi-fi] 💻 ♻ ℹ

Services: 🔌 🧼 🍷 🛢 🍽 🛍 🍼 ⚓

Within 3 miles: ⛳ 🚣 🎬 🎣 ◎ 🏄 [$] 🧼 🐴

Notes: No tents, no cycling, no scooters. Dogs must be kept on leads. Boat launching.

►►►► 82% Hill of Oaks & Blakeholme *(SD386899)*

LA12 8NR

☎ **015395 31578**

e-mail: enquiries@hillofoaks.co.uk
web: www.hillofoaks.co.uk
dir: *M6 junct 36, A590 towards Barrow. At rdbt signed Bowness turn right onto A592. Site approx 3m on left*

🚐 🚙

Open Mar-14 Nov

Last departure noon

A secluded, heavily wooded park on the shores of Lake Windermere. Pretty lakeside picnic areas, woodland walks and a play area make this a delightful park for families, with excellent serviced pitches, a licensed shop and a heated toilet block. Watersports include sailing and canoeing, with private jetties for boat launching. 31 acre site. 43 touring pitches. 43 hardstandings. Caravan pitches. Motorhome pitches. 215 statics.

AA Pubs & Restaurants nearby: Eagle & Child Inn, Staveley 01539 821320

Jerichos, Windermere 015394 42522

Leisure: ⚁ ✪

Facilities: ⌢ ☉ ⌐ ✶ ⅍ ⓒ ⑤ 🖥 ⊼ WiFi 🖳 ♻ ❻

Services: 🔌 ⑤ 🔋 T ↧

Within 3 miles: ↓ ⳻ ⵠ ⌁ ◎ ⅍ 🛍 🛒 ∪

Notes: No tents (except trailer tents), no groups. Dogs must be kept on leads.

SERVICES: 🔌 Electric hook up   ⑤ Launderette   🍷 Licensed bar   🔋 Calor Gas   ⌀ Camping Gaz   T Toilet fluid   🍽 Café/Restaurant   🍔 Fast Food/Takeaway   🔋 Battery charging
🍼 Baby care   ↯ Motorvan service point   **ABBREVIATIONS:** BH/bank hols-bank holidays   Etr-Easter   Whit-Whitsun   dep-departure   fr-from   hrs-hours   m-mile   mdnt-midnight
rdbt-roundabout   rs-restricted service   wk-week   wknd-weekend   ⊗ No credit cards   ⊗ no dogs   See page 7 for details of the AA Camping Card Scheme

Derbyshire

Think of Derbyshire and you instantly think of
the Peak District, the first of Britain's glorious and
much-loved National Parks and still the most popular.
This is where the rugged, sometimes inhospitable
landscape of north England meets the gentler beauty
of the Midland counties.

Within the National Park lies the upland country of the Dark Peak, shaped over the centuries by silt from the region's great rivers, and where gritstone outcrops act as monuments to the splendour and magic of geology. History was made in this corner of Derbyshire in 1932 when 500 ramblers spilled on to Kinder Scout to argue for the right of public access to the countryside.

Southern landscape

To the south is the White Peak, different in both character and appearance. This is a land of limestone, of deep wooded gorges, underground caves and high pastures crisscrossed by traditional drystone walls. There are dales, too – the most famous among them being Dovedale, the haunt of countless writers and artists over the years. Not surprisingly, Wordsworth and Tennyson sought inspiration here and much of it retains a rare, magical quality.

Fine buildings

Look in and around the Peak District National Park and you'll find an impressive range of fine

▶

buildings. Calke Abbey (NT) is not an abbey at all but a magnificent baroque mansion dating back to the beginning of the 18th century.

World-famous Chatsworth, the palatial home of the Duke of Devonshire, is one of Derbyshire's most cherished visitor attractions. Work began on the original building in 1549 and the house has been substantially altered and enlarged over the years. The 1,000-acre park is the jewel in Chatsworth's crown; designed by 'Capability' Brown, it includes rare trees, a maze and the highest gravity-fed fountain in the world.

Towns and villages

As well as the county's palatial houses, there is an impressive array of quaint villages and historic towns. Chesterfield is known for the crooked spire of its church, while Buxton is acknowledged as one of the country's loveliest spa towns. Bakewell introduced the tradition of the Bakewell Pudding and the villagers of Tissington still maintain the old custom of well dressing on Ascension Day.

• Dove Dale

Walking and Cycling

Derbyshire is just the place for exhilarating walking where almost every person you pass is pleasant and friendly. The Peak District offers more demanding and adventurous routes, including the High Peak Trail, which runs from Hurdlow to Cromford, and the Monsal Trail, which extends from Haddon Park to Topley Pike. There is also the 26-mile (42km) Limestone Way from Matlock to Castleton and the 35-mile (56km) Gritstone Trail from Disley to Kidsgrove. Derbyshire's most famous walk is undoubtedly the Pennine Way, which starts at Edale in the Peak District and runs north for 251 miles (404km) to Kirk Yetholm in Scotland.

In common with other parts of the country, the Peak District includes a number of disused railway tracks that have been adapted to user-friendly cycle trails. Among many popular cycle trails are several family routes around Derwent reservoir, where 617 Squadron, 'The Dambusters', famously practised low-level flying during the Second World War.

Festivals and Events

Among many fixtures are the following:

- The Ashbourne Shrovetide Football on Shrove Tuesday and Ash Wednesday.
- The Bamford Sheep Dog Trials, the Chatsworth Horse Trials and the Castleton Garland Ceremony in May.
- In July there is the Bakewell Carnival, the Padley Pilgrimage and the Buxton Festival.
- September sees the Matlock Bath Illuminations and Firework Display and December the Castleton Christmas Lights and the Boxing Day Raft Race at Matlock Bath.

● View from Mam Tor to Hollins Cross

DERBYSHIRE

See Walk 3 & Cycle Ride 3 in the Walks & Cycle Rides section at the end of the guide

ASHBOURNE   Map 10 SK14

Places to visit

Kedleston Hall, KEDLESTON HALL 01332 842191 www.nationaltrust.org.uk

Wirksworth Heritage Centre, WIRKSWORTH 01629 825225 www.storyofwirksworth.co.uk

Great for kids: Crich Tramway Village, CRICH 01773 854321 www.tramway.co.uk

AA CAMPING CARD SITE

►► 83% Carsington Fields Caravan Park (SK251493)

Millfields Ln, Nr Carsington Water DE6 3JS
☎ 01335 372872 & 07546 210956
e-mail: bookings@carsingtoncaravaning.co.uk
dir: From Belper towards Ashbourne on A517, right approx 0.25m past Hulland Ward into Dog Ln. 0.75m right at x-roads signed Carsington. Site on right approx 0.75m

* 🚐 £15-£20 🚎 £15-£20 ▲ £15-£20

Open Mar-Oct

Last arrival 21.00hrs Last departure 18.00hrs

A very well presented and spacious park with a good toilet block, open views and a large fenced pond that attracts plenty of wildlife. The popular tourist attraction of Carsington Water is a short stroll away, with its variety of leisure facilities including fishing, sailing, windsurfing and children's play area. The park is also a good base for walkers. 6 acre site. 55 touring pitches. 12 hardstandings. Caravan pitches. Motorhome pitches. Tent pitches.

AA Pubs & Restaurants nearby: The Coach & Horses Inn, Fenny Bentley 01335 350246

Bentley Brook Inn, Fenny Bentley 01335 350278

The Dining Room, Ashbourne 01335 300666

Facilities: 🌣⊙🅿✳&🌂 📶 ♻ ❶
Services: �'❏ Within 3 miles: ✦🐾🛱👣❶∪

Notes: No large groups or group bookings, no noise after 23.00hrs. Dogs must be kept on leads. Fish & chip van Fri 20.00hrs, Indian takeaway deliver to site free of charge.

BAKEWELL   Map 16 SK26

Places to visit

Chatsworth, CHATSWORTH 01246 565300 www.chatsworth.org

Chesterfield Museum and Art Gallery, CHESTERFIELD 01246 345727 www.visitchesterfield.info

AA CAMPING CARD SITE

►►► 78% Greenhills Holiday Park (SK202693)

Crowhill Ln DE45 1PX
☎ 01629 813052 & 813467
e-mail: info@greenhillsholidaypark.co.uk
web: www.greenhillsholidaypark.co.uk
dir: 1m NW of Bakewell on A6. Signed before Ashford-in-the-Water, 50yds along unclassified road on right

* 🚐 fr £15 🚎 fr £15 ▲ fr £15

Open Feb-Nov (rs Feb-Apr & Oct-Nov bar & shop closed)

Last arrival 22.00hrs Last departure noon

A well-established park set in lovely countryside within the Peak District National Park. Many pitches enjoy uninterrupted views, and there is easy accessibility to all facilities. A clubhouse, shop and children's playground are popular features. 8 acre site. 172 touring pitches. 30 hardstandings. Caravan pitches. Motorhome pitches. Tent pitches. 73 statics.

AA Pubs & Restaurants nearby: Bull's Head, Bakewell 01629 812931

Piedaniel's, Bakewell 01629 812687

Leisure: 🅼☺🎵
Facilities: 🌣⊙🅿✳&☺🛱🌂 📶 💻 ♻ ❶
Services: 🚐🗑🛒🔋⊘Ⓣ🍴🛒↯
Within 3 miles: ⌂🐾◎🛱❶∪

BIRCHOVER   Map 16 SK26

Places to visit

Haddon Hall, HADDON HALL 01629 812855 www.haddonhall.co.uk

The Heights of Abraham Cable Cars, Caverns & Hilltop Park, MATLOCK BATH 01629 582365 www.heightsofabraham.com

►►►► 81% Barn Farm Campsite (SK238621)

Barn Farm DE4 2BL
☎ 01629 650245
e-mail: gilberthh@msn.com
dir: From A6 take B5056 towards Ashbourne. Follow brown signs to site

* 🚐 £20-£22 🚎 £20-£22 ▲ £10-£15

Open Apr-Oct

Last arrival 21.00hrs Last departure noon

An interesting park on a former dairy farm with the many and varied facilities housed in high quality conversions of old farm buildings. Three large and well maintained touring fields offer sweeping views across the Peak National Park. There is an excellent choice in the provision of privacy cubicles, including shower and wash basin cubicles and even a shower and sauna. There are five stylish camping barns for hire. 15 acre site. 50 touring pitches. Caravan pitches. Motorhome pitches. Tent pitches.

AA Pubs & Restaurants nearby: The Peacock at Rowsley, Rowsley 01629 733518

Leisure: 🅼☺🔍🖵
Facilities: 🌣⊙🅿✳&☺🛱🌂🛒💻♻❶
Services: 🚐🗑🔋Ⓣ🛒
Within 3 miles: ⌂🐎🐾◎🛱❶∪

Notes: No music after 22.30hrs, minimum noise 22.30hrs-07.00hrs. Dogs must be kept on leads.

BUXTON — Map 16 SK07

Places to visit

Eyam Hall, EYAM 01433 631976
www.eyamhall.com

Poole's Cavern (Buxton Country Park), BUXTON
01298 26978 www.poolescavern.co.uk

►►►► 83% Lime Tree Park (SK070725)

Dukes Dr SK17 9RP
☎ 01298 22988
e-mail: info@limetreeparkbuxton.co.uk
dir: 1m S of Buxton, between A515 & A6

* 🚐 £22-£25 🚐 £22-£25 ▲ £15-£18

Open Mar-Oct

Last arrival 21.00hrs Last departure noon

A most attractive and well-designed site, set on the side of a narrow valley in an elevated location, with separate, neatly landscaped areas for statics, tents, touring caravans and motorhomes. There's good attention to detail throughout including the clean toilets and showers. Its backdrop of magnificent old railway viaduct and views over Buxton and the surrounding hills, make this a sought-after destination. There are eight static caravans, a pine lodge and two apartments available for holiday lets. 10.5 acre site. 106 touring pitches. 22 hardstandings. Caravan pitches. Motorhome pitches. Tent pitches. 43 statics.

AA Pubs & Restaurants nearby: Queen Anne Inn, Buxton 01298 871246

Leisure: 🎢 🐟 🖵
Facilities: 🐾 ⊙ 🅿 ⚹ 🕭 ⊕ 🗑 🛒
Services: 🔌 🗄 ⌀ 🅣 🛒
Within 3 miles: ⌘ ◎ 🎣 🗑 🗄 ∪

►►►► 87% Clover Fields Touring Caravan Park (SK075704)

1 Heath View, Harpur Hill SK17 9PU
☎ 01298 78731
e-mail: cloverfields@tiscali.co.uk
dir: A515, B5053, then immediately right. Site 0.5m on left

🚐 £20-£22.50 🚐 £20-£22.50 ▲ £18-£22.50

Open all year

Last departure 18.00hrs

A developing and spacious adults-only park with very good facilities, including an upmarket, timber chalet-style toilet block, just over a mile from the attractions of Buxton. All pitches are fully serviced including individual barbecues, and are set out on terraces, each with extensive views over the countryside. Swathes of natural meadow grasses and flowers cloak the terraces and surrounding fields. 12 acre site. 25 touring pitches. 25 hardstandings. Caravan pitches. Motorhome pitches. Tent pitches.

AA Pubs & Restaurants nearby: Queen Anne Inn, Buxton 01298 871246

Facilities: 🐾 ⊙ ⚹ 🕭 ⊕ 🗑 🛒 ♻ ❼
Services: 🔌 🗄 🛢 🅣 🛠
Within 3 miles: ⌘ 🎣 🗑 🗄 ∪

Notes: Adults only. No commercial vehicles. Dogs must be kept on leads. Small fishing pond, boules area.

►►► 85% Beech Croft Farm (SK122720)

Beech Croft, Blackwell in the Peak SK17 9TQ
☎ 01298 85330
e-mail: mail@beechcroftfarm.co.uk
dir: Exit A6 midway between Buxton & Bakewell. Site signed

* 🚐 £16-£20 🚐 £16-£20 ▲ £12.50-£15

Open all year (rs Mar)

Last arrival 21.30hrs

A small terraced farm site with lovely Peak District views. There's a fine stone-built toilet block with ultra-modern fittings, underfloor heating and additional unisex facilities, 31 fully-serviced hardstanding pitches (11 in the camping field), gravel roads, electric points, and a super tarmac pathway leading from the camping field to the toilet block. New for the 2012 season is a campers' shelter with a vending machine. This makes an ideal site for those touring or walking in the Peak District. 3 acre site. 30 touring pitches. 30 hardstandings. Caravan pitches. Motorhome pitches. Tent pitches.

AA Pubs & Restaurants nearby: Queen Anne Inn, Buxton 01298 871246

Facilities: 🐾 ⊙ ⚹ 🕭 🗑 🎛 🛒 📶 ♻ ❼
Services: 🔌 🗄 🛢 ⌀ 🅣
Notes: No noise after 23.00hrs.

HOPE — Map 16 SK18

Places to visit

Speedwell Cavern, CASTLETON 01433 620512
www.speedwellcavern.co.uk

Peveril Castle, CASTLETON 01433 620613
www.english-heritage.org.uk

►►► 77% Pindale Farm Outdoor Centre (SK163825)

Pindale Rd S33 6RN
☎ 01433 620111
e-mail: pindalefarm@btconnect.com
dir: From A6187 in Hope take turn signed Pindale between church & Woodroffe Arms. Centre 1m on left

▲

Open Mar-Oct

Set around a 13th-century farmhouse and a former lead mine pump house (now converted to a self-contained bunkhouse for up to 60 people), this simple, off-the-beaten track site is an ideal base for walking, climbing, caving and various outdoor pursuits. Around the farm are several deeply wooded closes available for tents, and old stone buildings that have been well converted to house modern toilet facilities. 4 acre site. 60 touring pitches. Tent pitches.

AA Pubs & Restaurants nearby: Cheshire Cheese Inn, Hope 01433 620381

Ye Olde Nags Head, Castleton 01433 620248

The Peaks Inn, Castleton 01433 620247

Facilities: 🐾 ⊙ ⚹ 📶
Services: 🔌 🗄
Within 3 miles: 🗑 ∪

Notes: No anti-social behaviour & noise must be kept to minimum after 21.00hrs, no fires, charge for use of Wi-fi. Dogs must be kept on leads.

MATLOCK — Map 16 SK35

Places to visit

Peak District Mining Museum, MATLOCK BATH 01629 583834 www.peakmines.co.uk

Haddon Hall, HADDON HALL 01629 812855 www.haddonhall.co.uk

Great for kids: The Heights of Abraham Cable Cars, Caverns & Hilltop Park, MATLOCK BATH 01629 582365 www.heightsofabraham.com

►►►► 80% Lickpenny Caravan Site

(SK339597)

Lickpenny Ln, Tansley DE4 5GF
☎ **01629 583040**
e-mail: lickpennycp@btinternet.com
dir: *From Matlock take A615 towards Alfreton for 3m. Site signed to left, into Lickpenny Ln, right into site near end of road*

* ⛺ £15-£25 🚐 £15-£25

Open all year

Last arrival 20.00hrs Last departure noon

A picturesque site in the grounds of an old plant nursery with areas broken up and screened by a variety of shrubs, and spectacular views, which are best enjoyed from the upper terraced areas. Pitches, several fully serviced, are spacious, well screened and well marked, and facilities are to a very good standard. The bistro/coffee shop is popular with visitors. 16 acre site. 80 touring pitches. 80 hardstandings. 20 seasonal pitches. Caravan pitches. Motorhome pitches.

AA Pubs & Restaurants nearby: Red Lion, Matlock 01629 584888

Stones Restaurant, Matlock 01629 56061

Leisure: 🛝

Facilities: 🖍️☉🅿️♿🛁🚿🪒🚻💻♻️ℹ️

Services: 🔌🛢️🚽🛒⚕️

Within 3 miles: ↕️✈️🎣⛳🛒🅿️⛺

Notes: Dogs must be kept on leads. Child bath available.

NEWHAVEN — Map 16 SK16

Places to visit

Middleton Top Engine House, MIDDLETON 01629 823204 www.derbyshire.gov.uk/countryside

Peak District Mining Museum, MATLOCK BATH 01629 583834 www.peakmines.co.uk

►►► 78% Newhaven Caravan & Camping Park *(SK167602)*

SK17 0DT
☎ **01298 84300**
e-mail: newhavencaravanpark@btconnect.com
web: www.newhavencaravanpark.co.uk
dir: *Between Ashbourne & Buxton at A515 & A5012 junct*

* ⛺ £14.50-£18.75 🚐 £14.50-£18.75
🅰 £11.25-£15

Open Mar-Oct

Last arrival 21.00hrs

Pleasantly situated within the Peak District National Park, this park has mature trees screening the three touring areas. Very good toilet facilities cater for touring vans and a large tent field, and there's a restaurant adjacent to the site. 30 acre site. 125 touring pitches. 18 hardstandings. 40 seasonal pitches. Caravan pitches. Motorhome pitches. Tent pitches. 73 statics.

AA Pubs & Restaurants nearby: Red Lion Inn, Birchover 01629 650363

Druid Inn, Birchover 01629 650302

Leisure: 🛝🎣

Facilities: 🖍️☉🅿️❄️🛁🚿🚻♻️ℹ️

Services: 🔌🛢️🚿🚽🛒

Within 3 miles: ✈️🎣🛒🅿️⛺

Notes: Dogs must be kept on leads.

RIPLEY — Map 16 SK35

Places to visit

Midland Railway Butterley, RIPLEY 01773 747674 www.midlandrailwaycentre.co.uk

Denby Pottery Visitor Centre, DENBY 01773 740799 www.denbyvisitorcentre.co.uk

►►►► 80% Golden Valley Caravan & Camping Park

(SK408513)

Coach Rd DE55 4ES
☎ **01773 513881 & 746786**
e-mail: enquiries@goldenvalleycaravanpark.co.uk
web: www.goldenvalleycaravanpark.co.uk
dir: *M1 junct 26, A610 to Codnor. Right at lights, then right into Alfreton Rd. In 1m left into Coach Rd, park on left. (NB it is advised that Sat Nav is ignored for last few miles & guide directions are followed)*

* ⛺ £22-£30 🚐 £22-£30 🅰 £15-£27.50

Open all year (rs Wknds only in low season bar & café open, childrens activities)

Last arrival 21.00hrs Last departure noon

This superbly landscaped park is set within 30 acres of woodland in the Amber Valley. The fully-serviced pitches are set out in informal groups in clearings amongst the trees. The park has a cosy bar and bistro with outside patio, a fully stocked fishing lake, an innovative and well-equipped play area, an on-site jacuzzi and fully equipped fitness suite. There is also a wildlife pond and a nature trail. 30 acre site. 45 touring pitches. 45 hardstandings. Caravan pitches. Motorhome pitches. Tent pitches. 1 static.

AA Pubs & Restaurants nearby: Santo's Higham Farm Hotel, Higham 01773 833812

Leisure: 🏋️🛝🎣📺

Facilities: 🛁🖍️☉🅿️❄️♿🛁🚿🚻📶💻♻️ℹ️

Services: 🔌🛢️🍴🚿🛢️🚽🍽️🛒🛍️🚜⚕️

Within 3 miles: ↕️🎠🎣🛒🅿️⛺

Notes: No open fires or disposable BBQs, no noise after 22.30hrs, no vehicles on grass. Dogs must be kept on leads. Jacuzzi, zip slide, donkey rides, tractor train, water walking balls, log flume ride.

LEISURE: 🏊 Indoor swimming pool 🏊 Outdoor swimming pool 🛝 Children's playground 🪁 Kid's club 🎾 Tennis court 🎯 Games room 📺 Separate TV room ⛳ 9/18 hole golf course 🚣 Boats for hire 🎬 Cinema 🎵 Entertainment 🎣 Fishing ◉ Mini golf 🏄 Watersports 🏋️ Gym 🏟️ Sports field Spa ⛺ Stables
FACILITIES: 🛁 Bath 🚿 Shower ☉ Electric shaver 🅿️ Hairdryer ❄️ Ice Pack Facility ♿ Disabled facilities 🕐 Public telephone 🛒 Shop on site or within 200yds 🚐 Mobile shop (calls at least 5 days a week) 🍖 BBQ area 🌲 Picnic area 📶 Wi-fi 💻 Internet access ♻️ Recycling ℹ️ Tourist info 🐕 Dog exercise area

ROSLISTON · Map 10 SK21

Places to visit

Sudbury Hall and Museum of Childhood, SUDBURY 01283 585305 www.nationaltrust.org.uk

Ashby-de-la-Zouch Castle, ASHBY-DE-LA-ZOUCH 01530 413343 www.english-heritage.org.uk

Great for kids: Conkers, MOIRA 01283 216633 www.visitconkers.com

►►► 81% Beehive Woodland Lakes (SK249161)

DE12 8HZ
☎ 01283 763981
e-mail: info@beehivefarm-woodlandlakes.co.uk
dir: From A444 in Castle Gresley into Mount Pleasant Rd, follow Rosliston signs for 3.5m through Linton to T-junct. Left signed Beehive Farms

* ➔ £14-£22 ➔ £14-£22 ▲ £14-£22

Open Mar-Nov

Last arrival 20.00hrs Last departure noon

A small, informal and rapidly developing caravan area secluded from an extensive woodland park in the heart of the National Forest National Park. Toilet facilities include four family rooms. Young children will enjoy the on-site animal farm and playground, whilst anglers will appreciate fishing the three lakes within the park; bikes can be hired. For the 2012 season new hardstandings and an adults-only area have been added. The Honey Pot tearoom provides snacks and is open most days. 2.5 acre site. 46 touring pitches. 46 hardstandings. Caravan pitches. Motorhome pitches. Tent pitches.

AA Pubs & Restaurants nearby: The Waterfront, Barton-under-Needwood 01283 711500

Leisure: ⚲
Facilities: ⬟⊙⊡❄⬥⚑⬚⬛ 🅱
Services: ⬟⬚⬛⬛
Within 3 miles: ⬛⬛⬛⬛⬚⬚

Notes: Last arrival time 18.00hrs low season. Dogs must be kept on leads. 3 coarse fishing lakes, takeaway food delivered to site.

ROWSLEY · Map 16 SK26

Places to visit

Hardwick Hall, HARDWICK HALL 01246 850430 www.nationaltrust.org.uk/main/w-hardwickhall

Temple Mine, MATLOCK BATH 01629 583834 www.peakmines.co.uk

Great for kids: The Heights of Abraham Cable Cars, Caverns & Hilltop Park, MATLOCK BATH 01629 582365 www.heightsofabraham.com

►►► 73% *Grouse & Claret* (SK258660)

Station Rd DE4 2EB
☎ 01629 733233
e-mail: grouseandclaret.matlock@marstons.co.uk
dir: M1 junct 29. Site on A6, 5m from Matlock & 3m from Bakewell

➔ ➔ ▲

Open all year

Last arrival 20.00hrs Last departure noon

A well-designed, purpose-built park at the rear of an eating house on the A6 between Bakewell and Chatsworth, and adjacent to the New Peak Shopping Village. The park comprises a level grassy area running down to the river, and all pitches have hardstandings and electric hook-ups. 2.5 acre site. 26 touring pitches. 26 hardstandings. Caravan pitches. Motorhome pitches. Tent pitches.

AA Pubs & Restaurants nearby: Grouse & Claret (on site); Peacock at Rowsley 01629 733518

Leisure: ⚲
Facilities: ⬟⊙⚑⬛
Services: ⬟⬛⬚⬛⬛
Within 3 miles: ⬛⬚⬚⬚

Notes: No cars by tents. Dogs must be kept on leads.

SHARDLOW · Map 11 SK43

Places to visit

Melbourne Hall & Gardens, MELBOURNE 01332 862502 www.melbournehall.com

►►► 67% Shardlow Marina Caravan Park (SK444303)

London Rd DE72 2GL
☎ 01332 792832
e-mail: admin@shardlowmarina.co.uk
dir: M1 junct 24a, A50 signed Derby. Exit junct 1 at rdbt signed Shardlow. Site 1m on right

➔ ➔ ▲

Open Mar-Jan (rs Mar-Jan office closed between 13.00-14.00hrs)

Last arrival 17.00hrs Last departure noon

A large marina site with restaurant facilities, situated on the Trent/Merseyside Canal. Pitches are on grass surrounded by mature trees, and for the keen angler the site offers fishing within the marina. The attractive grass touring area overlooks the marina. 25 acre site. 35 touring pitches. 10 hardstandings. 10 seasonal pitches. Caravan pitches. Motorhome pitches. Tent pitches. 73 statics.

AA Pubs & Restaurants nearby: Old Crown Inn, Shardlow 01332 792392

Priest House Hotel, Castle Donington 0845 072 7502

Facilities: ⬟⊙❄⬥⚑🅱
Services: ⬟⬚⬛⬛⬛⬚⬛⬛⬛
Within 3 miles: ⬛⬛⬛⬚⬚⬚

Notes: Max 2 dogs & 1 child per unit. Dogs must not be left unattended or tied up outside, and must be kept on leads.

Devon

With two magnificent coastlines, two historic
cities and a world-famous national park, Devon
sums up all that is best about the British landscape.
For centuries it has been a fashionable and much-loved
holiday destination – especially south Devon's glorious
English Riviera.

The largest and most famous seaside resort on the southern coast is Torquay, created in the 19th century and still retaining a tangible air of Victorian charm mixed with a pleasing hint of the Mediterranean. Palm trees grace the bustling harbour where colourful yachts and cabin cruisers vie for space and the weather is pleasantly warm and sunny for long hours in the summer.

In and around Torquay

In recent years television and literature have helped to boost Torquay's holiday image. The hotel that was the inspiration for *Fawlty Towers*, starring the incomparable John Cleese, is located in the town, while Agatha Christie, the Queen of Crime, was born and raised in Torquay. A bust of her, unveiled in 1990 to mark the centenary of her birth, stands near the harbour and tourist information centre.

Greenway, Christie's splendid holiday home, now managed by the National Trust and open to the public, lies outside the town, overlooking a glorious sweep of the River Dart. By taking a nostalgic ride on the Paignton and Dartmouth

▶

Steam Railway you can wallow in the world of Poirot and Miss Marple, Christie's famous sleuths, passing close to the house and its glorious grounds.

Dartmoor

One of Agatha Christie's favourite Devon landscapes was Dartmoor. The National Park which contains it covers 365 square miles and includes vast moorland stretches, isolated granite tors and two summits exceeding 2,000 feet. This bleak and brooding landscape is the largest tract of open wilderness left in southern England. More than 100 years ago Sir Arthur Conan Doyle gave Dartmoor something of a boost when he set his classic and most famous Sherlock Holmes' story, *The Hound of the Baskervilles*, in this romantic and adventurous area.

● Sutton Harbour, Plymouth

South Devon

Plymouth lies in Devon's south-west corner and is a fine city and naval port with a wide range of visitor attractions, including the Plymouth Mayflower, overlooking Sutton Harbour, an interactive exhibition explaining the city's history. There is particular emphasis on the Spanish Armada and the voyage of the Pilgrim Fathers to America. The ancient city of Exeter can also occupy many hours of sightseeing. As well as the famous cathedral with its Norman twin towers, there is the Guildhall, which includes a Mayor's Parlour with five original Tudor windows, and the Quay House Visitor Centre where the history of the city is illustrated.

Walking and Cycling

The beauty of Devon, of course, is also appreciated on foot. The Dart Valley Trail offers views of the river at its best, while at Dartmouth you can join the South West Coast Path, renowned for its stunning views and breezy cliff-top walking. The trail heads along the coast to South Hams, a rural farming district where gently rolling hills sweep down to the majestic coastline. One of the area's great landmarks is Salcombe, a bustling fishing port with a magnificent natural harbour.

Another popular trail is the 103-mile (164km) Two Moors Way which begins at Ivybridge and crosses Dartmoor before passing through the delightful hidden landscape of R.D.Blackmoor's classic novel *Lorna Doone* to reach Exmoor, which straddles the Devon/Somerset border. On reaching picturesque Lynton and Lynmouth you can link up with the South Coast Path again to explore north Devon's stunning coastline. Don't miss the Valley of Rocks, an extraordinary

● Clapper Bridge, East Dart River

collection of peaks and outcrops which add a wonderful sense of drama to this stretch of coast.

There are various leaflets and booklets on cycling available from tourist information centres throughout the county. The Dartmoor Way is a great introduction to the National Park with a choice of off-road cycle routes; there is also a range of cycle trails in the Exmoor National Park.

Festivals and Events
- The Ashburton Carnival takes place at Ashburton in early July.
- Chagford has an Agricultural and Flower show in August.
- During July, Honiton hosts a Fair with the Hot Pennies ceremony; in August there is an Agricultural Show and in October a carnival.

DEVON

ASHBURTON Map 3 SX77

Places to visit

Compton Castle, COMPTON 01803 842382 www.nationaltrust.org.uk/devoncornwall

Tuckers Maltings, NEWTON ABBOT 01626 334734 www.tuckersmaltings.com

Great for kids: Prickly Ball Farm and Hedgehog Hospital, NEWTON ABBOT 01626 362319 www.pricklyballfarm.com

AA CAMPING CARD SITE

►►►► 85% River Dart Country Park *(SX734700)*

Holne Park TQ13 7NP
☎ 01364 652511
e-mail: info@riverdart.co.uk
web: www.riverdart.co.uk
dir: *M5 junct 31, A38 towards Plymouth. In Ashburton at Peartree junct follow brown site signs. Site 1m on left. (NB Peartree junct is 2nd exit at Ashburton - do not exit at Linhay junct as narrow roads are unsuitable for caravans)*

* 🚐 £18-£30 🚙 £18-£30 ⛺ £18-£30

Open Apr-Sep (rs Low season café bar restricted opening hours)

Last arrival 21.00hrs Last departure 11.00hrs

Set in 90 acres of magnificent parkland that was once part of a Victorian estate, with many specimen and exotic trees, this peaceful, hidden away touring park occupies several camping areas, all served with good quality toilet facilities. In spring the park is a blaze of colour from the many azaleas and rhododendrons. There are numerous outdoor activities for all ages including abseiling, caving and canoeing, plus high quality, well-maintained facilities. The open moorland of Dartmoor is only a few minutes away. 90 acre site. 170 touring pitches. 23 hardstandings. Caravan pitches. Motorhome pitches. Tent pitches.

AA Pubs & Restaurants nearby: Dartbridge Inn, Buckfastleigh 01364 642214

Agaric, Ashburton 01364 654478

Leisure: 🛝 🎾 🏓

Facilities: 🛁 🚿 ⊙ 💨 ❄ ♿ ✆ $ 🪑 🐕 Wi-fi ♻ ℹ

Services: 🚐 🧺 🍷 🔒 🧪 [T] 🍽 🥡 🧺 ⛽

Within 3 miles: ⛳ 🎣 $ 🧺 U

Notes: Dogs must be kept on leads. Adventure playground, climbing, canoeing.

AA CAMPING CARD SITE

►►►► 84% Parkers Farm Holiday Park *(SX779713)*

Higher Mead Farm TQ13 7LJ
☎ 01364 654869
e-mail: parkersfarm@btconnect.com
dir: *From Exeter on A38, 2nd left after Plymouth/26m sign, signed Woodland & Denbury. From Plymouth on A38 take A383 Newton Abbot exit, turn right across bridge, rejoin A38, then as above*

🚐 £11-£25 🚙 £11-£25 ⛺ £11-£20

Open Etr-end Oct (rs Out of season bar & restaurant open wknds only)

Last arrival 22.00hrs Last departure 10.00hrs

A well-developed site terraced into rising ground with stunning views across rolling countryside to the Dartmoor tors. Part of a working farm, this park offers excellent fully serviced hardstanding pitches, which make the most of the fine views, beautifully maintained and good quality toilet facilities, and a popular games room and a bar/

LEISURE: 🏊 Indoor swimming pool 🏊 Outdoor swimming pool 🛝 Children's playground 👋 Kid's club 🎾 Tennis court 🏓 Games room 📺 Separate TV room ⛳ 9/18 hole golf course ⛵ Boats for hire 🎬 Cinema 🎵 Entertainment 🎣 Fishing ◎ Mini golf 🌊 Watersports 🏋 Gym ⚽ Sports field **Spa** U Stables
FACILITIES: 🛁 Bath 🚿 Shower ⊙ Electric shaver 💨 Hairdryer ❄ Ice Pack Facility ♿ Disabled facilities ✆ Public telephone $ Shop on site or within 200yds 🚚 Mobile shop (calls at least 5 days a week) 🍖 BBQ area 🪑 Picnic area Wi-fi Wi-fi 💻 Internet access ♻ Recycling ℹ Tourist info 🐕 Dog exercise area

restaurant that serves excellent meals. Large family rooms with two shower cubicles, a large sink and a toilet are especially appreciated by families with small children. There are regular farm walks when all the family can meet and feed the various animals. 25 acre site. 100 touring pitches. 20 hardstandings. Caravan pitches. Motorhome pitches. Tent pitches. 18 statics.

AA Pubs & Restaurants nearby: Dartbridge Inn, Buckfastleigh 01364 642214

Agaric, Ashburton 01364 654478

Leisure: 🅐💥🐕🔍⬜♫

Facilities: 📵⊙💥🖐🌡️🅢🗑️🏪⛟

Services: 🔌🅢🍽️🛢️🚿🅣🍴🛒🛄🛒⛽

Within 3 miles: 🏌️🅢🅢

Notes: Large field for dog walking.

AXMINSTER
Map 4 SY29

Places to visit

Branscombe - The Old Bakery, Manor Mill and Forge, BRANSCOMBE 01752 346585 www.nationaltrust.org.uk

Allhallows Museum, HONITON 01404 44966 www.honitonmuseum.co.uk

Great for kids: Pecorama Pleasure Gardens, BEER 01297 21542 www.pecorama.info

►►►► 83% Andrewshayes Caravan Park (ST248088)

Dalwood EX13 7DY
☎ **01404 831225**
e-mail: info@andrewshayes.co.uk
web: www.andrewshayes.co.uk
dir: *3m from Axminster (towards Honiton) on A35, right at Taunton Cross signed Dalwood & Stockland. Site 150mtrs on right*

* 🚐 £14-£22 🚐 £14-£22 ▲ £14-£22

Open Mar-Nov (rs Sep-Nov shop, bar hours limited, pool closed Sep-mid May)

Last arrival 22.00hrs Last departure 11.00hrs

An attractive family park within easy reach of Lyme Regis, Seaton, Branscombe and Sidmouth in an ideal touring location. This popular park offers modern toilet facilities, an outdoor swimming pool and a quiet, cosy bar with a wide-screen TV. 12 acre site. 150 touring pitches. 105 hardstandings. 100 seasonal pitches. Caravan pitches. Motorhome pitches. Tent pitches. 80 statics.

AA Pubs & Restaurants nearby: Tuckers Arms, Dalwood 01404 881342

Leisure: 🏊🅐⚽🔍⬜

Facilities: 📵⊙💥🖐🌡️🅢🗑️🏪♿🛒🗑️❓

Services: 🔌🅢🍽️🛢️🚿🛄🛒🛒

Within 3 miles: 🏌️🅢🅢

Notes: Dogs must be kept on leads.

AA CAMPING CARD SITE

►►► 81% Hawkchurch Country Park
(SY344985)

Hawkchurch EX13 5UL
☎ **08442 729502**
e-mail: enquiries@hawkchurchpark.co.uk
dir: *From Axminster towards Charmouth on A35 left onto B3165. Left into Wareham Rd, site on left, follow signs. (NB the lanes near Hawkchurch are narrow)*

🚐 🚐 ▲

Open 15 Feb-4 Jan

Last arrival 21.00hrs Last departure 10.00hrs

This peaceful park is set in mature woodlands right on the Devon and Dorset border, with easy access to the Jurassic Coast Heritage Site, Lyme Regis, Charmouth and West Bay. The site has huge potential, with hardstandings plus tent and rally fields. 30 acre site. 369 touring pitches. 225 hardstandings. Caravan pitches. Motorhome pitches. Tent pitches.

AA Pubs & Restaurants nearby: The Mariners, Lyme Regis 01297 442753

Pilot Boat Inn, Lyme Regis 01297 443157

Leisure: 🅐🔍♫

Facilities: 📵⊙💥🖐🌡️🅢🛒❓

Services: 🔌🅢🍽️🛢️🚿🅣🍴

Within 3 miles: 🏌️🍴🎣🏌️◎🛥️🅢🅢

Notes: Quiet period 22.00hrs-08.00hrs. Dogs must be kept on leads.

BERRYNARBOR
Map 3 SS54

Places to visit

Arlington Court, ARLINGTON 01271 850296 www.nationaltrust.org.uk/main/w-arlingtoncourt

Exmoor Zoological Park, BLACKMOOR GATE 01598 763352 www.exmoorzoo.co.uk

Great for kids: Combe Martin Wildlife Park & Dinosaur Park, COMBE MARTIN 01271 882486 www.dinosaur-park.com

►►► 84% Mill Park (SS559471)

Mill Ln EX34 9SH
☎ **01271 882647**
e-mail: millparkdevon@btconnect.com
dir: *M5 junct 27, A361 towards Barnstaple. Right onto A399 towards Combe Martin. At Sawmills Inn take turn opposite Berrynarbor sign*

* 🚐 £7-£22 🚐 £7-£22 ▲ £6.50-£22

Open Mar-30 Oct (rs Low season on-site facilities closed)

Last arrival 22.00hrs Last departure 10.00hrs

This family owned and run park is set in an attractive wooded valley with a stream running into a lake where coarse fishing is available. There is a quiet bar/restaurant with a family room, and the park now has two lakeside cocoons and a four bedroom apartment for hire. The park is two miles from Combe Martin and Ilfracombe and just a stroll across the road from the small harbour at Watermouth. 23 acre site. 178 touring pitches. 20 hardstandings. Caravan pitches. Motorhome pitches. Tent pitches. 2 wooden pods.

AA Pubs & Restaurants nearby: George & Dragon, Ilfracombe 01271 863851

11 The Quay, Ilfracombe 01271 868090

Leisure: 🅐🔍

Facilities: 📵⊙💥🖐🌡️🅢🗑️🛒❓🖥️🗑️❓

Services: 🔌🅢🍽️🛢️🚿🅣🍴🛒

Within 3 miles: 🏌️🍴📅🏌️◎🛥️🅢🅢∪

Notes: No large groups. Beauty therapy room.

BICKINGTON (NEAR ASHBURTON) Map 3 SX87

Places to visit

Bradley Manor, NEWTON ABBOT 01803 843235
www.nationaltrust.org.uk/devoncornwall

Great for kids: Living Coasts, TORQUAY
01803 202470 www.livingcoasts.org.uk

►►►► 81% Lemonford Caravan Park (SX793723)

TQ12 6JR
☎ **01626 821242**
e-mail: info@lemonford.co.uk
web: www.lemonford.co.uk
dir: From Exeter on A38 take A382, then 3rd exit at rdbt, follow Bickington signs

* ⊞ £13.50-£22.50 ⇔ £13.50-£22.50
▲ £13.50-£20.50

Open all year

Last arrival 22.00hrs Last departure 11.00hrs

Small, secluded and well-maintained park with a good mixture of attractively laid out pitches. The friendly owners pay a great deal of attention to detail, and the toilets in particular are kept spotlessly clean. This good touring base is only one mile from Dartmoor and ten miles from the seaside at Torbay. The bus to Exeter, Plymouth and Torbay stops outside the park. 7 acre site. 82 touring pitches. 55 hardstandings. Caravan pitches. Motorhome pitches. Tent pitches. 44 statics.

AA Pubs & Restaurants nearby: Wild Goose Inn, Combeinteignhead 01626 872241

Agaric, Ashburton 01364 654478

Lemonford Caravan Park

Leisure: ⚊

Facilities: ⚊🚿⊙☂✳🛁🅂🅰♻🛈

Services: 🖲🗑🔌📺🛒🖳

Within 3 miles: ♨🎣🅂🛒🖳U

Notes: No noise after 23.00hrs. Dogs must be kept on leads. Clothes drying area.

see advert on opposite page

BRAUNTON Map 3 SS43

Places to visit

Marwood Hill Gardens, BARNSTAPLE
01271 342528 www.marwoodhillgarden.co.uk

Great for kids: Combe Martin Wildlife Park & Dinosaur Park, COMBE MARTIN 01271 882486
www.dinosaur-park.com

PREMIER PARK
►►►►► 85% Hidden Valley Park (SS499408)

Best of British

West Down EX34 8NU
☎ **01271 813837**
dir: Direct access from A361, 8m from Barnstaple & 2m from Mullacott Cross

⊞ £9-£37 ⇔ £9-£37 ▲ £9-£40

Open all year

Last arrival 21.00hrs Last departure 10.30hrs

A delightful, well-appointed family site set in a wooded valley, with superb facilities and a café. The park is set in a very rural, natural location not far from the beautiful coastline around Ilfracombe. The woodland is now home to nesting buzzards and woodpeckers, and otters have taken up residence by the lake. Wi-fi is now available. There are three fully equipped timber cabins for hire. 32 acre site. 100 touring pitches. 50 hardstandings. 15 seasonal pitches. Caravan pitches. Motorhome pitches. Tent pitches. 3 statics.

AA Pubs & Restaurants nearby: The Williams Arms, Braunton 01271 812360

Leisure: ⚊

Facilities: ⚊🚿⊙☂✳🛁🅂🅰♻🛈

Services: 🖲🗑🔌🛒🖳

Within 3 miles: ♨🎣🅂🛒🖳U

►►► 79% Lobb Fields Caravan & Camping Park (SS475378)

Saunton Rd EX33 1HG
☎ **01271 812090**
e-mail: info@lobbfields.com
dir: At x-rds in Braunton take B3231 to Croyde. Site signed on right leaving Braunton

* ⊞ £12-£28 ⇔ £12-£28 ▲ £11-£28

Open 22 Mar-3 Nov

Last arrival 22.00hrs Last departure 10.30hrs

A bright, tree-lined park with the gently-sloping grass pitches divided into two open areas and a camping field in August. Braunton is an easy walk away, and the golden beaches of Saunton Sands and Croyde are within easy reach. 14 acre site. 180 touring pitches. 6 hardstandings. Caravan pitches. Motorhome pitches. Tent pitches.

AA Pubs & Restaurants nearby: The Williams Arms, Braunton 01271 812360

Leisure: ⚊

Facilities: 🚿⊙☂✳🛁🅂♻🛈

Services: 🖲🗑🔌🛒🖳

Within 3 miles: ♨🎣🅂🛒🖳U

Notes: No under 18s unless accompanied by an adult. Dogs must be kept on leads. Surfing, boards & wet suits for hire, wet suit washing areas.

LEISURE: 🏊 Indoor swimming pool 🏊 Outdoor swimming pool ⚊ Children's playground 🪁 Kid's club 🎾 Tennis court 🎱 Games room ▢ Separate TV room ⛳ 9/18 hole golf course ⛵ Boats for hire 🎬 Cinema 🎵 Entertainment 🎣 Fishing ◎ Mini golf 🏄 Watersports 🏋 Gym 🅂 Sports field Spa U Stables
FACILITIES: 🛁 Bath 🚿 Shower ⊙ Electric shaver ☂ Hairdryer ✳ Ice Pack Facility 🛁 Disabled facilities ☎ Public telephone 🅂 Shop on site or within 200yds 🛒 Mobile shop (calls at least 5 days a week) 🍖 BBQ area 🅰 Picnic area 🖳 Wi-fi 🖳 Internet access ♻ Recycling 🛈 Tourist info 🐕 Dog exercise area

BRIDESTOWE — Map 3 SX58

Places to visit

Lydford Castle and Saxon Town, LYDFORD
0870 333 1181 www.english-heritage.org.uk

Museum of Dartmoor Life,
OKEHAMPTON 01837 52295
www.museumofdartmoorlife.eclipse.co.uk

Great for kids: Tamar Otter & Wildlife Centre,
LAUNCESTON 01566 785646
www.tamarotters.co.uk

►►► 75% Bridestowe Caravan Park

(SX519893)

EX20 4ER
☎ 01837 861261
e-mail: ali.young53@btinternet.com
dir: *Exit A30 at A386/Sourton Cross junct, follow B3278 signed Bridestowe, left in 3m. In village centre, left down unclassified road for 0.5m*

✱ ⚏ £13-£18 ⚏ £13-£18 ▲ £10-£15

Open Mar-Dec

Last arrival 22.30hrs Last departure noon

A small, well-established park in a rural setting close to Dartmoor National Park. This mainly static park has a small, peaceful touring space, and there are many activities to enjoy in the area including fishing and riding. Part of the National Cycle Route 27 - the Devon coast to coast - passes close to this park. 1 acre site. 13 touring pitches. 3 hardstandings. Caravan pitches. Motorhome pitches. Tent pitches. 40 statics.

AA Pubs & Restaurants nearby: Highwayman Inn, Sourton 01837 861243

Lewtrenchard Manor, Lewdown 01566 783222

Leisure: ⛰ 🎣 Facilities: 🐕 ☉ ✳ 🅂 ♻ ❶
Services: ⊞ 🅂 🛢 ⟋ 🅃 🔋
Within 3 miles: 🎣 🅂 🅂

Notes: ⊗ Dogs must be kept on leads.

BRIDGERULE — Map 2 SS20

AA CAMPING CARD SITE

►►► 82% Hedleywood Caravan & Camping Park *(SS262013)*

EX22 7ED
☎ 01288 381404
e-mail: alan@hedleywood.co.uk
dir: *M5 south to Exeter, A30 to Launceston, B3254 towards Bude. Left into Tackbear Rd signed Marhamchurch & Widemouth (at Devon/Cornwall border). Site on right*

✱ ⚏ £13.50-£20 ⚏ £13.50-£20 ▲ £13.50-£20

Open all year (rs Main hols bar & restaurant open)

Last arrival anytime Last departure anytime

Set in a very rural location about four miles from Bude, this relaxed family-owned site has a peaceful, easy-going atmosphere. Pitches are in separate paddocks, some with extensive views, and this wooded park is quite sheltered in the lower areas. The refurbished restaurant/club house is a popular place to relax. 16.5 acre site. 120 touring pitches. 30 hardstandings. Caravan pitches. Motorhome pitches. Tent pitches. 16 statics.

AA Pubs & Restaurants nearby: The Bickford Arms, Holsworthy 01409 221318

Bay View Inn, Widemouth Bay 01288 361273

Hedleywood Caravan & Camping Park

Leisure: ⛰ 🎣 ▢
Facilities: 🐕 ☉ 🄿 ✳ 🕭 🕓 🅂 🚻 🛶 Ⓦ 🖥 ♻ ❶
Services: ⊞ 🅂 🍽 🛢 ⟋ 🅃 🍴 🔋 🛒 ⚡
Within 3 miles: 🎣 🅂 🅂 ♻

Notes: ⊗ Dogs must be kept on leads. Dog kennels, nature trail & dog walk, caravan storage.

BRIDGERULE *continued*

►► 89% Highfield House Camping & Caravanning (SS279035)

Holsworthy EX22 7EE
☎ 01288 381480
e-mail: njt@btinternet.com
dir: *Exit A3072 at Red Post x-rds onto B3254 towards Launceston. Direct access just over Devon border on right*

🚐 🚙 Å

Open all year

Set in a quiet and peaceful rural location, this park has extensive views over the valley to the sea at Bude, five miles away. The friendly owners, with children of their own, offer a relaxing holiday for families, with the simple facilities carefully looked after. 4 acre site. 20 touring pitches. Caravan pitches. Motorhome pitches. Tent pitches. 8 statics.

AA Pubs & Restaurants nearby: The Bickford Arms, Holsworthy 01409 221318

Bay View Inn, Widemouth Bay 01288 361273

Facilities: 📵 ☉ ✳ ♿ 🛒 ♻

Services: 📞 🔄

Within 3 miles: ⌇ ≑ 日 𝒫 ◎ ≋ 🛒 🔄 ∪

Notes: 🐾 Dogs must be kept on leads.

BRIXHAM	Map 3 SX95

Places to visit

Greenway, CHURSTON FERRERS 01803 842382 www.nationaltrust.org.uk/devoncornwall

Great for kids: Paignton Zoo Environmental Park, PAIGNTON 0844 474 2222 www.paigntonzoo.org.uk

AA CAMPING CARD SITE

►►►► 79% Galmpton Touring Park (SX885558)

Greenway Rd TQ5 0EP
☎ 01803 842066
e-mail: enquiries@galmptontouringpark.co.uk
dir: *Signed from A3022 (Torbay to Brixham road) at Churston*

* 🚐 £13-£28 🚙 £13-£28 Å £13-£21.50

Open May-Sep

Last arrival 21.00hrs Last departure 11.00hrs

Experienced owners run this stunningly located site, set on high ground overlooking the River Dart and with outstanding views of the creek and anchorage. The park looks smart and pitches are set on level terraces. The toilet block has been upgraded to provide good quality amenities. 10 acre site. 120 touring pitches. 15 hardstandings. Caravan pitches. Motorhome pitches. Tent pitches.

AA Pubs & Restaurants nearby: Quayside Hotel, Brixham 01803 855751

Leisure: ⚠

Facilities: 📵 ☉ 𝒫 ✳ ♿ 🛒 🎪 ♻ **ℹ**

Services: 📞 🔄 🔒 ⊘ 🖥 ⬇

Within 3 miles: ⌇ ≑ 日 𝒫 ◎ ≋ 🛒 🔄

Notes: Families & couples only, no dogs during peak season. Late arrival time requires prior notice. Dogs must be kept on leads. Bathroom for under 5s (charges apply). Free Wi-Fi in local pub.

BROADWOODWIDGER	Map 3 SX48

Places to visit

Museum of Dartmoor Life, OKEHAMPTON 01837 52295 www.museumofdartmoorlife.eclipse.co.uk

Finch Foundry, STICKLEPATH 01837 840046 www.nationaltrust.org.uk

►►► 77% *Roadford Lake* (SX421900)

Lower Goodacre PL16 0JL
☎ 01409 211507
e-mail: info@swlakestrust.org.uk
dir: *Exit A30 between Okehampton & Launceston at Roadford Lake signs, across dam wall, site 0.25m on right*

🚐 🚙 Å

Open Apr-Oct

Located right at the edge of Devon's largest inland water, this popular rural park is well screened by mature trees and shrubs. It boasts a good toilet block and an excellent watersports school (sailing, windsurfing, rowing and kayaking) with hire and day launch facilities, and is an ideal location for fly fishing for brown trout. Plans include running a ferry service to the excellent café/restaurant on the opposite side of the lake. One yurt is available for hire. 1.5 acre site. 30 touring pitches. 4 hardstandings. Caravan pitches. Motorhome pitches. Tent pitches.

AA Pubs & Restaurants nearby: Arundell Arms, Lifton 01566 784666

Facilities: 📵 ☉ 𝒫 ✳ ♿ 🛒 ♻ **ℹ**

Services: 📞 🔄 🍽

Within 3 miles: ≑ 𝒫 ≋ 🛒

Notes: Dogs must be kept on leads.

BUCKFASTLEIGH	Map 3 SX76

Places to visit

Buckfast Abbey, BUCKFASTLEIGH 01364 645500 www.buckfast.org.uk

Great for kids: Buckfast Butterfly Farm & Dartmoor Otter Sanctuary, BUCKFASTLEIGH 01364 642916 www.ottersandbutterflies.co.uk

► 88% Churchill Farm Campsite (SX743664)

TQ11 0EZ
☎ 01364 642844 & 07964 730578
e-mail: apedrick@btinternet.com
dir: *From A38 Dart Bridge exit for Buckfastleigh/ Totnes towards Buckfast Abbey. Pass Abbey entrance, up hill, left at x-roads to site opposite Holy Trinity Church*

🚐 🚙 Å

Open Etr-Sep

Last arrival 22.00hrs

A working family farm in a relaxed and peaceful setting, with keen, friendly owners. Set on the hills above Buckfast Abbey, this attractive park is maintained to a good standard. The spacious pitches in the neatly trimmed paddock enjoy extensive country views towards Dartmoor, and the clean, simple toilet facilities include smart showers. This is a hidden gem for those who love traditional camping. Close to a local bus service and within walking distance of Buckfastleigh, the Abbey and the South Devon Steam Railway. 3 acre site. 25 touring pitches. Caravan pitches. Motorhome pitches. Tent pitches.

AA Pubs & Restaurants nearby: Dartbridge Inn, Buckfastleigh 01364 642214

Facilities: 📵 ☉ ✳ ♿ ♻ **ℹ**

Services: 📞 🛒

Within 3 miles: 🛒

Notes: 🐾 No ball games. Dogs must be kept on leads. Within a Site of Special Scientific Interest.

LEISURE: 🏊 Indoor swimming pool 🏊 Outdoor swimming pool ⚠ Children's playground 👶 Kid's club 🎾 Tennis court 🎱 Games room 📺 Separate TV room ⌇ 9/18 hole golf course ⚓ Boats for hire 🎬 Cinema 🎵 Entertainment 𝒫 Fishing ◎ Mini golf ≋ Watersports 💪 Gym ⚽ Sports field Spa ∪ Stables
FACILITIES: 🛁 Bath 🚿 Shower ☉ Electric shaver 𝒫 Hairdryer ✳ Ice Pack Facility ♿ Disabled facilities ☎ Public telephone 🛒 Shop on site or within 200yds 🛒 Mobile shop (calls at least 5 days a week) 🍖 BBQ area 🎪 Picnic area 📶 Wi-fi ■ Internet access ♻ Recycling ℹ Tourist info 🐾 Dog exercise area

► 84% Beara Farm Caravan & Camping Site *(SX751645)*

Colston Rd TQ11 0LW
☎ 01364 642234
dir: *From Exeter take Buckfastleigh exit at Dart Bridge, follow South Devon Steam Railway/ Butterfly Farm signs. 200mtrs past entrance to South Devon Steam Railway 1st left into Old Totnes Rd, 0.5m right at red brick cottages signed Beara Farm. Approx 1m to site*

🚃 🚐 ⛺

Open all year

A very good farm park with clean unisex facilities and very keen and friendly owners. A well-trimmed camping field offers peace and quiet. Close to the River Dart and the Dart Valley steam railway line, within easy reach of the sea and moors. Please note that the approach to the site is narrow, with passing places, and care needs to be taken. 3.63 acre site. 30 touring pitches. 1 hardstanding. Caravan pitches. Motorhome pitches. Tent pitches.

AA Pubs & Restaurants nearby: Dartbridge Inn, Buckfastleigh 01364 642214

Facilities: 🚿 ⊙ ✲ 🪑 🐕 ♻

Services: 🔋

Within 3 miles: 🎣 [S]

Notes: 💳 Dogs must be kept on leads.

BUDLEIGH SALTERTON	Map 3 SY08

Places to visit

Otterton Mill, OTTERTON 01395 568521 www.ottertonmill.com

Great for kids: Bicton Park Botanical Gardens, BICTON 01395 568465 www.bictongardens.co.uk

AA CAMPING CARD SITE

►►► 80% Pooh Cottage Holiday Park *(SY053831)*

Bear Ln EX9 7AQ
☎ 01395 442354 & 07875 685595
e-mail: info@poohcottage.co.uk
web: www.poohcottage.co.uk
dir: *M5 junct 30, A376 towards Exmouth. Left onto B3179 towards Woodbury & Budleigh Salterton. Left into Knowle onto B3178. Through village, at brow of hill take sharp left into Bear Lane. Site 200yds*

🚃 🚐 ⛺

Open 15 Mar-Oct

Last arrival 21.00hrs Last departure 11.30hrs

A rural park with widespread views of the sea and surrounding peaceful countryside. Expect a friendly welcome to this attractive site, with its lovely play area, and easy access to plenty of walks, as well as the Buzzard Cycle Way. On site cycle hire, and there's a bus stop within walking distance. 8 acre site. 10 touring pitches. 45 seasonal pitches. Caravan pitches. Motorhome pitches. Tent pitches. 3 statics.

AA Pubs & Restaurants nearby: The Blue Ball, Sidford 01395 514062

Salty Monk, Sidford 01395 513174

Leisure: 🛝

Facilities: 🚿 ⊙ ✲ ♿ 🪑 🐕 [Wi-fi] ♻ ℹ

Services: 🔌 🧺 🛢 🔥 [T]

Within 3 miles: ⛳ ⛵ 🏋 🎣 🎯 🏄 [S] 🧺 🐎

Notes: Dogs must be kept on leads. Cycle track, bike hire.

CHAPMANS WELL	Map 3 SX39

Places to visit

Launceston Steam Railway, LAUNCESTON 01566 775665 www.launcestonsr.co.uk

Launceston Castle, LAUNCESTON 01566 772365 www.english-heritage.org.uk

Great for kids: Tamar Otter & Wildlife Centre, LAUNCESTON 01566 785646 www.tamarotters.co.uk

AA CAMPING CARD SITE

►►► 84% Chapmanswell Caravan Park *(SX354931)*

St Giles-on-the-Heath PL15 9SG
☎ 01409 211382
e-mail: george@chapmanswellcaravanpark.co.uk
web: www.chapmanswellcaravanpark.co.uk
dir: *Take A338 from Launceston towards Holsworthy, 6m. Site on left at Chapmans Well*

* 🚃 £13.50-£18 🚐 £13.50-£18 ⛺ £10.50-£25.50

Open all year

Last arrival anytime (by prior agreement) Last departure anytime (by prior agreement)

Set on the borders of Devon and Cornwall in peaceful countryside, this park is just waiting to be discovered. It enjoys extensive views towards Dartmoor from level pitches, and is within easy driving distance of Launceston (7 miles) and the golden beaches at Bude (14 miles). 10 acre site. 50 touring pitches. 35 hardstandings. 32 seasonal pitches. Caravan pitches. Motorhome pitches. Tent pitches. 50 statics.

AA Pubs & Restaurants nearby: The Bickford Arms, Holsworthy 01409 221318

Blagdon Manor, Ashwater 01409 211224

Leisure: 🛝 ♫

Facilities: 🚿 ⊙ ✲ ♿ [S] [Wi-fi] ♻ ℹ

Services: 🔌 🧺 🍷 🛢 🔥 [T] 🍴 🔋 🍔 🚰

Within 3 miles: ⛳ ⛵ 🎣 🏄 [S] 🧺 🐎

Notes: Dogs must be kept on leads.

CHUDLEIGH — Map 3 SX87

Places to visit

Canonteign Falls, CHUDLEIGH 01647 252434
www.canonteignfalls.co.uk

Exeter's Underground Passages, EXETER
01392 665887 www.exeter.gov.uk/passages

Great for kids: Prickly Ball Farm and Hedgehog
Hospital, NEWTON ABBOT 01626 362319
www.pricklyballfarm.com

►►► 83% Holmans Wood Holiday Park (SX881812)

Harcombe Cross TQ13 0DZ
☎ **01626 853785**
e-mail: enquiries@holmanswood.co.uk
dir: *M5 junct 31, A38. After racecourse at top of Haldon Hill left at BP petrol station signed Chudleigh, site entrance on left of slip road*

* ♠ £19-£25 ♠ £19-£25 ▲ £12-£16

Open mid Mar-end Oct

Last arrival 22.00hrs Last departure 11.00hrs

A delightful small park set back from the A38 in a secluded wooded area, handy for touring Dartmoor National Park, and the lanes and beaches of South Devon. The facilities are bright and clean, and the grounds are attractively landscaped. 12 acre site. 73 touring pitches. 71 hardstandings. Caravan pitches. Motorhome pitches. Tent pitches. 34 statics.

AA Pubs & Restaurants nearby: The Cridford Inn, Trusham 01626 853694

Leisure: ⚠
Facilities: ↖⊙℗✳❄⚒☉☎wifi ❶
Services: 🔌🔋💧∅
Within 3 miles: 🍴🛒U
Notes: No pets.

CLYST ST MARY — Map 3 SX99

Places to visit

Exeter Cathedral, EXETER 01392 285983
www.exeter-cathedral.org.uk

Exeter's Underground Passages, EXETER
01392 665887 www.exeter.gov.uk/passages

Great for kids: Crealy Adventure Park, CLYST ST MARY 01395 233200 www.crealy.co.uk

The World of Country Life, EXMOUTH
01395 274533 www.worldofcountrylife.co.uk

PREMIER PARK

NEW ►►►►► 82% Crealy Meadows Caravan and Camping Park (SY001906)

Sidmouth Rd EX5 1DR
☎ **01395 234888**
e-mail: stay@crealymeadows.co.uk
dir: *M5 junct 30, A3052 signed Exmouth. At rdbt take A3052 signed Seaton. Follow brown Crealy Great Adventure Park signs. Turn right*

* ♠ £22.50 ♠ £22.50 ▲ £17.50

Open Mar-Oct

Last arrival 22.00hrs Last departure 10.00hrs

A brand new quality park with excellent toilet facilities, spacious fully serviced pitches and good security, adjacent to the popular Crealy Adventure Park, with free or discounted entry available for all campers. The park is within a short drive of Exeter and the seaside attractions at Sidmouth. Free Wi-Fi is available and free kennels can be used on request. Pre-erected luxury safari tents are for hire, and also in the Camelot Village there are medieval pavillion tents for a real glamping holiday. For children there is a unique 'own pony' experience. 14.65 acre site. 120 touring pitches. 21 hardstandings. Caravan pitches. Motorhome pitches. Tent pitches. 18 bell tents/yurts.

AA Pubs & Restaurants nearby: Black Horse Inn, Sowton 01392 366649

Bridge Inn, Topsham 01392 873862

Leisure: ⚠ ⊕ ♫
Facilities: ↖℗⚒☉🍴🚿❄wifi 🖥 ♻ ❶
Services: 🔌🔋🚰💧∅T🍽♨🚮
Within 3 miles: 🌳🏌️🍴🛒
Notes: Dogs must be kept on leads.

COMBE MARTIN — Map 3 SS54

See also Berrynarbor

Places to visit

Arlington Court, ARLINGTON 01271 850296
www.nationaltrust.org.uk/main/w-arlingtoncourt

Great for kids: Combe Martin Wildlife Park & Dinosaur Park, COMBE MARTIN 01271 882486
www.dinosaur-park.com

►►►► 88% Stowford Farm Meadows (SS560427)

Berry Down EX34 0PW
☎ **01271 882476**
e-mail: enquiries@stowford.co.uk
dir: *M5 junct 27, A361 to Barnstaple. Take A39 from town centre towards Lynton, in 1m left onto B3230. Right at garage at Lynton Cross onto A3123, site 1.5m on right*

* ♠ £8.90-£23.20 ♠ £9.90-£24.20
▲ £8.90-£23.20

Open all year (rs Some of winter bars & catering closed)

Last arrival 20.00hrs Last departure 10.00hrs

Very gently sloping, grassy, sheltered and south-facing site approached down a wide, well-kept driveway. This large farm park is set in 500 acres, and offers many quality amenities, including a large swimming pool, horse riding and crazy golf. A 60-acre wooded nature trail is an added attraction, as is the mini zoo with its stock of friendly animals. 100 acre site. 700 touring pitches. 115 hardstandings. Caravan pitches. Motorhome pitches. Tent pitches.

AA Pubs & Restaurants nearby: George & Dragon, Ilfracombe 01271 863851

Fox & Goose, Parracombe 01598 763239

11 The Quay, Ilfracombe 01271 868090

Leisure: 🏊⚠⊕♣♫
Facilities: 🛁↖⊙℗✳❄⚒☉🍴🐾wifi ♻ ❶
Services: 🔌🔋🚰💧🍴∅T🍽♨⛟♨
Within 3 miles: 🏌️🎣◎🍴🛒U
Notes: Dogs must be kept on leads. Caravan accessory shop, storage, workshop & sales.

LEISURE: 🏊 Indoor swimming pool ⚐ Outdoor swimming pool ⚠ Children's playground 🚩 Kid's club ⚲ Tennis court ♣ Games room ▭ Separate TV room ⚑ 9/18 hole golf course ⚓ Boats for hire 🎬 Cinema ♫ Entertainment ℘ Fishing ◎ Mini golf ⚓ Watersports 🏋 Gym ⊕ Sports field Spa U Stables
FACILITIES: 🛁 Bath ↖ Shower ⊙ Electric shaver ℘ Hairdryer ✳ Ice Pack Facility ❄ Disabled facilities ☉ Public telephone 🍴 Shop on site or within 200yds 🏪 Mobile shop (calls at least 5 days a week) 🍖 BBQ area 🔥 Picnic area wifi Wi-fi 🖥 Internet access ♻ Recycling ❶ Tourist info 🐾 Dog exercise area

AA CAMPING CARD SITE

►►►► 85% Newberry Valley Park (SS576473)

GOLD

Woodlands EX34 0AT
☎ 01271 882334
e-mail: relax@newberryvalleypark.co.uk
dir: M5 junct 27, A361 to North Aller rdbt. Right onto A399, through Combe Martin to sea. Left into site

🚐 £15-£38 🚙 £15-£38 ⛺ £12-£38

Open Apr-Oct

Last arrival 20.45hrs (dusk in winter) Last departure 10.00hrs

A family owned and run touring park on the edge of Combe Martin, with all its amenities just a five-minute walk away. The park is set in a wooded valley with its own coarse fishing lake and has a stunning toilet block with underfloor heating and excellent unisex privacy cubicles. The safe beaches of Newberry and Combe Martin are reached by a short footpath opposite the park entrance, where the South West Coast Path is located. 20 acre site. 120 touring pitches. 18 hardstandings. 20 seasonal pitches. Caravan pitches. Motorhome pitches. Tent pitches.

AA Pubs & Restaurants nearby: George & Dragon, Ilfracombe 01271 863851

Fox & Goose, Parracombe 01598 763239

11 The Quay, Ilfracombe 01271 868090

Leisure: ⛰

Facilities: ⛽📶☉🅿✳♿🛉🕙🕹🚿🐕🔄ℹ

Services: 🔌🗑 T 🔋

Within 3 miles: ⚓🎣🛒🗑🗑

Notes: No camp fires. Dogs must be kept on leads.

CROYDE — Map 3 SS43

Places to visit

Marwood Hill Gardens, BARNSTAPLE 01271 342528 www.marwoodhillgarden.co.uk

Great for kids: Watermouth Castle & Family Theme Park, ILFRACOMBE 01271 863879 www.watermouthcastle.com

►►► 80% Bay View Farm Caravan & Camping Park (SS443388)

EX33 1PN
☎ 01271 890501
dir: M5 junct 27, A361, through Barnstaple to Braunton, left onto B3231. Site at entry to Croyde village

🚐 🚙 ⛺

Open Mar-Oct

Last arrival 21.30hrs Last departure 11.00hrs

A very busy and popular park close to surfing beaches and rock pools, with a public footpath leading directly to the sea. Set in a stunning location with views out over the Atlantic to Lundy Island, it is just a short stroll from Croyde. Facilities are clean and well maintained; a family bathroom is available. There is a fish and chip shop on site. Please note that no dogs are allowed. 10 acre site. 70 touring pitches. 38 hardstandings. 10 seasonal pitches. Caravan pitches. Motorhome pitches. Tent pitches. 3 statics.

AA Pubs & Restaurants nearby: The Williams Arms, Braunton 01271 812360

George & Dragon, Ilfracombe 01271 863851

11 The Quay, Ilfracombe 01271 868090

Leisure: ⛰

Facilities: 📶☉🅿✳♿🕙🔄ℹ

Services: 🔌🗑🪫⚡ T 🍴🔋🏪

Within 3 miles: ⚓🎠🚲◎🛒🗑🗑⛳

Notes: 🚫🐕

CROYDE BAY — Map 3 SS43

84% Ruda Holiday Park (SS438397)

GOLD

EX33 1NY
☎ 0844 335 3756
e-mail: touringandcamping@parkdeanholidays.com
web: www.parkdeantouring.com
dir: M5 junct 27, A361 to Braunton. Left at main lights, follow Croyde signs

✱ 🚐 £15-£47 🚙 £15-£47 ⛺ £12-£44

Open mid Mar-Oct

Last arrival 21.00hrs Last departure 10.00hrs

A spacious, well-managed park with its own glorious award-winning sandy beach, a surfer's paradise. Set in well-landscaped grounds, and with a full leisure programme plus daytime and evening entertainment for all the family. Cascades tropical adventure pool and an entertainment lounge are very popular features. The local bus stops outside the park. 220 acre site. 312 touring pitches. Caravan pitches. Motorhome pitches. Tent pitches. 312 statics.

AA Pubs & Restaurants nearby: The Williams Arms, Braunton 01271 812360

George & Dragon, Ilfracombe 01271 863851

11 The Quay, Ilfracombe 01271 868090

Leisure: 🏊⛰♨🎮♣🔴🎱🎯🎵

Facilities: ⛽📶☉🅿✳♿🕙🔄🚿 WiFi

Services: 🔌🗑🪫⚡⚡🍴🔋🏪

Within 3 miles: 🎣🗑🗑⛳

Notes: No pets. Children's clubs, Coast Bar & Kitchen.

CULLOMPTON

See Kentisbeare

DARTMOUTH Map 3 SX85

Places to visit

Dartmouth Castle, DARTMOUTH 01803 833588 www.english-heritage.org.uk

Coleton Fishacre House & Garden, KINGSWEAR 01803 752466 www.nationaltrust.org.uk

Great for kids: Woodlands Family Theme Park, DARTMOUTH 01803 712598 www.woodlandspark.com

AA CAMPING CARD SITE

PREMIER PARK

►►►►► 89% Woodlands Grove Caravan & Camping Park *(SX813522)*

Blackawton TQ9 7DQ
☎ 01803 712598
e-mail: holiday@woodlandsgrove.com
web: www.woodlands-caravanpark.com
dir: *4m from Dartmouth on A3122. From A38 take turn for Totnes & follow brown tourist signs*

* 🚃 £13.50-£23 🚐 £13.50-£23 ⛺ £13.50-£23

Open 22 Mar-3 Nov

Last departure 11.00hrs

A quality caravan or tent park with smart toilet facilities (including excellent family rooms), spacious pitches, including decent hardstandings, and good attention to detail throughout, all set in an extensive woodland environment with a terraced grass camping area. Free entry to the adjoining Woodlands Theme Park makes an excellent package holiday for families, but also good for adults travelling without children who are perhaps seeking a low season break. 16 acre site. 350 touring pitches. 113 hardstandings. Caravan pitches. Motorhome pitches. Tent pitches.

AA Pubs & Restaurants nearby: The Seahorse, Dartmouth 01803 835147

Jan and Freddies Brasserie, Dartmouth 01803 832491

Woodlands Grove Caravan & Camping Park

Leisure: 🛝🎮📺🎵

Facilities: 🛁🚿🪒💨❄♿📞🛒🧺🐕[Wi-fi]💻ℹ

Services: 🔧🧼 🛢🍃[T]🍽🔋🛍

Within 3 miles: ⛳🛒🧼

Notes: No open fires, fire pits or chimeneas. Dogs must be kept on leads. Falconry centre, woodland walk, mini golf. Discount available at local golf course & spa.

see advert on opposite page

►►►► 84% Little Cotton Caravan Park *(SX858508)*

Little Cotton TQ6 0LB
☎ 01803 832558
e-mail: enquiries@littlecotton.co.uk
dir: *Exit A38 at Buckfastleigh, A384 to Totnes, A381 to Halwell, take A3122 (Dartmouth Rd), site on right at entrance to town*

* 🚃 £13-£16 🚐 £15.50-£18.50 ⛺ £19-£22

Open 15 Mar-Oct

Last arrival 22.00hrs Last departure 11.00hrs

A very good grassy touring park set on high ground above Dartmouth, with quality facilities, and park-and-ride to the town from the gate. The immaculate toilet blocks are heated and superbly maintained. Spacious hardstandings are available. The friendly owners offer high levels of customer care and are happy to offer advice on touring in this pretty area. Excellent base for visiting Totnes, Slapton Sands and Kingsbridge. 7.5 acre site. 95 touring pitches. 42 hardstandings. Caravan pitches. Motorhome pitches. Tent pitches.

AA Pubs & Restaurants nearby: The Seahorse, Dartmouth 01803 835147

Jan and Freddies Brasserie, Dartmouth 01803 832491

Facilities: 🚿🪒💨❄♿📞🛒🐕[Wi-fi]♻ℹ

Services: 🔧🧼 🛢🍃[T]🔋

Within 3 miles: ⛳⛵🎬🎣◎🏄🛒🧼

Notes: No noise after 22.30hrs, no footballs. Dogs must be kept on leads.

DAWLISH Map 3 SX97

Places to visit

Kents Cavern, TORQUAY 01803 215136 www.kents-cavern.co.uk

Powderham Castle, POWDERHAM 01626 890243 www.powderham.co.uk

Great for kids: Babbacombe Model Village, TORQUAY 01803 315315 www.model-village.co.uk

83% Lady's Mile Holiday Park *(SX968784)*

EX7 0LX
☎ 0845 026 7252
e-mail: info@ladysmile.co.uk
dir: *1m N of Dawlish on A379*

* 🚃 £13-£27.50 🚐 £13-£27.50 ⛺ £13-£27.50

Open all year (rs Facilities open 23 Mar-Oct)

Last arrival 20.00hrs Last departure 11.00hrs

A holiday site with a wide variety of touring pitches, including some fully serviced pitches. There are plenty of activities for everyone, including two swimming pools with waterslides, a children's splash pool, a well-equipped gym, and sauna in the main season, a large adventure playground, and a bar with entertainment in high season all add to the enjoyment of a stay here. Facilities are kept very clean, and the surrounding beaches are easily accessed. Holiday homes and two, high quality glamping pods are also available. 18 acre site. 570 touring pitches. 30 hardstandings. 70 seasonal pitches. Caravan pitches. Motorhome pitches. Tent pitches. 100 statics. 2 wooden pods.

AA Pubs & Restaurants nearby: The Elizabethan Inn, Luton 01626 775425

Anchor Inn, Cockwood 01626 890203

Leisure: 🏊🌊🏋🛝✋⚽🎮🎵

Facilities: 🛁🚿🪒♿🛒🚚🧺🐕[Wi-fi]♻ℹ

Services: 🔧🧼 🍷🛢🍃[T]🍽🔋🛍

Within 3 miles: ⛳⛵🎬🎣◎🏄🛒🧼🐎

Notes: No noise after mdnt. 'Splashzone'.

LEISURE: 🏊 Indoor swimming pool 🌊 Outdoor swimming pool 🛝 Children's playground ✋ Kid's club 🎾 Tennis court 🎮 Games room 📺 Separate TV room ⛳ 9/18 hole golf course ⛵ Boats for hire 🎬 Cinema 🎵 Entertainment 🎣 Fishing ◎ Mini golf 🏄 Watersports 🏋 Gym ⚽ Sports field Spa 🐎 Stables
FACILITIES: 🛁 Bath 🚿 Shower 🪒 Electric shaver 💨 Hairdryer ❄ Ice Pack Facility ♿ Disabled facilities 📞 Public telephone 🛒 Shop on site or within 200yds 🚚 Mobile shop (calls at least 5 days a week) 🍖 BBQ area 🧺 Picnic area [Wi-fi] Wi-fi 💻 Internet access ♻ Recycling ℹ Tourist info 🐕 Dog exercise area

SERVICES: Electric hook up Launderette Licensed bar Calor Gas  Camping Gaz  Toilet fluid  Café/Restaurant Fast Food/Takeaway Battery charging
 Baby care Motorvan service point   ABBREVIATIONS: BH/bank hols-bank holidays Etr-Easter Whit-Whitsun dep-departure fr-from hrs-hours m-mile mdnt-midnight
rdbt-roundabout rs-restricted service wk-week wknd-weekend No credit cards no dogs   See page 7 for details of the AA Camping Card Scheme

DAWLISH *continued*

AA CAMPING CARD SITE

PREMIER PARK

▶▶▶▶▶ **84% Cofton Country Holidays** *(SX967801)*

Starcross EX6 8RP
☎ **01626 890111 & 0800 085 8649**
e-mail: info@coftonholidays.co.uk
dir: On A379 (Exeter/Dawlish road) 3m from Dawlish

* ⊟ £12-£36.50 ⊟ £12-£36.50 ▲ £12-£29.50

Open all year (rs Spring BH-mid Sep; Etr-end Oct pool, bar & shop open)

Last arrival 20.00hrs Last departure 11.00hrs

This park is set in a rural location surrounded by spacious open grassland, with plenty of well-kept flowerbeds throughout. Most pitches overlook either the outdoor swimming pool complex or the fishing lakes and woodlands. A purpose-built toilet block offers smart modern facilities and the on-site pub serves drinks, meals and snacks for all the family, and a mini-market caters for most shopping needs. Following major investment in 2012 a new leisure complex will open for 2013, featuring an indoor swimming pool, a steam room, gym and a stunning first-floor sitting area, replete with open fire, bar and coffee shop.

AA Pubs & Restaurants nearby: The Elizabethan Inn, Luton 01626 775425

Anchor Inn, Cockwood 01626 890203

Cofton Country Holidays

Leisure: ⊟ ⊟ ♈ ⋔ ☉ ◕

Facilities: ⊨ ⋔ ☉ ℱ ✲ ⅄ ⑭ ☺ ☷ ⋒ WI-FI 🖰 🛈

Services: ⑭ ◎ 🔧 ⋒ ⧄ ⊤ ⑩ 📥 ⧄ ▦ ↺

Within 3 miles: ⅃ ♈ ℘ ◎ ↳ 🖸 🖸

Notes: Dogs must be kept on leads. Coarse fishing, pub serving meals, soft play, sauna & steam room.

see advert below

LEISURE: ⊜ Indoor swimming pool ⊜ Outdoor swimming pool ⋔ Children's playground ⅃ Kid's club ⅃ Tennis court ◕ Games room ▭ Separate TV room ⅃ 9/18 hole golf course ♈ Boats for hire 🄷 Cinema ♫ Entertainment ℘ Fishing ◎ Mini golf ⅃ Watersports ♈ Gym ☉ Sports field **Spa** ↺ Stables
FACILITIES: ⊨ Bath ⋔ Shower ☉ Electric shaver ℱ Hairdryer ✲ Ice Pack Facility ⅄ Disabled facilities ⑭ Public telephone ☺ Shop on site or within 200yds 🖰 Mobile shop (calls at least 5 days a week) ☷ BBQ area ⋒ Picnic area WI-FI Wi-fi ▦ Internet access ↺ Recycling 🛈 Tourist info ⋒ Dog exercise area

AA CAMPING CARD SITE

►►► 81% Leadstone Camping

(SX974782)

Warren Rd EX7 0NG
☎ 01626 864411
e-mail: info@leadstonecamping.co.uk
web: www.leadstonecamping.co.uk
dir: *M5 junct 30, A379 to Dawlish. Before village turn left on brow of hill, signed Dawlish Warren. Site 0.5m on right*

* 🚐 £19-£24 🚌 £15-£20 ⛺ £15-£20

Open 14 Jun-1 Sep

Last arrival 22.00hrs Last departure noon

A traditional, mainly level, grassy camping park approximately a half-mile walk from the sands and dunes at Dawlish Warren, an Area of Outstanding Natural Beauty. This mainly tented park has been run by the same friendly family for many years, and is an ideal base for touring south Devon. A regular bus service from outside the gate takes in a wide area. The smart, new, well-equipped timber cabin toilet facility is now installed and includes some privacy cubicles. There is a pub a short walk away. 8 acre site. 137 touring pitches. 14 seasonal pitches. Caravan pitches. Motorhome pitches. Tent pitches.

AA Pubs & Restaurants nearby: The Elizabethan Inn, Luton 01626 775425

Anchor Inn, Cockwood 01626 890203

Leisure: 🛝

Facilities: 🚿 ⊙ 💨 ❄ ♿ 📞 🛒 [Wi-fi] ♻ ℹ

Services: 🔌 🧺 🛢 🍃 🔋

Within 3 miles: ⛳ 🎣 ◎ 🛒 🧺

Notes: No noise after 23.00hrs. Dogs must be kept on leads. Portable/disposable BBQs allowed.

DREWSTEIGNTON Map 3 SX79

Places to visit

Castle Drogo, DREWSTEIGNTON 01647 433306 www.nationaltrust.org.uk/main

Finch Foundry, STICKLEPATH 01837 840046 www.nationaltrust.org.uk

►►►► 84% Woodland Springs Adult Touring Park *(SX695912)*

Venton EX6 6PG
☎ 01647 231695
e-mail: enquiries@woodlandsprings.co.uk
web: www.woodlandsprings.co.uk
dir: *Exit A30 at Whiddon Down junct onto A382 towards Moretonhampstead. Site 1.5m on left*

🚐 £19-£22 🚌 £19-£22 ⛺ £16-£22

Open all year

Last arrival 20.00hrs Last departure 11.00hrs

An attractive park in a rural area within Dartmoor National Park. This site is surrounded by woodland and farmland, and is very peaceful. The toilet block offers superb facilities, including some for the disabled. There is a caravan available to hire. Please note that children are not accepted. 4 acre site. 81 touring pitches. 45 hardstandings. 17 seasonal pitches. Caravan pitches. Motorhome pitches. Tent pitches.

AA Pubs & Restaurants nearby: The Drewe Arms, Drewsteignton 01647 281224

The Old Inn, Drewsteignton 01647 281276

Facilities: 🚿 ⊙ 💨 ❄ ♿ 🛒 ⊓ 🐕 [Wi-fi] ♻ ℹ

Services: 🔌 🧺 🛢 🍃 [T] 🔋 ⤓

Within 3 miles: ⛳ 🎣 🛒 🐴

Notes: Adults only. No fires, no noise 23.00hrs-08.00hrs. Dogs must be kept on leads. Day kennels, freezer, coffee vending machine.

EAST ANSTEY Map 3 SS82

Places to visit

Quince Honey Farm, SOUTH MOLTON 01769 572401 www.quincehoney.com

Tiverton Museum of Mid Devon Life, TIVERTON 01884 256295 www.tivertonmuseum.org.uk

►►►► 86% Zeacombe House Caravan Park *(SS860240)*

Blackerton Cross EX16 9JU
☎ 01398 341279
e-mail: enquiries@zeacombeadultretreat.co.uk
dir: *M5 junct 27, A361 signed Barnstaple, right at next rdbt onto A396 signed Dulverton & Minehead. In 5m at Exeter Inn left, 1.5m, at Black Cat junct left onto B3227 towards South Molton, site 7m on left*

* 🚐 £14-£20 🚌 £14-£20 ⛺ £14-£20

Open 7 Mar-Oct

Last arrival 21.00hrs Last departure noon

Set on the southern fringes of Exmoor National Park, this sheltered, adult-only, 'garden' park is nicely landscaped in a tranquil location and enjoys panoramic views towards Exmoor. There is a choice of grass or hardstanding pitches and a unique restaurant-style meal service allowing you to eat a home-cooked evening meal in the comfort of your own unit. 5 acre site. 50 touring pitches. 12 hardstandings. Caravan pitches. Motorhome pitches. Tent pitches.

AA Pubs & Restaurants nearby: Masons Arms, Knowstone 01398 341231

Woods Bar & Dining Room, Dulverton 01398 324007

Facilities: 🚿 ⊙ 💨 ❄ ♿ 🛒 🐕 ℹ

Services: 🔌 🧺 🛢 🍃 [T] 🔋 🍔 ⤓

Within 3 miles: 🎣 🛒 🧺 🐴

Notes: Adults only. No awning ground sheets. Dogs must be kept on leads. Caravan store & stay system.

EAST WORLINGTON · Map 3 SS71

▶▶▶▶ 80% Yeatheridge Farm Caravan Park (SS768110)

EX17 4TN
☎ **01884 860330**
e-mail: yeatheridge@talk21.com
dir: *M5 junct 27, A361, at 1st rdbt at Tiverton take B3137 for 9m towards Witheridge. Fork left 1m past Nomansland onto B3042. Site on left in 3.5m. (NB do not enter East Worlington)*

🚐 £9-£18.50 🚐 £9-£18.50 ▲ £9-£18.50

Open 15 Mar-end Sep

Last arrival 22.00hrs Last departure 10.00hrs

A gently sloping grass site with mature trees, set in meadowland in rural Devon. There are good views of distant Dartmoor, and the site is of great appeal to families with its two play areas, farm animals, horse riding, and two indoor swimming pools, one with a flume. The onsite bar/restaurant serves good food at reasonable prices. There are many attractive villages in this area and the park is within easy reach of Exeter, Barnstaple and South Molton. 9 acre site. 85 touring pitches. Caravan pitches. Motorhome pitches. Tent pitches. 12 statics.

AA Pubs & Restaurants nearby: The Grove Inn, Kings Nympton 01769 580406

Leisure: 🏊 ⚓ 🎠 ✎

Facilities: 🛁 🍴 ☺ 🏈 ✳ ♿ ⓢ 🛎 📮 WiFi ♻ ❶

Services: 🔌 🔯 💧 🛢 ✎ ⊤ ⓞ 🛒 ♨ ♥ ↯

Within 3 miles: ✎ ⓢ 🏌 ∪

Notes: Dogs must be kept on leads. Fishing, pool table.

EXETER

See Kennford

EXMOUTH · Map 3 SY08

See also Woodbury Salterton

Places to visit

A la Ronde, EXMOUTH 01395 265514
www.nationaltrust.org.uk

Bicton Park Botanical Gardens, BICTON 01395 568465 www.bictongardens.co.uk

Great for kids: The World of Country Life, EXMOUTH 01395 274533
www.worldofcountrylife.co.uk

90% Devon Cliffs Holiday Park (SY036807)

Sandy Bay EX8 5BT
☎ **0871 231 0870**
e-mail: devoncliffs@haven.com
web: www.haven.com/devoncliffs
dir: *M5 junct 30/A376 towards Exmouth, follow brown signs to Sandy Bay*

🚐 🚐

Open mid Mar-end Oct (rs mid Mar-May & Sep-Oct some facilities may be reduced)

Last arrival anytime Last departure 10.00hrs

A large and exciting holiday park on a hillside setting close to Exmouth, with spectacular views across Sandy Bay. The all-action park offers a superb entertainment programme for all ages throughout the day, with the very modern sports and leisure facilities available for everyone. An internet café is just one of the quality amenities, and though some visitors may enjoy relaxing and watching others play, the temptation to join in is overpowering. The new South Beach Café, which overlooks the sea, is well worth a visit. Please note that this park does not accept tents. 163 acre site. 43 touring pitches. 43 hardstandings. Caravan pitches. Motorhome pitches. 1800 statics.

AA Pubs & Restaurants nearby: Globe Inn, Lympstone 01395 263166

Les Saveurs, Exmouth 01395 269459

Leisure: 🏊 ⚓ ✓ ⚓ ⚓ 🎵 Spa

Facilities: 🛁 🍴 ☺ 🏈 ♿ ⓢ 🛎 🛒 ♨ WiFi ♻

Services: 🔌 🔯 🛢 💧 🍴 ⓞ 🛒

Within 3 miles: 🏌 🚶 ✎ ⓞ ⚓ ⓢ ∪

Notes: Max 2 dogs per booking, certain dog breeds banned, no dogs on beach May-Sep. Dogs must be kept on leads. No commercial vehicles, no bookings by under 21s unless a family booking. Crazy golf, fencing, archery, bungee trampoline, aqua jets.

see advert on page 154

HOLSWORTHY · Map 3 SS30

Places to visit

Dartington Crystal, GREAT TORRINGTON 01805 626242 www.dartington.co.uk

RHS Garden Rosemoor, GREAT TORRINGTON 01805 624067 www.rhs.org.uk/rosemoor

Great for kids: The Milky Way Adventure Park, CLOVELLY 01237 431255
www.themilkyway.co.uk

AA CAMPING CARD SITE

▶▶▶ 77% Headon Farm Caravan Site (SS367023)

Headon Farm, Hollacombe EX22 6NN
☎ **01409 254477**
e-mail: reader@headonfarm.co.uk
dir: *From Holsworthy A388 signed Launceston. 0.5m, at hill brow left into Staddon Rd. 1m, (follow site signs) right signed Ashwater. 0.5m, left at hill brow. Site 25yds*

✱ 🚐 £14-£16 🚐 £14-£16

Open all year

Last arrival 19.00hrs Last departure noon

Set on a working farm in a quiet rural location. All pitches have extensive views of the Devon countryside, yet the park is only two and a half miles from the market town of Holsworthy, and within easy reach of roads to the coast and beaches of north Cornwall. 2 acre site. 19 touring pitches. 5 hardstandings. Caravan pitches. Motorhome pitches.

AA Pubs & Restaurants nearby: The Bickford Arms, Holsworthy 01409 221318

Leisure: ⚙ ☺

Facilities: ⌂ ☉ ✳ ✲ ☶ ⌘ ♻ ❶

Services: ⊡ ⛟

Within 3 miles: ↯ ☌ 🏊 🛈 ♨ U

Notes: Breathable groundsheets only. Dogs must be kept on leads. Secure caravan & motorhome storage.

▶▶ 77% Tamarstone Farm (SS286056)

Bude Rd, Pancrasweek EX22 7JT
☎ **01288 381734**
e-mail: camping@tamarstone.co.uk
dir: A30 to Launceston, then B3254 towards Bude, approx 14m. Right onto A3072 towards Holsworthy, approx 1.5m, site on left

🚐 £10-£15 �঎ £10-£15 ▲ £10-£15

Open Etr-end Oct

Last arrival 22.00hrs Last departure noon

Four acres of river-bordered meadow and woodland providing a wildlife haven for those who enjoy peace and seclusion. The wide, sandy beaches of Bude are just five miles away, and free coarse fishing is provided on site for visitors. 1 acre site. 16 touring pitches. Caravan pitches. Motorhome pitches. Tent pitches. 1 static.

AA Pubs & Restaurants nearby: The Bickford Arms, Holsworthy 01409 221318

Leisure: ⚲

Facilities: ⌂ ☉ ✳ ☶ ⌘ ♻ ❶

Services: ⊡

Within 3 miles: ↯ ☌ 🛈

Notes: ⊗ Dogs must be kept on leads.

▶ 75% Noteworthy Caravan and Campsite (SS303052)

Noteworthy, Bude Rd EX22 7JB
☎ **01409 253731**
e-mail: enquiries@noteworthy-devon.co.uk
dir: On A3072 between Holsworthy & Bude. 3m from Holsworthy on right

🚐 £10-£15 🚩 £10-£15 ▲ £10-£15

Open all year

Last departure 11.00hrs

This campsite is owned by a friendly young couple with their own children. There are good views from the quiet rural location, and simple toilet

---

facilities. The local bus stops outside the gate on request. 5 acre site. 5 touring pitches. Caravan pitches. Motorhome pitches. Tent pitches. 3 statics.

AA Pubs & Restaurants nearby: The Bickford Arms, Holsworthy 01409 221318

Leisure: ⚙

Facilities: ⌂ ☉ ✳ ☾ ⌘ ♻

Services: ⊡ ⛟

Within 3 miles: ↯ ☌ 🏊 🛈 🛈 U

Notes: ⊗ No open fires, no noise after 22.30hrs. Dogs must be kept on leads. Dog grooming.

ILFRACOMBE   Map 3 SS54

See also Berrynarbor

Places to visit

Arlington Court, ARLINGTON 01271 850296 www.nationaltrust.org.uk/main/w-arlingtoncourt

Exmoor Zoological Park, BLACKMOOR GATE 01598 763352 www.exmoorzoo.co.uk

Great for kids: Watermouth Castle & Family Theme Park, ILFRACOMBE 01271 863879 www.watermouthcastle.com

---

▶▶▶▶ 84% Hele Valley Holiday Park (SS533472)

GOLD

Hele Bay EX34 9RD
☎ **01271 862460**
e-mail: holidays@helevalley.co.uk
dir: M5 junct 27 onto A361. Through Barnstaple & Braunton to Ilfracombe. Take A399 towards Combe Martin. Follow brown Hele Valley signs. In 400mtrs sharp right, to T-junct. Park on left

* 🚐 £20-£32 🚩 £15-£32 ▲ £15-£34

Open Etr-Oct

Last arrival 21.00hrs Last departure 11.00hrs

A deceptively spacious park set in a picturesque valley with glorious tree-lined hilly views from most pitches. High quality toilet facilities are provided, and the park is within walking distance of a lovely beach and on a regular bus route. The harbour and other attractions of Ilfracombe are just a mile away. 17 acre site. 50 touring pitches. 18 hardstandings. Caravan pitches. Motorhome pitches. Tent pitches. 80 statics.

AA Pubs & Restaurants nearby: George & Dragon, Ilfracombe 01271 863851

11 The Quay, Ilfracombe 01271 868090

Leisure: ⚙ Spa

Facilities: ⌂ ☉ ☞ ✳ ☖ ⚲ ☶ ⌘ ♻ ❶

Services: ⊡ ☑ ⬙ ⛟ T ⛟ ⛟ ⛟

Within 3 miles: ↯ ✿ ☷ ☌ ◉ 🏊 🛈 🛈 U

Notes: Groups & motorhomes/tourers by arrangement only. Dogs must be kept on leads. Post collection, nature trail.

KENNFORD   Map 3 SX98

Places to visit

St Nicholas Priory, EXETER 01392 665858 www.exeter.gov.uk/priory

Quay House Visitor Centre, EXETER 01392 271611 www.exeter.gov.uk/quayhouse

Great for kids: Crealy Adventure Park, CLYST ST MARY 01395 233200 www.crealy.co.uk

---

▶▶▶▶ 79% Kennford International Caravan Park (SX912857)

EX6 7YN
☎ **01392 833046**
e-mail: ian@kennfordinternational.com
web: www.kennfordinternational.co.uk
dir: At end of M5, take A38, site signed at Kennford slip road

* 🚐 £16-£19 🚩 £16-£19 ▲ £15-£19

Open all year (rs Winter arrival times change)

Last arrival 21.00hrs Last departure 11.00hrs

Screened from the A38 by trees and shrubs, this park offers many pitches divided by hedging for privacy. A high quality toilet block complements the park's facilities. A good, centrally-located base for touring the coast and countryside of Devon, and Exeter is easily accessible via buses that stop nearby. 15 acre site. 56 touring pitches. 2 hardstandings. Caravan pitches. Motorhome pitches. Tent pitches. 56 statics.

AA Pubs & Restaurants nearby: The Bridge Inn, Topsham 01392 873862

Leisure: ⚙ ⚲

Facilities: ⛟ ⌂ ☉ ☖ ☾ ⌘ Wi-Fi ❶

Services: ⊡ ☑ ⬙ ☰ T ⛟ ⛟ ⛟

Within 3 miles: ↯ ✿ ☷ ☌ 🛈 🛈 U

Notes: Dogs must be kept on leads.

KENTISBEARE Map 3 ST00

Places to visit

Killerton House & Garden, KILLERTON
01392 881345 www.nationaltrust.org.uk

Allhallows Museum, HONITON 01404 44966
www.honitonmuseum.co.uk

Great for kids: Diggerland, CULLOMPTON
0871 227 7007 www.diggerland.com

AA CAMPING CARD SITE

▶▶▶▶ 80% **Forest Glade Holiday Park**

(ST101073)

EX15 2DT
☎ 01404 841381
e-mail: enquiries@forest-glade.co.uk
dir: *Tent traffic: from A373 turn left past Keepers Cottage Inn (2.5m E of M5 junct 28). (NB due to narrow roads, touring caravans & larger motorhomes must approach from Honiton direction. Please phone for access details)*

🚐 £15.50-£21.50 🚙 £15.50-£21.50
⛺ £13.50-£17.50

Forest Glade Holiday Park

Open mid Mar-end Oct (rs Low season limited shop hours)

Last arrival 21.00hrs Last departure noon

A quiet, attractive park in a forest clearing with well-kept gardens and beech hedge screening. One of the main attractions is the immediate proximity of the forest, which offers magnificent hillside walks with surprising views over the valleys. Please telephone for suitable route details. 15 acre site. 80 touring pitches. 40 hardstandings. 28 seasonal pitches. Caravan pitches. Motorhome pitches. Tent pitches. 57 statics.

AA Pubs & Restaurants nearby: Five Bells Inn, Clyst Hydon 01884 277288

Forest Glade Holiday Park

Leisure: 🏊 ⛰ ⚽ 😊 🎱
Facilities:
Services: 🚐 🔧 🏪 🧺 🚽 🛒 🚮 ⚓
Within 3 miles: 🎣 🛒 🛍 ⛴ ♨

Notes: Families & couples only. Dogs must be kept on leads. Adventure & soft play area, wildlife information room, paddling pool.

see advert below

KINGSBRIDGE
Map 3 SX74

Places to visit

Kingsbridge Cookworthy Museum,
KINGSBRIDGE 01548 853235
www.kingsbridgemuseum.org.uk

Overbeck's, SALCOMBE 01548 842893
www.nationaltrust.org.uk

PREMIER PARK

**NEW ►►►►► 74% Parkland
Caravan and Camping Site** (SX728462)

Sorley Green Cross TQ7 4AF
☎ 01548 852723 & 07968 222008
e-mail: enquiries@parklandsite.co.uk
dir: A384 to Totnes, A381 towards Kingsbridge.
12m, at Stumpy Post Cross rdbt turn right, 1m.
Site 200yds on left after Sorley Green Cross.

🚐 £14.50-£20 🚌 £14.50-£20 ▲ £14.50-£20

Open all year

Last arrival 22.00hrs Last departure 11.30hrs

Expect a high level of customer care at this
family-run park set in the glorious South Hams
countryside, with panoramic views over Salcombe
and rolling countryside towards Dartmoor.
Immaculately maintained grounds offer generous
grass pitches, hardstandings and super pitches.
New for 2013 are the seasonal on-site shop selling
local produce and pre-ordered hampers, and
upgraded toilet facilities featuring quality fully
serviced cubicles and family washrooms, plus a
bathroom and fully fitted disabled suite. A bus
stops close to the site entrance, handy for
exploring the local towns and villages. 3 acre site.
50 touring pitches. 30 hardstandings. 15 seasonal
pitches. Caravan pitches. Motorhome pitches.
Tent pitches.

AA Pubs & Restaurants nearby: Fortescue Arms,
East Allington 01548 521215

Crabshell Inn, Kingsbridge 01548 852345

Leisure: ⚑ ⚓

Facilities: 🛏 📷 ☉ 🍴 ✳ ⚿ 🕙 ⑤ 🗛 [Wi-Fi] 🖥 ♻ ❼

Services: 🔌 ⑤ 🚰 ⊘ 🗓 🎦 🛒 ♿

Within 3 miles: ⬇ ☇ 日 ✐ 🏄 🏵 🎱 🎿 U

Notes: ⊛ ⊗ No camp fires, no noise after
23.00hrs, children to be accompanied when using
facilities. Fridge freezers, storage facility, 200yds
from bus stop.

LYNTON
Map 3 SS74

See also Oare (Somerset)

Places to visit

Arlington Court, ARLINGTON 01271 850296
www.nationaltrust.org.uk/main/w-arlingtoncourt

Great for kids: Exmoor Zoological Park,
BLACKMOOR GATE 01598 763352
www.exmoorzoo.co.uk

AA CAMPING CARD SITE

**►►►► 71% Channel View
Caravan and Camping Park**
(SS724482)

Manor Farm EX35 6LD
☎ 01598 753349
e-mail: relax@channel-view.co.uk
web: www.channel-view.co.uk
dir: A39 E for 0.5m on left past Barbrook

* 🚐 £12-£20 🚌 £12-£20 ▲ £12-£14

Open 15 Mar-15 Nov

Last arrival 22.00hrs Last departure noon

On the top of the cliffs overlooking the Bristol
Channel, a well-maintained park on the edge of
Exmoor, and close to both Lynton and Lynmouth.
Pitches can be selected from either those in a
hidden hedged area or those with panoramic
views over the coast. 6 acre site. 76 touring
pitches. 15 hardstandings. Caravan pitches.
Motorhome pitches. Tent pitches. 31 statics.

AA Pubs & Restaurants nearby: The Rising Sun
Hotel, Lynmouth 01598 753223

Rockford Inn, Brendon 01598 741214

Leisure: ⚑

Facilities: 🛏 📷 ☉ 🍴 ✳ ⚿ 🕙 ⑤ 🗛 [Wi-Fi] ♻ ❼

Services: 🔌 ⑤ 🚰 ⊘ 🗓 🎦 🛒 ♿

Within 3 miles: 日 ✐ 🏵 🏄 🎱 🎿 U

Notes: Groups by prior arrangement only. Dogs
must be kept on leads. Parent & baby room.

►►► 76% Sunny Lyn Holiday Park
(SS719486)

Lynbridge EX35 6NS
☎ 01598 753384
e-mail: info@caravandevon.co.uk
web: www.caravandevon.co.uk
dir: M5 junct 27, A361 to South Molton. Right onto
A399 to Blackmoor Gate, right onto A39, left onto
B3234 towards Lynmouth. Site 1m on right

🚐 🚌 ▲

Open Mar-Oct

Last arrival 20.00hrs Last departure 11.00hrs

Set in a sheltered riverside location in a wooded
combe within a mile of the sea, in Exmoor National
Park. This family-run park offers good facilities
including an excellent café. 4.5 acre site. 9
touring pitches. 5 hardstandings. Caravan
pitches. Motorhome pitches. Tent pitches. 7
statics.

AA Pubs & Restaurants nearby: The Rising Sun
Hotel, Lynmouth 01598 753223

Rockford Inn, Brendon 01598 741214

Facilities: 📷 ☉ 🍴 ✳ ⚿ 🕙 ⑤ [Wi-Fi] 🖥 ♻ ❼

Services: 🔌 ⑤ 🚰 ⊘ 🎦 🛒 🖿

Within 3 miles: ⬇ 日 ✐ 🏵 🎱 🎿 U

Notes: No cars by tents. No wood fires, quiet after
22.30hrs.

SERVICES: 🔌 Electric hook up ⑤ Launderette 🍷 Licensed bar 🚰 Calor Gas ⊘ Camping Gaz 🗓 Toilet fluid 🍴 Café/Restaurant 🛒 Fast Food/Takeaway 🖿 Battery charging 🍼 Baby care ♿ Motorvan service point **ABBREVIATIONS:** BH/bank hols-bank holidays Etr-Easter Whit-Whitsun dep-departure fr-from hrs-hours m-mile mdnt-midnight rdbt-roundabout rs-restricted service wk-week wknd-weekend ⊛ No credit cards ⊗ no dogs

See page 7 for details of the AA Camping Card Scheme

MODBURY — Map 3 SX65

Places to visit

Kingsbridge Cookworthy Museum, KINGSBRIDGE 01548 853235 www.kingsbridgemuseum.org.uk

Overbeck's, SALCOMBE 01548 842893 www.nationaltrust.org.uk

Great for kids: National Marine Aquarium, PLYMOUTH 01752 275200 www.national-aquarium.co.uk

▶▶▶ 81% Pennymoor Camping & Caravan Park (SX685516)

PL21 0SB
☎ 01548 830542
e-mail: enquiries@pennymoor-camping.co.uk
dir: Exit A38 at Wrangaton Cross. Left & straight over x-roads. 4m, pass petrol station, 2nd left. Site 1.5m on right

* ♫ £10-£18 ♫ £10-£18 ▲ £10-£18

Open 15 Mar-15 Nov (rs 15 Mar-mid May one toilet & shower block only open)

Last arrival 20.00hrs Last departure 10.00hrs

A well-established rural park on part level, part gently sloping grass with good views over distant Dartmoor and the countryside in between. The park has been owned and run by the same family since 1935, and is very carefully tended, with clean, well maintained toilets and a relaxing atmosphere. 12.5 acre site. 119 touring pitches. Caravan pitches. Motorhome pitches. Tent pitches. 76 statics.

AA Pubs & Restaurants nearby: California Country Inn, Modbury 01548 821449

Rose & Crown, Yealmpton 01752 880223

Leisure: ⚠

Facilities: ⬛☉☞✳⬤☉⬛⬛WiFi ♻ ❶

Services: ♫⬛▮⬕⬛⬛⬛

Within 3 miles: ⬛⬛

Notes: No skateboards. Dogs must be kept on leads.

MOLLAND — Map 3 SS82

Places to visit

Quince Honey Farm, SOUTH MOLTON 01769 572401 www.quincehoney.com

Cobbaton Combat Collection, CHITTLEHAMPTON 01769 540740 www.cobbatoncombat.co.uk

▶▶▶ 75% Yeo Valley Holiday Park (SS788265)

The Blackcock Inn EX36 3NW
☎ 01769 550297
e-mail: info@yeovalleyholidays.co.uk
dir: From A361 onto B3227 towards Bampton. Follow brown signs for Blackcock Inn. Site opposite

* ♫ £14-£19.50 ♫ £14-£19.50 ▲ £12-£19.50

Open Mar-Nov

Last arrival 20.30hrs Last departure 10.30hrs

Set in a beautiful secluded valley on the edge of Exmoor National Park, this family-run park has easy access to both the moors and the north Devon coastline. The park is adjacent to the Blackcock Inn, which is under the same ownership and serves a variety of locally sourced meals, including breakfast to order. The pub also has a good heated indoor swimming pool and there is fishing close by. 8 acre site. 36 touring pitches. 16 hardstandings. Caravan pitches. Motorhome pitches. Tent pitches. 5 statics.

Leisure: ⬛⚠⬤⬛

Facilities: ⬛☉☞✳⬤⬛♻ ❶

Services: ♫⬛⬛⬛⬛⬛⬛

Within 3 miles: ⬛⬛⬛⬛⬛

Notes: Dogs must be kept on leads.

MORTEHOE — Map 3 SS44

See also Woolacombe

Places to visit

Marwood Hill Gardens, BARNSTAPLE 01271 342528 www.marwoodhillgarden.co.uk

Great for kids: Watermouth Castle & Family Theme Park, ILFRACOMBE 01271 863879 www.watermouthcastle.com

AA CAMPING CARD SITE

85% Twitchen House Holiday Village (SS465447)

Mortehoe Station Rd EX34 7ES
☎ 01271 870848
e-mail: goodtimes@woolacombe.com
dir: From Mullacott Cross rdbt take B3343 (Woolacombe road) to Turnpike Cross junct. Take right fork, site 1.5m on left

♫ ♫ ▲

Open Mar-Oct (rs mid May & mid Sep outdoor pool closed)

Last arrival mdnt Last departure 10.00hrs

A very attractive park with good leisure facilities. Visitors can use the amenities at all three of Woolacombe Bay holiday parks, and a bus service connects them all with the beach. The touring area features pitches (many fully serviced, including 80 for tents) with either sea views or a woodland countryside outlook. 45 acre site. 334 touring pitches. 110 hardstandings. Caravan pitches. Motorhome pitches. Tent pitches. 278 statics.

AA Pubs & Restaurants nearby: George & Dragon, Ilfracombe 01271 863851

11 The Quay, Ilfracombe 01271 868090

Leisure: ⬛⬛⚠⬤⬛⬛♫

Facilities: ⬛☉☞✳⬤☉⬛⬛WiFi ⬛ ♻

Services: ♫⬛⬛⬛⬛⬛⬛⬛⬛

Within 3 miles: ⬛⬛⬛⬛☞⬤⬛⬛⬛

Notes: Table tennis, sauna, swimming & surfing lessons, climbing wall, bungee trampoline.

LEISURE: ⬛ Indoor swimming pool ⬛ Outdoor swimming pool ⚠ Children's playground ⬛ Kid's club ⬛ Tennis court ⬤ Games room ⬛ Separate TV room ⬛ 9/18 hole golf course ⬛ Boats for hire ⬛ Cinema ♫ Entertainment ⬛ Fishing ◎ Mini golf ⬛ Watersports ⬛ Gym ⬛ Sports field **Spa** ⬛ Stables
FACILITIES: ⬛ Bath ⬛ Shower ☉ Electric shaver ☞ Hairdryer ✳ Ice Pack Facility ⬤ Disabled facilities ☉ Public telephone ⬛ Shop on site or within 200yds ⬛ Mobile shop (calls at least 5 days a week) ⬛ BBQ area ⬛ Picnic area WiFi Wi-fi ⬛ Internet access ♻ Recycling ❶ Tourist info ⬛ Dog exercise area

AA CAMPING CARD SITE

▶▶▶▶ 83% Warcombe Farm Caravan & Camping Park

(SS478445)

GOLD

Station Rd EX34 7EJ
☎ 01271 870690
e-mail: info@warcombefarm.co.uk
web: www.warcombefarm.co.uk
dir: On B3343 towards Woolacombe turn right towards Mortehoe. Site less than 1m on right

* ⬛ £12.50-£39 ⬛ £12.50-£39 ▲ £12.50-£39

Open 15 Mar-Oct (rs Low season no takeaway food)

Last arrival 21.00hrs Last departure 11.00hrs

Extensive views over the Bristol Channel can be enjoyed from the open areas of this attractive park, while other pitches are sheltered in paddocks with maturing trees. The site has 14 excellent super pitches with hardstandings. The superb sandy beach with a Blue Flag award at Woolacombe Bay is only a mile and a half away, and there is a fishing lake with direct access from some pitches. The local bus stops outside the park entrance. 19 acre site. 250 touring pitches. 10 hardstandings. Caravan pitches. Motorhome pitches. Tent pitches.

AA Pubs & Restaurants nearby: George & Dragon, Ilfracombe 01271 863851

11 The Quay, Ilfracombe 01271 868090

Leisure: /⚲

Facilities: ⬛ ⬛ ⬛ ⬛ ⬛ ⬛ ⬛ ⬛ ⬛ ⬛ ⬛ WI-FI ⬛ ⬛ ⬛

Services: ⬛ ⬛ ⬛ ⬛ T ⬛ ⬛ ⬛

Within 3 miles: ⬛ ⬛ ⬛ ⬛ ⬛ ⬛ ⬛ U

Notes: No groups unless booked in advance. Dogs must be kept on leads. Private fishing.

▶▶▶▶ 82% North Morte Farm Caravan & Camping Park (SS462455)

North Morte Rd EX34 7EG
☎ 01271 870381
e-mail: info@northmortefarm.co.uk
dir: From B3343 into Mortehoe, right at post office. Site 500yds on left

⬛ ⬛ ▲

Open Apr-Oct

Last arrival 22.30hrs Last departure noon

Set in spectacular coastal countryside close to National Trust land and 500 yards from Rockham Beach. This attractive park is very well run and maintained by friendly family owners, and the quaint village of Mortehoe with its cafés, shops and pubs, is just a five-minute walk away. 22 acre site. 180 touring pitches. 25 hardstandings. Caravan pitches. Motorhome pitches. Tent pitches. 73 statics.

AA Pubs & Restaurants nearby: George & Dragon, Ilfracombe 01271 863851

11 The Quay, Ilfracombe 01271 868090

Leisure: /⚲

Facilities: ⬛ ⬛ ⬛ ⬛ ⬛ ⬛ ⬛ ⬛ ⬛ WI-FI ⬛ ⬛

Services: ⬛ ⬛ ⬛ ⬛ T ⬛ ⬛

Within 3 miles: ⬛ ⬛ ⬛ ⬛ ⬛ U

Notes: No large groups. Dogs must be kept on leads.

AA CAMPING CARD SITE

▶▶▶ 80% Easewell Farm Holiday Village (SS465455)

Mortehoe Station Rd EX34 7EH
☎ 01271 871400
e-mail: goodtimes@woolacombe.com
dir: B3343 to Mortehoe. Turn right at fork, site 2m on right

⬛ ⬛ ▲

Open Mar-Nov (rs Etr)

Last arrival 22.00hrs Last departure 10.00hrs

A peaceful cliff-top park with full facility pitches for caravans and motorhomes, and superb views. The park offers a range of activities including indoor bowling and a 9-hole golf course, and all the facilities at the three other nearby holiday centres within this group are open to everyone. 17 acre site. 302 touring pitches. 50 hardstandings. Caravan pitches. Motorhome pitches. Tent pitches. 1 static.

AA Pubs & Restaurants nearby: George & Dragon, Ilfracombe 01271 863851

11 The Quay, Ilfracombe 01271 868090

Leisure: ⬛ ⬛ ⬛ ⬛ ⬛ ⬛

Facilities: ⬛ ⬛ ⬛ ⬛ ⬛ ⬛ ⬛ ⬛ ⬛ ⬛ ⬛ ⬛

Services: ⬛ ⬛ ⬛ ⬛ T ⬛ ⬛ ⬛

Within 3 miles: ⬛ ⬛ ⬛ ⬛ ⬛ ⬛ ⬛ ⬛ ⬛ U

Notes: Indoor bowls, snooker.

NEWTON ABBOT
Map 3 SX87

See also Bickington

Places to visit

Tuckers Maltings, NEWTON ABBOT 01626 334734
www.tuckersmaltings.com

Bradley Manor, NEWTON ABBOT 01803 843235
www.nationaltrust.org.uk/devoncornwall

Great for kids: Prickly Ball Farm and Hedgehog
Hospital, NEWTON ABBOT 01626 362319
www.pricklyballfarm.com

AA CAMPING CARD SITE

PREMIER PARK

▶▶▶▶▶ 96% Ross
Park (SX845671)

Park Hill Farm, Ipplepen TQ12 5TT
☎ 01803 812983
e-mail: enquiries@rossparkcaravanpark.co.uk
web: www.rossparkcaravanpark.co.uk
dir: N of Ipplepen on A381 follow brown site signs
(and sign fo Woodland) opposite Texaco garage

* ⬛ £15-£28.20 ⬛ £15-£28.50 ▲ £14-£27.20

Open Mar-2 Jan (rs Nov-Jan & 1st 3 wks in Mar
restaurant/bar closed (ex Xmas/New Year))

Last arrival 21.00hrs Last departure 10.00hrs

A top-class park in every way, with large secluded
pitches, high quality toilet facilities (which
include excellent family rooms) and colourful
flower displays throughout - note the wonderful
floral walk to the toilets. The beautiful tropical
conservatory also offers a breathtaking show of
colour. There's a conservation walk through
glorious wild flower meadows, replete with nature
trail, a dog shower/grooming area, and six fully-
serviced pitches. This very rural park enjoys
superb views of Dartmoor, and good quality meals
to suit all tastes and pockets are served in the
restaurant. Expect high levels of customer care -
this park gets better each year. Home-grown
produce and honey are sold in the shop. A bus,
which stops close to the entrance, runs to Totnes
and Newton Abbot. 32 acre site. 110 touring
pitches. 101 hardstandings. Caravan pitches.
Motorhome pitches. Tent pitches.

AA Pubs & Restaurants nearby: The Church House
Inn, Marldon 01803 558279

Union Inn, Denbury 01803 812595

Leisure: ⚠ ☼ ⚲ ▢

Facilities: ↾ ☉ ℱ ⚹ ⚭ ⊙ 🛋 ℙ ⏦ ⊞ 💧 ❸ ❶

Services: ⚇ 🅖 🔧 🛢 ⬛ Ⓣ ⊙ 🚲 🖐 ↴

Within 3 miles: ↧ 🗄 ℘ 🛋 🗄 ∪

Notes: Bikes, skateboards/scooters allowed only
on leisure field. Snooker, table tennis, badminton.

AA CAMPING CARD SITE

PREMIER PARK

▶▶▶▶▶ 94%
Dornafield (SX838683)

Dornafield Farm, Two Mile Oak TQ12 6DD
☎ 01803 812732
e-mail: enquiries@dornafield.com
web: www.dornafield.com
dir: From Newton Abbot take A381 signed Totnes
for 2m. At Two Mile Oak Inn right, left at x-roads in
0.5m. Site on right

* ⬛ £16.50-£34.20 ⬛ £16.50-£34.20 ▲ £15-£30

Open 14 Jan-4 Jan

Last arrival 22.00hrs Last departure 11.00hrs

An immaculately kept park in a tranquil wooded
valley between Dartmoor and Torbay, divided into
three areas. At the heart of the 30-acre site is
Dornafield, a 14th-century farmhouse, adapted for
campers' use but still retaining much charm. The
friendly family owners are always available for
help or advice. The site has superb facilities in
two ultra modern toilet blocks. On-site there is the
Quarry Café which provides takeaway fish & chips
or jacket potatoes daily. This is a quiet and
peaceful location convenient for Torbay, Dartmoor
and the charming coastal villages of the South
Hams. A bus service to Totnes or Newton Abbot
runs nearby. 30 acre site. 135 touring pitches. 119
hardstandings. 13 seasonal pitches. Caravan
pitches. Motorhome pitches. Tent pitches.

AA Pubs & Restaurants nearby: The Church House
Inn, Marldon 01803 558279

Union Inn, Denbury 01803 812595

Leisure: ⚠ ⚱ ⚲

Facilities: ↾ ☉ ℱ ⚹ ⚭ ⊙ 🛋 ⏦ ⊞ 🖥 ❸ ❶

Services: ⚇ 🅖 🛢 ⬛ Ⓣ 🚲 🖐 ↴

Within 3 miles: ↧ 🗄 ℘ 🗄 🗄

Notes: Dogs must be kept on leads. Caravan
storage (all year).

▶▶▶ 78% Twelve Oaks Farm Caravan
Park (SX852737)

Teigngrace TQ12 6QT
☎ 01626 335015
e-mail: info@twelveoaksfarm.co.uk
dir: A38 from Exeter left signed Teigngrace (only),
0.25m before Drumbridges rdbt. 1.5m, through
village, site on left. Or from Plymouth pass
Drumbridges rdbt, take slip road for Chudleigh
Knighton. Right over bridge, rejoin A38 towards
Plymouth. Left for Teigngrace (only), then as above

* ⬛ £10-£17.50 ⬛ £10-£17.50 ▲ £10-£17.50

Open all year

Last arrival 21.00hrs Last departure 10.30hrs

An attractive small park on a working farm close
to Dartmoor National Park, and bordered by the
River Teign. The tidy pitches are located amongst
trees and shrubs, and the modern facilities are

very well maintained. There are two well-stocked fishing lakes and children will enjoy all the farm animals. Close by is Stover Country Park and also the popular Templar Way walking route. 2 acre site. 50 touring pitches. 25 hardstandings. 15 seasonal pitches. Caravan pitches. Motorhome pitches. Tent pitches.

AA Pubs & Restaurants nearby: Elizabethan Inn, Luton (near Chudleigh) 01626 775425

Union Inn, Denbury 01803 812595

Leisure: ⛵ 🏔

Facilities: 🌳⊙📷✳♿☺💲🚻♿️♻ ❶

Services: 🔌🗑🛢🚿🚽♿

Within 3 miles: ↓🏇🎯📷◎💲🍴🛒∪

Notes: No noise after 23.00hrs. Dogs must be kept on leads.

PAIGNTON

Places to visit

Dartmouth Steam Railway & River Boat Company, PAIGNTON 01803 555872
www.dartmouthrailriver.co.uk

Kents Cavern, TORQUAY 01803 215136
www.kents-cavern.co.uk

Great for kids: Paignton Zoo Environmental Park, PAIGNTON 0844 474 2222
www.paigntonzoo.org.uk

PAIGNTON   Map 3 SX86

89% Beverley Parks Caravan & Camping Park *(SX886582)*

Goodrington Rd TQ14 7JE
☎ **01803 661979**
e-mail: info@beverley-holidays.co.uk
dir: *On A380, A3022, 2m S of Paignton left into Goodrington Rd. Beverley Park on right*

* 🚐 £16.70-£40.10 🚌 £16.70-£40.10
🛖 £13.60-£33.10

Open all year

Last arrival 21.00hrs Last departure 10.00hrs

A high quality family-run park with extensive views of the bay and plenty of on-site amenities. The park boasts indoor and outdoor heated swimming pools, plus tasteful bars and restaurants. The toilet facilities are modern and very clean and include excellent fully serviced family rooms. The park complex is attractively laid out with the touring areas divided into nicely screened areas. 12 acre site. 172 touring pitches. 49 hardstandings. Caravan pitches. Motorhome pitches. Tent pitches.

AA Pubs & Restaurants nearby: Church House Inn, Marldon 01803 558279

Cary Arms, Babbacombe 01803 327110

Elephant Restaurant & Brasserie, Torquay 01803 200044

Leisure: 🏊⛵⛳🏔♟🎱🎵 Spa
Facilities: 🛁🌳⊙📷✳♿☺💲🚻♿️🖥 ♻❶
Services: 🔌🗑🛒🛢🚿🚽🍴🛒♿
Within 3 miles: ↓🏇🎯📷◎💲🍴🛒∪
Notes: No pets. Table tennis, sauna, crazy golf, letter box trail.

▶▶▶▶ **79%** *Widend Touring Park (SX852619)*

Berry Pomeroy Rd, Marldon TQ3 1RT
☎ **01803 550116**
dir: *Signed from A380 (Torquay ring road) through Marldon. Site approx 1.5m on right*

🚐 🚌 🛖

Open Apr-end Sep (rs Apr-mid May & mid-end Sep swimming pool & club house closed)

Last arrival 20.00hrs Last departure 10.00hrs

A terraced grass park divided into paddocks and screened on high ground overlooking Torbay with views of Dartmoor. This attractive park is well laid out, divided up by mature trees and bushes but with plenty of open grassy areas. Facilities are of a high standard and offer a heated outdoor swimming pool with sunbathing area, a small lounge bar and a well-stocked shop. A local bus service to Torquay or Totnes runs from end of drive and a railway station is just two miles away. 22 acre site. 207 touring pitches. 6 hardstandings. Caravan pitches. Motorhome pitches. Tent pitches. 16 statics.

AA Pubs & Restaurants nearby: Church House Inn, Marldon 01803 558279

Cary Arms, Babbacombe 01803 327110

Elephant Restaurant & Brasserie, Torquay 01803 200044

Leisure: ⛵🏔🎱
Facilities: 🌳⊙✳♿☺💲🚻
Services: 🔌🗑🛒🛢🚿🚽🍴
Within 3 miles: ↓🏇🎯📷◎💲🍴🛒∪
Notes: No dogs mid Jul-Aug.

SERVICES: 🔌 Electric hook up   🗑 Launderette   🛒 Licensed bar   🛢 Calor Gas   🔥 Camping Gaz   T Toilet fluid   🍴 Café/Restaurant   🛒 Fast Food/Takeaway   🔋 Battery charging
🍼 Baby care   ♿ Motorvan service point   **ABBREVIATIONS:** BH/bank hols-bank holidays   Etr-Easter   Whit-Whitsun   dep-departure   fr-from   hrs-hours   m-mile   mdnt-midnight
rdbt-roundabout   rs-restricted service   wk-week   wknd-weekend   🚫 No credit cards   🚫 no dogs   See page 7 for details of the AA Camping Card Scheme

PAIGNTON *continued*

►►► 85% Whitehill Country Park *(SX857588)*

Stoke Rd TQ4 7PF
☎ 01803 782338
e-mail: info@whitehill-park.co.uk
dir: *A385 through Totnes towards Paignton. Turn right by Parkers Arms into Stoke Rd towards Stoke Gabriel. Site on left after approx 1.5m*

🚐 🚌 ⛺

Open Etr-Sep

Last arrival 21.00hrs Last departure 10.00hrs

A family-owned and run park set in rolling countryside, with many scenic beaches just a short drive away. This extensive country park covers 40 acres with woodland walks, and plenty of flora and fauna, and features an excellent outdoor swimming pool, a café, plus a bar/restaurant with summer entertainment. It offers ideal facilities, including luxury lodges and camping pods, for an excellent holiday. 40 acre site. 260 touring pitches. Caravan pitches. Motorhome pitches. Tent pitches. 60 statics. 5 wooden pods.

AA Pubs & Restaurants nearby: Church House Inn, Marldon 01803 558279

Cary Arms, Babbacombe 01803 327110

Elephant Restaurant & Brasserie, Torquay 01803 200044

Leisure: 🏊 🛝 🎱 📺

Facilities: 🚿 💇 ❄ ♿ 📞 🏪 🐕 [Wi-fi] 💻 ♻ ℹ

Services: 🔧 🫧 🍷 🔒 🍃 🍽 🛍 ⚓

Within 3 miles: ⛳ ⛵ 🎬 🎣 ◎ 🏄 🏪 🫧 🐴

Notes: Dogs only allowed 28 Mar-23 May, 3 Jun-19 Jul & 2-27 Sep. Dogs must be kept on leads. Walking & cycling trails, letter box trail, craft room, table tennis.

PLYMOUTH — Map 3 SX45

Places to visit

Plymouth City Museum & Art Gallery, PLYMOUTH 01752 304774 www.plymouthmuseum.gov.uk

The Elizabethan House, PLYMOUTH 01752 304774 www.plymouth.gov.uk/museums

Great for kids: National Marine Aquarium, PLYMOUTH 01752 275200 www.national-aquarium.co.uk

►►►► 83% Riverside Caravan Park *(SX515575)*

Leigham Manor Dr PL6 8LL
☎ 01752 344122
e-mail: office@riversidecaravanpark.com
dir: *A38 follow signs at Marsh Mills rdbt, take 3rd exit, then left. 400yds turn right (keep River Plym on right) to site*

* 🚐 £14-£22 🚌 £16-£28 ⛺ £10.50-£20

Open all year (rs Oct-Etr bar, restaurant, takeaway & pool closed)

Last arrival 22.00hrs Last departure 10.00hrs

A well-groomed site on the outskirts of Plymouth on the banks of the River Plym, in a surprisingly peaceful location surrounded by woodland. The toilet facilities are to a very good standard, and include private cubicles, plus there's a good games room and bar/restaurant serving food. This park is an ideal stopover for the ferries to France and Spain, and makes an excellent base for touring Dartmoor and the coast. The local bus stop is just a ten-minute walk from the site. 11 acre site. 259 touring pitches. Caravan pitches. Motorhome pitches. Tent pitches. 22 statics.

AA Pubs & Restaurants nearby: Fishermans Arms, Plymouth 01752 661457

Tanners Restaurant, Plymouth 01752 252001

Artillery Tower Restaurant, Plymouth 01752 257610

Leisure: 🏊 🛝 🎱 📺

Facilities: 🚿 🪒 💇 ❄ ♿ 📞 🏪 🐕 ♻ ℹ

Services: 🔧 🫧 🍷 🔒 🍃 [T] 🍽 🛏 🛍 ⚓

Within 3 miles: ⛳ ⛵ 🎬 🎣 ◎ 🏄 🏪 🫧 🐴

Notes: Dogs must be kept on leads.

SALCOMBE — Map 3 SX73

Places to visit

Overbeck's, SALCOMBE 01548 842893 www.nationaltrust.org.uk

Kingsbridge Cookworthy Museum, KINGSBRIDGE 01548 853235 www.kingsbridgemuseum.org.uk

►►► 84% *Karrageen Caravan & Camping Park* *(SX686395)*

Bolberry, Malborough TQ7 3EN
☎ 01548 561230
e-mail: phil@karrageen.co.uk
dir: *At Malborough on A381, sharp right through village, in 0.6m right again, 0.9m, site on right*

🚐 🚌 ⛺

Open Etr-Sep

Last arrival 21.00hrs Last departure 11.30hrs

A small friendly, family-run park with secluded hidden dells for tents and terraced grass pitches giving extensive sea and country views. There is a well-stocked shop and an excellent, refurbished toilet block that has two cubicled units, one suitable for families and less able visitors. This park is just one mile from the beach and pretty hamlet of Hope Cove and is a really peaceful park from which to explore the South Hams coast. 7.5 acre site. 70 touring pitches. Caravan pitches. Motorhome pitches. Tent pitches. 25 statics.

AA Pubs & Restaurants nearby: Victoria Inn, Salcombe 01548 842604

Soar Mill Cove Hotel, Salcombe 01548 561566

Facilities: 🚿 🪒 💇 ❄ ♿ 📞 🏪 ♻ ℹ

Services: 🔧 🫧 🔒 🍃 [T] 🛏 🛍

Within 3 miles: ⛳ ⛵ 🎣 🏄 🏪

Notes: 🚫 Dogs must be kept on leads.

LEISURE: ♨ Indoor swimming pool 🏊 Outdoor swimming pool 🛝 Children's playground 👋 Kid's club 🎾 Tennis court 🎱 Games room 📺 Separate TV room ⛳ 9/18 hole golf course ⛵ Boats for hire 🎬 Cinema 🎵 Entertainment 🎣 Fishing ◎ Mini golf 🏄 Watersports 🏋 Gym ⚽ Sports field **Spa** 🐴 Stables
FACILITIES: 🛁 Bath 🚿 Shower 🪒 Electric shaver 💇 Hairdryer ❄ Ice Pack Facility ♿ Disabled facilities 📞 Public telephone 🏪 Shop on site or within 200yds 🚚 Mobile shop (calls at least 5 days a week) 🍖 BBQ area 🧺 Picnic area [Wi-fi] Wi-fi 💻 Internet access ♻ Recycling ℹ Tourist info 🐕 Dog exercise area

►►► 79% Higher Rew Caravan & Camping Park *(SX714383)*

Higher Rew, Malborough TQ7 3BW
☎ 01548 842681
e-mail: enquiries@higherrew.co.uk
dir: *A381 to Malborough. Right at Townsend Cross, follow signs to Soar for 1m. Left at Rew Cross*

* 🚐 £14-£20 🚙 £14-£20 ⛺ £13-£18

Open Etr-Oct

Last arrival 22.00hrs Last departure noon

A long-established park in a remote location within sight of the sea. The spacious, open touring field has some tiered pitches in the sloping grass, and there are lovely countryside or sea views from every pitch. Friendly family owners are continually improving the facilities. 5 acre site. 85 touring pitches. Caravan pitches. Motorhome pitches. Tent pitches.

AA Pubs & Restaurants nearby: Victoria Inn, Salcombe 01548 842604

Soar Mill Cove Hotel, Salcombe 01548 561566

Leisure: 🏊 🎾

Facilities: 🚿 ⊙ 💨 ✲ ☎ 🛍 🐕 💻

Services: 🔌 🧺 🛢 🔥 [T] 🔋

Within 3 miles: ⛵ 🎣 🌊 🛍 🧺

Notes: 💳 Minimum noise after 23.00hrs. Tennis court, play barn.

►►► 76% Bolberry House Farm Caravan & Camping Park *(SX687395)*

Bolberry TQ7 3DY
☎ 01548 561251
e-mail: enquiries@bolberryparks.co.uk
dir: *At Malborough on A381 turn right signed Hope Cove/Bolberry. Take left fork after village signed Soar/Bolberry. Right in 0.6m. Site signed in 0.5m*

* 🚐 £12-£22 🚙 £12-£22 ⛺ £9-£24

Open Etr-Oct

Last arrival 20.00hrs Last departure 11.30hrs

A very popular park in a peaceful setting on a coastal farm with sea views, fine cliff walks and nearby beaches. Customers are assured of a warm welcome and the nicely tucked away portaloo facilities are smart and beautifully maintained. A mobile fish and chip van calls weekly and takeaways can be delivered to park. There's a super dog-walking area. 6 acre site. 70 touring pitches. Caravan pitches. Motorhome pitches. Tent pitches. 10 statics.

AA Pubs & Restaurants nearby: Victoria Inn, Salcombe 01548 842604

Soar Mill Cove Hotel, Salcombe 01548 561566

Leisure: 🛝

Facilities: 🚿 ⊙ 💨 ✲ ☎ 🛍 🐕 ♻ ℹ

Services: 🔌 🧺 🔋

Within 3 miles: ⛳ ⛵ 🏠 🎣 ◎ 🌊 🛍 🧺 🐎

Notes: 💳

►► 69% Alston Camping and Caravan Site *(SX716406)*

Malborough, Kingsbridge TQ7 3BJ
☎ 01548 561260 & 0780 803 0921
e-mail: info@alstoncampsite.co.uk
dir: *1.5m W of town off A381 towards Malborough*

🚐 🚙 ⛺

Open 15 Mar-Oct

An established farm site in a rural location adjacent to the Kingsbridge/Salcombe estuary. The site is well sheltered and screened, and approached down a long, well-surfaced narrow farm lane with passing places. The toilet facilities are basic. 16 acre site. 90 touring pitches. Caravan pitches. Motorhome pitches. Tent pitches. 58 statics.

AA Pubs & Restaurants nearby: Victoria Inn, Salcombe 01548 842604

Soar Mill Cove Hotel, Salcombe 01548 561566

Leisure: 🛝

Facilities: 🚿 ⊙ 💨 ✲ ♿ ☎ 🛍 🐕 Wi-fi ♻ ℹ

Services: 🔌 🧺 🛢 🔥 [T] 🔋

Within 3 miles: ⛳ ⛵ 🏠 🎣 🌊 🛍 🧺

Notes: Dogs must be kept on leads.

SAMPFORD PEVERELL Map 3 ST01

Places to visit

Tiverton Castle, TIVERTON 01884 253200 www.tivertoncastle.com

Tiverton Museum of Mid Devon Life, TIVERTON 01884 256295 www.tivertonmuseum.org.uk

Great for kids: Diggerland, CULLOMPTON 0871 227 7007 www.diggerland.com

►►►► 88% Minnows Touring Park *(SS042148)*

Holbrook Ln EX16 7EN
☎ 01884 821770
dir: *M5 junct 27, A361 signed Tiverton & Barnstaple. In 600yds take 1st slip road, then right over bridge, site ahead*

* 🚐 £13.80-£25.90 🚙 £13.80-£25.90 ⛺ £13.40-£16.70

Open 4 Mar-4 Nov

Last arrival 20.00hrs Last departure 11.30hrs

A small, well-sheltered park, peacefully located amidst fields and mature trees. The toilet facilities are of a high quality in keeping with the rest of the park, and there is a good laundry. The park has direct gated access to the canal towpath - a brisk 20-minute walk and there is a choice of pubs plus a farm shop, and the bus stop is 15 minutes away. All pitches are hardstanding with some large enough for American RVs. Wi-fi is now available. 5.5 acre site. 59 touring pitches. 59 hardstandings. Caravan pitches. Motorhome pitches. Tent pitches. 1 static.

AA Pubs & Restaurants nearby: The Butterleigh Inn, Butterleigh 01884 855433

Leisure: 🛝

Facilities: 🚿 ⊙ 💨 ✲ ♿ ☎ 🛍 🪑 Wi-fi 💻 ♻ ℹ

Services: 🔌 🧺 🛢 🔥 [T] 🔋 ⚓

Within 3 miles: ⛳ 🎣 🌊 🛍

Notes: No cycling, no groundsheets on grass. Dogs must be kept on leads. Caravan storage, fully serviced pitches, RVs welcome.

See page 7 for details of the AA Camping Card Scheme

SHALDON — Map 3 SX97

Places to visit

Bradley Manor, NEWTON ABBOT 01803 843235
www.nationaltrust.org.uk/devoncornwall

'Bygones', TORQUAY 01803 326108
www.bygones.co.uk

Great for kids: Babbacombe Model Village,
TORQUAY 01803 315315
www.model-village.co.uk

NEW 76% Coast View Holiday Park (SX935716)

Torquay Rd TQ14 0BG
☎ 01626 818350
e-mail: holidays@coastview.co.uk
dir: M5 junct 31, A38 then A380 towards
Torquay. Then A381 towards Teignmouth. Right
in 4m at lights, over Shaldon Bridge. 0.75m, up
hill, site on right

* ☐ £20-£40 ☐ £20-£40 ▲ £16-£26

Open mid Mar-end Oct

Last arrival 20.00hrs Last departure 10.00hrs

This park has stunning sea views from its
spacious pitches. The family-run park has a full
entertainment programme every night for all
the family, plus outdoor and indoor activities
for children; this site will certainly appeal to
lively families. 30 acre site. 67 touring pitches.
6 hardstandings. 10 seasonal pitches. Caravan
pitches. Motorhome pitches. Tent pitches. 27
statics.

AA Pubs & Restaurants nearby: ODE, Shaldon
01626 873977

Leisure: 🏊 🅰 🎣 🎵
Facilities: 🚿 ⊙ �🅵 ✳ 🕙 🔋 🎋 📶
💻 ♻ ❻
Services: 🔌 🔋 🚽 🛢 🍴 🛒 🚮 ↯
Within 3 miles: ⬇ 🎣 🎯 🏌 ◎ ⛴ 🔋 🛒

Notes: No noise after 23.00hrs. Dogs must be
kept on leads.

SIDMOUTH — Map 3 SY18

Places to visit

Branscombe - The Old Bakery, Manor Mill and
Forge, BRANSCOMBE 01752 346585
www.nationaltrust.org.uk

Otterton Mill, OTTERTON 01395 568521
www.ottertonmill.com

Great for kids: Pecorama Pleasure Gardens,
BEER 01297 21542 www.pecorama.info

AA CAMPING CARD SITE

PREMIER PARK

▶▶▶▶▶ 92% Oakdown Country Holiday Park (SY167902)

Best of British
GOLD

Gatedown Ln, Weston EX10 0PT
☎ 01297 680387
e-mail: enquiries@oakdown.co.uk
web: www.oakdown.co.uk
dir: Exit A3052, 2.5m E of junct with A375

* ☐ £15.80-£28.60 ☐ £15.80-£28.60
▲ £11.75-£22.90

Open Apr-Oct

Last arrival 22.00hrs Last departure 10.30hrs

A quality, friendly, well-maintained park with good
landscaping and plenty of maturing trees that
makes it well screened from the A3052. Pitches
are grouped in groves surrounded by shrubs, with
a 50-pitch development replete with an upmarket
toilet block. The park has excellent facilities
including a 9-hole par 3 golf course and a good
shop and café. The park's conservation areas,
with their natural flora and fauna, offer attractive
walks, and there is a hide by the Victorian reed
bed for bird watchers. A delightful park in every
respect. 16 acre site. 150 touring pitches. 90
hardstandings. Caravan pitches. Motorhome
pitches. Tent pitches. 62 statics.

AA Pubs & Restaurants nearby: The Blue Ball,
Sidford 01395 514062

Dukes, Sidmouth 01395 513320

Leisure: 🅰 🎣 🖵
Facilities: 🛁 🚿 ⊙ 🅵 ✳ 🕙 🔋 🎋 📶
💻 ♻ ❻
Services: 🔌 🔋 🛢 ✎ 🗊 🍴 🛒 ↯
Within 3 miles: ⬇ 🎣 🎯 🏌 ◎ ⛴ 🔋 🛒 ⛎

Notes: No bikes, skateboards or kite flying. Dogs
must be kept on leads. Use of microwave, field
trail to donkey sanctuary.

AA CAMPING CARD SITE

▶▶▶ 83% Salcombe Regis Caravan & Camping Park (SY153892)

Salcombe Regis EX10 0JH
☎ 01395 514303
e-mail: contact@salcombe-regis.co.uk
web: www.salcombe-regis.co.uk
dir: Exit A3052 1m E of junct with A375. From
opposite direction turn left past Donkey Sanctuary

* ☐ £12-£22 ☐ £12-£22 ▲ £12-£22

Open Etr-end Oct

Last arrival 20.15hrs Last departure 10.30hrs

Set in quiet countryside with glorious views, this
spacious park has well-maintained facilities, and
a good mix of grass and hardstanding pitches. A
footpath runs from the park to the coastal path
and the beach. There is a self-catering holiday
cottage and static caravans for hire. 16 acre site.
100 touring pitches. 40 hardstandings. 26
seasonal pitches. Caravan pitches. Motorhome
pitches. Tent pitches. 10 statics.

AA Pubs & Restaurants nearby: The Blue Ball,
Sidford 01395 514062

The Salty Monk, Sidford 01395 513174

Dukes, Sidmouth 01395 513320

Leisure: 🅰
Facilities: 🛁 🚿 ⊙ 🅵 ✳ 🕙 🔋 🎋 📶 ♻ ❻
Services: 🔌 🔋 🛢 ✎ 🗊 🛒 ↯
Within 3 miles: ⬇ 🎣 🎯 🏌 ◎ ⛴ 🔋 🛒 ⛎

Notes: Quiet 22.00hrs, no noise 23.00hrs. Dogs
must be kept on leads. Putting.

LEISURE: 🏊 Indoor swimming pool 🏊 Outdoor swimming pool 🅰 Children's playground 🧒 Kid's club 🎾 Tennis court 🎱 Games room 🖵 Separate TV room
⬇ 9/18 hole golf course 🚣 Boats for hire 🎬 Cinema 🎵 Entertainment 🎣 Fishing ◎ Mini golf 🏄 Watersports 💪 Gym 🔋 Sports field Spa ⛎ Stables
FACILITIES: 🛁 Bath 🚿 Shower ⊙ Electric shaver 🅵 Hairdryer ✳ Ice Pack Facility ♿ Disabled facilities 🕙 Public telephone 🛒 Shop on site or within 200yds
🏪 Mobile shop (calls at least 5 days a week) 🍴 BBQ area 🎋 Picnic area 📶 Wi-fi 🖥 Internet access ♻ Recycling ❻ Tourist info 🐕 Dog exercise area

▶▶▶ 77% Kings Down Tail Caravan & Camping Park (SY173907)

Salcombe Regis EX10 0PD
☎ 01297 680313
e-mail: info@kingsdowntail.co.uk
dir: Exit A3052 3m E of junct with A375

* 🚐 £17.50-£19.50 🚍 £17.50-£19.50
🛆 £17.50-£19.50

Open 15 Mar-15 Nov

Last arrival 22.00hrs Last departure noon

A well-kept site on level ground in a tree-sheltered spot on the side of the Sid Valley. This neat family-run park makes a good base for exploring the east Devon coast. 5 acre site. 102 touring pitches. 61 hardstandings. Caravan pitches. Motorhome pitches. Tent pitches.

AA Pubs & Restaurants nearby: The Blue Ball, Sidford 01395 514062

The Salty Monk, Sidford 01395 513174

Dukes, Sidmouth 01395 513320

Kings Down Tail Caravan & Camping Park

Leisure: 🗚 🏊
Facilities: 🖍⊙🍴※🕭🔄🏧🛒🗑️ℹ️
Services: 🔌🗄️🍴🚿Ⓣ🔋
Within 3 miles: 🛶🕯️🎡🅿️🛒🗄️↺
Notes: Dogs must be kept on leads.

see advert below

SOURTON CROSS

Places to visit

Lydford Gorge, LYDFORD 01822 820320
www.nationaltrust.org.uk/lydfordgorge

Okehampton Castle, OKEHAMPTON 01837 52844
www.english-heritage.org.uk

Great for kids: Tamar Otter & Wildlife Centre, LAUNCESTON 01566 785646
www.tamarotters.co.uk

SOURTON CROSS   Map 3 SX59

▶▶▶ 79% Bundu Camping & Caravan Park (SX546916)

EX20 4HT
☎ 01837 861611 & 861747
e-mail: bundu@btconnect.com
dir: W on A30, past Okehampton. Take A386 to Tavistock. Take 1st left & left again

🚐 £13-£16.50 🚍 £13-£16.50 🛆 £8-£12.50

Open all year

Last arrival 23.30hrs Last departure 14.00hrs

Welcoming, friendly owners set the tone for this well-maintained site, ideally positioned on the border of the Dartmoor National Park. Along with fine views, well maintained toilet facilities and level grassy pitches, the Granite Way cycle track from Lydford to Okehampton along the old railway line (part of the Devon Coast to Coast cycle trail) passes the edge of the park. There is a bus stop and cycle hire a few minute's walk away. Dogs are accepted. 4.5 acre site. 38 touring pitches. 11 hardstandings. Caravan pitches. Motorhome pitches. Tent pitches.

AA Pubs & Restaurants nearby: Highwayman Inn, Sourton 01837 861243

Facilities: 🖍⊙🍴※🕭🏧🖥️🔄ℹ️
Services: 🔌🗄️🍴🚿Ⓣ🔋
Within 3 miles: 🛶🎡🅿️🗄️
Notes: Dogs must be kept on leads.

SOUTH MOLTON Map 3 SS72

Places to visit

Quince Honey Farm, SOUTH MOLTON 01769 572401 www.quincehoney.com

Cobbaton Combat Collection, CHITTLEHAMPTON 01769 540740 www.cobbatoncombat.co.uk

Great for kids: Exmoor Zoological Park, BLACKMOOR GATE 01598 763352 www.exmoorzoo.co.uk

AA CAMPING CARD SITE

►►►► 88% Riverside Caravan & Camping Park *(SS723274)*

Marsh Ln, North Molton Rd EX36 3HQ
☎ 01769 579269
e-mail: relax@exmoorriverside.co.uk
web: www.exmoorriverside.co.uk
dir: *M5 junct 27, A361 towards Barnstaple. Site signed 1m before South Molton on right*

* 🚐 £15-£25 🚌 £15-£25 ⛺ £10-£20

Open all year

Last arrival 22.00hrs Last departure 11.00hrs

A family-run park, set alongside the River Mole, where supervised children can play, and fishing is available. This is an ideal base for exploring Exmoor, as well as north Devon's golden beaches. The site has an award for the excellence of the toilets. The local bus stops at park entrance. 40 acre site. 42 touring pitches. 42 hardstandings. Caravan pitches. Motorhome pitches. Tent pitches. 2 statics.

Leisure: 🛝 ⚽ ♫

Facilities: 🚿 ⊙ 💨 ❄ ♿ ☎ 🛒 ⛩ 🐕 📶 ♻ ℹ

Services: 🔌 🧺 🍷 🔒 🍃 Ⓣ 🍽 🛏 🛍 ⛽

Within 3 miles: ⛳ 🎬 🎣 🌊 🛒 🛍 🐎

Notes: Dogs must be kept on leads. Fishing.

STARCROSS

See Dawlish

STOKE GABRIEL Map 3 SX85

Places to visit

Berry Pomeroy Castle, TOTNES 01803 866618 www.english-heritage.org.uk

Totnes Museum, TOTNES 01803 863821 www.devonmuseums.net/totnes

Great for kids: Paignton Zoo Environmental Park, PAIGNTON 0844 474 2222 www.paigntonzoo.org.uk

►►► 84% Higher Well Farm Holiday Park *(SX857577)*

Waddeton Rd TQ9 6RN
☎ 01803 782289
e-mail: higherwell@talk21.com
dir: *From Exeter A380 to Torbay, turn right onto A385 for Totnes, in 0.5m left for Stoke Gabriel, follow signs*

🚐 £11.50-£19 🚌 £11.50-£19 ⛺ £11.50-£19

Open 23 Mar-3 Nov

Last arrival 22.00hrs Last departure 10.00hrs

Set on a quiet farm yet only four miles from Paignton, this rural holiday park is on the outskirts of the picturesque village of Stoke Gabriel. A toilet block, with some en suite facilities, is an excellent amenity, and tourers are housed in an open field with some very good views. 10 acre site. 80 touring pitches. 3 hardstandings. Caravan pitches. Motorhome pitches. Tent pitches. 19 statics.

AA Pubs & Restaurants nearby: Durant Arms, Ashprington 01803 732240

Steam Packet Inn,Totnes 01803 863880

White Hart, Totnes 01803 847111

Facilities: 🚿 ⊙ 💨 ❄ ♿ ☎ 🛒 🐕 ♻ ℹ

Services: 🔌 🧺 🔒 🍃 Ⓣ 🛏 ⛽

Within 3 miles: ⛳ 🎣 🛒 🛍

Notes: No commercial vehicles, pets must not be left unattended in caravans. Dogs must be kept on leads.

►►► 80% Broadleigh Farm Park *(SX851587)*

Coombe House Ln, Aish TQ9 6PU
☎ 01803 782422
e-mail: enquiries@broadleighfarm.co.uk
web: www.broadleighfarm.co.uk
dir: *From Exeter on A38 then A380 towards Torbay. Right onto A385 for Totnes. In 0.5m right at Whitehill Country Park. Site approx 0.75m on left*

🚐 🚌 ⛺

Open Mar-Oct

Last arrival 21.00hrs Last departure 11.30hrs

Set in a very rural location on a working farm bordering Paignton and Stoke Gabriel. The large sloping field with a timber-clad toilet block in the centre is sheltered and peaceful, surrounded by rolling countryside but handy for the beaches. There is also an excellent rally field with good toilets and showers. 7 acre site. 80 touring pitches. Caravan pitches. Motorhome pitches. Tent pitches.

AA Pubs & Restaurants nearby: Rumour, Totnes 01803 864682

Royal Seven Stars Hotel, Totnes 01803 862125

Facilities: 🚿 ⊙ 💨 ❄ ♿ 🐕 ♻ ℹ

Services: 🔌 🧺 🛏

Within 3 miles: ⛳ 🎬 🎣 ◎ 🌊 🛒 🛍

Notes: 🚫 Dogs must be kept on leads.

STOKENHAM Map 3 SX84

Places to visit

Kingsbridge Cookworthy Museum, KINGSBRIDGE 01548 853235 www.kingsbridgemuseum.org.uk

►►► 80% *Old Cotmore Farm* *(SX804417)*

TQ7 2LR
☎ 01548 580240
e-mail: info@holiday-in-devon.com
dir: *From Kingsbridge take A379 towards Dartmouth, through Frogmore & Chillington to mini rdbt at Stokenham. Right towards Beesands, site 1m on right*

🚐 🚌 ⛺

Open 15 Mar-Oct

Last arrival 20.00hrs Last departure 11.00hrs

A small and peaceful, family run touring caravan and campsite well located in the South Hams

LEISURE: 🏊 Indoor swimming pool 🌊 Outdoor swimming pool 🛝 Children's playground ✋ Kid's club 🎾 Tennis court ♣ Games room 📺 Separate TV room ⛳ 9/18 hole golf course ⛵ Boats for hire 🎬 Cinema ♫ Entertainment 🎣 Fishing ◎ Mini golf 🌊 Watersports 🏋 Gym ⚽ Sports field Spa 🐎 Stables
FACILITIES: 🛁 Bath 🚿 Shower ⊙ Electric shaver 💨 Hairdryer ❄ Ice Pack Facility ♿ Disabled facilities ☎ Public telephone 🛒 Shop on site or within 200yds 🛍 Mobile shop (calls at least 5 days a week) 🍖 BBQ area ⛩ Picnic area 📶 Wi-fi 💻 Internet access ♻ Recycling ℹ Tourist info 🐕 Dog exercise area

region of Devon, close to Slapton and within easy reach of Salcombe and Dartmouth. Facilities are very clean and well maintained and there is a basic shop and small play area. Sought-after tent pitches overlook fields and rolling fields. Pebble and sandy beaches with cliff walks through woods and fields are within walking distance. Self-catering cottages are available. 22 acre site. 30 touring pitches. 25 hardstandings. Caravan pitches. Motorhome pitches. Tent pitches.

AA Pubs & Restaurants nearby: Start Bay Inn, Torcross 01548 580553

The Cricket Inn, Beesands 01548 580215

Leisure: 🅰 🔍

Facilities: 🛁 ✱ & ⛴ 🚿 🚽 wifi 🖥 ♻ ❶

Services: 🔌 🖨 🧺 🚰 🔋

Within 3 miles: ⚓ 🎣 ⛳ 🛒 🏪

Notes: Dogs must be kept on leads.

| TAVISTOCK | Map 3 SX47 |

Places to visit

Morwellham Quay, MORWELLHAM 01822 832766 www.morwellham-quay.co.uk

Yelverton Paperweight Centre, YELVERTON 01822 854250 www.paperweightcentre.co.uk

Great for kids: National Marine Aquarium, PLYMOUTH 01752 275200 www.national-aquarium.co.uk

AA CAMPING CARD SITE

PREMIER PARK

►►►►► 85% Woodovis Park

(SX431745)

Gulworthy PL19 8NY
☎ 01822 832968
e-mail: info@woodovis.com
dir: A390 from Tavistock signed Callington & Gunnislake. At hill top right at rdbt signed Lamerton & Chipshop. Site 1m on left

🚐 £17-£38 🚙 £17-£38 ⛺ £17-£38

Open 22 Mar-3 Nov

Last arrival 20.00hrs Last departure 11.00hrs

A well-kept park in a remote woodland setting on the edge of the Tamar Valley. Peacefully located park at the end of a private, half-mile, tree-lined drive, it offers superb on-site facilities and high levels of customer care from hands-on owners. The toilets are immaculate and well maintained,

plus there is an indoor swimming pool, sauna and a good information/games room, all in a friendly, purposeful atmosphere. There is a wooden pod and a tipee with a woodburning stove for hire. 14.5 acre site. 50 touring pitches. 33 hardstandings. 8 seasonal pitches. Caravan pitches. Motorhome pitches. Tent pitches. 35 statics. 1 tipi. 1 wooden pod.

AA Pubs & Restaurants nearby: Dartmoor Inn, Lydford 01822 820221

Leisure: 🏊 🅰 🅿 🔍

Facilities: 🛁 🏪 ☉ ⛴ ✱ & 🕓 🧴 🚽 wifi 🖥 ♻ ❶

Services: 🔌 🖨 🚻 🧺 🚰 T 🚂 🔋 ⚡

Within 3 miles: ⬆ 🎣 🛒 🏪 ⛳

Notes: Dogs must be kept on leads. Archery, water-walking, physiotherm infra-red therapy cabin, petanque court, outdoor table tennis.

AA CAMPING CARD SITE

►►►► 84% Langstone Manor Camping & Caravan Park

SILVER

(SX524738)

Moortown PL19 9JZ
☎ 01822 613371
e-mail: jane@langstone-manor.co.uk
web: www.langstone-manor.co.uk
dir: Take B3357 from Tavistock to Princetown. Approx 1.5m turn right at x-rds, follow signs. Over bridge, cattle grid, up hill, left at sign, left again. Follow lane to park

✱ 🚐 £13-£18 🚙 £13-£18 ⛺ £13-£18

Open 15 Mar-Oct (rs 15 Mar-Oct bar & restaurant closed wkdays (excl BH & school hols))

Last arrival 22.00hrs Last departure 11.00hrs

A secluded and very peaceful site set in the well-maintained grounds of a manor house in Dartmoor National Park. Many attractive mature trees provide a screen within the park, yet the west-facing terraced pitches on the main park enjoy the

superb summer sunsets. Toilet facilities were completely refurbished and extended for the 2012 season and there is a popular lounge bar with an excellent menu of reasonably priced evening meals, and camping pods to hire. Plenty of activities and places of interest can be found within the surrounding moorland. Dogs are accepted. 6.5 acre site. 40 touring pitches. 10 hardstandings. 5 seasonal pitches. Caravan pitches. Motorhome pitches. Tent pitches. 25 statics. 5 wooden pods.

AA Pubs & Restaurants nearby: Dartmoor Inn, Lydford 01822 820221

Leisure: 🅰 🔍

Facilities: 🛁 🏪 ☉ ⛴ ✱ & 🕓 🚿 wifi ♻ ❶

Services: 🔌 🖨 🚻 🧺 🚰 T 🍽 🚂 🔋 ⚡

Within 3 miles: ⬆ 🎣 ◎ 🛒 🏪 ⛳

Notes: No skateboards, scooters, cycles, ball games. Dogs must be kept on leads. Baguettes, croissants etc available.

►►►► 79% Harford Bridge Holiday Park (SX504767)

GOLD

Peter Tavy PL19 9LS
☎ 01822 810349 & 07773 251457
e-mail: stay@harfordbridge.co.uk
web: www.harfordbridge.co.uk
dir: 2m N of Tavistock, off A386 Okehampton Rd, take Peter Tavy turn, entrance 200yds on right

✱ 🚐 £13.50-£21.55 🚙 £13.50-£21.55
⛺ £13.50-£21.55

Open all year (rs Nov-Mar statics only & 5 hardstandings)

Last arrival 21.00hrs Last departure noon

This beautiful spacious park is set beside the River Tavy in the Dartmoor National Park. Pitches are located beside the river and around the copses, and the park is very well equipped for the holidaymaker. An adventure playground and games room entertain children, and there is fly-fishing and a free tennis court. A lovely, authentic

continued

TAVISTOCK *continued*

shepherd's hut complete with furniture, fridge and woodburner is available to let. 16 acre site. 120 touring pitches. 5 hardstandings. 5 seasonal pitches. Caravan pitches. Motorhome pitches. Tent pitches. 80 statics.

AA Pubs & Restaurants nearby: The Peter Tavy Inn, Peter Tavy 01822 810348

Leisure: ⚓🏊♨🎱🖵

Facilities: 🏕☉🅿❄♿🕙🚿🛏📶♻❗

Services: 🔌🔋🛢🗑T🛒🛁↧

Within 3 miles: ↧🏇🎯🎣🎿🛒🛍🛍♺

Notes: Expedition groups welcome by prior arrangement. Dogs must be kept on leads. Fly fishing. Baguettes, croissants, snacks, sweets available.

TEDBURN ST MARY　Map 3 SX89

Places to visit

Finch Foundry, STICKLEPATH 01837 840046 www.nationaltrust.org.uk

Castle Drogo, DREWSTEIGNTON 01647 433306 www.nationaltrust.org.uk/main

Great for kids: Prickly Ball Farm and Hedgehog Hospital, NEWTON ABBOT 01626 362319 www.pricklyballfarm.com

AA CAMPING CARD SITE

▶▶▶▶ 81% Springfield Holiday Park (SX788935)

EX6 6EW
☎ 01647 24242
e-mail: enquiries@springfieldholidaypark.co.uk
dir: M5 junct 31, A30 towards Okehampton, exit at junct, signed to Cheriton Bishop. Follow brown tourist signs to site. (For Sat Nav use postcode EX6 6JN)

* 🚐 £15-£20 🚏 £15-£20 ▲ £10-£20

Open 15 Mar-15 Nov

Last arrival 22.00hrs Last departure noon

Set in a quiet rural location with countryside views, this park continues to be upgraded to a smart standard. There is a very inviting heated outdoor swimming pool. It has the advantage of being located close to Dartmoor National Park, with village pubs and stores less than a mile

away. 9 acre site. 48 touring pitches. 38 hardstandings. 25 seasonal pitches. Caravan pitches. Motorhome pitches. Tent pitches. 49 statics.

AA Pubs & Restaurants nearby: The Drewe Arms, Drewsteignton 01647 281224

The Old Inn, Drewsteignton 01647 281276

Leisure: ⚓🏊🎱

Facilities: 🏕☉❄🚿🛏📶♻❗

Services: 🔌🔋🛢🗑↧

Within 3 miles: ↧🎣🛒🛍

Notes: Dogs must be kept on leads.

TIVERTON

See East Worlington

TORQUAY　Map 3 SX96

See also Newton Abbot

Places to visit

Torre Abbey, TORQUAY 01803 293593 www.torre-abbey.org.uk

'Bygones', TORQUAY 01803 326108 www.bygones.co.uk

▶▶▶▶ 83% Widdicombe Farm Touring Park (SX876643)

Marldon TQ3 1ST
☎ 01803 558325
e-mail: info@widdicombefarm.co.uk
dir: On A380, midway between Torquay & Paignton ring road

🚐 🚏 ▲

Open mid Mar-end Oct

Last arrival 20.00hrs Last departure 11.00hrs

A friendly family-run park on a working farm with good quality facilities, extensive views and easy access as there are no narrow roads. The level pitches are terraced to take advantage of the views towards the coast and Dartmoor. This is the only adult touring park within Torquay, and is also handy for Paignton and Brixham. There's a bus service from the park to the local shopping centre and Torquay's harbour. There is a small shop, a restaurant and a lounge bar with entertainment from Easter to the end of September. Club Wi-fi is available throughout the park and The Nippy Chippy

van now calls regularly. 2013 marks the site's 40th anniversary and Ruby celebrations will be held, mainly in May. 8 acre site. 180 touring pitches. 180 hardstandings. 20 seasonal pitches. Caravan pitches. Motorhome pitches. Tent pitches. 3 statics.

AA Pubs & Restaurants nearby: Church House Inn, Marldon 01803 558279

Cary Arms, Babbacombe 01803 327110

Elephant Restaurant & Brasserie, Torquay 01803 200044

Leisure: 🎵

Facilities: 🏕☉🅿❄♿🛏🚿📶♻❗

Services: 🔌🔋🍴🛢🗑T🍽🛒🍺↧

Within 3 miles: ↧🏇🎯🎣◎🎿🛒🛍

Notes: Adults only. Most dog breeds accepted. Dogs must be kept on leads. Bus service to Torquay operates Mon-Fri excl BH.

WOODBURY SALTERTON　Map 3 SY08

Places to visit

The World of Country Life, EXMOUTH 01395 274533 www.worldofcountrylife.co.uk

A la Ronde, EXMOUTH 01395 265514 www.nationaltrust.org.uk

Great for kids: Crealy Adventure Park, CLYST ST MARY 01395 233200 www.crealy.co.uk

▶▶▶ 87% Browns Farm Caravan Park (SY016885)

Browns Farm EX5 1PS
☎ 01395 232895
dir: M5 junct 30, A3052 for 3.7m. Right at White Horse Inn, follow sign to Woodbury. At junct with Village Rd turn right, site on left

* 🚐 £11-£14 🚏 £11-£15 ▲ £11-£14

Open all year

Last departure 11.00hrs

A small farm park adjoining a 14th-century thatched farmhouse, and located in a quiet village. Pitches back onto hedgerows, and friendly owners keep the excellent facilities very clean. The tourist information and games room, with table tennis, chess etc, is housed in a purpose-built building. The park is just a mile from the historic heathland of Woodbury Common with its superb views. The local bus to Exeter and Exmouth stops

continued

LEISURE: 🏊 Indoor swimming pool　🏊 Outdoor swimming pool　🛝 Children's playground　🧒 Kid's club　🎾 Tennis court　🎱 Games room　🖵 Separate TV room
🏌 9/18 hole golf course　🚣 Boats for hire　🎬 Cinema　🎵 Entertainment　🎣 Fishing　◎ Mini golf　🏄 Watersports　💪 Gym　♻ Sports field　Spa　🛁 Stables
FACILITIES: 🛁 Bath　🚿 Shower　☉ Electric shaver　🅿 Hairdryer　❄ Ice Pack Facility　♿ Disabled facilities　🕙 Public telephone　🛒 Shop on site or within 200yds
🛍 Mobile shop (calls at least 5 days a week)　🍽 BBQ area　🏕 Picnic area　📶 Wi-fi　🖥 Internet access　♻ Recycling　❗ Tourist info　🐕 Dog exercise area

SERVICES: Electric hook up Launderette Licensed bar Calor Gas Camping Gaz Toilet fluid Café/Restaurant Fast Food/Takeaway Battery charging Baby care Motorvan service point **ABBREVIATIONS:** BH/bank hols-bank holidays Etr-Easter Whit-Whitsun dep-departure fr-from hrs-hours m-mile mdnt-midnight rdbt-roundabout rs-restricted service wk-week wknd-weekend No credit cards no dogs

See page 7 for details of the AA Camping Card Scheme

WOODBURY SALTERTON *continued*

at site entrance. 2.5 acre site. 29 touring pitches. 24 hardstandings. Caravan pitches. Motorhome pitches. Tent pitches.

AA Pubs & Restaurants nearby: The Digger's Rest, Woodbury Salterton 01395 232375

Golden Lion Inn, Tipton St John 01404 812881

Moores' Restaurant & Rooms, Newton Poppleford 01395 568100

Leisure: 🔴 🖵

Facilities: 🏕 ⊙ 🅿 🕆 ✳ ⅁ ① ✆

Services: 🔌 🗑 🔥 🧺 🚰

Within 3 miles: ⌕ 🖉 🝙 ∪

Notes: ⊘ No ground sheets in awnings, no music. Dogs must be kept on leads. Hardstandings for winter period, caravan storage.

WOOLACOMBE   Map 3 SS44

See also Mortehoe

Places to visit

Arlington Court, ARLINGTON 01271 850296 www.nationaltrust.org.uk/main/w-arlingtoncourt

Great for kids: Watermouth Castle & Family Theme Park, ILFRACOMBE 01271 863879 www.watermouthcastle.com

AA CAMPING CARD SITE

80% Golden Coast Holiday Village (SS482436)

Station Rd EX34 7HW
☎ **01271 872000**
e-mail: goodtimes@woolacombe.com
dir: *From Mullacott Cross towards Woolacombe Bay, site 1.5m on left*

🚐 🚃 🛆

Open Feb-Dec (rs mid Sep-May outdoor water park closed)

Last arrival mdnt Last departure 10.00hrs

A holiday village offering excellent leisure facilities together with the amenities available at the other Woolacombe Bay holiday parks. There is a neat touring area with a unisex toilet

---

block, maintained to a high standard. Ten-pin bowling, high ropes course, climbing wall, surfing simulator, surf school with equipment hire and adventure golf are just a few of the many activities on offer. 10 acre site. 91 touring pitches. 53 hardstandings. Caravan pitches. Motorhome pitches. Tent pitches. 444 statics.

AA Pubs & Restaurants nearby: George & Dragon, Ilfracombe 01271 863851

11 The Quay, Ilfracombe 01271 868090

The Williams Arms, Braunton 01271 812360

Leisure: 🔄 🐬 🅰 ↓ ⊛ ⊙ 🔴 🖵 ♫

Facilities: 🏕 ⊙ 🅿 🕆 ✳ ⅁ ① 🔋 🏕 🎌 📶 🖥 ♻

Services: 🔌 🗑 🔥 🧺 📺 🍴 🛒 🚰 ⚓

Within 3 miles: ⌕ 🎣 🖉 ◎ 🔆 🝙 🍴 ∪

Notes: No pets on touring pitches. Sauna, solarium, fishing, snooker, cinema, swimming & surfing lessons.

AA CAMPING CARD SITE

80% Woolacombe Bay Holiday Village (SS465442)

Sandy Ln EX34 7AH
☎ **01271 870221**
e-mail: goodtimes@woolacombe.com
dir: *From Mullacott Cross rdbt take B3343 (Woolacombe road) to Turnpike Cross junct. Right towards Mortehoe, site approx 1m on left*

🚐 🚃 🛆

Open Mar-Oct (rs Mar-mid May, mid Sep-Oct no touring, camping only available)

Last arrival mdnt Last departure 10.00hrs

A well-developed touring section in a holiday complex with a full entertainment and leisure programme. This park offers excellent facilities including a steam room and sauna. For a small charge a bus takes holidaymakers to the other Woolacombe Bay holiday centres where they can take part in any of the activities offered, and there is also a bus to the beach. 8.5 acre site. 180 touring pitches. Caravan pitches. Motorhome pitches. Tent pitches. 237 statics.

AA Pubs & Restaurants nearby: George & Dragon, Ilfracombe 01271 863851

11 The Quay, Ilfracombe 01271 868090

The Williams Arms, Braunton 01271 812360

Leisure: 🔄 🐬 🅰 ↓ ⊛ ⊙ 🔴 🖵 ♫ Spa

Facilities: 🏕 ⊙ 🅿 🕆 ✳ ⅁ ① 🔋 🏕 🎌 📶 🖥 ♻

Services: 🔌 🗑 🔥 🧺 📺 🛒 🚰

Within 3 miles: ⌕ 🔆 🝙 🖉 ◎ 🔆 🍴 🝙 ∪

Notes: Health suite, surfing & swimming lessons.

see advert on page 181 & inside front cover

AA CAMPING CARD SITE

78% Woolacombe Sands Holiday Park (SS471434)

Beach Rd EX34 7AF
☎ **01271 870569**
e-mail: lifesabeach@woolacombe-sands.co.uk
dir: *M5 junct 27, A361 to Barnstaple. Follow Ilfracombe signs to Mullacott Cross. Left onto B3343 to Woolacombe. Site on left*

🚐 🚃 🛆

Open Mar-Nov

Last arrival 22.00hrs Last departure 10.00hrs

Set in rolling countryside with grass and hardstanding terraced pitches, most with spectacular views overlooking the sea at Woolacombe. The lovely Blue Flag beach can be accessed directly by footpath in 10-15 minutes, and there is a full entertainment programme for all the family in high season. 20 acre site. 200 touring pitches. 75 hardstandings. 50 seasonal pitches. Caravan pitches. Motorhome pitches. Tent pitches. 80 statics.

LEISURE: 🔄 Indoor swimming pool 🐬 Outdoor swimming pool 🅰 Children's playground ↓ Kid's club ⊛ Tennis court 🔴 Games room 🖵 Separate TV room ⌕ 9/18 hole golf course 🔆 Boats for hire ☐ Cinema ♫ Entertainment 🖉 Fishing ◎ Mini golf 🐬 Watersports 🝙 Gym ⊙ Sports field Spa ∪ Stables
FACILITIES: 🛁 Bath 🏕 Shower ⊙ Electric shaver 🅿 Hairdryer ✳ Ice Pack Facility ⅁ Disabled facilities ① Public telephone 🔋 Shop on site or within 200yds 🏕 Mobile shop (calls at least 5 days a week) 🍴 BBQ area 🎌 Picnic area 📶 Wi-fi 🖥 Internet access ♻ Recycling ✆ Tourist info 🐕 Dog exercise area

AA Pubs & Restaurants nearby: George & Dragon, Ilfracombe 01271 863851

11 The Quay, Ilfracombe 01271 868090

The Williams Arms, Braunton 01271 812360

Woolacombe Sands Holiday Park

Leisure: 🏊🏖️🎠🎢🏀🔍🎱🎵

Facilities: 🚿⊙📮✳️♿🕐🛢️🍴🚮WiFi 🖥️ ♻️ ℹ️

Services: 🔌🗄️🍺🛢️🚿T🍽️🛒🚮🛒♿

Within 3 miles: 🚣🎣🛝🏌️◎🛥️🏪🛒U

Notes: Crazy golf, woodland walk, footpath to beach.

see advert below

▶▶▶ 77% Europa Park *(SS475435)*

Beach Rd EX34 7AN
☎ 01271 871425

e-mail: europaparkwoolacombe@yahoo.co.uk
dir: *M5 junct 27, A361 through Barnstaple to Mullacott Cross. Left onto B3343 signed Woolacombe. Site on right at Spa shop/garage*

🚐 🚙 ⛺

Open all year

Last arrival 23.00hrs Last departure 10.00hrs

A very lively family-run site handy for the beach at Woolacombe, and catering well for surfers but maybe not suitable for a quieter type of stay (please make sure the site is suitable for you before making your booking). Set in a stunning location high above the bay, it provides a wide range of accommodation including surf cabins, camping pods and generous touring pitches. Visitors can enjoy the indoor pool and sauna, games room, restaurant/café/bar and clubhouse. 16 acre site. 200 touring pitches. 20 hardstandings. Caravan pitches. Motorhome pitches. Tent pitches. 22 statics.

AA Pubs & Restaurants nearby: George & Dragon, Ilfracombe 01271 863851

11 The Quay, Ilfracombe 01271 868090

The Williams Arms, Braunton 01271 812360

Leisure: 🏊🎠🔍🖥️

Facilities: 🚿⊙✳️🕐🛢️

Services: 🔌🗄️🍺🛢️T🍽️🛒🚮♿

Within 3 miles: 🚣🛝🏌️◎🛥️🏪🛒U

Notes: Beer deck, off licence, pub, big screen TV.

SERVICES: 🔌 Electric hook up 🗄️ Launderette 🍺 Licensed bar 🛢️ Calor Gas 🅖 Camping Gaz T Toilet fluid 🍽️ Café/Restaurant 🍔 Fast Food/Takeaway 🔋 Battery charging 🍼 Baby care ♿ Motorvan service point ABBREVIATIONS: BH/bank hols-bank holidays Etr-Easter Whit-Whitsun dep-departure fr-from hrs-hours m-mile mdnt-midnight rdbt-roundabout rs-restricted service wk-week wknd-weekend 🚫 No credit cards 🚫 no dogs See page 7 for details of the AA Camping Card Scheme

Dorset

Dorset means rugged varied coastline and high chalk downland,
with more than a hint of Thomas Hardy, its most famous son.
The coastal grandeur is breathtaking with two famous local
landmarks, Lulworth Cove and Durdle Door, shaped and sculpted
to perfection by the elements. Squeezed in among the cliffs
and set amid some of Britain's most beautiful scenery is a chain
of picturesque villages and occasionally seaside towns.

Most prominent among these seaside towns is Lyme Regis, with its sturdy breakwater, known as the Cobb, made famous by Jane Austen in *Persuasion*, and John Fowles in *The French Lieutenant's Woman*. It's the sort of place where Georgian houses and quaint cottages jostle with historic pubs and independently run shops. With its blend of architectural styles and old world charm, Lyme looks very much like a film set, and fans of Austen and Fowles and the big-screen adaptations of their work flock to point their cameras and enjoy its beauty. Before the era of sea-bathing and Victorian respectability, the town was a haunt of smugglers.

Chesil Beach
In sharp contrast to Lyme's steep streets and dramatic inclines is Chesil Beach, a long shingle reef extending for 10 miles (16.1km) between Abbotsbury and Portland. The beach is covered by a vast wall of shingle resulting from centuries of violent weather-influenced activity along the Devon and Dorset coastline. The novelist Ian McEwan chose the setting for his recent novel *On Chesil Beach*. ▶

Thomas Hardy

Rural Dorset is where you can be 'far from the madding crowd'- to quote Thomas Hardy. For fans of this popular and much-admired writer there is the chance to visit two National Trust properties - the cob-and-thatch cottage in Higher Bockhampton where he was born and lived until the age of 34, and Max Gate in Dorchester, his home for 40 years and where he wrote some of his best-known works.

Walking and Cycling

For the true walker, however, there is nowhere to beat the magnificent Dorset coastline, particularly in the vicinity of Charmouth and Bridport where the domed Golden Cap stands tall and proud amid the cliffs. At 619ft it is the highest cliff on the south coast. Getting there, however, involves about 0.75 mile (1.2km) of steep walking. The Golden Cap is part of Dorset's spectacular Jurassic Coast, a World Heritage Site. This designated coastline stretches to East Devon.

The South West Coast Path, one of Britain's great walks, extends the length of the Dorset coast, from Lyme Regis to Studland Bay and Poole Harbour, and offers constant uninterrupted views of the coast and the Channel. Away from the sea there are miles of rolling downland walks which are no less impressive than the coastal stretches. The Purbeck Hills, between Weymouth and Poole Harbour, are great for exploring on foot. Cranborne Chase, to the north of Blandford Forum and once a royal forest, is a remote, rural backwater where the walker can feel totally at home.

The National Cycle Network offers the chance to ride from Dorchester through the heart of Dorset to Lyme Regis or north to Sherborne, taking in some of the county's most picturesque villages. There is also the chance to tour the ancient hill forts of Pilsdon Pen, Coneys Castle and Lamberts Castle around Charmouth and the Marshwood Vale – among a wide choice of Dorset cycle routes.

Festivals and Events

- Among numerous live shows, exhibitions, flower festivals and craft fairs, is the Great Dorset Steam Fair in September. This famous event draws many visitors who come to look at vintage and classic vehicles. There are also heavy horse shows and rural crafts.
- Also in September is the two-day Dorset County Show which includes over 450 trade stands, exciting main ring attractions and thousands of animals.
- For something a bit more light-hearted – but perhaps a little uncomfortable - there is the annual Nettle Eating Contest in June, which attracts fans from all over Europe.

● Promenade, Bournemouth

● Durdle Door and Bat's Head

DORSET

See Walk 4 in the Walks & Cycle Rides section at the end of the guide

ALDERHOLT   Map 5 SU11

Places to visit

Furzey Gardens, MINSTEAD 023 8081 2464
www.furzey-gardens.org

Breamore House & Countryside Museum,
BREAMORE 01725 512468
www.breamorehouse.com

Great for kids: Rockbourne Roman Villa,
ROCKBOURNE 0845 603 5635
www.hants.gov.uk/rockbourne-roman-villa

AA CAMPING CARD SITE

PREMIER PARK

►►►►► 80% **Hill Cottage Farm Camping and Caravan Park** (SU119133)

Sandleheath Rd SP6 3EG
☎ 01425 650513 & 07714 648690
e-mail:
hillcottagefarmcaravansite@supanet.com
dir: *Take B3078 W of Fordingbridge. Exit at Alderholt, site 0.25m on left after railway bridge*

Open Mar-Oct
Last arrival 19.00hrs Last departure 11.00hrs

Set within extensive grounds this rural, beautifully landscaped park offers all fully-serviced pitches set in individual hardstanding bays with mature hedges between giving adequate pitch privacy. The modern toilet block is kept immaculately clean, and there's a good range of leisure facilities. In high season there is an area available for tenting. Rallies are very welcome and there is a rally field. Function room with skittle alley available. 40 acre site. 75 touring pitches. 35 hardstandings. Caravan pitches. Motorhome pitches. Tent pitches.

AA Pubs & Restaurants nearby: The Augustus John, Fordingbridge 01425 652098

Leisure: 🏓 🎣

Facilities: 🐾 ⊙ ℗ ✳ 🏌 🕐 🛏 🚿 📮 WiFi 💻 ♻ 🅭

Services: 🚐 🔋 🛢 🧴 🚽

Within 3 miles: ⬇ 🎿 🎣 🛒 🏇 ∪

Notes: No noise after 22.30hrs. Dogs must be kept on leads.

BERE REGIS

Places to visit

Kingston Lacy, WIMBORNE 01202 883402 (Mon-Fri) www.nationaltrust.org.uk

Priest's House Museum and Garden, WIMBORNE 01202 882533 www.priest-house.co.uk

Great for kids: Monkey World-Ape Rescue Centre, WOOL 01929 462537 www.monkeyworld.org

BERE REGIS   Map 4 SY89

►►► 81% *Rowlands Wait Touring Park* (SY842933)

Rye Hill BH20 7LP
☎ 01929 472727
e-mail: enquiries@rowlandswait.co.uk
web: www.rowlandswait.co.uk
dir: *On approach to Bere Regis follow signs to Bovington Tank Museum. At top of Rye Hill, 0.75m from village turn right. 200yds to site*

🚐 🚉 🏕

Open mid Mar-Oct (winter by arrangement)
Last arrival 21.00hrs Last departure noon

This park lies in a really attractive setting overlooking Bere Regis and the Dorset countryside, set amongst undulating areas of trees and shrubs. The toilet facilities include two family rooms. Located within a few miles of the Tank Museum with its mock battles, and is also very convenient for visiting the Dorchester, Poole and Swanage areas. 8 acre site. 71 touring pitches. 2 hardstandings. 23 seasonal pitches. Caravan pitches. Motorhome pitches. Tent pitches.

LEISURE: 🏊 Indoor swimming pool 🏊 Outdoor swimming pool 🛝 Children's playground 🧒 Kid's club 🎾 Tennis court 🎱 Games room 📺 Separate TV room 🏌 9/18 hole golf course ⛵ Boats for hire 🎬 Cinema 🎵 Entertainment 🎣 Fishing ⛳ Mini golf 🏄 Watersports 🏋 Gym 🌳 Sports field Spa ∪ Stables
FACILITIES: 🛁 Bath 🚿 Shower ⊙ Electric shaver 🗲 Hairdryer ✳ Ice Pack Facility ♿ Disabled facilities 🕐 Public telephone 🛒 Shop on site or within 200yds 🛒 Mobile shop (calls at least 5 days a week) 🍖 BBQ area 🪑 Picnic area WiFi Wi-fi 💻 Internet access ♻ Recycling 🅭 Tourist info 🐕 Dog exercise area

AA Pubs & Restaurants nearby: Botany Bay Inne, Winterborne Zelston 01929 459227

Leisure: /Λ ⚲

Facilities: ⬥⊙🅟☀♿🖻🚿⚡♻🛈

Services: ⚡🖬🛢🖉🅣🔌⚰

Within 3 miles: ↓🏌🎯⊙🛍🐴U

Notes: No open fires. Dogs must be kept on leads.

BLANDFORD FORUM

Places to visit

Kingston Lacy, WIMBORNE 01202 883402 (Mon-Fri) www.nationaltrust.org.uk

Old Wardour Castle, TISBURY 01747 870487 www.english-heritage.org.uk

Great for kids: Monkey World-Ape Rescue Centre, WOOL 01929 462537 www.monkeyworld.org

---

BLANDFORD FORUM Map 4 ST80

▶▶▶▶ **81% The Inside Park**

(ST869046)

Down House Estate DT11 9AD
☎ **01258 453719**
e-mail: mail@theinsidepark.co.uk
dir: *From town, over River Stour, follow Winterborne Stickland signs. Site in 1.5m*

* 🚐 £15.50-£23.45 🚐 £15.50-£23.45
▲ £15.50-£23.45

Open Etr-Oct

Last arrival 22.00hrs Last departure noon

An attractive, well-sheltered and quiet park, half a mile off a country lane in a wooded valley. Spacious pitches are divided by mature trees and shrubs, and amenities are housed in an 18th-century coach house and stables. There are some lovely woodland walks within the park, an excellent fenced play area for children and a dog-free area. 12 acre site. 125 touring pitches. Caravan pitches. Motorhome pitches. Tent pitches.

AA Pubs & Restaurants nearby: Crown Hotel, Blandford Forum 01258 456626

Anvil Inn, Blandford Forum 01258 453431

Leisure: /Λ ⚲

Facilities: ⬥⊙🅟☀♿🕐🖻🚿♻🛈

Services: ⚡🖬🛢🖉🅣🛒

Within 3 miles: ↓🏌🛍🐴U

Notes: Dogs must be kept on leads. Kennels for hire.

BRIDPORT | Map 4 SY49

AA HOLIDAY CENTRE OF THE YEAR 2013

 91% Freshwater Beach Holiday Park (SY493892)

Burton Bradstock DT6 4PT
☎ 01308 897317
e-mail: office@freshwaterbeach.co.uk
web: www.freshwaterbeach.co.uk
dir: *Take B3157 from Bridport towards Burton Bradstock. Site 1.5m from Crown rdbt on right*

* ⛺ £16-£42 🚐 £16-£42 ⛺ £16-£42

Open mid Mar-mid Nov

Last arrival 22.00hrs Last departure 10.00hrs

A family holiday centre sheltered by a sand bank and enjoying its own private beach. The park offers a wide variety of leisure and entertainment programmes for all the family; plus the Jurassic Fun Centre with indoor pool, gym, 6-lane bowling alley, restaurant and bar is excellent. The park is well placed at one end of the Weymouth/Bridport coast with spectacular views of Chesil Beach. There are three immaculate toilet blocks, with excellent private rooms. 40 acre site. 500 touring pitches. 25 hardstandings. Caravan pitches. Motorhome pitches. Tent pitches. 250 statics. See also page 22.

AA Pubs & Restaurants nearby: Shave Cross Inn, Bridport 01308 868358

Riverside Restaurant, Bridport 01308 422011

Anchor Inn, Chideock 01297 489215

Freshwater Beach Holiday Park

Leisure: 🏊‍♂️ 🏊 ⛳ 🎢 🎡 🔫 🎵 Spa
Facilities: 🔫 ⊙ 🍴 ❄ ♿ 🛒 🕹 🔥 📶 💻 ℹ️
Services: 🚐 🔲 🛢 🚿 🍴 🛒 🍴 🛒 🛒
Within 3 miles: ⚓ 🏇 ⛳ 🎣 ⊙ 🛒 🛒 U

Notes: Families & couples only. Dogs must be kept on leads. Large TV, entertainment & kids' club in high season & BHs.

see advert on opposite page

LEISURE: 🏊 Indoor swimming pool 🏊 Outdoor swimming pool 🛝 Children's playground 🎣 Kid's club 🎾 Tennis court 🎱 Games room 📺 Separate TV room ⛳ 9/18 hole golf course ⛵ Boats for hire 🎬 Cinema 🎵 Entertainment 🎣 Fishing ⊙ Mini golf 🏄 Watersports 🏋 Gym 🏟 Sports field Spa U Stables
FACILITIES: 🛁 Bath 🚿 Shower ⊙ Electric shaver 🖐 Hairdryer ❄ Ice Pack Facility ♿ Disabled facilities 📞 Public telephone 🛒 Shop on site or within 200yds 🏪 Mobile shop (calls at least 5 days a week) 🍴 BBQ area 🪑 Picnic area 📶 Wi-fi 💻 Internet access ♻ Recycling ℹ️ Tourist info 🐕 Dog exercise area

Freshwater Beach
HOLIDAY PARK

- Exclusive private beach
- Jurassic Fun Centre including: 10-pin bowling, indoor family pools, water slides, hot tub, sauna & steam room, restaurants
- Fabulous entertainment*
- Outdoor family pools
- Children's activities during school holidays
- Caravan holiday homes for hire
- Large touring and camping field and much more....

Great family holidays on Dorset's World Heritage Coast.

Facilities will be reduced outside the main holiday periods
* Spring Bank Holiday to mid September

Wi Fi

01308 897 317 **freshwaterbeach.co.uk**

BRIDPORT *continued*

84% West Bay Holiday Park *(SY461906)*

GOLD

West Bay DT6 4HB
☎ 0844 335 3756
e-mail: touringandcamping@parkdeanholidays.com
web: www.parkdeantouring.com
dir: *From A35 (Dorchester road), W towards Bridport, take 1st exit at 1st rdbt, 2nd exit at 2nd rdbt into West Bay, site on right*

* ⊡ £15-£48 ⊟ £15-£48 ▲ fr £12

Open Mar-Oct

Last arrival 23.00hrs Last departure 10.00hrs

Overlooking the pretty little harbour at West Bay, and close to the shingle beach, this park offers a full entertainment programme for all ages. There are children's clubs and an indoor pool with flume for all the family, and plenty of evening fun with shows and cabaret etc. The large adventure playground is very popular. The terraced touring section, with its own reception and warden offers excellent sea views and has hardstandings and super pitches. 6 acre site. 116 touring pitches. Caravan pitches. Motorhome pitches. Tent pitches. 298 statics.

AA Pubs & Restaurants nearby: George Hotel, Bridport 01308 423187

West Bay, Bridport 01308 422157

Riverside Restaurant, Bridport 01308 422011

Leisure: 🏊 🎪 ↘ 🎱
Facilities: 🛁 🏠 ⊙ 🖅 ✳ 🕭 🕒 🅂 🎌 WiFi
Services: 🔌 🗄 🔧 🧺 ⚗ T 🍴 🛒 🏪 ⚘
Within 3 miles: ↘ ⚓ 🎣 ◎ 🖼 🅂 U
Notes: No skateboards.

▶▶▶▶ 89% Highlands End Holiday Park *(SY454913)*

Best of British
GOLD

Eype DT6 6AR
☎ 01308 422139 & 426947
e-mail: holidays@wdlh.co.uk
dir: *1m W of Bridport on A35, turn south for Eype. Site signed*

⊡ ⊟ ▲

Open 16 Mar-4 Nov

Last arrival 22.00hrs Last departure 11.00hrs

A well-screened site with magnificent cliff-top views over the Channel and Dorset coast, adjacent to National Trust land and overlooking Lyme Bay. The pitches are mostly sheltered by hedging and well spaced on hardstandings. The excellent facilities include a tasteful bar and resturant, indoor pool, leisure centre and The Cowshed, a very good coffee shop, which opened in 2012. There is a mixture of statics and tourers, but the tourers enjoy the best cliff-top positions. 9 acre site. 195 touring pitches. 45 hardstandings. Caravan pitches. Motorhome pitches. Tent pitches. 160 statics.

AA Pubs & Restaurants nearby: Shave Cross Inn, Bridport 01308 868358

Riverside Restaurant, Bridport 01308 422011

Anchor Inn, Chideock 01297 489215

Highlands End Holiday Park

Leisure: 🏊 ⛵ 🎪 🎱 ◎ ⚓ 🎣 🎵
Facilities: 🏠 ⊙ 🖅 ✳ 🕭 🕒 🅂 🎌 WiFi ♻ 🛈
Services: 🔌 🗄 🔧 🧺 ⚗ T 🍴 🛒 🏪 ⚘
Within 3 miles: ↘ 🎣 🅂 ◎
Notes: Dogs must be kept on leads. Steam room, sauna, pitch & putt.

see advert on opposite page

▶▶▶▶ 86% Bingham Grange Touring & Camping Park *(SY478963)*

Melplash DT6 3TT
☎ 01308 488234
e-mail: enquiries@binghamgrange.co.uk
dir: *From A35 at Bridport take A3066 N towards Beaminster. Site on left after 3m*

⊡ ⊟ ▲

Open 16 Mar-end Oct (rs Wed (eve high season), Tue-Wed (mid-low season) restaurant & bar closed)

Set in a quiet rural location but only five miles from the Jurassic Coast, this adults-only park enjoys views over the west Dorset countryside. The mostly level pitches are attractively set amongst shrub beds and ornamental trees. There is an excellent restaurant with lounge bar and takeaway, and all facilities are of a high quality. A very dog-friendly site. 20 acre site. 150 touring pitches. 85 hardstandings. 40 seasonal pitches. Caravan pitches. Motorhome pitches. Tent pitches.

AA Pubs & Restaurants nearby: George Hotel, Bridport 01308 423187

West Bay, Bridport 01308 422157

Riverside Restaurant, Bridport 01308 422011

Facilities: ⌂ ☉ ℙ ❋ ᕽ ☾ ⓢ ⊣ ⌁ ᴡɪ-ꜰɪ ♻ ❶

Services: 🔌 🔲 🍺 🛢 ⌀ Ⓣ 🍴 ⛽

Within 3 miles: ↕ 🏇 🌳 ⓢ 🔲 ∪

Notes: Adults only. No under 18s may stay or visit, no noise after 23.00hrs. Dogs must be kept on leads. Woodland walks & dog exercise trail leading to river banks.

CERNE ABBAS

Places to visit

Athelhampton House & Gardens, ATHELHAMPTON 01305 848363 www.athelhampton.co.uk

Hardy's Cottage, DORCHESTER 01305 262366 www.nationaltrust.org.uk

Great for kids: Maiden Castle, DORCHESTER 0870 333 1181 www.english-heritage.org.uk

---

CERNE ABBAS   Map 4 ST60

▶▶▶ 86% Lyons Gate Caravan and Camping Park *(ST660062)*

Lyons Gate DT2 7AZ
☎ 01300 345260
e-mail: info@lyons-gate.co.uk
dir: *Signed with direct access from A352, 3m N of Cerne Abbas*

* 🚐 fr £14 🚐 fr £14 ⛺ fr £14

Open all year

Last arrival 20.00hrs Last departure 11.30hrs

A peaceful park with pitches set out around the four attractive coarse fishing lakes. It is surrounded by mature woodland, with many footpaths and bridleways. Other easily accessible attractions include the Cerne Giant carved into the hills, the old market town of Dorchester, and the superb sandy beach at Weymouth. Holiday homes are now available for sale. 10 acre site. 90 touring pitches. 24 hardstandings. Caravan pitches. Motorhome pitches. Tent pitches. 14 statics.

AA Pubs & Restaurants nearby: The Piddle Inn, Piddletrenthide 01300 348468

Poachers Inn, Piddletrenthide 01300 348358

Leisure: ⚙ 🎣 🔲

Facilities: ⌂ ☉ ℙ ❋ ᕽ ☾ ⓢ ⊣ ⌁ ᴡɪ-ꜰɪ ❶

Services: 🔌 🔲 🍺 ⌀

Within 3 miles: ↕ 🌳 🔲 ∪

Notes: Dogs must be kept on leads.

▶▶ 69% Giants Head Caravan & Camping Park *(ST675029)*

Giants Head Farm, Old Sherborne Rd DT2 7TR
☎ 01300 341242
e-mail: holidays@giantshead.co.uk
dir: *From Dorchester into town avoiding by-pass, at Top O'Town rdbt take A352 (Sherborne road), in 500yds right fork at BP (Loder's) garage, site signed*

* 🚐 £8-£16 🚐 £8-£16 ⛺ £8-£16

Open Etr-Oct (rs Etr shop & bar closed)

Last arrival anytime Last departure 13.00hrs

A pleasant, though rather basic, park set in Dorset downland near the Cerne Giant (the famous landmark figure cut into the chalk) with stunning views. This is a good stopover site, ideal for tenters and backpackers on the Ridgeway route. Holiday chalets to let. 4 acre site. 50 touring pitches. Caravan pitches. Motorhome pitches. Tent pitches.

AA Pubs & Restaurants nearby: Greyhound Inn, Sydling St Nicholas 01300 341303

Facilities: ⌂ ☉ ℙ ❋ ᕽ ⊣ ⌁ ♻ ❶

Services: 🔌 🔲 🍺 ⌀ 🔋

Within 3 miles: 🌳 ⓢ 🔲

Notes: 🐕 Dogs must be kept on leads.

CHARMOUTH   Map 4 SY39

Places to visit

Forde Abbey, CHARD 01460 221290
www.fordeabbey.co.uk

Dorset County Museum, DORCHESTER
01305 262735 www.dorsetcountymuseum.org

Great for kids: Abbotsbury Swannery,
ABBOTSBURY 01305 871858
www.abbotsbury-tourism.co.uk

PREMIER PARK

►►►►► 91% Wood Farm Caravan & Camping Park

(SY356940)

Axminster Rd DT6 6BT
☎ 01297 560697
e-mail: holidays@woodfarm.co.uk
web: www.woodfarm.co.uk
dir: *Site entered directly from A35 rdbt, on Axminster side of Charmouth*

* 🚐 £15.50-£33.50 🚏 £15.50-£33.50
▲ £15.50-£28

Open Etr-Oct

Last arrival 19.00hrs Last departure noon

This top quality park, the perfect place to relax, is set amongst mature native trees with the various levels of the site falling away into a beautiful valley below. The park offers excellent facilities including family rooms and fully serviced pitches. The facilities throughout the park are spotless. At the bottom end of the park there is an excellent indoor swimming pool and leisure complex, plus the licensed, conservatory-style Offshore Café. There's a good children's play room plus tennis courts and a well-stocked, coarse-fishing lake. The park is well positioned on the Heritage Coast near Lyme Regis. Static holiday homes are also available for hire. 13 acre site. 175 touring pitches. 175 hardstandings. 20 seasonal pitches. Caravan pitches. Motorhome pitches. Tent pitches. 92 statics.

AA Pubs & Restaurants nearby: Pilot Boat Inn, Lyme Regis 01297 443157

Leisure: 🏊⚲🎢🎣⛳▢
Facilities: 🛁🕯☉🅿✳♿⛱🖊📶♻️❶
Services: 🔌🛢🚽💧🚰🅣🍽️🛒⚙️
Within 3 miles: ⚓🎣🅷🖊◎🛶🛥️🐎

Notes: No skateboards, scooters, roller skates or bikes. Dogs must be kept on leads.

►►►► 86% Newlands Caravan & Camping Park (SY374935)

DT6 6RB
☎ 01297 560259
e-mail: enq@newlandsholidays.co.uk
web: www.newlandsholidays.co.uk
dir: *4m W of Bridport on A35*

🚐🚏▲

Open 10 Mar-4 Nov

Last arrival 21.00hrs Last departure 10.00hrs

A very smart site with excellent touring facilities. The park offers a full cabaret and entertainment programme for all ages, and boasts an indoor swimming pool with spa and an outdoor pool with water slide. Set on gently sloping ground in hilly countryside near the sea. Lodges and apartments are available. 23 acre site. 240 touring pitches. 52 hardstandings. Caravan pitches. Motorhome pitches. Tent pitches. 86 statics.

AA Pubs & Restaurants nearby: Pilot Boat Inn, Lyme Regis 01297 443157

Leisure: 🏊⚲🎢♿🎣▢🎵
Facilities: 🕯☉🅿✳♿⛱🖊📶💻♻️❶
Services: 🔌🛢🚽💧🚰🅣🍽️🛒⚙️
Within 3 miles: ⚓🎣🅷🖊◎🛶🛥️🐎

Notes: Dogs must be kept on leads. Kids' club only during school holidays.

AA CAMPING CARD SITE

►►► 85% Manor Farm Holiday Centre (SY368937)

DT6 6QL
☎ 01297 560226
e-mail: enquiries@manorfarmholidaycentre.co.uk
dir: *W on A35 to Charmouth, site 0.75m on right*

* 🚐 £14-£28 🚏 £14-£28 ▲ £14-£28

Open all year (rs End Oct-mid Mar statics only)

Last arrival 20.00hrs Last departure 10.00hrs

Set just a short walk from the safe sand and shingle beach at Charmouth, this popular family park offers a good range of facilities. Children enjoy the activity area and outdoor swimming pool (so do their parents!), and the park also offers a lively programme in the extensive bar and entertainment complex. There is an excellent outdoor/indoor swimming pool, plus café, sun terrace and gym complex. 1- to 5-bedroom

cottages are available for hire. 30 acre site. 400 touring pitches. 80 hardstandings. 100 seasonal pitches. Caravan pitches. Motorhome pitches. Tent pitches. 29 statics.

AA Pubs & Restaurants nearby: Pilot Boat Inn, Lyme Regis 01297 443157

Leisure: 🏊⚲🎢♿🎣🎵 Spa
Facilities: 🕯☉🅿✳♿⛱🖊📶♻️❶
Services: 🔌🛢🚽💧🚰🅣🍽️🛒⚙️
Within 3 miles: ⚓🎣🅷🖊◎🛶🛥️🐎

Notes: No skateboards. Dogs must be kept on leads.

CHIDEOCK   Map 4 SY49

Places to visit

Branscombe - The Old Bakery, Manor Mill and Forge, BRANSCOMBE 01752 346585
www.nationaltrust.org.uk

Mapperton, BEAMINSTER 01308 862645
www.mapperton.com

Great for kids: Pecorama Pleasure Gardens, BEER 01297 21542 www.pecorama.info

►►►► 83% Golden Cap Holiday Park (SY422919)

Seatown DT6 6JX
☎ 01308 422139 & 426947
e-mail: holidays@wdlh.co.uk
dir: *On A35, in Chideock follow Seatown signs, site signed*

🚐🚏▲

Open 22 Mar-3 Nov

Last arrival 22.00hrs Last departure 11.00hrs

A grassy site, overlooking sea and beach and surrounded by National Trust parkland. This uniquely placed park slopes down to the sea, although pitches are generally level. A slight dip hides the view of the beach from the back of the park, but this area benefits from having trees, scrub and meadows, unlike the barer areas closer to the sea which do have a spectacular outlook. This makes an ideal base for touring Dorset and Devon. 11 acre site. 108 touring pitches. 24 hardstandings. Caravan pitches. Motorhome pitches. Tent pitches. 234 statics.

LEISURE: 🏊 Indoor swimming pool ⚲ Outdoor swimming pool 🎢 Children's playground 🎣 Kid's club 🎾 Tennis court 🎯 Games room ▢ Separate TV room ⛳ 9/18 hole golf course 🚣 Boats for hire 🎬 Cinema 🎵 Entertainment 🎣 Fishing ◎ Mini golf 🛥️ Watersports 💪 Gym 🏟️ Sports field Spa 🐎 Stables
FACILITIES: 🛁 Bath 🕯 Shower ☉ Electric shaver 🅿 Hairdryer ✳ Ice Pack Facility ♿ Disabled facilities 🕐 Public telephone 🛢 Shop on site or within 200yds 🏪 Mobile shop (calls at least 5 days a week) ⛱ BBQ area 🌲 Picnic area 📶 Wi-fi 💻 Internet access ♻️ Recycling ❶ Tourist info 🖊 Dog exercise area

AA Pubs & Restaurants nearby: George Hotel, Bridport 01308 423187

West Bay, Bridport 01308 422157

Riverside Restaurant, Bridport 01308 422011

Leisure: ⚁

Facilities: 🏕☉🏟✻🅱🛈🏪🚻🚽🎮🚮🛈

Services: 🔌🗑🛢🛒🕿🅃🍽🔋

Within 3 miles: 🚶🏌🛒🛍

Notes: Dogs must be kept on leads. Fishing lake.

CHRISTCHURCH — Map 5 SZ19

Places to visit

Red House Museum & Gardens, CHRISTCHURCH 01202 482860 www.hants.gov.uk/museum/redhouse

Hurst Castle, HURST CASTLE 01590 642344 www.english-heritage.org.uk

Great for kids: Oceanarium, BOURNEMOUTH 01202 311993 www.oceanarium.co.uk

PREMIER PARK

▶▶▶▶▶ 85% Meadowbank Holidays (SZ136946)

Stour Way BH23 2PQ
☎ 01202 483597
e-mail: enquiries@meadowbank-holidays.co.uk
web: www.meadowbank-holidays.co.uk
dir: A31 onto A338 towards Bournemouth. Take 1st exit after 5m then left towards Christchurch on B3073. Right at 1st rdbt into St Catherine's Way/River Way. Stour Way 3rd right, site at end of road

* 🚐 £10-£31 🚑 £10-£31

Open Mar-Oct

Last arrival 21.00hrs Last departure noon

A very smart park on the banks of the River Stour, with a colourful display of hanging baskets and flower-filled tubs placed around the superb reception area. The facility block is excellent. Visitors can choose between the different pitch

sizes, including luxury fully-serviced ones. There is also an excellent play area and a good shop on site. Statics are available for hire. 2 acre site. 41 touring pitches. 22 hardstandings. Caravan pitches. Motorhome pitches. 180 statics.

AA Pubs & Restaurants nearby: Ship in Distress, Christchurch 01202 485123

Splinters Restaurant, Christchurch 01202 483454

Leisure: ⚁🎣

Facilities: 🛁🏕☉🏟🅱🛈🏪🚻🎮🖥🚮🛈

Services: 🔌🗑🛢🛒🅃🔋🚰

Within 3 miles: 🚶🏌🛒🛍🔌🚣🛍U

Notes: No pets. Fishing on site.

CORFE CASTLE — Map 4 SY98

Places to visit

Corfe Castle, CORFE CASTLE 01929 481294 www.nationaltrust.org.uk

Brownsea Island, BROWNSEA ISLAND 01202 707744 www.nationaltrust.org.uk

Great for kids: Swanage Railway, SWANAGE 01929 425800 www.swanagerailway.co.uk

▶▶▶▶ 86% Corfe Castle Camping & Caravanning Club Site (SY953818)

Bucknowle BH20 5PQ
☎ 01929 480280 & 0845 130 7633
dir: From Wareham A351 towards Swanage. In 4m turn right at foot of Corfe Castle signed Church Knowle. 0.75m right to site on left at top of lane

🚐🚑🅰

Open Mar-Oct

Last arrival 20.00hrs Last departure noon

This lovely campsite, where non-members are also very welcome, is set in woodland near to the famous Corfe Castle at the foot of the Purbeck Hills. It has a stone reception building, on-site shop and modern toilet and shower facilities, which are spotless. Although the site is sloping, pitches are level and include spacious hardstandings. The site is perfect for visiting the many attractions of the Purbeck area, including the award-winning beaches at Studland and Swanage, and the seaside towns of Poole, Bournemouth and Weymouth. There is also the station at Corfe for the Swanage Steam Railway. The site is pet friendly. 6 acre site. 80 touring pitches. 33 hardstandings. Caravan pitches. Motorhome pitches. Tent pitches.

AA Pubs & Restaurants nearby: Greyhound Inn, Corfe Castle 01929 480205

New Inn, Church Knowle 01929 480357

Leisure: ⚁

Facilities: 🏕☉🏟✻🅱🛈🏪🚮🛈

Services: 🔌🗑🛢🛒🅃🔋🚽

Within 3 miles: 🚶🏌🛒🔌🚣🛍U

Notes: Site gates closed between 23.00hrs-07.00hrs, any arrival time after 20.00hrs by prior arrangement. Dogs must be kept on leads.

▶▶▶ 80% Woody Hyde Camp Site (SY974804)

Valley Rd BH20 5HT
☎ 01929 480274
e-mail: camp@woodyhyde.fsnet.co.uk
dir: From Corfe Castle towards Swanage on A351, site approx 1m on right

* 🚑 £14 🅰 £14

Open Mar-Oct

A large grassy campsite in a sheltered location for tents and motorhomes only, set into three paddocks - one is dog free. There is a well-stocked shop on site, and a regular bus service located near the site entrance. This site offers traditional camping in a great location on Purbeck. Electric hook-ups and some hardstandings are now available. A new toilet and shower block opened for the 2012 season. 13 acre site. 150 touring pitches. Motorhome pitches. Tent pitches.

AA Pubs & Restaurants nearby: Greyhound Inn, Corfe Castle 01929 480205

New Inn, Church Knowle 01929 480357

Facilities: 🏕🏟✻🅱🛍🚮

Services: 🔌🛢🛒

Within 3 miles: 🛍🛍

Notes: No noise after 23.00hrs, no open fires. Dogs must be kept on leads.

DORCHESTER

See Cerne Abbas

DRIMPTON
Map 4 ST40

Places to visit

Forde Abbey, CHARD 01460 221290
www.fordeabbey.co.uk

Mapperton, BEAMINSTER 01308 862645
www.mapperton.com

▶▶▶▶ **81% Oathill Farm Touring and Camping Site** (ST404055)

Oathill TA18 8PZ
☎ **01460 30234**
e-mail: oathillfarm@btconnect.com
dir: From Crewkerne take B3165. Site on left just after Clapton

* ⊞ £17.50-£22.50 ⇔ £17.50-£22.50
Å £16.50-£18.00

Open all year

Last arrival 20.00hrs Last departure noon

This small peaceful park is located on the borders of Somerset and Devon, with the Jurassic coast of Lyme Regis, Charmouth and Bridport only a short drive away. The modern facilities are spotless and there are hardstandings and fully-serviced pitches available. Lucy's Tea Room serves breakfast and meals. Well stocked, landscaped fishing ponds are now open. Three luxury lodges are available for hire. 10 acre site. 13 touring pitches. 13 hardstandings. 3 seasonal pitches. Caravan pitches. Motorhome pitches. Tent pitches. 3 statics.

AA Pubs & Restaurants nearby: The Wild Garlic, Beaminster 01308 861446

Leisure: ✪
Facilities: ♠ ☉ ☔ ✳ ⓘ ☵ ☴ WiFi 🖥 ♲ 🛈
Services: 🖉 ⊡ 🍴 🙂 ⏦ ⊤ 🍲 ⊞ ⛟
Within 3 miles: ♨ ♪ ⓢ ⓢ ♺

Notes: No washing lines, no quad bikes, no noise after 23.00hrs. Separate recreational areas.

FERNDOWN
Map 5 SU00

Places to visit

Poole Museum, POOLE 01202 262600
www.boroughofpoole.com/museums

Kingston Lacy, WIMBORNE 01202 883402
(Mon-Fri) www.nationaltrust.org.uk

Great for kids: Oceanarium, BOURNEMOUTH
01202 311993 www.oceanarium.co.uk

AA CAMPING CARD SITE

▶▶▶ **77% St Leonards Farm Caravan & Camping Park** (SU093014)

Ringwood Rd, West Moors BH22 0AQ
☎ **01202 872637**
e-mail: enquiries_stleonards@yahoo.co.uk
web: www.stleonardsfarm.biz
dir: From E (Ringwood): entrance directly off A31, after crossing rdbt, opposite Texaco garage. From W: U-turn at rdbt after Texaco garage, turn left into site

* ⊞ £11-£21 ⇔ £11-£21 Å £11-£21

Open Apr-Sep

Last departure 14.00hrs

A private road off the A31 leads to this well-screened park divided into paddocks, with spacious pitches; the site now has a new children's play fort. This is one of the nearest parks to Bournemouth which has many holiday amenities. 12 acre site. 151 touring pitches. 30 seasonal pitches. Caravan pitches. Motorhome pitches. Tent pitches. 6 statics.

Leisure: ⚠
Facilities: ♠ ☉ ✳ ☵ ☴ 🛈
Services: 🖉 ⊡ 🍴 ♺
Within 3 miles: ♨ ♪ ⓢ ⓢ

Notes: No large groups, no noise after 23.00hrs, no disposable BBQs, no gazebos. Dogs must be kept on leads.

HOLTON HEATH
Map 4 SY99

Places to visit

Royal Signals Museum, BLANDFORD FORUM
01258 482248 www.royalsignalsmuseum.com

Larmer Tree Gardens, TOLLARD ROYAL
01725 516228 www.larmertreegardens.co.uk

Great for kids: Moors Valley Country Park,
RINGWOOD 01425 470721
www.moors-valley.co.uk

 84% Sandford Holiday Park (SY939916)

Organford Rd BH16 6JZ
☎ **0844 335 3756 & 01202 631600**
e-mail:
touringandcamping@parkdeanholidays.com
web: www.parkdeantouring.com
dir: A35 from Poole towards Dorchester, at lights onto A351 towards Wareham. Right at Holton Heath. Site 100yds on left

* ⊞ £15.50-£45 ⇔ £15.50-£45 Å £12.50-£38

Open Mar-Oct (rs 4 May-16 Sep outdoor pool open)

Last arrival 20.00hrs Last departure 10.00hrs

With touring pitches set individually in 20 acres surrounded by woodland, this park offers a full range of leisure activities and entertainment for the whole family. The touring area, situated at the far end of the park, is neat and well maintained, and there are children's clubs in the daytime and nightly entertainment. A reception area with lounge, bar, café and restaurant creates an excellent and attractive entrance, with a covered area outside with tables and chairs and well-landscaped gardens. Static holiday homes are available for hire or purchase. 64 acre site. 353 touring pitches. 20 hardstandings. 79 seasonal pitches. Caravan pitches. Motorhome pitches. Tent pitches. 344 statics.

AA Pubs & Restaurants nearby: Greyhound Inn, Corfe Castle 01929 480205

New Inn, Church Knowle 01929 480357

Leisure: ⚓🏊⛰🛶🎣🎮🎵

Facilities: ➤🏕☉🅿✳♿🕐🔥🚿🚐Wi-Fi 🖥♻ ❶

Services: 🔌🗑🍴💷🚿🚽🍽🏪🔋⚡

Within 3 miles: 🏇🛶🎯🎣🟰◎🚲🏪🗑U

Notes: No noise after 23.00hrs, no motorised scooters or carts, max 2 dogs per pitch. Dogs must be kept on leads. Bowling, crazy golf, bike hire, adventure playground.

Places to visit

Red House Museum & Gardens, CHRISTCHURCH 01202 482860
www.hants.gov.uk/museum/redhouse

Oceanarium, BOURNEMOUTH 01202 311993
www.oceanarium.co.uk

►► 85% Fillybrook Farm Touring Park *(SZ128997)*

Matchams Ln BH23 6AW
☎ 01202 478266
e-mail: enquiries@fillybrookfarm.co.uk
web: www.fillybrookfarm.co.uk
dir: *M27 junct 1, A31 to Ringwood. Continue towards Poole, left immediately after Texaco Garage signed Verwood & B3081, left into Hurn Ln signed Matchams. Site on right in 4m*

🚐 £15-£18 🚍 £15-£18 ▲ £15-£18

Open Etr-Oct

Last arrival 20.00hrs Last departure 11.00hrs

A small adults-only park well located on the edge of Hurn Forest, with Bournemouth, Christchurch, Poole and the New Forest within easy reach. The facilities are both modern and very clean. A dry-ski slope, with an adjoining restaurant and small bar, is a short walk from the site. There is also a separate rally field. 1 acre site. 18 touring pitches. Caravan pitches. Motorhome pitches. Tent pitches.

AA Pubs & Restaurants nearby: The Three Tuns Country Inn, Bransgore 01425 672232

Facilities: 🏕☉🅿✳🔥♻ ❶

Services: 🔌🔋🏪 **Within 3 miles:** 🏇🎣🗑🏪U

Notes: Adults only. ⊘ No large groups, no commercial vehicles. Dogs must be kept on leads.

See also Charmouth

Places to visit

Marwood Hill Gardens, BARNSTAPLE
01271 342528 www.marwoodhillgarden.co.uk

Pecorama Pleasure Gardens, BEER
01297 21542 www.pecorama.info

Great for kids: The World of Country Life, EXMOUTH 01395 274533
www.worldofcountrylife.co.uk

►►►► 87% Shrubbery Touring Park *(SY300914)*

Rousdon DT7 3XW
☎ 01297 442227
e-mail: info@shrubberypark.co.uk
web: www.shrubberypark.co.uk
dir: *3m W of Lyme Regis on A3052 (coast road)*

* 🚐 £12-£17 🚍 £12-£17 ▲ £12-£17

Open 22 Mar-Oct

Last arrival 21.00hrs Last departure 11.00hrs

Mature trees enclose this peaceful park, which has distant views of the lovely countryside. The modern facilities are well kept, the hardstanding pitches are spacious, and there is plenty of space for children to play in the grounds. This park is right on the Jurassic Coast bus route, which is popular with visitors to this area. 23 acre site. 120 touring pitches. 23 hardstandings. Caravan pitches. Motorhome pitches. Tent pitches.

AA Pubs & Restaurants nearby: Pilot Boat Inn, Lyme Regis 01297 443157

Leisure: 🅰

Facilities: 🏕☉🅿✳♿🔥♻ ❶

Services: 🔌🗑🍴⚡

Within 3 miles: 🏇🛶🎯🎣◎🚲🏪🗑

Notes: No motor scooters, roller skates or skateboards, no groups (except rallies). Dogs must be kept on leads. Crazy golf.

►►► 84% Hook Farm Caravan & Camping Park *(SY323930)*

Gore Ln, Uplyme DT7 3UU
☎ 01297 442801
e-mail: information@hookfarm-uplyme.co.uk
dir: *A35 onto B3165 towards Lyme Regis & Uplyme at Hunters Lodge pub. In 2m right into Gore Ln, site 400yds on right*

🚐 🚍 ▲

Open 15 Mar-Oct (rs Low season shop closed)

Last arrival 21.00hrs Last departure 11.00hrs

Set in a peaceful and very rural location, the popular farm site enjoys lovely views of Lym Valley and is just a mile from the seaside at Lyme Regis. There are modern toilet facilities and good on-site amenities. Most pitches are level due to excellent terracing - a great site for tents. 5.5 acre site. 100 touring pitches. 4 hardstandings. Caravan pitches. Motorhome pitches. Tent pitches. 17 statics.

AA Pubs & Restaurants nearby: Pilot Boat Inn, Lyme Regis 01297 443157

Leisure: 🅰

Facilities: 🏕☉🅿✳♿🕐🚿🔥

Services: 🔌🗑⚡🏪

Within 3 miles: 🏇🛶🎯🎣◎🚲🏪🗑U

Notes: ⊘ No groups of 6 adults or more, no dangerous dog breeds.

LYTCHETT MATRAVERS — Map 4 SY99

Places to visit

Brownsea Island, BROWNSEA ISLAND
01202 707744 www.nationaltrust.org.uk

Poole Museum, POOLE 01202 262600
www.boroughofpoole.com/museums

Great for kids: Swanage Railway, SWANAGE
01929 425800 www.swanagerailway.co.uk

►►► 78% Huntick Farm Caravan Park (SY955947)

Huntick Rd BH16 6BB
☎ 01202 622222

e-mail: huntickcaravans@btconnect.com
dir: Between Lytchett Minster & Lytchett Matravers. From A31 take A350 towards Poole. Follow Lytchett Minster signs, then Lytchett Matravers signs. Huntick Rd by Rose & Crown pub

* 🚐 £14.25-£20.50 🚐 £14.25-£20.50
🛆 £13.25-£19.25

Open Apr-Oct

Last arrival 21.00hrs Last departure noon

A really attractive little park nestling in rural surroundings edged by woodland, a mile from the village amenities of Lytchett Matravers. This neat grassy park is divided into three paddocks offering a peaceful location, yet it is close to the attractions of Poole and Bournemouth. 4 acre site. 30 touring pitches. Caravan pitches. Motorhome pitches. Tent pitches.

AA Pubs & Restaurants nearby: Botany Bay Inne, Winterborne Zelston 01929 459227

Leisure: 🛝 ⚽

Facilities: 🌂 ☉ ✳ 🚿 🚽 📶 ♻ ❶

Services: 🚽 🔒 🛒

Within 3 miles: 🛒

Notes: No ball games on site.

LYTCHETT MINSTER — Map 4 SY99

Places to visit

Clouds Hill, BOVINGTON CAMP 01929 405616
www.nationaltrust.org.uk

Poole Museum, POOLE 01202 262600
www.boroughofpoole.com/museums

Great for kids: Monkey World-Ape Rescue Centre, WOOL 01929 462537
www.monkeyworld.org

AA CAMPING CARD SITE

PREMIER PARK

►►►►► 92% South Lytchett Manor Caravan & Camping Park (SY954926)

Best of British

Dorchester Rd BH16 6JB
☎ 01202 622577

e-mail: info@southlytchettmanor.co.uk
dir: Exit A35 onto B3067, 1m E of Lytchett Minster, 600yds on right after village

* 🚐 £16.50-£29 🚐 🛆

Open Mar-2 Jan

Last arrival 21.00hrs Last departure 11.00hrs

Situated in the grounds of a historic manor house the park has modern facilities, which are spotless and well maintained. A warm and friendly welcome awaits at this lovely park which is well located for visiting Poole and Bournemouth; the Jurassic X53 bus route (Exeter to Poole) has a stop just outside the park. This park continues to improve each year. 22 acre site. 150 touring pitches. 80 hardstandings. Caravan pitches. Motorhome pitches. Tent pitches.

AA Pubs & Restaurants nearby: The Rising Sun, Poole 01202 771246

Guildhall Tavern, Poole 01202 671717

Leisure: 🛝 ⚽ 🎱 ⬜

Facilities: 🌂 ☉ 📻 ✳ 🦽 ☎ 🛒 🚿 📶 🖥 ♻ ❶

Services: 🚽 🔋 🔒 🖊 T 🛒 ✂

Within 3 miles: ⛳ 🎣 💆 🛒 🐎 ♨

Notes: No camp fires or Chinese lanterns. Dogs must be kept on leads.

ORGANFORD — Map 4 SY99

Places to visit

Tolpuddle Martyrs Museum, TOLPUDDLE
01305 848237 www.tolpuddlemartyrs.org.uk

Kingston Lacy, WIMBORNE 01202 883402
(Mon-Fri) www.nationaltrust.org.uk

Great for kids: Farmer Palmer's Farm Park, ORGANFORD 01202 622022
www.farmerpalmers.co.uk

►►►► 84% Pear Tree Holiday Park (SY938915)

Organford Rd, Holton Heath BH16 6LA
☎ 0844 272 9504

e-mail: enquiries@peartreepark.co.uk
web: www.peartreepark.co.uk
dir: From Poole take A35 towards Dorchester, onto A351 towards Wareham, at 1st lights turn right, site 300yds on left

🚐 🚐 🛆

Open Mar-Oct

Last arrival 19.00hrs Last departure 11.00hrs

A quiet, sheltered country park with many colourful flowerbeds, and toilet facilities that offer quality and comfort. The touring area is divided into terraces with mature hedges for screening, with a separate level tenting area on the edge of woodland. The friendly atmosphere at this attractive park help to ensure a relaxing holiday. A bridle path leads into Wareham Forest. 9 acre site. 154 touring pitches. 82 hardstandings. Caravan pitches. Motorhome pitches. Tent pitches. 40 statics.

AA Pubs & Restaurants nearby: Botany Bay Inne, Winterborne Zelston 01929 459227

Leisure: 🛝

Facilities: 🌂 ☉ 📻 ✳ 🦽 ☎ 🛒 🚿 ♻ ❶

Services: 🚽 🔋 🔒 🖊 T 🛒

Within 3 miles: ☉

Notes: No noise after 22.30hrs. Dogs must be kept on leads.

LEISURE: 🏊 Indoor swimming pool 🏊 Outdoor swimming pool 🛝 Children's playground 🧒 Kid's club ⚲ Tennis court 🎱 Games room ⬜ Separate TV room ⛳ 9/18 hole golf course ⛵ Boats for hire 🎬 Cinema 🎵 Entertainment 🎣 Fishing ⛳ Mini golf 🏄 Watersports 🏋 Gym ♨ Sports field Spa ♨ Stables
FACILITIES: 🛁 Bath 🚿 Shower ☉ Electric shaver 📻 Hairdryer ✳ Ice Pack Facility 🦽 Disabled facilities ☎ Public telephone 🛒 Shop on site or within 200yds 🚐 Mobile shop (calls at least 5 days a week) 🍖 BBQ area 🌲 Picnic area 📶 Wi-fi 🖥 Internet access ♻ Recycling ❶ Tourist info 🐕 Dog exercise area

OWERMOIGNE · Map 4 SY78

Places to visit

RSPB Nature Reserve Radipole Lake, WEYMOUTH 01305 778313 www.rspb.org.uk

Clouds Hill, BOVINGTON CAMP 01929 405616 www.nationaltrust.org.uk

Great for kids: Weymouth Sea Life Adventure Park & Marine Sanctuary, WEYMOUTH 0871 423 2110 www.sealifeeurope.com

▶▶▶ 77% Sandyholme Holiday Park (SY768863)

Moreton Rd DT2 8HZ
☎ 01308 422139 & 426947
e-mail: holidays@wdlh.co.uk
web: www.wdlh.co.uk
dir: From A352 (Wareham to Dorchester road) turn right to Owermoigne for 1m. Site on left

Open 22 Mar-3 Nov (rs Etr)

Last arrival 22.00hrs Last departure 11.00hrs

A pleasant quiet site surrounded by trees and within easy reach of the coast at Lulworth Cove, and handy for several seaside resorts, including Weymouth, Portland, Purbeck and Swanage. The facilities are good, including a children's play area, small football pitch, a shop and tourist information. 6 acre site. 46 touring pitches. Caravan pitches. Motorhome pitches. Tent pitches. 52 statics.

AA Pubs & Restaurants nearby: Smugglers Inn, Osmington Mills 01305 833125

Lulworth Cove Inn, West Lulworth 01929 400333

Castle Inn, West Lulworth 01929 400311

Leisure: ⚙ ☺ ⚲
Facilities: ⚙ ☺ ✱ ✶ ✚ ⚙ ⚙ 🚿 ♿ WiFi ♻ ⚙
Services: 🔌 ⚙ 🔧 ⚙ T 🚻 ⚙
Within 3 miles: ✎ 💲⚙

Notes: Dogs must be kept on leads. Table tennis, wildlife lake.

POOLE · Map 4 SZ09

See also Lytchett Minster, Organford & Wimborne Minster

Places to visit

Compton Acres Gardens, CANFORD CLIFFS 01202 700778 www.comptonacres.co.uk

Brownsea Island, BROWNSEA ISLAND 01202 707744 www.nationaltrust.org.uk

Great for kids: Oceanarium, BOURNEMOUTH 01202 311993 www.oceanarium.co.uk

86% Rockley Park (SY982909)

Hamworthy BH15 4LZ
☎ 0871 231 0880
e-mail: rockleypark@haven.com
web: www.haven.com/rockleypark
dir: M27 junct 1, A31 to Poole centre, then follow signs to site

Open mid Mar-end Oct (rs mid Mar-May & Sep-Oct some facilities may be reduced)

Last departure 10.00hrs

A complete holiday experience, including a wide range of day and night entertainment, and plenty of sports and leisure activities, notably watersports. There is also mooring and launching from the park. The touring area has 60 fully serviced pitches and an excellent toilet and shower block. A great base for all the family set in a good location to explore Poole or Bournemouth. 105 holiday homes are available for hire. 90 acre site. 60 touring pitches. 60 hardstandings. Caravan pitches. Motorhome pitches. Tent pitches. 1077 statics.

AA Pubs & Restaurants nearby: The Rising Sun, Poole 01202 771246

Guildhall Tavern, Poole 01202 671717

Leisure: ⚙ ⚙ ♿ ⬇ ⚙ ⚲ ♫ Spa
Facilities: ⚙ ☺ ⚙ ✱ ⚙ ♿ ⚙ 🚿 WiFi ♻ ⚙
Services: 🔌 ⚙ 🔧 T 🍴 ⚙
Within 3 miles: ⚙ ⛳ 🏇 ✎ ⚙ ⚙ 💲⚙

Notes: Max 2 dogs per booking, certain dog breeds banned, no commercial vehicles, no bookings by persons under 21yrs unless a family booking. Dogs must be kept on leads. Sailing school.

see advert on page 188

▶▶▶ 75% Beacon Hill Touring Park (SY977945)

Blandford Road North BH16 6AB
☎ 01202 631631
e-mail: bookings@beaconhilltouringpark.co.uk
dir: On A350, 0.25m N of junct with A35, 3m NW of Poole

Open Etr-end Oct (rs Low & mid season some services closed/restricted opening)

Last arrival 23.00hrs Last departure 11.00hrs

Set in an attractive, wooded area with conservation very much in mind. There are two large ponds for coarse fishing within the grounds, and the terraced pitches, with fine views, are informally sited so that visitors can choose their favourite spot. The outdoor swimming pool and tennis court are popular during the summer period. 30 acre site. 170 touring pitches. 10 hardstandings. Caravan pitches. Motorhome pitches. Tent pitches.

AA Pubs & Restaurants nearby: The Rising Sun, Poole 01202 771246

Guildhall Tavern, Poole 01202 671717

Leisure: ⚙ ⚙ ⚲ ⚙ □
Facilities: ⚙ ☺ ⚙ ✱ ♿ ⚙ 🚿 WiFi
Services: 🔌 ⚙ 🔧 T 🍴 ⚙ ⚙
Within 3 miles: ♪ ⚙ ⛳ ✎ ⚙ ⚙ 💲⚙ ∪

Notes: Groups of young people not accepted during high season.

PORTESHAM
Map 4 SY68

Places to visit

Tutankhamun Exhibition,
DORCHESTER 01305 269571
www.tutankhamun-exhibition.co.uk

Maiden Castle, DORCHESTER 0870 333 1181
www.english-heritage.org.uk

Great for kids: Teddy Bear Museum,
DORCHESTER 01305 266040
www.teddybearmuseum.co.uk

►►►► 80% Portesham Dairy Farm Campsite (SY602854)

Weymouth DT3 4HG
☎ 01305 871297
e-mail: info@porteshamdairyfarm.co.uk
dir: *From Dorchester on A35 towards Bridport. In 5m left at Winterbourne Abbas, follow Portesham signs. Through village, left at Kings Arms pub, site 350yds on right*

* ⌂ £12-£24 ⌂ £12-£24 Å £12-£24

Open Apr-Sep

Last arrival 18.30hrs Last departure 11.00hrs

Located at the edge of the picturesque village of Portesham close to the Dorset coast. This family run, level park is part of a small working farm in a quiet rural location. Fully serviced and seasonal pitches are available. Near the site entrance is a pub where meals are served, and it has a garden for children to play in. 8 acre site. 90 touring pitches. 61 hardstandings. Caravan pitches. Motorhome pitches. Tent pitches.

AA Pubs & Restaurants nearby: Manor Hotel, West Bexington 01308 897660

Leisure: ⚲

Facilities: ⌂⊙⌂✱⌂➔⌂❶

Services: ⌂⌂🔒

Within 3 miles: ⌂ ⑤

Notes: No commercial vehicles, no groups, no campfires, minimal noise after 22.00hrs. Dogs must be kept on leads. Caravan storage.

PUNCKNOWLE
Map 4 SY58

Places to visit

Dinosaur Museum, DORCHESTER 01305 269880
www.thedinosaurmuseum.com

Hardy's Cottage, DORCHESTER 01305 262366
www.nationaltrust.org.uk

Great for kids: Abbotsbury Swannery,
ABBOTSBURY 01305 871858
www.abbotsbury-tourism.co.uk

AA CAMPING CARD SITE

►► 85% Home Farm Caravan and Campsite (SY535887)

Home Farm, Rectory Ln DT2 9BW
☎ 01308 897258
dir: *From Dorchester towards Bridport on A35, left at start of dual carriageway, at hill bottom right to Litton Cheney. Through village, 2nd left to Puncknowle (Hazel Ln). Left at T-junct, left at phone box. Site 150mtrs on right. Caravan route: approach via A35 Bridport, then Swyre on B3157, continue to Swyre Lane & Rectory Lane*

⌂ ⌂ Å

Open Apr-Oct

Last arrival 21.00hrs Last departure noon

This quiet site hidden away on the edge of a little hamlet is an excellent place to camp. It offers sweeping views of the Dorset countryside from most pitches, and is just five miles from Abbotsbury, and one and a half miles from the South West Coastal Footpath. A really good base from which to tour this attractive area. 6.5 acre site. 47 touring pitches. 14 seasonal pitches. Caravan pitches. Motorhome pitches. Tent pitches.

AA Pubs & Restaurants nearby: Crown Inn, Puncknowle 01308 897711

Manor Hotel, West Bexington 01308 897660

Facilities: ⌂⊙⌂✱⊙⌂♻❶

Services: ⌂❶⌂⌂⌂

Within 3 miles: ⌂

Notes: ⊘ No cats. No wood burning fires, skateboards, rollerblades, loud music or motorised toys. Last arrival time by arrangement. Dogs must be kept on leads. Calor gas exchange only.

ST LEONARDS
Map 5 SU10

Places to visit

Rockbourne Roman Villa,
ROCKBOURNE 0845 603 5635
www.hants.gov.uk/rockbourne-roman-villa

Red House Museum & Gardens,
CHRISTCHURCH 01202 482860
www.hants.gov.uk/museum/redhouse

Great for kids: Moors Valley Country Park,
RINGWOOD 01425 470721
www.moors-valley.co.uk

AA CAMPING CARD SITE

PREMIER PARK

►►►►► 84% Shamba Holidays (SU105029)

230 Ringwood Rd BH24 2SB
☎ 01202 873302
e-mail: enquiries@shambaholidays.co.uk
web: www.shambaholidays.co.uk
dir: *From Poole on A31, pass Texaco garage on left, straight on at next 2 rdbts, 100yds, left into Eastmoors Lane. Site 0.25m on right (just past Woodman Inn)*

* ⌂ £22-£32 ⌂ £22-£32 Å £22-£32

Open Mar-Oct (rs Low season some facilities only open at wknds)

Last arrival 20.00hrs Last departure 11.00hrs

This top quality park has excellent modern facilities particularly suited to families. You can be certain of a warm welcome from the friendly staff. There is a really good indoor/outdoor heated pool, plus a tasteful bar supplying a good range of meals. The park is well located for visiting the south coast, which is just a short drive away, and also for the New Forest National Park. 7 acre site. 150 touring pitches. 40 seasonal pitches. Caravan pitches. Motorhome pitches. Tent pitches.

LEISURE: ⚲ Indoor swimming pool ⚲ Outdoor swimming pool ⚲ Children's playground ⚲ Kid's club ⚲ Tennis court ⚲ Games room ⚲ Separate TV room ⚲ 9/18 hole golf course ⚲ Boats for hire ⚲ Cinema ⚲ Entertainment ⚲ Fishing ⚲ Mini golf ⚲ Watersports ⚲ Gym ⚲ Sports field **Spa** ⚲ Stables
FACILITIES: ⚲ Bath ⚲ Shower ⚲ Electric shaver ⚲ Hairdryer ⚲ Ice Pack Facility ⚲ Disabled facilities ⚲ Public telephone ⚲ Shop on site or within 200yds ⚲ Mobile shop (calls at least 5 days a week) ⚲ BBQ area ⚲ Picnic area ⚲ Wi-fi ⚲ Internet access ⚲ Recycling ⚲ Tourist info ⚲ Dog exercise area

AA Pubs & Restaurants nearby: Old Beams Inn, Ibsley 01425 473387

Shamba Holidays

Leisure: 🏊 ⛵ 🎢 ⚽ 🎣

Facilities: 🚽 ⚡ ☉ ℙ ✳ ♿ ⊙ 🛢 🚲 ♻ ❶

Services: 🔌 🔲 🍴 🔒 ⊘ T 🍽 🚮 ⚒ ⬇

Within 3 miles: 🔎 📍 🛒 🛢 ∪

Notes: No large groups, no commercial vehicles. Dogs must be kept on leads. Phone card top-up facility.

see advert below

▶▶▶▶ 83% Back of Beyond Touring Park *(SU103034)*

234 Ringwood Rd BH24 2SB
☎ **01202 876968**
e-mail: melandsuepike@aol.com
web: www.backofbeyondtouringpark.co.uk
dir: *From E: on A31 over Little Chef rdbt, pass St Leonard's Hotel, at next rdbt U-turn into lane immediately left to site at end of lane. From W: on A31 pass Texaco garage & Woodman Inn, immediately left to site*

* 🚐 £18-£26 🚌 £18-£26 ▲ £18-£26

Open Mar-Oct

Last arrival 19.00hrs Last departure noon

Set well off the beaten track in natural woodland surroundings, with its own river and lake, yet close to many attractions. This tranquil park is run by keen, friendly owners, and the quality facilities are for adults only. This park is a haven for wildlife. 28 acre site. 80 touring pitches. 40 seasonal pitches. Caravan pitches. Motorhome pitches. Tent pitches.

AA Pubs & Restaurants nearby: Old Beams Inn, Ibsley 01425 473387

Facilities: ⚡ ☉ ℙ ✳ ♿ 🛢 🚲 🚮 ♻ ❶

Services: 🔌 🔲 🔒 ⊘ T 🚮 ⬇

Within 3 miles: 🔎 📍 ◎ 🛢 🛒 ∪

Notes: Adults only. No commercial vehicles. Lake & river fishing, 9-hole pitch & putt course, boules.

SERVICES: 🔌 Electric hook up 🔲 Launderette 🍴 Licensed bar 🛢 Calor Gas ⊘ Camping Gaz T Toilet fluid 🍽 Café/Restaurant 🚮 Fast Food/Takeaway ⬆ Battery charging 🚼 Baby care ⬇ Motorvan service point ABBREVIATIONS: BH/bank hols-bank holidays Etr-Easter Whit-Whitsun dep-departure fr-from hrs-hours m-mile mdnt-midnight rdbt-roundabout rs-restricted service wk-week wknd-weekend 📧 No credit cards 🚫 no dogs   See page 7 for details of the AA Camping Card Scheme

ST LEONARDS *continued*

▶▶▶ 79% *Forest Edge Touring Park*

(SU104024)

229 Ringwood Rd BH24 2SD
☎ 01590 648331
e-mail: holidays@shorefield.co.uk
dir: *From E: on A31 over 1st rdbt (Little Chef),
pass St Leonards Hotel, left at next rdbt into
Boundary Ln, site 100yds on left. From W: on A31
pass Texaco garage & Woodman Inn, right at rdbt
into Boundary Ln*

🏕 🚐 🛖

Open Feb-3 Jan (rs School & summer hols pool
open)

Last arrival 21.00hrs Last departure 10.00hrs

A tree-lined park set in grassland with plenty of
excellent amenities for all the family, including an
outdoor heated swimming pool and toddlers' pool,
an adventure playground, and two launderettes.
Visitors are invited to use the superb leisure club
plus all amenities and entertainment at the sister
site of Oakdene Forest Park, which is less than a
mile away. Holiday homes are available for hire.
9 acre site. 72 touring pitches. 29 seasonal
pitches. Caravan pitches. Motorhome pitches. Tent
pitches. 30 statics.

AA Pubs & Restaurants nearby: Old Beams Inn,
Ibsley 01425 473387

Leisure: 🏊 🎢 🔍
Facilities: 🛁 ⊙ 𝓟 ✳ ☺ 🛒 ♻ ❶
Services: 🔌 🔋 🔧 ⊘ 🗑 🅣
Within 3 miles: ↕ 🎣 ◎ 🛒 🗑 ∪

Notes: Families & couples only. 1 dog & 1 car per
pitch, no gazebos. Rallies welcome. Dogs must be
kept on leads.

see advert on page 211

SHAFTESBURY — Map 4 ST82

Places to visit

Shaftesbury Abbey Museum & Garden,
SHAFTESBURY 01747 852910
www.shaftesburyheritage.org.uk

Royal Signals Museum, BLANDFORD FORUM
01258 482248 www.royalsignalsmuseum.com

Great for kids: Sherborne Castle,
SHERBORNE 01935 813182 (office)
www.sherbornecastle.com

▶▶▶ 84% Blackmore Vale Caravan & Camping Park (ST835233)

Sherborne Causeway SP7 9PX
☎ 01747 851523 & 01225 290924
e-mail: info@dche.co.uk
dir: *From Shaftesbury's Ivy Cross rdbt take A30
signed Sherborne. Site 2m on right*

🏕 🚐 🛖

Open all year

Last arrival 21.00hrs

This developing touring park now has a new toilet
and shower block plus an excellent Glamping
section which includes tipis, yurts, shepherd huts,
bell tents and a pod. Special activities also take
place such as wine tasting, paint balling etc. The
fishing lake is now fully open. There are also static
homes and three shepherd's huts for hire. 5 acre
site. 26 touring pitches. 6 hardstandings. Caravan
pitches. Motorhome pitches. Tent pitches. 20
statics. 6 tipis. 8 bell tents/yurts. 1 wooden pod.

AA Pubs & Restaurants nearby: Kings Arms Inn,
Gillingham 01747 838325

Coppleridge Inn, Motcombe 01747 851980

Leisure: 🎣
Facilities: 🛁 ⊙ 𝓟 ✳ ⅄ ☺ 🛒 🗑 ♻ ❶
Services: 🔌 🔋 🔧 ⊘ 🅣 🚏 🛒
Within 3 miles: 🎣 🛒 ∪

Notes: No noise after mdnt. Dogs must be kept on
leads. Caravan sales & accessories.

SIXPENNY HANDLEY — Map 4 ST91

Places to visit

Larmer Tree Gardens, TOLLARD ROYAL
01725 516228 www.larmertreegardens.co.uk

Shaftesbury Abbey Museum & Garden,
SHAFTESBURY 01747 852910
www.shaftesburyheritage.org.uk

Great for kids: Moors Valley Country Park,
RINGWOOD 01425 470721
www.moors-valley.co.uk

▶▶▶▶ 84% *Church Farm Caravan & Camping Park* (ST994173)

The Bungalow, Church Farm, High St SP5 5ND
☎ 01725 552563 & 07766 677525
e-mail: churchfarmcandcpark@yahoo.co.uk
dir: *1m S of Handley Hill rdbt. Exit for Sixpenny
Handley, right by school, site 300yds by church*

🏕 🚐 🛖

Open all year (rs Nov-Mar 10 vans max)

Last arrival 21.00hrs Last departure 11.00hrs

A spacious park located within the Cranborne
Chase in an Area of Outstanding Natural Beauty;
the site is split into several camping areas
including one for adults only. There is a first-class
facility block with good private facilities and an
excellent café/restaurant. The pretty village of
Sixpenny Handley with all its amenities is just 200
yards away. 10 acre site. 35 touring pitches. 4
hardstandings. 5 seasonal pitches. Caravan
pitches. Motorhome pitches. Tent pitches. 2
statics.

AA Pubs & Restaurants nearby: Museum Inn, Farnham 01725 516261

Drovers Inn, Gussage All Saints 01258 840084

Leisure:

Facilities:

Services:

Within 3 miles:

Notes: Quiet after 23.00hrs. Dogs must be kept on leads. Caravan storage, use of fridge/freezer & microwave.

SWANAGE

Places to visit

Corfe Castle, CORFE CASTLE 01929 481294 www.nationaltrust.org.uk

Brownsea Island, BROWNSEA ISLAND 01202 707744 www.nationaltrust.org.uk

Great for kids: Swanage Railway, SWANAGE 01929 425800 www.swanagerailway.co.uk

SWANAGE — Map 5 SZ07

►►►► 85% Ulwell Cottage Caravan Park *(SZ019809)*

SILVER

Ulwell Cottage, Ulwell BH19 3DG

☎ 01929 422823

e-mail: enq@ulwellcottagepark.co.uk

web: www.ulwellcottagepark.co.uk

dir: *From Swanage N for 2m on unclassified road towards Studland*

Open Mar-7 Jan (rs Mar-Spring BH & mid Sep-early Jan takeaway closed, shop open variable hrs)

Last arrival 22.00hrs Last departure 11.00hrs

Nestling under the Purbeck Hills and surrounded by scenic walks, this park is only two miles from the beach. A family-run park that caters well for families and couples, and offers a toilet and shower block complete with good family rooms, all appointed to a high standard. There is a good indoor swimming pool and village inn offering a good range of meals. 13 acre site. 77 touring pitches. 19 hardstandings. Caravan pitches. Motorhome pitches. Tent pitches. 140 statics.

AA Pubs & Restaurants nearby: Bankes Arms Hotel, Studland 01929 450225

Square and Compass, Worth Matravers 01929 439229

Ulwell Cottage Caravan Park

Leisure:

Facilities:

Services:

Within 3 miles:

Notes: No bonfires or fireworks. Dogs must be kept on leads.

see advert below

SWANAGE *continued*

AA CAMPING CARD SITE

►►► 77% Herston Caravan & Camping Park *(SZ018785)*

Washpond Ln BH19 3DJ
☎ 01929 422932
e-mail: office@herstonleisure.co.uk
dir: *From Wareham on A351 towards Swanage. Washpond Ln on left just after 'Welcome to Swanage' sign*

* ⊕ £15-£42 ⊠ ▲

Open all year

Set in a rural area, with extensive views of the Purbecks, this tree-lined park has fully serviced pitches plus large camping areas. Herston Halt is within walking distance, a stop for the famous Swanage steam railway between the town centre and Corfe Castle. There are also yurts available for hire. 10 acre site. 100 touring pitches. 71 hardstandings. Caravan pitches. Motorhome pitches. Tent pitches. 5 statics. 6 bell tents/yurts.

AA Pubs & Restaurants nearby: Bankes Arms Hotel, Studland 01929 450225

Square and Compass, Worth Matravers 01929 439229

Leisure: 🅰

Facilities: 🜨☉🅿✳♿🚿🚽🅣📶♻🛈

Services: 🔌🔋🛢💧🚐🍽🛒🎈🚮

Within 3 miles: 🚴🏇🎣🍴📵⛳🐎🎯🏪🎳🎯U

Notes: No noise after 23.00hrs. Dogs must be kept on leads.

►► 73% Acton Field Camping Site

(SY991785)

Acton Field, Langton Matravers BH19 3HS
☎ 01929 424184 & 439424
e-mail: enquiries@actonfieldcampsite.co.uk
dir: *From A351 right after Corfe Castle onto B3069 to Langton Matravers, 2nd right after village sign (bridleway)*

* ⊕ £14 ⊠ £10-£14 ▲ £8-£14

Open mid Jul-early Sep (rs Apr-Oct open for organised groups)

Last arrival 22.00hrs Last departure noon

The informal campsite, bordered by farmland on the outskirts of Langton Matravers, with good upgraded toilet facilities. There are superb views of the Purbeck Hills and towards the Isle of Wight, and a footpath leads to the coastal path. The site occupies what was once a stone quarry, and rock pegs may be required. 7 acre site. 80 touring pitches. Caravan pitches. Motorhome pitches. Tent pitches.

AA Pubs & Restaurants nearby: Bankes Arms Hotel, Studland 01929 450225

Square and Compass, Worth Matravers 01929 439229

Facilities: 🜨☉✳🅿♻

Services: 🛒

Within 3 miles: 🚴🏇🎣📵⛳🐎🎯🏪🎳U

Notes: 🚭 No open fires, no noise after mdnt. Dogs must be kept on leads.

►►►► 80% Woolsbridge Manor Farm Caravan Park

(SU099052)

GOLD

BH21 6RA
☎ 01202 826369
e-mail: woolsbridge@btconnect.com
web: www.woolsbridgemanorcaravanpark.co.uk
dir: *From Ringwood take A31 westward. Approx 1m follow signs for Three Legged Cross & Horton. Site 2m on right*

* ⊕ £17.50-£24.50 ⊠ £17.50-£24.50 ▲ £17.50-£24.50

Open Mar-Oct

Last arrival 20.00hrs Last departure 10.30hrs

A small farm site with spacious pitches on a level field. This quiet site is an excellent central base for touring the New Forest, Salisbury and the south coast, and is close to Moors Valley Country Park for outdoor family activities. Facilities are good and very clean and there are excellent family rooms available. 6.75 acre site. 60 touring pitches. Caravan pitches. Motorhome pitches. Tent pitches.

AA Pubs & Restaurants nearby: Old Beams Inn, Ibsley 01425 473387

Woolsbridge Manor Farm Caravan Park

Leisure: ⚂

Facilities: ⬤⊙🅿✳♿🖄🚿🏕♻ ❶

Services: ⬤🔲🔋🚗🚽🔌

Within 3 miles: ⬇🚲🏪🛒∪

Notes: Dogs must be kept on leads.

see advert below

WAREHAM   Map 4 SY98

Places to visit

Compton Acres Gardens, CANFORD CLIFFS
01202 700778 www.comptonacres.co.uk

Brownsea Island, BROWNSEA ISLAND
01202 707744 www.nationaltrust.org.uk

Great for kids: Oceanarium, BOURNEMOUTH
01202 311993 www.oceanarium.co.uk

AA CAMPING CARD SITE

PREMIER PARK

▶▶▶▶▶ **93% Wareham**   Best of British
Forest Tourist Park   GOLD

(SY894912)

North Trigon BH20 7NZ
☎ **01929 551393**
e-mail: holiday@warehamforest.co.uk
dir: *Telephone for directions*

* 🚐 £16.50-£35.20 ⛺ £16.50-£35.20
🅰 £13.70-£28.45

Open all year (rs Off-peak season limited services)

Last arrival 21.00hrs Last departure 11.00hrs

A woodland park within the tranquil Wareham Forest, with its many walks and proximity to Poole, Dorchester and the Purbeck coast. Two luxury blocks, with combined washbasin and toilets for total privacy, maintain a high standard of cleanliness. A heated outdoor swimming pool, off licence, shop and games room add to the pleasure of a stay on this top quality park. 55 acre site. 200 touring pitches. 70 hardstandings. 70 seasonal pitches. Caravan pitches. Motorhome pitches. Tent pitches.

AA Pubs & Restaurants nearby: Kemps Country House, Wareham 0845 862 0315

Greyhound Inn, Corfe Castle 01929 480205

New Inn, Church Knowle 01929 480357

Leisure: ⬤⚂🔍

Facilities: ⬤⊙🅿✳♿🕒🖄🚿🏕WIFI ♻ ❶

Services: ⬤🔲🔋🚗🚽🔌🔽

Within 3 miles: ⬇🍴🏪🚲🏪🛒∪

Notes: Families & couples only, no group bookings. Dogs must be kept on leads.

SERVICES: ⬤ Electric hook up   🔲 Launderette   🍺 Licensed bar   🔋 Calor Gas   ⊘ Camping Gaz   🅃 Toilet fluid   🍽 Café/Restaurant   🍔 Fast Food/Takeaway   🔌 Battery charging
🚼 Baby care   🔽 Motorvan service point   **ABBREVIATIONS:** BH/bank hols-bank holidays   Etr-Easter   Whit-Whitsun   dep-departure   fr-from   hrs-hours   m-mile   mdnt-midnight
rdbt-roundabout   rs-restricted service   wk-week   wknd-weekend   🚫 No credit cards   🚫 no dogs   See page 7 for details of the AA Camping Card Scheme

WAREHAM *continued*

AA CAMPING CARD SITE

►►►► 79% Birchwood Tourist Park

(SY896905)

Bere Rd, Coldharbour BH20 7PA
☎ 01929 554763
e-mail: birchwoodtouristpark@hotmail.com
dir: *From Poole (A351) or Dorchester (A352) on N side of railway line at Wareham, follow Bere Regis signs (unclassified). 2nd park after 2.25m*

* 🚐 £17-£28.50 🚗 ⛺ £10.50-£21.50

Open 13 Dec-23 Nov (rs 31 Oct-1 Mar shop/ reception open for 2-3 hrs daily in winter)

Last arrival 21.00hrs Last departure 11.30hrs

Set in 50 acres of parkland located within Wareham Forest, this site offers direct access into ideal areas for walking, mountain biking, and horse and pony riding. This is a spacious open park with plenty of room for young people to play games or football. The modern facilities are in two central locations and are very clean. There is a good security barrier system. 25 acre site. 175 touring pitches. 25 hardstandings. Caravan pitches. Motorhome pitches. Tent pitches.

AA Pubs & Restaurants nearby: Kemps Country House, Wareham 0845 862 0315

Greyhound Inn, Corfe Castle 01929 480205

New Inn, Church Knowle 01929 480357

Leisure: 🛝 ⚽ 🔍

Facilities: 🚿 ⊙ 💇 ✳ 📞 🛒 🧺 🐕 Wi-fi ♻ ℹ

Services: 🔌 🧺 🔒 🧯 [T] 🍴 🚰

Within 3 miles: ⛳ ⛵ 🎬 🎣 🛒

Notes: No generators, no groups on BHs, no camp fires. Dogs must be kept on leads. Pitch & putt, paddling pool.

see advert below

►►► 84% Lookout Holiday Park

(SY927858)

Stoborough BH20 5AZ
☎ 01929 552546
e-mail: enquiries@caravan-sites.co.uk
web: www.caravan-sites.co.uk
dir: *Take A351 through Wareham, after crossing River Frome & through Stoborough, site signed on left*

* 🚐 £18-£32 🚗 £18-£32 ⛺ £14-£26

Open all year (rs Closed for camping 4 Jan-22 Mar)

Last arrival 22.00hrs Last departure noon

Divided into two paddocks and set well back from the Swanage road, this touring park is separated from the static part of the operation (32 static holiday homes are for hire). There are very good facilities; a superb children's playground and plenty of other attractions make this an ideal centre for families. The site is very convenient for visiting Corfe and Swanage. 15 acre site. 150 touring pitches. 99 hardstandings. Caravan pitches. Motorhome pitches. Tent pitches. 89 statics.

AA Pubs & Restaurants nearby: Kemps Country House, Wareham 0845 862 0315

Greyhound Inn, Corfe Castle 01929 480205

New Inn, Church Knowle 01929 480357

Lookout Holiday Park

Leisure: 🏊 🎣

Facilities: 🐕 ☉ ☂ ✳ ⚓ ⏰ Ⓢ WiFi ♻ ❶

Services: ⚡ ⛽ 🅿 🖉 Ⓣ 🔌 ⚒

Within 3 miles: ↓ ⛳ 🎯 🐾 🚲 🏪 Ⓢ ∪

Notes: No pets.

see advert below

▶▶▶ 82% East Creech Farm Campsite *(SY928827)*

East Creech Farm, East Creech BH20 5AP
☎ **01929 480519 & 481312**
e-mail: east.creech@virgin.net
dir: *From Wareham on A351 S towards Swanage. On bypass at 3rd rdbt take Furzebrook/Blue Pool Rd exit, approx 2m site on right*

🚐 £12-£19.50 � £12-£19.50 ▲ £12-£19.50

Open Apr-Oct

Last arrival 20.00hrs Last departure noon

A grassy park set in a peaceful location beneath the Purbeck Hills, with extensive views towards Poole and Brownsea Island. The park boasts a woodland play area, bright, clean toilet facilities, and a farm shop selling milk, eggs and bread. There are also three coarse fishing lakes teeming with fish. The park is close to the Norden Station on the Swanage to Norden steam railway, and is well located for visiting Corfe Castle, Swanage and the Purbeck coast. 4 acre site. 80 touring pitches. Caravan pitches. Motorhome pitches. Tent pitches.

AA Pubs & Restaurants nearby: Kemps Country House, Wareham 0845 862 0315

Greyhound Inn, Corfe Castle 01929 480205

New Inn, Church Knowle 01929 480357

Leisure: 🏊

Facilities: 🐕 ☉ ☂ ✳ ♻ ❶

Services: ⚡ ⛽

Within 3 miles: ↓ ⛳ 🎯 🐾 🏪 Ⓢ

Notes: 🚫 No camp fires, no loud noise. Dogs must be kept on leads.

▶▶▶ 78% Ridge Farm Camping & Caravan Park *(SY939868)*

Barnhill Rd, Ridge BH20 5BG
☎ **01929 556444**
e-mail: info@ridgefarm.co.uk
web: www.ridgefarm.co.uk
dir: *From Wareham take B3075 towards Corfe Castle, cross river to Stoborough, then left to Ridge. Follow site signs for 1.5m*

🚐 � ▲

Open Etr-Sep

Last arrival 21.00hrs Last departure noon

A quiet rural park, adjacent to a working farm and surrounded by trees and bushes. This away-from-it-all park is ideally located for touring this part of Dorset, and especially for birdwatchers, or those who enjoy walking and cycling. This site is perfect for visiting the Arne Nature Reserve. 3.47 acre site. 60 touring pitches. 2 hardstandings. Caravan pitches. Motorhome pitches. Tent pitches.

AA Pubs & Restaurants nearby: Kemps Country House, Wareham 0845 862 0315

Greyhound Inn, Corfe Castle 01929 480205

New Inn, Church Knowle 01929 480357

Facilities: 🐕 ☉ ☂ ✳ ⏰ Ⓢ ♻ ❶

Services: ⚡ ⛽ 🅿 🖉 Ⓣ ⚒

Within 3 miles: ↓ ⛳ 🎯 🐾 🏪 Ⓢ ∪

Notes: 🚫 No dogs Jul-Aug. Dogs must be kept on leads.

SERVICES: ⚡ Electric hook up ⛽ Launderette 🍺 Licensed bar ⚓ Calor Gas 🖉 Camping Gaz Ⓣ Toilet fluid 🍽 Café/Restaurant 🍟 Fast Food/Takeaway ⚒ Battery charging
🍼 Baby care ⛽ Motorvan service point **ABBREVIATIONS:** BH/bank hols-bank holidays Etr-Easter Whit-Whitsun dep-departure fr-from hrs-hours m-mile mdnt-midnight
rdbt-roundabout rs-restricted service wk-week wknd-weekend 🚫 No credit cards 🚫 no dogs   See page 7 for details of the AA Camping Card Scheme

WEYMOUTH
Map 4 SY67

Places to visit

RSPB Nature Reserve Radipole Lake, WEYMOUTH 01305 778313 www.rspb.org.uk

Portland Castle, PORTLAND 01305 820539 www.english-heritage.org.uk

Great for kids: Weymouth Sea Life Adventure Park & Marine Sanctuary, WEYMOUTH 0871 423 2110 www.sealifeeurope.com

86% Littlesea Holiday Park (SY654783)

Lynch Ln DT4 9DT
☎ 0871 231 0879
e-mail: littlesea@haven.com
web: www.haven.com/littlesea
dir: A35 onto A354 signed Weymouth. Right at 1st rdbt, 3rd exit at 2nd rdbt towards Chickerell. Left into Lynch Lane after lights. Site at far end of road

Open end Mar-end Oct (rs end Mar-May & Sep-Oct facilities may be reduced)

Last arrival mdnt Last departure 10.00hrs

Just three miles from Weymouth with its lovely beaches and many attractions, Littlesea has a cheerful family atmosphere and fantastic facilities. Indoor and outdoor entertainment and activities are on offer for all the family, and the toilet facilities on the touring park are of a good quality. The touring section of this holiday complex is at the far end of the site adjacent to the South West Coastal Path in a perfect location. 100 acre site. 120 touring pitches. Caravan pitches. Motorhome pitches. Tent pitches. 720 statics.

AA Pubs & Restaurants nearby: Old Ship Inn, Weymouth 01305 812522

Leisure: 🏊⛱️🛝🎣🎱🎵
Facilities: 🛁📺☀️🔌✂️♿🕐🛒🐾🏠📶♻️ℹ️
Services: 🔌🛒🚽🔋🧺🛢️📞🍴🛍️
Within 3 miles: 🎣⛳️🎬📽️🎣🏊🛍️🏇

Notes: Max 2 dogs per booking, certain dog breeds banned, no commercial vehicles, no bookings by persons under 21yrs unless a family booking, no boats.

see advert on page 189

83% Seaview Holiday Park (SY707830)

Preston DT3 6DZ
☎ 0871 231 0877
e-mail: seaview@haven.com
web: www.haven.com/seaview
dir: A354 to Weymouth, signs for Preston/ Wareham onto A353. Site 3m on right just after Weymouth Bay Holiday Park

Open mid Mar-end Oct (rs mid Mar-May & Sep-Oct facilities may be reduced)

Last arrival mdnt Last departure 10.00hrs

A fun-packed holiday centre for all the family, with plenty of activities and entertainment during the day and evening. Terraced pitches are provided for caravans, and there is a separate field for tents. The park is close to Weymouth and other coastal attractions. There's a smart toilet and shower block, plus fully-serviced hardstanding pitches. Holiday homes available for hire. 20 acre site. 87 touring pitches. 24 hardstandings. Caravan pitches. Motorhome pitches. Tent pitches. 259 statics.

AA Pubs & Restaurants nearby: Old Ship Inn, Weymouth 01305 812522

Smugglers Inn, Osmington Mills 01305 833125

Leisure: 🏊⛱️🛝🎣🎱🎵
Facilities: 🛁📺☀️🔌✂️♿🕐🛒🐾🏠📶♻️ℹ️
Services: 🔌🛒🚽🔋🍴🛍️
Within 3 miles: 🎣⛳️🎬📽️🎣🏊🛍️🏇

Notes: Max 2 dogs per booking, certain dog breeds banned, no commercial vehicles, no bookings by persons under 21yrs unless a family booking.

see advert on page 189

PREMIER PARK

▶▶▶▶▶ 87% **East Fleet Farm Touring Park** (SY640797)

Chickerell DT3 4DW
☎ 01305 785768
e-mail: enquiries@eastfleet.co.uk
dir: On B3157 (Weymouth-Bridport road), 3m from Weymouth

* �caravan £14-£25 �MH £14-£25 ⛺ £14-£25

Open 16 Mar-Oct

Last arrival 22.00hrs Last departure 10.30hrs

Set on a working organic farm overlooking Fleet Lagoon and Chesil Beach, with a wide range of amenities and quality toilet facilities with family rooms in a Scandinavian log cabin and facility block. The friendly owners, celebrating 25 years at the park, are welcoming and helpful; their family bar serving meals and takeaway food is open from Easter and has glorious views from the patio area. There is also a good accessory shop. 21 acre site. 400 touring pitches. 50 hardstandings. Caravan pitches. Motorhome pitches. Tent pitches.

AA Pubs & Restaurants nearby: Old Ship Inn, Weymouth 01305 812522

Leisure: 🛝🎱🎣
Facilities: 🛁📺☀️✂️♿🕐🛒🐾📶💻♻️ℹ️
Services: 🔌🛒🚽🔋🧺📞🍴🛒🛍️🚽
Within 3 miles: 🎣⛳️🎬📽️🎣🏊🛍️🏇

Notes: Dogs must be kept on leads.

LEISURE: 🏊 Indoor swimming pool 🏖️ Outdoor swimming pool 🛝 Children's playground 🎣 Kid's club 🎾 Tennis court 🎱 Games room 🖥️ Separate TV room
⛳ 9/18 hole golf course 🚣 Boats for hire 🎬 Cinema 🎵 Entertainment 🎣 Fishing 🏌️ Mini golf 🏄 Watersports 🏋️ Gym 🏟️ Sports field **Spa** 🏇 Stables
FACILITIES: 🛁 Bath 🚿 Shower ⊙ Electric shaver 🪮 Hairdryer ❄️ Ice Pack Facility ♿ Disabled facilities 🕐 Public telephone 🛒 Shop on site or within 200yds
🏪 Mobile shop (calls at least 5 days a week) 🍴 BBQ area 🪑 Picnic area 📶 Wi-fi 💻 Internet access ♻️ Recycling ℹ️ Tourist info 🐾 Dog exercise area

►►►► 83% Bagwell Farm Touring Park (SY627816)

Knights in the Bottom, Chickerell DT3 4EA
☎ 01305 782575
e-mail: aa@bagwellfarm.co.uk
web: www.bagwellfarm.co.uk
dir: *From A354 follow signs for Weymouth town centre, then B3157 to Chickerell & Abbotsbury, 1m past Chickerell left into site 500yds after Victoria Inn*

* 🚐 £16.50-£30 🚐 £16.50-£30 ▲ £13-£22

Open all year (rs Winter bar closed)

Last arrival 21.00hrs Last departure 11.00hrs

This well located park is set in a small valley with access to the South West Coastal Path and is very convenient for visiting Weymouth and Portland. It has excellent facilities including a good shop, pets' corner, children's play area plus the Red Barn bar and restaurant. 14 acre site. 320 touring pitches. 25 hardstandings. 70 seasonal pitches. Caravan pitches. Motorhome pitches. Tent pitches.

AA Pubs & Restaurants nearby: Old Ship Inn, Weymouth 01305 812522

Leisure: 🅰
Facilities: 🛏👤☺🆎✳🔥🔔🅱🛒🎠✂📶 ♻ ❶
Services: 🔌🅾🍴🔋🖊🚻🍽🏧🚮⚡
Within 3 miles: 🔔🅱🛒↻

Notes: Families & couples only, no noise after 23.00hrs. Dogs must be kept on leads. Wet suit shower, campers' shelter.

►►► 87% West Fleet Holiday Farm (SY625811)

Fleet DT3 4EF
☎ 01305 782218
e-mail: aa@westfleetholidays.co.uk
web: www.westfleetholidays.co.uk
dir: *From Weymouth take B3157 towards Abbotsbury for 3m. Past Chickerell turn left at mini-rdbt to Fleet, site 1m on right*

* 🚐 ▲ £13-£26

Open Etr-Sep (rs May-Sep clubhouse & pool available daily)

Last arrival 21.00hrs Last departure 11.00hrs

A spacious farm site with both level and sloping pitches divided into paddocks, and screened with hedging. Good views of the Dorset countryside, and a relaxing site for a family holiday. There is a new spacious clubhouse with bar, restaurant and entertainment area. Wi-fi also available. 12 acre site. 250 touring pitches. Motorhome pitches. Tent pitches.

AA Pubs & Restaurants nearby: Old Ship Inn, Weymouth 01305 812522

Leisure: ♨🅰🎠🎵
Facilities: 🛏👤☺🆎✳🔥🔔🅱🛒📶 ♻ ❶
Services: 🔌🅾🍴🔋🖊🚻🍽🏧🚮⚡
Within 3 miles: 🔔🅱🛒↻

Notes: Non-family groups by arrangement only, dogs restricted to certain areas. Dogs must be kept on leads.

►►► 84% *Pebble Bank Caravan Park* (SY659775)

Camp Rd, Wyke Regis DT4 9HF
☎ 01305 774844
dir: *From Weymouth take Portland road. At last rdbt turn right, then 1st left to Army Tent Camp. Site opposite*

🚐 🚐 ▲

Open Etr-mid Oct (rs High season & wknds only bar open)

Last arrival 21.00hrs Last departure 11.00hrs

This site, although only one and a half miles from Weymouth, is in a peaceful location overlooking Chesil Beach and the Fleet. There is a friendly little bar, which offers even better views. The toilet and shower block is very modern and spotlessly clean. 4 acre site. 40 touring pitches. Caravan pitches. Motorhome pitches. Tent pitches. 80 statics.

AA Pubs & Restaurants nearby: Old Ship Inn, Weymouth 01305 812522

Leisure: 🅰
Facilities: 👤☺🆎✳🔥📶 ❶
Services: 🔌🅾🍴🖊🏧
Within 3 miles: 🔔🍴🚲🅱🛒◎🚢🔔🅱↻

►►► 80% Rosewall Camping (SY736820)

East Farm Dairy, Osmington Mills DT3 6HA
☎ 01305 832248
e-mail: holidays@weymouthcamping.com
dir: *Take A353 towards Weymouth. At Osmington Mills sign (opposite garage) turn left, 0.25m, site on 1st right*

🚐 ▲

Open Etr-Oct (rs Apr, May & Oct shop opening times)

Last arrival 22.00hrs Last departure 10.00hrs

This well positioned, sloping tent site is close to the coast and the South West Coastal Path and has great views of Weymouth Bay. There are good toilet and shower blocks at the top and bottom of the site, and also a good shop. This site is a spacious place to camp and very suitable for families. 13 acre site. 225 touring pitches. Motorhome pitches. Tent pitches.

AA Pubs & Restaurants nearby: Old Ship Inn, Weymouth 01305 812522

Smugglers Inn, Osmington Mills 01305 833125

Leisure: 🅰 Facilities: 👤☺✳🔥🔔🅱 ♻ ❶
Services: 🅾🔋🖊🏧
Within 3 miles: 🔔🍴🚲🔔🅱🛒↻

Notes: Families & couples only. Dogs must be kept on leads. Riding stables & coarse fishing.

►►► 78% Sea Barn Farm (SY625807)

Fleet DT3 4ED
☎ 01305 782218
e-mail: aa@seabarnfarm.co.uk
web: www.seabarnfarm.co.uk
dir: *From Weymouth take B3157 towards Abbotsbury for 3m. Past Chickerell turn left at mini-rdbt towards Fleet. Site 1m on left*

* 🚐 ▲ £12-£23

Open 15 Mar-Oct (rs Mar-Jun & Sep-Oct use of facilities at West Fleet)

Last arrival 21.00hrs Last departure 11.00hrs

This site is set high on the Dorset coast and has spectacular views over Chesil Beach, The Fleet and Lyme Bay, and it is also on the South West Coastal Path. Optional use of the clubhouse and swimming pool at West Fleet Holiday Farm is available. Pitches are sheltered by hedging, and there is an excellent toilet facility block, and plenty of space for games. 12 acre site. 250

continued

SERVICES: 🔌 Electric hook up 🅾 Launderette 🍴 Licensed bar 🔋 Calor Gas ✎ Camping Gaz 🅃 Toilet fluid 🍽 Café/Restaurant 🏧 Fast Food/Takeaway ⚡ Battery charging 🛏 Baby care ⚡ Motorvan service point **ABBREVIATIONS:** BH/bank hols-bank holidays Etr-Easter Whit-Whitsun dep-departure fr-from hrs-hours m-mile mdnt-midnight rdbt-roundabout rs-restricted service wk-week wknd-weekend 🚫 No credit cards 🚫 no dogs See page 7 for details of the AA Camping Card Scheme

WEYMOUTH *continued*

touring pitches. Motorhome pitches. Tent pitches. 1 static.

AA Pubs & Restaurants nearby: Old Ship Inn, Weymouth 01305 812522

Leisure: 📷

Facilities: 🚽 ⚟ ⊙ ℙ ✳ ⅋ 🛉 📶 ♻ ❶

Services: 🖙 🗑 🔌 ⌀ T 🚽

Within 3 miles: ⅃ 🏪 U

Notes: Non-family groups by prior arrangement only. Dogs must be kept on leads.

---

hh U **Weymouth Bay Holiday Park**
(SY705830)

Preston DT3 6BQ
☎ **01305 832271**
e-mail: weymouthbay@haven.com
web: www.haven.com/weymouthbay
dir: *From A35 towards Dorchester take A354 signed Weymouth. Follow towards Preston signs onto A353. At Chalbury rdbt 1st left into Preston Rd. Park on right*

Open Mar-Oct

Overlooking Weymouth, yet only a short distance from the beach, this fun and activity packed park combines well with its sister park, Seaview Holiday Park (see entry) to offer more sport, leisure and entertainment activities. There are a good range of holiday caravans and apartments. At the time of going to press the quality rating for this site had not been confirmed. For up-to-date information please see the AA website: theAA.com.

Change over day: Mon, Fri, Sat **Arrival and departure times:** Please contact the site

Statics 83 **Sleeps** 6-8 **Bedrms** 2-3 **Bathrms** 1-2 **Toilets** 1-2 **Freezer** TV Sky/FTV **Elec** included **Gas** included **Grass** area **Parking**

Children 🧒 **Cots** **Dogs** Max 2 on leads No dangerous dogs (see page 12)

Leisure: 🏊 🏖 ✋ 📷

AA Pubs & Restaurants nearby: The Old Ship Inn, Weymouth 01305 812522

see advert on page 190

WIMBORNE MINSTER   Map 5 SZ09

Places to visit

Kingston Lacy, WIMBORNE 01202 883402 (Mon-Fri) www.nationaltrust.org.uk

Priest's House Museum and Garden, WIMBORNE 01202 882533 www.priest-house.co.uk

Great for kids: Moors Valley Country Park, RINGWOOD 01425 470721 www.moors-valley.co.uk

---

PREMIER PARK

▶▶▶▶▶ 85% *Merley Court*

(SZ008984)

Merley BH21 3AA
☎ **01590 648331**
e-mail: holidays@shorefield.co.uk
dir: *Site signed on A31, Wimborne by-pass & Poole junct rdbt*

🚐 🚚 Å

Open 6 Feb-2 Jan (rs Low season pool closed & bar, shop open limited hrs)

Last arrival 21.00hrs Last departure 10.00hrs

A superb site in a quiet rural position on the edge of Wimborne, with woodland on two sides and good access roads. The park is well landscaped and offers generous individual pitches in sheltered grassland. There are plenty of amenities for all the family, including a heated outdoor pool, tennis court and adventure playground plus a tastefully refurbished bar and restaurant. This park tends to get busy in summer and therefore advance booking is advised. Two Eurotents are now available for hire. 20 acre site. 160 touring pitches. 50 hardstandings. Caravan pitches. Motorhome pitches. Tent pitches. 2 statics.

AA Pubs & Restaurants nearby: Les Bouviers, Wimborne Minster 01202 889555

Botany Bay Inne, Winterborne Zelston 01929 459227

Leisure: 🏊 📷 🎾 ⊙ 🔍

Facilities: 🚽 ⚟ ⊙ ℙ ✳ ⅋ 🛉 📷 🚻 ⅋ ♻ ❶

Services: 🖙 🗑 🍴 🍺 ⌀ T 🍴 🛒 🛒 🚮

Within 3 miles: ⅃ 🐟 🎣 📷 ⊙ 🛍 🗑 U

Notes: Families & couples only, rallies welcome. Dogs must be kept on leads. Use of facilities at Oakdene Forest Park (7m).

see advert on opposite page

PREMIER PARK

▶▶▶▶▶ 85% *Wilksworth Farm Caravan Park* *(SU004018)*

SILVER

Cranborne Rd BH21 4HW
☎ **01202 885467**
e-mail: rayandwendy@ wilksworthfarmcaravanpark.co.uk
web: www.wilksworthfarmcaravanpark.co.uk
dir: *1m N of Wimborne on B3078*

🚐 🚚 Å

Open Apr-Oct (rs Oct no shop)

Last arrival 20.00hrs Last departure 11.00hrs

A popular and attractive park peacefully set in the grounds of a listed house in the heart of rural Dorset. The spacious site has much to offer visitors, including an excellent heated swimming pool, takeaway and café, a tastefully refurbished bar and restaurant plus a games room. The modern toilet facilities contain en suite rooms and good family rooms. 11 acre site. 85 touring pitches. 20 hardstandings. Caravan pitches. Motorhome pitches. Tent pitches. 77 statics.

AA Pubs & Restaurants nearby: Les Bouviers, Wimborne Minster 01202 889555

Botany Bay Inne, Winterborne Zelston 01929 459227

Leisure: 🏊 📷 🎾 🔍

Facilities: 🚽 ⚟ ⊙ ℙ ✳ ⅋ ⊙ 🛉 ⚟ ⅋

Services: 🖙 🗑 ⌀ T 🍴 🛒 🛒 🚮

Within 3 miles: ⅃ 🐟 📷 🛍 🗑

Notes: Max 2 dogs per pitch. Dogs must be kept on leads. Paddling pool, volley ball, mini football pitch.

LEISURE: 🏊 Indoor swimming pool 🏖 Outdoor swimming pool 📷 Children's playground 🪁 Kid's club 🎾 Tennis court 🔍 Games room 🖵 Separate TV room
⅃ 9/18 hole golf course 🚤 Boats for hire 🎦 Cinema 🎵 Entertainment 🎣 Fishing ⊙ Mini golf 🏄 Watersports 🏋 Gym ⊙ Sports field Spa U Stables
FACILITIES: 🚽 Bath ⚟ Shower ⊙ Electric shaver ℙ Hairdryer ✳ Ice Pack Facility ⅋ Disabled facilities 🕐 Public telephone 🛍 Shop on site or within 200yds
🛒 Mobile shop (calls at least 5 days a week) 🍴 BBQ area 🛒 Picnic area 📶 Wi-fi 🖥 Internet access ♻ Recycling ❶ Tourist info 🛉 Dog exercise area

SERVICES: Electric hook up Launderette Licensed bar Calor Gas Camping Gaz Toilet fluid Café/Restaurant Fast Food/Takeaway Battery charging Baby care Motorvan service point **ABBREVIATIONS:** BH/bank hols-bank holidays Etr-Easter Whit-Whitsun dep-departure fr-from hrs-hours m-mile mdnt-midnight rdbt-roundabout rs-restricted service wk-week wknd-weekend No credit cards no dogs   See page 7 for details of the AA Camping Card Scheme

WIMBORNE MINSTER *continued*

►►► 83% Springfield Touring Park
(SY987989)

Candys Ln, Corfe Mullen BH21 3EF
☎ **01202 881719**
e-mail: john.clark18@btconnect.com
dir: *From Wimborne on Wimborne by-pass (A31) at W end turn left after Caravan Sales, follow brown sign*

🚐 £18-£20 🚎 £18-£20 ▲ £14-£20

Open Apr-14 Oct

Last arrival 21.00hrs Last departure 11.00hrs

A small touring park with extensive views over the Stour Valley and a quiet and friendly atmosphere. It is well positioned for visiting Poole, Bournemouth or the really lovely town of Wimborne. The park is maintained immaculately, and has a well-stocked shop. 3.5 acre site. 45 touring pitches. 30 hardstandings. Caravan pitches. Motorhome pitches. Tent pitches.

AA Pubs & Restaurants nearby: Les Bouviers, Wimborne Minster 01202 889555

Botany Bay Inne, Winterborne Zelston 01929 459227

Leisure: ⚠
Facilities: 🅿️☉🄿❄️♿🅂♻️❓
Services: 🄯🅂🛒🚽
Within 3 miles: 🎣🚣🏌️🦌🍴🅂🛒U
Notes: 🅢 No skateboards. Dogs must be kept on leads.

►►► 80% Charris Camping & Caravan Park *(SY992988)*

Candy's Ln, Corfe Mullen BH21 3EF
☎ **01202 885970**
e-mail: bookings@charris.co.uk
web: www.charris.co.uk
dir: *From E, exit Wimborne bypass (A31) W end. 300yds after Caravan Sales, follow brown sign. From W on A31, over A350 rdbt, take next turn after B3074, follow brown signs*

* 🚐 £13.50-£18.25 🚎 £13.50-£18.25 ▲ £12.50-£18.25

Open all year

Last arrival 21.00hrs Last departure 11.00hrs

A sheltered park of grassland lined with trees on the edge of the Stour Valley. The owners are friendly and welcoming, and they maintain the park facilities to a good standard. Social get-togethers are held for customers including barbecues which are very popular. 3.5 acre site. 45 touring pitches. 12 hardstandings. 10 seasonal pitches. Caravan pitches. Motorhome pitches. Tent pitches.

AA Pubs & Restaurants nearby: Les Bouviers, Wimborne Minster 01202 889555

Botany Bay Inne, Winterborne Zelston 01929 459227

Facilities: 🅿️☉🄿❄️🅂📶♻️❓
Services: 🄯🅂🛒🚿🅃🚽
Within 3 miles: 🎣🍴🅂🛒U
Notes: Earliest arrival time 11.00hrs. Dogs must be kept on leads.

►►►► 81% Whitemead Caravan Park *(SY841869)*

East Burton Rd BH20 6HG
☎ **01929 462241**
e-mail: whitemeadcp@aol.com
dir: *Signed from A352 at level crossing on Wareham side of Wool*

* 🚐 £14.50-£22 🚎 £14.50-£22 ▲ £11.75-£19.25

Open mid Mar-Oct

Last arrival 22.00hrs Last departure noon

A well laid-out site in the valley of the River Frome, close to the village of Wool, and surrounded by woodland. A shop and games room enhance the facilities here, and the spotless, modern toilets are heated, providing an excellent amenity. Only a short walk away are the shops and pubs, plus the main bus route and mainline station to Poole, Bournemouth and Weymouth. 5 acre site. 95 touring pitches. 20 seasonal pitches. Caravan pitches. Motorhome pitches. Tent pitches.

AA Pubs & Restaurants nearby: New Inn, Church Knowle 01929 480357

Leisure: ⚠ 🎱
Facilities: 🅿️☉🄿❄️♿🅂🚼📶♻️❓
Services: 🄯🅂🛒🚿🅃🚽
Within 3 miles: 🎣🍴🅂🛒U
Notes: Dogs must be kept on leads.

CO DURHAM

BARNARD CASTLE — Map 19 NZ01

Places to visit

Barnard Castle, BARNARD CASTLE 01833 638212
www.english-heritage.org.uk

The Bowes Museum, BARNARD CASTLE
01833 690606 www.thebowesmuseum.org.uk

Great for kids: Raby Castle, STAINDROP
01833 660202 www.rabycastle.com

►►► 79% Pecknell Farm Caravan Park (NZ028178)

Lartington DL12 9DF
☎ 01833 638357

dir: 1.5m from Barnard Castle. From A66 take B6277. Site on right 1.5m from junct with A67

🚐 £12-£18 🚏 £12-£18

Open Apr-Oct

Last arrival 20.00hrs Last departure noon

A small well laid out site on a working farm in beautiful rural meadowland, with spacious marked pitches on level ground. There are many walking opportunities that start directly from this friendly site. 1.5 acre site. 20 touring pitches. 5 hardstandings. Caravan pitches. Motorhome pitches.

AA Pubs & Restaurants nearby: Fox and Hounds, Cotherstone 01833 650241

Morritt Arms Hotel, Barnard Castle 01833 627232

Rose & Crown, Romaldkirk 01833 650213

Facilities: 🅿 ☉ 🅿 🕑 ♻

Services: 🔌 🚑

Within 3 miles: ↓ 🐾 ☉ 🛒 🛢 ∪

Notes: 🐕 Maximum 2 dogs, no noise after 22.30hrs. Dogs must be kept on leads.

BEAMISH — Map 19 NZ25

Places to visit

Tanfield Railway, TANFIELD 0191 388 7545
www.tanfieldrailway.co.uk

Beamish Museum, BEAMISH 0191 370 4000
www.beamish.org.uk

Great for kids: Diggerland, LANGLEY PARK
0871 227 7007 www.diggerland.com

►►► 78% Bobby Shafto Caravan Park (NZ232545)

Cranberry Plantation DH9 0RY
☎ 0191 370 1776

dir: From A693 signed Beamish to sign for Beamish Museum. Take approach road, turn right immediately before museum, left at pub to site 1m on right

* 🚐 £21-£24 🚏 £21-£24 ▲ £21-£24

Open Mar-Oct

Last arrival 23.00hrs Last departure 11.00hrs

A tranquil rural park surrounded by trees, with very clean and well organised facilities. The suntrap touring area has plenty of attractive hanging baskets, and there is a clubhouse with bar, TV and pool. The hardstandings and the 28 fully serviced pitches enhance the amenities. 9 acre site. 83 touring pitches. 47 hardstandings. Caravan pitches. Motorhome pitches. Tent pitches. 54 statics.

AA Pubs & Restaurants nearby: Stables Pub & Brewery (Best Western Beamish Hall Hotel), Beamish 01207 288750

Leisure: 🎡 🎣 ⬚

Facilities: 🅿 ☉ 🅿 ✳ 🕭 🕑 🖫 🛜

Services: 🔌 🛢 🍽 🌡 🕑 🛢 🚑

Within 3 miles: ↓ 🐾 🎻 🐾 🛢 ∪

BLACKHALL COLLIERY — Map 19 NZ43

Places to visit

Hartlepool's Maritime Experience,
HARTLEPOOL 01429 860077
www.hartlepoolsmaritimeexperience.com

Auckland Castle, BISHOP AUCKLAND
01388 602576 www.auckland-castle.co.uk

Great for kids: Captain Cook Birthplace Museum, MIDDLESBROUGH 01642 311211
www.captcook-ne.co.uk

79% Crimdon Dene (NZ477378)

Coast Rd TS27 4BN
☎ 0871 664 9737
e-mail: crimdon.dene@park-resorts.com
web: www.park-resorts.com
dir: From A19 just S of Peterlee, take B1281 signed Blackhall. Through Castle Eden, left in 0.5m signed Blackhall. Approx 3m right at T-junct onto A1086 towards Crimdon. Site in 1m signed on left, by Seagull pub

🚐 🚏

Open Apr-Oct

Last arrival 23.00hrs Last departure 10.00hrs

A large, popular coastal holiday park, handily placed for access to Teeside, Durham and Newcastle. The park contains a full range of holiday centre facilities for both children and their parents. Touring facilities are appointed to a very good standard. 44 touring pitches. 44 hardstandings. 12 seasonal pitches. Caravan pitches. Motorhome pitches. 586 statics.

Leisure: 🏊 🎡 🛝 🎣 🎵

Facilities: 🅿 ☉ 🅿 🕑 🛢 🚻 🛜 ♻ ❶

Services: 🔌 🛢 🍽 🍽 🖿

Within 3 miles: ↓ 🎻 🐾 🛢 🛢 ∪

Notes: No cars by caravans. No quad bikes. Dogs must be kept on leads.

CONSETT — Map 19 NZ15

Places to visit

Beamish Museum, BEAMISH 0191 370 4000
www.beamish.org.uk

Tanfield Railway, TANFIELD 0191 388 7545
www.tanfieldrailway.co.uk

Great for kids: Gibside,
ROWLANDS GILL 01207 541820
www.nationaltrust.org.uk/gibside

▶▶▶ **75% Byreside Caravan Site**

(NZ122560)

Hamsterley NE17 7RT
☎ 01207 560280
dir: From A694 onto B6310 & follow signs

🚐 fr £14 🚐 fr £14 ▲ fr £12

Open all year

Last arrival 22.00hrs Last departure noon

A small, secluded family-run site on a working farm, with well-maintained facilities. It is immediately adjacent to the coast-to-coast cycle track so makes an ideal location for walkers and cyclists. Handy for Newcastle and Durham; the Roman Wall and Northumberland National Park are within an hour's drive. 1.5 acre site. 31 touring pitches. 29 hardstandings. Caravan pitches. Motorhome pitches. Tent pitches.

AA Pubs & Restaurants nearby: Manor House Inn, Carterway Heads 01207 255268

Facilities: 🌳 ⊙ ✳ ⅖ 🅖 ⋈ ♻ ❶

Services: 🚑 🔋 Ⓣ 🚮

Within 3 miles: ⅃ 🎬 🛒

Notes: No ball games. Dogs must be kept on leads. Caravan storage.

ESSEX

CANEWDON

Places to visit

RHS Garden Hyde Hall, CHELMSFORD
01245 402006 www.rhs.org.uk

Southend's Pier Museum,
SOUTHEND-ON-SEA 01702 611214
www.southendpiermuseum.co.uk

Great for kids: Southend Museum and Planetarium, SOUTHEND-ON-SEA 01702 434449
www.southendmuseums.co.uk

CANEWDON — Map 7 TQ99

AA CAMPING CARD SITE

▶▶▶ **79% Riverside Village Holiday Park** (TQ929951)

Creeksea Ferry Rd, Wallasea Island SS4 2EY
☎ 01702 258297
e-mail: riversidevillage@tiscali.co.uk
dir: M25 junct 29, A127, towards Southend-on-Sea. Take B1013 towards Rochford. Follow signs for Wallasea Island & Baltic Wharf

✳ 🚐 fr £22 🚐 fr £22 ▲ £16-£25

Open Mar-Oct

Next to a nature reserve beside the River Crouch, this holiday park is surrounded by wetlands but only eight miles from Southend. A modern toilet block with disabled facilities is provided for tourers and there's a handsome reception area. Several restaurants and pubs are within a short distance. 25 acre site. 60 touring pitches. Caravan pitches. Motorhome pitches. Tent pitches. 159 statics.

Leisure: 🄰

Facilities: 🌳 ⊙ 🅿 ✳ ⅖ 🅛 🅖 🚿 ⋈ 📶 ♻ ❶

Services: 🚑 🔋 🔋 ⊘ Ⓣ

Within 3 miles: ⅃ 🎣 🎬 🛒 ↻

Notes: No dogs in tents. Dogs must be kept on leads. Freshwater fishing, mobile newspaper vendor Sun & BH.

LEISURE: 🏊 Indoor swimming pool 🏊 Outdoor swimming pool 🄰 Children's playground 🎪 Kid's club 🎾 Tennis court 🎱 Games room 📺 Separate TV room ⅃ 9/18 hole golf course 🚣 Boats for hire 🎬 Cinema 🎵 Entertainment 🎣 Fishing ◎ Mini golf 🏄 Watersports 🏋 Gym 🅖 Sports field Spa ↻ Stables
FACILITIES: 🛁 Bath 🚿 Shower ⊙ Electric shaver 🅿 Hairdryer ✳ Ice Pack Facility ⅖ Disabled facilities 🅛 Public telephone 🛒 Shop on site or within 200yds 🛒 Mobile shop (calls at least 5 days a week) 🍖 BBQ area 🎪 Picnic area 📶 Wi-fi 💻 Internet access ♻ Recycling ❶ Tourist info 🐕 Dog exercise area

CLACTON-ON-SEA   Map 7 TM11

Places to visit

Harwich Redoubt Fort, HARWICH 01255 503429
www.harwich-society.com

The Beth Chatto Gardens, COLCHESTER
01206 822007 www.bethchatto.co.uk

Great for kids: Colchester Zoo, COLCHESTER
01206 331292 www.colchester-zoo.com

78% *Highfield Grange*
(TM173175)

London Rd CO16 9QY
☎ 0871 664 9746
e-mail: highfield.grange@park-resorts.com
web: www.park-resorts.com
dir: *A12 to Colchester, A120 (Harwich), A133 to Clacton-on-Sea. Site on B1441 clearly signed on left*

🚐 🚃

Open Apr-Oct

Last arrival mdnt Last departure 10.00hrs

The modern leisure facilities at this attractively planned park make it an ideal base for a lively family holiday. The swimming complex with both indoor and outdoor pools and a huge water shoot is especially popular. There are fully serviced touring pitches, each with its own hardstanding, located at the heart of the park. The nearby resorts of Walton on the Naze, Frinton and Clacton all offer excellent beaches and a wide range of popular seaside attractions. 30 acre site. 43 touring pitches. 43 hardstandings. Caravan pitches. Motorhome pitches. 509 statics.

AA Pubs & Restaurants nearby: Rose & Crown, Colchester 01206 866677

Whalebone, Fingringhoe 01206 729307

Leisure: 🗸🏊⚑🎢⊙♣🎵
Facilities: ⊓⊙🅿🔥⚓🕒🚻♿🛁 📺
Services: 🔌🔲🍽🍴🥤
Within 3 miles: 🏇🎣🗓🔗🎯🏛🎣🛒🗓⛳🗙
Notes: No fold-in campers or trailer tents.

75% *Martello Beach Holiday Park* (TM136128)

Belsize Av, Jaywick CO15 2LF
☎ 0871 664 9782 & 01442 830100
e-mail: martello.beach@park-resorts.com
web: www.park-resorts.com
dir: *Telephone for directions*

🚐 🚃 ⚕

Open Apr-Oct

Last arrival 21.30hrs Last departure 10.00hrs

Direct access to a seven-mile long Blue Flag beach is an undoubted attraction at this holiday park. The touring area is next to the leisure complex, where an indoor and outdoor swimming pool, shops, cafés and bars and evening entertainment are all provided. 40 acre site. 100 touring pitches. Caravan pitches. Motorhome pitches. Tent pitches. 294 statics.

AA Pubs & Restaurants nearby: Rose & Crown, Colchester 01206 866677

Whalebone, Fingringhoe 01206 729307

Leisure: 🗸🏊⚑🎢⊙♣🎵
Facilities: ⊓⊙🅿🔥⚓🕒🚻♿🛁 📺
Services: 🔌🔲🍽🍴🥤
Within 3 miles: 🔗🎣🛒🗓⛳🗙
Notes: 🗙 Water sports.

COLCHESTER

Places to visit

Colchester Castle Museum, COLCHESTER
01206 282939 www.colchestermuseums.org.uk

Layer Marney Tower, LAYER MARNEY
01206 330784 www.layermarneytower.co.uk

Great for kids: Colchester Zoo, COLCHESTER
01206 331292 www.colchester-zoo.com

COLCHESTER   Map 13 TL92

▶▶▶▶ 85% *Colchester Holiday Park*
(TL971252)

Cymbeline Way, Lexden CO3 4AG
☎ 01206 545551
e-mail: enquiries@colchestercamping.co.uk
dir: *Follow tourist signs from A12, then A133 Colchester Central slip road*

🚐 🚃 ⚕

Open all year

Last arrival 20.30hrs Last departure noon

A well-designed campsite on level grassland, on the west side of Colchester near the town centre. Close to main routes to London (A12) and east coast. There is good provision for hardstandings, and the owner's attention to detail is reflected in the neatly trimmed grass and well-cut hedges. Toilet facilities are housed in three buildings, two of which are modern and well equipped. 12 acre site. 168 touring pitches. 44 hardstandings. Caravan pitches. Motorhome pitches. Tent pitches.

AA Pubs & Restaurants nearby: Rose & Crown, Colchester 01206 866677

Whalebone, Fingringhoe 01206 729307

Swan Inn, Chappel 01787 222353

Leisure: ⚑
Facilities: ⊓⊙🅿🔥⚓🕒🛁🐕🚻
Services: 🔌🔲🍴🥤📺🛒🗙
Within 3 miles: 🏇🗓🔗🎣🏛🎣🛒🗓⛳🗙
Notes: No commercial vehicles. Badminton court.

SERVICES: 🔌 Electric hook up 🔲 Launderette 🍽 Licensed bar 🛢 Calor Gas 🔥 Camping Gaz 🔲 Toilet fluid 🍴 Café/Restaurant 🥤 Fast Food/Takeaway 🔋 Battery charging
🍼 Baby care ⛟ Motorvan service point **ABBREVIATIONS:** BH/bank hols-bank holidays Etr-Easter Whit-Whitsun dep-departure fr-from hrs-hours m-mile mdnt-midnight
rdbt-roundabout rs-restricted service wk-week wknd-weekend 🚫 No credit cards 🚫 no dogs   See page 7 for details of the AA Camping Card Scheme

MERSEA ISLAND Map 7 TM01

Places to visit

Layer Marney Tower, LAYER MARNEY
01206 330784 www.layermarneytower.co.uk

80% Waldegraves Holiday Park *(TM033133)*

CO5 8SE
☎ 01206 382898
e-mail: holidays@waldegraves.co.uk
web: www.waldegraves.co.uk
dir: *A12 junct 26, B1025 to Mersea Island across The Strood. Left to East Mersea, 2nd right, follow tourist signs to site*

* 🚐 £16-£26 🚙 £16-£26 ⛺ £16-£26

Open Mar-Nov (rs Mar-Jun & Sep-Nov (excl BH & school half terms) pool, shop & clubhouse reduced opening hrs, pool open May-Sep weather permitting)

Last arrival 22.00hrs Last departure 15.00hrs

A spacious and pleasant site, located between farmland and its own private beach on the Blackwater Estuary. Facilities include two freshwater fishing lakes, heated swimming pool, club, amusements, café and golf, and there is generally good provision for families. 25 acre site. 60 touring pitches. 30 seasonal pitches. Caravan pitches. Motorhome pitches. Tent pitches. 250 statics.

AA Pubs & Restaurants nearby: Peldon Rose, Peldon 01206 735248

Waldegraves Holiday Park

Leisure: 🏊 🛝 ✋ ⚽ 🎱 ♫
Facilities: 🚿 ⊙ 💨 ✲ ♿ $ ⛩ 🐕 Wi-fi ♻ ℹ
Services: 🔧 🗑 🍷 🔒 🍃 [T] 🍽 🍟 🛒 🛒
Within 3 miles: ⛳ 🎣 ◎ 🌊 $ 🗑
Notes: No large groups or groups of under 21s. Dogs must be kept on leads. Boating/slipway, pitch & putt/driving range.

see advert below

LEISURE: 🏊 Indoor swimming pool 🏊 Outdoor swimming pool 🛝 Children's playground ✋ Kid's club 🎾 Tennis court 🎱 Games room 📺 Separate TV room ⛳ 9/18 hole golf course ⛵ Boats for hire 🎬 Cinema ♫ Entertainment 🎣 Fishing ◎ Mini golf 🌊 Watersports 🏋 Gym ⚽ Sports field **Spa** ∪ Stables
FACILITIES: 🛁 Bath 🚿 Shower ⊙ Electric shaver 💨 Hairdryer ✲ Ice Pack Facility ♿ Disabled facilities 📞 Public telephone $ Shop on site or within 200yds 🚚 Mobile shop (calls at least 5 days a week) 🔥 BBQ area ⛩ Picnic area Wi-fi Wi-fi 💻 Internet access ♻ Recycling ℹ Tourist info 🐕 Dog exercise area

ST LAWRENCE — Map 7 TL90

Places to visit

RHS Garden Hyde Hall, CHELMSFORD
01245 402006 www.rhs.org.uk

Kelvedon Hatch Secret Nuclear Bunker,
BRENTWOOD 01277 364883
www.secretnuclearbunker.co.uk

Great for kids: Hadleigh Castle, HADLEIGH
01760 755161 www.english-heritage.org.uk

79% *Waterside St Lawrence Bay* (TL953056)

Main Rd CM0 7LY
☎ 0871 664 9794
e-mail: waterside@park-resorts.com
web: www.park-resorts.com
dir: A12 towards Chelmsford, A414 signed
Maldon. Follow B1010 & signs to Latchingdon,
then signs for Mayland/Steeple/St Lawrence.
Left towards St Lawrence. Site on right

Open Apr-Oct (rs Wknds)

Last arrival 22.00hrs Last departure 10.00hrs

Waterside occupies a scenic location
overlooking the Blackwater estuary. In addition
to the range of on-site leisure facilities there
are opportunities for beautiful coastal walks
and visits to the attractions of Southend. Tents
are welcome on this expansive site, which
has some touring pitches with electricity and
good toilet facilities. The park has its own boat
storage and slipway onto the Blackwater. 72
touring pitches. Caravan pitches. Motorhome
pitches. Tent pitches. 271 statics.

AA Pubs & Restaurants nearby: Ye Olde White
Harte Hotel, Burnham-on-Crouch
01621 782106

Ferryboat Inn, North Fambridge 01621 740208

Leisure:
Facilities:
Services:
Within 3 miles:
Notes: Sauna, spa pool.

ST OSYTH — Map 7 TM11

Places to visit

Harwich Redoubt Fort, HARWICH 01255 503429
www.harwich-society.com

Colchester Castle Museum, COLCHESTER
01206 282939 www.colchestermuseums.org.uk

Great for kids: Colchester Zoo, COLCHESTER
01206 331292 www.colchester-zoo.com

79% The Orchards Holiday Park (TM125155)

CO16 8LJ
☎ 0871 231 0861
e-mail: theorchards@haven.com
web: www.haven.com/theorchards
dir: From Clacton-on-Sea take B1027 towards
Colchester. Left after petrol station, then
straight on at x-rds in St Osyth. Follow signs to
Point Clear. Park in 3m

Open end Mar-end Oct (rs mid Mar-May &
Sep-Oct some facilities may be reduced)

Last arrival anytime Last departure 10.00hrs

The Orchards offers good touring facilities with
a quality toilet block which includes a laundry,
play area and two very spacious family rooms.
The touring pitches are generously sized.
There's also direct access to all the leisure,
entertainment and dining outlets available
on this large popular holiday park on the
Essex coast. 140 acre site. 69 touring pitches.
Caravan pitches. Tent pitches. 1000 statics.

AA Pubs & Restaurants nearby: Rose & Crown,
Colchester 01206 866677

Whalebone, Fingringhoe 01206 729307

Leisure:
Facilities:
Services:
Within 3 miles:
Notes: No cars by tents. Max 2 dogs per
booking, certain dog breeds banned, no
commercial vehicles, no bookings by persons
under 21yrs unless a family booking.

see advert on page 214

WALTON ON THE NAZE — Map 7 TM22

Places to visit

Ipswich Museum, IPSWICH 01473 433550
www.ipswich.gov.uk

Harwich Redoubt Fort, HARWICH 01255 503429
www.harwich-society.com

73% Naze Marine (TM255226)

Hall Ln CO14 8HL
☎ 0871 664 9755
e-mail: naze.marine@park-resorts.com
web: www.park-resorts.com
dir: A12 to Colchester. Then A120 (Harwich
road) then A133 to Weeley. Take B1033 to
Walton seafront. Site on left

* £8-£42 £8-£42

Open Apr-Oct

Last arrival anytime Last departure 10.00hrs

With its modern indoor swimming pool, show
bar, bar/restaurant and amusements, this
park offers a variety of on-site attractions.
The park is within easy access of the beaches
and attractions of Walton on the Naze, Frinton
and Clacton, and the more historic places of
interest inland. Please note that this site does
not cater for tents. 46 acre site. 41 touring
pitches. Caravan pitches. Motorhome pitches.
540 statics.

Leisure:
Facilities:
Services:
Within 3 miles:
Notes: Dogs must be kept on leads. Nature
walk, natural meadow.

WEST MERSEA   Map 7 TM01

Places to visit

Layer Marney Tower, LAYER MARNEY
01206 330784 www.layermarneytower.co.uk

Great for kids: Colchester Zoo, COLCHESTER
01206 331292 www.colchester-zoo.com

►►► 79% *Seaview Holiday Park*

(TM025125)

Seaview Av CO5 8DA
☎ **01206 382534**
e-mail: seaviewholidaypark@googlemail.com
dir: *From A12 (Colchester), onto B1025 (Mersea Island), cross causeway, left towards East Mersea, 1st right, follow signs*

Open Apr-Oct

Last arrival 18.00hrs Last departure noon

With sweeping views across the Blackwater estuary, this interesting, well established park has its own private beach, complete with boat slipway and photogenic beach cabins, a modern shop, café and a stylish clubhouse which offers evening meals and drinks in a quiet family atmosphere. The touring area is well maintained and has 40 fully serviced pitches. 30 acre site. 106 touring pitches. 40 hardstandings. 30 seasonal pitches. Caravan pitches. Motorhome pitches. 240 statics.

AA Pubs & Restaurants nearby: The Peldon Rose, Peldon 01206 735248

Facilities: ♠ ◐ ⑤ ⌨ ⊘ ❶

Services: ⊕ ⑤ ⌨ ⑩ ⊞

Within 3 miles: ↨ ↗ ⑤ ⑥ ∪

Notes: No noise after mdnt. Phone site if late arrival expected. Dogs must be kept on leads.

GLOUCESTERSHIRE

BERKELEY   Map 4 ST69

Places to visit

Dr Jenner's House, BERKELEY 01453 810631
www.jennermuseum.com

WWT Slimbridge, SLIMBRIDGE 01453 891900
www.wwt.org.uk

Great for kids: Berkeley Castle & Butterfly House, BERKELEY 01453 810332
www.berkeley-castle.com

►►► 76% Hogsdown Farm Caravan & Camping Park *(ST710974)*

Hogsdown Farm, Lower Wick GL11 6DD
☎ **01453 810224**
dir: *M5 junct 14 (Falfield), take A38 towards Gloucester. Through Stone & Woodford. After Newport turn right signed Lower Wick*

⛺ ⛟ ▲

Open all year

Last arrival 21.00hrs Last departure 16.00hrs

A pleasant site with good toilet facilities, located between Bristol and Gloucester. It is well positioned for visiting Berkeley Castle and the Cotswolds, and makes an excellent overnight stop when travelling to or from the West Country. 5 acre site. 45 touring pitches. 12 hardstandings. Caravan pitches. Motorhome pitches. Tent pitches.

AA Pubs & Restaurants nearby: Malt House, Berkeley 01453 511177

Anchor Inn, Oldbury-on-Severn 01454 413331

Leisure: ⚠

Facilities: ♠ ☉ ✳ ♻ ❶

Services: ⊕ ⑤ ⌨

Within 3 miles: ↨ ↗ ⑤ ⑥ ∪

Notes: ⊕ No skateboards or bicycles. Dogs must be kept on leads.

CHELTENHAM   Map 10 SO92

Places to visit

Holst Birthplace Museum, CHELTENHAM
01242 524846 www.holstmuseum.org.uk

Sudeley Castle, Gardens & Exhibitions,
WINCHCOMBE 01242 602308
www.sudeleycastle.co.uk

Great for kids: Gloucester City Museum & Art Gallery, GLOUCESTER 01452 396131
www.gloucester.gov.uk/citymuseum

►►►► 80% Briarfields Motel & Touring Park *(SO909218)*

Gloucester Rd GL51 0SX
☎ **01242 235324**
e-mail: briarfields@hotmail.co.uk
dir: *M5 junct 11, A40 towards Cheltenham. At rdbt left onto B4063, site 150mtrs on left*

* ⛟ £15-£18 ⛟ £15-£18 ▲ £11-£15

Open all year

A well-designed level park, with a motel, where the facilities are modern and very clean. The park is well-positioned between Cheltenham and Gloucester, with easy access to the Cotswolds. And, being close to the M5, it makes a perfect overnight stopping point. 5 acre site. 72 touring pitches. 72 hardstandings. Caravan pitches. Motorhome pitches. Tent pitches.

AA Pubs & Restaurants nearby: Gloucester Old Spot, Cheltenham 01242 680321

Royal Oak Inn, Cheltenham 01242 522344

Facilities: ♠ ℙ ✳ ⚙ ⌨ ♻ ❶

Services: ⊕ ⑤

Within 3 miles: ↨ 目 ↗ ◎ ⑤ ⑥ ∪

Notes: No noise after 23.00hrs. Dogs must be kept on leads.

LEISURE: 🏊 Indoor swimming pool   🏊 Outdoor swimming pool   ⚠ Children's playground   ✋ Kid's club   ♨ Tennis court   ♠ Games room   ▭ Separate TV room
↨ 9/18 hole golf course   ⚓ Boats for hire   🎬 Cinema   🎭 Entertainment   ◔ Fishing   ◎ Mini golf   ⛴ Watersports   🏋 Gym   ♻ Sports field   **Spa**   ∪ Stables
FACILITIES: 🛁 Bath   ♠ Shower   ☉ Electric shaver   ℙ Hairdryer   ✳ Ice Pack Facility   ⚙ Disabled facilities   ◐ Public telephone   ⑤ Shop on site or within 200yds
⑤ Mobile shop (calls at least 5 days a week)   🍖 BBQ area   🌲 Picnic area   **Wi-Fi** Wi-fi   🖥 Internet access   ♻ Recycling   ❶ Tourist info   ⌨ Dog exercise area

CIRENCESTER — Map 5 SP00

Places to visit

Corinium Museum, CIRENCESTER 01285 655611
www.coriniummuseum.cotswold.gov.uk

Chedworth Roman Villa,
CHEDWORTH 01242 890256
www.nationaltrust.org.uk/chedworth

Great for kids: Prinknash Abbey, CRANHAM
01452 812066 www.prinknashabbey.org.uk

►►►► 80% Mayfield Touring Park

(SP020055)

Cheltenham Rd GL7 7BH
☎ **01285 831301**
e-mail: mayfield-park@cirencester.fsbusiness.co.uk
dir: *From Cirencester bypass take Burford road/
A429 junct exit towards Cirencester, then follow
brown signs to site (approx 3.5m)*

* ⊞ £15-£23 ⊟ £15-£23 ▲ £13-£23

Open all year

Last arrival 20.00hrs Last departure noon

A gently sloping park on the edge of the
Cotswolds, with level pitches and a warm
welcome. Popular with couples and families, it
offers a good licensed shop selling a wide
selection of home-cooked takeaway food. This
lovely park makes an ideal base for visiting the
Cotswolds and the many attractions of the area.
The trees have now matured and consequently the
traffic noise is reduced. 12 acre site. 72 touring
pitches. 31 hardstandings. 10 seasonal pitches.
Caravan pitches. Motorhome pitches. Tent pitches.
33 statics.

AA Pubs & Restaurants nearby: The Crown of
Crucis, Cirencester 01285 851806

Hare & Hounds, Chedworth 01285 720288

Facilities: ♠⊙℮⚡⚹⚓⚘⚙☐♨☐🔌♻🛈

Services: ⚡🗑🔋⚗☐📶

Within 3 miles: ⚓♨⚙

Notes: Dogs only by prior arrangement. No cycles
or skateboards. Dogs must be kept on leads. Off
licence.

GLOUCESTER — Map 10 SO81

Places to visit

Gloucester Folk Museum,
GLOUCESTER 01452 396868
www.gloucester.gov.uk/folkmuseum

Nature in Art, GLOUCESTER 01452 731422
www.nature-in-art.org.uk

Great for kids: The National Waterways
Museum, GLOUCESTER 01452 318200
www.nwm.org.uk

►►► 73% Red Lion Caravan & Camping Park *(SO849258)*

Wainlode Hill, Norton GL2 9LW
☎ **01452 731810 & 01299 400787**
dir: *Exit A38 at Norton, follow road to river*

⊞ ⊟ ▲

Open all year

Last arrival 22.00hrs Last departure 11.00hrs

An attractive meadowland park, adjacent to a
traditional pub, with the River Severn just across
a country lane. This is an ideal touring and fishing
base. 24 acre site. 60 touring pitches. 10
hardstandings. 60 seasonal pitches. Caravan
pitches. Motorhome pitches. Tent pitches. 85
statics.

AA Pubs & Restaurants nearby: Queens Head,
Gloucester 01452 301882

Queens Arms, Ashleworth 01452 700395

Boat Inn, Ashleworth 01452 700272

Leisure: ⚠

Facilities: ♠⊙℮⚹⚓⚙☐♨🔌

Services: ⚡🗑🔋⚗☐🍽

Within 3 miles: ⚓♨⚙⚓

Notes: Freshwater fishing & private lake.

NEWENT — Map 10 SO72

Places to visit

Odda's Chapel, DEERHURST 0870 333 1181
www.english-heritage.org.uk

Westbury Court Garden, WESTBURY-ON-SEVERN
01452 760461 www.nationaltrust.org.uk

Great for kids: The National Birds of Prey
Centre, NEWENT 0870 9901992 www.nbpc.co.uk

►►► 82% Pelerine Caravan and Camping *(SO645183)*

Ford House Rd GL18 1LQ
☎ **01531 822761**
e-mail: pelerine@hotmail.com
dir: *1m from Newent*

⊞ fr £18 ⊟ fr £18 ▲ fr £18

Open Mar-Nov

Last arrival 22.00hrs Last departure 16.00hrs

A pleasant, French-themed site divided into
separate areas (Rue de Pelerine and Avenue des
Families), plus one for adults-only; there are some
hardstandings and electric hook-ups in each area.
Facilities are very good, especially for families. It
is close to several vineyards, and well positioned
in the north of the Forest of Dean with Tewkesbury,
Cheltenham and Ross-on-Wye within easy reach. 5
acre site. 35 touring pitches. 2 hardstandings.
Caravan pitches. Motorhome pitches. Tent pitches.

AA Pubs & Restaurants nearby: Yew Tree Inn,
Cliffords Mesne 01531 820719

Penny Farthing Inn, Aston Crews 01989 750366

Facilities: ♠⊙℮⚹⚓⚘📶♻🛈

Services: ⚡🗑📶

Within 3 miles: ⚓⊞♨⚙⚓

Notes: ⊛ Dogs must be kept on leads.
Woodburners, chimneas, burning pits available.

SERVICES: ⚡ Electric hook up 🗑 Launderette 🍷 Licensed bar ⛽ Calor Gas ⚗ Camping Gaz ☐ Toilet fluid 🍽 Café/Restaurant 🍔 Fast Food/Takeaway 🔋 Battery charging
🛒 Baby care ⛟ Motorvan service point **ABBREVIATIONS:** BH/bank hols-bank holidays Etr-Easter Whit-Whitsun dep-departure fr-from hrs-hours m-mile mdnt-midnight
rdbt-roundabout rs-restricted service wk-week wknd-weekend ⊛ No credit cards ⊗ no dogs See page 7 for details of the AA Camping Card Scheme

SLIMBRIDGE
Map 4 SO70

Places to visit

Dean Forest Railway, LYDNEY 01594 843423 (info) www.dfr.co.uk

Berkeley Castle & Butterfly House, BERKELEY 01453 810332 www.berkeley-castle.com

Great for kids: WWT Slimbridge, SLIMBRIDGE 01453 891900 www.wwt.org.uk

►►►► 86% Tudor Caravan & Camping (SO728040)
GOLD

Shepherds Patch GL2 7BP
☎ **01453 890483**
e-mail: aa@tudorcaravanpark.co.uk
web: www.tudorcaravanpark.com
dir: *M5 juncts 13 & 14 follow WWT Wetlands Wildlife Centre-Slimbridge signs. Site at rear of Tudor Arms pub*

* ⬡ £11.50-£20.50 ⬡ £11.50-£20.50
▲ £11.50-£20.50

Open all year

Last arrival 20.00hrs Last departure 11.00hrs

This park benefits from one of the best locations in the county, situated right alongside the Sharpness to Gloucester canal and just a short walk from the famous Wildfowl & Wetlands Trust at Slimbridge. The site has two areas, one for adults only, and a more open area with a facility block. There are both grass and gravel pitches complete with electric hook ups. Being next to the canal, there are excellent walks plus national cycle route 41 can be accessed from the site. There is a pub and restaurant adjacent to the site. 8 acre site. 75 touring pitches. 48 hardstandings. Caravan pitches. Motorhome pitches. Tent pitches.

AA Pubs & Restaurants nearby: Old Passage Inn, Arlingham 01452 740547

Facilities: ⬡⬡⬡⬡⬡⬡⬡⬡⬡⬡⬡⬡
Services: ⬡⬡⬡⬡⬡⬡⬡⬡⬡⬡
Within 3 miles: ⬡⬡⬡⬡⬡⬡

Notes: Debit cards only accepted. Dogs must be kept on leads.

STONEHOUSE
Map 4 SO80

Places to visit

Painswick Rococo Garden, PAINSWICK 01452 813204 www.rococogarden.org.uk

WWT Slimbridge, SLIMBRIDGE 01453 891900 www.wwt.org.uk

►►►► 81% Apple Tree Park Caravan and Camping Site (SO766063)

A38, Claypits GL10 3AL
☎ **01452 742362 & 07708 221457**
e-mail: appletreepark@hotmail.co.uk
dir: *M5 junct 13, A38. Take 1st exit at rdbt. Site 0.7m on left, 400mtrs beyond filling station*

* ⬡ £13-£18 ⬡ £13-£18 ▲ £13-£18

Open Feb-Nov

Last arrival 21.00hrs Last departure noon

This is a family owned park conveniently located on the A38, not far from the M5. A peaceful site with glorious views of the Cotswolds, it offers modern and spotlessly clean toilet facilities with under-floor heating. The park is well located for visiting Slimbridge Wildfowl & Wetlands Trust, and makes an excellent stopover for M5 travellers. There is a bus stop directly outside the park which is handy for those with motorhomes wishing to visit nearby Gloucester and Cheltenham. This site is very much a hidden gem. 6.5 acre site. 65 touring pitches. 14 hardstandings. 10 seasonal pitches. Caravan pitches. Motorhome pitches. Tent pitches.

AA Pubs & Restaurants nearby: George Inn, Stonehouse 01453 822302

Leisure: ⬡
Facilities: ⬡⬡⬡⬡⬡⬡⬡⬡⬡⬡⬡⬡
Services: ⬡⬡⬡⬡⬡⬡
Within 3 miles: ⬡⬡⬡⬡

Notes: Minimum noise after 22.30hrs. Dogs must be kept on leads.

GREATER MANCHESTER

LITTLEBOROUGH
Map 16 SD91

Places to visit

Imperial War Museum North, MANCHESTER 0161 836 4000 www.iwm.org.uk

Manchester Art Gallery, MANCHESTER 0161 235 8888 www.manchestergalleries.org

Great for kids: Heaton Park, PRESTWICH 0161 773 1085 www.heatonpark.org.uk

►►► 70% Hollingworth Lake Caravan Park (SD943146)

Round House Farm, Rakewood Rd, Rakewood OL15 0AT
☎ **01706 378661 & 373919**
dir: *From Littleborough or Milnrow (M62 junct 21), follow Hollingworth Lake Country Park signs to Fishermans Inn/The Wine Press. Take 'No Through Road' to Rakewood, then 2nd on right*

* ⬡ £14-£16 ⬡ £14-£16 ▲ £8-£16

Open all year

Last arrival 20.00hrs Last departure noon

A popular park adjacent to Hollingworth Lake, at the foot of the Pennines, within easy reach of many local attractions. Backpackers walking the Pennine Way are welcome at this family-run park, and there are also large rally fields. 5 acre site. 50 touring pitches. 25 hardstandings. Caravan pitches. Motorhome pitches. Tent pitches. 53 statics.

AA Pubs & Restaurants nearby: The White House, Littleborough 01706 378456

Facilities: ⬡⬡⬡⬡⬡⬡
Services: ⬡⬡⬡⬡⬡⬡
Within 3 miles: ⬡⬡⬡⬡⬡⬡⬡⬡
Notes: ⬡ ⬡ Family groups only. Pony trekking.

LEISURE: ⬡ Indoor swimming pool ⬡ Outdoor swimming pool ⬡ Children's playground ⬡ Kid's club ⬡ Tennis court ⬡ Games room ⬡ Separate TV room ⬡ 9/18 hole golf course ⬡ Boats for hire ⬡ Cinema ⬡ Entertainment ⬡ Fishing ⬡ Mini golf ⬡ Watersports ⬡ Gym ⬡ Sports field Spa ⬡ Stables
FACILITIES: ⬡ Bath ⬡ Shower ⬡ Electric shaver ⬡ Hairdryer ⬡ Ice Pack Facility ⬡ Disabled facilities ⬡ Public telephone ⬡ Shop on site or within 200yds ⬡ Mobile shop (calls at least 5 days a week) ⬡ BBQ area ⬡ Picnic area ⬡ Wi-fi ⬡ Internet access ⬡ Recycling ⬡ Tourist info ⬡ Dog exercise area

HAMPSHIRE

See Cycle Ride 4 in the Walks & Cycle Rides section at the end of the guide

BRANSGORE
Map 5 SZ19

Places to visit

Sammy Miller Motorcycle Museum, NEW MILTON 01425 620777 www.sammymiller.co.uk

Red House Museum & Gardens, CHRISTCHURCH 01202 482860 www.hants.gov.uk/museum/redhouse

Great for kids: Moors Valley Country Park, RINGWOOD 01425 470721 www.moors-valley.co.uk

►►► 84% Harrow Wood Farm Caravan Park (SZ194978)

Harrow Wood Farm, Poplar Ln BH23 8JE
☎ 01425 672487

e-mail: harrowwood@caravan-sites.co.uk
dir: From Ringwood take B3347 towards Christchurch. At Sopley, left for Bransgore, to T-junct. Turn right. Straight on at x-rds. Left in 400yds (just after garage) into Poplar Lane

* ➡ £17-£28.25 ⇌ £17-£28.25 ▲ £17-£28.25

Open Mar-6 Jan

Last arrival 22.00hrs Last departure noon

A well laid-out, well-drained and spacious site in a pleasant rural position adjoining woodland and fields. Free on-site coarse fishing is available at this peaceful park. Well located for visiting Christchurch, the New Forest National Park and the south coast. 6 acre site. 60 touring pitches. 60 hardstandings. Caravan pitches. Motorhome pitches. Tent pitches. 14 bell tents/yurts.

AA Pubs & Restaurants nearby: Three Tuns Country Inn, Bransgore 01425 672232

Facilities: ↖☉🅿✳&☉ 📶 ❼
Services: 🔌🅕🔋📤⛽
Within 3 miles: ✎🅢 **Notes:** ⊗ No open fires.

FORDINGBRIDGE
Map 5 SU11

Places to visit

Rockbourne Roman Villa, ROCKBOURNE 0845 603 5635 www.hants.gov.uk/rockbourne-roman-villa

Breamore House & Countryside Museum, BREAMORE 01725 512468 www.breamorehouse.com

Great for kids: Moors Valley Country Park, RINGWOOD 01425 470721 www.moors-valley.co.uk

 92% Sandy Balls Holiday Centre (SU167148)

Sandy Balls Estate Ltd, Godshill SP6 2JZ
☎ 0845 270 2248
e-mail: post@sandyballs.co.uk
web: www.sandyballs.co.uk
dir: M27 junct 1 onto B3078, B3079, 8m to Godshill. Site 0.25m after cattle grid

➡⇌▲

Open all year (rs Nov-Feb pitches reduced, no activities)

Last arrival 21.00hrs Last departure 11.00hrs

A large, mostly wooded New Forest holiday complex with good provision of touring facilities on terraced, well laid-out fields. Pitches are fully serviced with shingle bases, and groups can be sited beside the river and away from the main site. There are excellent sporting, leisure and entertainment facilities for the whole family, a bistro and information centre, and ready erected tents and lodges for hire. 120 acre site. 233 touring pitches. 233 hardstandings. Caravan pitches. Motorhome pitches. Tent pitches. 233 statics. 4 bell tents/yurts.

AA Pubs & Restaurants nearby: The Augustus John, Fordingbridge 01425 652098

Leisure: 🏊⬦👕🅰☉⚓🎵 Spa
Facilities: 🛒↖☉🅿✳&☉🅕🄿📶 ♻❼
Services: 🔌🅕🍴🅣🍽🔋🔧⛽
Within 3 miles: ✎⬦🅢⛳U

Notes: Groups only by arrangement, no gazebos, no noise after 23.00hrs. Dogs must be kept on leads. Jacuzzi, sauna, beauty therapy, gym, horse riding, bistro.

HAMBLE-LE-RICE
Map 5 SU40

Places to visit

Royal Armouries Fort Nelson, FAREHAM 01329 233734 www.royalarmouries.org

Southampton City Art Gallery, SOUTHAMPTON 023 8083 2277 www.southampton.gov.uk/art

Great for kids: Southampton Maritime Museum, SOUTHAMPTON 023 8022 3941 www.southampton.gov.uk/leisure

AA CAMPING CARD SITE

►►►► 80% Riverside Holidays (SU481081)

21 Compass Point, Ensign Way SO31 4RA
☎ 023 8045 3220
e-mail: enquiries@riversideholidays.co.uk
web: www.riversideholidays.co.uk
dir: M27 junct 8, follow signs to Hamble on B3397. Left into Satchell Lane, site in 1m

➡⇌▲

Open Mar-Oct

Last arrival 22.00hrs Last departure 11.00hrs

A small, peaceful park next to the marina, and close to the pretty village of Hamble. The park is neatly kept, and there are two toilet and shower blocks complete with good family rooms. A pub and restaurant are very close by and there are good river walks alongside the Hamble. Lodges and static caravans are available for hire. 6 acre site. 77 touring pitches. Caravan pitches. Motorhome pitches. Tent pitches. 45 statics.

AA Pubs & Restaurants nearby: The Bugle, Hamble-le-Rice 023 8045 3000

continued

HAMBLE-LE-RICE *continued*

Riverside Holidays

Facilities: ⬅🏠⊙🅿✳♿📷❶

Services: 🔌🔲🛒🛗

Within 3 miles: ⬇🚤🛶🏊🛍⊙♻

Notes: Dogs must be kept on leads. Bike hire, baby-changing facilities.

see advert below

LINWOOD

Places to visit

The New Forest Centre, LYNDHURST
023 8028 3444 www.newforestmuseum.org.uk

Furzey Gardens, MINSTEAD 023 8081 2464
www.furzey-gardens.org

Great for kids: Paultons Park, OWER
023 8081 4442 www.paultonspark.co.uk

LINWOOD · Map 5 SU10

▶▶▶ **84% Red Shoot Camping Park**

(SU187094)

BH24 3QT
☎ 01425 473789

e-mail: enquiries@redshoot-campingpark.com
dir: *A31 onto A338 towards Fordingbridge & Salisbury. Right at brown signs for caravan park towards Linwood on unclassified roads, site signed*

* 🚐 £23-£33 🚐 £23-£33 ⚠ £17-£27

Open Mar-Oct

Last arrival 20.30hrs Last departure 13.00hrs

Located behind the Red Shoot Inn in one of the most attractive parts of the New Forest, this park is in an ideal spot for nature lovers and walkers. It is personally supervised by friendly owners, and offers many amenities including a children's play area. There are modern and spotless facilities plus a smart reception and shop. 3.5 acre site. 130 touring pitches. Caravan pitches. Motorhome pitches. Tent pitches.

AA Pubs & Restaurants nearby: High Corner Inn, Linwood 01425 473973

Leisure: 🎢

Facilities: 🏠⊙🅿✳♿⊙🛍

Services: 🔌🔲🍴🛒🗑📧🍽🛗

Within 3 miles: 🛶🏊🛍⊙♻

Notes: Quiet after 22.30hrs. Dogs must be kept on leads.

MILFORD ON SEA · Map 5 SZ29

Places to visit

Buckler's Hard, BUCKLERS HARD 01590 616203
www.bucklershard.co.uk

Exbury Gardens & Railway, EXBURY
023 8089 1203 www.exbury.co.uk

Great for kids: Beaulieu, BEAULIEU
01590 612345 www.beaulieu.co.uk

▶▶▶▶ **84% *Lytton Lawn Touring Park*** *(SZ293937)*

Lymore Ln SO41 0TX
☎ 01590 648331

e-mail: holidays@shorefield.co.uk
dir: *From Lymington A337 to Christchurch for 2.5m to Everton. Left onto B3058 to Milford on Sea. 0.25m, left into Lymore Lane*

🚐🚐⚠

Open 6 Feb-2 Jan (rs Low season shop/reception limited hrs. No grass pitches)

Last arrival 22.00hrs Last departure 10.00hrs

A pleasant well-run park with good facilities, located near the coast. The park is peaceful and quiet, but the facilities of a sister park 2.5 miles away are available to campers, including swimming pool, tennis courts, bistro and bar/carvery, and large club with family entertainment. Fully-serviced pitches provide good screening, and standard pitches are on gently-sloping grass. 8 acre site. 136 touring pitches. 53 hardstandings. Caravan pitches. Motorhome pitches. Tent pitches.

LEISURE: 🏊 Indoor swimming pool 🏊 Outdoor swimming pool 🎢 Children's playground 🧒 Kid's club 🎾 Tennis court ♣ Games room 📺 Separate TV room ⬇ 9/18 hole golf course 🚤 Boats for hire 🎬 Cinema 🎵 Entertainment 🎣 Fishing ◎ Mini golf 🏄 Watersports 🏋 Gym ⚽ Sports field Spa ♻ Stables
FACILITIES: 🛁 Bath 🏠 Shower ⊙ Electric shaver 🅿 Hairdryer ✳ Ice Pack Facility ♿ Disabled facilities 🕐 Public telephone 🛍 Shop on site or within 200yds 📱 Mobile shop (calls at least 5 days a week) 🍖 BBQ area 🎍 Picnic area 📶 Wi-fi 📧 Internet access ♻ Recycling ❶ Tourist info 🐕 Dog exercise area

AA Pubs & Restaurants nearby: Royal Oak, Downton 01590 642297

Leisure: 🅰 🅾 🔍

Facilities: 🌂 ☉ 🅿 ✳ 🕓 🅢 🛒 🖥 ♻ 🅘

Services: 🔌 🅢 🅰 🛢 🚽 🛒

Within 3 miles: 🚶 🏌 ◎ 🏊 🅢 🅢 ∪

Notes: Families & couples only. Rallies welcome. Dogs must be kept on leads. Free use of Shorefield Leisure Club (2.5m).

see advert on page 211

RINGWOOD

See St Leonards (Dorset)

ROMSEY

Places to visit

The Sir Harold Hillier Gardens, AMPFIELD 01794 369318 www.hilliergardens.org.uk

Avington Park, AVINGTON 01962 779260 www.avingtonpark.co.uk

Great for kids: Longdown Activity Farm, ASHURST 023 8029 2837 www.longdownfarm.co.uk

---

ROMSEY	Map 5 SU32

PREMIER PARK

▶▶▶▶▶ 84% Hill Farm Caravan Park *(SU287238)*

Branches Ln, Sherfield English SO51 6FH
☎ 01794 340402
e-mail: gjb@hillfarmpark.com
dir: *Signed from A27 (Salisbury to Romsey road) in Sherfield English, 4m NW of Romsey & M27 junct 2*

* 🚐 £16-£30 🚙 £16-£30 ▲ £16-£30

Open Mar-Oct

Last arrival 20.00hrs Last departure noon

A small, well-sheltered park peacefully located amidst mature trees and meadows. The two toilet blocks offer smart unisex showers as well as a fully en suite family/disabled room and plenty of privacy in the washrooms. Bramleys, a good café/restaurant, with an outside patio, serves a wide range of snacks and meals. This attractive park is well placed for visiting Salisbury and the New Forest National Park, and the south coast is only a short drive away, making it an appealing holiday location. 10.5 acre site. 70 touring pitches. 60 hardstandings. Caravan pitches. Motorhome pitches. Tent pitches. 6 statics.

AA Pubs & Restaurants nearby: Dukes Head, Romsey 01794 514450

The Cromwell Arms, Romsey 01794 519515

Three Tuns, Romsey 01794 512639

Leisure: 🅰 🅾

Facilities: 🌂 ☉ 🅿 ✳ 🕓 🅢 🅢 🛒 🖥 📶 ♻

Services: 🔌 🅢 🅰 🛢 🚽 🅣 🍽 🔋 🛒

Within 3 miles: 🚶 🖪 🏌 ◎ 🅢 🅢 ∪

Notes: 🔇 Minimum noise at all times & no noise after 23.00hrs. One unit per pitch. Unsuitable for teenagers. 9-hole pitch & putt.

see advert below

ROMSEY *continued*

NEW ▶▶▶ 78% Green Pastures Farm Camping & Touring Park

(SU321158)

Ower SO51 6AJ
☎ 023 8081 4444

e-mail: enquiries@greenpasturesfarm.com
dir: *M27 junct 2. Follow Salisbury signs for 0.5m. Then follow brown tourist signs for Green Pastures. Also signed from A36 & A3090 at Ower*

🚐 £18 🚎 £18 ▲ £13-£26

Open 13 Mar-Oct

Last arrival 20.30hrs Last departure 11.00hrs

This pleasent site, now under new ownership, is well located for visiting Paultons Theme Park, Southampton or the New Forest. Being close to the M27 it is convenient for overnight stops. There are also new kennels where dogs can be left while you visit the theme park or go shopping. 6 acre site. 53 touring pitches. 6 hardstandings. Caravan pitches. Motorhome pitches. Tent pitches.

AA Pubs & Restaurants nearby: Sir John Barleycorn, Cadnam 023 8081 2236

Facilities: 🜂 ✳ ⛱ 🛉 ♻ ❼

Services: 🔌 🗑 🔋 🅣 🛒

Within 3 miles: 🛁 🖉 🏧

Notes: No water games, BBQs off ground only. Dogs must be kept on leads.

WARSASH   Map 5 SU40

Places to visit

Explosion Museum of Naval Firepower, GOSPORT 023 9250 5600 www.explosion.org.uk

Portchester Castle, PORTCHESTER 023 9237 8291 www.english-heritage.org.uk

Great for kids: Blue Reef Aquarium, PORTSMOUTH 023 9287 5222 www.bluereefaquarium.co.uk

▶▶▶▶ 82% Dibles Park *(SU505060)*

Dibles Rd SO31 9SA
☎ 01489 575232

e-mail: dibles.park@btconnect.com
dir: *M27 junct 9, at rdbt 5th exit (Parkgate A27), 3rd rdbt 1st exit, 4th rdbt 2nd exit. Site 500yds on left. Or M27 junct 8, at rdbt 1st exit (Parkgate), next rdbt 3rd exit (Brook Ln), 4th rdbt 2nd exit. Site 500yds on left*

🚐 🚎 ▲

Open all year

Last arrival 20.30hrs Last departure 11.00hrs

A small peaceful touring park adjacent to a private residential park. The facilities are excellent and spotlessly clean. A warm welcome awaits visitors to this well-managed park, which is very convenient for the Hamble, the Solent and the cross-channel ferries. Excellent information on local walks from the site is available. 0.75 acre site. 14 touring pitches. 14 hardstandings. Caravan pitches. Motorhome pitches. Tent pitches. 46 statics.

AA Pubs & Restaurants nearby: The Jolly Farmer Country Inn, Warsash 01489 572500

Facilities: 🜂 ⊙ 🅟 ✳ 🕙 ♻ ❼

Services: 🔌 🗑 🔋 ⚲

Within 3 miles: 🜄 🖉 🛁 🏧 🗑 U

Notes: Dogs must be kept on leads.

HEREFORDSHIRE

See Walk 5 in the Walks & Cycle Rides section at the end of the guide

EARDISLAND   Map 9 SO45

Places to visit

Berrington Hall, ASHTON 01568 615721 www.nationaltrust.org.uk/main/w-berringtonhall

Hergest Croft Gardens, KINGTON 01544 230160 www.hergest.co.uk

▶▶▶ 88% Arrow Bank Holiday Park

(SO419588)

Nun House Farm HR6 9BG
☎ 01544 388312

e-mail: enquiries@arrowbankholidaypark.co.uk
dir: *From Leominster A44 towards Rhayader. Right to Eardisland, follow signs*

* 🚐 £18-£20 🚎 £18-£20 ▲ £15-£18

Open Mar-7 Jan

Last arrival 17.00hrs Last departure noon

This peaceful, adults-only park is set in the beautiful 'Black and White' village of Eardisland with its free exhibitions, tea rooms and heritage centre. The park is well positioned for visiting the many local attractions, as well as those further afield such as Ludlow Castle, Ross-on-Wye, Shrewsbury and Wales. The modern toilet facilities are spotlessly clean. 65 acre site. 38 touring pitches. 38 hardstandings. 16 seasonal pitches. Caravan pitches. Motorhome pitches. Tent pitches. 60 statics. 4 bell tents/yurts.

AA Pubs & Restaurants nearby: New Inn, Pembridge 01544 388427

The Bateman Arms, Shobdon 01568 708374

Stagg Inn & Restaurant, Titley 01544 230221

Facilities: 🜂 ⊙ 🅟 🛉 🕙 🐾 📶 ❼

Services: 🔌 🗑 🅣

Within 3 miles: 🖉 🏧 🗑

Notes: Adults only. No ball games, no skateboards or cycles in park. Dogs must be kept on leads.

LEISURE: 🏊 Indoor swimming pool 🏊 Outdoor swimming pool 🛝 Children's playground 🛝 Kid's club 🎾 Tennis court 🎱 Games room 📺 Separate TV room 🏌 9/18 hole golf course 🚣 Boats for hire 🎬 Cinema 🎵 Entertainment 🎣 Fishing ⛳ Mini golf 🏄 Watersports 🏋 Gym 🏟 Sports field **Spa** U Stables
FACILITIES: 🛁 Bath 🚿 Shower ⊙ Electric shaver 🅟 Hairdryer ✳ Ice Pack Facility ♿ Disabled facilities 🕙 Public telephone 🏧 Shop on site or within 200yds 🛒 Mobile shop (calls at least 5 days a week) 🍖 BBQ area 🪑 Picnic area 📶 Wi-fi 💻 Internet access ♻ Recycling ❼ Tourist info 🐾 Dog exercise area

HEREFORD Map 10 SO53

Places to visit

Cider Museum & King Offa Distillery, HEREFORD 01432 354207 www.cidermuseum.co.uk

Great for kids: Goodrich Castle, GOODRICH 01600 890538 www.english-heritage.org.uk

► 69% Ridge Hill Caravan and Campsite *(SO509355)*

HR2 8AG

☎ 01432 351293

e-mail: ridgehill@fsmail.net

dir: *From Hereford on A49, take B4399 signed Rotherwas. At 1st rdbt follow Dinedor/Little Dewchurch signs, in 1m signed Ridge Hill/Twyford turn right. Right at phone box, 200yds, site on right*

* 🚐 £7 🚙 £7 ⛺ £6

Open Mar-Oct

Last departure noon

A simple, basic site set high on Ridge Hill a few miles south of Hereford. This peaceful site offers outstanding views over the countryside. It does not have toilets or showers, and therefore own facilities are essential, although toilet tents can be supplied on request at certain times of the year. (NB Please do not rely on Sat Nav directions to this site - guidebook directions should be used for caravans and motorhomes). 1.3 acre site. 5 touring pitches. Caravan pitches. Motorhome pitches. Tent pitches.

Facilities: ♻ ℹ

Within 3 miles: ⛳ 🏊 🎣 [S] [L]

Notes: 💳 Dogs must be kept on leads.

MORETON ON LUGG Map 10 SO54

Places to visit

The Weir Gardens, SWAINSHILL 01981 590509 www.nationaltrust.org.uk

Brockhampton Estate, BROCKHAMPTON 01885 482077 www.nationaltrust.org.uk/brockhampton

►► 82% Cuckoo's Corner Campsite *(SO501456)*

Cuckoo's Corner HR4 8AH

☎ 01432 760234

e-mail: cuckooscorner@gmail.com

dir: *Direct access from A49. From Hereford 2nd left after Moreton on Lugg sign. From Leominster 1st right (non gated road) after brown sign. Right just before island*

🚐 £13 🚙 £13 ⛺ £13

Open all year

Last arrival 21.00hrs Last departure 13.00hrs

This small adults-only site is well positioned just north of Hereford, with easy access to the city. The site has two areas, and offers hardstandings and some electric pitches. It is an ideal spot for an overnight stop or longer stay to visit the attractions of the area. There's a bus stop just outside the site and a full timetable is available from the reception office. 3 acre site. 19 touring pitches. 15 hardstandings. Caravan pitches. Motorhome pitches. Tent pitches.

AA Pubs & Restaurants nearby: England's Gate Inn, Bodenham 01568 797286

The Wellington, Wellington 01432 830367

Facilities: 🚿 ⊙ ✲ 🐕 Wi-fi 💻 ♻ ℹ

Services: 🔌 [L] 🍔

Within 3 miles: ⛳ 🎣 [S]

Notes: Adults only. 💳 No large groups, no noise after 22.30hrs. Dogs must be kept on leads. DVD library, books & magazines.

PEMBRIDGE Map 9 SO35

Places to visit

The Weir Gardens, SWAINSHILL 01981 590509 www.nationaltrust.org.uk

Brockhampton Estate, BROCKHAMPTON 01885 482077 www.nationaltrust.org.uk/brockhampton

PREMIER PARK

►►►►► 87% *Townsend Touring Park* *(SO395583)*

Best of British

Townsend Farm HR6 9HB

☎ 01544 388527

e-mail: info@townsend-farm.co.uk

dir: *A44 through Pembridge. Site 40mtrs from 30mph on E side of village*

🚐 🚙 ⛺

Open Mar-mid Jan

Last arrival 22.00hrs Last departure noon

This outstanding park is spaciously located on the edge of one of Herefordshire's most beautiful Black and White villages. The park offers excellent facilities, and all hardstanding pitches are fully serviced, and it has its own award-winning farm shop and butchery. Course fishing is possible on the site's lake. It also makes an excellent base from which to explore the area, including Ludlow Castle and Ironbridge. There are four camping pods available for hire. 12 acre site. 60 touring pitches. 23 hardstandings. Caravan pitches. Motorhome pitches. Tent pitches.

AA Pubs & Restaurants nearby: New Inn, Pembridge 01544 388427

The Bateman Arms, Shobdon 01568 708374

Stagg Inn & Restaurant, Titley 01544 230221

Leisure: ⛺

Facilities: 🛁 🚿 ⊙ 🚿 ♿ 📞 [S] 🪑 🐕

Services: 🔌 [L] ⛽ ⛛

Within 3 miles: [S] [L] U

STANFORD BISHOP   Map 10 SO65

►►► 81% Boyce Caravan Park

(SO692528)

WR6 5UB
☎ **01886 884248**
e-mail: enquiries@boyceholidaypark.co.uk
web: www.boyceholidaypark.co.uk
dir: *From A44 take B4220. In Stanford Bishop take 1st left signed Linley Green, then 1st right into private driveway*

* 🚐 £19-£23 🚐 £19-£23 ▲ £19

Open Feb-Dec (static) (rs Mar-Oct (touring))

Last arrival 18.00hrs Last departure noon

A friendly and peaceful park with access allowed onto the 100 acres of farmland. Coarse fishing is also available in the grounds, and there are extensive views over the Malvern and Suckley Hills. There are many walks to be enjoyed. 10 acre site. 14 touring pitches. 3 hardstandings. 18 seasonal pitches. Caravan pitches. Motorhome pitches. Tent pitches. 200 statics.

AA Pubs & Restaurants nearby: Three Horseshoes Inn, Little Cowarne 01885 400276

Leisure: 🪁 ⚽
Facilities: 🛁 ⊙ 🧴 ✳ 🔥 🧑‍🦽 ⚓ 🛒 🏇 🧹 ❶
Services: 🔌 🗑 🛍 ⚎
Within 3 miles: 🎣 🛒 🗑

Notes: Certain dog breeds are not accepted (call for details). Dogs must be kept on leads. Farm walks.

SYMONDS YAT (WEST)   Map 10 SO51

Places to visit

The Nelson Museum & Local History Centre, MONMOUTH 01600 710630

Great for kids: Goodrich Castle, GOODRICH 01600 890538 www.english-heritage.org.uk

►►► 85% Doward Park Camp Site

(SO539167)

Great Doward HR9 6BP
☎ **01600 890438**
e-mail: enquiries@dowardpark.co.uk
dir: *A40 from Monmouth towards Ross-on-Wye. In 2m left signed Crockers Ash, Ganarew & The Doward. Cross over A40, 1st left at T-junct, in 0.5m 1st right signed The Doward. Follow park signs up hill (NB do not follow Sat Nav for end of journey)*

🚐 ▲

Open Mar-Oct

Last arrival 20.00hrs Last departure 11.30hrs

This delightful little park is set in peaceful woodlands on the hillside above the Wye Valley. It is ideal for campers and motorhomes but not caravans due to the narrow twisting approach roads. A warm welcome awaits and the facilities are kept spotless. 1.5 acre site. 28 touring pitches. 6 seasonal pitches. Motorhome pitches. Tent pitches.

AA Pubs & Restaurants nearby: Mill Race, Walford 01989 562891

Leisure: 🪁
Facilities: 🛁 ⊙ 🧴 ✳ 🧑‍🦽 ⑤ 📶 ❶
Services: 🔌 🗑 🛍 ⚎ ⚎
Within 3 miles: 🎣 🛶 🗓 🎣 ◉ ⚓ ⑤ 🗑

Notes: No fires, quiet after 22.00hrs. Dogs must be kept on leads.

KENT

ASHFORD   Map 7 TR04

Places to visit

Leeds Castle, MAIDSTONE 01622 765400
www.leeds-castle.com

Great for kids: Thorpe Park, CHERTSEY 0870 444 4466 www.thorpepark.com

PREMIER PARK

►►►►► 86% Broadhembury Caravan & Camping Park

(TR009387)

Steeds Ln, Kingsnorth TN26 1NQ
☎ **01233 620859**
e-mail: holidaypark@broadhembury.co.uk
web: www.broadhembury.co.uk
dir: *M20 junct 10, A2070. Left at 2nd rdbt signed Kingsnorth, left at 2nd x-roads in village*

🚐 🚐 ▲

Open all year

Last arrival 22.00hrs Last departure noon

A well-run and well-maintained small family park surrounded by open pasture; it is neatly landscaped with pitches sheltered by mature hedges. There is a well-equipped campers' kitchen adjacent to the spotless toilet facilities and children will love the play areas, games room and football pitch. The adults-only area, close to the excellent reception building, includes popular fully serviced hardstanding pitches; this area has its own first-class, solar heated toilet block. 10 acre site. 110 touring pitches. 20 hardstandings. Caravan pitches. Motorhome pitches. Tent pitches. 25 statics.

AA Pubs & Restaurants nearby: Wife of Bath, Wye 01233 812232

The New Flying Horse, Wye 01233 812297

Leisure: 🪁 ⚽ 🎱 🖥
Facilities: 🛁 ⊙ 🧴 ✳ 🧑‍🦽 ⑤ 🏇 📶 🖥 ♻ ❶
Services: 🔌 🗑 🛍 ⚎ ⊤ ⚎ ⇊
Within 3 miles: 🎣 🗓 🎣 ◉ ⑤ 🗑 ⛲

Notes: No noise after 23.00hrs. Dogs must be kept on leads.

LEISURE: 🏊 Indoor swimming pool   🏊 Outdoor swimming pool   🪁 Children's playground   👦 Kid's club   🎾 Tennis court   🎱 Games room   🖥 Separate TV room   ⛳ 9/18 hole golf course   🚣 Boats for hire   🎬 Cinema   🎵 Entertainment   🎣 Fishing   ◉ Mini golf   🏄 Watersports   🏋 Gym   ⚽ Sports field   **Spa**   ⛲ Stables
FACILITIES: 🛁 Bath   🚿 Shower   ⊙ Electric shaver   💈 Hairdryer   ✳ Ice Pack Facility   🧑‍🦽 Disabled facilities   🕐 Public telephone   ⑤ Shop on site or within 200yds   🚐 Mobile shop (calls at least 5 days a week)   🍖 BBQ area   🧺 Picnic area   📶 Wi-fi   🖥 Internet access   ♻ Recycling   ❶ Tourist info   🏇 Dog exercise area

BELTRING
Map 6 TQ64

►► 73% The Hop Farm Touring & Camping Park (TQ674469)

Maidstone Rd TN12 6PY
☎ 01622 870838
e-mail: touring@thehopfarm.co.uk
dir: *M20 junct 4, M25 junct 5 onto A21 S, follow brown tourist signs*

Open Mar-Oct (rs Major Hop Farm events - camping occasionally closed)

Last arrival 19.00hrs Last departure 14.00hrs

Occupying a large field (for tents) and neat paddocks close to a collection of Victorian oast houses and its surrounding family attractions, which include indoor and outdoor play areas, animal farm, shire horses and restaurant, this popular touring park makes a great base for families. One paddock has good hardstanding pitches and the older-style toilet facilities are kept clean and tidy. 16 acre site. 106 touring pitches. 25 hardstandings. Caravan pitches. Motorhome pitches. Tent pitches. 12 statics.

AA Pubs & Restaurants nearby: The Poacher, Tudeley 01732 358934

Facilities: ⬆⊙🅿♿⚙🏪🎡🚿⛍

Services: 🔌🔋⚗

Within 3 miles: ⬆🅿🏪🏬

Notes: No open fires, no large or 'same age' groups, no mini motors or quad bikes. Dogs must be kept on leads. Site campers entitled to half price entry to Hop Farm Family Park.

BIRCHINGTON
Map 7 TR36

Places to visit
Reculver Towers & Roman Fort, RECULVER 01227 740676 www.english-heritage.org.uk

Great for kids: Richborough Roman Fort & Amphitheatre, RICHBOROUGH 01304 612013 www.english-heritage.org.uk

AA CAMPING CARD SITE

►►► 83% Two Chimneys Caravan Park (TR320684)

Shottendane Rd CT7 0HD
☎ 01843 841068 & 843157
e-mail: info@twochimneys.co.uk
dir: *From A28 to Birchington Sq, right into Park Lane (B2048). Left at Manston Rd (B2050), 1st left*

* 🚐 £15-£31 🚙 £15-£31 ⛺ £15-£31

Open Mar-Oct (rs Mar-May & Sep-Oct shop, bar, pool & takeaway restricted)

Last arrival 22.00hrs Last departure 11.00hrs

An impressive entrance leads into this busy, family-run site, which boasts two swimming pools, a fully-licensed clubhouse, and a new café/bistro. Other attractions include a tennis court and children's play area, and the immaculately clean toilet facilities fully meet the needs of this popular family park. 60 acre site. 250 touring pitches. 5 hardstandings. 20 seasonal pitches. Caravan pitches. Motorhome pitches. Tent pitches. 200 statics.

AA Pubs & Restaurants nearby: The Ambrette, Margate 01843 231504

Leisure: 🏊🎱🎯🎮🎵

Facilities: ⬆⊙🅿✳♿🕐🔥🚿WiFi♻🅰

Services: 🔌🔋🍺⚗🅣🍴🏬🔋⛽

Within 3 miles: ⬆🍴🗓🅿◎⛳🏪🏬🅕⛵

Notes: ⊗ No gazebos, no noise between 23.00hrs-07.00hrs, no bikes after dusk. Amusement arcade, bus service.

BIRCHINGTON *continued*

►►► 81% Quex Caravan Park

(TR321685)

Park Rd CT7 0BL
☎ **01843 841273**
e-mail: quex@keatfarm.co.uk
dir: *From Birchington (A28) turn SE into Park Rd to site in 1m*

Open Mar-Nov

Last arrival 18.00hrs Last departure noon

A small parkland site in a quiet and secluded woodland glade, with a very clean toilet block, an excellent café and informative boards around the site describing the wildlife to be seen. This picturesque, well managed site is just one mile from the village of Birchington, while Ramsgate, Margate and Broadstairs are all within easy reach. 11 acre site. 48 touring pitches. Caravan pitches. Motorhome pitches. 180 statics.

AA Pubs & Restaurants nearby: The Ambrette, Margate 01843 231504

Leisure: ⋔ ☉

Facilities: ⋔ ☉ ℱ ⚟ ⚙ 🕐 👖 Wi-fi 💻 ♻ ⓘ

Services: ⊞ ⊠ 🔋 ⊘ 🗂 🍴 🍽 🚮

Within 3 miles: ⅃ ⚓ 🎋 ⸸ ℱ ◎ 🏊 🏌 🏬 ∪

Notes: Dogs must be kept on leads.

DOVER   Map 7 TR34

Places to visit

The White Cliffs of Dover, DOVER 01304 202756
www.nationaltrust.org.uk

Walmer Castle & Gardens, DEAL 01304 364288
www.english-heritage.org.uk

Great for kids: Dover Castle & Secret Wartime Tunnels, DOVER 01304 211067
www.english-heritage.org.uk

►►►► 80% Hawthorn Farm Caravan Park *(TR342464)*

Station Rd, Martin Mill CT15 5LA
☎ **01304 852658** & 852914
e-mail: hawthorn@keatfarm.co.uk
dir: *Signed from A258*

* ⊞ £14-£21 ⇔ ⚠

Open all year (rs 18 Dec-7 Jan reception closed)

Last arrival 22.00hrs Last departure noon

This pleasant rural park set in 28 acres of beautifully-landscaped gardens is screened by young trees and hedgerows, in grounds which include woods and a rose garden. A popular night-halt to and from the cross-channel ferry port, it has decent facilities including a shop/café, an excellent new reception area, and good hardstanding pitches. 28 acre site. 147 touring pitches. 15 hardstandings. Caravan pitches. Motorhome pitches. Tent pitches. 163 statics.

AA Pubs & Restaurants nearby: Bay Restaurant (White Cliffs Hotel), St Margaret's at Cliffe 01304 852229

Facilities: ⋔ ☉ ℱ 🕐 🕐 👖 Wi-fi 💻 ♻ ⓘ

Services: ⊞ ⊠ 🔋 ⊘ 🗂 🍴 🚮

Within 3 miles: ⅃ ⚓ 🎋 ⸸ ℱ ◎ 🏊 🏌 🏬 ∪

Notes: No noise after 22.00hrs. Dogs must be kept on leads.

EASTCHURCH   Map 7 TQ97

Places to visit

Upnor Castle, UPNOR 01634 718742
www.english-heritage.org.uk

The Historic Dockyard Chatham, CHATHAM 01634 823807 www.thedockyard.co.uk

74% *Warden Springs Caravan Park* *(TR019722)*

Warden Point ME12 4HF
☎ **01795 880216**
e-mail: warden.springs@park-resorts.com
web: www.park-resorts.com
dir: *M2 junct 5 (Sheerness/Sittingbourne), A249 for 8m, right onto B2231 to Eastchurch. In Eastchurch left after church, follow park signs*

⊞ ⇔ ⚠

Open Apr-Oct (rs BH & peak wks)

Last arrival 22.00hrs Last departure noon

Panoramic views from the scenic cliff-top setting can be enjoyed at their best from the touring area of this holiday park. All of the many and varied leisure activities provided by the park are included in the pitch tariff, ie the heated outdoor swimming pool, adventure playground, family entertainment and a good choice of food outlets. 66 touring pitches. Caravan pitches. Motorhome pitches. Tent pitches. 198 statics.

Leisure: ⇔ ⋔ 👋 ♫

Facilities: ⋔ ☉ ℱ ⚙ 🕐 👖 Wi-fi 💻

Services: ⊠ 🍴 🍽 🚮

Within 3 miles: ℱ 🏬 🏬 ∪

Notes: No cars by caravans or tents.

FOLKESTONE — Map 7 TR23

Places to visit
Dymchurch Martello Tower, DYMCHURCH 01304 211067 www.english-heritage.org.uk
Great for kids: Port Lympne Wild Animal Park, LYMPNE 0844 842 4647 www.aspinallfoundation.org

►►► 84% Little Satmar Holiday Park (TR260390)

Winehouse Ln, Capel Le Ferne CT18 7JF
☎ 01303 251188
e-mail: satmar@keatfarm.co.uk
dir: Signed off B2011

🚐 🚍 ⛺

Open Mar-Nov

Last arrival 21.00hrs Last departure 12.00hrs

A quiet, well-screened site well away from the road and statics, with clean and tidy facilities. A useful base for visiting Dover and Folkestone, or as an overnight stop for the Channel Tunnel and ferry ports, and it's just a short walk from the Battle of Britain War Memorial, cliff paths with their views of the Channel, and sandy beaches below. 5 acre site. 47 touring pitches. Caravan pitches. Motorhome pitches. Tent pitches. 75 statics.

AA Pubs & Restaurants nearby: Rocksalt Restaurant, Folkestone 01303 212070

Leisure: 🏕
Facilities: 🛁⊙🍴☀🕐👣🚱🛒♻🚿🛡🛒ℹ
Services: 🔌🗑🔋🧺🚽
Within 3 miles: ↕�⛳ℹ🏧🗑🖕
Notes: No noise after 22.00hrs. Dogs must be kept on leads.

►► 75% Little Switzerland Camping & Caravan Site (TR248380)

Wear Bay Rd CT19 6PS
☎ 01303 252168
e-mail: btony328@aol.com
dir: Signed from A20 E of Folkestone. Approaching from A259 or B2011 on E outskirts of Folkestone follow signs for Wear Bay/Martello Tower, then tourist sign to site, follow signs to country park

🚐 🚍 ⛺

Open Mar-Oct

Last arrival mdnt Last departure noon

Set on a narrow plateau below the white cliffs, this unusual site has sheltered camping in secluded dells and enjoys fine views across Wear Bay and the Strait of Dover. The licensed café with an alfresco area is popular; please note that the basic toilet facilities are unsuitable for disabled visitors. 3 acre site. 32 touring pitches. Caravan pitches. Motorhome pitches. Tent pitches. 13 statics.

AA Pubs & Restaurants nearby: Rocksalt Restaurant, Folkestone 01303 212070

Facilities: 🛁⊙☀🕐🚱🛒WiFi
Services: 🔌🗑🔋🧺🍴🛒🖕🛒
Within 3 miles: ↕🛒🏧🗑🖕
Notes: No open fires. Dogs must be kept on leads.

LEYSDOWN-ON-SEA — Map 7 TR07

►►► 71% Priory Hill (TR038704)

Wing Rd ME12 4QT
☎ 01795 510267
e-mail: touringpark@prioryhill.co.uk
dir: M2 junct 5, A249 signed Sheerness, then B2231 to Leysdown, follow brown tourist signs

* 🚐 £14-£28 🚍 £14-£26 ⛺ £14-£26

Open Mar-Oct (rs Low season shorter opening times for pool & club)

Last arrival 20.00hrs Last departure noon

A small well-maintained touring area on an established family-run holiday park close to the sea, with views of the north Kent coast. Amenities include a clubhouse and a swimming pool. The pitch price includes membership of the clubhouse with live entertainment, and use of indoor swimming pool. 1.5 acre site. 37 touring pitches. Caravan pitches. Motorhome pitches. Tent pitches.

Leisure: 🏊☺⚽🖥
Facilities: 🛁⊙🍴☀🕐🚱🛒WiFiℹ
Services: 🔌🗑🍴🖕
Within 3 miles: 🛒🏧🗑
Notes: Dogs must be kept on leads.

MARDEN — Map 6 TQ74

PREMIER PARK

►►►►► 88% Tanner Farm Touring Caravan & Camping Park (TQ732415)

Tanner Farm, Goudhurst Rd TN12 9ND
☎ 01622 832399 & 831214
e-mail: enquiries@tannerfarmpark.co.uk
dir: From A21 or A229 onto B2079. Midway between Marden & Goudhurst

* 🚐 £13.85-£24.10 🚍 £13.85-£24.10 ⛺ £14.25-£24.10

Open all year (rs Nov-Feb shop opening hours restricted)

Last arrival 20.00hrs Last departure noon

At the heart of a 150-acre Wealden farm, replete with oast house, this extensive, long-established touring park is peacefully tucked away down a quiet farm drive deep in unspoilt Kentish countryside, yet close to Sissinghurst Castle and within easy reach of London (Marden station 3 miles). Perfect for families, with its farm animals, two excellent play areas and recreation room (computer/TV), it offers quality toilet blocks with privacy cubicles, a good shop, spacious hardstandings (12 fully serviced), and high levels of security and customer care. 15 acre site. 100 touring pitches. 33 hardstandings. 10 seasonal pitches. Caravan pitches. Motorhome pitches. Tent pitches.

AA Pubs & Restaurants nearby: Bull Inn, Linton 01622 743612

Star & Eagle Inn, Goudhurst 01580 211512

Green Cross Inn, Goudhurst 01580 211200

Leisure: 🏕☺⚽🖥
Facilities: 🛁🛁⊙🍴☀🕐🚱🛒WiFi🖥♻ℹ
Services: 🔌🗑🔋🧺🚽🛒🖕
Within 3 miles: 🛒🏧🗑
Notes: No groups, 1 car per pitch, no commercial vehicles. Dogs must be kept on leads.

ROCHESTER   Map 6 TQ76

Places to visit

Guildhall Museum, ROCHESTER 01634 848717
www.medway.gov.uk

Upnor Castle, UPNOR 01634 718742
www.english-heritage.org.uk

Great for kids: Diggerland, STROOD
0871 227 7007 www.diggerland.com

 NEW Allhallows Holiday Park
(TQ841784)

Allhallows-on-Sea ME3 9QD
☎ **01634 270385**
e-mail: allhallows@haven.com
web: www.haven.com/allhallows
dir: *M25 junct 2, A2 signed Rochester, A289 signed Gillingham. A228 signed Grain. Follow site signs*

Open Mar-Oct

Located in a peaceful country park setting close to Rochester in Kent, Allhallows is a static-only holiday park offering a wide range of sporting and leisure activities for all the family, including swimming pools, tennis courts, coarse fishing, a 9-hole golf course and fencing. Children will love the kids' club and play area, and there is a restaurant and bar with evening entertainment for adults. At the time of going to press the quality rating for this site had not been confirmed. For up-to-date information please see the AA website: theAA.com.

Change over day: Mon, Fri, Sat **Arrival & departure times:** Please contact the site

Statics 101 Sleeps 6-8 Bedrms 2-3 Bathrms 1-2 Toilets 1-2 Dishwasher Freezer TV Sky/FTV Elec inc Gas inc Grass area Parking

Children ♦♦ Cots inc **Dogs** Max 2 on leads No dangerous dogs (see page 12)

Leisure: 🏊 🏖 ⚓ U ⚐ ⚑ 🎢

see advert on page 227

ST NICHOLAS AT WADE   Map 7 TR26

Places to visit

Reculver Towers & Roman Fort, RECULVER
01227 740676 www.english-heritage.org.uk

Great for kids: Richborough Roman Fort & Amphitheatre, RICHBOROUGH 01304 612013
www.english-heritage.org.uk

►► **76% St Nicholas Camping Site**
(TR254672)

Court Rd CT7 0NH
☎ **01843 847245**
dir: *Signed from A299 & A28, site at W end of village near church*

* 🚐 £19-£22 🚐 £19-£20 ▲ £16-£25

Open Etr-Oct

Last arrival 22.00hrs Last departure 14.00hrs

A gently-sloping field with mature hedging, on the edge of the village close to the shop. This pretty site offers good facilities, including a family/disabled room, and is conveniently located close to primary routes and the north Kent coast. 3 acre site. 75 touring pitches. 6 seasonal pitches. Caravan pitches. Motorhome pitches. Tent pitches.

Leisure: 🛝

Facilities: ⚐ ☉ ⚑ ☀ ♿ 🎢 ❶

Services: 🚽 🛁 🗑 🚿 🗑

Within 3 miles: ⚐ 🏪 U

Notes: 🚭 No music after 22.30hrs. Dogs must be kept on leads. Baby changing area.

WHITSTABLE   Map 7 TR16

Places to visit

Royal Engineers Museum, Library & Archive, GILLINGHAM 01634 822839
www.re-museum.co.uk

Canterbury West Gate Towers, CANTERBURY 01227 789576
www.canterbury-museum.co.uk

Great for kids: Howletts Wild Animal Park, BEKESBOURNE 0844 842 4647
www.aspinallfoundation.org

►►►► **84% Homing Park**
(TR095645)

Church Ln, Seasalter CT5 4BU
☎ **01227 771777**
e-mail: info@homingpark.co.uk
dir: *Exit A299 for Whitstable & Canterbury, left at brown camping-caravan sign into Church Ln. Site entrance has 2 large flag poles*

* 🚐 £19.50-£27 🚐 £19.50-£27 ▲ £19.50-£27

Open Etr-Oct

Last arrival 20.00hrs Last departure 11.00hrs

A small touring park close to Seasalter Beach and Whitstable, which is famous for its oysters. All pitches are generously sized and fully serviced, and most are separated by hedging and shrubs. A clubhouse and swimming pool are available on site with a small cost for the use of the swimming pool. 12.6 acre site. 43 touring pitches. Caravan pitches. Motorhome pitches. Tent pitches. 195 statics.

AA Pubs & Restaurants nearby: The Sportsman, Whitstable 01227 273370

Crab & Winkle Seafood Restaurant, Whitstable 01227 779377

Leisure: 🏊 🛝 ⚓

Facilities: ⚐ ☉ ⚑ ☀ ♿ 📶 ♻ ❶

Services: 🚽 🗑 🗑 🛁 🚿

Within 3 miles: ⚑ 🗓 ⚐ 🎣 🏪 U

Notes: No commercial vehicles, no tents greater than 8 berth or 5mtrs, no unaccompanied minors, no cycles/scooters. Dogs must be kept on leads.

WROTHAM HEATH   Map 6 TQ65

AA CAMPING CARD SITE

▶▶▶ 78% Gate House Wood Touring Park (TQ635585)

Ford Ln TN15 7SD
☎ 01732 843062
e-mail: contact@gatehousewoodtouringpark.com
dir: M26 junct 2a, A20 S towards Maidstone, through lights at Wrotham Heath. 1st left signed Trottiscliffe, left at next junct into Ford Ln. Site 100yds on left

* ⊕ £16-£20 ⇔ £16-£20 ▲ £14-£18

Open Mar-Oct

Last arrival 21.00hrs Last departure noon

A well-sheltered and mature site in a former quarry surrounded by tall deciduous trees and gorse banks. The well-designed facilities include reception, shop and smart toilets, and there is good entrance security. The colourful flower beds and hanging baskets are impressive and give a positive first impression. Conveniently placed for the M20 and M25. 3.5 acre site. 55 touring pitches. Caravan pitches. Motorhome pitches. Tent pitches.

AA Pubs & Restaurants nearby: The Bull, Wrotham 01732 789800

Leisure: ⋀
Facilities: ⋔☉ꝯ✳⅄⊙⑤ᴡᴴ ♺ ❶
Services: ⊡⑤⬛∅ᵀ⬇
Within 3 miles: ↓⅄ℓ⬇⑤∪
Notes: ⊛⊗ No commercial vehicles, no noise after 23.00hrs.

LANCASHIRE

See also sites under Greater Manchester & Merseyside

BLACKPOOL   Map 18 SD33

See also Lytham St Annes & Thornton

Places to visit

Blackpool Zoo, BLACKPOOL 01253 830830
www.blackpoolzoo.org.uk

 83% Marton Mere Holiday Village
(SD347349)

GOLD

Mythop Rd FY4 4XN
☎ 0871 231 0881
e-mail: martinmere@haven.com
web: www.haven.com/martonmere
dir: M55 junct 4, A583 towards Blackpool. Right at Clifton Arms lights, onto Mythop Rd. Site 150yds on left

⊕ ⇔

Open mid Mar-end Oct (rs Mar-end May & Sep-Oct reduced facilities, splash zone closed)

Last arrival 22.00hrs Last departure 10.00hrs

A very attractive holiday centre in an unusual setting on the edge of the mere, with plenty of birdlife to be spotted. The on-site entertainment is directed at all ages, and includes a superb show bar. There's a regular bus service into Blackpool for those who want to explore further afield. The separate touring area is well equipped with hardstandings and electric pitches, and there are good quality facilities, including a superb amenities block. 30 acre site. 84 touring pitches. 84 hardstandings.

Caravan pitches. Motorhome pitches. 700 statics.

AA Pubs & Restaurants nearby: Jali Fine Indian Dining, Blackpool 01253 622223

Leisure: ⋩⋀⋔♪
Facilities: ⋔⋔☉ꝯ✳⅄⊙⑤⋔⬛ ♺ ❶
Services: ⊡⑤⋕∅⬛∅⬛∅ᴵ◑⬛
Within 3 miles: ↓⅄⊟ℓ☉⬇⑤⑤∪

Notes: Max 2 dogs per booking, certain dog breeds banned, no commercial vehicles, no bookings by persons under 21yrs unless a family booking.

see advert on page 232

BOLTON-LE-SANDS   Map 18 SD46

Places to visit

Lancaster Maritime Museum, LANCASTER 01524 382264 www.lancashire.gov.uk/museums

Lancaster City Museum, LANCASTER 01524 64637 www.lancashire.gov.uk/museums

Great for kids: Lancaster Castle, LANCASTER 01524 64998 www.lancastercastle.com

▶▶▶ 86% Bay View Holiday Park (SD478683)

BRONZE

LA5 9TN
☎ 01524 701508
e-mail: info@holgatesleisureparks.co.uk
dir: W of A6, 1m N of Bolton-le-Sands

* ⊕ £20-£25 ⇔ £20-£25 ▲ £18-£23

Open all year (rs Mar-May shop & café hours restricted)

Last arrival 20.00hrs Last departure noon

A high quality, family-oriented seaside destination with fully-serviced all weather pitches, many of which have views across Morecombe Bay and the Cumbrian hills. A stylish bar/restaurant is just one of the park's amenities. and there is a wide range of activities and attractions on offer within a few miles. This makes a good choice for a family holiday by the sea. 10 acre site. 100 touring pitches. 50 hardstandings. 127 seasonal pitches. Caravan pitches. Motorhome pitches. Tent pitches. 100 statics. 2 wooden pods.

continued

BOLTON-LE-SANDS *continued*

AA Pubs & Restaurants nearby: Longland Inn & Restaurant, Carnforth 01524 781256

Hest Bank Hotel, Hest Bank 01524 824339

Leisure: ⚙️🐾🖵

Facilities: ↖️⊙❄️⚸🕓🖩🛪 WIFI ♻️ ❶

Services: 🔌🖸🕎🛢️🧺🅣🍴🚮🏧

Within 3 miles: ↨⛸️🖽 ⌀ 🖫🖥

Notes: Dogs must be kept on leads.

see advert on page 237

►►► 84% Sandside Caravan & Camping Park *(SD472681)*

The Shore LA5 8JS
☎ 01524 822311
e-mail: sandside@btconnect.com
dir: *M6 junct 35, A6 through Carnforth. Right after Far Pavillion in Bolton-le-Sands, over level crossing to site*

🚐🚮Å

Open Mar-Oct

Last arrival 20.00hrs Last departure 13.00hrs

A well-kept family park located in a pleasant spot overlooking Morecambe Bay, with distant views of the Lake District. The site is next to a West Coast railway line with a level crossing. The shop and reception are assets to this welcoming park. Booking is advisable at peak periods. 9 acre site. 70 touring pitches. 70 hardstandings. Caravan pitches. Motorhome pitches. Tent pitches. 33 statics.

AA Pubs & Restaurants nearby: Longland Inn & Restaurant, Carnforth 01524 781256

Hest Bank Hotel, Hest Bank 01524 824339

Facilities: ↖️⊙🖗🗦

Services: 🔌🖸

Within 3 miles: ↨🖽⌀🖫🖥🔄

►►► 80% Red Bank Farm *(SD472681)*

LA5 8JR
☎ 01524 823196
e-mail: mark.archer@hotmail.co.uk
dir: *Take A5105 (Morecambe road), after 200mtrs right on Shore Lane. At rail bridge turn right to site*

🚮Å

Open Mar-Oct

A gently sloping grassy field with mature hedges, close to the sea shore and a RSPB reserve. This farm site has smart toilet facilities, a superb view across Morecambe Bay to the distant Lake District hills, and is popular with tenters. Archers Café serves a good range of cooked food, including home reared marsh lamb. 3 acre site. 60 touring pitches. Motorhome pitches. Tent pitches.

AA Pubs & Restaurants nearby: Longland Inn & Restaurant, Carnforth 01524 781256

Hest Bank Hotel, Hest Bank 01524 824339

Facilities: ↖️⊙🖗❄️🔄

Services: 🔌🖸🧺

Within 3 miles: ↨⛸️🖽⌀◎⚓🖫🖥

Notes: Dogs must be kept on leads. Pets' corner.

►►►► 86% Old Hall Caravan Park *(SD533716)*

LA6 1AD
☎ 01524 733276
e-mail: info@oldhallcaravanpark.co.uk
web: www.oldhallcaravanpark.co.uk
dir: *M6 junct 35 follow signs to Over Kellet, left onto B6254, left at village green signed Capernwray. Site 1.5m on right*

* 🚐 fr £20 🚮 fr £20

Open Mar-Oct

Last departure noon

A lovely secluded park set in a clearing amongst trees at the end of a half-mile long drive. This peaceful park is home to a wide variety of wildlife, and there are marked walks in the woods. The facilities are well maintained by friendly owners, and booking is advisable. 3 acre site. 38 touring pitches. 38 hardstandings. 30 seasonal pitches. Caravan pitches. Motorhome pitches. 220 statics.

LEISURE: 🏊 Indoor swimming pool 🏊 Outdoor swimming pool ⚙️ Children's playground 🪁 Kid's club 🎾 Tennis court 🎱 Games room 🖵 Separate TV room ⛳ 9/18 hole golf course ⛵ Boats for hire 🎞️ Cinema 🎵 Entertainment 🎣 Fishing ◎ Mini golf 🏄 Watersports 🏋️ Gym ⚽ Sports field **Spa** ⛎ Stables

FACILITIES: 🛁 Bath 🚿 Shower ⊙ Electric shaver 🖗 Hairdryer ❄️ Ice Pack Facility ♿ Disabled facilities 🕿 Public telephone 🛍️ Shop on site or within 200yds 🛒 Mobile shop (calls at least 5 days a week) 🍴 BBQ area 🛪 Picnic area WIFI Wi-fi 🖥 Internet access ♻️ Recycling ❶ Tourist info 🐾 Dog exercise area

AA Pubs & Restaurants nearby: The Highwayman, Burrow 01524 273338

Lunesdale Arms, Tunstall 015242 74203

Leisure: 🎯

Facilities: 🐕☀️🌳🍴🕐♿🚿📶🖥️♻️❄️🛈

Services: 🔌🔲🔋🧴🔌

Within 3 miles: 🎣🏇🛒🎯🎱⛳U

Notes: No skateboards, rollerblades or roller boots. Dogs must be kept on leads.

COCKERHAM

Places to visit

Lancaster Maritime Museum, LANCASTER 01524 382264 www.lancashire.gov.uk/museums

Lancaster City Museum, LANCASTER 01524 64637 www.lancashire.gov.uk/museums

Great for kids: Blackpool Zoo, BLACKPOOL 01253 830830 www.blackpoolzoo.org.uk

COCKERHAM Map 18 SD45

▶▶▶▶ 82% Moss Wood Caravan Park *(SD456497)*

Crimbles Ln LA2 0ES
☎ 01524 791041
e-mail: info@mosswood.co.uk
dir: *M6 junct 33, A6, approx 4m to site. From Cockerham take W A588. Left into Crimbles Lane to site*

🚐 � Å

Open Mar-Oct

Last arrival 20.00hrs Last departure 16.00hrs

A tree-lined grassy park with sheltered, level pitches, located on peaceful Cockerham Moss. The modern toilet block is attractively clad in stained wood, and the facilities include cubicled washing facilities and a launderette. 25 acre site. 25 touring pitches. 25 hardstandings. Caravan pitches. Motorhome pitches. Tent pitches. 143 statics.

AA Pubs & Restaurants nearby: Bay Horse Inn, Forton 01524 791204

Leisure: ⚽

Facilities: 🐕☀️🌳🍴🕐♿🚿🏠🐕

Services: 🔌🔲🔋🧴🔲

Within 3 miles: 🎣🏇🛒U

Notes: Dogs must be kept on leads. Woodland walks.

CROSTON Map 15 SD41

Places to visit

Harris Museum & Art Gallery, PRESTON 01772 905427 www.harrismuseum.org.uk

AA CAMPING CARD SITE

▶▶▶ 83% Royal Umpire Caravan Park *(SD504190)*

Southport Rd PR26 9JB
☎ 01772 600257
e-mail: info@royalumpire.co.uk
dir: *From N M6 junct 28 (S junct 27). Take B5209, right onto B5250*

🚐 £9-£30 � £9-£30 Å £9-£21

Open all year

Last arrival 20.00hrs Last departure 16.00hrs

A large park with tree or hedge lined bays for touring caravans and motorhomes, and a large camping field in open countryside. There are many areas for children's activities and a choice of pubs and restaurants is within walking distance. 60 acre site. 195 touring pitches. 180 hardstandings. Caravan pitches. Motorhome pitches. Tent pitches.

AA Pubs & Restaurants nearby: Farmers Arms, Heskin Green 01257 451276

Leisure: 🎯☀️🎵

Facilities: 🐕☀️🌳✳️♿🕐🚿🏠🐕📶♻️🛈

Services: 🔌🔲🔋🧴🚽↕️

Within 3 miles: 🎣🎯🏇🛒🎱⛳U

Notes: Dogs must be kept on leads.

SERVICES: 🔌 Electric hook up 🔲 Launderette 🔲 Licensed bar 🔋 Calor Gas 🧴 Camping Gaz 🔲 Toilet fluid 🍴 Café/Restaurant 🍔 Fast Food/Takeaway 🔋 Battery charging 🍼 Baby care ↕️ Motorvan service point **ABBREVIATIONS:** BH/bank hols-bank holidays Etr-Easter Whit-Whitsun dep-departure fr-from hrs-hours m-mile mdnt-midnight rdbt-roundabout rs-restricted service wk-week wknd-weekend 🚫 No credit cards 🚫 no dogs

See page 7 for details of the AA Camping Card Scheme

FAR ARNSIDE — Map 18 SD47

ROGER ALMOND AWARD FOR THE MOST IMPROVED CAMPSITE 2013

►►►► 87% Hollins Farm Camping & Caravanning

(SD450764)

LA5 0SL
☎ 01524 701508
e-mail: reception@holgates.co.uk
dir: *M6 junct 35, A601/Carnforth. Left in 1m at rdbt to Carnforth. Right in 1m at lights signed Silverdale. Left in 1m into Sands Ln, signed Silverdale. 2.4m over auto-crossing, 0.3m to T-junct. Right, follow signs to site, approx 3m & take 2nd left after passing Holgates*

* ➡ fr £28 ➡ fr £28 ▲ fr £26

Open 14 Mar-7 Nov

Last arrival 20.00hrs Last departure noon

Hollins Farm is a long established park that continues to be upgraded by the owners. There are 50 fully serviced hardstanding pitches for tourers and 25 fully serviced tent pitches; the excellent amenities block provides very good facilities and privacy options. It has a traditional family camping feel and offers high standard facilities; most pitches offer views towards Morecambe Bay. The leisure and recreation facilities of the nearby, much larger, sister park (Silverdale Holiday Park) can be accessed by guests here. 30 acre site. 12 touring pitches. 12 hardstandings. 38 seasonal pitches. Caravan pitches. Motorhome pitches. Tent pitches. See also page 23.

Facilities: ♠ ☉ ✳ ❶

Services: 🚰 🛒 🐾

Within 3 miles: ↧ ↗ ◎ 🛍 🛒

Notes: No unaccompanied children. Dogs must be kept on leads.

see advert on page 237

FLEETWOOD — Map 18 SD34

🏠 ⓤ NEW Cala Gran Holiday Park
(SD330451)

Fleetwood Rd FY7 8JY
☎ 01253 872555
e-mail: calagran@haven.com
web: www.haven.com/calagran
dir: *M55 junct 3, A585 signed Fleetwood. At 4th rdbt (Nautical College on left) take 3rd exit. Park 250yds on left*

Open Mar-Oct

Cala Gran is a lively holiday park close to Blackpool with a range of quality holiday caravans and apartments. The park is all about fun and entertainment includes live music, comedy shows and resident DJs, while for children there are swimming pools and SplashZone. At the time of going to press the quality rating for this site had not been confirmed. For up-to-date information please see the AA website: theAA.com.

Change over day: Mon, Fri, Sat **Arrival & departure times:** Please contact the site

Statics (226) Sleeps 6-8 Bedrms 2-3 Bathrms 1-2 Toilets 1-2 Freezer TV Sky/FTV Elec included Gas included Grass area Parking

Children 🧒 Cots **Dogs** Max 2 on leads No dangerous dogs (see page 12)

Leisure: 🏊 🤸 ⅍

AA Pubs & Restaurants nearby: Twelve Restaurant and Lounge Bar, Thornton 01253 821212

see advert on page 233

GARSTANG — Map 18 SD44

Places to visit

Lancaster Maritime Museum, LANCASTER 01524 382264
www.lancashire.gov.uk/museums

Lancaster City Museum, LANCASTER 01524 64637 www.lancashire.gov.uk/museums

Great for kids: Lancaster Castle, LANCASTER 01524 64998 www.lancastercastle.com

►►►► 83% Claylands Caravan Park
(SD496485)

Cabus PR3 1AJ
☎ 01524 791242
e-mail: alan@claylands.com
dir: *From M6 junct 33 S to Garstang, approx 6m pass Quattros Restaurant, signed from A6 into Weavers Lane, follow lane to end, over cattle grid*

* ➡ £20-£27 ➡ £20-£27 ▲ £17-£22

Open Mar-Jan

Last arrival 23.00hrs Last departure noon

Colourful seasonal floral displays create an excellent first impression. A well-maintained site with lovely river and woodland walks and good views over the River Wyre towards the village of Scorton. This friendly park is set in delightful countryside where guests can enjoy fishing, and the atmosphere is very relaxed. The quality facilities and amenities are of a high standard, and everything is immaculately maintained. 14 acre site. 30 touring pitches. 30 hardstandings. Caravan pitches. Motorhome pitches. Tent pitches. 68 statics.

AA Pubs & Restaurants nearby: Owd Nell's Tavern, Bilsborrow 01995 640010

Leisure: ⅍ 🎵

Facilities: ♠ ☉ ✳ ♿ ☏ 🛍 🔥 ⊞ 📶 ♻ ❶

Services: 🚰 🛍 🔌 🐾 ⊤ 🍴 🍺 ⚒

Within 3 miles: ↧ ↟ ↗ 🛍 🛒 ⌂

Notes: No roller blades or skateboards. Dogs must be kept on leads.

LEISURE: 🏊 Indoor swimming pool ⍽ Outdoor swimming pool ⅍ Children's playground 🤸 Kid's club ♗ Tennis court ♞ Games room ▭ Separate TV room ↧ 9/18 hole golf course ⛵ Boats for hire ☰ Cinema 🎵 Entertainment ℘ Fishing ◎ Mini golf ⍽ Watersports 🏋 Gym ♛ Sports field **Spa** ⌂ Stables
FACILITIES: 🛁 Bath ♠ Shower ☉ Electric shaver ℘ Hairdryer ✳ Ice Pack Facility ♿ Disabled facilities ☏ Public telephone 🛍 Shop on site or within 200yds 🛒 Mobile shop (calls at least 5 days a week) 🔥 BBQ area 🪑 Picnic area 📶 Wi-fi ☷ Internet access ♻ Recycling ❶ Tourist info 🐕 Dog exercise area

AA CAMPING CARD SITE

►►► 78% Bridge House Marina & Caravan Park (SD483457)

Nateby Crossing Ln, Nateby PR3 0JJ
☎ **01995 603207**
e-mail: edwin@bridgehousemarina.co.uk
dir: *Exit A6 at pub & Knott End sign, immediately right into Nateby Crossing Ln, over canal bridge to site on left*

* 🚐 £19.75 🚏 £19.75

Open Feb-1 Jan

Last arrival 22.00hrs Last departure 13.00hrs

A well-maintained site in attractive countryside by the Lancaster Canal, with good views towards the Trough of Bowland. The boatyard atmosphere is interesting, and there is a good children's playground. 4 acre site. 30 touring pitches. 50 hardstandings. Caravan pitches. Motorhome pitches. 40 statics.

AA Pubs & Restaurants nearby: Owd Nell's Tavern, Bilsborrow 01995 640010

Leisure: 🄰

Facilities: 🅿️⊙🄿❆🄳🕘🄶 Wifi 🄾

Services: 🅿️🄸🄰🄼🅃🔋

Within 3 miles: 🚴‍♂️🔥🄿🄰🄸

Notes: Dogs must be kept on leads.

KIRKHAM   Map 18 SD43

Places to visit

Castle Howard, MALTON 01653 648333 www.castlehoward.co.uk

Duncombe Park, HELMSLEY 01439 778625 www.duncombepark.com

Great for kids: Eden Camp Modern History Theme Museum, MALTON 01653 697777 www.edencamp.co.uk

►►► 80% Little Orchard Caravan Park (SD399355)

Shorrocks Barn, Back Ln PR4 3HN
☎ **01253 836658**
e-mail: info@littleorchardcaravanpark.com
web: www.littleorchardcaravanpark.com
dir: *M55 junct 3, A585 signed Fleetwood. Left in 0.5m opposite Ashiana Tandoori restaurant into Greenhalgh Ln in 0.75m, right at T-junct, site entrance 1st left*

🚐 £17.50-£18.50 🚏 £17.50-£18.50
🅰 £14.50-£16.50

Open 14 Feb-1 Jan

Last arrival 20.00hrs Last departure noon

Set in a quiet rural location in an orchard, this attractive park welcomes mature visitors. The toilet facilities are to a very high standard but there is no laundry. Two excellent fisheries are within easy walking distance. The site advises that bookings should be made by phone only, not on-line. 7 acre site. 45 touring pitches. 45 hardstandings. 20 seasonal pitches. Caravan pitches. Motorhome pitches. Tent pitches.

AA Pubs & Restaurants nearby: The Ship at Elswick, 01995 672777

Facilities: 🅿️⊙🄿🄳🄰🄲 Wifi 🄲 🄾

Services: 🅿️🔋

Within 3 miles: 🄿◎🕈🄸🄶🅄

Notes: 🚫 No cars by tents. No ball games or skateboards, no dangerous dog breeds, no noise after 23.00hrs, children must be supervised in toilet blocks. Dogs must be kept on leads.

LANCASTER   Map 18 SD46

Places to visit

Lancaster Maritime Museum, LANCASTER 01524 382264 www.lancashire.gov.uk/museums

Lancaster City Museum, LANCASTER 01524 64637 www.lancashire.gov.uk/museums

Great for kids: Lancaster Castle, LANCASTER 01524 64998 www.lancastercastle.com

►►► 82% New Parkside Farm Caravan Park (SD507633)

Denny Beck, Caton Rd LA2 9HH
☎ **015247 70723**
dir: *M6 junct 34, A683 towards Caton/Kirkby Lonsdale. Site 1m on right*

🚐 £15-£18 🚏 £15-£18 🅰 £12-£15

Open Mar-Oct

Last arrival 20.00hrs Last departure 16.00hrs

Peaceful, friendly grassy park on a working farm convenient for exploring the historic city of Lancaster and the delights of the Lune Valley. Please note that there is no laundry at this site. 4 acre site. 40 touring pitches. 40 hardstandings. Caravan pitches. Motorhome pitches. Tent pitches. 16 statics.

AA Pubs & Restaurants nearby: Sun Hotel & Bar, Lancaster 01524 66006

The white Cross, Lancaster 01524 33999

The Stork Inn, Lancaster 01524 751234

Facilities: 🅿️⊙🄿🄳🄲 🄾

Services: 🅿️🄰

Within 3 miles: 🚴‍♂️🄷🄿🄸

Notes: 🚫 No football. Dogs must be kept on leads.

LYTHAM ST ANNES — Map 18 SD32

See also Kirkham

Places to visit

Blackpool Zoo, BLACKPOOL 01253 830830
www.blackpoolzoo.org.uk

►►► 78% Eastham Hall Caravan Park (SD379291)

Saltcotes Rd FY8 4LS
☎ 01253 737907
e-mail: info@easthamhall.co.uk
web: www.easthamhall.co.uk
dir: M55 junct 3. Straight over 3 rdbts onto B5259. Through Wrea Green & Moss Side, site 1m after level crossing

* ⚏ £15-£35 ⚏ £15-£35

Open Mar-Nov (rs Nov only hardstanding pitches available)

Last arrival 21.00hrs Last departure noon

A large family run park in a tranquil rural setting, surrounded by trees and mature shrubs. The pitch density is very good and some are fully serviced. 15 acre site. 160 touring pitches. 99 hardstandings. 133 seasonal pitches. Caravan pitches. Motorhome pitches. 150 statics.

AA Pubs & Restaurants nearby: Greens Bistro, St Annes-on-Sea 01253 789990

Eastham Hall Caravan Park

Leisure: ⚞ ⚽
Facilities: ⚟ ⊙ ℱ ✳ ⅃ ⌚ 🅂 🚿 ⅏ ♻ ❶
Services: ⚡ 🔄 🛢 ⌀ ⅁ 🆃
Within 3 miles: ⚿ ⚓ ℱ ◎ ⅁ 🅱 🅶 ⵁ

Notes: No tents, breathable groundsheets only in awnings. Dogs must be kept on leads. Football field, night touring pitches.

see advert below

MORECAMBE

Places to visit

Leighton Hall, LEIGHTON HALL 01524 734474
www.leightonhall.co.uk

MORECAMBE — Map 18 SD46

AA CAMPING CARD SITE

►►► 81% Venture Caravan Park (SD436633)

Langridge Way, Westgate LA4 4TQ
☎ 01524 412986
e-mail: mark@venturecaravanpark.co.uk
dir: From M6 junct 34 follow Morecambe signs. At rdbt follow signs for Westgate then site signs. 1st right after fire station

⚏ ⚏ ⚟

Open all year (rs Winter one toilet block open)

Last arrival 22.00hrs Last departure noon

A large family park close to the town centre, with good modern facilities, including a small indoor heated pool, a licensed clubhouse and a family room with children's entertainment. The site has many statics, some of which are for holiday hire. 17.5 acre site. 56 touring pitches. 40 hardstandings. Caravan pitches. Motorhome pitches. Tent pitches. 304 statics.

AA Pubs & Restaurants nearby: Hest Bank Hotel, Hest Bank 01524 824339

Leisure: ⚞ ⚟ ⚽ ⚞
Facilities: 🛁 ⚟ ⊙ ℱ ✳ ⅃ ⌚ 🅂 ♻
Services: ⚡ 🔄 🍴 🛢 🆃 ⅃ ⬛ ⬇
Within 3 miles: ⚿ 🍴 ℱ 🅱 🅶

Notes: Dogs must be kept on leads. Amusement arcade, off licence, bar & seasonal entertainment.

LEISURE: ⚞ Indoor swimming pool ⚝ Outdoor swimming pool ⚟ Children's playground ⚞ Kid's club ⚞ Tennis court ⚞ Games room ⚞ Separate TV room ⚞ 9/18 hole golf course ⚞ Boats for hire ⚞ Cinema ⚞ Entertainment ⚞ Fishing ◎ Mini golf ⚞ Watersports ⚞ Gym ⚞ Sports field **Spa** ⵁ Stables

FACILITIES: 🛁 Bath ⚟ Shower ⊙ Electric shaver ℱ Hairdryer ✳ Ice Pack Facility ⅃ Disabled facilities ⌚ Public telephone 🅂 Shop on site or within 200yds 🔄 Mobile shop (calls at least 5 days a week) 🍴 BBQ area 🔺 Picnic area ⚟ Wi-fi ⬛ Internet access ♻ Recycling ❶ Tourist info 🛏 Dog exercise area

ORMSKIRK Map 15 SD40

Places to visit

Astley Hall Museum & Art Gallery, CHORLEY 01257 515555 www.chorley.gov.uk

British Commercial Vehicle Museum, LEYLAND 01772 451011 www.bcvm.co.uk

Great for kids: Camelot Theme Park, CHARNOCK RICHARD 01257 452100 www.camelotthemepark.co.uk

▶▶▶▶ 79% *Abbey Farm Caravan Park* (SD434098)

Dark Ln L40 5TX
☎ **01695 572686**
e-mail: abbeyfarm@yahoo.com
dir: *M6 junct 27, A5209 to Burscough. 4m, left onto B5240. Immediately right into Hobcross Lane. Site 1.5m on right*

🚐 🚃 ▲

Open all year

Last arrival 21.00hrs Last departure noon

Delightful hanging baskets and flower beds brighten this garden-like rural park which is sheltered by hedging and mature trees. Modern, very clean facilities include a family bathroom, and there are suitable pitches, close to the toilet facilities, for disabled visitors. A superb recreation field caters for children of all ages, and there is an indoor games room, large library, fishing lake and dog walk. Tents have their own area with BBQ and picnic tables. 6 acre site. 56 touring pitches. Caravan pitches. Motorhome pitches. Tent pitches. 44 statics.

AA Pubs & Restaurants nearby: Eagle & Child, Parbold 01257 462297

Leisure: 🛝 😊 🔍

Facilities: 🚿 🍴 🎣 ☀ ⚕ 🕐 💲 🛒 🛗 ♻ ℹ

Services: 🔌 🗑 🔋 🚿 🗑 🔋

Within 3 miles: 🚴 ♿ 🛒 🛒 ↻

Notes: No camp fires. Off-licence, farm walk.

Make the discovery Holgates

Silverdale Caravan Park

Hard standing fully serviced 5 star pitches open all year

AA Campsite of the Year 2011

Hollins Farm

Beautiful secluded Farm site with hard standing fully serviced pitches

Bay View

Now fully serviced pitches with new extended year round season

SILVERDALE — Map 18 SD47

Places to visit

Leighton Hall, LEIGHTON HALL 01524 734474
www.leightonhall.co.uk

Great for kids: RSPB Leighton Moss Nature
Reserve, SILVERDALE 01524 701601
www.rspb.org.uk/leightonmoss

PREMIER PARK

▶▶▶▶▶ 95% Silverdale Caravan
Park (SD455762)

Middlebarrow Plain, Cove Rd LA5 0SH
☎ 01524 701508
e-mail: caravan@holgates.co.uk
dir: *M6 junct 35. 5m NW of Carnforth. From
Carnforth centre take unclassified Silverdale road
& follow tourist signs after Warton*

* 🚐 fr £32 🚃 fr £32 ⛺ fr £32

Open all year

Last arrival 20.00hrs Last departure noon

A superb family holiday park set in wooded
countryside next to the sea, which demonstrates
high quality in all areas, and offers a wide range of
leisure amenities. Its relaxing position overlooking
Morecambe Bay combined with excellent touring
facilities mark this park out as special. 100 acre
site. 80 touring pitches. 80 hardstandings. 2
seasonal pitches. Caravan pitches. Motorhome
pitches. Tent pitches. 339 statics.

AA Pubs & Restaurants nearby: Longland Inn &
Restaurant, Carnforth 01524 781256

The Wheatsheaf, Beetham 015395 62123

Leisure: 🏊 ⛳ 🎠 🎾 🔍

Facilities: ⬆️ ⊙ 🌀 ❄ ⛐ 🕐 🛁 📮 🛒 🔌 ♻ ❶

Services: 🔌 🛢 🍴 🛢 🧴 🚰 🍴 🛒 ⬇

Within 3 miles: ⬇ ⛵ ◎ 🛁 🛢 ⛴

Notes: No unaccompanied children. Dogs must be
kept on leads. Sauna, spa pool, steam room, mini-
golf.

see advert on page 237

THORNTON — Map 18 SD34

Places to visit

Blackpool Zoo, BLACKPOOL 01253 830830
www.blackpoolzoo.org.uk

PREMIER PARK

▶▶▶▶▶ 82% Kneps Farm Holiday
Park (SD353429)

River Rd, Stanah FY5 5LR
☎ 01253 823632
e-mail: enquiries@knepsfarm.co.uk
web: www.knepsfarm.co.uk
dir: *Exit A585 at rdbt onto B5412 to Little
Thornton. Right at mini-rdbt after school into
Stanah Rd, over 2nd mini-rdbt, leading to River
Rd*

* 🚐 £19–£20.50 🚃 £19–£20.50

Open Mar-mid Nov

Last arrival 20.00hrs Last departure noon

A quality park, quietly located, adjacent to the
River Wyre and the Wyre Estuary Country Park,
handily placed for the attractions of Blackpool and
the Fylde coast. This family-run park offers an
excellent toilet block with immaculate facilities,
and a mixture of hard and grass pitches (no
tents), plus there are six camping pods for hire. 10
acre site. 40 touring pitches. 40 hardstandings. 5
seasonal pitches. Caravan pitches. Motorhome
pitches. 40 statics. 6 wooden pods.

AA Pubs & Restaurants nearby: Twelve
Restaurant & Lounge Bar, Thornton 01253 821212

Leisure: 🛝

Facilities: ⬆️ ⬆️ ⊙ 🌀 ❄ 🕐 🛁 📮 🛒 🔌 ❶

Services: 🔌 🛢 🛢 🧴 🚰 🛒 ⬇

Within 3 miles: ⬇ 🏠 ⛵ ◎ 🛁 🛢

Notes: No commercial vehicles. Max 2 dogs
(chargeable) per group, and must be kept on
leads.

LEICESTERSHIRE

See also Wolvey, Warwickshire

CASTLE DONINGTON — Map 11 SK42

Places to visit

Twycross Zoo, TWYCROSS 0844 474 1777
www.twycrosszoo.org

National Space Centre, LEICESTER
0845 605 2001 www.spacecentre.co.uk

Great for kids: Snibston Discovery Museum,
COALVILLE 01530 278444 www.snibston.com

▶▶▶ 72% *Donington Park
Farmhouse* (SK414254)

Melbourne Rd, Isley Walton DE74 2RN
☎ 01332 862409
e-mail: info@parkfarmhouse.co.uk
dir: *M1 junct 24, pass airport to Isley Walton, right
towards Melbourne. Site 0.5m on right*

🚐 🚃 ⛺

Open Jan-23 Dec (rs Winter hardstanding only)

Last arrival 21.00hrs Last departure noon

A secluded touring site at the rear of a hotel
beside Donington Park motor racing circuit, which
is very popular on race days when booking is
essential. Both daytime and night flights from
nearby East Midlands Airport may cause
disturbance. 7 acre site. 60 touring pitches. 10
hardstandings. Caravan pitches. Motorhome
pitches. Tent pitches.

AA Pubs & Restaurants nearby: Priest House
Hotel, Castle Donington 0845 072 7502

Leisure: 🛝

Facilities: ⬆️ ⊙ ❄ 🕐 ⛐ 📮 🛒 🔌 ❶

Services: 🔌 🛢 🍴 🧴 🍴 ⬇

Within 3 miles: ⬇ ⛵ 🛁 🛢 ⛴

Notes: Dogs must be kept on leads. Bread & milk
sold, hotel on site for bar/dining.

LEISURE: 🏊 Indoor swimming pool 🏊 Outdoor swimming pool 🛝 Children's playground 🧒 Kid's club 🎾 Tennis court 🔍 Games room 📺 Separate TV room ⛳ 9/18 hole golf course ⛵ Boats for hire 🎬 Cinema 🎵 Entertainment 🎣 Fishing ◎ Mini golf 🏄 Watersports ⛳ Gym 🏟 Sports field Spa ⛴ Stables
FACILITIES: 🛁 Bath 🚿 Shower ⊙ Electric shaver 💈 Hairdryer ❄ Ice Pack Facility ⛐ Disabled facilities 🕐 Public telephone 🏪 Shop on site or within 200yds 🚐 Mobile shop (calls at least 5 days a week) 🍖 BBQ area 🍴 Picnic area 📶 Wi-fi 💻 Internet access ♻ Recycling ❶ Tourist info 🐕 Dog exercise area

LINCOLNSHIRE

See Walk 6 in the Walks & Cycle Rides section at the end of the guide

ANCASTER
Map 11 SK94

Places to visit

Belton House Park & Gardens, BELTON 01476 566116 www.nationaltrust.org.uk

Belvoir Castle, BELVOIR 01476 871002 www.belvoircastle.com

►►► 82% Woodland Waters

(SK979435)

Willoughby Rd NG32 3RT
☎ 01400 230888
e-mail: info@woodlandwaters.co.uk
web: www.woodlandwaters.co.uk
dir: On A153 W of junct with B6403

🚐 £16-£19.50 🚐 £16-£19.50 ▲ £16-£19.50

Open all year

Last arrival 20.00hrs Last departure noon

Peacefully set around five impressive fishing lakes, with a few log cabins in a separate area, this is a pleasant open park. The access road is through mature woodland, and there is an excellent heated toilet block, and a pub/club house with restaurant. 72 acre site. 128 touring pitches. 4 hardstandings. Caravan pitches. Motorhome pitches. Tent pitches.

AA Pubs & Restaurants nearby: Bustard Inn & Restaurant, South Rauceby 01529 488250

Brownlow Arms, Hough-on-the-Hill 01400 250234

Leisure: 🎬 🎣
Facilities: 🏪 ⊙ 🅿 🕭 🖪 🎋 🚻 ⅏
Services: 🔌 🗑 🍴 🛢 🍽 🎒 🎂
Within 3 miles: 🎣 🅿 🛒 🛍 ∪

Notes: No noise after 23.00hrs. Dogs must be kept on leads.

BOSTON
Map 12 TF34

Places to visit

Battle of Britain Memorial Flight Visitor Centre, CONINGSBY 01522 782040 www.lincolnshire.gov.uk/bbmf

Tattershall Castle, TATTERSHALL 01526 342543 www.nationaltrust.org.uk

AA CAMPING CARD SITE

►►►► 81% Long Acres Touring Park

(TF384531)

Station Rd, Old Leake PE22 9RF
☎ 01205 871555
e-mail: enquiries@longacres-caravanpark.co.uk
dir: From A16 take B1184 at Sibsey (by church); approx 1m at T-junct turn left. 1.5m, after level crossing take next right into Station Rd. Park entrance approx 0.5m on left

* 🚐 £17.50-£20 🚐 £17.50-£20 ▲ £17.50-£20

Open Mar-Oct

Last arrival 20.00hrs Last departure 11.00hrs

A small rural adults-only park in an attractive setting within easy reach of Boston, Spalding and Skegness. The park has a smart toilet block, which is very clean and has an appealing interior, with modern, upmarket fittings. Excellent shelter is provided by the high, mature boundary hedging. A holiday cottage is available to let. 2 acre site. 40 touring pitches. 40 hardstandings. Caravan pitches. Motorhome pitches. Tent pitches.

Facilities: 🏪 ⊙ 🅿 🕭 🖪 🎋 🚻 ⅏ ⅃
Services: 🔌 ⅂
Within 3 miles: 🅿 🛍

Notes: Adults only. Washing lines not permitted. Dogs must be kept on leads.

►►►► 81% Pilgrims Way Caravan & Camping Park *(TF358434)*

Church Green Rd, Fishtoft PE21 0QY
☎ 01205 366646 & 07973 941955
e-mail: pilgrimsway@caravanandcampingpark.com
dir: E from Boston on A52. In 1m, after junct with A16, at Ball House pub turn right. Follow tourist signs to site

* 🚐 £15-£22 🚐 £15-£22 ▲ £10-£25

Open all year

Last arrival 22.00hrs Last departure noon

A beautifully maintained and peaceful park within easy walking distance of the town centre that has many attractions. All pitches, named after birds species, are screened by well trimmed hedges to create optimum privacy; a lush tent field is also available. Regular barbacue evenings with entertainment are held during the warmer months. 2.5 acre site. 22 touring pitches. 15 hardstandings. Caravan pitches. Motorhome pitches. Tent pitches.

Leisure: 🎬 🎣
Facilities: 🏪 ⊙ 🅿 🕭 🖪 🎋 🚻 ⅏ 🎂 ⅃
Services: 🔌 🗑 🛢 ⅂
Within 3 miles: 🎣 🎋 🖪 🅿 ⊙ 🛒 🛍 🛍 ∪

Notes: 🚫 Last arrival time 21.00hrs summer. Dogs must be kept on leads. Tea house & sun terrace, day dog kennels.

LEISURE: Indoor swimming pool Outdoor swimming pool Children's playground Kid's club Tennis court Games room Separate TV room 9/18 hole golf course Boats for hire Cinema Entertainment Fishing Mini golf Watersports Gym Sports field Spa Stables
FACILITIES: Bath Shower Electric shaver Hairdryer Ice Pack Facility Disabled facilities Public telephone Shop on site or within 200yds Mobile shop (calls at least 5 days a week) BBQ area Picnic area Wi-fi Internet access Recycling Tourist info Dog exercise area

BOSTON *continued*

►►►► 80% Orchard Park

(TF274432)

Frampton Ln, Hubbert's Bridge PE20 3QU
☎ **01205 290328**
e-mail: info@orchardpark.co.uk
dir: *On B1192, between A52 (Boston-Grantham) & A1121 (Boston-Sleaford)*

* � £16 ⟷ £16 ▲ £8-£16

Open all year (rs Dec-Feb bar, shop & café closed)

Last arrival 22.30hrs Last departure 16.00hrs

Ideally located for exploring the unique fenlands, this rapidly improving park has two lakes - one for fishing and the other set aside for conservation. The very attractive restaurant and bar prove popular with visitors, and Sandy's Café offers a delivery service to fisherman at the lakeside. 51 acre site. 87 touring pitches. 15 hardstandings. Caravan pitches. Motorhome pitches. Tent pitches. 164 statics.

Leisure: ⊙ 🎣 🎵
Facilities: ➤ 🐾 ⊙ 🅿 ☼ ⅃ ⊙ 🗑 ⟷ 🏇 WiFi ♻ ❶
Services: ᠎ 🗑 🍺 🛢 ⌀ T ⊙ 🎮 🎮
Within 3 miles: ↕ 🗗 🅿 ⊙ 🗑 🗑 ∪

Notes: Adults only. ⊛ Washing lines not permitted. Dogs must be kept on leads.

CLEETHORPES
Map 17 TA30

Places to visit

Fishing Heritage Centre, GRIMSBY 01472 323345
www.nelincs.gov.uk/leisure/museums

Great for kids: Pleasure Island Family Theme Park, CLEETHORPES 01472 211511
www.pleasure-island.co.uk

83% Thorpe Park Holiday Centre

(TA321035)

DN35 0PW
☎ **0871 231 0885**
e-mail: thorpepark@haven.com
web: www.haven.com/thorpepark
dir: *Take unclassified road from A180 at Cleethorpes, signed Humberstone & Holiday Park*

➤ ⟷ ▲

Open mid Mar-end Oct (rs mid Mar-May & Sep-Oct some facilities may be reduced)

Last arrival anytime Last departure 10.00hrs

A large static site, adjacent to the beach, with touring facilities, including fully-serviced pitches and pitches with hardstandings. This holiday centre offers excellent recreational and leisure activities, including an indoor pool with bar, bowling greens, crazy golf, tennis courts, and a games area. Parts of the site overlook the sea. 300 acre site. 141 touring pitches. Caravan pitches. Motorhome pitches. Tent pitches. 1357 statics.

AA Pubs & Restaurants nearby: Ship Inn, Barnoldby le Beck 01472 822308

Leisure: 🏄 ⟋ ⚑ 🎿
Facilities: ➤ 🐾 ⊙ 🅿 ⅃ ⊙ 🗑 🏇 ⟷ WiFi 🖥 ♻ ❶
Services: ᠎ 🗑 🍺 🛢 ⌀ ⊙ 🎮 🎮
Within 3 miles: ↕ 🗗 🅿 ⊙ 🗑 🗑 🗑 ∪

Notes: Max 2 dogs per booking, certain dog breeds banned, no commercial vehicles, no bookings by persons under 21yrs unless a family booking. Pitch & putt, roller ring, fishing lakes.

see advert on opposite page

GREAT CARLTON
Map 17 TF48

►►► 82% West End Farm *(TF418842)*

Salters Way LN11 8BF
☎ **01507 450949** & **07766 278740**
e-mail: westendfarm@talktalkbusiness.net
dir: *From A157 follow Great Carlton signs at Gayton Top. Follow brown sign for West End Farm in 0.5m, right into site*

➤ £12-£15 ⟷ £12-£15 ▲ £12-£15

Open 28 Mar-2 Oct

Last arrival 20.30hrs Last departure 14.00hrs

A neat and well-maintained four-acre touring park situated on the edge of the Lincolnshire Wolds. Surrounded by mature trees and bushes and well away from the busy main roads, yet connected by footpaths ideal for walking and cycling, it offers enjoyable peace and quiet close to the popular holiday resort of Mablethorpe. Good clean facilities throughout. 4 acre site. 35 touring pitches. 4 seasonal pitches. Caravan pitches. Motorhome pitches. Tent pitches.

AA Pubs & Restaurants nearby: Kings Head Inn, Theddlethorpe All Saints 01507 339798

Leisure: ⚑
Facilities: 🐾 🅿 ☼ ⟷ 🖥 ❶
Services: ᠎ 🗑 🎮
Within 3 miles: ↕ 🅿 ⊙ 🗑 ∪

Notes: No fires, quiet after 22.30hrs. Dogs must be kept on leads. Fridge available.

SERVICES: ᠎ Electric hook up 🗑 Launderette 🍺 Licensed bar 🛢 Calor Gas ⌀ Camping Gaz T Toilet fluid 🎮 Café/Restaurant 🎮 Fast Food/Takeaway 🔋 Battery charging 🍼 Baby care ⚓ Motorvan service point **ABBREVIATIONS:** BH/bank hols-bank holidays Etr-Easter Whit-Whitsun dep-departure fr-from hrs-hours m-mile mdnt-midnight rdbt-roundabout rs-restricted service wk-week wknd-weekend ⊛ No credit cards ⊗ no dogs

See page 7 for details of the AA Camping Card Scheme

HOLBEACH — Map 12 TF32

Places to visit

Butterfly & Wildlife Park, SPALDING
01406 363833
www.butterflyandwildlifepark.co.uk

►►► 76% *Herons Cottage Touring Park* (TF364204)

BRONZE

Frostley Gate PE12 8SR
☎ 01406 540435
e-mail: simon@satleisure.co.uk
dir: *4m S of Holbeach on B1165 between Sutton St James & Whaplode St Catherine*

🚐 🚌 Å

Open all year

Last arrival 20.00hrs Last departure 11.00hrs

Under the same ownership as Heron's Mead Touring Park in Orby (see entry), this park is situated in the heart of the Fens beside the Little South Holland Drain, with its extremely good coarse fishing. There's excellent supervision and 18 fully-serviced pitches. 4.5 acre site. 52 touring pitches. 48 hardstandings. 40 seasonal pitches. Caravan pitches. Motorhome pitches. Tent pitches. 9 statics.

AA Pubs & Restaurants nearby: Ship Inn, Surfleet Seas End 01775 680547

Facilities: 🏕 ⚥ 🚿 ✂
Services: 🔌 🚽 💧 🗑 🛒 ⬇
Within 3 miles: 🎣 🏪

Notes: ⊘ Strictly no children under 12yrs. Dogs must be kept on leads.

MABLETHORPE — Map 17 TF58

Places to visit

The Village-Church Farm, SKEGNESS 01754 766658
www.churchfarmvillage.org.uk

Great for kids: Skegness Natureland Seal Sanctuary, SKEGNESS 01754 764345
www.skegnessnatureland.co.uk

80% Golden Sands Holiday Park (TF501861)

GOLD

Quebec Rd LN12 1QJ
☎ 0871 231 0884
e-mail: goldensands@haven.com
web: www.haven.com/goldensands
dir: *From centre of Mablethorpe turn left on seafront road towards north end. Site on left*

🚐 🚌 Å

Open mid Mar-end Oct

Last arrival anytime Last departure 10.00hrs

A large, well-equipped seaside holiday park with many all-weather attractions and a good choice of entertainment and eating options, The large touring area is serviced by two amenities blocks and is close to the mini market and laundry. 23 acre site. 234 touring pitches. Caravan pitches. Motorhome pitches. Tent pitches. 1500 statics.

AA Pubs & Restaurants nearby: Red Lion Inn, Partney 01790 752271

Leisure: 🏊 🏊 🎠 🎱
Facilities: 🛁 🏕 ☉ 🚿 ✂ ⚥ 🚻 🛒 WiFi
Services: 🔌 🚽 💧 ⊘ 🗑 🍴 🛒 ⬇
Within 3 miles: 🎣 🏇 🎣 ⛳ 🏪

Notes: Max 2 dogs per booking, certain dog breeds banned, no commercial vehicles, no bookings by persons under 21yrs unless a family booking. Mini bowling alley, snooker/pool, indoor fun palace.

see advert on page 240

AA CAMPING CARD SITE

►►► 77% Kirkstead Holiday Park (TF509835)

North Rd, Trusthorpe LN12 2QD
☎ 01507 441483
e-mail: mark@kirkstead.co.uk
dir: *From Mablethorpe town centre take A52 S towards Sutton-on-Sea. 1m, sharp right by phone box into North Rd. Site signed in 300yds*

* 🚐 £12-£26 🚌 £12-£26 Å £12-£26

Open Mar-Nov

Last arrival 22.00hrs Last departure 15.00hrs

A well-established family-run park catering for all age groups, just a few minutes' walk from Trusthorpe and the sandy beaches of Mablethorpe. The main touring area, which is serviced by good quality toilet facilities, has 37 fully-serviced pitches on what used to be the football pitch, and here portacabin toilets have been installed. The site is particularly well maintained. 12 acre site. 60 touring pitches. 3 hardstandings. 30 seasonal pitches. Caravan pitches. Motorhome pitches. Tent pitches. 70 statics.

Leisure: 🎠 ⚽ 🎱 🎵 🎶
Facilities: 🏕 ☉ 🚿 ✂ ⚥ 🚻 🛒 🪑 🐕 WiFi 💻 ♻ ⓘ
Services: 🔌 🚽 🗑 🍴 🛒 ⬇
Within 3 miles: 🎣 🏇 ⛳ 🏪 U

Notes: No dogs in tents. Dogs must be kept on leads.

MARSTON — Map 11 SK84

Places to visit

Belton House Park & Gardens, BELTON
01476 566116 www.nationaltrust.org.uk

Newark Air Museum, NEWARK-ON-TRENT
01636 707170 www.newarkairmuseum.org

NEW ►►►► 83% Wagtail Country Park (SK897412)

GOLD

Cliff Ln NG32 2HU
☎ 01400 251955 & 07814 481088 (bookings)
e-mail: info@wagtailcountrypark.co.uk
dir: *From A1 exit at petrol station signed Barkston & Marston, right signed Barkston onto Green Ln, follow park signs*

🚐 £17.50-£23 🚌 £17.50-£23

Open all year

LEISURE: 🏊 Indoor swimming pool 🏊 Outdoor swimming pool 🎠 Children's playground 🎣 Kid's club 🎾 Tennis court 🎱 Games room 📺 Separate TV room 🏌 9/18 hole golf course ⛵ Boats for hire 🎬 Cinema 🎵 Entertainment 🎣 Fishing ⛳ Mini golf 🏄 Watersports 🏋 Gym 🏟 Sports field Spa U Stables
FACILITIES: 🛁 Bath 🚿 Shower ☉ Electric shaver ✂ Hairdryer ❄ Ice Pack Facility ⚥ Disabled facilities 📞 Public telephone 🛒 Shop on site or within 200yds 🚐 Mobile shop (calls at least 5 days a week) 🍴 BBQ area 🪑 Picnic area WiFi Wi-fi 💻 Internet access ♻ Recycling ⓘ Tourist info 🐕 Dog exercise area

Last arrival 19.00hrs Last departure 16.00hrs

A peaceful site near the village of Marston, surrounded by trees with birdsong the only welcome distraction. The touring areas are neatly laid out and enhanced by mature shrubs and pretty seasonal flowers. There is a separate adults-only area, and coarse fishing is also available. 20 acre site. 49 touring pitches. 49 hardstandings. 10 seasonal pitches. Caravan pitches. Motorhome pitches.

AA Pubs & Restaurants nearby: The Brownlow Arms, Hough-on-the-Hill 01400 250234

Facilities: ♠ ♇ ♿ ⚘ ☕ ♻ 🅿

Services: ⊕ 🗑 🔒

Within 3 miles: ♨ 🎣 🛍

Notes: No noise after 23.00hrs. Fishing dawn-dusk. Dogs must be kept on leads.

OLD LEAKE Map 17 TF45

Places to visit

Lincolnshire Aviation Heritage Centre, EAST KIRKBY 01790 763207 www.lincsaviation.co.uk

Battle of Britain Memorial Flight Visitor Centre, CONINGSBY 01522 782040 www.lincolnshire.gov.uk/bbmf

►►► 75% *Old Leake Leisure Park*
(TF415498)

Shaw Ln PE22 9LQ
☎ 01205 870121
dir: *Just off A52, 7m NE of Boston, opposite B1184*

🚐 🚍 ⛺

A pleasant, well-maintained small touring park set down a rural lane just off the A52, surrounded by the tranquillity of the Fenlands. It makes a peaceful base for exploring Boston and the Lincolnshire coast, and there are two holiday statics for hire. 2.5 acre site. 30 touring pitches. Caravan pitches. Motorhome pitches. Tent pitches.

ORBY

Places to visit

The Village-Church Farm, SKEGNESS 01754 766658 www.churchfarmvillage.org.uk

Great for kids: Skegness Natureland Seal Sanctuary, SKEGNESS 01754 764345 www.skegnessnatureland.co.uk

ORBY Map 17 TF46

AA CAMPING CARD SITE

►►►► 80% Heron's Mead Fishing Lake & Touring Park
(TF508673)

Marsh Ln PE24 5JA
☎ 01754 811340 & 07876 025369
e-mail: mail@heronsmeadtouringpark.co.uk
dir: *From A158 (Lincoln to Skegness road) turn left at rdbt, through Orby for 0.5m*

✱ 🚐 £20 🚍 £20 ⛺ £15

Open Mar-1 Nov

Last arrival 21.00hrs Last departure noon

A pleasant fishing and touring park with coarse fishing and an eight-acre woodland walk. The owners continue to improve the facilities, which prove particularly appealing to quiet couples and more mature visitors. 16 acre site. 21 touring pitches. 14 hardstandings. 10 seasonal pitches. Caravan pitches. Motorhome pitches. Tent pitches. 50 statics.

Facilities: ♠ ♇ 🅿 ☀ ♿ ⚘ ☕ ♻ 🅿

Services: ⊕ 🗑 🔒 👶

Within 3 miles: ♨ 🎣 🛍 🛍 ⛳

Notes: No cars by caravans or tents. No ball games, no motorbikes. Carp lake.

SALTFLEET Map 17 TF49

 80% *Sunnydale*
(TF455941)

Sea Ln LN11 7RP
☎ 0871 664 9776
e-mail: sunnydale@park-resorts.com
web: www.park-resorts.com
dir: *From A16 towards Louth take B1200 through Manby & Saltfleetby. Left into Saltfleet. Sea Lane on right. Site in approx 400mtrs*

🚐 🚍

Open Mar-Oct (rs BH & peak wks)

Last arrival noon Last departure 10.00hrs

Set in a peaceful and tranquil location in the village of Saltfleet between the seaside resorts of Cleethorpes and Mablethorpe. This park offers modern leisure facilities including an indoor pool, the tavern bar with entertainment, amusements and a coarse fishing pond. There is also direct access to the huge expanse

of Saltfleet beach. The touring facilities are incorporated into the leisure complex, and are modern and well cared for. 38 touring pitches. Caravan pitches. Motorhome pitches. 260 statics.

AA Pubs & Restaurants nearby: Kings Head Inn, Theddlethorpe All Saints 01507 339798

Leisure: ♨ ⚑ ⛷ ♪

Facilities: ♠ ♿ ⚘ 🗑 🅿 ⚄ 🖥

Services: ⊕ 🗑 🍴 👶

Within 3 miles: 🎣 ◎ ⛷ 🛍 ⛳

SKEGNESS Map 17 TF56

Places to visit

Skegness Natureland Seal Sanctuary, SKEGNESS 01754 764345 www.skegnessnatureland.co.uk

The Village-Church Farm, SKEGNESS 01754 766658 www.churchfarmvillage.org.uk

 83% Southview Leisure Park (TF541645)

Burgh Rd PE25 2LA
☎ 01754 896001
e-mail: southview@park-resorts.com
web: www.park-resorts.com
dir: *A158 towards Skegness. Park on left*

🚐 🚍

Open Apr-Oct

Last arrival noon Last departure 10.00hrs

A well presented holiday and leisure park close to the resort of Skegness. The leisure and entertainment facilities are modern and well maintained, and are just a short walk from the touring area with its neat pitches and clean and tidy amenity block. The staff are friendly and efficient. 98 touring pitches. Caravan pitches. Motorhome pitches.

AA Pubs & Restaurants nearby: Best Western Vine Hotel, Skegness 01754 763018

Leisure: ♨ ⚑ ⚑ ⚑ ◎ ❤ ♪

Facilities: ⚓ ♠ ♿ ☕ 🗑 ⚄ 🖥 ♻ ⚘

Services: ⊕ 🗑 🍴 🆃 🍴 👶

Within 3 miles: ♨ 🏇 🎣 ◎ ⛷ 🛍 🛍

TATTERSHALL   Map 17 TF25

▶▶▶▶ 83% Tattershall Lakes Country Park (TF234587)

Sleaford Rd LN4 4LR
☎ 01526 348800
e-mail: tattershall.holidays@away-resorts.com
dir: A153 to Tattershall

🚐 £4-£42 🚐 £4-£42 ⛺ £4-£42

Open end Mar-end Oct

Last arrival 21.00hrs Last departure 10.00hrs

Set amongst woodlands, lakes and parkland on the edge of Tattershall in the heart of the Lincolnshire Fens, this mature country park has been created from old gravel pits and the flat, well-drained and maintained touring area offers plenty of space for campers. There's a lot to entertain the youngsters as well as the grown-ups, with good fishing on excellent lakes, an 18-hole golf course, water-ski and jet ski lakes and an indoor heated pool with spa facilities. There is a separate adults-only field. 365 acre site. 186 touring pitches. 20 hardstandings. 25 seasonal pitches. Caravan pitches. Motorhome pitches. Tent pitches. 500 statics. 3 bell tents/yurts.

AA Pubs & Restaurants nearby: Lea Gate Inn, Coningsby 01526 342370

Leisure: 🏊🏕️⛰️🎣🎡🎯🖥️🎵 Spa

Facilities: 🚿⊙📡♿🚼🚽🐕📶🖥️♻️ℹ️

Services: 🔌🗑️🚽🍴🛒

Within 3 miles: 🎣🚣🎬🐾🏇🎯🎱

Notes: No excessive noise after mdnt. Dogs must be kept on leads. Water & jet skiing. Family activities.

see advert below

WADDINGHAM   Map 17 SK99

Places to visit
Gainsborough Old Hall, GAINSBOROUGH
01427 612669 www.english-heritage.org.uk

▶▶▶ 76% *Brandy Wharf Leisure Park* (TF014968)

Brandy Wharf DN21 4RT
☎ 01673 818010
e-mail: brandywharflp@freenetname.co.uk
dir: From A15 onto B1205 through Waddingham. Site 3m from Waddingham

🚐🚐⛺

Brandy Wharf Leisure Park

Open all year (rs Nov-Etr no tents)

Last arrival dusk Last departure 17.00hrs

A delightful site in a very rural area on the banks of the River Ancholme, where fishing is available. The toilet block has unisex rooms with combined facilities as well as a more conventional ladies and gents with wash hand basins and toilets. All of the grassy pitches have electricity, and there's a playing and picnic area. The site attracts a lively clientele at weekends, and music around open fires is allowed until 1am. Advance booking is necessary for weekend pitches. 5 acre site. 50 touring pitches. Caravan pitches. Motorhome pitches. Tent pitches.

AA Pubs & Restaurants nearby: The George, Kirton in Lindsey 01652 640600

Leisure: ⛰️ Facilities: 🚿⊙❄️♿🚽🐕♻️ℹ️

Services: 🔌🗑️🛢️🧺🍴🛒🛒

Within 3 miles: 🎣🚣🐾🎱🎱⛳

Notes: 🚭 No disposable BBQs on grass, no music after 01.00hrs. Fishing, boat mooring, boat launching slipway, canoe hire, pedalos, pets' corner.

LEISURE: 🏊 Indoor swimming pool ⛱️ Outdoor swimming pool ⛰️ Children's playground 👶 Kid's club 🎾 Tennis court 🎱 Games room 📺 Separate TV room 🏌️ 9/18 hole golf course 🚣 Boats for hire 🎬 Cinema 🎵 Entertainment 🎣 Fishing ⛳ Mini golf 🏄 Watersports 💪 Gym 🏟️ Sports field Spa ♘ Stables
FACILITIES: 🛁 Bath 🚿 Shower ⊙ Electric shaver 📡 Hairdryer ❄️ Ice Pack Facility ♿ Disabled facilities 📞 Public telephone 🛒 Shop on site or within 200yds 🛒 Mobile shop (calls at least 5 days a week) 🍴 BBQ area 🪑 Picnic area 📶 Wi-fi 🖥️ Internet access ♻️ Recycling ℹ️ Tourist info 🐕 Dog exercise area

WOODHALL SPA
Map 17 TF16

Places to visit

Tattershall Castle, TATTERSHALL 01526 342543
www.nationaltrust.org.uk

Battle of Britain Memorial Flight Visitor Centre,
CONINGSBY 01522 782040
www.lincolnshire.gov.uk/bbmf

PREMIER PARK

REGIONAL WINNER - AA HEART OF ENGLAND CAMPSITE OF THE YEAR 2013

►►►►► 85% Woodhall Country Park (TF189643)

Stixwold Rd LN10 6UJ
☎ 01526 353710
e-mail: info@woodhallcountrypark.co.uk
dir: In Woodhall Spa at rdbt in High St take
Stixwold Rd. 1m, site on right, just before Village
Limits pub

* 🚐 £18-£22 🚐 £18-£22 ▲ £14-£16

Open Mar-Nov

Last arrival 20.00hrs Last departure noon

A peaceful and attractive, touring park situated
just a short walk from Woodhall Spa. The owners
transformed part of the woodland area into a
countryside retreat for campers who wish to
escape from a hectic lifestyle. Well organised and
well laid out, the park offers fishing lakes, three
log cabin amenity blocks, fully serviced pitches
and high levels of customer care. Bird hides and
three camping pods were added in 2012. 80 acre
site. 80 touring pitches. 80 hardstandings.
Caravan pitches. Motorhome pitches. Tent pitches.
3 wooden pods. See also page 21.

AA Pubs & Restaurants nearby: Village Limits
Country Pub & Restaurant, Woodall Spa
01526 353312

Leisure: ⚽

Facilities: 🌡☺🞆✳🛁🖕🏧🚪♻ ❶

Services: 🔌🌀🔋🗑

Within 3 miles: ⛳🏕🎣🛒🗑🎡

Notes: No cars by tents. No fires, chinese lanterns
or fireworks, no noise between 23.00hrs- 07.00hrs,
BBQs must be off ground. Dogs must be kept on
leads.

NEW ►►► 83% Glen Lodge Touring Park (TF190647)

Glen Lodge, Edlington Moor LN10 6UL
☎ 01526 353523
e-mail: glenlodge1@tiscali.co.uk
dir: From Woodhall Spa take B1190 (Stixwould
road) towards Bardney for 1m. At sharp left bend
turn right, site on left

* 🚐 fr £16 🚐 fr £16

Open Mar-Nov

Last arrival 21.00hrs Last departure 02.00hrs

Peacefully located within a few minutes' drive of
the village centre, this well established park is
surrounded by trees and colourful hedges. The
spacious pitches are immaculately maintained
and a warm welcome is assured. Please note, this
site does not accept tents. 4 acre site. 35 touring
pitches. 35 hardstandings. Caravan pitches.
Motorhome pitches.

AA Pubs & Restaurants nearby: Village Limits
Country Pub & Restaurant, Woodhall Spa
01526 353312

Facilities: 🌡☺✳🛁🖕♻

Services: 🔌🌀🔋

Within 3 miles: ⛳🏕🎣🛒🗑

Notes: 🚫 No noise after 23.00hrs. Dogs must be
kept on leads.

E4 CHINGFORD
Map 6 TQ39

►►►► 83% Lee Valley Campsite (TQ381970)

Sewardstone Rd, Chingford E4 7RA
☎ 020 8529 5689
e-mail:
sewardstonecampsite@leevalleypark.org.uk
dir: M25 junct 26, A112. Site signed

🚐🚐▲

Open Mar-Jan

Last arrival 21.00hrs Last departure noon

Overlooking King George's Reservoir and close to
Epping Forest, this popular and very peaceful park
features very good modern facilities and excellent
hardstanding pitches including nine that are able
to accommodate larger motorhomes. This
impressive park is maintained to a high standard
and there are camping pods in a separate shady
glade for hire, and timber cabins. A bus calls at
the site hourly to take passengers to the nearest
tube station, and Enfield is easily accessible. 12
acre site. 81 touring pitches. 65 hardstandings.
Caravan pitches. Motorhome pitches. Tent pitches.
46 statics. 17 wooden pods.

continued

SERVICES: 🔌 Electric hook up 🌀 Launderette 🍺 Licensed bar 🔋 Calor Gas 🛢 Camping Gaz ⊤ Toilet fluid 🍴 Café/Restaurant 🍔 Fast Food/Takeaway 🔋 Battery charging
🍼 Baby care 🔧 Motorvan service point **ABBREVIATIONS:** BH/bank hols-bank holidays Etr-Easter Whit-Whitsun dep-departure fr-from hrs-hours m-mile mdnt-midnight
rdbt-roundabout rs-restricted service wk-week wknd-weekend 🚫 No credit cards 🚫 no dogs   See page 7 for details of the AA Camping Card Scheme

E4 CHINGFORD *continued*

Lee Valley Campsite

Leisure: ⚐

Facilities: ⬧☉⬢⬩⬧⬥⬦◉⬡⬛⬣♻️ℹ️

Services: ⬒⬓⬔⬕⬖⬗

Within 3 miles: ⬧⬨⬩⬪⬫⬬

Notes: Under 18s must be accompanied by an adult, no commercial vehicles on site. Dogs must be kept on leads.

see advert below

N9 EDMONTON   Map 6 TQ39

▶▶▶▶ 83% **Lee Valley Camping & Caravan Park** *(TQ360945)*

Meridian Way N9 0AR
☎ **020 8803 6900**
e-mail: edmontoncampsite@leevalleypark.org.uk
dir: *M25 junct 25, A10 S, 1st left onto A1055, approx 5m to Leisure Complex. From A406 (North Circular), N on A1010, left after 0.25m, right (Pickets Lock Ln)*

⬕⬖⬗

Open all year

Last arrival 20.00hrs Last departure noon

A pleasant, open site within easy reach of London yet peacefully located close to two large reservoirs. Upgrading of the park includes renewing the internal lighting, creating new gravel roads to improve access to the camping field, complete refurbishment of the gents' toilets, and new signage throughout. The site has the advantage of being adjacent to a restaurant and bar, and a multi-screen cinema. There are also camping pods and timber cabins for hire. A bus stop provides direct access to central London. 7 acre site. 100 touring pitches. 54 hardstandings. Caravan pitches. Motorhome pitches. Tent pitches. 12 wooden pods.

Leisure: ⚐

Facilities: ⬧☉⬢⬩⬧⬥⬦◉⬡♻️ℹ️

Services: ⬒⬓⬔⬕⬖⬗⬗

Within 3 miles: ⬧⬨

Notes: Under 18s must be accompanied by an adult. Dogs must be kept on leads.

LEISURE: 🏊 Indoor swimming pool   🏊 Outdoor swimming pool   ⚐ Children's playground   Kid's club   Tennis court   Games room   Separate TV room   9/18 hole golf course   Boats for hire   Cinema   Entertainment   Fishing   Mini golf   Watersports   Gym   Sports field   **Spa**   Stables
FACILITIES: Bath   Shower   Electric shaver   Hairdryer   Ice Pack Facility   Disabled facilities   Public telephone   Shop on site or within 200yds   Mobile shop (calls at least 5 days a week)   BBQ area   Picnic area   Wi-fi   Internet access   Recycling   Tourist info   Dog exercise area

MERSEYSIDE

SOUTHPORT
Map 15 SD31

Places to visit

The British Lawnmower Museum, SOUTHPORT
01704 501336 www.lawnmowerworld.com

85% Riverside Holiday Park (SD405192)

Southport New Rd PR9 8DF
☎ 01704 228886
e-mail: reception@harrisonleisureuk.com
dir: M6 junct 27, A5209 towards Parbold/
Burscough, right onto A59. Left onto A565 at
lights in Tarleton. Continue to dual carriageway.
At rdbt straight across, site 1m on left

* 🚐 £15-£27 🚌 £15-£27 ▲ £15-£23

Open 14 Feb-Jan

Last arrival 17.00hrs Last departure 11.00hrs

A large popular holiday destination for couples
and families, with many indoor attractions
including entertainment, dancing and theme
nights. A well-equipped swimming pool area
also provides spa treatments; free Wi-fi is
available in the attractive café. 80 acre site.
260 touring pitches. 130 hardstandings.
Caravan pitches. Motorhome pitches. Tent
pitches. 355 statics.

AA Pubs & Restaurants nearby: Warehouse
Kitchen & Bar, Southport 01704 544662

Bistrot Vérité, Southport 01704 564199

V-Café & Sushi Bar, Southport 01704 883800

Leisure: 🏊 🧗 🎣 🐎 🎵
Facilities: 🚿 🍴 🏪 🕐 👶 📷 🎮 💻 ℹ️
Services: 🔌 🧺 🍺 🍴 🗑️ 🚽 🍽️ 🍔 🚼
Within 3 miles: 🚴 🎣 🛒 🏪 🎡 ⛳

Notes: One car per pitch. Dogs must be kept
on leads.

►►► 86% Willowbank Holiday Home & Touring Park (SD305110)

Coastal Rd, Ainsdale PR8 3ST
☎ 01704 571566
e-mail: info@willowbankcp.co.uk
web: www.willowbankcp.co.uk
dir: From A565 between Formby & Ainsdale exit at
Woodvale lights onto coast road, site 150mtrs on
left. From N: M6 junct 31, A59 towards Preston,
A565, through Southport & Ainsdale, right at
Woodvale lights

* 🚐 £14.50-£19.40 🚌 £14.50-£19.40

Open Mar-Jan

Last arrival 21.00hrs Last departure noon

Set in woodland on a nature reserve next to sand
dunes, this constantly improving park is a
peaceful and relaxing holiday destination with
mature trees, shrubs and colourful seasonal
flowers surrounding neat pitches and modern
amenities blocks. 8 acre site. 87 touring pitches.
61 hardstandings. Caravan pitches. Motorhome
pitches. 228 statics.

AA Pubs & Restaurants nearby: Warehouse
Kitchen & Bar, Southport 01704 544662

Bistrot Vérité, Southport 01704 564199

V-Café & Sushi Bar, Southport 01704 883800

Leisure: 🧗
Facilities: 🚿 🍴 🕐 ✳️ 🏪 🕐 🐕 ♻️ ℹ️
Services: 🔌 🧺 🍴 🗑️ 🚽
Within 3 miles: 🚴 🏇 🏕️ 🎣 🏌️ 🛒 🏪 🎡 ⛳

Notes: No dangerous dog breeds, cannot site
continental door entry units, no commercial
vehicles. Dogs must be kept on leads. Baby
changing facility.

►►► 80% Hurlston Hall Country Caravan Park (SD398107)

Southport Rd L40 8HB
☎ 01704 841064
e-mail: enquiries@hurlstonhallcaravanpark.co.uk
dir: On A570, 3m from Ormskirk towards Southport

🚐 🚌

Open Etr-Oct

Last arrival 20.30hrs Last departure 17.00hrs

A peaceful tree-lined touring park next to a static
site in attractive countryside about ten minutes'
drive from Southport. The park is maturing well,
with growing trees and a coarse fishing lake, and
the excellent on-site facilities include golf, a
bistro, a well-equipped health centre, a bowling
green and model boat lake. Please note that
neither tents nor dogs are accepted at this site. 5
acre site. 60 touring pitches. Caravan pitches.
Motorhome pitches. 68 statics.

AA Pubs & Restaurants nearby: Warehouse
Kitchen & Bar, Southport 01704 544662

Bistrot Vérité, Southport 01704 564199

V-Café & Sushi Bar, Southport 01704 883800

Leisure: 🎣 🧗
Facilities: 🚿 🍴 🍴 🏪 🕐
Services: 🔌 🧺 🍺 🏪 🍽️
Within 3 miles: 🚴 🎣 🏪 🎡

Notes: 🚫 Latest arrival time 18.30hrs at wknds.

Norfolk

Even today, with faster cars and improved road and rail systems, Norfolk still seems a separate entity, as if strangely detached from the rest of the country. There are those who would like it to stay that way. The renowned composer, actor and playwright, Noel Coward, famously described Norfolk as 'very flat' and he was right.

Top of the list of attractions is the North Norfolk Coast, designated an Area of Outstanding Natural Beauty, which has been described as a long way from anywhere, a place of traditions and ancient secrets. The coastline here represents a world of lonely beaches, vast salt marshes and extensive sand dunes stretching as far as the eye can see. It is the same today as it has always been, and is a stark reminder of how this area has been vulnerable to attack and enemy invasion.

Delightful villages

With its old harbour and quaint High Street, Wells-next-the-Sea is a popular favourite with regular visitors to Norfolk, as is Blakeney, famous for its mudflats and medieval parish church, dedicated to the patron saint of seafarers, standing guard over the village and the estuary of the River Glaven.

Cromer is a classic example of a good old fashioned seaside resort where rather grand Victorian hotels look out to sea; the writer and actor Stephen Fry once worked as a

▶

● Wells-Next-The-Sea

● Cliffs and lighthouse at Hunstanton

waiter at Cromer's Hotel de Paris. A pier, such a key feature of coastal towns, completes the scene.

Farther down the coast, among a string of sleepy villages, is Happisburgh, pronounced Hazeburgh. The Hill House pub here is where Sir Arthur Conan Doyle stayed at the beginning of the 20th century; the Sherlock Holmes' story *The Adventure of the Dancing Men* (1903) is set in a Norfolk where 'on every hand enormous square-towered churches bristled up from the flat, green landscape.' Explore this corner of the county today and the scene is remarkably unchanged.

The Broads and nearby area

No visit to Norfolk is complete without a tour of the popular Broads, a network of mostly navigable rivers and lakes. Located a little inland to the south of Happisburgh, the various linked rivers, streams and man-made waterways, offer about 200 miles of highly enjoyable sailing and cruising. Away from the Broads rural Norfolk stretches for miles. If you've the time, you could spend days exploring a network of quiet back roads and winding lanes, visiting en route a generous assortment of picturesque villages and quiet market towns, including Fakenham and Swaffham. Also well worth a look is Thetford, with its delightful Dad's Army Museum. The location filming for the much-loved BBC comedy series was completed in and around Thetford Forest, and fictional Walmington-on-Sea was in fact the town of Thetford.

Ideally, this itinerary should also include the village of Castle Acre, with its impressive monastic ruins, and, of course, Norwich, with its magnificent cathedral, one of the country's greatest examples of Norman cathedral architecture.

● River Bure and Stracey Arms Mill

Walking and Cycling

The 93-mile (150km) Peddars Way and North Norfolk Coast Path is one of Britain's most popular national trails. Consisting of two paths joined together to form one continuous route, the trail begins near Thetford on the Suffolk/Norfolk border and follows ancient tracks and stretches of Roman road before reaching the coast near Hunstanton. There are also good walks around the Burnham villages, Castle Acre and the National Trust's Blickling Hall.

Cycling in Norfolk offers variety and flexibility and the chance to tie it in with a bit of train travel. You can cycle beside the Bure Valley Railway on a 9-mile (14.5km) trail running from Aylsham to Wroxham and return to the start by train. Alternatively, combine an undemanding 5 miles (8km) of mostly traffic-free cycling with a trip on the North Norfolk Railway from Sheringham to Holt, starting and finishing at Kelling Heath. There is also the North Norfolk Coast Cycleway between King's Lynn and Cromer and a series of cycle trails around the Norfolk Broads.

Festivals and Events

- The Norfolk & Norwich Festival, held in May, is a celebration of creativity, innovation, jazz, comedy, dance and classical music.
- The Sandringham Game & Country Fair in September has falconry, fishing, wildfowling and archery among many other country sports and pursuits.
- The Little Vintage Lovers Fair takes place on different dates and at different venues around the county throughout the year and includes 30 stalls with the emphasis on quality vintage fashion, textiles and accessories.

NORFOLK

See Walk 7 in the Walks & Cycle Rides section at the end of the guide

BARNEY — Map 13 TF93

Places to visit

Baconsthorpe Castle, BACONSTHORPE 01799 322399 www.english-heritage.org.uk

Holkham Hall & Bygones Museum, HOLKHAM 01328 710227 www.holkham.co.uk

Great for kids: Dinosaur Adventure Park, LENWADE 01603 876310 www.dinosauradventure.co.uk

PREMIER PARK

▶▶▶▶▶ **88% The Old Brick Kilns** (TG007328)

Little Barney Ln NR21 0NL
☎ **01328 878305**
e-mail: enquiries@old-brick-kilns.co.uk
dir: *From A148 (Fakenham-Cromer) follow brown tourist signs to Barney, left into Little Barney Lane. Site at end of lane*

Open 15 Mar-15 Dec (rs Low season bar food & takeaway on selected nights only)

Last arrival 21.00hrs Last departure 11.00hrs

A secluded and peaceful park approached via a quiet leafy country lane. The park is on two levels with its own boating and fishing pool and many mature trees. Excellent, well-planned toilet facilities can be found in two beautifully refurbished blocks, and there is a short dog walk. Due to a narrow access road, no arrivals are accepted until after 1pm. B&B accommodation is available and there are four self-catering holiday cottages. 12.73 acre site. 65 touring pitches. 65 hardstandings. Caravan pitches. Motorhome pitches. Tent pitches.

AA Pubs & Restaurants nearby: Chequers Inn, Binham 01328 830297

Old Forge Seafood Restaurant, Thursford 01328 878345

Leisure: 🅰 🎱 🖵
Facilities: 🌳⊙🎣❄♿🕙🛝🚿🎯 ᴡɪꜰɪ
Services: 🔌🗑🚽🚿🛒🍴🛒⬇
Within 3 miles: 🎣🏪🛒
Notes: No gazebos. Outdoor draughts, chess, family games.

BELTON — Map 13 TG40

Places to visit

Burgh Castle, BURGH CASTLE 0870 333 1181 www.english-heritage.org.uk

Great for kids: Thrigby Hall Wildlife Gardens, FILBY 01493 369477 www.thrigbyhall.co.uk

 74% Wild Duck Holiday Park (TG475028)

Howards Common NR31 9NE
☎ **0871 231 0876**
e-mail: wildduck@haven.com
web: www.haven.com/wildduck
dir: *Phone for detailed directions*

🚐🚙⛺

Open 16 Mar-5 Nov (rs mid Mar-May & Sep-Oct some facilities may be reduced)

Last arrival 21.00hrs Last departure 10.00hrs

This a large holiday complex with plenty to do for all ages both indoors and out. This level grassy site has well laid-out facilities and is set in a forest with small, cleared areas for tourers. Clubs for children and teenagers, sporting activities and evening shows all add to the fun of a stay here. 97 acre site. 118 touring pitches. Caravan pitches. Motorhome pitches. Tent pitches. 560 statics.

AA Pubs & Restaurants nearby: Andover House, Great Yarmouth 01493 843490

Leisure: 🏊⛵🅰🎣
Facilities: 🌳⊙♿🕙🛝🚿🎯 ᴡɪꜰɪ ♻ ℹ
Services: 🔌🗑🚽🛒🍴🛒⬇
Within 3 miles: 🎣🏪🛒⊙🏪🛒
Notes: Max 2 dogs per booking, certain dog breeds banned, no commercial vehicles, no bookings by persons under 21yrs unless a family booking.

see advert on opposite page

AA CAMPING CARD SITE

PREMIER PARK

▶▶▶▶▶ **85% Rose Farm Touring & Camping Park** (TG488033)

Stepshort NR31 9JS
☎ **01493 780896**
dir: *Follow signs to Belton off A143, right at lane signed Stepshort, site 1st on right*

🚐🚙⛺

Open all year

A former railway line is the setting for this very peaceful site which enjoys rural views and is beautifully presented throughout. The newly refurbished toilet facilities are smart, spotlessly clean, inviting to use and include new family rooms, and the park is brightened with many flower and herb beds. The customer care here is truly exceptional and a quality café opened in 2012. 10 acre site. 145 touring pitches. 20 hardstandings. Caravan pitches. Motorhome pitches. Tent pitches.

AA Pubs & Restaurants nearby: Andover House, Great Yarmouth 01493 843490

Leisure: 🅰🎱🖵
Facilities: 🌳⊙❄♿🕙🛝🚿 ᴡɪꜰɪ
Services: 🔌🗑🚿🛒
Within 3 miles: 🎣🏪🎣⊙🏪🛒🛒🎣
Notes: No dog fouling. Café open in peak season only.

Wild Duck Holiday Park
Nr. Great Yarmouth, Norfolk

We've got the lot
- Heated indoor and outdoor pools
- Family entertainment and kids' clubs
- Sports activities and facilities
- Peaceful woodland setting
- Stay in our caravans, or bring your own tourer, motorhome, tent or trailer tent

Save up to **50%***
on 2013 self-catering & touring and camping holidays

To find out more, order a brochure and to book
Call: **0843 658 0484** Quote: AAWD Visit: **haven.com/aawd**
Calls cost 5p per minute plus network extras. Open 7 days a week, 9am-9pm
Haven

*Save up to 50% discount is available on selected spring and autumn dates in 2013. Full booking terms and conditions apply. Haven Holidays is a trading name of Bourne Leisure Limited, 1 Park Lane, Hemel Hempstead, HP2 4YL. Registered in England No. 04011660.

Caister Holiday Park
Great Yarmouth, Norfolk

We've got the lot
- Heated indoor pool with multi-lane slide
- Family entertainment and kids' clubs
- Sports activities and facilities
- Direct access to a large sandy beach
- Stay in our caravans, or bring your own tourer or motorhome

Save up to **50%***
on 2013 self-catering & touring and camping holidays

To find out more, order a brochure and to book
Call: **0843 658 0455** Quote: AACC Visit: **haven.com/aacc**
Calls cost 5p per minute plus network extras. Open 7 days a week, 9am-9pm
Haven

*Save up to 50% discount is available on selected spring and autumn dates in 2013. Full booking terms and conditions apply. Haven Holidays is a trading name of Bourne Leisure Limited, 1 Park Lane, Hemel Hempstead, HP2 4YL. Registered in England No. 04011660.

Seashore Holiday Park
Great Yarmouth, Norfolk

We've got the lot
- Heated indoor and outdoor pools and SplashZone
- Family entertainment and kids' clubs
- Sports activities and facilities
- Large sandy beach opposite our park
- Come and stay in one of our comfortable, roomy self-catering caravans

Save up to **50%*** on 2013 holidays

To find out more, order a brochure and to book
Call: **0843 658 0478** Quote: AASA Visit: **haven.com/aasa**
Calls cost 5p per minute plus network extras. Open 7 days a week, 9am-9pm
Haven

*Save up to 50% discount is available on selected spring and autumn dates in 2013. Full booking terms and conditions apply. Haven Holidays is a trading name of Bourne Leisure Limited, 1 Park Lane, Hemel Hempstead, HP2 4YL. Registered in England No. 04011660.

SERVICES: Electric hook up Launderette Licensed bar Calor Gas Camping Gaz Toilet fluid Café/Restaurant Fast Food/Takeaway Battery charging Baby care Motorvan service point **ABBREVIATIONS:** BH/bank hols-bank holidays Etr-Easter Whit-Whitsun dep-departure fr-from hrs-hours m-mile mdnt-midnight rdbt-roundabout rs-restricted service wk-week wknd-weekend No credit cards no dogs See page 7 for details of the AA Camping Card Scheme

BURGH CASTLE — Map 13 TG40

Places to visit

Burgh Castle, BURGH CASTLE 0870 333 1181
www.english-heritage.org.uk

Thrigby Hall Wildlife Gardens, FILBY
01493 369477 www.thrigbyhall.co.uk

Great for kids: Pettitts Animal Adventure Park,
REEDHAM 01493 700094
www.pettittsadventurepark.co.uk

 77% *Breydon Water*
(TG479042)

Butt Ln NR31 9QB
☎ 0871 664 9710
e-mail: breydon.water@park-resorts.com
web: www.park-resorts.com
dir: *From Gt Yarmouth on A12 towards
Lowestoft over 2 rdbts. Follow Burgh Castle
sign. Right at lights signed Diss & Beccles.
1.5m, right signed Burgh Castle & Belton. At
mini rdbt right onto Stepshort. Site on right*

Open Apr-Oct

Last arrival anytime Last departure 10.00hrs

This large park has two village areas just a
short walk apart. Yare Village offers touring
facilities, family fun and superb entertainment,
while Bure Village, which is a quieter base, is
now static caravans only. Although the villages
are separated, guests are more than welcome to
use facilities at both. Yare Village has modern,
well maintained toilets, and tents are welcome.
The park is are just a short drive from the bright
lights of Great Yarmouth and the unique Norfolk
Broads. 189 touring pitches. Caravan pitches.
Motorhome pitches. Tent pitches. 327 statics.

AA Pubs & Restaurants nearby: Andover House,
Great Yarmouth 01493 843490

Leisure: 🏊🏖️🎢🎣⚽🎱🎵
Facilities: 🚿🅿️♿⏱️💈📶🖥️
Services: 🔌📷🚽🧹🍽️
Within 3 miles: 🚴🎣🏇⛳📷◎⛵🏧🛒

CAISTER-ON-SEA — Map 13 TG51

 **86% Caister Holiday
Park** *(TG519132)*
SILVER

Ormesby Rd NR30 5NQ
☎ 0871 231 0873
e-mail: caister@haven.com
web: www.haven.com/caister
dir: *A1064 signed Caister-on-Sea. At rdbt take
2nd exit onto A149, at next rdbt take 1st exit
onto Caister by-pass, at 3rd rdbt take 3rd exit
to Caister-on-Sea. Park on left*

Open mid Mar-end Oct

Last arrival 18.00hrs Last departure 10.00hrs

An all-action holiday park located beside the
beach north of the resort of Great Yarmouth, yet
close to the attractions of the Norfolk Broads.
The touring area offers 46 fully serviced pitches
and a modern purpose-built toilet block.
Customer care is of an extremely high standard
with a full time, experienced and caring warden.
Please note that the park does not accept tents.
138 acre site. 46 touring pitches. Caravan
pitches. Motorhome pitches. 900 statics.

AA Pubs & Restaurants nearby: Fishermans
Return, Winterton-on-Sea 01493 393305

Leisure: 🏊🎢⚽🎣🎱🎵
Facilities: 🚿🅿️♿⏱️💈🏧📶♻️ℹ️
Services: 🔌📷🚽🧹🍽️🛒⛽🚮
Within 3 miles: 🚴🎣🏇⛳◎🏧🛒

Notes: Max 2 dogs per booking, certain dog
breeds banned, no commercial vehicles, no
bookings by persons under 21yrs unless a family
booking, no sleeping in awnings, no tents.

see advert on page 253

CLIPPESBY — Map 13 TG41

Places to visit

Fairhaven Woodland & Water Garden,
SOUTH WALSHAM 01603 270449
www.fairhavengarden.co.uk

Great for kids: Caister Roman Site,
CAISTER-ON-SEA 0870 333 1181
www.english-heritage.org.uk

AA CAMPING CARD SITE

PREMIER PARK

▶▶▶▶▶ **93% Clippesby Hall**
(TG423147) GOLD

Hall Ln NR29 3BL
☎ 01493 367800
e-mail: holidays@clippesby.com
web: www.clippesby.com
dir: *From A47 follow tourist signs for The Broads.
At Acle rdbt take A1064, in 2m left onto B1152,
0.5m left opposite village sign, site 400yds on
right*

🚐 £12.50-£32.50 🚍 £12.50-£32.50
⛺ £12.50-£32.50

Open all year

Last arrival 17.30hrs Last departure 11.00hrs

A lovely country house estate with secluded
pitches hidden among the trees or in sheltered
sunny glades. The toilet facilities are appointed to
a very good standard, providing a wide choice of
cubicles. Amenities include a coffee shop with
Wi-fi and wired internet access, family bar and
restaurant and family golf. Excellent new
hardstanding pitches have been added as the
park is now open all year. There are pine lodges
and holiday cottages available for holiday lets. 30
acre site. 120 touring pitches. 41 hardstandings.
Caravan pitches. Motorhome pitches. Tent pitches.

AA Pubs & Restaurants nearby: Fishermans Return, Winterton-on-Sea 01493 393305

Fur & Feather Inn, Woodbastwick 01603 720003

Leisure: ⏺⏺⏺⏺⏺

Facilities: ⏺⏺⏺⏺⏺⏺⏺⏺⏺⏺⏺⏺⏺⏺
⏺⏺⏺

Services: ⏺⏺⏺⏺⏺⏺⏺⏺⏺⏺

Within 3 miles: ⏺⏺⏺⏺⏺⏺⏺⏺

Notes: No noise after 23.00hrs, no campfires, no groups. Dogs must be kept on leads. Bicycle hire, family golf, volley ball.

CROMER Map 13 TG24

Places to visit

RNLI Henry Blogg Museum, CROMER 01263 511294 www.rnli.org.uk/henryblogg

Felbrigg Hall, FELBRIGG 01263 837444 www.nationaltrust.org.uk/main/w-felbrigghallgardenandpark

▶▶▶▶ 81% Forest Park

(TG233405)

Northrepps Rd NR27 0JR
☎ 01263 513290
e-mail: info@forest-park.co.uk
dir: A140 from Norwich, left at T-junct signed Cromer, right signed Northrepps, right then immediately left, left at T-junct, site on right

⏺⏺⏺

Open 15 Mar-15 Jan

Last arrival 21.00hrs Last departure 11.00hrs

Surrounded by forest, this gently sloping park offers a wide choice of pitches. Visitors have the use of a heated indoor swimming pool, and a large clubhouse with entertainment. 100 acre site. 262 touring pitches. Caravan pitches. Motorhome pitches. Tent pitches. 420 statics.

AA Pubs & Restaurants nearby: The Wheatsheaf, West Beckham 01263 822110

White Horse, Overstrand 01263 579237

Frazers, Sea Marge Hotel, Overstrand 01263 579579

Leisure: ⏺⏺⏺

Facilities: ⏺⏺⏺⏺⏺⏺⏺⏺⏺⏺

Services: ⏺⏺⏺⏺⏺⏺⏺⏺

Within 3 miles: ⏺⏺⏺⏺⏺⏺⏺⏺

▶▶▶▶ 79% Manor Farm Caravan & Camping Site (TG198416)

East Runton NR27 9PR
☎ 01263 512858 & 07760 324673
e-mail: manor-farm@ukf.net
dir: 1m W of Cromer, exit A148 or A149 (recommended towing route) at Manor Farm sign.

* ⏺ £18.50-£21 ⏺ £14-£21 ⏺ £14-£21

Open Etr-Sep

Last arrival 20.30hrs Last departure noon

A well-established family-run site on a working farm enjoying panoramic sea views. There are good modern facilities across the site, including three smart toilet blocks that include two quality family rooms and privacy cubicles, two good play areas and a large expanse of grass for games - the park is very popular with families. 17 acre site. 250 touring pitches. Caravan pitches. Motorhome pitches. Tent pitches.

AA Pubs & Restaurants nearby: The Wheatsheaf, West Beckham 01263 822110

White Horse, Overstrand 01263 579237

Frazers, Sea Marge Hotel, Overstrand 01263 579579

Leisure: ⏺⏺

Facilities: ⏺⏺⏺⏺⏺⏺⏺

Services: ⏺⏺⏺⏺⏺

Within 3 miles: ⏺⏺⏺⏺⏺⏺⏺

Notes: ⏺ No noise after 23.00hrs, no groups. 2 dog-free fields.

SERVICES: ⏺ Electric hook up ⏺ Launderette ⏺ Licensed bar ⏺ Calor Gas ⏺ Camping Gaz ⏺ Toilet fluid ⏺ Café/Restaurant ⏺ Fast Food/Takeaway ⏺ Battery charging ⏺ Baby care ⏺ Motorvan service point ABBREVIATIONS: BH/bank hols-bank holidays Etr-Easter Whit-Whitsun dep-departure fr-from hrs-hours m-mile mdnt-midnight rdbt-roundabout rs-restricted service wk-week wknd-weekend ⏺ No credit cards ⏺ no dogs See page 7 for details of the AA Camping Card Scheme

DOWNHAM MARKET
Map 12 TF60

►►► 86% *Lakeside Caravan Park & Fisheries* (TF608013)

Sluice Rd, Denver PE38 0DZ
☎ 01366 387074 & 07790 272978
e-mail: richesflorido@aol.com
web: www.westhallfarmholidays.co.uk
dir: *Exit A10 towards Denver, follow signs to Denver Windmill*

🚐 🚍 🛆

Open Mar-Oct

Last arrival 21.00hrs Last departure noon

A peaceful, rapidly improving park set around four pretty fishing lakes. Investment for 2012 included new electric hook-ups, improved lighting across the park, a new timber reception chalet, and plans include upgrading the toilet facilities. Several grassy touring areas are sheltered by mature hedging and trees, and there is a function room, shop and laundry. 30 acre site. 100 touring pitches. Caravan pitches. Motorhome pitches. Tent pitches. 1 static.

AA Pubs & Restaurants nearby: Hare Arms, Stow Bardolph 01366 382229

Leisure: /Ⱥ

Facilities: 🏕⊙🏴✳⅘🛅📶

Services: 🔌🗄🗑🍴🖤🇹📏

Within 3 miles: 🚶🐾🎡🖤🎿🛒🗄

Notes: Dogs must be kept on leads. Pool table, fishing tackle/bait, caravan accessories.

FAKENHAM
Map 13 TF92

Places to visit

Houghton Hall, HOUGHTON 01485 528569
www.houghtonhall.com

Great for kids: Pensthorpe Nature Reserve & Gardens, FAKENHAM 01328 851465
www.pensthorpe.co.uk

►►► 83% Fakenham Campsite
(TF907310)

Burnham Market Rd, Sculthorpe NR21 9SA
☎ 01328 856614
e-mail: fakenham.campsite@gmail.com
dir: *From Fakenham take A148 towards King's Lynn then right onto B1355 Burnham Market Road. Site on right in 400yds*

🚐 🚍 🛆

Open all year

Last arrival 20.00hrs Last departure noon

Enthusiastic owners are running this peaceful site that is surrounded by tranquil countryside and which is part of a 9-hole, par 3 golf complex and driving range. The toilet facilities are of good quality, and there is a golf shop and licensed bar. Please note there is no laundry. 4 acre site. 50 touring pitches. 13 hardstandings. Caravan pitches. Motorhome pitches. Tent pitches. 2 statics.

AA Pubs & Restaurants nearby: Blue Boar Inn, Great Ryburgh 01328 829212

Brisley Bell Inn & Restaurant, Brisley 01362 668686

Leisure: /Ⱥ

Facilities: 🏕✳⅘🛒🔁🛈

Services: 🔌🍴🖤

Within 3 miles: 🚶🎡🖤🛒

Notes: No noise after 22.30hrs. Dogs must be kept on leads.

►►► 79% Caravan Club M.V.C. Site
(TF926288)

Fakenham Racecourse NR21 7NY
☎ 01328 862388
e-mail: caravan@fakenhamracecourse.co.uk
dir: *From B1146, S of Fakenham follow brown Racecourse signs (with tent & caravan symbols) leads to site entrance*

* 🚐 £13.25-£18.25 🚍 £13.25-£18.25 🛆 fr £14

Open all year

Last arrival 21.00hrs Last departure noon

A very well laid-out site set around the racecourse, with a grandstand offering smart modern toilet facilities. Tourers move to the centre of the course on race days, and enjoy free racing, and there's a wide range of sporting activities in the club house. 11.4 acre site. 120 touring pitches. 25 hardstandings. Caravan pitches. Motorhome pitches. Tent pitches.

AA Pubs & Restaurants nearby: Blue Boar Inn, Great Ryburgh 01328 829212

Brisley Bell Inn & Restaurant, Brisley 01362 668686

Facilities: 🏕⊙🏴✳⅘🛅📏🛒📶🔁🛈

Services: 🔌🗄🗑🍴🖤🇹📏🤚

Within 3 miles: 🚶🐾🖤🎡🗄🛒🐴

Notes: Max 2 dogs per unit. Dogs must be kept on leads. TV aerial hook-ups.

►► 72% Crossways Caravan & Camping Park
(TF961321)

Crossways, Holt Rd, Little Snoring NR21 0AX
☎ 01328 878335
e-mail: joyholland@live.co.uk
dir: *From Fakenham take A148 towards Cromer. After 3m pass exit for Little Snoring. Site on A148 on left behind post office*

* 🚐 £10.50-£18.50 🚍 £10.50-£18.50
🛆 £7-£18.50

Open all year

Last arrival 22.00hrs Last departure noon

Set on the edge of the peaceful hamlet of Little Snoring, this level site enjoys views across the fields towards the north Norfolk coast some seven miles away. Visitors can use the health suite for a small charge, and there is a shop on site, and a good village pub. 2 acre site. 26 touring pitches. 10 hardstandings. 14 seasonal pitches. Caravan pitches. Motorhome pitches. Tent pitches. 1 static.

LEISURE: 🏊 Indoor swimming pool 🏊 Outdoor swimming pool /Ⱥ Children's playground 🎽 Kid's club 🎾 Tennis court 🎱 Games room 📺 Separate TV room 🏌 9/18 hole golf course ⛵ Boats for hire 🎬 Cinema 🎵 Entertainment ✒ Fishing ◉ Mini golf 🏄 Watersports 🏋 Gym 🎯 Sports field Spa ⛎ Stables
FACILITIES: 🛁 Bath 🚿 Shower ⊙ Electric shaver ✂ Hairdryer ✳ Ice Pack Facility ⅘ Disabled facilities ⏰ Public telephone 🛒 Shop on site or within 200yds 🚗 Mobile shop (calls at least 5 days a week) 🍴 BBQ area 🌳 Picnic area 📶 Wi-fi 💻 Internet access 🔁 Recycling 🛈 Tourist info 🐾 Dog exercise area

AA Pubs & Restaurants nearby: Blue Boar Inn, Great Ryburgh 01328 829212

Brisley Bell Inn & Restaurant, Brisley 01362 668686

Leisure: ⚽

Facilities: 🛒☉❄🕐🔥⛺📺♻🅸

Services: 🔌🅾💧🚿🆃

Within 3 miles: 🛝🎏ℓ◎🏧🛒🅾⛴

Notes: Dogs must be kept on leads.

GREAT YARMOUTH

Places to visit

Elizabethan House Museum, GREAT YARMOUTH 01493 855746 www.museums.norfolk.gov.uk

Great Yarmouth Row 111 Houses & Greyfriars' Cloister, GREAT YARMOUTH 01493 857900 www.english-heritage.org.uk

Great for kids: Merrivale Model Village, GREAT YARMOUTH 01493 842097 www.merrivalemodelvillage.co.uk

---

GREAT YARMOUTH   Map 13 TG50

 87% Vauxhall Holiday Park *(TG520083)*

SILVER

4 Acle New Rd NR30 1TB
☎ **01493 857231**
e-mail: info@vauxhallholidays.co.uk
web: www.vauxhall-holiday-park.co.uk
dir: On A47 approaching Great Yarmouth

* 🚐 £19-£44 🚏 £19-£44 Å £19-£44

Open Etr, mid May-Sep & Oct half term

Last arrival 21.00hrs Last departure 10.00hrs

A very large holiday complex with plenty of entertainment and access to beach, river, estuary, lake and the A47. The touring pitches

---

are laid out in four separate areas, each with its own amenity block, and all arranged around the main entertainment. 40 acre site. 220 touring pitches. Caravan pitches. Motorhome pitches. Tent pitches. 421 statics.

AA Pubs & Restaurants nearby: Andover House, Great Yarmouth 01493 843490

Vauxhall Holiday Park

Leisure: 🏊🎣🎯🎮🏐🎱☺🎾🎹🎵

Facilities: 🛒☉❄🕐🔥📺♻

Services: 🔌🅾💧🚿🆃🍽�🔋

Within 3 miles: 🛝🎏ℓ◎🛥🏧🛒🅾⛴

Notes: No pets. Children's pool, sauna, solarium.

see advert below

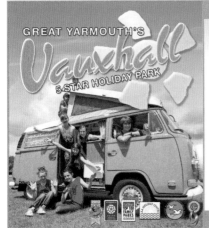

SERVICES: 🔌 Electric hook up 🅾 Launderette 🍷 Licensed bar 🛢 Calor Gas ⊘ Camping Gaz 🆃 Toilet fluid 🍽 Café/Restaurant 🍟 Fast Food/Takeaway 🔋 Battery charging 🍼 Baby care 🛠 Motorvan service point **ABBREVIATIONS:** BH/bank hols-bank holidays Etr-Easter Whit-Whitsun dep-departure fr-from hrs-hours m-mile mdnt-midnight rdbt-roundabout rs-restricted service wk-week wknd-weekend ⊛ No credit cards ⊗ no dogs   See page 7 for details of the AA Camping Card Scheme

GREAT YARMOUTH *continued*

AA CAMPING CARD SITE

▶▶▶▶ 80% The Grange Touring Park

(TG510142)

Yarmouth Rd, Ormesby St Margaret NR29 3QG
☎ 01493 730306 & 730023

e-mail: info@grangetouring.co.uk

dir: *From A419, 3m N of Great Yarmouth. Site at junct of A419 & B1159. Signed*

* ⛺ £12-£19 ⛺ £12-£19 ▲ £11-£19

Open Etr-Oct

Last arrival 21.00hrs Last departure 11.00hrs

A mature, ever improving park with plenty of trees, located just one mile from the sea, within easy reach of both coastal attractions and the Norfolk Broads. The level pitches have electric hook-ups and include 13 hardstanding pitches, and there are clean, modern toilets including three spacious family rooms. All pitches have Wi-Fi access. 3.5 acre site. 70 touring pitches. 7 hardstandings. Caravan pitches. Motorhome pitches. Tent pitches.

AA Pubs & Restaurants nearby: Andover House, Great Yarmouth 01493 843490

Leisure: ⚄

Facilities: ⎾ ☉ ☞ ⚒ ⚕ ⚬ ☏ Wi-Fi 🖳 𝒊

Services: ☎ ⬛ 🍽 🛢 ⌚ ⟲ 🚽 ↯

Within 3 miles: ↧ ⌖ ☉ 🛒 ☏ U

Notes: No football, no gazebos, no open fires. Dogs must be kept on leads.

  NEW Seashore Holiday Park

(TG653103)

North Denes NR30 4HG
☎ 01493 851131

e-mail: seashore@haven.com

web: www.haven.com/seashore

dir: *A149 from Great Yarmouth to Caister. Right at 2nd lights signed seafront & racecourse. Continue to sea, turn left. Park on left*

Open Mar-Oct

Bordered by sand dunes and with direct access to a sandy beach, Seashore Holiday Park is located in Great Yarmouth yet close to the peaceful Norfolk Broads for day trips. Facilities include excellent water activities and bike hire for kids and lively evening entertainment for adults. There are a good range of holiday caravans and apartments. At the time of going to press the quality rating for this site had not been confirmed. For up-to-date information please see the AA website: theAA.com.

Change over day: Mon, Fri, Sat **Arrival & departure times:** Please contact the site

Statics 322 Sleeps 6-8 Bedrms 2-3 Bathrms 1-2 Toilets 1-2 Freezer TV Sky/FTV Elec included Gas included Parking

Children ↟ Cots **Dogs** Max 2 on leads No dangerous dogs (see page 12)

Leisure: ☋ ⚴ ⚄

AA Pubs & Restaurants nearby: Andover House, Great Yarmouth 01493 843490

Imperial Hotel, Great Yarmouth 01493 842000

see advert on page 253

Places to visit

St Olave's Priory, ST OLAVES 0870 333 1181 www.english-heritage.org.uk

---

NEW Hopton Holiday Park

(TG531002)

NR31 9BW
☎ 01502 730214

e-mail: hopton@haven.com

web: www.haven.com/hopton

dir: *Site signed from A12 between Great Yarmouth & Lowestoft*

Open Mar-Oct

Located in the heart of Great Yarmouth, close to beaches and the town attractions, this lively holiday park offers excellent sport activities, including a 9-hole golf course and tennis coaching, and popular evening entertainment in the form of shows, music and dancing. There are a good range of holiday caravans and apartments. At the time of going to press the quality rating for this site had not been confirmed. For up-to-date information please see the AA website: theAA.com.

Change over day: Mon, Fri, Sat **Arrival & departure times:** Please contact the site

Statics 213 Sleeps 6-8 Bedrms 2-3 Bathrms 1-2 Toilets 1-2 Freezer TV Sky/FTV Elec included Gas included Grass area Parking

Children ↟ Cots **Dogs** Max 2 on leads No dangerous dogs (see page 12)

Leisure: ☋ ⚴ ⚲ ⚄ ⚄

see advert on page 255

HUNSTANTON — Map 12 TF64

Places to visit

Lynn Museum, KING'S LYNN 01553 775001
www.museums.norfolk.gov.uk

Norfolk Lavender, HEACHAM 01485 570384
www.norfolk-lavender.co.uk

Great for kids: Hunstanton Sea Life Sanctuary,
HUNSTANTON 01485 533576
www.sealsanctuary.co.uk

88% Searles Leisure Resort (TF671400)

South Beach Rd PE36 5BB
☎ 01485 534211
e-mail: bookings@searles.co.uk
web: www.searles.co.uk
dir: A149 from King's Lynn to Hunstanton. At
rdbt follow signs for South Beach. Straight on
at 2nd rdbt. Site on left

* 🚐 £11-£54 🚐 £11-£54 ▲ £11-£46

Open all year (rs Dec-Mar excl Feb half term
limited facilities & use of indoor pool & country
park only)

A large seaside holiday complex with well-
managed facilities, adjacent to sea and beach.
The tourers have their own areas, including
two excellent toilet blocks, and pitches are
individually marked by small maturing shrubs
for privacy. The bars and entertainment,
restaurant, bistro and takeaway, heated indoor
and outdoor pools, golf, fishing and bowling
green make this park popular throughout the
year. 50 acre site. 255 touring pitches. 91
hardstandings. Caravan pitches. Motorhome
pitches. Tent pitches. 158 statics.

AA Pubs & Restaurants nearby: King William IV
Country Inn & Restaurant, Hunstanton
01485 571765

Neptune Restaurant with Rooms, Hunstanton
01485 532122

Gin Trap Inn, Ringstead 01485 525264

Marco Pierre White The Lifeboat Inn, Thornham
01485 512236

Leisure: 🏊🏖🎾🎡🎿♨🐾⚽🎣🎵
Facilities: 🏪☀️🔥🔔🚿🚻✂️📶🖥️♨♻️ℹ️
Services: 🔌🗑️🍺🔋🔧🚽🍴🛒♿🔧
Within 3 miles: ⛳🎣⛵🛍️🎱🎯⛵
Notes: Dogs must be kept on leads.

AA CAMPING CARD SITE

80% Manor Park Holiday Village

(TF671399)

Manor Rd PE36 5AZ
☎ 01485 532300
e-mail: manor.park@park-resorts.com
web: www.park-resorts.com
dir: Take A149 (Lynn Rd) to Hunstanton, left
onto B1161 (Oasis Way)

* 🚐 £5-£33 🚐 £5-£33

Open Apr-Oct

Last arrival noon Last departure 10.00hrs

Situated just a few yards from the beach on
the outskirts of the lively resort of Hunstanton,
Manor Farm offers a range of leisure activities,
including two heated outdoor swimming
pools, children's playground, children's club,
amusement arcade, restaurant, bar and
cabaret. There are 64 electric, all-grass pitches
set out in the heart of the park and adjacent to
the leisure complex. Expect high standards of
customer care. 64 touring pitches. 10 seasonal
pitches. Caravan pitches. Motorhome pitches.
650 statics.

AA Pubs & Restaurants nearby: King William IV
Country Inn & Restaurant, Hunstanton
01485 571765

Neptune Restaurant with Rooms, Hunstanton
01485 532122

Leisure: 🏊🎡🎿♨⛱🎵
Facilities: 🏪♿☀️🚿✂️📶🖥️♨ℹ️
Services: 🔌🗑️🍺🔔🍴🛒♿
Within 3 miles: ⛳🎣⛵🎱🎯⛵
Notes: Dogs must be kept on leads. Bicycle
hire.

KING'S LYNN — Map 12 TF62

See also Stanhoe

Places to visit

Lynn Museum, KING'S LYNN 01553 775001
www.museums.norfolk.gov.uk

African Violet Centre,
KING'S LYNN 01553 828374
www.africanvioletandgardencentre.com

Great for kids: Castle Rising Castle, CASTLE
RISING 01553 631330
www.english-heritage.org.uk

▶▶▶▶ 79% King's Lynn Caravan and
Camping Park (TF645160)

New Rd, North Runcton PE33 0RA
☎ 01553 840004
e-mail: klcc@btconnect.com
web: www.kl-cc.co.uk
dir: From King's Lynn take A47 signed Swaffham &
Norwich, in 1.5m turn right signed North Runcton.
Site 100yds on left

* 🚐 fr £16 🚐 fr £16 ▲ fr £16

Open all year

Last arrival flexible Last departure flexible

Set in approximately 10 acres of parkland, this
developing camping park is situated on the edge
of North Runcton, just a few miles south of the
historic town of King's Lynn. There is an eco-
friendly toilet block which is powered by solar
panels and an air-sourced heat pump, plus it also
recycles rainwater; in itself this proves a source of
great interest. The three very extensive touring
fields are equipped with 150 electric hook-ups and
one field is reserved for rallies. 9 acre site. 150
touring pitches. 2 hardstandings. 20 seasonal
pitches. Caravan pitches. Motorhome pitches. Tent
pitches.

AA Pubs & Restaurants nearby: The Stuart House
Hotel, Bar & Restaurant, King's Lynn
01553 772169

Bank House Hotel, King's Lynn 01553 660492

Facilities: 🏪☉☀️♿🚿✂️📶♨ℹ️
Services: 🔌🗑️🔔🛢️🚽🛒♿
Within 3 miles: ⛳🎣🛍️🎱🎯⛵
Notes: No skateboards or fires. Dogs must be kept
on leads.

SERVICES: 🔌 Electric hook up 🗑️ Launderette 🍺 Licensed bar 🛢️ Calor Gas 🛢️ Camping Gaz 🚽 Toilet fluid 🍴 Café/Restaurant 🛒 Fast Food/Takeaway 🔋 Battery charging
🍼 Baby care 🔧 Motorvan service point **ABBREVIATIONS:** BH/bank hols-bank holidays Etr-Easter Whit-Whitsun dep-departure fr-from hrs-hours m-mile mdnt-midnight
rdbt-roundabout rs-restricted service wk-week wknd-weekend 🚫 No credit cards 🚫 no dogs See page 7 for details of the AA Camping Card Scheme

NORTH WALSHAM
Map 13 TG23

Places to visit

Blickling Hall, BLICKLING 01263 738030
www.nationaltrust.org.uk/blickling

Horsey Windpump, HORSEY 01263 740241
www.nationaltrust.co.uk

PREMIER PARK

►►►►► 85% Two Mills Touring Park (TG291286)

Best of British

Yarmouth Rd NR28 9NA
☎ 01692 405829
e-mail: enquiries@twomills.co.uk
dir: 1m S of North Walsham on Old Yarmouth road past police station & hospital on left

🚐 🚐 Å

Open Mar-3 Jan

Last arrival 20.30hrs Last departure noon

An intimate, beautifully presented park set in superb countryside in a peaceful, rural spot, which is also convenient for touring. The 'Top Acre' section is maturing and features fully serviced pitches, offering panoramic views over the site, an immaculate toilet block and good planting, plus the layout of pitches and facilities is excellent. The very friendly and helpful owners keep the park in immaculate condition. Please note this park is for adults only. 7 acre site. 81 touring pitches. 81 hardstandings. Caravan pitches. Motorhome pitches. Tent pitches.

AA Pubs & Restaurants nearby: Butchers Arms, East Ruston 01692 650237

Beechwood Hotel, North Walsham 01692 403231

Leisure: 🖵
Facilities: ⚲⊙☞✳⛺🕭🕭🖮🎋📶♻🛈
Services: 🔌🖩🍴⊘☐🖴
Within 3 miles: 🖉🏪

Notes: Adults only. Max 2 dogs per pitch. Dogs must be kept on leads. Library.

SCRATBY
Map 13 TG51

Places to visit

St Olave's Priory, ST OLAVES 0870 333 1181
www.english-heritage.org.uk

Time and Tide Museum of Great Yarmouth Life,
GREAT YARMOUTH 01493 743930
www.museums.norfolk.gov.uk

Great for kids: Caister Roman Site,
CAISTER-ON-SEA 0870 333 1181
www.english-heritage.org.uk

►►► 86% Scratby Hall Caravan Park (TG501155)

NR29 3SR
☎ 01493 730283
e-mail: scratbyhall@aol.com
dir: 5m N of Great Yarmouth. Exit A149 onto B1159, site signed

🚐 🚐 Å

Open Etr-end Sep

Last arrival 21.00hrs Last departure noon

A neatly-maintained site with a popular children's play area, well-equipped shop and outdoor swimming pool with sun terrace. The toilets are kept very clean. The beach and the Norfolk Broads are close by. 5 acre site. 85 touring pitches. Caravan pitches. Motorhome pitches. Tent pitches.

AA Pubs & Restaurants nearby: Fishermans Return, Winterton-on-Sea 01493 393305

Leisure: 🏊 ⛰
Facilities: ⚲⊙☞✳⛺🕭📶♻🛈
Services: 🔌🖩🍴⊘☐🖴
Within 3 miles: 🎣🚣🖉🏪🛒♨

Notes: No commercial vehicles. Dogs must be kept on leads. Food preparation room.

STANHOE
Map 13 TF83

Places to visit

Norfolk Lavender, HEACHAM 01485 570384
www.norfolk-lavender.co.uk

Walsingham Abbey Grounds & Shirehall Museum, LITTLE WALSINGHAM 01328 820510
www.walsinghamabbey.com

►►► 82% The Rickels Caravan & Camping Park (TF794355)

Bircham Rd PE31 8PU
☎ 01485 518671
dir: A148 from King's Lynn to Hillington. B1153 to Great Bircham. B1155 to x-rds, straight over, site on left

🚐 🚐 Å

Open Mar-Oct

Last arrival 21.00hrs Last departure 11.00hrs

Set in three acres of grassland, with sweeping country views and a pleasant, relaxing atmosphere fostered by being for adults only. The meticulously maintained grounds and facilities are part of the attraction, and the slightly sloping land has some level areas and sheltering for tents. 3 acre site. 30 touring pitches. Caravan pitches. Motorhome pitches. Tent pitches. 1 static.

AA Pubs & Restaurants nearby: Lord Nelson, Burnham Thorpe 01328 738241

The Hoste Arms, Burnham Market 01328 738777

Leisure: 🖵
Facilities: ⚲⊙✳🎋♻🛈
Services: 🔌🖩🍴⊘🖴
Within 3 miles: 🖉🏪

Notes: Adults only. ⊛ No ground sheets. Dogs must be kept on leads. Field available to hire for rallies.

LEISURE: 🏊 Indoor swimming pool 🏊 Outdoor swimming pool ⛰ Children's playground 🖐 Kid's club 🎾 Tennis court 🎱 Games room 🖵 Separate TV room ⛳ 9/18 hole golf course ⛵ Boats for hire 🎬 Cinema 🎵 Entertainment 🎣 Fishing ⦿ Mini golf 🏄 Watersports 🏋 Gym 🏵 Sports field Spa ♨ Stables
FACILITIES: 🛁 Bath 🚿 Shower ⊙ Electric shaver 🎋 Hairdryer ✳ Ice Pack Facility ♿ Disabled facilities ☎ Public telephone 🏪 Shop on site or within 200yds 🚚 Mobile shop (calls at least 5 days a week) 🍴 BBQ area 🪑 Picnic area 📶 Wi-fi 🖥 Internet access ♻ Recycling 🛈 Tourist info 🐾 Dog exercise area

SWAFFHAM
Map 13 TF80

Places to visit

Gressenhall Farm and Workhouse, GRESSENHALL
01362 860563 www.museums.norfolk.gov.uk

Great for kids: Castle Acre Priory and Castle,
CASTLE ACRE 01760 755394
www.english-heritage.org.uk

AA CAMPING CARD SITE

►►► 80% **Breckland Meadows Touring Park** *(TF809094)*

Lynn Rd PE37 7PT
☎ 01760 721246
e-mail: info@brecklandmeadows.co.uk
dir: *1m W of Swaffham on old A47*

* ⊞ £11.95-£13.95 ⊟ £11.95-£13.95
▲ £8-£11.50

Open all year

Last arrival 21.00hrs Last departure noon

An immaculate, well-landscaped little park on the edge of Swaffham. The impressive toilet block is well equipped, and there are hardstandings, full electricity and laundry equipment. Plentiful planting is resulting in attractive screening. 3 acre site. 45 touring pitches. 35 hardstandings. 5 seasonal pitches. Caravan pitches. Motorhome pitches. Tent pitches.

AA Pubs & Restaurants nearby: Canary & Linnet, Little Fransham 01362 687027

Facilities: ⌂⊙⋇⅊🖬🔥🚻🔌♻🛈

Services: ⊞🗑🔋⌀🅃🔋

Within 3 miles: ♨🎡⌀🛒🔋∪

Notes: Adults only. Dogs must be kept on leads. Newspaper deliveries.

SYDERSTONE
Map 13 TF83

Places to visit

Creake Abbey, NORTH CREAKE 0870 333 1181
www.english-heritage.org.uk

Great for kids: Castle Rising Castle,
CASTLE RISING 01553 631330
www.english-heritage.org.uk

►►► 77% **The Garden Caravan Site** *(TF812337)*

Barmer Hall Farm PE31 8SR
☎ 01485 578220 & 578178
e-mail: nigel@gardencaravansite.co.uk
dir: *Signed from B1454 at Barmer between A148 & Docking, 1m W of Syderstone*

* ⊞ £18.50-£20.50 ⊟ £18.50-£20.50
▲ £18.50-£20.50

Open Mar-Nov

Last arrival 21.00hrs Last departure noon

In the tranquil setting of a former walled garden beside a large farmhouse, with mature trees and shrubs, a secluded site surrounded by woodland. The site is run mainly on trust, with a daily notice indicating which pitches are available, and an honesty box for basic foods. An ideal site for the discerning camper, and well placed for touring north Norfolk. 3.5 acre site. 30 touring pitches. Caravan pitches. Motorhome pitches. Tent pitches.

AA Pubs & Restaurants nearby: Lord Nelson, Burnham Thorpe 01328 738241

The Hoste Arms, Burnham Market 01328 738777

Facilities: ⌂⊙⅌⋇⅊🕐🔥🛈

Services: ⊞🔋🛒⌃

Within 3 miles: 🛒

Notes: ⊘ Max 2 dogs per pitch. Dogs must be kept on leads. Cold drinks, ice creams & eggs available.

THREE HOLES
Map 12 TF50

Places to visit

African Violet Centre,
KING'S LYNN 01553 828374
www.africanvioletandgardencentre.com

Norfolk Lavender, HEACHAM 01485 570384
www.norfolk-lavender.co.uk

►►► 77% *Lode Hall Holiday Park* *(TF529989)*

Lode Hall, Silt Rd PE14 9JW
☎ 01354 638133
e-mail: dick@lode-hall.co.uk
dir: *From Wisbech take A1101 towards Downham Market. At Outwell continue on A1101 signed Littleport. Site signed from Three Holes. Right onto B1094 to site*

⊞⊟▲

Open Apr-Oct

Peace and tranquilly is assured at this deeply rural park in the grounds of Lode Hall. The toilet facilities are located in an imaginative restoration of a former cricket pavilion and include combined toilet/wash basin cubicles and unisex showers. Please note that this is an adults-only site. 5 acre site. 20 touring pitches. 8 hardstandings. Caravan pitches. Motorhome pitches. Tent pitches.

AA Pubs & Restaurants nearby: Hare Arms, Stow Bardolph 01366 382229

Facilities: ⌂⊙⋇⅊🚻🔥🖬

Services: ⊞🗑🔋

Within 3 miles: ⅊🛒∪

Notes: Adults only. ⊘

TRIMINGHAM — Map 13 TG23

Places to visit

RNLI Henry Blogg Museum, CROMER
01263 511294 www.rnli.org.uk/henryblogg

Cromer Museum, CROMER 01263 513543
www.norfolk.gov.uk/tourism/museums

▶▶▶ 77% Woodland Holiday Park (TG274388)

NR11 8AL
☎ 01263 579208
e-mail: info@woodland-park.co.uk
web: www.woodlandholidaypark.co.uk
dir: 4m SE on B1159 (coast road)

* ♠ £19-£29 ♣ £19-£29 ▲ £12-£16

Open Mar-Dec

Last arrival 23.00hrs Last departure noon

A secluded woodland site in an open enclosure, close to the sea but well sheltered from the winds by tall trees. Facilities include two bars, a restaurant, an indoor swimming pool, bowling green and sauna, and entertainment is provided in the clubhouse. There are holiday statics for hire and a large field is available for tents. 55 acre site. 11 touring pitches. Caravan pitches. Motorhome pitches. Tent pitches. 230 statics.

AA Pubs & Restaurants nearby: White Horse, Overstrand 01263 579237

Frazers, Sea Marge Hotel, Overstrand 01263 579579

Leisure: 🏊⛱️🎱🎯🎵
Facilities: � 🔁 ❶
Services: symbols
Within 3 miles: symbols

Notes: Dogs must be kept on leads.

WORTWELL — Map 13 TM28

Places to visit

Bressingham Steam Museum & Gardens, BRESSINGHAM 01379 686900
www.bressingham.co.uk

Great for kids: Banham Zoo, BANHAM
01953 887771 www.banhamzoo.co.uk

▶▶▶▶ 83% Little Lakeland Caravan Park (TM279849)

IP20 0EL
☎ 01986 788646
e-mail: information@littlelakeland.co.uk
dir: From W: exit A143 at sign for Wortwell. In village turn right 300yds past garage. From E: on A143, left onto B1062, then right. After 800yds turn left

♠ £15.50-£21 ♣ £15.50-£21 ▲ £15.50-£21

Open 15 Mar-Oct

Last arrival 22.00hrs Last departure noon

A well-kept and pretty site built round a fishing lake, and accessed by a lake-lined drive. The individual pitches are sited in hedged enclosures for complete privacy, and the purpose-built toilet facilities are excellent. 4.5 acre site. 38 touring pitches. 6 hardstandings. 17 seasonal pitches. Caravan pitches. Motorhome pitches. Tent pitches. 21 statics.

AA Pubs & Restaurants nearby: Dove Restaurant with Rooms, Alburgh 01986 788315

Fox & Goose Inn, Fressingfield 01379 586247

Leisure: 🎯
Facilities: symbols
Services: symbols
Within 3 miles: symbols

Notes: ⊘ No noise after 22.30hrs. Dogs must be kept on leads. Library.

NORTHUMBERLAND

BAMBURGH — Map 21 NU13

Places to visit

Chillingham Wild Cattle Park, CHILLINGHAM
01668 215250 www.chillinghamwildcattle.com

Great for kids: Bamburgh Castle, BAMBURGH
01668 214515 www.bamburghcastle.com

▶▶▶▶ 79% Waren Caravan Park (NU155343)

Waren Mill NE70 7EE
☎ 01668 214366
e-mail: waren@meadowhead.co.uk
dir: 2m E of town. From A1 onto B1342 signed Bamburgh. Take unclassified road past Waren Mill, signed Budle

* ♠ £14.50-£24.50 ♣ £14.50-£24.50
▲ £14.50-£30

Open Apr-Oct

Last arrival 20.00hrs Last departure noon

Attractive seaside site with footpath access to the beach, surrounded by a slightly sloping grassy embankment giving shelter to caravans. The park offers excellent facilities, including several family bathrooms, and the on-site restaurant serves a good breakfast. There are also wooden wigwams to rent. 4 acre site. 150 touring pitches. 24 hardstandings. Caravan pitches. Motorhome pitches. Tent pitches. 300 statics. 8 tipis.

AA Pubs & Restaurants nearby: Olde Ship Inn, Seahouses 01665 720200

Blue Bell Hotel, Belford 01668 213543

Grays Restaurant, Waren House Hotel, Bamburgh 01668 214581

Leisure: 🏊🎯🎱
Facilities: symbols
Services: symbols
Within 3 miles: symbols

Notes: Dogs must be kept on leads. 100 acres of private heathland.

LEISURE: 🏊 Indoor swimming pool ⛱️ Outdoor swimming pool 🎢 Children's playground 🪁 Kid's club 🎾 Tennis court 🎱 Games room 📺 Separate TV room ⛳ 9/18 hole golf course ⛵ Boats for hire 🎬 Cinema 🎵 Entertainment 🎣 Fishing ◎ Mini golf 🏄 Watersports 🏋️ Gym ⚽ Sports field Spa ∪ Stables
FACILITIES: 🛁 Bath 🚿 Shower ⊙ Electric shaver 🪮 Hairdryer ❄️ Ice Pack Facility ♿ Disabled facilities 📞 Public telephone 🏪 Shop on site or within 200yds 🚐 Mobile shop (calls at least 5 days a week) 🍖 BBQ area 🎋 Picnic area Wi-Fi Wi-fi 🌐 Internet access ♻️ Recycling ❶ Tourist info 🐕 Dog exercise area

SERVICES: Electric hook up 🔌 Launderette Licensed bar Calor Gas Camping Gaz Toilet fluid Café/Restaurant Fast Food/Takeaway Battery charging Baby care Motorvan service point **ABBREVIATIONS:** BH/bank hols-bank holidays Etr-Easter Whit-Whitsun dep-departure fr-from hrs-hours m-mile mdnt-midnight rdbt-roundabout rs-restricted service wk-week wknd-weekend No credit cards no dogs See page 7 for details of the AA Camping Card Scheme

BAMBURGH *continued*

▶▶▶ 84% Glororum Caravan Park

(NU166334)

Glororum Farm NE69 7AW
☎ 01670 860256
e-mail: enquiries@northumbrianleisure.co.uk
dir: *Exit A1 at junct with B1341 (Purdy's Lodge).
In 3.5m left onto unclassified road. Site 300yds
on left*

🚐 🚃

Open Mar-end Nov

Last arrival 18.00hrs Last departure noon

A pleasantly situated site in an open countryside
setting with good views of Bamburgh Castle. A
popular holiday destination where tourers have
their own separate area with 42 excellent well-
spaced, fully serviced pitches with a lush grass
area in addition to the hardstanding. This field,
opened in 2012, also has an excellent purpose-
built amenities block with a smart cladded interior
and modern, efficient fittings. 6 acre site. 42
touring pitches. 42 hardstandings. 20 seasonal
pitches. Caravan pitches. Motorhome pitches. 150
statics.

AA Pubs & Restaurants nearby: Olde Ship Inn,
Seahouses 01665 720200

Bamburgh Castle Inn, Seahouses 01665 720283

Blue Bell Hotel, Belford 01668 213543

Leisure: 🏟 ✪

Facilities: 🏕 ⊙ ⚑ ✳ ⅃ ◐ ⑤ 🚿 🕱 ❶

Services: ⚑ ⑤ ⌀ ⊤

Within 3 miles: ⅃ ⨠ ⌖ ⟱ ⑤ ⑤ ∪

Notes: No noise after 23.00hrs, no commercial
vehicles. Dogs must be kept on leads.

PREMIER PARK

▶▶▶▶▶ 80% Bellingham Camping & Caravanning Club Site *(NY835826)*

Brown Rigg NE48 2JY
☎ 01434 220175 & 0845 130 7633
dir: *From A69 take A6079 N to Chollerford &
B6320 to Bellingham. Pass Forestry Commission
land, site 0.5m S of Bellingham*

🚐 🚃 ⛺

Open 15 Mar-3 Nov

Last arrival 20.00hrs Last departure noon

A beautiful and peaceful campsite set in the
glorious Northumberland National Park.
Exceptionally well-managed, it continues to
improve and offers high levels of customer care,
maintenance and cleanliness - the excellent toilet
facilities are spotlessly clean. There are four
camping pods for hire. This is a perfect base for
exploring this undiscovered part of England, and it
is handily placed for visiting the beautiful
Northumberland coast. 5 acre site. 64 touring
pitches. 42 hardstandings. Caravan pitches.
Motorhome pitches. Tent pitches. 4 wooden pods.

AA Pubs & Restaurants nearby: Pheasant Inn,
Falstone 01434 240382

Leisure: 🏟

Facilities: 🏕 ⊙ ⚑ ✳ ⅃ ◐ ⑤ 🕱 🚿 Ⓦⓕ 🖥 ♻ ❶

Services: ⚑ ⑤ ⌀ ⊤ ⛟ ⬇

Within 3 miles: ⅃ ⌖ ⑤ ⑤

Notes: Site gates closed & quiet time
23.00hrs-07.00hrs. Dogs must be kept on leads.

BERWICK-UPON-TWEED   Map 21 NT95

80% Haggerston Castle *(NU041435)*

Beal TD15 2PA
☎ 0871 231 0865
e-mail: haggerstoncastle@haven.com
web: www.haven.com/haggerstoncastle
dir: *On A1, 7m S of Berwick-upon-Tweed, site
signed*

🚐 🚃

Open mid Mar-end Oct (rs mid Mar-May & Sep-
Oct some facilities may be reduced)

Last arrival anytime Last departure 10.00hrs

A large holiday centre with a very well equipped
touring park, offering comprehensive holiday
activities. The entertainment complex contains
amusements for the whole family, and there
are several bars, an adventure playground,
boating on the lake, a children's club, a
9-hole golf course, tennis courts, and various
eating outlets. Please note that this site does
not accept tents. 100 acre site. 132 touring
pitches. 132 hardstandings. Caravan pitches.
Motorhome pitches. 1200 statics.

AA Pubs & Restaurants nearby: Blue Bell Hotel,
Belford 01668 213543

Leisure: ⛱ 🏟 ⨲ ♨ 🎵

Facilities: 🏕 ⊙ ✳ ⅃ ⑤ 🕱 🚿 Ⓦⓕ 🖥 ♻ ❶

Services: ⚑ ⑤ ⛟ ⌀ ⬤ 🍽 ⬛

Within 3 miles: ⅃ ⨠ ◎ ⑤ ⑤ ∪

Notes: Max 2 dogs per booking, certain dog
breeds banned, no commercial vehicles, no
bookings by persons under 21yrs unless a
family booking.

see advert on page 263

LEISURE: 🏊 Indoor swimming pool 🏊 Outdoor swimming pool 🎠 Children's playground 🎪 Kid's club 🎾 Tennis court 🎱 Games room ⬛ Separate TV room
⛳ 9/18 hole golf course ⛵ Boats for hire 🎬 Cinema 🎵 Entertainment 🎣 Fishing ◎ Mini golf 🏄 Watersports 🏋 Gym ⚽ Sports field **Spa** ∪ Stables
FACILITIES: 🛁 Bath 🚿 Shower ⊙ Electric shaver ⚑ Hairdryer ✳ Ice Pack Facility ⅃ Disabled facilities ◐ Public telephone ⑤ Shop on site or within 200yds
🏪 Mobile shop (calls at least 5 days a week) 🍖 BBQ area 🕱 Picnic area Ⓦⓕ Wi-fi 🖥 Internet access ♻ Recycling ❶ Tourist info 🐕 Dog exercise area

►►►►► **82% Ord House Country Park**

(NT982515)

East Ord TD15 2NS
☎ **01289 305288**
e-mail: enquiries@ordhouse.co.uk
dir: *On A1, Berwick bypass, exit at 2nd rdbt at East Ord, follow 'Caravan' signs*

* ⊞ £17.50-£28 ⊞ £17.50-£28 ▲ £17.50-£28

Open all year

Last arrival 23.00hrs Last departure noon

A very well run park set in the pleasant grounds of an 18th-century country house. Touring pitches are marked and well spaced, some of them fully-serviced. The very modern toilet facilities include family bath and shower suites, and first class disabled rooms. There is an exceptional outdoor leisure shop with a good range of camping and caravanning spares, as well as clothing and equipment, and an attractive licensed club selling bar meals. 42 acre site. 79 touring pitches. 46 hardstandings. 30 seasonal pitches. Caravan pitches. Motorhome pitches. Tent pitches. 255 statics. 10 wooden pods.

AA Pubs & Restaurants nearby: Wheatsheaf at Swinton 01890 860257

Leisure: ⋀ ✺
Facilities: ⊷ ⋔ ⊙ ☇ ✳ ⅋ ⊙ ⓢ ⋔ ⚏ ⊠ ♻ ❶
Services: ⊡ ⊟ ⬓ ⬛ ⬚ ⊤ ⏱ ⚒ ⚓
Within 3 miles: ⤋ ⋈ ⊟ ⌁ ◎ ⓢ ⊟

Notes: No noise after mdnt. Dogs must be kept on leads. Crazy golf, table tennis.

►► **78% Old Mill Caravan Site**

(NU055401)

West Kyloe Farm, Fenwick TD15 2PG
☎ **01289 381279** & **07971 411625**
e-mail: teresamalley@westkyloe.demon.co.uk
dir: *A1 onto B6353, 9m S of Berwick-upon-Tweed. Road signed to Lowick/Fenwick. Site 1.5m signed on left*

* ⊞ £15-£20 ⊞ £15-£20 ▲ £15-£20

Open Etr-Oct

Last arrival 19.00hrs Last departure 11.00hrs

Small, secluded site accessed through a farm complex, and overlooking a mill pond complete with resident ducks. Some pitches are in a walled garden, and the amenity block is simple but well kept. Delightful walks can be enjoyed on the 600-acre farm. A holiday cottage is also available. 2.5 acre site. 12 touring pitches. Caravan pitches. Motorhome pitches. Tent pitches.

AA Pubs & Restaurants nearby: Black Bull, Etal 01890 820200

Blue Bell Hotel, Belford 01668 213543

Facilities: ⋔ ⊙ ☇ ⋔ ♻ ❶
Services: ⊡ ⚓
Within 3 miles: ⓢ

Notes: No gazebos or open fires. Dogs must be kept on leads.

 ⊔ **NEW Berwick Holiday Park**
(NT998535)

Magdalene Fields TD15 1NE
☎ **01289 307113**
e-mail: berwick@haven.com
web: www.haven.com/berwick
dir: *On A1, follow Berwick-upon-Tweed signs. At Morrisons/McDonalds rdbt take 2nd exit. At mini rdbt straight on, into North Rd (pass Shell garage on left). At next mini rdbt 1st exit into Northumberland Ave. Park at end*

Open Mar-Oct

This all-happening static-only holiday park has direct access to a beach on the edge of Berwick and offers exciting family activities and entertainment, including the FunWorks Amusement Centre and a multisports court. At the time of going to press the quality rating for this site had not been confirmed. For up-to-date information please see the AA website: theAA.com.

Change over day: Mon, Fri, Sat **Arrival & departure times:** Please contact the site

Statics 204 Sleeps 6-8 Bedrms 2-3 Bathrms 1-2 Toilets 1-2 Freezer TV Sky/FTV Elec included Gas included Grass area Parking

Children ⋔ Cots **Dogs** Max 2 on leads No dangerous dogs (see page 12)

Leisure: ⋐ ⋑ ⋓ ⋀

see advert on page 263

HEXHAM Map 21 NY96

Places to visit

Vindolanda (Chesterholm), BARDON MILL 01434 344277 www.vindolanda.com

Temple of Mithras (Hadrian's Wall), CARRAWBROUGH 0870 333 1181 www.english-heritage.org.uk

Great for kids: Housesteads Roman Fort, HOUSESTEADS 01434 344363 www.english-heritage.org.uk

►►► **64% Hexham Racecourse Caravan Site** *(NY919623)*

Hexham Racecourse NE46 2JP
☎ **01434 606847** & 606881
e-mail: hexrace.caravan@btconnect.com
dir: *From Hexham take B6305 signed Allendale/ Alston. Left in 3m signed to racecourse. Site 1.5m on right*

* ⊞ £14-£17 ⊞ £14-£17 ▲ fr £10

Open May-Sep

Last arrival 20.00hrs Last departure noon

A part-level and part-sloping grassy site situated on a racecourse overlooking Hexhamshire Moors. The facilities, although clean, are of an older but functional type. 4 acre site. 50 touring pitches. Caravan pitches. Motorhome pitches. Tent pitches.

AA Pubs & Restaurants nearby: Miners Arms Inn, Hexham 01434 603909

Dipton Mill, Hexham 01434 606577

Rat Inn, Hexham 01434 602814

Leisure: ⋀ ✺
Facilities: ⋔ ⊙ ☇ ✳ ⊙ ⋔ ⚏ ❶
Services: ⊡ ⊟ ⬛ ⬚ ⚒
Within 3 miles: ⤋ ⋈ ⊟ ⌁ ◎ ⓢ ⊟

Notes: No noise after 23.00hrs. Dogs must be kept on leads.

NORTH SEATON
Map 21 NZ28

Places to visit

Woodhorn, ASHINGTON 01670 528080
www.experiencewoodhorn.com

Morpeth Chantry Bagpipe Museum, MORPETH
01670 535163 www.experiencewoodhorn.com/
morpeth-bagpipe-museum

72% *Sandy Bay*

(NZ302858)

NE63 9YD
☎ 0871 664 9764
e-mail: sandy.bay@park-resorts.com
web: www.park-resorts.com
dir: *From A1 at Seaton Burn take A19 signed
Tyne Tunnel. Then A189 signed Ashington,
approx 8m, at rdbt right onto B1334 towards
Newbiggin-by-the-Sea. Site on right*

Open Apr-Oct

Last arrival anytime Last departure noon

A beach-side holiday park on the outskirts of
the small village of North Seaton, within easy
reach of Newcastle. The site is handily placed
for exploring the magnificent coastline and
countryside of Northumberland, but for those
who do not wish to travel, it offers the full range
of holiday centre attractions, both for parents
and their children. 48 touring pitches. Caravan
pitches. Motorhome pitches. 396 statics.

Leisure: 🏊 🅰 🛝 🎵
Facilities: 🖫 📶 🕐 §️ WiFi 💻
Services: 🔌 🗑 🎱 🍴 🏧
Within 3 miles: 🚲 §️ 🗑
Notes: Koi carp lake.

WOOLER
Map 21 NT92

Places to visit

Chillingham Castle, CHILLINGHAM 01668 215359
www.chillingham-castle.com

Great for kids: Chillingham Wild Cattle Park,
CHILLINGHAM 01668 215250
www.chillinghamwildcattle.com

⊔ NEW Riverside Leisure Park

(NT993279)

South Rd NE71 6NJ
☎ 01668 281447
e-mail: reception@riverside-wooler.co.uk
dir: *From S: A1 to Morpeth, A697 signed Wooler
& Coldstream. In Wooler, park on left. From N:
From Berwick-upon-Tweed on A1, 1st right signed
Wooler (B6525). Through Wooler on A697. Park
on right*

* 🚐 £25-£40 �RV £12-£25.50 ▲ £7-£11

Open all year

Last departure noon

The sister park to Thurston Manor Leisure Park at
Dunbar in East Lothian is set in the heart of
stunning Northumberland countryside on the edge
of Wooler Water. Very much family orientated, the
park offers excellent leisure facilities, including
swimming pools, a bar and restaurant with
weekend entertainment, and riverside and
woodland walks. Caravan pitches. Motorhome
pitches. Tent pitches. At the time of going to
press the rating for this park had not been
confirmed. For up-to-date information please the
AA website: theAA.com.

AA Pubs & Restaurants nearby: The Red Lion,
Milfield 01688 216224

NOTTINGHAMSHIRE

CHURCH LANEHAM
Map 17 SK87

Places to visit

Newark Air Museum, NEWARK-ON-TRENT
01636 707170 www.newarkairmuseum.org

Vina Cooke Museum of Dolls & Bygone
Childhood, NEWARK-ON-TRENT 01636 821364
www.vinasdolls.co.uk

Great for kids: Sherwood Forest Country Park &
Visitor Centre, EDWINSTOWE 01623 823202
www.nottinghamshire.gov.uk/sherwoodforestcp

AA CAMPING CARD SITE

▶▶▶ 81% **Trentfield Farm** (SK815774)

DN22 0NJ
☎ 01777 228651
e-mail: post@trentfield.co.uk
dir: *A1 onto A57 towards Lincoln for 6m. Left
signed Laneham, 1.5m, through Laneham &
Church Laneham (pass Ferryboat pub on left). Site
300yds on right*

🚐 fr £18 🚐 fr £18 ▲ fr £18

Open Etr-Nov

Last arrival 20.00hrs Last departure noon

A delightfully rural and level grass park tucked
away on the banks of the River Trent. The park has
its own river frontage with free coarse fishing
available to park residents. The cosy local pub,
which serves food, is under the same ownership.
34 acre site. 25 touring pitches. Caravan pitches.
Motorhome pitches. Tent pitches.

Facilities: 🖫 🕐 📶 ☀️ & §️ 🛒 🐕 WiFi
Services: 🔌 🗑 🛒 🔧
Within 3 miles: 🚲 🚲 §️ 🗑 ⛺
Notes: Dogs must be kept on leads. 24-hour mini
shop.

MANSFIELD

Places to visit

Sherwood Forest Country Park & Visitor Centre,
EDWINSTOWE 01623 823202
www.nottinghamshire.gov.uk/sherwoodforestcp

Great for kids: Vina Cooke Museum of Dolls &
Bygone Childhood, NEWARK-ON-TRENT
01636 821364 www.vinasdolls.co.uk

LEISURE: 🏊 Indoor swimming pool 🏊 Outdoor swimming pool 🅰 Children's playground 🛝 Kid's club 🎾 Tennis court 🎱 Games room 📺 Separate TV room
🏌 9/18 hole golf course ⛵ Boats for hire 🎦 Cinema 🎵 Entertainment 🎣 Fishing ⛳ Mini golf 🏄 Watersports 💪 Gym ⚽ Sports field Spa ♨ Stables
FACILITIES: 🛁 Bath 🚿 Shower ⚡ Electric shaver 💈 Hairdryer ❄ Ice Pack Facility 👤 Disabled facilities 📞 Public telephone §️ Shop on site or within 200yds
🛒 Mobile shop (calls at least 5 days a week) 🍖 BBQ area 🏕 Picnic area WiFi Wi-fi 💻 Internet access ♻ Recycling ❶ Tourist info 🐕 Dog exercise area

MANSFIELD — Map 16 SK56

►►► 78% Tall Trees Touring Park
(SK551626)

Old Mill Ln, Forest Town NG19 0JP
☎ 01623 626503 & 07770 661957
e-mail: info@talltreestouringpark.co.uk
dir: *A60 from Mansfield towards Worksop. After 1m turn right at lights into Old Mill Lane. Site approx 0.5m on left*

* ⊞ £12.50-£17.50 ⊟ £12.50-£17.50
▲ £12.50-£17.50

Open all year

Last arrival anytime Last departure anytime

A very pleasant park situated just on the outskirts of Mansfield and within easy walking distance of shops and restaurants. It is surrounded on three sides by trees and shrubs, and securely set at the back of the residential park. This site has a modern amenities block, a fishing lake to the rear of the site and an extra grassed area to give more space for caravans and tents. 10 acre site. 24 touring pitches. 10 hardstandings. Caravan pitches. Motorhome pitches. Tent pitches.

AA Pubs & Restaurants nearby: Forest Lodge, Edwinstowe 01623 824443

Fox & Hounds, Blidworth 01623 792383

Leisure: ☺
Facilities: ⋔☉☞⅃☂☷⊣⋔♻ ❶
Services: ⊞⊡ **Within 3 miles:** ⅃⊟☞⊞⊡

Notes: No noise after mdnt. Dogs must be kept on leads.

NEWARK

See Southwell

RADCLIFFE ON TRENT — Map 11 SK63

Places to visit

Nottingham Castle Museum & Art Gallery, NOTTINGHAM 0115 876 3356
www.mynottingham.gov.uk/nottinghamcastle

Wollaton Hall, Gardens & Deer Park, NOTTINGHAM 0115 915 3900
www.nottingham.gov.uk/wollatonhall

►►► 78% Thornton's Holt Camping Park *(SK638377)*

Stragglethorpe Rd, Stragglethorpe NG12 2JZ
☎ 0115 933 2125 & 933 4204
e-mail: camping@thorntons-holt.co.uk
web: www.thorntons-holt.co.uk
dir: *Take A52, 3m E of Nottingham. Turn S at lights towards Cropwell Bishop. Site 0.5m on left. Or A46 SE of Nottingham. N at lights. Site 2.5m on right*

* ⊞ £16-£19 ⊟ £16-£19 ▲ £13-£19

Open Apr-6 Nov

Last arrival 20.00hrs Last departure noon

A well-run family site in former meadowland, with pitches located among young trees and bushes for a rural atmosphere and outlook. The toilets are housed in converted farm buildings, and an indoor swimming pool is a popular attraction. 13 acre site. 155 touring pitches. 35 hardstandings. 20 seasonal pitches. Caravan pitches. Motorhome pitches. Tent pitches.

AA Pubs & Restaurants nearby: Ye Olde Trip to Jerusalem, Nottingham 0115 947 3171

Leisure: ☞ ⚞
Facilities: ⋔☉☞☀⅃☷⊣⋔♻ ❶
Services: ⊞⊡⊞⊘Ⓣ⌷⅄
Within 3 miles: ⅃≑⊟☞⋛⊞⊡Ս

Notes: Noise curfew at 22.00hrs. Dogs must be kept on leads.

SOUTHWELL — Map 17 SK65

Places to visit

Galleries of Justice Museum, NOTTINGHAM 0115 952 0555 www.galleriesofjustice.org.uk

The Workhouse, SOUTHWELL 01636 817250 www.nationaltrust.org.uk/main/w-theworkhouse

►►► 76% New Hall Farm Touring Park *(SK660550)*

New Hall Farm, New Hall Ln NG22 8BS
☎ 01623 883041
e-mail: enquiries@newhallfarm.co.uk
dir: *From A614 at White Post Modern Farm Centre, turn E signed Southwell. Immediately after Edingley turn S into New Hall Ln to site (0.5m)*

* ⊞ £12-£20 ⊟ £12-£20 ▲ £10-£18

Open Mar-Oct

Last arrival 21.00hrs Last departure 13.00hrs

A park on a working stock farm with the elevated pitching area enjoying outstanding panoramic views. It is within a short drive of medieval Newark and Sherwood Forest. A log cabin viewing gantry offers a place to relax and take in the spectacular scenery. 2.5 acre site. 25 touring pitches. 10 hardstandings. 7 seasonal pitches. Caravan pitches. Motorhome pitches. Tent pitches.

AA Pubs & Restaurants nearby: Tom Browns Brasserie, Gunthorpe 0115 966 3642

Facilities: ⋔☉☀☷⊣⋔♻ ❶
Services: ⊞⊡⛟
Within 3 miles: ⅃☞⊞⊡Ս

Notes: Adults only. Dogs must be kept on leads.

TEVERSAL — Map 16 SK46

Places to visit

Sherwood Forest Country Park & Visitor Centre, EDWINSTOWE 01623 823202
www.nottinghamshire.gov.uk/sherwoodforestcp

Hardwick Hall, HARDWICK HALL 01246 850430
www.nationaltrust.org.uk/main/w-hardwickhall

PREMIER PARK

►►►►► 89% Teversal Camping & Caravanning Club Site *(SK472615)*

Silverhill Ln NG17 3JJ
☎ 01623 551838
dir: *M1 junct 28, A38 towards Mansfield. Left at lights onto B6027. At top of hill straight over at lights & left at Tesco Express. Right onto B6014, left at Craven Arms, site on left*

* 🚃 £15-£28 🚐 £15-£28 ⛺ £15-£28

Open all year

Last arrival 20.00hrs Last departure noon

A top notch park with excellent purpose-built facilities and innovative, hands-on owners. Each pitch is spacious, the excellent toilet facilities are state-of-the-art, and there are views of and access to the countryside and nearby Silverhill Community Woods. The attention to detail and all-round quality are truly exceptional - guests can even hire a car for a day. A six-berth holiday caravan and two luxury ready-erected safari tents are available for hire, and there is a special area for washing dogs and bikes. The site has an on-site shop. Non-members are very welcome too. 6 acre site. 126 touring pitches. 92 hardstandings. Caravan pitches. Motorhome pitches. Tent pitches. 1 static. 2 bell tents/yurts.

AA Pubs & Restaurants nearby: The Shoulder at Hardstoft 01246 850276

Leisure: 🛝 ⚽

Facilities: 🚿 🪒 💨 ❄ ♿ 📞 🏪 📶 ♻ ℹ

Services: 🗨 🌀 🛍 🍃 [T] 🛒 ⚓

Within 3 miles: ⛳ 🎣 🏪 🐴

Notes: Site gates closed 23.00hrs-07.00hrs. Dogs must be kept on leads.

TUXFORD — Map 17 SK77

Places to visit

Museum of Lincolnshire Life, LINCOLN 01522 528448
www.lincolnshire.gov.uk/museumoflincolnshirelife

Great for kids: Lincoln Castle, LINCOLN 01522 511068
www.lincolnshire.gov.uk/lincolncastle

AA CAMPING CARD SITE

►►► 82% Orchard Park Touring Caravan & Camping Park *(SK754708)*

Marnham Rd NG22 0PY
☎ 01777 870228
e-mail: info@orchardcaravanpark.co.uk
dir: *Exit A1 at Tuxford onto A6075 towards Lincoln. 0.5m, right into Marnham Rd. Site 0.75m on right*

🚃 £17-£25 🚐 £17-£25 ⛺ £17-£25

Open mid Mar-Oct

Last arrival mdnt Last departure 18.00hrs

A rural site set in an old fruit orchard with spacious pitches arranged in small groups separated by shrubs; many of the pitches are served with water and electricity. A network of grass pathways and picnic clearings have been created in a woodland area, and there's a superb adventure playground. 7 acre site. 60 touring pitches. 30 hardstandings. Caravan pitches. Motorhome pitches. Tent pitches.

AA Pubs & Restaurants nearby: Mussel & Crab, Tuxford 01777 870491

Robin Hood Inn, Elkesley 01777 838259

Leisure: 🛝

Facilities: 🚿 🪒 💨 ❄ ♿ 📞 🏪 🧺 🐕 📶 💻 ♻ ℹ

Services: 🗨 🌀 🛍 🍃 [T] 🛒

Within 3 miles: 🎣 🏪 🐴

Notes: Dogs must be kept on leads.

WORKSOP — Map 16 SK57

Places to visit

Clumber Park, WORKSOP 01909 476592
www.nationaltrust.org.uk

►►► 80% Riverside Caravan Park

(SK582790)

Central Av S80 1ER
☎ 01909 474118
dir: *From A57 E of town, take B6040 signed Town Centre at rdbt. Follow international camping sign to site*

🚃 🚐 ⛺

Open all year

Last arrival 18.00hrs Last departure noon

A very well maintained park within the attractive market town of Worksop and next door to the cricket and bowls club where Riverside customers are made welcome. This is an ideal park for those wishing to be within walking distance of all amenities yet also within a 10-minute car journey of the extensive Clumber Park and numerous good garden centres. The towpath of the adjacent Chesterfield Canal provides excellent walking opportunities. 4 acre site. 60 touring pitches. 59 hardstandings. Caravan pitches. Motorhome pitches. Tent pitches.

Facilities: 🚿 🪒 ❄ ℹ

Services: 🗨 🛍 🍃 🛒 ⚓

Within 3 miles: ⛳ 🎬 🎣 🏪

Notes: No bikes around reception or in toilet block. Dogs must be kept on leads.

LEISURE: 🏊 Indoor swimming pool 🌊 Outdoor swimming pool 🛝 Children's playground 👋 Kid's club 🎾 Tennis court 🎱 Games room 📺 Separate TV room ⛳ 9/18 hole golf course ⛵ Boats for hire 🎬 Cinema 🎵 Entertainment 🎣 Fishing ◎ Mini golf 🏄 Watersports 🏋 Gym ⚽ Sports field **Spa** 🐴 Stables
FACILITIES: 🛁 Bath 🚿 Shower 🪒 Electric shaver 💨 Hairdryer ❄ Ice Pack Facility ♿ Disabled facilities 📞 Public telephone 🏪 Shop on site or within 200yds 🚚 Mobile shop (calls at least 5 days a week) 🍖 BBQ area 🧺 Picnic area 📶 Wi-fi 💻 Internet access ♻ Recycling ℹ Tourist info 🐕 Dog exercise area

OXFORDSHIRE

See Walk 8 in the Walks & Cycle Rides section at the end of the guide

BANBURY   Map 11 SP44

Places to visit

Banbury Museum, BANBURY 01295 753752
www.cherwell.gov.uk/banburymuseum

Great for kids: Deddington Castle, DEDDINGTON
0870 333 1181 www.english-heritage.org.uk

▶▶▶▶ 84% *Bo Peep Farm Caravan Park* (SP481348)

Bo Peep Farm, Aynho Rd, Adderbury OX17 3NP
☎ **01295 810605**
e-mail: warden@bo-peep.co.uk
dir: *1m E of Adderbury & A4260, on B4100
(Aynho road)*

🚐 🚙 Å

Open Mar-Oct

Last arrival 20.00hrs Last departure noon

A delightful park with good views and a spacious feel. Four well laid out camping areas including two with hardstandings and a separate tent field are all planted with maturing shrubs and trees. The two facility blocks are built in attractive Cotswold stone. There is a bay in which you can clean your caravan or motorhome. There are four miles of on-site walks including through woods and on the river bank. The site is well placed for visiting Banbury and the Cotswolds. 13 acre site. 104 touring pitches. Caravan pitches. Motorhome pitches. Tent pitches.

AA Pubs & Restaurants nearby: Ye Olde Reindeer Inn, Banbury 01295 264031

Wykham Arms, Banbury 01295 788808

Saye and Sele Arms, Broughton 01295 263348

Facilities: ⬆⊙☞※⅙⊙ⓢ🚽🚿 🏧
📺 ♻ ❼

Services: ⚡️🔋 ⊘T🍼↯

Within 3 miles: ↨ 🔗 ⓢ

AA CAMPING CARD SITE

▶▶▶▶ 83% **Barnstones Caravan & Camping Site** (SP455454)

Great Bourton OX17 1QU
☎ **01295 750289**
dir: *Take A423 from Banbury signed Southam. In 3m turn right signed Gt Bourton/Cropredy, site 100yds on right*

🚐 £12-£14 🚙 £12-£14 Å £8-£12

Open all year

A popular, neatly laid-out site with plenty of hardstandings, some fully serviced pitches, a smart up-to-date toilet block, and excellent rally facilities. Well run by a very personable owner, this is an excellent value park. The site is well positioned for stopovers or for visiting nearby Banbury. 3 acre site. 49 touring pitches. 44 hardstandings. Caravan pitches. Motorhome pitches. Tent pitches.

AA Pubs & Restaurants nearby: Ye Olde Reindeer Inn, Banbury 01295 264031

Wykham Arms, Banbury 01295 788808

Saye and Sele Arms, Broughton 01295 263348

Leisure: ⚞ ✪

Facilities: ⬆⊙※⅙⊙☞🚽🚿♻ ❼

Services: ⚡️🔋 ⊘🍼↯

Within 3 miles: ↨❄🗓🔗◎ 🥤ⓢⓢ∪

Notes: ⊜ Dogs must be kept on leads.

BLETCHINGDON

Places to visit

Rousham House, ROUSHAM 01869 347110
www.rousham.org

Museum of the History of Science, OXFORD
01865 277280 www.mhs.ox.ac.uk

Great for kids: Oxford University Museum of Natural History, OXFORD 01865 272950
www.oum.ox.ac.uk

BLETCHINGDON   Map 11 SP51

▶▶▶▶ 84% **Greenhill Leisure Park** (SP488178)

Greenhill Farm, Station Rd OX5 3BQ
☎ **01869 351600**
e-mail: info@greenhill-leisure-park.co.uk
web: www.greenhill-leisure-park.co.uk
dir: *M40 junct 9, A34 S for 3m. Take B4027 to Bletchingdon. Site 0.5m after village on left*

🚐 £17-£20 🚙 £17-£20 Å £15-£17

Open all year (rs Oct-Mar no dogs, shop & games room closed)

Last arrival 21.00 (20.00hrs winter) Last departure noon

An all-year round park set in open countryside near the village of Bletchingdon and well placed for visiting Oxford or the Cotswolds. Fishing is available in the nearby river or in the parks two well stocked lakes. Pitches are very spacious and the park is very family orientated and in keeping with the owner's theme of 'Where fun meets the countryside'. The facilities are also very good. 7 acre site. 92 touring pitches. 33 hardstandings. 20 seasonal pitches. Caravan pitches. Motorhome pitches. Tent pitches.

AA Pubs & Restaurants nearby: The Kings Arms, Woodstock 01993 813636

Feathers Hotel, Woodstock 01993 812291

Leisure: ⚞ 🎣

Facilities: ⬆⊙☞※⅙ⓢ🚽🚿📺♻ ❼

Services: ⚡️🔋 ⊘T🍼

Within 3 miles: ↨ 🔗 ⓢ

Notes: No camp fires. Pets' corner.

SERVICES: ⚡️ Electric hook up   🔋 Launderette   🍷 Licensed bar   🛢 Calor Gas   ⊘ Camping Gaz   T Toilet fluid   🍽 Café/Restaurant   🍟 Fast Food/Takeaway   🔌 Battery charging
🍼 Baby care   ↯ Motorvan service point   **ABBREVIATIONS:** BH/bank hols-bank holidays   Etr-Easter   Whit-Whitsun   dep-departure   fr-from   hrs-hours   m-mile   mdnt-midnight
rdbt-roundabout   rs-restricted service   wk-week   wknd-weekend   ⊜ No credit cards   ⊗ no dogs   See page 7 for details of the AA Camping Card Scheme

BLETCHINGDON *continued*

AA CAMPING CARD SITE

▶▶▶▶ 82% **Diamond Farm Caravan & Camping Park** *(SP513170)*

Islip Rd OX5 3DR
☎ 01869 350909
e-mail: warden@diamondpark.co.uk
dir: *M40 junct 9, A34 S for 3m, B4027 to Bletchingdon. Site 1m on left*

🚐 🚖 ⛺

Open all year

Last arrival dusk Last departure 11.00hrs

A well-run, quiet rural site in good level surroundings, and ideal for touring the Cotswolds, situated seven miles north of Oxford in the heart of the Thames Valley. This popular park has excellent facilities, and offers a heated outdoor swimming pool, a games room for children and a small bar. 3 acre site. 37 touring pitches. 20 hardstandings. Caravan pitches. Motorhome pitches. Tent pitches.

AA Pubs & Restaurants nearby: The Kings Arms, Woodstock 01993 813636

Feathers Hotel, Woodstock 01993 812291

Leisure: 🏊 ⅄ 🔍
Facilities: 🛁 🚿 ☉ 🖋 ✳ Ⓢ 📶 ♻ ❶
Services: 🔌 ▣ 🍽 🚽 🖉 Ⓣ 🍴 🛒 ⛽
Within 3 miles: ♨ 🎣 Ⓢ
Notes: 🐾 Dogs must be kept on leads.

CHARLBURY   Map 11 SP31

Places to visit

Blenheim Palace, WOODSTOCK 0800 849 6500
www.blenheimpalace.com

Minster Lovell Hall & Dovecote, MINSTER LOVELL 0870 333 1181 www.english-heritage.org.uk

Great for kids: Cogges Witney, WITNEY 01993 772602 www.cogges.org.uk

▶▶▶▶ 84% *Cotswold View Touring Park* *(SP365210)*

Enstone Rd OX7 3JH
☎ 01608 810314
e-mail: bookings@gfwiddows.co.uk
dir: *From A44 in Enstone take B4022 towards Charlbury. Follow site signs. Site 1m from Charlbury.*

🚐 🚖 ⛺

Open Etr or Apr-Oct

Last arrival 21.00hrs Last departure noon

A good Cotswold site, well screened and with attractive views across the countryside. The toilet facilities include fully-equipped family rooms and bathrooms, and there are spacious, sheltered pitches, some with hardstandings. Breakfasts and takeaway food are available from the shop. The site has camping pods for hire. This is the perfect location for exploring the Cotswolds and anyone heading for the Charlbury Music Festival. 10 acre site. 125 touring pitches. Caravan pitches. Motorhome pitches. Tent pitches.

AA Pubs & Restaurants nearby: Bull Inn, Charlbury 01608 810689

Crown Inn, Church Enstone 01608 677262

Leisure: ⅄ 🎾 🔍
Facilities: 🛁 🚿 ☉ 🖋 ✳ 🚿 Ⓢ 🖥 🎋 🐕
Services: 🔌 ▣ 🛢 🖉 Ⓣ 🛒 ⛽
Within 3 miles: 🖋 Ⓢ ▣
Notes: Off licence, skittle alley, chess, boules.

HENLEY-ON-THAMES   Map 5 SU78

Places to visit

Greys Court, HENLEY-ON-THAMES 01491 628529
www.nationaltrust.org.uk

River & Rowing Museum, HENLEY-ON-THAMES 01491 415600 www.rrm.co.uk

Great for kids: LEGOLAND Windsor, WINDSOR www.legoland.co.uk

PREMIER PARK

▶▶▶▶▶ 84% **Swiss Farm Touring & Camping** *(SU759837)*

Marlow Rd RG9 2HY
☎ 01491 573419
e-mail: enquiries@swissfarmcamping.co.uk
web: www.swissfarmcamping.co.uk
dir: *On A4155, N of Henley, next left after rugby club, towards Marlow*

* 🚐 £16-£24 🚖 £16-£27 ⛺ £13-£24

Open Mar-Oct (rs Mar-May & Oct pool closed)

Last arrival 21.00hrs Last departure noon

This park enjoys an excellent location within easy walking distance of Henley and is perfect for those visiting the Henley Regatta (but booking is essential). Pitches are spacious and well appointed, and include some that are fully serviced. There is a tasteful bar plus a nice outdoor swimming pool. 6 acre site. 140 touring pitches. 20 hardstandings. Caravan pitches. Motorhome pitches. Tent pitches. 6 statics.

AA Pubs & Restaurants nearby: Little Angel, Henley-on-Thames 01491 411008

Crooked Billet, Stoke Row, 01491 681048

Five Horseshoes, Maidensgrove, 01491 641282

Leisure: 🏊 ⅄
Facilities: 🚿 ☉ 🖋 ✳ 🚿 Ⓢ 🎋 📶 ❶
Services: 🔌 ▣ 🍽 🛢 🖉 Ⓣ
Within 3 miles: ♨ 🚣 🎋 🖋 Ⓢ ▣
Notes: No groups, no dogs during high season.

LEISURE: 🏊 Indoor swimming pool 🏊 Outdoor swimming pool ⅄ Children's playground 🪁 Kid's club 🎾 Tennis court 🔍 Games room 📺 Separate TV room ⛳ 9/18 hole golf course 🚣 Boats for hire 🎬 Cinema 🎵 Entertainment 🎣 Fishing ◎ Mini golf 🏄 Watersports 💪 Gym 🏟 Sports field Spa ♨ Stables
FACILITIES: 🛁 Bath 🚿 Shower ☉ Electric shaver 🖋 Hairdryer ✳ Ice Pack Facility ♿ Disabled facilities 📞 Public telephone Ⓢ Shop on site or within 200yds 🏪 Mobile shop (calls at least 5 days a week) 🍖 BBQ area 🌳 Picnic area 📶 Wi-fi 🌐 Internet access ♻ Recycling ❶ Tourist info 🐕 Dog exercise area

STANDLAKE
Map 5 SP30

Places to visit

Buscot Park, BUSCOT 01367 240786 www.buscotpark.com

Harcourt Arboretum, OXFORD 01865 343501 www.botanic-garden.ox.ac.uk

Great for kids: Cotswold Wildlife Park and Gardens, BURFORD 01993 823006 www.cotswoldwildlifepark.co.uk

AA CAMPING CARD SITE

PREMIER PARK

▶▶▶▶▶ **96% Lincoln Farm Park Oxfordshire** *(SP395028)*

 Best of British

High St OX29 7RH
☎ 01865 300239
e-mail: info@lincolnfarmpark.co.uk
web: www.lincolnfarmpark.co.uk
dir: *In village of Standlake exit A415 between Abingdon & Witney, 5m SE of Witney*

🚐 🚏 Å

Open Feb-Nov

Last arrival 20.00hrs Last departure noon

This attractively landscaped family-run park, located in a quiet village near the River Thames, offers a truly excellent camping or caravanning experience. There are top class facilities throughout the park. It has excellent leisure facilities in the Standlake Leisure Centre complete with two pools plus gym, sauna etc. This is the perfect base for visiting the many attractions in Oxfordshire and the Cotswolds. A warm welcome is assured from the friendly staff. 9 acre site. 90 touring pitches. 75 hardstandings. Caravan pitches. Motorhome pitches. Tent pitches.

AA Pubs & Restaurants nearby: Bear & Ragged Staff, Cumnor 01865 862329

The Vine Inn, Cumnor 01865 862567

Leisure: 🏊 🎠 🎣
Facilities: 🚻 📞 ⊙ 🐾 ☀ ♿ 🕐 🖥 🏪 🐕 WiFi
Services: 🔌 🛢 ⊘ 🚽 🔋 ↯
Within 3 miles: ↓ ✿ 🎣 ⛴ 🏬 ⛳

Notes: No gazebos, no noise after 23.00hrs. Dogs must be kept on leads. Putting green, outdoor chess.

UPPER HEYFORD
Map 11 SP42

▶▶▶ **79% Heyford Leys Camping Park** *(SP518256)*

Camp Rd OX25 5LX
☎ 01869 232048
e-mail: heyfordleys@aol.com
dir: *M40 junct 10 take B430 towards Middleton Stoney. Right after 1.5m marked The Heyford, follow brown signs to site*

🚐 🚏 Å

Open all year

Last arrival 22.00hrs Last departure 11.00hrs

This small peaceful park near the Cherwell Valley and the village of Upper Heyford is well positioned for visiting nearby Bicester, Oxford and Banbury, as well as being about a 15-minute drive from Silverstone. The facilities are very clean and guests will be assured of a warm welcome. A small fishing lake is also available to customers. 5 acre site. 25 touring pitches. 5 hardstandings. Caravan pitches. Motorhome pitches. Tent pitches.

AA Pubs & Restaurants nearby: Horse & Groom, Caulcott 01869 343257

Facilities: 📞 ⊙ 🐾 ☀ 🐕 WiFi ♻ ❶
Services: 🔌 🔋
Within 3 miles: ↓ ✿ 🎣 🏬 🛍
Notes: No groups, no noise after 20.00hrs.

RUTLAND

GREETHAM
Map 11 SK91

Places to visit

Rutland County Museum & Visitor Centre, OAKHAM 01572 758440 www.rutland.gov.uk/museum

Great for kids: Oakham Castle, OAKHAM 01572 758440 www.rutland.gov.uk/castle

▶▶▶▶ **83% Rutland Caravan & Camping** *(SK925148)*

Park Ln LE15 7FN
☎ 01572 813520
e-mail: info@rutlandcaravanandcamping.co.uk
dir: *From A1 onto B668 towards Greetham. Before Greetham turn right at x-rds, left to site*

🚐 🚏 Å

Open all year

Last arrival 20.00hrs

This pretty caravan park, built to a high specification and surrounded by well-planted banks, continues to improve due to the enthusiasm and vision of its owner. From the spacious reception and the innovative play area to the toilet block, everything is of a very high standard. The spacious grassy site is close to the Viking Way and other footpath networks, and well sited for visiting Rutland Water and the many picturesque villages in the area. 5 acre site. 130 touring pitches. 65 hardstandings. Caravan pitches. Motorhome pitches. Tent pitches.

AA Pubs & Restaurants nearby: Jackson Stops Country Inn, Stretton 01780 410237

Olive Branch, Clipsham 01780 410355

Leisure: 🎠 🎣
Facilities: 📞 ⊙ 🐾 ☀ ♿ 🖥 🐕 WiFi ♻ ❶
Services: 🔌 🛢 🪫 ⊘ 🚽 ↯
Within 3 miles: ↓ ✿ 🎣 ◎ ⛴ 🏬 ⛳
Notes: Dogs must be kept on leads. Dog shower.

WING
Map 11 SK80

Places to visit

Lyddington Bede House, LYDDINGTON
01572 822438 www.english-heritage.org.uk

Great for kids: Oakham Castle, OAKHAM
01572 758440 www.rutland.gov.uk/castle

►►► 71% Wing Lakes Caravan & Camping (SK892031)

Wing Hall LE15 8RY
☎ 01572 737283 & 737090
e-mail: winghall1891@aol.com
dir: From A1 take A47 towards Leicester, 14m, follow Morcott signs. In Morcott follow Wing signs. 2.5m, follow site signs

🚐 🚐 Å

Open all year

Last arrival 21.00hrs Last departure noon

A deeply tranquil and rural park set in the grounds of an old manor house. The four grassy fields with attractive borders of mixed, mature deciduous trees have exceptional views across the Rutland countryside and are within one mile of Rutland Water. There's a good shop, which specialises in locally sourced produce, a licensed café, and there are high quality showers and a fully-equipped laundry. Children and tents are very welcome in this safe environment where there is space to roam. 11 acre site. 250 touring pitches. 4 hardstandings. Caravan pitches. Motorhome pitches. Tent pitches.

AA Pubs & Restaurants nearby: Kings Arms, Wing 01572 737634

Facilities: ⬈ ℙ ☀ ⑤ ㏊ ㎞
Services: 🚐 🛢
Within 3 miles: ↓ ⌚ ✐ ⚓ ⑤ 🔯 ∪
Notes: ⊛ Farm shop, coarse fishing.

SHROPSHIRE

BRIDGNORTH
Map 10 SO79

Places to visit

Benthall Hall, BENTHALL 01952 882159
www.nationaltrust.org.uk/main/w-benthallhall

Great for kids: Dudmaston Estate, QUATT 01746 780866
www.nationaltrust.org.uk/main/w-dudmaston

PREMIER PARK

►►►►► 87% Stanmore Hall Touring Park (SO742923)

Stourbridge Rd WV15 6DT
☎ 01746 761761
e-mail: stanmore@morris-leisure.co.uk
dir: 2m E of Bridgnorth on A458

🚐 🚐 Å

Open all year

Last arrival 20.00hrs Last departure noon

An excellent park in peaceful surroundings offering outstanding facilities. The pitches, many fully serviced (with Freeview TV), are arranged around the lake close to Stanmore Hall. Handy for touring Ironbridge and the Severn Valley Railway, while Bridgnorth itself is an attractive old market town. 12.5 acre site. 131 touring pitches. 53 hardstandings. Caravan pitches. Motorhome pitches. Tent pitches.

AA Pubs & Restaurants nearby: Halfway House Inn, Eardington 01746 762670

Leisure: ⚠ ❀
Facilities: ⬈ ☉ ℙ ☀ ⚓ ⑤ ⑤ ㏊ ㎞ ❶
Services: 🚐 ⑤ 🛢 ⌀ Ⓣ 🛒 ⌄
Within 3 miles: ↓ ⌚ ⑤ ✐ 🔯 ⑤ ∪
Notes: Max of 2 dogs. Dogs must be kept on leads.

CRAVEN ARMS
Map 9 SO48

Places to visit

Stokesay Castle, STOKESAY 01588 672544
www.english-heritage.org.uk

Great for kids: Ludlow Castle, LUDLOW
01584 873355 www.ludlowcastle.com

►►► 79% Wayside Camping and Caravan Park (SO399816)

Aston on Clun SY7 8EF
☎ 01588 660218
e-mail: waysidecamping@hotmail.com
dir: From Craven Arms on A49, W onto B4368 (Clun road) towards Clun Valley. Site approx 2m on right just before Aston-on-Clun

* 🚐 £12-£18 🚐 £12-£18 Å £8-£18

Open Apr-Oct

A peaceful park with lovely views, close to excellent local walks and many places of interest. The modern toilet facilities provide a good level of comfort, and there are several electric hook-ups. You are assured of a warm welcome by the helpful owner. Out of season price reductions are available. Many places of interest are within easy reach including Stokesay Castle, Offa's Dyke and Ludlow. 2.5 acre site. 20 touring pitches. 4 hardstandings. Caravan pitches. Motorhome pitches. Tent pitches. 1 static.

AA Pubs & Restaurants nearby: Sun Inn, Corfton 01584 861239

Crown Country Inn, Munslow 01584 841205

Facilities: ⬈ ☉ ℙ ☀ ⚓ ❀ ❶
Services: 🚐 Ⓣ 🛒 ⌄
Within 3 miles: ↓ ✐ ⑤ 🔯
Notes: ⊛ Adults only on BHs, only 1 dog per unit. Dogs must be kept on leads. Seasonal organic vegetables on sale.

LEISURE: 🏊 Indoor swimming pool 🏊 Outdoor swimming pool ⚠ Children's playground 👶 Kid's club 🎾 Tennis court 🎱 Games room 🖵 Separate TV room ↓ 9/18 hole golf course ⛵ Boats for hire 🎬 Cinema 🎵 Entertainment 🎣 Fishing ⛳ Mini golf 🏄 Watersports 🏋 Gym ⚽ Sports field Spa ∪ Stables
FACILITIES: 🛁 Bath 🚿 Shower ⊙ Electric shaver ℙ Hairdryer ☀ Ice Pack Facility ♿ Disabled facilities ☎ Public telephone ⑤ Shop on site or within 200yds 🔯 Mobile shop (calls at least 5 days a week) 🍖 BBQ area 🞉 Picnic area ㎞ Wi-fi 🖳 Internet access ♻ Recycling ❶ Tourist info ㏊ Dog exercise area

ELLESMERE

See Lyneal

HUGHLEY
Map 10 SO59

Places to visit

Old Oswestry Hill Fort, OSWESTRY
0870 333 1181 www.english-heritage.org.uk

Great for kids: Hoo Farm Animal Kingdom,
TELFORD 01952 677917 www.hoofarm.com

▶▶▶ 79% Mill Farm Holiday Park (SO564979)

SY5 6NT
☎ 01746 785208
e-mail: myrtleroberts@hotmail.com
dir: On unclassified road off B4371 through
Hughley, 3m SW of Much Wenlock, 11m SW of
Church Stretton

* ⛺ fr £16 ⛺ fr £16 ▲ fr £16

Open all year

Last arrival 18.00hrs Last departure noon

A well-established farm site set in meadowland
adjacent to river, with mature trees and bushes
providing screening, and situated below Wenlock
Edge. Horse riding can be arranged at the riding
stables on the farm. 20 acre site. 60 touring
pitches. 6 hardstandings. 10 seasonal pitches.
Caravan pitches. Motorhome pitches. Tent pitches.
90 statics.

AA Pubs & Restaurants nearby: Wenlock Edge
Inn, Much Wenlock 01746 785678

George & Dragon, Much Wenlock 01952 727312

Talbot Inn, Much Wenlock 01952 727077

Leisure: ⚽

Facilities: ⌂⊙🅿✳🚻🔭🆚♻ ❶

Services: 🔌🛢⊘🚮↯

Within 3 miles: 🎣🛒U

Notes: Site more suitable for adults. Dogs must
be kept on leads. Fishing, horse riding.

LYNEAL (NEAR ELLESMERE)
Map 15 SJ43

Places to visit

Old Oswestry Hill Fort, OSWESTRY
0870 333 1181 www.english-heritage.org.uk

Great for kids: Hawkstone Historic Park &
Follies, WESTON-UNDER-REDCASTLE
01948 841700 www.principal-hayley.co.uk

▶▶▶▶ 81% Fernwood Caravan Park (SJ445346)

GOLD

SY12 0QF
☎ 01948 710221
e-mail: enquiries@fernwoodpark.co.uk
dir: From A495 in Welshampton take B5063, over
canal bridge, turn right as signed

* ⛺ £22-£29.50 ⛺ £22-£29.50

Open Mar-Nov (rs Mar & Nov shop closed)

Last arrival 21.00hrs Last departure 17.00hrs

A peaceful park set in wooded countryside, with a
screened, tree-lined touring area and coarse
fishing lake. The approach is past colourful
flowerbeds, and the static area which is tastefully
arranged around an attractive children's playing
area. There is a small child-free touring area for
those wanting complete relaxation, and the park
has 20 acres of woodland walks. 26 acre site. 60
touring pitches. 8 hardstandings. 30 seasonal
pitches. Caravan pitches. Motorhome pitches. 165
statics.

AA Pubs & Restaurants nearby: The Leaking Tap,
Cockshutt 01939 270636

Leisure: 🅰

Facilities: ⌂⊙🅿✳🔭🕙🛢🚮♻ ❶

Services: 🔌🛢🔒🅣↯

Within 3 miles: 🎣🛒🛒

Notes: Dogs must be kept on leads.

MINSTERLEY
Map 15 SJ30

Places to visit

Powis Castle & Garden, WELSHPOOL
01938 551920 www.nationaltrust.org.uk

Great for kids: Shrewsbury Castle and
Shropshire Regimental Museum, SHREWSBURY
01743 358516 www.shrewsburymuseums.com

AA CAMPING CARD SITE

▶▶ 92% The Old School Caravan Park (SO322977)

Shelve SY5 0JQ
☎ 01588 650410
e-mail: t.ward425@btinternet.com
dir: 6.5m SW of Minsterley on A488, site on left 2m
after village sign for Hope

⛺⛺▲

Open Mar-Jan

Last arrival 21.00hrs Last departure 11.00hrs

Situated in the Shropshire hills with many
excellent walks starting directly from the site, as
well as being close to many cycle trails. Although
a small site of just 1.5 acres it is well equipped.
This is a really beautiful park, often described as
'a gem', that has excellent facilities and offers all
the requirements for a relaxing countryside
holiday. The friendly owners, Terry and Jan, are
always on hand to help out with anything. There's
also a shooting range and leisure centre within six
miles, and Snailbreach Mine, one of the most
complete disused mineral mines in the country, is
nearby. 1.5 acre site. 22 touring pitches. 10
hardstandings. 6 seasonal pitches. Caravan
pitches. Motorhome pitches. Tent pitches.

AA Pubs & Restaurants nearby: Sun Inn, Marton
01938 561211

Lowfield Inn, Marton 01743 891313

Facilities: ⌂⊙✳🕙🚮♻ ❶

Services: 🔌🚮

Within 3 miles: 🛒🛒U

Notes: 🚫 No ball games or cycle riding. Dogs
must be kept on leads. TV aerial connection.

SHREWSBURY — Map 15 SJ41

Places to visit

Attingham Park, ATCHAM 01743 708123
www.nationaltrust.org.uk/attinghampark

Great for kids: Wroxeter Roman City, WROXETER
01743 761330 www.english-heritage.org.uk

AA CAMPING CARD SITE

PREMIER PARK

▶▶▶▶▶ **89% Beaconsfield Farm Caravan Park** *(SJ522189)*

Best of British

Battlefield SY4 4AA
☎ 01939 210370 & 210399
e-mail: mail@beaconsfield-farm.co.uk
web: www.beaconsfield-farm.co.uk
dir: At Hadnall, 1.5m NE of Shrewsbury. Follow sign for Astley from A49

* 🚐 £20-£26 🚙 £24-£26

Open all year

Last arrival 19.00hrs Last departure noon

A purpose-built family-run park on farmland in open countryside. This pleasant park offers quality in every area, including superior toilets, heated indoor swimming pool, luxury lodges for hire and attractive landscaping. Fly and coarse fishing are available from the park's own lake and The Bothy restaurant is excellent. Car hire is now available directly from the site, and there's a steam room, plus free Wi-fi. 12 luxury lodges are available for hire or sale. Only adults over 21 years are accepted. 16 acre site. 60 touring pitches. 50 hardstandings. 10 seasonal pitches. Caravan pitches. Motorhome pitches. 35 statics.

AA Pubs & Restaurants nearby: The Armoury, Shrewsbury 01743 340525

Plume of Feathers, Shrewsbury 01952 727360

Mytton & Mermaid, Shrewsbury 01743 761220

Beaconsfield Farm Caravan Park

Leisure: 🛶
Facilities: 🏕⊙🅿✳🐕🛁🕙🚻🍴🔌🖥♻🛈
Services: 🚱🔋🛢🍴🛒🛗
Within 3 miles: 🌿🚶🏌◎🛍🗄

Notes: Adults only. Dogs must be kept on leads. Cycle hire.

PREMIER PARK

▶▶▶▶▶ **88% Oxon Hall Touring Park** *(SJ455138)*

Best of British

Welshpool Rd SY3 5FB
☎ 01743 340868
e-mail: oxon@morris-leisure.co.uk
dir: Exit A5 (ring road) at junct with A458. Site shares entrance with 'Oxon Park & Ride'

🚐 🚙 ⛺

Open all year

Last arrival 21.00hrs

A delightful park with quality facilities, and a choice of grass and fully-serviced pitches. A warm welcome is assured from the friendly staff. An adults-only section proves very popular, and there is an inviting patio area next to reception and the shop, overlooking a small lake. This site is ideally located for visiting Shrewsbury and the surrounding countryside, and the site also benefits from the Oxon Park & Ride, a short walk through the park. 15 acre site. 105 touring pitches. 72 hardstandings. Caravan pitches. Motorhome pitches. Tent pitches. 60 statics.

AA Pubs & Restaurants nearby: The Armoury, Shrewsbury 01743 340525

Plume of Feathers, Shrewsbury 01952 727360

Mytton & Mermaid, Shrewsbury 01743 761220

Leisure: 🏔
Facilities: 🏕⊙🅿✳🐕🕙🛁🍴🚻🔌🖥♻🛈
Services: 🚱🔋🛢🚿🍴🛗
Within 3 miles: 🌿🚶🏌🛍🗄🛗

Notes: Max 2 dogs per pitch. Dogs must be kept on leads.

TELFORD — Map 10 SJ60

Places to visit

Lilleshall Abbey, LILLESHALL 0121 625 6820
www.english-heritage.org.uk

Ironbridge Gorge Museums, IRONBRIDGE
01952 884391 www.ironbridge.org.uk

PREMIER PARK

▶▶▶▶▶ **79% Severn Gorge Park** *(SJ705051)*

Bridgnorth Rd, Tweedale TF7 4JB
☎ 01952 684789
e-mail: info@severngorgepark.co.uk
dir: Signed off A442, 1m S of Telford

🚐 🚙

Open all year

Last arrival 22.00hrs Last departure 18.00hrs

A very pleasant wooded site in the heart of Telford, well-screened and well-maintained. The sanitary facilities are fresh and immaculate, and landscaping of the grounds is carefully managed. Although the touring section is small, this is a really delightful park to stay on, and it is also well positioned for visiting nearby Ironbridge and its museums. The Telford bus stops at the end of the drive. 6 acre site. 10 touring pitches. 10 hardstandings. Caravan pitches. Motorhome pitches. 120 statics.

AA Pubs & Restaurants nearby: All Nations Inn, Madeley 01952 585747

New Inn, Madeley 01952 601018

Facilities: 🏕⊙🅿✳🐕🛗
Services: 🚱🔋🍴🛒🛗🛗
Within 3 miles: 🌿🚶🏌◎🛍🗄🛗

Notes: Adults only. Well behaved dogs only.

LEISURE: 🏊 Indoor swimming pool 🏊 Outdoor swimming pool 🛝 Children's playground 🎏 Kid's club 🎾 Tennis court 🎱 Games room 📺 Separate TV room ⛳ 9/18 hole golf course ⛵ Boats for hire 🎬 Cinema 🎵 Entertainment 🎣 Fishing ◎ Mini golf 🏄 Watersports 🏋 Gym ⚽ Sports field **Spa** ☯ Stables
FACILITIES: 🛁 Bath 🚿 Shower ⊙ Electric shaver 🅿 Hairdryer ✳ Ice Pack Facility ♿ Disabled facilities ☎ Public telephone 🛍 Shop on site or within 200yds 🛒 Mobile shop (calls at least 5 days a week) 🍴 BBQ area 🏕 Picnic area 📶 Wi-fi 🖥 Internet access ♻ Recycling 🛈 Tourist info 🐕 Dog exercise area

WEM
Map 15 SJ52

Places to visit

Hawkstone Historic Park & Follies,
WESTON-UNDER-REDCASTLE 01948 841700
www.principal-hayley.co.uk

Attingham Park, ATCHAM 01743 708123
www.nationaltrust.org.uk/attinghampark

Great for kids: Shrewsbury Castle and
Shropshire Regimental Museum, SHREWSBURY
01743 358516 www.shrewsburymuseums.com

►►► 79% Lower Lacon Caravan Park

(SJ534304)

SY4 5RP
☎ 01939 232376
e-mail: info@llcp.co.uk
web: www.llcp.co.uk
dir: A49 onto B5065. Site 3m on right

Open all year (rs Winter)

Last arrival anytime Last departure 16.00hrs

A large, spacious park with lively club facilities
and an entertainments' barn, set safely away from
the main road. The park is particularly suited to
families, with an outdoor swimming pool and farm
animals. 57 acre site. 270 touring pitches. 30
hardstandings. 100 seasonal pitches. Caravan
pitches. Motorhome pitches. Tent pitches. 50
statics. 2 wooden pods.

AA Pubs & Restaurants nearby: Burlton Inn,
Burlton 01939 270284

Leisure: 🏊 🎱 🎣 🖵

Facilities: 🚼 📶 ⊙ 🎏 ☀ ♿ 🕙 🖥 🔧 📶 ♻ 🛈

Services: 🔌 🗑 🍽 🛢 🖉 T 🍴 🛁 🏪

Within 3 miles: 🚴 🖉 ◎ 🏌 🛒

Notes: No skateboards, no commercial vehicles,
no sign written vehicles. Dogs must be kept on
leads. Crazy golf.

WENTNOR
Map 15 SO39

Places to visit

Montgomery Castle, MONTGOMERY
01443 336000 www.cadw.wales.gov.uk

Glansevern Hall Gardens, BERRIEW
01686 640644 www.glansevern.co.uk

►►► 81% The Green Caravan Park (SO380932)

SY9 5EF
☎ 01588 650605
e-mail: karen@greencaravanpark.co.uk
dir: 1m NE of Bishop's Castle on A489. Right at
brown tourist sign

* 🚐 fr £14.50 🚗 fr £14.50 ▲ fr £13

Open Etr-Oct

Last arrival 21.00hrs Last departure 13.00hrs

A pleasant site in a peaceful setting convenient
for visiting Ludlow or Shrewsbury. Very family
orientated, with good facilities. The grassy pitches
are mainly level, and some hardstandings are
available. 15 acre site. 140 touring pitches. 5
hardstandings. Caravan pitches. Motorhome
pitches. Tent pitches. 20 statics.

AA Pubs & Restaurants nearby: Crown Inn,
Wentnor 01588 650613

Leisure: 🎱

Facilities: 📶 ⊙ 🎏 ☀ 🖥 🔧 ♻ 🛈

Services: 🔌 🗑 🍽 🛢 🖉 T 🍴 🏪

Within 3 miles: 🖉 🏌 🛒

Notes: Dogs must be kept on leads.

SERVICES: 🔌 Electric hook up 🗑 Launderette 🍽 Licensed bar 🛢 Calor Gas 🖉 Camping Gaz T Toilet fluid 🍴 Café/Restaurant 🏪 Fast Food/Takeaway 🔋 Battery charging
🛁 Baby care 🔧 Motorvan service point **ABBREVIATIONS:** BH/bank hols-bank holidays Etr-Easter Whit-Whitsun dep-departure fr-from hrs-hours m-mile mdnt-midnight
rdbt-roundabout rs-restricted service wk-week wknd-weekend 🚫 No credit cards 🚫 no dogs See page 7 for details of the AA Camping Card Scheme

Somerset

South of Bristol and north-east of the West Country lies Somerset, that most English of counties. You tend to think of classic traditions and renowned honey traps when you think of Somerset – cricket and cider, the ancient and mysterious Glastonbury Tor and the deep gash that is Cheddar Gorge.

Somerset means 'summer pastures' – appropriate given that so much of this old county is rural and unspoiled. At its heart are the Mendip Hills, 25 miles (40km) long by 5 miles (8km) wide. Mainly of limestone over old red sandstone, and rising to just over 1,000 ft (303m) above sea level, they have a striking character and identity and are not really like any of the other Somerset hills.

Landscape of contrasts

By contrast, to the south and south-west are the Somerset Levels, a flat fenland landscape that was the setting for the Battle of Sedgemoor in 1685, while close to the rolling acres of Exmoor National Park lie the Quantock Hills, famous for gentle slopes, heather-covered moorland stretches and red deer. From the summit, the Bristol Channel is visible where it meets the Severn Estuary; look to the east and you can see the Mendips.

The Quantocks were the haunt of several distinguished British poets. Coleridge wrote *The Ancient Mariner* and *Kubla Khan* while living in the area. Wordsworth and his sister visited on occasions and often accompanied Coleridge on his country walks. ▶

Along the coast

Somerset's fine coastline takes a lot of beating. Various old-established seaside resorts overlook Bridgwater Bay – among them Minehead, on the edge of Exmoor National Park, and classic Weston-Super-Mare, with its striking new pier (the previous one was destroyed by fire in 2008). Fans of the classic Merchant-Ivory film production of The Remains of the Day, starring Anthony Hopkins and Emma Thompson, will recognise the Royal Pier Hotel in Birnbeck Road as one of the locations. Weston has just about everything for the holidaymaker – including Marine Parade, which runs for 2 miles (3.2km).

Historic Wells

Inland – and not to be missed – is historic Wells, one of the smallest cities in the country, and with its period houses and superb cathedral, it is certainly one of the finest. Adorned with sculptures, Wells Cathedral's West Front is a masterpiece of medieval craftsmanship. Nearby are Vicar's Close, a delightful street of 14th-century houses, and the Bishop's Palace, which is 13th century and moated.

Walking and Cycling

The choice of walks in Somerset is plentiful, as is the range of cycle routes. One of the most attractive of long-distance trails is the 50-mile (80km) West Mendip Way, which runs from Weston to Frome. En route the trail visits Cheddar Gorge and Wells. The local tourist information centres throughout the county offer a varied mix of described walks and longer trails to suit all.

   One of Somerset's most popular cycling trails is the delightfully named Strawberry Line which links Yatton railway station with Cheddar and

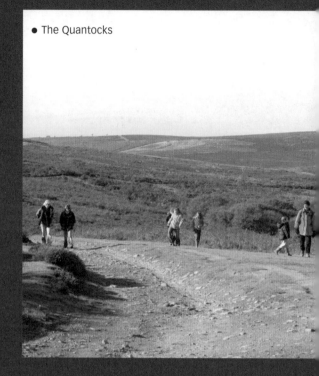

● The Quantocks

runs for 9 miles (14.5km) along the course of a disused track bed. The trail is relatively easy and along the way are various picnic spots and various public artworks.

Festivals and Events

- The Cheddar Ales Beer Festival in June is a celebration of real ale with a range of beers from micro-breweries across the country.
- The Priddy Sheep Fair in mid-August is a great occasion for country lovers and farming traditions.
- Between July and September there are amazing sand sculptures down on the beach at Weston-Super-Mare.
- The Autumn Steam Gala at the West Somerset Railway in Minehead during late September/early October is a must for steam train enthusiasts.

● Glastonbury Tor

SOMERSET

See Walk 9 in the Walks & Cycle Rides section at the end of the guide

BATH   Map 4 ST76

Places to visit

Roman Baths & Pump Room, BATH
01225 477785 www.romanbaths.co.uk

Bath Abbey, BATH 01225 422462
www.bathabbey.org

Great for kids: The Herschel Museum of Astronomy, BATH 01225 446865
www.bath-preservation-trust.org.uk

▶▶▶▶ **82%** *Newton Mill Holiday Park* (ST715649)

Newton Rd BA2 9JF
☎ 08442 729503
e-mail: enquiries@newtonmillpark.co.uk
dir: *From Bath W on A4 to rdbt by Globe Inn, immediately left, site 1m on left*

🚐 🚏 Å

Open all year (rs Wknds low season restaurant open)

Last arrival 21.30hrs Last departure 11.30hrs

An attractive, high quality park set in a sheltered valley and surrounded by woodland, with a stream running through. It offers excellent toilet facilities with private cubicles and family rooms, and there is an appealing restaurant and bar offering a wide choice of menus throughout the year. Additional hardstandings have been put in on the top area of the park. The City of Bath is easily accessible by bus or via the Bristol to Bath cycle path. 42 acre site. 106 touring pitches. 67 hardstandings. Caravan pitches. Motorhome pitches. Tent pitches.

AA Pubs & Restaurants nearby: Marlborough Tavern, Bath 01225 423731

King William, Bath 01225 428096

Hop Pole, Bath 01225 446327

Jamie's Italian, Bath 01225 432430

Leisure: 🎠 🎵
Facilities: 🛁 📷 ☺ 🏷 ✳ ⚓ ☪ 🖅 🍴 ♻ ❻
Services: 🔌 🔄 🍽 🔒 🧺 📞 🍴 ♿
Within 3 miles: ⚓ 🥾 🎏 🏌 🍴 🔄

Notes: No noise after 22.00hrs. Dogs must be kept on leads. Satellite TV hook up on selected pitches.

BREAN   Map 4 ST25

Places to visit

King John's Hunting Lodge, AXBRIDGE
01934 732012 www.nationaltrust.org.uk

North Somerset Museum,
WESTON-SUPER-MARE 01934 621028
www.n-somerset.gov.uk/museum

Great for kids: The Helicopter Museum,
WESTON-SUPER-MARE 01934 635227
www.helicoptermuseum.co.uk

91% *Holiday Resort Unity* (ST294539)

Coast Rd, Brean Sands TA8 2RB
☎ 01278 751235
e-mail: admin@hru.co.uk
dir: *M5 junct 22, B3140 through Burnham-on-Sea, through Berrow to Brean. Site on left just before Brean Leisure Park*

🚐 🚏 Å

Open Feb-Nov

Last arrival 21.00hrs Last departure 10.00hrs

This is an excellent, family-run holiday park offering very good touring facilities plus a wide range of family oriented activities, including bowling, RJ's entertainment club plus good eating outlets etc. Brean Leisure Park and a swimming pool complex are available directly from the touring park at a discounted entry price. Ready erected, fully-equipped tents are also available for hire. 200 acre site. 453 touring pitches. 158 hardstandings. 168 seasonal pitches. Caravan pitches. Motorhome pitches. Tent pitches. 650 statics. 8 bell tents/yurts.

Leisure: 🎠 🎣 ⛱ 🎾 🎠 🎣 ⚓ 🎵
Facilities: 🛁 📷 ☺ 🏷 ✳ ⚓ ☪ ☎ 🖅 🍴 🐾 🖧 💻 ♻ ❻
Services: 🔌 🔄 🍽 🔒 🧺 🍴 🛒
Within 3 miles: ⚓ 🎏 🏌 🔄 🍴 🔄 ♿

Notes: Family parties of 3 or more, must be over 21 (young persons policy applies). Dogs must be kept on leads. Fun City theme park, fishing lake.

90% Warren Farm Holiday Centre (ST297564)

Brean Sands TA8 2RP
☎ 01278 751227
e-mail: enquiries@warren-farm.co.uk
dir: *M5 junct 22, B3140 through Burnham-on-Sea to Berrow & Brean. Site 1.5m past Brean Leisure Park*

✳ 🚐 £7.50-£17 🚏 £7.50-£17 Å £7.50-£17

Open Apr-Oct

Last arrival 20.00hrs Last departure noon

A large family-run holiday park close to the beach, divided into several fields each with its own designated facilities. Pitches are spacious and level, and enjoy panoramic views of the Mendip Hills and Brean Down. A bar and restaurant are part of the complex, which provide entertainment for all the family, and there is also separate entertainment for children. The park has excellent modern facilities and a large caravan sales and service facility. 100 acre site. 575 touring pitches. Caravan pitches. Motorhome pitches. Tent pitches. 400 statics.

AA Pubs & Restaurants nearby: Crossways Inn, West Huntspill 01278 783756

Leisure: 🎠 ⚓ ⚓ 📺 🎵
Facilities: 🛁 📷 ☺ 🏷 ✳ ⚓ ☪ ☎ 🖅 🐾 🖧 💻
❻ **Services:** 🔌 🔄 🍽 🔒 🧺 🍴 🛒 ♿
Within 3 miles: ⚓ 🔄 🎏 🍴 🔄 ♿

Notes: No commercial vehicles. Fishing lake & ponds, indoor play area.

see advert on page 282

Burnham-on-Sea Holiday Village
Burnham-on-Sea, Somerset

We've got the lot
- Heated indoor and outdoor pools
- Family entertainment and kids' clubs
- Sports activities and facilities
- Sandy beach opposite our park
- Stay in our caravans, or bring your own tourer, motorhome, tent or trailer tent

Save up to 50%*
on 2013 self-catering & touring and camping holidays

To find out more, order a brochure and to book **Call: 0843 658 0454** Quote: AABR **Visit: haven.com/aabr** *Haven*

Calls cost 5p per minute plus network extras. Open 7 days a week, 9am-9pm

Doniford Bay Holiday Park
Watchet, Somerset

We've got the lot
- Heated indoor and outdoor pools
- Family entertainment and kids' clubs
- Sports activities and facilities
- Climbing wall, leap of faith and ropes course†
- Come and stay in one of our comfortable, roomy self-catering caravans

Save up to 50%* on 2013 holidays

To find out more, order a brochure and to book **Call: 0843 658 0461** Quote: AADF **Visit: haven.com/aadf** *Haven*

Calls cost 5p per minute plus network extras. Open 7 days a week, 9am-9pm

SERVICES: Electric hook up | Launderette | Licensed bar | Calor Gas | Camping Gaz | Toilet fluid | Café/Restaurant | Fast Food/Takeaway | Battery charging | Baby care | Motorvan service point **ABBREVIATIONS:** BH/bank hols-bank holidays Etr-Easter Whit-Whitsun dep-departure fr-from hrs-hours m-mile mdnt-midnight rdbt-roundabout rs-restricted service wk-week wknd-weekend No credit cards no dogs See page 7 for details of the AA Camping Card Scheme

LEISURE: 🛋 Indoor swimming pool 🏊 Outdoor swimming pool Children's playground 🧒 Kid's club 🎾 Tennis court Games room 📺 Separate TV room ⛳ 9/18 hole golf course 🚤 Boats for hire 🎬 Cinema 🎵 Entertainment 🎣 Fishing ⛳ Mini golf 🏄 Watersports 🏋 Gym Sports field Spa Stables
FACILITIES: 🛁 Bath 🚿 Shower Electric shaver Hairdryer Ice Pack Facility ♿ Disabled facilities 📞 Public telephone 🛒 Shop on site or within 200yds 🛒 Mobile shop (calls at least 5 days a week) BBQ area Picnic area Wi-fi 💻 Internet access ♻ Recycling ℹ Tourist info Dog exercise area

BREAN *continued*

►►►► 89% Northam Farm Caravan & Touring Park *(ST299556)*

TA8 2SE
☎ 01278 751244
e-mail: stay@northamfarm.co.uk
dir: *M5 junct 22, B3140 to Burnham-on-Sea & Brean. Park on right 0.5m past Brean Leisure Park*

* ⊕ £8.75-£26.25 ⊕ £8.75-£26.25
Å £8.75-£22.25

Open Mar-Oct (rs Mar-Oct shop, café, takeaway open limited hours)

Last arrival 20.00hrs Last departure 10.30hrs

An attractive site a short walk from the sea and a long sandy beach. This quality park also has lots of children's play areas, and also owns the Seagull Inn about 600 yards away, which includes a restaurant and entertainment. There is a fishing lake on the site, which proves very popular. Facilities on this park are excellent. A DVD of the site is available free of charge. 30 acre site. 350 touring pitches. 260 hardstandings. Caravan pitches. Motorhome pitches. Tent pitches.

Leisure: ᗩ ☺
Facilities: ☱ ♁ ⊙ ℱ ✿ ᘐ ⓢ ⓢ 冔 ♣ ♻ ❻
Services: ❷ ᱪ ♨ ⌀ ⊤ ᠀ ┷ ↯ ♻
Within 3 miles: ↥ ♪ ◎ ⓢ ⓢ ∪

Notes: Families & couples only, no motorcycles or commercial vehicles. Dogs must be kept on leads.
see advert on inside back cover

Places to visit
Dunster Castle, DUNSTER 01643 821314
www.nationaltrust.org.uk

Cleeve Abbey, WASHFORD 01984 640377
www.english-heritage.org.uk

►►►► 82% Exe Valley Caravan Site *(SS923333)*

Mill House TA22 9JR
☎ 01643 851432
e-mail: info@exevalleycamping.co.uk
dir: *Take A396 (Tiverton to Minehead road). Turn W in centre of Bridgetown, site 40yds on right*

⊕ £11-£17 ⊕ £11-£17 Å £11-£20

Open 15 Mar-21 Oct

Last arrival 22.00hrs Last departure 11.00hrs

Set in the Exmoor National Park, this adults-only park occupies an enchanting, peaceful spot in a wooded valley alongside the River Exe. There is free fly-fishing, and an abundance of wildlife, with excellent walks directly from the park. The inn opposite serves lunchtime and evening meals. 4 acre site. 50 touring pitches. 10 hardstandings. Caravan pitches. Motorhome pitches. Tent pitches.

AA Pubs & Restaurants nearby: Rest & Be Thankful Inn, Wheddon Cross 01643 841222

Facilities: ♁ ⊙ ℱ ✿ ᘐ ⓢ ⓢ 冔 ♣ ⱳ ♻ ❻
Services: ❷ ᱪ ♨ ⌀ ⊤ ┷ ↯
Within 3 miles: ↥ ♪ ◎ ⓢ ∪

Notes: Adults only. ⊛ 17th-century mill, cycle hire, TV sockets & cables.

Places to visit
Hestercombe Gardens, TAUNTON 01823 413923
www.hestercombe.com

Coleridge Cottage, NETHER STOWEY
01278 732662 www.nationaltrust.org.uk

Great for kids: Tropiquaria Animal and Adventure Park, WASHFORD 01984 640688
www.tropiquaria.co.uk

 ## 81% Mill Farm Caravan & Camping Park *(ST219410)*

Fiddington TA5 1JQ
☎ 01278 732286 web: www.millfarm.biz
dir: *From Bridgwater take A39 W, left at Cannington rdbt, 2m, right just beyond Apple Inn towards Fiddington. Follow camping signs*

* ⊕ £12-£24 ⊕ £12-£24 Å £12-£24

Open all year

Last arrival 23.00hrs Last departure 10.00hrs

A large holiday park with plenty to interest all the family, including indoor and outdoor pools, a boating lake, a gym and horse riding. There is also a clubhouse with bar, and a full entertainment programme in the main season. Although lively and busy in the main season, the park also offers a much quieter environment at other times; out of season some activities and entertainment may not be available. 6 acre site. 125 touring pitches. Caravan pitches. Motorhome pitches. Tent pitches.

AA Pubs & Restaurants nearby: Lemon Tree Restaurant (Walnut Tree Hotel), North Petherton 01278 662255

Leisure: ♒ ⇌ ᛟ ᗩ ☺ ☐ ♫
Facilities: ☱ ♁ ⊙ ℱ ✿ ᘐ ⓢ ⓢ 冔 ♣ 冚 ⱳ
♻ ❻ Services: ❷ ᱪ ᵺ ♨ ⌀ ⊤ ᠀ ┷
Within 3 miles: ↥ ♪ ◎ ⓢ ⓢ ∪

Notes: No noise after 23.00hrs. Dogs must be kept on leads. Canoeing, pool table, trampolines, pony rides, fitness classes, saunas.
see advert on opposite page

BURNHAM-ON-SEA — Map 4 ST34

Places to visit

Glastonbury Abbey, GLASTONBURY 01458 832267
www.glastonburyabbey.com

King John's Hunting Lodge, AXBRIDGE
01934 732012 www.nationaltrust.org.uk

Great for kids: Wookey Hole Caves & Papermill,
WOOKEY HOLE 01749 672243 www.wookey.co.uk

86% Burnham-on-Sea Holiday Village

(ST305485)

Marine Dr TA8 1LA
☎ **0871 231 0868**
e-mail: burnhamonsea@haven.com
web: www.haven.com/burnhamonsea
dir: M5 junct 22, A38 towards Highbridge. Over
mini rdbt, right onto B3139 to Burnham. After
Total Garage left into Marine Drive. Park 400yds
on left

Open mid Mar-end Oct (rs mid Mar-May & Sep-
Oct facilities may be reduced)

Last arrival anytime Last departure 10.00hrs

A large, family-orientated holiday village
complex with a separate touring park
containing 43 super pitches. There is a wide
range of activities, including excellent indoor
and outdoor pools, plus bars, restaurants and
entertainment for all the family. The coarse
fishing lake is very popular, and the seafront at
Burnham is only half a mile away. A wide range
of well laid out holiday homes are available
for hire. 94 acre site. 75 touring pitches. 44
hardstandings. Caravan pitches. Motorhome
pitches. Tent pitches. 700 statics.

AA Pubs & Restaurants nearby: Crossways Inn,
West Huntspill 01278 783756

Leisure: 🏊 🏊 🎪 ⚓ 🎾 🏐 🎵

Facilities: 🚿 📺 ☀ & 🕐 🛒 📶

Services: 🔌 🗑 🚽 🗑 🍴 🛒 🏪

Within 3 miles: 🎿 🎣 🚵 ⛳ 🛒 🛒 ⛵

Notes: No pets, no commercial vehicles, no
bookings by persons under 21yrs unless a
family booking.

see advert on page 281

BURTLE — Map 4 ST34

Places to visit

Glastonbury Abbey, GLASTONBURY 01458 832267
www.glastonburyabbey.com

The Bishop's Palace, WELLS 01749 988111
www.bishopspalace.org.uk

Great for kids: East Somerset Railway,
CRANMORE 01749 880417
www.eastsomersetrailway.com

AA CAMPING CARD SITE

▶ **76% Orchard Camping** (ST397434)

Ye Olde Burtle Inn, Catcott Rd TA7 8NG
☎ **01278 722269 & 722123**
e-mail: food@theinn.eu
dir: M5 junct 23, A39, in approx 4m left onto
unclassified road to Burtle, site by pub in village
centre

🏕

Open all year

Last arrival anytime

A simple campsite set in an orchard at the rear of
a lovely 17th-century family inn in the heart of the
Somerset Levels. The restaurant offers a wide
range of meals, and breakfast can be pre-ordered
by campers. The site has a shower and disabled
toilet which are available to campers outside pub
opening hours. Free internet access and Wi-fi are
available. 0.75 acre site. 30 touring pitches. Tent
pitches.

AA Pubs & Restaurants nearby: The Burcott Inn,
Wookey 01749 673874

Leisure: 🎪 🔫

Facilities: 🚿 ☀ & 🕐 🛒 📶 🎯

Services: 🔌 🍴 🛒 🏪

Within 3 miles: 🎣 🛒 ⛵

Notes: No cars by tents. Cycle & tent hire,
sleeping bags & equipment.

CHARD — Map 4 ST30

Places to visit

Forde Abbey, CHARD 01460 221290
www.fordeabbey.co.uk

Barrington Court, BARRINGTON 01460 241938
www.nationaltrust.org.uk

AA CAMPING CARD SITE

▶▶▶▶ **80% Alpine Grove Touring Park** (ST342071)

Forton TA20 4HD
☎ **01460 63479**
e-mail: stay@alpinegrovetouringpark.com
dir: Exit A30 between Chard & Crewkerne towards
Cricket St Thomas, follow signs. Site 2m on right

* 🚐 £14-£20 🚙 £14-£20 🏕 £11.50-£20

Open 1 wk before Etr-Sep

Last arrival 21.00hrs Last departure 10.30hrs

A warm welcome awaits at this attractive, quiet
wooded park that has both hardstandings and
grass pitches. The facilities are kept spotlessly
clean. Families particularly enjoy the small
swimming pool and terrace in summer. Log cabins
are also available for hire. This very dog-friendly
site offers a dog sitting service. 8.5 acre site. 40
touring pitches. 16 hardstandings. Caravan
pitches. Motorhome pitches. Tent pitches. 4
wooden pods.

AA Pubs & Restaurants nearby: George Inn,
Crewkerne 01460 73650

New Inn, Ilminster 01460 52413

Leisure: 🏊 🎪

Facilities: 🚿 📺 ☀ & 🕐 🛒 🏐 📶 ♻ 🎯

Services: 🔌 🗑 🚽 🍴 📺 🛒 🏪

Within 3 miles: 🎿 🎣 🛒 ⛵

Notes: No open fires. Dogs must be kept on leads.
Fire pits to hire.

LEISURE: 🏊 Indoor swimming pool 🏊 Outdoor swimming pool 🎪 Children's playground 🛝 Kid's club 🎾 Tennis court 🔫 Games room 📺 Separate TV room
🏌 9/18 hole golf course ⚓ Boats for hire 🎬 Cinema 🎵 Entertainment 🎣 Fishing 🏐 Mini golf 🌊 Watersports 🏋 Gym 🏐 Sports field **Spa** ⛵ Stables
FACILITIES: 🛁 Bath 🚿 Shower ⚡ Electric shaver 📺 Hairdryer ☀ Ice Pack Facility & Disabled facilities 🕐 Public telephone 🛒 Shop on site or within 200yds
🛒 Mobile shop (calls at least 5 days a week) 🍴 BBQ area 🎋 Picnic area 📶 Wi-fi 💻 Internet access ♻ Recycling 🎯 Tourist info 🐕 Dog exercise area

CHEDDAR — Map 4 ST45

Places to visit

Glastonbury Abbey, GLASTONBURY 01458 832267 www.glastonburyabbey.com

The Helicopter Museum, WESTON-SUPER-MARE 01934 635227 www.helicoptermuseum.co.uk

Great for kids: Wookey Hole Caves & Papermill, WOOKEY HOLE 01749 672243 www.wookey.co.uk

84% *Broadway House Holiday Park* (ST448547)

BRONZE

Axbridge Rd BS27 3DB
☎ 08442 729501
e-mail: enquiries@broadwayhousepark.co.uk
dir: From M5 junct 22 follow signs to Cheddar Gorge & Caves (8m). Site midway between Cheddar & Axbridge on A371

Open Mar-Oct (rs Mar-end May & Oct bar & pool closed, limited shop hours)

Last arrival 22.00hrs Last departure 11.00hrs

A well-equipped holiday park on the slopes of the Mendips with an exceptional range of activities for all ages. This is a busy and lively park in the main holiday periods, but can be quiet and peaceful off-peak. The park was due to close in September 2012 for a major re-development as a holiday lodge and static-only park, and it was not certain whether touring facilities would be maintained. 30 acre site. 342 touring pitches. 70 hardstandings. Caravan pitches. Motorhome pitches. Tent pitches. 35 statics.

AA Pubs & Restaurants nearby: Wookey Hole Inn, Wookey Hole 01749 676677

Leisure: ⌂ ⚓ 🎵

Facilities: ↻ ⊙ ℙ ⚒ ⚙ ⊙ 🛢 🚻 ♨ ❓

Services: 🔌 🛢 🍽 🍴 📶 ⊤ 🍴 🔋 🛠 ⚙

Within 3 miles: 🏌 ⊚ 🛢🛢

Notes: Children to be supervised at all times. Dogs must be kept on leads. Table tennis, skate park, BMX track.

▶▶▶▶ 86% Cheddar Bridge Touring Park (ST459529)

Draycott Rd BS27 3RJ
☎ 01934 743048
e-mail: enquiries@cheddarbridge.co.uk
dir: M5 junct 22 (Burnham-on-Sea), A38 towards Cheddar & Bristol, approx 5m. Right onto A371 at Cross, follow Cheddar signs. Through Cheddar village towards Wells, site on right just before Caravan Club site

Open Mar-Oct

Last arrival 22.00hrs Last departure 11.00hrs

A peaceful adults-only park on the edge of the village of Cheddar, with the River Yeo passing attractively through its grounds. It is handy for exploring Cheddar Gorge and Wookey Hole, Wells and Bath. The toilet and shower facilities are very good. There are camping pods, a gypsy wagon, seven statics and two apartments for hire. 4 acre site. 45 touring pitches. 10 hardstandings. Caravan pitches. Motorhome pitches. Tent pitches. 7 statics.

AA Pubs & Restaurants nearby: Wookey Hole Inn, Wookey Hole 01749 676677

Cheddar Bridge Touring Park

Facilities: ↻ ⊙ ℙ ⚒ ⚙ ⊙ 🛢 🚻

Services: 🔌 ⚙ ⚙

Within 3 miles: ↑ 🏌 ⊚ ⚓ 🛢🛢 ⛳

Notes: Adults only. Quiet 23.00hrs-08.00hrs.

see advert below

COWSLIP GREEN   Map 4 ST46

Places to visit

Clevedon Court, CLEVEDON 01275 872257
www.nationaltrust.org.uk

Bristol Museum & Art Gallery, BRISTOL
0117 922 3571 www.bristol.gov.uk/museums

Great for kids: HorseWorld, BRISTOL
01275 540173 www.horseworld.org.uk

►►► 83% *Brook Lodge Farm Camping & Caravan Park (Bristol)*
(ST486620)

BS40 5RB
☎ **01934 862311**
e-mail: info@brooklodgefarm.com
dir: *M5 junct 18 follow signs for Bristol Airport. Site 3m on left of A38 at bottom of hill. M5 junct 22 follow A38 to Churchill. Site 4m on right opposite Holiday Inn*

Open Mar-Oct

Last arrival 21.30hrs Last departure noon

A naturally sheltered country touring park nestling in a valley of the Mendip Hills, surrounded by trees and a historic walled garden. A friendly welcome is always assured by the family owners who are particularly keen on preserving the site's environment and have won a green tourism award. This park is particularly well placed for visiting the Bristol Balloon Festival, held in August, plus the many country walks in the area. 3.5 acre site. 29 touring pitches. 3 hardstandings. Caravan pitches. Motorhome pitches. Tent pitches.

AA Pubs & Restaurants nearby: The White Hart, Congresbury 01934 833303

Leisure: ⚴

Facilities: ⚐☺⚐⚒⚙⚗⚑

Services: ⚑⚑⚑⚑⚑

Within 3 miles: ⚑⚑⚑⚑⚑

Notes: Dogs by prior arrangement. Cycle hire, walking maps available.

CREWKERNE

See Drimpton, Dorset

CROWCOMBE   Map 3 ST13

Places to visit

Cleeve Abbey, WASHFORD 01984 640377
www.english-heritage.org.uk

Great for kids: Dunster Castle, DUNSTER
01643 821314 www.nationaltrust.org.uk

►►►► 86% *Quantock Orchard Caravan Park* (*ST138357*)

Flaxpool TA4 4AW
☎ **01984 618618**
e-mail: member@flaxpool.freeserve.co.uk
web: www.quantock-orchard.co.uk
dir: *Take A358 from Taunton, signed Minehead & Williton. In 8m turn left just past Flaxpool Garage. Park immediately on left*

Open all year (rs 10 Sep-20 May swimming pool closed)

Last arrival 22.00hrs Last departure noon

This small family run park is set at the foot of the beautiful Quantock Hills and makes an ideal base for touring Somerset, Exmoor and north Devon. It is also close to the West Somerset Railway. It has excellent facilities and there is a lovely heated outdoor swimming pool, plus gym and fitness centre; bike hire is also available. There are static homes for hire. 3.5 acre site. 69 touring pitches. 30 hardstandings. Caravan pitches. Motorhome pitches. Tent pitches. 8 statics.

AA Pubs & Restaurants nearby: White Horse, Stogumber 01984 656277

Blue Ball, Triscombe 01984 618242

Rising Sun Inn, West Bagborough 01823 432575

Leisure: ⚴⚴⚴⚴⚴ Spa

Facilities: ⚑⚐☺⚐⚒⚙⚗⚑⚑
⚑⚑⚑⚑

Services: ⚑⚑⚑⚑⚑⚑⚑

Within 3 miles: ⚑⚑⚑⚑⚑

Notes: Dogs must be kept on leads. Off-licence on site.

DULVERTON   Map 3 SS92

See also East Anstey (Devon)

Places to visit

Knightshayes Court,
KNIGHTSHAYES COURT 01884 254665
www.nationaltrust.org.uk/knightshayes

Killerton House & Garden, KILLERTON
01392 881345 www.nationaltrust.org.uk

Great for kids: Tiverton Castle, TIVERTON
01884 253200 www.tivertoncastle.com

►►► 80% *Wimbleball Lake* (*SS960300*)

Brompton Regis TA22 9NU
☎ **01398 371257 & 371460**
e-mail: wimbleball@swlakestrust.org.uk
dir: *From A396 (Tiverton-Minehead road) take B3222 signed Dulverton Services, follow signs to Wimbleball Lake. Ignore 1st entry (fishing) & take 2nd entry for tea room & camping. (NB care needed due to narrow roads)*

Open Mar-Oct

Last departure 11.30hrs

A grassy site overlooking Wimbleball Lake, set high up on Exmoor National Park. The camping area is adjacent to the Visitor Centre and café, which also includes the camping toilets and showers. The camping field, with 11 electric hook-ups and two hardstandings, is in a quiet and peaceful setting with good views of the lake, which is nationally renowned for its trout fishing, and boats can be hired with advance notice. 1.25 acre site. 30 touring pitches. 4 hardstandings. Caravan pitches. Motorhome pitches. Tent pitches.

AA Pubs & Restaurants nearby: Masons Arms, Knowstone 01398 341231

Leisure: ⚠

Facilities: �️☺️🏵️✳️⚃🕒🛁🚽♻️ ❼

Services: ⚡🛢️🍴

Within 3 miles: ≽ℓ⛟🛁🚽↻

Notes: Dogs must be kept on leads. Watersports & activity centre, bird watching, cycling, lakeside walks.

EMBOROUGH   Map 4 ST65

Places to visit

Glastonbury Abbey, GLASTONBURY 01458 832267 www.glastonburyabbey.com

King John's Hunting Lodge, AXBRIDGE 01934 732012 www.nationaltrust.org.uk

Great for kids: East Somerset Railway, CRANMORE 01749 880417 www.eastsomersetrailway.com

▶▶▶ 83% Old Down Touring Park

(ST628513)

Old Down House BA3 4SA
☎ **01761 232355**
e-mail: jsmallparkhomes@aol.com
dir: A37 from Farrington Gurney through Ston Easton. In 2m left onto B3139 to Radstock. Site opposite Old Down Inn

✳ 🚐 fr £18 🚍 fr £18 ⛺ fr £18

Open all year

Last arrival 20.00hrs Last departure noon

A small family-run site set in open parkland, surrounded by well-established trees. The excellent toilet facilities are well maintained as is every other aspect of the park. Children are welcome. 4 acre site. 30 touring pitches. 15 hardstandings. 6 seasonal pitches. Caravan pitches. Motorhome pitches. Tent pitches.

AA Pubs & Restaurants nearby: Moody Goose, Old Priory, Midsomer Norton 01761 416784

Facilities: �️☺️🏵️✳️🛁🚽♻️ ❼

Services: ⚡🛢️🍴🔌📦🔋

Within 3 miles: ⛳🎠ℓ🛁🚽↻

Notes: Dogs must be kept on leads.

EXFORD   Map 3 SS83

Places to visit

Dunster Castle, DUNSTER 01643 821314 www.nationaltrust.org.uk

West Somerset Railway, MINEHEAD 01643 704996 www.west-somerset-railway.co.uk

Great for kids: Exmoor Zoological Park, BLACKMOOR GATE 01598 763352 www.exmoorzoo.co.uk

▶▶ 84% Westermill Farm *(SS825398)*

TA24 7NJ
☎ **01643 831238**
e-mail: aa@westermill.com
dir: From Exford on Porlock road. Left in 0.25m, left to Westermill, sign on tree. Fork left (NB recommended route)

✳ 🚍 ⛺ fr £15.50

Open all year (rs Nov-May larger toilet block & shop closed)

An idyllic site for peace and quiet, in a sheltered valley in the heart of Exmoor, which has won awards for conservation. Highly recommended for traditional camping. There are four waymarked walks over the 500-acre working farm and self-catering accommodation is also available. Please note that the site should only be approached from Exford (other approaches are difficult). 6 acre site. 60 touring pitches. Motorhome pitches. Tent pitches.

AA Pubs & Restaurants nearby: Crown Hotel, Exford 01643 831554

Facilities: �️☺️🏵️✳️🕒🛁🔌📶♻️ ❼

Services: 🛢️🔋📦

Within 3 miles: ℓ🛁🚽

Notes: 🐕 Dogs must be kept on leads. Shallow river for fishing & bathing, waymarked walks.

FROME   Map 4 ST74

Places to visit

Stourhead, STOURHEAD 01747 841152 www.nationaltrust.org.uk/main/w-stourhead

Dyrham Park, DYRHAM 0117 937 2501 www.nationaltrust.org.uk

Great for kids: Longleat Safari & Adventure Park, LONGLEAT 01985 844400 www.longleat.co.uk

▶▶▶ 84% Seven Acres Caravan & Camping Site *(ST777444)*

Seven Acres, West Woodlands BA11 5EQ
☎ **01373 464222**
dir: A361 (Frome bypass) onto B3092 at rdbt, 0.75m to site

✳ 🚐 fr £16 🚍 fr £16 ⛺ fr £12

Open Mar-Oct

A level meadowland site beside the shallow River Frome, with a bridge across to an adjacent field, and plenty of scope for families. The facilities are spotless. Set on the edge of the Longleat Estate with its stately home, wildlife safari park, and many other attractions. 3 acre site. 16 touring pitches. 16 hardstandings. Caravan pitches. Motorhome pitches. Tent pitches.

AA Pubs & Restaurants nearby: The George at Nunney, Nunney 01373 836458

Vobster Inn, Lower Vobster 01373 812920

Leisure: ⚠

Facilities: �️☺️🏵️✳️🛁🔌♻️

Services: ⚡

Within 3 miles: ⛳🎠ℓ🛁🚽↻

Notes: 🐕 Dogs must be kept on leads.

GLASTONBURY — Map 4 ST53

Places to visit

Lytes Cary Manor, KINGSDON 01458 224471
www.nationaltrust.org.uk/
main/w-lytescarymanor

Great for kids: Haynes International Motor
Museum, SPARKFORD 01963 440804
www.haynesmotormuseum.co.uk

PREMIER PARK

ENGLAND & OVERALL WINNER OF THE AA BEST CAMPSITE OF THE YEAR 2013

►►►►► 97% The Old Oaks Touring Park (ST521394)

Best of British

Wick Farm, Wick BA6 8JS
☎ 01458 831437
e-mail: info@theoldoaks.co.uk
dir: M5 junct 23, take A39 to Glastonbury, then
A361 towards Shepton Mallet

Open 8 Feb-18 Nov (rs Feb-Mar & Oct-Nov reduced
shop & reception hours) Last arrival 20.00hrs
(18.00hrs low season) Last departure noon

An exceptional adults-only park offering larger
than average landscaped pitches, impeccably
maintained grounds and wonderful views. The
perfect 'get away from it all' spot where you can
enjoy walking, cycling, fishing and touring or
simply relaxing amid the abundant wildlife. The
top class facilities include a well-stocked shop,
stocking locally sourced produce and home-baked
cakes, a new shower block which was opened in
the 2012 season, quality, accessible facilities,
Wi-fi, free walking and cycling maps, a daily
minibus service to nearby towns, a half-acre
fishing lake and even a hot doggy shower!
Camping cabins are available for hire. 10 acre
site. 100 touring pitches. 99 hardstandings.
Caravan pitches. Motorhome pitches. Tent pitches.
6 wooden pods. See also page 18.

AA Pubs & Restaurants nearby: Ring O'Bells,
Ashcott 01458 210232

Facilities: ⊌ ♟ ⊙ ☂ ☀ ☃ ♿ ⓢ ⓢ ♖ ♠ ⓦ🖬
🖥 ♻ ❶ **Services:** ♥ ⓢ 🔓 ⊘ Ⓣ 🖿 ♨
Within 3 miles: ♟ ⓢ ⓢ

Notes: Adults only. Group or block bookings
accepted only at owners' discretion. Dogs must be
kept on leads. Fishing, cycle hire, off licence, dog
sitting, local produce boxes.

►►►► 79% Isle of Avalon Touring Caravan Park (ST494397)

Godney Rd BA6 9AF
☎ 01458 833618
dir: M5 junct 23, A39 to outskirts of Glastonbury,
2nd exit signed Wells at B&Q rdbt, straight over
next rdbt, 1st exit at 3rd rdbt (B3151), site 200yds
on right

Open all year

Last arrival 21.00hrs Last departure 11.00hrs

A popular site on the south side of this historic
town and within easy walking distance of the town
centre. This level park, with a separate tent field,
offers a quiet environment in which to stay and
explore the many local attractions including the
Tor, Wells, Wookey Hole and Clarks Village. 8 acre
site. 120 touring pitches. 70 hardstandings.
Caravan pitches. Motorhome pitches. Tent pitches.

AA Pubs & Restaurants nearby: Ring O'Bells,
Ashcott 01458 210232

Leisure: ⚠

Facilities: ♟ ⊙ ☂ ☀ ♿ Ⓛ ⓢ ♖

Services: ♥ ⓢ 🔓 ⊘ Ⓣ 🖿 ♨

Within 3 miles: 🖺 ♟ ⓢ ⓢ Ⓤ

Notes: Cycle hire.

LANGPORT — Map 4 ST42

Places to visit

Montacute House, MONTACUTE 01935 823289
www.nationaltrust.org.uk

Lytes Cary Manor, KINGSDON 01458 224471
www.nationaltrust.org.uk/
main/w-lytescarymanor

Great for kids: Fleet Air Arm Museum,
YEOVILTON 01935 840565 www.fleetairarm.com

►►► 84% Thorney Lakes Caravan Park (ST430237)

GOLD

Thorney Lakes, Muchelney TA10 0DW
☎ 01458 250811
e-mail: enquiries@thorneylakes.co.uk
dir: From A303 at Podimore rdbt take A372 to
Langport. At Huish Episcopi Church turn left for
Muchelney. In 100yds left (signed Muchelney
& Crewkerne). Site 300yds after John Leach Pottery

* 🚐 £12-£20 🚐 £12-£20 ▲ £12-£20

Open Etr-Oct

A small, basic but very attractive park set in a
cider apple orchard, with coarse fishing in the
three well-stocked, on-site lakes. Excellent family
facilities are available. The famous John Leach
pottery shop is close at hand, and The Lowland
Games are held nearby in July. 6 acre site. 36
touring pitches. Caravan pitches. Motorhome
pitches. Tent pitches.

AA Pubs & Restaurants nearby: Rose & Crown,
Huish Episcopi 01458 250494

Old Pound Inn, Langport 01458 250469

Devonshire Arms, Long Sutton 01458 241271

Halfway House, Pitney 01458 252513

Facilities: ♟ ⊙ ☀ ⓦ🖬 ♻ ❶

Services: ♥

Within 3 miles: ♟ ♟ ⓢ

Notes: 🐾

LEISURE: ≋ Indoor swimming pool ≋ Outdoor swimming pool ⚠ Children's playground ⚑ Kid's club ♨ Tennis court ♦ Games room ▭ Separate TV room
♟ 9/18 hole golf course ⚑ Boats for hire 🎬 Cinema ♫ Entertainment ♟ Fishing ◉ Mini golf ≋ Watersports ♙ Gym ♦ Sports field Spa ∪ Stables
FACILITIES: ⊌ Bath ♟ Shower ⊙ Electric shaver ☂ Hairdryer ☀ Ice Pack Facility ♿ Disabled facilities ⓛ Public telephone ⓢ Shop on site or within 200yds
🏪 Mobile shop (calls at least 5 days a week) ♖ BBQ area ♠ Picnic area ⓦ🖬 Wi-fi ∍ Internet access ♻ Recycling ❶ Tourist info ♖ Dog exercise area

MARTOCK
Map 4 ST41

Places to visit

Montacute House, MONTACUTE 01935 823289
www.nationaltrust.org.uk

Montacute House, MONTACUTE 01935 823289
www.nationaltrust.org.uk

Great for kids: Fleet Air Arm Museum,
YEOVILTON 01935 840565 www.fleetairarm.com

►►►► 82% Southfork Caravan Park *(ST448188)*

Parrett Works TA12 6AE
☎ **01935 825661**

e-mail: southforkcaravans@btconnect.com
dir: *8m NW of Yeovil, 2m off A303. From E, take
exit after Cartgate rdbt. From W, 1st exit off rdbt
signed South Petherton, follow camping signs*

* 🚐 £17-£26 🚐 £17-£26 ▲ £13-£22

Open all year

Last arrival 22.30hrs Last departure noon

A neat, level mainly grass park in a quiet rural area, just outside the pretty village of Martock. Some excellent spacious hardstandings are available. The facilities are always spotless and the whole site well cared for by the friendly owners, who will ensure your stay is a happy one, a fact borne out by the many repeat customers. The park is unique in that it also has a fully-approved caravan repair and servicing centre with accessory shop. There are also static caravans available for hire. 2 acre site. 27 touring pitches. 2 hardstandings. Caravan pitches. Motorhome pitches. Tent pitches. 3 statics.

AA Pubs & Restaurants nearby: Nag's Head Inn, Martock 01935 823432

Ilchester Arms, Ilchester 01935 840220

Southfork Caravan Park

Leisure: 🅐
Facilities: 🏕☉🅟✳🕒🅖🚣♻🄋
Services: 🔌🅖🅿🚿🚽🧰
Within 3 miles: 🥾🎣🅖

Notes: Dogs must be kept on leads.

MINEHEAD
Map 3 SS94

Places to visit

West Somerset Railway,
MINEHEAD 01643 704996
www.west-somerset-railway.co.uk

Dunster Castle, DUNSTER 01643 821314
www.nationaltrust.org.uk

Great for kids: Tropiquaria Animal and Adventure Park, WASHFORD 01984 640688
www.tropiquaria.co.uk

►►► 76% Minehead & Exmoor Caravan & Camping Park *(SS950457)*

Porlock Rd TA24 8SW
☎ **01643 703074**

e-mail: enquiries@mineheadandexmoorcamping.co.uk
dir: *1m W of Minehead town centre, take A39 towards Porlock. Site on right*

* 🚐 £14-£20 🚐 £14-£20 ▲ £14-£20

Open Mar-Oct (rs Nov-Feb open certain weeks only (phone to check))

Last arrival 22.00hrs Last departure noon

A small terraced park on the edge of Exmoor, spread over five small paddocks and screened by the mature trees that surround it. The level pitches provide a comfortable space for each unit on this family-run park. The site is very convenient for visiting nearby Minehead (where there is a laundrette) or the Exmoor National Park. 3 acre site. 50 touring pitches. 10 hardstandings. 10 seasonal pitches. Caravan pitches. Motorhome pitches. Tent pitches.

AA Pubs & Restaurants nearby: Luttrell Arms, Dunster 01643 821555

The Smugglers, Blue Anchor 01984 640385

Leisure: 🅐
Facilities: 🏕☉🅟✳🕒🅖🚣♻🄋
Services: 🔌🅖🅿🧰
Within 3 miles: 🥾🎣🎣◎🚣🅖🅖

Notes: ⊗ No open fires or loud music. Dogs must be kept on leads.

OARE
Map 3 SS74

Places to visit

Marwood Hill Gardens, BARNSTAPLE
01271 342528 www.marwoodhillgarden.co.uk

Great for kids: Exmoor Zoological Park, BLACKMOOR GATE 01598 763352
www.exmoorzoo.co.uk

►►► 77% Cloud Farm *(SS794467)*

EX35 6NU
☎ **01598 741278**

e-mail: stay@cloudfarmcamping.co.uk
web: www.cloudfarmcamping.com
dir: *M5 junct 24, A39 towards Minehead & Porlock then Lynton. Left in 6.5m, follow signs to Oare, right, site signed*

🚐 🚐 ▲

Open all year

A traditional campsite set in a stunning location in Exmoor's Doone Valley. This quiet, sheltered site is arranged over four riverside fields, with fairly basic but modern toilet and shower facilities. It offers a good shop and a café serving all-day food including breakfasts, with a large garden for outdoor eating. This is a great place to camp in a special area of the country. There are also several self-catering cottages for hire. 110 acre site. 70 touring pitches. 6 hardstandings. Caravan pitches. Motorhome pitches. Tent pitches.

AA Pubs & Restaurants nearby: Rockford Inn, Brendon 01598 741214

Facilities: 🏕☉🅟✳🕒🅖🚣📶🖥♻🄋
Services: 🔌🅖🅿◎🧰🚚
Within 3 miles: 🎣🚣🅖↺

PORLOCK Map 3 SS84

Places to visit

West Somerset Railway,
MINEHEAD 01643 704996
www.west-somerset-railway.co.uk

Great for kids: Tropiquaria Animal and
Adventure Park, WASHFORD 01984 640688
www.tropiquaria.co.uk

AA CAMPING CARD SITE

PREMIER PARK

►►►►► 83% Porlock
Caravan Park *(SS882469)*

GOLD

TA24 8ND
☎ 01643 862269
e-mail: info@porlockcaravanpark.co.uk
dir: *Through village fork right signed Porlock Weir,
site on right*

🚐 🚊 Å

Open 15 Mar-Oct

Last arrival 20.00hrs Last departure 11.00hrs

A sheltered touring park, attractively laid-out in
the centre of lovely countryside, on the edge of the
village of Porlock. The famous Porlock Hill which
starts a few hundred yards from the site, takes you
to some spectacular parts of Exmoor with stunning
views. The toilet facilities are superb, and there's
a popular kitchen area with microwave and freezer.
Holiday statics for hire. 3 acre site. 40 touring
pitches. 14 hardstandings. Caravan pitches.
Motorhome pitches. Tent pitches. 55 statics.

AA Pubs & Restaurants nearby: Ship Inn, Porlock
01643 862507

The Bottom Ship, Porlock 01643 863288

Facilities: 🖲⊙🅿✳🕭🕔🚿🚻🚾 ♻ 🅯
Services: 🚽🗑🔋⊘🔌⛽
Within 3 miles: 🕸🎣🗑🛍🖲U
Notes: No fires. Dogs must be kept on leads.

►►►► 86% Burrowhayes Farm
Caravan & Camping Site & Riding
Stables *(SS897460)*

West Luccombe TA24 8HT
☎ 01643 862463
e-mail: info@burrowhayes.co.uk
dir: *A39 from Minehead towards Porlock for 5m.
Left at Red Post to Horner & West Luccombe, site
0.25m on right, immediately before humpback
bridge*

* 🚐 £15-£20 🚊 £15-£20 Å £12-£17

Open 15 Mar-Oct (rs Mar-Apr caravan hire &
riding only from Etr)

Last arrival 22.00hrs Last departure noon

A delightful site on the edge of Exmoor, sloping
gently down to Horner Water. The farm buildings
have been converted into riding stables, from
where escorted rides onto the moors can be taken,
and the excellent toilet facilities are housed in
timber-clad buildings. Hardstandings are
available. There are many walks into the
countryside that can be directly accessed from the
site. 8 acre site. 120 touring pitches. 10
hardstandings. Caravan pitches. Motorhome
pitches. Tent pitches. 20 statics.

AA Pubs & Restaurants nearby: Ship Inn, Porlock
01643 862507

The Bottom Ship, Porlock 01643 863288

Facilities: 🖲⊙🅿✳🕭🕔🚿🚻🚾 💻 ♻ 🅯
Services: 🚽🗑🔋⊘🔌⛽
Within 3 miles: 🕸🎣🖲🛍🖲U
Notes: Pony trekking.

PRIDDY Map 4 ST55

Places to visit

Glastonbury Abbey, GLASTONBURY
01458 832267 www.glastonburyabbey.com

The Helicopter Museum, WESTON-SUPER-MARE
01934 635227 www.helicoptermuseum.co.uk

Great for kids: Wookey Hole Caves & Papermill,
WOOKEY HOLE 01749 672243 www.wookey.co.uk

►►►► 86% Cheddar Mendip Heights
Camping & Caravanning Club Site
(ST522519)

Townsend BA5 3BP
☎ 01749 870241 & 0845 130 7633
dir: *From A39 take B3135 to Cheddar. Left in
4.5m. Site 200yds on right*

🚐 🚊 Å

Open 15 Mar-5 Nov

Last arrival 20.00hrs Last departure noon

A gently sloping site set high on the Mendip Hills
and surrounded by trees. This excellent campsite
offers really good facilities, including top notch
family rooms and private cubicles which are
spotlessly maintained. Fresh bread is baked daily
and available from the well-stocked shop. The site
is well positioned for visiting local attractions
such as Cheddar, Wookey Hole, Wells and
Glastonbury, and is popular with walkers. Self-
catering caravans are now available for hire. 4.5
acre site. 90 touring pitches. 37 hardstandings.
Caravan pitches. Motorhome pitches. Tent pitches.
2 statics.

AA Pubs & Restaurants nearby: Wookey Hole Inn,
Wookey Hole 01749 676677

The Burcott Inn, Wookey 01749 673874

Leisure: ⚠
Facilities: 🖲⊙🅿✳🕭🕔🚿🚻🚾 ♻ 🅯
Services: 🚽🗑🔋⊘🔌⛽
Within 3 miles: 🕭🛍U
Notes: Site gates closed 23.00hrs-07.00hrs. Dogs
must be kept on leads.

SHEPTON MALLET — Map 4 ST64

Places to visit

Stourhead, STOURHEAD 01747 841152
www.nationaltrust.org.uk/main/w-stourhead

Westwood Manor, WESTWOOD 01225 863374
www.nationaltrust.org.uk

Great for kids: Longleat Safari & Adventure Park, LONGLEAT 01985 844400
www.longleat.co.uk

AA CAMPING CARD SITE

▶▶ 95% Greenacres Camping

(ST553417)

Barrow Ln, North Wootton BA4 4HL
☎ 01749 890497

e-mail: stay@greenacres-camping.co.uk
dir: Approx halfway between Glastonbury & Shepton Mallet on A361 turn at Steanbow Farm signed North Wootton. Or from A39 between Upper Coxley & Wells turn at Brownes Garden Centre into Woodford Ln. Follow North Wootton & site signs

* ⌂ £17 ▲ £17

Open Apr-Sep

Last arrival 21.00hrs Last departure 11.00hrs

An immaculately maintained site peacefully set within sight of Glastonbury Tor. Mainly family orientated with many thoughtful extra facilities provided, and there is plenty of space for children to play games in a very safe environment. There is even a 'glow worm safari' at certain times of the year. Facilities are exceptionally clean. 4.5 acre site. 40 touring pitches. Motorhome pitches. Tent pitches.

AA Pubs & Restaurants nearby: Bull Terrier, Croscombe 01749 343658

George Inn, Croscombe 01749 342306

Leisure:
Facilities:
Services:
Within 3 miles:
Notes: No caravans or large motorhomes. Free use of fridges & freezers, book library.

SPARKFORD — Map 4 ST62

Places to visit

Lytes Cary Manor, KINGSDON 01458 224471
www.nationaltrust.org.uk/main/w-lytescarymanor

Montacute House, MONTACUTE 01935 823289
www.nationaltrust.org.uk

▶▶▶▶ 82% Long Hazel Park

(ST602262)

High St BA22 7JH
☎ 01963 440002

e-mail: longhazelpark@hotmail.com
dir: Exit A303 at Hazlegrove rdbt, follow signs for Sparkford. Site 400yds on left

⌂ £18-£22 ⌂ £18-£22 ▲ £18-£22

Open all year

Last arrival 21.00hrs Last departure 11.00hrs

A very neat, adults-only park next to the village inn in the high street. This attractive park is run by friendly owners to a very good standard. Many of the spacious pitches have hardstandings. There are also luxury lodges on site for hire or purchase. 3.5 acre site. 50 touring pitches. 30 hardstandings. 21 seasonal pitches. Caravan pitches. Motorhome pitches. Tent pitches. 1 static.

AA Pubs & Restaurants nearby: Walnut Tree, West Camel 01935 851292

Queens Arms, Corton Denham 01963 220317

Facilities:
Services:
Within 3 miles:
Notes: Adults only. Dogs must be kept on leads and exercised off site. Picnic tables available, camping spares.

TAUNTON — Map 4 ST22

Places to visit

Hestercombe Gardens, TAUNTON 01823 413923
www.hestercombe.com

Barrington Court, BARRINGTON 01460 241938
www.nationaltrust.org.uk

Great for kids: Sunnycroft, WELLINGTON 01952 242884
www.nationaltrust.org.uk/sunnycroft

▶▶▶▶ 84% Cornish Farm Touring Park (ST235217)

Shoreditch TA3 7BS
☎ 01823 327746

e-mail: info@cornishfarm.com
web: www.cornishfarm.com
dir: M5 junct 25 towards Taunton. Left at lights. 3rd left into Ilminster Rd (follow Corfe signs). Right at rdbt, left at next rdbt. Right at T-junct, left into Killams Dr, 2nd left into Killams Ave. Over motorway bridge. Site on left, take 2nd entrance

* ⌂ £14-£18 ⌂ £14-£18 ▲ £14-£18

Open all year

Last arrival anytime Last departure 11.30hrs

This smart park provides really top quality facilities throughout. Although only two miles from Taunton, it is set in open countryside and is a very convenient base for visiting the many attractions of the area such as Clarks Village, Glastonbury and Cheddar Gorge. Also makes an excellent base for watching county cricket at the nearby Somerset County Ground. 3.5 acre site. 50 touring pitches. 25 hardstandings. Caravan pitches. Motorhome pitches. Tent pitches.

AA Pubs & Restaurants nearby: Hatch Inn, Hatch Beauchamp 01823 480245

Facilities:
Services:
Within 3 miles:
Notes: Dogs must be kept on leads.

SERVICES: Electric hook up Launderette Licensed bar Calor Gas Camping Gaz Toilet fluid Café/Restaurant Fast Food/Takeaway Battery charging Baby care Motorvan service point **ABBREVIATIONS:** BH/bank hols-bank holidays Etr-Easter Whit-Whitsun dep-departure fr-from hrs-hours m-mile mdnt-midnight rdbt-roundabout rs-restricted service wk-week wknd-weekend No credit cards no dogs

See page 7 for details of the AA Camping Card Scheme

TAUNTON *continued*

►►► 81% Ashe Farm Camping & Caravan Site *(ST279229)*

Thornfalcon TA3 5NW
☎ 01823 443764 & 07891 989482
e-mail: info@ashefarm.co.uk
dir: *M5 junct 25, A358 E for 2.5m. Right at Nags Head pub. Site 0.25m on right*

Open Apr-Oct

Last arrival 22.00hrs Last departure noon

A well-screened site surrounded by mature trees and shrubs, with two large touring fields. A modern facilities block includes toilets and showers plus a separate laundry room. Not far from the bustling market town of Taunton, and handy for both south and north coasts. Also makes a good stop over for people travelling on the nearby M5. 7 acre site. 30 touring pitches. 11 hardstandings. Caravan pitches. Motorhome pitches. Tent pitches. 3 statics.

AA Pubs & Restaurants nearby: Hatch Inn, Hatch Beauchamp 01823 480245

Willow Tree Restaurant, Taunton 01823 352835

Leisure: ⋀ ⌇
Facilities: ⬏ ⊙ ⌱ ⚹ ⛛ ⤳ ♻ ❶
Services: ⬚ ⬛
Within 3 miles: ⬒ Ḣ ⤳ ⬚ ⬛ ∪
Notes: ⊘ No camp fires. Baby changing facilities.

►►► 86% Home Farm Holiday Centre *(ST106432)*

St Audries Bay TA4 4DP
☎ 01984 632487
e-mail: dib@homefarmholidaycentre.co.uk
dir: *A39 for 17m to West Quantoxhead, B3191 after garage in village (signed Doniford), 1st right in 0.25m*

🚐 £12-£27.50 🚙 £12-£27.50 ⛺ £12-£27.50

Open all year (rs Nov-1 Mar camping, shop & bar closed)

Last arrival dusk Last departure noon

In a hidden valley beneath the Quantock Hills, this park overlooks its own private beach. The atmosphere is friendly and quiet, and there are lovely sea views from the level pitches. Flowerbeds, woodland walks, and a Koi carp pond all enhance this very attractive site, along with a lovely indoor swimming pool and a beer garden. 45 acre site. 40 touring pitches. 35 hardstandings. Caravan pitches. Motorhome pitches. Tent pitches. 230 statics.

AA Pubs & Restaurants nearby: The Smugglers, Blue Anchor 01984 640385

Leisure: ⬕ ⋀
Facilities: ⬏ ⊙ ⌱ ⚹ ⛛ ⦾ ⬚ ⤳ ♻ ❶
Services: ⬚ ⬛ ⬛ ⬛ ⬛ ⊤
Within 3 miles: ⤳ ⬚ ⬛
Notes: No cars by caravans or tents. No noise after mdnt. Dogs must be kept on leads. Site open all year for touring caravans.

🏠 ⓤ NEW Doniford Bay Holiday Park *(ST093432)*

TA23 0TJ
☎ 01984 632423
e-mail: donifordbay@haven.com
web: www.haven.com/donifordbay
dir: *M5 junct 23, A38 towards Bridgwater, A39 towards Minehead. 15m, at West Quantoxhead, right after St Audries garage. Park 1m on right*

Open Mar-Oct

Doniford Bay Holiday Park is a lively woodland park located above a rocky bay on the glorious north Somerset coast, with views of the Quantock Hills and Exmoor. Expect fun evening entertainment and excellent activities for children. There are a good range of holiday caravans and apartments. At the time of going to press the quality rating for this site had not been confirmed. For up-to-date information please see the AA website: theAA.com.

Change over day: Mon, Fri, Sat **Arrival & departure times:** Please contact the site

Statics 143 **Sleeps** 6-8 **Bedrms** 2-3 **Bathrms** 1-2 **Toilets** 1-2 **Freezer** **TV** Sky/FTV **Elec** included **Gas** included **Grass area** **Parking**

Children ⬩⬥ **Cots** **Dogs** Max 2 on leads No dangerous dogs (see page 12)

Leisure: ⬕ ⬔ ⬗ ⋀

AA Pubs & Restaurants nearby: The Hood Arms, Kilve 01278 741210

see advert on page 281

WELLINGTON — Map 3 ST12

Places to visit

Sunnycroft, WELLINGTON 01952 242884
www.nationaltrust.org.uk/sunnycroft

Hestercombe Gardens, TAUNTON 01823 413923
www.hestercombe.com

Great for kids: Diggerland, CULLOMPTON
0871 227 7007 www.diggerland.com

►►►► 82% Greenacres Touring Park (ST156001)

Haywards Ln, Chelston TA21 9PH
☎ 01823 652844

e-mail: enquiries@wellington.co.uk
dir: M5 junct 26, right at rdbt signed Wellington, approx 1.5m. At Chelston rdbt, take 1st left, signed A38 West Buckland Rd. In 500mtrs follow sign for site

Open Apr-end Sep

Last arrival 20.00hrs Last departure 11.00hrs

This attractively landscaped adults-only park is situated close to the Somerset/Devon border in a peaceful setting with great views of the Blackdown and Quantock Hills. It is in a very convenient location for overnight stays, being just one and half miles from the M5. This park is also well positioned for visiting both the north and south coasts, and it is also close to a local bus route. It has excellent facilities, which are spotlessly clean and well maintained. 2.5 acre site. 40 touring pitches. 30 hardstandings. Caravan pitches. Motorhome pitches.

AA Pubs & Restaurants nearby: White Horse Inn, Bradford-on-Tone 01823 461239

Facilities: ⚫⊙♿♨🐕♻ℹ
Services: ⚡ Within 3 miles: ♿🏇🎣🛒🏪⛪
Notes: Adults only. No RVs. Dogs must be kept on leads.

►►► 79% Gamlins Farm Caravan Park (ST083195)

Gamlins Farm House, Greenham TA21 0LZ
☎ 01823 672859 & 07967 683738

e-mail: nataliehowe@hotmail.com
dir: M5 junct 26, A38 towards Tiverton & Exeter. 5m, right for Greenham, site 1m on right

🚐 £10-£16 🚐 £10-£16 ▲ £5-£16

Open Mar-Oct

A well-planned site in a secluded position with panoramic views. The friendly owners keep the toilet facilities to a good standard of cleanliness. 4 acre site. 35 touring pitches. 6 hardstandings. Caravan pitches. Motorhome pitches. Tent pitches. 4 statics.

AA Pubs & Restaurants nearby: White Horse Inn, Bradford-on-Tone 01823 461239

Leisure: 🎣
Facilities: ⚫⊙♿♨☕♿🐕♻🛜📺♻ℹ
Services: ⚡🔌🛒 Within 3 miles: ♿🏇🛒🏪⛪
Notes: No loud noise after 22.00hrs. Dogs must be kept on leads. Free coarse fishing on site.

WELLS — Map 4 ST54

Places to visit

Glastonbury Abbey, GLASTONBURY 01458 832267
www.glastonburyabbey.com

PREMIER PARK

►►►►► 82% Wells Holiday Park (ST531459)

Haybridge BA5 1AJ
☎ 01749 676869
e-mail: jason@wellsholidaypark.co.uk
dir: A38 then follow signs for Axbridge, Cheddar & Wells

🚐🚐▲

Open all year

Last arrival 20.00hrs Last departure noon

This well established, adults-only holiday park has first-class toilet facilities and many hardstandings, all with electricity. A restful park set in countryside on the outskirts of Wells, it is within easy walking distance of the city, with its spectacular cathedral and Bishop's Palace. Cheddar Gorge and Caves, Bath, Bristol, Weston-Super-Mare, Wookey Hole and Glastonbury are all within easy driving distance. Holiday cottages are available for hire. 7.5 acre site. 72 touring pitches. 54 hardstandings. 20 seasonal pitches.

Caravan pitches. Motorhome pitches. Tent pitches. 20 bell tents/yurts.

AA Pubs & Restaurants nearby: City Arms, Wells 01749 673916

Fountains Inn & Boxer's Restaurant, Wells 01749 672317

Goodfellows, Wells 01749 673866

The Old Spot, Wells 01749 689099

Wells Holiday Park

Facilities: ⚫⊙♿♨☕♿🛒🛜♻ℹ
Services: ⚡🔌🛒♻📺🏪⛪♻
Within 3 miles: ♿🏇🎣◎🛒⛪
Notes: Adults only. No cars by tents. Dogs must be kept on leads. Pétanque, beauty salon.

►► 84% Homestead Park (ST532474)

Wookey Hole BA5 1BW
☎ 01749 673022
e-mail: homesteadpark@onetel.com
dir: 0.5m NW off A371 (Wells to Cheddar road). (NB weight limit on bridge into touring area now 1 tonne)

* ▲ £16-£19

Open Etr-Sep

Last arrival 20.00hrs Last departure noon

This attractive, small site for tents only is set on a wooded hillside and meadowland with access to the river and nearby Wookey Hole. This park is for adults only and the statics are residential caravans. 2 acre site. 30 touring pitches. Tent pitches. 28 statics.

AA Pubs & Restaurants nearby: City Arms, Wells 01749 673916

Fountains Inn & Boxer's Restaurant, Wells 01749 672317

Goodfellows, Wells 01749 673866

The Old Spot, Wells 01749 689099

Facilities: ⚫⊙♿♨ℹ **Services:** 🛒♻🏪
Within 3 miles: 🏇🎣♿🛒⛪
Notes: Adults only. Dogs must be kept on leads.

WESTON-SUPER-MARE — Map 4 ST36

Places to visit

North Somerset Museum,
WESTON-SUPER-MARE 01934 621028
www.n-somerset.gov.uk/museum

Great for kids: The Helicopter Museum,
WESTON-SUPER-MARE 01934 635227
www.helicoptermuseum.co.uk

►►► 90% Country View Holiday Park

(ST335647)

Sand Rd, Sand Bay BS22 9UJ
☎ 01934 627595
e-mail: info@cvhp.co.uk
dir: *M5 junct 21, A370 towards Weston-Super-Mare. Immediately into left lane, follow Kewstoke/Sand Bay signs. Straight over 3 rdbts onto Lower Norton Ln. At Sand Bay right into Sand Rd, site on right*

* 🚐 £15-£25 🚐 £15-£25 ▲ £15-£25

Open Mar-Jan

Last arrival 20.00hrs Last departure noon

A pleasant open site in a rural area a few hundred yards from Sandy Bay and the beach. The park is also well placed for energetic walks along the coast at either end of the beach and is only a short drive away from Weston-Super-Mare. There is now a completely new touring section for tents, caravans and motorhomes with a new toilet and shower block. There are 14 hardstanding pitches plus grass pitches all with electricity. The facilities are excellent and well maintained. 8 acre site. 120 touring pitches. 120 hardstandings. 90 seasonal pitches. Caravan pitches. Motorhome pitches. Tent pitches. 65 statics.

AA Pubs & Restaurants nearby: The Cove, Weston-Super-Mare 01934 418217

Leisure: 🏊🎢🎡🎣🎵
Facilities: 📷⊙🌡🖊✳️♿🕔🚿📶💻♻️ℹ️
Services: 🔌🗄🚫🚽T
Within 3 miles: ⚓🏇🏉🎣🎯◎⛷🚴🛝🐴↻

Notes: Dogs must be kept on leads.

►►► 82% West End Farm Caravan & Camping Park (ST354600)

Locking BS24 8RH
☎ 01934 822529
e-mail: robin@westendfarm.org
dir: *M5 junct 21 onto A370. Follow International Helicopter Museum signs. Right at rdbt, follow signs to site*

* 🚐 £14.50-£22.50 🚐 £14.50-£22.50
▲ £14.50-£22.50

Open all year

Last arrival 21.00hrs Last departure noon

A spacious and well laid out park bordered by hedges, with good landscaping, and well kept facilities. Fully serviced pitches are available. It is handily located next to a helicopter museum, and offers good access to Weston-Super-Mare and the Mendips. 10 acre site. 75 touring pitches. 10 hardstandings. 30 seasonal pitches. Caravan pitches. Motorhome pitches. Tent pitches. 11 statics.

AA Pubs & Restaurants nearby: The Cove, Weston-Super-Mare 01934 418217

Leisure: ☺
Facilities: 📷⊙♿🖊🚿♻️ℹ️
Services: 🔌🗄📶♻⤵
Within 3 miles: ⚓🏇🏉🎣◎⛷🚴🛝🐴↻
Notes: No noise after 22.00hrs. Dogs must be kept on leads.

WINSFORD — Map 3 SS93

Places to visit

Dunster Castle, DUNSTER 01643 821314
www.nationaltrust.org.uk

Cleeve Abbey, WASHFORD 01984 640377
www.english-heritage.org.uk

Great for kids: Tropiquaria Animal and Adventure Park, WASHFORD 01984 640688
www.tropiquaria.co.uk

►►► 79% Halse Farm Caravan & Camping Park

(SS894344)

TA24 7JL
☎ 01643 851259
e-mail: info@halsefarm.co.uk
web: www.halsefarm.co.uk
dir: *Signed from A396 at Bridgetown. In Winsford turn left, bear left past pub. 1m up hill, entrance on left immediately after cattle grid*

🚐 🚐 ▲

Open 16 Mar-Oct

Last arrival 22.00hrs Last departure noon

A peaceful little site on Exmoor overlooking a wooded valley with glorious views. This moorland site is quite remote, but it provides good modern toilet facilities which are kept immaculately clean. This is a good base for exploring the Exmoor National Park and Minehead, Porlock and Lynton are only a short drive away. 3 acre site. 44 touring pitches. Caravan pitches. Motorhome pitches. Tent pitches.

AA Pubs & Restaurants nearby: Crown Hotel, Exford 01643 831554

Leisure: 🎢
Facilities: 📷⊙🌡✳️♿🕔🖊📶♻️ℹ️
Services: 🔌🗄🔋♻
Within 3 miles: 🖊🛝↻
Notes: Dogs must be kept on leads.

LEISURE: 🏊 Indoor swimming pool 🏊 Outdoor swimming pool 🎢 Children's playground 🏌 Kid's club 🎾 Tennis court 🎱 Games room 📺 Separate TV room ⛳ 9/18 hole golf course 🚣 Boats for hire 🎬 Cinema 🎵 Entertainment 🎣 Fishing ◎ Mini golf 🏄 Watersports 🏋 Gym 🏟 Sports field Spa ↻ Stables
FACILITIES: 🛁 Bath 🚿 Shower ⊙ Electric shaver 🖊 Hairdryer ✳️ Ice Pack Facility ♿ Disabled facilities 🕔 Public telephone 🏪 Shop on site or within 200yds 🚙 Mobile shop (calls at least 5 days a week) 🍖 BBQ area 🏕 Picnic area 📶 Wi-fi 💻 Internet access ♻️ Recycling ℹ️ Tourist info 🐕 Dog exercise area

WIVELISCOMBE Map 3 ST02

Places to visit

Sunnycroft, WELLINGTON 01952 242884
www.nationaltrust.org.uk/sunnycroft

Hestercombe Gardens, TAUNTON 01823 413923
www.hestercombe.com

Great for kids: Tropiquaria Animal and
Adventure Park, WASHFORD 01984 640688
www.tropiquaria.co.uk

PREMIER PARK

►►►►► 86% Waterrow
Touring Park (ST053251)

 Best of British

TA4 2AZ
☎ 01984 623464
e-mail: info@waterrowpark.co.uk
dir: *M5 junct 25, A358 (signed Minehead)
bypassing Taunton, B3227 through Wiveliscombe.
Site in 3m at Waterrow, 0.25m past Rock Inn*

🚐 �90 Å

Open all year

Last arrival 19.00hrs Last departure 11.30hrs

This really delightful park for adults only has
spotless facilities and plenty of spacious
hardstandings. The River Tone runs along a valley
beneath the park, accessed by steps to a nature
area created by the owners, where fly-fishing is
permitted. Watercolour painting workshops and
other activities are available, and the local pub is
a short walk away. There is also a bus stop just
outside of the site. 6 acre site. 45 touring pitches.
38 hardstandings. Caravan pitches. Motorhome
pitches. Tent pitches.

AA Pubs & Restaurants nearby: White Hart,
Wiveliscombe 01984 623344

Rock Inn, Waterrow 01984 623293

Three Horseshoes, Langley Marsh 01984 623763

Facilities: 🅟⊙🅟⁕🅰🅒🅝🛒💻♻🅘
Services: 🅔🗑🔋🅣📥⚡
Within 3 miles: 🖊🏧🔢
Notes: Adults only. No gazebos, max 2 dogs per
unit. Dogs must be kept on leads. Frozen meals
available, watercolour painting holidays.

YEOVIL Map 4 ST51

Places to visit

Montacute House, MONTACUTE 01935 823289
www.nationaltrust.org.uk

Lytes Cary Manor, KINGSDON 01458 224471
www.nationaltrust.org.uk/
main/w-lytescarymanor

Great for kids: Fleet Air Arm Museum,
YEOVILTON 01935 840565 www.fleetairarm.com

►► 82% **Halfway Caravan & Camping
Park** (ST530195)

Trees Cottage, Halfway, Ilchester Rd BA22 8RE
☎ 01935 840342
e-mail: halfwaycaravanpark@earthlink.net
web: www.halfwaycaravanpark.com
dir: *On A37 between Ilchester & Yeovil*

🚐 £10-£12.50 �90 £10-£12.50 Å £10-£12.50

Open Apr-Oct

Last arrival 19.00hrs Last departure noon

An attractive little park near the Somerset and
Dorset border, and next to the Halfway House pub
and restaurant, which also has excellent AA-
graded accommodation. It overlooks a fishing lake
and is surrounded by attractive countryside. Dogs
are welcome here. 2 acre site. 20 touring pitches.
10 hardstandings. Caravan pitches. Motorhome
pitches. Tent pitches.

AA Pubs & Restaurants nearby: Masons Arms,
Yeovil 01935 862591

Helyar Arms, East Coker 01935 862332

Facilities: 🛁🅟🅒🅘
Services: 🅔🍴
Within 3 miles: ⚓🅗🖊🏧🔢
Notes: 🈲 Last arrival 21.00hrs on Fri. Dogs must
be kept on leads.

STAFFORDSHIRE

CHEADLE Map 10 SK04

Places to visit

Wedgwood Visitor Centre, STOKE-ON-TRENT
01782 282986
www.wedgwoodvisitorcentre.com

The Potteries Museum & Art Gallery,
STOKE-ON-TRENT 01782 232323
www.stoke.gov.uk/museums

Great for kids: Alton Towers Resort, ALTON
0871 222 3330 www.altontowers.com

Etruria Industrial Museum, STOKE-ON-TRENT
01782 233144 www.stokemuseums.org.uk

►►►► 73% **Quarry Walk Park**

(SK045405)

**Coppice Ln, Croxden Common, Freehay
ST10 1RQ**
☎ 01538 723412
e-mail: quarry@quarrywalkpark.co.uk
dir: *From A522 (Uttoxeter-Cheadle road) turn at
Crown Inn at Mabberley signed Freehay. In 1m at
rdbt by Queen pub turn to Great Gate. Site signed
on right in 1.25m*

🚐 �90 Å

Open all year

Last arrival 18.00hrs Last departure 11.00hrs

A pleasant park, close to Alton Towers, developed
in an old quarry with well-screened pitches, all
with water and electricity, and mature trees and
shrubs, which enhance the peaceful ambience of
the park. There are seven glades of varying sizes
used exclusively for tents, one with ten electric
hook-ups. There are timber lodges for hire, each
with its own hot tub. 46 acre site. 16 touring
pitches. 16 hardstandings. 13 seasonal pitches.
Caravan pitches. Motorhome pitches. Tent pitches.
1 wooden pod.

AA Pubs & Restaurants nearby: The Queens at
Freehay, Cheadle 01538 722383

Leisure: 🄰
Facilities: 🅟⊙🅟⁕🅒🅰🅝🛒💻♻🅘
Services: 🅔🗑🔋🅓
Within 3 miles: 🅗🖊◎🏧🔢∪
Notes: No cars by tents. Dogs must be kept on
leads.

SERVICES: 🅔 Electric hook up 🗑 Launderette 🍴 Licensed bar 🔋 Calor Gas ⚡ Camping Gaz 🅣 Toilet fluid 🍴 Café/Restaurant 🍔 Fast Food/Takeaway 📥 Battery charging
📥 Baby care ⚡ Motorvan service point **ABBREVIATIONS:** BH/bank hols-bank holidays Etr-Easter Whit-Whitsun dep-departure fr-from hrs-hours m-mile mdnt-midnight
rdbt-roundabout rs-restricted service wk-week wknd-weekend 🈲 No credit cards 🈲 no dogs See page 7 for details of the AA Camping Card Scheme

Suffolk

Suffolk's superb Heritage Coast is the jewel in the county's crown.
The beaches, often windswept and completely deserted, run for
miles, with the waves of the North Sea breaking beside them in
timeless fashion. But it is an ecologically fragile coastline with much
of it claimed by the sea over the years. The poet, George Crabbe,
perfectly summed up the fate of this area when he wrote:
'The ocean roar whose greedy waves devour the lessening shore.'

With its huge skies and sense of space and solitude, Suffolk's crumbling, time-ravaged coastline is highly evocative and wonderfully atmospheric. This is where rivers wind lazily to the sea and 18th-century smugglers hid from the excise men.

Suffolk's coast

Between Felixstowe and Lowestoft the coast offers something for everyone. For example, Orford Ness is a unique visitor attraction where ecology meets military history. This internationally important nature reserve - home to many breeding birds, including the avocet – was once the setting for a highly secret military testing site. These days, Orford Ness is managed by the National Trust.

Aldeburgh is all about the arts and in particular the Aldeburgh Music Festival. Benjamin Britten lived at nearby Snape and wrote *Peter Grimes* here. The Suffolk coast is where both the sea and the natural landscape have influenced generations of writers, artists and musicians.

The charm of Southwold, further north, is undimmed and reminiscent of a fashionable, genteel seaside resort from a bygone era. ▶

Inland towns and villages

But there is much more to Suffolk than its scenic coastline. Far away to the west lies Newmarket and the world of horseracing. Apart from its equine associations, the town boasts some handsome buildings and memorable views. Palace House in Palace Street was the home of Charles II while the High Street is the setting for the National Horseracing Museum, illustrating how this great sporting tradition has evolved over the last 400 years.

Bury St Edmunds, Sudbury and Ipswich also feature prominently on the tourist trail and the county's smaller towns offer a wealth of attractions, too. With their picturesque, timber-framed houses, Lavenham, Kersey and Debenham are a reminder of Suffolk's key role in the wool industry and the vast wealth it yielded for the merchants.

Constable's legacy

It was the artist John Constable who really put Suffolk's delightful countryside on the map. Son of a wealthy miller, Constable spent much of his early life sketching in the vicinity of Dedham Vale. Situated on the River Stour at Flatford,

● Sea gulls, Aldeburgh

Constable's mill is now a major tourist attraction in the area but a close look at the surroundings confirms rural Suffolk is little changed since the family lived here. Constable himself maintained that the Suffolk countryside *'made me a painter and I am grateful.'*

Walking and Cycling

With 3,300 miles of rights of way, walkers in the county have plenty of choice. There are many publicised trails and waymarked routes, including the Angles Way which runs along Norfolk and Suffolk's boundary in the glorious Waveney Valley. Hard to beat is the county's famous Suffolk Coast Path which runs for 50 miles (80km) between Felixstowe and Lowestoft and is the best way to explore Suffolk's dramatic eastern extremity.

The county offers plenty of potential for cycling, too. There is the Heart of Suffolk Cycle Route, which extends for 78 miles (125km), while the National Byway, a 4,000-mile (6,436km) cycle route around Britain takes in part of Suffolk and is a highly enjoyable way to tour the county.

Festivals and Events

- The popular Aldeburgh Literary Festival takes place in March.
- The Alde Valley Spring Festival is staged in April and May with a 4-week celebration of food, farming, landscape and the arts. The venue is Great Glemham near Saxmundham.
- There is the Lattitude Music Festival at Southwold in July.
- The 3-day Christmas Fayre at Bury St Edmunds showcases the ancient town and in recent years has attracted 70,000 visitors.

● Beach huts at Southwold

● River Stour, Dedham

SUFFOLK

See Walk 10 in the Walks & Cycle Rides section at the end of the guide

BUCKLESHAM   Map 13 TM24

Places to visit

Ipswich Museum, IPSWICH 01473 433550
www.ipswich.gov.uk

Christchurch Mansion, IPSWICH 01473 433554
www.ipswich.gov.uk

AA CAMPING CARD SITE

►►►► 87% Westwood Caravan Park

(TM253411)

Old Felixstowe Rd IP10 0BN
☎ 01473 659637 & 07814 570973
e-mail:
caroline.pleace@westwoodcaravanpark.co.uk
dir: *A14 towards Felixstowe, after junct 58
take 1st exit signed to Kirton. Follow road to
Bucklesham for 1.5m. Site on right*

* ⊞ £18-£20 ⊟ £18-£20 ▲ £18-£20

Open Mar-15 Jan

Last arrival 22.00hrs Last departure 15.00hrs

This site is in the heart of rural Suffolk in an idyllic, peaceful setting. All buildings are of traditional Suffolk style, and the toilet facilities are of outstanding quality. There is also a spacious room for disabled visitors, and plenty of space for children to play. 4.5 acre site. 100 touring pitches. 50 hardstandings. 45 seasonal pitches. Caravan pitches. Motorhome pitches. Tent pitches.

AA Pubs & Restaurants nearby: Ship Inn, Levington 01473 659573

Mariners, Ipswich 01473 289748

The Eaterie at Salthouse Harbour Hotel, Ipswich 01473 226789

Leisure: ⚙ ⚲

Facilities: ⚲ ☉ ⚒ ⚙ ⚙ ⚒ ⚒ wifi ♻ ❶

Services: ⚙ ⚙ ⚙ ⚒ ⚙ ⚙ ⚒

Within 3 miles: ⚙ ⚙ ⚙ ⚙ ⚙

Notes: Dogs must be kept on leads.

BUNGAY   Map 13 TM38

►►► 70% Outney Meadow Caravan Park *(TM333905)*

Outney Meadow NR35 1HG
☎ 01986 892338
e-mail: c.r.hancy@ukgateway.net
dir: *At Bungay, site signed from rdbt junction of
A143 & A144*

* ⊞ £14-£20 ⊟ £14-£20 ▲ £14-£20

Open Mar-Oct

Last arrival 21.00hrs Last departure 16.00hrs

Three pleasant grassy areas beside the River Waveney, with screened pitches. The central toilet block offers good modern facilities, especially in the ladies, and is open at all times. The views from the site across the wide flood plain could be straight out of a Constable painting. Canoeing and boating, coarse fishing and cycling are all available here. 6 acre site. 45 touring pitches. 8 hardstandings. 8 seasonal pitches. Caravan pitches. Motorhome pitches. Tent pitches. 30 statics.

Facilities: ⚲ ☉ ⚙ ⚒ ⚙ ♻ ❶

Services: ⚙ ⚙ ⚙ ⚒ ⚙ ⚙

Within 3 miles: ⚙ ⚒ ⚙ ⚙ ⚙ ⚙

Notes: Dogs must be kept on leads. Boat, canoe & cycle hire.

BURY ST EDMUNDS   Map 13 TL86

Places to visit

Moyse's Hall Museum, BURY ST EDMUNDS 01284 706183 www.moyseshall.org

Ickworth House, Park & Gardens, HORRINGER 01284 735270 www.nationaltrust.org.uk/ickworth

Great for kids: National Horseracing Museum and Tours, NEWMARKET 01638 667333 www.nhrm.co.uk

►►►► 85% Dell Touring Park

(TL928640)

Beyton Rd, Thurston IP31 3RB
☎ 01359 270121
e-mail: thedellcaravanpark@btinternet.com
dir: *Signed from A14 at Beyton/Thurston (4m E of
Bury St Edmunds) & from A143 at Barton/Thurston*

⊞ £16-£20 ⊟ £16 ▲ £13-£24

Open all year

Last arrival 20.00hrs Last departure noon

A small site with enthusiastic owners that has been developed to a high specification. Set in a quiet spot with lots of mature trees, the quality purpose-built toilet facilities include family rooms, dishwashing and laundry. This is an ideal base for exploring this picturesque area. 6 acre site. 50 touring pitches. 12 hardstandings. Caravan pitches. Motorhome pitches. Tent pitches.

AA Pubs & Restaurants nearby: Old Cannon Brewery, Bury St Edmunds 01284 768769

Linden Tree, Bury St Edmunds 01284 754600

Maison Bleue, Bury St Edmunds 01284 760623

Leaping Hare Restaurant & Country Store, Bury St Edmunds 01359 250287

Facilities: ⚙ ⚲ ☉ ⚙ ⚒ ⚙ ⚙ wifi ♻ ❶

Services: ⚙ ⚙ ⚙ ⚙

Within 3 miles: ⚙ ⚙

Notes: No footballs, no noise after 23.00hrs. Dogs must be kept on leads.

LEISURE: ⚙ Indoor swimming pool ⚙ Outdoor swimming pool ⚙ Children's playground ⚙ Kid's club ⚙ Tennis court ⚙ Games room ⚙ Separate TV room ⚙ 9/18 hole golf course ⚙ Boats for hire ⚙ Cinema ⚙ Entertainment ⚙ Fishing ⚙ Mini golf ⚙ Watersports ⚙ Gym ⚙ Sports field Spa ⚙ Stables
FACILITIES: ⚙ Bath ⚙ Shower ☉ Electric shaver ⚙ Hairdryer ⚙ Ice Pack Facility ⚙ Disabled facilities ⚙ Public telephone ⚙ Shop on site or within 200yds ⚙ Mobile shop (calls at least 5 days a week) ⚙ BBQ area ⚙ Picnic area wifi Wi-fi ⚙ Internet access ♻ Recycling ❶ Tourist info ⚙ Dog exercise area

DUNWICH Map 13 TM47

AA CAMPING CARD SITE

►► 71% Haw Wood Farm Caravan Park *(TM421717)*

Hinton IP17 3QT
☎ 01986 784248
e-mail: bookings@hawwoodfarm.co.uk
dir: *Exit A12, 1.5m N of Darsham level crossing at Little Chef. Site 0.5m on right*

🚐 🚌 ⛺

Open Mar-14 Jan

Last arrival 21.00hrs Last departure noon

An unpretentious family-orientated park set in two large fields surrounded by low hedges. The toilets are clean and functional, and there is plenty of space for children to play. 15 acre site. 60 touring pitches. Caravan pitches. Motorhome pitches. Tent pitches. 55 statics.

AA Pubs & Restaurants nearby: Westleton Crown, Westleton 01728 648777

The Ship at Dunwich 01728 648219

Queen's Head, Halesworth 01986 784214

Leisure: 🛝

Facilities: 🚿 ⊙ ✻ [$] 🐕 ℹ

Services: 🔌 🛢 🌿 [T]

Within 3 miles: ⛳ 🎣 [$] ∪

Notes: Ⓝ Dogs must be kept on leads.

FELIXSTOWE Map 13 TM33

Places to visit

Ipswich Museum, IPSWICH 01473 433550 www.ipswich.gov.uk

Christchurch Mansion, IPSWICH 01473 433554 www.ipswich.gov.uk

►►► 78% Peewit Caravan Park *(TM290338)*

Walton Av IP11 2HB
☎ 01394 284511
e-mail: peewitpark@aol.com
dir: *Signed from A14 in Felixstowe, 100mtrs past Dock Gate 1, 1st on left*

* 🚐 £14.50-£28.35 🚌 £14.50-£28.35 ⛺ £14-£30

Open Apr (or Etr if earlier)-Oct

Last arrival 21.00hrs Last departure 11.00hrs

A grass touring area fringed by trees, with well-maintained grounds and a colourful floral display. This handy urban site is not overlooked by houses, and the toilet and shower facilities are clean and well cared for. A function room contains a TV and library. The beach is a few minutes away by car. 13 acre site. 45 touring pitches. 4 hardstandings. Caravan pitches. Motorhome pitches. Tent pitches. 200 statics.

AA Pubs & Restaurants nearby: Ship Inn, Levington 01473 659573

Leisure: 🛝

Facilities: 🚿 ⊙ 🚰 ✻ ♿ 📞 🐕 Wi-fi ♻ ℹ

Services: 🔌 🧺 🛢 🔋

Within 3 miles: ⛳ 🎾 🎳 🎣 ◎ 🏊 [$] 🧺

Notes: Only foam footballs are permitted, 5mph speed restriction. Dogs must be kept on leads. Boules area, bowling green, adventure trail.

HOLLESLEY Map 13 TM34

Places to visit

Woodbridge Tide Mill, WOODBRIDGE 01728 746959 www.woodbridgetidemill.org.uk

Sutton Hoo, WOODBRIDGE 01394 389700 www.nationaltrust.org.uk/suttonhoo

Great for kids: Orford Castle, ORFORD 01394 450472 www.english-heritage.org.uk

►►► 85% Run Cottage Touring Park *(TM350440)*

Alderton Rd IP12 3RQ
☎ 01394 411309
e-mail: info@run-cottage.co.uk
dir: *From A12 (Ipswich-Saxmundham) onto A1152 at Melton. 1.5m, right at rdbt onto B1083. 0.75m, left to Hollesley. In Hollesley right into The Street, through village, down hill, over bridge, site 100yds on left*

* 🚐 fr £18 🚌 fr £18 ⛺ fr £15

Open all year

Last arrival 20.00hrs Last departure 11.00hrs

Located in the peaceful village of Hollesley on the Suffolk coast, this landscaped park is set behind the owners' house. The generously-sized pitches are serviced by a well-appointed and immaculately maintained toilet block. This site is handy for the National Trust's Sutton Hoo, and also by travelling a little further north, the coastal centre and beach at Dunwich Heath, and the RSPB bird reserve at Minsmere. 3.75 acre site. 45 touring pitches. 10 hardstandings. Caravan pitches. Motorhome pitches. Tent pitches.

AA Pubs & Restaurants nearby: The Crown at Woodbridge 01394 384242

Facilities: 🚿 ⊙ 🚰 ✻ ♿ 🐕 ♻ ℹ

Services: 🔌 🔋

Within 3 miles: ⛳ 🎣 🏊 [$] ∪

Notes: No groundsheets, ball games or cycles.

IPSWICH

See Bucklesham

KESSINGLAND   Map 13 TM58

Places to visit

East Anglia Transport Museum, LOWESTOFT
01502 518459 www.eatm.org.uk

Maritime Museum, LOWESTOFT 01502 561963
www.lowestoftmaritimemuseum.org.uk

Great for kids: Pleasurewood Hills, LOWESTOFT
01502 586000 (admin)
www.pleasurewoodhills.com

75% *Kessingland Beach Holiday Park*

(TM535852)

Beach Rd NR33 7RN
☎ 01502 740636
e-mail: holidaysales.kessinglandbeach
@park-resorts.com
web: www.park-resorts.com
dir: *From Lowestoft take A12 S. At Kessingland take 3rd exit at rdbt towards beach. Through village. At beach follow road to right. In 400yds fork left for park*

Open Apr-Oct

Last departure 10.00hrs

A large holiday centre with direct access onto the beach, and a variety of leisure facilities. The touring area is tucked away from the statics, and served by a clean and functional toilet block. A fish and chip shop and the Boat House Restaurant are popular features. 69 acre site. 90 touring pitches. Caravan pitches. Motorhome pitches. Tent pitches. 95 statics.

Leisure:

Facilities:

Services:

Within 3 miles:

Notes: Archery.

▶▶▶▶ **89% Heathland Beach Caravan Park** (TM533877)

London Rd NR33 7PJ
☎ 01502 740337
e-mail: heathlandbeach@btinternet.com
web: www.heathlandbeach.co.uk
dir: *1m N of Kessingland exit A12 onto B1437*

* 🚐 £20-£25 🚐 £20-£25 ⛺ £20-£30

Open Apr-Oct

Last arrival 21.00hrs Last departure 11.00hrs

A well-run and maintained park offering superb toilet facilities. The park is set in meadowland, with level grass pitches, and mature trees and bushes. There is direct access to the sea and beach, and good provisions for families on site with a heated swimming pool and three play areas. 5 acre site. 63 touring pitches. Caravan pitches. Motorhome pitches. Tent pitches. 200 statics.

Leisure:

Facilities:

Services:

Within 3 miles:

Notes: One dog only per unit. Dogs must be kept on leads. Freshwater & sea fishing.

LEISTON   Map 13 TM46

Places to visit

Long Shop Museum, LEISTON 01728 832189
www.longshopmuseum.co.uk

Leiston Abbey, LEISTON 01728 831354
www.leistonabbey.co.uk

Great for kids: Easton Farm Park, EASTON
01728 746475 www.eastonfarmpark.co.uk

▶▶▶ **86% Cakes & Ale** (TM432637)

Abbey Ln, Theberton IP16 4TE
☎ 01728 831655
e-mail: cakesandalepark@gmail.com
web: www.cakesandale.co.uk
dir: *From Saxmundham E on B1119. 3m follow minor road over level crossing, turn right, in 0.5m straight on at x-rds, entrance 0.5m on left*

* 🚐 £20-£24 🚐 £20-£24 ⛺ £20-£24

Cakes & Ale

Open Apr-Oct (rs Low season club, shop & reception limited hours)

Last arrival 20.00hrs Last departure 13.00hrs

A large, well spread out and beautifully maintained site with many trees and bushes on a former Second World War airfield. The spacious touring area includes plenty of hardstandings and super pitches, and there is a good bar and a well-maintained toilet block, a fully-serviced family/disabled room and a washing-up room. 45 acre site. 50 touring pitches. 50 hardstandings. Caravan pitches. Motorhome pitches. Tent pitches. 200 statics.

AA Pubs & Restaurants nearby: 152 Aldeburgh, Aldeburgh 01728 454594

Regatta Restaurant, Aldeburgh 01728 452011

Leisure:

Facilities:

Services:

Within 3 miles:

Notes: No group bookings, no noise between 21.00hrs-08.00hrs. Dogs must be kept on leads. Practice range/net, volleyball court, boules, football nets.

see advert on opposite page

LOWESTOFT

See Kessingland

SAXMUNDHAM
Map 13 TM36

Places to visit

Long Shop Museum, LEISTON 01728 832189
www.longshopmuseum.co.uk

Leiston Abbey, LEISTON 01728 831354
www.leistonabbey.co.uk

Great for kids: Museum of East Anglian Life,
STOWMARKET 01449 612229
www.eastanglianlife.org.uk

►►►► 85% Carlton Meres Country Park (TM372637)

Rendham Rd, Carlton IP17 2QP
☎ 01728 603344

e-mail: enquiries@carlton-meres.co.uk
dir: From A12, W of Saxmundham, take B1119
towards Framlingham. Site signed from A12

🚐 🚙

Open Etr-Oct

Last arrival 17.00hrs Last departure 10.00hrs

With two large fishing lakes, a modern fitness
suite, a beauty salon, sauna and steam rooms,
tennis court, a bar, and a heated outdoor
swimming pool, Carlton Meres offers a wealth of
leisure facilities, and all for the exclusive use for
those staying on the site (holiday statics and
lodges for hire). There is a modern heated toilet
block and excellent security. This site is well-
placed for all the Suffolk coast attractions. Please

note that this site does not accept tents. 52 acre
site. 96 touring pitches. 56 hardstandings.
Caravan pitches. Motorhome pitches.

AA Pubs & Restaurants nearby: 152 Aldeburgh,
Aldeburgh 01728 454594

Regatta Restaurant, Aldeburgh 01728 452011

Leisure: 🏊 🎣 🛝 **Facilities:** 🔗 ☀ ♿ 🐕 WiFi

Services: 🔌 🗑 🍴 🛢 🍴 ♨

Within 3 miles: ♿ 🎯 🎱 🎣 🏊 🛒 🗑 U

►►► 80% Whitearch Touring Caravan Park (TM379610)

Main Rd, Benhall IP17 1NA
☎ 01728 604646 & 603773
dir: At junct of A12 & B1121

* 🚐 fr £16.50 🚙 fr £16.50 ⛺ fr £13.50

Open Apr-Oct

Last arrival 20.00hrs

A small, maturing park set around an attractive
coarse-fishing lake, with good quality,
imaginatively appointed toilet facilities and
secluded pitches tucked away among trees and
shrubs. The park is popular with anglers; there is
some traffic noise from the adjacent A12. 14.5
acre site. 50 touring pitches. 50 hardstandings.
Caravan pitches. Motorhome pitches. Tent pitches.

AA Pubs & Restaurants nearby: 152 Aldeburgh,
Aldeburgh 01728 454594

Regatta Restaurant, Aldeburgh 01728 452011

Leisure: 🛝

Facilities: 🔗 ⊙ 🅿 ☀ ♿ 🛒 🗑 🐕 ♻ ❶

Services: 🔌 🗑 🛢 🚿 **Within 3 miles:** ♿ 🗑 🗑

Notes: 🚫 No cars by caravans. No bicycles. Dogs
must be kept on leads.

►► 82% Marsh Farm Caravan Site (TM385608)

Sternfield IP17 1HW
☎ 01728 602168
dir: A12 onto A1094 (Aldeburgh road), at Snape
x-roads left signed Sternfield, follow signs to site

* 🚐 £15-£19.50 🚙 £15-£19.50 ⛺ £10-£20

Open all year

Last arrival 21.00hrs Last departure 17.00hrs

A very pretty site overlooking reed-fringed lakes
which offer excellent coarse fishing. The facilities
are very well maintained, and the park is a truly
peaceful haven. 30 acre site. 45 touring pitches.
Caravan pitches. Motorhome pitches. Tent pitches.

AA Pubs & Restaurants nearby: 152 Aldeburgh,
Aldeburgh 01728 454594

Regatta Restaurant, Aldeburgh 01728 452011

Facilities: 🔗 ☀ 🗑 🛒 🐕 ♻ ❶

Services: 🔌 🛢

Within 3 miles: ♿ 🎯 🎣 🗑 U

Notes: 🅿 Campers must report to reception first.
Dogs must be kept on leads.

SERVICES: 🔌 Electric hook up 🗑 Launderette 🍴 Licensed bar 🛢 Calor Gas 🔥 Camping Gaz 🚽 Toilet fluid 🍴 Café/Restaurant 🍟 Fast Food/Takeaway 🔋 Battery charging
🍼 Baby care 🔧 Motorvan service point **ABBREVIATIONS:** BH/bank hols-bank holidays Etr-Easter Whit-Whitsun dep-departure fr-from hrs-hours m-mile mdnt-midnight
rdbt-roundabout rs-restricted service wk-week wknd-weekend 🚫 No credit cards 🚫 no dogs See page 7 for details of the AA Camping Card Scheme

SUDBURY Map 13 TL84

Places to visit

Melford Hall, LONG MELFORD 01787 379228
www.nationaltrust.org.uk/melfordhall

Kentwell Hall, LONG MELFORD 01787 310207
www.kentwell.co.uk

Great for kids: Colne Valley Railway &
Museum, CASTLE HEDINGHAM 01787 461174
www.colnevalleyrailway.co.uk

▶▶▶ 75% *Willowmere Caravan Park*
(TL886388)

Bures Rd, Little Cornard CO10 0NN
☎ 01787 375559 & 310422
e-mail: awillowmere@aol.com
dir: *1.5m S of Sudbury on B1508 (Bures road)*

🚐 🚏 ⛺

Open Etr-Oct

Last arrival anytime Last departure noon

A pleasant little site in a quiet location tucked
away beyond a tiny residential static area, offering
spotless facilities. 3 acre site. 40 touring pitches.
Caravan pitches. Motorhome pitches. Tent pitches.
9 statics.

AA Pubs & Restaurants nearby: White Hart, Great
Yeldham 01787 237250

Bell Inn, Castle Hedingham 01787 460350

Facilities: 🏪 ☉ ⚡ ⚹ ⚞ ⚟

Services: 🖭 🔋

Within 3 miles: ⚓ 🎣 ◎ 🏬 🛒 ♨

Notes: 🐾 Fishing.

WOODBRIDGE Map 13 TM24

Places to visit

Sutton Hoo, WOODBRIDGE 01394 389700
www.nationaltrust.org.uk/suttonhoo

Orford Castle, ORFORD 01394 450472
www.english-heritage.org.uk

Great for kids: Easton Farm Park, EASTON
01728 746475 www.eastonfarmpark.co.uk

PREMIER PARK

▶▶▶▶▶ 92% *Moon & Sixpence*
(TM263454)

Newbourn Rd, Waldringfield IP12 4PP
☎ 01473 736650
e-mail: info@moonandsixpence.eu
web: www.moonandsixpence.eu
dir: *Follow caravan & Moon & Sixpence signs from
A12 Ipswich (east bypass). 1.5m, left at x-roads*

* 🚐 £17-£33 🚏 £17-£33 ⛺ £17-£33

Open Apr-Oct (rs Low season club, shop, reception
open limited hours)

Last arrival 20.00hrs Last departure noon

A well-planned site, with tourers occupying a
sheltered valley position around an attractive
boating lake with a sandy beach. Toilet facilities
are housed in a smart Norwegian-style cabin, and
there is a laundry and dishwashing area. Leisure
facilities include two tennis courts, a bowling
green, fishing, boating and a games room. There
is an adult-only area, and a strict 'no groups and
no noise after 9pm' policy. 5 acre site. 65 touring
pitches. Caravan pitches. Motorhome pitches. Tent
pitches. 225 statics.

AA Pubs & Restaurants nearby: The Crown at
Woodbridge 01394 384242

Seckford Hall Hotel, Woodbridge 01394 385678

Leisure: 🎢 ⚽ ☺ 🔍

Facilities: 🛁 🏪 ☉ ⚡ ⚹ 🛒 🔧 📶 💻 ♻ ℹ

Services: 🖭 🔋 🍴 🛢 ✎ 🍽 🚚 ⬇

Within 3 miles: ⚓ 🎣 🚴 🏬 🛒

Notes: No group bookings or commercial vehicles,
quiet 21.00hrs-08.00hrs. Lake, cycle trail, 10-acre
sports area, 9-hole golf, tennis courts.

see advert on opposite page

▶▶▶ 85% Moat Barn Touring
Caravan Park *(TM269530)*

Dallinghoo Rd, Bredfield IP13 6BD
☎ 01473 737520
dir: *Exit A12 at Bredfield, 1st right at village
pump. Through village, 1m site on left*

* 🚐 £18 🚏 £18 ⛺ £18

Open Mar-15 Jan

Last arrival 22.00hrs Last departure noon

An attractive small park set in idyllic Suffolk
countryside, perfectly located for touring the
heritage coastline and for visiting the National
Trust's Sutton Hoo. The modern toilet block is well
equipped and maintained. There are ten tent
pitches and the park is located on the popular Hull
to Harwich cycle route. Cycle hire is available. 2
acre site. 34 touring pitches. Caravan pitches.
Motorhome pitches. Tent pitches.

AA Pubs & Restaurants nearby: The Crown at
Woodbridge 01394 384242

Seckford Hall Hotel, Woodbridge 01394 385678

Facilities: 🏪 ☉ ⚡ ⚹ 🛒 📶 ♻

Services: 🖭

Within 3 miles: ⚓ 🎣 🏬 🛒 ♨

Notes: Adults only. 🐾 No ball games, breatheable
groundsheets only. Dogs must be kept on leads.

LEISURE: 🏊 Indoor swimming pool 🏖 Outdoor swimming pool 🎢 Children's playground 🪁 Kid's club 🎾 Tennis court 🔍 Games room 📺 Separate TV room
⛳ 9/18 hole golf course 🚣 Boats for hire 🎬 Cinema 🎵 Entertainment 🎣 Fishing ◎ Mini golf 🏄 Watersports 🏋 Gym ☺ Sports field **Spa** ♨ Stables
FACILITIES: 🛁 Bath 🏪 Shower ☉ Electric shaver ⚡ Hairdryer ⚹ Ice Pack Facility ⚞ Disabled facilities ⚟ Public telephone 🛒 Shop on site or within 200yds
🛍 Mobile shop (calls at least 5 days a week) 🍴 BBQ area 🪑 Picnic area 📶 Wi-fi 💻 Internet access ♻ Recycling ℹ Tourist info 🐾 Dog exercise area

SERVICES: ⚡ Electric hook up 🔄 Launderette 🍺 Licensed bar 🔥 Calor Gas 🔥 Camping Gaz T Toilet fluid 🍽️ Café/Restaurant 🍔 Fast Food/Takeaway 🔋 Battery charging 🛒 Baby care 🚐 Motorvan service point **ABBREVIATIONS:** BH/bank hols-bank holidays Etr-Easter Whit-Whitsun dep-departure fr-from hrs-hours m-mile mdnt-midnight rdbt-roundabout rs-restricted service wk-week wknd-weekend 🚫 No credit cards 🚫 no dogs

See page 7 for details of the AA Camping Card Scheme

Sussex

Sussex, deriving its name from 'South Saxons' is divided into two -
East and West - but the name is so quintessentially English that we
tend to think of it as one entity. Mention its name anywhere in the
world and for those who are familiar with 'Sussex by the sea', images
of rolling hills, historic towns and villages and miles of spectacular
chalky cliffs immediately spring to mind. Perhaps it is the bare South
Downs with which Sussex is most closely associated.

This swathe of breezy downland represents some of the finest walking in southern England. Now a National Park, the South Downs provide country-loving locals and scores of visitors with a perfect natural playground. As well as walkers and cyclists, you'll find kite flyers, model aircraft enthusiasts and hang gliders.

Beaches and cliffs

The coast is one of the county's gems. At its western end lies sprawling Chichester harbour, with its meandering channels, creeks and sleepy inlets, and on the horizon is the imposing outline of the cathedral, small but beautiful. To the east are the seaside towns of Worthing, Brighton, Eastbourne, Bexhill and Hastings. Here, the South Downs sweep down towards the sea with two famous landmarks, Birling Gap and Beachy Head, demonstrating how nature and the elements have shaped the land over time.

The heart of the county

Inland is Arundel, with its rows of elegant Georgian and Victorian buildings standing in the shadow of the great castle, ancestral home of the Dukes of Norfolk, and the ▶

● Brighton Pier

BRIGHTON PIER

● Devil's Dyke

● West Wittering beach

magnificent French Gothic-style Roman Catholic cathedral. Mid Sussex is the setting for a chain of attractive, typically English towns, including Midhurst, Petworth, Pulborough, Billingshurst, Uckfield and Haywards Heath.

There are grand country houses, too. Parham, built during the reign of Henry VIII, was one of the first stately homes to open its doors to the public, while the National Trust's Petworth House, in 2,000 acres of parkland, retains the 13th-century chapel of an earlier mansion and has a fine art collection including works by Rembrandt and Van Dyck.

Walking and Cycling

In terms of walking, this county is spoilt for choice. Glancing at the map reveals innumerable paths and bridleways, while there are many more demanding and adventurous long-distance paths – a perfect way to get to the heart of rural East and West Sussex. The Sussex Border Path meanders along the boundary between

● Bodiam Castle

the two counties; the Monarch's Way broadly follows Charles II's escape route in 1651; the most famous of all of them, the South Downs Way, follows hill paths and clifftop tracks all the way from Winchester to Eastbourne; the West Sussex Literary Trail links Horsham with Chichester and recalls many literary figures associated with this area – Shelley, Tennyson and Wilde among them.

East and West Sussex offer exciting cycle rides through the High Weald, along the South Downs Way and via coastal routes between Worthing and Rye. Brighton to Hastings via Polegate is part of the Downs and Weald Cycle Route. There is also the Forest Way through East Grinstead to Groombridge and the Cuckoo Trail from Heathfield to Eastbourne. For glorious coastal views and stiff sea breezes, the very easy ride between Chichester and West Wittering is recommended. You can vary the return by taking the Itchenor Ferry to Bosham.

Festivals and Events

- March is the month for the Pioneer Motorcycle Run from Epsom Downs to Brighton. All the participating motorcycles are pre 1915 and the event offers a fascinating insight into the early history of these machines – 300 of which are on display.
- In early May there is the Sussex Food & South Downs Fair at the Weald and Downland Open Air Museum near Chichester.
- The 15th-century moated Herstmonceux Castle hosts England's Medieval Festival on August Bank Holiday weekend, complete with minstrels, magicians, lords, ladies and serfs.
- Goodwood is the venue for the Motor Circuit Revival Meeting in September. This is when fast cars and track legends celebrate the golden age of British motor sport from the 1940s and '50s.
- The same month – September – sees Uckfield Bonfire and Carnival Society's Annual Carnival with fancy dress and a torchlight procession.

SUSSEX, EAST

BATTLE
Map 7 TQ71

Places to visit

1066 Story in Hastings Castle, HASTINGS & ST LEONARDS 01424 781111 www.discoverhastings.co.uk/hastings-castle-1066/

Great for kids: Smugglers Adventure, HASTINGS & ST LEONARDS 01424 422964 www.discoverhastings.co.uk

▶▶▶ 80% *Brakes Coppice Park*
(TQ765134)

Forewood Ln TN33 9AB
☎ 01424 830322
e-mail: brakesco@btinternet.com
web: www.brakescoppicepark.co.uk
dir: *From Battle on A2100 towards Hastings. After 2m turn right for Crowhurst. Site 1m on left*

Open Mar-Oct
Last arrival 21.00hrs Last departure noon

A secluded farm site in a sunny meadow deep in woodland with a small stream and a coarse fishing lake. The toilet block has quality fittings and there's a good fully-serviced family/disabled room. Hardstanding pitches are neatly laid out on a terrace, and tents are pitched on grass edged by woodland. The hands-on owners offer high levels of customer care and this tucked away gem proves a peaceful base for exploring Battle and the south coast. 3 acre site. 30 touring pitches. 10 hardstandings. Caravan pitches. Motorhome pitches. Tent pitches.

AA Pubs & Restaurants nearby: Ash Tree Inn, Ashburnham Place 01424 892104

Wild Mushroom Restaurant, Westfield 01424 751137

Leisure: ⌂
Facilities: ⌂⊙♟※⅏☺⌂⌖⛟🛈
Services: ⌂⌂⌂⌂⌂⌂
Within 3 miles: ⌂⌂⌂⌂
Notes: No fires, footballs or kite flying. Dogs must be kept on leads.

▶▶▶ 71% Senlac Wood (TQ722153)

Catsfield Rd, Catsfield TN33 9LN
☎ 01424 773969
e-mail: senlacwood@xlninternet.co.uk
dir: *A271 from Battle onto B2204 signed Bexhill. Site on left*

* 🚐 £15-£17 🚐 £15-£17 ▲ £15-£17

Open Mar-Oct

Last arrival 22.00hrs Last departure noon

A woodland site with many secluded bays with hardstanding pitches, and two peaceful grassy glades for tents. The functional toilet facilities are clean and due for refurbishment, plus plans include the welcome addition of new portacabin toilets in the tent area. The site is ideal for anyone looking for seclusion and shade and is well placed for visiting nearby Battle and the south coast beaches. 20 acre site. 35 touring pitches. 16 hardstandings. Caravan pitches. Motorhome pitches. Tent pitches.

AA Pubs & Restaurants nearby: Ash Tree Inn, Ashburnham Place 01424 892104

Wild Mushroom Restaurant, Westfield 01424 751137

Leisure: ⌂⌂
Facilities: ⌂⊙♟※☺⌂⛟🅆🛈
Services: ⌂⌂⌂⌂⌂
Within 3 miles: ⌂⌂⌂⌂⌂
Notes: No camp fires, no noise after 23.00hrs. Caravan storage.

BEXHILL
Map 6 TQ70

Places to visit

Pevensey Castle, PEVENSEY 01323 762604
www.english-heritage.org.uk

1066 Story in Hastings Castle, HASTINGS & ST
LEONARDS 01424 781111 www.discover
hastings.co.uk/hastings-castle-1066/

Great for kids: The Observatory Science Centre,
HERSTMONCEUX 01323 832731
www.the-observatory.org

PREMIER PARK

REGIONAL WINNER - AA SOUTH EAST
ENGLAND CAMPSITE OF THE YEAR 2013

►►►►► 87% Kloofs Caravan Park
(TQ709091)

Sandhurst Ln TN39 4RG
☎ **01424 842839**
e-mail: camping@kloofs.com
dir: *NE of Bexhill exit A259 at Little Common rdbt,
N into Peartree Lane, left at x-rds, site 300mtrs
on left*

* 🚐 fr £24.50 🚎 fr £24.50 ▲ fr £24.50

Open all year

Last arrival anytime Last departure 11.00hrs

Hidden away down a quiet lane, just inland from
Bexhill and the coast, Kloofs is a friendly, family-
run park surrounded by farmland and oak
woodlands, with views extending to the South
Downs from hilltop pitches. Lovingly developed by
the owners over the past 17 years, the site is well
landscaped and thoughtfully laid out, with
excellent hardstandings (some large enough for
RVs), colourful flower beds, and spacious pitches,
each with mini patio, bench and barbecue stand.
Spotless, upmarket toilet facilities include a family
shower room and a unisex block with privacy
cubicles, a dog shower, a drying room, and a
dishwasher. 22 acre site. 50 touring pitches. 50
hardstandings. Caravan pitches. Motorhome
pitches. Tent pitches. 75 statics. See also page 20.

Leisure: /A 🔍 ▢
Facilities: 🌂 ⊙ 🄿 ✳ ᵬ ⑤ 🖻 🛏 🐿 ♻ ❶
Services: 🔌 ⑤ 🛢 ∅ Ⓣ 🔋 ⚡
Within 3 miles: ↓ ⃒ 🌢 ◎ ≥ 🖻 ⑤ ∪

Notes: No noise between 22.30hrs-07.00hrs. Dogs
must be kept on leads. Hanging/drying room,
kitchens, pet showers, baby changing.

►►► 79% Cobbs Hill Farm Caravan &
Camping Park *(TQ736102)*

Watermill Ln TN39 5JA
☎ **01424 213460 & 07708 958910**
e-mail: cobbshillfarmuk@hotmail.com
dir: *Exit A269 into Watermill Ln, park 1m on left
(NB it is advisable not to follow Sat Nav)*

🚐 £12-£14 🚎 £12-£14 ▲ £13-£15

Open Apr-Oct

Last arrival 20.00hrs Last departure noon

A well established farm site tucked away in
pleasant rolling countryside close to Bexhill and a
short drive from Battle, the South Downs and good
beaches. Neat, well maintained camping
paddocks, one with eight hardstanding pitches,
are sheltered by mature trees and hedging; the
toilet block is clean and freshly painted. Children
will love the menagerie of farm animals. 17 acre
site. 55 touring pitches. 8 hardstandings. 20
seasonal pitches. Caravan pitches. Motorhome
pitches. Tent pitches. 15 statics.

AA Pubs & Restaurants nearby: Ash Tree Inn,
Ashburton Place 01424 892104

Leisure: /A 🔍
Facilities: 🌂 ⊙ 🄿 ✳ ᵬ ⑤ 🖻 🛏 📶 ❶
Services: 🔌 ⑤ 🛢 ∅ Ⓣ 🔋
Within 3 miles: ↓ ⃒ 🌢 🖻 ⑤

Notes: No camp fires. Dogs must be kept on
leads.

CAMBER
Map 7 TQ91

Places to visit

Rye Castle Museum, RYE 01797 226728
www.ryemuseum.co.uk

Lamb House, RYE 01580 762334
www.nationaltrust.org.uk/main/w-lambhouse

Great for kids: 1066 Story in Hastings Castle,
HASTINGS & ST LEONARDS 01424 781111
www.discoverhastings.co.uk/hastings-
castle-1066/

 ### 66% *Camber Sands*
(TQ972184)

New Lydd Rd TN31 7RT
☎ **0871 664 9719**
e-mail: camber.sands@park-resorts.com
web: www.park-resorts.com
dir: *M20 junct 10 (Ashford International
Station), A2070 signed Brenzett. Follow
Hastings & Rye signs on A259. 1m before Rye,
left signed Camber. Site in 3m*

🚐 🚎 ▲

Open Apr-Oct

Last arrival anytime Last departure 10.00hrs

Located opposite Camber's vast sandy beach,
this large holiday centre offers a good range
of leisure and entertainment facilities. The
touring area is positioned close to the reception
and entrance, and is served by a clean and
functional toilet block. 110 acre site. 40 touring
pitches. 6 hardstandings. Caravan pitches.
Motorhome pitches. Tent pitches. 921 statics.

AA Pubs & Restaurants nearby: Mermaid Inn,
Rye 01797 223065

Globe Inn, Rye 01797 227918

Ypres Castle Inn, Rye 01797 223248

The George in Rye 01797 222114

Leisure: ⌇ /A 🛶 🌊 🎣 ♫ Spa
Facilities: 🌂 ⊙ ᬰ ⑤ 🖻 🛏 📶 🖥 ♻ ❶
Services: 🔌 ⑤ 🔋 🍽 🍴
Within 3 miles: ↓ ⃒ ◎ ≥ 🖻 ⑤

Notes: Quiet between 23.00hrs-7.00hrs. Dogs
must be kept on leads.

SERVICES: 🔌 Electric hook up 🄖 Launderette 🍺 Licensed bar 🛢 Calor Gas ∅ Camping Gaz Ⓣ Toilet fluid 🍽 Café/Restaurant 🍴 Fast Food/Takeaway 🔋 Battery charging
🚼 Baby care ⚡ Motorvan service point **ABBREVIATIONS:** BH/bank hols-bank holidays Etr-Easter Whit-Whitsun dep-departure fr-from hrs-hours m-mile mdnt-midnight
rdbt-roundabout rs-restricted service wk-week wknd-weekend ⊗ No credit cards ⊗ no dogs See page 7 for details of the AA Camping Card Scheme

FURNER'S GREEN — Map 6 TQ42

Places to visit

Sheffield Park Garden, SHEFFIELD PARK 01825 790231 www.nationaltrust.org.uk/main/w-sheffieldparkgarden

Nymans, HANDCROSS 01444 405250 www.nationaltrust.org.uk/nymans

►► 81% Heaven Farm (TQ403264)

TN22 3RG
☎ 01825 790226
e-mail: heavenfarmleisure@btinternet.com
dir: On A275 between Lewes & East Grinstead, 1m N of Sheffield Park Garden

* ⚐ fr £20 ⚐ fr £20 ▲ fr £20

Open all year (rs Nov-Mar no tents)

Last arrival 21.00hrs Last departure noon

A delightful, small, rural site on a popular farm complex incorporating a farm museum, craft shop, tea room and nature trail. Good clean toilet facilities are housed in well-converted outbuildings and chickens and duck roam freely around the site. Ashdown Forest, the Bluebell Railway and Sheffield Park Garden are nearby. 1.5 acre site. 25 touring pitches. 2 hardstandings. Caravan pitches. Motorhome pitches. Tent pitches.

AA Pubs & Restaurants nearby: Coach & Horses, Danehill 01825 740369

Griffin Inn, Fletching 01825 722890

Facilities: ⬤⊙✳♿🅂🚻⚡
Services: ⌇🅣🍴🛒🚮
Within 3 miles: ↡🖉🅂U
Notes: ⬤ Dogs must be kept on leads. Fishing.

HASTINGS — Map 7 TQ80

Places to visit

Shipwreck & Coastal Heritage Centre, HASTINGS & ST LEONARDS 01424 437452 www.shipwreck-heritage.org.uk

Great for kids: Blue Reef Aquarium, HASTINGS & ST LEONARDS 01424 718776 www.bluereefaquarium.co.uk

🏠 🅄 NEW Combe Haven Holiday hh Park (TQ779091)

Harley Shute Rd, St Leonards-on-Sea TN38 8BZ
☎ 01424 427891
e-mail: combehaven@haven.com
web: www.haven.com/combehaven
dir: A21 towards Hastings. In Hastings take A259 towards Bexhill. Park signed on right

Open Mar-Oct

Close to a beach and the resort attractions of Hastings, this newly upgraded holiday park has been designed with families in mind. Activities include a pirates adventure playground, heated swimming pools and a wealth of sports and outdoor activities. There are a good range of holiday caravans and apartments. At the time of going to press the quality rating for this site had not been confirmed. For up-to-date information please see the AA website: theAA.com.

Change over day: Mon, Fri, Sat Arrival & departure times: Please contact the site

Statics 284 Sleeps 6-8 Bedrms 2-3 Bathrms 1-2 Toilets 1-2 Freezer TV Sky/FTV Elec included Gas included Grass area Parking

Children ♦♦ Cots Dogs Max 2 on leads No dangerous dogs (see page 12)

Leisure: 🏊🏊♨/M

AA Pubs & Restaurants nearby: Jali Restaurant, Hastings 01424 457300

see advert on page 310

HEATHFIELD — Map 6 TQ52

Places to visit

Pashley Manor Gardens, TICEHURST 01580 200888 www.pashleymanorgardens.com

The Truggery, HERSTMONCEUX 01323 832314 www.truggery.co.uk

Great for kids: Bentley Wildfowl & Motor Museum, HALLAND 01825 840573 www.bentley.org.uk

►► 77% Greenviews Caravan Park (TQ605223)

Burwash Rd, Broad Oak TN21 8RT
☎ 01435 863531
dir: Through Heathfield on A265 for 1m. Site on left after Broad Oak sign

⚐⚐▲

Open Apr-Oct (rs Apr & Oct bookings only, subject to weather)

Last arrival 22.00hrs Last departure 10.30hrs

A small touring area adjoining a residential park, with a smart clubhouse. The facility block includes a room for disabled visitors. The owners always offer a friendly welcome, and they take pride in the lovely flower beds which adorn the park. 3 acre site. 10 touring pitches. Caravan pitches. Motorhome pitches. Tent pitches. 51 statics.

AA Pubs & Restaurants nearby: The Middle House, Mayfield 01435 872146

Best Beech Inn, Wadhurst 01892 782046

Facilities: ⬤⊙♿📞
Services: ⌇🅂🍴🍺🧴
Within 3 miles: 🅂
Notes: ⬤ 🚫

PEVENSEY BAY
Map 6 TQ60

Places to visit

"How We Lived Then" Museum of Shops & Social History, EASTBOURNE 01323 737143 www.how-we-lived-then.co.uk

Alfriston Clergy House, ALFRISTON 01323 871961 www.nationaltrust.org.uk/alfriston/

Great for kids: The Observatory Science Centre, HERSTMONCEUX 01323 832731 www.the-observatory.org

▶▶▶ **84% Bay View Park**

(TQ648028)

Old Martello Rd BN24 6DX
☎ 01323 768688
e-mail: holidays@bay-view.co.uk
web: www.bay-view.co.uk
dir: *Signed from A259 W of Pevensey Bay. On seaward side of A259 take private road towards beach*

* ⊞ £16-£24 ⊞ £16-£24 ▲ £16-£24

Open Mar-Oct

Last arrival 20.00hrs Last departure noon

A pleasant well-run site just yards from the beach, in an area east of Eastbourne town centre known as 'The Crumbles'. The level grassy site is very well maintained and the toilet facilities feature fully-serviced cubicles. The seasonal tent field now has marked pitches and improved portacabin toilet facilites with WC/WHB and WHB/tiled shower cubicles. 6 acre site. 94 touring pitches. 14 hardstandings. 15 seasonal pitches. Caravan pitches. Motorhome pitches. Tent pitches. 14 statics.

Leisure: ⋀

Facilities: ⬚⊙℘✳⬚⬚⬚⬚ ♻ ❶

Services: ⬚⬚⬚⬚⬚⬚⬚⬚

Within 3 miles: ⬚⬚℘◎⬚⬚⬚

Notes: Families & couples only, no commercial vehicles. Dogs must be kept on leads. 9-hole golf course.

SUSSEX, WEST

See Walk 11 in the Walks & Cycle Rides section at the end of the guide

ARUNDEL
Map 6 TQ00

Places to visit

Arundel Castle, ARUNDEL 01903 882173 www.arundelcastle.org

Harbour Park, LITTLEHAMPTON 01903 721200 www.harbourpark.com

Great for kids: Look & Sea! Visitor Centre, LITTLEHAMPTON 01903 718984 www.lookandsea.co.uk

AA CAMPING CARD SITE

▶▶ **79% Ship & Anchor Marina**

(TQ002040)

Station Rd, Ford BN18 0BJ
☎ 01243 551262
e-mail: enquiries@shipandanchormarina.co.uk
dir: *From A27 at Arundel take road S signed Ford. Site 2m on left after level crossing*

* ⊞ £15-£21 ⊞ £15-£21 ▲ £15-£21

Open Mar-Oct

Last arrival 21.00hrs Last departure noon

Neatly maintained by the enthusiastic, hard working owner, this small, well located site has dated but spotlessly clean toilet facilities, a secluded tent area, and enjoys a pleasant position beside the Ship & Anchor pub and the tidal River Arun. There are good walks from the site to Arundel and the coast. 12 acre site. 120 touring pitches. 11 hardstandings. Caravan pitches. Motorhome pitches. Tent pitches.

AA Pubs & Restaurants nearby: The Town House, Arundel 01903 883847

George & Dragon, Burpham 01903 883131

Leisure: ⋀

Facilities: ⬚⬚⊙℘✳⬚⬚⬚⬚ ❶

Services: ⬚⬚⬚⬚⬚⬚⬚⬚

Within 3 miles: ⬚⬚℘◎⬚⬚⬚ ∪

Notes: ⬚ No music audible to others. Dogs must be kept on leads. River fishing from site, pub on site.

BARNS GREEN Map 6 TQ12

Places to visit

Parham House & Gardens, PULBOROUGH
01903 744888 www.parhaminsussex.co.uk

Great for kids: Bignor Roman Villa & Museum, BIGNOR 01798 869259
www.bignorromanvilla.co.uk

►►►► 86% Sumners Ponds Fishery & Campsite *(TQ125268)*

Chapel Rd RH13 0PR
☎ 01403 732539
e-mail: info@sumnersponds.co.uk
dir: *From A272 at Coolham x-rds, N towards Barns Green. In 1.5m take 1st left at small x-rds. 1m, over level crossing. Site on left just after right bend*

🚐 🚌 ⛺

Open all year

Last arrival 20.00hrs Last departure noon

Diversification towards high quality camping continues at this working farm set in attractive surroundings on the edge of the quiet village of Barns Green. There are three touring areas; one continues to develop and includes camping pods, and another, which has a stunning new toilet block, has excellent pitches (and pods) on the banks of one of the well-stocked fishing lakes. A woodland walk has direct access to miles of footpaths. Horsham and Brighton are within easy reach. 40 acre site. 85 touring pitches. 45 hardstandings. Caravan pitches. Motorhome pitches. Tent pitches.

AA Pubs & Restaurants nearby: Cricketers Arms, Wisborough Green 01403 700369

Black Horse Inn, Nuthurst 01403 891272

White Horse, Maplehurst 01403 891208

Leisure: 🛝

Facilities: 🚿 🔌 💨 ❄ ♿ 🏪 🧺 🐕 [Wi-fi] ♻ ℹ

Services: 🚐 🫧 🔋 🔥 [T] 🍴 🍔 ⚡

Within 3 miles: ⛳ 🎣 🏄 🏪 🫧 🐴

Notes: Only one car per pitch. Cycling paths, cycle racks.

BILLINGSHURST Map 6 TQ02

Places to visit

Borde Hill Garden, HAYWARDS HEATH
01444 450326 www.bordehill.co.uk

Petworth Cottage Museum, PETWORTH 01798 342100
www.petworthcottagemuseum.co.uk

►► 74% Limeburners Arms Camp Site *(TQ072255)*

Lordings Rd, Newbridge RH14 9JA
☎ 01403 782311
e-mail: chippy.sawyer@virgin.net
dir: *From A29 take A272 towards Petworth for 1m, left onto B2133. Site 300yds on left*

🚐 🚌 ⛺

Open Apr-Oct

Last arrival 22.00hrs Last departure 14.00hrs

A secluded site in rural West Sussex, at the rear of the Limeburners Arms public house, and surrounded by fields. It makes a pleasant base for touring the South Downs and the Arun Valley. The toilets are basic but very clean. 2.75 acre site. 40 touring pitches. Caravan pitches. Motorhome pitches. Tent pitches.

AA Pubs & Restaurants nearby: Cricketers Arms, Wisborough Green 01403 700369

Black Horse Inn, Nuthurst 01403 891272

White Horse, Maplehurst 01403 891208

Leisure: 🛝

Facilities: 🚿 🔌 ❄ 📞

Services: 🚐 🍷 🍴 🛏 ⚡

Within 3 miles: ⛳ 🏪 🐴

Notes: Dogs must be kept on leads.

CHICHESTER Map 5 SU80

Places to visit

Chichester Cathedral, CHICHESTER
01243 782595 www.chichestercathedral.org.uk

Pallant House Gallery, CHICHESTER
01243 774557 www.pallant.org.uk

►►► 82% Ellscott Park *(SU829995)*

Sidlesham Ln, Birdham PO20 7QL
☎ 01243 512003
e-mail: camping@ellscottpark.co.uk
dir: *From Chichester take A286 for approx 4m, left at Butterfly Farm sign, site 500yds right*

🚐 🚌 ⛺

Open Apr-3rd wk in Oct

Last arrival daylight Last departure variable

A well-kept park set in sheltered meadowland behind the owners' nursery and van storage area. The park attracts a peace-loving clientele, has spotless, well maintained toilet facilities, and is handy for the beach, Chichester, Goodwood House, the racing at Goodwood and walking on the South Downs. Home-grown produce is for sale. 2.5 acre site. 50 touring pitches. 25 seasonal pitches. Caravan pitches. Motorhome pitches. Tent pitches.

AA Pubs & Restaurants nearby: Crab & Lobster, Sidlesham 01243 641233

Leisure: 🛝 ⚽

Facilities: 🚿 🔌 ❄ ♿ 🧺 🐕 ♻ ℹ

Services: 🚐 🫧 🔥 [T] 🛏

Within 3 miles: ⛳ 🚣 🎣 🏄 🏪 🫧 🐴

Notes: 🚫 Dogs must be kept on leads.

LEISURE: 🏊 Indoor swimming pool 🌊 Outdoor swimming pool 🛝 Children's playground ✋ Kid's club 🎾 Tennis court ♠ Games room 📺 Separate TV room ⛳ 9/18 hole golf course 🚣 Boats for hire 🎬 Cinema 🎵 Entertainment 🎣 Fishing ◎ Mini golf 🏄 Watersports 🏋 Gym ⚽ Sports field Spa 🐴 Stables
FACILITIES: 🛁 Bath 🚿 Shower 🔌 Electric shaver 💨 Hairdryer ❄ Ice Pack Facility ♿ Disabled facilities 📞 Public telephone 🏪 Shop on site or within 200yds 🚚 Mobile shop (calls at least 5 days a week) 🍖 BBQ area 🧺 Picnic area [Wi-fi] Wi-fi 💻 Internet access ♻ Recycling ℹ Tourist info 🐕 Dog exercise area

DIAL POST · Map 6 TQ11

Places to visit

Bignor Roman Villa & Museum, BIGNOR
01798 869259 www.bignorromanvilla.co.uk

Great for kids: Amberley Working Museum,
AMBERLEY 01798 831370
www.amberleymuseum.co.uk

►►►► 85% Honeybridge Park
(TQ152183)

Honeybridge Ln RH13 8NX
☎ 01403 710923
e-mail: enquiries@honeybridgepark.co.uk
dir: *10m S of Horsham, just off A24 at Dial Post.
Behind Old Barn Nursery*

* ⊕ £18.60-£26 ⇔ £18.60-£26 ▲ £15.60-£26

Open all year

Last arrival 19.00hrs Last departure noon

An attractive and very popular park on gently-sloping ground surrounded by hedgerows and mature trees. A comprehensive amenities building houses upmarket toilet facilities including luxury family and disabled rooms, as well as a laundry, shop and off-licence. There are plenty of hardstandings and electric hook-ups, a refurbished games room, and an excellent children's play area. 15 acre site. 130 touring pitches. 70 hardstandings. 20 seasonal pitches. Caravan pitches. Motorhome pitches. Tent pitches. 50 statics.

AA Pubs & Restaurants nearby: Countryman Inn, Shipley 01403 741383

George & Dragon, Shipley 01403 741320

Queens Head, West Chiltington 01798 812244

Leisure: ⚠ ✎ ▢

Facilities: ➡ ⌁ ☉ ☂ ⁑ ⅋ ⓑ ☷ ❶

Services: ⊕ ☷ ⌂ ⌀ T ᵀᴼᴵ ☷

Within 3 miles: ✐ ⤵ ⓑ ☷ U

Notes: No open fires. Dogs must be kept on leads. Fridges available.

HENFIELD · Map 6 TQ21

AA CAMPING CARD SITE

►► 72% Blacklands Farm Caravan & Camping (TQ231180)

Wheatsheaf Rd BN5 9AT
☎ 01273 493528 & 07773 792599
e-mail: info@blacklandsfarm.co.uk
dir: *A23, B2118, B2116 towards Henfield. Site approx 4m on right*

⊕ ⇔ ▲

Open Mar-Jan

Last arrival 20.00hrs Last departure noon

Tucked away off the B2116, east of Henfield, and well placed for visiting Brighton and exploring the South Downs National Park, this simple, grassy site has great potential, and the owners plan positive improvements that will not spoil the traditional feel of the campsite. There are spacious pitches down by fishing lakes and the basic portaloos are clean and tidy and have been smartly clad in wood. Future plans include building a new toilet block. 5 acre site. 75 touring pitches. Caravan pitches. Motorhome pitches. Tent pitches.

AA Pubs & Restaurants nearby: The Fountains Inn, Ashurst 01403 710219

The Royal Oak, Poynings 01273 857389

Leisure: ⚠ ⚽ ✇

Facilities: ⌁ ⌂ ☂ ⁑ ⅋ ⓑ ☷ ⤷ ♻ ❶

Services: ⊕

Within 3 miles: ↓ ✐ ⓑ ☷ U

Notes: No camp fires, no commercial vehicles. Dogs must be kept on leads. Coffee machine.

HORSHAM

See Barns Green & Dial Post

PAGHAM

Places to visit

Chichester Cathedral, CHICHESTER
01243 782595 www.chichestercathedral.org.uk

Great for kids: Haredown Mountain Boarding Centre, CHICHESTER 01243 81197
www.haredown.com

PAGHAM · Map 6 SZ89

⌂ U NEW Church Farm Holiday Park (SZ885974)

Church Ln PO21 4NR
☎ 01243 262635
e-mail: churchfarm@haven.com
web: www.haven.com/churchfarm
dir: *At rdbt on A27 (S of Chichester) take B2145 signed Hunston & Selsey. At mini rdbt take 1st left signed N Mundham, Pagham & Bognor Regis. Site in approx 3m*

Open Mar-Oct

Close to Portsmouth, Chichester and south coast beaches, this relaxing and fun-packed holiday park is located close to Pagham Harbour Nature Reserve. On-site activities include a 9-hole golf course, tennis coaching, shopping, kids play areas and evening entertainment. There are a range of holiday caravans and apartments. At the time of going to press the quality rating for this site had not been confirmed. For up-to-date information please see the AA website: theAA.com.

Change over day: Mon, Fri, Sat **Arrival & departure times:** Please contact the site

Statics 168 **Sleeps** 6-8 **Bedrms** 2-3 **Bathrms** 1-2 **Toilets** 1-2 **Freezer TV** Sky/FTV **Elec** included **Gas** included **Grass area Parking**

Children ✦ **Cots Dogs** Max 2 on leads No dangerous dogs (see page 12)

Leisure: ⌂ ⌂ ⌂ ✋ ⚠

AA Pubs & Restaurants nearby: The Bull's Head, Chichester 01243 839895

The Earl of March, Chichester 01243 533993

The Crab & Lobster, Sidlesham 01243 641233

see advert on page 313

SELSEY
Map 5 SZ89

Places to visit

Chichester Cathedral,
CHICHESTER 01243 782595
www.chichestercathedral.org.uk

Pallant House Gallery, CHICHESTER
01243 774557 www.pallant.org.uk

79% Warner Farm Touring Park (SZ845939)

Warner Ln, Selsey PO20 9EL
☎ 01243 604499
e-mail: touring@bunnleisure.co.uk
web: www.warnerfarm.co.uk
dir: From B2145 in Selsey turn right into School Lane & follow signs

🚐 £26.50-£43 🚌 £26.50-£43 ▲ £22.50-£39

Open Mar-Oct
Last arrival 17.30hrs Last departure 10.00hrs

A well-screened touring site that adjoins the three static parks under the same ownership. A courtesy bus runs around the complex to entertainment areas and supermarkets. The park backs onto open grassland, and the leisure facilities with bar, amusements and bowling alley, and swimming pool/sauna complex are also accessible to tourers. 10 acre site. 250 touring pitches. 60 hardstandings. 25 seasonal pitches. Caravan pitches. Motorhome pitches. Tent pitches.

AA Pubs & Restaurants nearby: Crab & Lobster, Sidlesham 01243 641233

Leisure: 🏊🏖️🎾🎣🛶🏐⚽♫
Facilities: 🔦⊙🖍️✳️♿🕐🚿🗑️🛁🐕 📶 🖥️ ♻️ 🛈
Services: 🚐🖪🔧🔌🚽🍴🏪🛒
Within 3 miles: 🚲🏇🎣◎🛍️🔥🛒🐴

Notes: Dogs must be kept on leads.

see advert below

TYNE & WEAR

SOUTH SHIELDS
Map 21 NZ36

Places to visit

Arbeia Roman Fort & Museum, SOUTH SHIELDS
0191 456 1369 www.twmuseums.org.uk/arbeia

Tynemouth Priory and Castle, TYNEMOUTH
0191 257 1090 www.english-heritage.org.uk

Great for kids: Blue Reef Aquarium, TYNEMOUTH
0191 258 1031 www.bluereefaquarium.co.uk

▶▶▶ **80% Lizard Lane Caravan & Camping Site** (NZ399648)

Lizard Ln NE34 7AB
☎ 0191 454 4982
e-mail: info@littlehavenhotel.com
dir: 2m S of town centre on A183 (Sunderland road)

🚐 🚌

Open Feb-28 Jan

Last arrival anytime Last departure 11.00hrs

This site is located in an elevated position with good sea views. All touring pitches are fully serviced and the modern smart amenities block is equipped with superb fixtures and fittings. A shop is also provided. Please note that tents are not

LEISURE: 🏊 Indoor swimming pool 🏖️ Outdoor swimming pool 𝔸 Children's playground 🪁 Kid's club 🎾 Tennis court 🎱 Games room ☐ Separate TV room 🏌️ 9/18 hole golf course 🚣 Boats for hire 🎬 Cinema ♫ Entertainment 🎣 Fishing ◎ Mini golf 🏄 Watersports 🏋️ Gym 🏐 Sports field Spa ♨ Stables
FACILITIES: 🛁 Bath 🚿 Shower ⊙ Electric shaver 🎀 Hairdryer ❄️ Ice Pack Facility ♿ Disabled facilities 🕐 Public telephone 🛒 Shop on site or within 200yds 🛒 Mobile shop (calls at least 5 days a week) 🔥 BBQ area 🪑 Picnic area 📶 Wi-fi 🖥️ Internet access ♻️ Recycling 🛈 Tourist info 🐕 Dog exercise area

accepted. 2 acre site. 47 touring pitches. Caravan pitches. Motorhome pitches. 70 statics.

Facilities: ⓝ⊙🅿✱🖢🕭🎱♻ ❶

Services: 🖭⊘🎘

Within 3 miles: ↨⅃日🖉🏊🖾🅱∪

Notes: Dogs must be kept on leads. 9-hole putting green.

WARWICKSHIRE

ASTON CANTLOW   Map 10 SP16

Places to visit

Mary Arden's Farm, WILMCOTE 01789 201844
www.shakespeare.org.uk

Charlecote Park, CHARLECOTE 01789 470277
www.nationaltrust.org.uk/
main/w-charlecotepark

Great for kids: Warwick Castle, WARWICK
0871 265 2000 www.warwick-castle.com

AA CAMPING CARD SITE

▶▶▶ **78% Island Meadow**
Caravan Park (SP137596)

The Mill House B95 6JP
☎ 01789 488273
e-mail: holiday@islandmeadowcaravanpark.co.uk
dir: From A46 or A3400 follow signs for Aston
Cantlow. Site signed 0.25m W off Mill Lane

* 🚐 £21 🚐 £21 ▲ £15-£20

Open Mar-Oct

Last arrival 21.00hrs Last departure noon

A small well-kept site bordered by the River Alne
on one side and its mill stream on the other.
Mature willows line the banks, and this is a very
pleasant place to relax and unwind. There are six
holiday statics for hire. 7 acre site. 24 touring
pitches. 14 hardstandings. Caravan pitches.
Motorhome pitches. Tent pitches. 56 statics.

AA Pubs & Restaurants nearby: The Stag, Red Hill
01789 764634

Blue Boar Inn, Temple Grafton 01789 750010

Facilities: ⓝ⊙🅿✱🖢🕭🅲🖾♻ ❶

Services: 🖭🅾🔋⊘🎘

Within 3 miles: ↨🖉◎🖾

Notes: Dogs must be kept on leads. Free fishing
for visitors.

HARBURY   Map 11 SP35

Places to visit

Warwick Castle, WARWICK 0871 265 2000
www.warwick-castle.com

Farnborough Hall, FARNBOROUGH 01295 690002
www.nationaltrust.org.uk

Great for kids: Stratford Butterfly Farm,
STRATFORD-UPON-AVON 01789 299288
www.butterflyfarm.co.uk

▶▶▶▶ **87% Harbury Fields** (SP352604)

Harbury Fields Farm CV33 9JN
☎ 01926 612457
e-mail: rdavis@harburyfields.co.uk
dir: M40 junct 12, B4451 (signed Kineton/
Gaydon). 0.75m, right signed Lightborne. 4m,
right at rdbt onto B4455 (signed Harbury). 3rd
right by petrol station, site in 700yds (by two
cottages)

* 🚐 £16-£22 🚐

Open Feb-19 Dec

Last arrival 20.00hrs Last departure noon

This developing park is in a peaceful farm setting
with lovely countryside views. All pitches have
hardstandings with electric and the facilities are
spotless. It is well positioned for visiting Warwick
and Leamington Spa as well as the exhibition
centres at NEC Birmingham and Stoneleigh Park.
Stratford is just ten miles away, and Upton House
(NT) and Compton Valley Art Gallery are nearby. 3
acre site. 32 touring pitches. 31 hardstandings.
Caravan pitches. Motorhome pitches.

AA Pubs & Restaurants nearby: Duck on the Pond,
Long Itchington 01926 815876

Facilities: ⓝ⊙🖢🎘🛒 ❶

Services: 🖭🅾🔋

Within 3 miles: ↨🖉🖾

Notes: No traffic noise between mdnt & 07.30hrs.

KINGSBURY   Map 10 SP29

Places to visit

Sarehole Mill, BIRMINGHAM 0121 777 6612
www.bmag.org.uk

Museum of the Jewellery Quarter, BIRMINGHAM
0121 554 3598 www.bmag.org.uk

AA CAMPING CARD SITE

▶ **70% Tame View Caravan Site**
(SP209979)

Cliff B78 2DR
☎ 01827 873853
dir: 400yds off A51 (Tamworth-Kingsbury road),
1m N of Kingsbury opposite pub. Signed Cliff Hall
Lane

🚐 🚐 ▲

Open all year

Last arrival 23.00hrs Last departure 23.00hrs

A secluded spot overlooking the Tame Valley and
river, sheltered by high hedges. Sanitary facilities
are minimal but clean on this small park. The site
is popular with many return visitors who like a
peaceful basic site. 5 acre site. 5 touring pitches.
Caravan pitches. Motorhome pitches. Tent pitches.

AA Pubs & Restaurants nearby: Chapel House
Restaurant with Rooms, Atherstone 01827 718949

Facilities: ✱🅲🎘🛒♻

Services: 🎘

Within 3 miles: ↨⅃日🖉◎🏊🖾🅱∪

Notes: 🚫 No noise after mdnt. Dogs must be kept
on leads. Fishing.

SERVICES: 🖭 Electric hook up 🅾 Launderette 🍺 Licensed bar 🅲 Calor Gas ⊘ Camping Gaz 🅣 Toilet fluid 🍴 Café/Restaurant 🍔 Fast Food/Takeaway 🔋 Battery charging
🚼 Baby care 🅥 Motorvan service point **ABBREVIATIONS:** BH/bank hols-bank holidays Etr-Easter Whit-Whitsun dep-departure fr-from hrs-hours m-mile mdnt-midnight
rdbt-roundabout rs-restricted service wk-week wknd-weekend 🚫 No credit cards 🚫 no dogs   See page 7 for details of the AA Camping Card Scheme

WOLVEY Map 11 SP48

Places to visit

Arbury Hall, NUNEATON 024 7638 2804 www.arburyestate.co.uk

Jaguar Daimler Heritage Centre, COVENTRY 024 7640 1291 www.jdht.com

Great for kids: Lunt Roman Fort, COVENTRY 024 7629 4734 www.theherbert.org

►►► 77% Wolvey Villa Farm Caravan & Camping Site *(SP428869)*

LE10 3HF

☎ 01455 220493 & 220630

dir: *M6 junct 2, B4065 follow Wolvey signs. Or M69 junct 1 & follow Wolvey signs*

🚐 £13-£16 🚌 £13-£16 ⛺ £13-£16

Open all year

Last arrival 22.00hrs Last departure noon

A level grass site surrounded by trees and shrubs, on the borders of Warwickshire and Leicestershire. This quiet country site has its own popular fishing lake, and is convenient for visiting the cities of Coventry and Leicester. 7 acre site. 110 touring pitches. 24 hardstandings. Caravan pitches. Motorhome pitches. Tent pitches.

AA Pubs & Restaurants nearby: Bell Inn, Monks Kirby 01788 832352

The Pheasant, Withybrook 01455 220480

Leisure: ⚽ 🔍

Facilities: 🚿 ⊙ 💇 ❄ ♿ 📞 🏪 🐕 ℹ

Services: 🔌 🧺 🔒 🧪 [T] 🍴

Within 3 miles: ⛳ 🎬 🎣 🏪 🧺 Ʊ

Notes: 🚫 No twin axles. Dogs must be kept on leads. Putting green, off licence.

WEST MIDLANDS

MERIDEN Map 10 SP28

Places to visit

Blakesley Hall, BIRMINGHAM 0121 464 2193 www.bmag.org.uk

Aston Hall, BIRMINGHAM 0121 464 2193 www.bmag.org.uk/aston-hall

AA CAMPING CARD SITE

►►►► 92% Somers Wood Caravan Park *(SP225824)*

Best of British

Somers Rd CV7 7PL

☎ 01676 522978

e-mail: enquiries@somerswood.co.uk

dir: *M42 junct 6, A45 signed Coventry. Keep left (do not take flyover). Then right onto A452 signed Meriden & Leamington. At next rdbt left onto B4102 (Hampton Lane). Site in 0.5m on left*

🚐 £18-£24 🚌 £18-£24

Open all year

Last arrival variable Last departure variable

A peaceful adults-only park set in the heart of England with spotless facilities. The park is well positioned for visiting the National Exhibition Centre (NEC), the NEC Arena and National Indoor Arena (NIA), and Birmingham is only 12 miles away. The park also makes an ideal touring base for Warwick, Coventry and Stratford-upon-Avon just 22 miles away. Please note that tents are not accepted. 4 acre site. 48 touring pitches. 48 hardstandings. Caravan pitches. Motorhome pitches.

AA Pubs & Restaurants nearby: White Lion Inn, Hampton-in-Arden 01675 442833

Facilities: 🚿 ⊙ 💇 ❄ ♿ 📞 [Wi-fi] ♻ ℹ

Services: 🔌 🔒 🧪 [T] 🍴

Within 3 miles: ⛳ 🎣 🏪 Ʊ

Notes: Adults only. No noise 22.30hrs-08.00hrs. Dogs must be kept on leads. Laundry service available.

SERVICES: ⚡ Electric hook up 🔲 Launderette 🍺 Licensed bar 🔥 Calor Gas 🌀 Camping Gaz T Toilet fluid 🍽 Café/Restaurant 🍟 Fast Food/Takeaway ⚡ Battery charging
🍼 Baby care ⚓ Motorvan service point **ABBREVIATIONS:** BH/bank hols-bank holidays Etr-Easter Whit-Whitsun dep-departure fr-from hrs-hours m-mile mdnt-midnight
rdbt-roundabout rs-restricted service wk-week wknd-weekend 🚫 No credit cards 🚫 no dogs   See page 7 for details of the AA Camping Card Scheme

Isle of Wight

Generations of visitors to the Isle of Wight consistently say the same
thing, that to go there is akin to stepping back to the 1950s and '60s.
The pace of life is still gentle and unhurried and the place continues to
exude that familiar salty tang of the sea we all remember from
childhood, when bucket and spade holidays were an integral part of
growing up. Small and intimate – just 23 miles by 13 miles – the Isle of
Wight is just the place to get away-from-it-all.

Being an island, it has a unique and distinctive identity. With its mild climate, long hours of sunshine and exuberant architecture, the Isle of Wight has something of a continental flavour. In the summer the place understandably gets very busy, especially during Cowes week in August – a key date in the country's sporting calendar. Elsewhere, seaside towns such as Ventnor, Shanklin and Sandown are popular during the season for their many and varied attractions.

Variety is the key on this delightful and much-loved holiday island. Queen Victoria made the place fashionable and popular when she and Prince Albert chose it as the setting for their summer home, Osborne House, and the island has never looked back. In recent years the steady increase in tourism has ushered in many new visitor attractions to meet the demands of the late 20th and early 21st centuries, but there are still the perennial old favourites. The Needles, the iconic series of chalk stacks, is a classic example, and just about everyone who has visited over the years can recall buying tubes of sand from nearby Alum Bay – a multi-coloured mix of white quartz, red iron oxide and yellow limonite.

▶

Walking and Cycling

Despite the large numbers of summer visitors, there are still plenty of places on the island where you can be alone and savour its tranquillity. The 65-mile Isle of Wight Coast Path allows walkers to appreciate the natural beauty and diversity of its coastal scenery. Much of the path in the southern half of the island is a relatively undemanding walk over sweeping chalk downs, and beyond Freshwater Bay the coast is often remote and essentially uninhabited. Completing the whole trail or just part of it is the ideal way to discover the island's coastline without the aggravation. Mostly, the route is over cliff-top paths, tracks, sea walls and esplanades. Nearly 40 miles of it is beside the coast, though the inland stretches are never far from the sea. However, beware of erosion and expect to find the path diverted in places. The Isle of Wight's hinterland may lack the sea views but the scenery is no less appealing. Here walkers can explore a vast and well publicised network of paths that reach the very heart of the island. In all, the Isle of Wight has more than 500 miles of public rights of way and more than half the island is recognised as an Area of Outstanding Natural Beauty.

For cyclists there is also a good deal of choice. The Round the Island Cycle Route runs for 49 miles and takes advantage of quiet roads and lanes. There are starting points at Yarmouth, Cowes and Ryde and the route is waymarked with official Cycle Route blue signs.

Festivals and Events

Among a host of festivals and events held on the Isle of Wight throughout the year are:-

- The Real Ale Festival in May
- The Isle of Wight Walking Festival in May and the Isle of Wight Weekend Walking Festival held in October
- The Cycling Festival in September
- The Garlic Festival in August

For more information visit
www.islandbreaks.co.uk

● The Needles

Shanklin Chine

WIGHT, ISLE OF

BEMBRIDGE

See Whitecliff Bay

COWES
Map 5 SZ49

Places to visit

Osborne House, OSBORNE HOUSE 01983 200022
www.english-heritage.org.uk

Bembridge Windmill, BEMBRIDGE 01983 873945
www.nationaltrust.org.uk/isleofwight

Great for kids: Robin Hill Country Park,
ARRETON 01983 527352 www.robin-hill.com

 85% *Thorness Bay Holiday Park* (SZ448928)

Thorness PO31 8NJ
☎ 01983 523109
e-mail: holidaysales.thornessbay
@park-resorts.com
web: www.park-resorts.com
dir: *On A3054 towards Yarmouth, 1st right after BMW garage, signed Thorness Bay*

Open Apr-1 Nov

Last arrival anytime Last departure 10.00hrs

Splendid views of The Solent can be enjoyed from this rural park located just outside Cowes. A footpath leads directly to the coast, while on site there is an all-weather sports court, entertainment clubs for children, and cabaret shows, and a bar for all the family. There are 23 serviced pitches, in the separate touring area, with TV boosters. 130 holiday homes are for hire. 148 acre site. 124 touring pitches. 21 hardstandings. 8 seasonal pitches. Caravan pitches. Motorhome pitches. Tent pitches. 560 statics.

AA Pubs & Restaurants nearby: Fountain Inn, Cowes 01983 292397

Duke of York Inn, Cowes 01983 295171

The Folly, Whippingham 01983 297171

Leisure: 🏊♨🎠🎲🎵
Facilities: 🚿🔫☉📷🛁⚲🔌🧴🚻📠♻🛈
Services: 🔌🛒🍴🛁🔧🚰🚽🎲🍴♿🛒
Within 3 miles: 🎣🛶🛒🛍

Notes: Dogs must be kept on leads. Water slide.

FRESHWATER
Map 5 SZ38

Places to visit

Colemans Farm Park, PORCHFIELD
01983 522831 www.colemansfarmpark.co.uk

Dimbola Lodge Museum, FRESHWATER
01983 756814 www.dimbola.co.uk

Great for kids: Blackgang Chine Fantasy Park,
BLACKGANG 01983 730330
www.blackgangchine.com

▶▶▶▶ **84% Heathfield Farm Camping** (SZ335879)

Heathfield Rd PO40 9SH
☎ 01983 407822
e-mail: web@heathfieldcamping.co.uk
dir: *2m W from Yarmouth ferry port on A3054, left to Heathfield Rd, entrance 200yds on right*

🚐🚍⛺

Open May-Sep

Last arrival 20.00hrs Last departure 11.00hrs

A very good quality park with friendly and welcoming staff. There are lovely views across the Solent to Hurst Castle. The toilet facilities, the amenities, which include an excellent backpackers' area, and the very well maintained grounds, make this park amongst the best on the island. 10 acre site. 60 touring pitches. Caravan pitches. Motorhome pitches. Tent pitches.

AA Pubs & Restaurants nearby: Red Lion, Freshwater 01983 754925

Leisure: ⚽
Facilities: 🚿☉📷✳⚲☉🔌🐕📠♻🛈
Services: 🔌🛒🚰🚽
Within 3 miles: 🎣🛶🛒◎🛍🍴🍴🛍U

Notes: Family camping only. Dogs must be kept on leads.

NEWBRIDGE
Map 5 SZ48

Places to visit

Newtown Old Town Hall,
NEWTOWN 01983 531785
www.nationaltrust.org.uk/isleofwight

Brighstone Shop and Museum,
BRIGHSTONE 01983 740689
www.nationaltrust.org.uk/isleofwight

Great for kids: Yarmouth Castle, YARMOUTH
01983 760678 www.english-heritage.org.uk

PREMIER PARK

▶▶▶▶▶ **92% The Orchards Holiday Caravan Park** (SZ411881)

Main Rd PO41 0TS
☎ 01983 531331 & 531350
e-mail: info@orchards-holiday-park.co.uk
web: www.orchards-holiday-park.co.uk
dir: *4m E of Yarmouth; 6m W of Newport on B3401. Take A3054 from Yarmouth, after 3m turn right at Horse & Groom Inn. Follow signs to Newbridge. Entrance opposite post office*

🚐🚍⛺

Open 11 Feb-2 Jan (rs Nov-Feb takeaway, shop, outdoor pool closed)

Last arrival 23.00hrs Last departure 11.00hrs

A really excellent, well-managed park set in a peaceful village location amid downs and meadowland, with glorious downland views. Pitches are terraced and offer a good provision of hardstandings, including water serviced pitches. There is a high quality facility centre offering excellent spacious showers and family rooms, plus there is access for disabled visitors to all site facilities and disabled toilets. The park has indoor and outdoor swimming pools, a shop, takeaway and licensed shop. Static homes are available for hire and 'ferry plus stay' packages are on offer. 15 acre site. 171 touring pitches. 74 hardstandings.

LEISURE: 🏊 Indoor swimming pool 🏊 Outdoor swimming pool 🛝 Children's playground 🧒 Kid's club 🎾 Tennis court 🎱 Games room 📺 Separate TV room 🏌 9/18 hole golf course 🚣 Boats for hire 🎬 Cinema 🎵 Entertainment 🎣 Fishing ◎ Mini golf 🏄 Watersports 💪 Gym ⚽ Sports field **Spa** ♨ Stables
FACILITIES: 🛁 Bath 🚿 Shower ☉ Electric shaver 📷 Hairdryer ✳ Ice Pack Facility ⚲ Disabled facilities ☎ Public telephone 🛒 Shop on site or within 200yds 🚐 Mobile shop (calls at least 5 days a week) 🍴 BBQ area 🪑 Picnic area 📶 Wi-fi 🌐 Internet access ♻ Recycling 🛈 Tourist info 🐕 Dog exercise area

Caravan pitches. Motorhome pitches. Tent pitches. 65 statics.

AA Pubs & Restaurants nearby: New Inn, Shalfleet 01983 531314

Leisure: 🌳🛶🎢🎣🎱🏓

Facilities: 🛁🚿⊙🍴❄️♿🛒🔥🏕️🐕 WiFi 🅿️

Services: 🔌🗑️🔋🚽🍴⬆️🚐♻️

Within 3 miles: 🚶🎣🛒

Notes: No cycling. Dogs must be kept on leads. Table tennis room, poolside coffee shop.

NEWPORT   Map 5 SZ58

Places to visit

Carisbrooke Castle, CARISBROOKE 01983 522107 www.english-heritage.org.uk

Osborne House, OSBORNE HOUSE 01983 200022 www.english-heritage.org.uk

▶▶▶ 74% *Riverside Paddock Camp Site* (SZ503911)

Dodnor Ln PO30 5TE
☎ **01983 821367 & 07962 400533**
e-mail: enquiries@riversidepaddock.co.uk
dir: *From Newport take dual carriageway towards Cowes. At 1st rdbt take 3rd exit, immediately left at next rdbt. Follow until road meets National Cycle Route. Site on left*

🚐🚋🏕️

Open all year

Last arrival 20.00hrs Last departure 11.00hrs

Although fairly close to Newport this quiet campsite offers a really peaceful environment and has direct access to the national cycle route from Newport to Cowes. The Medina River with its riverside walks is also nearby. The park's toilet facilities include two fully serviced unisex cubicles, and there are good hardstandings, many with electric; all facilities are spotless. The location of the park makes it perfect for people who like to walk or to ride their bikes. 8 acre site. 28 touring pitches. 18 hardstandings. Caravan pitches. Motorhome pitches. Tent pitches. 5 tipis.

AA Pubs & Restaurants nearby: White Lion, Arreton 01983 528479

Facilities: 🏕️❄️♿🐕 WiFi 💻♻️🅿️

Services: 🔌

Within 3 miles: 🚶🎣🎱🎢♻️🛒🍴🛒↻

Notes: Adults only. 🚫 No loud music, no generators. Dogs must be kept on leads.

RYDE   Map 5 SZ59

Places to visit

Nunwell House & Gardens, BRADING 01983 407240

Bembridge Windmill, BEMBRIDGE 01983 873945 www.nationaltrust.org.uk/isleofwight

Great for kids: Robin Hill Country Park, ARRETON 01983 527352 www.robin-hill.com

---

PREMIER PARK

▶▶▶▶▶ 91% Whitefield Forest Touring Park (SZ604893)

GOLD

Brading Rd PO33 1QL
☎ **01983 617069**
e-mail: pat&louise@whitefieldforest.co.uk
web: www.whitefieldforest.co.uk
dir: *From Ryde follow A3055 towards Brading, after Tesco rdbt site 0.5m on left*

* 🚐 £15-£22 🚋 £15-£22 🏕️ £15-£22

Open Etr-Oct

Last arrival 21.00hrs Last departure 11.00hrs

This park is beautifully laid out in Whitefield Forest, and offers a wide variety of pitches, all of which have electricity. It offers excellent modern facilities, which are spotlessly clean. The park takes great care in retaining the natural beauty of the forest, and is a haven for wildlife; red squirrels can be spotted throughout the park, including on the nature walk. 23 acre site. 80 touring pitches. 35 hardstandings. Caravan pitches. Motorhome pitches. Tent pitches.

AA Pubs & Restaurants nearby: Boathouse, Seaview 01983 810616

Leisure: 🎢

Facilities: 🏕️⊙❄️♿🛒 WiFi ♻️🅿️

Services: 🔌🗑️🔋🚽⬆️

Within 3 miles: 🚶🎣🎱🎢♻️🛒🍴

Notes: Dogs must be kept on leads.

▶▶▶ 84% *Roebeck Camping and Caravan Park* (SZ581903)

Gatehouse Rd, Upton Cross PO33 4BP
☎ **01983 611475 & 07930 992080**
e-mail: info@roebeck-farm.co.uk
dir: *Right from Fishbourne ferry terminal (west of Ryde). At lights left onto A3054 towards Ryde. In outskirts straight on at 'All Through Traffic' sign. At end of Pellhurst Rd right into Upton Rd. Site 50yds beyond mini-rdbt*

🚐🏕️

Open Apr-Nov

A quiet park in a country setting on the outskirts of Ryde offering very nice facilities, especially for campers, including an excellent dishwashing/kitchen cabin. The unique, ready-erected tipis, which are available for hire, add to the ambience of the site. There is also an excellent fishing lake. 4 acre site. 37 touring pitches. Caravan pitches. Tent pitches.

AA Pubs & Restaurants nearby: Lakeside Park Hotel, Ryde 01983 882266

Boathouse, Seaview 01983 810616

Seaview Hotel & Restaurant, Seaview 01983 612711

Facilities: 🏕️🛒❄️🔥🐕 WiFi

Services: 🔌🗑️

Within 3 miles: 🚶🎣🎱⊙♻️🛒🍴↻

ST HELENS Map 5 SZ68

Places to visit

Brading The Experience, BRADING 01983 407286 www.bradingtheexperience.co.uk

Bembridge Windmill, BEMBRIDGE 01983 873945 www.nationaltrust.org.uk/isleofwight

Great for kids: Lilliput Antique Doll & Toy Museum, BRADING 01983 407231 www.lilliputmuseum.org.uk

86% *Nodes Point Holiday Park* *(SZ636897)*

Nodes Rd PO33 1YA
☎ 01983 872401
e-mail: gm.nodespoint@park-resorts.com
web: www.park-resorts.com
dir: *From Ryde take B3330 signed Seaview/Puckpool. At junct for Puckpool bear right. 1m past Road Side Inn in Nettlestone, site on left*

🚐 🚌 ⛺

Open Apr-Oct

Last arrival 21.00hrs Last departure 10.00hrs

A well-equipped holiday centre on an elevated position overlooking Bembridge Bay with direct access to the beach. The touring area is mostly sloping with some terraces. Activities are organised for youngsters, and there is entertainment for the whole family. Buses pass the main entrance road. The touring area has very well appointed, ready-erected tents for hire. Holiday homes are also available for hire or purchase. 16 acre site. 150 touring pitches. 4 hardstandings. 4 seasonal pitches. Caravan pitches. Motorhome pitches. Tent pitches. 195 statics.

AA Pubs & Restaurants nearby: Windmill Inn, Bembridge 01983 872875

The Crab & Lobster Inn, Bembridge 01983 872244

Leisure: 🏊 🛝 ✋ ⚽ 🎵

Facilities: 🛁 🚿 ⊙ 💨 ❄ ♿ 📞 🛒 🪑 🐕 [Wi-fi] 💻

Services: 🔧 🫧 🍺 □ 🍃 🍽 🛍

Within 3 miles: ⛳ 🚣 🎬 🎣 ◎ 🏄 🛒 🫧 🐴

SANDOWN Map 5 SZ58

Places to visit

Nunwell House & Gardens, BRADING 01983 407240

Bembridge Windmill, BEMBRIDGE 01983 873945 www.nationaltrust.org.uk/isleofwight

Great for kids: Dinosaur Isle, SANDOWN 01983 404344 www.dinosaurisle.com

AA CAMPING CARD SITE

►►►► 79% Old Barn Touring Park *(SZ571833)*

Cheverton Farm, Newport Rd, Apse Heath PO36 9PJ
☎ 01983 866414
e-mail: oldbarn@weltinet.com
dir: *On A3056 from Newport, site on left after Apse Heath rdbt*

🚐 £17-£23 🚌 £17-£23 ⛺ £17-£23

Open May-Sep

Last arrival 21.00hrs Last departure noon

A terraced site with several secluded camping areas divided by hedges. This site is well positioned for visiting the eastern side of the island, and customers can be sure of a warm welcome from the friendly staff. Rallies are very welcome plus there are two ready erected tents for hire. 5 acre site. 60 touring pitches. 9 hardstandings. 6 seasonal pitches. Caravan pitches. Motorhome pitches. Tent pitches.

AA Pubs & Restaurants nearby: Windmill Inn, Bembridge 01983 872875

The Crab & Lobster Inn, Bembridge 01983 872244

Leisure: 🛝 ♠ 📺

Facilities: 🚿 ⊙ 💨 ❄ ♿ 🐕 [Wi-fi] 💻 ♻ ℹ

Services: 🔧 🫧 🔒 🍃 [T] 🛌 ⛛

Within 3 miles: ⛳ 🚣 🎣 ◎ 🏄 🛒 🫧 🐴

Notes: Dogs must be kept on leads.

► 78% Queenbower Dairy Caravan Park *(SZ567846)*

Alverstone Rd, Queenbower PO36 0NZ
☎ 01983 403840
e-mail: queenbowerdairy@btconnect.com
dir: *3m N of Sandown from A3056 right into Alverstone Rd, site 1m on left*

* 🚐 £6.50-£10 🚌 £6.50-£10 ⛺ £6.50-£10

Open May-Oct

A small site with basic amenities that will appeal to campers keen to escape the crowds and the busy larger sites. The enthusiastic owners keep the facilities very clean. 2.5 acre site. 20 touring pitches. Caravan pitches. Motorhome pitches. Tent pitches.

AA Pubs & Restaurants nearby: Windmill Inn, Bembridge 01983 872875

The Crab & Lobster Inn, Bembridge 01983 872244

Facilities: ❄ 🛒

Services: 🔧 🛌

Within 3 miles: ⛳ 🚣 🎣 ◎ 🏄 🛒 🫧

Notes: 🚭 Dogs must be kept on leads and exercised off site.

LEISURE: 🏊 Indoor swimming pool 🌊 Outdoor swimming pool 🛝 Children's playground ✋ Kid's club 🎾 Tennis court ♠ Games room 📺 Separate TV room ⛳ 9/18 hole golf course 🚣 Boats for hire 🎬 Cinema 🎵 Entertainment 🎣 Fishing ◎ Mini golf 🏄 Watersports 🏋 Gym ⚽ Sports field Spa 🐴 Stables
FACILITIES: 🛁 Bath 🚿 Shower ⊙ Electric shaver 💨 Hairdryer ❄ Ice Pack Facility ♿ Disabled facilities 📞 Public telephone 🛒 Shop on site or within 200yds 🚚 Mobile shop (calls at least 5 days a week) 🍖 BBQ area 🪑 Picnic area [Wi-fi] Wi-fi 💻 Internet access ♻ Recycling ℹ Tourist info 🐕 Dog exercise area

SHANKLIN — Map 5 SZ58

Places to visit

Shanklin Chine, SHANKLIN 01983 866432
www.shanklinchine.co.uk

Ventnor Botanic Garden, VENTNOR
01983 855397 www.botanic.co.uk

Great for kids: Dinosaur Isle, SANDOWN
01983 404344 www.dinosaurisle.com

 84% Lower Hyde Holiday Park (SZ575819)

Landguard Rd PO37 7LL
☎ 01983 866131
e-mail:
holidaysales.lowerhyde@park-resorts.com
web: www.park-resorts.com
dir: From Fishbourne ferry terminal follow
A3055 to Shanklin. Site signed just past lake

* ➡ fr £5.60 ➡ fr £6.40 ▲ fr £4.60

Open Mar-end Oct

Last arrival 17.00hrs Last departure noon

A popular holiday park on the outskirts of
Shanklin, close to the sandy beaches. There
is an outdoor swimming pool and plenty of
organised activities for youngsters of all ages.
In the evening there is a choice of family
entertainment. The touring facilities are located
in a quiet area away from the main complex,
with good views over the downs. Holiday homes
are available for hire or purchase. 65 acre
site. 151 touring pitches. 25 hardstandings.
Caravan pitches. Motorhome pitches. Tent
pitches.

AA Pubs & Restaurants nearby: Bonchurch Inn,
Bonchurch 01983 852611

The Taverners, Godshill 01983 840707

Leisure: 🌊🏊⚡🎮♦🎣🎵
Facilities: 🔧🐕✱👶🔥🛒🏃🔌 ♻ ❶
Services: 🔌🛢🍴🔋🚿🚮⬆⚡
Within 3 miles: ↓🐴🗓✏◎🏊🛒📮♨
Notes: Dogs must be kept on leads.

▶▶▶ 84% Ninham Country Holidays

(SZ573825)

Ninham PO37 7PL
☎ 01983 864243
e-mail: office@ninham-holidays.co.uk
dir: Signed from A3056 (Newport to Sandown road)

➡ £16.50-£25 ➡ £16.50-£25 ▲ £13-£23

Open May day BH-Sep

Last arrival 20.00hrs Last departure 10.00hrs

Enjoying a lofty rural position with fine country
views, this delightful, spacious park occupies two
separate, well-maintained areas in a country park
setting near the sea and beach. There's a good
outdoor swimming pool. At the time of our last
visit a new toilet block was under construction. 12
acre site. 98 touring pitches. 4 hardstandings.
Caravan pitches. Motorhome pitches. Tent pitches.

AA Pubs & Restaurants nearby: Bonchurch Inn,
Bonchurch 01983 852611

The Taverners, Godshill 01983 840707

Leisure: 🌊⚡😊🎣
Facilities: 🔧☀✱👶🔥🛒🌐 ♻ ❶
Services: 🔌🛢🍴🔋🚿⬆
Within 3 miles: ↓🐴✏◎🏊🛒📮♨
Notes: ⊗ Swimming pool & coarse fishing rules
apply. Fully serviced pitches. Late night/arrival
area available.

▶▶▶ 80% Landguard Camping

(SZ580825)

Manor Rd PO37 7PJ
☎ 01983 863100
e-mail:
holidaysales.landguard@park-resorts.com
web: www.park-resorts.com
dir: A3056 towards Sandown. After Morrisons on
left, turn right into Whitecross Ln. Follow brown
signs to site

➡ fr £4.80 ➡ fr £5.60 ▲

Open Mar-end Oct

Last arrival 17.00hrs Last departure noon

Now owned by Park Resorts, this peaceful and
secluded park offers good touring facilities.
Customers here also have the benefit of using the
swimming pool and entertainment facilities at
Lower Hyde Holiday Park nearby. 142 touring
pitches. 6 hardstandings. Caravan pitches.
Motorhome pitches. Tent pitches.

AA Pubs & Restaurants nearby: Bonchurch Inn,
Bonchurch 01983 852611

The Taverners, Godshill 01983 840707

Leisure: 🌊⚡🏕🎮♦🎵🎶
Facilities: 🔧✱👶🔥🛒🏃🔌🌐 ♻ ❶
Services: 🔌🛢🍴🔋🚿🚮⬆⚡
Within 3 miles: ↓🐴🗓✏◎🏊🛒📮♨
Notes: Dogs must be kept on leads.

TOTLAND BAY — Map 5 SZ38

Places to visit

Dimbola Lodge Museum, FRESHWATER
01983 756814 www.dimbola.co.uk

Mottistone Manor Garden,
MOTTISTONE 01983 741302
www.nationaltrust.org.uk/isleofwight

Great for kids: Yarmouth Castle, YARMOUTH
01983 760678 www.english-heritage.org.uk

▶▶▶ 76% Stoats Farm Caravan & Camping (SZ324865)

PO39 0HE
☎ 01983 755258 & 753416
e-mail: david@stoats-farm.co.uk
dir: On Alum Bay road, 1.5m from Freshwater &
0.75m from Totland

➡➡▲

Open Apr-Oct

A friendly, personally run site in a quiet country
setting close to Alum Bay, Tennyson Down and The
Needles. It has good laundry and shower facilities,
and the shop, although small, is well stocked.
Popular with families, walkers and cyclists, it
makes the perfect base for campers wishing to
explore this part of the island. 10 acre site. 100
touring pitches. Caravan pitches. Motorhome
pitches. Tent pitches.

AA Pubs & Restaurants nearby: Red Lion,
Freshwater 01983 754925

Facilities: 🔧☀✱👶🔥🛒🏃❶
Services: 🔌🛢🚿⬆
Within 3 miles: ↓🐴✏◎🏊🛒♨
Notes: No loud noise after 23.00hrs, no camp
fires. Dogs must be kept on leads. Campers' fridge
available.

WHITECLIFF BAY
Map 5 SZ68

84% Whitecliff Bay Holiday Park (SZ637862)

Hillway Rd, Bembridge PO35 5PL
☎ 01983 872671
e-mail: holiday.sales@away-resorts.com
dir: *1m S of Bembridge, signed from B3395 in village*

🚐 £4-£55 🚘 £4-£55 ⛺ £4-£43

Open Mar-end Oct
Last arrival 21.00hrs Last departure 10.30hrs

A large seaside complex on two sites, with camping on one and self-catering chalets and statics on the other. There is an indoor pool with flume and spa pool, and an outdoor pool with a kiddies' pool, a family entertainment club, and plenty of traditional on-site activities including crazy golf, an indoor soft play area and table tennis, plus a restaurant and a choice of bars. Activities include a 'My Active' programme for all the family in partnership with 'Fit4Life'.

Access to a secluded beach from the park. The Canvas Village has 12 ready-erected tents for hire. Dogs are welcome. 49 acre site. 400 touring pitches. 50 hardstandings. Caravan pitches. Motorhome pitches. Tent pitches. 227 statics. 12 bell tents/yurts.

AA Pubs & Restaurants nearby: Windmill Inn, Bembridge 01983 872875

Leisure: 🏊 🏊 ⛰ ⚽ 🔍 ▢ 🎵

Facilities: 🚿 ⊙ 🪒 ✳ 🔥 🚽 🛎 🏧 WiFi 💻 ♻ ❗

Services: 🚐 🗑 🍴 🔒 🚰 T 🍽 🛖 🏕 🐕 ⚡

Within 3 miles: ⤒ 🚣 🎣 ◎ ⛵ 🏧 🐴 U

Notes: Adults & families only. Dogs must be kept on leads. Sauna, sunbed, sports TV lounge.

see advert below

WOOTTON BRIDGE
Map 5 SZ59

Places to visit

Osborne House, OSBORNE HOUSE 01983 200022 www.english-heritage.org.uk

Bembridge Windmill, BEMBRIDGE 01983 873945 www.nationaltrust.org.uk/isleofwight

Great for kids: Robin Hill Country Park, ARRETON 01983 527352 www.robin-hill.com

►►► 85% Kite Hill Farm Caravan & Camping Park (SZ549906)

Firestone Copse Rd PO33 4LE
☎ 01983 882543 & 883261
e-mail: welcome@kitehillfarm.co.uk
dir: *Signed from A3054 at Wootton Bridge, between Ryde & Newport*

🚐 🚘 ⛺

Open all year
Last arrival anytime Last departure anytime

The park, on a gently sloping field, is tucked away behind the owners' farm, just a short walk from

LEISURE: 🏊 Indoor swimming pool 🏊 Outdoor swimming pool ⛰ Children's playground 🎣 Kid's club 🎾 Tennis court 🎯 Games room ▢ Separate TV room ⤒ 9/18 hole golf course 🚣 Boats for hire 🎬 Cinema 🎵 Entertainment 🎣 Fishing ◎ Mini golf 🏄 Watersports 🏋 Gym 🏐 Sports field Spa U Stables
FACILITIES: 🛁 Bath 🚿 Shower ⊙ Electric shaver 🪒 Hairdryer ✳ Ice Pack Facility ♿ Disabled facilities 📞 Public telephone 🛒 Shop on site or within 200yds 🏪 Mobile shop (calls at least 5 days a week) 🍴 BBQ area 🏕 Picnic area WiFi Wi-fi 💻 Internet access ♻ Recycling ❗ Tourist info 🐕 Dog exercise area

the village and attractive river estuary. The facilities are excellent and very clean. This park provides a nice relaxing atmosphere for a stay on the island. Rallies are welcome. 12.5 acre site. 50 touring pitches. 10 hardstandings. Caravan pitches. Motorhome pitches. Tent pitches.

AA Pubs & Restaurants nearby: The Folly, Whippingham 01983 297171

Fountain Inn, Cowes 01983 292397

Duke of York Inn, Cowes 01983 295171

Leisure: ⚏

Facilities: 🏕️⊙❄️&🕐➰🐾❶

Services: 🔌🗑️🧺🔋

Within 3 miles: ⚲🎏𝒫🛢️🛒🅾️

Notes: Owners must clean up after pets. Dogs must be kept on leads.

WROXALL   Map 5 SZ57

Places to visit

Appuldurcombe House, WROXALL 01983 852484 www.english-heritage.org.uk

Great for kids: Blackgang Chine Fantasy Park, BLACKGANG 01983 730330 www.blackgangchine.com

---

PREMIER PARK

▶▶▶▶▶ **84% Appuldurcombe Gardens Holiday Park** *(SZ546804)*

Appuldurcombe Rd PO38 3EP
☎ **01983 852597**
e-mail: info@appuldurcombegardens.co.uk
dir: *From Newport take A3020 towards Shanklin & Ventnor. Through Rookley & Godshill. Right at Whiteley Bank rdbt towards Wroxall village, then follow brown signs*

🚐 🚙 Å

Open Mar-Nov

Last arrival 21.00hrs Last departure 11.00hrs

This well-appointed park is set in a unique setting fairly close to the town of Ventnor. It has modern and spotless facilities including a new toilet and shower block, and a very tasteful lounge bar and function room. There is an excellent, screened outdoor pool and paddling pool plus café and shop. The site is close to cycle routes and is only 150 yards from the bus stop making it perfect for those with a motorhome or those not wanting to take the car out. Static caravans and apartments are also available for hire. 14 acre site. 130 touring pitches.

40 hardstandings. Caravan pitches. Motorhome pitches. Tent pitches. 40 statics.

AA Pubs & Restaurants nearby: Pond Café, Ventnor 01983 855666

Leisure: ⚤ ⚏ 🎣

Facilities: 🛏️🏕️⊙❄️🖊️&🛁🛡️🏊⚙️❶

Services: 🔌🗑️🍴🧺🚽🍽️🛒🚮♻️

Within 3 miles: ⚲🎏🎏𝒫🅾️⛴️🛢️🛢️🅾️

Notes: No skateboards. Dogs must be kept on leads. Entertainment in high season.

YARMOUTH

See Newbridge

WILTSHIRE

AMESBURY   Map 5 SU14

Places to visit

Stonehenge, STONEHENGE 0870 333 1181 www.english-heritage.org.uk

Heale Gardens, MIDDLE WOODFORD 01722 782504

Great for kids: Wilton House, WILTON [NEAR SALISBURY] 01722 746714 www.wiltonhouse.com

▶▶▶ **81% Stonehenge Touring Park** *(SU061456)*

Orcheston SP3 4SH
☎ **01980 620304**
e-mail: stay@stonehengetouringpark.com
dir: *From A360 towards Devizes turn right, follow lane, site at bottom of village on right*

🚐 £10-£16 🚙 £10-£16 Å £10-£27

Open all year

Last arrival 19.00hrs Last departure 11.00hrs

A quiet site adjacent to the small village of Orcheston near the centre of Salisbury Plain and four miles from Stonehenge. There's an excellent on-site shop. 2 acre site. 30 touring pitches. 12 hardstandings. Caravan pitches. Motorhome pitches. Tent pitches.

Leisure: ⚏

Facilities: 🏕️⊙❄️🖊️&🕐🛁🔌♻️❶

Services: 🔌🗑️🍴🧺🚽🛒🚮

Within 3 miles: 🛢️🛢️

Notes: No noise after 23.00hrs. Dogs must be kept on leads.

CALNE   Map 4 ST97

Places to visit

Avebury Manor & Garden, AVEBURY 01672 539250 www.nationaltrust.org.uk

Bowood House & Gardens, CALNE 01249 812102 www.bowood.org

Great for kids: Alexander Keiller Museum, AVEBURY 01672 539250 www.nationaltrust.org.uk

---

AA CAMPING CARD SITE

▶▶▶ **76% Blackland Lakes Holiday & Leisure Centre** *(ST973687)*

Stockley Ln SN11 0NQ
☎ **01249 810943**
e-mail: blacklandlakes.bookings@btconnect.com
web: www.blacklandlakes.co.uk
dir: *From Calne take A4 E for 1.5m, right at camp sign. Site 1m on left*

* 🚐 £7.50-£22.25 🚙 £7.50-£22.25 Å £7.50-£22.25

Open all year (rs 30 Oct-1 Mar pre-paid bookings only)

Last arrival 22.00hrs Last departure noon

A rural site surrounded by the North and West Downs. The park is divided into several paddocks separated by hedges, trees and fences, and there are two well-stocked carp fisheries for the angling enthusiast. There are some excellent walks close by, and the interesting market town of Devizes is just a few miles away. 15 acre site. 180 touring pitches. 16 hardstandings. 25 seasonal pitches. Caravan pitches. Motorhome pitches. Tent pitches.

AA Pubs & Restaurants nearby: Red Lion Inn, Lacock 01249 730456

George Inn, Lacock 01249 730263

Leisure: ⚏

Facilities: 🏕️⊙𝒫❄️&🛁🍴🏊

Services: 🔌🗑️🔋⚙️🛒🚮

Within 3 miles: ⚲𝒫🛢️🅾️

Notes: No noise after 23.00hrs, no loud music, no groups of under 25s. Dogs must be kept on leads. Wildfowl sanctuary, cycle trail.

LACOCK — Map 4 ST96

Places to visit

Lacock Abbey, Fox Talbot Museum & Village, LACOCK 01249 730459 www.nationaltrust.org.uk/lacock

Corsham Court, CORSHAM 01249 701610 www.corsham-court.co.uk

►►►► 82% Piccadilly Caravan Park

(ST913683)

Folly Lane West SN15 2LP
☎ 01249 730260
e-mail: piccadillylacock@aol.com
dir: *4m S of Chippenham just past Lacock. Exit A350 signed Gastard. Site 300yds on left*

⇌ £17-£19 ⇌ £17-£19 ▲ £17-£22.50

Open Etr/Apr-Oct

Last arrival 21.00hrs Last departure noon

A peaceful, pleasant site, well established and beautifully laid-out, close to the village of Lacock. Facilities and grounds are immaculately kept, and there is very good screening. A section of the park has been developed to provide spacious pitches, especially for tents, complete with a new toilet and shower block. 2.5 acre site. 41 touring pitches. 12 hardstandings. Caravan pitches. Motorhome pitches. Tent pitches.

AA Pubs & Restaurants nearby: Red Lion Inn, Lacock 01249 730456

George Inn, Lacock 01249 730263

Leisure: ⚲ ✿
Facilities: ⚐ ☉ 𝄞 ✳ ☾ 🚿 wifi ♻ ❶
Services: ⊞ 🗑 🛢 ∅ 🎟
Within 3 miles: ↓ 🎱 ✎ 🖺 🖻 U
Notes: ⊛ Dogs must be kept on leads.

LANDFORD — Map 5 SU21

Places to visit

Furzey Gardens, MINSTEAD 023 8081 2464 www.furzey-gardens.org

Mottisfont Abbey & Garden, MOTTISFONT 01794 340757 www.nationaltrust.org.uk/mottisfontabbey

Great for kids: Paultons Park, OWER 023 8081 4442 www.paultonspark.co.uk

►►►► 79% Greenhill Farm Caravan & Camping Park *(SU266183)*

Greenhill Farm, New Rd SP5 2AZ
☎ 01794 324117
e-mail: info@greenhillholidays.co.uk
dir: *M27 junct 2, A36 towards Salisbury, approx 3m after Hants/Wilts border, (Shoe Inn pub on right, BP garage on left) take next left into New Rd, signed Nomansland, 0.75m on left*

* ⇌ £17-£25 ⇌ £17-£25 ▲ £13.50-£25

Open all year

Last arrival 21.30hrs Last departure 11.00hrs

A tranquil, well-landscaped park hidden away in unspoilt countryside on the edge of the New Forest. Pitches overlooking the fishing lake include hardstandings and are for adults only. The other section of the park is for families and includes a play area, games room and an excellent new toilet and shower block for 2012. Well placed for visiting Paultons Park. 13 acre site. 160 touring pitches. 45 hardstandings. Caravan pitches. Motorhome pitches. Tent pitches.

AA Pubs & Restaurants nearby: Royal Oak, Fritham 023 8081 2606

Leisure: ⚲ ♦
Facilities: ⚐ ☉ 𝄞 ✳ ⚫ ☾ 🚿 🗑 ♻ ❶
Services: ⊞ 🗑 🛢 ∅ 🎟 ⚒ ⟱
Within 3 miles: ↓ ✎ ◎ 🖺 🖻 U
Notes: No noise after 23.00hrs. Dogs must be kept on leads. Disposable BBQs.

SALISBURY — Map 5 SU12

See also Amesbury

Places to visit

Salisbury & South Wiltshire Museum, SALISBURY 01722 332151 www.salisburymuseum.org.com

Salisbury Cathedral, SALISBURY 01722 555120 www.salisburycathedral.org.uk

Great for kids: The Medieval Hall, SALISBURY 01722 412472 www.medieval-hall.co.uk

►►►► 86% Coombe Touring Park

(SU099282)

Race Plain, Netherhampton SP2 8PN
☎ 01722 328451
e-mail: enquiries@coombecaravanpark.co.uk
dir: *A36 onto A3094, 2m SW, site adjacent to Salisbury racecourse*

⇌ ⇌ ▲

Open 3 Jan-20 Dec (rs Oct-May shop closed)

Last arrival 21.00hrs Last departure noon

A very neat and attractive site adjacent to the racecourse with views over the downs. The park is well landscaped with shrubs and maturing trees, and the very colourful beds are stocked from the owner's greenhouse. A comfortable park with a superb luxury toilet block, and four static holiday homes for hire. 3 acre site. 50 touring pitches. Caravan pitches. Motorhome pitches. Tent pitches. 4 statics.

AA Pubs & Restaurants nearby: Wig & Quill, Salisbury 01722 335665

Leisure: ⚲
Facilities: ⚐ ☉ 𝄞 ✳ ⚫ 🖺 ❶
Services: ⊞ 🗑 ∅ 🎟 ⚒ 🚐
Within 3 miles: ↓ 🖺 🖻 U
Notes: ⊛ No disposable BBQs or fires, no mini motorbikes, no noise between 23.00hrs-07.00hrs. Dogs must be kept on leads. Children's bathroom.

LEISURE: 🏊 Indoor swimming pool 🏊 Outdoor swimming pool ⚲ Children's playground 🪁 Kid's club 🎾 Tennis court 🎱 Games room 📺 Separate TV room ⛳ 9/18 hole golf course ⛵ Boats for hire 🎬 Cinema 🎵 Entertainment 🎣 Fishing ◎ Mini golf 🏄 Watersports 🏋 Gym ⚽ Sports field **Spa** U Stables
FACILITIES: 🛁 Bath 🚿 Shower ☉ Electric shaver 𝄞 Hairdryer ✳ Ice Pack Facility ⚫ Disabled facilities ☾ Public telephone 🖺 Shop on site or within 200yds 🖻 Mobile shop (calls at least 5 days a week) 🗑 BBQ area 🍴 Picnic area wifi Wi-fi ▦ Internet access ♻ Recycling ❶ Tourist info 🐕 Dog exercise area

►►► 79% *Alderbury Caravan & Camping Park* (SU197259)

Southampton Rd, Whaddon SP5 3HB
☎ 01722 710125
e-mail: alderbury@aol.com
dir: *Just off A36, 3m from Salisbury, opposite The Three Crowns*

Open all year

Last arrival 21.00hrs Last departure 12.30hrs

A pleasant, attractive park set in the village of Whaddon not far from Salisbury. The small site is well maintained by friendly owners, and is ideally positioned near the A36 for overnight stops to and from the Southampton ferry terminals. 2 acre site. 39 touring pitches. 12 hardstandings. Caravan pitches. Motorhome pitches. Tent pitches. 1 static.

AA Pubs & Restaurants nearby: Salisbury Seafood & Steakhouse, Salisbury 01722 417411

Old Mill, Salisbury 01722 327517

The Cloisters, Salisbury 01722 338102

Facilities: ♠☉✳♿✿
Services: ♨🗑🛢∅📶
Within 3 miles: ↨⚓🎣🏇🎣🏤🏪∪

Notes: No open fires. Dogs must be kept on leads. Microwave & electric kettle available.

TROWBRIDGE   Map 4 ST85

Places to visit

Great Chalfield Manor and Garden, BRADFORD-ON-AVON 01225 782239
www.nationaltrust.org.uk

The Courts Garden, HOLT 01225 782875
www.nationaltrust.org.uk

Great for kids: Longleat Safari & Adventure Park, LONGLEAT 01985 844400
www.longleat.co.uk

►► 74% *Stowford Manor Farm* (ST810577)

Stowford, Wingfield BA14 9LH
☎ 01225 752253
e-mail: stowford1@supanet.com
dir: *From Trowbridge take A366 W towards Radstock. Site on left in 3m*

♠☉✳

Open Etr-Oct

A very simple farm site set on the banks of the River Frome behind the farm courtyard. The owners are friendly and relaxed, and the park enjoys a similarly comfortable ambience. Farleigh & District Swimming Club, one of the few remaining river swimming clubs, is just half a mile from the site. 1.5 acre site. 15 touring pitches. Caravan pitches. Motorhome pitches. Tent pitches.

AA Pubs & Restaurants nearby: George Inn, Norton St Philip 01373 834224

Facilities: ♠☉✳🐾♲
Services: ♨🍴📶
Within 3 miles: ↨⚓🎣♿🏤🏪∪

Notes: No open fires. Dogs must be kept on leads. Fishing, boating, swimming in river.

WESTBURY   Map 4 ST85

Places to visit

Great Chalfield Manor and Garden, BRADFORD-ON-AVON 01225 782239
www.nationaltrust.org.uk

The Courts Garden, HOLT 01225 782875
www.nationaltrust.org.uk

AA CAMPING CARD SITE

►►►► 83% Brokerswood Country Park (ST836523)

GOLD

Brokerswood BA13 4EH
☎ 01373 822238
e-mail: info@brokerswoodcountrypark.co.uk
web: www.brokerswoodcountrypark.co.uk
dir: *M4 junct 17, S on A350. Right at Yarnbrook to Rising Sun pub at North Bradley, left at rdbt. Left on bend approaching Southwick, 2.5m, site on right*

* ♠ £12-£31 ♠ £12-£31 ♠ £12-£31

Open all year

Last arrival 21.30hrs Last departure 11.00hrs

A popular park on the edge of an 80-acre woodland park with nature trails and fishing lakes. An adventure playground offers plenty of fun for all ages, and there is a miniature railway, an indoor play centre, and a café. There are high quality toilet facilities and fully-equipped, ready-erected tents are available for hire. 5 acre site. 69 touring pitches. 21 hardstandings. Caravan pitches. Motorhome pitches. Tent pitches.

AA Pubs & Restaurants nearby: Full Moon, Rudge 01373 830936

Leisure: ⚒
Facilities: ⚓♠☉🅿✳♿🏪🏹🐾♲✿
Services: ♨🗑🍺🛢∅🅃🍴📶↯
Within 3 miles: ♿🏪

Notes: Families only. Dogs must be kept on leads.

WORCESTERSHIRE

HONEYBOURNE   Map 10 SP14

Places to visit

Kiftsgate Court Garden, MICKLETON
01386 438777 www.kiftsgate.co.uk

Hidcote Manor Garden,
MICKLETON 01386 438333
www.nationaltrust.org.uk/hidcote

Great for kids: Anne Hathaway's Cottage,
SHOTTERY 01789 201844
www.shakespeare.org.uk

PREMIER PARK

►►►►► 81% Ranch Caravan Park (SP113444)

GOLD

Station Rd WR11 7PR
☎ 01386 830744
e-mail: enquiries@ranch.co.uk
dir: *Through village x-rds towards Bidford, site 400mtrs on left*

* 🚐 £23-£27 🚐 £23-£27

Open Mar-Nov (rs Mar-May & Sep-Nov swimming pool closed, shorter club hours)

Last arrival 20.00hrs Last departure noon

An attractive and well-run park set amidst farmland in the Vale of Evesham and landscaped with trees and bushes. Tourers have their own excellent facilities in two locations, and the use of an outdoor heated swimming pool in peak season. There is also a licensed club serving meals. Please note that this site does not accept tents. 12 acre site. 120 touring pitches. 46 hardstandings. 20 seasonal pitches. Caravan pitches. Motorhome pitches. 218 statics.

AA Pubs & Restaurants nearby: Fleece Inn, Bretforton 01386 831173

Ebrington Arms, Ebrington 01386 593223

Leisure: 🏊 ⛳ 🎠 ⚽ 🔍 ▭ 🎵
Facilities: 🚿 ⊙ 🗄 ✳ 🦻 🕐 💲 📮 🖥 ♻ ❓
Services: 🚐 🗄 🍽 🛢 🧺 🇹 🍴 🛒 🏪 ↧
Within 3 miles: ↓ 🏌 🎣 💲 🗄 ⛁ ∪

Notes: No unaccompanied minors. Dogs must be kept on leads.

WORCESTER   Map 10 SO85

Places to visit

City Museum & Art Gallery,
WORCESTER 01905 25371
www.museumsworcestershire.org.uk

Great for kids: West Midland Safari & Leisure Park, BEWDLEY 01299 402114 www.wmsp.co.uk

►►► 87% Peachley Leisure Touring Park (SO807576)

Peachley Ln, Lower Broadheath WR2 6QX
☎ 01905 641309
e-mail: info@peachleyleisure.com
dir: *M5 junct 7, A44 (Worcester ring road) towards Leominster. Exit at sign for Elgar's Birthplace Museum. Pass museum, at x-roads turn right. In 0.75m at T-junct turn left. Park signed on right*

🚐 🚐 🛆

Open all year

Last arrival 21.30hrs Last departure noon

The park is set in its own area in the grounds of Peachley Farm. It has all hardstanding and fully-serviced pitches. There are two fishing lakes, and a really excellent quad bike course. The park provides a peaceful haven, and is an excellent base from which to explore the area, which includes the Elgar Museum, Worcester Races and Victorian Fayre; it is also convenient for Malvern's Three Counties Showground. 8 acre site. 82 touring pitches. 82 hardstandings. Caravan pitches. Motorhome pitches. Tent pitches.

AA Pubs & Restaurants nearby: The Talbot, Knightwick 01886 821235

Bear & Ragged Staff, Bransford 01886 833399

Leisure: ⚽
Facilities: 🚿 ⊙ ✳ 🦻 📮 🖥 ♻ 🚿
Services: 🚐 🗄 🛢 🍴
Within 3 miles: 🏊 🇭 🎣 💲 🗄 ⛁ ∪

Notes: No skateboards, no riding of motorbikes or scooters. Dogs must be kept on leads.

LEISURE: 🏊 Indoor swimming pool   🏊 Outdoor swimming pool   🎠 Children's playground   🧒 Kid's club   🎾 Tennis court   🎱 Games room   ▭ Separate TV room
♪ 9/18 hole golf course   🚣 Boats for hire   🎬 Cinema   🎵 Entertainment   🎣 Fishing   ◉ Mini golf   🏄 Watersports   🏋 Gym   ⚽ Sports field   **Spa**   ∪ Stables
FACILITIES: 🛁 Bath   🚿 Shower   ⊙ Electric shaver   💈 Hairdryer   ✳ Ice Pack Facility   🦻 Disabled facilities   🕐 Public telephone   💲 Shop on site or within 200yds
🛒 Mobile shop (calls at least 5 days a week)   🍖 BBQ area   🌲 Picnic area   📶 Wi-fi   🖥 Internet access   ♻ Recycling   ❓ Tourist info   🐕 Dog exercise area

SERVICES: 🔌 Electric hook up 🌀 Launderette 🍷 Licensed bar 🛢 Calor Gas 🔥 Camping Gaz T Toilet fluid 🍽 Café/Restaurant 🍟 Fast Food/Takeaway 🔋 Battery charging
🍼 Baby care 🚐 Motorvan service point **ABBREVIATIONS:** BH/bank hols-bank holidays Etr-Easter Whit-Whitsun dep-departure fr-from hrs-hours m-mile mdnt-midnight
rdbt-roundabout rs-restricted service wk-week wknd-weekend 🚫 No credit cards 🚫 no dogs   See page 7 for details of the AA Camping Card Scheme

Yorkshire

There is nowhere in the British Isles quite like
Yorkshire. By far the largest county, and with
such scenic and cultural diversity, it is almost a
country within a country. For sheer scale, size
and grandeur, there is nowhere to beat it.

Much of it in the spectacular Pennines, Yorkshire is a land of castles, grand houses, splendid rivers, tumbling becks and historic market towns. But it is the natural, unrivalled beauty of the Yorkshire Dales and the North York Moors that captures the heart and leaves a lasting impression. Surely no-one could fail to be charmed by the majestic landscapes of these two much-loved National Parks.

The Dales
Wherever you venture in the Yorkshire Dales, stunning scenery awaits you; remote emerald green valleys, limestone scars and timeless villages of charming stone cottages. The Dales, beautifully represented in the books of James Herriot, are characterised and complemented by their rivers – the Wharfe, Ribble, Ure, Nidd and Swale among them.

Touring this glorious region reveals the broad sweep of Wensleydale, the delights of Arkengarthdale and the charming little villages of Swaledale. There is also the spectacular limestone country of the western Dales – the land of the Three Peaks. Perhaps here, more than anywhere else in the area, ▶

there is a true sense of space and freedom. This is adventure country – a place of endless views and wild summits.

The Moors

To the east lies another sprawling landscape – the North York Moors. This is where the purple of the heather gives way to the grey expanse of the North Sea. Covering 554 square miles (1,436km) and acknowledged as an internationally important site for upland breeding birds, the North York Moors National Park is a vast, intricately-woven tapestry of heather moorland, narrow valleys, rolling dales, broad-leaved woodland and extensive conifer forests. Few places in Britain offer such variety and breadth of terrain.

Extending for 36 miles (58km), the North Yorkshire and Cleveland Heritage Coast forms the Park's eastern boundary. The popular holiday resorts of Whitby and Scarborough are the two largest settlements on this stretch of coastline, which is rich in fossils and minerals and protected for its outstanding natural beauty and historic interest.

Further south

To the south of the North York Moors is the beautiful city of York, its history stretching back 2,000 years. At its heart stands the minster, constructed between 1220 and 1470 and the largest medieval church in northern Europe. There is so much to see and do in this ancient, vibrant city that you can easily lose track of time.

Farther south, despite the relics of the county's industrial heritage, is Yorkshire's magical *Last of the Summer Wine* country. The BBC's long-running and much-loved comedy series, *Last of the Summer Wine*, ran for 37 years and was filmed in and around the town of Holmfirth, near Huddersfield.

Walking and Cycling

Not surprisingly, Yorkshire offers a myriad of circular walks and long-distance trails throughout the county. For the more ambitious walker there

● York Minster

is the Pennine Way, which runs through Yorkshire from top to bottom, from the Scottish Borders as far south as Derbyshire. The 81-mile (130km) Dales Way, another popular route, is a perfect way to explore the magnificent scenery of Wharfedale, Ribblesdale and Dentdale, while the 50-mile (80km) Calderdale Way offers a fascinating insight into the Pennine heartland of industrial West Yorkshire.

Yorkshire also boasts a great choice of cycle routes. You can cycle to York on the track bed of the former King's Cross to Edinburgh railway line, or ride along a 20-mile (32.2km) stretch of the former Whitby to Scarborough line, looping around Robin Hood's Bay. There are also cycle routes through the Yorkshire Wolds, Dalby Forest in the North York Moors National Park and around Castle Howard, the magnificent estate near Malton where Evelyn Waugh's *Brideshead Revisited* was filmed.

Festivals and Events

- The long established Jorvik Festival is held in York in February and lasts eight days. The festival celebrates Viking heritage with various lectures, arts and crafts and river events.
- Easter Monday is the date for Ossett's Coal Carrying Championships where competitors carry a sack of coal through the streets.
- November sees the three-day Northern Antiques Fair at Harrogate. This event includes various indoor stalls, as well as displays of glass and ceramics.
- The Yorkshire Dales has numerous events and festivals throughout the year, including the Masham Arts Festival in October every two years the Lunesdale Agricultural Show in August and the Grassington Festival of Music & Arts in June.

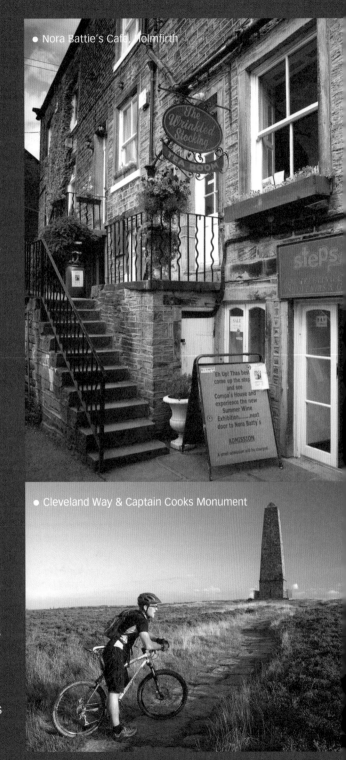

● Nora Battie's Café, Holmfirth

● Cleveland Way & Captain Cooks Monument

YORKSHIRE, EAST RIDING OF

BRANDESBURTON — Map 17 TA14

Places to visit

The Guildhall, BEVERLEY 01482 392783 www.eastriding.gov.uk/museums

Burton Constable Hall, SPROATLEY 01964 562400 www.burtonconstable.com

Great for kids: 'Streetlife' - Hull Museum of Transport, KINGSTON UPON HULL 01482 613902 www.hullcc.gov.uk

►►► 85% Blue Rose Caravan Country Park *(TA110464)*

DAVID BELLAMY CONSERVATION AWARD SILVER

Star Carr Ln YO25 8RU
☎ 01964 543366 & 07504 026899
e-mail: info@bluerosepark.com
dir: *From A165 at rdbt into New Rd signed Brandesburton (becomes Star Carr Ln). Approx 1m, site on left*

* 🚐 £15-£22 🚙 £15-£22

Open all year

Last arrival 20.00hrs Last departure noon

A neat and well maintained adult-only site well placed for visiting Hornsea and the Yorkshire coastline. The park is within walking distance of Brandesburton and offers an idyllic stopover for caravanners wanting a peaceful break in the countryside. 12 acre site. 58 touring pitches. 58 hardstandings. 44 seasonal pitches. Caravan pitches. Motorhome pitches. 36 statics.

Leisure: 📺

Facilities: 🚿 ⊙ 💨 ♿ ☎ 🧺 🐕 ♻ ℹ

Services: 🗨 🫧 🛢 🍃 [T] ψ

Within 3 miles: ⛳ ⛵ 🎣 ◎ 🏄 🛒 🫧 🐴

Notes: Adults only. Dogs must be kept on leads.

►►► 82% Dacre Lakeside Park *(TA118468)*

YO25 8RT
☎ 0800 1804556 & 01964 543704
e-mail: dacrepark@btconnect.com
dir: *Off A165 bypass, midway between Beverley & Hornsea*

🚐 🚙 ⛺

Open Mar-Oct

Last arrival 21.00hrs Last departure noon

A large lake popular with watersports enthusiasts is the focal point of this grassy site. The clubhouse offers indoor activities; there's a fish and chip shop, a pub and a Chinese takeaway in the village, which is within walking distance. The six-acre lake is used for windsurfing, sailing, kayaking, canoeing and fishing. Camping pods are available for hire. 8 acre site. 120 touring pitches. 110 seasonal pitches. Caravan pitches. Motorhome pitches. Tent pitches. 110 statics. 9 wooden pods.

Leisure: 🎾 ⚽ ♠ 🎵

Facilities: 🚿 ⊙ 💨 ❄ ♿ 🐕 📶 💻

Services: 🗨 🫧 🍷 🍃 [T] 🍴

Within 3 miles: ⛳ ⛵ 🎣 🏄 🛒 🫧 🐴

Notes: No noise 23.00hrs-08.00hrs, no craft with engines on lake. Fishing, canoeing, sailing & tennis.

BRIDLINGTON — Map 17 TA16

See also Rudston

Places to visit

Sewerby Hall & Gardens, BRIDLINGTON 01262 673769 www.sewerby-hall.co.uk

Hornsea Museum, HORNSEA 01964 533443 www.hornseamuseum.com

Great for kids: Flamingo Land Theme Park & Zoo, KIRBY MISPERTON 01653 668287 www.flamingoland.co.uk

►►► 82% Fir Tree Caravan Park *(TA195702)*

Jewison Ln, Sewerby YO16 6YG
☎ 01262 676442
e-mail: info@flowerofmay.com
dir: *1.5m from centre of Bridlington. Left onto B1255 at Marton Corner. Site 600yds on left*

🚐

Open Mar-Oct (rs Early & late season bar & entertainment restrictions)

Last arrival dusk Last departure noon

Fir Tree Park has a well laid out touring area with its own facilities within a large, mainly static park. It has an excellent swimming pool complex, and the adjacent bar-cum-conservatory serves meals. There is also a family bar, games room and outdoor children's play area. 22 acre site. 45 touring pitches. 45 hardstandings. 45 seasonal pitches. Caravan pitches. 400 statics.

AA Pubs & Restaurants nearby: Seabirds Inn, Flamborough 01262 850242

Old Star Inn, Kilham 01262 420619

Leisure: 🏊 🛝 ♠ 🎵

Facilities: 🚿 ⊙ ❄ ♿ ☎ 🛒 🐕 📶 ♻ ℹ

Services: 🗨 🫧 🍷 🛢 🍴

Within 3 miles: ⛳ ⛵ 🎬 🎣 ◎ 🏄 🛒 🫧 🐴

Notes: Dogs accepted by prior arrangement only, no noise after mdnt. Dogs must be kept on leads.

KINGSTON UPON HULL

See Sproatley

RUDSTON — Map 17 TA06

Places to visit

Sewerby Hall & Gardens, BRIDLINGTON 01262 673769 www.sewerby-hall.co.uk

►►► 86% Thorpe Hall Caravan & Camping Site *(TA108677)*

DAVID BELLAMY CONSERVATION AWARD GOLD

Thorpe Hall YO25 4JE
☎ 01262 420393 & 420574
e-mail: caravansite@thorpehall.co.uk
dir: *5m from Bridlington on B1253 (West)*

* 🚐 £16-£32.50 🚙 £16-£32.50 ⛺ £11.50-£28.50

Open Mar-Oct

Last arrival 22.00hrs Last departure noon

A delightful, peaceful small park within the walled gardens of Thorpe Hall yet within a few miles of the bustling seaside resort of Bridlington. The site offers a games field, its own coarse fishery, pitch and putt, and a games and TV lounge. There are numerous walks locally. 4.5 acre site. 92 touring pitches. Caravan pitches. Motorhome pitches. Tent pitches.

AA Pubs & Restaurants nearby: Old Star Inn, Kilham 01262 420619

Leisure: 🛝 ⚽ ♠ 📺

Facilities: 🛁 🚿 ⊙ 💨 ❄ ♿ ☎ 🛒 🧺 🐕 📶 ♻ ℹ

Services: 🗨 🫧 🛢 🍃 [T] 🍴

Within 3 miles: 🎣 🛒 🫧 🐴

Notes: No ball games (field provided), no noise between 23.00hrs-08.00hrs. Dogs must be kept on leads and be well behaved. Golf practice area (4.5 acres).

SKIPSEA — Map 17 TA15

Places to visit

Hornsea Museum, HORNSEA 01964 533443
www.hornseamuseum.com

Sewerby Hall & Gardens, BRIDLINGTON
01262 673769 www.sewerby-hall.co.uk

AA CAMPING CARD SITE

 85% Skirlington Leisure Park (TA188528)

SILVER

YO25 8SY
☎ 01262 468213 & 468466
e-mail: info@skirlington.com
dir: From M62 towards Beverley then Hornsea. Between Skipsea & Hornsea on B1242

Open Mar-Oct

A large well-run seaside park set close to the beach in partly-sloping meadowland with young trees and shrubs. The site has five toilet blocks, a supermarket and an amusement arcade, with occasional entertainment in the clubhouse. The wide range of family amenities includes an indoor heated swimming pool complex with sauna, jacuzzi and sunbeds. A 10-pin bowling alley and indoor play area for children are added attractions. 24 acre site. 285 touring pitches. 15 hardstandings. Caravan pitches. Motorhome pitches. 450 statics.

Leisure: 🏊 🎾 🎮 🎣 ▢ 🎵
Facilities: 🛁 🚿 ⊙ 🅿 ✳ 🕹 🕐 🛍 🎢 🐕 ♻ ❶
Services: 🔌 🗑 🍴 🛢 🍽 🛒 🚮
Within 3 miles: 🚶 🚲 🅿 ⊙ 🛍 🍴 🔵 ⛳

Notes: Dogs must be on leads. Putting green.

 80% *Skipsea Sands* (TA176563)

GOLD

Mill Ln YO25 8TZ
☎ 01262 468210
e-mail: skipsea.sands@park-resorts.com
web: www.park-resorts.com
dir: From A165 (Bridlington to Kingston upon Hull road) 8m S of Bridlington take B1242 to Skipsea. Follow Skipsea Sands signed to left just after sharp left bend

🏕 🚐 Å

Open Apr-Oct

Last arrival noon Last departure 10.00hrs

A busy and popular holiday park just a stone's throw from the beach, and offering an excellent range of leisure and entertainment facilities for families and couples. There's a good, well maintained touring area with clean toilets and neat grass pitches. A dedicated team ensure that standards are high across the park. 91 touring pitches. Caravan pitches. Motorhome pitches. Tent pitches.

SPROATLEY — Map 17 TA13

Places to visit

Maritime Museum, LOWESTOFT 01502 561963
www.lowestoftmaritimemuseum.org.uk

Great for kids: The Deep, KINGSTON UPON HULL 01482 381000 www.thedeep.co.uk

AA CAMPING CARD SITE

▶▶▶▶ **82% Burton Constable Holiday Park & Arboretum** (TA186357)

 GOLD

Old Lodges HU11 4LJ
☎ 01964 562508
e-mail: info@burtonconstable.co.uk
dir: A165 onto B1238 to Sproatley. Follow signs to site

* 🏕 £16.50-£29 🚐 £16.50-£29 Å £16.50-£23.50

Open Mar-mid Feb (rs Mar-Oct tourers & tents)

Last arrival 22.00hrs Last departure 14.00hrs

Within the extensive estate of Constable Burton Hall, this large and secluded holiday destination provides a wide range of attractions including fishing and boating on the lakes, a snooker room, and a licensed bar with a designated family room. The grounds are immaculately maintained and generous pitch density offers good privacy. 90 acre site. 140 touring pitches. 14 hardstandings.

---

14 seasonal pitches. Caravan pitches. Motorhome pitches. Tent pitches. 350 statics.

Leisure: 🎮 🏊 🎣 🎵
Facilities: 🛁 ⊙ 🅿 🕹 🕐 🛍 🎢 ♻ ❶
Services: 🔌 🗑 🍴 🛢 🔋 🍽 🛒 🚮
Within 3 miles: 🚶 🅿 🛍 🔵 ⛳

Notes: No skateboards or rollerblades. Dogs must be kept on leads. Two 10-acre fishing lakes, snooker table.

TUNSTALL — Map 17 TA33

Places to visit

Burton Constable Hall, SPROATLEY
01964 562400 www.burtonconstable.com

 NEW 80% Sand le Mere Holiday Village (TA305318)

Southfield Ln HU12 0TY
☎ 01964 670403
e-mail: info@sand-le-mere.co.uk
dir: From Hull A1033 signed Withernsea, B1362 (Hull Rd) signed Hedon. In Hedon continue on B3162 towards Withernsea. Turn left signed Roos. In Roos take B1242. Turn left at brown sign for site. In Tunstall right at T-junct, right into Seaside Ln to site

🏕 🚐 Å

Open Mar-Nov

Last arrival 23.00hrs Last departure 11.00hrs

Ideally located between Withernsea and Bridlington, this £4 million development provides first-class indoor leisure facilities with swimming pool, entertainment and a kiddies'

continued

TUNSTALL *continued*

soft ball area. The touring pitches are level and surrounded by maturing trees and shrubs. 135 acre site. 72 touring pitches. 51 hardstandings. Caravan pitches. Motorhome pitches. Tent pitches.

Sand le Mere Holiday Village

Leisure: 🏊 🏋 🛝 ✋ ⚽ 🎱 📺 🎵 Spa

Facilities: 🚿 💨 ✳ ♿ ☎ [S] Wi-fi 💻 ♻ ℹ

Services: 🚐 🧺 🍷 🔒 🍽 🛒 ⚓

Within 3 miles: 🎣 [S] 🧺

Notes: No noise after 23.00hrs, speed limits around site, no camp fires. Dogs must be kept on leads.

see advert below

WITHERNSEA Map 17 TA32

Places to visit

Wilberforce House, KINGSTON UPON HULL
01482 613902 www.hullcc.gov.uk

Maister House, KINGSTON UPON HULL
01723 879900 www.nationaltrust.org.uk

Great for kids: The Deep, KINGSTON UPON HULL
01482 381000 www.thedeep.co.uk

76% *Withernsea Sands* *(TA335289)*

AA HOLIDAY CENTRE · DAVID BELLAMY CONSERVATION AWARD SILVER

Waxholme Rd HU19 2BS
☎ 0871 664 9803
e-mail: withernsea.sands@park-resorts.com
web: www.park-resorts.com
dir: *M62 junct 38, A63 through Hull. At end of dual carriageway, right onto A1033, follow Withernsea signs. Through village, left at mini-rdbt onto B1242. 1st right at lighthouse. Site 0.5m on left*

🚐 🚗 ⛺

Open Apr-Oct (rs BH & peak wknds sports available)

Last arrival 22.00hrs Last departure noon

Touring is very much at the heart of this holiday park's operation, with 100 all-electric pitches and additional space for tents. The owners, Park Resorts, continue to upgrade the facilities and attractions, and the leisure complex with its futuristic design is especially impressive. 115 touring pitches. Caravan pitches. Motorhome pitches. Tent pitches. 400 statics.

Leisure: 🏊 🛝 ✋ ⚽ 🎱 🎵

Facilities: 🛁 🚿 ⊙ 💨 ✳ ♿ ☎ [S] 🧺 🐕 Wi-fi 💻 ♻

Services: 🚐 🧺 🍷 🔒 🌿 [T] 🍽 🛒

Within 3 miles: ⛳ 🎣 [S] 🧺 U

Notes: No noise between 23.00hrs & 07.00hrs. Dogs must be kept on leads. Extension leads & utilities from reception.

LEISURE: 🏊 Indoor swimming pool 🏊 Outdoor swimming pool 🛝 Children's playground ✋ Kid's club 🎾 Tennis court 🎱 Games room 📺 Separate TV room ⛳ 9/18 hole golf course ⛵ Boats for hire 🎬 Cinema 🎵 Entertainment 🎣 Fishing ◎ Mini golf 🏄 Watersports 🏋 Gym ⚽ Sports field **Spa** U Stables
FACILITIES: 🛁 Bath 🚿 Shower ⊙ Electric shaver 💨 Hairdryer ✳ Ice Pack Facility ♿ Disabled facilities ☎ Public telephone [S] Shop on site or within 200yds [S] Mobile shop (calls at least 5 days a week) 🍖 BBQ area 🧺 Picnic area Wi-fi Wi-fi 💻 Internet access ♻ Recycling ℹ Tourist info 🐕 Dog exercise area

YORKSHIRE, NORTH

See Walk 12 & Cycle Ride 5 in the Walks & Cycle Rides section at the end of the guide

ACASTER MALBIS
Map 16 SE54

Places to visit

Yorkshire Museum, YORK 01904 551800 www.yorkshiremuseum.org.uk

York Art Gallery, YORK 01904 687687 www.york.trust.museum

Great for kids: Jorvik Viking Centre, YORK 01904 615505 www.jorvik-viking-centre.com

▶▶▶ 78% Moor End Farm *(SE589457)*

YO23 2UQ

☎ 01904 706727 & 07860 405872

e-mail: moorendfarm@acaster99.fsnet.co.uk

dir: *Follow signs to Acaster Malbis from junct of A64 & A1237 at Copmanthorpe*

* ⚐ £16-£20 ⚐ £16-£20 ▲ £15-£22

Open Etr or Apr-Oct

Last arrival 22.00hrs Last departure 12.00hrs

A very pleasant farm site with modernised facilities including a heated family/disabled shower room. A riverboat pickup to York is 150 yards from the site entrance, and the village inn and restaurant are a short stroll away. A very convenient site for visiting York Racecourse. 1 acre site. 12 touring pitches. Caravan pitches. Motorhome pitches. Tent pitches. 6 statics.

AA Pubs & Restaurants nearby: Ye Old Sun Inn, Colton 01904 744261

Leisure: ⚐

Facilities: ⚐⚐⚐⚐⚐⚐⚐⚐

Services: ⚐⚐⚐

Within 3 miles: ⚐⚐⚐⚐⚐⚐

Notes: ⚐ Dogs must be kept on leads. Use of fridge, freezer & microwave.

ALLERSTON
Map 19 SE88

Places to visit

Scarborough Castle, SCARBOROUGH 01723 372451 www.english-heritage.org.uk

Pickering Castle, PICKERING 01751 474989 www.english-heritage.org.uk

Great for kids: Sea Life & Marine Sanctuary, SCARBOROUGH 01723 373414 www.sealife.co.uk

AA CAMPING CARD SITE

PREMIER PARK

REGIONAL WINNER - AA NORTH EAST ENGLAND CAMPSITE OF THE YEAR 2013

▶▶▶▶▶ 82% Vale of Pickering Caravan Park

(SE879808)

Carr House Farm YO18 7PQ

☎ 01723 859280

e-mail: tony@valeofpickering.co.uk

dir: *On B1415, 1.75m from A170 (Pickering-Scarborough road)*

* ⚐ £16-£27 ⚐ £16-£27 ▲ £13-£22

Open 5 Mar-3 Jan (rs Mar)

Last arrival 21.00hrs Last departure 11.30hrs

A well-maintained, spacious family park with excellent facilities including a well-stocked shop and immaculate toilet facilities, and an interesting woodland walk. Younger children will enjoy the attractive play area, while the large ball sports area will attract older ones. The park is set in open countryside bounded by hedges, has manicured grassland and stunning seasonal floral displays, and is handy for the North Yorkshire Moors and the attractions of Scarborough. 13 acre site. 120 touring pitches. 100 hardstandings. Caravan pitches. Motorhome pitches. Tent pitches. See also page 22.

AA Pubs & Restaurants nearby: New Inn, Thornton le Dale 01751 474226

Coachman Inn, Snainton 01723 859231

Cayley Arms, Brompton-by-Sawdon 01723 859372

Leisure: ⚐⚐

Facilities: ⚐⚐⚐⚐⚐⚐⚐⚐⚐⚐⚐⚐

Services: ⚐⚐⚐⚐⚐⚐

Within 3 miles: ⚐⚐⚐⚐⚐⚐

Notes: Microwave available.

ALNE
Map 19 SE46

Places to visit

Castle Howard, MALTON 01653 648333 www.castlehoward.co.uk

Great for kids: National Railway Museum, YORK 01904 621261 www.nrm.org.uk

PREMIER PARK

▶▶▶▶▶ 79% Alders Caravan Park

(SE497654)

Home Farm YO61 1RY

☎ 01347 838722

e-mail: enquiries@homefarmalne.co.uk

dir: *From A19 exit at Alne sign, in 1.5m left at T-junct, 0.5m site on left in village centre*

* ⚐ £18-£20 ⚐ fr £18 ▲ fr £18

Open Mar-Oct

Last arrival 21.00hrs Last departure 14.00hrs

A tastefully developed park on a working farm with screened pitches laid out in horseshoe-shaped areas. This well designed park offers excellent toilet facilities including a bathroom and fully-serviced washing and toilet cubicles. A woodland area and a water meadow are pleasant places to walk. 12 acre site. 87 touring pitches. 6 hardstandings. 71 seasonal pitches. Caravan pitches. Motorhome pitches. Tent pitches. 2 wooden pods.

AA Pubs & Restaurants nearby: Black Bull Inn, Boroughbridge 01423 322413

The Dining Room Restaurant, Boroughbridge 01423 326426

Facilities: ⚐⚐⚐⚐⚐⚐⚐⚐⚐⚐⚐⚐

Services: ⚐⚐⚐⚐⚐ **Within 3 miles:** ⚐⚐⚐⚐

Notes: Max 2 dogs per pitch. Dogs must be kept on leads. Summer house. Bread, eggs, milk & other farm produce for sale.

LEISURE: Indoor swimming pool Outdoor swimming pool Children's playground Kid's club Tennis court Games room Separate TV room 9/18 hole golf course Boats for hire Cinema Entertainment Fishing Mini golf Watersports Gym Sports field **Spa** Stables

FACILITIES: Bath Shower Electric shaver Hairdryer Ice Pack Facility Disabled facilities Public telephone Shop on site or within 200yds Mobile shop (calls at least 5 days a week) BBQ area Picnic area Wi-fi Internet access Recycling Tourist info Dog exercise area

BISHOP MONKTON — Map 19 SE36

Places to visit

Newby Hall & Gardens, RIPON 01423 322583
www.newbyhall.com

Fountains Abbey & Studley Royal, RIPON
01765 643197 www.fountainsabbey.org.uk

Great for kids: Stump Cross Caverns, PATELEY
BRIDGE 01756 752780
www.stumpcrosscaverns.co.uk

▶▶▶ 75% Church Farm Caravan Park (SE328660)

Knaresborough Rd HG3 3QQ
☎ 01765 676578 & 07861 770164
e-mail: churchfarmcaravan@btinternet.com
dir: From A61 at x-rds follow Bishop Monkton
signs. 1.25m to village. At x-rds right into
Knaresborough Rd, site approx 500mtrs on right

🚐 £13-£15 🚘 £13-£15 ▲ £12-£17

Open Mar-Oct

Last arrival 22.30hrs Last departure 15.30hrs

A very pleasant rural site on a working farm, on
the edge of the attractive village of Bishop
Monkton with its well-stocked shop and pubs.
Whilst very much a place to relax, there are many
attractions close by, including Fountains Abbey,
Newby Hall, Ripon and Harrogate. 4 acre site. 45
touring pitches. 3 hardstandings. Caravan
pitches. Motorhome pitches. Tent pitches.
3 statics.

AA Pubs & Restaurants nearby: Black Bull Inn,
Boroughbridge 01423 322413

The Dining Room Restaurant, Boroughbridge
01423 326426

Facilities: 🌣⊙✻🛇🗑♻🕉 **❶**
Services: 🔌🛒⚓
Within 3 miles: 🕹🖉🗓🗑U
Notes: ⊕ No ball games. Dogs must be kept on
leads.

BOLTON ABBEY — Map 19 SE05

Places to visit

RHS Garden Harlow Carr, HARROGATE
01423 565418 www.rhs.org.uk/harlowcarr

Parcevall Hall Gardens,
GRASSINGTON 01756 720311
www.parcevallhallgardens.co.uk

Great for kids: Stump Cross Caverns, PATELEY
BRIDGE 01756 752780
www.stumpcrosscaverns.co.uk

▶▶▶ 83% Howgill Lodge (SE064592)

GOLD

Barden BD23 6DJ
☎ 01756 720655
e-mail: info@howgill-lodge.co.uk
dir: From Bolton Abbey take B6160 signed
Burnsall. In 3m at Barden Tower right signed
Appletreewick. 1.5m at phone box right into lane
to site

✱ 🚐 £18-£26.50 🚘 £18-£24 ▲ £18-£30.50

Open mid Mar-Oct

Last arrival 20.00hrs Last departure noon

A beautifully-maintained and secluded site
offering panoramic views of Wharfedale. The
spacious hardstanding pitches are mainly
terraced, and there is a separate tenting area with
numerous picnic tables. There are three toilet
facilities spread throughout the site, with the
main block (including private, cubicled wash
facilities) appointed to a high standard. There is
also a well stocked shop. 4 acre site. 40 touring
pitches. 20 hardstandings. Caravan pitches.
Motorhome pitches. Tent pitches.

AA Pubs & Restaurants nearby: The Fleece,
Addingham 01943 830491

Craven Arms, Appletreewick 01756 720270

Leisure: 🎾
Facilities: 🌣⊙✱✻🛇🗓🛒Wi-fi ♻ **❶**
Services: 🔌🗓⚓⊘🇹⚓
Within 3 miles: 🖉🗓🗓
Notes: Dogs must be kept on leads.

CONSTABLE BURTON — Map 19 SE19

Places to visit

Middleham Castle, MIDDLEHAM 01969 623899
www.english-heritage.org.uk

Great for kids: Bedale Museum, BEDALE
01677 427516

▶▶▶▶ 80% Constable Burton Hall Caravan Park (SE158907)

DL8 5LJ
☎ 01677 450428
e-mail: caravanpark@constableburton.com
dir: Off A684

🚐 £19-£24 🚘 £19-£24

Open Apr-Oct

Last arrival 20.00hrs Last departure noon

A pretty site in the former deer park of the
adjoining Constable Burton Hall, screened from
the road by the deer park walls and surrounded by
mature trees in a quiet rural location. The laundry
is housed in a converted 18th-century deer barn,
there is a pub and restaurant opposite, and
seasonal pitches are available. Wi-fi is available
from the 2013 season. Please note that this site
does not accept tents. 10 acre site. 120 touring
pitches. Caravan pitches. Motorhome pitches.

AA Pubs & Restaurants nearby: Sandpiper Inn,
Leyburn 01969 622206

White Swan, Middleham 01969 622093

Black Swan, Middleham 01969 622221

Wensleydale Heifer, West Witton 01969 622322

Facilities: 🌣⊙✻✱🛇🗓🛒Wi-fi 💻 ♻
Services: 🔌🗓⚓⚓
Within 3 miles: 🕹🗓
Notes: No commercial vehicles, no games. Dogs
must be kept on leads.

FILEY
Map 17 TA18

Places to visit

Scarborough Castle, SCARBOROUGH
01723 372451 www.english-heritage.org.uk

Sea Life & Marine Sanctuary, SCARBOROUGH
01723 373414 www.sealife.co.uk

90% Flower of May Holiday Park (TA085835)

Lebberston Cliff YO11 3NU
☎ 01723 584311
e-mail: info@flowerofmay.com
dir: Signed from A165

* ⊕ £15-£21 ⇌ £15-£21 ▲ £15-£21

Open Etr-Oct (rs Early & late season restricted opening in café, shop & bars)

Last arrival dusk Last departure noon

A well-run, high quality family holiday park with top class facilities. This large landscaped park offers a full range of recreational activities, with plenty to occupy everyone. Grass and hard pitches are available, all on level ground, and arranged in avenues screened by shrubs. Enjoy the 'Scarborough Fair' museum, with its collection of restored fairground attractions, including rides, organs and vintage cars. 13 acre site. 300 touring pitches. 250 hardstandings. 100 seasonal pitches. Caravan pitches. Motorhome pitches. Tent pitches. 193 statics.

AA Pubs & Restaurants nearby: Cayley Arms, Brompton-by-Sawdon 01723 859372

Leisure: 🏊 🎠 ⚽ 🎱 🖵 🎵
Facilities: 🌲 ☉ ✳ 🚿 ⚕ 📞 🅂 📮 🛉 📶 ♻ ❓
Services: 🔌 🖵 🍴 🧺 🚿 🛒 🕿 🍽 🚽 ⌣
Within 3 miles: 🎣 🚤 🏌 🌊 ◎ 🛒 🅂 🐎 ♘

Notes: 1 dog per pitch by arrangement only, no noise after mdnt. Dogs must be kept on leads. Squash, bowling, 9-hole golf, basketball court, skate park. *see advert on opposite page*

81% Primrose Valley Holiday Park (TA123778)
GOLD

YO14 9RF
☎ 0871 231 0892
e-mail: primrosevalley@haven.com
web: www.haven.com/primrosevalley
dir: Signed from A165 (Scarborough-Bridlington road), 3m S of Filey

⊕ ⇌

Open mid Mar-end Oct

Last arrival anytime Last departure 10.00hrs

A large all-action holiday centre with a wide range of sports and leisure activities to suit everyone from morning until late in the evening. The touring area is completely separate from the main park with its own high quality amenity block. All touring pitches are fully-serviced hardstandings with grassed awning strips. The touring area has its own reception and designated warden. 160 acre site. 50 touring pitches. 50 hardstandings. Caravan pitches. Motorhome pitches. 1514 statics.

AA Pubs & Restaurants nearby: Cayley Arms, Brompton-by-Sawdon 01723 859372

Leisure: 🏊 🏖 🎠 🛝 🎾 ☉ 🎱 🎵
Facilities: 🛁 🌲 🅿 🚿 ☉ 🅂 📮 🛉 📶 🖥 ♻ ❓
Services: 🔌 🖵 🍴 🧺 🚿 🕿 🍽 🛒
Within 3 miles: 🎣 🚤 🏌 ◎ 🅂 🅂

Notes: Max 2 dogs per booking, certain dog breeds banned, no commercial vehicles, no bookings by persons under 21yrs unless a family booking. *see advert on page 342*

79% Blue Dolphin Holiday Park (TA095829)
GOLD

Gristhorpe Bay YO14 9PU
☎ 0871 231 0893
e-mail: bluedolphin@haven.com
web: www.haven.com/bluedolphin
dir: On A165, 2m N of Filey

⊕ ⇌ ▲

Open mid Mar-end Oct (rs mid Mar-May & Sep-Oct some facilities may be reduced & outdoor pool closed)

Last arrival mdnt Last departure 10.00hrs

There are great cliff-top views to be enjoyed from this fun-filled holiday centre with an extensive and separate touring area. The emphasis is on non-stop entertainment, with organised sports and clubs, all-weather leisure facilities, heated swimming pools (with multi-slide), and plenty of well-planned amusements. Pitches are mainly on level or gently-sloping grass plus there are some fully-serviced hardstandings. The beach is just two miles away. 85 acre site. 320 touring pitches. 20 seasonal pitches. Caravan pitches. Motorhome pitches. Tent pitches. 850 statics.

AA Pubs & Restaurants nearby: Cayley Arms, Brompton-by-Sawdon 01723 859372

Leisure: 🏊 🏖 🎠 ⚽ ☉ 🎵
Facilities: 🌲 ☉ ✳ 🚿 🅂 📮 🛉 📶 ♻ ❓
Services: 🔌 🖵 🍴 🧺 🚿 🕿 🍽 🛒 ⌣
Within 3 miles: 🎣 🏌 ◎ 🅂 🅂

Notes: Max 2 dogs per booking, certain dog breeds banned, no commercial vehicles, no bookings by persons under 21yrs unless a family booking. Dogs must be kept on leads. *see advert on page 342*

LEISURE: 🏊 Indoor swimming pool 🏖 Outdoor swimming pool 🎠 Children's playground 🛝 Kid's club ☉ Tennis court 🎱 Games room 🖵 Separate TV room 🏌 9/18 hole golf course 🚤 Boats for hire 🎬 Cinema 🎵 Entertainment 🎣 Fishing ◎ Mini golf 🌊 Watersports 🏋 Gym ☉ Sports field Spa 🐎 Stables
FACILITIES: 🛁 Bath 🌲 Shower ☉ Electric shaver 🅿 Hairdryer ✳ Ice Pack Facility ⚕ Disabled facilities ⏲ Public telephone 🅂 Shop on site or within 200yds 🅂 Mobile shop (calls at least 5 days a week) 🍴 BBQ area 🪑 Picnic area 📶 Wi-fi 🖥 Internet access ♻ Recycling ❓ Tourist info 🛉 Dog exercise area

---

SERVICES: 🔌 Electric hook up 🧺 Launderette 🍷 Licensed bar 🛢 Calor Gas ⌀ Camping Gaz Ⓣ Toilet fluid 🍽 Café/Restaurant 🏪 Fast Food/Takeaway 🔋 Battery charging
🍼 Baby care ⚡ Motorvan service point **ABBREVIATIONS:** BH/bank hols-bank holidays Etr-Easter Whit-Whitsun dep-departure fr-from hrs-hours m-mile mdnt-midnight
rdbt-roundabout rs-restricted service wk-week wknd-weekend 🚫 No credit cards 🚫 no dogs   See page 7 for details of the AA Camping Card Scheme

FILEY *continued*

77% Reighton Sands Holiday Park *(TA142769)*

Reighton Gap YO14 9SH
☎ 0871 231 0894
e-mail: reightonsands@haven.com
web: www.haven.com/reightonsands
dir: *On A165, 5m S of Filey at Reighton Gap, signed*

🚐 🚚 ⛺

Open mid Mar-end Oct (rs mid Mar-May & Sep-Oct some facilities may be reduced)

Last arrival 22.00hrs Last departure 10.00hrs

A large, lively holiday centre with a wide range of entertainment and all-weather leisure facilities, located just a 10-minute walk from a long sandy beach. There are good all-weather pitches and a large tenting field. The site is particularly geared towards families with young children. 229 acre site. 238 touring pitches. 5 seasonal pitches. Caravan pitches. Motorhome pitches. Tent pitches. 800 statics.

AA Pubs & Restaurants nearby: Cayley Arms, Brompton-by-Sawdon 01723 859372

Leisure: 🏊 🛝 🎱

Facilities: 🛁 🚿 🪒 💨 ♿ 📞 🏪 🧺 🐕 [Wi-fi] 💻 ♻ ℹ

Services: ⚙ 🫧 🍷 [T] 🍽 🍔 ⚓

Within 3 miles: ⛳ 🎬 🎣 ◎ 🏪 🫧 🐴

Notes: Max 2 dogs per booking, certain dog breeds banned, no commercial vehicles, no bookings by persons under 21yrs unless a family booking. Indoor play area.

see advert on page 342

►►►► 86% Lebberston Touring Park *(TA077824)*

Filey Rd YO11 3PE
☎ 01723 585723
e-mail: info@lebberstontouring.co.uk
dir: *Off A165 (Filey to Scarborough road). Site signed*

🚐 £15.50-£27 🚚

Open Mar-Oct

Last arrival 20.00hrs Last departure 11.00hrs

A peaceful family park in a gently-sloping rural area, where the quality facilities are maintained to a high standard of cleanliness. The keen owners are friendly and helpful, and create a relaxing atmosphere. A natural area offers views of the surrounding countryside through the shrubbery. Please note that this park does not accept tents. 7.5 acre site. 125 touring pitches. 25 hardstandings. 50 seasonal pitches. Caravan pitches. Motorhome pitches.

AA Pubs & Restaurants nearby: Cayley Arms, Brompton-by-Sawdon 01723 859372

Facilities: 🛁 🚿 🪒 💨 ❄ ♿ 🏪 🐕 [Wi-fi] ♻ ℹ

Services: ⚙ 🫧 🔥 🍃 [T]

Within 3 miles: ⛳ ⛵ 🎣 ◎ 🏄 🏪 🫧 🐴

Notes: No noise after 22.00hrs. Dogs must be kept on leads.

►►►► 80% Crows Nest Caravan Park *(TA094826)*

Gristhorpe YO14 9PS
☎ 01723 582206
e-mail: enquires@crowsnestcaravanpark.com
dir: *5m S of Scarborough & 2m N of Filey. On seaward side of A165, signed from rdbt, near petrol station*

* 🚐 £15-£30 🚚 £15-£30 ⛺ £15-£30

Open Mar-Oct

Last departure noon

A beautifully situated park on the coast between Scarborough and Filey, with excellent panoramic views. This large and mainly static park offers lively entertainment, and two bars. A small touring area is close to the attractions, and the main touring and camping section is at the top of the park overlooking the sea - this area is equipped with some excellent fully serviced pitches and a superb amenities block. 20 acre site. 49 touring pitches. 49 hardstandings. Caravan pitches. Motorhome pitches. Tent pitches. 217 statics.

AA Pubs & Restaurants nearby: Cayley Arms, Brompton-by-Sawdon 01723 859372

Leisure: 🏊 🛝 ⚽ 🎱 🎵

Facilities: 🚿 🪒 💨 ❄ ♿ 📞 🏪 🐕 [Wi-fi] 💻 ♻ ℹ

Services: ⚙ 🫧 🍷 🔥 🍃 [T] 🍔 👶 ⚓

Within 3 miles: ⛳ 🎣 ◎ 🏄 🏪 🫧 🐴

Notes: Dogs must be kept on leads.

see advert on page 357

LEISURE: 🏊 Indoor swimming pool 🌊 Outdoor swimming pool 🛝 Children's playground ✋ Kid's club 🎾 Tennis court 🎱 Games room 📺 Separate TV room ⛳ 9/18 hole golf course ⛵ Boats for hire 🎬 Cinema 🎵 Entertainment 🎣 Fishing ◎ Mini golf 🏄 Watersports 🏋 Gym ⚽ Sports field **Spa** 🐴 Stables
FACILITIES: 🛁 Bath 🚿 Shower 🪒 Electric shaver 💨 Hairdryer ❄ Ice Pack Facility ♿ Disabled facilities 📞 Public telephone 🏪 Shop on site or within 200yds 🛒 Mobile shop (calls at least 5 days a week) 🍖 BBQ area 🧺 Picnic area [Wi-fi] Wi-fi 💻 Internet access ♻ Recycling ℹ Tourist info 🐕 Dog exercise area

▶▶▶▶ 79% Orchard Farm Holiday Village (TA105779)

Stonegate, Hunmanby YO14 0PU
☎ 01723 891582

e-mail: info@orchardfarmholidayvillage.co.uk
dir: *A165 from Scarborough towards Bridlington. Turn right signed Hunmanby, site on right just after rail bridge*

🚐 £14-£22 🚐 £14-£22 ▲ £14-£22

Open Mar-Oct (rs Off peak some facilities restricted)

Last arrival 23.00hrs Last departure 11.00hrs

Pitches are arranged around a large coarse fishing lake at this grassy park. The enthusiastic owners are friendly, and offer a wide range of amenities including an indoor heated swimming pool and a licensed bar. 14 acre site. 91 touring pitches. 34 hardstandings. Caravan pitches. Motorhome pitches. Tent pitches. 46 statics.

Leisure: 🏊 🗚 🎣 ▢

Facilities: 🌇 ⊙ 🍴 ⚒ 🕭 🛒 🚿 🛗 🚽

Services: 🔌 🛢 🍴 🚰

Within 3 miles: 🎣 🛝 🛒 🎤 🛢 🛒

Notes: 🐕 Dogs must be kept on leads. Miniature railway.

▶▶▶ 79% Centenary Way Camping & Caravan Park (TA115798)

Muston Grange YO14 0HU
☎ 01723 516415 & 512313

dir: *Just off A1039 near A165 junct towards Bridlington*

* 🚐 £11-£18 🚐 £11-£18 ▲ £8-£18

Open Mar-Oct

Last arrival 21.00hrs Last departure noon

A well set-out family-owned park, with footpath access to nearby beach. Close to the seaside resort of Filey, and caravan pitches enjoy views over open countryside. 3 acre site. 75 touring

pitches. 25 hardstandings. Caravan pitches. Motorhome pitches. Tent pitches.

AA Pubs & Restaurants nearby: Cayley Arms, Brompton-by-Sawdon 01723 859372

Leisure: 🗚 **Facilities:** 🌇 ⊙ ⚒ 🕭 🛢 🚿 🛒 🐕

Services: 🔌 🛢 🚰

Within 3 miles: 🎣 🛝 🎤 🛒 🎤

Notes: 🐕 No group bookings in peak period, no 9-12 berth tents, no gazebos. Dogs must be kept on leads.

▶▶▶ 77% Filey Brigg Touring Caravan & Country Park (TA115812)

North Cliff YO14 9ET
☎ 01723 513852

e-mail: fileybrigg@scarborough.gov.uk
dir: *0.5m from Filey town centre on coast road from Scarborough, A165*

🚐 🚐 ▲

Open Etr-2 Jan

Last arrival 18.00hrs Last departure noon

A municipal park overlooking Filey Brigg with splendid views along the coast, and set in a country park. The beach is just a short walk away, as is the resort of Filey. There is a good quality amenity block, and 50 all-weather pitches are available. An excellent children's adventure playground is adjacent to the touring areas. 9 acre site. 158 touring pitches. 82 hardstandings. Caravan pitches. Motorhome pitches. Tent pitches.

Leisure: 🗚 🎡

Facilities: 🌇 ⊙ ⚒ 🕭 🕭 🛢 🛒 🐕 🐕

Services: 🔌 🛢 🇹 🍴 🚰

Within 3 miles: 🎣 🛝 🎤 🛒 🛢 🛒 ∪

Notes: Dogs must be kept on leads.

HARROGATE   Map 19 SE35

PREMIER PARK

▶▶▶▶▶ 80% Rudding Holiday Park
(SE333531)

Follifoot HG3 1JH
☎ 01423 870439

e-mail: holiday-park@ruddingpark.com
web: www.ruddingholidaypark.co.uk
dir: *From A1 take A59 to A658 signed Bradford. 4.5m then right, follow signs*

* 🚐 £15-£38 🚐 £15-£38 ▲ £15-£36

Open Mar-Jan (rs Nov-Jan shop & Deer House Pub - limited opening, summer open times only for outdoor swimming pool)

Last arrival 23.00hrs Last departure 11.00hrs

A spacious park set in beautiful 200 acres of mature parkland and walled gardens of Rudding Park. The setting has been tastefully enhanced with terraced pitches and dry-stone walls. A separate area houses super pitches where all services are supplied including a picnic table and TV connection, and there are excellent toilets. An 18-hole golf course, a 6-hole short course, driving range, golf academy, heated outdoor swimming pool, the Deer House Family Pub, and a children's play area complete the amenities. 50 acre site. 141 touring pitches. 20 hardstandings. 50 seasonal pitches. Caravan pitches. Motorhome pitches. Tent pitches. 57 statics.

AA Pubs & Restaurants nearby: Clocktower (Rudding Park Hotel, Spa & Golf), Harrogate 01423 871350

Leisure: 🏊 🗚 🎡 🎣 🎵 Spa

Facilities: 🛁 🌇 ⊙ 🍴 ⚒ 🕭 🕭 🛢 🚿 🛒 📶 🖥 🐕

Services: 🔌 🛢 🍴 🛢 🇹 🍴 🚰 🛒 🛗

Within 3 miles: 🎣 🏇 🎤 🛢 🛒 ∪

Notes: Under 18s must be accompanied by an adult.

HARROGATE *continued*

PREMIER PARK

▶▶▶▶▶ 75% Ripley Caravan Park *(SE289610)*

GOLD

Knaresborough Rd, Ripley HG3 3AU
☎ 01423 770050
e-mail: ripleycaravanpark@talk21.com
web: www.ripleycaravanpark.com
dir: *3m N of Harrogate on A61. Right at rdbt onto B6165 signed Knaresborough. Site 300yds left*

* 🚐 £16.50-£19.50 🚌 £16.50-£19.50 ⛺ £16.50-£21.50

Open Etr-Oct

Last arrival 21.00hrs Last departure noon

A well-run rural site in attractive meadowland which has been landscaped with mature tree plantings. The resident owners lovingly maintain the facilities, and there is a heated swimming pool and sauna, a TV and games room, and a covered nursery playroom for small children. 18 acre site. 100 touring pitches. 50 hardstandings. 35 seasonal pitches. Caravan pitches. Motorhome pitches. Tent pitches. 50 statics.

AA Pubs & Restaurants nearby: van Zeller, Harrogate 01423 508762

Malt Shovel Inn, Brearton 01423 862929

General Tarleton, Knaresborough 01423 340284

Leisure: 🏊 🛝 ⚽ 🏓

Facilities: 🚿 ⊙ 💨 ❄ ♿ 📞 🛒 🐕 ♻ ℹ

Services: 💬 🧼 ⛽ 🍃 [T] 🔋 ⬇

Within 3 miles: ⛳ 🚣 🎞 🎣 ◎ 🛒 🧼 🐴

Notes: Family camping only, BBQs must be off ground, no skateboards or rollerblades, no open fires. Dogs must be kept on leads. Football, volley ball, sauna.

▶▶▶▶ 80% High Moor Farm Park *(SE242560)*

Skipton Rd HG3 2LT
☎ 01423 563637 & 564955
e-mail: highmoorfarmpark@btconnect.com
dir: *4m W of Harrogate on A59 towards Skipton*

* 🚐 £22-£27 🚌 £22-£27

Open Etr or Apr-Oct

Last arrival 23.30hrs Last departure 15.00hrs

An excellent site with very good facilities, set beside a small wood and surrounded by thorn hedges. The numerous touring pitches are located in meadowland fields, each area with its own toilet block. A large heated indoor swimming pool, games room, 9-hole golf course, full-sized crown bowling green, and a bar serving meals and snacks are all popular. Please note that this park does not accept tents. 15 acre site. 320 touring pitches. 51 hardstandings. 57 seasonal pitches. Caravan pitches. Motorhome pitches. 158 statics.

AA Pubs & Restaurants nearby: van Zeller, Harrogate 01423 508762

General Tarleton, Knaresborough 01423 340284

Leisure: 🏊 🛝 ⚽ 🏓

Facilities: 🛁 🚿 ⊙ 💨 ❄ ♿ 📞 🛒 🪑 🐕 ♻ ℹ

Services: 💬 🧼 🍷 ⛽ 🍃 [T] 🍽 🔋 🧺

Within 3 miles: ⛳ 🎞 🎣 🛒 🧼 🐴

Notes: Dogs must be kept on leads. Coarse fishing.

▶▶▶ 76% Bilton Park *(SE317577)*

Village Farm, Bilton Ln HG1 4DH
☎ 01423 565070
e-mail: welcome@biltonpark.co.uk
dir: *In Harrogate, exit A59 (Skipton Rd) at Skipton Inn into Bilton Lane. Site approx 1m*

* 🚐 £16-£19 🚌 fr £16 ⛺ £13-£16

Open Apr-Oct

An established family-owned park in open countryside yet only two miles from the shops and tearooms of Harrogate. The spacious grass pitches are complemented by a well-appointed toilet block with private facilities. The Nidd Gorge is right on the doorstep. 4 acre site. 25 touring pitches. 10 hardstandings. 16 seasonal pitches. Caravan pitches. Motorhome pitches. Tent pitches. 40 statics.

AA Pubs & Restaurants nearby: van Zeller, Harrogate 01423 508762

Malt Shovel Inn, Brearton 01423 862929

General Tarleton, Knaresborough 01423 340284

Leisure: 🛝

Facilities: 🚿 ⊙ 💨 ❄ 🛒 ♻ ℹ

Services: 💬 🧼 ⛽ 🍃 [T] 🔋

Within 3 miles: ⛳ 🚣 🎞 🎣 ◎ 🏄 🛒 🧼

Notes: ⊘ Dogs must be kept on leads. Water point.

AA CAMPING CARD SITE

▶▶▶ 69% Shaws Trailer Park

(SE325557)

Knaresborough Rd HG2 7NE
☎ 01423 884432
dir: On A59 1m from town centre. 0.5m SW of Starbeck railway crossing, by Johnsons (dry cleaners)

* ♠ fr £13 ♠ fr £13 ▲ £12-£16

Open all year

Last arrival 20.00hrs Last departure 14.00hrs

A long-established site just a mile from the centre of Harrogate. The all-weather pitches are arranged around a carefully kept grass area, and the toilets are basic but functional and clean. The entrance is on the bus route to Harrogate. 11 acre site. 60 touring pitches. 24 hardstandings. Caravan pitches. Motorhome pitches. Tent pitches. 146 statics.

AA Pubs & Restaurants nearby: van Zeller, Harrogate 01423 508762

Malt Shovel Inn, Brearton 01423 862929

General Tarleton, Knaresborough 01423 340284

Facilities: ♿ ↑ ⊙ ᕦ ᕮ 𝓲
Services: 🔌 ᕮ ᕦ
Within 3 miles: ↨ ✚ ⱨ ℓ ᕮ ᕮ ↻

Notes: Adults only. ⊗ Dogs must be kept on leads.

HAWES   Map 18 SD88

Places to visit

Dales Countryside Museum & National Park Centre, HAWES 01969 666210
www.yorkshiredales.org.uk/dcm

▶▶▶ 76% Bainbridge Ings Caravan & Camping Site *(SD879895)*

DL8 3NU
☎ 01969 667354
e-mail: janet@bainbridge-ings.co.uk
dir: Approaching Hawes from Bainbridge on A684, left at Gayle sign, site 300yds on left

♠ £18 ♠ £15-£18 ▲ £15

Open Apr-Sep

Last arrival 22.00hrs Last departure noon

A quiet, well-organised site in open countryside close to Hawes in the heart of Upper Wensleydale, popular with ramblers. Pitches are sited around the perimeter of several fields, each bounded by traditional stone walls. 5 acre site. 70 touring pitches. 8 hardstandings. Caravan pitches. Motorhome pitches. Tent pitches. 15 statics.

AA Pubs & Restaurants nearby: Moorcock Inn, Hawes 01969 667488

Facilities: ↑ ⊙ ᕮ ✲ 🛜 ᕮ 𝓲
Services: 🔌 ᕮ ᕦ ⊘ ⫶ ᕮ
Within 3 miles: ℓ ᕮ ᕮ

Notes: ⊗ No noise after 23.00hrs. Dogs must be kept on leads.

HELMSLEY   Map 19 SE68

Places to visit

Duncombe Park, HELMSLEY 01439 778625
www.duncombepark.com

Helmsley Castle, HELMSLEY 01439 770442
www.english-heritage.org.uk

Great for kids: Flamingo Land Theme Park & Zoo, KIRBY MISPERTON 01653 668287
www.flamingoland.co.uk

AA CAMPING CARD SITE

PREMIER PARK

▶▶▶▶▶ 78% Golden Square Touring Caravan Park *(SE604797)*

GOLD

Oswaldkirk YO62 5YQ
☎ 01439 788269
e-mail: reception@goldensquarecaravanpark.com
dir: From York take B1363 to Oswaldkirk. Left onto B1257, 2nd left onto unclassified road signed Ampleforth, site 0.5m on right. Or A19 from Thirsk towards York. Left, follow 'Caravan Route avoiding Sutton Bank' signs, through Ampleforth to site in 1m

* ♠ £16-£20 ♠ £16-£20 ▲ £14-£20

Open Mar-Oct

Last arrival 21.00hrs Last departure noon

An excellent, popular and spacious site with very good facilities. This friendly, immaculately maintained park is set in a quiet rural situation with lovely views over the North York Moors. Terraced on three levels and surrounded by mature trees, it caters particularly for families, with excellent play areas and space for ball games. Country walks and mountain bike trails start here and an attractive holiday home area is also available. 12 acre site. 129 touring pitches. 10 hardstandings. 50 seasonal pitches. Caravan pitches. Motorhome pitches. Tent pitches. 10 statics.

AA Pubs & Restaurants nearby: The Star Inn, Harome 01439 770397

Leisure: 🎱 ⊙ 🔍
Facilities: ♿ ↑ ⊙ ᕮ ✲ ᕦ ᕮ ⊙ ᕦ ⤢ 🖥 ᕮ 𝓲
Services: 🔌 ᕮ ᕦ ⊘ ⱦ ⫶ ᕮ
Within 3 miles: ↨ ⱨ ℓ ⊙ ᕮ ↻

Notes: No skateboards or fires. Dogs must be kept on leads. Microwave available.

▶▶▶ 75% Foxholme Caravan Park

(SE658828)

Harome YO62 5JG
☎ 01439 771904
dir: A170 from Helmsley towards Scarborough, right signed Harome, left at church, through village, follow signs

♠ £20 ♠ £20 ▲ £20

Open Etr-Oct

Last arrival 23.00hrs Last departure noon

A quiet park set in secluded wooded countryside, with well-shaded pitches in individual clearings divided by mature trees. The facilities are well maintained, and the site is ideal as a touring base or a place to relax. Please note that caravans are prohibited on the A170 at Sutton Bank between Thirsk and Helmsley. 6 acre site. 60 touring pitches. 30 seasonal pitches. Caravan pitches. Motorhome pitches. Tent pitches.

AA Pubs & Restaurants nearby: The Star Inn, Harome 01439 770397

Facilities: ♿ ↑ ⊙ ᕮ ✲ ᕦ ᕮ ⤢ 𝓲
Services: 🔌 ᕮ ᕦ ⊘ ⱦ ⫶ ᕮ
Within 3 miles: ↨ ᕮ ᕮ ↻
Notes: Adults only. ⊗

HIGH BENTHAM — Map 18 SD66

Places to visit

Lancaster Maritime Museum, LANCASTER 01524 382264 www.lancashire.gov.uk/museums

Lancaster City Museum, LANCASTER 01524 64637 www.lancashire.gov.uk/museums

Great for kids: Lancaster Castle, LANCASTER 01524 64998 www.lancastercastle.com

PREMIER PARK

▶▶▶▶▶ **80% Riverside Caravan Park** (SD665688) Best of British GOLD

LA2 7FJ
☎ 015242 61272
e-mail: info@riversidecaravanpark.co.uk
dir: Exit B6480, signed from High Bentham town centre

* 🚐 £19.25-£25 🚃 £19.25-£25

Open Mar-16 Dec

Last arrival 20.00hrs Last departure noon

A well-managed riverside park developed to a high standard, with level grass pitches set in avenues separated by trees, and there are excellent facilities for children, who are made to feel as important as the adults! It has an excellent, modern amenity block, including a family bathroom, and an excellent shop, laundry and information room. The superb games room and adventure playground are hugely popular, and the market town of High Bentham is close by. Please note that this site does not accept tents. Bentham Golf Club (within one mile) is also under same ownership with facilities available for Riverside customers. 12 acre site. 61 touring pitches. 27 hardstandings. 50 seasonal pitches. Caravan pitches. Motorhome pitches. 206 statics.

AA Pubs & Restaurants nearby: The Traddock, Austwick 015242 51224

Game Cock Inn, Austwick 015242 51226

Leisure: 🎦 🔍
Facilities: 🍴 ☉ 🗜 ⚿ 🕔 ⌷ 🐕 Wi-fi 💻 ♲ ❶
Services: 🔌 🗐 🛢 🚿 🔟 🛒 ⬇
Within 3 miles: ↕ ✎ 🏧 🛒 ⛳

Notes: Dogs must be kept on leads. Permits for private fishing (chargeable), discounted golf green fees.

▶ **81% Lowther Hill Caravan Park** (SD696695)

LA2 7AN
☎ 015242 61657 & 07985 478750
web: www.caravancampingsites.co.uk/northyorkshire/lowtherhill.htm
dir: From A65 at Clapham onto B6480 signed Bentham. 3m to site on right

* 🚐 £15-£16.50 🚃 £15-£16.50 ⛺ £10

Open Mar-Nov

Last arrival 21.00hrs Last departure 14.00hrs

A simple site with stunning panoramic views from every pitch. Peace reigns on this little park, though the tourist villages of Ingleton, Clapham and Settle are not far away. All pitches have electricity, and there is a heated toilet/washroom and dishwashing facilities. 1 acre site. 9 touring pitches. 4 hardstandings. Caravan pitches. Motorhome pitches. Tent pitches.

AA Pubs & Restaurants nearby: The Traddock, Austwick 015242 51224

Game Cock Inn, Austwick 015242 51226

Facilities: 🍴 🗜 🐕 ♲
Services: 🔌
Within 3 miles: ↕ ✎ 🏧 🛒

Notes: ⊚ Payment on arrival. Dogs must be kept on leads.

HUTTON-LE-HOLE — Map 19 SE79

Places to visit

Nunnington Hall, NUNNINGTON 01439 748283 www.nationaltrust.org.uk

Rievaulx Abbey, RIEVAULX 01439 798228 www.english-heritage.org.uk

Great for kids: Pickering Castle, PICKERING 01751 474989 www.english-heritage.org.uk

▶▶▶▶ **80% Hutton-le-Hole Caravan Park** (SE705895)

Westfield Lodge YO62 6UG
☎ 01751 417261
e-mail: rwstrickland@farmersweekly.net
dir: From A170 at Keldholme follow Hutton-le-Hole signs. Approx 2m, over cattle grid, left in 500yds into Park Drive, site signed

🚐 🚃 ⛺

Open Etr-Oct

Last arrival 21.00hrs Last departure noon

A small high quality park on a working farm in the North York Moors National Park. The purpose-built toilet block offers en suite family rooms, and there is a choice of hardstanding or grass pitches within a well-tended area surrounded by hedges and shrubs. The village facilities are a 10-minute walk away. Please note that caravans are prohibited from the A170 at Sutton Bank between Thirsk and Helmsley. 5 acre site. 42 touring pitches. 36 hardstandings. Caravan pitches. Motorhome pitches. Tent pitches.

AA Pubs & Restaurants nearby: Blacksmiths Arms, Lastingham 01751 417247

The Moors Inn, Appleton-le-Moors 01751 417435

Facilities: 🍴 ☉ 🗜 ⚿ 🕔 🐕 ♲ ❶
Services: 🔌 🛢 🔟 🛒
Within 3 miles: ↕ ⊚ 🏧 ⛳

Notes: Farm walks.

LEISURE: 🏊 Indoor swimming pool 🏊 Outdoor swimming pool 🎦 Children's playground 🎪 Kid's club 🎾 Tennis court 🔍 Games room 📺 Separate TV room
↕ 9/18 hole golf course 🚣 Boats for hire 🎬 Cinema 🎵 Entertainment ✎ Fishing ◎ Mini golf ⛵ Watersports 🏋 Gym 🏟 Sports field **Spa** ⛳ Stables
FACILITIES: 🛁 Bath 🍴 Shower ☉ Electric shaver 🗜 Hairdryer ✳ Ice Pack Facility ⚿ Disabled facilities 🕔 Public telephone 🏧 Shop on site or within 200yds
🚐 Mobile shop (calls at least 5 days a week) 🍖 BBQ area 🎍 Picnic area Wi-fi Wi-fi 💻 Internet access ♲ Recycling ❶ Tourist info 🐕 Dog exercise area

KNARESBOROUGH — Map 19 SE35

Places to visit

RHS Garden Harlow Carr, HARROGATE
01423 565418 www.rhs.org.uk/harlowcarr

The Royal Pump Room Museum,
HARROGATE 01423 556188
www.harrogate.gov.uk/museums

Great for kids: Knaresborough Castle &
Museum, KNARESBOROUGH 01423 556188
www.harrogate.gov.uk/museums

AA CAMPING CARD SITE

▶▶▶ **75% Kingfisher Caravan Park**

(SE343603)

Low Moor Ln, Farnham HG5 9JB
☎ 01423 869411
dir: *From Knaresborough take A6055. Left in 1m
towards Farnham, left in village signed Scotton.
Site 1m on left*

* 🚐 fr £14 🚛 fr £14 ▲ fr £14

Open Mar-Oct

Last arrival 21.00hrs Last departure 16.00hrs

A large grassy site with open spaces set in a
wooded area in rural countryside. Whilst
Harrogate, Fountains Abbey and York are within
easy reach, anglers will want to take advantage of
on-site coarse and fly fishing lakes. The park has
a separate flat tenting field with electric hook-ups
available. 14 acre site. 35 touring pitches.
Caravan pitches. Motorhome pitches. Tent pitches.
80 statics.

AA Pubs & Restaurants nearby: General Tarleton,
Knaresborough 01423 340284

Leisure: 🛝

Facilities: 🖍️⊙🏳️✳️🔥🕙🖐️🚿🚻🚮❂

Services: 🔌🗑️🅿️🗑️ ✓

Within 3 miles: 🐕‍🦺🚶♨️🎣🏊🔥🚵⛳️

Notes: ⊗ Pets must be kept under strict adult
control, no football.

MARKINGTON — Map 19 SE26

Places to visit

Fountains Abbey & Studley Royal, RIPON
01765 643197 www.fountainsabbey.org.uk

Norton Conyers, RIPON 01765 640333
www.weddingsatnortonconyers.co.uk

Great for kids: Stump Cross Caverns, PATELEY
BRIDGE 01756 752780
www.stumpcrosscaverns.co.uk

▶▶▶ **77% Yorkshire Hussar Inn
Holiday Caravan Park** (SE288650)

High St HG3 3NR
☎ 01765 677327 & 677715
e-mail: yorkshirehussar@yahoo.co.uk
dir: *From A61 between Harrogate & Ripon at
Wormald Green follow Markington signs, 1m, left
past Post Office into High Street. Site signed on
left behind The Yorkshire Hussar Inn*

* 🚐 £16.50-£22 🚛 £16.50-£22 ▲ £10-£22

Open Etr-Oct

Last arrival 19.00hrs Last departure noon

A terraced site behind the village inn with well-
kept grass. This pleasant site offers spacious
pitches with some hardstandings and electricity,
and there are a few holiday statics for hire.
Although the pub does not provide food, an
alternative food pub is available within walking
distance. 5 acre site. 20 touring pitches. 2
hardstandings. 12 seasonal pitches. Caravan
pitches. Motorhome pitches. Tent pitches. 73
statics.

AA Pubs & Restaurants nearby: Sawley Arms,
Sawley 01765 620642

Leisure: 🛝

Facilities: 🖍️⊙🏳️✳️🔥🚮❂

Services: 🔌🗑️🍺🅿️🛒

Within 3 miles: 🎣🔥🚵⛳️

Notes: ⊗ Dogs must be kept on leads. Paddling
pool.

MASHAM — Map 19 SE28

Places to visit

Theakston Brewery & Visitor Centre, MASHAM
01765 680000 www.theakstons.co.uk

Norton Conyers, RIPON 01765 640333
www.weddingsatnortonconyers.co.uk

Great for kids: Lightwater Valley Theme Park,
NORTH STAINLEY 0871 720 0011
www.lightwatervalley.co.uk

▶▶▶ **80% Old Station Holiday Park**

(SE232812)

Old Station Yard, Low Burton HG4 4DF
☎ 01765 689569
e-mail: oldstation@tiscali.co.uk
dir: *A1 onto B6267 signed Masham & Thirsk. In
8m left onto A6108. In 100yds left into site*

🚐🚛▲

Open Mar-Nov (rs Mar-Nov café closed wkdays)

Last arrival 20.00hrs Last departure noon

An interesting site on a former station. The
enthusiastic and caring family owners have
maintained the railway theme in creating a park
with high quality facilities. The small town of
Masham with its Theakston and Black Sheep
breweries are within easy walking distance of the
park. The reception/café in a carefully restored
wagon shed provides a range of meals using local
produce. 3.75 acre site. 50 touring pitches.
Caravan pitches. Motorhome pitches. Tent pitches.
12 statics.

AA Pubs & Restaurants nearby: Black Sheep
Brewery, Masham 01765 680101

Vennell's, Masham 01765 689000

Facilities: 🖍️⊙🏳️✳️🔥🕙🖐️🚿🚻📶💻🚮❂

Services: 🔌🗑️🅿️🚽🍽️🛒🚚🚐

Within 3 miles: 🐕‍🦺🎣🔥🚵⛳️

Notes: No fast cycling around site, no campfires.
Dogs must be kept on leads.

SERVICES: 🔌 Electric hook up 🗑️ Launderette 🍺 Licensed bar 🅿️ Calor Gas 🛢️ Camping Gaz 🚽 Toilet fluid 🍽️ Café/Restaurant 🏪 Fast Food/Takeaway 🔋 Battery charging
🚼 Baby care ⚙️ Motorvan service point **ABBREVIATIONS:** BH/bank hols-bank holidays Etr-Easter Whit-Whitsun dep-departure fr-from hrs-hours m-mile mdnt-midnight
rdbt-roundabout rs-restricted service wk-week wknd-weekend ⊗ No credit cards ⊗ no dogs   See page 7 for details of the AA Camping Card Scheme

NABURN Map 16 SE54

Places to visit

Clifford's Tower, YORK 01904 646940 www.english-heritage.org.uk

Fairfax House, YORK 01904 655543 www.fairfaxhouse.co.uk

Great for kids: Jorvik Viking Centre, YORK 01904 615505 www.jorvik-viking-centre.com

►►►► 80% Naburn Lock Caravan Park *(SE596446)*

GOLD

YO19 4RU

☎ 01904 728697

e-mail: wilks@naburnlock.co.uk

dir: *From A64 (McArthur Glen designer outlet) take A19 N, turn left signed Naburn on B1222, site on right 0.5m past village*

* 🚐 fr £17 🚌 fr £17 ⛺ fr £17

Open Mar-6 Nov

Last arrival 20.00hrs Last departure 13.00hrs

A family park where the enthusiastic owners are steadily improving its quality. The mainly grass pitches are arranged in small groups separated by mature hedges. The park is close to the River Ouse, and the river towpath provides excellent walking and cycling opportunities. The river bus to nearby York leaves from a jetty beside the park. 7 acre site. 100 touring pitches. 22 hardstandings. Caravan pitches. Motorhome pitches. Tent pitches.

AA Pubs & Restaurants nearby: Lamb & Lion Inn, York 01904 612078

Blue Bell, York 01904 654904

Lysander Arms, York 01904 640845

Facilities: 🚿 ⊙ 💨 ❄ ♿ $ ⛩ 🐕 ♻ ℹ

Services: 🔧 🧺 🔒 🌿 [T] 🏪 ⚓

Within 3 miles: ⛵ 🎣 $ 🧺 🐎

Notes: Adults-only section, quiet 23.00hrs-07.00hrs. River fishing.

NETHERBY Map 16 SE34

Places to visit

Abbey House Museum, LEEDS 0113 230 5492 www.leeds.gov.uk

Royal Armouries Museum, LEEDS 0113 220 1866 www.royalarmouries.org

►►►► 82% *Maustin Caravan Park* *(SE332470)*

Kearby with Netherby LS22 4DA

☎ 0113 288 6234

e-mail: info@maustin.co.uk

dir: *From A61 (Leeds-Harrogate road) follow signs for Kirkby Overblow. Right towards Kearby, pass farm buildings to x-rds. Right to site*

🚐 🚌 ⛺

Open Mar-28 Jan

A secluded park for adults only, with pitches set around a well-tended grassed area. Adjacent to the pitching area, the amenity block offers a high standard of facilities. The charming Stables Restaurant, with its cosy bar and patio, is open at weekends and bank holidays, and the park has its own flat bowling green where competitions are held throughout the season. 8 acre site. 25 touring pitches. Caravan pitches. Motorhome pitches. Tent pitches. 70 statics.

AA Pubs & Restaurants nearby: Windmill Inn, Linton 01937 582209

Facilities: 🚿 ⊙ 💨 ❄ 📶

Services: 🔧 🧺 🍷 🍴

Within 3 miles: ⛳ 🎣 $ 🐎

Notes: Adults only.

NORTHALLERTON Map 19 SE39

Places to visit

Mount Grace Priory, OSMOTHERLEY 01609 883494 www.english-heritage.org.uk

Theakston Brewery & Visitor Centre, MASHAM 01765 680000 www.theakstons.co.uk

Great for kids: Falconry UK - Birds of Prey Centre, THIRSK 01845 587522 www.falconrycentre.co.uk

►►►► 79% *Otterington Park* *(SE378882)*

GOLD

Station Farm, South Otterington DL7 9JB

☎ 01609 780656

e-mail: info@otteringtonpark.com

dir: *From A168 midway between Northallerton & Thirsk onto unclassified road signed South Otterington. Site on right just before South Otterington*

🚐 🚌

Open Mar-Oct

Last arrival 21.00hrs Last departure 13.00hrs

A high quality park on a working farm with open outlooks across the Vale of York. It enjoys a peaceful location with a lovely nature walk and on-site fishing, which is very popular. Young children will enjoy the play area. Toilet facilities are very good. The attractions of Northallerton and Thirsk are a few minutes' drive away. 6 acre site. 62 touring pitches. 62 hardstandings. Caravan pitches. Motorhome pitches. 3 wooden pods.

Leisure: 🛝 ⚽

Facilities: 🛁 🚿 ⊙ 💨 ❄ ♿ ☎ $ ⛩ 🐕 📶 ♻ ℹ

Services: 🔧 🧺 🔒 🏪

Within 3 miles: ⛳ 🎬 🎣 ◎ $ 🧺

Notes: Hot tub, fitness equipment.

LEISURE: 🏊 Indoor swimming pool 🌞 Outdoor swimming pool 🛝 Children's playground ✋ Kid's club 🎾 Tennis court 🎱 Games room 📺 Separate TV room ⛳ 9/18 hole golf course ⛵ Boats for hire 🎬 Cinema 🎵 Entertainment 🎣 Fishing ◎ Mini golf 🌊 Watersports 🏋 Gym ⚽ Sports field **Spa** 🐎 Stables
FACILITIES: 🛁 Bath 🚿 Shower ⊙ Electric shaver 💨 Hairdryer ❄ Ice Pack Facility ♿ Disabled facilities ☎ Public telephone $ Shop on site or within 200yds 🚚 Mobile shop (calls at least 5 days a week) 🍖 BBQ area ⛩ Picnic area 📶 Wi-fi 💻 Internet access ♻ Recycling ℹ Tourist info 🐕 Dog exercise area

NORTH STAINLEY
Map 19 SE27

Places to visit

Norton Conyers, RIPON 01765 640333
www.weddingsatnortonconyers.co.uk

Falconry UK - Birds of Prey Centre, THIRSK
01845 587522 www.falconrycentre.co.uk

Great for kids: Lightwater Valley Theme Park,
NORTH STAINLEY 0871 720 0011
www.lightwatervalley.co.uk

►►►► 76% Sleningford Watermill Caravan Camping Park *(SE280783)*

HG4 3HQ
☎ **01765 635201**
web: www.sleningfordwatermill.co.uk
dir: *Adjacent to A6108. 5m N of Ripon & 1m N of North Stainley*

Open Etr & Apr-Oct

Last arrival 21.00hrs Last departure 12.30hrs

The old watermill and the River Ure make an attractive setting for this touring park which is laid out in two areas. Pitches are placed in meadowland and close to mature woodland, and the park has two enthusiastic managers. This is a popular place with canoeists. 14 acre site. 140 touring pitches. 8 hardstandings. 47 seasonal pitches. Caravan pitches. Motorhome pitches. Tent pitches.

AA Pubs & Restaurants nearby: Bruce Arms, West Tanfield 01677 470325

Black Sheep Brewery, Masham 01765 680101

Vennell's, Masham 01765 689000

Leisure: ✪ **Facilities:** ⌂⊙☞✳৬ৈ⊣♻❶
Services: ⊟☒🛢⌀🔋
Within 3 miles: ↓☞🔒☒

Notes: Groups by prior arrangement only, booked through organisations or associations. Dogs must be kept on leads. Fly fishing & outdoor activities.

OSMOTHERLEY
Map 19 SE49

Places to visit

Mount Grace Priory, OSMOTHERLEY
01609 883494 www.english-heritage.org.uk

Gisborough Priory, GUISBOROUGH 01287 633801
www.english-heritage.org.uk

Great for kids: Falconry UK - Birds of Prey Centre, THIRSK 01845 587522
www.falconrycentre.co.uk

PREMIER PARK

►►►►► 79% Cote Ghyll Caravan & Camping Park *(SE459979)*

DL6 3AH
☎ **01609 883425**
e-mail: hills@coteghyll.com
dir: *Exit A19 dual carriageway at A684 (Northallerton junct). Follow signs to Osmotherley. Left in village centre. Site entrance 0.5m on right*

* ⊟ £17.50-£22.50 ⊠ £17.50-£22.50
▲ £17.50-£22.50

Open Mar-Oct

Last arrival 21.00hrs Last departure noon

A quiet, peaceful site in a pleasant valley on the edge of moors, close to the village. The park is divided into terraces bordered by woodland, and the extra well-appointed amenity block is a welcome addition to this attractive park. Mature trees, shrubs and an abundance of fresh seasonal floral displays create a relaxing and peaceful atmosphere and the whole park is immaculately maintained. There are pubs and shops nearby and holiday statics for hire. 7 acre site. 77 touring pitches. 22 hardstandings. Caravan pitches. Motorhome pitches. Tent pitches. 18 statics.

AA Pubs & Restaurants nearby: Golden Lion, Osmotherley 01609 883526

Leisure: ⚠

Facilities: ⊯⌂⊙☞✳৬◐🗑⊣ WIFI
▣♻❶

Services: ⊟☒🛢⌀T🍽🔋�

Within 3 miles: ☞🔒☒∪

Notes: Dogs must be kept on leads.

PICKERING
Map 19 SE78

Places to visit

Pickering Castle, PICKERING 01751 474989
www.english-heritage.org.uk

North Yorkshire Moors Railway, PICKERING
01751 472508 www.nymr.co.uk

Great for kids: Flamingo Land Theme Park & Zoo, KIRBY MISPERTON 01653 668287
www.flamingoland.co.uk

►►►► 78% Wayside Holiday Park *(SE764859)*

Wrelton YO18 8PG
☎ **01751 472608**
e-mail: wrelton@waysideholidaypark.co.uk
web: www.waysideparks.co.uk
dir: *2.5m W of Pickering off A170, follow signs at Wrelton*

⊟ £20-£25 ⊠ £20-£25

Open Apr-Oct

Last arrival 22.00hrs Last departure noon

Located in the village of Wrelton, this well-maintained mainly seasonal touring and holiday home park is divided into small paddocks by mature hedging. The amenity block has smart, modern facilities. The village pub and restaurant are within a few minutes' walk of the park. Please note that caravans are prohibited from the A170 at Sutton Bank between Thirsk and Helmsley. 10 acre site. 40 touring pitches. 2 hardstandings. Caravan pitches. Motorhome pitches. 122 statics.

AA Pubs & Restaurants nearby: Fox & Hounds Country Inn, Sinnington, 01751 431577

White Swan Inn, Pickering 01751 472288

Leisure: ✪ **Facilities:** ⌂⊙☞৬◐⊣
Services: ⊟☒⌀T🔋
Within 3 miles: ↓☷☞🔒☒∪

Notes: Dogs must be kept on leads. Internet access for statics only.

RICHMOND   Map 19 NZ10

Places to visit

Green Howards Museum, RICHMOND
01748 826561 www.greenhowards.org.uk

Bolton Castle, CASTLE BOLTON 01969 623981
www.boltoncastle.co.uk

Great for kids: Richmond Castle, RICHMOND
01748 822493 www.english-heritage.org.uk

►►►► 79% Brompton Caravan Park

(NZ199002)

Brompton-on-Swale DL10 7EZ
☎ 01748 824629
e-mail: brompton.caravanpark@btconnect.com
dir: *Exit A1 signed Catterick. Take B6271 to
Brompton-on-Swale, site 1m on left*

Open mid Mar-Oct

Last arrival 21.00hrs Last departure noon

An attractive and well-managed family park where
pitches have an open outlook across the River
Swale. There is a good children's playground, an
excellent family recreation room, a takeaway food
service, and fishing is available on the river. Three
river view camping pods and holiday apartments
can also be hired. 14 acre site. 177 touring
pitches. 2 hardstandings. Caravan pitches.
Motorhome pitches. Tent pitches. 22 statics. 3
wooden pods.

AA Pubs & Restaurants nearby: Charles Bathurst
Inn, Arkengarthdale 01748 884567

Leisure: ⚑ ◤

Facilities: ⬆ ⊙ ◔ ✳ ⬆ ⬆ ⬆ ⬆ ⬆ ♻ ⬆

Services: ⬆ ⬆ ⬆ ⬆ ⬆ ⬆ ⬆

Within 3 miles: ⬆ ⬆ ⬆ ⬆ ⬆ ⬆ ⬆

Notes: No gazebos, no motor, electric cars or
scooters, no group bookings, open fires or wood
burners, no electricity for tents. Quiet at mdnt.

►►► 76% *Swale View Caravan Park*

(NZ134013)

Reeth Rd DL10 4SF
☎ 01748 823106 & 07736 820283
e-mail: swaleview@teesdaleonline.co.uk
dir: *3m W of Richmond on A6108 (Reeth to
Leyburn road)*

Open Mar-15 Jan

Last arrival 21.00hrs Last departure noon

Shaded by trees and overlooking the River Swale is
this attractive, mainly grassy site, which has a
number of attractive holiday homes and seasonal
tourers. The park, run by enthusiastic owners,
offers facilities for 30 tourers, all with electric and
hardstandings. It is a short distance from
Richmond, and well situated for exploring
Swaledale and Wensleydale. A luxury cottage is
also available for hire. 13 acre site. 30 touring
pitches. 30 hardstandings. 15 seasonal pitches.
Caravan pitches. Motorhome pitches. Tent pitches.
100 statics.

AA Pubs & Restaurants nearby: Charles Bathurst
Inn, Arkengarthdale 01748 884567

Leisure: ⚑

Facilities: ⬆ ⊙ ◔ ⬆ ⬆ ⬆ ⬆ ⬆ ⬆ ♻ ⬆

Services: ⬆ ⬆ ⬆ ⬆ ⬆ ⬆ ⬆ ⬆

Within 3 miles: ⬆ ⬆ ⬆ ⬆ ⬆ ⬆

Notes: 1 dog per pitch. Dogs must be kept on
leads. Vending machine.

RIPON   Map 19 SE37

See also North Stainley

Places to visit

Fountains Abbey & Studley Royal, RIPON
01765 643197 www.fountainsabbey.org.uk

Norton Conyers, RIPON 01765 640333
www.weddingsatnortonconyers.co.uk

Great for kids: Falconry UK - Birds of Prey
Centre, THIRSK 01845 587522
www.falconrycentre.co.uk

►►►► 78% Riverside Meadows
Country Caravan Park *(SE317726)*

Ure Bank Top HG4 1JD
☎ 01765 602964
e-mail: info@flowerofmay.com
dir: *On A61 at N end of bridge out of Ripon, W
along river (do not cross river). Site 400yds,
signed*

✱ ⬆ £15-£21 ⬆ £15-£21 ⬆ £15-£21

Open Etr-Oct (rs Low-mid season bar open wknds
only)

Last arrival dusk Last departure noon

This pleasant, well-maintained site stands on
high ground overlooking the River Ure, one mile
from the town centre. The site has an excellent
club with family room and quiet lounge. There is
no access to the river from the site. 28 acre site.
80 touring pitches. 40 hardstandings. 40 seasonal
pitches. Caravan pitches. Motorhome pitches. Tent
pitches. 269 statics.

AA Pubs & Restaurants nearby: Sawley Arms,
Sawley 01765 620642

Leisure: ⚑ ◤ ⬚ ♫

Facilities: ⬆ ⊙ ✳ ⬆ ⬆ ⬆ ⬆ ⬆ ⬆ ♻ ⬆

Services: ⬆ ⬆ ⬆ ⬆ ⬆ ⬆ ⬆

Within 3 miles: ⬆ ⬆ ⬆ ⬆ ⬆ ⬆ ⬆

Notes: No noise after mdnt. Dogs by prior
arrangement only. Dogs must be kept on leads.

see advert on page 345

ROBIN HOOD'S BAY Map 19 NZ90

See also Whitby

Places to visit

Whitby Abbey, WHITBY 01947 603568 www.english-heritage.org.uk

Scarborough Castle, SCARBOROUGH 01723 372451 www.english-heritage.org.uk

Great for kids: Sea Life & Marine Sanctuary, SCARBOROUGH 01723 373414 www.sealife.co.uk

AA CAMPING CARD SITE

►►►► 84% Grouse Hill Caravan Park *(NZ928002)*

Flask Bungalow Farm, Fylingdales YO22 4QH
☎ 01947 880543 & 880560
e-mail: info@grousehill.co.uk
dir: *Off A171 (Whitby-Scarborough road), entered via loop road at Flask Inn*

* 🚐 £15-£30 🚌 ⛺

Open Mar-Oct (rs Etr-May shop & reception restricted)

Last arrival 20.30hrs Last departure noon

A spacious family park on a south-facing slope with attractive, mostly level, terraced pitches overlooking The North Yorkshire National Park. The site has quality toilet blocks, a treatment plant to ensure excellent drinking water, security barriers, CCTV, Wi-fi and camping pods. This is an ideal base for walking and touring. 14 acre site. 175 touring pitches. 30 hardstandings. Caravan pitches. Motorhome pitches. Tent pitches. 1 static. 8 wooden pods.

AA Pubs & Restaurants nearby: Laurel Inn, Robin Hood's Bay 01947 880400

Magpie Café, Whitby 01947 602058

Grouse Hill Caravan Park

Leisure: ⛺ 🔍

Facilities: 🛁 🚿 ⊙ 🚿 ✳ ♿ ☎ $ 🐕 Wi-fi ♻ ℹ

Services: 🔌 🧺 🛢 🔥 [T] 🔋 ⛛

Within 3 miles: ⛳ $ 🧺 U

Notes: No noise after 22.30hrs. Dogs must be kept on leads.

see advert below

►►►► 81% Middlewood Farm Holiday Park *(NZ945045)*

GOLD

Middlewood Ln, Fylingthorpe YO22 4UF
☎ 01947 880414
e-mail: info@middlewoodfarm.com
dir: *From A171 towards Robin Hood's Bay & into Fylingthorpe. Site signed from A171*

🚐 🚌 ⛺

Open Mar-Oct

Last arrival 20.00hrs Last departure 11.00hrs

A peaceful, friendly family park enjoying panoramic views of Robin Hood's Bay in a picturesque fishing village. The park has two toilet blocks with private facilities. The village pub is a five-minute walk away, and the beach can be reached via a path leading directly from the site, which is also accessible by wheelchair users. 7 acre site. 100 touring pitches. 19 hardstandings. Caravan pitches. Motorhome pitches. Tent pitches. 30 statics.

continued

ROBIN HOOD'S BAY *continued*

AA Pubs & Restaurants nearby: Laurel Inn, Robin Hood's Bay 01947 880400

Magpie Café, Whitby 01947 602058

Middlewood Farm Holiday Park

Leisure: 🛝

Facilities: 🛁 🚿 🪒 💨 ❄ ♿ 🧺 🐕 [Wi-fi] ♻ ℹ

Services: 🚐 🧼 🔒 🍃 🛏 🍖 🛒 ⬇

Within 3 miles: ⛳ 🚣 🎣 🛒 🧼 ∪

Notes: Dangerous dog breeds are not accepted, no radios or noise after 22.00hrs. Dogs must be kept on leads.

see advert below

ROSEDALE ABBEY — Map 19 SE79

Places to visit

North Yorkshire Moors Railway, PICKERING 01751 472508 www.nymr.co.uk

Great for kids: Flamingo Land Theme Park & Zoo, KIRBY MISPERTON 01653 668287 www.flamingoland.co.uk

►►►► 80% Rosedale Caravan & Camping Park *(SE725958)*

YO18 8SA
☎ 01751 417272
e-mail: info@flowerofmay.com
dir: *From Pickering take A170 towards Sinnington for 2.25m. At Wrelton turn right onto unclassified road signed Cropton & Rosedale, 7m. Site on left in village*

* 🚐 £15-£21 🚙 £15-£21 ⛺ £15-£21

Open Mar-Oct

Last arrival dusk Last departure noon

Set in a sheltered valley in the centre of the North Yorkshire Moors National Park, and divided into separate areas for tents, tourers and statics. A very popular park, with well-tended grounds, and close to the pretty village of Rosedale Abbey. Two toilet blocks offer private, combined facilities. There are six camping pods situated by the river. 10 acre site. 100 touring pitches. 20 seasonal pitches. Caravan pitches. Motorhome pitches. Tent pitches. 35 statics. 6 wooden pods.

AA Pubs & Restaurants nearby: Blacksmiths Arms, Lastingham 01751 417247

Leisure: 🛝

Facilities: 🚿 🪒 ❄ ♿ 📞 🛒 🧺 🐕 ℹ

Services: 🚐 🧼 🔒 🍃 [T] 🛏

Within 3 miles: ⛳ 🎣 🛒 🧼 ∪

Notes: Dogs by prior arrangement only, no noise after mdnt. Dogs must be kept on leads.

see advert on page 345

SCARBOROUGH — Map 17 TA08

See also Filey & Wykeham

Places to visit

Scarborough Castle, SCARBOROUGH 01723 372451 www.english-heritage.org.uk

Pickering Castle, PICKERING 01751 474989 www.english-heritage.org.uk

Great for kids: Sea Life & Marine Sanctuary, SCARBOROUGH 01723 373414 www.sealife.co.uk

PREMIER PARK

►►►►► 75% Jacobs Mount Caravan Park *(TA021868)*

Jacobs Mount, Stepney Rd YO12 5NL
☎ 01723 361178
e-mail: jacobsmount@yahoo.co.uk
dir: *Direct access from A170*

* 🚐 £11-£21 🚙 £11-£21 ⛺ £11-£21

LEISURE: 🏊 Indoor swimming pool 🏊 Outdoor swimming pool 🛝 Children's playground ✋ Kid's club 🎾 Tennis court 🎱 Games room 📺 Separate TV room ⛳ 9/18 hole golf course 🚣 Boats for hire 🎬 Cinema 🎵 Entertainment 🎣 Fishing ◎ Mini golf 🏄 Watersports 🏋 Gym ⚽ Sports field Spa ∪ Stables
FACILITIES: 🛁 Bath 🚿 Shower 🪒 Electric shaver 💨 Hairdryer ❄ Ice Pack Facility ♿ Disabled facilities 📞 Public telephone 🛒 Shop on site or within 200yds 🚚 Mobile shop (calls at least 5 days a week) 🍖 BBQ area 🧺 Picnic area [Wi-fi] Wi-fi 💻 Internet access ♻ Recycling ℹ Tourist info 🐕 Dog exercise area

Jacobs Mount Caravan Park

Open Mar-Nov (rs Mar-May & Oct limited hours at shop & bar)

Last arrival 22.00hrs Last departure noon

An elevated family-run park surrounded by woodland and open countryside, yet only two miles from the beach. Touring pitches are terraced gravel stands with individual services. The Jacobs Tavern serves a wide range of appetising meals and snacks, and there is a separate well-equipped games room for teenagers. 18 acre site. 156 touring pitches. 131 hardstandings. Caravan pitches. Motorhome pitches. Tent pitches. 60 statics.

AA Pubs & Restaurants nearby: Cayley Arms, Brompton-by-Sawdon 01723 859372

Anvil Inn, Sawdon 01723 859896

Leisure: ⚓ ❧ ▢ ♫

Facilities: 🛁 ⚲ ☉ ℉ ☀ ♿ 🕒 🖐 🐾 Wi-Fi ▪ 🔧

Services: 🔌 🔥 🍴 📶 🛢 🚿 🔋 🛗 ⚙

Within 3 miles: ⚐ ⚑ 🗓 ✎ ◎ ⛵ 🔒 🔵 ∪

Notes: Dogs must be kept on leads. Food preparation area.

NEW ▶▶▶▶ 82% Cayton Village Caravan Park *(TA063838)*

 GOLD

Mill Ln, Cayton Bay YO11 3NN
☎ **01723 583171**
e-mail: info@caytontouring.co.uk
dir: *From Scarborough A64, B1261 signed Filey. In Cayton 2nd left after Blacksmiths Arms into Mill Ln. Site 150yds on left. Or from A165 from Scarborough towards Filey right at Cayton Bay rdbt into Mill Ln. Site 0.5m right. (NB it is advisable to follow guide directions not Sat Nav)*

* 🚐 £13.50-£35 🚙 £15.50-£35 Å £13.50-£28

Open Mar-Oct

Last arrival 18.00hrs Last departure noon

A long established, quietly located holiday destination close to all the major coastal attractions. The immaculately maintained grounds provide excellent pitch density and many areas are hedge-screened to create privacy. The latest touring field, The Laurels, is equipped with fully serviced hardstanding pitches that include TV hook-up and free Wi-Fi. 23 acre site. 310 touring pitches. 94 hardstandings. 180 seasonal pitches. Caravan pitches. Motorhome pitches. Tent pitches.

AA Pubs & Restaurants nearby: Marmalade's at Beiderbecke's Hotel, Scarborough 01723 365766

Leisure: ⚓ ☺

Facilities: ⚲ ☉ ℉ ☀ ♿ 🕒 🐾 Wi-Fi ♻ 🔧

Services: 🔌 🔥 🛢 📶 🛗

Within 3 miles: ⚐ ⚑ 🗓 ✎ ◎ ⛵ 🔒 🔵

Notes: No noise after 23.00hrs. Dogs must be kept on leads.

▶▶▶▶ 78% Scalby Close Park
(TA020925)

Burniston Rd YO13 0DA
☎ **01723 365908**
e-mail: info@scalbyclosepark.co.uk
web: www.scalbyclosepark.co.uk
dir: *2m N of Scarborough on A615 (coast road), 1m from junct with A171*

🚐 🚙

Open Mar-Oct

Last arrival 22.00hrs Last departure noon

An attractive park with enthusiastic owners. The site has a shower block, a laundry and fully-serviced pitches, and the landscaping is also very good. This is an ideal base from which to explore the nearby coast and countryside. 3 acre site. 42 touring pitches. 42 hardstandings. Caravan pitches. Motorhome pitches. 5 statics.

AA Pubs & Restaurants nearby: Cayley Arms, Brompton-by-Sawdon 01723 859372

Anvil Inn, Sawdon 01723 859896

Facilities: ⚲ ☉ ℉ ☀ ♿ 🕒 🖐

Services: 🔌 🔥 📶 🛗 ⚙

Within 3 miles: ⚐ ⚑ 🗓 ✎ 🔒 🔵 ∪

Notes: 🚫

SCARBOROUGH *continued*

AA CAMPING CARD SITE

►►► 80% Killerby Old Hall *(TA063829)*

Killerby YO11 3TW
☎ 01723 583799
e-mail: killerbyhall@btconnect.com
dir: *Direct access via B1261 at Killerby, near Cayton*

* ⊞ £16.50-£23 ⊟

Open 14 Feb-4 Jan

Last arrival 20.00hrs Last departure noon

A small secluded park, well sheltered by mature trees and shrubs, located at the rear of the old hall. Use of the small indoor swimming pool is shared by visitors to the hall's holiday accommodation. There is a children's play area. 2 acre site. 20 touring pitches. 20 hardstandings. Caravan pitches. Motorhome pitches.

AA Pubs & Restaurants nearby: Cayley Arms, Brompton-by-Sawdon 01723 859372

Anvil Inn, Sawdon 01723 859896

Leisure: 🏊 🛝 😊 🎱
Facilities: 📶 ⊙ 𝒫 🛏 🚻 📶 🚮 𝓲
Services: 🔌 🖥
Within 3 miles: 🚴 𝒫 ◎ ⛵ 🏧 🛒 🎠
Notes: Dogs must be kept on leads.

►►► 79% Arosa Caravan & Camping Park *(TA014830)*

Ratten Row, Seamer YO12 4QB
☎ 01723 862166 & 07858 694077
e-mail: info@arosacamping.co.uk
dir: *A64 towards Scarborough onto B1261. On entering village 1st left at rdbt signed Seamer. From Pickering on A171 right at Seamer rdbt. Last right in village*

⊞ ⊟ ▲

Open Mar-4 Jan

Last arrival 21.00hrs Last departure by arrangement

A mature park in a secluded location, but with easy access to costal attractions. Touring areas are hedge-screened to provide privacy, and a well stocked bar serving food is also available. Barbecues and hog roasts are a feature during the warmer months. 9 acre site. 118 touring pitches. 25 hardstandings. 40 seasonal pitches. Caravan pitches. Motorhome pitches. Tent pitches. 8 statics.

AA Pubs & Restaurants nearby: Cayley Arms, Brompton-by-Sawdon 01723 859372

Coachman Inn, Snainton 01723 859231

Leisure: 🛝 🎱 🎵
Facilities: 📶 𝒫 ❄ 🛁 🕐 📶 🖥 𝓲
Services: 🔌 🖥 🍴 🛢 ⊘ 🚽 🔌 🛒 🏧
Within 3 miles: 🚴 𝒫 🏧 🛒 🎠
Notes: No noise after 23.00hrs, no generators, no powered bikes or scooters. Dogs must be kept on leads.

SCOTCH CORNER   Map 19 NZ20

Places to visit
Green Howards Museum, RICHMOND
01748 826561 www.greenhowards.org.uk

Bolton Castle, CASTLE BOLTON 01969 623981
www.boltoncastle.co.uk

Great for kids: Raby Castle, STAINDROP
01833 660202 www.rabycastle.com

►►► 75% Scotch Corner Caravan Park *(NZ210054)*

DL10 6NS
☎ 01748 822530 & 07977 647722
e-mail: marshallleisure@aol.com
dir: *From Scotch Corner junct of A1 & A66 take A6108 towards Richmond. 250mtrs, cross central reservation, return 200mtrs to site entrance*

* ⊞ £16-£20 ⊟ £16-£20 ▲ £16

Open Etr-Oct

Last arrival 22.30hrs Last departure noon

A well-maintained site with good facilities, ideally situated as a stopover, and an equally good location for touring. The Vintage Hotel, which serves food, can be accessed from the rear of the site. 7 acre site. 96 touring pitches. 4 hardstandings. Caravan pitches. Motorhome pitches. Tent pitches. 1 static.

AA Pubs & Restaurants nearby: Shoulder of Mutton Inn, Kirby Hill 01748 822772

Facilities: 📶 ⊙ 𝒫 ❄ 🛁 🕐 🛏 🚮 🚻 𝓲
Services: 🔌 🖥 🍴 🛢 ⊘ 🚽 🔌 🛒 🏧
Within 3 miles: 🚴 𝒫 🏧 🛒 🎠
Notes: 🐕 Dogs must be kept on leads. Recreation area for children, soft ball.

SHERIFF HUTTON   Map 19 SE66

Places to visit
Kirkham Priory, KIRKHAM 01653 618768
www.english-heritage.org.uk

Sutton Park, SUTTON-ON-THE-FOREST
01347 810249 www.statelyhome.co.uk

AA CAMPING CARD SITE

NEW ►►►► 78% York Meadows Caravan Park *(SE644653)*

York Rd YO60 6QP
☎ 01347 878508
e-mail: reception@yorkmeadowscaravanpark.com
dir: *From York take A64 towards Scarborough. Left signed Flaxton & Sheriff Hutton. At West Lilling left signed Strensall. Site opposite junct*

* ⊞ £16-£20 ⊟ £16-£20 ▲ £14-£20

Open Mar-Oct

Last arrival 21.00hrs Last departure noon

Peacefully located in open countryside and surrounded by mature trees, shrubs and wildlife areas, this park, newly opened in 2012, provides all level pitches and a modern, well equipped amenities block. 7 acre site. 50 touring pitches. 35 hardstandings. 15 seasonal pitches. Caravan pitches. Motorhome pitches. Tent pitches. 10 statics.

AA Pubs & Restaurants nearby: Blackwell Ox Inn, Sutton-on-the-Forest 01347 810328

Rose & Crown, Sutton-on-the-Forest
01347 811333

Leisure: 🛝
Facilities: 🛁 📶 𝒫 ❄ 🛁 🛏 🚮 🚻 𝓲
Services: 🔌 🖥 🛁 ⊘ 🚽 🛒 🏧
Within 3 miles: 🚴 🎡 🛒
Notes: No fires. Max of 5 in a group or 6 in a unit. Dogs must be kept on leads.

LEISURE: 🏊 Indoor swimming pool 🏊 Outdoor swimming pool 🛝 Children's playground 🪁 Kid's club 🎾 Tennis court 🎱 Games room 📺 Separate TV room 🏌 9/18 hole golf course ⛵ Boats for hire 🎬 Cinema 🎵 Entertainment 🎣 Fishing ◎ Mini golf 🏄 Watersports 🏋 Gym ⚽ Sports field Spa 🎠 Stables
FACILITIES: 🛁 Bath 🚿 Shower ⊙ Electric shaver 𝒫 Hairdryer ❄ Ice Pack Facility 👨‍🦽 Disabled facilities 🕐 Public telephone 🛒 Shop on site or within 200yds 🏪 Mobile shop (calls at least 5 days a week) 🍴 BBQ area 🪑 Picnic area 📶 Wi-fi ⌨ Internet access ♻ Recycling 𝓲 Tourist info 🐕 Dog exercise area

SLINGSBY
Map 19 SE67

Places to visit

Nunnington Hall, NUNNINGTON 01439 748283
www.nationaltrust.org.uk

Castle Howard, MALTON 01653 648333
www.castlehoward.co.uk

►►►► 80% Robin Hood Caravan & Camping Park (SE701748)

Green Dyke Ln YO62 4AP
☎ 01653 628391
e-mail: info@robinhoodcaravanpark.co.uk
dir: Access from B1257 (Malton to Helmsley road)

* ⌂ £18-£25 ⌂ £18-£25 ▲ £18-£25

Open Mar-Oct

Last arrival 18.00hrs Last departure noon

A pleasant, well-maintained grassy park, in a good position for touring North Yorkshire. Situated on the edge of the village of Slingsby, the park has hardstandings and electricity for every pitch. The toilet block was completely refurbished for the 2012 season. 2 acre site. 32 touring pitches. 22

hardstandings. Caravan pitches. Motorhome pitches. Tent pitches. 35 statics.

AA Pubs & Restaurants nearby: Worsley Arms Hotel, Hovingham 01653 628234

Malt Shovel, Hovingham 01653 628264

Royal Oak Inn, Nunnington 01439 748271

Leisure: ⚑

Facilities: ⎙☉℘✳&⏱⑤🚿📶🖥♻❶

Services: ⚡⑤🗐🍺⊘Ⓣ🎫🛒

Within 3 miles: ⌀🗄∪

Notes: No noise after 23.00hrs. Dogs must be kept on leads. Caravan hire, off-licence.

see advert below

SNAINTON

Places to visit

Scarborough Castle, SCARBOROUGH 01723 372451 www.english-heritage.org.uk

Pickering Castle, PICKERING 01751 474989 www.english-heritage.org.uk

Great for kids: Sea Life & Marine Sanctuary, SCARBOROUGH 01723 373414 www.sealife.co.uk

SNAINTON
Map 17 SE98

AA CAMPING CARD SITE

►►►► 87% Jasmine Caravan Park
(SE928813)

Cross Ln YO13 9BE
☎ 01723 859240
e-mail: enquiries@jasminepark.co.uk
dir: Turn S from A170 in Snainton, then follow signs

* ⌂ £20-£35 ⌂ £20-£35 ▲ £20-£35

Open Mar-Oct

Last arrival 20.00hrs Last departure noon

A peaceful and beautifully-presented park on the edge of a pretty village, and sheltered by high hedges. The toilet block with individual wash cubicles is maintained to a very high standard, and there is a licensed shop. This picturesque park lies midway between Pickering and Scarborough on the southern edge of the North Yorkshire Moors. Please note there is no

continued

SERVICES: ⚡ Electric hook up ⑤ Launderette 🍺 Licensed bar ⬛ Calor Gas ⊘ Camping Gaz Ⓣ Toilet fluid 🍴 Café/Restaurant 🍟 Fast Food/Takeaway 🔋 Battery charging 🚼 Baby care ⎚ Motorvan service point **ABBREVIATIONS:** BH/bank hols-bank holidays Etr-Easter Whit-Whitsun dep-departure fr-from hrs-hours m-mile mdnt-midnight rdbt-roundabout rs-restricted service wk-week wknd-weekend ⊗ No credit cards ⊗ no dogs   See page 7 for details of the AA Camping Card Scheme

SNAINTON *continued*

motorhome service point but super pitches for motorhomes are available. 5 acre site. 68 touring pitches. 42 hardstandings. 42 seasonal pitches. Caravan pitches. Motorhome pitches. Tent pitches. 16 statics.

AA Pubs & Restaurants nearby: Coachman Inn, Snainton 01723 859231

New Inn, Thornton le Dale 01751 474226

Cayley Arms, Brompton-by-Sawdon 01723 859372

Leisure: ⚠ ⊕ ⚽

Facilities: ⛟ ♁ ⊙ ℙ ✳ ⚄ ⊙ 🖺 ⊞ 🗛 WIFI 🖥 ♻ ❶

Services: 🔌 🗑 🔋 🚰 T

Within 3 miles: ↓ ✎ ◎ 🖺 🗑 ∪

Notes: No noise after 23.00hrs. Dogs must be kept on leads. Baby changing unit.

STAINFORTH   Map 18 SD86

Places to visit

Brodsworth Hall & Gardens, DONCASTER 01302 722598 www.english-heritage.org.uk

Doncaster Museum & Art Gallery, DONCASTER 01302 734293 www.doncaster.gov.uk/museums

Great for kids: The Yorkshire Waterways Museum, GOOLE 01405 768730 www.waterwaysmuseum.org.uk

►►►► 78% Knight Stainforth Hall Caravan & Campsite *(SD816672)*

BD24 0DP
☎ 01729 822200
e-mail: info@knightstainforth.co.uk
dir: *From W, on A65 take B6480 for Settle, left before swimming pool signed Little Stainforth. From E, through Settle on B6480, over bridge to swimming pool, turn right*

* 🚐 £16-£22 🚙 £16-£22 ▲ £16-£22

Open Mar-Oct

Last arrival 22.00hrs Last departure noon

Located near Settle and the River Ribble in the Yorkshire Dales National Park, this well-maintained family site is sheltered by mature woodland. It is an ideal base for walking or touring in the beautiful surrounding areas. The toilet block is appointed to a very high standard. 6 acre site. 100 touring pitches. 30 hardstandings.

Caravan pitches. Motorhome pitches. Tent pitches. 60 statics.

AA Pubs & Restaurants nearby: Black Horse Hotel, Giggleswick 01729 822506

Game Cock Inn, Austwick 015242 51226

The Traddock, Austwick 015242 51224

Leisure: ⚠ ⊕ ♜ ⚽

Facilities: ♁ ⊙ ℙ ✳ ⚄ ⊙ 🖺 🗛 ⊞ WIFI 🖥 ♻ ❶

Services: 🔌 🗑 🔋 🚰 T 🖕 ⚊

Within 3 miles: ↓ ✎ 🖺 🗑 ∪

Notes: No groups of unaccompanied minors. Dogs must be kept on leads. Fishing.

STILLINGFLEET   Map 16 SE54

Places to visit

Merchant Adventurers' Hall, YORK 01904 654818 www.theyorkcompany.co.uk

Mansion House, YORK 01904 613161 www.mansionhouseyork.co.uk

Great for kids: National Railway Museum, YORK 01904 621261 www.nrm.org.uk

►►► 72% Home Farm Caravan & Camping *(SE595427)*

Moreby YO19 6HN
☎ 01904 728263
e-mail: home_farm@hotmail.co.uk
dir: *6m from York on B1222, 1.5m N of Stillingfleet*

🚐 🚙 ▲

Open Feb-Dec

Last arrival 22.00hrs

A traditional meadowland site on a working farm bordered by parkland on one side and the River Ouse on another. Facilities are in converted farm buildings, and the family owners extend a friendly welcome to tourers. An excellent site for relaxing and unwinding, yet only a short distance from the attractions of York. There are four log cabins for holiday hire. 5 acre site. 25 touring pitches. Caravan pitches. Motorhome pitches. Tent pitches.

Facilities: ♁ ⊙ ℙ ✳ ⊙ 🗛 ♻ ❶

Services: 🔌 🔋 🚰 T 🖕

Within 3 miles: ✎ ∪

Notes: ⊛ Dogs must be kept on leads. Family washroom.

SUTTON-ON-THE-FOREST   Map 19 SE56

Places to visit

Sutton Park, SUTTON-ON-THE-FOREST 01347 810249 www.statelyhome.co.uk

Treasurer's House, YORK 01904 624247 www.nationaltrust.org.uk

Great for kids: Jorvik Viking Centre, YORK 01904 615505 www.jorvik-viking-centre.com

PREMIER PARK

►►►►► 80% Goosewood Caravan Park *(SE595636)*

YO61 1ET
☎ 01347 810829
e-mail: enquiries@goosewood.co.uk
dir: *From A1237 take B1363. After 5m turn right. Right after 0.5m, site on right*

* 🚐 £15-£21 🚙 £15-£21

Open Mar-2 Jan (rs Low season shop, bar & pool reduced hours)

Last arrival dusk Last departure noon

A relaxing and immaculately maintained park with its own lake and seasonal fishing, set in attractive woodland just six miles north of York. Mature shrubs and stunning seasonal floral displays at the entrance create an excellent first impression and the well located toilet facilities are kept spotlessly clean. The generous patio pitches are randomly spaced throughout the site, providing optimum privacy, and in addition to an excellent outdoor children's play area, a new indoor swimming pool, club house, games room and bar/bistro will open for the 2013 season. 20 acre site. 100 touring pitches. 75 hardstandings. 50 seasonal pitches. Caravan pitches. Motorhome pitches. 35 statics.

AA Pubs & Restaurants nearby: Blackwell Ox Inn, Sutton-on-the-Forest 01347 810328

Rose & Crown, Sutton-on-the-Forest 01347 811333

Leisure: 🏊 ⚠ ♜

Facilities: ♁ ⊙ ℙ ✳ ⚄ ⊙ 🖺 🗛 🗛 WIFI ♻ ❶

Services: 🔌 🗑 ⚒ 🔋 T 🖕 ⚊

Within 3 miles: ↓ 🏇 ✎ 🖺 🗑

Notes: Dogs by arrangement only, no noise after mdnt. Dogs must be kept on leads.

see advert on page 345

LEISURE: 🏊 Indoor swimming pool 🏊 Outdoor swimming pool ⚠ Children's playground 🪁 Kid's club ⚼ Tennis court ♜ Games room 🖵 Separate TV room ↓ 9/18 hole golf course ⚓ Boats for hire 🎬 Cinema 🎵 Entertainment ✎ Fishing ◎ Mini golf 🏄 Watersports 🏋 Gym 🏇 Sports field Spa ∪ Stables
FACILITIES: ⛟ Bath 🚿 Shower ⊙ Electric shaver 🖈 Hairdryer ✳ Ice Pack Facility ⚄ Disabled facilities 🕿 Public telephone 🖺 Shop on site or within 200yds 🏪 Mobile shop (calls at least 5 days a week) 🍴 BBQ area 🗛 Picnic area WIFI Wi-fi 🖥 Internet access ♻ Recycling ❶ Tourist info 🗛 Dog exercise area

THIRSK — Map 19 SE48

Places to visit

Monk Park Farm Visitor Centre, THIRSK 01845 597730 www.monkparkfarm.co.uk

Norton Conyers, RIPON 01765 640333 www.weddingsatnortonconyers.co.uk

Great for kids: Falconry UK - Birds of Prey Centre, THIRSK 01845 587522 www.falconrycentre.co.uk

AA CAMPING CARD SITE

▶▶▶▶ 81% Hillside Caravan Park *(SE447889)*

Canvas Farm, Moor Rd, Knayton YO7 4BR
☎ **01845 537349 & 07711 643652**
e-mail: info@hillsidecaravanpark.co.uk
dir: *From Thirsk take A19 N. Left at Knayton sign. In 0.25m right (crossing bridge over A19), through village. Site on left in approx 1.5m*

* ⚏ £18-£30 ⚏ £18-£30

Open 4 Feb-4 Jan

Last arrival 21.00hrs Last departure noon

A high quality, spacious park with first-class facilities, set in open countryside. It is an excellent base for walkers and for those wishing to explore the Thirsk area. Please note that the park does not accept tents. 5 acre site. 35 touring pitches. 35 hardstandings. Caravan pitches. Motorhome pitches.

AA Pubs & Restaurants nearby: Black Swan at Oldstead 01347 868387

Leisure: 🅰 ✪
Facilities: 🅝 ☉ 🅟 ♿ 🏕 🛒 🚾 ♻ ⓘ
Services: 🔌 🔆 🛒 🔋
Within 3 miles: ⚓ 🔆 ♒
Notes: 🐕 Dogs must be kept on leads.

▶▶▶ 76% Thirkleby Hall Caravan Park *(SE472794)*

Thirkleby YO7 3AR
☎ **01845 501360 & 07799 641815**
e-mail: greenwood.parks@virgin.net
web: www.greenwoodparks.com
dir: *3m S of Thirsk on A19. Turn E through arched gatehouse into site*

⚏ ⚏ ⚑

Open Mar-Oct

Last arrival 20.00hrs Last departure 14.30hrs

A long-established site in the grounds of the old hall, with statics in wooded areas around a fishing lake and tourers based on slightly sloping grassy pitches. There is a quality amenities block and laundry. This well-screened park has superb views of the Hambledon Hills. 53 acre site. 50 touring pitches. 3 hardstandings. 20 seasonal pitches. Caravan pitches. Motorhome pitches. Tent pitches. 185 statics.

AA Pubs & Restaurants nearby: Black Swan at Oldstead 01347 868387

Leisure: 🅰 ✪
Facilities: 🅝 ☉ 🅟 ✳ ♿ 🏕 🛒 ♻
Services: 🔌 🔆 🛒 🔋 🔋
Within 3 miles: ⚓ 🅷 ♒ 🔆 🔆
Notes: 🐕 No noise after 23.00hrs. Dogs must be kept on leads. 12-acre woods.

TOLLERTON — Map 19 SE56

Places to visit

The York Brewery Co Ltd, YORK 01904 621162 www.yorkbrew.co.uk

Yorkshire Museum, YORK 01904 551800 www.yorkshiremuseum.org.uk

Great for kids: Jorvik Viking Centre, YORK 01904 615505 www.jorvik-viking-centre.com

▶▶▶▶ 76% Tollerton Holiday Park *(SE513643)*

Station Rd YO61 1RD
☎ **01347 838313**
e-mail: greenwood.parks@virgin.net
dir: *From York take A19 towards Thirsk. At Cross Lanes left towards Tollerton. 1m to Chinese restaurant just before rail bridge. Site entrance through restaurant car park*

⚏ ⚏ ⚑

Open Mar-Oct

Last arrival 20.00hrs Last departure 15.00hrs

Set in open countryside within a few minutes' walk of Tollerton and just a short drive from the Park & Ride for York, this is a small park. There's an amenities block of real quality, which includes a family bathroom and laundry. There is little disturbance from the East Coast mainline which passes near to the park. 5 acre site. 50 touring pitches. 6 hardstandings. 18 seasonal pitches. Caravan pitches. Motorhome pitches. Tent pitches. 75 statics.

AA Pubs & Restaurants nearby: Blackwell Ox Inn, Sutton-on-the-Forest 01347 810328

Rose & Crown, Sutton-on-the-Forest 01347 811333

Leisure: 🅰
Facilities: 🅝 ☉ 🅟 ✳ ♿ 🕭 🏕 🛒 ♻ ⓘ
Services: 🔌 🔆 🍴 🔋 🔋
Within 3 miles: ⚓ ♒ 🔆 🔆
Notes: 🐕 No groups. Dogs must be kept on leads. Small fishing lake, large recreation field.

TOWTHORPE
Map 19 SE65

Places to visit

Malton Museum, MALTON 01653 695136
www.maltonmuseum.co.uk

Wolds Way Lavender, MALTON 01944 758641
www.woldswaylavender.co.uk

Great for kids: Eden Camp Modern History
Theme Museum, MALTON 01653 697777
www.edencamp.co.uk

AA CAMPING CARD SITE

▶▶▶▶ 77% York Touring Caravan
Site *(SE648584)*

Greystones Farm, Towthorpe Moor Ln YO32 9ST
☎ 01904 499275
e-mail: info@yorkcaravansite.co.uk
web: www.yorkcaravansite.co.uk
dir: *From A64 follow Strensall & Haxby signs, site
1.5m on left*

* ⊞ £17-£22 ⊞ £17-£22 ▲ £16-£22

Open 8 Feb-3 Jan

Last arrival 21.00hrs Last departure noon

This purpose-built golf complex and caravan park
is situated just over five miles from York. There is
a 9-hole golf course, crazy golf, driving range and
golf shop with a coffee bar/café. The generous
sized, level pitches are set within well-manicured
grassland with a backdrop of trees and shrubs. 6
acre site. 44 touring pitches. 12 hardstandings.
Caravan pitches. Motorhome pitches. Tent pitches.

AA Pubs & Restaurants nearby: Blackwell Ox Inn,
Sutton-on-the-Forest 01347 810328

Rose & Crown, Sutton-on-the-Forest
01347 811333

Leisure: ⊗
Facilities: ↖⊙🄵✳🄻🄰🄷🅆📶♻🄸
Services: 🄴🄶🄰🅄🄾↻
Within 3 miles: ↓🄿◎🄵🄵

Notes: No noise after 23.00hrs, no commercial
vehicles. Dogs must be kept on leads.

WEST KNAPTON
Map 19 SE87

Places to visit

Pickering Castle, PICKERING 01751 474989
www.english-heritage.org.uk

North Yorkshire Moors Railway, PICKERING
01751 472508 www.nymr.co.uk

Great for kids: Eden Camp Modern History
Theme Museum, MALTON 01653 697777
www.edencamp.co.uk

▶▶▶▶ 80% Wolds Way Caravan and
Camping *(SE896743)*

West Farm YO17 8JE
☎ 01944 728463 & 728180
dir: *Signed between Rillington & West Heslerton
on A64 (Malton to Scarborough road). Site 1.5m*

⊞ ⊞ ▲

Open Mar-Oct

Last arrival 22.30hrs Last departure 19.00hrs

A park on a working farm in a peaceful, high
position on the Yorkshire Wolds, with magnificent
views over the Vale of Pickering. This is an
excellent walking area, with the Wolds Way
passing the entrance to the park. A pleasant one
and a half mile path leads to a lavender farm,
with its first-class coffee shop. 7.5 acre site. 70
touring pitches. 5 hardstandings. Caravan
pitches. Motorhome pitches. Tent pitches.

AA Pubs & Restaurants nearby: Coachman Inn,
Snainton 01723 859231

New Inn, Thornton le Dale 01751 474226

Cayley Arms, Brompton-by-Sawdon 01723 859372

Leisure: ⚠
Facilities: ↖↖⊙✳🄻🄰🄷🄷📶♻🄸
Services: 🄴🄶📱🅃🖴
Within 3 miles: 🄿🄵

Notes: Free use of microwave, toaster & TV.
Drinks machine, fridge & freezer.

WHITBY
Map 19 NZ81

See also Robin Hood's Bay

Places to visit

Whitby Abbey, WHITBY 01947 603568
www.english-heritage.org.uk

Scarborough Castle, SCARBOROUGH
01723 372451 www.english-heritage.org.uk

Great for kids: Sea Life & Marine Sanctuary,
SCARBOROUGH 01723 373414 www.sealife.co.uk

▶▶▶▶ 81% Ladycross
Plantation Caravan Park
(NZ821080)

Egton YO21 1UA
☎ 01947 895502
e-mail: enquiries@ladycrossplantation.co.uk
dir: *From A171 (Whitby-Teesside road) onto
unclassified road (site signed)*

⊞ £19-£25 ⊞ £19-£25 ▲ £19-£25

Open Mar-Nov

Last arrival 21.00hrs Last departure noon

A unique forest setting creates an away-from-it-
all feeling at this peaceful touring park set in 30
acres of woodland and under enthusiastic
ownership. Pitches are sited in small groups in
clearings around two smartly appointed amenity
blocks, which offer excellent facilities - under floor
heating, no-touch infra-red showers, cubicles,
kitchen prep areas and laundry facilities. The site
is well placed for visiting Whitby and exploring the
North York moors. Children will enjoy exploring the
woodland and new nature walk. Oak Lodges are
available for hire or sale in 2013. 30 acre site. 130
touring pitches. 33 hardstandings. 60 seasonal
pitches. Caravan pitches. Motorhome pitches. Tent
pitches. 2 wooden pods.

AA Pubs & Restaurants nearby: Wheatsheaf Inn, Egton 01947 895271

Horseshoe Hotel, Egton Bridge 01947 895245

Magpie Café, Whitby 01947 602058

Facilities: 🏕⊙🅿✳🚻🛁🕐🖵🅱📶♻🛈

Services: 🔌🖸🔋🧺🚽🛒🔧

Within 3 miles: ⌦🚴🌳🛒◎🍴🛒

Notes: Lodges open all year. Dogs must be kept on leads.

WYKEHAM   Map 17 SE98

Places to visit

Scarborough Castle, SCARBOROUGH 01723 372451 www.english-heritage.org.uk

Pickering Castle, PICKERING 01751 474989 www.english-heritage.org.uk

Great for kids: Sea Life & Marine Sanctuary, SCARBOROUGH 01723 373414 www.sealife.co.uk

PREMIER PARK

►►►►► 83% St Helens Caravan Park (SE967836)

YO13 9QD
☎ 01723 862771
e-mail: caravans@wykeham.co.uk
dir: On A170 in village, 150yds on left beyond Downe Arms Hotel towards Scarborough

* 🚐 £15.90-£24 🚐 £15.90-£24 ▲ £11-£21

Open 15 Feb-15 Jan (rs Nov-Jan shop/laundry closed)

Last arrival 22.00hrs Last departure 17.00hrs

Set on the edge of the North York Moors National Park this delightfully landscaped park is immaculately maintained and thoughtfully laid out with top quality facilities and a high level of customer care. The site is divided into terraces with tree-screening creating smaller areas, including an adults' zone, and the stunning floral displays around the park are impressive. There are six camping pods for hire. A cycle route leads through the surrounding Wykeham Estate, and there is a short pathway to the adjoining Downe Arms country pub. 25 acre site. 250 touring pitches. 40 hardstandings. Caravan pitches. Motorhome pitches. Tent pitches. 6 wooden pods.

AA Pubs & Restaurants nearby: Coachman Inn, Snainton 01723 859231

New Inn, Thornton le Dale 01751 474226

Cayley Arms, Brompton-by-Sawdon 01723 859372

Leisure: 🄰

Facilities: 🛏🏕⊙🅿✳🚻🛁🕐🖵🚻🛒📶♻🛈

Services: 🔌🖸🔋🧺🚽🍴🛒🔧🛒

Within 3 miles: ⌦🚴🌳◎🛒🛒🛒◎

Notes: No noise after 22.00hrs. Dogs must be kept on leads. Caravan storage, adult-only super pitches with water & drainage.

YORKSHIRE, SOUTH

WORSBROUGH   Map 16 SE30

Places to visit

Monk Bretton Priory, BARNSLEY 0870 333 1181 www.english-heritage.org.uk

Millennium Gallery, SHEFFIELD 0114 278 2600 www.museums-sheffield.org.uk

Great for kids: Magna Science Adventure Centre, ROTHERHAM 01709 720002 www.visitmagna.co.uk

►► 74% Greensprings Touring Park (SE330020)

Rockley Abbey Farm, Rockley Ln S75 3DS
☎ 01226 288298
dir: M1 junct 36, A61 to Barnsley. Left after 0.25m signed Pilley. Site 1m at bottom of hill

* 🚐 fr £15 🚐 fr £15 ▲ fr £10

Open Apr-30 Oct

Last arrival 21.00hrs Last departure noon

A secluded and attractive farm site set amidst woods and farmland, with access to the river and several good local walks. There are two touring areas, one gently sloping. Although not far from the M1, there is almost no traffic noise, and this site is convenient for exploring the area's industrial heritage, as well as the Peak District. 4 acre site. 65 touring pitches. 5 hardstandings. 22 seasonal pitches. Caravan pitches. Motorhome pitches. Tent pitches.

Leisure: 🅾 **Facilities:** 🏕⊙✳🚻🛈

Services: 🔌🔋

Within 3 miles: ⌦🅗🌳◎🛒🛒◎

Notes: 🚫 Dogs must be kept on leads.

YORKSHIRE, WEST

BARDSEY   Map 16 SE34

Places to visit

Bramham Park, BRAMHAM 01937 846000 www.bramhampark.co.uk

Thackray Museum, LEEDS 0113 244 4343 www.thackraymuseum.org

Great for kids: Leeds Industrial Museum at Armley Mills, LEEDS 0113 263 7861 www.leeds.gov.uk/armleymills

►►► 83% Glenfield Caravan Park (SE351421)

120 Blackmoor Ln LS17 9DZ
☎ 01937 574657
e-mail: glenfieldcp@aol.com
web: www.ukparks.co.uk/glenfield/
dir: From A58 at Bardsey into Church Ln, past church, up hill. 0.5m, site on right

* 🚐 fr £15 🚐 fr £15 ▲ £10-£20

Open all year

Last arrival 21.00hrs Last departure noon

A quiet family-owned rural site in a well-screened, tree-lined meadow. The site has an excellent toilet block complete with family room. A convenient touring base for Leeds and the surrounding area. Discounted golf and food are both available at the local golf club. 4 acre site. 30 touring pitches. 30 hardstandings. Caravan pitches. Motorhome pitches. Tent pitches. 1 static.

AA Pubs & Restaurants nearby: Windmill Inn, Linton 01937 582209

Facilities: 🏕⊙🅿✳🚻🕐🖵

Services: 🔌🖸🛒🔧

Within 3 miles: ⌦🅗🌳◎🛒◎

Notes: 🚫 Children must be supervised. Dogs must be kept on leads.

LEEDS Map 19 SE23

Places to visit

Leeds Art Gallery, LEEDS 0113 247 8256
www.leeds.gov.uk/artgallery

Temple Newsam Estate, LEEDS 0113 264 7321
(House) www.leeds.gov.uk/templenewsam

AA CAMPING CARD SITE

▶▶▶ 85% Moor Lodge Park (SE352423)

Blackmoor Ln, Bardsey LS17 9DZ
☎ 01937 572424
e-mail: rodatmlcp@aol.com
dir: From A1(M) take A659 (S of Wetherby) signed
Otley. Left onto A58 towards Leeds for 5m. Right
after New Inn pub (Ling Lane), right at x-rds, 1m.
Site on right

🚐 £16.50 🚍 £16.50 ⛺ £16.50

Open all year

Last arrival 20.00hrs Last departure noon

A warm welcome is assured at this well-kept site
set in a peaceful and beautiful setting, close to
Harewood House and only 25 minutes' drive from
York and the Dales; the centre of Leeds is just 15
minutes away. The touring area is for adults only.
7 acre site. 12 touring pitches. Caravan pitches.
Motorhome pitches. Tent pitches. 60 statics.

AA Pubs & Restaurants nearby: Windmill Inn,
Linton 01937 582209

Facilities: 🅵 ⊙ 🅿 ✳ ⓢ 🎋 wifi ♻ ❶
Services: 🔋 🖸 🏧 🖉 🛒
Within 3 miles: ⚓ 🎣 ◎ 🛍 ⛵ ∪

Notes: Adults only. Dogs must be kept on leads.

▶▶▶ 78% St Helena's Caravan Park
(SE240421)

Otley Old Rd, Horsforth LS18 5HZ
☎ 0113 284 1142
dir: From A658 follow signs for Leeds/Bradford
Airport. Then follow site signs

🚐 🚍 ⛺

Open Apr-Oct

Last arrival 19.30hrs Last departure 14.00hrs

A well-maintained parkland setting surrounded by
woodland yet within easy reach of Leeds with its
excellent shopping and cultural opportunities,
Ilkley, and the attractive Wharfedale town of Otley.
Some visitors may just want to relax in this
adults-only park's spacious and pleasant
surroundings. 25 acre site. 60 touring pitches. 31
hardstandings. Caravan pitches. Motorhome
pitches. Tent pitches. 40 statics.

Facilities: 🎋 🅵 ⊙ 🅿 ✳ ⓢ 🎋 🐎
Services: 🔋 🖸 🆃
Within 3 miles: ⚓ 🎣 🛍 🖸 **Notes:** Adults only.

CHANNEL ISLANDS

GUERNSEY

CASTEL Map 24

Places to visit

Sausmarez Manor, ST MARTIN 01481 235571
www.sausmarezmanor.co.uk

Fort Grey Shipwreck Museum, ROCQUAINE BAY
01481 265036 www.museum.gov.gg

▶▶▶▶ 85% Fauxquets Valley
Campsite

GY5 7QL
☎ 01481 255460 & 07781 413333
e-mail: info@fauxquets.co.uk
dir: From pier, take 2nd exit off rdbt. At top of hill
left into Queens Rd. 2m. Right into Candie Rd. Site
opposite sign for German Occupation Museum

🚍 ⛺

Open 3 May-3 Sep

A beautiful, quiet farm site in a hidden valley
close to the sea. The friendly and helpful owners,
who understand campers' needs, offer good
quality facilities and amenities, including
spacious pitches, an outdoor swimming pool, bar/
restaurant (limited opening times), a nature trail
and sports areas. Fully equipped tents and two

lodges are available for hire. Motorhomes up to
6.9 metres are allowed on Guernsey - contact the
site for details and a permit. 3 acre site. 120
touring pitches. Motorhome pitches. Tent pitches.

AA Pubs & Restaurants nearby: Fleur du Jardin,
Castel 01481 257996

Cobo Bay Hotel, Castel 01481 257102

Leisure: 🏊 🎠 ♟ 🎱 🖵
Facilities: 🅵 ⊙ 🅿 ✳ ⓢ ⓢ 🎋 🐎 wifi ♻ ❶
Services: 🔋 🖸 🏧 🖉 🆃 🍴 🛒 🛒
Within 3 miles: ⚓ 🏌 ⌛ 🎣 ◎ ⛵ 🛍 🖸 ∪

Notes: Dogs must be kept on leads. Birdwatching.

ST SAMPSON Map 24

Places to visit

Sausmarez Manor, ST MARTIN 01481 235571
www.sausmarezmanor.co.uk

Castle Cornet, ST PETER PORT 01481 721657
www.museums.gov.gg

▶▶▶ 85% Le Vaugrat Camp Site

Route de Vaugrat GY2 4TA
☎ 01481 257468
e-mail: enquiries@vaugratcampsite.com
web: www.vaugratcampsite.com
dir: From main coast road on NW of island, site
signed at Port Grat Bay into Route de Vaugrat,
near Peninsula Hotel

* 🚍 fr £21 ⛺ fr £21

Open May-mid Sep

Overlooking the sea and set within the grounds of
a lovely 17th-century house, this level grassy park
is backed by woodland, and is close to the lovely
sandy beaches of Port Grat and Grand Havre. It is
run by a welcoming family who pride themselves
on creating magnificent floral displays. The
facilities here are excellent. Motorhomes up to 6.9
metres are allowed on Guernsey - contact the site
for details and permit. A 'round the island' bus

LEISURE: 🏊 Indoor swimming pool 🏊 Outdoor swimming pool 🎠 Children's playground 🎯 Kid's club ♟ Tennis court 🎱 Games room 🖵 Separate TV room
⚓ 9/18 hole golf course ⛵ Boats for hire 🎬 Cinema 🎵 Entertainment 🎣 Fishing ◎ Mini golf 🏄 Watersports 🏋 Gym 🛍 Sports field **Spa** ∪ Stables
FACILITIES: 🎋 Bath 🅵 Shower ⊙ Electric shaver 🅿 Hairdryer ✳ Ice Pack Facility ⓢ Disabled facilities ⓢ Public telephone 🛍 Shop on site or within 200yds
🖸 Mobile shop (calls at least 5 days a week) 🍴 BBQ area 🎋 Picnic area wifi Wi-fi 🖥 Internet access ♻ Recycling ❶ Tourist info 🐎 Dog exercise area

stops very close to the site. 6 acre site. 150 touring pitches. Motorhome pitches. Tent pitches.

AA Pubs & Restaurants nearby: The Admiral de Saumarez, St Peter Port 01481 721431

The Absolute End, St Peter Port 01481 723822

Mora Restaurant & Grill, St Peter Port 01481 715053

Leisure: 🖵

Facilities: 🏲 ☉ 🎢 ✳ ⚒ ☉ 🖥 🎠 ♻ ❶

Services: 🔌 🗑 🔒 ⊘ 🛒

Within 3 miles: ⅃🞢 🝓 ◎ ≥ 🛢 🗑 ㄣ

Notes: No animals.

JERSEY

ST MARTIN　　　　　　Map 24

Places to visit

Mont Orgueil Castle, GOREY 01534 853292 www.jerseyheritage.org

Maritime Museum & Occupation Tapestry Gallery, ST HELIER 01534 811043 www.jerseyheritage.org

Great for kids: Elizabeth Castle, ST HELIER 01534 723971 www.jerseyheritage.org

PREMIER PARK

▶▶▶▶▶ 84% *Beuvelande Camp Site*

Beuvelande JE3 6EZ
☎ 01534 853575
e-mail: info@campingjersey.com
web: www.campingjersey.com
dir: *Take A6 from St Helier to St Martin & follow signs to site before St Martins Church*

🚐 🚏 Å

Open Apr-Sep (rs Apr-May & Sep pool & restaurant closed, shop hours limited)

A well-established site with excellent toilet facilities, accessed via narrow lanes in peaceful countryside close to St Martin. An attractive bar/restaurant is the focal point of the park, especially in the evenings, and there is a small swimming pool and playground. Motorhomes and towed caravans will be met at the ferry and escorted to the site if requested when booking. There are fully-equipped tents and two yurts available for hire. 6

acre site. 150 touring pitches. Caravan pitches. Motorhome pitches. Tent pitches. 75 statics.

AA Pubs & Restaurants nearby: Royal Hotel, St Martin 01534 856289

Leisure: ⚓ 🎢 🐦 🖵

Facilities: 🏲 ☉ 🎢 ✳ ⚒ ☉ 🖥 🎠

Services: 🔌 🗑 🍴 🔒 ⊘ T 🔋 🛒 ㄣ

Within 3 miles: ⅃ 🞢 🝓 ≥ 🛢 🗑 ㄣ

▶▶▶▶ 88% *Rozel Camping Park*

Summerville Farm JE3 6AX
☎ 01534 855200
e-mail: rozelcampingpark@jerseymail.co.uk
web: www.rozelcamping.co.uk
dir: *Take A6 from St Helier through Five Oaks to St Martins Church, turn right onto A38 towards Rozel, site on right*

🚐 🚏 Å

Open May-mid Sep

Last departure noon

Customers can be sure of a warm welcome at this delightful family run park. Set in the north east of the island, it offers large spacious pitches, many with electric, for tents, caravans and motorhomes. The lovely Rozel Bay is just a short distance away and spectacular views of the French coast can be seen from one of the four fields on the park. The site also offers excellent facilities including a swimming pool. Motorhomes and caravans will be met at the ferry and escorted to the park by arrangement when booking. Fully equipped, ready-erected tents available for hire. 4 acre site. 100 touring pitches. Caravan pitches. Motorhome pitches. Tent pitches. 20 statics.

AA Pubs & Restaurants nearby: Royal Hotel, St Martin 01534 856289

Leisure: ⚓ 🎢 🐦 🖵

Facilities: 🏲 ☉ 🎢 ✳ ⚒ ☉ 🖥

Services: 🔌 🗑 🔒 ⊘ T 🛒 ㄣ ㄣ

Within 3 miles: ⅃ 🞢 🝓 ≥ 🛢 🗑 ㄣ

Notes: Mini golf.

ISLE OF MAN

KIRK MICHAEL　　　　Map 24 SC39

Places to visit

Peel Castle, PEEL 01624 648000 www.storyofmann.com

House of Manannan, PEEL 01624 648000 www.storyofmann.com

Great for kids: Curraghs Wild Life Park, BALLAUGH 01624 897323 www.gov.im/wildlife

▶▶▶ 72% *Glen Wyllin Campsite*

(SC302901)

IM6 1AL
☎ 01624 878231 & 878836
e-mail: michaelcommissioners@manx.net
dir: *From Douglas take A1 to Ballacraine, right at lights onto A3 to Kirk Michael. Left onto A4 signed Peel. Site 100yds on right*

🚏 Å

Open mid Apr-mid Sep

Last departure noon

Set in a beautiful wooded glen with bridges over a pretty stream dividing the camping areas. A gently-sloping tarmac road gives direct access to a good beach. Hire tents are available. 9 acre site. 90 touring pitches. Motorhome pitches. Tent pitches. 18 statics.

AA Pubs & Restaurants nearby: The Creek Inn, Peel 01624 842216

Leisure: 🎢 🖵

Facilities: 🏲 ☉ 🎢 ✳ ⚒ ☉ 🖥 🎠

Services: 🔌 🗑 🔒 ⊘ 🍴 🛒 🛒

Within 3 miles: 🝓 🛢 🗑 ㄣ

Notes: No excess noise after midnight, dogs must be kept on leads and under control.

Scotland

West Highland Way & the Hills of Crianlarich

Scotland

It is virtually impossible to distil the spirit and essence of Scotland in a few short sentences. It is a country with a particular kind of beauty and something very special to offer. Around half the size of England but with barely one fifth of its population, the statistics alone are enough to make you want to rush there and savour its solitude and sense of space.

The Borders, maybe the most obvious place to begin a tour of Scotland, was for so long one of Britain's most bitterly contested frontiers. The border has survived the years of lawlessness, battle and bloodshed, though few crossing it today would probably give its long and turbulent history a second thought. Making up 1,800 square miles of dense forest, rolling hills and broad sweeps of open heather, this region includes some of the most spectacular scenery anywhere in the country. Next door is Dumfries & Galloway, where just across the English/Scottish border is Gretna Green, famous for the 'anvil marriages' of eloping couples.

Travelling north and miles of open moorland and swathes of forest stretch to the Ayrshire coast where there are views towards the islands of Bute and Arran.

The country's two great cities, Glasgow and Edinburgh, include innumerable historic sites, popular landmarks and innovative visitor attractions. To the north lies a landscape of tranquil lochs, fishing rivers, wooded glens and the cities of Perth and Dundee. There's also the superb scenery of the Trossachs, ▶

• Ben Macdui from Glen Lui

Highlands and Islands

The beauty of the Western Highlands and the islands has to be seen to be believed. It is, without question, one of Europe's wildest and most spectacular regions, evoking a truly breathtaking sense of adventure. There are a great many islands, as a glance at the map will reveal – Skye, Mull, Iona, Coll, Jura and Islay to name but a few; all have their own individual character and identity. The two most northerly island groups are Orkney and the Shetlands, which, incredibly, are closer to the Arctic Circle than London.

Walking and Cycling

There are numerous excellent walks in Scotland. Among the best is the 95-mile (152km) West Highland Way, Scotland's first long-distance path. The trail runs from Glasgow to Fort William. The Southern Upland Way and St Cuthbert's Way explore the best of the Scottish Borders, which is also the northerly terminus for the 250-mile (402km) Pennine Way.

Scotland's majestic landscapes are perfect for exploring by bike. There are scores of popular routes and trails – among them a ride through Dumfries & Galloway to Drumlanrig Castle and the museum where blacksmith, Kirkpatrick MacMillan, invented the bicycle. Alternatively, there's the chance to get away from the city and head for the coast along disused railway lines; perhaps the route from Edinburgh to Cramond, with good views of the Firth of Forth.

Festivals and Events

• The Viking Festival is staged at Largs on the Ayrshire coast during the August Bank Holiday week. This is where the last Viking invasion of

Loch Lomond and Stirling, which, with its wonderful castle perched on a rocky crag, is Scotland's heritage capital.

Further north

The country's prominent north-east shoulder is the setting for the mountain landscape of the Cairngorms and the Grampians, while Aberdeenshire and the Moray coast enjoy a pleasantly mild, dry climate with plenty of sunshine. Here, the River Spey, one of Scotland's great rivers and a mecca for salmon anglers, winds between lush pastures to the North Sea. Various famous distilleries can be found along its banks, some offering visitors the chance to sample a wee dram!

The remote far north is further from many parts of England than a good many European destinations. Names such as Pentland Firth, Sutherland, Caithness and Ross and Cromarty spring to mind, as does Cape Wrath, Britain's most northerly outpost. The stunning coast is known for its spectacular sea cliffs and deserted beaches – the haunt of some of the rarest mammals.

Britain took place in 1263. There are birds of prey displays, battle re-enactments, fireworks and the ritual burning of a longship.

- Also in August is the internationally famous Edinburgh Military Tattoo, which draws numerous visitors and participants from many parts of the world.
- The Highland Games, another classic fixture in the Scottish calendar, run from May onwards; the most famous being the Braemar gathering in September.

● Red deer

● West Highland Way with the Hills of Crianlarich

ABERDEENSHIRE

ABOYNE — Map 23 NO59

Places to visit

Alford Valley Railway, ALFORD 019755 64236 www.alfordvalleyrailway.org.uk

Crathes Castle Garden & Estate, CRATHES 0844 4932166 www.nts.org.uk

Great for kids: Craigievar Castle, ALFORD 0844 493 2174 www.nts.org.uk

►►► 71% Aboyne Loch Caravan Park *(NO538998)*

AB34 5BR
☎ 013398 86244 & 82589
e-mail: heatherreid24@yahoo.co.uk
dir: *On A93, 1m E of Aboyne*

🚐 🚌 ⛺

Open 31 Mar-Oct

Last arrival 20.00hrs Last departure 11.00hrs

Located on the outskirts of Aboyne on a small outcrop which is almost surrounded by Loch Aboyne, this is a mature site within scenic Royal Deeside. The facilities are well maintained, and pitches are set amongst mature trees with most having views over the loch. Boat hire and fishing are available and there is a regular bus service from the site entrance. 6 acre site. 20 touring pitches. 25 hardstandings. Caravan pitches. Motorhome pitches. Tent pitches. 120 statics.

AA Pubs & Restaurants nearby: Milton Restaurant, Crathes 01330 844566

Leisure: 🛝 ♞

Facilities: 🚿 🪒 💨 ❄ ♿ ☎ [$] 🐕 ♻ ℹ

Services: 🚐 🧺 🔒 🍃 [T] ⚓

Within 3 miles: ⛳ 🚣 🎣 ◎ 🏄 [$] 🧺 🐎

Notes: ⊘ Coarse & pike fishing, boats for hire.

ALFORD — Map 23 NJ51

Places to visit

Alford Valley Railway, ALFORD 019755 64236 www.alfordvalleyrailway.org.uk

Craigievar Castle, ALFORD 0844 493 2174 www.nts.org.uk

NEW ►►► 69% *Haughton House Holiday Park* *(NJ577168)*

Montgarrie Rd AB33 8NA
☎ 01975 562107
e-mail: enquiries@haughtonhouse.co.uk
dir: *Follow signs in Alford for Haughton Country House*

* 🚐 £17.50-£20 🚌 £17.50-£20 ⛺ £10-£12

Open Apr-Oct

Last arrival 21.30hrs Last departure noon

Located on the outskirts of Alford this site is set within a large country park with good countryside views. Now under the same ownership as Huntly Castle Caravan Park (Huntly), this park will receive the same attention to detail to ensure facilities are brought up to the highest standards. The existing facilities are clean and well maintained. The pitches are set amongst mature trees and the tenting area is within the old walled garden. There is plenty to do on site and within the country park which has various activities for children, including a narrow gauge railway that runs to the Grampian Transport Museum in nearby Alford. 18 acre site. 70 touring pitches. Caravan pitches. Motorhome pitches. Tent pitches.

FORDOUN — Map 23 NO77

Places to visit

Edzell Castle and Garden, EDZELL 01356 648631 www.historic-scotland.gov.uk

House of Dun, MONTROSE 0844 493 2144 www.nts.org.uk

►►► 74% Brownmuir Caravan Park *(NO740772)*

AB30 1SJ
☎ 01561 320786
e-mail: brownmuircaravanpark@talk21.com
web: www.brownmuircaravanpark.co.uk
dir: *From N: A90 take B966 signed Fettercairn, site 1.5m on left. From S: A90, exit 4m N of Laurencekirk signed Fordoun, site 1m on right*

* 🚐 £16-£18 🚌 £16.50-£18.50 ⛺ £9-£15

Open Apr-Oct

Last arrival 23.00hrs Last departure noon

With easy access to the A90, this peaceful site, formerly a Polish RAF base, is ideal for either a longer holiday or just an overnight stop. The Howe of Mearns is a perfect area for cyclists and walkers, and there are numerous golf courses nearby. Royal Deeside and seaside towns and villages are an easy drive away; there is an award-winning farm shop and café nearby. 7 acre site. 11 touring pitches. 7 hardstandings. 7 seasonal pitches. Caravan pitches. Motorhome pitches. Tent pitches. 49 statics.

AA Pubs & Restaurants nearby: Tolbooth Restaurant, Stonehaven 01569 762287

Carron Art Deco Restaurant, Stonehaven 01569 760460

Leisure: 🛝

Facilities: 🚿 🪒 💨 ❄ ♿ ☎ ⛱ 🐕 [Wi-fi] ♻ ℹ

Services: 🚐 🧺

Within 3 miles: ⛳ 🎣 [$]

Notes: ⊘ No noise after 23.30hrs. Dogs must be kept on leads.

HUNTLY   Map 23 NJ53

Places to visit

Leith Hall, Garden & Estate, RHYNIE
0844 493 2175 www.nts.org.uk

Glenfiddich Distillery, DUFFTOWN 01340 820373
www.glenfiddich.com

Great for kids: Archaeolink Prehistory Park,
OYNE 01464 851500 www.archaeolink.co.uk

AA CAMPING CARD SITE

PREMIER PARK

►►►►► 87% Huntly Castle
Caravan Park (NJ525405)

The Meadow AB54 4UJ
☎ 01466 794999
e-mail: enquiries@huntlycastle.co.uk
web: www.huntlycastle.co.uk
dir: From Aberdeen on A96 to Huntly. 0.75m after
rdbt (on outskirts of Huntly) right towards town
centre, left into Riverside Drive

* ➡ £17.80-£23.45 ➡ £17.80-£23.45
▲ £13.50-£17

Open Apr-Oct (rs Wknds & school hols indoor
activity centre open)

Last arrival 20.00hrs Last departure noon

A quality parkland site within striking distance of
the Speyside Malt Whisky Trail, the beautiful
Moray coast, and the Cairngorm Mountains. The
park provides exceptional toilet facilities, and
there are some fully serviced pitches. The indoor
activity centre provides a wide range of games;
the attractive town of Huntly is only a five-minute
walk away, with its ruined castle plus a wide
variety of restaurants and shops. 15 acre site. 90
touring pitches. 51 hardstandings. 10 seasonal
pitches. Caravan pitches. Motorhome pitches. Tent
pitches. 40 statics.

Leisure: ⚑
Facilities: ⚑⊙⚑☀⚿🚿📶♻❶
Services: ⚑🗑🛢🛒⚡⚙
Within 3 miles: ⚑⚑🗑🗑

Notes: Dogs must be kept on leads. Indoor
activity centre, indoor children's play area,
snooker table.

KINTORE   Map 23 NJ71

Places to visit

Pitmedden Garden, PITMEDDEN 0844 493 2177
www.nts.org.uk

Tolquhon Castle, PITMEDDEN 01651 851286
www.historic-scotland.gov.uk

Great for kids: Castle Fraser, KEMNAY
0844 493 2164 www.nts.org.uk

AA CAMPING CARD SITE

►►►► 77% Hillhead Caravan Park
(NJ777163)

AB51 0YX
☎ 01467 632809 & 0870 413 0870
e-mail: enquiries@hillheadcaravan.co.uk
dir: 1m from village & A96 (Aberdeen-Inverness
road). From A96 follow signs to site on B994, then
unclassified road

➡ ➡ ▲

Open all year

Last arrival 21.00hrs Last departure 13.00hrs

An attractive, nicely landscaped site, located on
the outskirts of Kintore in the River Dee valley with
excellent access to forest walks and within easy
reach of the many attractions in rural
Aberdeenshire. The toilet facilities are of a high
standard. There are good play facilities for smaller
children and a modern lodge-style games room,
with TV and internet access, for older teenagers.
1.5 acre site. 29 touring pitches. 14
hardstandings. Caravan pitches. Motorhome
pitches. Tent pitches.

AA Pubs & Restaurants nearby: Cock & Bull,
Balmedie 01358 743249

Old Blackfriars, Aberdeen 01224 581922

La Stella, Aberdeen 01224 211414

The Silver Darling, Aberdeen 01224 576229

Leisure: ⚑
Facilities: ⚑⊙⚑☀⚿🕐🗑🚿⚿🖥
Services: ⚑🗑⚑🛢🍽🛒
Within 3 miles: ⚑⚑🗑🗑

Notes: Caravan storage, accessories shop.

MACDUFF   Map 23 NJ76

Places to visit

Duff House, BANFF 01261 818181
www.historic-scotland.gov.uk

Banff Museum, BANFF 01771 622807
www.aberdeenshire.gov.uk/museums

►► 65% Wester Bonnyton Farm Site
(NJ741638)

Gamrie AB45 3EP
☎ 01261 832470
e-mail: westerbonnyton@fsmail.net
dir: From A98 (1m S of Macduff) take B9031
signed Rosehearty. Site 1.25m on right

* ➡ £10-£15 ➡ £10-£15 ▲ £10-£20

Open Mar-Oct

A spacious farm site, with level touring pitches,
overlooking the Moray Firth. The small,
picturesque fishing villages of Gardenstown and
Crovie and the larger town of Macduff, which has
a marine aquarium, are all within easy reach. All
the touring pitches have good views of the
coastline. Families with children are welcome. 8
acre site. 8 touring pitches. 5 hardstandings.
Caravan pitches. Motorhome pitches. Tent pitches.
60 statics.

Leisure: ⚑🎣
Facilities: ⚑⊙⚑🗑🚿⚿📶♻❶
Services: ⚑🗑🛢🛒
Within 3 miles: ⚑⚑⚑🏊🗑🗑

Notes: Dogs must be kept on leads. Children's
playbarn.

MINTLAW — Map 23 NJ94

Places to visit

Aberdeenshire Farming Museum, MINTLAW 01771 624590
www.aberdeenshire.gov.uk/museums

Deer Abbey, OLD DEER 01667 460232
www.historic-scotland.gov.uk

NEW ►►► 78% Aden Caravan and Camping Park (NJ981479)

Aden Country Park AB42 5FQ
☎ 01771 623460
e-mail: info@adencaravanandcamping.co.uk
dir: From Mintlaw take A950 signed New Pitsligo & Aden Country Park. Park on left

* ⊞ fr £22 ⊞ fr £22 ▲ £16.50-£19.25

Open Apr-Oct

Last arrival 18.00hrs Last departure 13.00hrs

Situated in the heart of Buchan in Aberdeenshire and within Aden Country Park, this is a small tranquil site offering excellent facilities. It is ideally located for visiting the many tourist attractions in this beautiful north-east coastal area, not least of which is the 230-acre country park itself. The site is only a short drive from the busy fishing towns of Fraserburgh and Peterhead, and as it is only an hour from Aberdeen's city centre, this is an ideal spot for a short stay or a longer holiday. The country park plays host to numerous events throughout the year, including pipe band championships, horse events and various ranger-run activities. This is a site for all ages. 11.1 acre site. 66 touring pitches. Caravan pitches. Motorhome pitches. Tent pitches.

NORTH WATER BRIDGE — Map 23 NO66

►►► 77% Dovecot Caravan Park (NO648663)

AB30 1QL
☎ 01674 840630
e-mail: adele@dovecotcaravanpark.co.uk
dir: Take A90, 5m S of Laurencekirk. At Edzell Woods sign turn left. Site 500yds on left

* ⊞ £15-£17 ⊞ £15-£17 ▲ £12-£20

Open Apr-Oct

Last arrival 20.00hrs Last departure noon

A level grassy site in a country area close to the A90, with mature trees screening one side and the River North Esk on the other. The immaculate toilet facilities make this a handy overnight stop in a good touring area. 6 acre site. 25 touring pitches. 8 hardstandings. 8 seasonal pitches. Caravan pitches. Motorhome pitches. Tent pitches. 44 statics.

Leisure: ⚠ 🔍
Facilities: 🖍 ⊙ ⏚ ✳ 🌡 🕙 ⏁ 🚽 ᴡɪ⊡ ♻ 🛈
Services: 🖭 🔒 🚽 ⏚

Notes: Dogs must be kept on leads.

PORTSOY — Map 23 NJ56

Places to visit

Banff Museum, BANFF 01771 622807
www.aberdeenshire.gov.uk/museums

Duff House, BANFF 01261 818181
www.historic-scotland.gov.uk

Great for kids: Macduff Marine Aquarium, MACDUFF 01261 833369
www.macduff-aquarium.org.uk

NEW ►►► 70% Portsoy Links Caravan Park (NJ591660)

Links Rd, Portsoy AB45 2RQ
☎ 01261 842695
e-mail: contact@portsoylinks.co.uk
dir: At Portsoy from A98 into Church St. 2nd right into Institute St (follow brown camping sign). At T-junct right, down slope to site

* ⊞ £15.50-£16.50 ⊞ £15.50-£16.50 ▲ £8.50-£9.50

Open 30 Mar-Oct

Last arrival 20.00hrs Last departure noon

Taken into community ownership under the auspices of the Scottish Traditional Boats Festival, this is a lovely links-type site with stunning views across the bay. There is a large, safe fenced play area for smaller children and the toilet facilities are kept clean and well maintained. Portsoy is a typical small fishing port and has various eateries and shops; it is very convenient for visiting the other small fishing villages on the North East Scotland's Coastal Trail. 0.8 acre site. 51 touring pitches. Caravan pitches. Motorhome pitches. Tent pitches.

ST CYRUS — Map 23 NO76

Places to visit

House of Dun, MONTROSE 0844 493 2144
www.nts.org.uk

Pictavia Visitor Centre, BRECHIN 01356 626241
www.pictavia.org.uk

Great for kids: Brechin Town House Museum, BRECHIN 01356 625536
www.angus.gov.uk/history/museum

►►►► 79% East Bowstrips Caravan Park (NO745654)

DD10 0DE
☎ 01674 850328
e-mail: tully@bowstrips.freeserve.co.uk
web: www.caravancampingsites.co.uk/aberdeenshire/eastbowstrips.htm
dir: From S on A92 (coast road) into St Cyrus. Pass hotel on left. 1st left then 2nd right signed

* ⊞ £14-£18 ⊞ £14-£18 ▲ £9-£10

Open Etr or Apr-Oct

Last arrival 20.00hrs Last departure noon

A quiet rural site on the edge of St Cyrus, which is a small seaside village with a large sandy beach and a National Nature Reserve. This is a well maintained site with excellent toilet facilities. The touring pitches are in two separate areas behind mature trees and hedges and some have views of the sea. 4 acre site. 32 touring pitches. 22 hardstandings. 13 seasonal pitches. Caravan pitches. Motorhome pitches. Tent pitches. 17 statics.

Facilities: 🖍 ⊙ ⏚ ✳ 🌡 🕙 🛒 🚽 🛈
Services: 🖭 🔥 🔒 ⊘
Within 3 miles: 🖉 🛍

Notes: ⊗ If camping no dogs allowed & if touring, dogs must always be kept on leads. Separate garden with boule pitch.

LEISURE: 🏊 Indoor swimming pool 🏊 Outdoor swimming pool ⚠ Children's playground 🪁 Kid's club ♨ Tennis court 🔍 Games room ▭ Separate TV room
🏌 9/18 hole golf course ⚓ Boats for hire 🎬 Cinema 🎵 Entertainment 🎣 Fishing ◉ Mini golf 🏄 Watersports 🏋 Gym ☉ Sports field **Spa** ♌ Stables
FACILITIES: 🛁 Bath 🖍 Shower ⊙ Electric shaver ⏚ Hairdryer ✳ Ice Pack Facility 🕙 Disabled facilities ☏ Public telephone 🛍 Shop on site or within 200yds
🛒 Mobile shop (calls at least 5 days a week) 🍖 BBQ area 🚽 Picnic area ᴡɪ⊡ Wi-fi 🖥 Internet access ♻ Recycling 🛈 Tourist info 🐕 Dog exercise area

STRACHAN   Map 23 NO69

Places to visit

Banchory Museum, BANCHORY 01771 622807
www.aberdeenshire.gov.uk/museums

Crathes Castle Garden & Estate, CRATHES
0844 4932166 www.nts.org.uk

Great for kids: Go Ape! Crathes Castle,
CRATHES 0845 643 9215
www.goape.co.uk/sites/crathes-castle

NEW ►►►► 78% Feughside
Caravan Park (NO636913)

AB31 6NT
☎ 01330 850669
e-mail: info@feughsidecaravanpark.co.uk
dir: From Banchory take B974 to Strachan, 3m,
then B976, 2m to Feughside Inn, follow site signs

* ⊞ fr £20 ⊞ fr £20 ▲ £16-£20

Open Apr-Oct

Last arrival 22.00hrs Last departure noon

A small, well maintained family run site, set
amongst mature trees and hedges and located
five miles from Banchory. The site is ideally suited
to those wishing for a peaceful location that is
within easy reach of scenic Royal Deeside. 5.5
acre site. 27 touring pitches. 10 hardstandings.
12 seasonal pitches. Caravan pitches. Motorhome
pitches. Tent pitches. 54 statics.

AA Pubs & Restaurants nearby: Raemoir House
Hotel, Banchory 01330 824884

Leisure: ⚙

Facilities: ⬤⊙🅿✳🔥⛲☎💧♻🛈

Services: 🔌🔲🔋🪒🔌

Within 3 miles: 🎣🚴⛵🎯🔲🛒⛳

Notes: No cars by caravans or tents. Quiet
after 22.00hrs, no open fires. Dogs must be kept
on leads and exercised off-site.

TURRIFF   Map 23 NJ75

Places to visit

Fyvie Castle, TURRIFF 0844 493 2182
www.nts.org.uk

NEW ►►► 74% Turriff Caravan Park
(NJ727492)

Station Rd AB53 4ER
☎ 01888 562205
e-mail: turriffcaravanpark@btconnect.com
dir: On A947, S of Turriff

* ⊞ £17.50-£20 ⊞ £17.50-£20 ▲ £9-£9.50

Open Apr-Oct

Last arrival 18.00hrs Last departure noon

Located on the outskirts of Turriff on the site of an
old railway station, this site is owned by the local
community. The pitches are level and the
attractive landscaping is well maintained. The
site also has a rally field. There is a large public
park close to the site which has a boating pond
and a large games park where the annual
agricultural show is held. The town is only five
minutes' walk through the park and has a good
variety of shops to suit all tastes. This is an ideal
base for touring rural Aberdeenshire and the
nearby Moray coastline with its traditional fishing
villages. 5 acre site. 70 touring pitches. Caravan
pitches. Motorhome pitches. Tent pitches.

AA Pubs & Restaurants nearby: The Redgarth,
Oldmeldrum 01651 872353

ANGUS

MONIFIETH   Map 21 NO43

Places to visit

Barry Mill, BARRY 0844 493 2140
www.nts.org.uk

HM Frigate Unicorn, DUNDEE 01382 200900
www.frigateunicorn.org

Great for kids: Discovery Point & RRS
Discovery, DUNDEE 01382 309060 www.
rrsdiscovery.com

►►►► 79% Riverview
Caravan Park (NO502322)

Marine Dr DD5 4NN
☎ 01382 535471 & 817979
e-mail: info@riverview.co.uk
web: www.riverview.co.uk
dir: From Dundee on A930 follow signs to
Monifieth, past supermarket, right signed golf
course, left under rail bridge. Site signed on left

⊞ ⊞

Open Mar-Jan

Last arrival 22.00hrs Last departure 12.30hrs

A well-landscaped seaside site with individual
hedged pitches, and direct access to the beach.
The modernised toilet block has excellent facilities
which are immaculately maintained. Amenities
include a multi-gym, sauna and steam rooms. 5.5
acre site. 49 touring pitches. 45 hardstandings.
Caravan pitches. Motorhome pitches. 46 statics.

AA Pubs & Restaurants nearby: Royal Arch Bar,
Broughty Ferry, 01382 779741

Dalhousie Restaurant at Carnoustie Golf Hotel,
Carnoustie 01241 411999

Leisure: 🎾⚙☺🎣

Facilities: ⬤⊙🅿✳⛲☎🔥✂☎💻💧♻🛈

Services: 🔌🔲🔋🅣🔌

Within 3 miles: ✈🏋🚴◎⛵🔲🛒⛳

Notes: Dogs must be kept on leads.

ARGYLL & BUTE

CARRADALE — Map 20 NR83

►►► 85% *Carradale Bay Caravan Park* (NR815385)

PA28 6QG
☎ 01583 431665
e-mail: info@carradalebay.com
dir: *A83 from Tarbert towards Campbeltown, left onto B842 (Carradale road), right onto B879. Site 0.5m*

Open Apr-Sep

Last arrival 22.00hrs Last departure noon

A beautiful, natural site on the sea's edge with superb views over Kilbrannan Sound to the Isle of Arran. Pitches are landscaped into small bays broken up by shrubs and bushes, and backed by dunes close to the long sandy beach. The toilet facilities are appointed to a very high standard. An environmentally-aware site that requires the use of green toilet chemicals - available on the site. Lodges and static caravans for holiday hire. 8 acre site. 74 touring pitches. Caravan pitches. Motorhome pitches. Tent pitches. 15 statics.

Facilities: ⟦icons⟧
Services: ⟦icons⟧
Within 3 miles: ⟦icons⟧

GLENDARUEL — Map 20 NR98

Places to visit

Benmore Botanic Garden, BENMORE
01369 706261 www.rbge.org.uk

►►► 77% *Glendaruel Caravan Park* (NR005865)

PA22 3AB
☎ 01369 820267
e-mail: mail@glendaruelcaravanpark.com
web: www.glendaruelcaravanpark.com
dir: *A83 onto A815 to Strachur, 13m to site on A886. By ferry from Gourock to Dunoon then B836, then A886 for approx 4m N. (NB this route not recommended for towing vehicles - 1:5 uphill gradient on B836)*

Open Apr-Oct

Last arrival 22.00hrs Last departure noon

Glendaruel Gardens, with an arboretum, is the peaceful setting for this 22-acre, wooded site in a valley surrounded by mountains. It is set back from the main road and screened by trees so that a peaceful stay is ensured. This very pleasant, well-established site has level grass and hardstanding pitches. A regular local bus service and a ferry at Portavadie (where there are new retail outlets and eateries) make a day trip to the Mull of Kintyre a possibility. The Cowal Way, a long distance path, and a national cycle path pass the site. Static caravans, and a camping lodge, are available for hire. 6 acre site. 27 touring pitches. 15 hardstandings. 12 seasonal pitches. Caravan pitches. Motorhome pitches. Tent pitches. 32 statics. 1 wooden pod.

AA Pubs & Restaurants nearby: Kilfinan Hotel Bar, Kilfinan 01700 821201

Leisure: ⟦icons⟧
Facilities: ⟦icons⟧
Services: ⟦icons⟧
Within 3 miles: ⟦icons⟧

Notes: Dogs must be kept on leads. Sea trout & salmon fishing, woodland walks, 24-hour emergency phone available.

OBAN — Map 20 NM82

Places to visit

Dunstaffnage Castle and Chapel, OBAN
01631 562465 www.historic-scotland.gov.uk

Bonawe Historic Iron Furnace, TAYNUILT
01866 822432 www.historic-scotland.gov.uk

►►► 75% *Oban Caravan & Camping Park* (NM831277)

Gallanachmore Farm, Gallanach Rd PA34 4QH
☎ 01631 562425
e-mail: info@obancaravanpark.com
dir: *From Oban centre follow signs for Mull Ferry. After terminal follow Gallanach signs. 2m to site*

* ⟦icon⟧ £16-£19.50 ⟦icon⟧ £16-£19.50 ▲ £14-£15

Open Etr & Apr-Oct

Last arrival 23.00hrs Last departure noon

A tourist park in an attractive location close to the sea and ferries. This family park is a popular base for walking, sea-based activities and for those who just want to enjoy the peace and tranquillity. There are self-catering holiday lodges for hire. 15 acre site. 120 touring pitches. 35 hardstandings. 10 seasonal pitches. Caravan pitches. Motorhome pitches. Tent pitches. 17 statics.

AA Pubs & Restaurants nearby: Coast, Oban 01631 569900

Leisure: ⟦icons⟧
Facilities: ⟦icons⟧
Services: ⟦icons⟧
Within 3 miles: ⟦icons⟧

Notes: No commercial vehicles, no noise after 23.00hrs. Dogs must be kept on leads. Indoor kitchen for tent campers.

TAYINLOAN — Map 20 NR64

NEW ►►► 74% *Point Sands Camping & Caravan Park* (NR707484)

Rhunahaorine PA29 6XG
☎ 01583 441263
e-mail: info@pointsands.com
dir: *From A83 S of Tarbert site signed on right (opposite school) (NB Sat Nav directions cannot be guaranteed from Lochgilphead on A83)*

⟦icon⟧ £15-£20 ⟦icon⟧ £15-£20 ▲ £15-£20

Open Apr-Oct

Last departure noon

Located on the Kintyre peninsular the site has direct access to a sandy beach overlooking the islands of Gigha, Islay, Jura and Colonsay. Ideally located for all the ferries to these islands and also for Tarbert (to Portavadie) and Claonaig (to Lochranza, Isle of Arran). While perhaps one of the quieter areas of Scotland it is by no means inaccessible as there is a regular bus service that travels round the Mull of Kintyre and stops at the ferry terminals making day trips a relatively simple affair. The ageing toilet block, while providing good clean facilities, is being replaced, so for the 2013 season temporary facilities may be in use. 10 acre site. 40 touring pitches. 15 seasonal pitches. Caravan pitches. Motorhome pitches. Tent pitches. 50 statics.

Leisure: ⟦icon⟧
Facilities: ⟦icons⟧
Services: ⟦icons⟧
Within 3 miles: ⟦icons⟧

Notes: No jet skis, fireworks or Chinese lanterns.

LEISURE: 🏊 Indoor swimming pool 🏊 Outdoor swimming pool Ⓐ Children's playground Kid's club Tennis court Games room Separate TV room 9/18 hole golf course Boats for hire Cinema Entertainment Fishing Mini golf Watersports Gym Sports field Spa Stables
FACILITIES: Bath Shower Electric shaver Hairdryer Ice Pack Facility Disabled facilities Public telephone Shop on site or within 200yds Mobile shop (calls at least 5 days a week) BBQ area Picnic area Wi-fi Internet access Recycling Tourist info Dog exercise area

DUMFRIES & GALLOWAY

ANNAN
Map 21 NY16

Places to visit

Ruthwell Cross, RUTHWELL 0131 550 7612
www.historic-scotland.gov.uk

Great for kids: Caerlaverock Castle,
CAERLAVEROCK 01387 770244
www.historic-scotland.gov.uk

▶▶ **74% Galabank Caravan &
Camping Group** (NY192676)

North St DG12 5DQ
☎ 01461 203539 & 204108
dir: Enter site via North Street

🚐 🚎 ⛺

Open Apr-early Sep

Last departure noon

A tidy, well-maintained grassy little park with
spotless facilities close to the centre of town but
with pleasant rural views, and skirted by River
Annan. 1 acre site. 30 touring pitches. Caravan
pitches. Motorhome pitches. Tent pitches.

AA Pubs & Restaurants nearby: Smiths of Gretna
Green, Gretna 01461 337007

Facilities: 📻 ⚡ 📷 🔥 📙

Services: 🔌

Within 3 miles: ⬇ 🗓 ✏ 📷

Notes: 🐕 Dogs must be kept on leads. Social club
adjacent.

BARGRENNAN
Map 20 NX37

▶▶▶ **78% Glentrool Holiday Park**

(NX350769)

DG8 6RN
☎ 01671 840280
e-mail: enquiries@glentroolholidaypark.co.uk
dir: Exit Newton Stewart on A714 towards Girvan,
right at Bargrennan towards Glentrool. Site on left
before village

🚐 🚎 ⛺

Open Mar-Oct

Last arrival 21.00hrs Last departure noon

A small park close to the village of Glentrool, and
bordered by the Galloway Forest Park. Both the
touring and static areas, with vans for hire, are
immaculately presented and the amenity block is
clean and freshly painted. The on-site shop is well
stocked. The Southern Upland Way, a long
distance coast to coast path runs through the site
and Galloway Forest Park Visitor Centre, providing
numerous walking and cycling tracks, is one mile
away. The site is within the official Dumfries &
Galloway Dark Sky Zone and provides ideal star
gazing opportunities. A regular bus stops at the
site entrance. 6 acre site. 16 touring pitches. 13
hardstandings. 3 seasonal pitches. Caravan
pitches. Motorhome pitches. Tent pitches. 26
statics.

AA Pubs & Restaurants nearby: Creebridge House
Hotel, Newton Stewart 01671 402121

Galloway Arms Hotel, Newton Stewart
01671 402653

Kirroughtree House, Minnigaff, Newton Stewart
01671 402141

Leisure: 🎿

Facilities: 📻 ☉ ⚡ ✳ ⬇ 🕐 📷 ♻ 🔧

Services: 🔌 📷 🔧 🔋 ✏ 🔋

Within 3 miles: ∪

Notes: 🐕 No cars by tents, no ball games, no
groups. Dogs must be kept on leads.

BRIGHOUSE BAY
Map 20 NX64

PREMIER PARK

▶▶▶▶▶ **79% Brighouse Bay
Holiday Park** (NX628453)

Best of
British

DG6 4TS
☎ 01557 870267
e-mail: info@gillespie-leisure.co.uk
dir: From Gatehouse-of-Fleet take A75 towards
Castle Douglas, onto B727 (signed Kirkcudbright
& Borgue). Or from Kirkcudbright take A755 onto
B727. Site signed

🚐 🚎 ⛺

Open all year (rs Nov-Mar leisure club closed 3
days each week)

Last arrival 21.00hrs Last departure 11.30hrs

This top class park has a country club feel and
enjoys a marvellous coastal setting adjacent to
the beach and has superb views. Pitches have
been imaginatively sculpted into the meadowland,
with stone walls and hedges blending in with the
site's mature trees. These features, together with
the large range of leisure activities, make this an
excellent park for families who enjoy an active
holiday. Many of the facilities are at an extra
charge. A range of self-catering units is available
for hire. 120 acre site. 190 touring pitches. 100
hardstandings. 50 seasonal pitches. Caravan
pitches. Motorhome pitches. Tent pitches. 285
statics.

AA Pubs & Restaurants nearby: Selkirk Arms
Hotel, Kirkcudbright 01557 330402

Leisure: 🏊 🎯 🎱 🎣 🎵

Facilities: 🛁 📻 ☉ ⚡ ✳ ⬇ 🕐 📷 🔥 📡 🔧

Services: 🔌 📷 🔧 🔋 ✏ 🔤 🍽 🔋 🚽 ⬇

Within 3 miles: ⬇ ✏ ☉ 📷 📙 ∪

Notes: No motorised scooters, jet skis or own
quad bikes. Dogs must be kept on leads. Mini golf,
18-hole golf, quad bikes for hire, horse riding,
fishing, outdoor bowling green, jacuzzi.

CREETOWN — Map 20 NX46

Places to visit

Cardoness Castle, CARDONESS CASTLE
01557 814427 www.historic-scotland.gov.uk

Great for kids: Creetown Gem Rock Museum,
CREETOWN 01671 820357 www.gemrock.net

AA CAMPING CARD SITE

PREMIER PARK

▶▶▶▶▶ 83% Castle Cary Holiday Park (NX475576)

DG8 7DQ
☎ 01671 820264
e-mail: enquiries@castlecarypark.f9.co.uk
web: www.castlecary-caravans.com
dir: Signed with direct access from A75, 0.5m S of village

* 🚐 £15.40-£19.20 🚙 £15.40-£19.20
▲ £15.40-£19.20

Open all year (rs Oct-Mar reception/shop, no heated outdoor pool)

Last arrival anytime Last departure noon

This attractive site in the grounds of Cassencarie House is sheltered by woodlands, and faces south towards Wigtown Bay. The park is in a secluded location with beautiful landscaping and excellent facilities. The bar/restaurant is housed in part of an old castle, and enjoys extensive views over the River Cree estuary. 12 acre site. 50 touring pitches. 50 hardstandings. Caravan pitches. Motorhome pitches. Tent pitches. 26 statics. 2 bell tents/yurts.

AA Pubs & Restaurants nearby: Creebridge House Hotel, Newton Stewart 01671 402121

Galloway Arms Hotel, Newton Stewart
01671 402653

Kirroughtree House, Minnigaff, Newton Stewart
01671 402141

Cally Palace Hotel, Gatehouse-of-Fleet
01557 814341

Leisure: 🏊 🏖 /A ⚽ 🎱 ▭
Facilities: 🚿 🌂 ☉ 🍴 ✳ ♿ ⏰ 🖃 🎍 📶 🖥 ❶
Services: 🚰 🗑 🗄 🔒 🚿 T 🍴 🍴 🎍
Within 3 miles: ↧ 🏌 ◎ 🔢 🗄

Notes: Dogs must be kept on leads. Crazy golf, coarse fishing, full size football pitch.

DALBEATTIE — Map 21 NX86

Places to visit

Threave Garden & Estate, CASTLE DOUGLAS
0844 493 2245 www.nts.org.uk

Orchardton Tower, PALNACKIE
www.historic-scotland.gov.uk

▶▶▶▶ 81% Glenearly Caravan Park

(NX838628)

DG5 4NE
☎ 01556 611393
e-mail: glenearlycaravan@btconnect.com
dir: From Dumfries take A711 towards Dalbeattie. Site entrance after Edingham Farm on right (200yds before boundary sign)

* 🚐 £15-£17 🚙 £15-£17 ▲ £15-£17

Open all year

Last arrival 19.00hrs Last departure noon

An excellent small park set in open countryside with panoramic views of Long Fell, Maidenpap and Dalbeattie Forest. The park is located in 84 beautiful acres of farmland which visitors are invited to enjoy. The attention to detail here is of the highest standard, and this is most notable in the presentation of the amenity block. There is a regular bus service on the main road, making trips to the surrounding towns easy, and Dalbeattie is only a 10-minute walk away. The site is also convenient for visiting the Solway coast which provides good beaches and a variety of walks. Static holiday caravans are for hire.
10 acre site. 39 touring pitches. 33 hardstandings. Caravan pitches. Motorhome pitches. Tent pitches. 74 statics.

Leisure: /A 🎱
Facilities: 🌂 ☉ 🍴 ✳ ♿ ⏰ 🎍 ❶
Services: 🚰 🗑 🎍 🎍
Within 3 miles: ↧ ✦ 🏌 ◎ 🔢 🗄 🗄 ∪

Notes: No commercial vehicles. Dogs must be kept on leads.

ECCLEFECHAN — Map 21 NY17

Places to visit

Robert Burns House, DUMFRIES 01387 255297
www.dumgal.gov.uk/museums

Old Bridge House Museum, DUMFRIES
01387 256904 www.dumgal.gov.uk/museums

Great for kids: Dumfries Museum & Camera Obscura, DUMFRIES 01387 253374
www.dumgal.gov.uk/museums

PREMIER PARK

▶▶▶▶▶ 79% Hoddom Castle Caravan Park (NY154729)

Hoddom DG11 1AS
☎ 01576 300251
e-mail: hoddomcastle@aol.com
dir: M74 junct 19, follow signs to site. From A75, W of Annan, take B723 for 5m, follow signs to site

🚐 🚙 ▲

Open Etr or Apr-Oct

Last arrival 21.00hrs Last departure 14.00hrs

The peaceful, well-equipped park can be found on the banks of the River Annan, and offers a good mix of grassy and hard pitches, beautifully landscaped and blending into the surroundings. There are signed nature trails, maintained by the park's countryside ranger, a 9-hole golf course, trout and salmon fishing, and plenty of activity ideas for children. 28 acre site. 200 touring pitches. 150 hardstandings. 100 seasonal pitches. Caravan pitches. Motorhome pitches. Tent pitches. 54 statics. 9 wooden pods.

Leisure: /A 🎱 🎵
Facilities: 🚿 🌂 ☉ 🍴 ✳ ♿ ⏰ 🖃 🎍 📶 🖥 ❶
Services: 🚰 🗑 🗄 🚿 T 🍴 🎍 🎍 ↯
Within 3 miles: ↧ 🏌 ◎ 🗄 🗄

Notes: No electric scooters, no gazebos, no fires. Visitor centre.

LEISURE: 🏊 Indoor swimming pool 🏖 Outdoor swimming pool /A Children's playground 🧑 Kid's club 🎾 Tennis court 🎱 Games room ▭ Separate TV room ↧ 9/18 hole golf course 🚣 Boats for hire 🎬 Cinema 🎵 Entertainment 🎣 Fishing ◎ Mini golf 🏄 Watersports 🏋 Gym 🏟 Sports field Spa ∪ Stables
FACILITIES: 🚿 Bath 🌂 Shower ☉ Electric shaver 🍴 Hairdryer ✳ Ice Pack Facility ♿ Disabled facilities ⏰ Public telephone 🗄 Shop on site or within 200yds 🗄 Mobile shop (calls at least 5 days a week) 🎍 BBQ area 🌲 Picnic area 📶 Wi-fi 🖥 Internet access ♻ Recycling ❶ Tourist info 🐕 Dog exercise area

GATEHOUSE OF FLEET — Map 20 NX55

Places to visit

MacLellan's Castle, KIRKCUDBRIGHT
01557 331856 www.historic-scotland.gov.uk

Great for kids: Galloway Wildlife Conservation
Park, KIRKCUDBRIGHT 01557 331645
www.gallowaywildlife.co.uk

89% Auchenlarie Holiday Park (NX536522)

DG7 2EX
☎ 01556 506200 & 206201
e-mail: enquiries@auchenlarie.co.uk
web: www.auchenlarie.co.uk
dir: Direct access from A75, 5m W of Gatehouse
of Fleet

🚐 🚐 🛆

Open Mar-Oct

Last arrival 20.00hrs Last departure noon

A well-organised family park set on cliffs
overlooking Wigtown Bay, with its own sandy
beach. The tenting area, in sloping grass
surrounded by mature trees, has its own
sanitary facilities, while the marked caravan
pitches are in paddocks, with open views
and the provision of high quality toilets. The
leisure centre includes a swimming pool, gym,
solarium and sports hall. There are six self-
catering holiday apartments for let. 32 acre
site. 49 touring pitches. 52 hardstandings.
Caravan pitches. Motorhome pitches. Tent
pitches. 400 statics.

AA Pubs & Restaurants nearby: Cally Palace
Hotel, Gatehouse-of-Fleet 01557 814341

Leisure: 🏊 ♈ ⛰ ⬇ ◎ 🎣 🎵
Facilities: 🖐 ♈ ⊙ 🎡 ✳ ⅄ 🕙 🅂 🎡 🐶 📶
🖥 ❶
Services: 🔌 🅂 🍴 🛢 🖊 🚽 🍽 🎪 🚮 ⬇
Within 3 miles: ⬇ 🖊 ◎ 🅂 🛒 ∪

Notes: Dogs must be kept on leads. Baby
changing facilities, crazy golf.

►►►► 80% Anwoth Caravan Site

(NX595563)

DG7 2JU
☎ 01557 814333 & 01556 506200
e-mail: enquiries@auchenlarie.co.uk
dir: From A75 into Gatehouse of Fleet, site on right
towards Stranraer. Signed from town centre

🚐 £16-£22 🚐 £16-£22 🛆 £16-£22

Open Mar-Oct

Last arrival 20.00hrs Last departure noon

A very high quality park in a peaceful sheltered
setting within easy walking distance of the
village, ideally placed for exploring the scenic
hills, valleys and coastline. Grass, hardstanding
and fully serviced pitches are available and
guests may use the leisure facilities at the sister
site, Auchenlarie Holiday Park. 2 acre site. 28
touring pitches. 13 hardstandings. Caravan
pitches. Motorhome pitches. Tent pitches. 44
statics.

AA Pubs & Restaurants nearby: Cally Palace
Hotel, Gatehouse-of-Fleet 01557 814341

Facilities: 🖐 ♈ ⊙ 🎡 ✳ ⅄ 🕙 🎡 📶
Services: 🔌 🅂 🖊
Within 3 miles: ⬇ 🖊 🛒 🅂

GRETNA — Map 21 NY36

Places to visit

Carlisle Cathedral, CARLISLE 01228 535169
www.carlislecathedral.org.uk

Tullie House Museum & Art Gallery Trust,
CARLISLE 01228 618718 www.tulliehouse.co.uk

Great for kids: Carlisle Castle, CARLISLE
01228 591992 www.english-heritage.org.uk

►►►► 78% Braids Caravan Park

(NY313674)

Annan Rd DG16 5DQ
☎ 01461 337409
e-mail: enquiries@thebraidscaravanpark.co.uk
dir: On B721, 0.5m from village on right, towards
Annan

* 🚐 £17-£20 🚐 £17-£20

Open all year

Last arrival 21.00hrs (20.00hrs in winter) Last
departure noon

A very well-maintained park conveniently located
on the outskirts of Gretna village. Within walking
distance is Gretna Gateway Outlet Village, and
Gretna Green with the World Famous Old
Blacksmith's Shop is nearby. It proves a
convenient stop-over for anyone travelling to and
from both the north of Scotland, and Northern
Ireland (via the ferry at Stranraer). The park has
first-class toilet facilities and generous-sized all-
weather pitches. Please note that tents are not
accepted. A rally field and a meeting room are
available. 6 acre site. 93 touring pitches. 46
hardstandings. Caravan pitches. Motorhome
pitches.

Facilities: ♈ ⊙ 🎡 ✳ ⅄ 🕙 ♻
Services: 🔌 🅂 🍴 🖊 🚽 ⬇
Within 3 miles: 🅂

Notes: Dogs must be kept on leads.

GRETNA *continued*

►►►► 76% King Robert the Bruce's Cave Caravan & Camping Park

(NY266705)

Cove Estate, Kirkpatrick Fleming DG11 3AT
☎ 01461 800285 & 07779 138694
e-mail: enquiries@brucescave.co.uk
web: www.brucescave.co.uk
dir: *Exit A74(M) junct 21 for Kirkpatrick Fleming, follow N through village, pass Station Inn, left at Bruce's Court. Over rail crossing to site*

* ➡ £14-£20 ➡ £14-£20 ▲ £10-£22

Open Apr-Nov (rs Nov shop closed, water restriction)

Last arrival 22.00hrs Last departure 16.00hrs

The lovely wooded grounds of an old castle and mansion are the setting for this pleasant park. The mature woodland is a haven for wildlife, and there is a riverside walk to Robert the Bruce's Cave. A toilet block with en suite facilities is especially useful to families. The site is convenient for the M74 and there is a good local bus service available nearby; the site is also on a National Cycle Route. 80 acre site. 75 touring pitches. 60 hardstandings. Caravan pitches. Motorhome pitches. Tent pitches. 35 statics.

AA Pubs & Restaurants nearby: Smiths of Gretna Green, Gretna 01461 337007

Leisure: ⚠ ☺ 🎱 ⏹
Facilities: ➡ ⚓ ☉ ☔ ✱ ⟲ ⓢ 🏠 ⎚ 🕙 ♿ 🐕 wifi 📺 ♻ 🚻
Services: 🔌 ⑤ 🛢 ⟲ T ⓘⓞⓛ 🚽
Within 3 miles: ↓ ☰ ✎ ⟲ ⓢ ⓢ ⓤ

Notes: No noise after 23.00hrs. Dogs must be kept on leads. BMX bike hire, coarse fishing, first aid available.

Places to visit
Orchardton Tower, PALNACKIE
www.historic-scotland.gov.uk

AA CAMPING CARD SITE

►►► 76% Kippford Holiday Park *(NX844564)*

Best of British GOLD

DG5 4LF
☎ 01556 620636
e-mail: info@kippfordholidaypark.co.uk
dir: *From Dumfries take A711 to Dalbeattie, left onto A710 (Solway coast road) for 3.5m. Park 200yds beyond Kippford turn on right*

➡ £22-£29 ➡ £22-£29 ▲ £19-£27

Open all year

Last arrival 21.30hrs Last departure noon

An attractively landscaped park set in hilly countryside close to the Urr Water estuary and a sand/shingle beach, and with spectacular views. The level touring pitches are on grassed hardstands with private garden areas, and many are fully serviced; there are attractive lodges for hire. The Doon Hill and woodland walks separate the park from the lovely village of Kippford. 18 acre site. 45 touring pitches. 35 hardstandings. 15 seasonal pitches. Caravan pitches. Motorhome pitches. Tent pitches. 119 statics.

AA Pubs & Restaurants nearby: Balcary Bay Hotel, Auchencairn 01556 640217

Kippford Holiday Park

Leisure: ⚠ ☺
Facilities: ⚓ ☉ ☔ ✱ ⟲ ⓢ 🏠 ⎚ 🕙 ♿ 🐕 wifi 📺 ♻ 🚻
Services: 🔌 ⑤ 🛢 ⟲ T 🚽 🚽
Within 3 miles: ↓ ✎ ◎ ⟲ ⓢ ⓢ ⓤ

Notes: No camp fires. Dogs must be kept on leads. Golf, fishing, nature walk, cycle hire.

see advert on opposite page

Places to visit
Stewartry Museum,
KIRKCUDBRIGHT 01557 331643
www.dumgal.gov.uk/museums

Tolbooth Art Centre, KIRKCUDBRIGHT
01557 331556 www.dumgal.gov.uk/museums

Great for kids: Broughton House & Garden,
KIRKCUDBRIGHT 0844 493 2246 www.nts.org.uk

►►►► 83% *Seaward Caravan Park*

(NX662494)

Dhoon Bay DG6 4TJ
☎ 01557 870267 & 331079
e-mail: info@gillespie-leisure.co.uk
dir: *2m SW off B727 (Borgue road)*

➡ ➡ ▲

Open Mar-Oct (rs Mar-mid May & mid Sep-Oct swimming pool closed)

Last arrival 21.30hrs Last departure 11.30hrs

An attractive park with outstanding views over Kirkcudbright Bay which forms part of the Dee Estuary. Access to a sandy cove with rock pools is just across the road. Facilities are well organised and neatly kept, and the park offers a very peaceful atmosphere. The leisure facilities at the other Gillespie Parks are available to visitors to Seaward Caravan Park. 23 acre site. 26 touring pitches. 20 hardstandings. Caravan pitches. Motorhome pitches. Tent pitches. 54 statics.

AA Pubs & Restaurants nearby: Selkirk Arms Hotel, Kirkcudbright 01557 330402

Leisure: ⚓ 🅰 🔍

Facilities: 🚻 🖫 ⊙ ℱ ⚡ ♿ ⓛ ⓢ 🚿 🈂

Services: 🔌 🗑 🔋 ⊘ Ⓣ

Within 3 miles: ⚓ ℱ ◎ 🖫 🛒 U

Notes: No motorised scooters or bikes (except disabled vehicles), no jet skis or own quad bikes. Dogs must be kept on leads. Pitch & putt, volley ball, badminton, table tennis.

LANGHOLM Map 21 NY38

Places to visit

Hermitage Castle, HERMITAGE 01387 376222 www.historic-scotland.gov.uk

►► 65% Ewes Water Caravan & Camping Park (NY365855)

Milntown DG13 0BG
☎ 013873 80386
dir: Access directly from A7 approx 0.5m N of Langholm. Site in Langholm Rugby Club

🚐 🚃 ⛺

Open Apr-Sep

Last departure noon

On the banks of the River Esk, this attractive park lies in a sheltered wooded valley close to an unspoilt Borders' town. 2 acre site. 24 touring pitches. Caravan pitches. Motorhome pitches. Tent pitches.

Facilities: 🖫 ⊙ ⚡ ♿ ⓛ 🚿 🈂

Services: 🔌 🔋 ⊘ 🛒

Within 3 miles: ⚓ ℱ 🖫

Notes: 🈂 Large playing area.

LOCKERBIE

See Ecclefechan

NEWTON STEWART Map 20 NX46

►►► 67% Creebridge Caravan Park

(NX415656)

Minnigaff DG8 6AJ
☎ 01671 402324 & 402432
e-mail: john_sharples@btconnect.com
dir: 0.25m E of Newton Stewart at Minnigaff on bypass, signed off A75

🚐 £12-£19 🚃 £12-£19 ⛺ £9-£13

Open all year (rs Mar only one toilet block open)

Last arrival 20.00hrs Last departure 10.30hrs

A small family-owned site a short walk from the town's amenities. The site is surrounded by mature trees, and the toilet facilities are clean and functional. 5.5 acre site. 26 touring pitches. 9 hardstandings. Caravan pitches. Motorhome pitches. Tent pitches. 60 statics.

AA Pubs & Restaurants nearby: Creebridge House Hotel, Newton Stewart 01671 402121

Galloway Arms Hotel, Newton Stewart 01671 402653

Kirroughtree House, Minnigaff, Newton Stewart 01671 402141

Leisure: 🅰

Facilities: 🖫 ⊙ ℱ ⚡ ♿ ⓛ ⓢ 🚿 🈂 ♲ 🈂

Services: 🔌 🔋 ⊘ 🛒

Within 3 miles: ⚓ 🎫 ℱ ⛵ 🖫 🛒 U

Notes: Dogs must be kept on leads. Security lighting.

SERVICES: 🔌 Electric hook up 🖫 Launderette 🍺 Licensed bar 🔋 Calor Gas ⊘ Camping Gaz Ⓣ Toilet fluid 🍽 Café/Restaurant 🍔 Fast Food/Takeaway 🔋 Battery charging 🍼 Baby care 🔧 Motorvan service point ABBREVIATIONS: BH/bank hols-bank holidays Etr-Easter Whit-Whitsun dep-departure fr-from hrs-hours m-mile mdnt-midnight rdbt-roundabout rs-restricted service wk-week wknd-weekend 🈂 No credit cards 🈂 no dogs See page 7 for details of the AA Camping Card Scheme

PALNACKIE — Map 21 NX85

Places to visit

Orchardton Tower, PALNACKIE
www.historic-scotland.gov.uk

▶▶▶ 79% Barlochan Caravan Park

(NX819572)

DG7 1PF
☎ 01556 600256 & 01557 870267
dir: *On A711, N of Palnackie, signed*

* 🚐 £16.50-£21.50 🚐 £16.50-£21.50 ▲ £13-£18

Open Apr-Oct (rs Apr-May & Sep-Oct swimming pool closed)

Last arrival 21.30hrs Last departure 11.30hrs

A small terraced park with quiet landscaped pitches in a level area backed by rhododendron bushes. There are spectacular views over the River Urr estuary, and the park has its own coarse fishing loch nearby. The amenity block includes combined wash facilities. The leisure facilities at Brighouse Bay are available. 9 acre site. 20 touring pitches. 10 hardstandings. Caravan pitches. Motorhome pitches. Tent pitches. 65 statics.

AA Pubs & Restaurants nearby: Balcary Bay Hotel, Auchencairn 01556 640217

Leisure: ◈ ⚠ 🎣 ▭
Facilities: 🖳 ♂ ✳ & ☺ 🖻 🗗 🖈 ♻ 🛈
Services: 🚐 🖲 ⚡ ▯ 🛒
Within 3 miles: ↓ ♪ ◎ 🖻 🖸
Notes: Dogs must be kept on leads. Pitch & putt.

PARTON — Map 20 NX67

Places to visit

The Rum Story, WHITEHAVEN 01946 592933
www.rumstory.co.uk

The Beacon, WHITEHAVEN 01946 592302
www.thebeacon-whitehaven.co.uk

▶▶▶ 86% *Loch Ken Holiday Park* (NX687702)

DG7 3NE
☎ 01644 470282
e-mail: office@lochkenholidaypark.co.uk
web: www.lochkenholidaypark.co.uk
dir: *On A713, N of Parton. (NB do not follow Sat Nav directions. Site on main road)*

🚐 🚐 ▲

Open Mar-mid Nov (rs Mar (ex Etr) & Nov restricted shop hours)

Last departure noon

Run with energy, enthusiasm and commitment by the hands-on Bryson family, this busy and popular park, with a natural emphasis on water activities, is set on the eastern shores of Loch Ken. With superb views, it is in a peaceful and beautiful spot opposite the RSPB reserve, with direct access to the loch for fishing and boat launching. The park offers a variety of watersports, as well as farm visits and nature trails. Static caravans are available for hire. 15 acre site. 40 touring pitches. 12 hardstandings. 12 seasonal pitches. Caravan pitches. Motorhome pitches. Tent pitches. 35 statics.

Leisure: ⚠ ⚽ ☺
Facilities: 🖳 ☺ ♂ ✳ & ☺ 🖻 🗗 🖈 📶 ♻ 🛈
Services: 🚐 🖲 🖲 ⚡ ▯ 🛒
Within 3 miles: ✳ ♪ ◈ 🖻 🖸
Notes: No noise after 22.00hrs. Dogs must be kept on leads. Bike, boat & canoe hire, water skiing, sailing.

PORT WILLIAM — Map 20 NX34

Places to visit

Glenluce Abbey, GLENLUCE 01581 300541
www.historic-scotland.gov.uk

▶▶▶ 78% Kings Green Caravan Site

(NX340430)

South St DG8 9SG
☎ 01988 700489
dir: *Direct access from A747 at junct with B7085, towards Whithorn*

* 🚐 £11-£13 🚐 £11-£13 ▲ £11-£13

Open mid Mar-Oct

Last arrival 20.00hrs Last departure noon

Located on the edge of Port William, with beautiful views across Luce Bay as far as the Isle of Man, this is a community run site which offers good facilities and large grass pitches with direct access to the pebble shore where otters have been seen. The road which runs along the coast is relatively traffic free so does not detract from the tranquillity of this small site. Two public boat launches are available. There are several good shops in the village and a local bus, with links to Whithorn, Garlieston and Newton Stewart, runs

past the site. 3 acre site. 30 touring pitches. Caravan pitches. Motorhome pitches. Tent pitches.

AA Pubs & Restaurants nearby: Steam Packet Inn, Isle of Whithorn 01988 500334

Facilities: 🖳 ☺ ♂ & ☺ 🖻 🗗 🖈 📶 🛈
Services: 🚐 🖲
Within 3 miles: ↓ ♪ ♨ 🖻
Notes: ⊘ No golf or fireworks permitted on site. Dogs must be kept on leads. Free book lending.

SANDHEAD — Map 20 NX04

Places to visit

Glenwhan Gardens, STRANRAER 01581 400222
www.glenwhangardens.co.uk

Great for kids: Castle Kennedy & Gardens, STRANRAER 01776 702024
www.castlekennedygardens.co.uk

▶▶▶▶ 80% Sands of Luce Holiday Park (NX103510)

Sands of Luce DG9 9JN
☎ 01776 830456
e-mail: info@sandsofluceholidaypark.co.uk
web: www.sandsofluceholidaypark.co.uk
dir: *From S & E: left from A75 onto B7084 signed Drummore. Site signed at junct with A716. From N: A77 through Stranraer towards Portpatrick, 2m, follow A716 signed Drummore, site signed in 5m*

* 🚐 £20-£25 🚐 £20-£25 ▲ £15-£22

Open Mar-Jan

Last arrival 20.00hrs Last departure noon

This is a large, well managed holiday park overlooking Luce Bay. The site has a private boat launch and direct access to a wide sandy beach, which is proving popular with kite surfers. There is a small café, two games rooms and a nice play area for children; adults might like to visit the Lighthouse Bar at the site's entrance. A bus stops at the site entrance so this makes an ideal base for exploring the Mull of Galloway, and Port Logan Botanical Gardens is within easy driving distance. The site is tailored mainly for statics but touring customers are well catered for. 30 acre site. 100 touring pitches. Caravan pitches. Motorhome pitches. Tent pitches. 250 statics.

AA Pubs & Restaurants nearby: Knockinaam Lodge, Portpatrick 01776 810471

LEISURE: 🏊 Indoor swimming pool 🏊 Outdoor swimming pool ⚠ Children's playground ⚓ Kid's club ⚲ Tennis court 🎣 Games room ▭ Separate TV room ⛳ 9/18 hole golf course 🚣 Boats for hire 🎬 Cinema 🎵 Entertainment 🎣 Fishing ◎ Mini golf 🏄 Watersports 🏋 Gym ⚽ Sports field **Spa** ♨ Stables
FACILITIES: 🛁 Bath 🚿 Shower ⚡ Electric shaver ♂ Hairdryer ✳ Ice Pack Facility & Disabled facilities 🕔 Public telephone 🖻 Shop on site or within 200yds 🖸 Mobile shop (calls at least 5 days a week) 🍖 BBQ area 🪑 Picnic area 📶 Wi-fi ⌨ Internet access ♻ Recycling 🛈 Tourist info 🖈 Dog exercise area

Leisure: △◉🔍♫
Facilities: 🌾◉🅿✳🔥👤🛁🚻🚮WiFi 🖥♻ ❶
Services: 🔌🛢🍴🍽🚰🔋
Within 3 miles: 🥾🎣⛵🚲🏇🏌⛳

Notes: Dog fouling must be cleared up by owners. No quad bikes. Dogs must be kept on leads. Boat launching.

SANDYHILLS Map 21 NX85

Places to visit
Threave Garden & Estate, CASTLE DOUGLAS 0844 493 2245 www.nts.org.uk

Orchardton Tower, PALNACKIE www.historic-scotland.gov.uk

Great for kids: Threave Castle, CASTLE DOUGLAS 07711 223101 www.historic-scotland.gov.uk

▶▶▶▶ 75% Sandyhills Bay Leisure Park (NX892552)

DG5 4NY
☎ 01557 870267 & 01387 780257
e-mail: info@gillespie-leisure.co.uk
dir: On A710, 7m from Dalbeattie, 6.5m from Kirkbean

* 🚐 £17-£22.50 ➡ £17-£22.50 ⛺ £13.50-£19

Open Apr-Oct

Last arrival 21.30hrs Last departure 11.30hrs

A well-maintained park in a superb location beside a beach, and close to many attractive villages. The level, grassy site is sheltered by woodland, and the south-facing Sandyhills Bay and beach are a treasure trove for all the family, with their caves and rock pools. The leisure facilities at Brighouse Bay are available to visitors here. Two wigwams with TV, fridge, kettle and microwave are available for hire. 15 acre site. 24 touring pitches. Caravan pitches. Motorhome pitches. Tent pitches. 32 statics. 2 tipis.

AA Pubs & Restaurants nearby: Cavens, Kirkbean 01387 880234

Leisure: △
Facilities: 🌾◉🅿✳🕐🛁🚻🏇❶
Services: 🔌🛢🍴🚽🔋🔋
Within 3 miles: 🎣🏇⛳🚲⛳

Notes: No motorised scooters, jet skis or own quad bikes. Dogs must be kept on leads.

SHAWHEAD Map 21 NX87

Places to visit
Robert Burns House, DUMFRIES 01387 255297 www.dumgal.gov.uk/museums

Old Bridge House Museum, DUMFRIES 01387 256904 www.dumgal.gov.uk/museums

AA CAMPING CARD SITE

NEW ▶▶▶ 76% Barnsoul Caravan Park (NX876778)

Irongray DG2 9SQ
☎ 01557 814351 & 07921 910088
e-mail: info@barnsoulcaravanpark.co.uk
web: www.barnsoulcaravanpark.co.uk
dir: Exit A75 between Dumfries & Crocketford at site sign onto unclassified road signed Shawhead. Right at T-junct, immediate left. Site 1m on left, follow Barnsoul signs

🚐 £20-£25 ➡ £20-£25 ⛺ fr £15

Open Mar-Oct

Last arrival 23.00hrs Last departure 11.00hrs

A lovely site set in a quiet valley only two miles from the A75 and seven miles from the busy town of Dumfries. Set in 250 acres of woodland, parkland and farmland, it is an ideal centre for touring the surrounding unspoilt countryside. The new owner has already made significant improvements, with a new reception at the site entrance and a fabulous camp kitchen. There are two lochans on site with free fishing and walks to suit all capabilities; visitors can also just sit and watch the wildlife that abounds on the park and in the nearby woods. There are wigwam mountain bothies for hire. 100 acre site. 35 touring pitches. 12 hardstandings. 15 seasonal pitches. Caravan pitches. Motorhome pitches. Tent pitches. 11 statics.

Facilities: 🌾◉🅿✳🛁🚻🏇❶
Services: 🔌🛢🔋🚽
Within 3 miles: 🏇⛳🚲⛳

Notes: No unbooked groups, no loud noise after 23.00hrs, 2-axle caravans must pre-book. Dogs must be kept on leads.

SOUTHERNESS Map 21 NX95

83% Southerness Holiday Village
(NX976545)

Off Sandy Ln DG2 8AZ
☎ 0844 335 3756
e-mail: touringandcamping@parkdeanholidays.com
web: www.parkdeantouring.com
dir: From S: A75 from Gretna to Dumfries. From N: A74, exit at A701 to Dumfries. Take A710 (coast road), approx 16m, site easily visible

* 🚐 £14-£39 ➡ £14-£39 ⛺ £12-£31

Open Mar-Oct

Last arrival 21.00hrs Last departure 10.00hrs

There are stunning views across the Solway Firth from this holiday park at the foot of the Galloway Hills. A sandy beach on the Solway Firth is accessible directly from the park. The emphasis is on family entertainment, and facilities include an indoor pool, show bar, coast bar and kitchen. A very well organised park with excellent all-weather, fully-serviced pitches and five Star Pitches (grass or hardstanding) with electricity, water supply and direct drainage system for showers and sinks. 50 acre site. 99 touring pitches. Caravan pitches. Motorhome pitches. Tent pitches. 611 statics.

AA Pubs & Restaurants nearby: Cavens, Kirkbean 01387 880234

Leisure: 🏊△🎿🔍♫
Facilities: 🌾◉🅿✳🛁🕐🛁🚻🔥WiFi
Services: 🔌🛢🍴🚿🚽🍽🔋
Within 3 miles: 🏇⛳◎⛳🛁

Notes: Amusements centre, live entertainment.

STRANRAER — Map 20 NX06

Places to visit

Ardwell House Gardens, ARDWELL 01776 860227

►►►► 81% Aird Donald Caravan Park (NX075605)

London Rd DG9 8RN
☎ 01776 702025
e-mail: enquiries@aird-donald.co.uk
dir: *From A75 left on entering Stranraer (signed). Opposite school, site 300yds*

Open all year

Last departure 16.00hrs

A spacious touring site set behind mature trees and within a five-minute walk of Stranraer town centre at the head of Loch Ryan. It is an ideal base to tour the 'Rinns of Galloway', to visit Port Logan Botanical Gardens or the lighthouse at the Mull of Galloway. It provides a very convenient stop over for the Cairnryan ferry to Ireland, but there's plenty to do in the area if staying longer. A 25 pitch rally field is available. 12 acre site. 100 touring pitches. 50 hardstandings. Caravan pitches. Motorhome pitches. Tent pitches.

AA Pubs & Restaurants nearby: Knockinaam Lodge, Portpatrick 01776 810471

Leisure: /Å\
Facilities: ➀⊙ℙ& ➔ ❶
Services: ➋ ➄ ➊ ⊘ ➤ ➥
Within 3 miles: ➢ ➤ ➀ ⌂ ℙ ➄ ➄ ∪
Notes: ⊕ Dogs must be kept on leads.

WIGTOWN — Map 20 NX45

AA CAMPING CARD SITE

►►► 85% Drumroamin Farm Camping & Touring Site (NX444512)

1 South Balfern DG8 9DB
☎ 01988 840613 & 07752 471456
e-mail: enquiry@drumroamin.co.uk
dir: *A75 towards Newton Stewart, onto A714 for Wigtown. Left on B7005 through Bladnock, A746 through Kirkinner. Take B7004 signed Garlieston, 2nd left opposite Kilsture Forest, site 0.75m at end of lane*

* ➦ £17 ➦ £17 Å £14–£17

Open all year

Last arrival 21.00hrs Last departure noon

An open, spacious site overlooking Wigtown Bay and the Galloway Hills. Located near Wigtown and Newton Stewart, this is an easily accessible site for those wishing to stay in a rural location. The toilet and other facilities are maintained in an exemplary manner. There is a large and separate tent field with a well-equipped day room, while the touring pitches can easily accommodate rally events. The RSPB's Crook of Baldoon Reserve is located a 10-minute walk away. There is a good bus service at the top of the road which goes to Newton Stewart, Wigtown and Whithorn. There are three statics on site with two for hire. 5 acre site. 48 touring pitches. Caravan pitches. Motorhome pitches. Tent pitches. 3 statics.

AA Pubs & Restaurants nearby: Creebridge House Hotel, Newton Stewart 01671 402121

Galloway Arms Hotel, Newton Stewart 01671 402653

Kirroughtree House, Minnigaff, Newton Stewart 01671 402141

Leisure: /Å\ ◆
Facilities: ➀⊙ℙ✳& ➔ ➆ ❶
Services: ➋ ➄ ➤ ➥
Within 3 miles: ➢ ℙ ➄
Notes: No fires. Dogs must be kept on leads. Ball games area.

EAST LOTHIAN

ABERLADY — Map 21 NT47

Places to visit

Dirleton Castle and Gardens, DIRLETON 01620 850330 www.historic-scotland.gov.uk

Hailes Castle, EAST LINTON www.historic-scotland.gov.uk

Great for kids: Myreton Motor Museum, ABERLADY 01875 870288

►► 77% Aberlady Caravan Park (NT482797)

Haddington Rd EH32 0PZ
☎ 01875 870666
e-mail: aberladycaravanpark@hotmail.co.uk
dir: *From Aberlady take A6137 towards Haddington. Right in 0.25m, site on right*

* ➦ fr £19.50 ➦ fr £19.50 Å fr £12

Open Mar-Oct

Last arrival 22.00hrs Last departure noon

A small family-run site located within the grounds of the old Aberlady railway station. It is pleasantly landscaped with an open outlook towards the nearby hills, and within easy reach of many seaside towns, beaches, golf courses and other attractions including the National Museum of Flight. The A1 is nearby and Edinburgh is just a short drive away. 4.5 acre site. 22 touring pitches. 12 hardstandings. Caravan pitches. Motorhome pitches. Tent pitches. 3 wooden pods.

AA Pubs & Restaurants nearby: La Potinière, Gullane 01620 843214

Macdonald Marine Hotel & Spa, North Berwick 0844 879 9130

Leisure: 🅰

Facilities: 🏕⊙🏁⚒✳🎣🛒 Wi-Fi ♻ ❶

Services: 🔌🅾💷🛢🧺Ⓣ🍴🔋⛽

Within 3 miles: ⚓🏌⊚🎣🛒⛳⭕

Notes: ⊛ No ball games, no loud music. Dogs must be kept on leads.

DUNBAR — Map 21 NT67

Places to visit

Preston Mill & Phantassie Doocot, EAST LINTON 0844 493 2128 www.nts.org.uk

Great for kids: Tantallon Castle, NORTH BERWICK 01620 892727 www.historic-scotland.gov.uk

---

PREMIER PARK

▶▶▶▶▶ **86%** *Thurston Manor Leisure Park* (NT712745)

Innerwick EH42 1SA

☎ 01368 840643

e-mail: holidays@thurstonmanor.co.uk

dir: *4m S of Dunbar, signed off A1*

🚐🚏⛺

Open Mar-7 Jan (rs 1-22 Dec site open wknds only)

Last arrival 23.00hrs Last departure noon

A pleasant park set in 250 acres of unspoilt countryside. The touring and static areas of this large park are in separate areas. The main touring area occupies an open, level position, and the toilet facilities are modern and exceptionally well maintained. The park boasts a well-stocked fishing loch, a heated indoor swimming pool, steam room, sauna, jacuzzi, mini-gym and fitness room plus seasonal entertainment. There is a superb family toilet block. 250 acre site. 120 touring pitches. 53 hardstandings. Caravan pitches. Motorhome pitches. Tent pitches. 490 statics.

AA Pubs & Restaurants nearby: Macdonald Marine Hotel & Spa, North Berwick 0844 879 9130

Leisure: ☂🏹🅰🔍⛱🎵

Facilities: 🏕⊙🏁✳🛝⛵🅗🎣🛒 Wi-Fi 💻♻❶

Services: 🔌🅾💷🛢⊘Ⓣ🍴🧺⛽🔋

Within 3 miles: 🏌🅗⭕

Notes: Dogs must be kept on leads.

▶▶▶ **75%** **Belhaven Bay Caravan & Camping Park**

(NT661781)

(gold award logo)

Belhaven Bay EH42 1TS

☎ 01368 865956

e-mail: belhaven@meadowhead.co.uk

dir: *A1 onto A1087 towards Dunbar. Site (1m) in John Muir Park*

* 🚐 £15-£27.50 £15-£27.50 ⛺ £18-£26

Open Mar-13 Oct

Last arrival 20.00hrs Last departure noon

Located on the outskirts of Dunbar, this is a sheltered park within walking distance of the beach. There is a regular bus service to Dunbar which is also one of the main east coast railway stations. The site is convenient for the A1 and well placed to visit the area's many seaside towns and the various visitor attractions. A new amenity block is being installed for the 2013 season and will provide self-contained units. There is a large children's play area. 40 acre site. 52 touring pitches. 11 hardstandings. Caravan pitches. Tent pitches. 64 statics.

AA Pubs & Restaurants nearby: Macdonald Marine Hotel & Spa, North Berwick 0844 879 9130

Leisure: 🅰

Facilities: 🛁🏕⊙🏁✳🅗⛵🅗🎣🛒 Wi-Fi 💻♻❶

Services: 🔌🅾Ⓣ🚐⛽

Within 3 miles: ⚓🏌⊚🎣🛒🅗⭕

Notes: No rollerblades or skateboards, no open fires, no noise 23.00hrs-07.00hrs. Dogs must be kept on leads.

SERVICES: 🔌 Electric hook up 🅾 Launderette 💷 Licensed bar 🛢 Calor Gas ⊘ Camping Gaz Ⓣ Toilet fluid 🍴 Café/Restaurant 🧺 Fast Food/Takeaway 🔋 Battery charging 🚐 Baby care ⛽ Motorvan service point **ABBREVIATIONS:** BH/bank hols-bank holidays Etr-Easter Whit-Whitsun dep-departure fr-from hrs-hours m-mile mdnt-midnight rdbt-roundabout rs-restricted service wk-week wknd-weekend ⊛ No credit cards ⊗ no dogs See page 7 for details of the AA Camping Card Scheme

LONGNIDDRY
Map 21 NT47

Places to visit

Crichton Castle, CRICHTON 01875 320017
www.historic-scotland.gov.uk

72% Seton Sands Holiday Village

(NT420759)

GOLD

EH32 0QF
☎ **0871 231 0867**
e-mail: setonsands@haven.com
web: www.haven.com/setonsands
dir: *A1 to A198 exit, then B6371 to Cockenzie. Right onto B1348. Site 1m on right*

Open mid Mar-end Oct (rs mid Mar-May & Sep-Oct some facilities may be reduced)

Last arrival 22.00hrs Last departure 10.00hrs

A well-equipped holiday centre with plenty of organised entertainment, clubs and bars, restaurants, and sports and leisure facilities. A multi-sports court, heated swimming pool, and various play areas ensure that there is plenty to do, and there is lots to see and do in and around Edinburgh which is nearby; there is a regular bus service from the site entrance, which makes Edinburgh easily accessible. The touring field is in a small area to the side of the entertainment complex and has all grass pitches. 1.75 acre site. 34 touring pitches. Caravan pitches. Motorhome pitches. Tent pitches. 635 statics.

AA Pubs & Restaurants nearby: La Potinière, Gullane 01620 843214

Leisure:
Facilities:
Services:
Within 3 miles:

Notes: Max 2 dogs per booking, certain dog breeds banned, no commercial vehicles, no bookings by persons under 21yrs unless a family booking. Dogs must be kept on leads.

see advert on page 385

MUSSELBURGH
Map 21 NT37

Places to visit

Dalmeny House, SOUTH QUEENSFERRY
0131 331 1888 www.dalmeny.co.uk

AA CAMPING CARD SITE

▶▶▶▶ **82% Drum Mohr Caravan Park** *(NT373734)*

Levenhall EH21 8JS
☎ **0131 665 6867**
e-mail: admin@drummohr.org
web: www.drummohr.org
dir: *Exit A1 at A199 junct through Wallyford, at rdbt onto B1361 signed Prestonpans. 1st left, site 400yds*

Open all year (rs Winter arrivals by arrangement)

Last arrival 18.00hrs Last departure noon

This attractive park is sheltered by mature trees on all sides, and carefully landscaped within. The park is divided into separate areas by mature hedging and planting of trees and ornamental shrubs. The pitches are generous in size, and there are a number of fully serviced pitches plus first-class amenities. The site is ideally located to explore East Lothian, with numerous seaside towns and the National Museum of Flight at East Fortune. It is also very convenient for the A1 and Edinburgh which is an easy drive, or alternatively, there is a regular service bus which passes near the site. 9 acre site. 120 touring pitches. 50 hardstandings. Caravan pitches. Motorhome pitches. Tent pitches. 12 statics. 10 wooden pods.

AA Pubs & Restaurants nearby: The Kitchen, Leith, Edinburgh 0131 555 1755

Plumed Horse, Leith 0131 554 5556

Leisure:
Facilities:
Services:
Within 3 miles:

Notes: Max 2 dogs per pitch. Dogs must be kept on leads. Freshly baked bread & croissants, tea & coffee.

FIFE

ST ANDREWS
Map 21 NO51

Places to visit

St Andrews Castle, ST ANDREWS 01334 477196
www.historic-scotland.gov.uk

British Golf Museum, ST ANDREWS
01334 460046 www.britishgolfmuseum.co.uk

Great for kids: St Andrews Aquarium,
ST ANDREWS 01334 474786
www.standrewsaquarium.co.uk

PREMIER PARK

▶▶▶▶▶ **91% Cairnsmill Holiday Park** *(NO502142)*

GOLD

Largo Rd KY16 8NN
☎ **01334 473604**
e-mail: cairnsmill@aol.com
dir: *A915 from St Andrews towards Lathones. Approx 2m, site on right*

* 🚐 £26 🚐 £24 ▲ £16-£18

Open all year (rs Winter prior bookings only)

Last arrival flexible Last departure 11.00hrs

Hidden behind mature trees and hedging in open countryside on the outskirts of St Andrews, this top quality park is ideally placed for visiting St Andrews and exploring the Fife area. It is a family owned and run site providing high levels of customer care and excellent facilities, including a swimming pool, licensed bar and café, numerous play areas for children and a small fishing lochan, stocked annually with rainbow trout. Toilet

---

LEISURE: 🏊 Indoor swimming pool 🏊 Outdoor swimming pool 🛝 Children's playground 🧒 Kid's club 🎾 Tennis court 🎱 Games room 📺 Separate TV room ⛳ 9/18 hole golf course 🚣 Boats for hire 🎬 Cinema 🎵 Entertainment 🎣 Fishing ⛳ Mini golf 🏄 Watersports 💪 Gym 🏅 Sports field Spa ♨ Stables
FACILITIES: 🛁 Bath 🚿 Shower 🪒 Electric shaver 💇 Hairdryer ❄ Ice Pack Facility ♿ Disabled facilities 📞 Public telephone 🛒 Shop on site or within 200yds 🚚 Mobile shop (calls at least 5 days a week) 🍖 BBQ area 🪑 Picnic area 📶 Wi-fi 💻 Internet access ♻ Recycling ℹ Tourist info 🐕 Dog exercise area

facilities are first class, and the tent area has its own amenity block and outdoor kitchen area. Bunk house accommodation is available as well as five static homes for hire. The local bus to St Andrews stops at the site entrance. 27 acre site. 62 touring pitches. 33 hardstandings. 24 seasonal pitches. Caravan pitches. Motorhome pitches. Tent pitches. 194 statics.

AA Pubs & Restaurants nearby: The Inn at Lathones, Largoward 01334 840494

Cairnsmill Holiday Park

Leisure: 🌊 🄐 🎱 ▢ 🎵 Spa
Facilities: 🚿 ⊙ 🗜 ✳ 🕭 🕒 🎍 🗚 WiFi 🖥 ♻ ❶
Services: 🔌 🗑 🍴 🔥 ⊘ T 🍴 🔋 ⚘
Within 3 miles: 🖊 ⚴ ⊞ 🎣 ◎ 🍴 🏌 🎱 🗄 ∪
Notes: Dogs must be kept on leads.

▶▶▶▶▶ **91% Craigtoun Meadows Holiday Park** *(NO482150)*

Mount Melville KY16 8PQ
☎ **01334 475959**
e-mail: craigtoun@aol.com
web: www.craigtounmeadows.co.uk
dir: *M90 junct 8, A91 to St Andrews. Just after Guardbridge right for Strathkinness. At 2nd x-rds left for Craigtoun*

* 🚐 £20-£25.50 🚐 £20-£25.50 ▲ £17-£20

Open 15 Mar-Oct (rs Mar-Etr & Sep-Oct no shop & restaurant open shorter hours)

Last arrival 21.00hrs Last departure 11.00hrs

An attractive site set unobtrusively in mature woodlands, with large pitches in spacious hedged paddocks. All pitches are fully serviced, and there are also some patio pitches and a summerhouse containing picnic tables and chairs. The modern toilet block provides cubicled en suite facilities as well as spacious showers, baths, disabled facilities and baby changing areas. The licensed restaurant and coffee shop are popular, and there is a takeaway, indoor and outdoor games areas and a launderette. Located three miles from St Andrews which has sandy beaches, shops and restaurants, and being 'the home of golf', there are, of course, various golf courses including The Dukes, which borders the site. 32 acre site. 57 touring pitches. 57 hardstandings. 3 seasonal pitches. Caravan pitches. Motorhome pitches. Tent pitches. 199 statics.

AA Pubs & Restaurants nearby: Jigger Inn, St Andrews 01334 474371

Inn at Lathones, Largoward 01334 840494

Leisure: 🄐 ♻ 🎱
Facilities: ⚒ 🚿 ⊙ 🗜 🕒 🕭 🗚 WiFi 🖥 ♻ ❶
Services: 🔌 🗑 🍴 🔋 🚿 ⚘ ⚱
Within 3 miles: 🖊 ⊞ 🎣 ◎ 🍴 🏌 🗄 🗄 ∪
Notes: No groups of unaccompanied minors, no pets. Putting green.

See Walk 13 in the Walks & Cycle Rides section at the end of the guide

ARISAIG Map 22 NM68

Places to visit

Glenfinnan Monument, GLENFINNAN 0844 493 2221 www.nts.org.uk

NEW ▶▶▶ **72% Camusdarach Campsite** *(NM664916)*

Camusdarach PH39 4NT
☎ **01687 450221**
dir: *From Fort William take A830 towards Mallaig. At Arisaig take B8008, 2m to site*

* 🚐 £21 🚐 £21 ▲ £18

Open 15 Mar-15 Oct

Under new ownership this family owned site offers personal attention. The touring pitches are in two large areas and occupy only a small part of this large site which has good access through woodland and sand dunes to beautiful secluded sandy beaches. The facilities, including the toilets, are well maintained. It is only four miles from Mallaig, a small port with regular ferries to the islands, including Rhum, Eigg and Skye. It is also the end station for the famous Jacobite steam train (featured in the Harry Potter films) which passes Glenfinnan en route to Fort William. There are two large holiday flats for let in a Victorian farmhouse. 2.8 acre site. 21 touring pitches. Caravan pitches. Motorhome pitches. Tent pitches.

AA Pubs & Restaurants nearby: Cnoc-na-Faire, Arisaig 01687 450249

BALMACARA Map 22 NG82

Places to visit

Balmacara Estate & Lochalsh Woodland Garden, BALMACARA 0844 493 2233 www.nts.org.uk

▶▶▶ **78% Reraig Caravan Site** *(NG815272)*

IV40 8DH
☎ **01599 566215**
e-mail: warden@reraig.com
dir: *On A87, 3.5m E of Kyle, 2m W of junct with A890*

* 🚐 £15.40 🚐 £15.40 ▲ £13

Open May-Sep

Last arrival 22.00hrs Last departure noon

A lovely site, on the saltwater Sound of Sleet, set back from the main road amongst mature trees in a garden-type environment. It is located near the Skye Bridge and very handy for exploring the surrounding area including Plockton. There is a regular bus that stops at the site entrance. 2 acre site. 40 touring pitches. 36 hardstandings. Caravan pitches. Motorhome pitches. Tent pitches.

AA Pubs & Restaurants nearby: Waterside Seafood Restaurant, Kyle of Lochalsh 01599 534813

Plockton Inn & Seafood Restaurant, Plockton 01599 544222

Plockton Hotel, Plockton 01599 544274

Facilities: 🚿 ⊙ 🗜 🗄 WiFi ♻ ❶
Services: 🔌 ⚘
Within 3 miles: 🗄
Notes: No awnings Jul & Aug. Only small tents permitted. Dogs must be kept on leads. Ramp access to block.

CORPACH
Map 22 NN07

Places to visit

West Highland Museum,
FORT WILLIAM 01397 702169
www.westhighlandmuseum.org.uk

Great for kids: Inverlochy Castle, FORT WILLIAM
www.historic-scotland.gov.uk

AA CAMPING CARD SITE

PREMIER PARK

▶▶▶▶▶ **85% Linnhe Lochside**
Holidays (NN074771)
GOLD

PH33 7NL
☎ 01397 772376
e-mail: relax@linnhe-lochside-holidays.co.uk
dir: On A830, 1m W of Corpach, 5m from Fort
William

🚐 £17.75-£21.75 🚍 £17.75-£21.75 ▲ £12-£18

Open 15 Dec-30 Oct (rs Dec-Etr shop closed out of
season, unisex showers during peak season only)

Last arrival 21.00hrs Last departure 11.00hrs

An excellently maintained site in a beautiful
setting on the shores of Loch Eil, with Ben Nevis to
the east and the mountains and Sunart to the
west. The owners have worked in harmony with
nature to produce an idyllic environment, where
the highest standards of design and maintenance
are evident. 5.5 acre site. 85 touring pitches. 63
hardstandings. 20 seasonal pitches. Caravan
pitches. Motorhome pitches. Tent pitches. 20
statics.

AA Pubs & Restaurants nearby: Inverlochy Castle
Hotel, Fort William 01397 702177

Moorings Hotel, Fort William 01397 772797

Lime Tree Hotel & Restaurant, Fort William
01397 701806

Linnhe Lochside Holidays

Leisure: ⚙

Facilities: 🛁 🚿 ☉ 🅿 ✳ ♿ Ⓢ 🛒 🏇 🐕 📶 ♻ ℹ

Services: 🔌 🔄 🍴 🚽 🏕 ♨

Within 3 miles: 🎣 🚣 ℘ ◎ ⛸ 🏪 🛒

Notes: No cars by tents. No large groups.
Launching slipway, free fishing.

see advert on opposite page

DORNOCH
Map 23 NH78

Places to visit

Dunrobin Castle, GOLSPIE 01408 633177
www.dunrobincastle.co.uk

 77% Grannie's Heilan
Hame Holiday Park
GOLD

(NH818924)

Embo IV25 3QD
☎ 0844 335 3756
e-mail: touringandcamping@parkdeanholidays.
com
web: www.parkdeantouring.com
dir: A949 to Dornoch, left in square. Follow
Embo signs

* 🚐 £12-£36 🚍 £12-£36 ▲ £10-£27

Open Mar-Oct

Last arrival 21.00hrs Last departure 10.00hrs

A 60-acre holiday park situated in Embo that
has direct access to the beach on the Dornoch
Firth. Within a few miles of the historic town
of Dornoch and with easy access to the A9 and
regular bus services, this makes an excellent
touring base. There is a swimming pool, spa
and solarium, a children's club, a bar and
bistro and a good shop. The main amenity block
provides good facilities and is well maintained.
60 acre site. 125 touring pitches. Caravan
pitches. Motorhome pitches. Tent pitches. 273
statics.

AA Pubs & Restaurants nearby: Dornoch Castle
Hotel, Dornoch 01862 810216

Leisure: 🏊 ⚙ 🛝 👶 🎱 🎵

Facilities: 🚿 ☉ 🅿 ✳ ♿ Ⓢ 🛒 🏇 📶 💻 ♻ ℹ

Services: 🔌 🔄 🍴 🛢 ℘ 🚽 🍴 🏪 🛒

Within 3 miles: 🎣 ℘ ◎ 🏪 🛒

Notes: No noise after mdnt. Dogs must be kept
on leads. Mini ten-pin bowling, sauna.

DUROR
Map 22 NM95

►►►► 78% Achindarroch Touring Park (NM997554)

PA38 4BS
☎ **01631 740329**
e-mail: stay@achindarrochtp.co.uk
dir: *A82 onto A828 at Ballachulish Bridge then towards Oban for 5.2m. In Duror site on left, signed*

* ⊞ fr £18 ⊞ fr £18 ▲ fr £18

Open 24 Jan-16 Jan

Last departure 11.00hrs

A long established, well-laid out park which continues to be upgraded to a high standard by an enthusiastic and friendly family team. There is a well-appointed heated toilet block and spacious all-weather pitches and there are also 2- and 4-person camping pods for hire. The park is well placed for visits to Oban, Fort William and Glencoe. A wide variety of outdoor sports is available in the area. 5 acre site. 40 touring pitches. 21 hardstandings. 10 seasonal pitches. Caravan pitches. Motorhome pitches. Tent pitches. 2 wooden pods.

Facilities: ♠⊙🅿✳⚙🕭🖂🎇📶♻️ⓘ
Services: 🔌🖸🅿⚙🛒♨
Within 3 miles: 🎣∪

Notes: Groups by prior arrangement only. Dogs must be kept on leads. Campers' kitchen (freezer, toaster, kettle, microwave, boot dryer).

FORT WILLIAM
Map 22 NN17

See also Corpach

Places to visit

West Highland Museum,
FORT WILLIAM 01397 702169
www.westhighlandmuseum.org.uk

Great for kids: Inverlochy Castle, FORT WILLIAM
www.historic-scotland.gov.uk

►►►► 88% *Glen Nevis Caravan & Camping Park* (NN124722)

Glen Nevis PH33 6SX
☎ **01397 702191**
e-mail: holidays@glen-nevis.co.uk
web: www.glen-nevis.co.uk
dir: *On northern outskirts of Fort William follow A82 to mini-rdbt. Exit for Glen Nevis. Site 2.5m on right*

⊞ ⊞ ▲

Open 13 Mar-9 Nov (rs Mar & mid Oct-Nov limited shop & restaurant facilities)

Last arrival 22.00hrs Last departure noon

A tasteful site with well-screened enclosures, at the foot of Ben Nevis in the midst of some of the most spectacular Highland scenery; an ideal area for walking and touring. The park boasts a restaurant which offers a high standard of cooking and provides good value for money. 30 acre site. 380 touring pitches. 150 hardstandings. Caravan pitches. Motorhome pitches. Tent pitches. 30 statics.

AA Pubs & Restaurants nearby: Inverlochy Castle Hotel, Fort William 01397 702177

Moorings Hotel, Fort William 01397 772797

Lime Tree Hotel & Restaurant, Fort William 01397 701806

Leisure: ⚲
Facilities: ♠⊙🅿✳⚙🕭🖂🎇🐾
Services: 🔌🖸🍴⚙🛒T🍽🛒♨
Within 3 miles: ⚑🎣☕📷🖸
Notes: Quiet 23.00hrs-08.00hrs.

Corpach, Fort William PH33 7NL
www.linnhe-lochside-holidays.co.uk
01397-772376

Luxury Chalets, Centrally heated
Linen & towels included, Sleeps 4-6 people

Luxury Caravans, Double glazing option.
book fantastic views, Sleeps up to 6 people.

AA Scottish campsite Winner 2011

Touring & Camping, Terraced touring pitches,
Heated facilities.

Open from 15th December till 30th October. Book online at our website or telephone For more details.

GAIRLOCH   Map 22 NG87

Places to visit

Gairloch Heritage Museum,
GAIRLOCH 01445 712287
www.gairlochheritagemuseum.org

Inverewe Garden, POOLEWE 0844 493 2225
www.nts.org.uk

AA CAMPING CARD SITE

▶▶▶ **79% Gairloch Caravan Park**
(NG798773)

Strath IV21 2BX
☎ **01445 712373**
e-mail: info@gairlochcaravanpark.com
dir: *From A832 take B8021 signed Melvaig towards Strath. In 0.5m turn right, just after Millcroft Hotel. Immediately right again*

* 🚐 £14-£15 🚌 £14-£15 ▲ £14-£15

Open Etr-Oct

Last arrival 21.00hrs Last departure noon

A clean, well-maintained site on flat coastal grassland close to Loch Gairloch. The owners and managers are hard working and well organised and continued investment in recent years has seen significant improvements around the park, including the hardstandings, good shrub and flower planting, and the building of a bunkhouse that provides accommodation for families. 6 acre site. 70 touring pitches. 13 hardstandings. 8 seasonal pitches. Caravan pitches. Motorhome pitches. Tent pitches.

AA Pubs & Restaurants nearby: Old Inn, Gairloch 01445 712006

Facilities: 🍴 ⊙ 📛 ✳ 🚿 🕐 🖐 [s] [wifi] ♻ ❶

Services: 🔌 🔘 [T] 🍴

Within 3 miles: ↓ 🎣 ◎ 💧 [s] [5] ∪

Notes: No noise after 23.00hrs. Dogs must be kept on leads.

GLENCOE   Map 22 NN15

Places to visit

Glencoe & Dalness, GLENCOE 0844 493 2222
www.nts.org.uk

Great for kids: Glencoe & North Lorn Folk Museum, GLENCOE 01855 811664
www.glencoemuseum.com

▶▶▶▶ **83% Invercoe Caravan & Camping Park** (NN098594)

PH49 4HP
☎ **01855 811210**
e-mail: holidays@invercoe.co.uk
web: www.invercoe.co.uk
dir: *Exit A82 at Glencoe Hotel onto B863 for 0.25m*

🚐 £22-£25 🚌 £22-£25 ▲ £20-£22

Open all year

Last departure noon

A level grass site set on the shore of Loch Leven, with excellent mountain views. The area is ideal for both walking and climbing, and also offers a choice of several freshwater and saltwater lochs. Convenient for the good shopping in Fort William. 5 acre site. 60 touring pitches. Caravan pitches. Motorhome pitches. Tent pitches. 4 statics. 2 wooden pods.

AA Pubs & Restaurants nearby: Loch Leven Hotel, North Ballachulish 01855 821236s

Leisure: ⚠

Facilities: 🍴 ⊙ 📛 ✳ 🖐 🕐 [s] 🍽 ↗ [wifi]

Services: 🔌 🔘 ⟋ [T] 🍴 ⬆

Within 3 miles: ↓ ⫞ 🎣 [s] [5]

Notes: No large group bookings.

JOHN O'GROATS   Map 23 ND37

Places to visit

The Castle & Gardens of Mey, THURSO
01847 851473 www.castleofmey.org.uk

▶▶▶ **79% John O'Groats Caravan Site** (ND382733)

KW1 4YR
☎ **01955 611329** & **07762 336359**
e-mail: info@johnogroatscampsite.co.uk
dir: *At end of A99*

* 🚐 £16.50-£19.50 🚌 £16.50-£19.50 ▲ £13-£16

Open Apr-Sep

Last arrival 22.00hrs Last departure 11.00hrs

An attractive site in an open position above the seashore and looking out towards the Orkney Islands. Nearby is the passenger ferry that makes day trips to the Orkneys, and there are grey seals to watch, and sea angling can be organised by the site owners. 4 acre site. 90 touring pitches. 30 hardstandings. Caravan pitches. Motorhome pitches. Tent pitches.

Facilities: 🍴 ⊙ 📛 ✳ 🖐 🕐 ↗ [wifi] ♻ ❶

Services: 🔌 🔘 ⟋ 🍴 ⬆

Within 3 miles: 🎣 [s] [5]

Notes: ⊘ Dogs must be kept on leads.

LAIRG   Map 23 NC50

▶▶▶ **74% Dunroamin Caravan and Camping Park** (NC585062)

Main St IV27 4AR
☎ **01549 402447**
e-mail: enquiries@lairgcaravanpark.co.uk
dir: *300mtrs from centre of Lairg on S side of A839*

🚐 🚌 ▲

Open Apr-Oct

Last arrival 21.00hrs Last departure noon

An attractive little park with clean and functional facilities, adjacent to a licensed restaurant. The park is close to the lower end of Loch Shin. 4 acre site. 40 touring pitches. 8 hardstandings. Caravan

---

LEISURE: 🏊 Indoor swimming pool 🏊 Outdoor swimming pool ⚠ Children's playground 🛝 Kid's club ⚲ Tennis court 🎱 Games room ▭ Separate TV room ↓ 9/18 hole golf course ⛵ Boats for hire 🎬 Cinema ♫ Entertainment 🎣 Fishing ◎ Mini golf 💧 Watersports 💪 Gym ◯ Sports field **Spa** ∪ Stables
FACILITIES: 🛁 Bath 🚿 Shower ⊙ Electric shaver 📛 Hairdryer ✳ Ice Pack Facility 🖐 Disabled facilities 🕐 Public telephone [s] Shop on site or within 200yds 🛒 Mobile shop (calls at least 5 days a week) 🍽 BBQ area ↗ Picnic area [wifi] Wi-fi 🖥 Internet access ♻ Recycling ❶ Tourist info ↗ Dog exercise area

pitches. Motorhome pitches. Tent pitches. 9 statics.

Facilities: ⚒ ⊙ ☐ ⁂ Wifi ♻ ❶

Services: 🔌 🔥 🔒 🗑 T ⑴ 🛏 🍴 🛁

Within 3 miles: ⚑ 🏌 🚣 🛒 🗑

Notes: No vehicles to be driven on site between 21.00hrs-07.00hrs. Dogs must be kept on leads.

►►► 67% Woodend Caravan & Camping Site (NC551127)

Achnairn IV27 4DN
☎ 01549 402248
dir: *4m N of Lairg exit A836 onto A838, signed at Achnairn*

* 🚐 £10-£12 🚃 £10-£12 ⛺ £8-£10

Open Apr-Sep

Last arrival 23.00hrs

A clean, simple site set in hilly moors and woodland with access to Loch Shin. The area is popular with fishing and boating enthusiasts, and there is a choice of golf courses within a 30 mile radius. A spacious campers' kitchen is a useful amenity. There's also a holiday cottage to hire. 4 acre site. 55 touring pitches. 5 hardstandings. Caravan pitches. Motorhome pitches. Tent pitches.

Leisure: 🎱
Facilities: ⚒ ⊙ ☐ ⁂
Services: 🔌 🗑
Within 3 miles: ⚑ 🏌 🗑
Notes: 🐾

NAIRN
Places to visit
Sueno's Stone, FORRES 01667 460232
www.historic-scotland.gov.uk
Dallas Dhu Distillery, FORRES 01309 676548
www.historic-scotland.gov.uk
Great for kids: Brodie Castle, BRODIE CASTLE
0844 493 2156 www.nts.org.uk

NAIRN Map 23 NH85

76% Nairn Lochloy Holiday Park (NH895574)
East Beach IV12 5DE
☎ 0844 335 3756
e-mail: touringandcamping@parkdeanholidays.com
web: www.parkdeantouring.com
dir: *From A96 (Bridge St) in Nairn follow site signs onto unclassified road at Bridgemill Direct shop*
* 🚐 £13-£35 🚃 £13-£35 ⛺ £11-£32.50

Open Mar-Oct
Last arrival 21.00hrs Last departure 10.00hrs

A small touring site situated within a popular holiday park with a wide range of leisure facilities including heated pool, sauna, spa bath, children's play-area and clubs, crazy golf, amusements, bars, restaurant and mini supermarket. A small, well-maintained toilet block exclusively serves the touring area where all pitches have electricity. Handily placed in the centre of Nairn, only minutes from the beach and within striking distance of Inverness and the Highlands. 15 acre site. 13 touring pitches. Caravan pitches. Motorhome pitches. Tent pitches. 263 statics.

AA Pubs & Restaurants nearby: Cawdor Tavern, Cawdor 01667 404777
Boath House, Nairn 01667 454896
Newton Hotel, Nairn 01667 453144
Golf View Hotel & Leisure Club, Nairn 01667 452301
Leisure: ⚓ 🎱 🏊 🎣 🎵
Facilities: 🚿 ⚒ ⊙ ☐ 🛒 🕐 Ⓢ Wifi
Services: 🔌 🗑 🍴 🔒 🗑 ⑴ 🛏
Within 3 miles: ⚑ 🏌 ◎ 🚣 🛒 🗑 U

ULLAPOOL Map 22 NH19
►►► **74% Broomfield Holiday Park** (NH123939)
West Shore St IV26 2UT
☎ 01854 612020 & 612664
e-mail: sross@broomfieldhp.com
web: www.broomfieldhp.com
dir: *Take 2nd right past harbour*
* 🚐 £17-£21 🚃 £16-£20 ⛺ £10-£18

Open Etr or Apr-Sep
Last departure noon

Set right on the water's edge of Loch Broom and the open sea, with lovely views of the Summer Isles. This clean, well maintained and managed park is close to the harbour and town centre with their restaurants, bars and shops. The Ullapool ferry allows easy access to the Hebridian islands for day trips or longer visits. 12 acre site. 140 touring pitches. Caravan pitches. Motorhome pitches. Tent pitches.

Leisure: 🎱
Facilities: ⚒ ⊙ ⁂ ♿ 🛁 Wifi
Services: 🔌 🗑 🛏 🛁
Within 3 miles: ⚓ 🏌 🗑 🗑
Notes: No noise at night. Dogs must be kept on leads.

MORAY

ABERLOUR   Map 23 NJ24

Places to visit

Balvenie Castle, DUFFTOWN 01340 820121
www.historic-scotland.gov.uk

►►► 80% Aberlour Gardens Caravan Park

(NJ282434)

AB38 9LD
☎ 01340 871586
e-mail: info@aberlourgardens.co.uk
dir: *Midway between Aberlour & Craigellachie on A95 turn onto unclassified road. Site signed. (NB vehicles over 10' 6" use A941 (Dufftown to Craigellachie road) where park is signed)*

* ➡ £18.75-£23.40 ⛺ £18.75-£23.40
▲ £14.80-£23.40

Open Mar-27 Dec (rs Winter park opening dates weather dependant)

Last arrival 19.00hrs Last departure noon

This attractive parkland site is set in the five-acre walled garden of the Victorian Aberlour House, surrounded by the full range of spectacular scenery from the Cairngorm National Park, through pine clad glens, to the famous Moray coastline; the park is also well placed for the world renowned Speyside Malt Whisky Trail. It offers a small, well-appointed toilet block, laundry and small licensed shop. 5 acre site. 34 touring pitches. 16 hardstandings. 10 seasonal pitches. Caravan pitches. Motorhome pitches. Tent pitches. 32 statics.

AA Pubs & Restaurants nearby: Craigellachie Hotel, Craigellachie 01340 881204

Archiestown Hotel, Archiestown 01340 810218

Leisure: 🅰
Facilities: ⬤☉🅿✳♿⏱🆂📶 ♻ ❶
Services: 🔌🗑💧🚿🅣⬇
Within 3 miles: ⬇🏌🎣🆂

Notes: No ball games, max 5mph speed limit, no noise after 23.00hrs. Dogs must be kept on leads.

ALVES   Map 23 NJ16

Places to visit

Pluscarden Abbey, ELGIN 01343 890257
www.pluscardenabbey.org

Elgin Museum, ELGIN 01343 543675
www.elginmuseum.org.uk

Great for kids: Duffus Castle, DUFFUS
01667 460232 www.historic-scotland.gov.uk

►►► 67% *North Alves Caravan Park*

(NJ122633)

IV30 8XD
☎ 01343 850223
dir: *From Elgin towards Forres on A96, follow signs for site (sign in Alves), turn right onto unclassified road. Approx 1m site on right*

➡ ⛺ ▲

Open Apr-Oct

Last arrival 23.00hrs Last departure noon

A quiet rural site in attractive rolling countryside within three miles of a good beach. The site is on a former farm, and the stone buildings are quite unspoilt. 10 acre site. 45 touring pitches. Caravan pitches. Motorhome pitches. Tent pitches. 45 statics.

Leisure: 🅰⚽🎣🖵
Facilities: ⬤☉🅿✳🐾
Services: 🔌🗑🅣🏪
Within 3 miles: ⬇🍴🎬🏌🆂♨

Notes: 🚫 Dogs must be kept on leads.

FOCHABERS   Map 23 NJ35

Places to visit

Strathisla Distillery, KEITH 01542 783044
www.chivas.com

Glen Grant Distillery, ROTHES 01340 832118
www.glengrant.com

►►►► 76% Burnside Caravan Park

(NJ350580)

IV32 7ET
☎ 01343 820511
e-mail: burnside7et@googlemail.com
dir: *0.5m E of town off A96*

* ➡ fr £22 ⛺ fr £22 ▲ fr £10

Open all year

Last departure noon

An attractive site in a tree-lined, sheltered valley with a footpath to the village and owned by the garden centre on the opposite side of the A96. The site has fully serviced pitches and there is a camping area for 20 tents, all with water and electricity. 9 acre site. 76 touring pitches. 31 hardstandings. 10 seasonal pitches. Caravan pitches. Motorhome pitches. Tent pitches. 108 statics.

AA Pubs & Restaurants nearby: Gordon Arms Hotel, Fochabers 01343 820508

Leisure: 🏊🅰🎣🖵
Facilities: ⬤☉🅿♿⏱🆂📮♨📶 ♻ ❶
Services: 🔌🗑💧🅣⬇
Within 3 miles: ⬇🏌◎🆂♨

Notes: Dogs must be kept on leads. Jacuzzi & sauna.

LEISURE: 🖼 Indoor swimming pool 🏊 Outdoor swimming pool 🅰 Children's playground ⬇ Kid's club ⬤ Tennis court 🎣 Games room 🖵 Separate TV room ⬇ 9/18 hole golf course 🚣 Boats for hire 🎬 Cinema 🎵 Entertainment 🎣 Fishing ◎ Mini golf 🏄 Watersports 🏋 Gym 🆂 Sports field **Spa** ♨ Stables
FACILITIES: 🛁 Bath 🚿 Shower ☉ Electric shaver 🅿 Hairdryer ✳ Ice Pack Facility ♿ Disabled facilities ⏱ Public telephone 🆂 Shop on site or within 200yds 📮 Mobile shop (calls at least 5 days a week) 🍴 BBQ area 🅿 Picnic area 📶 Wi-fi 🖥 Internet access ♻ Recycling ❶ Tourist info 🐾 Dog exercise area

NORTH AYRSHIRE

SALTCOATS
Map 20 NS24

Places to visit

North Ayrshire Heritage Centre, SALTCOATS 01294 464174
www.north-ayrshire.gov.uk/museums

Kelburn Castle and Country Centre, LARGS
01475 568685 www.kelburnestate.com

Great for kids: Scottish Maritime Museum, IRVINE 01294 278283
www.scottishmaritimemuseum.org

80% *Sandylands*
(NS258412)

James Miller Crescent, Auchenharvie Park KA21 5JN
☎ **0871 664 9767**
e-mail: sandylands@park-resorts.com
web: www.park-resorts.com
dir: From Glasgow take M77 & A77 to Kilmarnock, A71 towards Irvine. Follow signs for Ardrossan. Take A78 follow Stevenston signs. Through Stevenston, past Auchenharvie Leisure Centre, 1st left follow signs to site on left

Open Apr-Oct

Last arrival mdnt Last departure 10.00hrs

A holiday centre with on-site recreational and entertainment facilities for all ages, including an indoor swimming pool. There is a links golf course nearby. With good transport links and easy access to the ferry terminal in Ardrossan, day trips to the Isle of Arran are possible. A new amenity block has been built for the 2012 season and provides touring customers with modern facilities. 55 acre site. 20 touring pitches. 20 hardstandings. Caravan pitches. Motorhome pitches. Tent pitches. 438 statics.

Leisure:
Facilities:
Services:
Within 3 miles:

PERTH & KINROSS

BLAIR ATHOLL
Map 23 NN86

Places to visit

Blair Castle, BLAIR ATHOLL 01796 481207
www.blair-castle.co.uk

Killiecrankie Visitor Centre, KILLIECRANKIE
0844 493 2194 www.nts.org.uk

PREMIER PARK

►►►►► **88% Blair Castle Caravan Park** *(NN874656)*

PH18 5SR
☎ **01796 481263**
e-mail: mail@blaircastlecaravanpark.co.uk
dir: From A9 junct with B8079 at Aldclune, then NE to Blair Atholl. Site on right after crossing bridge in village

* ⊕ £17.50-£20.50 ⊕ £17.50-£20.50
▲ £17.50-£20.50

Open Mar-Nov

Last arrival 21.30hrs Last departure noon

An attractive site set in impressive seclusion within the Atholl estate, surrounded by mature woodland and the River Tilt. Although a large park, the various groups of pitches are located throughout the extensive parkland, and each has its own sanitary block with all-cubicled facilities of a very high standard. There is a choice of grass pitches, hardstandings, or fully-serviced pitches. This park is particularly suitable for the larger type of motorhome. 32 acre site. 241 touring pitches. Caravan pitches. Motorhome pitches. Tent pitches. 107 statics.

AA Pubs & Restaurants nearby: Killiecrankie House Hotel, Killiecrankie 01796 473220

Leisure:
Facilities:
Services:
Within 3 miles:

Notes: Family park, no noise after 23.00hrs. Dogs must be kept on leads.

PREMIER PARK

►►►►► **81% River Tilt Caravan Park** *(NN875653)*

PH18 5TE
☎ **01796 481467**
e-mail: stuart@rivertilt.co.uk
dir: 7m N of Pitlochry on A9, take B8079 to Blair Atholl & site at rear of Tilt Hotel

⊕ fr £21 ⊕ fr £19 ▲ £10-£21

Open 16 Mar-12 Nov

Last arrival 21.00hrs Last departure noon

An attractive park with magnificent views of the surrounding mountains, idyllically set in hilly woodland country on the banks of the River Tilt, adjacent to the golf course. There is also a leisure complex with heated indoor swimming pool, sun lounge area, spa pool and multi-gym, all available for an extra charge; outdoors there is a short tennis court. The toilet facilities are very good. 2 acre site. 30 touring pitches. Caravan pitches. Motorhome pitches. Tent pitches. 69 statics.

AA Pubs & Restaurants nearby: Killiecrankie House Hotel, Killiecrankie 01796 473220

Leisure: Spa
Facilities:
Services:
Within 3 miles:

Notes: Sauna, solarium, steam room.

DUNKELD   Map 21 NO04

Places to visit

The Ell Shop & Little Houses, DUNKELD
0844 493 2192 www.nts.org.uk

Castle Menzies, WEEM 01887 820982
www.menzies.org

▶▶▶ **80% Inver Mill Farm Caravan Park** (NO015422)

Inver PH8 0JR
☎ 01350 727477
e-mail: invermill@talk21.com
dir: *A9 onto A822 then immediately right to Inver*

🚐 🚃 Å

Open end Mar-Oct

Last arrival 22.00hrs Last departure noon

A peaceful park on level former farmland, located on the banks of the River Braan and surrounded by mature trees and hills. The active resident owners keep the park in very good condition. 5 acre site. 65 touring pitches. Caravan pitches. Motorhome pitches. Tent pitches.

Facilities: 🏧 ⊙ ℱ ✳ ⟐ ℂ
Services: 🔌 🔲 🖉 🛒
Within 3 miles: ↨ ℘ 🛒 🛍
Notes: 🐾

KINLOCH RANNOCH   Map 23 NN65

▶ **74% *Kilvrecht Campsite*** (NN623567)

PH16 5QA
☎ 01350 727284
e-mail: tay.fd@forestry.gsi.gov.uk
dir: *3m along S shore of Loch Rannoch. Approach via unclassified road along Loch, with Forestry Commission signs*

🚐 🚃 Å

Open Apr-Oct

Last arrival 22.00hrs Last departure 10.00hrs

Set within a large forest clearing, approximately half mile from the road to Kinloch Rannoch which runs along the loch. This is a beautifully maintained site, with good clean facilities, for those who wish for a peaceful break. It also makes an ideal base for those who prefer the more active outdoor activities of hill walking (Schiehallion is within easy reach) or mountain biking; it is a great spot to observe the multitude of birds and wildlife in the area. Please note the site has no electricity. 17 acre site. 60 touring pitches. Caravan pitches. Motorhome pitches. Tent pitches.

AA Pubs & Restaurants nearby: Dunalistair Hotel, Kinloch Rannoch 01882 632323

Facilities: ⟐ 🅿 🛈
Within 3 miles: ⚓ ℘ 🛍
Notes: 🚭 No fires. Dogs must be kept on leads.

PITLOCHRY

Places to visit

Edradour Distillery, PITLOCHRY 01796 472095
www.edradour.co.uk

Great for kids: Scottish Hydro Electric Visitor Centre, Dam & Fish Pass, PITLOCHRY
01796 473152

LEISURE: 🏊 Indoor swimming pool   🏊 Outdoor swimming pool   🎢 Children's playground   👶 Kid's club   🎾 Tennis court   🎱 Games room   📺 Separate TV room   ⛳ 9/18 hole golf course   🚣 Boats for hire   🎬 Cinema   🎵 Entertainment   🎣 Fishing   🔵 Mini golf   🏄 Watersports   💪 Gym   ⚽ Sports field   **Spa**   ⛎ Stables
FACILITIES: 🛁 Bath   🚿 Shower   ⊙ Electric shaver   ℱ Hairdryer   ✳ Ice Pack Facility   ⟐ Disabled facilities   ℂ Public telephone   🛍 Shop on site or within 200yds   🛒 Mobile shop (calls at least 5 days a week)   🍖 BBQ area   🅿 Picnic area   📶 Wi-fi   💻 Internet access   ♻ Recycling   🛈 Tourist info   🐾 Dog exercise area

PITLOCHRY Map 23 NN95

AA CAMPSITE OF THE YEAR FOR SCOTLAND 2013

►►►► 88% Milton of Fonab Caravan Site *(NN945573)*

Bridge Rd PH16 5NA
☎ 01796 472882
e-mail: info@fonab.co.uk
dir: *0.5m S of town off A924*

* 🚙 £18-£23 🚐 £18-£23 ⛺ £18-£23

Open Apr-Oct

Last arrival 21.00hrs Last departure 13.00hrs

Set on the bank of the River Tummel on the outskirts of Pitlochry, with extensive views over countryside and hills. This family-owned site has excellent toilet facilities and large spacious pitches on hardstanding, or grass which is maintained to golf course standard. Pitlochry Festival Theatre is a short walk away and also plenty shops. This makes an ideal base to tour rural Perthshire. 15 acre site. 154 touring pitches. Caravan pitches. Motorhome pitches. Tent pitches. 34 statics. See also page 19.

AA Pubs & Restaurants nearby: Killiecrankie House Hotel, Killiecrankie 01796 473220

Facilities: 🛁 🚿 ⊙ 💨 ❄ ♿ ☎ 🏪 🐕 [Wi-fi] ♻ ℹ

Services: 🔌 🧺 🛢 🔥

Within 3 miles: ⛳ 🎣 🏌 ◎ 🏪 🧺

Notes: 💳 Couples & families only, no motor cycles. Free trout fishing.

►►►► 81% Faskally Caravan Park *(NN916603)*

PH16 5LA
☎ 01796 472007
e-mail: info@faskally.co.uk
dir: *1.5m N of Pitlochry on B8019*

* 🚙 £19.50-£21.50 🚐 £19.50-£21.50 ⛺ £19.50-£21.50

Open 15 Mar-Oct

Last arrival 23.00hrs Last departure 11.00hrs

A large park near Pitlochry, which is divided into smaller areas by mature trees and set within well-tended grounds. This family-owned site has two large amenity blocks and an entertainment complex with a heated swimming pool, bar, restaurant and indoor games area. There are numerous walks from the site and it is ideal for either a longer stay to explore the area or as a convenient stop over. A regular bus service is available at the site entrance. 27 acre site. 300 touring pitches. Caravan pitches. Motorhome pitches. Tent pitches. 130 statics.

AA Pubs & Restaurants nearby: Killiecrankie House Hotel, Killiecrankie 01796 473220

Leisure: 🏊 🛝 🎾 ♫ **Spa**

Facilities: 🚿 ⊙ 💨 ❄ ♿ ☎ 🏪 [Wi-fi] ♻

Services: 🔌 🧺 🍷 🛢 🔥 [T] 🍴 🍼

Within 3 miles: ⛳ 🎣 🏌 🏪 🧺 🐎

Notes: Dogs must be kept on leads.

see advert on opposite page

TUMMEL BRIDGE Map 23 NN75

80% Tummel Valley Holiday Park *(NN764592)*

PH16 5SA
☎ 0844 335 3756
e-mail: touringandcamping@parkdeanholidays.com
web: www.parkdeantouring.com
dir: *From Perth take A9 N to bypass Pitlochry. 3m after Pitlochry take B8019 signed Tummel Bridge. Site 11m on left*

* 🚙 £13.50-£37 🚐 £13.50-£37

Open Mar-Oct

Last arrival 21.00hrs Last departure 10.00hrs

A well-developed site amongst mature forest in an attractive valley, beside the famous bridge on the banks of the River Tummel. Play areas and the bar are sited alongside the river, and there is an indoor pool, children's clubs and live family entertainment. This is an ideal base in which to relax. Please note that this park does not accept tents or trailer tents. 55 acre site. 26 touring pitches. 28 hardstandings. Caravan pitches. Motorhome pitches. 169 statics.

AA Pubs & Restaurants nearby: Dunalistair Hotel, Kinloch Rannoch 01882 632323

Killiecrankie House Hotel, Killiecrankie 01796 473220

Leisure: 🏊 🛝 ✋ 🎾 ♫

Facilities: 🛁 🚿 ⊙ 💨 ❄ ♿ ☎ 🏪 🪑 [Wi-fi]

Services: 🔌 🧺 🍷 🛢 🍴 🍔

Within 3 miles: 🏌 ◎ 🏪 🧺

Notes: Sports courts, sauna, solarium, toddlers' pool, amusements, rod hire.

SCOTTISH BORDERS

EYEMOUTH
Map 21 NT96

Places to visit

Manderston, DUNS 01361 883450
www.manderston.co.uk

Great for kids: Eyemouth Museum, EYEMOUTH
018907 50678

 74% Eyemouth
(NT941646)

SILVER

Fort Rd TD14 5BE
☎ **0871 664 9740**
e-mail: eyemouth@park-resorts.com
web: www.park-resorts.com
dir: *From A1, approx 6m N of Berwick-upon-Tweed take A1107 to Eyemouth. On entering town, site signed. Right after petrol station, left at bottom of hill into Fort Rd*

Open Apr-Oct

Last arrival mdnt Last departure 10.00hrs

A cliff-top holiday park on the outskirts of the small fishing village of Eyemouth, within easy reach of Edinburgh and Newcastle. The site is handily placed for exploring the beautiful Scottish Borders, and the magnificent coastline and countryside of north Northumberland. 22 acre site. 17 touring pitches. 7 hardstandings. 17 seasonal pitches. Caravan pitches. Motorhome pitches. 276 statics.

Leisure: 🅰 🌡 🌞 🎱 🎵
Facilities: 🌳 🌂 🍳 👶 🚿 📶 🔲 ♻ 🛈
Services: 🚽 🔄 🍽 🍴 🛒
Within 3 miles: ✚ 🎣 🛒 📮
Notes: Dogs must be kept on leads.

KELSO

Places to visit

Kelso Abbey, KELSO 0131 668 8800
www.historic-scotland.gov.uk

Smailholm Tower, SMAILHOLM 01573 460365
www.historic-scotland.gov.uk

Great for kids: Floors Castle, KELSO
01573 223333 www.floorscastle.com

KELSO
Map 21 NT73

▶▶▶▶ **80% Springwood Caravan Park** *(NT720334)*

TD5 8LS
☎ **01573 224596**
e-mail: admin@springwood.biz
dir: *1m E of Kelso on A699, signed Newtown St Boswells*

🚐 🚙

Open 25 Mar-17 Oct

Last arrival 23.00hrs Last departure noon

Set in a secluded position on the banks of the tree-lined River Teviot, this well-maintained site enjoys a pleasant and spacious spot in which to relax. It offers a high standard of modern toilet facilities, which are mainly contained in cubicled units. Floors Castle and the historic town of Kelso are close by. 2 acre site. 20 touring pitches. 20 hardstandings. Caravan pitches. Motorhome pitches. 180 statics.

AA Pubs & Restaurants nearby: Roxburghe Hotel & Golf Course, Kelso 01573 450331

Leisure: 🅰 🎱
Facilities: 🌳 ⊙ 🍳 🚿 👶 🛗 🌂 ✈ ♻ 🛈
Services: 🚽 🔄 🛒
Within 3 miles: ✚ 🎣 🛒 📮 🛒 ⛵
Notes: Dogs must be kept on leads.

LAUDER
Map 21 NT54

Places to visit

Abbotsford, MELROSE 01896 752043
www.scottsabbotsford.co.uk

Harmony Garden, MELROSE 0844 493 2251
www.nts.org.uk

Great for kids: Thirlestane Castle, LAUDER
01578 722430 www.thirlestanecastle.co.uk

▶▶▶ **76% Thirlestane Castle Caravan & Camping Site** *(NT536473)*

Thirlestane Castle TD2 6RU
☎ **01578 718884 & 07976 231032**
e-mail: thirlestanepark@btconnect.com
dir: *Signed from A68 & A697, just S of Lauder*

* 🚐 £14-£17 🚙 £16-£17 ▲ £10-£17

Open Apr-1 Oct

Last arrival 20.30hrs Last departure noon

Located on the outskirts of Lauder, close to the A68 and within the grounds of Thirlestane Castle, this is an ideal site from which to explore the many attractions in the Scottish Borders. The amenity block is immaculately maintained and the pitches are behind the estate boundary wall to provide a secluded and peaceful location. There is a regular service bus near the site entrance. 5 acre site. 60 touring pitches. 22 hardstandings. 30 seasonal pitches. Caravan pitches. Motorhome pitches. Tent pitches. 27 statics.

AA Pubs & Restaurants nearby: Black Bull, Lauder 01578 722208

Facilities: 🌳 ⊙ 🍳 🚿 🛒 🔲 ♻ 🛈
Services: 🚽 🔄 🛒
Within 3 miles: ✚ 🎣 🛒 📮
Notes: 🐕 Dogs must be kept on leads.

PEEBLES
Map 21 NT24

Places to visit

Kailzie Gardens, PEEBLES 01721 720007
www.kailziegardens.com

Robert Smail's Printing Works, INNERLEITHEN
0844 493 2259 www.nts.org.uk

Great for kids: Culzean Castle & Country Park, CULZEAN CASTLE 0844 493 2149 www.nts.org.uk

▶▶▶▶ **79% Crossburn Caravan Park** *(NT248417)*

Edinburgh Rd EH45 8ED
☎ **01721 720501**
e-mail: enquiries@crossburncaravans.co.uk
web: www.crossburn-caravans.com
dir: *0.5m N of Peebles on A703*

* 🚐 £24-£26 🚙 £24-£26 ▲ £20-£24

Open Apr-Oct

LEISURE: 🏊 Indoor swimming pool 🏊 Outdoor swimming pool 🅰 Children's playground 👦 Kid's club 🎾 Tennis court 🎱 Games room 📺 Separate TV room 🏌 9/18 hole golf course ⛵ Boats for hire 🎬 Cinema 🎵 Entertainment 🎣 Fishing ⛳ Mini golf 🏄 Watersports 🏋 Gym 🏟 Sports field **Spa** ⛲ Stables
FACILITIES: 🛁 Bath 🚿 Shower ⊙ Electric shaver 🪮 Hairdryer ❄ Ice Pack Facility 👶 Disabled facilities 📞 Public telephone 🏪 Shop on site or within 200yds 🏪 Mobile shop (calls at least 5 days a week) 🍖 BBQ area 🌲 Picnic area 📶 Wi-fi 🔲 Internet access ♻ Recycling 🛈 Tourist info 🐕 Dog exercise area

Last arrival 21.00hrs Last departure 14.00hrs

A peaceful, family run park, on the edge of Peebles and within easy driving distance for Edinburgh and the Scottish Borders. The park is divided by well maintained landscaping and mature trees and has good views over the countryside. There is a regular bus service at the site entrance and Peebles has a wide range of shops and attractions. The facilities are maintained to a high standard. There is also a main caravan dealership on site and a large stock of spares and accessories are available. 6 acre site. 45 touring pitches. 15 hardstandings. Caravan pitches. Motorhome pitches. Tent pitches. 85 statics.

AA Pubs & Restaurants nearby: Cringletie House, Peebles 01721 725750

Renwicks at Macdonald Cardrona Hotel, Peebles 0844 879 9024

Leisure: ⚑ ◣

Facilities: ⛺ ⅌ ⊙ ⌚ & ⚓ ♻ ❶

Services: ⊡ ⓢ 🛢 ⊘ T ⚌ ⬇

Within 3 miles: ↧ ⌔ ⬆ ∪

Notes: Dogs must be kept on leads.

SOUTH AYRSHIRE

AYR — Map 20 NS32

 78% Craig Tara Holiday Park (NS300184) GOLD

KA7 4LB
☎ 0871 231 0866 & 01292 265141
e-mail: craigtara@haven.com
web: www.haven.com/craigtara
dir: Take A77 towards Stranraer, 2nd right after Bankfield rdbt. Follow signs for A719 & to park

🚐 🚃

Open mid Mar-end Oct (rs mid Mar-May & Sep-Oct some facilities may be limited)

Last arrival 20.00hrs Last departure 10.00hrs

A large, well-maintained holiday centre with on-site entertainment and sporting facilities to suit all ages. The touring area is set apart from the main complex at the entrance to the park, and campers can use all the facilities, including a water world, soft play areas, sports zone, show bars, and supermarket with in-house bakery. There is a bus service to Ayr. 213 acre site. 39 touring pitches. 39 hardstandings. Caravan pitches. Motorhome pitches. 1100 statics.

AA Pubs & Restaurants nearby: Fairfield House Hotel, Ayr 01292 267461

Western House Hotel, Ayr 0870 055 5510

Leisure: ⚓ ⚑ ⬇ ⊙ ♫

Facilities: ⅌ ⊙ & ⓒ 🛢 ⌐ WiFi ♻ ❶

Services: ⊡ ⓢ ⛽ 🛢 🍽 ⚌

Within 3 miles: ↧ ⊞ ⌔ ◎ 🛢 ⬆ ∪

Notes: Max 2 dogs per booking, certain dog breeds banned, no commercial vehicles, no bookings by persons under 21yrs unless a family booking. Access to beach from park.

see advert below

SERVICES: ⊡ Electric hook up ⓢ Launderette ⅌ Licensed bar 🛢 Calor Gas ⊘ Camping Gaz T Toilet fluid 🍽 Café/Restaurant ⬛ Fast Food/Takeaway ⚌ Battery charging 🛁 Baby care ⬇ Motorvan service point **ABBREVIATIONS:** BH/bank hols-bank holidays Etr-Easter Whit-Whitsun dep-departure fr-from hrs-hours m-mile mdnt-midnight rdbt-roundabout rs-restricted service wk-week wknd-weekend ⊗ No credit cards ⊗ no dogs See page 7 for details of the AA Camping Card Scheme

BARRHILL
Map 20 NX28

▶▶▶▶ 78% Barrhill Holiday Park
(NX216835)

KA26 0PZ
☎ 01465 821355
e-mail: barrhillholidaypark@gmail.com
dir: On A714 (Newton Stewart to Girvan road). 1m N of Barrhill

Open Mar-Jan

Last arrival 22.00hrs Last departure 10.00hrs

A small, friendly park in a tranquil rural location, screened from the A714 by trees. The park is terraced and well landscaped, and a high quality amenity block includes disabled facilities. A local bus to Girvan stops at the site entrance. 6 acre site. 30 touring pitches. 30 hardstandings. Caravan pitches. Motorhome pitches. Tent pitches. 42 statics.

Leisure: ⚑
Facilities: ⚑☉⚑✳⚑☉⚑⚑☺⚑
Services: ⚑⚑⚑⚑⚑⚑⚑
Within 3 miles: ⚑⚑
Notes: ⚑ No noise after 23.00hrs.

COYLTON
Map 20 NS41

81% Sundrum Castle Holiday Park (NS405208)

GOLD

KA6 5JH
☎ 0844 335 3756
e-mail:
touringandcamping@parkdeanholidays.com
web: www.parkdeantouring.com
dir: Just off A70, 4m E of Ayr near Coylton

* ⚑ £16-£40 ⚑ £16-£40 ⚑ £14-£31.50

Open Mar-Oct

Last arrival 21.00hrs Last departure 10.00hrs

A large family holiday park, in rolling countryside and just a 10-minute drive from the centre of Ayr, with plenty of on-site entertainment. Leisure facilities include an indoor swimming pool complex with flume, crazy golf, clubs for young children and teenagers. The touring pitch areas and amenity block have been appointed to a high standard. 30 acre site. 30 touring pitches. Caravan pitches. Motorhome pitches. Tent pitches. 247 statics.

AA Pubs & Restaurants nearby: Browne's @ Enterkine, Annbank 01292 520580

Leisure: ⚑⚑⚑⚑⚑⚑⚑
Facilities: ⚑☉⚑⚑☉⚑⚑
Services: ⚑⚑⚑⚑⚑⚑⚑
Within 3 miles: ⚑⚑⚑☉⚑⚑⚑
Notes: No cars by tents. Adventure play area, nature trail.

SOUTH LANARKSHIRE

ABINGTON
Map 21 NS92

Places to visit

Moat Park Heritage Centre,
BIGGAR 01899 221050
www.biggarmuseumtrust.co.uk

Gladstone Court Museum, BIGGAR
01899 221050 www.biggarmuseumtrust.co.uk

Great for kids: National Museum of Rural Life,
EAST KILBRIDE 0300 123 6789
www.nms.ac.uk/rural

▶▶▶ 77% Mount View Caravan Park
(NS935235)

ML12 6RW
☎ 01864 502808
e-mail: info@mountviewcaravanpark.co.uk
dir: M74 junct 13, A702 S into Abington. Left into Station Rd, over river & railway. Site on right

* ⚑ £14-£17 ⚑ £14-£17 ⚑ £8-£24

Open Mar-Oct

Last arrival 20.45hrs Last departure 11.30hrs

A delightfully maturing family park, surrounded by the Southern Uplands and handily located between Carlisle and Glasgow. It is an excellent stopover site for those travelling between Scotland and the south, and the West Coast Railway passes beside the park. 5.5 acre site. 50 touring pitches. 50 hardstandings. Caravan pitches. Motorhome pitches. Tent pitches. 20 statics.

Leisure: ⚑
Facilities: ⚑☉⚑⚑⚑
Services: ⚑⚑⚑
Within 3 miles: ⚑⚑⚑
Notes: Dogs must be kept on leads and walked off-site, 5mph speed limit. Emergency phone.

LEISURE: 🏊 Indoor swimming pool 🏊 Outdoor swimming pool ⚑ Children's playground 🏐 Kid's club 🎾 Tennis court 🎱 Games room 🖵 Separate TV room ⛳ 9/18 hole golf course 🚤 Boats for hire 🎬 Cinema 🎵 Entertainment 🎣 Fishing ⊙ Mini golf 🏄 Watersports 🏋 Gym 🏟 Sports field **Spa** ⚑ Stables
FACILITIES: 🛁 Bath 🚿 Shower ☉ Electric shaver ⚑ Hairdryer ✳ Ice Pack Facility ⚑ Disabled facilities ⚑ Public telephone 🅂 Shop on site or within 200yds 🚗 Mobile shop (calls at least 5 days a week) 🍖 BBQ area ⚑ Picnic area WiFi Wi-fi 🖳 Internet access ⚑ Recycling ⚑ Tourist info ⚑ Dog exercise area

STIRLING

ABERFOYLE — Map 20 NN50

Places to visit

Inchmahome Priory, PORT OF MENTEITH
01877 385294 www.historic-scotland.gov.uk

PREMIER PARK

▶▶▶▶▶ 82% **Trossachs Holiday Park** (NS544976)

FK8 3SA
☎ 01877 382614
e-mail: info@trossachsholidays.co.uk
web: www.trossachsholidays.co.uk
dir: Access on E side of A81, 1m S of junct A821 & 3m S of Aberfoyle

🚐 🚃 Å

Open Mar-Oct

Last arrival 21.00hrs Last departure noon

An attractively landscaped and peaceful park with outstanding views towards the hills, including the Munro, Ben Lomond. Set within the Loch Lomond National Park, boating, walking, cycling and beautiful drives over the Dukes Pass through the Trossachs are just some of the attractions within easy reach. Bikes can be hired from the reception and there is an internet café that sells home baking. There are lodges for hire. 40 acre site. 66 touring pitches. 46 hardstandings. Caravan pitches. Motorhome pitches. Tent pitches. 84 statics.

Trossachs Holiday Park

Leisure: 🅰 🎣 ▢
Facilities: 🌀 ⊙ 🅿 ※ 🕓 🖪 🚿 🛝 Wifi 💻
Services: 🔌 🖪 🛒 🅣 🍴 🔋
Within 3 miles: 🎣 🛶 ℘ 🎯 🛒 🎡 ♻
Notes: Groups by prior arrangement only.

see advert below

AUCHENBOWIE

Places to visit

Stirling Old Town Jail, STIRLING 01786 450050
www.oldtownjail.com

Stirling Smith Art Gallery & Museum, STIRLING 01786 471917
www.smithartgallery.demon.co.uk

Great for kids: Stirling Castle, STIRLING 01786 450000 www.stirlingcastle.gov.uk

AUCHENBOWIE — Map 21 NS78

▶▶▶ 66% *Auchenbowie Caravan & Camping Site* (NS795880)

FK7 8HE
☎ 01324 823999
dir: From M9 junct 9 or M80 follow A872/Denny signs. 0.5m, site signed

🚐 🚃 Å

Open Apr-Oct

Last departure noon

A pleasant little site in a rural location, with mainly level grassy pitches. The friendly warden creates a relaxed atmosphere, and given its position close to the junction of the M9 and M80, this is a handy stopover spot for tourers. 3.5 acre site. 60 touring pitches. Caravan pitches. Motorhome pitches. Tent pitches. 12 statics.

Leisure: 🅰 **Facilities:** 🌀 ⊙ 🅿 🕓 🛝 🟢
Services: 🔌 🛒 ⌀
Within 3 miles: 🎣 🎡 ℘ 🎯 🛒 ♻
Notes: Dogs must be kept on leads.

see advert on page 400

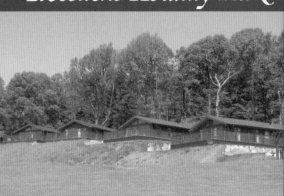

SERVICES: 🔌 Electric hook up 🖪 Launderette 🍺 Licensed bar 🔴 Calor Gas ⌀ Camping Gaz 🅣 Toilet fluid 🍴 Café/Restaurant 🍔 Fast Food/Takeaway 🔋 Battery charging 🚼 Baby care ⚡ Motorvan service point **ABBREVIATIONS:** BH/bank hols-bank holidays Etr-Easter Whit-Whitsun dep-departure fr-from hrs-hours m-mile mdnt-midnight rdbt-roundabout rs-restricted service wk-week wknd-weekend 🚫 No credit cards 🚫 no dogs   See page 7 for details of the AA Camping Card Scheme

BLAIRLOGIE — Map 21 NS89

Places to visit

The Regimental Museum of the Argyll & Sutherland Highlanders, STIRLING 01786 475165 www.argylls.co.uk

►►►► 86% Witches Craig Caravan & Camping Park

GOLD

(NS821968)

FK9 5PX
☎ 01786 474947
e-mail: info@witchescraig.co.uk
dir: *3m NE of Stirling on A91 (Hillfoots to St Andrews road)*

* ⛺ fr £20 🚐 fr £20 ▲ fr £16.50

Open Apr-Oct

Last arrival 20.00hrs Last departure noon

In an attractive setting with direct access to the lower slopes of the dramatic Ochil Hills, this is a well-maintained family-run park. It is in the centre of 'Braveheart' country, with easy access to historical sites and many popular attractions. 5 acre site. 60 touring pitches. 60 hardstandings. 6 seasonal pitches. Caravan pitches. Motorhome pitches. Tent pitches.

Leisure: 🅰

Facilities: 🖤⊙🅟✳🧺🚿🛒 WiFi ♻ 🛈

Services: 🔌🗑🍴🚿🅣📧🛗

Within 3 miles: 🦆🎏🏇◎🛒🍴🍺U

Notes: Dogs must be kept on leads. Food preparation area, baby bath & changing area.

CALLANDER — Map 20 NN60

Places to visit

Doune Castle, DOUNE 01786 841742 www.historic-scotland.gov.uk

►►►► 84% Gart Caravan Park

(NN643070)

The Gart FK17 8LE
☎ 01877 330002
e-mail: enquiries@theholidaypark.co.uk
dir: *1m E of Callander on A84*

* 🚐 £23-£25 🚐 £23-£25

Open Etr or Apr-15 Oct

Last arrival 22.00hrs Last departure 11.30hrs

A very well appointed and spacious parkland site within easy walking distance of the tourist and outdoor activity friendly town of Callander. The site is in an excellent location for touring the area; Loch Katrine where there are trips on the SS *Sir Walter Scott*, the Trossachs and the Rob Roy Centre are only a few of the many nearby attractions. Free fishing is available on the River Teith which runs along the edge of the site. The statics vans are in a separate area. Please note that tents are not accepted. 26 acre site. 128 touring pitches. Caravan pitches. Motorhome pitches. 66 statics.

AA Pubs & Restaurants nearby: Roman Camp Country House Hotel, Callander 01877 330003

Callander Meadows, Callander 01877 330181

Leisure: 🅰 🌳

Facilities: 🖤⊙✳🧺🕒🚿♻ 🛈

Services: 🔌🗑🍴🛗

Within 3 miles: 🦆🎏🏇🚣🍺🍴U

Notes: No commercial vehicles. Dogs must be kept on leads.

LUIB — Map 20 NN42

Places to visit

Balmacara Estate & Lochalsh Woodland Garden, BALMACARA 0844 493 2233 www.nts.org.uk

►►►► 73% Glendochart Holiday Park *(NN477278)*

FK20 8QT
☎ 01567 820637
e-mail: info@glendochart-caravanpark.co.uk
dir: *On A85 (Oban to Stirling road), midway between Killin & Crianlarich*

🚐 🚐 ▲

Open Mar-Nov

Last arrival 21.00hrs Last departure noon

A small site located on the A85 some eight miles from Killin, with boating and fishing available on Loch Tay. It is also convenient for Oban, Fort William and Loch Lomond. Hill walkers have direct access to numerous walks to suit all levels including the nearby Munro of Ben More. There is a regular bus service at the site entrance and nearby Crianlarich provides access to the West Highland Railway known as Britain's most scenic

LEISURE: 🏊 Indoor swimming pool 🏊 Outdoor swimming pool 🅰 Children's playground 🧒 Kid's club 🎾 Tennis court 🎱 Games room 📺 Separate TV room 🏌 9/18 hole golf course ⛵ Boats for hire 🎬 Cinema 🎵 Entertainment 🎣 Fishing ◎ Mini golf 🚣 Watersports 🏋 Gym ⊕ Sports field **Spa** U Stables
FACILITIES: 🛁 Bath 🚿 Shower ⊙ Electric shaver 🅟 Hairdryer ✳ Ice Pack Facility 🕒 Disabled facilities 🕙 Public telephone 🅢 Shop on site or within 200yds 🛒 Mobile shop (calls at least 5 days a week) 🍴 BBQ area 🌲 Picnic area WiFi Wi-fi 💻 Internet access ♻ Recycling 🛈 Tourist info 🐕 Dog exercise area

rail route, and also the West Highland Way. An ideal site as a stop over to the west coast or for a longer holiday. 15 acre site. 35 touring pitches. 28 hardstandings. Caravan pitches. Motorhome pitches. Tent pitches. 60 statics.

Facilities: ⚲ ⊙ 🄿 ✳ & ⌚ 🛋 🚐 ❼

Services: 🔌 🔄 🔒 🗑 🛒

Within 3 miles: ✎

Notes: Dogs must be kept on leads.

STIRLING

See Auchenbowie & Blairlogie

STRATHYRE   Map 20 NN51

▶▶▶ *74% Immervoulin Caravan and Camping Park* (NN560164)

FK18 8NJ
☎ **01877 384285**
dir: *Off A84, approx 1m S of Strathyre*

🚐 🚃 🛆

Open Mar-Oct

Last arrival 22.00hrs

A family run park on open meadowland beside the River Balvaig, where fishing, canoeing and other water sports can be enjoyed. A riverside walk leads to Loch Lubnaig, and the small village of Strathyre has various pubs offering food. Located on the A84, the site is ideally located for exploring this lovely area. The park has a modern well-appointed amenity block. 5 acre site. 50 touring pitches. Caravan pitches. Motorhome pitches. Tent pitches.

AA Pubs & Restaurants nearby: Creagan House, Strathyre 01877 384638

Roman Camp Country House Hotel, Callander 01877 330003

Callander Meadows, Callander 01877 330181

Facilities: ⚲ ⊙ 🄿 ✳ & ⌚ 🔟 🛋 ♻ ❼

Services: 🔌 🔄 🔒 🗑 Ⓣ 🛒 🚽

Within 3 miles: ✎ 🔟

Notes: No noise after 23.00hrs.

WEST DUNBARTONSHIRE

BALLOCH   Map 20 NS38

Places to visit

Finlaystone Country Estate, LANGBANK
01475 540505 www.finlaystone.co.uk

The Tall Ship at Glasgow Harbour, GLASGOW
0141 222 2513 www.thetallship.com

▶▶▶▶ **81% Lomond Woods Holiday Park** (NS383816)

Old Luss Rd G83 8QP
☎ **01389 755000**
e-mail: lomondwoods@holiday-parks.co.uk
web: www.holiday-parks.co.uk
dir: *From A82, 17m N of Glasgow, take A811 (Stirling to Balloch road). Left at 1st rdbt, follow holiday park signs, 150yds on left*

🚐 £20-£26 🚃 £20-£26

Open all year

Last arrival 20.00hrs Last departure noon

This site is ideally placed on the southern end of the UK's largest inland water, Loch Lomond which is also a National Park. This site has something to suit all tastes from the most energetic visitor to those who just wish to relax. There are loch cruises, boats to hire, plus retail outlets, superstores and eateries within easy walking distance. A drive or cycle ride along Loch Lomond provides breathtaking views. There are two large boat storage areas. Please note that this site does not accept tents. 13 acre site. 100 touring pitches. 100 hardstandings. Caravan pitches. Motorhome pitches. 35 statics.

AA Pubs & Restaurants nearby: Cameron Grill 01389 755565 & Martin Wishart Loch Lomond 01389 722504 - both at Cameron House Hotel, Balloch

Leisure: ⚙ 🎣 ⛶

Facilities: 🍼 ⚲ ⊙ 🄿 ✳ & 🔟 🛋 🚐 📶 ♻ ❼

Services: 🔌 🔄 🔒 🗑 Ⓣ 🛒 🚽

Within 3 miles: 🔻 ⚓ ✎ 🚵 🔟 🔟 ⛳

Notes: No jet skis. Dogs must be kept on leads.

WEST LOTHIAN

EAST CALDER   Map 21 NT06

Places to visit

Suntrap Garden, GOGAR 0131 339 7283
www.suntrap-garden.org.uk

Malleny Garden, BALERNO 0844 493 2123
www.nts.org.uk

▶▶▶▶ **82% Linwater Caravan Park** (NT104696)

West Clifton EH53 0HT
☎ **0131 333 3326**
e-mail: linwater@supanet.com
dir: *M9 junct 1, signed to B7030 or from Wilkieston on A71*

🚐 £16-£22 🚃 £16-£22 🛆 £14-£19

Open late Mar-late Oct

Last arrival 21.00hrs Last departure noon

A farmland park in a peaceful rural area within easy reach of Edinburgh. The very good facilities are housed in a Scandinavian-style building, and are well maintained by resident owners; they are genuinely caring hosts and nothing is too much trouble. There are 'timber tents' for hire and nearby are plenty of pleasant woodland walks. 5 acre site. 60 touring pitches. 18 hardstandings. Caravan pitches. Motorhome pitches. Tent pitches. 4 wooden pods.

AA Pubs & Restaurants nearby: Bridge Inn, Ratho 0131 333 1320

Leisure: ⚙

Facilities: ⚲ ⊙ 🄿 ✳ & ⌚ 🛋 📶 ♻ ❼

Services: 🔌 🔄 🔒 🗑 Ⓣ 🛒

Within 3 miles: 🔻 ✎ 🔟 🔄

Notes: No noise after 23.00hrs. Dogs must be kept on leads.

LINLITHGOW Map 21 NS97

Places to visit

Linlithgow Palace, LINLITHGOW 01506 842896
www.historic-scotland.gov.uk

House of The Binns, LINLITHGOW 0844 493 2127
www.nts.org.uk

Great for kids: Blackness Castle, LINLITHGOW
01506 834807 www.historic-scotland.gov.uk

►►►► 81% Beecraigs Caravan & Camping Site (NT006746)

**Beecraigs Country Park, The Visitor Centre
EH49 6PL**
☎ 01506 844516 & 848943
e-mail: mail@beecraigs.com
web: www.beecraigs.com
*dir: From Linlithgow on A803 or from Bathgate
on B792, follow signs to country park. Reception
within restaurant or visitor centre*

* ⊞ £17-£21 ⊞ £17-£21 ▲ £14-£21

Open all year (rs 25-26 Dec, 1-2 Jan no new
arrivals)

Last arrival 21.00hrs Last departure noon

A wildlife enthusiast's paradise where even the
timber facility buildings are in keeping with the
environment. Beecraigs is situated peacefully in
the open countryside of the Bathgate Hills. Small
bays with natural shading offer intimate pitches,
and there's a restaurant serving lunch and
evening meals. The smart toilet block on the main
park includes en suite facilities, and there is a
luxury toilet block for tenters. 6 acre site. 36
touring pitches. 36 hardstandings. Caravan
pitches. Motorhome pitches. Tent pitches.

AA Pubs & Restaurants nearby: The Chop & Ale
House, Champany Inn, Linlithgow 01506 834532

Beecraigs Caravan & Camping Site

Leisure: ⚠

Facilities: ⬅ ⋔ ☉ ☕ ✳ ⚕ ⚓ ⌂ ⊞ ♻ ❶

Services: 🔌 🔲 🚰 🔲 🍴

Within 3 miles: ↕ ⚲ ≥ 🔲 🔲 ∪

Notes: No cars by tents. No ball games near
caravans, no noise after 22.00hrs. Dogs must be
kept on leads. Children's bath, country park
facilities.

SCOTTISH ISLANDS

ISLE OF ARRAN

KILDONAN Map 20 NS02

Places to visit

Brodick Castle, Garden & Country Park, BRODICK
0844 493 2152 www.nts.org.uk

Isle of Arran Heritage Museum, BRODICK
01770 302636 www.arranmuseum.co.uk

AA CAMPING CARD SITE

NEW ►►►► 78% Sealshore Camping and Touring Site (NS024210)

KA27 8SE
☎ 01770 820320
e-mail: enquiries@campingarran.com
*dir: From ferry terminal in Brodick turn left, 12m,
through Lamlash & Whiting Bay. Left to Kildonan,
site on left*

* ⊞ £18.50-£19.50 ⊞ £18.50-£19.50 ▲ £14

Open Mar-Oct

Last arrival 21.00hrs Last departure noon

On the south coast of Arran and only 12 miles
from the ferry at Brodick, this is a peaceful,
family-run site with direct access to a sandy
beach. There are fabulous views across the water
to Pladda Island and Ailsa Craig, and an
abundance of wildlife. The site is suited for all
types of touring vehicles but caters very well for
non-motorised campers. The resident owner, also
a registered fisherman, sells fresh lobster and
crab, and on request will give fishing lessons on a
small, privately owned lochan. There is an
undercover BBQ, campers' kitchen and day room
with TV. A bus, which stops on request, travels
around the island. 3 acre site. 43 touring pitches.
8 hardstandings. Caravan pitches. Motorhome
pitches. Tent pitches.

Leisure: ✎ ⊡

Facilities: ⋔ ☉ ☕ ✳ ⚕ 🔲 ⌂ ⊞ ♻ ❶

Services: 🔌 🔲 ⬌ 🔲 ⬌ ⬆

Within 3 miles: ↕ ⚲ ◎ 🔲 🔲

Notes: ⊗ No cars by tents. No fires, no noise after
22.00hrs. Dogs must be kept on leads.

ISLE OF MULL

CRAIGNURE
Map 20 NM73

Places to visit

Mull & West Highland Narrow Gauge Railway, CRAIGNURE 01680 812494 (in season) www.mullrail.co.uk

►►►► 80% Shieling Holidays
(NM724369)

PA65 6AY
☎ **01680 812496 & 0131 556 0068**
e-mail: sales@shielingholidays.co.uk
web: www.shielingholidays.co.uk
dir: From ferry left onto A849 to Iona. 400mtrs left at church, follow site signs towards sea

* 🚐 fr £16.50 🚐 fr £16.50 ▲ fr £15.50

Open 8 Mar-4 Nov

Last arrival 22.00hrs Last departure noon

A lovely site on the water's edge with spectacular views, and less than one mile from the ferry landing. Hardstandings and service points are provided for motorhomes, and there are astro-turf pitches for tents. The park also offers unique, en suite cottage tents for hire and bunkhouse accommodation for families. There is also a wildlife trail on site. 7 acre site. 90 touring pitches. 30 hardstandings. Caravan pitches. Motorhome pitches. Tent pitches. 15 statics.

Leisure: 🎢 🎣 🖵
Facilities: 🚌 🌣 ⊙ 🅿 ⚘ ☇ 🚻 🕭 ⚲ 🌳 🛒 🛜 ♻ ❶
Services: 🔌 🗑 🛢 🚿 🚾 🔋 ⚒
Within 3 miles: 🚶 ✐ 🖪 🗑

Notes: Dogs must be kept on leads. Bikes available.

ISLE OF SKYE

EDINBANE
Map 22 NG35

►►►► 85% Skye Camping & Caravanning Club Site (NG345527)

Loch Greshornish, Borve, Arnisort IV51 9PS
☎ **01470 582230**
e-mail: skye.site@thefriendlyclub.co.uk
dir: Approx 12m from Portree on A850 (Dunvegan road). Site by loch shore

🚐 🚐 ▲

Open Apr-Oct

Last arrival 22.00hrs Last departure noon

Situated on the beautiful Isle of Skye, this campsite stands out for its stunning waterside location and glorious views, the generous pitch density, the overall range of facilities, and the impressive ongoing improvements under enthusiastic franchisee owners. The layout maximises the beauty of the scenery and genuine customer care is very evident with an excellent tourist information room and campers' shelter being just two examples. The amenities block has that definite 'wow' factor with smart, modern fittings, including excellent showers, a generously proportioned disabled room and a family bathroom. This is a green site that uses only green toilet fluids, which are available on site. There is an on-site shop, two camping pods to let, plus car hire is available on the site. Non-members are very welcome too. 7.5 acre site. 105 touring pitches. 36 hardstandings. Caravan pitches. Motorhome pitches. Tent pitches. 2 wooden pods.

AA Pubs & Restaurants nearby: Stein Inn, Stein 01470 592362

Loch Bay Seafood Restaurant, Stein 01470 592235

Three Chimneys Restaurant, Colbost 01470 511258

Facilities: 🌣 ⊙ 🅿 ⚘ ☇ 🕭 🖪 🚻 🕭 🛜 ♻ ❶
Services: 🔌 🗑 🛢 🚿 🚾 🔋 ⚒
Within 3 miles: ✐ 🖪 🗑

Notes: Dogs must be kept on leads.

STAFFIN
Map 22 NG46

►►► 77% Staffin Camping & Caravanning (NG492670)

IV51 9JX
☎ **01470 562213**
e-mail: staffincampsite@btinternet.com
dir: On A855, 16m N of Portree. Turn right before 40mph signs

🚐 🚐 ▲

Open Apr-Oct

Last arrival 22.00hrs Last departure 11.00hrs

A large sloping grassy site with level hardstandings for motorhomes and caravans, close to the village of Staffin. The toilet block is appointed to a very good standard and the park has a laundry. Mountain bikes are available for hire. 2.5 acre site. 50 touring pitches. 18 hardstandings. Caravan pitches. Motorhome pitches. Tent pitches.

AA Pubs & Restaurants nearby: The Glenview, Staffin 01470 562248

Flodigarry Country House Hotel, Staffin 01470 552203

Facilities: 🌣 ⊙ 🅿 ⚘ ☇ 🕭 🚻 🛜 ♻ ❶
Services: 🔌 🗑 🛢 🚿 🔋
Within 3 miles: 🚶 ✐ 🖪 🗑

Notes: ⊗ No music after 22.00hrs. Dogs must be kept on leads. Picnic tables, kitchen area, campers' bothy.

Wales

Snowdonia National Park, Llynau Mymbyr lake

Wales

Wales may be small but it certainly packs a punch.
Its scenery is a matchless mix of magnificent mountains,
rolling green hills and craggy coastlines. But it is not just
the landscape that makes such a strong impression -
Wales is renowned for its prominent position in the world
of culture and the arts.

This is a land of ancient myths and traditions, of male voice choirs, exceptionally gifted singers and leading actors of stage and screen. Richard Burton hailed from the valleys in south Wales, Anthony Hopkins originates from Port Talbot and Tom Jones, born Thomas Jones Woodward, comes from Pontypridd. One man who is inextricably linked to Wales is the poet Dylan Thomas. Born in Swansea in 1914, he lived at the Boat House in Laugharne, on the Taf and Tywi estuaries, overlooking Carmarthen Bay. He is buried in the local churchyard.

The valleys
East of here are the old industrial valleys of the Rhondda, once a byword for hardship and poverty and the grime of the local coal and iron workings, it has been transformed into now a very different place. Also vastly altered and improved by the passage of time are the great cities of Swansea and Cardiff, the latter symbolising New Labour's 'Cool Britannia' philosophy with its café culture and Docklands-style apartments.

▶

Going west and north

Tenby in west Wales still retains the charm of a typical seaside resort while the Pembrokeshire coast, overlooking Cardigan Bay, is one of the country's scenic treasures. Lower Fishguard has a connection with Dylan Thomas. In 1971, less than 20 years after his death, some of the theatre's greatest names – Richard Burton and Peter O'Toole among them – descended on this picturesque village to film *Under Milk Wood*, which Thomas originally wrote as a radio play.

Farther north is Harlech Castle, built by Edward I around 1283, with the peaks of Snowdonia in the distance. The formidable Caernarfon Castle, the setting for the investiture of the Prince of Wales in 1969, stands in the north-west corner of the country. Both castles are part of a string of massive strongholds built by Edward to establish a united Britain.

The mountains

With its many attractions and miles of natural beauty, the coast of Wales is an obvious draw for its many visitors but ultimately it is the country's spectacular hinterland that people make for. Snowdonia, with its towering summits and craggy peaks, is probably top of the list of adventure destinations. Heading back south reveals still more scenic landscapes – the remote country of the Welsh Borders and the stunning scenery of the dramatic Brecon Beacons among them.

Walking and Cycling

With mile upon mile of natural beauty, it's hardly surprising that Wales offers so much potential for walking. There's the Cistercian Way, which circles the country by incorporating its Cistercian abbeys; the Glyndwr's Way, named after the 15th-

● Offa's Dyke

century warrior statesman; and the Pembrokeshire Coast Path, which is a great way to explore the Pembrokeshire National Park.

Cycling is understandably very popular here but be prepared for some tough ascents and dramatic terrain. Try the Taff Trail, which runs north from Cardiff to Caerphilly and includes three castles en route; it's a fairly easy trail, quite flat and largely free of traffic.

For something completely different, cycle from Swansea to Mumbles, enjoying memorable views of the Gower Peninsula.

Festivals and Events

- May is the month for the Royal Welsh Smallholder & Garden Festival, held on the Royal Welsh Showground at Llanelwedd. The event features all manner of farming and horticultural activities.
- The August Bank Holiday weekend sees the Summer Harp Festival at the National Botanic Garden of Wales at Llanarthne in Carmarthenshire. There are concerts, talks and workshops.
- The Abergavenny Food Festival takes place in September with more than 80 events, including masterclasses, tutored tastings, talks and debates.

● Pentre Ifan on the Preseli Hills

ANGLESEY, ISLE OF

See Walk 14 in the Walks & Cycle Rides section at the end of the guide

DULAS — Map 14 SH48

PREMIER PARK

►►►►► 85% Tyddyn Isaf Caravan Park *(SH486873)*

Lligwy Bay LL70 9PQ
☎ 01248 410203 & 410667
e-mail: mail@tyddynisaf.co.uk
dir: *Take A5025 through Benllech to Moelfre rdbt, left towards Amlwch to Brynrefail. Turn right to Lligwy at phone box. Site 0.5m down lane on right*

🚐 🚗 Å

Open Mar-Oct (rs Mar-Jul & Sep-Oct bar & shop opening limited)

Last arrival 21.30hrs Last departure 11.00hrs

A beautifully situated, very spacious family park on rising ground adjacent to a sandy beach, with magnificent views overlooking Lligwy Bay. A private footpath leads directly to the beach and there is an excellent nature trail around the park. The site has very good toilet facilities, including a block with under-floor heating and excellent unisex privacy cubicles, a well-stocked shop, and café/bar serving meals, which are best enjoyed on the terrace with its magnificent coast and sea views. 16 acre site. 30 touring pitches. 50 hardstandings. 40 seasonal pitches. Caravan pitches. Motorhome pitches. Tent pitches. 56 statics.

AA Pubs & Restaurants nearby: The Ship Inn, Red Wharf Bay 01248 852568

Ye Olde Bulls Head Inn, Beaumaris 01248 810329

Bishopsgate House Hotel, Beaumaris 01248 810302

Leisure: 🏕 ☐
Facilities: 🍴 ☉ 🖤 ♬ ⚹ ⅙ ⓒ 🖫 🎏 📶 ♻ ❶
Services: 🔌 🖾 🛞 🖤 ♨ T 🍴 🎪 ♨ 🛢
Within 3 miles: ↕ 🚴 🖉 🖫 🖫 U

Notes: 🐾 No groups, loud music or open fires, maximum 3 units together. Dogs must be kept on leads. Baby changing unit, nature walk.

MARIAN-GLAS — Map 14 SH58

Places to visit

Bryn Celli Ddu Burial Chamber, BRYNCELLI DDU 01443 336000 www.cadw.wales.gov.uk

PREMIER PARK

►►►►► 93% Home Farm Caravan Park *(SH498850)*

LL73 8PH
☎ 01248 410614
e-mail: enq@homefarm-anglesey.co.uk
web: www.homefarm-anglesey.co.uk
dir: *On A5025, 2m N of Benllech. Site 300mtrs beyond church*

* 🚐 £19.50-£33.50 🚗 £19.50-£33.50 Å £15-£23

Open Apr-Oct

Last arrival 21.00hrs Last departure noon

A first-class park, run with passion and enthusiasm, set in an elevated and secluded position sheltered by trees, with good planting and landscaping. The peaceful rural setting affords views of farmland, the sea, and the mountains of Snowdonia. The modern toilet blocks are spotlessly clean and well maintained, and there are excellent play facilities for children both indoors and out. Improvements include a super visitors' parking area, a stunning water feature, a children's play area with top-notch equipment, and a smart reception and shop. The area is blessed with sandy beaches, and local pubs and shops cater for everyday needs. 12 acre site. 102 touring pitches. 65 hardstandings. Caravan pitches. Motorhome pitches. Tent pitches. 84 statics.

AA Pubs & Restaurants nearby: The Ship Inn, Red Wharf Bay 01248 852568

Ye Olde Bulls Head Inn, Beaumaris 01248 810329

Bishopsgate House Hotel, Beaumaris 01248 810302

Leisure: 🏕 🏊 ☺ 🎱 ☐
Facilities: 🛁 🍴 ☉ 🖤 ♬ ⚹ ⅙ ⓒ 🖫 🎏 📶
🖥 ♻ ❶
Services: 🔌 🖾 🛞 T 🎪 🛢
Within 3 miles: ↕ 🖉 🖫 🖫 U

Notes: No roller blades, skateboards or scooters. Indoor adventure playground.

PENTRAETH — Map 14 SH57

Places to visit

Bryn Celli Ddu Burial Chamber, BRYNCELLI DDU 01443 336000 www.cadw.wales.gov.uk

Plas Newydd, PLAS NEWYDD 01248 714795 www.nationaltrust.org.uk/main/plasnewydd

►►► 78% Rhos Caravan Park *(SH517794)*

Rhos Farm LL75 8DZ
☎ 07788 772268
web: www.rhoscaravanparkanglesey.co.uk
dir: *Site on A5025, 1m N of Pentraeth*

🚐 🚗 Å

Open Mar-Oct

Last arrival 22.00hrs Last departure 16.00hrs

A warm welcome awaits families at this spacious park on level, grassy ground with easy access to the main road to Amlwch. A 200-acre working farm that has two play areas and farm animals to keep children amused, with good beaches, pubs, restaurants and shops nearby. The two toilet blocks are kept to a good standard by enthusiastic owners who are constantly improving the facilities. The tent field re-opened in 2012. 15 acre site. 98 touring pitches. Caravan pitches. Motorhome pitches. Tent pitches. 66 statics.

AA Pubs & Restaurants nearby: The Ship Inn, Red Wharf Bay 01248 852568

Ye Olde Bulls Head Inn, Beaumaris 01248 810329

Bishopsgate House Hotel, Beaumaris 01248 810302

LEISURE: 🏊 Indoor swimming pool 🏊 Outdoor swimming pool 🎠 Children's playground 🎣 Kid's club 🎾 Tennis court 🎱 Games room ☐ Separate TV room
↕ 9/18 hole golf course ⛵ Boats for hire 🎬 Cinema 🎵 Entertainment 🎣 Fishing ◎ Mini golf 🏄 Watersports 🏋 Gym 🏅 Sports field Spa U Stables
FACILITIES: 🛁 Bath 🍴 Shower ☉ Electric shaver 🖤 Hairdryer ⚹ Ice Pack Facility ⅙ Disabled facilities ⓒ Public telephone 🖫 Shop on site or within 200yds
🖼 Mobile shop (calls at least 5 days a week) 🍴 BBQ area 🎏 Picnic area 📶 Wi-fi 🖥 Internet access ♻ Recycling ❶ Tourist info 🎏 Dog exercise area

Leisure: 🛝

Facilities: ♠☉☼⚲★❸

Services: 🔌🗑🧴🚿🔋

Within 3 miles: ⚓✈🏌🏄🎣🎬🏌↻

Notes: 🚫🐕

RHOS LLIGWY   Map 14 SH48

►►► 68% Ty'n Rhos Caravan Park

(SH495867)

Lligwy Bay, Moelfre LL72 8NL
☎ **01248 852417**
e-mail: robert@bodafonpark.co.uk
dir: *Take A5025 from Benllech to Moelfre rdbt, right to T-junct in Moelfre. Left, approx 2m, pass x-roads leading to beach, site 50mtrs on right*

* 🚐 £18-£25 �: £18-£25 ▲ £16-£25

Open Mar-Oct

Last arrival 21.00hrs Last departure noon

A family park close to the beautiful beach at Lligwy Bay, and cliff walks along the Heritage Coast. Historic Din Lligwy, and the shops at picturesque Moelfre are nearby. All the touring pitches have water, electric hook-up and TV connection. Please note that guests should register at Bodafon Caravan Park in Benllech where detailed directions will be given and pitches allocated. 10 acre site. 30 touring pitches. 4 hardstandings. 48 seasonal pitches. Caravan pitches. Motorhome pitches. Tent pitches. 80 statics. 20 bell tents/yurts.

AA Pubs & Restaurants nearby: The Ship Inn, Red Wharf Bay 01248 852568

Ye Olde Bulls Head Inn, Beaumaris 01248 810329

Bishopsgate House Hotel, Beaumaris 01248 810302

Facilities: ♠☉☼⚲🐕🛁Wi-Fi 🖥❸
Services: 🔌🗑🧴
Within 3 miles: ⚓✈🏄🎣🎬↻
Notes: No campfires, no noise after 23.00hrs. Dogs must be kept on leads.

RHOSNEIGR   Map 14 SH37

►►► 77% Ty Hen (SH327738)

Station Rd LL64 5QZ
☎ **01407 810331**
e-mail: info@tyhen.com
web: www.tyhen.com
dir: *From A55 junct 5 follow signs to Rhosneigr, at clock turn right. Entrance (red gate post) 50mtrs before Rhosneigr railway station*

* 🚐 £15-£20 �: £15-£20 ▲ £5-£10

Open mid Mar-Oct

Last arrival 21.00hrs Last departure noon

This site is in an attractive seaside location near a large fishing lake and riding stables. Surrounded by lovely countryside, this former working farm is close to RAF Valley, which is great for plane spotters, but expect some aircraft noise during the day. The friendly owners are always on hand. 7.5 acre site. 38 touring pitches. 5 hardstandings. 33 seasonal pitches. Caravan pitches. Motorhome pitches. Tent pitches. 42 statics.

AA Pubs & Restaurants nearby: Ye Olde Bulls Head Inn, Beaumaris 01248 810329

Bishopsgate House Hotel, Beaumaris 01248 810302

Leisure: ⚓🛝🎣🎵
Facilities: ♠☉🐕🛁🐕★Wi-Fi ♻❸
Services: 🔌🗑🛁🔋
Within 3 miles: ⚓🏄🎬🏌🎬
Notes: 1 motor vehicle per pitch, children must not be out after 22.00hrs. Dogs must be kept on leads. Fishing, family room, walks.

BRIDGEND

PORTHCAWL   Map 9 SS87

Places to visit

Newcastle, BRIDGEND 01443 336000
www.cadw.wales.gov.uk

Coity Castle, COITY 01443 336000
www.cadw.wales.gov.uk

►► 73% Brodawel Camping & Caravan Park (SS816789)

Moor Ln, Nottage CF36 3EJ
☎ **01656 783231**
e-mail: info@brodawelcamping.co.uk
dir: *M4 junct 37, A4229 towards Porthcawl. Site on right off A4229*

* 🚐 fr £13.50 �: fr £13.50 ▲ fr £13.50

Open Apr-Sep

Last arrival 19.00hrs Last departure 11.00hrs

A family run park catering mainly for families, on the edge of the village of Nottage. It is very convenient for Porthcawl and the Glamorgan Heritage Coast, each is within a five-minute drive. 4 acre site. 100 touring pitches. 4 hardstandings. 40 seasonal pitches. Caravan pitches. Motorhome pitches. Tent pitches.

AA Pubs & Restaurants nearby: Prince of Wales Inn, Kenfig 01656 740356

Leisure: 🛝🎣
Facilities: 🛁♠☉☼🐕🛁🖥🎬♻❸
Services: 🔌🗑🧴🚿T
Within 3 miles: ⚓✈🎣🏌🎬🏄🎬↻
Notes: Dogs must be kept on leads.

CARMARTHENSHIRE

HARFORD   Map 8 SN64

►►► 88% Springwater Lakes

(SN637430)

SA19 8DT
☎ **01558 650788**
dir: *4m E of Lampeter on A482, entrance well signed on right*

🚐🚚▲

Open Mar-Oct

Last arrival 20.00hrs Last departure 11.00hrs

In a rural setting overlooked by the Cambrian Mountains, this park is adjoined on each side by four spring-fed and well-stocked fishing lakes. All pitches (some beside one of the lakes) have hardstandings, electricity and TV hook-ups, and there is a small and very clean toilet block and a shop. 20 acre site. 30 touring pitches. 30 hardstandings. Caravan pitches. Motorhome pitches. Tent pitches.

Facilities: ♠☉🐕☼🛁🖥🎬★♻❸
Services: 🔌🧴🚿🔋
Within 3 miles: 🎬🏌↻
Notes: 🚫🐕 Children must be supervised around lakes, no cycling on site, no ball games. Dogs must be kept on leads. Bait & tackle shop.

LLANDOVERY — Map 9 SN73

Places to visit

Dolaucothi Gold Mines, PUMSAINT 01558 650177
www.nationaltrust.org.uk/
main/w-dolaucothigoldmines

PREMIER PARK

▶▶▶▶▶ 83% *Erwlon Caravan* Best of British
& Camping Park (SN776343)

Brecon Rd SA20 0RD
☎ 01550 721021 & 720332
e-mail: peter@erwlon.co.uk
dir: 0.5m E of Llandovery on A40

🚐 🚎 ▲

Open all year

Last arrival anytime Last departure noon

A long-established, family-run site set beside a brook in the Brecon Beacons foothills. The town of Llandovery and the hills overlooking the Towy Valley are a short walk away. The superb, Scandinavian-style facilities block has cubicled washrooms, family and disabled rooms and is an impressive feature. 8 acre site. 75 touring pitches. 15 hardstandings. Caravan pitches. Motorhome pitches. Tent pitches.

AA Pubs & Restaurants nearby: The Kings Head, Llandovery 01550 720393

Leisure: 🅰

Facilities: 🌰⊙🅿✳💧⊙🛉🚿🚾💧 ❸ ❼

Services: 🔋🔲🖉⌀🎀🔄

Within 3 miles: ⌀🖉🏧🛒🔵⟳

Notes: 😊 Quiet after 22.30hrs. Dogs must be kept on leads. Fishing, cycle storage & hire.

▶▶ 77% Llandovery Caravan Park
(SN762342)

Church Bank SA20 0DT
☎ 01550 721993 & 07970 650 606
e-mail: drovers.rfc@btinternet.com
dir: A40 from Carmarthen, over rail crossing, past junct with A483 (Builth Wells). Turn right for Llangadog, past church, 1st right signed Rugby Club & Camping

* 🚐 £12-£14 🚎 £12-£14 ▲ £10-£12

Open all year

Last arrival 20.00hrs Last departure 20.00hrs

A level, spacious and developing small site adjacent to the rugby club on the outskirts of Llandovery. Toilets facilities are adequate but plans continue to upgrade and improve the facilities. 8 acre site. 100 touring pitches. 32 hardstandings. Caravan pitches. Motorhome pitches. Tent pitches.

AA Pubs & Restaurants nearby: The Kings Head, Llandovery 01550 720393

Leisure: 🅰⚽🖵

Facilities: 🌰⊙🛉🚿🔄 ❼

Services: 🔋🖿🔒🛁

Within 3 miles: ⌀🖉🏧🛒🔵⟳

Notes: 😊 Dogs must be kept on leads.

LLANGADOG — Map 9 SN72

Places to visit

Dinefwr Park and Castle,
LLANDEILO 01558 823902
www.nationaltrust.org.uk/main/w-dinefwrpark

Carreg Cennen Castle, CARREG CENNEN CASTLE
01558 822291 www.cadw.wales.gov.uk

▶▶▶ 77% Abermarlais Caravan Park
(SN695298)

SA19 9NG
☎ 01550 777868 & 777797
dir: On A40 midway between Llandovery & Llandeilo, 1.5m NW of Llangadog

🚐 🚎 ▲

Open 15 Mar-15 Nov (rs Mar & Nov 1 toilet block, water point no hot water)

Last arrival 23.00hrs Last departure noon

An attractive, well-run site with a welcoming atmosphere. This part-level, part-sloping park is in a wooded valley on the edge of the Brecon Beacons National Park, beside the River Marlais. 17 acre site. 88 touring pitches. 2 hardstandings. Caravan pitches. Motorhome pitches. Tent pitches.

AA Pubs & Restaurants nearby: The Red Lion, Llangadog 01550 777357

Leisure: 🅰

Facilities: 🌰⊙✳💧⊙🛒🛉 ❼

Services: 🔋🔒🖉🇹🛁

Within 3 miles: 🖉🏧🛒🔵⟳

Notes: No open fires, quiet from 23.00hrs-08.00hrs. Dogs must be kept on leads. Volleyball, badminton court, softball tennis net.

LLANWRDA

See Harford

NEWCASTLE EMLYN — Map 8 SN34

Places to visit

Cilgerran Castle, CILGERRAN 01239 621339
www.cadw.wales.gov.uk

Castell Henllys Iron Age Fort, CRYMYCH
01239 891319 www.castellhenllys.com

Great for kids: Felinwynt Rainforest Centre,
FELINWYNT 01239 810882
www.butterflycentre.co.uk

AA CAMPING CARD SITE

PREMIER PARK

▶▶▶▶▶ 85% Cenarth Falls
Holiday Park (SN265421)

Cenarth SA38 9JS
☎ 01239 710345
e-mail: enquiries@cenarth-holipark.co.uk
dir: Off A484 on outskirts of Cenarth towards Cardigan

🚐 £17-£27 🚎 £17-£27 ▲ £17-£27

Open Mar-Nov (rs Off peak bar & meals restricted to wknds only)

Last arrival 20.00hrs Last departure 11.00hrs

A high quality park with excellent facilities, close to the village of Cenarth where the River Teifi (famous for its salmon and sea trout) cascades through the Cenarth Falls Gorge. A well-landscaped park with an indoor heated swimming pool and fitness suite, and a restaurant and bar. 2 acre site. 30 touring pitches. 30 hardstandings. Caravan pitches. Motorhome pitches. Tent pitches. 89 statics.

AA Pubs & Restaurants nearby: Nags Head Inn, Abercych 01239 841200

Webley Waterfront Inn & Hotel, St Dogmaels 01239 612085

Leisure: ♨ ⚲ ⚡ 🏔 🎣 🎵

Facilities: 🌂 ⊙ 🥖 ☀ ♿ 🕒 WiFi ♻ 🛈

Services: 🔌 🗑 🍽 🔋 ⊘ 🍴 🔋 ⚡

Within 3 miles: 🎯 ✎ 🐾 🛒 🎣

Notes: No skateboards. Dogs must be kept on leads. Pool table, health & leisure complex.

AA CAMPING CARD SITE

►►► 85% Argoed Meadow Caravan and Camping Site *(SN268415)*

Argoed Farm SA38 9JL
☎ **01239 710690**
dir: From Newcastle Emlyn on A484 towards Cenarth, take B4332. Site 300yds on right

🚐 🚏 ⛺

Open all year

Last arrival anytime Last departure noon

Pleasant open meadowland on the banks of the River Teifi, very close to Cenarth Falls gorge, this site has a modern toilet block which adds to the general appeal of this mainly adults-only park. 3 acre site. 30 touring pitches. 5 hardstandings. Caravan pitches. Motorhome pitches. Tent pitches. 5 statics.

AA Pubs & Restaurants nearby: Nags Head Inn, Abercych 01239 841200

Webley Waterfront Inn & Hotel, St Dogmaels 01239 612085

Facilities: 🌂 ⊙ 🥖 ☀ ♿ 🕒 🛁 🔥 ♻ 🛈

Services: 🔌 🗑 🔋 ⊘ 🔋 🐾

Within 3 miles: 🎯 ✎ 🛒 🎣 ∪

Notes: ⊘ No bikes or skateboards. Dogs must be kept on leads.

►►► 82% Moelfryn Caravan & Camping Park *(SN321370)*

Ty-Cefn, Pant-y-Bwlch SA38 9JE
☎ **01559 371231**
e-mail: moelfryn@moelfryncaravanpark.co.uk
dir: A484 from Carmarthen towards Cynwyl Elfed. Pass Blue Bell Inn on right, 200yds take left fork onto B4333 towards Hermon. In 7m follow brown sign on left. Turn left, site on right

* 🚐 fr £12.50 🚏 fr £12.50 ⛺ fr £11

Open Mar-10 Jan

Last arrival 22.00hrs Last departure noon

A small, beautifully maintained, family-run park in a glorious elevated location overlooking the valley of the River Teifi. Pitches are level and spacious, and well screened by hedging and mature trees. Facilities are spotlessly clean and tidy, and the playing field is well away from the touring area. 3 acre site. 25 touring pitches. 16 hardstandings. 12 seasonal pitches. Caravan pitches. Motorhome pitches. Tent pitches.

AA Pubs & Restaurants nearby: Nags Head Inn, Abercych 01239 841200

Webley Waterfront Inn & Hotel, St Dogmaels 01239 612085

Leisure: 🏔

Facilities: 🌂 ⊙ 🥖 ☀ 🛁 WiFi ♻ 🛈

Services: 🔌 🗑 🔋 ⊘ 🔋

Within 3 miles: 🎯 🛒 🎯 ✎ 🛒 🎣 🎣 ∪

Notes: Games to be played in designated area only. Dogs must be kept on leads. Caravan storage.

►►► 78% Afon Teifi Caravan & Camping Park *(SN338405)*

Pentrecagal SA38 9HT
☎ **01559 370532**
e-mail: afonteifi@btinternet.com
dir: Signed from A484, 2m E of Newcastle Emlyn

* 🚐 £18-£20 🚏 £18-£20 ⛺ £10-£20

Open Apr-Oct

Last arrival 23.00hrs

Set on the banks of the River Teifi, a famous salmon and sea trout river, this park is secluded with good views. Family owned and run, and only two miles from the market town of Newcastle Emlyn. 6 acre site. 110 touring pitches. 22 hardstandings. 25 seasonal pitches. Caravan pitches. Motorhome pitches. Tent pitches. 15 statics.

AA Pubs & Restaurants nearby: Nags Head Inn, Abercych 01239 841200

Webley Waterfront Inn & Hotel, St Dogmaels 01239 612085

Leisure: 🏔 ⚽ 🎣

Facilities: 🚿 🌂 ⊙ 🥖 ☀ ♿ 🕒 🛁 🔥 🔨 ♻ 🛈

Services: 🔌 🗑 🔋 ⊘ T 🔋

Within 3 miles: 🎯 ✎ 🛒 🎯 🎣 ∪

Notes: ⊘ Dogs must be kept on leads. 15 acres of woodland, fields & walks.

CEREDIGION

ABERAERON
Map 8 SN46

Places to visit

Llanerchaeron, ABERAERON 01545 570200
www.nationaltrust.org.uk

►►► 88% Aeron Coast Caravan Park

(SN460631)

North Rd SA46 0JF
☎ 01545 570349

e-mail: enquiries@aeroncoast.co.uk
web: www.aeroncoast.co.uk
dir: *On A487 (coast road) on N edge of Aberaeron, signed. Filling station at entrance*

🚐 £17-£27 🚍 £17-£27 ▲ £17-£27

Open Mar-Oct

Last arrival 23.00hrs Last departure 11.00hrs

A well-managed family holiday park on the edge of the attractive resort of Aberaeron, with direct access to the beach. The spacious pitches are all level. On-site facilities include an extensive outdoor pool complex, a multi-activity outdoor sports area, an indoor children's play area, a small lounge bar which serves food, a games room and an entertainment suite. 22 acre site. 100 touring pitches. 30 hardstandings. Caravan pitches. Motorhome pitches. Tent pitches. 200 statics.

AA Pubs & Restaurants nearby: Harbourmaster, Aberaeron 01545 570755

Ty Mawr Mansion, Aberaeron 01570 470033

Leisure: 🌊♨🏊🎣🎱♩
Facilities: 🛁⊙☂✳☕♿⊙🔗🚻❄️
Services: 🚐🔌💷🔨🚽🍽🚮🛒🚽
Within 3 miles: 🎣🚣💷💷○

Notes: Families only, no motorcycles. Dogs must be kept on leads.

ABERYSTWYTH
Map 8 SN58

Places to visit

The National Library of Wales, ABERYSTWYTH
01970 632800 www.llgc.org.uk

►►► 82% Ocean View Caravan Park

(SN592842)

North Beach, Clarach Bay SY23 3DT
☎ 01970 828425 & 623361

e-mail: enquiries@oceanviewholidays.com
dir: *Exit A487 in Bow Street. Straight on at next x-roads. Site 2nd on right*

* 🚐 £17.50-£22 🚍 ▲

Open Mar-Oct

Last arrival 20.00hrs Last departure noon

This site is in a sheltered valley on gently sloping ground, with wonderful views of both the sea and the countryside. The beach of Clarach Bay is just 200 yards away, and this welcoming park is ideal for all the family. There is a children's football field and dog walking area. Campers may use the pool, gym, restaurant and bar at Clarach Bay which is within walking distance of the site. 9 acre site. 24 touring pitches. 15 hardstandings.

Caravan pitches. Motorhome pitches. Tent pitches. 56 statics.

Leisure: ♨
Facilities: 🛁⊙☂✳🔗🚻♻️❄️
Services: 🚐🔌🔨🚻
Within 3 miles: 🎣🏇🎣◎🚣💷💷○

Notes: Dogs must be kept on leads.

BORTH
Map 14 SN69

Places to visit

The National Library of Wales, ABERYSTWYTH
01970 632800 www.llgc.org.uk

74% *Brynowen Holiday Park* (SN608893)

SY24 5LS
☎ 01970 871366

e-mail: brynowen@park-resorts.com
web: www.park-resorts.com
dir: *Signed from B4353, S of Borth*

🚐 🚍

Open Apr-Oct

Last arrival mdnt Last departure 10.00hrs

Enjoying spectacular views across Cardigan Bay and the Cambrian Mountains, a small touring park in a large and well-equipped holiday centre. The well-run park offers a wide range of organised activities and entertainment for all the family from morning until late in the evening. A long sandy beach is a few minutes'

LEISURE: 🏊 Indoor swimming pool 🌊 Outdoor swimming pool 🎠 Children's playground 🧸 Kid's club ♨ Tennis court 🎱 Games room 🖵 Separate TV room
🏌 9/18 hole golf course 🚣 Boats for hire 🎬 Cinema ♩ Entertainment 🎣 Fishing ◎ Mini golf 🏄 Watersports 🏋 Gym ⊙ Sports field **Spa** ∪ Stables
FACILITIES: 🛁 Bath 🚿 Shower ⊙ Electric shaver ☂ Hairdryer ✳ Ice Pack Facility ♿ Disabled facilities ☎ Public telephone 🛒 Shop on site or within 200yds
🏪 Mobile shop (calls at least 5 days a week) 🍖 BBQ area 🎍 Picnic area � Wi-fi ■ Internet access ♻️ Recycling 🛈 Tourist info 🐕 Dog exercise area

drive away. 52 acre site. 16 touring pitches. 16 hardstandings. 4 seasonal pitches. Caravan pitches. Motorhome pitches. 480 statics.

Leisure: 🏊🎱🎣🎿⚽🎯🎵

Facilities: 🌳⊙♿🛁🚻⬆️🚿WiFi ▆ ♻️

Services: 🔌🗑🍺🍴🍽🔋

Within 3 miles: ⚓🐎🗑

Notes: No cars by caravans. Dogs must be kept on leads. Mini ten-pin bowling.

LLANON
Map 8 SN56

Places to visit

The National Library of Wales, ABERYSTWYTH 01970 632800 www.llgc.org.uk

AA CAMPING CARD SITE

►►► 75% Woodlands Caravan Park
(SN509668)

SY23 5LX
☎ 01974 202342 & 202454

e-mail: info@woodlandsholidayparkllanon.co.uk
dir: *Between Aberystwyth & Aberaeron (S of Llanon) follow brown camping sign onto unclassified road towards coast. Site 280yds right*

🚐 £15-£20 🚍 £15-£20 ⛺ £15-£20

Open Mar-Oct

Last arrival 21.30hrs Last departure noon

A well maintained, mainly grass site surrounded by mature trees and shrubs near woods and meadowland, adjacent to the sea and a stony beach. The park is half a mile from the village. 4 acre site. 40 touring pitches. 10 hardstandings. Caravan pitches. Motorhome pitches. Tent pitches. 59 statics.

AA Pubs & Restaurants nearby: Harbourmaster, Aberaeron 01545 570755

Ty Mawr Mansion, Aberaeron 01570 470033

Facilities: 🌳⊙🅿️♻️ ❶

Services: 🔌🗑🍺🗑🧴T🔋

Within 3 miles: ⚓🐎◎🗑🗑

Notes: Dogs must be kept on leads.

NEW QUAY
Map 8 SN35

Places to visit

Llanerchaeron, ABERAERON 01545 570200 www.nationaltrust.org.uk

hh ⓊU NEW Quay West Holiday Park
(SN397591)

SA45 9SE
☎ 01545 560477

e-mail: quaywest@haven.com
web: www.haven.com/quaywest
dir: *From Cardigan on A487 left onto A486 into New Quay. Or from Aberystwyth on A487 right onto B4342 into New Quay*

Open Mar-Oct

Quay West Holiday Park enjoys a stunning clifftop position overlooking picturesque New Quay and Cardigan Bay. It's an easy walk to a glorious sandy beach and the all-action on-site activities include heated swimming pools, SplashZone, football, archery and fencing (with professional tuition). New for 2012 - the Aqua Bar and terrace. There are a good range of holiday caravans and apartments. At the time of going to press the quality rating for this site had not been confirmed. For up-to-date information please see the AA website: theAA.com.

Change over day: Mon, Fri, Sat **Arrival & departure times:** Please contact the site

Children 👶 Cots **Dogs** Max 2 on leads No dangerous dogs (see page 12)

Statics 125 Sleeps 6-8 Bedrms 2-3 Bathrms 1-2 Toilets 1-2 Freezer TV Sky/FTV Elec included Gas included Grass area Parking

Leisure: 🏊🏖🎣🎿🅰️

AA Pubs & Restaurants nearby: The Crown Inn & Restaurant, Llwyndafydd 01545 560396

The Harbourmaster, Aberaeron 01545 570755

Ty Mawr Mansion, Aberaeron 01570 470033

see advert on opposite page

CONWY

BETWS-YN-RHOS
Map 14 SH97

Places to visit

Denbigh Castle, DENBIGH 01745 813385 www.cadw.wales.gov.uk

AA CAMPING CARD SITE

►►►► 80% Hunters Hamlet Caravan Park
(SH928736)

Sirior Goch Farm LL22 8PL
☎ 01745 832237 & 07721 552106

e-mail: huntershamlet@aol.com
web: www.huntershamlet.co.uk
dir: *From A55 W'bound, A547 junct 24 into Abergele. At 2nd lights turn left by George & Dragon pub, onto A548. 2.75m right at x-rds onto B5381. Site 0.5m on left*

* 🚐 £18-£26 🚍 £18-£26

Open Mar-Oct

Last arrival 22.00hrs Last departure noon

A warm welcome is assured at this long established family run working farm park next to owners' Georgian farmhouse. Well spaced pitches, including 15 with water, electric and TV hook-up, are within two attractive hedge-screened grassy paddocks. The well maintained amenities block, includes unisex bathrooms. Please note that this site does not accept tents. 2 acre site. 30 touring pitches. 30 hardstandings. Caravan pitches. Motorhome pitches.

AA Pubs & Restaurants nearby: Wheatsheaf Inn, Betws-Yn-Rhos 01492 680218

Leisure: 🅰️

Facilities: 🚿🌳⊙🅿️❄️♿🚻WiFi ♻️ ❶

Services: 🔌🗑📧🔋

Within 3 miles: ⚓🐎🗑

Notes: No football, dogs must be kept on leads and not be left unattended. Baby bath & changing facilities.

BETWS-YN-RHOS *continued*

►►►► 80% Plas Farm Caravan Park *(SH897744)*

LL22 8AU

☎ 01492 680254 & 07831 482176

e-mail: info@plasfarmcaravanpark.co.uk

dir: *A547 Abergele, right into Rhyd y Foel Rd, 3m, left signed B5381, 1st farm on right*

🚐 £17.50-£27.50 🚐 £17.50-£27.50 ▲ £10-£25

Open Mar-Oct

Last departure 11.00hrs

A quiet caravan park on a working farm, surrounded by rolling countryside and farmland. This constantly improving park features hardstanding pitches, 45 of which are fully serviced with electric, water supply and TV hook up. New for the 2012 season is a laundry and campers' kitchen with microwave, kettles and toasters. There's a secluded tenting field, conveniently placed for the amenities blocks. The park is close to Bodnant Gardens and glorious beaches. 10 acre site. 54 touring pitches. 54 hardstandings. Caravan pitches. Motorhome pitches. Tent pitches.

AA Pubs & Restaurants nearby: Wheatsheaf Inn, Betws-Yn-Rhos 01492 680218

Leisure: ⚠

Facilities: ⬧☉☂⚒&⚒☉⚧⚒ WiFi ♻ ❼

Services: ⚡⚒❏T⚒⚒⚒⚒

Within 3 miles: ⚒☐⚒⚒⚒

Notes: Quiet after 23.00hrs, no campfires. Dogs must be kept on leads. Dog kennels available, woodland walk.

►►► 78% Peniarth Bach Farm *(SH926737)*

Roadside LL22 8PL

☎ 07545 572744

e-mail: geoff-wilson@btinternet.com

dir: *A55 junct 25, left into Abergele. Left at lights onto B5381 towards Llanfairth. Right after 3m signed Betws-yn-Rhos. Site signed on right*

🚐 🚐 ▲

Open Mar-Oct

Last arrival flexible Last departure 11.00hrs

Opened just a couple of year's ago and part of a working farm which also offers quality stone holiday cottages for hire. Most pitches are hardstanding, with electric hook-up and water supply, and the smart purpose-built amenities block provides modern and efficient facilities. 40 acre site. 38 touring pitches. 15 hardstandings. Caravan pitches. Motorhome pitches. Tent pitches.

AA Pubs & Restaurants nearby: Wheatsheaf Inn, Betws-Yn-Rhos 01492 680218

Hawk & Buckle Inn, Llannefydd 01745 540249

Kinmel Arms, Abergele 01745 832207

Facilities: ⬧☉☂⚒&⚒⚒⚒ WiFi ♻ ❼

Services: ⚡⚒T⚒⚒

Within 3 miles: ⚒⚒☐⚒☉⚒⚒⚒⚒

Notes: ⊘ No noise after mdnt. Dogs must be kept on leads. Family room.

LLANDDULAS Map 14 SH97

PREMIER PARK

►►►►► 83% Bron-Y-Wendon Caravan Park *(SH903785)*

Wern Rd LL22 8HG

☎ 01492 512903

e-mail: stay@northwales-holidays.co.uk

dir: *Take A55 W. Turn right at sign for Llanddulas A547 junct 23, then sharp right. 200yds, under A55 bridge. Park on left*

* 🚐 £20-£24 🚐 £20-£24

Open all year

Last arrival anytime Last departure 11.00hrs

A top quality site in a stunning location, with panoramic sea views from every pitch and excellent purpose-built toilet facilities including heated shower blocks. Pitch density is excellent, offering a high degree of privacy, and the grounds are beautifully landscaped and immaculately maintained. Staff are helpful and friendly, and everything from landscaping to maintenance has a stamp of excellence. An ideal seaside base for touring Snowdonia and visiting Colwyn Bay, Llandudno and Conwy. 8 acre site. 130 touring pitches. 85 hardstandings. Caravan pitches. Motorhome pitches.

AA Pubs & Restaurants nearby: Pen-y-Bryn, Colwyn Bay 01492 533360

Leisure: 🔍

Facilities: ⬧☉☂⚒&☉⚒⚒ WiFi ▦ ♻ ❼

Services: ⚡⚒🔒⚒⚒

Within 3 miles: ⚒⚒⚒⚒☉⚒⚒

Notes: Dogs must be kept on leads.

LLANRWST
Map 14 SH86

PREMIER PARK

▶▶▶▶▶ 85% Bron Derw Touring
Caravan Park (SH798628)

LL26 0YT ☎ 01492 640494
e-mail: bronderw@aol.com
web: www.bronderw-wales.co.uk
dir: A55 onto A470 for Betws-y-Coed & Llanrwst.
In Llanrwst left into Parry Rd signed Llanddoged.
Left at T-junct, site signed at 1st farm entrance
on right

🚐 £19-£21 🚐 £19-£21

Open Mar-Oct

Last arrival 22.00hrs Last departure 11.00hrs

Surrounded by hills and beautifully landscaped
from what was once a dairy farm, Bron Derw has
been built to a very high standard and is fully
matured, with stunning flora and fauna displays.
All pitches are fully serviced, and there is a
heated, stone-built toilet block with excellent and
immaculately maintained facilities. The Parc
Derwen adults-only field has 28 fully serviced
pitches and its own designated amenities block.
CCTV security cover the whole park. 4.5 acre site.
48 touring pitches. 48 hardstandings. 20 seasonal
pitches. Caravan pitches. Motorhome pitches.

AA Pubs & Restaurants nearby: Ty Gwyn Inn,
Betws-Y-Coed 01690 710383

Facilities: 🐾⊙🅿🔥🌡🔵🕂🐕♻ 🛈

Services: 🔌🛢🍼↯⚓ Within 3 miles: 📎🔒🛒

Notes: Children must be supervised, no bikes,
scooters or skateboards. Dogs must be on leads.

▶▶▶▶ 81% Bodnant Caravan Park
(SH805609)

Nebo Rd LL26 0SD ☎ 01492 640248
e-mail: ermin@bodnant-caravan-park.co.uk
dir: S in Llanrwst, at lights exit A470 opposite
Birmingham garage onto B5427 signed Nebo. Site
300yds on right, opposite leisure centre

🚐 £18-£19.50 🚐 £18-£19.50 ⛺ £14-£17

Open Mar-end Oct

Last arrival 21.00hrs Last departure 11.00hrs

This well maintained and stunningly attractive
park is filled with flower beds, and the landscape
includes shrubberies and trees. The statics are
unobtrusively sited and the quality, spotlessly
clean toilet blocks have fully serviced private
cubicles. All caravan pitches are multi-service,
and the tent pitches serviced. There is a separate
playing field and rally field, and there are lots of
farm animals on the park to keep children
entertained, and Victorian farming implements
are on display around the touring fields. 5 acre
site. 54 touring pitches. 20 hardstandings.
Caravan pitches. Motorhome pitches. Tent pitches.
2 statics.

AA Pubs & Restaurants nearby: Ty Gwyn Inn,
Betws-Y-Coed 01690 710383

Facilities: 🐾⊙🅿🔥🔵🕂🐕♻ 🛈

Services: 🔌🛢🍼

Within 3 miles: 🔱📎🔒🛒

Notes: No bikes, skateboards or camp fires. Main
gates locked 23.00hrs-08.00hrs, no noise after
23.00hrs. Dogs must be kept on leads.

TAL-Y-BONT (NEAR CONWY)
Map 14 SH76

Places to visit

Bodnant Garden, TAL-Y-CAFN 01492 650460
www.bodnant-garden.co.uk

Great for kids: Smallest House, CONWY
01492 593484

▶ 89% Tynterfyn Touring Caravan
Park (SH768695)

LL32 8YX ☎ 01492 660525
dir: 5m S of Conwy on B5106, signed Tal-y-Bont,
1st on left

* 🚐 £12.80 🚐 £13.50 ⛺ fr £5

Open Mar-Oct (rs 28 days in year tent pitches
only)

Last arrival 22.00hrs Last departure noon

A quiet, secluded little park set in the beautiful
Conwy Valley, and run by family owners. The
grounds are tended with care, and the older-style
toilet facilities sparkle. There is lots of room for
children and dogs to run around. 2 acre site. 15
touring pitches. 4 hardstandings. Caravan
pitches. Motorhome pitches. Tent pitches.

AA Pubs & Restaurants nearby: The Old Ship,
Trefriw 01492 640013

Leisure: 🅰♨

Facilities: 🐾⊙🅿✳🕂♻ 🛈

Services: 🔌🛢↯⚓

Within 3 miles: 🔱📎🛒

Notes: 🐕 Dogs must be kept on leads.

TOWYN (NEAR ABERGELE)
Map 14 SH97

Places to visit

Rhuddlan Castle, RHUDDLAN 01745 590777
www.cadw.wales.gov.uk

Great for kids: Welsh Mountain Zoo, COLWYN
BAY 01492 532938 www.welshmountainzoo.org

 75% Ty Mawr Holiday
Park (SH965792)

Towyn Rd LL22 9HG
☎ 01745 832079
e-mail: admin.tymawr@parkresorts.com
web: www.park-resorts.com
dir: On A548, 0.25m W of Towyn

🚐🚐⛺

Open Apr-Oct (rs Apr (excluding Etr))

Last arrival mdnt Last departure 10.00hrs

Located between Chester and the Isle of
Anglesey and close to many attractions
including the lively resort of Rhyl. A very large
coastal holiday park with extensive leisure
facilities including sports and recreational
amenities. Touring areas are within two level
grassy fields and all amenities blocks are
centrally located. The entertainment facilities
are ideal for both adults and families and a
choice of eating outlets is available. 18 acre
site. 406 touring pitches. Caravan pitches.
Motorhome pitches. Tent pitches. 464 statics.

AA Pubs & Restaurants nearby: Kinmel Arms,
Abergele 01745 832207

Barratt's at Ty'n Rhyl, Rhyl 01745 344138

Leisure: 🏊🅰🏐⊙❓🎵

Facilities: 🐾⊙🔵❓🅱🕂🐕 📶 💻

Services: 🔌🛢🍷🍽🛗

Within 3 miles: 🔱🅟📎⊚🅱🛒↻

SERVICES: 🔌 Electric hook up 🅾 Launderette 🍷 Licensed bar 🛢 Calor Gas 🅶 Camping Gaz Ⓣ Toilet fluid 🍽 Café/Restaurant 🛗 Fast Food/Takeaway 🔋 Battery charging
🍼 Baby care ↯ Motorvan service point ABBREVIATIONS: BH/bank hols-bank holidays Etr-Easter Whit-Whitsun dep-departure fr-from hrs-hours m-mile mdnt-midnight
rdbt-roundabout rs-restricted service wk-week wknd-weekend 🚫 No credit cards 🚫 no dogs   See page 7 for details of the AA Camping Card Scheme

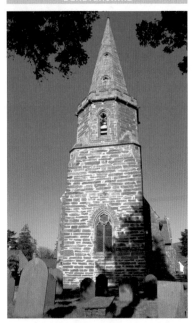

DENBIGHSHIRE

AA CAMPING CARD SITE

▶▶▶ 79% Hendwr Country Park

(SJ042386)

LL21 0SN

☎ 01490 440210

dir: *From Corwen (A5) take B4401 for 4m. Right at Hendwr sign. Site 0.5m on right down tree-lined drive. Or follow brown signs from A5 at Corwen*

🚐 £18-£20 🚃 £18-£20 ▲ £18-£20

Open Apr-Oct

Last arrival 22.00hrs Last departure 16.00hrs

Surrounded by the Berwen Mountains, this well established site has a stream meandering through it - the sound of running water and birdsong are the only distractions. A tree-lined drive welcomes visitors on to the immaculately maintained pitches. Fly fishing instruction can be arranged on the river which borders the park. Scandinavian-style lodges are available. 11 acre site. 40 touring pitches. 3 hardstandings. 26 seasonal pitches. Caravan pitches. Motorhome pitches. Tent pitches. 80 statics.

Facilities: 🏳🔆❄🛢�🐾 WiFi ♻ 🕖

Services: 🔌🔟🛒🛢🚽I🏪🛗

Within 3 miles: 🏌🛒

Notes: Dogs must be kept on leads. Wet weather camping facilities.

LLANDRILLO Map 15 SJ03

Places to visit

Chirk Castle, CHIRK 01691 777701
www.nationaltrust.org.uk/main/w-chirkcastle

Rug Chapel, CORWEN 01490 412025
www.cadw.wales.gov.uk

LLANGOLLEN Map 15 SJ24

Places to visit

Valle Crucis Abbey, LLANGOLLEN 01978 860326
www.cadw.wales.gov.uk

Great for kids: Llangollen Railway, LLANGOLLEN 01978 860979 www.llangollen-railway.co.uk

▶▶ 76% *Ty-Ucha Caravan Park*

(SJ232415)

Maesmawr Rd LL20 7PP

☎ 01978 860677

dir: *Take A5 from Llangollen. In approx 1m follow brown site signs. Right, to site in 250yds*

🚐 🚃

Open Etr-Oct

Last arrival 22.00hrs Last departure 13.00hrs

A very spacious site in beautiful unspoilt surroundings, with a small stream on site, and superb views. Ideal for country and mountain walking, and handily placed near the A5. Pitch density is excellent, facilities are clean and well maintained, and there is a games room with table tennis. Please note that this site does not accept tents. 4 acre site. 40 touring pitches. Caravan pitches. Motorhome pitches.

Leisure: ⚽🎾 **Facilities:** 🏳🔆🕖

Services: 🔌

Within 3 miles: 🎿🔆🎡🏌🚣🛒🔟🗘

Notes: 🐾 Dogs must be kept on leads.

LEISURE: 🏊 Indoor swimming pool 🏊 Outdoor swimming pool 🛝 Children's playground 🧒 Kid's club 🎾 Tennis court 🎱 Games room 📺 Separate TV room 🏌 9/18 hole golf course ⛵ Boats for hire 🎬 Cinema 🎭 Entertainment 🎣 Fishing ⛳ Mini golf 🏄 Watersports 💪 Gym ⚽ Sports field Spa ♨ Stables
FACILITIES: 🛁 Bath 🚿 Shower 🔌 Electric shaver 💨 Hairdryer ❄ Ice Pack Facility ♿ Disabled facilities 📞 Public telephone 🛒 Shop on site or within 200yds 🛒 Mobile shop (calls at least 5 days a week) 🍖 BBQ area 🪑 Picnic area WiFi Wi-fi 🌐 Internet access ♻ Recycling 🕖 Tourist info 🐾 Dog exercise area

PRESTATYN Map 15 SJ08

Places to visit

Basingwerk Abbey, HOLYWELL 01443 336000 www.cadw.wales.gov.uk

80% Presthaven Sands Holiday Park *(SJ091842)*

GOLD

Gronant LL19 9TT
☎ 0871 231 0888
e-mail: presthavensands@haven.com
web: www.haven.com/presthavensands
dir: *A548 from Prestatyn towards Gronant. Site signed. (NB For Sat Nav use LL19 9ST)*

🚐 🚙

Open mid Mar-end Oct (rs mid Mar-May & Sep-Oct facilities may be reduced)

Last arrival 20.00hrs Last departure 10.00hrs

Set beside two miles of superb sandy beaches and dunes (with donkeys on site at weekends) this constantly improving holiday park provides a wide range of both indoor and outdoor attractions. The site can boast happy returning visitors. The small touring field at park entrance offers good electric pitches - the majority are hardstandings and include five super pitches. The centrally located entertainment area includes two indoor swimming pools, excellent children's activities and a choice of eating outlets. 21 acre site. 34 touring pitches. Caravan pitches. Motorhome pitches. 1052 statics.

Leisure: 🏊 🏊 ⛺ ✋

Facilities: 🚿 ⊙ ♿ ✆ [$] [Wi-fi]

Services: 🔌 🧺 🍷 🍴 🍔 🚰

Within 3 miles: ⛳ 🎣 ◎ [$] 🧺 U

Notes: Max 2 dogs per booking, certain dog breeds banned, no commercial vehicles, no bookings by persons under 21yrs unless a family booking. Dogs must be kept on leads.

see advert on opposite page

RHUALLT Map 15 SJ07

Places to visit

Rhuddlan Castle, RHUDDLAN 01745 590777 www.cadw.wales.gov.uk

Bodelwyddan Castle, BODELWYDDAN 01745 584060 www.bodelwyddan-castle.co.uk

Great for kids: Denbigh Castle, DENBIGH 01745 813385 www.cadw.wales.gov.uk

AA CAMPING CARD SITE

►►►► 89% Penisar Mynydd Caravan Park *(SJ093770)*

Caerwys Rd LL17 0TY
☎ 01745 582227 & 07831 408017
e-mail: contact@penisarmynydd.co.uk
web: www.penisarmynydd.co.uk
dir: *From A55 junct 29 follow Dyserth & brown caravan signs. Site 500yds on right*

🚐 🚙 ⛺

Open Mar-15 Jan

Last arrival 21.00hrs Last departure 21.00hrs

A very tranquil, attractively laid-out park set in three grassy paddocks with superb facilities block including a disabled room and dishwashing area. The majority of pitches are super pitches. Everything is immaculately maintained, and the amenities of the seaside resort of Rhyl are close by. 6.6 acre site. 75 touring pitches. 75 hardstandings. Caravan pitches. Motorhome pitches. Tent pitches.

AA Pubs & Restaurants nearby: Plough Inn, St Asaph 01745 585080

Leisure: ⚽

Facilities: 🚿 ⊙ ✲ ♿ ✆ 🏪 ⛱ 🐕 [Wi-fi] ♻ ℹ

Services: 🔌 🧺 🛢 🔋 🚰

Within 3 miles: ⛳ 🎣 ◎ 🌊 [$] 🧺 U

Notes: 💳 No cycling. Dogs must be kept on leads. Rally area.

RUABON Map 15 SJ34

Places to visit

Plas Newydd, LLANGOLLEN 01978 861314 www.denbighshire.gov.uk

Valle Crucis Abbey, LLANGOLLEN 01978 860326 www.cadw.wales.gov.uk

Great for kids: Horse Drawn Boats Centre, LLANGOLLEN 01978 860702 www.horsedrawnboats.co.uk

►►► 73% James' Caravan Park *(SJ300434)*

LL14 6DW
☎ 01978 820148
e-mail: ray@carastay.demon.co.uk
dir: *Approach on A483 South, at rdbt with A539 turn right (signed Llangollen), over dual carriageway bridge, site 500yds on left*

🚐 🚙

Open all year

Last arrival 21.00hrs Last departure 11.00hrs

A well-landscaped park on a former farm, with modern heated toilet facilities. Old farm buildings house a collection of restored original farm machinery, and the village shop, four pubs, takeaway and launderette are a 10-minute walk away. 6 acre site. 40 touring pitches. 4 hardstandings. Caravan pitches. Motorhome pitches.

Facilities: 🚿 ⊙ 🌀 ✲ ♿ ✆ 🐕

Services: 🔌 🛢 🍃 🔋

Within 3 miles: ⛳ [$] 🧺

Notes: 💳 No fires. Dogs must be kept on leads. Chest freezer available.

SERVICES: 🔌 Electric hook up 🧺 Launderette 🍷 Licensed bar 🛢 Calor Gas 🍃 Camping Gaz [T] Toilet fluid 🍴 Café/Restaurant 🍔 Fast Food/Takeaway 🔋 Battery charging 🍼 Baby care 🚰 Motorvan service point **ABBREVIATIONS:** BH/bank hols-bank holidays Etr-Easter Whit-Whitsun dep-departure fr-from hrs-hours m-mile mdnt-midnight rdbt-roundabout rs-restricted service wk-week wknd-weekend 💳 No credit cards 🚫 no dogs

See page 7 for details of the AA Camping Card Scheme

GWYNEDD

ABERSOCH
Map 14 SH32

Places to visit

Plas-yn-Rhiw, PLAS YN RHIW 01758 780219
www.nationaltrust.org.uk

Penarth Fawr, PENARTH FAWR 01443 336000
www.cadw.wales.gov.uk

Great for kids: Criccieth Castle, CRICCIETH
01766 522227 www.cadw.wales.gov.uk

►►►► 81% Beach View Caravan Park *(SH316262)*

Bwlchtocyn LL53 7BT
☎ 01758 712956
dir: *Through Abersoch & Sarn Bach. Over x-rds, next left signed Porthtocyn Hotel. Pass chapel to another Porthtocyn Hotel sign. Turn left, site on left*

🚐 🚎 Å

Open mid Mar-mid Oct

Last arrival 19.00hrs Last departure 11.00hrs

A compact family park run by a very enthusiastic owner who makes continual improvements. Just a six-minute walk from the beach, the site's immaculately maintained grounds, good hardstanding pitches (mostly seasonal) and excellent facilities are matched by great sea and country views. 4 acre site. 47 touring pitches. Caravan pitches. Motorhome pitches. Tent pitches.

AA Pubs & Restaurants nearby: Porth Tocyn Hotel, Abersoch 01758 713303

Facilities: 🐾 ⊙ 🗗 🛏

Services: 🔌 🗐 🐾

Within 3 miles: ♨ ⚓ 🗜 🛶 🛒 🎣 ∪

Notes: 🐾 Dogs must be kept on leads.

►►►► 80% Deucoch Touring & Camping Park *(SH301269)*

Sarn Bach LL53 7LD
☎ 01758 713293 & 07740 281770
e-mail: info@deucoch.com
dir: *From Abersoch take Sarn Bach road, at x-rds turn right, site on right in 800yds*

🚐 🚎 Å

Open Mar-Oct

Last arrival 22.00hrs Last departure 11.00hrs

A colourful, sheltered site with stunning views of Cardigan Bay and the mountains, and situated just a mile from Abersoch and a long sandy beach. The friendly, enthusiastic, hands-on proprietors make year-on-year improvements to enhance their visitors' experience. Facilities include outside hot showers, a superb dish washing facility, housed in an attractive log cabin, and caravan repairs. 5 acre site. 70 touring pitches. 10 hardstandings. Caravan pitches. Motorhome pitches. Tent pitches.

AA Pubs & Restaurants nearby: Porth Tocyn Hotel, Abersoch 01758 713303

Leisure: 🎱 🎣

Facilities: 🐾 ⊙ 🗗 ✳ ♿ ♻ 🛈

Services: 🔌 🗐 ♿

Within 3 miles: ♨ ⚓ 🗜 🛶 🛒 🎣 ∪

Notes: 🐾 Families only.

►►► 82% Tyn-y-Mur Touring & Camping *(SH304290)*

Lon Garmon LL53 7UL
☎ 01758 712328
e-mail: info@tyn-y-mur.co.uk
dir: *From Pwllheli into Abersoch on A499, sharp right at Land & Sea Garage. Site approx 0.5m on left*

🚐 £25 🚎 £25 Å £18-£25

Open Apr-Oct

Last arrival 22.00hrs Last departure 11.00hrs

A family-only park in a glorious hill-top location overlooking a lush valley and with views extending across Abersoch to the mountains beyond

LEISURE: 🏊 Indoor swimming pool 🏊 Outdoor swimming pool 🎢 Children's playground 🪁 Kid's club 🎾 Tennis court 🎱 Games room 📺 Separate TV room ⛳ 9/18 hole golf course ⛵ Boats for hire 🎬 Cinema 🎵 Entertainment 🎣 Fishing ⛳ Mini golf 🏄 Watersports 💪 Gym 🏅 Sports field Spa ∪ Stables
FACILITIES: 🛁 Bath 🚿 Shower ⊙ Electric shaver 🗗 Hairdryer ✳ Ice Pack Facility ♿ Disabled facilities 📞 Public telephone 🛒 Shop on site or within 200yds 🏪 Mobile shop (calls at least 5 days a week) 🍖 BBQ area 🎍 Picnic area WI-FI Wi-fi 💻 Internet access ♻ Recycling 🛈 Tourist info 🐾 Dog exercise area

Cardigan Bay. Good, clean modernised toilet facilities and spacious tent pitches in a level grassy field. The beach at Abersoch is just a short walk away and the park offers boat storage facilities. 22 acre site. 50 touring pitches. 37 hardstandings. Caravan pitches. Motorhome pitches. Tent pitches.

AA Pubs & Restaurants nearby: Porth Tocyn Hotel, Abersoch 01758 713303

Tyn-y-Mur Touring & Camping

Leisure: 🅰 🌀

Facilities: 🏮 ☉ ✳ ☕ ⛱ 🔥 ♻ ❶

Services: 🔌 🔲 🔒 ⏴ T 🛒 🔋

Within 3 miles: 🛴 ✛ 🎣 🏊 🎱 🎬 U

Notes: ⓧ No open fires, no motorcycles, no noisy activity after 23.00hrs, 1 dog per unit. Dogs must be kept on leads.

►►► 80% Bryn Bach Caravan & Camping Site *(SH315258)*

Tyddyn Talgoch Uchaf, Bwlchtocyn LL53 7BT
☎ 01758 712285 & 07789 390808
e-mail: brynbach@abersochcamping.co.uk
dir: *From Abersoch take Sarn Bach road for approx 1m, left at sign for Bwlchtocyn. Site approx 1m on left*

🚐 🚗 Å

Open Mar-Oct

Last arrival 20.00hrs Last departure 11.00hrs

This well-run, elevated park overlooks Abersoch Bay, with lovely sea views towards the Snowdonia mountain range. Pitches are well laid out in sheltered paddocks, with well-placed modern facilities. Fishing, watersports, golf and beach access are all nearby. 4 acre site. 8 touring pitches. 1 hardstanding. 30 seasonal pitches. Caravan pitches. Motorhome pitches. Tent pitches. 2 statics.

AA Pubs & Restaurants nearby: Porth Tocyn Hotel, Abersoch 01758 713303

Leisure: 🅰 🌀

Facilities: 🏮 ☉ 🅿 ✳ ☕ 🔥 📶 ♻ ❶

Services: 🔌 🔲 🔒 ⏴ T 🔋

Within 3 miles: 🛴 ✛ 🎣 🏊 🎱 🎬 U

Notes: Families & couples only. Dogs must be kept on leads. Private shortcut to beach, boat storage.

►►► 70% *Tanrallt Farm (SH296288)*

Tanrallt, Llangian LL53 7LN
☎ 01758 713527
e-mail: www.abersoch-holiday.co.uk
dir: *A499 to Abersoch, right up hill, follow signs for Llangian. Site in village on left*

🚐 🚗 Å

Open Etr-end Oct

Last arrival 21.30hrs Last departure 10.30hrs

Tanrallt Farm site is in a secluded valley on a working farm. Friendly owners make their guests feel welcome, providing a BBQ area, very clean and serviceable toilets, a laundry room with washer, dryer, spin dryer, iron and ironing board plus a drying area for wet clothing. There are also three bunk rooms and a kitchen. 1.5 acre site. 12 touring pitches. 12 hardstandings. Caravan pitches. Motorhome pitches. Tent pitches.

AA Pubs & Restaurants nearby: Porth Tocyn Hotel, Abersoch 01758 713303

Facilities: 🏮 ✳ ☕ 🔥 ⛱ **Services:** 🔌 🔲 🛒 🔋

Within 3 miles: 🛴 ✛ 🎣 ◎ 🏊 🎱 🎬 U

Notes: ⓧ Families & couples only. No noise after 23.00hrs.

ABERSOCH *continued*

►►► 69% *Rhydolion* (SH283276)

Rhydolion, Llangian LL53 7LR
☎ **01758 712342**
e-mail: enquiries@rhydolion.co.uk
dir: *From A499 take unclassified road to Llangian for 1m, turn left, through Llangian. Site 1.5m after road forks towards Hell's Mouth/Porth Neigwl*

🚐🏕

Open Mar-Oct

Last arrival 22.00hrs Last departure noon

A peaceful small site with good views, on a working farm close to the long sandy surfers beach at Hell's Mouth. The simple toilet facilities are kept to a high standard by the friendly owners, and nearby Abersoch is a mecca for boat owners and water sports enthusiasts. 1.5 acre site. 28 touring pitches. Caravan pitches. Tent pitches.

AA Pubs & Restaurants nearby: Porth Tocyn Hotel, Abersoch 01758 713303

Leisure: 🏊🎯 **Facilities:** 🏾☉✳🕭♻ ❻
Services: 🔌🗑🛒
Within 3 miles: ↓🛶🏌◎🛥💲🛍🍴🅄
Notes: 🐾 Families & couples only, dogs by arrangement only. Dogs must be kept on leads. 3 fridge freezers.

BALA   Map 14 SH93

Places to visit

Bala Lake Railway, LLANUWCHLLYN
01678 540666 www.bala-lake-railway.co.uk

Rug Chapel, CORWEN 01490 412025
www.cadw.wales.gov.uk

Great for kids: Ewe-Phoria Sheepdog Centre, CORWEN 01490 460369 www.ewe-phoria.co.uk

---

AA CAMPING CARD SITE

►►►► 81% Pen-y-Bont Touring Park
(SH932350)

Llangynog Rd LL23 7PH
☎ **01678 520549**
e-mail: penybont-bala@btconnect.com
dir: *From A494 take B4391. Site 0.75m on right*

🚐🚏🏕

Open Mar-Oct

Last arrival 21.00hrs Last departure noon

A family run attractively landscaped park in a woodland country setting. Set close to Bala Lake and the River Dee, with plenty of opportunities for water sports including kayaking and white water rafting. The park offers good facilities including a motorhome service point, and many pitches have water and electricity. Around the park are superb large wood carvings of birds and mythical creatures depicting local legends. 6 acre site. 95 touring pitches. 47 hardstandings. 20 seasonal pitches. Caravan pitches. Motorhome pitches. Tent pitches. 1 bell tents/yurts. 2 wooden pods.

Facilities: 🏾☉🅿✳🕭🕓🗑🏄🎣🚿🛁📶♻❻
Services: 🔌🗑💧🚰Ⓣ🛒🔧
Within 3 miles: ↓🛶🏌🎣🛥💲🛍🍴🅄
Notes: No camp fires, BBQs must be kept off ground, quiet after 22.30hrs. Dogs must be kept on leads.

►►►► 79% Tyn Cornel Camping & Caravan Park (SH895400)

Frongoch LL23 7NU
☎ **01678 520759**
e-mail: tyncornel@mail.com
dir: *From Bala take A4212 (Porthmadog road) for 4m. Site on left before National White Water Centre*

* 🚐 £12-£20 🚏 £12-£20 🏕 £8-£30

Open Etr-Oct

Last arrival 20.00hrs Last departure 11.00hrs

A delightful riverside park with mountain views, popular with those seeking a base for river kayaks and canoes, with access to the nearby White Water Centre and riverside walk with tearoom. The resident owners are always improving the very well maintained and colourful grounds. 10 acre site. 67 touring pitches. 10 hardstandings. 14 seasonal pitches. Caravan pitches. Motorhome pitches. Tent pitches.

Leisure: 🎯
Facilities: 🏾☉🅿✳🕭🕓🏄🎣📶♻❻
Services: 🔌🗑💧🚰🔧
Within 3 miles: ↓🛶🏌🎣🛥💲🛍🍴🅄
Notes: Quiet after 23.00hrs, no cycling, no camp fires or wood burning. Dogs must be kept on leads. Fridge, freezer & tumble dryer available.

BANGOR   Map 14 SH57

Places to visit

Penrhyn Castle, BANGOR 01248 353084
www.nationaltrust.org.uk

Plas Newydd, PLAS NEWYDD 01248 714795
www.nationaltrust.org.uk/main/plasnewydd

Great for kids: Greenwood Forest Park, Y FELINHELI 01248 670076
www.greenwoodforestpark.co.uk

►►► 68% Treborth Hall Farm Caravan Park (SH554707)

The Old Barn, Treborth Hall Farm LL57 2RX
☎ **01248 364399**
e-mail: enquiries@treborthleisure.co.uk
dir: *A55 junct 9, 1st left at rdbt, straight over 2nd rdbt, site approx 800yds on left*

🚐 £23-£26 🚏 £23-£26 🏕 £12-£20

Open Etr-end Oct

Last arrival 22.30hrs Last departure 10.30hrs

Set in eight acres of beautiful parkland with its own trout fishing lake and golf course, this park offers serviced pitches in a sheltered, walled orchard. Tents have a separate grass area, and there is a good clean toilet block. This is a useful base for families, with easy access for the Menai Straits, Anglesey beaches, Snowdon and the Lleyn peninsula. 8 acre site. 34 touring pitches. 34 hardstandings. Caravan pitches. Motorhome pitches. Tent pitches. 4 statics.

Leisure: 🏊
Facilities: 🏾🕓🏄❻
Services: 🔌
Within 3 miles: ↓🎣🛥💲🛍🍴
Notes: Dogs must be kept on leads.

LEISURE: 🏊 Indoor swimming pool 🏊 Outdoor swimming pool 🎢 Children's playground Ⓚ Kid's club 🎾 Tennis court 🎱 Games room 📺 Separate TV room 🏌 9/18 hole golf course 🛶 Boats for hire 🎬 Cinema 🎵 Entertainment 🎣 Fishing ◎ Mini golf 🌊 Watersports 🏋 Gym 🏟 Sports field **Spa** 🅄 Stables
FACILITIES: 🛁 Bath 🚿 Shower ☉ Electric shaver 🅿 Hairdryer ✳ Ice Pack Facility 🕭 Disabled facilities 🕓 Public telephone 🛍 Shop on site or within 200yds 🛒 Mobile shop (calls at least 5 days a week) 🍴 BBQ area 🏄 Picnic area 📶 Wi-fi 💻 Internet access ♻ Recycling ❻ Tourist info 🐾 Dog exercise area

BARMOUTH
Map 14 SH61

Places to visit

Harlech Castle, HARLECH 01766 780552
www.cadw.wales.gov.uk

Cymer Abbey, CYMER ABBEY 01443 336000
www.cadw.wales.gov.uk

Great for kids: Fairbourne Railway, FAIRBOURNE
01341 250362 www.fairbournerailway.com

PREMIER PARK

▶▶▶▶▶ 92% Trawsdir
Touring Caravans & Camping
Park (SH596198)

Best of British

Llanaber LL42 1RR
☎ 01341 280611 & 280999
e-mail: enquiries@barmouthholidays.co.uk
web: www.barmouthholidays.co.uk
dir: 3m N of Barmouth on A496, just past Wayside
pub on right

* ⚏ £18-£32 ⚏ £18-£32 ▲ £12-£28

Open Mar-Jan

Last arrival 20.00hrs Last departure noon

Well run by the owners, this quality park enjoys
spectacular views to the sea and hills, and is very
accessible to motor traffic. The facilities are
appointed to a very high standard, and include
spacious cubicles containing showers and
washbasins, individual showers, smart toilets
with sensor-operated flush, and under-floor
heating. Tents and caravans have their own
designated areas divided by dry-stone walls (both
have spacious fully serviced pitches) and the site
is very convenient for large recreational vehicles.
There is an excellent children's play area, plus
glorious seasonal floral displays and an
illuminated dog walk that leads directly to the
nearby pub! There are five wooden pods for hire.
15 acre site. 70 touring pitches. 70
hardstandings. Caravan pitches. Motorhome
pitches. Tent pitches. 5 wooden pods.

Leisure: ⚏
Facilities: ⚏⚏⚏⚏⚏⚏⚏⚏⚏⚏⚏⚏
Services: ⚏⚏⚏⚏⚏⚏⚏⚏⚏
Within 3 miles: ⚏⚏⚏⚏

Notes: Families & couples only. Dogs must be
kept on leads. Milk/bread etc available from
reception, takeaway food can be delivered from
sister site.

PREMIER PARK

▶▶▶▶▶ 82% Hendre Mynach
Touring Caravan & Camping Park
(SH605170)

Llanaber Rd LL42 1YR
☎ 01341 280262
e-mail: mynach@lineone.net
web: www.hendremynach.co.uk
dir: 0.75m N of Barmouth on A496

⚏⚏▲

Open Mar-9 Jan (rs Nov-Jan shop closed)

Last arrival 22.00hrs Last departure noon

A lovely site with enthusiastic owners and
immaculate facilities, just off the A496 and near
the railway, with almost direct access to the
promenade and beach. Caravanners should not be
put off by the steep descent, as park staff are
always on hand to help if needed. Spacious
pitches have TV and satellite hook-up as well as
water and electricity. A small café serves light
meals and takeaways. 10 acre site. 240 touring
pitches. 75 hardstandings. 23 seasonal pitches.
Caravan pitches. Motorhome pitches. Tent pitches.
1 static.

Leisure: ⚏
Facilities: ⚏⚏⚏⚏⚏⚏⚏⚏⚏⚏⚏⚏
Services: ⚏⚏⚏⚏⚏⚏⚏⚏
Within 3 miles: ⚏⚏⚏⚏⚏

Notes: Dogs must be kept on leads.

BETWS GARMON
Map 14 SH55

Places to visit

Snowdon Mountain Railway, LLANBERIS
01286 870223 www.snowdonrailway.co.uk

Great for kids: Dolbadarn Castle, LLANBERIS
01443 336000 www.cadw.wales.gov.uk

▶▶▶▶ 80% Bryn Gloch Caravan &
Camping Park (SH534574)

LL54 7YY
☎ 01286 650216
e-mail: eurig@bryngloch.co.uk
web: www.campwales.co.uk
dir: On A4085, 5m SE of Caernarfon

* ⚏ £15-£30 ⚏ £15-£30 ▲ £15-£30

Open all year

Last arrival 23.00hrs Last departure 17.00hrs

An excellent family-run site with immaculate
modern facilities, and all level pitches in beautiful
surroundings. The park offers the best of two
worlds, with its bustling holiday atmosphere and
the peaceful natural surroundings. The 28 acres of
level fields are separated by mature hedges and
trees, guaranteeing sufficient space for families
wishing to spread themselves out. There are static
holiday caravans for hire and plenty of walks in
the area. 28 acre site. 160 touring pitches. 60
hardstandings. 50 seasonal pitches. Caravan
pitches. Motorhome pitches. Tent pitches. 17
statics.

AA Pubs & Restaurants nearby: Snowdonia Parc
Brewpub, Waunfawr 01286 650409

Leisure: ⚏⚏⚏
Facilities: ⚏⚏⚏⚏⚏⚏⚏⚏⚏⚏⚏⚏⚏⚏⚏⚏⚏⚏
Services: ⚏⚏⚏⚏⚏⚏⚏⚏
Within 3 miles: ⚏⚏⚏⚏⚏⚏⚏

Notes: Dogs must be kept on leads. Family
bathroom, mother & baby room.

SERVICES: ⚏ Electric hook up ⚏ Launderette ⚏ Licensed bar ⚏ Calor Gas ⚏ Camping Gaz ⚏ Toilet fluid ⚏ Café/Restaurant ⚏ Fast Food/Takeaway ⚏ Battery charging
⚏ Baby care ⚏ Motorvan service point **ABBREVIATIONS:** BH/bank hols-bank holidays Etr-Easter Whit-Whitsun dep-departure fr-from hrs-hours m-mile mdnt-midnight
rdbt-roundabout rs-restricted service wk-week wknd-weekend ⚏ No credit cards ⚏ no dogs See page 7 for details of the AA Camping Card Scheme

CAERNARFON   Map 14 SH46

See also Dinas Dinlle & Llandwrog

Places to visit

Segontium Roman Museum, CAERNARFON
01286 675625 www.segontium.org.uk

Welsh Highland Railway, CAERNARFON
01766 516024 www.festrail.co.uk

Great for kids: Caernarfon Castle, CAERNARFON
01286 677617 www.cadw.wales.gov.uk

▶▶▶▶ 86% Llys Derwen Caravan & Camping Site (SH539629)

Ffordd Bryngwyn, Llanrug LL55 4RD
☎ 01286 673322
e-mail: llysderwen@aol.com
dir: A55 junct 13 (Caernarfon) onto A4086 to
Llanberis, through Llanrug, turn right at pub, site
60yds on right

* ⊞ £17-£19 ⇔ £17-£19 ▲ £17-£19

Open Mar-Oct

Last arrival 22.00hrs Last departure noon

On the outskirts of the village of Llanrug, three
miles from Caernarfon on the way to Llanberis and
Snowdon. A beautifully maintained site with
enthusiastic owners who are constantly investing
to improve their customers' experience. The
amenities block was totally refurbished to a high
standard for the 2012 season and the
immaculately maintained grounds are equipped
with an abundance of colourful shrubs and
seasonal flowers. 5 acre site. 20 touring pitches.
Caravan pitches. Motorhome pitches. Tent pitches.
2 statics.

AA Pubs & Restaurants nearby: Seiont Manor
Hotel, Llanrug 01286 673366

Facilities: ⋔⊙𝒫☀⅋♿ₓ♺𝒊
Services: ⊟🗓🛒
Within 3 miles: ⅃⅌𝒫⅚🖫🛒∪

Notes: ⊛ No open fires, no noise after 22.00hrs,
no ball games. Dogs must be kept on leads.

▶▶▶▶ 84% Riverside Camping (SH505630)

Seiont Nurseries, Pont Rug LL55 2BB
☎ 01286 678781
e-mail: brenda@riversidecamping.co.uk
web: www.riversidecamping.co.uk
dir: 2m from Caernarfon on right of A4086
towards Llanberis, follow signs

* ⊞ £18-£21 ⇔ £19-£24 ▲ £13-£21

Open Etr-end Oct

Last arrival anytime Last departure noon

Set in the grounds of a former garden centre and
enjoying a superb location along the River Seiont,
this park is approached by an impressive tree-
lined drive. Immaculately maintained by the
owners, there are a mixture of riverside grassy
pitches and fully serviced pitches for caravans
and motorhomes. In addition to smart amenities
blocks, other facilities include an excellent café/
restaurant, a volley ball court and boules pitch.
River fishing permits are available. 13
hardstanding pitches have electric hook up, water,
drainage and TV connection (especially suitable
for motorhomes). A haven of peace close to
Caernarfon, Snowdonia and some great walking
opportunities. 5 acre site. 73 touring pitches. 15
hardstandings. 10 seasonal pitches. Caravan
pitches. Motorhome pitches. Tent pitches.

AA Pubs & Restaurants nearby: Seiont Manor
Hotel, Llanrug 01286 673366

Rhiwafallen Restaurant with Rooms, Llandwrog
01286 830172

Leisure: 🛝
Facilities: ⋔⊙𝒫☀♿ₓ♺𝒊
Services: ⊟🗓🍽🛒🍺
Within 3 miles: ⅃⅌𝒫◎⅚🖫🛒∪

Notes: No fires, no loud music. Dogs must be kept
on leads. Family shower room, baby changing
facilities.

▶▶▶ 80% Plas Gwyn Caravan & Camping Park (SH520633)

Llanrug LL55 2AQ
☎ 01286 672619
e-mail: info@plasgwyn.co.uk
web: www.plasgwyn.co.uk
dir: A4086, 3m E of Caernarfon, site on right.
Between River Seiont & Llanrug

* ⊞ £17.50-£21 ⇔ £17.50-£21 ▲ £10.50-£25

Open Mar-Oct

Last arrival 22.00hrs Last departure 11.30hrs

A secluded park in an ideal location for visiting
the glorious nearby beaches, historic Caernarfon,
the Snowdonia attractions and walking
opportunities. The site is set within the grounds of
Plas Gwyn House, a Georgian property with
colonial additions, and the friendly owners
constantly improve facilities to enhance their
visitors' experience. A 'breakfast butty' service
with fresh tea or coffee is available for delivery to
individual pitches. The all-electric pitches include
hardstandings and five are fully serviced. Two
timber camping tents and five statics are also
available for hire. 3 acre site. 42 touring pitches.
8 hardstandings. 8 seasonal pitches. Caravan
pitches. Motorhome pitches. Tent pitches. 18
statics. 2 wooden pods.

AA Pubs & Restaurants nearby: Seiont Manor
Hotel, Llanrug 01286 673366

Rhiwafallen Restaurant with Rooms, Llandwrog
01286 830172

Facilities: ⋔⊙𝒫☀🖫ₓ♿🖳💻♺𝒊
Services: ⊟🗓🛢⌀🅣🛒⅄
Within 3 miles: ⅃⅌𝒫⅚🖫🛒∪

Notes: Minimal noise between 22.00hrs-mdnt,
complete quiet between mdnt-08.00hrs.

►►► 79% Cwm Cadnant Valley

(SH487628)

Cwm Cadnant Valley, Llanberis Rd LL55 2DF
☎ 01286 673196
e-mail: aa@cwmcadnant.co.uk
web: www.cwmcadnant.co.uk
dir: *On outskirts of Caernarfon on A4086 towards Llanberis, next to fire station*

⌂ £14-£22 ⌂ £14-£22 Å £10-£18

Open 14 Mar-3 Nov

Last arrival 22.00hrs Last departure 11.00hrs

Set in an attractive wooded valley with a stream is this terraced site with secluded pitches, a good camping area for backpackers and clean, modernised toilet facilities. It is located on the outskirts of Caernarfon in a rural location, close to the main Caernarfon-Llanberis road and just a 10-minute walk from the castle and town centre. 4.5 acre site. 60 touring pitches. 9 hardstandings. 5 seasonal pitches. Caravan pitches. Motorhome pitches. Tent pitches.

AA Pubs & Restaurants nearby: Rhiwafallen Restaurant with Rooms, Llandwrog 01286 830172

Leisure: ⌂

Facilities: ⌂⊙ℓ✳⌂⌂⌂⌂ ⌂ ⌂

Services: ⌂⌂⌂⌂⌂⌂⌂

Within 3 miles: ⌂⌂ℓ⌂⌂⌂⌂∪

Notes: No noise after 23.00hrs, no wood fires. Dogs must be kept on leads. Family room with baby changing facilities.

►►► 77% Ty'n yr Onnen Caravan Park *(SH533588)*

Waunfawr LL55 4AX
☎ 01286 650281 & 07503 702886
e-mail: tynronnen.farm@btconnect.com
dir: *At Waunfawr on A4085, onto unclassified road opposite church. Site signed*

⌂ £14-£22 ⌂ £14-£22 Å £14-£22

Open Apr-Oct

Last arrival 22.00hrs Last departure noon

A gently sloping site on a 200-acre sheep farm set in magnificent surroundings close to Snowdon and enjoying stunning mountain views. This secluded park is well equipped and has quality toilet facilities. Access is via a narrow, unclassified road. 3.5 acre site. 20 touring pitches. Caravan pitches. Motorhome pitches. Tent pitches.

AA Pubs & Restaurants nearby: Snowdonia Parc Brewpub, Waunfawr 01286 650409

Leisure: ⌂⌂⌂

Facilities: ⌂⊙✳⌂⌂⌂⌂⌂ ⌂

Services: ⌂⌂⌂

Within 3 miles: ⌂⌂ℓ⌂⌂⌂⌂∪

Notes: ⌂ No music after 23.00hrs. Dogs must be kept on leads - working farm.

CRICCIETH	Map 14 SH43

Places to visit

Portmeirion, PORTMEIRION 01766 770000 www.portmeirion-village.com

Great for kids: Ffestiniog Railway, PORTHMADOG 01766 516000 www.festrail.co.uk

---

►►►► 82% Eisteddfa *(SH518394)*

Eisteddfa Lodge, Pentrefelin LL52 0PT
☎ 01766 522696
e-mail: eisteddfa@criccieth.co.uk
dir: *From Porthmadog take A497 towards Criccieth. Approx 3.5m, through Pentrefelin, site signed 1st right after Plas Gwyn Nursing Home*

⌂ ⌂ Å

Open Mar-Oct

Last arrival 22.30hrs Last departure 11.00hrs

A quiet, secluded park on elevated ground, sheltered by the Snowdonia Mountains and with lovely views of Cardigan Bay; Criccieth is nearby. The owners are carefully improving the park whilst preserving its unspoilt beauty, and are keen to welcome families, who will appreciate the cubicled facilities. There's a field and play area, woodland walks, a cocoon pod, two tipis, six superb slate-based hardstandings, three static holiday caravans for hire, and a three-acre coarse fishing lake adjacent to the park. 24 acre site. 100 touring pitches. 17 hardstandings. Caravan pitches. Motorhome pitches. Tent pitches. 3 statics. 2 tipis. 1 wooden pod.

AA Pubs & Restaurants nearby: Bron Eifion Country House Hotel, Criccieth 01766 522385

Leisure: ⌂⌂⌂

Facilities: ⌂⊙ℓ✳⌂⌂⌂⌂⌂ ⌂ ⌂

Services: ⌂⌂⌂⌂⌂

Within 3 miles: ⌂⌂⌂ℓ⌂⌂⌂⌂∪

Notes: No noise after 22.30hrs. Dogs must be kept on leads. Baby bath available.

►► 82% Llwyn-Bugeilydd Caravan & Camping Site *(SH498398)*

LL52 0PN
☎ 01766 522235 & 07714 196137
e-mail: cazzyanne1@hotmail.com
dir: *From Porthmadog on A497, 1m N of Criccieth on B4411. Site 1st on right. From A55 take A487 through Caernarfon. After Bryncir right onto B4411, site on left in 3.5m*

*⌂ fr £18 ⌂ fr £18 Å fr £14

Open Mar-Oct

Last arrival anytime Last departure 11.00hrs

A quiet rural site with stunning scenery and well tended grass pitches, enhanced by shrubs and seasonal flowers. Well located for touring Snowdonia and coastal areas. The smartly presented amenities block is kept spotlessly clean. 6 acre site. 45 touring pitches. 2 hardstandings. Caravan pitches. Motorhome pitches. Tent pitches.

AA Pubs & Restaurants nearby: Bron Eifion Country House Hotel, Criccieth 01766 522385

Plas Bodegroes, Pwllheli 01758 612363

Leisure: ⌂⌂

Facilities: ⌂⊙ℓ✳⌂⌂ ⌂

Services: ⌂⌂

Within 3 miles: ⌂⌂ℓ⌂⌂⌂⌂∪

Notes: ⌂ No skateboards. Dogs must be kept on leads.

DINAS DINLLE
Map 14 SH45

Places to visit

Snowdon Mountain Railway, LLANBERIS 01286 870223 www.snowdonrailway.co.uk

St Cybi's Well, LLANGYBI 01443 336000 www.cadw.wales.gov.uk

Great for kids: Dolbadarn Castle, LLANBERIS 01443 336000 www.cadw.wales.gov.uk

▶▶▶▶ 86% *Dinlle Caravan Park*

(SH438568)

LL54 5TW
☎ 01286 830324
e-mail: enq@thornleyleisure.co.uk
dir: S on A499 turn right at sign for Caernarfon Airport. 2m W of Dinas Dinlle coast

Open Mar-Oct

Last arrival 23.00hrs Last departure noon

A very accessible, well-kept grassy site, adjacent to a sandy beach, with good views to Snowdonia. The park is situated in acres of flat grassland, with plenty of room for even the largest groups. The lounge bar and family room are comfortable places in which to relax, and children are well provided for with an exciting adventure playground. The beach road gives access to the golf club, a nature reserve, and to Air World at Caernarfon Airport. The man-made dunes offers campers additional protection from sea breezes. 20 acre site. 175 touring pitches. 20 hardstandings. Caravan pitches. Motorhome pitches. Tent pitches. 167 statics.

AA Pubs & Restaurants nearby: Rhiwafallen Restaurant with Rooms, Llandwrog 01286 830172

Leisure:

Facilities:

Services:

Within 3 miles:

Notes: No skateboards.

DYFFRYN ARDUDWY
Map 14 SH52

Places to visit

Cymer Abbey, CYMER ABBEY 01443 336000 www.cadw.wales.gov.uk

Great for kids: Harlech Castle, HARLECH 01766 780552 www.cadw.wales.gov.uk

▶▶▶ 79% Murmur-yr-Afon Touring Park (SH586236)

LL44 2BE
☎ 01341 247353
e-mail: murmuryrafon1@btinternet.com
dir: On A496 N of village

* 🚐 £13-£24 🚍 £13-£24 ▲ £11.50-£22

Open Mar-Oct

Last arrival 22.00hrs Last departure 11.00hrs

A pleasant family-run park alongside a wooded stream on the edge of the village, and handy for large sandy beaches. Expect good, clean facilities, and lovely views of rolling hills and mountains. 6 acre site. 77 touring pitches. 37 hardstandings. Caravan pitches. Motorhome pitches. Tent pitches.

AA Pubs & Restaurants nearby: Victoria Inn, Llanbedr 01341 241213

Leisure:

Facilities:

Services:

Within 3 miles:

Notes: Dogs must be kept on leads.

LLANDWROG
Map 14 SH45

Places to visit

Sygun Copper Mine, BEDDGELERT 01766 890595 www.syguncoppermine.co.uk

Great for kids: Caernarfon Castle, CAERNARFON 01286 677617 www.cadw.wales.gov.uk

AA CAMPING CARD SITE

▶▶▶▶ 79% White Tower Caravan Park (SH453582)

LL54 5UH
☎ 01286 830649 & 07802 562785
e-mail: whitetower@supanet.com
web: www.whitetowerpark.co.uk
dir: 1.5m from village on Tai'r Eglwys road. From Caernarfon take A487 (Porthmadog road). Cross rdbt, 1st right. Site 3m on right

🚐 £18-£25 🚍 £18-£25 ▲ £18-£25

Open Mar-10 Jan (rs Mar-mid May & Sep-Oct bar open wknds only)

Last arrival 23.00hrs Last departure noon

There are lovely views of Snowdonia from this park located just two miles from the nearest beach at Dinas Dinlle. A well-maintained toilet block has key access, and the hardstanding pitches have water and electricity. Popular amenities include an outdoor heated swimming pool, a lounge bar with family room, and a games and TV room. 6 acre site. 68 touring pitches. 68 hardstandings. 58 seasonal pitches. Caravan pitches. Motorhome pitches. Tent pitches. 68 statics.

AA Pubs & Restaurants nearby: Rhiwafallen Restaurant with Rooms, Llandwrog 01286 830172

Leisure:

Facilities:

Services:

Within 3 miles:

Notes: Dogs must be kept on leads.

LEISURE: 🏊 Indoor swimming pool 🏊 Outdoor swimming pool Ⓐ Children's playground 🪁 Kid's club ⚲ Tennis court 🎱 Games room 🖵 Separate TV room 🏌 9/18 hole golf course ⚓ Boats for hire 🎬 Cinema 🎵 Entertainment 🎣 Fishing ◎ Mini golf 🏄 Watersports 🏈 Gym ⚽ Sports field **Spa** ♨ Stables
FACILITIES: 🛁 Bath 🚿 Shower ⊙ Electric shaver 🖊 Hairdryer ❄ Ice Pack Facility ♿ Disabled facilities ☏ Public telephone 🏪 Shop on site or within 200yds 🏪 Mobile shop (calls at least 5 days a week) 🍖 BBQ area 🎋 Picnic area 📶 Wi-fi 💻 Internet access ♻ Recycling 🛈 Tourist info 🐕 Dog exercise area

PONT-RUG

See Caernarfon

PORTHMADOG   Map 14 SH53

Places to visit

Inigo Jones Slateworks, GROESLON
01286 830242 www.inigojones.co.uk

Great for kids: Ffestiniog Railway, PORTHMADOG
01766 516000 www.festrail.co.uk

82% Greenacres Holiday Park *(SH539374)*

**Black Rock Sands, Morfa Bychan
LL49 9YF**
☎ 0871 231 0886
e-mail: greenacres@haven.com
web: www.haven.com/greenacres
dir: *From Porthmadog High Street follow Black Rock Sands signs between The Factory Shop & Post Office. Park 2m on left at end of Morfa Bychan*

Open mid Mar-end Oct (rs mid Mar-May & Sep-Oct some facilities may be reduced)

Last arrival anytime Last departure 10.00hrs

A quality holiday park on level ground just a short walk from Black Rock Sands, and set against a backdrop of Snowdonia National Park. All touring pitches are on hardstandings surrounded by closely-mown grass, and near the entertainment complex. A full programme of entertainment, organised clubs, indoor and outdoor sports and leisure, pubs, shows and cabarets all add to a holiday experience here. A bowling alley and a large shop/bakery are useful amenities. 121 acre site. 48 touring pitches. 48 hardstandings. Caravan pitches. Motorhome pitches. 900 statics.

AA Pubs & Restaurants nearby: Royal Sportsman Hotel, Porthmadog 01766 512015

Hotel Portmeirion, Portmeirion Village, Penrhyndeudraeth 01766 770000

Castell Deudraeth, Portmeirion Village 01766 772400

Leisure: 🏊♨️🎣🎯🎱🎵
Facilities: 🛝☕️🏪♿🛇🚿🛒📶♻️🔧
Services: 🔌🗑️🍴🔋🧺🍽️🔧
Within 3 miles: 🚶🎣🏊🛒🚣⛳

Notes: Max 2 dogs per booking, certain dog breeds banned, no commercial vehicles, no bookings by persons under 21yrs unless a family booking.

see advert on page 420

PWLLHELI   Map 14 SH33

Places to visit

Penarth Fawr, PENARTH FAWR 01443 336000 www.cadw.wales.gov.uk

Plas-yn-Rhiw, PLAS YN RHIW 01758 780219 www.nationaltrust.org.uk

Great for kids: Criccieth Castle, CRICCIETH 01766 522227 www.cadw.wales.gov.uk

87% Hafan Y Môr Holiday Park *(SH431368)*

LL53 6HJ
☎ 0871 231 0887
e-mail: hafanymor@haven.com
web: www.haven.com/hafanymor
dir: *From Caernarfon take A499 to Pwllheli. A497 to Porthmadog. Park on right, approx 3m from Pwllheli. Or from Telford, A5, A494 to Bala. Right for Porthmadog. Left at rdbt in Porthmadog signed Criccieth & Pwllheli. Park on left 3m from Criccieth*

Hafan Y Môr Holiday Park

Open mid Mar-end Oct (rs mid Mar-May & Sep-Oct reduced facilities)

Last arrival 21.00hrs Last departure 10.00hrs

Located between Pwllheli and Criccieth and surrounded by mature trees that attracts wildlife, this popular holiday centre has undergone major investment in recent years to provide a wide range of all weather attractions. Activities include a sports hall, an ornamental boating lake, a large indoor swimming pool and show bar, to name but a few. There are also great eating options including the Mash & Barrel bar and bistro, fish & chips and a Starbucks café. New for 2012 is the £1.1m redevelopment of the touring area; there's now 75 fully serviced all-weather pitches and a top notch, air-conditioned amenities block. 500 acre site. 75 touring pitches. 75 hardstandings. Caravan pitches. Motorhome pitches. 800 statics.

AA Pubs & Restaurants nearby: Plas Bodegroes, Pwllheli 01758 612363

Leisure: 🏊♨️🎣🖐️
Facilities: 🛝☕️♿🛇🕐🚿📶
Services: 🔌🗑️🍴🔋🍽️🔧
Within 3 miles: 🚶🏇🏊🚴🛒🚣⛳

Notes: Max 2 dogs per booking, certain dog breeds banned, no commercial vehicles, no bookings by persons under 21yrs unless a family booking.

see advert on page 421

PWLLHELI continued

►►► 71% Abererch Sands Holiday Centre (SH403359)

LL53 6PJ
☎ 01758 612327
e-mail: enquiries@abererch-sands.co.uk
dir: On A497 (Porthmadog to Pwllheli road), 1m from Pwllheli

Open Mar-Oct

Last arrival 21.00hrs Last departure 21.00hrs

Glorious views of Snowdonia and Cardigan Bay can be enjoyed from this very secure, family-run site adjacent to a railway station and a four-mile stretch of sandy beach. A large heated indoor swimming pool, snooker room, pool room, fitness centre and children's play area make this an ideal holiday venue. 85 acre site. 70 touring pitches. 70 hardstandings. Caravan pitches. Motorhome pitches. Tent pitches. 90 statics.

AA Pubs & Restaurants nearby: Plas Bodegroes, Pwllheli 01758 612363

Leisure: 🎱 ⛰ 🔍
Facilities: 🛁 ☉ ☀ ⚙ 🕙 🖩 🐕 WiFi
Services: 🔌 🗑 💧 🚮 🚰 ♻
Within 3 miles: ↨ ⚓ ✚ 🏊 ⛵ 🛍 🎱 U

TALSARNAU

Places to visit

Portmeirion, PORTMEIRION 01766 770000
www.portmeirion-village.com

Harlech Castle, HARLECH 01766 780552
www.cadw.wales.gov.uk

Great for kids: Ffestiniog Railway, PORTHMADOG 01766 516000 www.festrail.co.uk

TALSARNAU   Map 14 SH63

AA CAMPING CARD SITE

►►►► 83% Barcdy Touring Caravan & Camping Park (SH620375)

LL47 6YG
☎ 01766 770736
e-mail: anwen@barcdy.co.uk
dir: From Maentwrog take A496 for Harlech. Site 4m on left

* 🚐 £18-£24 🚍 £16-£24 ⛺ £12-£18

Open Apr-Oct (rs Selected dates 2nd facility building closed (excl high season & school hols))

Last arrival 21.00hrs Last departure noon

A quiet picturesque park on the edge of the Vale of Ffestiniog near the Dwryd estuary. Two touring areas serve the park, one near the park entrance, and the other with improved and more secluded terraced pitches beside a narrow valley. The tent area is secluded and peaceful, and the toilet facilities are clean and tidy. Footpaths through adjacent woodland lead to small lakes and an established nature trail. 12 acre site. 80 touring pitches. 40 hardstandings. 15 seasonal pitches. Caravan pitches. Motorhome pitches. Tent pitches. 30 statics.

AA Pubs & Restaurants nearby: Hotel Portmeirion, Portmeirion Village, Penrhyndeudraeth 01766 770000

Castell Deudraeth, Portmeirion Village 01766 772400

Facilities: 🛁 ☉ 🗲 ☀ 🛋 WiFi ♻ 🛈
Services: 🔌 🗑 💧 ∅
Within 3 miles: ↨ 🎣 🛍 U

Notes: ⊗ No noisy parties, quiet families & couples only, no groups except Duke of Edinburgh award students.

TAL-Y-BONT   Map 14 SH52

Places to visit

Cymer Abbey, CYMER ABBEY 01443 336000
www.cadw.wales.gov.uk

Great for kids: Fairbourne Railway, FAIRBOURNE 01341 250362 www.fairbournerailway.com

AA CAMPING CARD SITE

PREMIER PARK

►►►►► 89% Islawrffordd Caravan Park (SH584215)

LL43 2AQ
☎ 01341 247269
e-mail: jane@islawrffordd.co.uk
dir: On seaward side of A496 (coast road), 4m N of Barmouth, 6m S of Harlech

* 🚐 £25-£33.50 🚍 £25-£33.50 ⛺ £20-£33.50

Open Mar-1 Nov

Last arrival 20.00hrs Last departure noon

Situated on the coast between Barmouth and Harlech, and within the Snowdonia National Park, with clear views of Cardigan Bay, the Lleyn Peninsula and the Snowdonia and Cader Idris mountain ranges, this excellent, family-run and family-friendly park has seen considerable investment over recent years. Fully matured, the touring area boasts fully serviced pitches, a superb toilet block with under-floor heating and top-quality fittings, and the park has private access to miles of sandy beach. 25 acre site. 105 touring pitches. 75 hardstandings. Caravan pitches. Motorhome pitches. Tent pitches. 201 statics.

AA Pubs & Restaurants nearby: Victoria Inn, Llanbedr 01341 241213

LEISURE: 🎱 Indoor swimming pool 🏊 Outdoor swimming pool ⛰ Children's playground ⚲ Kid's club 🎾 Tennis court 🔍 Games room 🖵 Separate TV room ↨ 9/18 hole golf course ⚓ Boats for hire 🎬 Cinema 🎵 Entertainment 🎣 Fishing ◎ Mini golf ⛵ Watersports 🏋 Gym 🏟 Sports field Spa U Stables

FACILITIES: 🛁 Bath 🚿 Shower ☉ Electric shaver 🗲 Hairdryer ☀ Ice Pack Facility ⚙ Disabled facilities 🕙 Public telephone 🛍 Shop on site or within 200yds 🖩 Mobile shop (calls at least 5 days a week) 🍖 BBQ area 🎋 Picnic area WiFi Wi-fi 💻 Internet access ♻ Recycling 🛈 Tourist info 🐕 Dog exercise area

Islawrffordd Caravan Park

Leisure: 🏊 ⛰ 🎣 ▢
Facilities: 🛒 ⊙ 🅿 ⚒ ☀ & ⏰ 💷 ♻ ❓
Services: 🔌 🗄 🍽 🛢 🗑 📋 ⓣ 🍴 🔋 ⚐ ⚒
Within 3 miles: 🛁 ⚐ ◎ ⚓ 🏧 📮 ∪

Notes: Strictly families & couples only, no groups. Dogs must be kept on leads.

see advert on page 430

TYWYN Map 14 SH50

Places to visit

Talyllyn Railway, TYWYN 01654 710472
www.talyllyn.co.uk

Castell-y-Bere, LLANFIHANGEL-Y-PENNANT
01443 336000 www.cadw.wales.gov.uk

Great for kids: King Arthur's Labyrinth,
MACHYNLLETH 01654 761584
www.kingarthurslabyrinth.co.uk

►►►► 81% Ynysymaengwyn Caravan Park *(SH602021)*

LL36 9RY
☎ 01654 710684
e-mail: rita@ynysy.co.uk
dir: *On A493, 1m N of Tywyn, towards Dolgellau*

* 🚐 £18-£26 ⛺ £18-£23 ▲ £12-£25

Open Etr or Apr-Oct

Last arrival 23.00hrs Last departure noon

A lovely park set in the wooded grounds of a former manor house, with designated nature trails through 13 acres of wildlife-rich woodland, scenic river walks, fishing and a sandy beach nearby. The attractive stone amenity block is clean and well kept, and this smart municipal park is ideal for families. 4 acre site. 80 touring pitches. Caravan pitches. Motorhome pitches. Tent pitches. 115 statics.

Leisure: ⛰
Facilities: 🛒 ⊙ 🅿 ☀ & ⏰ ♻ 🏐 🚼 🏸
Services: 🔌 🗄 🍽 🗑 ⚒
Within 3 miles: 🛁 🏧 ⚐ ◎ ⚓ 🏧 📮 ∪
Notes: 🐕 Dogs must be kept on leads.

MONMOUTHSHIRE

ABERGAVENNY Map 9 SO21

Places to visit

White Castle, WHITE CASTLE 01600 780380
www.cadw.wales.gov.uk

Hen Gwrt, LLANTILIO CROSSENNY 01443 336000
www.cadw.wales.gov.uk

Great for kids: Raglan Castle, RAGLAN
01291 690228 www.cadw.wales.gov.uk

►►► 79% Pyscodlyn Farm Caravan & Camping Site *(SO266155)*

Llanwenarth Citra NP7 7ER
☎ 01873 853271 & 07816 447942
e-mail: pyscodlyn.farm@virgin.net
dir: *From Abergavenny take A40 (Brecon road), site 1.5m from entrance of Nevill Hall Hospital, on left 50yds past phone box*

* 🚐 £14-£15 ⛺ £14-£15 ▲ £14-£15

Open Apr-Oct

With its outstanding views of the mountains, this quiet park in the Brecon Beacons National Park makes a pleasant venue for country lovers. The Sugarloaf Mountain and the River Usk are within easy walking distance and, despite being a working farm, dogs are welcome. Please note that credit cards are not taken on this site. 4.5 acre site. 60 touring pitches. Caravan pitches. Motorhome pitches. Tent pitches. 6 statics.

AA Pubs & Restaurants nearby: Angel Hotel, Abergavenny 01873 857121

Llansantffraed Court Hotel, Llanvihangel Gobion, Abergavenny 01873 840678

Facilities: 🛒 ⊙ ☀ & 🏸 ♻ ❓
Services: 🔌 🗄 🍽 🗑
Within 3 miles: 🛁 🏧 ⚐ ◎ 🏧 ∪
Notes: 🐕 Dogs must be kept on leads.

DINGESTOW Map 9 SO41

Places to visit

Raglan Castle, RAGLAN 01291 690228
www.cadw.wales.gov.uk

Tintern Abbey, TINTERN PARVA 01291 689251
www.cadw.wales.gov.uk

Great for kids: The Nelson Museum & Local History Centre, MONMOUTH 01600 710630

AA CAMPING CARD SITE

►►► 82% Bridge Caravan Park & Camping Site *(SO459104)*

Bridge Farm NP25 4DY
☎ 01600 740241
e-mail: info@bridgecaravanpark.co.uk
dir: *Telephone site for detailed directions*

* 🚐 £15-£18 ⛺ £15-£18 ▲ £15-£18

Open Etr-Oct

Last arrival 22.00hrs Last departure 16.00hrs

The River Trothy runs along the edge of this quiet village park, which has been owned by the same family for many years. Touring pitches are both grass and hardstanding, and there is a backdrop of woodland. The quality facilities are enhanced by good laundry equipment. Dog walking area. There is a village shop within 100 yards and a play field within 200 yards. 4 acre site. 94 touring pitches. 15 hardstandings. Caravan pitches. Motorhome pitches. Tent pitches.

AA Pubs & Restaurants nearby: Beaufort Arms Coaching Inn & Brasserie, Raglan 01291 690412

Facilities: 🛒 ⊙ 🅿 ☀ & ⏰ 🏧 🚼 🏸 ♻ ❓
Services: 🔌 🗄 🍽 🗑 ⚒
Within 3 miles: 🛁 ⚓ 🏧 ⚐ 🏧 ∪
Notes: 🐕 Dogs must be kept on leads. Fishing.

ISLAWRFFORDD CARAVAN PARK

TALYBONT, NR BARMOUTH, GWYNEDD, LL43 2AQ, NORTH WALES

01341 247269

Email: info@islawrffordd.co.uk   www.islawrffordd.co.uk

A family owned park Est. 1957

"AA CAMPSITE OF THE YEAR 2012"

Family owned and run since being established in 1957, Islawrffordd Caravan Park offers the very best in quality which you are immediately aware of when entering the award winning reception building now to be complimented in 2011 with similar architectural design to the laundry, bar and amusement/take-away facilities.

Situated at the southern end of the magnificent Snowdonia National Park coastline in the village of Talybont, Islawrffordd offers 201 holiday home bases, 75 touring caravan/motorhome plots and 30 camping pitches all benefitting from the very best facilities, including a heated indoor swimming pool/sauna/jacuzzi and tanning suite.

Nigel Mansell, O.B.E. & 1992 Formula 1 World Champion & Indy Car World Champion 1993 has a Holiday Home association with Islawrffordd that stretches back from the present day to his childhood and his opinion of the Snowdonia Coastline area and our park is still the same "It's absolutely fantastic".

Choice of a Champion

LEISURE: Indoor swimming pool Outdoor swimming pool Children's playground Kid's club Tennis court Games room Separate TV room 9/18 hole golf course Boats for hire Cinema Entertainment Fishing Mini golf Watersports Gym Sports field **Spa** Stables
FACILITIES: Bath Shower Electric shaver Hairdryer Ice Pack Facility Disabled facilities Public telephone Shop on site or within 200yds Mobile shop (calls at least 5 days a week) BBQ area Picnic area **WI-Fi** Wi-fi Internet access Recycling Tourist info Dog exercise area

USK
Map 9 SO30

Places to visit

Caerleon Roman Baths, CAERLEON
01663 422518 www.cadw.wales.gov.uk

Big Pit National Coal Museum, BLAENAVON
01495 790311 www.museumwales.ac.uk

Great for kids: Greenmeadow Community
Farm, CWMBRAN 01633 647662
www.greenmeadowcommunityfarm.org.uk

PREMIER PARK

►►►►► 85% Pont Kemys Caravan & Camping Park (SO348058)

Chainbridge NP7 9DS
☎ 01873 880688
e-mail: info@pontkemys.com
web: www.pontkemys.com
dir: From Usk take B4598 towards Abergavenny. Approx 4m, over river bridge, bear right, 300yds to site. For other routes contact site for detailed directions

* ⚏ £15-£19 ⚏ £15-£19 Å £15-£19

Open Mar-Oct

Last arrival 21.00hrs Last departure noon

A peaceful park next to the River Usk, offering an excellent standard of toilet facilities with family rooms. A section of the park has fully serviced pitches. The park is in a rural area with mature trees and country views, and attracts quiet visitors who enjoy the many attractions of this area. The local golf club is open during the day and serves breakfast and lunches. 8 acre site. 65 touring pitches. 29 hardstandings. 25 seasonal pitches. Caravan pitches. Motorhome pitches. Tent pitches.

AA Pubs & Restaurants nearby: Raglan Arms, Llandenny 01291 690800

Nags Head Inn, Usk 01291 672820

Three Salmons Hotel, Usk 01291 672133

Leisure: ✪ ▢
Facilities: ⬤ ☉ ℙ ✳ ⬤ ⬤ ⬤ ⬤ ⬤ 🚻 ♻ ❶
Services: ⬤ ⬤ ⬤ ⬤ ⬤ ⬤
Within 3 miles: ⬤ ⬤ ⬤ ⬤

Notes: No music allowed on site. Dogs must be kept on leads. Mother & baby room, kitchen facilities for groups.

PEMBROKESHIRE

See Walk 15 in the Walks & Cycle Rides section at the end of the guide

BROAD HAVEN
Map 8 SM81

Places to visit

Pembroke Castle, PEMBROKE 01646 681510
www.pembrokecastle.co.uk

Llawhaden Castle, LLAWHADEN 01443 336000
www.cadw.wales.gov.uk

Great for kids: Scolton Manor Museum & Country Park, SCOLTON 01437 731328 (Museum)

►►► 86% Creampots Touring Caravan & Camping Park (SM882131)

Broadway SA62 3TU
☎ 01437 781776
e-mail: creampots@btconnect.com
dir: From Haverfordwest take B4341 to Broadway. Turn left, follow brown tourist signs to site

⚏ ⚏ Å

Open Mar-Jan

Last arrival 21.00hrs Last departure noon

Set just outside the Pembrokeshire National Park, this quiet site is just one and a half miles from a safe sandy beach at Broad Haven, and the coastal footpath. The park is well laid out and carefully maintained, and the toilet block offers a good standard of facilities. The owners welcome families. 8 acre site. 72 touring pitches. 20

hardstandings. Caravan pitches. Motorhome pitches. Tent pitches. 1 static.

AA Pubs & Restaurants nearby: Swan Inn, Little Haven 01437 781880

Facilities: ⬤ ☉ ℙ ✳ ⬤ ⬤ 🚻 ♻ ❶
Services: ⬤ ⬤ ⬤ ⬤ ⬤
Within 3 miles: ⬤ ⬤ ⬤ ⬤ ⬤ ⬤ ⬤

Notes: Dogs must be kept on leads.

►►► 77% South Cockett Caravan & Camping Park (SM878136)

South Cockett SA62 3TU
☎ 01437 781296 & 781760
e-mail: esmejames@hotmail.co.uk
dir: From Haverfordwest take B4341 to Broad Haven, at Broadway turn left, site 300yds

⚏ ⚏ Å

Open Etr-Oct

Last arrival 22.30hrs

A small park on a working farm, with touring areas divided into neat paddocks by high, well-trimmed hedges. Good toilet facilities, and in a convenient location for the lovely beach at nearby Broad Haven. 6 acre site. 73 touring pitches. Caravan pitches. Motorhome pitches. Tent pitches.

AA Pubs & Restaurants nearby: Swan Inn, Little Haven 01437 781880

Facilities: ⬤ ☉ ✳ ⬤ ♻
Services: ⬤ ⬤ ⬤ ⬤ ⬤
Within 3 miles: ⬤ ⬤ ⬤ ⬤ ⬤ ⬤ ⬤

Notes: ⊗ Dogs must be kept on leads.

FISHGUARD — Map 8 SM93

Places to visit

Pentre Ifan Burial Chamber, NEWPORT
01443 336000 www.cadw.wales.gov.uk

Tredegar House & Park, NEWPORT
01633 815880 www.newport.gov.uk

Great for kids: OceanLab, FISHGUARD
01348 874737 www.ocean-lab.co.uk

►►► 89% Fishguard Bay Caravan & Camping Park (SM984383)

Garn Gelli SA65 9ET
☎ 01348 811415
e-mail: enquiries@fishguardbay.com
web: www.fishguardbay.com
dir: If approaching Fishguard from Cardigan on A487 ignore Sat Nav to turn right. Turn at campsite sign onto single track road

* 🚐 £18-£22 🚙 £18-£22 ▲ £17-£21

Open Mar-9 Jan
Last arrival anytime Last departure noon

Set high up on cliffs with outstanding views of Fishguard Bay, and the Pembrokeshire Coastal Path running right through the centre. The park is extremely well kept, with three good toilet blocks, a common room with TV, a lounge/library, decent laundry, and well-stocked shop. 5 acre site. 50 touring pitches. 4 hardstandings. Caravan pitches. Motorhome pitches. Tent pitches. 50 statics.

AA Pubs & Restaurants nearby: Sloop Inn, Porthgain 01348 831449

The Shed, Porthgain 01348 831518

Salutation Inn, Felindre Farchog 01239 820564

Fishguard Bay Caravan & Camping Park

Leisure: 🅰 🎱 ▢
Facilities: 🍴 ⊙ 🏠 ☀ 🕓 🧴 🎪 Wi-Fi ♻ 🛈
Services: 🚐 📮 🛢 🧺 T 🍴
Within 3 miles: ⚓ 🎣 ⛳ 🚣 🛒 🛍 ♻
Notes: Dogs must be kept on leads.

►►► 75% Gwaun Vale Touring Park (SM977356)

Llanychaer SA65 9TA
☎ 01348 874698
e-mail: margaret.harries@talk21.com
dir: B4313 from Fishguard. Site 1.5m on right

🚐 🚙 ▲

Open Apr-Oct

Last arrival anytime Last departure 11.00hrs

Located at the opening of the beautiful Gwaun Valley, this well-kept park is set on the hillside with pitches tiered on two levels. There are lovely views of the surrounding countryside, and good facilities. 1.6 acre site. 29 touring pitches. 5 hardstandings. Caravan pitches. Motorhome pitches. Tent pitches. 1 static.

AA Pubs & Restaurants nearby: Sloop Inn, Porthgain 01348 831449

The Shed, Porthgain 01348 831518

Salutation Inn, Felindre Farchog 01239 820564

Leisure: 🅰
Facilities: 🍴 ⊙ 🏠 ☀ 🕓 🧴 🎪 🚻
Services: 🚐 📮 🧺
Within 3 miles: ⚓ 🎣 ⛳ 🛒 🛍 ♻
Notes: No skateboards. Dogs must be kept on leads. Guidebooks available.

LEISURE: 🏊 Indoor swimming pool 🏊 Outdoor swimming pool 🅰 Children's playground 🪁 Kid's club 🎾 Tennis court 🎱 Games room ▢ Separate TV room 🏌 9/18 hole golf course ⚓ Boats for hire 🎬 Cinema 🎵 Entertainment 🎣 Fishing ◎ Mini golf 🏄 Watersports 🏋 Gym 🏟 Sports field **Spa** ⛎ Stables
FACILITIES: 🛁 Bath 🚿 Shower ⊙ Electric shaver 🪮 Hairdryer ☀ Ice Pack Facility ♿ Disabled facilities 🕓 Public telephone 🛍 Shop on site or within 200yds 🛒 Mobile shop (calls at least 5 days a week) 🍴 BBQ area 🎪 Picnic area Wi-Fi Wi-fi ▬ Internet access ♻ Recycling 🛈 Tourist info 🐕 Dog exercise area

HASGUARD CROSS   Map 8 SM80

Places to visit

Pembroke Castle, PEMBROKE 01646 681510
www.pembrokecastle.co.uk

AA CAMPING CARD SITE

►►► 82% Hasguard Cross Caravan Park *(SM850108)*

SA62 3SL
☎ **01437 781443**
e-mail: hasguard@aol.com
dir: *From Haverfordwest take B4327 towards Dale. In 7m right at x-rds. Site 1st right*

* ⌖ £25-£29 ⌖ £25-£29 ▲ £15-£19

Open all year (rs Aug tent field for 28 days)

Last arrival 21.00hrs Last departure 10.00hrs

A very clean, efficient and well-run site in the Pembrokeshire National Park, just one and a half miles from the sea and beach at Little Haven, and with views of the surrounding hills. The toilet and shower facilities are immaculately clean, and there is a licensed bar (evenings only) serving a good choice of food. 4.5 acre site. 12 touring pitches. 3 hardstandings. Caravan pitches. Motorhome pitches. Tent pitches. 42 statics.

AA Pubs & Restaurants nearby: Swan Inn, Little Haven 01437 781880

Leisure: ✪

Facilities: ⍾☉☂✳⚸⍉⤢⊐⌂♻ ❶

Services: ⌖⍾⍾⌾⍾⍾⍾⤢⛶⟱

Within 3 miles: ↓⌖⟲⟲⌾⍾⍾U

Notes: Dogs must be kept on leads.

HAVERFORDWEST   Map 8 SM91

Places to visit

Llawhaden Castle, LLAWHADEN 01443 336000
www.cadw.wales.gov.uk

Carew Castle & Tidal Mill, CAREW
01646 651782 www.carewcastle.com

Great for kids: Oakwood Theme Park, NARBERTH
01834 891373 www.oakwoodthemepark.co.uk

AA CAMPING CARD SITE

►► 81% Nolton Cross Caravan Park *(SM879177)*

Nolton SA62 3NP
☎ **01437 710701**
e-mail: info@noltoncross-holidays.co.uk
web: www.noltoncross-holidays.co.uk
dir: *1m from A487 (Haverfordwest to St Davids road) at Simpson Cross, towards Nolton & Broadhaven*

* ⌖ £8.50-£15.50 ⌖ £8.50-£15.50
▲ £8.50-£15.50

Open Mar-Dec

Last arrival 22.00hrs Last departure noon

High grassy banks surround the touring area of this park next to the owners' working farm. It is located on open ground above the sea and St Bride's Bay (within one and a half miles), and there is a coarse fishing lake close by - equipment for hire and reduced permit rates for campers are available. 4 acre site. 15 touring pitches. Caravan pitches. Motorhome pitches. Tent pitches. 30 statics.

AA Pubs & Restaurants nearby: Swan Inn, Little Haven 01437 781880

Leisure: ⋒

Facilities: ⍾☉✳⍉⌾⊐▥ ♻ ❶

Services: ⌖⍾⍾T⤢

Within 3 miles: ⟲⌾⍾⍾U

Notes: No youth groups. Dogs must be kept on leads.

LITTLE HAVEN

See Hasguard Cross

ROSEBUSH   Map 8 SN02

Places to visit

Cilgerran Castle, CILGERRAN 01239 621339
www.cadw.wales.gov.uk

OceanLab, FISHGUARD 01348 874737
www.ocean-lab.co.uk

Great for kids: Llawhaden Castle, LLAWHADEN
01443 336000 www.cadw.wales.gov.uk

►► 73% Rosebush Caravan Park *(SN073293)*

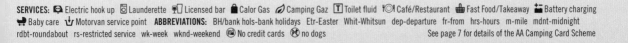

Rhoslwyn SA66 7QT
☎ **01437 532206 & 07831 223166**
dir: *From A40, near Narberth, take B4313, between Haverfordwest & Cardigan take B4329, site 1m*

⌖⌖▲

Open 14 Mar-Oct

Last arrival 23.00hrs Last departure noon

A most attractive park with a large ornamental lake at its centre and good landscaping. Situated off the main tourist track, it offers lovely views of the Preseli Hills which can be reached by a scenic walk. Rosebush is a quiet village with a handy pub, and the park owner also runs the village shop. Please note that due to the deep lake on site, children are not accepted. 12 acre site. 65 touring pitches. Caravan pitches. Motorhome pitches. Tent pitches. 15 statics.

AA Pubs & Restaurants nearby: Tafarn Sinc, Rosebush 01437 532214

Facilities: ⍾☉☂✳⌾⊐♻ ❶

Services: ⌖⤢

Within 3 miles: ⟲◎

Notes: Adults only. ⊗

ST DAVIDS   Map 8 SM72

Places to visit

St Davids Bishop's Palace, ST DAVIDS
01437 720517 www.cadw.wales.gov.uk

St Davids Cathedral, ST DAVID'S 01437 720202
www.stdavidscathedral.org.uk

Great for kids: Oakwood Theme Park, NARBERTH
01834 891373 www.oakwoodthemepark.co.uk

PREMIER PARK

AA CAMPSITE OF THE YEAR FOR WALES 2013

►►►►► 86% Caerfai Bay Caravan & Tent Park (SM759244)

Caerfai Bay SA62 6QT
☎ 01437 720274
e-mail: info@caerfaibay.co.uk
web: www.caerfaibay.co.uk
dir: At St Davids exit A487 at Visitor Centre/Grove Hotel. Follow signs for Caerfai Bay. Right at end of road

🚐 £14-£18.50 🚎 £12-£18.50 ▲ £12-£16.50

Open Mar-mid Nov

Last arrival 21.00hrs Last departure 11.00hrs

Magnificent coastal scenery and an outlook over St Bride's Bay can be enjoyed from this delightful site, located just 300 yards from a bathing beach. The excellent toilet facilities include four family rooms, which are a huge asset to the park, and ongoing improvements include a second, solar-heated wet suit shower room, upgraded roadways, and modernised water points. There is an excellent farm shop just across the road. 10 acre site. 106 touring pitches. 24 hardstandings. Caravan pitches. Motorhome pitches. Tent pitches. 33 statics. See also page 19.

AA Pubs & Restaurants nearby: Cwtch, St Davids 01437 720491

Sloop Inn, Porthgain 01348 831449

The Shed, Porthgain 01348 831518

Cambrian Inn, Solva 01437 721210

Facilities: 🍴☉🏈🛠️☀️👥🛈🧺📶💻♻️❂
Services: 🔌🔲💧🗑️🛒🔄
Within 3 miles: 🎣🏇🚣♨️🏊🅿️📖

Notes: No dogs in tent field mid Jul-Aug, no skateboards or rollerblades. Dogs must be kept on leads. Family washrooms.

►►► 81% Hendre Eynon Camping & Caravan Site (SM771284)

SA62 6DB
☎ 01437 720474
e-mail: hendreeynoninfo@gmail.com
dir: Take A487 (Fishguard road) from St Davids, left at rugby club signed Llanrhian. Site 2m on right (NB do no take turn to Whitesands)

* 🚐 £14-£20 🚎 £14-£20 ▲ £14-£20

Open Apr-Sep

Last arrival 21.00hrs Last departure noon

A peaceful country site on a working farm, with a modern toilet block including family rooms. Within easy reach of many lovely sandy beaches, and two miles from the cathedral city of St Davids. 7 acre site. 50 touring pitches. 20 seasonal pitches. Caravan pitches. Motorhome pitches. Tent pitches.

AA Pubs & Restaurants nearby: Cwtch, St Davids 01437 720491

Sloop Inn, Porthgain 01348 831449

The Shed, Porthgain 01348 831518

Cambrian Inn, Solva 01437 721210

Facilities: 🍴☉☀️👥🛈🏇❂
Services: 🔌🔲💧🗑️🛒
Within 3 miles: 🎣🏇🚣♨️🏊🅿️📖↻

Notes: ❂ Maximum 2 dogs per unit. Dogs must be kept on leads.

►►► 80% *Tretio Caravan & Camping Park* (SM787292)

SA62 6DE
☎ 01437 781600
e-mail: info@tretio.com
dir: *From St Davids take A487 towards Fishguard, left at Rugby Football Club, straight on for 3m. Site signed, left to site*

🚐 🚎 ▲

Open Mar-Oct

Last arrival 20.00hrs Last departure 10.00hrs

An attractive site in a very rural spot with distant country views, and beautiful local beaches. A mobile shop calls daily at peak periods, and the tiny cathedral city of St Davids is only three miles away. 6.5 acre site. 40 touring pitches. 8 seasonal pitches. Caravan pitches. Motorhome pitches. Tent pitches. 30 statics.

AA Pubs & Restaurants nearby: Cwtch, St Davids 01437 720491

Sloop Inn, Porthgain 01348 831449

The Shed, Porthgain 01348 831518

Cambrian Inn, Solva 01437 721210

Leisure: 🏓❂
Facilities: 🍴☉🏈☀️👥🏞️🏇♻️❂
Services: 🔌🔲🗑️🔤🛒
Within 3 miles: 🎣🏇🚣♨️◎🏊🅿️📖

Notes: Dogs must be kept on leads. Pitch & putt.

TENBY

Places to visit

Tudor Merchant's House, TENBY 01834 842279 www.nationaltrust.org.ukmain-w-tudormerchantshouse

Tenby Museum & Art Gallery, TENBY 01834 842809 www.tenbymuseum.org.uk

Great for kids: Colby Woodland Garden, AMROTH 01834 811885 www.nationaltrust.org.uk/main

---

TENBY
Map 8 SN10

85% Kiln Park Holiday Centre (SN119002)

Marsh Rd SA70 7RB
☎ 0871 231 0889
e-mail: kilnpark@haven.com
web: www.haven.com/kilnpark
dir: Follow A477, A478 to Tenby for 6m, then follow signs to Penally, site 0.5m on left

Open mid Mar-end Oct (rs mid Mar-May & Sep-Oct some facilities may be reduced)

Last arrival dusk Last departure 10.00hrs

A large holiday complex complete with leisure and sports facilities, and lots of entertainment for all the family. There are bars and cafés, and plenty of security. This touring, camping and static site is on the outskirts of town, with a short walk through dunes to the sandy beach. The well-equipped toilet block is very clean. 103 acre site. 130 touring pitches. Caravan pitches. Motorhome pitches. Tent pitches. 703 statics.

AA Pubs & Restaurants nearby: Stackpole Inn, Stackpole 01646 672324

New Inn, Amroth 01834 812368

Leisure: 🏊⚽🎾 ♨🎣🎮♪
Facilities: ⛺📶✳🔥🔌👶📷🚻♿
Services: 🔌🗑🍺💧🧺📷🍴🚮
Within 3 miles: 🎣🚤🏌🐎🛒◎🌊🎱🎯⛳

Notes: Max 2 dogs per booking, certain dog breeds banned, no commercial vehicles, no bookings by persons under 21yrs unless a family booking. Entertainment complex, bowling & putting green.

see advert on page 432

►►►► 87% Trefalun Park (SN093027)

Devonshire Dr, St Florence SA70 8RD
☎ 01646 651514
e-mail: trefalun@aol.com
dir: 1.5m NW of St Florence & 0.5m N of B4318

* 🚐 £14.50-£25 🚙 £14.50-£22 ⛺ £14.50-£22

Open Etr-Oct

Last arrival 19.00hrs Last departure noon

Set within 12 acres of sheltered, well-kept grounds, this quiet country park offers well-maintained level grass pitches separated by bushes and trees, with plenty of space to relax in. Children can feed the park's friendly pets. Plenty of activities are available at the nearby Heatherton Country Sports Park, including go-karting, indoor bowls, golf and bumper boating. 12 acre site. 90 touring pitches. 54 hardstandings. 45 seasonal pitches. Caravan pitches. Motorhome pitches. Tent pitches. 10 statics.

AA Pubs & Restaurants nearby: Stackpole Inn, Stackpole 01646 672324

New Inn, Amroth 01834 812368

Leisure: ♨
Facilities: ⛺☉✳🔥🔌👶🚻📶♿🅿
Services: 🔌🗑💧🧺🅃🚮🚮♿
Within 3 miles: 🎣🚤🏌◎🌊🎱🎯

Notes: No motorised scooters. Dogs must be kept on leads.

see advert on page 436

AA CAMPING CARD SITE

►►►► 81% Well Park Caravan & Camping Site (SN128028)

SA70 8TL
☎ 01834 842179
e-mail: enquiries@wellparkcaravans.co.uk
dir: A478 towards Tenby. At rdbt at Kilgetty follow Tenby/A478 signs. 3m to next rdbt, take 2nd exit, site 2nd right

* 🚐 £14-£27 🚙 £14-£27 ⛺ £14-£20

Open Mar-Oct (rs Mar-mid Jun & mid Sep-Oct bar may be closed)

Last arrival 22.00hrs Last departure 11.00hrs

An attractive, well-maintained park with good landscaping from trees, ornamental shrubs, and flower borders. The amenities include a launderette and indoor dishwashing, games room with table tennis, and an enclosed play area. The park is ideally situated between Tenby and Saundersfoot; Tenby just a 15-minute walk away, or the town can be reached via a traffic-free cycle track. 10 acre site. 100 touring pitches. 16 hardstandings. Caravan pitches. Motorhome pitches. Tent pitches. 42 statics.

AA Pubs & Restaurants nearby: Stackpole Inn, Stackpole 01646 672324

New Inn, Amroth 01834 812368

Leisure: ♨🎣🎮
Facilities: ⛺☉✳🔥🔌👶📷🚻📶♿🅿
Services: 🔌🗑🍺💧🧺📷🚮♿
Within 3 miles: 🎣🚤🏌◎🌊🎱🎯⛳

Notes: Family groups only. Dogs must be kept on leads. TV hook-ups.

TENBY *continued*

AA CAMPING CARD SITE

▶▶▶ **76% Wood Park Caravans**

(SN128025)

New Hedges SA70 8TL
☎ **01834 843414** & **0844 4141464 (winter)**
e-mail: info@woodpark.co.uk
dir: *At rdbt 2m N of Tenby follow A478 towards Tenby, take 2nd right & right again*

* 🚐 £15-£25 🚃 £15-£25 ⛺ £14-£23

Open Spring BH-Sep (rs May & mid-end Sep bar, laundrette & games room may not be open)

Last arrival 22.00hrs Last departure 10.00hrs

Situated in beautiful countryside between the popular seaside resorts of Tenby and Saundersfoot, and with Waterwynch Bay just a 15-minute walk away, this peaceful site provides a spacious and relaxing atmosphere for holidays. The slightly sloping touring area is partly divided by shrubs into three paddocks. 10 acre site. 60 touring pitches. 40 hardstandings. 10 seasonal pitches. Caravan pitches. Motorhome pitches. Tent pitches. 90 statics.

AA Pubs & Restaurants nearby: Stackpole Inn, Stackpole 01646 672324

New Inn, Amroth 01834 812368

Leisure: 🅰 🔍
Facilities: 🐾 ⊙ 𝒫 ✳ ♻ 🛈
Services: 🖳 🗄 🍴 🎒 ∅ 🛒
Within 3 miles: ⌕ ⫯ 🌊 ⊚ 🛶 🏬

Notes: 🐕 No groups. 1 car per unit, only small dogs accepted, no dogs Jul-Aug & BHs. Dogs must be kept on leads.

FRIENDLY FAMILY HOLIDAYS

HOLIDAY HOMES TOURING VANS CAMPING

Trefalun Park

RING FOR FREE COLOUR BROCHURE
01646 651514
ST. FLORENCE, TENBY, PEMBROKESHIRE SA70 8RD
www.trefalunpark.co.uk

MEMBER   EXCELLENT

LEISURE: 🏊 Indoor swimming pool 🏊 Outdoor swimming pool 🅰 Children's playground 🪁 Kid's club 🎾 Tennis court 🔍 Games room ▭ Separate TV room ⌕ 9/18 hole golf course ⛵ Boats for hire 🎬 Cinema 🎵 Entertainment 🎣 Fishing ⊚ Mini golf 🌊 Watersports 🏋 Gym ⚽ Sports field **Spa** ∪ Stables
FACILITIES: 🛁 Bath 🚿 Shower ⊙ Electric shaver 𝒫 Hairdryer ✳ Ice Pack Facility ♿ Disabled facilities ☎ Public telephone 🛒 Shop on site or within 200yds 🏪 Mobile shop (calls at least 5 days a week) 🍴 BBQ area ⛱ Picnic area 📶 Wi-fi 💻 Internet access ♻ Recycling 🛈 Tourist info 🐾 Dog exercise area

POWYS

BRECON Map 9 SO02

Places to visit

Brecknock Museum & Art Gallery, BRECON 01874 624121 www.powys.gov.uk/breconmuseum

Regimental Museum of The Royal Welsh, BRECON 01874 613310 www.rrw.org.uk

PREMIER PARK

►►►►► 88% Pencelli Castle Caravan & Camping Park *(SO096248)*

Pencelli LD3 7LX
☎ 01874 665451
e-mail: pencelli@tiscali.co.uk
dir: *Exit A40 2m E of Brecon onto B4558, follow signs to Pencelli*

🚐 🚙 ⛺

Open Feb-27 Nov (rs 30 Oct-Etr shop closed)

Last arrival 22.00hrs Last departure noon

Lying in the heart of the Brecon Beacons National Park, this charming park offers peace, beautiful scenery and high quality facilities. It is bordered by the Brecon and Monmouth Canal. The attention to detail is superb, and the well-equipped heated toilets with en suite cubicles are matched by a drying room for clothes and boots, full laundry, and a shop. Regular buses stop just outside the gate and go to Brecon, Abergavenny and Swansea. 10 acre site. 80 touring pitches. 40 hardstandings. Caravan pitches. Motorhome pitches. Tent pitches.

AA Pubs & Restaurants nearby: Felin Fach Griffin, Felin Fach 01874 620111

White Swan Inn, Llanfrynach 01874 665276

Leisure: 🛝

Facilities: 🚿 ☉ 💨 ✱ ♿ ☎ 🛍 ⛩ [Wi-fi] ♻ ℹ

Services: 🔌 🧺 🛢 🔥 [T] 🔋 ⚓

Within 3 miles: ⛵ 🎣 ⛳ 🛍 🧺 U

Notes: Assistance dogs only. No radios, music or campfires. Cycle hire.

BRONLLYS Map 9 SO13

Places to visit

Brecknock Museum & Art Gallery, BRECON 01874 624121 www.powys.gov.uk/breconmuseum

Regimental Museum of The Royal Welsh, BRECON 01874 613310 www.rrw.org.uk

AA CAMPING CARD SITE

►►►► 80% Anchorage Caravan Park *(SO142351)*

LD3 0LD
☎ 01874 711246 & 711230
dir: *8m NE of Brecon in village centre*

🚐 fr £12 🚙 fr £12 ⛺ fr £12

Open all year (rs Nov-Mar TV room closed)

Last arrival 23.00hrs Last departure 18.00hrs

A well-maintained site with a choice of south-facing, sloping grass pitches and superb views of the Black Mountains, or a more sheltered lower area with a number of excellent super pitches. The site is a short distance from the water sports centre at Llangorse Lake. 8 acre site. 110 touring pitches. 8 hardstandings. 60 seasonal pitches. Caravan pitches. Motorhome pitches. Tent pitches. 101 statics.

AA Pubs & Restaurants nearby: Castle Inn, Talgarth 01874 711353

Old Black Lion, Hay-on-Wye 01497 820841

Kilverts Inn, Hay-on-Wye 01497 821042

Leisure: 🛝 □

Facilities: 🚿 ☉ 💨 ✱ ♿ ☎ 🛍 ⛩ 🐕 ♻ ℹ

Services: 🔌 🧺 🛢 🔥 [T] 🔋

Within 3 miles: ⛳ 🛍 🧺 U

Notes: Dogs must be kept on leads. Post office, hairdresser.

BUILTH WELLS Map 9 SO05

►►►► 80% *Fforest Fields Caravan & Camping Park*

(SO100535)

Hundred House LD1 5RT
☎ 01982 570406
e-mail: office@fforestfields.co.uk
web: www.fforestfields.co.uk
dir: *From town follow New Radnor signs on A481. 4m to signed entrance on right, 0.5m before Hundred House village*

🚐 🚙 ⛺

Open Etr & Apr-Oct

Last arrival 21.00hrs Last departure 18.00hrs

A sheltered park in a hidden valley with wonderful views and plenty of wildlife. Set in unspoilt countryside, this is a peaceful park with delightful hill walks beginning on site. The historic town of Builth Wells and the Royal Welsh Showground are only four miles away, and there are plenty of outdoor activities in the vicinity. 12 acre site. 60 touring pitches. 17 hardstandings. Caravan pitches. Motorhome pitches. Tent pitches.

AA Pubs & Restaurants nearby: Laughing Dog, Howey 01597 822406

Facilities: 🚿 ☉ 💨 ✱ ☎ 🐕 [Wi-fi]

Services: 🔌 🧺 🛢 🔥 🔋

Within 3 miles: 🎣 ⛵ ⛳ 🛍 🧺

Notes: 🚫💳 No loud music or revelry. Bread, dairy produce & cured bacon available.

CRICKHOWELL Map 9 SO21

Places to visit

Tretower Court & Castle, TRETOWER
01874 730279 www.cadw.wales.gov.uk

Big Pit National Coal Museum, BLAENAVON
01495 790311 www.museumwales.ac.uk

Great for kids: Grosmont Castle, GROSMONT
01981 240301 www.cadw.wales.gov.uk

►►► 80% Riverside Caravan & Camping Park (SO215184)

New Rd NP8 1AY
☎ 01873 810397
dir: On A4077, well signed from A40

* ⊞ fr £15 ⊞ fr £15 ▲ fr £12

Open Mar-Oct

Last arrival 21.00hrs

A very well tended adults-only park in delightful countryside on the edge of the small country town of Crickhowell. The adjacent riverside park is an excellent facility for all, including dog-walkers. Crickhowell has numerous specialist shops including a first-class delicatessen. Within a few minutes' walk of the park are several friendly pubs with good restaurants. 3.5 acre site. 35 touring pitches. Caravan pitches. Motorhome pitches. Tent pitches. 20 statics.

AA Pubs & Restaurants nearby: Bear Hotel, Crickhowell 01873 810408

Nantyffin Cider Mill Inn, Crickhowell
01873 810775

Facilities: ♠ ⊙ ℉ ✳ ⑤ ❶
Services: ⊞ ➊ ➤
Within 3 miles: ↧ ✦ ⑤ ∪

Notes: Adults only. ⊘ No hangliders or paragliders. Dogs must be kept on leads. Large canopied area for drying clothes, cooking & socialising.

LLANDRINDOD WELLS Map 9 SO06

Places to visit

The Judge's Lodging, PRESTEIGNE 01544 260650
www.judgeslodging.org.uk

►►► 81% Disserth Caravan & Camping Park (SO035583)

Disserth, Howey LD1 6NL
☎ 01597 860277
e-mail: disserthcaravan@btconnect.com
dir: 1m from A483, between Newbridge-on-Wye & Howey, by church. Follow brown signs from A483 or A470

⊞ £13.50-£16 ⊞ £13.50-£16 ▲ £7-£25

Open Mar-Oct

Last arrival sunset Last departure noon

A delightfully secluded and predominantly adult park nestling in a beautiful valley on the banks of the River Ithon, a tributary of the River Wye. This little park is next to a 13th-century church, and has a small bar open at weekends and busy periods. The chalet toilet block offers spacious, combined cubicles. 4 acre site. 30 touring pitches. 6 hardstandings. Caravan pitches. Motorhome pitches. Tent pitches. 25 statics. 1 wooden pod.

AA Pubs & Restaurants nearby: Laughing Dog, Howey 01597 822406

Bell Country Inn, Llanyre 01597 823959

Facilities: ♠ ⊙ ℉ ✳ ⅙ ⅲⅰ ♻ ❶
Services: ⊞ ⑤ ⬚ ➊ ⦸ ⓣ ➤ ⬆
Within 3 miles: ↧ ☐ ℘ ⑤ ⑤ ∪

Notes: ⊘ Dogs must be kept on leads. Private trout fishing.

AA CAMPING CARD SITE

►► 82% Dalmore Camping & Caravanning Park (SO045568)

Howey LD1 5RG
☎ 01597 822483
dir: 3m S of Llandrindod Wells off A483. 4m N of Builth Wells, at top of hill

* ⊞ £8-£11 ⊞ £8-£11 ▲ £8-£11

Open Mar-Oct

Last arrival 22.00hrs Last departure noon

An intimate and well laid out adults-only park. Pitches are attractively terraced to ensure that all enjoy the wonderful views from this splendidly landscaped little park. Please note, dogs are not allowed on this site. 3 acre site. 20 touring pitches. 12 hardstandings. 6 seasonal pitches. Caravan pitches. Motorhome pitches. Tent pitches. 20 statics.

AA Pubs & Restaurants nearby: Laughing Dog, Howey 01597 822406

Bell Country Inn, Llanyre 01597 823959

Facilities: ♠ ⊙ ℉ ✳ ⊙ ⌂ ❶
Services: ⊞ ➊ ⦸ ➤ ⬆
Within 3 miles: ↧ ✦ ☐ ℘ ◎ ⑤ ⑤

Notes: Adults only. ⊞ ⊗ Gates closed 23.00hrs-07.00hrs, no ball games. Male & female washing areas, no cubicles.

LEISURE: 🏊 Indoor swimming pool 🏊 Outdoor swimming pool 🎢 Children's playground 🧒 Kid's club 🎾 Tennis court 🎱 Games room 📺 Separate TV room
↧ 9/18 hole golf course ⛵ Boats for hire 🎬 Cinema 🎵 Entertainment 🎣 Fishing ◎ Mini golf 🏄 Watersports 🏋 Gym ⚽ Sports field **Spa** ∪ Stables
FACILITIES: 🛁 Bath ♠ Shower ⊙ Electric shaver ℉ Hairdryer ✳ Ice Pack Facility ⅙ Disabled facilities ⊙ Public telephone ⑤ Shop on site or within 200yds
⑤ Mobile shop (calls at least 5 days a week) 🍴 BBQ area 🏓 Picnic area ⅲⅰ Wi-fi 💻 Internet access ♻ Recycling ❶ Tourist info ✦ Dog exercise area

LLANGORS   Map 9 SO12

Places to visit

Llanthony Priory, LLANTHONY 01443 336000
www.cadw.wales.gov.uk

Great for kids: Tretower Court & Castle,
TRETOWER 01874 730279
www.cadw.wales.gov.uk

►►► 76% *Lakeside Caravan Park*

(SO128272)

LD3 7TR
☎ **01874 658226**
e-mail: holidays@llangorselake.co.uk
dir: *Exit A40 at Bwlch onto B4560 towards
Talgarth. Site signed towards lake in Llangors
centre*

🚐 🚗 Å

Open Etr or Apr-Oct (rs Mar-May & Oct clubhouse,
restaurant, shop limited)

Last arrival 21.30hrs Last departure 10.00hrs

Adjacent to the common and lake in Llangors, this
attractive park has launching and mooring
facilities and is an ideal centre for water sports
enthusiasts. Popular with families, and offering a
clubhouse/bar, with a well-stocked shop and café/
takeaway next door. Boats, bikes and windsurfing
equipment can be hired on site. 2 acre site. 40
touring pitches. 8 hardstandings. Caravan
pitches. Motorhome pitches. Tent pitches. 72
statics.

AA Pubs & Restaurants nearby: Usk Inn,
Talybont-on-Usk 01874 676251

Star Inn, Talybont-on-Usk 01874 676635

Leisure: ⚓ ⚲

Facilities: 🖍 ☉ 🅿 ☀ 🖐 🛒 🚂 ♻ ❶

Services: 🔌 🗓 🍽 🔋 🧺 🚰 🚽 🍴 ♨

Within 3 miles: ≠ 🏌 🛶 🎣 🗓 🛒 ∪

Notes: No open fires. Dogs must be kept on leads.
Boat hire during summer season.

MIDDLETOWN   Map 15 SJ31

Places to visit

Powis Castle & Garden, WELSHPOOL
01938 551920 www.nationaltrust.org.uk

Great for kids: Old Oswestry Hill Fort, OSWESTRY
0870 333 1181 www.english-heritage.org.uk

►►► 79% Bank Farm Caravan Park

(SJ293123)

SY21 8EJ
☎ **01938 570526**
e-mail: bankfarmcaravans@yahoo.co.uk
dir: *13m W of Shrewsbury, 5m E of Welshpool on
A458*

* 🚐 fr £15 🚗 fr £15 Å fr £13

Open Mar-Oct

Last arrival 20.00hrs

An attractive park on a small farm, maintained to
a high standard. There are two touring areas, one
on either side of the A458, and each with its own
amenity block, and immediate access to hills,
mountains and woodland. A pub serving good
food, and a large play area are nearby. 2 acre site.
40 touring pitches. Caravan pitches. Motorhome
pitches. Tent pitches. 33 statics.

AA Pubs & Restaurants nearby: Old Hand &
Diamond Inn, Coedway 01743 884379

Leisure: ⚓ ⚲

Facilities: 🖍 ☉ ☀ 🖐 🛒 🚂 ♻ ❶

Services: 🔌 🗓 🔋 🧺

Within 3 miles: 🛶 🎣

Notes: ⊗ Dogs must be kept on leads. Coarse
fishing, jacuzzi, snooker room.

RHAYADER   Map 9 SN96

Places to visit

Blaenavon Ironworks, BLAENAVON 01495 792615
www.cadw.wales.gov.uk

White Castle, WHITE CASTLE 01600 780380
www.cadw.wales.gov.uk

Great for kids: Raglan Castle, RAGLAN
01291 690228 www.cadw.wales.gov.uk

►►► 75% Wyeside Caravan &
Camping Park *(SO967690)*

Llangurig Rd LD6 5LB
☎ **01597 810183**
e-mail: wyesidecc@powys.gov.uk
dir: *400mtrs N of Rhayader town centre on A470*

* 🚐 £17-£20 🚗 £17-£20 Å £14-£17

Open Mar-Oct

Last arrival 20.00hrs Last departure noon

With direct access from the A470, the park sits on
the banks of the River Wye. Situated just 400
metres from the centre of the market town of
Rhayader, and next to a recreation park with
tennis courts, bowling green and children's
playground. There are good riverside walks from
here, though the river is fast flowing and
unfenced, and care is especially needed when
walking with children. 6 acre site. 120 touring
pitches. 22 hardstandings. 21 seasonal pitches.
Caravan pitches. Motorhome pitches. Tent pitches.
39 statics.

AA Pubs & Restaurants nearby: Bell Country Inn,
Llanyre 01597 823959

Facilities: 🖍 ☉ 🅿 ☀ 🖐 🛒 🕐 🆆 ♻ ❶

Services: 🔌 🗓 🔋 🧺 🚰 🚽 ♨

Within 3 miles: 🎣 ◎ 🛶 🗓 🛒 ∪

Notes: No noise after 23.00hrs. Dogs must be
kept on leads.

SWANSEA

PONTARDDULAIS Map 8 SN50

Places to visit

The National Botanic Garden of Wales, LLANARTHNE 01558 668768 www.gardenofwales.org.uk

Glynn Vivain Art Gallery, SWANSEA 01792 516900 www.glynnviviangallery.org

Great for kids: Plantasia, SWANSEA 01792 474555 www.plantasia.org

►►►► 89% River View Touring Park *(SN578086)*

The Dingle, Llanedi SA4 0FH
☎ 01269 844876
e-mail: info@riverviewtouringpark.com
web: www.riverviewtouringpark.com
dir: *M4 junct 49, A483 signed Llandeilo. 0.5m, 1st left after lay-by, follow lane to site*

* 🚐 £15-£22 🚌 £15-£22 ⛺ £15-£22

Open Mar-late Nov

Last arrival 20.00hrs Last departure noon

This peaceful park is set on one lower and two upper levels in a sheltered valley with an abundance of wild flowers and wildlife. The River Gwli flows around the bottom of the park where fishing for brown trout is possible. The excellent toilet facilities are an added bonus. This park is ideally situated for visiting the beaches of south Wales, The Black Mountains and the Brecon Beacons. 6 acre site. 60 touring pitches. 43 hardstandings. 18 seasonal pitches. Caravan pitches. Motorhome pitches. Tent pitches.

Leisure: ⚽

Facilities: 🚿 🪒 💨 ❄ ♿ [S] 🐕 [Wi-fi] ♻ ℹ

Services: 🔌 🧺 🛢 🌿 [T]

Within 3 miles: ⛳ 🎬 🎣 [S] 🧺 🐴

Notes: Dogs must be kept on leads.

PORT EYNON Map 8 SS48

Places to visit

Weobley Castle, LLANRHIDIAN 01792 390012 www.cadw.wales.gov.uk

Gower Heritage Centre, PARKMILL 01792 371206 www.gowerheritagecentre.co.uk

Great for kids: Oxwich Castle, OXWICH 01792 390359 www.cadw.wales.gov.uk

►►► 82% Carreglwyd Camping & Caravan Park *(SS465863)*

SA3 1NL
☎ 01792 390795
dir: *A4118 to Port Eynon, site adjacent to beach*

🚐 🚌 ⛺

Open Mar-Dec

Last arrival 18.00hrs Last departure 15.00hrs

Set in an unrivalled location alongside the safe sandy beach of Port Eynon on the Gower Peninsula, this popular park is an ideal family holiday spot. Close to an attractive village with pubs and shops, most pitches offer sea views. The sloping ground has been partly terraced, and facilities are excellent. 12 acre site. 150 touring pitches. Caravan pitches. Motorhome pitches. Tent pitches.

AA Pubs & Restaurants nearby: Fairyhill, Reynoldston 01792 390139

King Arthur Hotel, Reynoldston 01792 390775

Facilities: 🚿 🪒 ♿ [S] 🐕 [Wi-fi] ♻ ℹ

Services: 🔌 🧺 🛢 🌿 [T] 🚰

Within 3 miles: 🎣 🌊 [S] 🐴

Notes: Dogs must be kept on leads.

RHOSSILI Map 8 SS48

Places to visit

Weobley Castle, LLANRHIDIAN 01792 390012 www.cadw.wales.gov.uk

Gower Heritage Centre, PARKMILL 01792 371206 www.gowerheritagecentre.co.uk

Great for kids: Oxwich Castle, OXWICH 01792 390359 www.cadw.wales.gov.uk

►►► 87% *Pitton Cross Caravan & Camping Park* *(SS434877)*

SA3 1PH
☎ 01792 390593
e-mail: admin@pittoncross.co.uk
web: www.pittoncross.co.uk
dir: *2m W of Scurlage on B4247*

🚐 🚌 ⛺

Open all year (rs Nov-Mar no bread, milk or papers)

Last arrival 20.00hrs Last departure 11.00hrs

Surrounded by farmland close to sandy Menslade Bay, which is within walking distance across the fields, this grassy park is divided by hedging into paddocks; hardstandings for motorhomes are available. Rhossili Beach which is popular with surfers and the Wales Coastal Path are nearby. Performance kites are sold, and instruction in flying is given. Geo-caching and paragliding are possible too. 6 acre site. 100 touring pitches. 25 hardstandings. Caravan pitches. Motorhome pitches. Tent pitches.

AA Pubs & Restaurants nearby: Fairyhill, Reynoldston 01792 390139

King Arthur Hotel, Reynoldston 01792 390775

Kings Head, Llangennith 01792 386212

Leisure: /‖\

Facilities: ⬅☉☂☼⛱⊙🛁♻ ❶

Services: 🔌🗑🛢🧴T

Within 3 miles: ✐⛵🛒🛍

Notes: Quiet at all times, charcoal BBQs must be off ground. Dogs must be kept on leads. Baby bath available.

SWANSEA
Map 9 SS69

Places to visit

Swansea Museum, SWANSEA 01792 653763 www.swanseaheritage.net

Glynn Vivain Art Gallery, SWANSEA 01792 516900 www.glynnviviangallery.org

Great for kids: Plantasia, SWANSEA 01792 474555 www.plantasia.org

75% *Riverside Caravan Park*
(SS679991)

Ynys Forgan Farm, Morriston SA6 6QL
☎ 01792 775587
e-mail: reception@riversideswansea.com
dir: *Exit M4 junct 45 towards Swansea. Left into private road signed to site*

🚐🚚🅰

Open all year (rs Winter months pool & club closed)

Last arrival mdnt Last departure noon

A large and busy park close to the M4 but in a quiet location beside the River Taw. This friendly, family orientated park has a licensed club and bar with a full high-season entertainment programme. There is a choice of eating outlets - the clubhouse restaurant, takeaway and chip shop. The park has a good indoor pool. 5 acre site. 90 touring pitches. Caravan pitches. Motorhome pitches. Tent pitches. 256 statics.

AA Pubs & Restaurants nearby: Hanson at the Chelsea Restaurant, Swansea 01792 464068

Leisure: 🏊/‖\🎣⛶

Facilities: ⬅☉☂☼⛱⊙🛁🏐WiFi

Services: 🔌🗑🍴🛢🧴T🔋🚮

Within 3 miles: ⚓⛵🎣✐🛒🛍⛳

Notes: Dogs by arrangement only (no aggressive dog breeds permitted). Fishing on site by arrangement.

LLANTWIT MAJOR
Map 9 SS96

Places to visit

Old Beaupre Castle, ST HILARY 01443 336000 www.cadw.wales.gov.uk

Great for kids: Ogmore Castle, OGMORE 01443 336000 www.cadw.wales.gov.uk

▶▶▶ 83% Acorn Camping & Caravan Site *(SS973678)*

Ham Lane South CF61 1RP
☎ 01446 794024
e-mail: info@acorncamping.co.uk
dir: *B4265 to Llantwit Major, follow camping signs. Approach site through Ham Manor residential park*

* 🚐 £16-£17 🚚 £16-£17 🅰 £11.80-£14

Open Feb-Nov

Last arrival 21.00hrs Last departure 11.00hrs

A peaceful country site in level meadowland, with some individual pitches divided by hedges and shrubs. It is about one mile from the beach, which can be reached via a cliff top walk, and the same distance from the historic town of Llantwit Major. An internet station and a full-size snooker table are useful amenities. 5.5 acre site. 90 touring pitches. 10 hardstandings. Caravan pitches. Motorhome pitches. Tent pitches. 25 statics.

AA Pubs & Restaurants nearby: Illtud's 216, Llantwit Major 01446 793800

Plough & Harrow, Monknash 01656 890209

Blue Anchor Inn, East Aberthaw 01446 750329

Leisure: /‖\🔍

Facilities: ⬅☉☂☼⛱⊙🛁WiFi♻ ❶

Services: 🔌🗑🛢🧴T🍴🔋🚮🚮

Within 3 miles: ⚓✐🛒🛍⛳

Notes: No noise 23.00hrs-07.00hrs. Dogs must be kept on leads.

EYTON
Map 15 SJ34

Places to visit

Erddig, WREXHAM 01978 355314 www.nationaltrust.org.uk

Chirk Castle, CHIRK 01691 777701 www.nationaltrust.org.uk/main/w-chirkcastle

AA CAMPING CARD SITE

PREMIER PARK

▶▶▶▶▶ 93% The Plassey Leisure Park
(SJ353452)

The Plassey LL13 0SP
☎ 01978 780277
e-mail: enquiries@plassey.com
web: www.plassey.com
dir: *From A483 at Bangor-on-Dee exit onto B5426 for 2.5m. Site entrance signed on left*

* 🚐 £16.50-£26.50 🚚 £16.50-£26.50 🅰 £16.50-£26.50

Open Feb-Nov

Last arrival 20.30hrs Last departure noon

A lovely park set in several hundred acres of quiet farm and meadowland in the Dee Valley. The superb toilet facilities include individual cubicles for total privacy and security, while the Edwardian farm buildings have been converted into a restaurant, coffee shop, beauty studio, and various craft outlets. There is plenty here to entertain the whole family, from scenic walks and swimming pool to free fishing, and use of the 9-hole golf course. 10 acre site. 90 touring pitches. 45 hardstandings. 60 seasonal pitches. Caravan pitches. Motorhome pitches. Tent pitches. 15 statics.

AA Pubs & Restaurants nearby: Hanmer Arms, Hanmer 01948 830532

Leisure: 🏊⛳/‖\🔍

Facilities: ⬅☉☂☼⛱⊙🛁🏐WiFi♻ ❶

Services: 🔌🗑🍴🛢🧴T🍴🔋🚮🚮🚮

Within 3 miles: ⚓✐◎🛒🛍⛳

Notes: No footballs or skateboards. Dogs must be kept on leads. Sauna, badminton & table tennis.

Ireland

Belfast

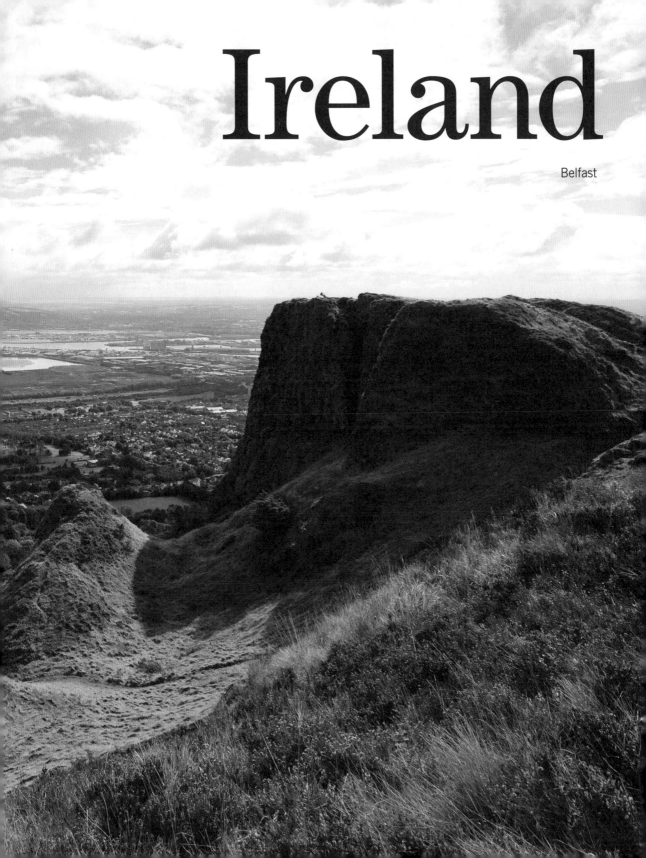

NORTHERN IRELAND

CO ANTRIM

ANTRIM | Map 1 D5

Places to visit

Antrim Round Tower, ANTRIM 028 9023 5000
www.ehsni.gov.uk

Bonamargy Friary, BALLYCASTLE 028 9023 5000
www.ehsni.gov.uk

Great for kids: Belfast Zoological Gardens,
BELFAST 028 9077 6277 www.belfastzoo.co.uk

▶▶▶ 83% Six Mile Water Caravan Park (J137870)

Lough Rd BT41 4DG
☎ 028 9446 4963 & 9446 3113
e-mail: sixmilewater@antrim.gov.uk
web: www.antrim.gov.uk/caravanpark
dir: *From A6 (Dublin road) into Lough Rd signed Antrim Forum & Loughshore Park. Site at end of road on right*

* ⚍ £21-£23 ⚍ £21-£23 ▲ £15-£22

Open Mar-Oct (rs Feb & Nov wknds only)

Last arrival 21.45hrs Last departure noon

A pretty tree-lined site in a large municipal park, within walking distance of Antrim and the Antrim Forum leisure complex yet very much in the countryside. The modern toilet block is well equipped, and other facilities include a laundry and electric hook-ups. All the pitches are precisely set on generous plots. 9.61 acre site. 45 touring pitches. 37 hardstandings. Caravan pitches. Motorhome pitches. Tent pitches.

AA Pubs & Restaurants nearby: Galgorm Resort & Spa, Ballymena 028 2588 1001

Leisure: ⚈ ⊡
Facilities: ⋔ ⊙ ℙ ⅋ ⚍ wi-fi ♻ 𝒊
Services: ⊡ ⊡ ⊙ ⊞ ⅋
Within 3 miles: ⌁ ⊟ ⅋ ⊚ ⚄ 𝔰 𝔰

Notes: Max stay 14 nights, no noise between 22.00hrs-08.00hrs. Dogs must be kept on leads. Watersports, angling stands.

BALLYCASTLE | Map 1 D6

Places to visit

Bonamargy Friary, BALLYCASTLE 028 9023 5000
www.ehsni.gov.uk

Great for kids: Dunluce Castle, PORTBALLINTRAE
028 2073 1938 www.ehsni.gov.uk

AA CAMPING CARD SITE

▶▶▶ 74% Watertop Farm (D115407)

188 Cushendall Rd BT54 6RN
☎ 028 2076 2576
e-mail: watertopfarm@aol.com
dir: *Take A2 from Ballycastle towards Cushendall. Site opposite Ballypatrick forest*

* ⚍ fr £22 ⚍ fr £22 ▲ fr £10

Open Etr-Oct (rs Etr-Jun & Sep-Oct farm activities not available)

Last departure 14.00hrs

Located on a family hill sheep farm set in the glens of Antrim, the farm offers a range of activities and attractions including pony trekking, boating, pedal go-karts, farm tours, tea room and lots more. The touring facilities consist of three individual sections, two reserved for caravans and the other for tents. The toilets are housed in a converted traditional Irish cottage, and the attached small rural museum serves as a night time social area. 0.5 acre site. 14 touring pitches. 9 hardstandings. Caravan pitches. Motorhome pitches. Tent pitches.

AA Pubs & Restaurants nearby: Frances Anne Restaurant, Londonderry Arms Hotel, Carnlough 028 2888 5255

Leisure: ⚎ ⚈
Facilities: ⋔ ⊙ ✳ ⚍ 🐾 ♻
Services: ⊡ ⊡ ⊙ ⊞ ⊙ ⚍ ⅋
Within 3 miles: ⌁ ⅋ ⅋ ⚄ 𝔰 𝔰 ∪

Notes: No camp fires, no BBQ trays on grass. Dogs must be kept on leads.

BALLYMONEY | Map 1 C6

Places to visit

Leslie Hill Open Farm, BALLYMONEY
028 2766 6803 www.lesliehillopenfarm.co.uk

Bonamargy Friary, BALLYCASTLE 028 9023 5000
www.ehsni.gov.uk

Great for kids: Dunluce Castle, PORTBALLINTRAE
028 2073 1938 www.ehsni.gov.uk

PREMIER PARK

▶▶▶▶▶ 78% Drumaheglis Marina & Caravan Park (C901254)

36 Glenstall Rd BT53 7QN
☎ 028 2766 0280 & 2766 0227
e-mail: drumaheglis@ballymoney.gov.uk
dir: *Signed from A26, approx 1.5m from Ballymoney towards Coleraine. Also accessed from B66, S of Ballymoney*

⚍ £24-£25 ⚍ £24-£25 ▲ £17

Open 17 Mar-Oct

Last arrival 20.00hrs Last departure 13.00hrs

Exceptionally well-designed and laid out park beside the Lower Bann River, with very spacious pitches (all fully serviced) and two quality toilet blocks. Ideal base for touring Antrim and for watersports enthusiasts. 16 acre site. 55 touring pitches. 55 hardstandings. 20 seasonal pitches. Caravan pitches. Motorhome pitches. Tent pitches.

Leisure: ⚎
Facilities: ⋔ ⊙ ℙ ✳ ⅋ ⊙ ⚍ 🐾 wi-fi ♻ 𝒊
Services: ⊡ ⊡ ⚍ ⅋
Within 3 miles: ⌁ ⅋ ⚄ 𝔰 𝔰

Notes: Dogs must be kept on leads. Marina berths. Table tennis & volleyball.

LEISURE: ⚈ Indoor swimming pool ⚎ Outdoor swimming pool ⚍ Children's playground ⚑ Kid's club ⚈ Tennis court ⚈ Games room ⊡ Separate TV room ⌁ 9/18 hole golf course ⚌ Boats for hire ⊟ Cinema ⚆ Entertainment ℙ Fishing ⊚ Mini golf ⚄ Watersports ⚇ Gym ⚈ Sports field Spa ∪ Stables
FACILITIES: ⚍ Bath ⋔ Shower ⊙ Electric shaver ℙ Hairdryer ✳ Ice Pack Facility ⅋ Disabled facilities ⊙ Public telephone 𝔰 Shop on site or within 200yds ⊞ Mobile shop (calls at least 5 days a week) ⚍ BBQ area ⚍ Picnic area wi-fi Wi-fi ⊟ Internet access ♻ Recycling 𝒊 Tourist info 🐾 Dog exercise area

BUSHMILLS
Map 1 C6

Places to visit

Old Bushmills Distillery, BUSHMILLS
028 2073 1521 www.bushmills.com

Great for kids: Belfast Zoological Gardens,
BELFAST 028 9077 6277 www.belfastzoo.co.uk

AA CAMPING CARD SITE

PREMIER PARK

▶▶▶▶▶ 88% Ballyness
Caravan Park *(C944397)*

GOLD

40 Castlecatt Rd BT57 8TN
☎ 028 2073 2393
e-mail: info@ballynesscaravanpark.com
web: www.ballynesscaravanpark.com
dir: 0.5m S of Bushmills on B66, follow signs

🚐 🚃

Open 17 Mar-Oct

Last arrival 21.00hrs Last departure noon

A quality park with superb toilet and other facilities, on farmland beside St Columb's Rill, the stream that supplies the famous nearby Bushmills Distillery. The friendly owners built this park with the discerning camper in mind, and they continue to improve it to ever higher standards. There is a pleasant walk around several ponds, and the park is peacefully located close to the beautiful north Antrim coast. There is a a new and spacious play

barn and a holiday cottage to let. 16 acre site. 48 touring pitches. 48 hardstandings. Caravan pitches. Motorhome pitches. 65 statics.

AA Pubs & Restaurants nearby: Bushmills Inn Hotel, Bushmills 028 2073 3000

Leisure: 🅰 🎣 🖵

Facilities: 🛁 🚻 ☉ 🅿 ✳ 🚿 🕒 💲 🛒 📶 🖥 ♻ ❶

Services: 🚐 🖬 🛢 💧 🚽 🛗 ⛽

Within 3 miles: 🚲 🥾 💲

Notes: No skateboards or roller blades. Dogs must be kept on leads. Library.

BELFAST

DUNDONALD

Places to visit

Mount Stewart House & Gardens, NEWTOWNARDS
028 4278 8387 www.nationaltrust.org.uk

Giant's Ring, BELFAST 028 9023 5000
www.ehsni.gov.uk

Great for kids: Belfast Zoological Gardens,
BELFAST 028 9077 6277 www.belfastzoo.co.uk

DUNDONALD
Map 1 D5

▶▶▶ 77% Dundonald Touring
Caravan Park *(J410731)*

111 Old Dundonald Rd BT16 1XT
☎ 028 9080 9123 & 9080 9129
e-mail: sales@castlereagh.gov.uk
dir: From Belfast city centre follow M3 & A20 to City Airport. Then A20 to Newtownards, follow signs to Dundonald & Ulster Hospital. At hospital right at sign for Dundonald Ice Bowl. Follow to end, turn right (Ice Bowl on left)

* 🚐 £22 🚃 £8-£23 ▲ £15

Open 14 Mar-Oct (rs Nov-Mar Aire de Service restricted to motorhomes)

Last arrival 23.00hrs Last departure noon

A purpose-built park in a quiet corner of Dundonald Leisure Park on the outskirts of Belfast. This peaceful park is ideally located for touring County Down and exploring the capital. In the winter it offers an 'Aire de Service' for motorhomes. 1.5 acre site. 22 touring pitches. 22 hardstandings. Caravan pitches. Motorhome pitches. Tent pitches.

continued

DUNDONALD *continued*

Dundonald Touring Caravan Park

Facilities: 🏠⊙🅿✳☕⊙🚿🌳🚻 📺 ❶

Services: 🔌🗑 🍴⛟↯

Within 3 miles: ⚓🏊🎣◎🛍🏊🛍∪

Notes: No commercial vehicles. Dogs must be kept on leads. Bowling, indoor play area, Olympic ice rink (additional charges apply).

see advert on page 445

CO FERMANAGH

BELCOO — Map 1 C5

PREMIER PARK

►►►►► **83%** *Rushin House Caravan Park* (H835047)

Holywell BT93 5DY
☎ 028 6638 6519
e-mail: enquiries@rushinhousecaravanpark.com
dir: *From Enniskillen take A4 W for 13m to Belcoo. Right onto B52 towards Garrison for 1m. Site signed*

🚐🚏⛺

Open mid Mar-Oct (rs Nov-Mar Aire de Service facilities available)

Last arrival 21.00hrs Last departure 13.00hrs

This park occupies a scenic location overlooking Lough MacNean, close to the picturesque village of Belcoo, and is the product of meticulous planning and execution. There are 24 very generous, fully-serviced pitches standing on a terrace overlooking the lough, with additional tenting pitches below; all are accessed by excellent wide tarmac roads. Play facilities include a lovely well-equipped play area and a hard surface and fenced five-a-side football pitch. There is a slipway providing boat access to the lough and, of course, fishing. Excellent toilet facilities are housed in a purpose-built structure and include family rooms. 5 acre site. 38 touring pitches. 38 hardstandings. Caravan pitches. Motorhome pitches. Tent pitches.

Leisure: 🏓⚓🎯🖵

Facilities: 🏠⊙🅿✳☕⊙🌳🚻 📶 🐾 ❶

Services: 🔌🗑 🍷🏬↯

Within 3 miles: ⚓🏊🛶🛍🛍

Notes: No cars by tents. Dogs must be kept on leads. Lakeside walk.

IRVINESTOWN — Map 1 C5

Places to visit

Castle Coole, ENNISKILLEN 028 6632 2690
www.nationaltrust.org.uk

Great for kids: Castle Balfour, LISNASKEA
028 9023 5000 www.ehsni.gov.uk

►►►► **82% Castle Archdale Caravan Park & Camping Site** (H176588)

Lisnarick BT94 1PP
☎ 028 6862 1333
e-mail: info@castlearchdale.com
dir: *From Irvinestown take B534 signed Lisnarick. Left onto B82 signed Enniskillen. Approx 1m right by church (site signed)*

* 🚐 £25-£30 🚏 £25-£30 ⛺ £20-£40

Open Apr-Oct (rs Apr-Jun & Sep-Oct shop, restaurant & bar open wknds only)

Last departure noon

This park is located within the grounds of Castle Archdale Country Park on the shores of Lough Erne which boasts stunning scenery, forest walks and also war and wildlife museums. The site is ideal for watersport enthusiasts with its marina and launching facilities. Also on site are a shop, licenced restaurant, takeaway and play park. There are 56 fully serviced, hardstanding pitches. 11 acre site. 158 touring pitches. 120 hardstandings. Caravan pitches. Motorhome pitches. Tent pitches. 139 statics.

AA Pubs & Restaurants nearby: Catalina Restaurant, Lough Erne Resort, Enniskillen 028 6632 3230

Leisure: 🏓

Facilities: 🏠⊙✳☕⊙🛍🌳🚻 📶 ❶

Services: 🔌🗑 🍷🏬📺🍴🏬↯

Within 3 miles: ⚓🏊🎣🛶🛍🛍

Notes: No open fires. Dogs must be kept on leads.

LISNASKEA — Map 1 C5

Places to visit

Castle Balfour, LISNASKEA 028 9023 5000
www.ehsni.gov.uk

Florence Court, ENNISKILLEN 028 6634 8249
www.nationaltrust.org.uk

Great for kids: Castle Coole, ENNISKILLEN
028 6632 2690 www.nationaltrust.org.uk

►►► **81%** *Lisnaskea Caravan Park* (H297373)

BT92 0NZ
☎ 028 6772 1040
dir: *From Lisnaskea take B514 signed Carry Bridge, site signed*

🚐🚏⛺

Open Mar-Sep

Last arrival 21.00hrs Last departure 14.00hrs

A pretty riverside site set in peaceful countryside, with well-kept facilities and friendly owners. Fishing is available on the river, and this quiet area is an ideal location for touring the lakes of Fermanagh. 6 acre site. 43 touring pitches. 43 hardstandings. Caravan pitches. Motorhome pitches. Tent pitches. 8 statics.

AA Pubs & Restaurants nearby: Catalina Restaurant, Lough Erne Resort, Enniskillen 028 6632 3230

Leisure: 🏓

Facilities: 🏠⊙✳☕🚿

Services: 🔌🗑 🍷

Within 3 miles: ⚓🏊🎣🛍🛍∪

Notes: 🐾

LEISURE: 🏊 Indoor swimming pool 🏊 Outdoor swimming pool 🎠 Children's playground 🪁 Kid's club 🎾 Tennis court 🎱 Games room 🖵 Separate TV room 🏌 9/18 hole golf course 🚣 Boats for hire 🎬 Cinema 🎵 Entertainment 🎣 Fishing ◉ Mini golf 🚤 Watersports 🏋 Gym 🎯 Sports field **Spa** ∪ Stables
FACILITIES: 🛁 Bath 🚿 Shower ⊙ Electric shaver 🅿 Hairdryer ✳ Ice Pack Facility 🦽 Disabled facilities 📞 Public telephone 🛍 Shop on site or within 200yds 🏪 Mobile shop (calls at least 5 days a week) 🍖 BBQ area 🌳 Picnic area 📶 Wi-fi 🖥 Internet access ♻ Recycling ❶ Tourist info 🐾 Dog exercise area

CO TYRONE

DUNGANNON   Map 1 C5

Places to visit

The Argory, MOY 028 8778 4753
www.nationaltrust.org.uk

Greencastle, KILKEEL 028 9181 1491
www.ehsni.gov.uk

Great for kids: Mountjoy Castle, MOUNTJOY
028 9023 5000 www.ehsni.gov.uk

▶▶▶ 81% **Dungannon Park** *(H805612)*

Moy Rd BT71 6DY
☎ 028 8772 8690
e-mail: dpreception@dungannon.gov.uk
dir: *M1 junct 15, A29, left at 2nd lights*

* 🚐 £12-£15 🚐 £12-£15 ▲ fr £10

Open Mar-Oct

Last arrival 20.30hrs Last departure 14.00hrs

A modern caravan park in a quiet area of a
stunning public park with fishing lake and
excellent facilities, especially for disabled visitors.
2 acre site. 20 touring pitches. 12 hardstandings.
Caravan pitches. Motorhome pitches. Tent pitches.

Leisure: 🎱 ⚓ 🐾 ⚽ ▭

Facilities: 🕯 ⊙ 🛉 ✳ ⚅ 🕙 🖄 🎋 ➊

Services: 🔌 🗄 🔋

Within 3 miles: ↨ ✦ 日 🖉 🖄 🗄 ∪

Notes: Dogs must be kept on leads. Hot & cold
drinks, snacks available.

REPUBLIC OF IRELAND

CO CORK

BALLINSPITTLE   Map 1 B2

Places to visit

Cork City Gaol, CORK 021 4305022
www.corkcitygaol.com

Blarney Castle & Rock Close, BLARNEY
021 4385252 www.blarneycastle.ie

Great for kids: Muckross House, Gardens &
Traditional Farms, KILLARNEY 064 6670144
www.muckross-house.ie

▶▶▶▶ 80% *Garrettstown House
Holiday Park* *(W588445)*

☎ 021 4778156 & 4775286
e-mail: reception@garrettstownhouse.com
dir: *6m from Kinsale, through Ballinspittle, past
school & football pitch on main road to beach.
Beside stone estate entrance*

🚐 🚐 ▲

Open 4 May-9 Sep (rs Early season-1 Jun shop
closed)

Last arrival 22.00hrs Last departure noon

Elevated holiday park with tiered camping areas
and superb panoramic views. Plenty of on-site
amenities, and close to beach and forest park. 7
acre site. 60 touring pitches. 20 hardstandings.
Caravan pitches. Motorhome pitches. Tent pitches.
80 statics.

Leisure: 🎯 🎱 ⚓ 🐾 🔍 ▭ ♫

Facilities: 🕯 ⊙ 🛉 ✳ ⚅ 🕙 🖄 🎋 🍴 📶 ♻ ➊

Services: 🔌 🗄 🔋 🛢 🚿 T 🚼 🛒 ⚡

Within 3 miles: ↨ ✦ 🖉 ◎ 🛶 🖄 🗄 ∪

Notes: 🚫 Dogs must be kept on leads. Crazy golf,
video shows, snooker, adult reading lounge, tots'
playroom.

BALLYLICKEY   Map 1 B2

Places to visit

Muckross House, Gardens & Traditional Farms,
KILLARNEY 064 6670144
www.muckross-house.ie

Great for kids: Fota Wildlife Park,
CARRIGTWOHILL 021 4812678
www.fotawildlife.ie

▶▶▶▶ 85% **Eagle Point Caravan and
Camping Park** *(V995535)*

☎ 027 50630
e-mail: eaglepointcamping@eircom.net
dir: *N71 to Bandon, then R586 to Bantry, then
N71, 4m to Glengarriff, opposite petrol station*

🚐 €26-€35 🚐 €26-€35 ▲ €26-€35

Open 19 Apr-23 Sep

Last arrival 21.00hrs Last departure noon

An immaculate park set in an idyllic position on a
headland overlooking the rugged Bantry Bay and
the mountains of West Cork. There are boat
launching facilities, small and safe pebble
beaches, a football field, tennis court, a small
playground, and TV rooms for children and adults
on the park. There is an internet café at reception
and a shop and petrol station across from the
park entrance. Nearby are two golf courses, riding
stables, a sailing centre and cycle hire facilities.
20 acre site. 125 touring pitches. 20
hardstandings. 60 seasonal pitches. Caravan
pitches. Motorhome pitches. Tent pitches.

AA Pubs & Restaurants nearby: Sea View House
Hotel, Ballylickey 027 50073

Leisure: 🎱 ⚓ ⚽ ▭

Facilities: 🕯 ⊙ ✳ 🕙 🖄 📶 🖥 ♻ ➊

Services: 🔌 🗄 🔋 ⚡

Within 3 miles: ↨ 日 🖉 🖄 🗄

Notes: 🚫 No commercial vehicles, bikes, skates,
scooters or jet skis.

SERVICES: 🔌 Electric hook up 🗄 Launderette 🍺 Licensed bar 🛢 Calor Gas 🚿 Camping Gaz T Toilet fluid 🍴 Café/Restaurant 🛒 Fast Food/Takeaway 🔋 Battery charging
🚼 Baby care ⚡ Motorvan service point **ABBREVIATIONS:** BH/bank hols-bank holidays Etr-Easter Whit-Whitsun dep-departure fr-from hrs-hours m-mile mdnt-midnight
rdbt-roundabout rs-restricted service wk-week wknd-weekend 🚫 No credit cards 🚫 no dogs   See page 7 for details of the AA Camping Card Scheme

CO DUBLIN

CLONDALKIN — Map 1 D4

Places to visit

Castletown, CELBRIDGE 01 6288252
www.heritageireland.ie

Irish Museum of Modern Art, DUBLIN
01 6129900 www.imma.ie

Great for kids: Dublin Zoo, DUBLIN 01 4748900
www.dublinzoo.ie

►►►► 81% *Camac Valley Tourist Caravan & Camping Park* (0056300)

Naas Rd, Clondalkin
☎ 01 4640644
e-mail: info@camacvalley.com
dir: *M50 junct 9, W on N7, site on right of dual carriageway after 2km. Site signed from N7*

Open all year

Last arrival anytime Last departure noon

A pleasant, lightly wooded park with good facilities, security and layout, situated within an hour's drive, or a bus ride, from city centre. 15 acre site. 163 touring pitches. 113 hardstandings. Caravan pitches. Motorhome pitches. Tent pitches.

AA Pubs & Restaurants nearby: Finnstown Country House Hotel, Lucan 01 6010700

Leisure:

Facilities:

Services:

Within 3 miles:

CO MAYO

CASTLEBAR — Map 1 B4

Places to visit

King House - Georgian Mansion & Military Barracks, BOYLE 071 9663242
www.kinghouse.ie

►►►► 80% Lough Lannagh Caravan Park (M140890)

Old Westport Rd
☎ 094 9027111
e-mail: info@loughlannagh.ie
web: www.loughlannagh.ie
dir: *N5, N60, N84 to Castlebar. At ring road follow signs for Westport. Signs for Lough Lannagh Village on all approach roads to Westport rdbt*

€21-€25 €21-€25 €21-€25

Open 22 Mar-31 Aug

Last arrival 18.00hrs Last departure 10.00hrs

This park is part of the Lough Lannagh Village which is situated in a wooded area a short walk from Castlebar. Leisure facilities include a purpose-built fitness and relaxation centre, tennis courts, children's play area and café. 2.5 acre site. 20 touring pitches. 20 hardstandings. Caravan pitches. Motorhome pitches. Tent pitches.

AA Pubs & Restaurants nearby: Knockranny House Hotel, Westport 098 28600

Bluewave Restaurant, Carlton Atlantic Coast Hotel, Westport 098 29000

Leisure:

Facilities:

Services:

Within 3 miles:

Notes: No pets Jul & Aug. Dogs by prior arrangement only. Fitness club, table tennis, boules, Wi-fi in café.

KNOCK — Map 1 B4

Places to visit

King House - Georgian Mansion & Military Barracks, BOYLE 071 9663242
www.kinghouse.ie

AA CAMPING CARD SITE

►►►► 76% Knock Caravan and Camping Park (M408828)

Claremorris Rd
☎ 094 9388100
e-mail: caravanpark@knock-shrine.ie
dir: *From rdbt in Knock, through town. Site entrance on left 1km, opposite petrol station*

€20-€22 €20-€22 €20-€22

Open Mar-Nov

Last arrival 22.00hrs Last departure noon

A pleasant, very well maintained camping park within the grounds of Knock Shrine, offering spacious terraced pitches and excellent facilities. 10 acre site. 88 touring pitches. 88 hardstandings. Caravan pitches. Motorhome pitches. Tent pitches. 12 statics.

Leisure:

Facilities:

Services:

Within 3 miles:

Notes: Dogs must be kept on leads.

LEISURE: Indoor swimming pool Outdoor swimming pool Children's playground Kid's club Tennis court Games room Separate TV room 9/18 hole golf course Boats for hire Cinema Entertainment Fishing Mini golf Watersports Gym Sports field Spa Stables
FACILITIES: Bath Shower Electric shaver Hairdryer Ice Pack Facility Disabled facilities Public telephone Shop on site or within 200yds Mobile shop (calls at least 5 days a week) BBQ area Picnic area Wi-fi Internet access Recycling Tourist info Dog exercise area

CO ROSCOMMON

BOYLE Map 1 B4

Places to visit

King House - Georgian Mansion & Military Barracks, BOYLE 071 9663242 www.kinghouse.ie

Florence Court, ENNISKILLEN 028 6634 8249 www.nationaltrust.org.uk

▶▶▶ 74% *Lough Key Caravan & Camping Park* (G846039)

Lough Key Forest Park
☎ 071 9662212
e-mail: info@loughkey.ie
web: www.loughkey.ie
dir: *3km E of Boyle on N4. Follow Lough Key Forest Park signs, site within grounds. Approx 0.5km from entrance*

Open Apr-20 Sep

Last arrival 18.00hrs Last departure noon

Peaceful and very secluded site within the extensive grounds of a beautiful forest park. Lough Key offers boat trips and waterside walks, and there is a viewing tower. 15 acre site. 72 touring pitches. 52 hardstandings. Caravan pitches. Motorhome pitches. Tent pitches.

Leisure: ⚄

Facilities: ⚄

Services: ⚄

Within 3 miles: ⚄

Notes: No cars by tents.

● Walkers on Coppett Hill

WALKS & CYCLE RIDES
Contents

WALKS & CYCLE RIDES
Walking and cycling in safety

WALKING

All the walks are suitable for families, but less experienced family groups, especially those with younger children, should try the shorter or easier walks first. Route finding is usually straightforward, but the maps are for guidance only and we recommend that you always take the suggested Ordnance Survey map with you.

Risks

Although each walk has been researched with a view to minimising any risks, no walk in the countryside can be considered to be completely free from risk. Walking in the outdoors will always require a degree of common sense and judgement to ensure safety, especially for young children.

- Be particularly careful on cliff paths and in upland terrain, where the consequences of a slip can be serious.
- Remember to check tidal conditions before walking on the seashore.
- Some sections of routes are by, or cross, busy roads. Remember traffic is a danger even on minor country lanes.
- Be careful around farmyard machinery and livestock.
- Be aware of the consequences of changes in the weather and check the forecast before you set out. Ensure the whole family is properly equipped, wearing appropriate clothing and a good pair of boots or sturdy walking shoes. Take waterproof clothing with you and carry spare clothing and a torch if you are walking in the winter months. Remember the weather can change quickly at any time of the year, and in moorland and heathland areas, mist and fog can make route finding much harder. In summer, take account of the heat and sun by wearing a hat and carrying enough water.
- On walks away from centres of population you should carry a whistle and survival bag. If you do have an accident requiring emergency services, make a note of your position as accurately as possible and dial 999.

CYCLING

Cycling is a fun activity which children love, and teaching your child to ride a bike, and going on family cycling trips, are rewarding experiences. Not only is cycling a great way to travel, but as a regular form of exercise it can make an invaluable contribution to a child's health and fitness, and increase their confidence and independence.

The growth of motor traffic has made Britain's roads increasingly dangerous and unattractive to cyclists. Cycling with children is an added responsibility and, as with everything, there is a risk when taking them out cycling. However, in recent years measures have been taken to address this, including the on-going development of the National Cycle Network (more than 12,600 miles utilising quiet lanes and traffic-free paths) and local designated off-road routes for families, such as converted railway lines, canal tow paths and forest tracks.

In devising the cycle rides included in this guide, every effort has been made to use these designated cycle paths, or to link them with quiet country lanes and waymarked byways and bridleways. Unavoidably, in a few cases, some relatively busy B-roads link the quieter, more attractive routes.

Taking care on the road

- Ride in single file on narrow and busy roads.
- Be alert, look and listen for traffic, especially on narrow lanes and blind bends and be extra careful when descending steep hills, as loose gravel can lead to an accident.
- In wet weather make sure you keep a good distance between you and other riders.
- Make sure you indicate your intentions clearly.
- Brush up on The Highway Code before venturing out on to the road.

Off-road safety code of conduct

- Only ride where it is legal to do so. It is forbidden to cycle on public footpaths. The only 'rights of way' open to cyclists are bridleways and unsurfaced tracks, known as byways, which are open to all traffic.
- Canal tow paths: you need a permit to cycle on some stretches of tow path (**www.waterscape.com**). Remember that access paths can be steep and slippery and always get off and push your bike under low bridges and by locks.
- Always yield to walkers and horses, giving adequate warning of your approach.
- Don't expect to cycle at high speeds.

- Keep to the main trail to avoid any unnecessary erosion to the area beside the trail and to prevent skidding, especially if it is wet.
- Remember the Countryside Code. (**www.naturalengland.org.uk**)

Cycling with children

Children can use a child seat from the age of eight months, or from the time they can hold themselves upright. A number of child seats fit on the front or rear of a bike, and it's worth investigating towable two-seat trailers. 'Trailer bicycles', suitable for five- to ten-year-olds, can be attached to the rear of an adult's bike, so that the adult has control, allowing the child to pedal if he/she wishes. Family cycling can be made easier by using a tandem, as it can carry a child seat and tow trailers. 'Kiddy-cranks' for shorter legs can be fitted to the rear seat tube, enabling either parent to take their child out cycling. For older children it is better to purchase the right size bike: an oversized bike will be difficult to control, and potentially dangerous.

Preparing your bicycle

Basic routine includes checking the wheels for broken spokes or excess play in the bearings, and checking for punctures, undue tyre wear and the correct tyre pressures. Ensure that the brake blocks are firmly in place and not worn, and that cables are not frayed or too slack. Lubricate hubs, pedals, gear mechanisms and cables. Make sure you have a pump, a bell, a rear rack to carry panniers and, if cycling at night, a set of working lights.

Preparing yourself

Equipping the family with cycling clothing need not be expensive; comfort is the key. Essential items for cycling are padded cycling shorts, warm stretch leggings (avoid tight-fitting and seamed trousers like jeans or baggy tracksuit trousers that may become caught in the chain), stiff-soled training shoes, and a wind/waterproof jacket. Fingerless gloves are comfortable.

A cycling helmet provides essential protection and are essential for young children learning to cycle.

Wrap your child up with several layers in colder weather. Make sure you and those with you are easily visible by all road users, by wearing light-coloured or luminous clothing in daylight and reflective strips or sashes in failing light and when it is dark.

What to take with you

Invest in a pair of medium-sized panniers (rucksacks can affect balance) to carry the necessary gear for the day. Take extra clothes with you, the amount depending on the season, and always pack a light wind/waterproof jacket. Carry a basic tool kit (tyre levers, adjustable spanner, a small screwdriver, puncture repair kit, a set of Allen keys) and practical spares, such as an inner tube, a universal brake/gear cable, and a selection of nuts and bolts. Also, always take a pump and a strong lock.

Cycling, especially in hilly terrain and off-road, saps energy, so take enough food and drink. Always carry plenty of water, especially in hot and humid weather. Consume high-energy snacks like cereal bars, cake or fruits, eating little and often to combat feeling weak and tired. Remember that children get thirsty (and hungry) much more quickly than adults so always have food and diluted juices available for them.

And finally, the most important advice of all – enjoy yourselves!

Useful cycling websites

- National Cycle Network: **www.sustrans.org.uk**
- British Waterways (tow path cycling): **www.waterscape.com**
- Forestry Commission (for cycling on Forestry Commission woodland): **www.forestry.gov.uk**
- Cyclists Touring Club: **www.ctc.org.uk**

▷

WALKS & CYCLE RIDES

continued

Each walk and cycle ride starts with a panel giving essential information, including the distance, terrain, nature of the paths, and where to park your car.

WALKS AND CYCLE ROUTES

Minimum time: The time stated for each route is the estimated minimum time that a reasonably fit family group would take to complete the circuit. This does not include rest or refreshment stops.

Maps: Each main route is shown on a detailed map. However, some detail is lost because of the scale. For this reason, we always recommend that you use the maps alongside the suggested Ordnance Survey (OS) map.

Start/Finish: Indicates the start and finish point and parking. The six-figure grid reference prefixed by two letters refers to a 100km square of the National Grid. You'll find more information on grid references on most OS maps.

Level of difficulty: The walks and cycle rides have been graded from 1 to 3. Easier routes, such as those with little total ascent, on easy footpaths or level trails, or those covering shorter distances are graded 1. The hardest routes, either because they include a lot of ascent, greater distances, or are in hilly, more demanding terrains, are graded 3.

Parking: Local parking information for the walks.

Tourist information: A contact number for the nearest tourist information office may be provided to help find local information.

Cycle hire: For the cycle rides, this lists, within reason, the nearest cycle hire shop/centre.

❗ This highlights at a glance any potential difficulties or hazards along the route. If a particular route is suitable for older, fitter children it says so here.

All the walks and cycle rides featured in this guide appear in the *AA 365 Pub Walks and Cycle Rides*. This is a comprehensive ring-binder format directory offering a vast collection of routes for the whole family. See the AA website for more details
http://shop.theaa.com/store/anywhere-and-everywhere

WALK 1
The Serpentine Route to Cadgwith

A wandering route between coast and countryside through the serpentine rock landscape of the Lizard Peninsula.

Minimum time:	3hrs
Walk length:	4.5 miles (7.2km)
Ascent/gradient:	230ft (70mtrs) ▲▲▲
Difficulty level:	✚✚✚
Paths:	Very good. Occasionally rocky in places. Rock can be slippery when wet.
Landscape:	Landlocked lanes and woodland tracks, coastal footpaths high above the sea
Map:	OS Explorer 103 The Lizard
Start/finish:	Grid reference: SW 720146
Dog friendliness:	Can let dogs off lead on coastal paths, but please keep under strict control on field paths
Parking:	Cadgwith car park. About 350yds (320mtrs) from Cadgwith. Busy in summer
Public toilets:	Ruan Minor and Cadgwith

● Cadgwith

The serpentine rock of the Lizard Peninsula is fascinating by name and by nature. Its geological label, serpentinite, is a word that fails to slither quite so easily off the tongue as does its popular usage 'serpentine'. The name derives from the sinuous veins of green, red, yellow and white that wriggle across the dark green or brownish red surface of the rock. The best quality serpentine is easily carved and shaped and can be polished to a beautiful sheen.

Height of Fashion

In the 19th century serpentine furnishings were the height of fashion and the material was used for shop fronts and fireplaces. The industry declined during the 1890s however, due to the vagaries of fashion but also because the colourful, curdled stone of the Lizard decayed quickly in polluted urban atmospheres. Serpentine became less popular for use in shop fronts and monuments as cheaper, more resilient marble from Italy and Spain began to dominate the market. Today serpentine craftsmen still operate in little workshops on the Lizard and you can buy serpentine souvenirs at Lizard Village. Throughout this walk there are stiles built of

serpentine; their surfaces are mirror-smooth and slippery from use. Admire, but take care when they are wet.
The walk first takes a fittingly wandering route inland to the sleepy village of Ruan Minor from where a narrow lane leads down to the Poltesco Valley. At the mouth of the valley is Carleon Cove, once the site of water wheels, steam engines, machine shops, storehouses and a factory where serpentine was processed. Only a few ruins remain. A narrow harbour pool, almost stagnant now, is dammed on the seaward side by a deep shingle bank where once there was an outlet to the sea. From here, during the heyday of Carleon's serpentine industry, barges loaded with finished pieces were towed out during spells of fine weather to cargo ships awaiting offshore.

Thatched Cottages

From Carleon Cove the coast path is followed to Cadgwith, an archetypal Cornish fishing village. Cadgwith has a number of thatched cottages, a rare sight in windy Cornwall, although a covering of wire-mesh is a wise precaution against storm damage. Cadgwith still supports a fleet of fishing boats and is given an enduring identity because of it. Beyond the village the coast path leads to the Devil's Frying Pan, a vast gulf in the cliffs caused by the collapse of a section of coast that had been undermined by the sea. From here the path leads along the edge of the cliffs before the route turns inland to the Church of the Holy Cross at Grade. Beyond the church you find the ancient St Ruan's Well and the road back to the start.

Walk Directions

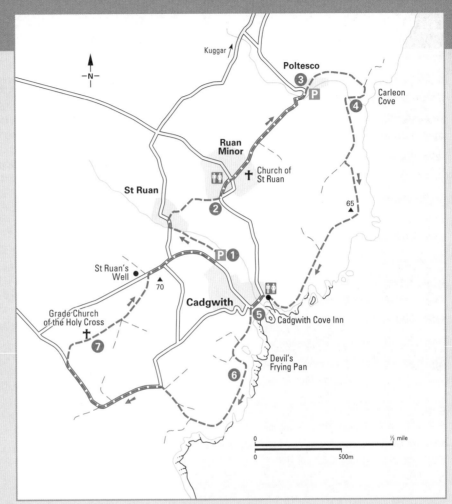

1 Go left along a grassy ride below the car park, to a stile. Continue through a gate and into woodland. Turn right at a lane, then on the corner, go up a track and continue to the main road at Ruan Minor.

2 Go left and, just beyond the shop, turn left down a surfaced path. Rejoin the main road by a thatched cottage (there are toilets just before the road). Cross diagonally right, then go down a lane past the Church of St Ruan.

3 In 0.3 mile (500mtrs), just past an old mill and a bridge, go right at a T-junction to reach the car park at Poltesco. From the far end of the car park follow a track, signposted 'Carleon Cove'. Go right at a junction.

4 Go over a wooden bridge above the cove, then turn left at a T-junction and again turn left in 0.25 mile (400mtrs) where the path branches. Go through a kissing gate and continue along the cliff-edge path to Cadgwith. At the road, turn left.

5 Follow a narrow path, signposted 'Coast Path'. By a house gateway, go left up a surfaced path, signposted 'Devil's Frying Pan'. At an open area turn left, pass Townplace Cottage, cross a meadow and reach the Devil's Frying Pan itself.

6 Keep on the coast path and at a junction, just past a chalet studio, follow a path inland to a T-junction with a rough track. Turn left and then, at a public lane, go left again and after 0.5 mile (800mtrs) turn right along a track to Grade Church.

7 Follow the left-hand field-edge behind the church, then go over a stile into the next field to reach a lane. St Ruan's Well is opposite diagonally left. Turn right for 200yds (183mtrs), then branch off right between stone pillars to return to the car park.

what to look out for...

Water is often slow to drain on the soil of the Cadgwith and Lizard areas due to the impermeable nature of the underlying rock. This results in the development of many marshy areas known as wet flushes, that support moisture-loving plants. There are several places where you should see the greater horsetail, an attractive, exotic looking plant that has long feathery branches and segmented flower stalks. On the coast proper look for the sturdy tree mallow, a tall plant with hairy stem and purple flowers.

A gentle ride along the Taw estuary from historic Braunton to Barnstaple's old quayside.

Minimum time:	1hr 30min
Ride length:	11 miles/17.7km
Difficulty level:	✦✦✦
Map:	OS Explorer 139 Bideford, Ilfracombe & Barnstaple
Start/finish:	Braunton car park (contributions), grid ref: SS 486365
Trails/tracks:	Level tarmac and gritty former railway track
Landscape:	Townscape, estuary
Public toilets:	At start and in Barnstaple
Tourist information:	Barnstaple, tel 01271 375000
Cycle hire:	Otter Cycle Hire, tel 01271 813339; Tarka Trail Cycle Hire, Barnstaple, tel 01271 324202
❗	Busy crossing of A361 on route to the Williams Arms

Getting to the start

Braunton lies on the A361 Barnstaple to Ilfracombe road in north Devon. The car park is signed from the traffic lights in the centre of the village. If approaching from Barnstaple, turn left, and 100yds (91mtrs) later turn left into the car park.

Why do this cycle ride?

Visiting Barnstaple by car at the height of the tourist season can be something of a trial as this north Devon market town, the oldest borough in the country, can get pretty choked by traffic. So what better way to get into the heart of Barnstaple than by cycling from Braunton via the Tarka Trail along the edge of the Taw estuary?

did you know?

An air-sea rescue Sea King helicopter from Chivenor was the first to arrive at Boscastle when the village was hit by floods in 2004. It helped rescue 55 people in the UK's largest peacetime emergency operation, and the crew were decorated for bravery.

while you're there...

The 18-acre (7ha) Marwood Hill Gardens contain three small lakes and rare trees and shrubs. There are bog gardens, a walled garden, collections of clematis, camellias, and eucalyptus. Alpine plants are also a feature, and there is a plant shop.

Braunton Burrows

As you set off along the Tarka Trail from Braunton look right and in the distance you'll see a ridge of sand dunes (dating from the last Ice Age) – those nearest the sea are around 100ft (over 30mtrs) high. This is Braunton Burrows, the second largest dune system in the UK, designated as an UNESCO International Biosphere Reserve in November 2002. The whole dune system is moving gradually inland, in some places as much as 10ft (3mtrs) per year, and is well worth exploring. There are areas of managed meadowland, grassland, marsh and sandy habitats. Almost 500 different species of flowering plant have been identified, including 11 orchids. Sustainable tourism is the keyword here, and access for visitors is managed carefully so that fragile parts of the site are protected. The area is easily accessible by road or bike.

Braunton has a fascinating agricultural history, too. Between the village and the Burrows lies Braunton Great Field, a rare example of medieval strip farming. This area once lay beneath the sea and is extremely fertile. There's also an area of tidal saltmarsh, enclosed in the early 19th century for grazing cattle.

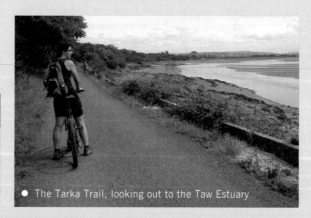

● The Tarka Trail, looking out to the Taw Estuary

The Ride

1 The car park marks the site of the old Braunton railway station, closed in 1965. The line – Barnstaple to Ilfracombe – was opened in 1874, and the last train ran in 1970. Cycle to the far end of the car park and turn right into the overflow area. Bear left and leave the car park by the police station (right). Bear right onto Station Road and cycle down it, passing the cycle hire on the left. Turn right into Station Close and then immediately left down a tarmac way. At the end cross the lane; keep ahead through black bollards to cross another lane, with a roundabout right.

2 Follow signs left to pick up the old railway line. Pass a wetland conservation area (left) and pass round a staggered barrier to cross a lane (the wire fences right mark the boundary of RAF Chivenor).

3 (Note: For The Williams Arms turn left here; at the end of the lane cross the A361 with care; the pub is on the other side.) Cycle on to reach a roundabout at the entrance to RAF Chivenor. The church ahead left is St Augustine's at Heanton Punchardon, built by Richard Puncharden (owner of Heanton estate) after his return from the Crusades in 1290. The village, formerly Heanton (Saxon Hantona – High Town) took on his name from that time. Cross the road by the roundabout and keep ahead through a wooded section.

4 Emerge suddenly from woodland onto the Taw Estuary, with far-reaching views. Listen for the oystercatcher's piping call, and watch out for curlew too. In winter thousands of migrant birds feed on the broad sandbanks here. Pass castellated Heanton Court on the left, a refuge for Royalists in the Civil War. The then owner of the Heanton estate, Colonel Albert Basset, fought for Barnstaple, which eventually fell to the Parliamentarians. Continue along the banks of the Taw to pass the football club (left).

5 Cross arched Yeo Bridge, a swing bridge over a tributary of the Taw, and pass the Civic Centre on the left (cyclists and pedestrians separate here). Bear left away from the river to meet the road. Turn right along the cycle path past old Barnstaple Town Station on the right (the railway reached the south side of the river in 1854, and this side in the early 1870s). Bear right as signed, then left along the quay (note: there is no wall along the edge).

6 Continue on to pass Barnstaple Heritage Centre (left), with its elaborate statue of Queen Anne. The River Front Café (with cycle racks) lies a few yards along on the left, just before Barnstaple's Long Bridge over the Taw (there has been a bridge here since the 13th century). There is evidence of a settlement at Barnstaple from early Saxon times; trade via the Taw was vital to the town's prosperity for centuries.

A fine linear walk from Ravenglass to Eskdale Green, returning on La'al Ratty.

Minimum time:	2hrs 30min
Walk length:	6 miles (9.7km)
Ascent/gradient:	730ft (220mtrs) ▲▲▲
Difficulty level:	✚✚✚
Paths:	Clear tracks and paths, muddy after rain, 1 stile
Landscape:	Woodlands, moderately rugged fell and gentle valley
Map:	OS Explorer OL6 The English Lakes (SW)
Start:	Grid reference: SD 085964
Finish:	Grid reference: SD 145998
Dog friendliness:	Under close control where sheep are grazing
Parking:	Village car park at Ravenglass, close to station
Public toilets:	Ravenglass village and Ravenglass and Eskdale Station

La'al Ratty

Muncaster Fell is a long and knobbly fell of no great height. The summit rises to 758ft (231mtrs), but is a little off the route described. A winding path negotiates the fell from end to end and this can be linked with other paths and tracks to offer a fine walk from Ravenglass to Eskdale Green. It's a linear walk, but when the Ravenglass and Eskdale Railway is in full steam, a ride back on the train is simply a joy.

Affectionately known as La'al Ratty, the Ravenglass and Eskdale Railway has a history of fits and starts. It was originally opened as a standard gauge track in 1875 to serve a granite quarry and was converted to narrow gauge between 1915 and 1917. After a period of closure it was bought by enthusiasts in 1960, overhauled and re-opened, and is now a firm favourite. The line runs from Ravenglass to Dalegarth Station, near Boot at the head of Eskdale. The railway runs almost all year, but there are times in the winter when there are no services. Obtain a timetable and study it carefully. When the trains are running, there are few Lakeland journeys to compare with a trip both ways.

The Romans operated an important port facility at Ravenglass. Fortifications were built all the way around the Cumbrian coast to link with Hadrian's Wall and a Roman road cut through Eskdale, over the passes to Ambleside, then along the crest of High Street to link with the road network near Penrith. Some people think the Romans planned to invade Ireland from Ravenglass, though this is a subject of debate. The mainline railway sliced through the old Roman fort in 1850, leaving only the bathouse intact, though even this ruin is among the tallest Roman remains in Britain. The Romans also operated a tileworks on the lower slopes of Muncaster Fell.

Surrounded by luxuriant rhododendrons, Muncaster Castle is almost completely hidden from view. It has been the home of the Pennington family since about 1240, though they occupied a nearby site even earlier than that. The estate around the castle includes a church that was founded in 1170, as well as a network of paths and tracks to explore. Owls are bred and reared at Muncaster, then released into the wild.

what to look out for...

The Ravenglass estuary is a haunt of wildfowl and waders. Oystercatchers and curlews probe the mudflats and there are sometimes raucous gulls. On Muncaster Fell there may be grouse in the heather and it's usual to see buzzards overhead.

Walk Directions

1 Leave the car park by crossing the mainline and miniature railway line, using the footbridges, then follow a narrow path to a road junction. Turn right on a footpath by the side of a narrow road, signposted 'Walls Castle'. The bathouse is soon on the left.

2 Continue along the access road and turn left along a track signposted 'Newtown'. Turn left again before the cottage and follow another track up a little wooded valley. Go through four gates, following the track from the wood, across fields and into another wood. Turn left to reach Home Farm and a busy main road.

3 Cross the road and turn right, passing Muncaster Castle car park and the Muncaster Country Guest House. The road leads up to a bend, where Fell Lane is signposted uphill. Ascend the clear track, cross a little wooded dip, then fork right and left, noticing Muncaster Tarn on the left. Go through a gate at the top of the lane to reach Muncaster Fell.

4 A path forges through boggy patches along the edge of a coniferous plantation, then the path runs free across the slopes of Muncaster Fell. A path rising to the left leads to the summit, otherwise keep right to continue.

5 Views develop as the path winds about on the slope overlooking Eskdale. A panorama of fells opens up as a curious

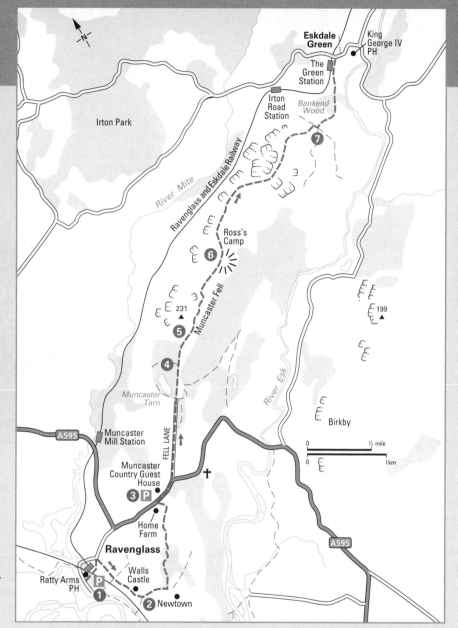

structure is reached at Ross's Camp. Here, a large stone slab was turned into a picnic table for a shooting party in 1883.

6 Continue along the footpath, looping round a broad and boggy area to reach a corner of a dry-stone wall. Go down through

a gateway and bear in mind that the path can be muddy. There is a short ascent on a well-buttressed stretch, then the descent continues on a sparsely wooded slope, through a gate, ending on a track near another gate.

7 Go through the gate and then

turn left, crossing a field to reach a stone wall seen at the edge of Bankend Wood. Walk on keeping to the right side of the wall to reach a stile and a stream. A narrow track continues, becoming better as it draws close to a road. Turn left at the end of the road to reach The Green Station.

Along the peaceful western shore of England's largest lake.

Minimum time:	1 hour
Ride length:	5.75 miles (9.2km)
Difficulty level:	✦✦✦
Map:	OS Explorer OL7 The English Lakes (SE)
Start/finish:	Car park near Windermere Ferry; grid ref: SD 387958
Trails/tracks:	Mostly easy tracks, some stony sections
Landscape:	Rich woodland and lakeshore
Public toilets:	None on route
Tourist information:	Bowness-on-Windermere, tel 015394 42895
Cycle hire:	Wheelbase, Staveley, tel 015398 21443; Biketreks, Ambleside, tel 015394 31245; Ghyllside Cycles, Ambleside, tel 015394 33592; Grizedale Mountain Bikes, Grizedale Forest, tel 01229 860369
❗	Mostly easy but one rough steep climb and descent. Suitability: children 8+. Mountain bike recommended, or walk some sections. Shorter ride from Red Nab, all ages

● Lake Windermere

Getting to the start

Road access to Windermere's mid-western shore is via Far Sawrey or on minor roads from the south. Follow the B5285 towards the ferry terminal, turning left before the terminal itself, to a National Trust car park. Or bring your bikes over by ferry from Bowness-on-Windermere.

Why do this cycle ride?

This is a perfect ride for taking a picnic. The full ride is surprisingly challenging. For a shorter ride, go from the car park at Red Nab. Then follow the bridleway to High Wray Bay.

Windermere

Water traffic includes yachts of all sizes, windsurfers, canoes, rowing boats and the traditional launches and steamers which ply up and down throughout the year. Power-boating and water-skiing are popular activities on the lake; there is a 10 knots (11.5mph; 18.5km/h) speed limit for all powered craft on the lake which makes this ride fairly peaceful.

An attractive feature, the privately owned Belle Isle is said to have been used since Roman times. Today it is supplied by a little boat, which serves the 38 acre (15ha) estate. Belle Isle's circular house, rebuilt after extensive fire damage, was originally built by a Mr English in 1774. Apparently William Wordsworth accredited Mr English with the honour of being the first man to settle in the Lake District for the sake of the scenery. The woodland here is typical of the Lake District. Before clearances for agriculture, notably sheep-grazing, there were many more similar woods. The predominant species is the sessile oak, which in times past provided timber for local industry and bark for tanning. It is a close relative of the 'English' oak of more southern counties, and it is not easy to tell them apart, but on closer inspection you will see that the acorns have no stalks to speak of. These woods are also rich in mosses and ferns, but often the most striking plant is the foxglove, which fills the clearings.

The Ride

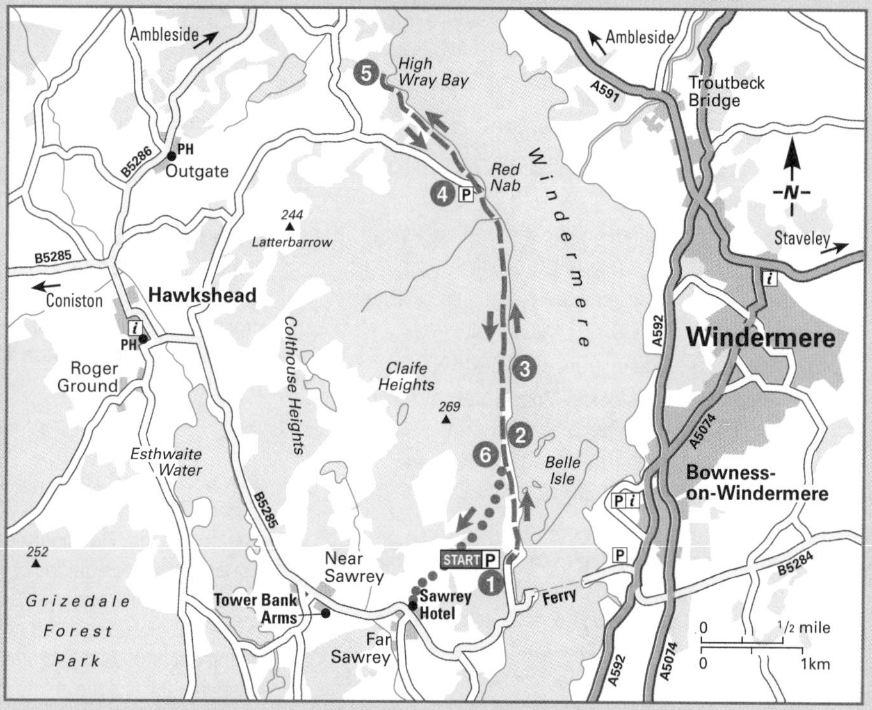

1 Leave the car park and turn left on a surfaced lane. There are views along here of moored yachts, Belle Isle and the lake, with a backdrop of high fells. The shapely peak is Ill Bell. Follow the lane past lay-bys to reach a gate and cattle grid.

2 The road beyond is marked 'Unsuitable for Motor Vehicles'. Keep left past the entrance to Strawberry Gardens. Beyond this the track becomes considerably rougher, and soon begins to climb quite steeply. It's worth persevering!

3 Once over the crest and just as you begin to descend, look out on the left for a wildlife viewing platform. There are squirrel feeders scattered in the trees, and you may spot roe deer. Take great care on the descent – there are loose stones and several rocky steps, and it may be safer to walk down. The track levels out for a short distance, then continues its descent, finally levelling out just above the lakeshore. The going is easier now, generally level. Pass several small shingle beaches. Keep left (almost straight ahead) at a fork and then, where a bridleway climbs off to the left, keep right (signed to Red Nab and Wray) along a smoother gravel track. At a gate, emerge onto a tarmac track but almost immediately fork right, signposted 'Bridleway Wray Castle'. Continue into the Red Nab car park.

4 Go round a low barrier on to the bridleway. This is level, easy riding all the way along to a gate by a boathouse, beyond which you emerge to the curve of High Wray Bay. The bridleway now veers away from the lake. The bay is a popular picnic spot, with people arriving both by land and by water. Walk the bikes round to the grassy slope above the further shore.

5 Retrace your route to Point **2**.

6 A bridleway rises off to the right here. It offers the option of a direct route to the pub at Far Sawrey, but the climb is longer, steeper and rougher than what you have encountered so far – so unless you found that all too easy, it's best to ignore it and simply return to the car park. The road route to the pub requires riding for 1 mile (1.6km) on the B5285, which can be busy at times, and also involves a steep climb midway.

what to look out for...

St Martin's Church, an impressive building surrounded by ancient yew trees, is the parish church of Bowness, built in 1483 and restored and enlarged in 1870. It is well worth taking a look inside. Behind the church is the oldest area of Bowness, known as Lowside, where an intriguing web of narrow streets thread between buildings of dark slate.

WALK 3
Through Monsal Dale, the Valley of the Gods

Following the ever-changing River Wye from Ashford-in-the-Water through lovely Monsal Dale.

Minimum time:	3hrs 30min
Walk length:	5.5 miles (8.8km)
Ascent/gradient:	656ft (200mtrs) ▲▲▲
Difficulty level:	✦✦✦
Paths:	Well-defined paths and tracks throughout, lots of stiles
Landscape:	Limestone dales and high pasture
Map:	OS Explorer OL24 White Peak
Start/finish:	Grid reference: SK 194696
Dog friendliness:	Livestock in Monsal Dale, dogs should be on leads
Parking:	Ashford-in-the-Water car park
Public toilets:	At car park

The Wye is a chameleon among rivers. Rising as a peaty stream from Axe Edge, it rushes downhill, only to be confined by the concrete and tarmac of Buxton, a spa town, and the quarries to the east. Beyond Chee Dale it gets renewed vigour and cuts a deep gorge through beds of limestone, finally to calm down again among the gentle fields and hill slopes of Bakewell. The finest stretch of the river valley must be around Monsal Head, and the best approach is that from Ashford-in-the-Water, one of Derbyshire's prettiest villages found just off the busy A6.

Monsal Dale

After passing through Ashford's streets the route climbs to high pastures that give no clue as to the whereabouts of Monsal Dale. But suddenly you reach the last wall and the ground falls away into a deep wooded gorge. John Ruskin was so taken with this beauty that he likened it to the Vale of Tempe: 'you might have seen the Gods there morning and evening – Apollo and the sweet Muses of light – walking in fair procession on the lawns of it and to and fro among the pinnacles of its crags'.

The Midland Railway

It's just a short walk along the rim to reach one of Derbyshire's best-known viewpoints, where the Monsal Viaduct spans the gorge. Built in 1867 as part of the Midland

Railway's line to Buxton, the five-arched, stone-built viaduct is nearly 80ft (25mtrs) high. But the building of this railway angered Ruskin. He continued, 'you blasted its rocks away, heaped thousands of tons of shale into its lovely stream. The valley is gone and the Gods with it'.

The line closed in 1968 and the rails were ripped out, leaving only the trackbed and the bridges. Ironically, today's conservationists believe that those are worth saving and have slapped a conservation order on the viaduct. The trackbed is used as a recreational route for walkers and cyclists – the Monsal Trail. The walk continues over the viaduct, giving bird's-eye views of the river and the lawn-like surrounding pastures. It then descends to the river bank, following it westwards beneath the prominent peak of Fin Cop. The valley curves like a sickle, while the path weaves in and out of thickets, and by wetlands where tall bulrushes and irises grow. After crossing the A6 the route takes you into the mouth of Deep Dale then the shade of Great Shacklow Wood. Just past some pools filled with trout there's an entrance to the Magpie Mine Sough. The tunnel was built in 1873 to drain the Magpie Lead Mines at nearby Sheldon. Magpie was worked intermittently for over 300 years before finally closing in the 1960s. It's believed to be haunted by the ghosts of miners from the neighbouring Redsoil Mine who tragically died underground in a dispute with the Magpie men.

Looking back on the beauty of the day's walk it's hard to believe that the gods haven't returned, or at least given the place a second look.

Walk Directions

1 From Ashford-in-the-Water car park, walk out to the road and turn right to walk along Vicarage Lane. After 100yds (91mtrs), a footpath on the left doubles back left, then swings sharp right to continue along a ginnel behind a row of houses. Beyond a stile the path enters a field.

2 Head for a stile in the top left corner, then veer slightly right to locate a stile allowing the route to go on to Pennyunk Lane. This walled stony track winds among high pastures. At its end go left uphill along a field-edge. At the top it joins another track, heading north (right) towards the rim of Monsal Dale. The path runs along the top edge of the deep wooded dale to reach the car park at Monsal Head.

3 Take the path marked 'Viaduct and Monsal Trail' here – this way you get to walk across the viaduct. On the other side of the viaduct go through a gate on the left. Ignore the path climbing west up the hillside, but descend south-west on a grassy path raking through scrub woods down into the valley. This shouldn't be confused with the steep eroded path plummeting straight down to the foot of the viaduct.

4 Now you walk down the pleasant valley. The right of way is well away from the river at first but most walkers trace the river bank to emerge at Lees Bottom and a roadside stile.

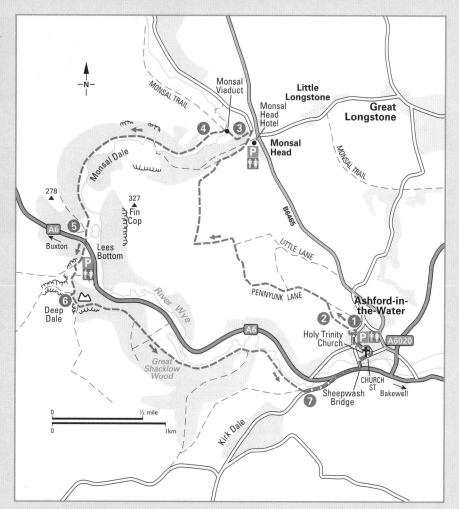

5 Cross the A6 with great care and go through the White Lodge car park on the path the other side, where the route back to Ashford begins. Beyond the gate carry on along the path, ignoring the turning to Toddington. Go over a wall stile and then up to a rocky path, forking left for the path into Great Shacklow Wood, signposted 'Ashford'.

6 The path now climbs steeply through the trees and stony ground to another gate. Ignore the turning right for Sheldon and continue straight ahead, following a fine ledge path along the steep wooded slopes. Eventually the path comes down to the river, past an old mill, before joining a minor road at the bottom of Kirk Dale.

7 Turn left along the road, down to the A6 and turn right towards Ashford. Leave the road to cross Sheepwash Bridge. Turn right along Church Street, then left along Court Lane to the car park.

CYCLE 3
The White Peak Plateau

From the High Peak Trail and excellent by-roads to timeless villages and old churches.

Minimum time:	4hrs
Ride length:	11.5 miles/18.4km
Difficulty level:	✚✚✚
Map:	OS Explorer OL24 White Peak
Start/finish:	Hurdlow car park, High Peak Trail, grid ref SK 128660
Trails/tracks:	Old railway track, back lanes with light traffic
Landscape:	Small walled fields, views across the White Peak plateau
Public toilets:	Parsley Hay
Tourist information:	Buxton, tel 01298 25106
Cycle hire:	Parsley Hay 01298 84493, www.derbyshire.gov.uk/countryside
❗	Two direct crossings of an A road need care. Suitable for older children and/or fitter cyclists, one long climb of around 0.5 miles (800m) requires regular rest stops

● Chelmorton

Getting to the start

Hurdlow car park (named Sparklow on OS maps) on the High Peak Trail, is signposted off the A515 Buxton to Ashbourne road about 6 miles (9.7km) south of Buxton. At the crossroads signed for Monyash in one direction and Crowdecote/Longnor in the other, turn towards Longnor to the car park.

Why do this cycle ride?

This is an easy, flowing route along quiet back roads and a section of the Pennine Bridleway. Largely level, quiet, minor roads skim between walled fields to charming villages. Rising gently to Monyash, lanes then rise steeply to the White Peak plateau before an exhilarating ride back to the start.

Ancient Walls

One of the great characteristics of the White Peak are the miles of dry-stone walls that thread the landscape from valley bottom to the very tops of the plateau. You can pass them by without giving them a second thought, but they have a fascinating history that goes back to medieval times when the great monastic estates controlled huge tracts of land and boundaries were established between these religious holdings and the lands of the great families.

As the monasteries disappeared, their lands were gradually parcelled up, and a further phase of wall building occurred. These walls are often winding and uneven. Huge areas still remained open however. As well as the wealthy estates, poor villagers also were permitted to farm dispersed strips of land near their homes. These initially were separated by low earth embankments. From the early 1700s onwards land reform saw such holdings consolidated into larger areas, each separated by a stone wall. These small strip fields can be seen at Chelmorton.

The Enclosure Awards of, largely, the 18th century, saw the great, unwalled estates split up into regular 'Parliamentary' fields (each Enclosure Award needed an Act of Parliament); it is these regular, geometric walls that form the mosaic that dominate today's landscape. Some walls were even built by French prisoners during the Napoleonic Wars.

what to look out for...

The area around Lathkill Dale, a National Nature Reserve, is rich in wild flowers in late spring and early summer, such as orchids, cowslips and the rare Jacob's ladder.

The Ride

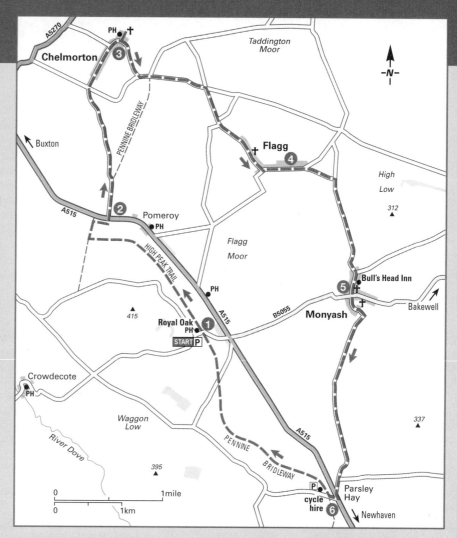

1 Ride north along the old railway, leaving the Royal Oak on your left. The current end of the High Peak Trail at Dowlow is soon reached; turn right here along a surfaced track for Chee Dale that heads for the A515. This is marked on the OS map as a footpath, but has been upgraded as part of the development of the Pennine Bridleway project and is open to pedal cycles. A fenced path beside the A515 then takes you right to a crossing point. Take great care crossing directly over here and join a lane heading north.

2 This peaceful lane undulates across the limestone uplands, with grand vistas all around across a patchwork of old stone walls and hay meadows. Where the Pennine Bridleway joins a rough lane, you remain on the tarred road. A lengthy downhill freewheel brings you to a crossroads. Carefully cross straight over and continue along the lane, rising very gradually up the one street that makes up Chelmorton. Continue to the end to find the old church.

3 Drop back downhill again slightly to reach a left turn; take this and start a lengthy but shallow climb back up on to the breezy uplands. At the T-junction turn left, signposted 'Flagg and Taddington', joining a largely flat road with excellent sight lines. Again, there are great views and there is little traffic to disturb your enjoyment. At the next

junction turn right, signed Flagg, starting a good long descent into the village. Keep left at a bend, dropping along the straggling main street of the village and past the little church.

4 Continue to a right turn for Monyash, joining a rather bumpy surfaced lane and soon a long, easy descent to a T-junction. Here turn right, signed Monyash, to another long downhill cruise to the outskirts of Monyash. A short

climb brings you to the village centre crossroads, village green and the Bull's Head Inn.

5 Carefully cross directly over, taking Rakes Road, signposted 'Newhaven and Youlgreave' and continue with a long ascent out of Monyash. Allow plenty of time to pause and take in the superb panorama across the southern stretches of the Peak District, easily visible over the low limestone walls. The

road gradually levels out before dropping to the A515.

6 Take care crossing here, as the traffic can be fast despite restrictions. Go diagonally across to the lane signposted Parsley Hay car park. Just along the lane turn right along the access road to the car park. Pick up the High Peak Trail here and follow it north (signed as the Pennine Bridleway towards Peak Forest) to return to the car park.

WALK 4
Dorset's Other Hardy

Rolling farmland and a high vantage point above Abbotsbury, where Nelson's fighting companion is remembered.

Minimum time:	3hrs 30min
Walk length:	7 miles (11.3km)
Ascent/gradient:	784ft (228mtrs) ▲▲▲
Difficulty level:	+++
Paths:	Field tracks, quiet roads, woodland tracks, 15 stiles
Landscape:	Rolling hills and escarpments above Abbotsbury
Map:	OS Explorer OL15 Purbeck & South Dorset
Start/finish:	Grid reference: SY 613876
Dog friendliness:	Some unfriendly stiles and electric fences
Parking:	By Hardy Monument, signed off road between Portesham and Winterbourne Abbas; additional parking by barrier
Public toilets:	None en route; nearest in Back Street, Abbotsbury

Admiral Hardy is best remembered today as the close friend of Admiral Lord Horatio Nelson, who attended the great naval hero in the hour of his death after the Battle of Trafalgar. He was a hero in his own right, his features decorating jugs and tankards of the time. Compared to his literary namesake, you'll find few signboards and memorials to this Hardy in his home county, but there is one monument – and it's a big one.

The Sea in his Veins

Thomas Masterman Hardy was born in 1769 at Kingston Russell, near Long Bredy, and from the age of nine raised at Portesham House in Portesham, a practical sort of village tucked well back under the hill of Black Down. At 12 he experienced his first taste of life at sea, but was sent home for further schooling. After three more years on land he escaped to sea again, this time slipping secretly aboard a merchantman, where he served before the mast and in the galley before enlisting. His naval career was to be illustrious.

In 1796 he had been put in charge of a captured foreign vessel when he witnessed two frigates under the command of Nelson in severe and imminent danger from a Spanish squadron. In a courageous and selfless act, Hardy hoisted the British flag, drawing the Spanish fire to his own vessel. He was captured, but was later returned to the Royal Navy in an exchange of prisoners. Some months later he and Nelson were involved in another near-death adventure, when Nelson stopped the flight of his ship to wait for Hardy, who had gone to the rescue of a drowning seaman. His bold action so surprised his Spanish pursuers that they stopped in their tracks.

Brothers in Arms

The friendship of the two men was to be deep and lasting. Hardy became the captain of Nelson's flagships and served with him at many of his most famous battles, including the Nile in 1798. In 1805, as captain of HMS *Victory*, he was at Nelson's side in that man's greatest hour and, when Nelson was mortally wounded, Hardy took command of the fleet. Nelson's last words were a blessing addressed to his friend. Hardy continued in his career and stayed in the navy for another 30 years. His final service was as Governor of Greenwich Hospital, where he died and was buried in 1839.

Solid and Reliable

Set high on Black Down hill, the Hardy Monument, solid and reliable as Hardy himself, looks like a Victorian chimney. You can climb up inside on summer weekends, but even if it is closed, the views from here over a sea of green fields and on down to Portland are superb.

while you're there...

Abbotsbury Swannery is a unique sanctuary. Mute swans have lived on the Fleet for 600 years, since they were introduced as a food source for the abbey, and their nest site is now protected. Come in April to see them nesting and from mid-May to see cygnets. The tithe barn near by houses the Smuggler's Barn and Children's Farm. Just outside the village are the Subtropical Gardens.

Walk Directions

1 Facing the road, turn left down a path by the entrance to the monument, signposted 'Inland Route'. Follow the broad track down through the woods. At the bottom fork right, then turn right opposite a ruin, and immediately bear left, over a stile. Walk up the edge of two fields. At the corner go over a stone stile and immediately cross the right-hand of two stiles. Walk alongside the fence to the hedge.

2 Turn left on to the road and right towards a farm, where you take a gate on the left and go up a track, then through another gate and bear right. Pass Hampton Stone Circle and keep straight on. Cross a stile and bear along the fence, signposted 'West Bexington'. Follow the path along the hillside and up through a gate to a road.

3 Turn right and take the first road left. Soon, at a cattlegrid, bear right along a track. Go through a gate (blue marker) and walk ahead down the hedge. Keep straight on through three fields.

4 Go through a gate to a junction of tracks. Bear right across the field, passing Kingston Russell Stone Circle. Go through a gate and bear slightly left over the hill, passing grassy earthworks (remains of prehistoric round huts) on the left. At the bottom go straight on down to a gate. Go through and bear left, then go through a gate to your right and down the hill.

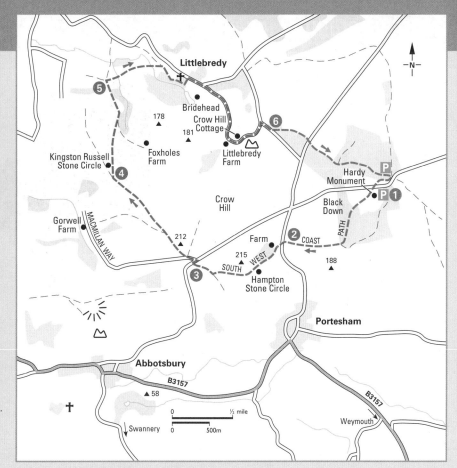

5 In the middle of the field turn right. Cross a footbridge to go through a gate. Cross a stream and walk straight ahead up the field. Bear left along the hedge. Cross a double stile and head diagonally left. Cross another footbridge over a stream. Turn right, bear left up through some trees, then go up to the right, to a stile. Cross and go over the hill towards Littlebredy. Cross a stile by a fingerpost and go straight on. Pass the church, go left through a gate and turn right on to the road. Bear right at the junction, at the cycle route sign. Continue past Crow Hill

Cottage and up a long hill. At the junction turn right.

6 Just after a bridleway sign, turn left on a track which leads beside woods and past a barn. Cross the road and go straight

ahead. Descend through the woods and, where the track divides, turn up to the right. After 0.5 mile (800mtrs), turn right and at the road take a rising path on the right to reach the road opposite the Hardy Monument.

what to look out for...

There are two prehistoric stone circles on this route. The first is Hampton Stone Circle, where the nine flinty stone lumps are well used by cattle as scratching posts. The stone the circle is made of is a natural phenomenon, with flint gravel cemented by silica, laid down over 40 million years ago. The more numerous lumps of the Kingston Russell Stone Circle are mottled with lichen.

CYCLE 4
A circuit around Linwood

Venture off the beaten track and mix with wildlife in the heart of the New Forest.

Minimum time:	1hr 45min
Ride length:	7 miles/11.3km
Difficulty level:	+++
Map:	OS Explorer OL22 New Forest
Start/finish:	Spring Bushes car park, Linwood; grid ref: SU 196107
Trails/tracks:	Gravelled forest tracks, two short sections on rural lanes
Landscape:	Broadleaf and coniferous woodland interspersed with open heathland
Public toilets:	None on route
Tourist information:	Lyndhurst, tel: 023 8028 2269
Cycle hire:	Ringwood Bicycle Hire, tel: 07510 734 367
!	Moderate hills, some uneven and stony tracks. Suitable for older children, off-road riding experience useful.

Getting to the start

Linwood is a village on a minor road north east of Ringwood. Spring Bushes car park is on the road that runs west from Emery Down, near Lyndhurst, to Rockford, just north of Ringwood.

Why do this cycle ride?

This relatively remote ride offers peace and quiet, and the opportunity to see the New Forest at its best. You'll follow waymarked Forestry Commission off-road cycle tracks deep into the heart of the Forest, with two short sections on tarred roads where you will need to watch out for the occasional car. There are plenty of opportunities for birdwatching or studying the other wildlife.

New Forest deer

You'll often see deer along this trail, especially early in the morning or around dusk – go quietly for the best chance of seeing these timid woodland residents in their natural habitat. Keep an eye out for roe deer in the cultivated fields close to Dockens Water, between the start of the ride and the point where you join the tarred lane leading up to the Red Shoot

● Linwood, New Forest National Park

Inn. These graceful creatures are 24–28 inches (61–71cm) high at the shoulder and the males have short, forked antlers. Roe deer have rich reddish-brown coats from May to September, but turn greyer in winter and develop a white patch on the rump.

You'll occasionally spot red deer in the same area, especially on the open heath near Black Barrow. These are our largest native species, and a fully-grown male with his splendid russet coat and impressive antlers may stand nearly 4ft (1.2mtrs) tall at the shoulder. The males are at their boldest when competing for females during the mating season in early autumn.

Fallow deer may pop up almost anywhere on the ride, but a favourite haunt is in Broomy Bottom, off to your right as you cross Broomy Plain. With their reddish-fawn coats dappled with white spots, these appealing animals have white rumps and a black line running up the tail. The males have broad antlers and stand up to 3ft (0.9mtrs) tall at the shoulder.

while you're there...

More common in Spain and Portugal than in England, the Dartford warbler is not a frequent sight. The best time to spot one is on a fine sunny morning, when the male will perch singing on a bush.

The Ride

1 Turn right out of the car park and pass the end of the gravel track which leads up to the High Corner Inn.

2 At Woodford Bottom bear left at the wooden barrier on your right and pass the ford across the Dockens Water stream, also on your right. Keep to the waymarked cycle route as it follows the gravelled track that winds across the open heath, past a few scattered houses and the tree-capped mound of Black Barrow. A few smaller tracks lead off to left and right, but the main gravelled trail is easy enough to follow. Keep straight on as a similar track leads in from your left near the thatched Bogmyrtle Cottage, until you join a tarred lane. Almost at once the lane turns sharp left through a tiny ford and climbs gently up to the road junction at the Red Shoot Inn.

3 Turn left opposite the post-box, still following the waymarked cycle route, and continue to climb until the road levels off and swings to the left at Amie's Corner. Fork

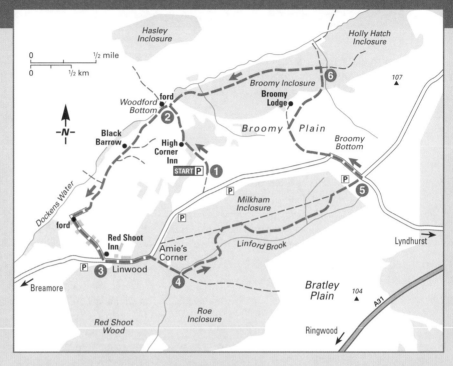

right here, sticking with the waymarked cycle route as it joins a gravelled forest track. The trail dives into Milkham Inclosure through wooden gates beside an attractive whitewashed cottage, then drops to a bridge over the Linford Brook.

4 A few yards further on turn left at the numbered waymark post 5, then follow the track as it winds

through open mixed woodland and re-crosses the Linford Brook. Continue as the track bears right at the next waymark post, then right again in front of a pair of wooden gates where you enter an area of mainly coniferous woodland. A pair of wooden gates punctuates your progress to the top of the hill, where further gates lead you out into the Forestry Commission's Milkham car park. Go through here, cross the car park, and stop at the road junction.

5 Turn left towards Linwood and follow the narrow tarred lane for 500yds (457mtrs) until it bears away to the left. Fork right here on to the waymarked cycle trail that follows the gravel track towards Broomy Lodge and Holly Hatch. Here your route crosses the high heathland plateau of

Broomy Plain. This is a good spot to see Dartford warblers, meadow pipits and stonechats, and you'll also enjoy long views towards Cranborne Chase and the Wiltshire Downs. Bear right at the next fork and follow the trail down into Holly Hatch Inclosure.

6 At the foot of the hill, numbered waymark post 3 stands at the forest crossroads. Turn left here, on to a lovely tree-shaded track with soft green verges that leads you through the oak woods. Two pairs of wooden gates mark your progress through the inclosure, and at length the oaks give way to conifers. Follow the waymarked trail until you rejoin your outward route at a low wooden barrier. Turn left here, and climb the short hill back to the High Corner Inn.

Did you know?

In March 2005 the Rural Affairs Minister confirmed the New Forest National Park (Designation) Order, and thus created a new National Park. For centuries the New Forest has been administered partly by the Verderers, who sit in open court every two months in the Verderers Hall in Lyndhurst. Their duties are largely political and judicial, concerning common rights, conservation issues and the implementation of local by-laws.

This peaceful walk in a popular corner of Herefordshire includes an energetic climb, rewarded with fine views.

Minimum time:	2hrs 45min
Walk length:	6.75 miles (10.9km)
Ascent/gradient:	855ft (260mtrs) ▲▲▲
Difficulty level:	+++
Paths:	Quiet lanes, riverside meadows, woodland paths, 2 stiles
Landscape:	Much-photographed river valley
Map:	OS Explorer OL14 Wye Valley & Forest of Dean
Start/finish:	Grid reference: SO 575196
Dog friendliness:	Good, but dogs forbidden in castle grounds
Parking:	Goodrich Castle pay-and-display car park open daily, times vary with the season
Public toilets:	At start

The well-preserved remains of Goodrich Castle seen today are of building work carried out in the 12th and 13th centuries, replacing those from the early 12th century. Some gory traps and ruses kept would-be intruders away. The most often quoted is a tunnel beneath the gate tower that could be blocked by a portcullis; doomed attackers would then be scalded with hot water from above or, better still, burned to death with molten lead (presumably recyclable).

Ghost Story

The castle eventually succumbed to Parliamentarians in 1646 during the Civil War, led by Colonel John Birch, who had successfully attacked the city of Hereford the previous December. The story goes that the colonel's niece, Alice, and Charles Clifford, her lover, fled from the battle, only to meet their deaths trying to cross the River Wye. So watch out for their ghosts on a phantom horse. Goodrich Castle is open daily from 10am to 5pm, except between November and March, when the opening days are Wednesday to Sunday, and the hours are 10am to 1pm and 2pm to 4pm.

A Simple Price

The oddly named Welsh Bicknor was once a detached parish of Monmouthshire. Welsh Bicknor Youth Hostel, a former Victorian rectory, is just one of approximately 225 in England and Wales. The Youth Hostels Association (YHA) began with 73 buildings, many donated, in 1931. The organisation arose to meet the increasing demand from ramblers, cyclists and, in particular, youth organisations for simple, inexpensive accommodation. The YHA has, in relative terms, remained true to this concept, but it has also moved with the times – some would say too slowly, others would say too quickly – improving the quality of its accommodation in line with the relentlessly rising expectations of the recreational public. It seems cherished by the minority that uses it, yet overlooked (inexplicably?) by the majority that doesn't.

On Location

The area around Symonds Yat has, in recent years, attracted film buffs who wanted to see the locations used for Richard Attenborough's film, *Shadowlands*, the stars of which were Debra Winger, Anthony Hopkins and Symonds Yat. The film was based on the life of C S Lewis, author of *The Chronicles of Narnia*. Coppet Hill Nature Reserve is managed by a trust. It earned Local Nature Reserve status in 2000 after 14 years of conservation management.

while you're there...

For a 35-minute river cruise, try Kingfisher Cruises at Symonds Yat East, where you'll also find the Saracen's Head (a former cider mill) and the hand ferry. The aMazing Hedge Puzzle maze are at Symonds Yat West.

what to look out for...

One hundred yards (91mtrs) from Point ❹ are some partly covered kilns, marked by a clump of trees growing on top. As you climb Coppet Hill, look for formerly coppiced woodland, where the trees were 'let go' when the demand for coppice wood petered out.

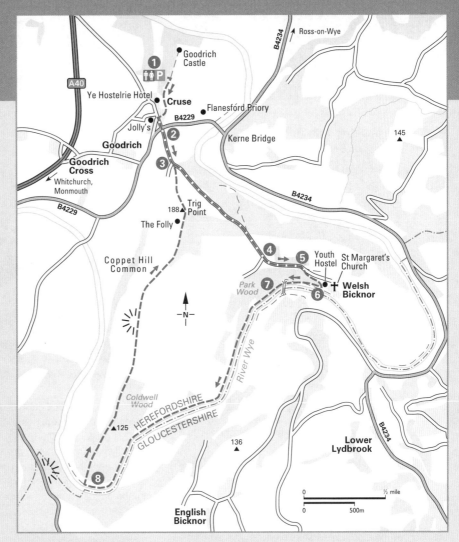

Walk Directions

1 Walk back to the castle access road junction and turn immediately left. In 110yds (100mtrs) cross a bridge over the B4229.

2 Go up a further 400yds (366mtrs). Ignore another road branching off to the right, but enjoy the view of Kerne Bridge. Opposite, between the two roads, a sign 'Coppet Hill Common' indicates your return route. Go on a few paces.

3 Go 0.5 mile (800mtrs) up this dead end, to reach a cattle grid. Here, at the brow, the woods give way to parkland. Go straight ahead for another 325yds (297mtrs) to a solitary horse chestnut tree at a right turn.

4 Keep ahead for 400yds (366mtrs), bending left and dipping down, the road once again tree-lined. The road curves right a fraction, while a gravel track goes up a ramp and fractionally left.

5 Curve right. Ignore the pillared driveway but begin down the youth hostel's driveway. At a welcome sign take a footpath that runs initially parallel to it. Descend wooden steps and a sometimes muddy path to a T-junction beside the River Wye.

6 Turn right, following the Wye Valley Walk (turn left to visit the church first). In 350yds (320mtrs) you'll reach an old, iron girder railway bridge, which now carries the Wye Valley Walk across the river, but stay this side, passing underneath the bridge. In about 160yds (146mtrs) look carefully for narrow yellow bands of 'rights of way' tape on a tree.

7 Take the path closest to the river. Continue for about 1.25miles (2km). Enter Coldwell Wood to walk beside the river for a further 0.25 mile (400mtrs). On leaving, keep by the river in preference to a path that follows the woodland's edge. In about 350yds (320mtrs) you'll reach a stile beside a fallen willow.

8 Turn right, signposted 'Coppet Hill', passing through the line of trees to a stile. Soon begin the arduous woodland ascent. The path levels, later rising to The Folly, then goes down (not up!) to a triangulation point. Follow the clear green sward ahead, becoming a narrow rut then a stepped path, down to the road, close to Point **3**. Retrace your steps to the castle car park.

where to eat and drink...

A visitor centre beside the castle car park has hot food and drinks. Jolly's of Goodrich is the village store and post office. The Hostelrie at Goodrich serves coffee, tea and lunchtime bar food.

WALK 6
A Taste for Lincolnshire

Work up an appetite with this scenic walk through the Wolds west of Louth.

Minimum time:	3hrs
Walk length:	6 miles (9.7km)
Ascent/gradient:	410ft (125mtrs) ▲▲▲
Difficulty level:	✚✚✚
Paths:	Bridleways and lanes, field paths, may be boggy, 10 stiles
Landscape:	Broad, rounded hills and shallow river valley
Map:	OS Explorer 282 Lincolnshire Wolds North
Start/finish:	Grid reference: TF 236829
Dog friendliness:	Some livestock, plenty of off-lead potential
Parking:	Main Road, Donington on Bain
Public toilets:	None on route (nearest in Louth)

● Horncastle Canal at Kirkby on Bain

Lincolnshire is well known as one of the foremost English counties for food production. The fertile soils of the Fens in the south support vast and seemingly endless fields of arable crops, such as potatoes, onions, cabbages and sugar beet. The county is the leading producer of cereals and it's also the world's largest producer of daffodils.

The 'Tastes of Lincolnshire' initiative was launched within the county to promote Lincolnshire produce; its members include tea rooms, B&Bs, pubs and restaurants, as well as many of the local producers themselves. Look out for the stickers and leaflets.

what to look out for...

Unless it's misty, you can't miss Belmont Transmitting Station. Built in 1964 by the Independent Television Authority, it was originally 1,265ft (385mtrs) high, which at that time made it the second tallest communications mast in Europe. It then gained a further 7ft (2.1mtrs) when meteorological equipment was added. Since it stands pencil-thin, only 9ft (2.7mtrs) in diameter, you feel that all it needs to round it off is a giant flag.

This walk starts and finishes near The Black Horse Inn in Donington on Bain, and there's no better place to try the county's produce after a bracing ramble.

In villages and market towns such as Louth, Horncastle, Boston and Spalding, a visit to the local baker will reveal yet another subtle variation of the famous Lincolnshire plumbread, delicious spread with butter and accompanied by a cup of strong tea. Also look out for Grantham gingerbread and Lincolnshire curd tart. Other regional recipes include Lincolnshire dripping cake, traditionally eaten for lunch during harvest time.

Lincolnshire's hand-made poacher cheese has long been famous, and recently sheep's milk products have been reintroduced, with herds of ewes now generating a growing supply of cheese, milk and yogurt. Another return to the county's pastures are Lincoln Reds, a traditional breed of beef cattle with a handsome deep-red coat.

The county is also well-known for haslet – a loaf of cooked, minced pig's offal eaten cold – and chine. Stuffed chine harks back to an 18th-century way of cooking ham, peculiar to Lincolnshire, whereby gashes in the ham are stuffed with parsley, mint, thyme and other herbs before boiling. It is traditionally served cold, sliced, with vinegar and a salad. Finally, don't forget about a drink to accompany all this decent food, and what better than Batemans 'good honest ales', brewed at Wainfleet.

Walk Directions

1 Walk out of the village northwards, past the Norman church and the post office, on to Mill Road. At the first junction turn right, signposted 'Hallington' and 'Louth', then in a few paces go left, over a stile. Walk along the bottom of successive fields, with the River Bain on your left and the lofty Belmont Transmitting Station dominating the skyline further west. After 0.75 mile (1.2km), and having passed a fishing lake, you reach a footbridge.

2 Cross over the footbridge to reach Biscathorpe's isolated little church, rebuilt in the mid-1800s in a medieval Gothic style. Walk around its perimeter wall, then continue past a house and across a lane to cross another footbridge ahead.

3 Now head half left across the bumpy outline of a deserted medieval village. The ditches, ridges and mounds give some indication of its layout, and there are more abandoned settlements to the north of the A157. Head towards the top of the hill and go through a gate for a path through a small plantation. Turn right on a lane and walk along this for 550yds (503mtrs).

4 Go over a stile on the right for a signposted public footpath down the side of disused workings, then left across a wide field, aiming for the far corner down by the stream. Go over a footbridge, then follow the farm track round

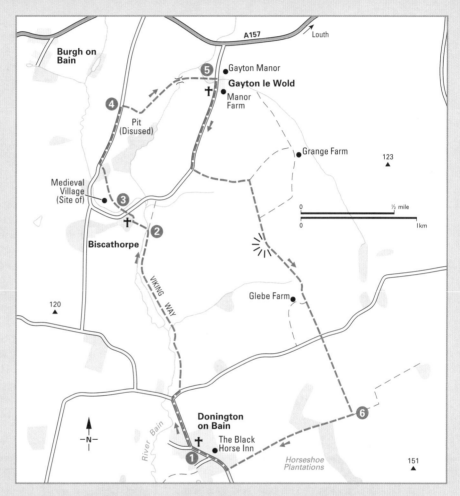

to the left before crossing another footbridge and walking across a meadow to reach the lane at Gayton le Wold.

5 Turn right and walk along the lane past Manor Farm's whitewashed buildings and another miniature church, then out across the hilltop fields. In 0.5 mile (800mtrs), where the lane bends right, go left on a broad track indicated 'public bridleway'. Veer right into the field at the top and follow this obvious and waymarked route alongside huge fields. There are delightful views down across the Bain Valley to your right, back towards Donington. Continue around and above the back of Glebe Farm, by a thick hedge, and go straight over a lane.

6 In just under 0.5 mile (800mtrs) from the road crossing, turn right where a signpost points to a public footpath downhill behind a hedge. Follow this wide track gradually down via Horseshoe Plantations, then a hedge by fields of grazing horses from the stable near by. Turn right on to the road at the bottom to return to the centre of Donington on Bain.

Enjoy some of the loveliest scenery in Norfolk as you stroll through the grounds of Blickling Hall.

Minimum time:	3hrs
Walk length:	6.5 miles (10.4km)
Ascent/gradient:	98ft (30mtrs) ▲▲▲
Difficulty level:	✦✦✦
Paths:	Paved lanes and some footpaths
Landscape:	Stately house grounds and pretty agricultural land
Map:	OS Explorer 252 Norfolk Coast East
Start/finish:	Grid reference: TG 176285
Dog friendliness:	Dogs must be on lead in grounds of hall
Parking:	Blickling Hall car park on Aylsham Road (free for NT members)
Public toilets:	Visitor centre at Blickling Hall; also in Aylsham town centre

For the walker, Blickling Hall is probably the best of the many National Trust properties found in Norfolk. The River Bure meanders pleasantly to the north of its grounds, which are full of shady mature trees, there is a quiet lake to stroll around and the grounds are full of fascinating buildings and monuments.

A Chequered History

The ancient manor of Blickling once belonged to King Harold who built the first house here. He was defeated at Hastings by William the Conqueror in 1066, who seized Blickling for himself, then passed it to a man who later became Bishop of Thetford. The manor remained in the hands of successive bishops until it passed to a line of soldiers. One of these, Nicholas Dagworth, built a moated house here in the 1390s. Eventually, Blickling came into the possession of Sir John Fastolf, widely believed to be the inspiration for Shakespeare's Falstaff, and then passed to the Boleyn family, where it remained until Anne Boleyn's execution by Henry VIII. The Boleyns lost a good deal of property after Anne's dramatic fall from grace and Blickling eventually came into the hands of the Hobart family in 1616.

The Hobarts made drastic changes, almost completely rebuilding the house between 1618 and 1629. Instead of following the contemporary craze for new Classical architecture, the Hobarts remained firmly traditional, and as a result the house is one of the finest examples of Jacobean architecture in the country. It was designed by Robert Lyminge, who also built Hatfield House in Essex. The building is made of brick with stone dressings, and has a pair of handsome corner towers.

From Russia With Love

Blickling is a veritable treasure house. Perhaps its most famous acquisition is the magnificent tapestry that hangs in the Peter-the-Great Room. This belonged to John Hobart, who was described by Horace Walpole as painfully transparent. He therefore appears an odd choice to appoint as Ambassador to Catherine of Russia, but to Russia he went and he seems to have made a success of his posting. It was during this sojourn that he bought the remarkable tapestry depicting the Tsar prancing along on his horse with the carnage of Poltava in the background.

The park has its origins in the 18th century and was once much bigger, before financial considerations forced its owners to sell off parcels of it. There was already a lake on the land, but the Hobarts had it enlarged in 1762. They built themselves a racecourse in 1773. It still stands on the Aylsham Road and is known as the Tower House (privately owned). Enjoy the lake and the 4,777 acres (1,935ha) of beautiful woods and gardens, as this walk takes you on a pleasant amble up to the north of the hall.

● Blickling Hall

Walk Directions

1 Go towards the National Trust visitor centre and take the gravel path to its left, past the Buckinghamshire Arms. At the drive, turn left signed to the park and lake. Keep right and go through gates into Blickling Park. Keep ahead at a fork and follow the Weavers' Way, eventually to go through a gate into The Beeches. Continue ahead at a crossing of paths along the right-hand field-edge. On nearing a house, follow the path right, then left to a lane.

2 Turn left at the lane, following its winding path until you pass Mill Cottage, complete with mill pond, on your right and Mill Farm on your left. The mixed deciduous Great Wood on your left belongs to the National Trust. Leave the woods and walk through the pretty Bure Valley for about 700yds (640mtrs) until you see a footpath on your left (although the sign is on the right).

3 Turn left down this overgrown track, with hedgerows to the right and trees to the left. Go up a slope to Bunker's Hill Plantation (also

protected by the National Trust), skirting around the edge of this before the footpath merges with a farm track. It eventually comes out on to a road.

4 Turn left and then right, on to New Road, which is signposted for Cawston and Oulton Street. This wide lane runs as straight as an arrow for about 0.75 mile (1.2km), before reaching a crossroads at the village sign for Oulton Street.

5 Turn left by the RAF memorial and its bench. The lane starts off wide, but soon narrows to a peaceful rural track. Continue along this for 1.5 miles (2.4km), passing through the thin line of trees known as the Oulton Belt and eventually arriving at Abel Heath, a small conservation area owned by the National Trust.

6 Turn left by the oak tree, then left at the T-junction towards

Abel Heath Farm. The lane winds downhill until you reach the red-brick cottages of the little hamlet of Silvergate. You are now on the Weavers' Way long distance footpath. Pass a cemetery on your right and continue until you see St Andrew's Church (partly 14th century, but mostly Victorian). Continue on until you reach the main road.

7 Turn left, passing the Buckinghamshire Arms and the pretty 18th- and 19th-century estate cottages at the park gates on your right. Continue walking until you see signs for the car park, where you turn right.

what to look out for...

Blickling Hall holds many treasures, but in particular you should not miss the grand South Drawing Room with its superb plaster ceiling; the Brown Drawing Room, which was a chapel in the 17th century; and the sumptuous Peter-the-Great Room and State Bedroom. In the grounds, look for the early 18th-century temple and fountain, and the 1782 Orangery.

A fine walk in peaceful countryside to one of Britain's top country houses.

Minimum time:	3hrs
Walk length:	7 miles (11.3km)
Ascent/gradient:	150ft (46mtrs) ▲▲▲
Difficulty level:	✦✦✦
Paths:	Field paths and tracks, parkland paths and estate drives. Some quiet road walking, 2 stiles
Landscape:	Farmland and parkland
Map:	OS Explorer 180 Oxford
Start/finish:	Grid reference: SP 412159
Dog friendliness:	On lead in grounds of Blenheim Palace
Parking:	Spaces in centre of Combe
Public toilets:	Blenheim Palace, for visitors; otherwise none en route

When King George III first set eyes on Blenheim Palace, he remarked, 'We have nothing to equal this.' Few would disagree with him. The views of the palace, the lake and the Grand Bridge from the waterside path on this delightful walk are stunning. Set in a magnificent 2,000-acre (810ha) park landscaped by 'Capability' Brown, the great Baroque house covers a staggering 7 acres (2.8ha) and is England's largest stately home.

Blenheim Palace took nearly 20 years to build and was finally completed in 1722. The architect John Vanbrugh was commissioned to design the house for John Churchill, 1st Duke of Marlborough (1650–1722), following his victory over the French at Blenheim in 1704. Inside, there are

while you're there...

Have a look at Combe church. The original building, which was in the valley about 1 mile (1.6km) from its present site, was built during the Norman period. The present church was built in about 1395, about 50 years after the villagers moved their homes out of the valley. The design of the church is an example of the Early Perpendicular style, with a stone pulpit and medieval stained glass.

various state rooms and tapestries, the Long Library – considered by many to be the finest room in the house – and the room where Winston Churchill was born in 1874.

A Just Reward

It was Queen Anne who decided that John Churchill's efforts in battle should be suitably rewarded, reflecting the high regard in which the nation held him. But what exactly did Churchill do to earn such respect? As a soldier and as a statesman, he was responsible for supressing Louis XIV's imperialist ambitions in Europe. His spirit and determination resulted in a humiliating defeat of the French at Blenheim on 13 August 1704.

In gratitude, Queen Anne conferred the Royal Manor of Woodstock on the Duke of Marlborough and his heirs in perpetuity, and a sum of £500,000 was voted by parliament for the building of Blenheim Palace. But problems lay ahead. The Duke's wife, Sarah, was Princess Anne's favourite companion before she became Queen in 1702. Sarah used her close friendship and her influence in royal circles to secure a dukedom for her husband, and it was she, not the Duke of Marlborough, who approved the plans and then supervised the building work. Proving just how ruthless and determined she could be, Sarah rejected Sir Christopher Wren's designs in favour of those produced by John Vanbrugh.

A Sweet House

The Duchess remained a thorn in the side of builders and architects for some time, insisting that all she wanted was a 'clean, sweet house and garden, be it ever so small.' Parliament complained about the spiralling cost, money gradually ran out and the Duchess forbade Vanbrugh from seeing the finished building in 1725, refusing him entry to the grounds.

Characterised by ornament and exuberance, creating a memorable skyline, Blenheim Palace is not to everyone's taste, though the immense scale of the house has to be seen as a tribute to the skill and ingenuity of its creators. The vast parkland and gardens, too, are renowned for their beauty and range with Vanbrugh's Grand Bridge as the focal point.

Walk Directions

1 From the green, take the road signposted 'East End'. Swing right by the village pump into the churchyard and keep left of the church. Exit through the gap in the boundary wall, flanked by two gravestones, and begin skirting the right-hand edge of the sports field. After about 50yds (46mtrs), branch off into the trees, then head diagonally across the field. Cross into the next field and keep to the right edge of the wood. In the next field, turn left (trees on the left) and go up to the woodland corner. Pass through a gap in the hedge and cross the field.

2 Exit to the road, turn left and keep right at the next junction. Walk to Combe Gate. Go through the large kissing gate into the grounds of Blenheim Palace, keep left at the junction and follow the drive through the parkland. As it sweeps left to a cattle grid, veer to the right by a Public Footpath sign. Follow the grassy path to a stile. Keep right when the path divides and walk beside the western arm of The Lake.

3 Eventually you reach a tarmac drive. Turn right and walk down towards the Grand Bridge. As you approach it, turn sharp left, passing between mature trees with Queen Pool on your right. Cross a cattle grid and keep ahead through the park. With the Column of Victory on your left, follow the drive as it sweeps to the right.

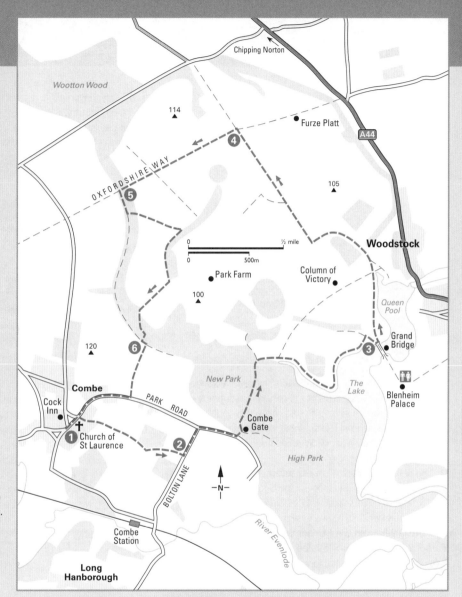

4 Turn left at the second cattle grid, in line with Furze Platt (right). Join the Oxfordshire Way, go through a gate and follow the grassy track beside trees, then along a gravel track between fields. At length cross a track and continue towards woodland. Enter, and turn left after a few paces to join a clear track.

5 After about 150yds (137mtrs) first left, crossing a footbridge to reach a field edge. Keep right here, following the obvious path across a large field beside fencing. When you reach a track, turn right. Keep alongside trees to a junction. Turn right and follow the grassy track down to and through a wood, then diagonally left across a strip of pasture to an opening. Go up to a track and cross it to a ladder stile.

6 Turn left to a hedge, then turn right, keeping it and a ditch on your right. Skirt a field to the road, turn right and walk back into Combe.

WALK 9
Horner's Corners

On the trail of Exmoor's red deer in the woodlands under Dunkery Beacon.

Minimum time:	2hrs 30min
Walk length:	4.5 miles (7.2km)
Ascent/gradient:	1,000ft (305mtrs) ▲▲▲
Difficulty level:	+++
Paths:	Broad paths, with some stonier ones, steep in places, no stiles
Landscape:	Dense woodland in steep-sided stream valleys
Map:	OS Explorer OL 9 Exmoor
Start/finish:	Grid reference: SS 898455
Dog friendliness:	Off lead, but be aware of deer and horse-riders
Parking:	National Trust car park (free) at Horner
Public toilets:	At car park

Horner takes its name from the Saxon 'hwrnwr', a wonderfully expressive word meaning snorer, that here describes the rumble of the stream in its enclosed valley. Above the treetops, Webber's Post is a splendid viewpoint out across the Bristol Channel. What Mr Webber stood there to view, though, was the hunting of red deer.

The herd on Exmoor numbers several thousand. Although this is small compared to those in the Scottish Highlands, the Exmoor stag himself is the UK's biggest wild deer. This is simply because his life is slightly easier – farmed deer are larger again. On Exmoor, as in the rest of Northern Europe outside Scotland, the deer remains a forest animal. Exmoor's mix of impenetrable woodland with areas of open grazing, even with all its houses, farms and fields, remains good deer country.

The calf is born dappled for camouflage under the trees, and lies in shelter during the day while the hind feeds. If you do come across a deer calf, leave it alone – it hasn't been abandoned. During the summer the stags and hinds run in separate herds. In the Scottish Highlands deer graze on high ground during the day to escape from midges, and descend to the forest at night; on Exmoor the main annoying pest is the human, so the deer graze the moor at dawn and dusk, and spend the day in the trees.

Stag Nights

In September and October comes the spectacular rut, when stags roar defiance at each other, and, if that fails, do battle with antlers for mating privileges. During this time they eat only occasionally, fight a lot and mate as often as possible. The stag with a mighty roar and a hard head can gather a harem of a dozen hinds. Your best chance of seeing one is very early or very late in the day – or else in the forest. You may well smell the deer, even though it probably smelled you first and has already gone quietly away. Look closely, too, at the small brown cows two fields away – they may well actually turn out to be deer – binoculars are a must.

While deer are thriving, it is the Exmoor stag hunters that are in danger of extinction. Just one pack of the traditional staghounds remains. Following pressure from its own members, the National Trust banned hunting from its land, and the national government has now criminalised it along with fox-hunting.

what to look out for...

Multiple tree trunks growing from a single point show where the woodland has formerly been coppiced. Every ten years the new shoots would be cut back to the original stump. This method of harvesting a woodland is more productive than clear-felling and replanting, whether what you're after is oak bark for the tanning industry or just firewood. Coppicing has also allowed the original woodland plants to survive through the centuries.

while you're there...

Dunster Castle has everything – battlements and gardens, a wooded hill setting with an ancient village below, a working watermill, the national collection of strawberry trees (*Arbutus unedo*) and even a somewhat implausible King Arthur legend – he helped St Carantoc tame the local dragon.

Walk Directions

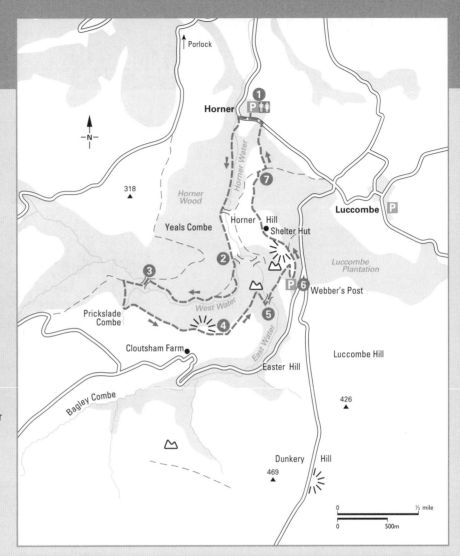

1 Leave the National Trust car park in Horner village past the toilets and turn right to the track leading into Horner Wood. This crosses a bridge and passes a field before rejoining Horner Water. You can take a footpath alongside the stream instead of the track, they lead to the same place. Ignore the first footbridge, and continue along the obvious track to where a sign, 'Dunkery Beacon', points to the left towards a second footbridge.

2 Ignore this footbridge as well. Keep on the track for another 100yds (91mtrs), then fork left on a path alongside West Water. This rejoins the track, and after another 0.5mile (800mtrs) alongside the track is another footbridge.

3 Cross to a path that slants up to the right. After 200yds (183mtrs) turn left into a smaller path that turns uphill alongside Prickslade Combe. The path reaches the combe's little stream at a cross-path, with the wood top visible above. Here turn left, across the stream, on a path contouring through the top of the wood. After a dip and climb, it emerges into the open and arrives at a fine view over the top of the woodlands to Porlock Bay. It joins a bridleway near a lone pine with a bench.

4 Continue ahead on the bridleway's grassy track, with the car park of Webber's Post visible ahead. Alas, the deep valley of

the East Water lies between you and your destination. So, in 55yds (50mtrs), fork down left on a clear path back into birchwoods. This zig-zags down to meet a larger track in the valley bottom.

5 Turn downstream, crossing a footbridge over the East Water, beside a ford. After about 60yds (55mtrs) bear right on to an ascending path. At the top of the steep section turn right on a small sunken path that climbs to the right to Webber's Post car park.

6 Walk to the left, round the car park, to a path to Horner. (Or you could take the pink-surfaced, easy-access path immediately to the right.) The path runs immediately below the 'easy access' one with its stone bench. Just after the concrete sculpture where easy access turns back, bear left on a wider path, soon passing a wooden shelter hut. Again fork left on a wider path to keep ahead down a wide, gentle spur, with the deep valley

of the Horner Water on your left. As the spur steepens, the footpath meets a crossing track signposted 'Windsor Path'.

7 Turn right for perhaps 30 paces, then take a descending path signposted 'Horner'. Narrow at first, this widens and finally meets a wide, horse-mangled track with wooden steps; turn left down this into Horner.

A walk along the River Deben from a historic riverside town, with views of England's last working tide mill.

Minimum time:	1hr 30min
Walk length:	4 miles (6.4km)
Ascent/gradient:	164ft (50mtrs) ▲▲▲
Difficulty level:	✦✦✦
Paths:	River wall, riverside paths, town streets, some steps
Landscape:	Woodbridge and River Deben
Map:	OS Explorer 197 Ipswich, Felixstowe & Harwich or 212 Woodbridge & Saxmundham
Start/finish:	Grid reference: TM 271485
Dog friendliness:	Riverside paths suitable for dogs
Parking:	The Avenue car park, Woodbridge
Public toilets:	On riverside near start of walk

River Deben at Woodbridge

Woodbridge is one of those places that would have appealed to the water rat in *Wind in the Willows*, who declared that there was nothing, absolutely nothing, half so much worth doing as simply messing about in boats. Situated at the head of the Deben estuary, at the point where the river is navigable to the sea, Woodbridge attracts a sailing crowd who hang around its cafés and yacht club in summer, enthusiastically comparing mast sizes and discussing wind speeds like the people of Newmarket discuss horses and form.

Along the River Deben

This short walk takes you out along the River Deben among the sailing boats, marshes and mudflats. Seagulls swoop for fish and boats bob on the quayside, enhancing the nautical feel. On the way back you have the opportunity for a closer look at Woodbridge. The town owes much to Thomas Seckford, a courtier and legal adviser to Elizabeth I, who left the proceeds of his Clerkenwell Estate to Woodbridge. This generous bequest has been used to fund everything from hospitals to schools and playing fields and the Seckford Foundation continues to be administered for the benefit of the people of Woodbridge today. Seckford is buried in St Mary's Church, close to the abbey and the Shire Hall, which he built.

Tide Mill

There is also the chance to visit the Tide Mill, whose elegant white weatherboarded façade dominates the quay. A mill has stood on this site since at least the 12th century, although the present building dates from 1793 and was England's last working tide mill when it finally stopped turning in 1957. The mill was sold at auction in 1968, restored and opened to the public, and you can once again see the giant waterwheel turning at low tide. The old mill pond is now a marina, but a smaller pond has been dug to collect the water at high tide and release it when the tide has gone out. The times of the display, obviously, vary with the tides, but the wheel usually turns for an hour or so each day in summer, and if the tide is low enough you can see the channel created by the mill race as it flows back into the sea.

Kept Alive

Even if you struggle to understand the technology, this is still a fascinating example of Industrial Revolution machinery, kept alive by a team of dedicated volunteers. There are good views over the harbour and river from the upper floors.

Walk Directions

1 Leave the car park on The Avenue and cross the railway line to continue to the boatyard at the end of the lane. Turn right to walk along the river wall, passing the slipways of Deben Yacht Club. Continue along the river wall on an easy section of the walk, on a tarmac path with lovely views out over the meadows to your right, to enter the National Trust-owned land at Kyson Hill.

2 Turn left at a three-way junction to drop down to the beach and continue the walk along the foreshore beneath a canopy of oak trees. (If the tide is high, you may have to turn right instead, picking up the route at Point **4**.) Keep right at some wooden railings and follow this path round to Martlesham Creek, where you scramble up the embankment and follow a peaceful riverside path.

3 Turn right at the end of the creek and walk around a sewage works to Sandy Lane. Turn right beneath the brick-arched railway bridge and stay on this road as it climbs steadily for about 700yds (640mtrs). At the top of a rise, turn right on to Broom Heath.

4 When the road bends round to the right, turn left past a gate leading to some Woodland Trust woods (Porter's Wood). (The short cut rejoins from the right here.) Stay on the path on the outside of the woods to return to Sandy Lane. Turn right here and right again when you get to the main road, then cross the road and climb the steps on the far side after 50yds (46mtrs). Keep straight ahead to the end of this footpath and cross a road to reach Portland Crescent.

5 Keep straight ahead to drop down a hill and climb up the other side. Continue along Fen Walk, enclosed by black railings with graveyards to either side. Fork left at a junction of paths to drop down a grassy slope with views of the church tower up ahead. Keep straight ahead and climb the steps to Seckford Street.

6 Turn right and stay on this road to reach Market Hill. An alleyway on the right-hand side leads you to the churchyard. Turn left through the churchyard on to Church Street, emerging alongside the site of the old abbey, now a private school. Walk down Church Street and cross over The Thoroughfare, an attractive pedestrian shopping street, on your left-hand side. Continue walking along Quay Street and cross the station yard to take the footbridge over the railway line. Once over, turn left to visit the Tide Mill or right to return to the start of the walk.

what to look out for...

Market Hill is the historic centre of Woodbridge and is surrounded by medieval buildings and interesting shops. Look for the parish pump. It was erected in 1876 and has separate troughs designed to provide drinking water for horses and dogs.

WALK 11
Treasures in Trust on the Slindon Estate

Tour and explore a sprawling National Trust estate on this glorious woodland walk which offers fine views of Sussex.

Minimum time:	2hrs
Walk length:	4 miles (6.4km)
Ascent/gradient:	82ft (25mtrs) ▲▲▲
Difficulty level:	+++
Paths:	Woodland, downland paths and tracks, 4 stiles
Landscape:	Sweeping downland and woodland
Map:	OS Explorer 121 Arundel & Pulborough
Start/finish:	Grid reference: SU 960076
Dog friendliness:	Unless signed otherwise, off lead, except in Slindon village
Parking:	Free National Trust car park in Park Lane, Slindon
Public toilets:	None on route

It all began in 1895, the year the National Trust was founded by three far-sighted, visionary Victorians whose objective was to acquire sites of historic interest and natural beauty for the benefit of the nation.

Trust in Future Generations

The Trust has come a long way since those early, pioneering days. More than 100 years after its foundation, it is the country's biggest landowner, depending on donations and legacies and the annual subscriptions of its two million members for much of its income. The statistics are awesome. Over the years it has acquired 600,000 acres (243,000ha) of countryside, much of which is freely open to everyone, 550 miles (891km) of coastline, over 300 historic houses and more than 150 gardens, all of which it aims to preserve and protect for future generations. It is some achievement.

Slindon Estate

Much of the West Sussex village of Slindon is part of the National Trust's 3,500-acre (1,419ha) Slindon Estate, which is situated on the southern slopes of the South Downs between Arundel and Chichester. The estate, the setting for this lovely walk, was originally designed and developed as an integrated community and it is the Trust's

aim to maintain this structure as far as possible.

Take a stroll through Slindon village as you end the walk and you can see that many of the cottages are built of brick and flint, materials typical of chalk country. During the medieval period, long before the National Trust was established, Slindon was an important estate of the Archbishops of Canterbury. Even earlier it was home to Neolithic people who settled at Barkhale, a hilltop site at its northern end.

Downland Scenery

As well as the village, the estate consists of a large expanse of sweeping downland dissected by dry valleys, a folly, several farms and a stretch of Roman road. Glorious hanging beechwoods on the scarp enhance the picture, attracting walkers and naturalists in search of peace and solitude. Parts of the estate were damaged in the storms of 1987 and 1990, though the woods are regenerating, with saplings and woodland plants flourishing in the lighter glades. Typical ground plants of the beechwoods include bluebell, dog's mercury, greater butterfly orchid and wood sedge.

To help celebrate its centenary in 1995, the National Trust chose the Slindon Estate to launch its 100 Paths Project, a scheme designed to enhance access to its countryside properties by creating or improving paths. This glorious, unspoiled landscape offers many miles of footpaths and bridleways, making it an excellent choice for a country walk.

● Brick and flint estate cottage in Slindon

Walk Directions

1 From the car park walk towards the road and turn right at a 'No riding' sign, passing through the gate to join a wide straight path cutting between trees and bracken. The path runs alongside sunny glades and clearings and between lines of attractive beech and silver birch trees before reaching a crossroads.

2 Turn right to a second crossroads and continue ahead here, keeping the grassy bank and ditch, all that remains of the Park Pale, on your right. Follow the broad path as it begins a wide curve to the right and the boundary ditch is still visible here, running parallel to the path. On reaching a kissing gate, continue ahead, soon skirting fields. As you approach the entrance to Slindon campsite, swing left and follow the track down to the road.

3 Turn left and follow the road through the woodland. Pass Slindon Bottom Road and turn right after a few paces to join a bridleway. Follow the path as it cuts between fields and look for a path on the right.

4 Cross the stile, go down the field, up the other side to the next stile and join a track. Turn right and follow it as it immediately bends left. Walk along to Row's Barn and continue ahead on the track. Nore folly can be seen over to the left.

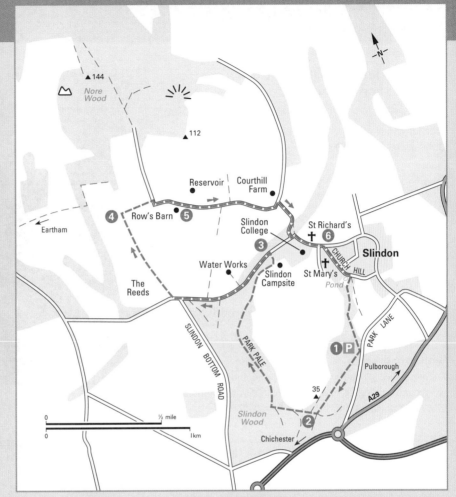

5 Continue straight ahead along the track, following it down to some double gates and a stile. Pass to the right of Courthill Farm, turn right and follow the lane or soon branch left on to a parallel woodland path to the next road. Bear left and pass Slindon College on the right and St Richard's Catholic Church on the left before reaching Church Hill.

6 Fork right into Church Hill, pass the church and make for the pond, a familiar weeping willow reaching down to the water's edge. Look for mallard ducks here. Turn right around the far end of the pond on the obvious waterside path to enter the wood. On reaching a fork, by a National Trust sign for the Slindon Estate, keep left and walk through the trees, to return to the car park.

while you're there...

Have a look at the Church of St Mary, which is partly Norman and greatly restored. Inside is a rare wooden effigy to Sir Anthony St Leger who died in 1539. Slindon House, now part of a college, was one of the rest-houses of the Archbishops of Canterbury during the Middle Ages.

CYCLE 5
The Harland Way

Follow a picturesque railway line to discover Yorkshire's forgotten fortress.

Minimum time:	2hrs
Ride length:	8 miles/12.9km
Difficulty level:	✛✛✛
Map:	OS Explorer 289 Leeds
Start/finish:	Sicklinghall Road, Wetherby; grid ref: SE 397483
Trails/tracks:	Well compacted gravel railway trackbed, lanes and smooth bridleways
Landscape:	Landscape: pastureland and village
Public toilets:	None en route
Tourist information:	Wetherby, tel 01937 582151
Cycle hire:	None locally
❶	A short section of main road through Spofforth village

Getting to the start
From the A661 Wetherby to Harrogate road turn off on the westbound Sicklinghall Road then after 300yds (274mtrs) a blue cycleway sign points to the car park on the right.

Why do this cycle ride?
The Harland Way forms the basis of a delightful rural ride following in the tracks of the steam trains and visiting one of Yorkshire's most fascinating Norman castles.

Around Spofforth
Lying among the peaceful pastures of the Crimple Valley, Spofforth is an idyllic backwater for a Sunday afternoon ride. Go back in time to the medieval era and things were very different. A year after the Battle of Hastings, William the Conqueror's friend, William de Percy, made Spofforth his headquarters. The original dwelling would have been a fortified hall, of which nothing remains, but by the 13th century the castle was taking shape, built into the rock on which it stood. Subsequent alterations of the 14th and 15th centuries gave the castle its powerful walls and that strong Gothic look.

In 1309 Henry de Percy bought the Manor of Alnwick in Northumberland and made that his main residence, but the family's alliances were to land them in trouble on several

Spofforth Castle

occasions – after their rebellion against King Henry IV in 1408, and their support in the Wars of the Roses. On both occasions the Crown confiscated Spofforth Castle. The castle lay waste for around a hundred years until Henry, Lord Percy restored it in 1559. Within another hundred years, however, it was sacked by Oliver Cromwell's forces during fierce fighting of the Civil War. Stand on the green today, and you can still feel the presence and imagine the times of turmoil endured by this rugged historic building.

did you know?

Gardens through Time at RHS Garden Harlow Carr, consists of seven themed gardens reflecting trends in horticulture from the Regency period through to a 21st-century garden designed by Diarmuid Gavin. Each garden displays the most popular and influential features and techniques of that period, many of which are still used. The gardens also reflect national events such as Queen Victoria's Golden Jubilee and the Festival of Britain.

The Ride

1 With your back to the car park entrance, turn right along the railway trackbed, highlighted by a Harland Way fingerpost. The line has been exploded through the bedrock to reveal limestone crags, now hung with pleasant woodland that offers excellent shade on hot summer days.

2 Take the left fork at the junction that used to be known as the Wetherby Triangle. You're soon joined from the right by another branch of the line and together the routes head west towards Spofforth. Halfway along the track you have to dismount to get through a metal gateway, then again almost immediately at another gate. The trackbed forges through an avenue of beech, hawthorn, ash, and rowan before coming out into the open. Now you'll see thickets of wild roses and bramble, with scabious and purple vetch among the numerous wild flowers of the verges. There are wide views across cornfields, and soon the tower of Spofforth church comes into view ahead.

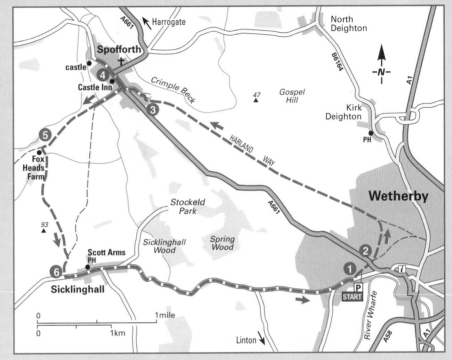

3 The Harland Way ends beyond a gate just short of the village. A gravel path veers right across a green on to East Park Road. This threads through modern housing to come to the main road where you should turn right. If you have young children it might be better to dismount to cross the road, and use the pavements to get to The Castle inn.

4 Just beyond the pub, where the road bends right, take the lane on the left, which heads for the castle. When you've seen the castle retrace your route past the pub then turn right along Park Road. Beyond the houses this becomes a stony bridleway, rising gently across the fields.

5 Ignore turn-offs until you come to Fox Heads Farm. Turn left along the track here, passing left of the farmhouse. The dirt and stone track descends to a bridge over a stream, then climbs again past an old quarry. Though there are a few climbs the track is still quite easy, being smooth-surfaced and fairly well drained. Often it's lined with

bramble, ferns and foxgloves, with the odd tree. Just beyond the summit of the hill the track bends right. After being joined from the right by another farm track it comes to the road, just to the west of Sicklinghall village.

6 Turn left along the road into the village. On the right there's a pond with lilies and coots, then on the left there's another pub, the Scott Arms. The winding road makes a long but gradual descent towards Wetherby. Ignore the right turn 'to Linton'. After passing through housing in the Wetherby suburbs watch out for the blue cyclists' sign. This marks the access road back to the car park.

did you know?

The Harland Way, the Spofforth to Wetherby cycle/footpath route, lies on part of the York and West Midland Railway Company's Church Fenton to Harrogate line and the former Leeds to Scarborough route from Crossgates to Wetherby. The railway was closed to passengers in 1964.

WALK 12
Richmond's Drummer Boy

Following in the steps of the Richmond Drummer, to Easby Abbey.

Minimum time:	2hrs 20min
Walk length:	6 miles (9.7km)
Ascent/gradient:	656ft (200mtrs) ▲▲▲
Difficulty level:	✦✦✦
Paths:	Field and riverside paths, a little town walking, 15 stiles
Landscape:	Valley of River Swale and its steep banks
Map:	OS Explorer 304 Darlington & Richmond
Start/finish:	Grid reference: NZ 168012
Dog friendliness:	Dogs should be on lead for most of walk
Parking:	Friars Close long-stay car park
Public toilets:	Friars Close car park, Richmond town centre and Round Howe car park

● River Swale and Richmond Castle

The first part of the walk follows much of the route taken by the legendary Richmond Drummer Boy. At the end of the 18th century, the story says, soldiers in Richmond Castle discovered a tunnel that was thought to lead from there to Easby Abbey. They sent their drummer boy down it, beating his drum so they could follow from above ground. His route went under the Market Square and along to Frenchgate, then beside the river towards the abbey. At the spot now marked by the Drummer Boy Stone, the drumming stopped. The Drummer Boy was never seen again. A version of the story is found in William Maynes's novel *Earthfasts*. The Green Howards Regimental Museum in the Market Square can tell you more about the drummer boy and his regiment.

while you're there...

Visit Richmond Castle, which looms over the Swale Valley. Its keep, more than 100ft (30mtrs) high, was complete by 1180. Now in the care of English Heritage, the castle's central ward is surrounded by high curtain walls with towers. Inside the keep are unique drawings done in the First World War by conscientious objectors. They were imprisoned here in squalid conditions.

Abbey and Church

Easby Abbey, whose remains are seen on the walk, was founded for Premonstratensian Canons in 1155 by the Constable of Richmond Castle. Although not much of the church remains, some of the other buildings survive well, including the gatehouse, built about 1300. The refectory is also impressive, and you can see the infirmary, the chapter house and the dormitory. Just by the abbey ruins is the parish church, St Agatha's. It contains a replica of the Anglo-Saxon Easby Cross (the original is in the British Museum) and a set of medieval wall paintings showing Old Testament scenes of Adam and Eve, on the north wall, and the life of Jesus on the south, as well as depictions of activities such as pruning and hawking.

After the abbey, you'll cross the River Swale on the old railway bridge, and follow the track bed. This was part of the branch line from Richmond to Darlington, which opened in 1846. It was closed in 1970. The station has been restored as a cinema and shopping centre, with a café. Look right over Richmond Bridge after you have passed below the castle to see how the stonework differs from one end to the other. It was built by different contractors, one working for Richmond Council and one for the North Riding of Yorkshire. In the hillside below Billy Bank Wood, which you enter beyond the bridge, were copper mines dating back to the 15th century. After you have climbed the hill and crossed the 12 stiles (between Points ❺ and ❻), you're following the old route of the Swale, which thousands of years ago changed its course and formed the hill known as Round Howe.

Walk Directions

1 Leave the Friars Close car park and turn right, then left at the T-junction. At the roundabout, go straight on, down Ryder's Wynd. At the bottom turn left, then go right into Station Road. Just past the church, take Lombards Wynd left.

2 Turn right at the next junction and follow the track, passing to the right of the Drummer Boy Stone along the path to a gate. Bear right after the gate, still parallel with the river, bearing right again to a gate then along beside the abbey in the village of Easby.

3 Just beyond the car park turn right, along the track. Follow the wall on the left to Love Lane House. Turn right over the old railway bridge. Follow the track bed, crossing a metalled lane, to the station. Go to the left of the station building to the road.

4 Turn left, up the road, then turn right up Priory Villas, bearing right to go in front of the houses. Go through three waymarked gates, keeping parallel to the river. Cross some playing fields and pass a clubhouse to a road.

5 Cross the road and take a signed path opposite, to the left of the cottage. Climb steeply through the woodland, through a gate and straight on to a stile. At the end of the woodland, bend right, then left to pass a stile in a former crossing fence. Follow the signed path over

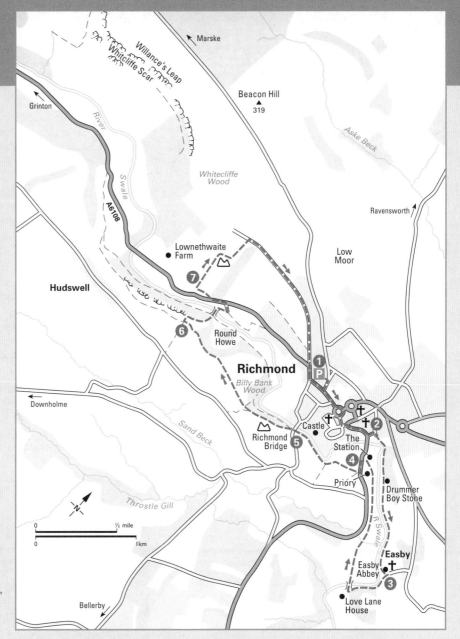

12 more stiles. After the last, bear right over another stile, turn left to follow the wall, then go over another stile.

6 Turn right to go through a gate. Follow the track as it bends downhill, through a gate, to a

bridge. Cross it and walk to the lane. Go left and left again at the main road. After 200yds (183mtrs), go right up a bridleway-signed track, to a junction.

7 Turn right and follow the track uphill, bearing right, then

left near the farmhouse, to reach a metalled lane. Turn right and follow the lane back into Richmond. Go ahead at the main road and follow it as it bends left to the garage, where you turn left back to the car park.

WALK 13
Grey Mare's Tail and Mamore Lodge

A waterfall, a shooting lodge and a ramble down the West Highland Way.

Minimum time:	2hrs 15min
Walk length:	3.5 miles (5.7km)
Ascent/gradient:	984ft (300mtrs) ▲▲▲
Difficulty level:	+++
Paths:	Well-made paths, one steep, rough ascent, no stiles
Landscape:	Birchwoods leading to long views along Loch Leven
Map:	OS Explorer 384 Glen Coe & Glen Etive or 392 Ben Nevis & Fort William
Start/finish:	Grid reference: NN 187622 on OS Explorer 384
Dog friendliness:	Off lead unless sheep near by
Parking:	Grey Mare's Tail car park, Kinlochleven
Public toilets:	Kinlochleven, at bridge over River Leven

Aluminium is a very common metal: around eight per cent of the earth's crust is made up of it. But, it's very reactive, which means that it's extremely difficult to extract the aluminium atoms out of the ore called bauxite. There is no chemical method for this process. Instead, it's done by dissolving the ore in molten cryolite (a fluoride mineral) and applying vast quantities of electricity. As a result, aluminium processing doesn't take place where you find the bauxite, but where you find the electricity, with lots of water coming down steep hillsides, and a deep-water harbour at the bottom, such as Kinlochleven.

The village of Kinlochleven was built around the smelter. Two lochs above have been dammed for hydro-electricity, and six huge pipes bring the water down from a control station above the Devil's Staircase footpath.

Pipeline or Path

A pipeline on the OS Landranger map is a dotted line, rather like a path. And it may be that the path of this walk happened by mistake, as walkers mistook the pipeline for a path, walked along it and so created the path that they thought was there in the first place.

The pipeline path leads from the outflow of Loch Eilde Mor, around the head of Loch Leven along the 1,100ft (335mtrs) contour, giving superb views towards the Pap of Glencoe and the loch's foot. Eventually, it carries Loch Eilde's water to the Blackwater Reservoir.

Why has the water from Loch Eilde been taken all the way round this hillside to the Blackwater Reservoir, instead of straight down to the turbines where it's actually needed? You need to glance across the valley at the six descending pipes for the answer. At the foot of those huge reinforced pipes the water is under 30 tons per square foot (300 tonnes/sq mtr) of pressure. A second such set from Loch Eilde would cost far more than the much longer, unpressurised pipe to the other reservoir.

The Kinlochmore smelter started as one of the largest in the world, but by the end of the 1900s it was the world's smallest. It closed in 2000, although its turbines continue to generate electricity, which is now diverted to the smelter at Fort William or into the National Grid. The smelter had been the reason for Kinlochleven, and its main employer. Projects to keep Kinlochleven alive include the fine, path system and the visitor centre on the site where carbon electrical connectors were once made.

● Pap of Glen Coe and Loch Leven

Walk Directions

1 A smooth gravel path leads up out of the car park to multicoloured waymarkers pointing left. The path rises to a view through trees of the Grey Mare's Tail waterfall, then descends to a footbridge. Here turn left (blue waymarker) to visit the foot of the spectacular waterfall, then return to take the path on the right (white, yellow and green waymarker). Follow the stream up for 100yds (91mtrs), then turn left at a waymarker. The path, quite steep and loose, zig-zags up through birches to reach more open ground.

2 Here the path forks. Take the right-hand branch, with a yellow and green waymarker, to pass under power lines. The path runs through scattered birch to a gate in a deer fence, then bends left to cross over two streams. Immediately after the second stream is another junction.

3 The confusing waymarker here has eight arrows in four colours. Turn left, following a white arrow slightly downhill, to cross a footbridge above a waterfall and red granite rocks. The path leads up under birches. Here the ground cover includes the aromatic bog myrtle, which can be used to discourage midges. When the path reaches a track, turn left. Below the track is a tin deer used by stalkers for target practice: it's more convenient than the real thing as it doesn't wander off just when you're creeping up on

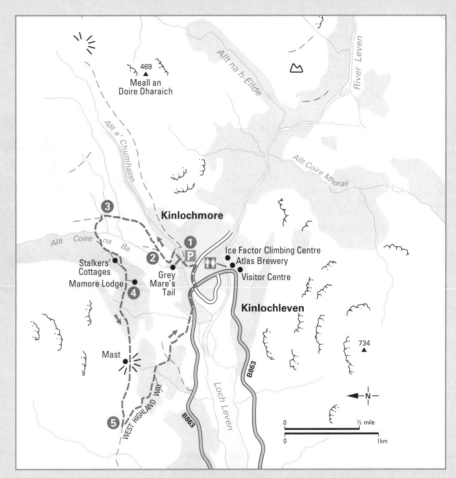

it. A signed footpath bypasses the Stalkers' Cottages on the left, then rejoins the track beyond, to a junction above Mamore Lodge.

4 Keep ahead, above the lodge, climbing gently past two tin huts, self-catering accommodation labelled 'stable' and 'bothy'. At the high point of the track there is a TV mast on the right, a bench on the left and a view along Loch Leven ahead. The track descends

gently, with slabs of whitish quartzite above. The wide path of the West Highland Way (WHW) can be seen below and gradually rises to join the track, with a large waymarker planted in a cairn.

5 Turn left down the West Highland Way path, which drops into the woods below. Watch out for a junction where the main path seems to double back to the right; take the smaller path, continuing

ahead with a WHW waymarker. After crossing the tarred access track of Mamore Lodge, the path fords a small stream to reach the village. Turn left along the pavement and fork left into Wades Road to regain the car park.

Walk along Anglesey's beautiful east coast and discover a remarkably intact ancient village.

Minimum time:	3hrs
Walk length:	5 miles (8km)
Ascent/gradient:	541ft (165mtrs) ▲▲▲
Difficulty level:	✚✚✚
Paths:	Well-defined coastal and field paths, 5 stiles
Landscape:	Sea cliffs and coastal pasture
Map:	OS Explorer 263 Anglesey East
Start/finish:	Grid reference: SH 511862
Dog friendliness:	Can be off lead on coastal path
Parking:	Car park at entrance to village
Public toilets:	In car park and by harbour

● Neolithic Lligwy burial chamber, Moelfre

Being in Moelfre is like being in Cornwall. The pebble beach, the whitewashed cottages looking down from the cliff tops, small boats in a tiny harbour, and there's that same bracing quality of the wave-wafted air. As you stroll along the rocky coastline above the low cliffs, past the two lifeboat stations and the Moelfre Seawatch Centre, all thoughts are on ships and the ocean. If it's sunny and the breeze is only slight, everything appears so picturesque and peaceful, but as you read the inscriptions on the *Royal Charter* memorial, you get a different story…

A Ship in Distress

The monument remembers the night of 26 October 1859. A proud British cutter, the *Royal Charter* was on the last stretch of its long homeward journey from Hobson's Bay in Melbourne to Liverpool. Sailing past Ireland there had not been a hint of wind, but as night fell, a savage storm ensued. Captain Taylor signalled for a pilot, but none would come on such a night. In deep trouble, he set anchor, but at 1:30am the chain parted. At daybreak two locals saw the wreck being pounded against the rocks.

Gallant Seamen

To their horror they saw a man shimmy down a rope from the decks and into the furious sea. He had volunteered to try to swim with a hawser for shore, the only means to secure the ship and save the lives of the crew and passengers. Twice he

failed, but Joseph Rogers, an able seaman from Malta, finally made it and lashed the ship to a rock. The gallant seaman and the men of Moelfre made a human chain into the breakers. They managed to rescue 18 passengers, 5 riggers and 18 crew, but on that day 452 people, including all the officers and 28 men from Moelfre, lost their lives. The ship also carried gold and, though most of it was recovered, some must still be buried among the barnacles and tangled seaweed in that watery graveyard you see below.

An Ancient Village

On the way back to Moelfre you leave the sea and follow country lanes through peaceful pastures. Through the hedges you'll spot a roofless 12th-century chapel, which you pass en route to Din Lligwy, an ancient village hidden in the woods. This is a wonderfully preserved Celtic settlement dating back to the last years of the Roman Empire in the 4th century AD.

Burial Chamber

In a field further down the lane are the remains of a neolithic burial chamber. The Lligwy tomb has a massive capstone weighing 25 tons. The excavation in 1909 revealed the remains of 15 to 30 people and Beaker and grooved ware pottery.

Walk Directions

1 From the car park, follow the main road (A5108) down to the shore. The road winds behind the bay before swinging left. Leave the road at that point for a shoreline path on the right.

2 Pass the the Moelfre Seawatch Centre and the lifeboat station and ignore the footpath signs pointing inland. Instead follow a clear coast path that looks across to the island of Ynys Moelfre. After passing to the right of terraced cottages and going through a couple of kissing gates the path crosses a small caravan site. It then goes through another kissing gate and climbs past the *Royal Charter* memorial.

3 Swinging left into Porth Forllwyd, the path ends beside a cottage, Moryn. Follow a track to a gate, turning before it along a fenced path into a field. Keep ahead to rejoin the coast, which turns in above the large bay of Traeth Lligwy.

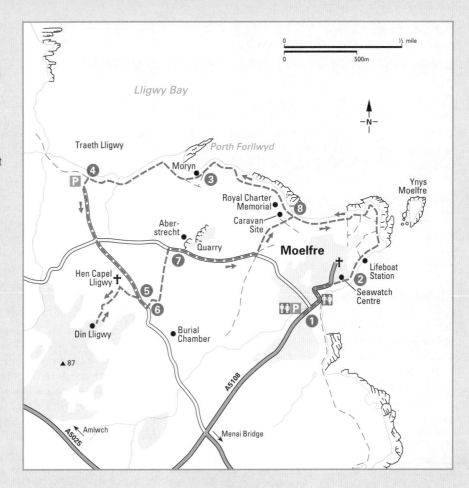

4 On reaching the beach car park, turn left along the narrow lane before going straight ahead at the next crossroads.

5 Take the next path on the right, signposted to Din Lligwy ancient village. First, turn half-right across the field to see the old chapel. Then bear left across two fields and into a wood concealing Din Lligwy. Return to the lane and turn right along it.

6 Leave after 50yds (46mtrs) over a ladder stile on the left. Follow the doglegging boundary right to a stile, over which turn left, walking downfield to emerge by a roadside quarry at Aber-strecht.

7 Follow the lane right to the edge of the village and go left on a waymarked track. Around the first bend, swing left through a gate, keeping right at a fork to walk through the caravan site again.

8 Follow the shoreline path back to the start.

what to look out for...

At Din Lligwy you enter the foundations of the old settlement through thick rubble walls, which would have been added as protection against the Romans. The circular huts inside were the living quarters, while the large rectangular hut in the top right-hand corner would have been the smelting workshop – the remains of a charcoal hearth were excavated here.

WALK 15
Broad Haven and the Haroldston Woods

A winding path through mixed woodland and an easy stroll above the Haroldston cliffs.

Minimum time:	1hr 30min
Walk length:	3.5 miles (5.7km)
Ascent/gradient:	290ft (88mtrs) ▲▲▲
Difficulty level:	✦✦✦
Paths:	Woodland trail, country lanes and coast path, no stiles
Landscape:	Mixed woodland and lofty cliffs above broad beach
Map:	OS Explorer OL36 South Pembrokeshire
Start/finish:	Grid reference: SM 863140
Dog friendliness:	Poop scoop around car park and beach, care needed on cliff tops
Parking:	Car park by tourist information centre in Broad Haven
Public toilets:	Between car park and beach

Woodland walking is something of a rarity along the Pembrokeshire Coast Path, so this short stretch of permissive path, which sneaks through a narrow strip of woodland separating Broad Haven from Haroldston, makes a refreshing diversion from the usual salty air and the cries of the seabirds. This walk has an almost billiard table-level section of coast path, some of which has been surfaced for access by wheelchair users. The artificial path, however, takes nothing away from the quality of the scenery, which is magnificent.

Eroding Cliffs

The cliffs here are of softer shales and millstone grit making them prone to erosion and subsidence, as you'll witness firsthand along the way. Amazingly, this whole stretch of coast sits on top of huge coal reserves, but the last colliery, which was situated further north in Nolton Haven, actually closed down in the early 1900s. As you progress south you'll pass the crumpled remains of an Iron Age fort on Black Point – although this is rapidly becoming separated from the main cliff by a landslide – and also a diminutive standing stone, known as the Harold Stone, which is tucked away in a field on the left as you approach Broad Haven. It's said to mark the spot where Harold, the Earl of Wessex, defeated the Welsh in the 11th century, but it's actually more likely to be Bronze Age.

Coastal Resort

Broad Haven is about as close as you'll get to a traditional seaside resort in north Pembrokeshire. The town's popularity as a holiday destination blossomed in the early 1800s, but recent years have seen an acceleration in development that has resulted in almost wall-to-wall caravan parks and a significant rise in the number of residential properties. The beach is beautiful, with gently sloping sands encased in brooding dark cliffs. As well as the usual selection of family holiday-makers, it's a popular place with windsurfers. This is due partly to a shop and rental centre behind the beach, and because the prevalent south-westerlies that blow across and onshore from the left make it a safe but fun place to play in the sometimes sizeable surf.

Rock Formations

At low tide it's possible to walk south along the beach to the charming village of Little Haven. A walk northwards will reveal some fascinating rock formations beneath the headland. These include Den's Door, an impressive double arch in a rugged sea stack; the Sleek Stone, a humpback rock forced into its contorted position by a geological fault; and Shag Rock and Emmet Rock. Contorted layers of rock are also clearly visible in the main cliffs.

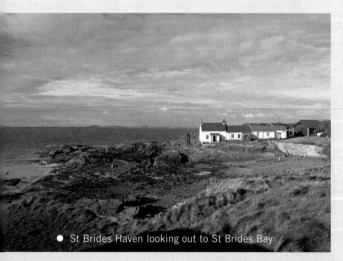

● St Brides Haven looking out to St Brides Bay

Walk Directions

1 From anywhere in the car park, walk towards the National Park information centre and follow a waymarked path that runs between the information centre and the coastguard rescue building. Fork left at the junction with the holiday park path and continue to a kissing gate, where you cross a small footbridge to another junction with a path from the holiday park. Turn half right, through a kissing gate, to continue with the stream on your left.

2 Cross the stream by another bridge and now, with the stream and valley floor to your right, continue easily upwards until you reach a T-junction of paths by a fingerpost. Turn right here, past a bench on the right, and then swing left to continue upwards to another junction of paths by a small chapel.

3 Turn left to the road and then right on to it to walk uphill, with the church on your right. Keep ahead at the T-junction, then take the first left, towards Druidston Haven. Follow this over a cattle-

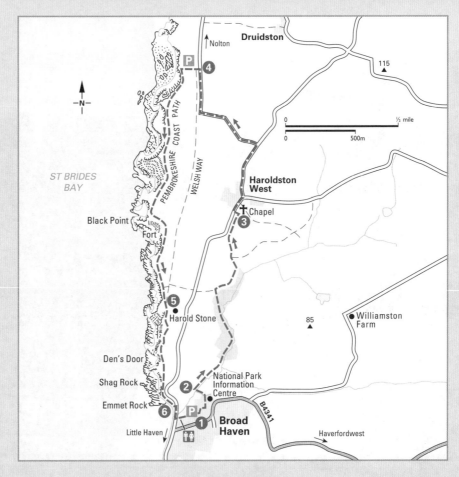

grid to a sharp right-hand bend. Continue for another 300yds (274mtrs) to the Haroldston Chin parking area and a gate on the left.

4 Go through the gate and follow the well-surfaced track down towards the coast. On reaching the cliff tops, bear around to the left and continue past Black Point.

5 After passing the Harold Stone on your left, the path starts to drop, generally quite easily but there is one steep step. Follow the path down to meet the road and keep right to drop to the walkway above the beach.

6 Cross over the bridge and then, just before the road you are on merges into the main road, turn left on to a tarmac footpath that leads through a green and back to the car park.

---

what to look out for...

As you turn the sharp right-hand bend on the road at Point **3** you'll see a good track running parallel to the road in the field on your left. This is an ancient trade route, known as the Welsh Way, that runs from Monk's Haven – more commonly known as St Ishmael's – to Whitesands Beach. It was considered a safer mode of transport than sailing across the waters of the bay.

Maps

County Maps

The county map shown here will help you identify the counties within each country. You can look up each county in the guide using the county names at the top of each page. To find towns featured in the guide use the atlas and the index.

England

1 Bedfordshire
2 Berkshire
3 Bristol
4 Buckinghamshire
5 Cambridgeshire
6 Greater Manchester
7 Herefordshire
8 Hertfordshire
9 Leicestershire
10 Northamptonshire
11 Nottinghamshire
12 Rutland
13 Staffordshire
14 Warwickshire
15 West Midlands
16 Worcestershire

Scotland

17 City of Glasgow
18 Clackmannanshire
19 East Ayrshire
20 East Dunbartonshire
21 East Renfrewshire
22 Perth & Kinross
23 Renfrewshire
24 South Lanarkshire
25 West Dunbartonshire

Wales

26 Blaenau Gwent
27 Bridgent
28 Caerphilly
29 Denbighshire
30 Flintshire
31 Merthyr Tydfil
32 Monmouthshire
33 Neath Port Talbot
34 Newport
35 Rhondda Cynon Taff
36 Torfaen
37 Vale of Glamorgan
38 Wrexham

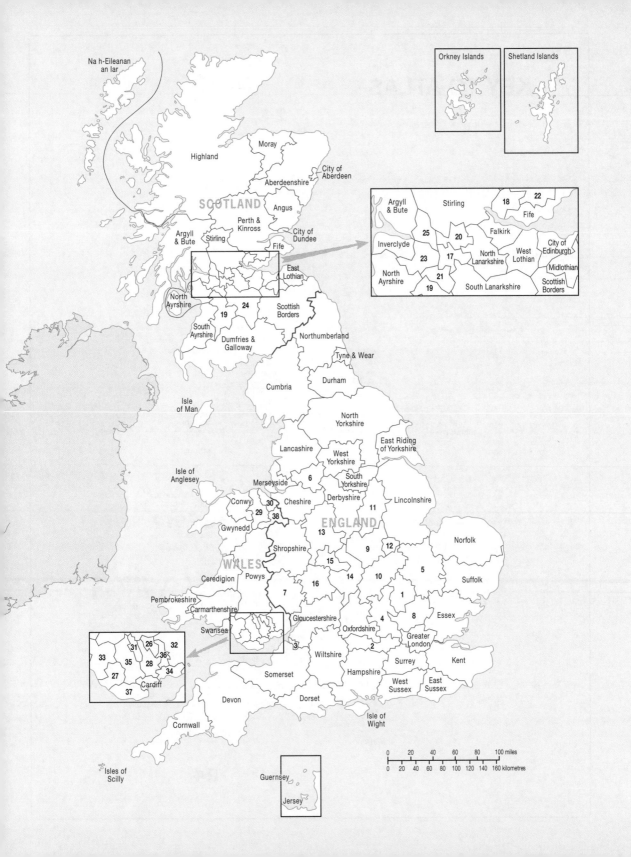

Orkney Islands

Shetland Islands

Na h-Eileanan
an Iar

Highland

Moray

Aberdeenshire

City of
Aberdeen

SCOTLAND

Angus

Perth &
Kinross

City of
Dundee

Argyll
& Bute

Stirling

Fife

East
Lothian

North
Ayrshire

24

Scottish
Borders

South
Ayrshire

19

Dumfries &
Galloway

Argyll
& Bute

Stirling

18

22

Fife

Inverclyde

25

20

Falkirk

North
Ayrshire

23

17

North
Lanarkshire

West
Lothian

City of
Edinburgh

Midlothian

North
Ayrshire

21

19

South Lanarkshire

Scottish
Borders

Northumberland

Tyne & Wear

Durham

Cumbria

Isle
of Man

North
Yorkshire

Lancashire

West
Yorkshire

East Riding
of Yorkshire

Isle of
Anglesey

Merseyside

6

South
Yorkshire

Conwy

30

Cheshire

Derbyshire

11

Lincolnshire

29

38

ENGLAND

Gwynedd

13

Shropshire

9

12

Norfolk

WALES

15

5

Powys

14

10

Suffolk

Ceredigion

16

1

Pembrokeshire

7

Essex

Carmarthenshire

Gloucestershire

8

Swansea

3

Oxfordshire

Greater
London

26

32

Wiltshire

2

Kent

31

36

Surrey

33

28

34

Somerset

Hampshire

West
Sussex

East
Sussex

27

35

Cardiff

37

Devon

Dorset

Isle of
Wight

Cornwall

Isles of
Scilly

Guernsey

Jersey

0   20   40   60   80   100 miles

0 20 40 60 80 100 120 140 160 kilometres

KEY TO ATLAS

Shetland Islands

24

Orkney Islands

22

23

Inverness

Aberdeen

Fort William

Perth

Glasgow

Edinburgh

20

21

Londonderry

Larne

Stranraer

Newcastle upon Tyne

Belfast

Carlisle

Middlesbrough

Isle of Man

Kendal

18

19

24

Leeds

York

Kingston upon Hull

1

Manchester

16

17

Galway

Dublin

Liverpool

Sheffield

Lincoln

Holyhead

14

15

Limerick

Nottingham

Rosslare

Aberystwyth

Birmingham

Norwich

Cork

10

11

12

13

8

9

Cambridge

Carmarthen

Gloucester

Colchester

Cardiff

Oxford

LONDON

Bristol

Guildford

6

7

Barnstaple

4

5

Maidstone

Dover

Taunton

Southampton

2

3

Bournemouth

Brighton

Exeter

Plymouth

Penzance

Isles of Scilly

Channel Islands

24

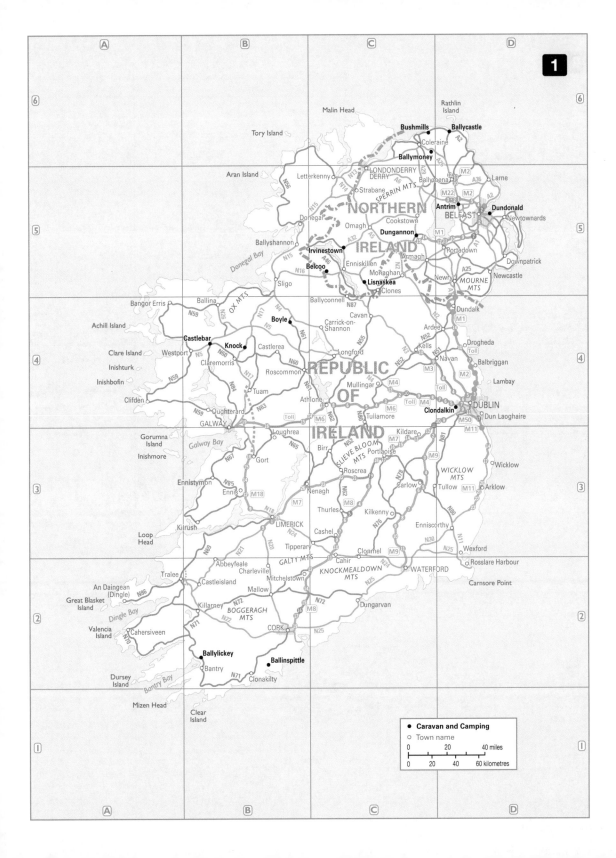

2

Legend

M6	Motorway/toll motorway
	Motorway junction full/restricted. Service area
A49	Primary route single/dual carriageway
A34	Other A road single/dual carriageway
B3400	B road
	Unclassified road
⊸V⊸	Vehicle ferry
⊸C⊸	Fast vehicle ferry or catamaran
● Ashbourne	Caravan and Camping
● St Davids	AA Campsite Award Winner
○ Oundle	Town/Village name
	National boundary
ESSEX	English county name & boundary
CONWY	Welsh county name & boundary
MORAY	Scottish county name & boundary
	National Park

ISLES OF SCILLY

Bryher
New Grimsby
St Martin's
Tresco
Higher Town
Hugh Town
St Mary's
Old Town
Middle Town
St Agnes
ISLES OF SCILLY
SV

SW

Lundy

Hartland Point
Hartland

Morwenstow

Kilkhampton

Bude
Bude Bay
Stratton
Widemouth Bay
Bridgerule
Week St Mary
Crackington Haven
Jacobstow
Boscastle
Otterham
Tintagel
Delabole
Camelford
Port Isaac
Pendoggett
Polzeath
St Minver
St Tudy
Bolventor
BODMIN MOOR
Rock
Harlyn
St Merryn
Padstow
Blisland
Porthcothan
Wadebridge
Rumford
Ruthernbridge
CORNWALL
St Cleer
Mawgan Porth
St Mawgan
Bodmin
Watergate Bay
St Columb Major
Lanivet
Dobwalls
Newquay
Roche
A3059
Liskeard
West Pentire
St Keyne
Holywell Bay
Cubert
Bugle
Luxulyan
Lostwithiel
Rejerrah
Indian Queens
Summercourt
St Blazey Gate
St Blazey
Pelynt
Perranporth
Goonhavern
Roche
St Austell
Fowey
Ladock
St Stephen
Carlyon Bay
Looe
St Agnes
St Allen
Grampound
Polruan
Polperro
Porthtowan
Blackwater
Marazanvose
Pentewan
Portreath
St Day
Truro
Tregony
Mevagissey
Gorran
St Ives Bay
Carnon Downs
Gorran Haven
St Ives
Gwithian
Redruth
Portloe
Zennor
Camborne
St Just-in-Roseland
Lelant
Hayle
Leedstown
Penryn
Portscatho
St Just
St Hilary
Edgcumbe
Falmouth
St Mawes
Penzance
Marazion
Ashton
Helston
Constantine
Newlyn
Rosudgeon
Praa Sands
Mawnan Smith
Land's End
St Buryan
Mousehole
Porthleven
Gweek
Sennen
Treen
Porthcurno
Manaccan
St Keverne
Mullion
Coverack
Kennack Sands
Cadgwith
Lizard
Lizard Point

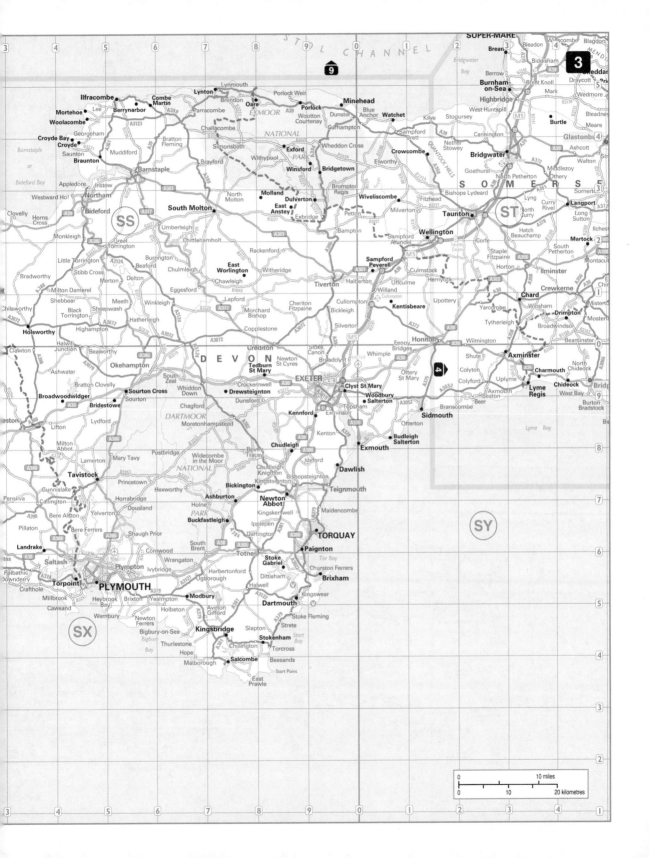

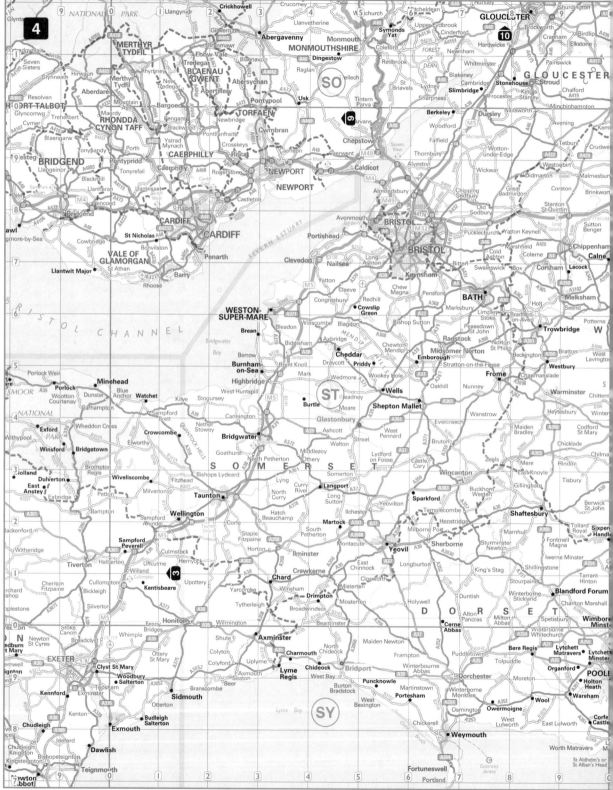

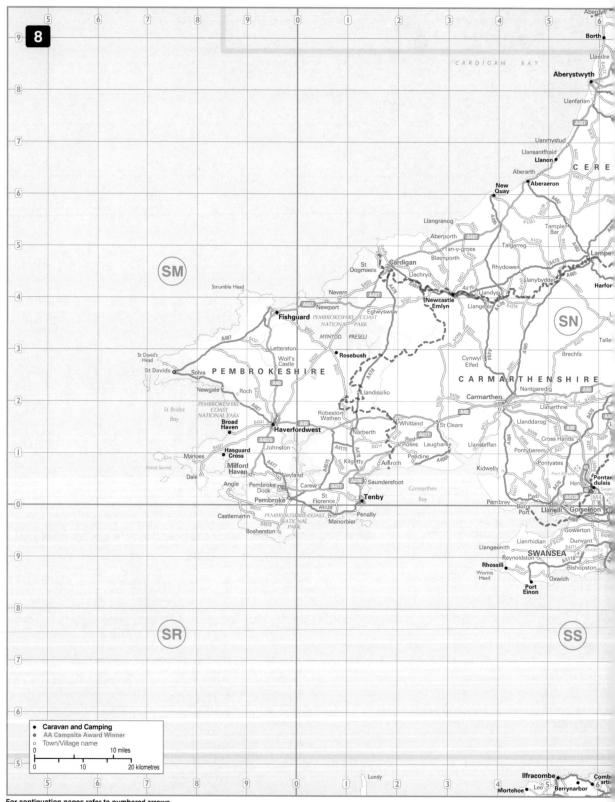

CARDIGAN BAY

Borth
Llandre
Aberystwyth
Llanfarian
Llanrhystud
Llansantffraid
Llanon
Aberarth
New Quay
Aberaeron
CERE
Llangranog
Aberporth
Tan-y-groes
Blaenporth
Talgarreg
Temple Bar
Rhydowen
Lampe
Llanybydder
Harfor
St Dogmaels
Cardigan
Llechryd
Llandysul
Nevern
Newcastle Emlyn
Llangeler
Talle
Strumble Head
Eglwyswrw
Fishguard
PEMBROKESHIRE COAST NATIONAL PARK
Letterston
MYNYDD PRESELI
Cynwyl Elfed
Brechfa
St David's Head
Wolf's Castle
Rosebush
St Davids
CARMARTHENSHIRE
Solva
Nantgaredig
PEMBROKESHIRE
Llandissilio
Carmarthen
Newgale
Roch
Llanarthne
St Brides Bay
Robeston Wathen
Whitland
St Clears
Llanddarog
Cross Hands
PEMBROKESHIRE COAST NATIONAL PARK
Broad Haven
Haverfordwest
Narberth
Red Roses
Laugharne
Llansteffan
Pontyberem
Pontyates
Hasguard Cross
Johnston
Kilgetty
Amroth
Pendine
Kidwelly
Marloes
Milford Haven
Pontar dulais
Broad Sound
Dale
Angle
Neyland
Carew
Saundersfoot
Henry
Pembroke Dock
St Florence
Tenby
Pembrey
Burry Port
Llanelli
Gorseinon
M4
Pembroke
Penally
Carmarthen Bay
Pembroke
Castlemartin
Manorbier
Gowerton
Bosherston
Llangennith
Llanrhidian
Dunvant
Reynoldston
SWANSEA
Bishopston
Rhossili
Worms Head
Oxwich
Port Einon

SM
SN
SR
SS

- ● **Caravan and Camping**
- ● **AA Campsite Award Winner**
- ○ Town/Village name

0 ——————— 10 miles
0 ———— 10 ———— 20 kilometres

Lundy
Ilfracombe
Comb arti
Mortehoe
Lee
Berrynarbor

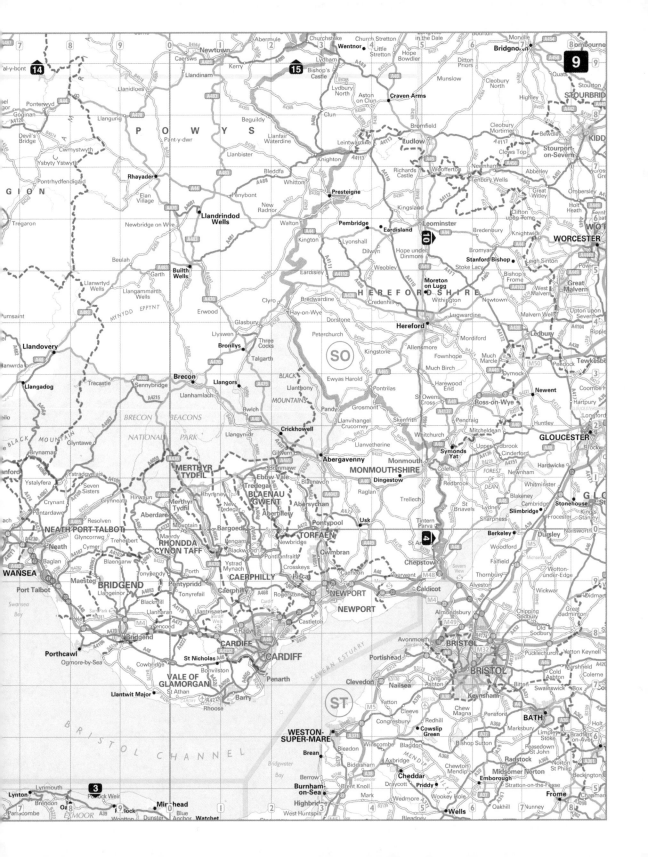

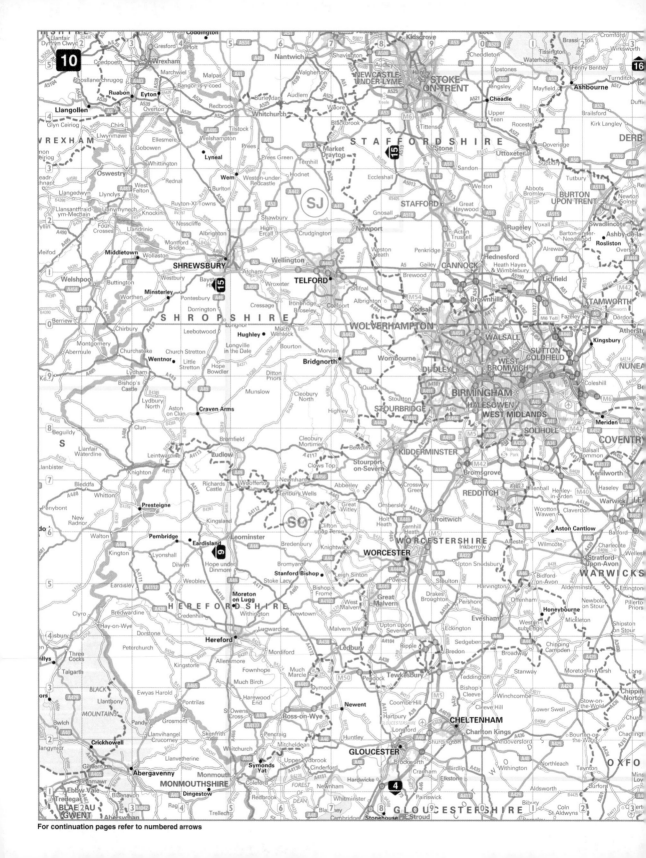

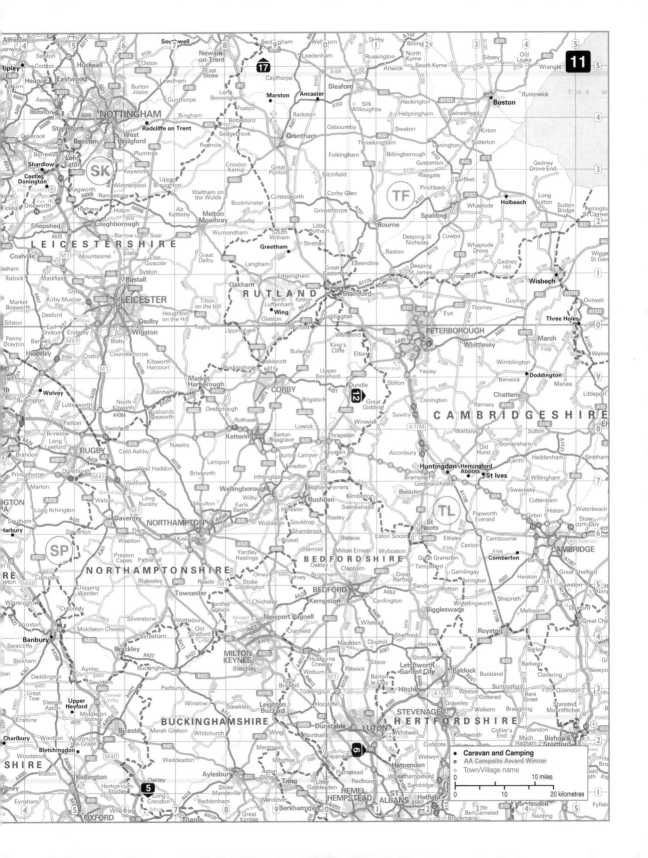

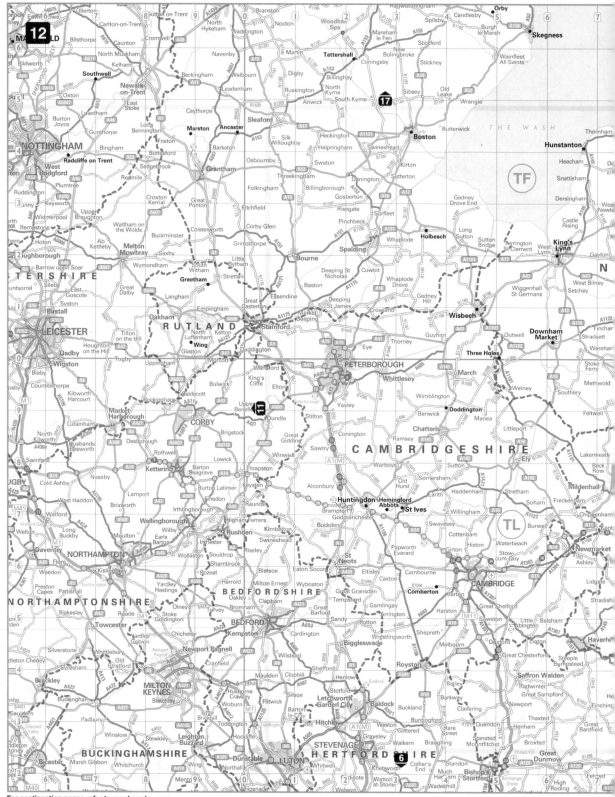

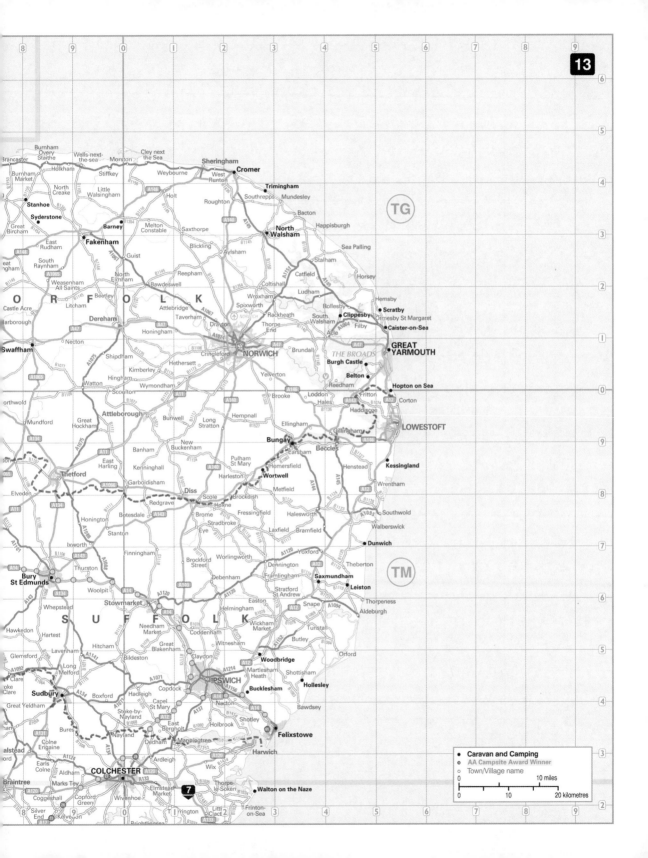

ISLE OF
ANGLESEY

Cemaes
Amlwch
Dulas
Rhôs Lligwy
Marian-Glas
Llanerchymedd
Llanfachraeth
Benllech
Red Wharf
Bay
Pentraeth
Holyhead
Llangoed
Deganwy
Llandudno
Rhôs-
on-Sea
Colwyn Bay
Towyn
Rhy
Trearddur Bay
Penmaenmawr
Conwy
Llanddulas
Abergele
Holy
Island
Llangefni
Beaumaris
Llanfairfechan
Llansanffraid
Glan Conwy
Betws-yn-Rhos
Llannef
Rhosneigr
Menai
Bridge
Bangor
Llanfairfechan
Tal-y-Cafn
Llanfair
Talhaiarn
Llansannan
Her
Aberffraw
Y Felinheli
Llanfair
P G
Llanllechid
Bethesda
Tal-y-Bont
Llangernyw
Bylchau
Newborough
Caernarfon
Llanrug
Llanberis
Trefriw
Llanrwst
CONWY
Bontnewydd
Capel Curig
Dinas Dinlle
Llanwnda
Betws Garmon
Betws-y-Coed
Llandwrog
Penygroes
Rhyd-Ddu
Dolwyddelan
Penmachno
Pentrefoelas
Cerrigydrudion
Clynnog-fawr
Caernarfon
Bay
SH
Beddgelert
SNOWDONIA
Blaenau Ffestiniog
Y Maen
Llanaelhaearn
Prenteg
Ffestiniog
Morfa Nefyn
PENINSULA
Tremadog
Maentwrog
Nefyn
Llanystumdwy
Porthmadog
Penrhyndeudraeth
NATIONAL
Bala
Bodfuan
LLEYN
Criccieth
Borth-y-Gest
Talsarnau
Sarn
Trawsfynydd
Pwllheli
Harlech
GWYNEDD
Llanbedrog
PARK
Llanuwchllyn
Aberdaron
Y Rhiw
Abersoch
Llanbedr
Bardsey
Island
Dyffryn Ardudwy
Ganllwyd
Tal-y-bont
Dinas-Mawddwy
Barmouth
Dolgellau
Mallwyd
Llangadfa
Fairbourne
MOUNTAIN
Llwyngwril
Corris
Cemmaes
Road
Llanbrynmair
Bryncrug
Pennal
Tywyn
Machynlleth
Carno
SN
Aberdyfi
Borth
Tal-y-bont
Llandre
Llanidloes
CARDIGAN BAY
Aberystwyth
Capel
Bangor
Ponterwyd

Legend
- ● Caravan and Camping
- ● AA Campsite Award Winner
- ○ Town/Village name

0   10 miles
0   10   20 kilometres

9

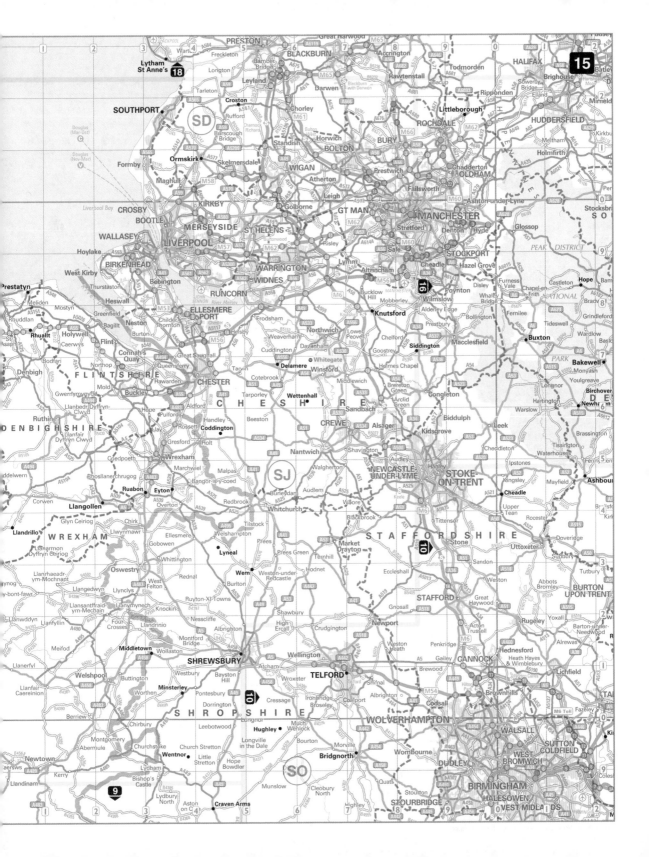

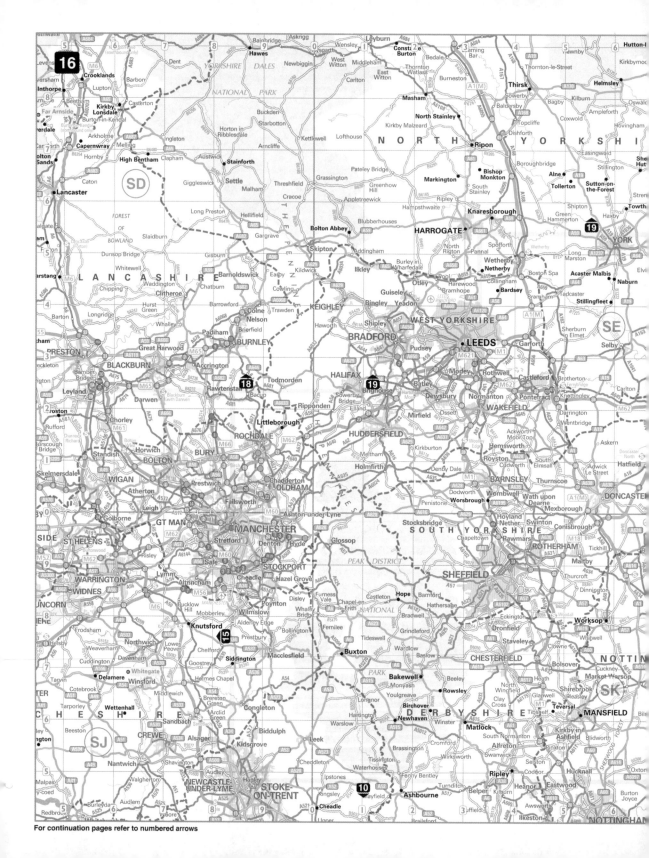

18

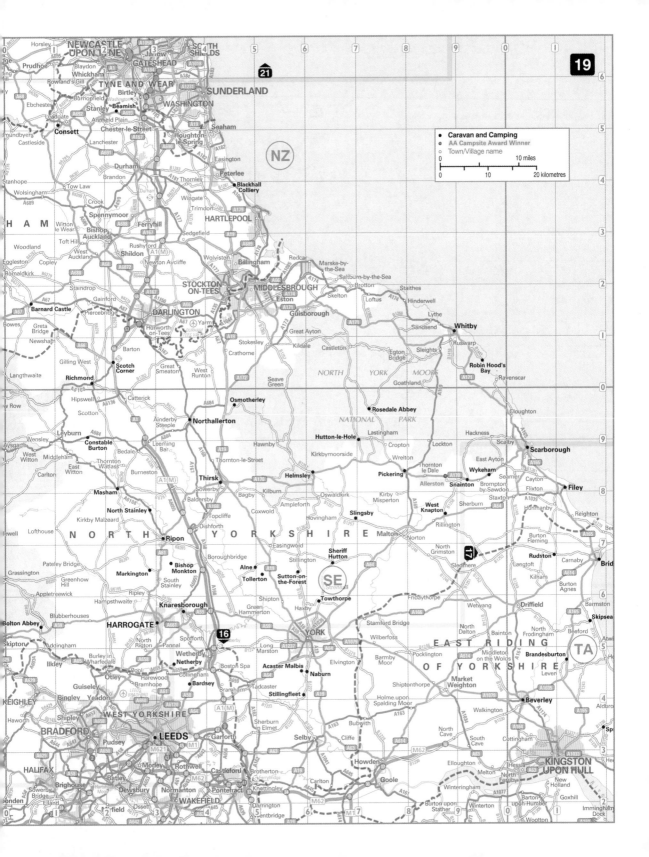

19

Caravan and Camping
AA Campsite Award Winner
Town/Village name

0   10 miles
0   10   20 kilometres

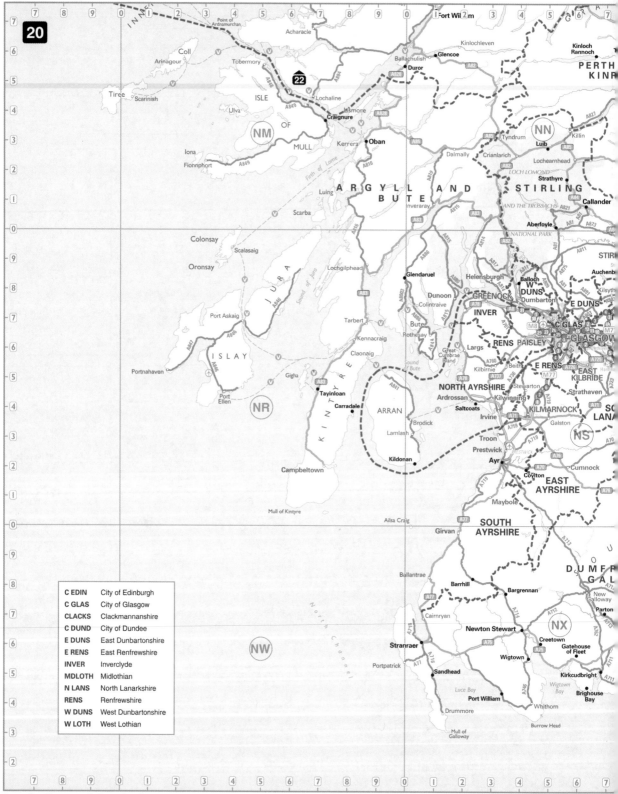

Point of Ardnamurchan
Acharacle
Fort Wil 2m
Kinlochleven
Kinloch Rannoch
PERTH
KINR

Coll
Arinagour
Tobermory
Ballachulish
Glencoe
Duror

Tiree
Scarinish
ISLE
Lochaline
Lismore
22

Ulva
OF
MULL
Craignure
Tyndrum
Luib
Killin
NN

Iona
Fionnphort
Kerrera
Oban
Dalmally
Crianlarich
Lochearnhead

Firth of Lorne
Strathyre
STIRLING

Luing
ARGYLL AND BUTE
Inveraray
LOCH LOMOND
Callander

Scarba
AND THE TROSSACHS
Aberfoyle
STIR

Colonsay
NATIONAL PARK

Scalasaig
Lochgilphead
Glendaruel
Helensburgh
Auchenb

Oronsay
Dunoon
Balloch
W DUNS
Kilsyth

JURA
Colintraive
GREENOCK
Dumbarton
E DUNS

Sound of Jura
Bute
INVER
C GLAS

Port Askaig
Tarbert
Rothesay
GLASGOW

Portnahaven
ISLAY
Kennacraig
Great Cumbrae Island
RENS PAISLEY

Claonaig
Sound of Bute
EAST KILBRIDE

Port Ellen
NR
Gigha
Tayinloan
Largs
Beith
E RENS
M77

Carradale
ARRAN
Kilbirnie
NORTH AYRSHIRE
Strathaven

Brodick
Ardrossan
Stewarton
NS
SO LANA

KINTYRE
Lamlash
Saltcoats
Kilwinning
KILMARNOCK

Campbeltown
Kildonan
Irvine
Galston

Troon
Prestwick
A76

Mull of Kintyre
Ailsa Craig
Ayr
Cumnock

Maybole
Coylton
EAST AYRSHIRE

North Channel
SOUTH AYRSHIRE
Girvan

DUMFR GAL

Ballantrae
Barrhill
Bargrennan
New Galloway
Parton

Cairnryan
NX

NW
Newton Stewart
Creetown
Gatehouse of Fleet

Stranraer
Wigtown
Kirkcudbright

Portpatrick
Sandhead
Brighouse Bay

Luce Bay
Wigtown Bay

Port William
Whithorn

Drummore
Burrow Head

Mull of Galloway

C EDIN	City of Edinburgh
C GLAS	City of Glasgow
CLACKS	Clackmannanshire
C DUND	City of Dundee
E DUNS	East Dunbartonshire
E RENS	East Renfrewshire
INVER	Inverclyde
MDLOTH	Midlothian
N LANS	North Lanarkshire
RENS	Renfrewshire
W DUNS	West Dunbartonshire
W LOTH	West Lothian

OUTER HEBRIDES

NA

NB

Cape Wrath

Rudha Rhobhanais
(Butt of Lewis)
Port Nis
(Port of Ness)

Cellar Head

LEWIS

A857

A858

Great Bernera

Carlabhagh
(Carloway)

Tiumpan Head

Handa Island
Scourie

ISLE

Steornabhagh
(Stornoway)

A857

A859

STORNOWAY

A858

A866

A894

NA H-EILEANAN
AN IAR

Lochinver

Inchnadamph

A837

A859

Scarp

THE MINCH

A837

Taransay

Tairbeart
(Tarbert)

HARRIS

A859

Scalpay

Gruinard Bay

Ullapool

A835

Pabbay

THE AARON

Gairloch

A832

Boreray

Berneray

A859

Kinlochewe

Achnasheen

A832

NORTH UIST

Loch nam Madadh
(Lochmaddy)

A867

A865

THE LITTLE MINCH

Uig

A855

Dunvegan

Edinbane

A850

NG

Portree

A87

Raasay

Inner Sound

A896

A890

Cannich

Benbecula

A865

Ronay

Wiay

NF

ISLE

A863

A87

Scalpay

Kyle of Lochalsh

Balmacara

OF

Drynoch

SOUTH UIST

A865

SKYE

A87

NORTH WEST HIGHLANDS

Loch Baghasdail
(Lochboisdale)

Soay

Eriskay

Canna

Ardvasar

Sound of Sleat

A851

A87

A887

A82

Invergarry

BARRA

Cuillin Sound

Point of Ardnamurchan

Rùm

Mallaig

INNER HEBRIDES

Eigg

A830

Arisaig

A82

Bagh a Chaisteil
(Castlebay)

A888

Sandray

Mingulay

Muck

Corpach

A861

Spean Bridge

Fort William

A861

A830

Kinlochleven

NL

NM

Acharacle

Coll

Tobermory

A884

A861

Ballachulish

Glencoe

A82

Arinagour

Duror

A828

20

Lismore

A849

Tiree

Scarinish

ISLE

Lochaline

A828

A849

Craignure

Kerrera

Oban

Ulva

OF

MULL

Iona
Fionnphort

A849

Dalmally

Crianlarich

Tyr

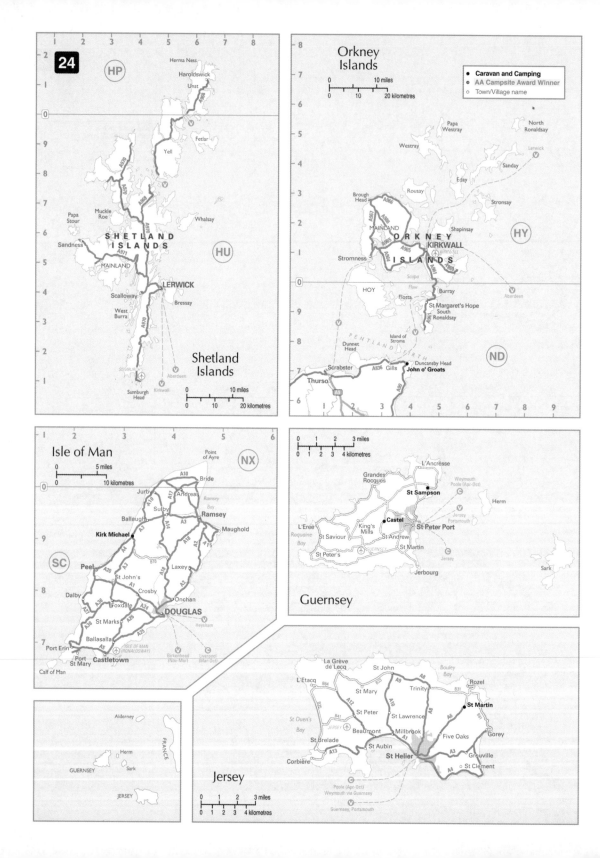

24

HP

Herma Ness
Haroldswick
Unst
A968

Fetlar
Yell
A970

Muckle Roe
Papa Stour
Whalsay
HU

SHETLAND ISLANDS
Sandness
MAINLAND
A971
LERWICK
Scalloway
Bressay
West Burra
A970
SUMBURGH
Aberdeen
Kirkwall
Sumburgh Head

Shetland Islands

0   10 miles
0   10   20 kilometres

Orkney Islands

Caravan and Camping
AA Campsite Award Winner
Town/Village name

0   10 miles
0   10   20 kilometres

Papa Westray
Westray
North Ronaldsay
Lerwick
Sanday
Eday
Rousay
Stronsay
Brough Head
A966
MAINLAND
A986
Shapinsay
A965
KIRKWALL
ORKNEY
A964
Stromness
ISLANDS
A961
HY
Scapa Flow
HOY
Burray
Aberdeen
St Margaret's Hope
South Ronaldsay
PENTLAND FIRTH
Island of Stroma
Dunnet Head
ND
Scrabster
A836   Gills
Duncansby Head
John o' Groats
Thurso
A9

Isle of Man

Point of Ayre
NX

0   5 miles
0   10 kilometres

A10
Bride
Jurby
A10
A17
Andreas
Ramsey Bay
Sulby
Ballaugh
A14
Ramsey
A3
A1
Kirk Michael
A18
Maughold
A2
A15
SC
A3
Laxey
A4
Peel
A20
St John's
B10
A1
A2
Dalby
A36
Crosby
A5
A24
Foxdale
St Marks
A25
Onchan
DOUGLAS
A3
Heysham
Ballasalla
ISLE OF MAN (RONALDSWAY)
Birkenhead (Nov-Mar)
Liverpool (Mar-Oct)
Port Erin
A5
Port St Mary
Castletown
Calf of Man

0   1   2   3 miles
0   1   2   3   4 kilometres

Grandes Rocques
L'Ancresse
Weymouth Poole (Apr-Oct)
Herm
St Sampson
L'Erée
Castel
King's Mills
St Peter Port
Jersey Portsmouth
L'Eree
Roquaine Bay
St Saviour
St Andrew
St Peter's
GUERNSEY
St Martin
Jersey
Jerbourg
Sark

Guernsey

Alderney
FRANCE
Herm
GUERNSEY
Sark
JERSEY

La Grève de Lecq
St John
Bouley Bay
Rozel
L'Etacq
B64
St Mary
A9
Trinity
B31
A12
B33
St Peter
St Lawrence
A6
St Martin
St Ouen's Bay
JERSEY
B31
Beaumont
A1
Millbrook
Five Oaks
Gorey
St Brelade
St Aubin
A3
Grouville
Corbière
A13
St Helier
A4
St Clement
Poole (Apr-Oct)
Weymouth via Guernsey
Guernsey, Portsmouth

Jersey

0   1   2   3 miles
0   1   2   3   4 kilometres

AA Camping Card Sites

The following list shows AA rated campsites that accept the AA Camping Card which is valid until 31st January 2014. See page 7 for further details of the card.

ENGLAND

CORNWALL
BODMIN
Mena Caravan & Camping Park
BUDE
Pentire Haven Holiday Park
CAMELFORD
Lakefield Caravan Park
HAYLE
Higher Trevaskis Caravan
  & Camping Park
HELSTON
Poldown Caravan Park
Skyburriowe Farm
LOOE
Tencreek Holiday Park
LOSTWITHIEL
Eden Valley Holiday Park
MAWGAN PORTH
Sun Haven Valley Holiday Park
MEVAGISSEY
Seaview International Holiday Park
NEWQUAY
Hendra Holiday Park
Trethiggey Touring Park
PERRANPORTH
Higher Golla Touring & Caravan Park
REDRUTH
Stithians Lake Country Park
ST AGNES
Beacon Cottage Farm Touring Park
ST AUSTELL
Meadow Lakes
ST BURYAN
Treverven Touring Caravan
  & Camping Park
ST HILARY
Wayfarers Caravan & Camping Park

ST JUST [NEAR LAND'S END]
Secret Garden Caravan & Camping Park
ST MINVER
Gunvenna Caravan Park
TORPOINT
Whitsand Bay Lodge & Touring Park
WATERGATE BAY
Watergate Bay Touring Park

CUMBRIA
APPLEBY-IN-WESTMORLAND
Wild Rose Park
KESWICK
Burns Farm Caravan Park
PENRITH
Flusco Wood
PENTON
Twin Willows
POOLEY BRIDGE
Park Foot Caravan & Camping Park
SILLOTH
Hylton Caravan Park
Stanwix Park Holiday Centre
WATERMILLOCK
Cove Caravan & Camping Park

DERBYSHIRE
ASHBOURNE
Carsington Fields Caravan Park
BAKEWELL
Greenhills Holiday Park

DEVON
ASHBURTON
Parkers Farm Holiday Park
River Dart Country Park
AXMINSTER
Hawkchurch Country Park
BRIDGERULE
Hedleywood Caravan & Camping Park
BRIXHAM
Galmpton Touring Park
BUDLEIGH SALTERTON
Pooh Cottage Holiday Park
CHAPMANS WELL
Chapmanswell Caravan Park

COMBE MARTIN
Newberry Valley Park
DARTMOUTH
Woodlands Grove Caravan
  & Camping Park
DAWLISH
Cofton Country Holidays
Leadstone Camping
HOLSWORTHY
Headon Farm Caravan Site
KENTISBEARE
Forest Glade Holiday Park
LYNTON
Channel View Caravan and Camping Park
MORTEHOE
Easewell Farm Holiday Park
Twitchen House Holiday Park
Warcombe Farm Caravan
  & Camping Park
NEWTON ABBOT
Dornafield
Ross Park
SIDMOUTH
Oakdown Country Holiday Park
Salcombe Regis Caravan & Camping Park
SOUTH MOLTON
Riverside Caravan & Camping Park
TAVISTOCK
Woodovis Park
Langstone Manor Camping
  & Caravan Park
TEDBURN ST MARY
Springfield Holiday Park
WOOLACOMBE
Golden Coast Holiday Park
Woolacombe Bay Holiday Park
Woolacombe Sands Holiday Park

DORSET
ALDERHOLT
Hill Cottage Farm Camping
  and Caravan Park
CHARMOUTH
Manor Farm Holiday Centre
FERNDOWN
St Leonards Farm Caravan
  & Camping Park

AA Camping Card Sites *continued*

LYME REGIS
Hook Farm Caravan & Camping Park
LYTCHETT MINSTER
South Lytchett Manor Caravan
  & Camping Park
PUNCKNOWLE
Home Farm Caravan and Campsite
ST LEONARDS
Shamba Holidays
SWANAGE
Herston Caravan & Camping Park
WAREHAM
Birchwood Tourist Park
Wareham Forest Tourist Park
WIMBORNE MINSTER
Charris Camping & Caravan Park

ESSEX
CANEWDON
Riverside Village Holiday Park

HAMPSHIRE
HAMBLE
Riverside Holidays

KENT
BIRCHINGTON
Two Chimneys Caravan Park
WROTHAM HEATH
Gate House Wood Touring Park

LANCASHIRE
CROSTON
Royal Umpire Caravan Park
GARSTANG
Bridge House Marina & Caravan Park
MORECAMBE
Venture Caravan Park

LINCOLNSHIRE
BOSTON
Long Acres Touring Park
MABLETHORPE
Kirkstead Holiday Park
ORBY
Heron's Mead Fishing Lake
  & Touring Park

NORFOLK
BELTON
Rose Farm Touring & Camping Park
CLIPPESBY
Clippesby Hall
GREAT YARMOUTH
The Grange Touring Park
HUNSTANTON
Manor Park Holiday Village
SWAFFHAM
Breckland Meadows Touring Park

NOTTINGHAMSHIRE
CHURCH LANEHAM
Trentfield Farm
TUXFORD
Orchard Park Touring Caravan
  & Camping Park

OXFORDSHIRE
BANBURY
Barnstones Caravan & Camping Site
BLETCHINGDON
Diamond Farm Caravan & Camping Park

SHROPSHIRE
MINSTERLEY
The Old School Caravan Park
SHREWSBURY
Beaconsfield Farm Caravan Park

SOMERSET
BURTLE
Orchard Camping
CHARD
Alpine Grove Touring Park
PORLOCK
Porlock Caravan Park
SHEPTON MALLET
Greenacres Camping

SUFFOLK
BUCKLESHAM
Westwood Caravan Park
DARSHAM
Haw Wood Farm Caravan Park

SUSSEX, WEST
ARUNDEL
Ship & Anchor Marina
HENFIELD
Blacklands Farm Caravan & Camping

WARWICKSHIRE
ASTON CANTLOW
Island Meadow Caravan Park
KINGSBURY
Tame View Caravan Site

WEST MIDLANDS
MERIDEN
Somers Wood Caravan Park

WIGHT, ISLE OF
SANDOWN
Old Barn Touring Park

WILTSHIRE
CALNE
Blackland Lakes Holiday & Leisure Centre
WESTBURY
Brokerswood Country Park

YORKSHIRE, EAST RIDING OF
SKIPSEA
Skirlington Leisure Park
SPROATLEY
Burton Constable Holiday Park
  & Arboretum

YORKSHIRE, NORTH
ALLERSTON
Vale of Pickering Caravan Park
HARROGATE
Shaws Trailer Park
HELMSLEY
Golden Square Touring Caravan Park
KNARESBOROUGH
Kingfisher Caravan Park
ROBIN HOOD'S BAY
Grouse Hill Caravan Park
SCARBOROUGH
Killerby Old Hall

SHERIFF HUTTON
York Meadows Caravan Park
SNAINTON
Jasmine Caravan Park
THIRSK
Hillside Caravan Park
TOWTHORPE
York Touring Caravan Site

YORKSHIRE, WEST
LEEDS
Moor Lodge Park

SCOTLAND

ABERDEENSHIRE
HUNTLY
Huntly Castle Caravan Park
KINTORE
Hillhead Caravan Park

DUMFRIES & GALLOWAY
CREETOWN
Castle Cary Holiday Park
KIPPFORD
Kippford Holiday Park
SHAWHEAD
Barnsoul Caravan Park
WIGTOWN
Drumroamin Farm Camping
  & Touring Site

EAST LOTHIAN
MUSSELBURGH
Drum Mohr Caravan Park

HIGHLAND
CORPACH
Linnhe Lochside Holidays
GAIRLOCH
Gairloch Caravan Park

SCOTTISH ISLANDS

ISLE OF ARRAN
KILDONAN
Sealshore Camping and Touring Site

WALES

CARMARTHENSHIRE
NEWCASTLE EMLYN
Argoed Meadow Caravan
  and Camping Site
Cenarth Falls Holiday Park

CEREDIGION
LLANON
Woodlands Caravan Park

CONWY
BETWS-YN-RHOS
Hunters Hamlet Caravan Park

DENBIGHSHIRE
LLANDRILLO
Hendwr Country Park
RHUALLT
Penisar Mynydd Caravan Park

GWYNEDD
BALA
Pen-y-Bont Touring Park
CAERNARFON
Plas Gwyn Caravan & Camping Park
Riverside Camping
LLANDWROG
White Tower Caravan Park
TALSARNAU
Barcdy Touring Caravan & Camping Park
TAL-Y-BONT
Islawrffordd Caravan Park

MONMOUTHSHIRE
DINGESTOW
Bridge Caravan Park & Camping Site

PEMBROKESHIRE
HASGUARD CROSS
Hasguard Cross Caravan Park
HAVERFORDWEST
Nolton Cross Caravan Park
TENBY
Well Park Caravan & Camping Site
Wood Park Caravans

POWYS
BRONLLYS
Anchorage Caravan Park
LLANDRINDOD WELLS
Dalmore Camping & Caravanning Park

WREXHAM
EYTON
The Plassey Leisure Park

NORTHERN IRELAND

CO ANTRIM
BALLYCASTLE
Watertop Farm
BUSHMILLS
Ballyness Caravan Park

REPUBLIC OF IRELAND

CO MAYO
KNOCK
Knock Caravan and Camping Park

Index

Entries are listed alphabetically by town name, then campsite name. The following abbreviations have been used: C&C – Caravan & Camping; HP – Holiday Park; CP – Caravan Park; C&C Club – Camping & Caravanning Club Site

Acknowledgments

AA Media would like to thank the following photographers, companies and picture libraries for their assistance in the preparation of this book.

Abbreviations for the picture credits are as follows – (t) top; (b) bottom; (c) centre; (l) left; (r) right; (AA) AA World Travel Library

001c AA/James Tims; 002l AA/Nigel Hicks; 003tl AA/James Tims; 009b AA/James Tims; 010b AA/James Tims; 016 AA/Nigel Hicks; 016tr AA/James Tims; 018l AA/Jonathan Smith; 023r AA/David Clapp; 024 Eskdale Camping & Caravanning Club Site; 026 Eskdale Camping & Caravanning Club Site; 027 Eskdale Camping & Caravanning Club Site; 028 Eskdale Camping & Caravanning Club Site; 29 Eskdale Camping & Caravanning Club Site; 030/031 Charlie Hamp; 032t Charlie Hamp; 032b Charlie Hamp; 034 David Hancock; 035t David Hancock; 035b Charlie Hamp; 036/037 The Quiet Site; 039 The Camping & Caravanning Club; 040 The Quiet Site; 041t South Penquite Farm; 041b Teversal Camping & Caravanning Club Site; 046 AA/Adam Burton; 048 AA/James Tims; 049 AA/James Tims; 050/051 AA/Michael Moody; 079 AA/Adam Burton; 141 AA/Tom Mackie; 190 AA/Wyn Voysey; 237 AA/Steve Day; 240 AA/Peter Baker; 263 AA/Jeff Beazley; 275 AA/Mike Hayward; 281 AA/James Tims; 305 AA/Tom Mackie; 318/319 AA; 332/333 AA/Richard Surman; 366/367 AA/Jim Henderson; 388 AA/Richard Elliott; 398 AA/Ken Paterson; 404/405 AA/Steve Watkins; 418 AA/Jonathan Welsh; 437 AA/Michael Moody; 442/443 AA/Chris Hill; 449 AA/Liam Blake; 496/497 AA/Adam Burton; 513 AA/David Clapp; 540 AA/Tom Mackie.

County Introductions/Walks & Cycle Rides

Cornwall AA/Adam Burton; AA/John Wood; AA/John Wood; Cumbria AA/Steve Day; AA/Tom Mackie; AA/Anna Mockford & Nick Bonetti; AA/Tom Mackie; Derbyshire AA/Tom Mackie; AA/Andrew Midgley; AA/Tom Mackie; Devon AA/Caroline Jones; AA/Nigel Hicks; AA/Guy Edwardes; AA/Adam Burton; Dorset AA/Andrew Newey; AA/Andrew Newey; AA/Max Jourdan; Norfolk AA/Tom Mackie; AA/Tom Mackie; AA/Tom Mackie; AA/Tom Mackie; Somerset AA/Adam Burton; AA/James Tims; AA/James Tims; Suffolk AA/Tom Mackie; AA/Tom Mackie; AA/Tom Mackie; AA/Tom Mackie; Sussex AA/John Miller; AA/Laurie Noble; AA/John Miller; AA/John Miller; AA/Laurie Noble; Isle of Wight AA/Adam Burton; AA/Andrew Newey; AA/Andrew Newey; Yorkshire AA/Mike Kipling; AA/David Clapp; AA/Tom Mackie; AA/Mike Kipling; Scotland AA/Stephen Whitehorne; AA/Mark Hamblin; AA/David W Robertson; AA/David W Robertson; Wales AA/Nick Jenkins; AA/Dan Santillo; AA/Chris Warren; Walks &Cycle Routes AA/Caroline Jones; AA/James Tims; AA/James Tims; Walk 1 AA/John Wood; Walk 2 AA/Peter Sharpe; Walk 6 AA/Peter Baker; Walk 7 AA/S&O Mathews; Walk 10 AA/S&O Mathews; Walk 11 AA/Tony Souter; Walk 12 AA/Peter Baker; Walk 13 AA/Sue Anderson; Walk 14 AA/Alan Grierley; Walk 15 AA/Chris Warren; Cycle 1 AA/Sue Viccars; Cycle 2 AA/Adrian Baker; Cycle 3 AA/Malc Birkitt; Cycle 4 AA/John O'Carroll; Cycle 5 AA/Linda Whitwam.

Every effort has been made to trace the copyright holders, and we apologise in advance for any unintentional omissions or errors. We would be pleased to apply any corrections in a following edition of this publication.

Readers' Report Form

Please send this form to:–
Editor, AA Caravan & Camping,
Lifestyle Guides,
AA Media,
Fanum House,
Basingstoke RG21 4EA

e-mail: lifestyleguides@theAA.com

Please use this form to tell us about any site that you have visited, whether it is in the guide or not currently listed. Feedback from readers helps us to keep our guide accurate and up to date. However, if you have a complaint during your visit, we recommend that you discuss the matter with the management there and then, so that they have a chance to put things right before your visit is spoilt.

Please note that the AA does not undertake to arbitrate between you and the establishment, or to obtain compensation or engage in protracted correspondence.

Date

Your name (BLOCK CAPITALS)

Your address (BLOCK CAPITALS)

Post code

E-mail address

Name of site/park

Location

Comments

(please attach a separate sheet if necessary)

Please tick here ☐ if you DO NOT wish to receive details of AA offers or products

PTO

Readers' Report Form *continued*

Have you bought this guide before? ☐ YES ☐ NO

How often do you visit a caravan park or camp site? (tick one choice)
Once a year ☐   Twice a year ☐   Three times a year ☐
More than three times a year ☐

How long do you generally stay at a park or site? (tick one choice)
One night ☐   Up to a week ☐   1 week ☐
2 weeks ☐   Over 2 weeks ☐

Do you have a: (tick all that apply)
Tent ☐   Caravan ☐   Motorhome ☐

Please answer these questions to help us make improvements to the guide:
Which of these factors are the most important when choosing a site? (tick one choice)
Location ☐   Toilet/washing facilities ☐   Personal Recommendation ☐
Leisure facilities ☐
Other (please state)

Do you read the editorial features in the guide? ☐ YES ☐ NO

Do you use the location atlas?   ☐ YES ☐ NO

What elements of the guide do you find most useful when choosing a site/park? (tick all that apply)
Description ☐   Photo ☐   Advertisement ☐

Is there any other information you would like to see added to this guide?

Readers' Report Form

Please send this form to:–
Editor, AA Caravan & Camping,
Lifestyle Guides,
AA Media,
Fanum House,
Basingstoke RG21 4EA

e-mail: lifestyleguides@theAA.com

Please use this form to tell us about any site that you have visited, whether it is in the guide or not currently listed. Feedback from readers helps us to keep our guide accurate and up to date. However, if you have a complaint during your visit, we recommend that you discuss the matter with the management there and then, so that they have a chance to put things right before your visit is spoilt.

Please note that the AA does not undertake to arbitrate between you and the establishment, or to obtain compensation or engage in protracted correspondence.

Date

Your name (BLOCK CAPITALS)

Your address (BLOCK CAPITALS)

Post code

E-mail address

Name of site/park

Location

Comments

(please attach a separate sheet if necessary)

Please tick here ☐ if you DO NOT wish to receive details of AA offers or products

PTO

Readers' Report Form *continued*

Have you bought this guide before? ☐ YES ☐ NO

How often do you visit a caravan park or camp site? (tick one choice)
Once a year ☐   Twice a year ☐   Three times a year ☐
More than three times a year ☐

How long do you generally stay at a park or site? (tick one choice)
One night ☐   Up to a week ☐   1 week ☐
2 weeks ☐   Over 2 weeks ☐

Do you have a: (tick all that apply)
Tent ☐   Caravan ☐   Motorhome ☐

Please answer these questions to help us make improvements to the guide:
Which of these factors are the most important when choosing a site? (tick one choice)
Location ☐   Toilet/washing facilities ☐   Personal Recommendation ☐
Leisure facilities ☐
Other (please state)

Do you read the editorial features in the guide? ☐ YES ☐ NO

Do you use the location atlas?   ☐ YES ☐ NO

What elements of the guide do you find most useful when choosing a site/park? (tick all that apply)
Description ☐   Photo ☐   Advertisement ☐

Is there any other information you would like to see added to this guide?